International Economics

Thought-provoking and clearly explained, the new edition of this outstanding textbook provides students of international economics and international business with a rigorous explanation of global economic theory and policy, both current trends and historic developments. Improving on the popular success of previous editions, this superb title explores key models through case studies and review questions, enabling students to challenge the reporting of economic events by press and government alike.

Split into two parts – International Trade and International Finance – the text explains conceptual building blocks before applying them to current events and controversies. The International Finance section develops progressively more realistic macroeconomic models of open economies. Key issues discussed include:

- the influence of transportation costs
- economies of scale and the new economic geography
- the evaluation of preferential trade agreements
- expansion of the European Union and of the European Economic and Monetary Union
- the integration of international financial markets and the crucial need for a new financial architecture
- international financial crises
- the economics of reserve accumulation by China and other emerging economies

Fully illustrated with tables and figures to allow students to visualize the issues discussed, the lively prose gives this book a refreshing approach. It is the ideal companion for any module on International Economics, and an invaluable reference tool for students throughout their Economics or Business degree course. An accompanying website also provides context and coverage of the international financial crisis of October 2008, including the "credit crunch" and the collapse of some banking institutions.

Theo S. Eicher is Professor and Robert R. Richards Distinguished Scholar in the Department of Economics at the University of Washington, Seattle, USA. He is also an affiliate professor at Ludwig-Maximilians-Universität, Munich, Germany.

John H. Mutti is the Sidney Meyer Professor International Economics at Grinnell College, Iowa, USA. His experience in government includes the US Treasury Office of International Taxation and the President's Council of Economic Advisers. His research focuses on international trade, taxation, and foreign direct investment.

Michelle H. Turnovsky is Senior Lecturer in the Department of Economics at the University of Washington, Seattle, USA where she has overseen the Undergraduate Program for twenty years mostly as Director.

International Economics

7th edition

Theo S. Eicher, John H. Mutti, and Michelle H. Turnovsky

 Routledge
Taylor & Francis Group

LONDON AND NEW YORK

First published 2009 by Routledge
2 Park Square, Milton Park, Abingdon, Oxon, OX14 4RN

Simultaneously published in the USA and Canada by Routledge
270 Madison Avenue, New York, NY 10016

Routledge is an imprint of the Taylor & Francis Group

© 2009 Theo S. Eicher, John H. Mutti, and Michelle H. Turnovsky

Typeset in Berling by
Keystroke, 28 High Street, Tettenhall, Wolverhampton
Printed and bound in the US by
Edwards Brothers Inc.

British Library Cataloguing in Publication Data
A catalogue record for this book is available from the British Library

Library of Congress Cataloging in Publication Data
Eicher, Theo S.
    International economics.—7th ed./Theo S. Eicher, John H. Mutti, and Michelle H. Turnovsky.
        p. cm.
    Rev. ed. of: International economics/Dunn, Robert M. 6th ed. 2004.
    ISBN 978–0–415–77285–3 (hardback)—ISBN 978–0–415–77286–0 (pbk.)
    1. International economic relations. I. Mutti, John H. II. Turnovsky, Michelle H.
    III. Dunn, Robert M. Inernational economics. IV. Title.
    HF1359.D86 2009
    337—dc22   2008044877

ISBN10: 0–415–77285–0 (hbk)
ISBN10: 0–415–77286–9 (pbk)
ISBN10: 0–203–87861–2 (ebk)

ISBN13: 978–0–415–77286–0 (pbk)
ISBN13: 978–0–415–77285–3 (hbk)
ISBN13: 978–0–203–87861–3 (ebk)

Contents

20 Perfectly Flexible Prices and Exchange Rate Dynamics 595

21 The International Monetary System: A Brief History 626

22 European Monetary Integration 659

List of case studies

List of boxes

Chapter 6

Chapter 7

Chapter 8

Chapter 9

Chapter 10

Chapter 11

Chapter 12

Chapter 13

Chapter 14

Chapter 15

Chapter 16

Chapter 17

Chapter 23

List of figures

List of tables

Preface

This book is an introduction to international economics, intended for students who are taking their first course in the subject. The level of exposition assumes that students have completed courses in intermediate microeconomic and macroeconomic theory, so that the economist's toolkit of indifference curves, isoquants, and the *IS–LM* model are familiar. However, because that material may not be so fresh in every student's mind, we review these concepts before using them to develop the additional insights relevant in an international setting.

The primary purpose of this book is to present a clear, straightforward, and current account of the main topics in international economics. We have tried to keep the student's perspective constantly in mind and to make the explanations clear at both an intuitive level and also in a more rigorous fashion. To provide this analytical framework, we primarily rely on the grand graphical tradition refined by generations of economists who were drawn to the challenges of representing complex international economic relationships in understandable ways. We include some more formal mathematical models in appendices, when including them provides a useful bridge to understanding some of the suggested readings listed at the conclusion of each chapter. Throughout the book we hope to communicate the ferment and controversy that continues to arise in the development, evaluation, and application of economic models to explain economic performance internationally.

This is the 7th edition of this textbook, and it marks another transition in authorship. Theo Eicher and Michelle Turnovsky of the University of Washington, Seattle, replace Robert Dunn as co-authors and join John Mutti in preparing this edition. The current authors are deeply appreciative of those responsible for the successful progression to this edition. James Ingram, who is now Emeritus at the University of North Carolina, Chapel Hill, authored the first two editions alone, and subsequently coauthored the next two with Robert Dunn of George Washington University. With the fifth edition, John Mutti replaced Ingram as a co-author, and Dunn and Mutti wrote the 6th edition. Both Jim Ingram and Bob Dunn have generously given permission to carry over portions of the material they wrote for previous editions. Their insights still represent important contributions to this edition, even as a new team brings fresh ideas to the goal of helping students understand the causes of economic events and consequences of economic policies in the international arena.

The book is divided into two main parts, International Trade and Trade Policy (Part I) and International Finance and Open Economy Macroeconomics (Part II). In each part we develop the basic models and principal analytical approaches used by international economists, and apply them to recent policy issues and historical episodes. We try to draw examples that will be familiar to readers both in Europe and North America, without limiting our attention to those two areas.

Changes in the Coverage of International Trade

The most visible change in the first half of the book is the integration of more formal graphical tools of analysis into the body of the text. Many of these concepts were included in appendices or separate boxes in previous editions. The text still provides intuitive explanations of important theoretical concepts, but the current organization provides a more concise treatment of the material and what we hope is a logical transition to the more complete graphical presentations.

Chapter 1 does not serve as a comprehensive overview of the text, but instead is intended to be suggestive of the way a familiar item from student life, an iPod digital music player, embodies many complicated international trade relationships that a student can understand much better by studying the chapters that follow.

The contributions of Adam Smith, David Ricardo, and John Stuart Mill are treated in Chapter 2, and the more formal conceptual models developed by neoclassical economists are now treated separately in Chapter 3. Because the writers cited in Chapter 2 based their analysis on labor productivity and the labor theory of value, however, we include more recent information on the way this basic framework must be modified to take into account transportation costs and their relationship to wages.

The factor endowments theory of Eli Heckscher and Bertil Ohlin is still the heart of Chapter 4, but we pay more attention to how it relates to the specific factors model of trade and the plight of nations who worry about a resource curse when they discover new deposits of oil or gold. We also include more of the ongoing effort to explain why the factor endowments theory overpredicts the amount of trade that should be occurring between industrialized and developing countries.

The discussion of economies of scale and imperfect competition in Chapter 5 includes greater treatment of the models of monopolistic competition. Extensions of that approach in the new economic geography include the role of transportation in spatial economies, which provide suggestive explanations for the reason per capita incomes vary across countries.

The Chapter 6 discussion of trade restrictions updates information on the costs of protection in the E.U., changes in E.U. sugar policy, and the response to the elimination of the Multifiber Arrangement. Chapter 7 pays additional attention to more nuanced arguments for protection, the rise of protectionist action through antidumping duties, and the way trade policy decisions are made in democratic governments. Issues that arise under actual dumping cases are illustrated with E.U. actions in the footwear industry and U.S. restrictions on shrimp imports.

Chapter 8 now contains material on immigration, capital mobility, and multinational corporations. Presenting this information before discussions of customs unions or multilateral trade agreements seems desirable, because those agreements have come to address these additional issues. New data on international migration allow a more complete discussion of the movement of skilled versus unskilled workers. Material on tax competition and capital mobility has been moved into this chapter, and the discussion of multinational corporations broadened to include recent work that tries to identify positive externalities from hosting MNC affiliates.

We examine preferential trade agreements in Chapter 9. The expansion of the E.U. since the last edition of this book provides a strong reason to focus more attention on issues of convergence and the need for financial assistance to lagging regions. Also, we consider recent empirical analysis using the gravity model to assess the consequences of trade blocs on members and non-members, as well as a recent assessment of the Canadian fear that it would lose its industrial base as a consequence of a free trade agreement with the United States.

If countries gain from unilateral free trade, what is left that must be accomplished multilaterally instead? Chapter 10 begins with this basic question. The presentation is now organized around lessons that may be drawn from past negotiations, and reviews the way the dispute resolution mechanism has functioned, including the WTO ruling against U.S. agricultural subsidies for cotton.

Chapter 11 examines the relationship between growth and trade. The discussion of trade policy in developing countries includes more recent insights beyond the two poles of import substitution industrialization and export-led growth. A case study considers what lessons can be drawn from the experience of China's rapid industrialization. The chapter also includes material about the consequences of growth and the negative environmental externalities that industrialization generates.

Changes in the Coverage of International Finance and Open Economy Macroeconomics

The second part of the book has an entirely new feel. It is organized around three main topics: the balance of payments and the exchange rate; open economy models and policy; and international monetary developments. First, we explain the mechanics of the basic international accounting device, the balance of payments. We then discuss the different kinds of exchange rates and explain how they are determined on the foreign exchange market. We also present the various exchange rate regimes and describe their adjustment mechanisms, which depend on the extent of monetary sterilization that a government chooses.

The second section focuses on modeling the open economy. Because models can get very complex, we use assumptions to organize our analysis. We start with fixed exchange rates and continue the discussion under flexible exchange rates. At first, we assume no capital mobility and then extend the models to allow varying degrees of capital mobility, eventually reaching perfect capital mobility. Similarly with respect to macroeconomic policy, we usually look at the impact of monetary and fiscal policy in isolation and then we raise the question of the appropriate policy mix. We also start by considering a small open-economy model, i.e. an economy that is too small to affect its trade partners, so it is a price taker on the world markets. Then we extend the analysis to large open economies and consider their interactions (repercussions). Finally, with respect to prices, we first look at short-run sticky price types of models. Eventually, the monetarist views are acknowledged and flexible prices are introduced. However, we also present models where prices adjust in the medium-run.

The third section takes us through history to track the evolution of the international monetary system from the nineteenth century's gold standard to the present. Among the notable developments of recent years, the creation of the European Economic and Monetary Union is discussed and its potential success appraised. The history chapter illustrates that the main causes for international financial upheavals in the past were connected with, or were the consequences of, world armed conflicts. However none has taken place in the past sixty years, but serious international financial crises have rocked the smooth functioning of the international order. These crises are usually localized, but they do spread from one country to its neighbour in a specific region. We analyze the causes of these crises and explain what steps countries are taking to insure themselves against such upheavals.

Among the more salient features of the new edition, we would like to point out some specific aspects. We try to be as up-to-date as possible with some of the main developments in international finance. We present an extensive chapter on international capital markets that tracks the recent explosion of international capital flows all over the world. In this chapter, some of the latest innovations introduced in these markets are raised: derivatives, technical analysis, carry trade. Later on, we discuss at length the new international financial architecture and how to regulate it. The sprouting of new stateless financial entities coupled with new international financial instruments that cannot be regulated on the national level has made it essential to review the desirability of stricter international financial regulation. We devote a whole chapter to the development and implications of the new European Economic and Monetary Union. Finally, we cover the issue of currency crises. We address the different origins of these crises over the past three decades in various countries/regions and explain how the nature of the crises has changed. The open economy models are presented in a very logical manner; their complexity gradually increases as we adapt the assumptions to eventually depict a model closest to today's world. All the chapters end with one or two case studies: readings from the press covering an issue or an event that has relevance to the material in the chapter and some suggested questions for discussion.

Recommendations to Users of the Book

For those teaching a year-long course that covers both international trade and international finance, you will be able to cover the material of this book, and may choose to supplement it with the suggested readings given at the end of each chapter. For those teaching a course that covers both parts of the discipline but lasts a single semester or quarter, you will need to make choices regarding the material to assign. You have considerable flexibility in doing so, because the basic models and analytical tools are presented in the early chapters of each part. The core explanations of trade and a country's trade policy choices are contained in Chapters 2 through 6. A fundamental understanding of international financial markets and open economy macroeconomic issues is given in Chapters 12 through 19.

You will recognize that not all chapters are of the same length, or even if they are of the same length, they may require a different intensity of effort to master the concepts presented. This reality does thwart any plan to assign a chapter a week to students on the supposition that all chapters can be treated equally. In the first part of book, we particularly flag Chapter 4 as one that includes more analytical material than others and one that deserves extra time.

Acknowledgements

In writing this book, we have accumulated a number of obligations: to our students and colleagues, and to international economists too numerous to mention whose work is drawn upon in preparing a textbook such as this. We also gratefully acknowledge the economics editors and outside reviewers who have helped in the preparation of previous editions of this book. We limit our acknowledgements of individuals to those involved with the development of this edition. At Routledge we are pleased to recognize the editorial team of Harriet Brinton, Russell George, and Robert Langham who encouraged this major revision, and we appreciate the many helpful suggestions made by our outside reviewers. Especially helpful colleagues include Richard Kim of Cleary Gottlieb, Andrew McCallum of the University of Michigan, Yuchin Chen, Haideh Salehi-Esfahani, Stephen J. Turnovsky, and Ying Tang of the University of Washington, Goncalo Monteiro at Suny-Buffalo, Stefan Schubert, University of Bözen-Bolzano, Dale Hultengren, Bank of America, Florian Pfister of the University of Munich, Andreas Leukert of USB, Bryan Morales of Lehman Brothers, and Julio Saavedra of the ifo Institute at the University of Munich. Patty Dale at Grinnell College was instrumental in compiling the separate chapters of the three authors in a consistent format.

Finally, we thank users of the first six editions of the book who made useful comments and suggestions.

Theo S. Eicher, University of Washington, Seattle, Washington
John H. Mutti, Grinnell College, Grinnell, Iowa
Michelle H. Turnovsky, University of Washington, Seattle, Washington
October, 2008

Introduction

Life in an International Economy

Why study international economics? For one, it is difficult to read a newspaper today without references to "globalization," and its effects on firm profits and employment. What are the fundamental catalysts of globalization and how does international economics help us understand these drivers? Often a mental picture is worth a thousand words, and, in this general introduction to our textbook, we take the concrete example of the Apple iPod to highlight the many facets of the international economy. We will use this ultra popular portable media player to trace its production and sales patterns and introduce the forces of globalization and how they relate to the principles of international economics.

Apple Inc., a master of marketing, has used a global advertising campaign with its dark silhouetted characters dancing against bright-colored backgrounds to sell the iPod successfully worldwide. Introduced in 2001, iPod sales reached 100 million by 2007, and the product diversified quickly from music to videos, podcasting, and most recently to the ubiquitous iPhone. Some (lucky) students even receive free iPods from their universities to complete their assignments!

While iPods are closely associated with Apple Inc. – the American company that brought you the iMac – the product is actually not "Made in the USA." Turn over your iPod, and you find that it carries the text *"Designed in California, Made in China."* Strictly speaking, this statement is far from true! A recent study of iPod components shows the final product contains major intermediate inputs that are sourced from at least 5 countries, as shown in Table 1.1, and the share accounted for by China is a small part of the total.

Clearly, Apple does not produce each iPod in the country where it is sold, so it must be traded internationally. Table 1.1 also shows that companies from all over the world are responsible for the various components used in an iPod; but the company whose name is stamped on a component may not generate all of its innovative ideas in the country where it is headquartered and it may well produce the component in some third country. For example, Toshiba, based in Japan, has a fabled research laboratory in Cambridge, U.K., that has been involved in many of the company's creative innovations, but it produces the crucial iPod hard drive in the Philippines or China.

Different companies seem to make different choices about the best location for production. This textbook explains why. While iPod production may involve a handful of countries, its distribution is

TABLE 1.1 A Geographic Breakdown of the Value of the Fifth Generation iPod, 2005
The Most Expensive Parts

Component	Supplier company	Company HQ location	Manufacturing location	Percentage of all parts
Hard drive	Toshiba	Japan	China	51
Display module	Toshiba–Matsushita	Japan	Japan	14
Video/multimedia processor	Broadcom	U.S.	Taiwan or Singapore	6
Portal player CPU	Portal player	U.S.	U.S. or Taiwan	3
Insertion, test and assembly	Inventec	Taiwan	China	3
Battery pack	Unknown			2
Display driver	Renesas	Japan	Japan	2
Mobile SDRAM memory	Samsung	Korea	Korea	2
Back enclosure	Unknown			2
Mainboard PCB	Unknown			1
The ten most expensive parts				85

Source: Adapted from Linden, G., Kraemer, K., and Dedrick, J. (2008).

truly global – this is why Apple Inc. has been able to generate a staggering iPod revenue stream of $20 billion (so far!). Obviously the iPod trade is a far cry from the good old days when a commodity was produced and sold exclusively in one country. But then again, we live in a world where countries have long leveraged the gains from trade to improve national welfare.

What Determines Where a Product is Produced?

The first chapters of this book consider alternative theories that economists have developed over time to explain patterns of production and trade. The most fundamental reasons to engage in international trade are differences in climates, natural resources, or know-how. These factors contribute to the substantial differences in production costs observed across countries. Note that these theories do not necessarily focus on one firm (aka Apple Inc.), but on a *country*. Trade theory is based on the welfare of an entire nation, and a central tenet is the possibility for mutual gains of trade for each country.

Not everyone within a country may gain from trade, however, so we must also understand how the gains to some potentially offset the losses to others.

In the early twentieth century, two Swedish economists, Eli Heckscher and Bertil Ohlin, proposed a trade theory that focused on the availability of factors of production within a country (unskilled/skilled labor or capital) and differences in factor requirements in the production of goods. Their framework, the Heckscher–Ohlin model, still serves today as a powerful tool to develop intuition about why countries engage in trade. The fact that some iPod components are produced in so called "high-wage countries" contradicts assertions in the popular press that firms thrive by ruthlessly exploiting low-wage workers. Rather, the production of many commodities requires a good amount of skilled labor. Trade theory suggests how the mix of factor inputs required at each stage of a production process, together with the comparative costs of those inputs, influences the production location decision. When the supply chain is as fragmented as in the case of the iPod, inputs are sourced from many different countries, and we examine when outsourcing of production becomes an attractive option for firms and countries.

The fact that the iPod spawned a whole industry of subsequent products (such as the iPod Nano or the Microsoft Zune) suggests that our study of international trade must also account for the introduction of new products. Innovations require upfront costs of research and development (R&D). This implies that a company like Apple must have some market power to recover its R&D outlays. To do so, it must be able to charge a price that exceeds the unit cost of production. Subsequent chapters examine how trade is affected when markets are not competitive and firms have ownership or location advantages that allow them to differentiate their product, segment the market, and charge a price that exceeds marginal costs.

Multinational Corporations and Trade

Even if there were no differences in wages and interest rates across countries, Apple would be unlikely to locate a production plant in every single country where it sold iPods. Rather, firms seek to achieve economies of scale by concentrating production in just a few locations in order to spread the fixed costs of production over more units of output. Then the product is shipped internationally.

Yet, why does Apple outsource iPod production in the first place? Even if the company realizes that there are gains from trade and that it is advantageous to produce inputs in different countries, why doesn't Apple produce all the inputs itself? Is its most profitable strategy just to design and market products, not to produce them? When Apple assembles iPods in China, it does not do so in a factory owned by Apple. Rather, it contracts with a third party to produce according to the specifications it provides.

Actually, much of international trade does take place among affiliates and/or subsidiaries across the globe. No one pattern describes the production decision of all companies. When does a multinational seek to keep its production processes secret, and when can it risk outsourcing production? We devote a chapter to addressing such questions concerning the movement of companies across borders, and we additionally consider related incentives for the migration of labor and the flow of capital and technology.

How do Governments Influence International Trade?

Imagine the European Union imposed a 10 percent tariff on Japanese cars (well, actually it has) or that Canada imposed a $75 tax on iPods (as it attempted in January 2008, but the Canadian high court ruled the tariff was unconstitutional). One might jump to the conclusion that this action would simply add 10 percent to the price of Japanese cars in Europe, but things are more complicated than that. Prices are determined by the interaction between supply and demand, and the tariff may have induced Japanese companies to locate production plants within the European Union. The price of an iPod in Canada undoubtedly would have risen if the tax had been imposed, and Canadians would have lived with less music in their lives, unless they drove across the border to buy their iPods in the United States.

Starting in Chapter 6, we examine how government trade policies affect national welfare. Generally, the consequences for economic efficiency are negative. This immediately raises the question why governments choose to intervene in international trade in the first place. This question cannot be answered satisfactorily without formulating political economy models that consider not only the action of firms (such as Apple), but also the incentives of the owners of factors (such as workers) and the interests of politicians who serve specific interest groups or try to maximize their prospects of staying in office.

A further dimension of trade policy becomes apparent when we notice that all of Apple's suppliers are members of the World Trade Organization (WTO). Is this an accident? It turns out that multilateral tariff reductions via the WTO (or its predecessor the General Agreement on Tariffs and Trade, GATT) have been accompanied by enormous expansions of international trade. Why do countries join multilateral tariff reduction agreements, and how do these agreements contribute to the more intricate supply chains and marketing decisions of multinationals like Apple Inc.? Not all agreements are made within the halls of the WTO in Geneva, however. Some countries reduce their trade restrictions on a preferential basis for just some countries, as is done for fellow members of the European Union or the North American Free Trade Agreement. In those situations, does such trade liberalization help the members, but hurt those that are not members? We address these questions about alternative forms of government trade policy intervention in the chapters that follow our initial treatment of unilateral trade policy choices made by a single country.

Assembly of the iPod and other consumer electronics in China typically takes place in special enterprise zones where taxes on imports are waived as long as the final goods are exported. What makes that arrangement attractive to Chinese policy makers and to Apple? Debate over the appropriate trade policy for developing countries remains contentious. Even the claim that exports have been critical to the amazing growth of several Asian economies is disputed by some economists. You will be asked to assess those claims in the chapters ahead.

International Finance – Exchange Rates

Table 1.1 shows that at least seven companies in five countries are involved in iPod production. Each of these countries has its own national currency. How does Apple pay its trading partners in foreign countries? Where and how does it obtain foreign currency and at what price? Do foreign companies perhaps accept U.S. dollars, or do they seek payments in currencies that they can in turn use to purchase their own inputs? These are some of the questions we address in the second part of this textbook when we explicitly examine macroeconomic aspects of the international economy.

One building block that economists use to keep track of the sources of demand and supply of a currency internationally is a balance of payments sheet. The nature of Apple's iPod production and distribution should warn us that focusing on a balance of imports and exports with a single country, such as the U.S. trade balance with China, can be highly misleading, because only a small share of the value of an iPod is actually produced in China. Apple also has an incentive to declare its profits in locales where it can minimize its tax burden, which is likely to further influence the price it assigns to the assembled products it brings into the United States. In spite of these complications, which make it more difficult to interpret balance of payments entries than in previous eras, we still will find that they provide useful insights about what fundamental factors influence the market for a country's currency.

International trade involves the use of various currencies. A key question is to determine how we measure the price of foreign currency (i.e. the exchange rate), first when only one other country is involved and then when we account for the reality of a world with many trade partners and potential investors abroad. We should not be surprised that the price Apple Inc. has to pay for foreign currency directly influences its bottom line. The cost of a foreign component varies not only with the price quoted in a foreign currency, but also with the exchange rate. Indeed Apple's quarterly report to the U.S. Securities and Exchange Commission on July 23, 2008 indicates that:

> In general, the Company is a net receiver of currencies other than the U.S. dollar. Accordingly, changes in exchange rates, and in particular a strengthening of the U.S. dollar, will negatively affect the Company's net sales and gross margins as expressed in U.S. dollars.

How countries choose to intervene to influence their exchange rate is a basic national choice that impacts Apple's dealings in various markets. When Apple trades with a Japanese company, for example, the exchange rate can change from day to day (second by second, in fact). In contrast, the Chinese central bank plays a much more direct role in determining its exchange rate. Until July 2005, its policy was to fix the price it charged to exchange Chinese currency for U.S. dollars. In that setting, Apple could confidently forecast the Chinese/U.S. exchange rate weeks in advance!

Why would a country fix its exchange rate and what are the actual mechanics involved in such a "fix"? This type of government intervention sounds like price controls that you may have encountered in your introductory economics class (for example in agricultural markets). The international macroeconomics section of this textbook discusses in detail how exchange rate fluctuations can have a profound and, at times, adverse impact on the domestic economy. Hence it might be in the interest of a country to manage exchange rate fluctuations. Once we have developed a basic framework to analyze the open economy, we can examine how fiscal and monetary policies affect the exchange rate and output in a global economy. Then we can assess the costs and benefits associated with the different ways a central bank may choose to manage the value of its currency.

Open Economy Models and Policy

We begin our analysis of open economies by formulating simple models where there are no international capital flows. That is a far cry from the world confronting Apple, but that background helps us sort out the additional implications that capital flows introduce. When we allow for such flows, the many new innovations in international financial markets with respect to futures, forwards, swaps, and options play a significant role, and we devote a chapter to explaining the economic significance of that specialized collection of international financial instruments.

For a sample of what these financial innovations mean for Apple, consider another passage from its July 2008 report, which states that the company:

> may enter into foreign currency forward and option contracts with financial institutions to protect against foreign exchange risks associated with existing assets and liabilities, certain firmly committed transactions, forecasted future cash flows, and net investments in foreign subsidiaries. Generally, the Company's practice is to hedge a majority of its material foreign exchange exposures, typically for 3 to 6 months.

At this point, much of what Apple seems to be doing to insulate itself from foreign exchange risk may sound a bit like financial gibberish. We will demonstrate how those strategies help Apple limit the foreign exchange risks it faces and lock in future profits earned in different countries.

International financial flows have not only spawned financial innovations, but they also influence whether a government's monetary and fiscal policy is successful in stabilizing its economic performance. So the models of the earlier chapters must be extended to take into account these international flows of capital. For example, U.S. policy makers may favor very low interest rates to encourage more demand for housing and to promote recovery of the construction industry. When international capital flows are possible, the lower interest rate is likely to result in a capital outflow and a weaker dollar. That may spur U.S. exports and have a more immediate effect on U.S. output than any recovery in the housing market. With respect to the prospects of a single company such as Apple, the weaker dollar also means that its euro earnings translate into more dollars and allows it to report a higher profit rate to its stockholders.

The progression of models we use also allows for the effects of rising prices. While developing countries in particular have been remarkably more successful in controlling inflation in this decade than in previous decades, the implications of rising prices can be ignored only with great peril. A company such as Apple has a particular stake in China successfully managing to keep its economy from overheating and generating higher inflation rates; whether China maintains its billing as the workshop of the world depends importantly upon that answer.

International Monetary Developments

Over the past century or so, the financial monetary system has seen great changes. We have now reached an era with near perfect capital mobility and a host of new international financial entities, practices, and instruments, e.g. offshore operations, derivatives. These activities cannot be regulated at the national level, and international agencies need to scrutinize and police them. Multinationals such as Apple strive to do business in countries with a minimal level of regulations to maximize their profit, but this must be balanced against the risk of an international financial meltdown that would have dire consequences on their business.

Any text in international macroeconomics must address the European monetary integration. A large group of important countries sharing a common currency and instituting common financial regulations will certainly facilitate business dealings for a multinational such as Apple. Foreign exchange risk and accounting costs are reduced. On the other hand, the increase in transparency means that it will be easier for the currency union to impose its rules and scrutinize foreign multinationals. Apple has no choice but to adapt to the situation if it wants to serve the rising E.U. market.

We conclude with a chapter that shines a spotlight on the dark sides of international financial markets: International Currency Crises. More than a dozen countries have experienced severe financial market disturbances as the value of their currencies teeter on the edge of the abyss. Indeed currency crises are the scourge of multinationals. They have assets in many countries and their potential losses can be considerable. Two of the countries subject to speculative attacks at the time of the Asian currency crises, Korea and Taiwan, are now listed as main partners in the making of the iPods. In addition, the fact that these crises have a tendency to spread to neighboring countries makes them even more threatening for the iPod trade.

References and Suggestions for Further Reading

Apple Inc. (2008) *United States Securities and Exchange Commission, Form 10-Q, for the quarter ended 28 June 2008.* Available at http://www.secinfo.com/d14D5a.t4XXa.htm or http://www.sec.gov/Archives/edgar/data/320193/000119312508156421/d10q.htm (accessed 12 August 2008).

Linden, G., Kraemer, K., and Dedrick, J. (2008) "Who Captures Value in a Global Innovation System? The Case Apple's iPod," Personal Computing Industry Center, University of California, Irvine.

European Commission, Taxation and Customs Union, Databases, TARIC home page (2008). Available at http://ec.europa.eu/taxation_customs/dds/tarhome_en.htm (accessed 12 August 2008).

Fisher, K., (2008) "'iPod Tax' smacked down in Canada," *Arts Tecnica*. Available at http://arstechnica.com/news.ars/post/20080113-ipod-tax-smacked-down-in-canada.html (accessed 12 August 2008).

Part I

International Trade and Trade Policy

Why do we separate the material in this book into two distinct sections? Patterns of international trade and investment sometimes vary considerably from year to year, but they also demonstrate general trends over time. Factors that determine the volatility in the short run often differ from factors that determine the long-run trends. In the first half of this book, we pay primary attention to the longer-run determinants of these trends in international trade and investment. Economists often refer to these relationships as pertaining to the "real side of the economy." The goods a country trades are typically independent of whether the country fixes the value of its national currency in terms of gold, or euros, or the dollar. Likewise, a country's choice of monetary policy is not likely to have a permanent impact on whether it exports airplanes and imports shoes. Although such financial relationships are a significant part of our discussion of international finance in the second half of this book, we largely ignore them in our treatment of trade theory and trade policy.

Chapter 2 is based on the ideas classical economists Adam Smith and David Ricardo presented 200 years ago to support the claim that there are mutual gains from trade. That position was a major contrast to the prevailing mercantilistic view that exports allow a country gain while imports represent a loss. The principle of comparative advantage is fundamental to understanding why trade is not a zero sum game where the benefit to one country must come at the expense of the other country. Yet, this powerful insight does not tell us exactly how these gains are divided. Although we consider John Stuart Mill's approach to answering that question in Chapter 2, we provide a more complete answer in Chapter 3, which introduces the role of individual and community preferences, as well as production conditions, based on the graphical toolkit of the neoclassical economists.

Although the classical framework assumed that differences in labor productivity across countries caused differences in costs and created the basis for trade, two Swedish economists, Eli Heckscher and Bertil Ohlin, proposed an alternative reason for costs to differ across countries: differences in the availability of factor inputs. For example, countries that are relatively abundant in labor will export labor-intensive goods. That theory is presented in Chapter 4. Economists have found this a useful approach, not only to predict how a country's pattern of trade may change as its factor endowments change, but also to make strong predictions about the consequences of trade on the distribution of income: trade benefits abundant factors used intensively in export production and hurts scarce factors used intensively in import-competing production. The theoretical completeness of this model makes it an attractive one for economists to use, but when economists try to test its implications empirically, they often discover that it does not explain trade that well. We include these developments in Chapter 4.

The factor endowments model also assumes perfectly competitive markets, a condition that does not characterize much of the trade between industrialized countries, where imperfect competition and economies of scale play an important role. Chapter 5 presents several alternative partial-equilibrium explanations of production and trade with imperfectly competitive markets. Gains from trade still exist and often are likely to be magnified. To look at the effects of trade allowing for adjustments outside any single industry is more difficult when not all markets are competitive. Economists have had the most success assuming that markets are characterized by monopolistic competition, with lots of product varieties and low barriers to enter the industry. In one set of these models, trade has less drastic implications for the distribution of income, because trade does not cause relative prices to change. When that framework is altered to take into account the cost of transporting goods from one country to another, however, economists suggest that an advanced core of countries and a laggard periphery may develop.

Chapters 6 and 7 examine the consequences of trade barriers that reduce but do not eliminate trade. In a world with competitive markets, trade barriers reduce economic efficiency and leave a small country worse off, as shown in Chapter 6. When a country is large enough to affect prices internationally or when distortions in the domestic economy exist, an activist trade policy using trade barriers and subsidies may make a country better off on theoretical grounds, as analyzed in Chapter 7. To successfully implement such a policy in a political setting where there are many competing claimants for protection is a tall order indeed. In fact, we may be surprised that trade is as open as it is, given the responsiveness of politicians in countries like the U.S. to special interests.

Although the factor endowments theory of trade in goods and services ignored any movement of labor and capital across borders, in Chapter 8 we allow for those possibilities. We develop the reasons that many countries have sought to encourage the immigration of skilled labor but discourage the immigration of unskilled labor. Conversely, we examine the argument that developing countries lose from a brain drain, as the return they expect from greater public expenditures on education may not materialize. In the case of capital mobility internationally, we find world production can become more efficient, but again, in a setting where public expenditures and taxation are considered, not all countries may gain. Finally, we consider the operations of multinational corporations, and make important distinctions between horizontal and vertical integration in predicting what conditions will attract such activity. We also examine what evidence economists have found to judge whether there are benefits from attracting MNC operations.

Regional trade blocs, such as the European Union or the North American Free Trade Area, are agreements to reduce trade barriers on a preferential or discriminatory basis for members only. Chapter 9 assesses whether such blocs are likely to increase welfare, because they liberalize trade, or reduce welfare, because they divert production to less efficient producers. Advocates of multilateral trade liberalization fear the losses from such trade diversion. They point to the benefits of a trade system open to all countries, especially a rule-based system that disciplines the practices of large countries that otherwise could gain at the expense of smaller countries. Chapter 10 considers the rationale for acting multilaterally. It examines the successes and shortcomings of the General Agreement on Tariffs and Trade, and its successor, the World Trade Organization, in removing barriers to trade and enforcing the members' commitments.

Chapter 11 examines the way growth affects trade and vice versa. For most industrialized countries the most important source of growth has been rising factor productivity. Therefore, models that explain why factor productivity rises are necessary. By extending the learning by doing the model of dynamic economies of scale familiar from Chapter 5, we find that multiple answers are possible regarding the possibility for developing countries to catch up with industrialized countries. No single policy prescription emerges. The role of trade policy in promoting economic development has long been controversial, and we review two poles of that debate: import substitution industrialization and export-led growth. We then turn to more recent interpretations of what lessons can be distilled from countries that have grown successfully over several decades. The chapter also includes material on growth, industrialization, and the negative environmental externalities generated. Some externalities are local, while others are not limited to a single country, as illustrated by the case of global warming. We review aspects of both situations and point to some of the challenges in addressing them successfully.

Chapter 2

Why Do Nations Trade? Some Early Answers

LEARNING OBJECTIVES

By the end of this chapter you should be able to explain:

- how both countries gain from trade based on absolute advantage
- how both countries gain from trade based on comparative advantage
- how demand conditions help determine international prices or the ratio in which goods are exchanged
- how the comparative advantage model appears to predict patterns of trade successfully

Nations (more accurately, individuals and firms in different nations) trade with each other because they benefit from it. Other motives may be involved, of course, but the basic motivation for international trade is the gain to the participants. In this chapter, we examine the fundamental insights of classical economists who wrote in the late eighteenth and early nineteenth centuries. They noted that gains from international trade arise because specialization enables resources to be allocated to their most productive uses in each trading nation. Everyone recognizes that it would be foolish for a town or a province to try to be self-sufficient, but we often fail to recognize that the benefits of specialization and the division of labor also exist in international trade. The political boundaries that divide geographic areas into nations do not change the fundamental nature of trade, nor do they remove the benefits it confers on the trading partners. Our goal in this chapter is to establish and illustrate this basic truth.

ABSOLUTE ADVANTAGE

Adam Smith's original statement of the case for trade, contained in *The Wealth of Nations* (1776), was couched in terms of absolute cost differences between countries. That is, Smith assumed that each country could produce one or more commodities at a lower real cost than its trading partners. It then follows that each country will benefit from specialization in those commodities in which it has an **absolute advantage** (i.e. can produce at lower real cost than another country), exporting them and importing other commodities that it produces at a higher real cost than does another country.

The Labor Theory of Value

"Real cost," for Smith, meant the amount of labor time required to produce a commodity. His analysis was based on the labor theory of value, which treats labor as the only factor of production and holds that commodities exchange for one another in proportion to the number of hours required for their production. For example, if 10 hours of labor are required to produce a shirt, and 40 hours to produce a pair of shoes, then four shirts will exchange for one pair of shoes. The labor embodied in four shirts equals the labor embodied in one pair of shoes. Costs can be expressed without any reference to money or gold. This approach holds as long as labor can move freely from one industry to another.

Within a single country, competition ensures that commodities exchange in the market in proportion to their labor cost. In our example of shirts and shoes, if an individual is quoted a price of 6 shirts to acquire 1 pair of shoes, she will refuse such a trade. In the time she must spend to make 6 shirts, she can make 1.5 pairs of shoes. For that reason she will be unwilling to offer more than 4 shirts in exchange for a pair of shoes, because with 40 hours of labor she can produce either 4 shirts or 1 pair of shoes. Similarly, she will not accept fewer than 4 shirts in exchange for 1 pair of shoes. If all workers in a country have the same productivity as the one considered above (the labor force is homogeneous), and they can move freely between the two industries, shirts and shoes will be exchanged in proportion to their labor cost.

Because of legal and cultural restrictions, however, labor does not move freely between nations. To simplify the analysis, we make the classical economists' assumption that labor is completely immobile between nations. If labor requirements differ across countries, then in the absence of trade, prices of goods will differ across countries. Adam Smith ignored the way an equilibrium price might be reached among trading nations. He instead demonstrated the proposition that a nation benefits from trade in which it exports those commodities it can produce at lower real cost than other countries, and imports those commodities it produces at a higher real cost than other countries.

Comparing Costs across Countries

An arithmetical example helps to illustrate the case of absolute cost differences. Suppose that, as shown in Table 2.1, in Scotland it takes 30 days to produce a bolt of cloth and 120 days to produce a barrel of wine, whereas in Italy it takes 100 days to produce a bolt of cloth and only 20 days to produce a barrel of wine. (Each commodity is assumed to be identical in both countries, which ignores the problem of the likely quality of Scottish wine.) Scottish producers have an absolute advantage in cloth production – they can produce a bolt of cloth at a lower real cost than can producers in Italy – whereas Italian producers have an absolute advantage in wine production. Consequently, each country will benefit if its producers specialize in the commodity in which they have an absolute advantage, obtaining the other commodity through trade. The benefit derives from obtaining the imported commodity at a lower real cost through trade than through direct production at home.

In the absence of trade, in Scotland one barrel of wine will exchange for four bolts of cloth; in Italy one barrel of wine will exchange for one-fifth of a bolt of cloth. Scottish producers benefit if they can trade less than four bolts of cloth for one barrel of wine, while Italian producers benefit if they can obtain more than one-fifth of a bolt of cloth for one barrel of wine. Clearly, both countries can gain at an intermediate ratio such as one barrel of wine for one bolt of cloth. At that price ratio, Scottish producers see the price of a bolt of cloth rise from one quarter of a barrel of wine to 1 barrel of wine.

TABLE 2.1 An Example of Absolute Advantage

Days of labor required to produce	Italy	Scotland
Wine (1 barrel)	20	120
Cloth (1 bolt)	100	30

TABLE 2.2 The Gain in Output from Trade with an Absolute Advantage

	Italy	Scotland	Total
Wine (barrels)	30	–5	25
Cloth (bolts)	–6	20	14

They have an incentive to expand cloth production because the international price ratio exceeds the domestic cost of production. Correspondingly, Italian producers see the price of a barrel of wine rise from one fifth of a bolt of cloth to 1 bolt of cloth. Because the international price exceeds their domestic cost of production, Italian producers will increase their output of wine.

The possible efficiency gains for the combined economies of Scotland and Italy in this situation can be seen by noting what will happen if each country shifts 600 days of labor from the production of the commodity in which it is inefficient toward one it produces efficiently. If Scotland moves 600 labor days from wine production to cloth, while Italy shifts 600 labor days in the opposite direction, the production changes shown in Table 2.2 will occur in each country. With no increase in labor inputs, the combined economy of the two countries gains 14 bolts of cloth and 25 barrels of wine. These gains in the production of both goods resulted from merely shifting 600 labor days in each country toward more efficient uses. If 1,200 labor days were shifted by each country instead of 600, the gains would be twice as large.

This explanation, based on absolute advantage, certainly suffices to account for important segments of international trade. Brazil can produce coffee at a lower real cost than can Germany; Florida can produce oranges at a lower real cost than Iceland; Australia can produce wool at a lower real cost than Switzerland. But what if a nation (or an individual) does not have an absolute advantage in any line of production? Does trade then offer it no benefit?

COMPARATIVE ADVANTAGE

David Ricardo, in his *Principles of Political Economy and Taxation* (1817), showed that the gains from trade hold in a more general set of circumstances and do not depend upon a country or an individual having an absolute cost advantage. Instead, trade will benefit both nations, provided only that their relative costs, that is, the ratios of their real costs in terms of labor inputs, are different for two or more commodities. In short, trade depends on comparative advantage, and one nation can profitably trade with another even though its real costs are higher (or lower) in every commodity. This point can best be explained through a numerical example.

Ricardo presented the case of potential trade in wine and cloth between Portugal and England. His original example assumed that producers in Portugal were more efficient than the English in producing both goods, circumstances that undoubtedly caught the attention of his readers. We consider a slightly different example here to demonstrate the same point. Table 2.3 presents the costs of producing a bolt of cloth or a barrel of wine in each of the two countries, measured in terms of days

TABLE 2.3 An Example of Comparative Advantage

Days of labor required to produce	Portugal	England
Wine (1 barrel)	3	2
Cloth (1 bolt)	10	4

of labor. Here, the English are more efficient at the production of both goods. Less labor is required to produce either good in England than in Portugal. To explain the pattern of trade, however, that fact is irrelevant. What is important is that Portugal has a comparative advantage in wine, whereas England has a comparative advantage in cloth.

The English can produce either two barrels of wine or one bolt of cloth with the same amount of labor (4 days). By shifting labor from wine to cloth production, they can transform two barrels of wine into one bolt of cloth. The Portuguese, however, can produce either 3.33 barrels of wine or one bolt of cloth with the same labor (10 days). Therefore by shifting labor from cloth to wine production, the Portuguese can transform one bolt of cloth into 3.33 barrels of wine. In comparative terms, cloth is inexpensive in England and expensive in Portugal, whereas wine is cheap in Portugal and costly in England. A bolt of cloth costs only two barrels of wine in England, but the same bolt of cloth costs 3.33 barrels of wine in Portugal. When viewed from the perspective of wine, we see that a barrel costs one-half of a bolt of cloth in England, but only one-third of a bolt of cloth in Portugal. These differences in the relative costs of one good in terms of the other create Portugal's comparative advantage in wine and England's in cloth.

Trade with Comparative Advantage

The efficiency gains that this pattern of comparative advantage makes possible can be seen by imagining that Portugal shifts 60 days of labor from the production of cloth to employment in the wine industry, whereas England shifts 36 days of labor in the opposite direction, that is, from wine to cloth production. Given the labor costs presented in Table 2.3, the result of these shifts of labor use would be as shown in Table 2.4. Total output of both goods rises when Portugal shifts 60 labor days from cloth to wine production and England shifts 36 labor days from wine to cloth production. The combined economies of Portugal and England can drink two more barrels of wine and wear clothes using three more bolts of cloth, even though there has been no increase in labor use. Note that to guarantee that total output of both goods rises, Portugal must shift more labor days than England because Portugal produces less efficiently in absolute terms. If both countries had shifted the same number of labor days, there would have been a far larger increase in cloth production and a small reduction in wine output.

Another way to understand the nature of these gains from applying comparative advantage is to imagine that someone had the monopoly right to trade between London and Lisbon. If the labor costs

TABLE 2.4 The Gain in Output From Trade with Comparative Advantage

	Portugal	England	Total
Wine (barrels)	20	−18	2
Cloth (bolts)	−6	9	3

presented in Table 2.3 prevailed and labor were the only input, the price ratios faced by the monopoly trader in the two countries would be as shown in Table 2.5. In Portugal a bolt of cloth is 3.33 times as expensive as a barrel of wine, whereas in England cloth is only twice as costly as wine. The difference in these two **barter exchange ratios** creates an enormously profitable opportunity for the monopoly trader. Starting out with 100 bolts of cloth in London, the trader ships that merchandise to Lisbon, where it can be exchanged for 333.3 barrels of wine. The 333.3 barrels are put on the ship back to London, where they are bartered for 166.7 bolts of cloth. The trader started out with 100 bolts of cloth and now has 166.7 bolts, thereby earning a return of 66.7 percent minus shipping costs by simply trading around in a circle between London and Lisbon.[1]

The monopoly trader merely took advantage of the differing price ratios in England and Portugal, which were based on differing relative labor costs, and made an enormous profit. Now imagine that the monopoly has been eliminated and that anyone who wishes to do so can trade between London and Lisbon. As large numbers of people purchase cloth in London, with the intention of shipping it to Lisbon, they will drive the English price of cloth up. When these same people arrive in Lisbon and sell this large amount of cloth, they will depress the price. As these same traders buy large amounts of Portuguese wine to ship to London, they will drive the Lisbon price of wine up. When they all arrive in London to sell that wine, they will push the price down.

TABLE 2.5 Domestic Exchange Ratios in Portugal and England

	Portugal	England
Wine (barrels)	3.33	2
Cloth (bolts)	1	1

---

1 Such monopolies existed in the sixteenth, seventeenth, and eighteenth centuries as European governments gave corporations, such as the British East India Company, the sole right to trade between the home country and a foreign area or colony. The resulting profits were typically shared with the government through taxes, although such tax payments were in part compensation for the government's use of its navy to provide security for the corporation's ships.

As a result of trade, the price ratios are converging. As the price of cloth rises in London and falls in Lisbon, while the price of wine rises in Portugal and falls in England, the large profits previously earned by the traders decline. In a competitive equilibrium, the differences in the price ratios would be just sufficient to cover transport costs and provide a minimum competitive rate of return for the traders. For simplicity we will ignore transport costs and the minimum return for the traders; free trade will result in a single price ratio that prevails in both countries. That price ratio will be somewhere between the two initial price ratios in Portugal and England.

Gains from Trade versus No Trade

Does this mean that the gains from trade, which were previously concentrated in the profits of the monopoly trader, have disappeared? No, it merely means that these gains have been shifted away from the trader and toward the societies of Portugal and England through changes in the price ratios. When the monopolist controlled trade between the two countries, England had to export one bolt of cloth to get two barrels of wine. Now that competition prevails, the English price of cloth has risen while the price of wine has declined. Consequently, a bolt of cloth exported by England will pay for considerably more wine, or significantly less exported cloth will pay for the same amount of wine. England now has an improved standard of living because it can have more wine, or more cloth, or both. A similar outcome arises in Portugal. In Lisbon the price of wine has risen and the price of cloth has declined; thus the same amount of wine exported will purchase more cloth, or the same amount of cloth can be purchased with less wine. Portugal also has an improved standard of living because it can consume more cloth, or more wine, or both.

This demonstration, that the gain from trade arises from differences in comparative cost, has been hailed as one of the greatest achievements of economic analysis. It may seem to be a rather small point to warrant such extravagant praise, but it has proven to have a great many applications in economics and in other fields of study as well. Ricardo presented the following common-sense application in another of his examples:

> Two men can make both shoes and hats, and one is superior to the other in both employments, but in making hats he can only exceed his competitor by one-fifth or 20 per cent, and in making shoes he can excel him by one-third or 33 per cent; – will it not be for the interest of both that the superior man should employ himself exclusively in making shoes, and the inferior man in making hats? (p.83)

It is the principle of comparative advantage that underlies the gain from a division of labor, whether between individuals, firms, regions, or nations. We specialize in those activities in which we have a relative advantage, depending on others to supply us with other goods and services. Because of this specialization, real income increases.

RECIPROCAL DEMAND AND PRICES INTERNATIONALLY

The classical economist John Stuart Mill extended the analysis of Smith and Ricardo to consider the additional question of how the equilibrium international price or ratio of exchange is established. He introduced demand considerations into the analysis by noting that at the equilibrium ratio of exchange, the amount of the export good one country offers must exactly equal the amount the other country is willing to purchase. He referred to this equilibrium as one characterized by equal reciprocal demands. If trade is to balance, as we assume here, this condition must be met for each country's export good.

Consider an example from Mill. Suppose a given amount of labor, say a man-day, will produce the amounts of broadcloth and linen shown in Table 2.6. Note that Mill has changed the way of stating the relationship between cost and output. Instead of giving the amount of labor required to produce a given output, as Ricardo did, he states the output that can be produced by a given input of labor. Based on the labor theory of value, 10 meters of cloth will exchange for 15 meters of linen in England; 10 meters of cloth will exchange for 20 meters of linen in Germany. England has a comparative advantage in cloth and Germany has a comparative advantage in linen.

With the opening of trade between England and Germany, England will benefit from trade if it can obtain more than 15 linen for 10 cloth, while Germany will benefit if it can obtain 10 cloth for less than 20 linen. Thus, the range within which the actual barter terms of trade will lie extends from $10C:15L$ to $10C:20L$. Mill then observed that the willingness of each country to trade will depend on the barter terms of trade. At a ratio very near $10C:15L$, England will gain little and thus will not offer much cloth for export. Germany will find that ratio attractive and will demand a large amount of cloth and offer much linen in exchange. In that case, German demand for cloth imports will exceed the English supply of cloth exports, and the price of cloth in terms of linen will have to rise. As the real exchange ratio rises, to $10C:16L$ or $10C:17L$, England will tend to offer more cloth and to demand more linen, whereas Germany will tend to demand less cloth and hence offer less linen.

Mill showed that, within the terms set by the initial cost conditions in each country, the barter terms of trade will be determined by the demand in each country for the other country's export. In his chapter on international value, Mill analyzed the influence of the elasticity of demand, country size, changes in technology, and other factors on the terms of trade, and some of those possibilities are addressed in the problems at the end of the chapter.

TABLE 2.6 Another Example of Comparative Advantage, Based on Output Per Man-Day

Country	Sq. meters of Broadcloth	Sq. meters of Linen
England	10	15
Germany	10	20

Reciprocal Demand through Demand and Supply Curves

The classical economists did not use the supply and demand framework familiar to students of introductory economics classes today. Nevertheless, we can represent their ideas in such a framework to better indicate the market adjustments they had in mind as an equilibrium price is established. We illustrate that framework in Figure 2.1 for the cloth market. With no money in the economy, however, all prices must be expressed as a barter exchange ratio, such as 1.5 meters of linen per meter of cloth. Furthermore, the labor theory of value, together with constant productivity of labor, imply a horizontal supply curve, until all available labor is employed in cloth production. At that point the supply curve becomes vertical because a higher price cannot attract any more labor into cloth production.

For Mill's example, the corresponding demand and supply representation is given by the three panels of Figure 2.1. The left panel represents supply and demand conditions in England, the right panel the supply and demand conditions in Germany, and the center panel the market for cloth traded internationally. The demand curves represent the hypothetical preferences of consumers in each country. The intersection of the demand curve with the horizontal section of the country's supply curve demonstrates how much cloth is demanded in each country if no trade is allowed.

If England were to produce only cloth at the 1.5 price, then the difference between its total output of cloth, C_{max}, and the amount that consumers demand at home, C_0, would be the amount of cloth its firms could export in exchange for linen. Its consumers would not gain from such trade, however, because the amount of linen obtained would be exactly the same as when the labor used in export production of cloth was transferred into linen production in England. Only if the international price rises above the domestic cost of 1.5 will England gain. If the price rises above 1.5, say to 1.7, then English consumers choose to buy less cloth, at C^*. A greater quantity of cloth is available to export, and English consumers benefit from the opportunity to acquire linen more cheaply in exchange for the cloth that they give up.

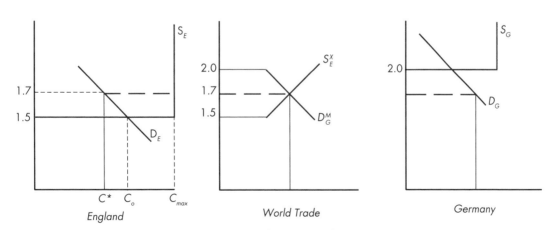

FIGURE 2.1 A Supply–Demand Representation of the Market for Cloth

At a price of 1.7, the quantity of cloth English firms want to export just equals the quantity of cloth German consumers want to import.

Conversely, in Germany at any price below 2 meters of linen, German producers find it unattractive to produce any cloth at all. German consumers will import all their cloth from England. As the price falls further below 2, German consumers will increase the quantity of cloth that they demand. The price 1.7 will be an equilibrium if the quantity of cloth English firms want to export exactly matches the quantity of cloth German consumers want to import. That outcome is shown in the center panel, where the English export supply curve and the German import demand curve have been derived from the difference between the quantity produced and the quantity consumed at each price in both countries.

We have only shown the equilibrium in the cloth market, but in a two-good world, that is sufficient to guarantee that the linen market is in equilibrium, too. Recognize that the English supply of cloth also represents a demand for linen. At a price of 1.7, an English supply of 100 meters of cloth represents a demand for 170 meters of linen. Correspondingly, in Germany a demand for 100 meters of cloth represents a willingness to supply 170 meters of linen.

Transport Costs and the Effect on Trade

Transport costs influence what goods are traded internationally and how much a country gains from trade. In terms of the example given in Figure 2.1, suppose that the amount of labor necessary to transport 10 square meters of cloth from England to Germany was 0.5 man days. Under those circumstances, the price of English cloth in Germany rises and the export supply curve must be shifted up. Not only must 1.5 meters of linen be given up in order to produce an extra meter of cloth, but transporting it to Germany would divert additional labor that could have produced 0.75 meters of linen. Thus, an English producer would only be willing to export to Germany if the price were 2.25 meters of linen or higher. Because Germany can produce its own cloth at a cost of only 2 meters of linen, the imported English cloth is no longer attractive, and cloth becomes a nontraded good.

When transport costs fall relative to the value of the good being transported, more goods are likely to become tradable. Historically, this ratio of trade costs fell substantially in the latter half of the nineteenth century up to World War I, as steam ships replaced sailing ships and input costs of coal and metal-hulled shipping fell. Saif Mohammed and Jeffrey Williamson (2004) document these trends, as shown in Figure 2.2. While the declining cost of ocean freight is especially important in explaining the first wave of globalization before 1914, in the more recent wave of globalization ocean freight rates have not declined nearly as rapidly as air freight.

The additional competition posed by greater merchandise trade in the late nineteenth century often resulted in political pressure to impose other barriers to trade in continental Europe, Latin America, and former British colonies. We examine the causes and consequences of trade policy in subsequent chapters.

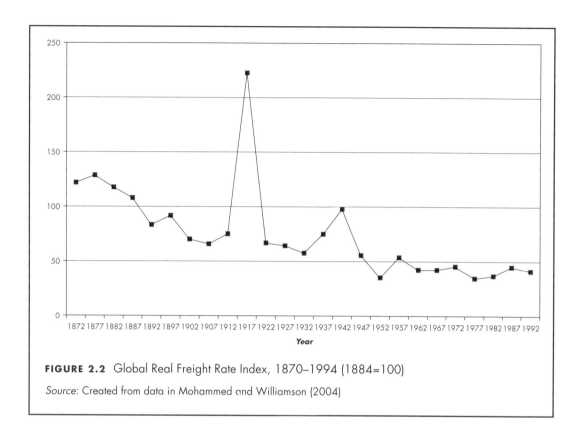

FIGURE 2.2 Global Real Freight Rate Index, 1870–1994 (1884=100)

Source: Created from data in Mohammed and Williamson (2004)

COMPARATIVE ADVANTAGE WITH MANY GOODS

Thus far we have presented comparative advantage for only two countries and two goods, with the assumption of no transport costs. The real world, of course, includes thousands of goods, almost 200 countries, and significant transport costs. How is a country's trade pattern established in this more realistic situation?

For a single country in a world with many goods, consider a rank-ordering of those products, from a country's greatest comparative advantage to its greatest comparative disadvantage. We want this ranking to represent the marginal cost of production in Country A relative to the marginal cost of production in Country B (which represents the rest of the world), for each of the many goods that can be produced. Under the labor theory of value, this ranking of relative costs will depend upon the ratio of labor productivities in each country, assuming labor earns the same wage wherever it is employed within the country.

To generate such a ranking for Country A, begin by recognizing that the marginal cost of cloth production (MC_c) equals the wage rate (w) times the amount of labor required per unit output (L/Q_c):

$$MC_C^A = w^A \ (L/Q)_C^A \tag{2.1}$$

In a barter economy, the price of cloth is the amount of another good, say oats, given up to buy one unit of cloth. Wages also are measured by this same standard, the amount of oats that labor receives per hour of work. With respect to the expression for marginal cost, we can see that A's marginal cost of production will be higher when its wage rate is higher and lower when its labor productivity is higher, because labor productivity (output per hour of labor input) is just the inverse of labor required per unit of output. We can write the same relationship for country B:

$$MC_C^B = w^B \ (L/Q)_C^B \tag{2.2}$$

and form the ratio of these two marginal cost terms:

$$\frac{MC_C^A = w^A \ (L/Q)_C^A}{MC_C^B = w^B \ (L/Q)_C^B} \tag{2.3}$$

It is the ranking of these ratios across all goods that we want to consider in predicting the pattern of trade that will emerge.

Establishing the Competitiveness of Different Goods

Suppose we can calculate this ratio of marginal costs for cloth, oats, and steel, and the ranking turns out to be:

$$\frac{w^A \ (L/Q)_C^A}{w^B \ (L/Q)_C^B} < \frac{w^A \ (L/Q)_O^A}{w^B \ (L/Q)_O^B} < \frac{w^A \ (L/Q)_S^A}{w^B \ (L/Q)_S^B} \tag{2.4}$$

We can see that A has the greatest productivity advantage in cloth production, which gives it a relatively lower marginal cost in cloth, and the least advantage in steel. As long as there is a single wage rate in each country, the ratio (w^A/w^B) is simply a constant term that does not affect the comparative advantage ranking across industries; relative labor productivities determine the ranking.

From our discussion of reciprocal demand and the determination of equilibrium prices internationally when each country's trade must be balanced, we have the necessary framework to determine the demand for output and labor in each country and the ratio of wages in A and B. The greater the world demand for cloth, for example, where Country A has a comparative advantage, the higher the wage in Country A will be relative to Country B. Correspondingly, Country A will be more likely to import both steel and oats from Country B.

Distinguishing between Traded and Nontraded Goods

From the standpoint of a single country considering what to trade with the rest of the world, we predict that it will export goods at the top of the list and import goods at the bottom of the list. Most small countries will export large amounts of a few goods and import smaller amounts of many goods. A country will tend to trade primarily with those countries that normally import its strongest comparative-advantage goods and/or export its strongest comparative-disadvantage goods. Trade volumes will be larger with countries that represent particularly large markets for exports or sources of imports, that is, countries with large populations and high levels of GNP per capita. There will be a number of goods, most likely in the middle of a country's comparative-advantage rank-ordering, that it will neither export nor import, becase its comparative advantage or disadvantage in these products is too slight to overcome transport costs. Such products will be produced domestically in sufficient volume for local consumption. The heavier or bulkier products are, the more likely they are to be nontradables: for example, very few countries export or import gravel and sand. Transport costs will also mean that a country will tend to trade more with its neighbors and less with more distant countries.

Air Transport, Trade, and Wages

The two-good, two-country examples of Smith, Ricardo, and Mill imply a certain symmetry – what one country exports the other must import – that does not hold when more than two countries exist. When additional countries exist, however, they are unlikely to be equidistant from each other and transport costs will have a separate influence on the pattern of trade and wages.

James Harrigan (2005) presents a three-country Ricardian model with many goods and a role for transport costs. Producers have the opportunity to rely on more timely but more expensive air freight as well as surface transport. He suggests thinking of the U.S., Mexico, and China in this framework, and he addresses the types of goods Mexico and China may export to the U.S. He notes the importance of relative labor productivities and relative wage rates in Mexico and China, but he derives additional implications for the pattern of trade from the existence of transportation costs, especially the cost of air freight relative to surface transport. Here are some of his major predictions:

- For similar productivities in both countries, China's wages must be lower than Mexico's to allow China to export a given good;
- All else equal, China will export lighter goods that have greater value per kilo, while Mexico will have a comparative advantage in heavier goods with lower values per kilo;
- A decline in the relative cost of air transport will allow China to export goods with a lower value per kilo, and the greater demand for Chinese labor will raise its wage rate;
- A decline in the relative cost of air transport will cause Mexico to produce and export a narrower range of heavy goods, and the reduced demand for Mexican labor will lower its wage rate.

In a real world application, there are more than two source countries, and therefore finding evidence of these relationships is more complex. Based on U.S. trade data for the period 1990–2003, Harrigan finds that the share of imports sent by air has remained essentially zero for Canada and Mexico, but risen from 20 percent to 30 percent for East Asia, over a time period when the cost of air freight fell by 40 percent relative to surface transport. The reliance on air freight is particularly high for electronic components and machinery, pharmaceuticals, and labor-intensive manufactures such as apparel, but low for raw materials and capital-intensive basic metals, such as petroleum and steel.

He performs a more formal test by estimating how the value of a unit of U.S. imports differs by country for very narrowly defined categories of goods (10-digit HS code). (A unit value is just the value of imports divided by the quantity of imports, as in dollars per kilogram.) He explains these import values as a function of distance and the share of imports that arrive by air, as well as additional factors that may contribute to a country's ability to charge a higher price for its goods. He predicts that within a given product category, more distant countries will have a higher unit value of their exports and ship them by air, while neighboring countries will specialize in low-value goods. Also, when shipping costs and tariffs are a large share of the delivered value of a product, those charges are likely to result in a lower unit value measured at the point of embarkation. That is, producers (and workers in a Ricardian model) bear part of the burden of the transport costs, because producers must reduce their costs to be competitive with goods from countries that are closer.

Harrigan finds that if he divides countries into two groups, those greater than 4,000 kilometers from the U.S. and those that are closer, the consequence of being a more distant country is that its unit values will be 140 to 170 percent higher than the closer countries. If he also controls on the share of shipments that arrive by air, that variable has a particularly large effect, yielding unit values 300 to 500 percent higher than for surface trade. Finally, countries that export goods that face higher transport costs and tariffs offer a slightly lower export price.

EMPIRICAL VERIFICATION IN A WORLD WITH MANY GOODS

Attempts to test the predictions of the models discussed in this chapter have rested on the many-goods framework just discussed. The classical labor theory of value with constant labor productivities suggests a very direct test of the comparative-advantage model: countries will export goods in which their productivity relative to other countries is high. The prediction is clear-cut in the classical case, because costs of production will be the same before and after trade occurs. The fact that economists do not observe relative costs of production before trade occurs does not matter, because the same relative cost rankings will prevail after trade occurs.

One of the earliest systematic tests was reported by G.D.A. MacDougall (1951). He based his analysis on labor productivity in 25 different U.S. and British industries and their exports in 1937, which were largely made to third-country markets. MacDougall found that for 97 percent of the trade covered in his data set, the U.K. exported more than the United States whenever the U.S. advantage in labor productivity was less than twice U.K. productivity, whereas the United States exported more than the U.K. whenever the U.S. labor productivity was more than twice U.K. productivity. Because the U.S. wage rate on average was twice the British rate at that time, this relationship confirmed that relative labor costs determined the pattern of trade, as suggested by the chain of comparative advantage presented above. For example, U.S. labor productivity in cotton spinning and weaving was 1.5 times U.K. productivity, but with U.S. wages 1.7 times U.K. wages, U.S. producers had a price disadvantage relative to U.K. producers. British exports in this industry were nine times U.S. exports. The relationship MacDougall found was linear when expressed in logarithms or shown on a logarithmic scale as in Figure 2.3.

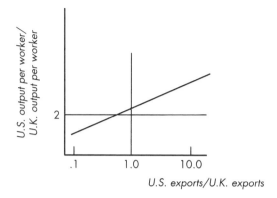

FIGURE 2.3 An Empirical Demonstration of the Relationship between Relative Labor Productivities and Trade

For a greater U.S. productivity advantage relative to the U.K., U.S. exports relative to U.K. exports tend to rise.

This outcome (the greater the relative U.S. productivity advantage, the greater the U.S./U.K. export ratio) is not particularly what the pure classical model would predict. In a world with constant costs, the country with the lower relative cost of producing a good should be its only producer. MacDougall's result does make sense if we relax some of the assumptions of the classical model. For example, if we allow for transportation costs internationally or quality differences in the goods produced by different countries, we can justify the existence of more than one producer. France may choose to import from the U.K. while Canada may choose to import from the United States if U.K. and U.S. labor costs are similar and any production cost difference is offset by a greater difference in transportation costs. Or, differences in product qualities may play a role if some French consumers prefer American cigarettes while other French consumers prefer British cigarettes. Nevertheless, we can see why a progressively larger U.S. productivity advantage, and consequently more favorable price, could come to overshadow transport costs or quality differences and result in a larger U.S. share of the export market.

A final result to note is that even though the United States had an absolute advantage in all of the industries examined, that did not prevent the U.K. from having a comparative advantage in some industries. The U.S. cost was higher in British export industries, such as cotton textiles, because of the high demand for U.S. labor in other industries where its relative productivity was much greater, such as automobiles. The high demand for labor in auto production bid up U.S. wage rates and raised the cost of producing U.S. cotton textiles.

The fact that the model of comparative advantage based on the labor theory of value predicts trade so well is rather remarkable. Some of the simplifying assumptions made, such as a nationwide wage rate or the existence of only a single factor of production, seem extreme. We must remind ourselves, however, that economists do not judge a model by the reasonableness of its assumptions, but by its ability to explain observed behavior and predict future behavior. From that standpoint, the classical model has shortcomings because it allows us to ask only a limited set of questions. For instance, it does not address why differences in productivity arise across countries or how they might change in the future. There is no basis for considering whether a government can affect the country's autarky cost conditions. A favorable climate may provide a permanent basis for comparative advantage in some industries. However, a more general appeal to differences in technology, which for some reason exist but cannot be transferred from one country to another, is not likely to give us much insight into likely changes in what is traded internationally. In subsequent chapters we present models that can better address these issues and also raise other issues that are overlooked in the classical approach.

Summary of Key Concepts

1. Adam Smith demonstrated that gains from specialization are possible when countries trade.
2. A country that can produce more output of a good per unit of input than other countries can have an absolute advantage in producing that good and should export it. The country should import those goods where it has an absolute disadvantage and produces less per unit of input than other countries can.
3. Trade makes it possible for world output and consumption to rise, even though individuals are working no harder than before trade.
4. David Ricardo demonstrated that the basis for gains from trade is the existence of comparative advantage, not absolute advantage.
5. A country that is less productive in producing both goods still gains from trade by exporting the good in which its relative disadvantage is smaller.
6. A country that has an absolute advantage in both goods still gains from trade by exporting the good in which its relative advantage is greater.
7. John Stuart Mill considered how an equilibrium price internationally is established. In a two-good world, a country's export supply of one good also represents its readiness to import the other good.
8. An equilibrium price internationally must ensure that the quantity of a good that consumers in one country want to import exactly equals the quantity that producers in the rest of the world want to export.
9. If we form the ratio of labor productivity in one country to labor productivity in another country for many different goods, the ratio of wages in the two countries allows us to distinguish goods that a country will export from those that it will import.
10. Tests of the classical model based on labor productivities in different countries suggest that patterns of commodity trade can be explained by the principle of comparative advantage.
11. Classical theory does not explain why labor productivities differ across countries.

CASE STUDY

Rising Productivity: A Guarantee of Manufacturing Success?

Classical theory highlights the role of labor productivity as the key determinant of comparative advantage. The first column of Table 2.7 presents figures for the annual rate of change in output per hour worked (labor productivity) in the manufacturing sector for Italy, Taiwan, and the United States. If we had not read Chapter 2, we might be tempted to use this column to predict which countries gained competitiveness in manufacturing and which lost competitiveness over the 1979–2006 period shown. In order to apply the logic of Ricardo's model to this setting, however, we need information to show changes in productivity elsewhere in each economy. Unfortunately, such data are not available on a comparable basis. Nevertheless, another useful comparison is possible based on a measure of unit labor cost in manufacturing (ULC), given by:

$$ULC = w \cdot (L/Q) \qquad (2.5)$$

where w is the wage rate, L is labor hours of input, and Q is manufacturing output. Note that L/Q is just the inverse of labor productivity, Q/L.

If wages are a good indication of the value of labor's productivity elsewhere in the economy, we can infer the way comparative advantage in manufacturing may be changing by comparing unit labor cost in the three countries. To make such a comparison, we need to introduce one more variable, the rate at which one country's currency exchanges for another, in order to express all wage rates in a common currency. (See the appendix to Chapter 3 for an elaboration of these concepts for economies that operate with money prices, not barter prices.) We can use the following framework to show whether U.S. unit labor costs have risen less rapidly than in Italy:

$$ULC_{us} = w_{us} \cdot (L/Q)_{us} \leq ULC_I = w_I \cdot E \cdot (L/Q)_I \quad (2.6)$$

where E is the number of dollars per unit of currency used by Italy (the lira and more recently the euro), and the subscripts $_I$ and $_{us}$ denote Italy and the U.S. This relationship can be represented in percentage change form as:

$$\Delta ULC/ULC_{us} = \Delta w/w_{us} - \Delta(Q/L)/(Q/L)_{us}$$
$$\leq \Delta w/w_I + \Delta E/E_I - \Delta(Q/L)/(Q/L)_I = \Delta ULC/ULC_I \quad (2.7)$$

TABLE 2.7 Annual Rates of Change in Productivity, Wages, and Unit Labor Cost in Manufacturing, 1979–2006

	Labor productivity	Wages	Exchange rate	Unit labor cost
Italy	1.7	6.8	–2.3	2.6
Taiwan	5.7	7.3	0.4	1.8
United States	3.9	4.7	—	0.8

Source: U.S. Department of Labor, Bureau of Labor Statistics (2008).

As shown by the right hand side terms, Italy's unit labor cost rises as wages increase and the value of its currency increases, but falls if its labor productivity rises.[2]

The final column of Table 2.7 reports the annual rate of increase in unit labor cost. This ranking differs from the ranking by labor productivity in column one. While Italy has the highest increase in unit labor cost and the lowest increase in labor productivity, the positions of Taiwan and the United States shift. The rate of increase in Taiwanese wages and the increase in the value of the New Taiwan Dollar relative to the U.S. dollar cause unit labor cost to rise more rapidly in Taiwan than in the United States.

CASE STUDY QUESTIONS

1. If you were to find from an analysis of trade data that Taiwanese manufacturing became more competitive relative to U.S. manufacturing in spite of a more rapid increase in unit labor cost, what potential problems might cause our reliance on unit labor cost in Table 2.7 to be misleading?

2. How would you characterize the extent of the fall in the value of the lira as a determinant of the competitiveness of Italian manufacturing?

3. Check the data source for Table 2.7 (http://www.bls.gov/news.release/pdf/prod4.pdf) for the most recent data that suggest how the change in ULC for Italy compares to the change in ULC for France and for Germany, and explain what problems this may pose for Italy.

4. For Norway, a major producer of petroleum, unit labor cost in manufacturing measured in U.S. dollars rose by 3.3 percent annually over this same period. Relative to the countries presented above, explain what this comparison indicates about Norway's international competitiveness in petroleum production versus manufacturing.

Questions for Study and Review

1. "China's wage rate is one tenth of the E.U. wage rate. Therefore, the E.U. will be unable to compete in the Chinese market."
"China is far behind E.U. levels of productivity and has an absolute disadvantage in all goods compared to E.U. firms. Therefore, E.U. firms currently are safe from Chinese competition."

These two statements indicate confusion over Ricardo's principle of comparative advantage. Based on that principle, correct each statement and convert it into an accurate characterization of the competitive positions of E.U. and Chinese producers, paying particular attention to the distinction between the competitiveness of producers in an industry versus the competitiveness of an entire economy.

---

2 An exact version of this expression can be derived by taking logarithms of each side of equation (2.6) and totally differentiating the resulting equation. For small changes, equation (2.7) will be an appropriate approximation.

2.   French output per worker in electronic assembly is 20 computers per hour, while in Indonesia it is 4 computers per hour. If output per worker in the French bicycle industry is 10 bicycles per hour, what range of productivity values for the Indonesian bicycle industry must exist for Indonesia to have a comparative advantage in assembling computers? . . . for France to have an absolute advantage in bicycle production?

3.   Assume a classical world of two goods and two countries where labor is the only input. The amount of labor required per ton of output in the production of sugar and coffee for Countries A and B is given in the table below.

Country	Sugar	Coffee
A	16	8
B	10	20

   a. Explain the pattern of comparative advantage that exists, and calculate the cost of coffee in each country.

   b. Suppose 20 individuals in B shift from producing coffee to producing sugar, and they are able to sell that sugar at A's domestic price ratio. How much more coffee would B gain compared to the amount of coffee those 20 individuals initially produced in B?

   c. If B is much smaller than A, why is B more likely to experience a large gain from trade?

4.   Again, assume a classical world of two goods and two countries where labor is the only input, but consider the relevant labor productivity information in a slightly different form. The table below shows what outputs of cloth and wheat one day of labor will produce in Inlandia and Outlandia.

Country	Cloth (square meters)	Wheat (kilograms)
Inlandia	20	30
Outlandia	4	5

   a. What pattern of comparative advantage exists?

   b. Outlandia has an absolute disadvantage in each good. Nevertheless, it can still gain from trade. If the equilibrium exchange ratio is 1.4 kilograms of wheat per 1 square meter of cloth, explain how Outlandia gains from trade.

   c. Why are demand factors important in determining equilibrium trading prices even under the labor theory of value? If there is a worldwide increase in demand for cloth due to rising fashion consciousness on university campuses, how will that affect wages and the gains from trade in Inlandia and Outlandia?

   d. If Outlandia discovers a new way of producing wheat and its labor productivity rises to 6 kilograms per day, how does that affect the potential gains from trade?

5. Why is a small country likely to export a lot of a few goods but import a little of many goods? What role do constant costs play in your explanation? Given the kinked supply curves that apply in the classical world, on what segment of the curve will the economy be operating when it trades internationally?

6. Suppose labor is the only cost of production and labor productivities (output per unit of labor input) in Japan and India are as follows:

Country	Nails (kg)	Oranges (kg)	Rice (kg)
Japan	10	10	30
India	1	2	5

   a. If these are the only two nations who trade, and consumers in both countries demand all three goods (the only ones that are available), explain what you can conclude about the comparative advantage of each country.

   b. Within what limits must the ratio of Japanese wages to Indian wages settle when trade is possible? If that ratio turns out to be 5.5, what goods will each country export and import?

7. Use the labor productivity information in the problem above to consider the role that transportation costs play in determining what Japan and India will trade. Suppose it takes 0.04 units of labor to transport a kilogram of any of the goods in either direction. (Consequently, the cost of Japan supplying nails to India becomes 0.1 units of labor to produce a kilo of nails plus 0.04 units of labor to transport them, while Indian costs of serving the domestic market remain 1.0 unit of labor.)

   a. Explain whether India now has an incentive to become self-sufficient in nail production (nails become a nontraded good) or whether India will still choose to import nails from Japan.

   b. Determine how this transportation cost affects trade in oranges and rice. Why does this additional cost make a bigger difference to the relative cost of rice than oranges in international trade?

References and Suggestions for Further Reading

The classical economists whose writings are presented in this chapter are as follows:

Mill, J.S. (1848) *Principles of Political Economy*. Reprinted Ashley edn, London: Longman, Green, 1921, book 3, ch. 18.

Ricardo, D. (1817) *Principles of Political Economy and Taxation*. Reprinted London: J.M. Dent, 1911.

Smith, A. (1776) *An Inquiry into the Nature and Causes of the Wealth of Nations*. Reprinted Modern Library edn, New York: Random House, 1937.

For commentary on the context in which these authors wrote, as well as controversies over the pedigree of the ideas presented, see:

Allen, W.R. (1965) *International Trade Theory: Hume to Ohlin*, New York: Random House.

Chipman, J. (1965) "A Survey of the Theory of International Trade, Part I: The Classical Theory," *Econometrica* 33: 477–519.

Heilbroner, R. (1953) *The Worldly Philosophers*, New York: Simon and Schuster.

Viner, J. (1937) *Studies in the Theory of International Trade*, New York: Harper.

For the development of a complete model of trade and demand based on Ricardian production conditions, see:

Dornbusch, R., Fischer, S., and Samuelson, P. (1977) "Comparative Advantage, Trade, and Payments in a Ricardian Model with a Continuum of Goods," *American Economic Review* 67: 823–39.

For empirical analysis of trade patterns based on the Ricardian model, see:

Balassa, B. (1963) "An Empirical Demonstration of Classical Comparative Cost Theory," *Review of Economics and Statistics* 45: 231–8.

Carlin, W., Glyn, A., and Van Reenen, J. (2001) "Export Market Performance of OECD Countries: An Empirical Examination of the Role of Cost Competitiveness," *Economic Journal* 111: 231–38.

MacDougall, G.D.A. (1951) "British and American Exports: A Study Suggested by the Theory of Comparative Costs," *The Economic Journal* 61: 697–724, reprinted in R. Caves and H.G. Johnson (eds) (1968) *Readings in International Economics*, Homewood, IL: Richard D. Irwin.

Stern, R. M. (1962) "British and American Productivity and Comparative Costs in International Trade," *Oxford Economic Papers* 14: 275–96.

For attention to the measurement and role of transportation costs, as well as other data cited in the chapter, see:

Anderson, J. and Van Wincoop, E. (2004) "Trade Costs," *Journal of Economic Literature* 42: 691–751.

Harrigan, J. (2005) "Airplanes and Comparative Advantage," *NBER Working Paper* No. 11688.

Hummels, D. (2007) "Transportation Costs and International Trade in the Second Wave of Globalization," *Journal of Economic Perspectives* 21: 131–54.

Mohammed, S. and Williamson, J. (2004) "Freight rates and productivity gains in British tramp shipping 1869–1950," *Exploration in Economic History* 41: 172–203.

North, D. (1958) "Ocean Freight Rates and Economic Development," *Journal of Economic History* 18: 537–55.

U.S. Department of Labor, Bureau of Labor Statistics (2008) *International Comparisons of Manufacturing Productivity and Unit Labor Cost Trends 2006, Revised*, Table B. Available at http://www.bls.gov/news.release/pdf/prod4.pdf (accessed 2 September 2008).

Chapter 3

Why Do Nations Trade? Some Later Answers

LEARNING OBJECTIVES

By the end of this chapter you should be able to demonstrate:

- why individuals gain from trade when either their tastes or endowments of goods differ and they value goods differently before trade occurs

- how a country's willingness to trade is based on its consumption preferences, represented by community indifference curves, and its domestic production capabilities, represented by its production-possibility curve

- how prices are determined internationally and how those prices determine the division of the gains from trade among countries

In this chapter we introduce the somewhat more formal framework developed by economists who followed the early classical writers, but we retain our focus on the same basic question: why do nations trade? We extend the analysis of Chapter 2 in two important ways: we examine demand conditions and consumer preferences more carefully; and we consider an economy's production capabilities in greater detail. By combining these two perspectives, we can better explain what determines the volume of goods and services traded and the international prices established.

Classical economists were not writing textbooks for university students, but rather were trying to influence public opinion and public policy on key issues of the day. Adam Smith argued against the mercantilist doctrine that a country only gained by exporting more than it imported. David Ricardo pressed the case that Britain would benefit by eliminating its protection of agricultural producers who had no comparative advantage internationally. They were not particularly concerned about developing formal models that could easily be applied to answer several related questions about trade, growth, and income distribution. In this course we remain interested in how to apply their reasoning to current controversies over the threats posed by globalization and greater openness to trade. But in order to be prepared to address many related questions about trade, we first consider the basis for potential gains from trade more systematically. To do so we make use of the more comprehensive approaches developed by the neoclassical economists who wrote in the late nineteenth and early twentieth centuries.

CONSUMER PREFERENCES AND THE GAINS FROM TRADE

The potential to gain from trade is not restricted to the case where the productivity of individuals differs in different activities. Individuals may choose to trade because they have different preferences. We can demonstrate this in a simple setting where there is no production at all. To do so, we will find it useful to introduce an analytical technique developed by Francis Edgeworth (1881) and Arthur Bowley (1924), the **Edgeworth–Bowley box**, as applied to the allocation of goods between two individuals. To develop this line of reasoning, however, we first review some basics about consumer preferences and indifference curves for a single individual.

Representing the Preferences of One Individual with Indifference Curves

The curve labeled i_1 in Figure 3.1 shows the alternative combinations of two goods, here chosen to be shampoo and rahman noodles as two possible items in a frugal student's budget, that give an

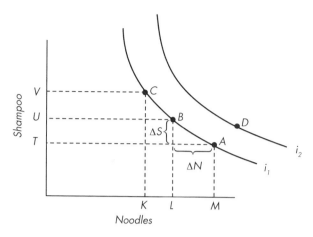

FIGURE 3.1 Consumer Indifference Curves

A consumer is equally satisfied with any combination of food and clothing along i_1. The curvature of that line demonstrates a diminishing marginal rate of substitution, because the amount of noodles the consumer will give up to get an additional bottle of shampoo becomes smaller as she moves from A to B to C.

individual the same level of satisfaction, well-being, or utility. Suppose the individual initially consumes the bundle of shampoo and noodles represented by point A.

Now suppose that one box of noodles (LM in Figure 3.1) is taken away from our consumer, thus reducing her level of satisfaction or utility. How much additional shampoo would it take to restore her to the same level of satisfaction or utility enjoyed at point A? If that amount is TU units of shampoo, as shown in Figure 3.1, then at point B the consumer will be just as well satisfied as at A. We can say that she is indifferent between the two commodity bundles represented by points A and B, and therefore these two points lie on the same indifference curve, i_1. Proceeding in a similar way, we can locate other points on i_1. Conceptually, we wish simply to determine the amount of one commodity that will exactly compensate the consumer for the loss of a given amount of the other commodity.

By that same procedure, we can generate a complete set of indifference curves. Starting at point A, suppose we give the consumer more of both commodities, moving her to point D. Since both commodities yield satisfaction, D represents a higher level of utility than does A – that is, it lies on a higher indifference curve, i_2. We can then proceed as before to locate other points on i_2. Movement to a higher indifference curve implies a higher level of welfare. Furthermore, because D lies along i_2, we can conclude that the individual is better off than at B, which lies along i_1, even though she has less shampoo at D than at B.

Note also that indifference curves are convex to the origin – that is, they bend in toward the origin. This curvature simply represents the fact that as the consumer gives up more noodles, it takes increasingly more shampoo to compensate her and to maintain the same level of satisfaction. Or, as indicated in Figure 3.1, to receive another bottle of shampoo, shown by a movement from B to C, she is willing to give up progressively fewer noodles. We can state this in terms of the marginal rate of substitution (MRS) of shampoo for noodles, which is the ratio of VU to KL for the movement from C to B or the ratio of TU to LM for the movement from B to A: the MRS falls as the consumer moves down the indifference curve.

We can also think of the MRS in the following way. As a consumer moves along an indifference curve and gives up $-\Delta N$ of noodles to get an additional ΔS of shampoo, she must place the same *value* on the noodles given up as on the shampoo gained. This can be expressed as $-\Delta N \cdot MU_n = \Delta S \cdot MU_s$, where MU represents marginal utility, which is the value a consumer places on an additional unit of a product. We can rearrange these terms and express the absolute value of the slope of the indifference curve as:

$$\frac{\Delta S = MU_n}{\Delta N = MU_s} \tag{3.1}$$

Thus the slope of the indifference curve, or the MRS, equals the ratio of the marginal utilities of the two goods.[1]

A consumer confronted with a given set of market prices will maximize her utility (reach the highest possible indifference curve) by allocating her budget such that her MRS just equals the market price ratio. That situation is shown in Figure 3.2, where the budget is shown by the straight line YY. Its slope represents the relative price of noodles, (P_n/P_s). The consumer can buy any combination of goods along YY. But, she will choose point A rather than any other point, such as B. At B, the slope of her indifference curve, the MRS, is much lower than the slope of the budget line. She puts a lower value on noodles than the market price, and therefore can become better off by buying fewer noodles and more shampoo. That comparison of the MRS and the market price ratio implies that she should move from B up to A, where the two are equal.

Finally, recall another important characteristic of the set of indifference curves: one curve should not intersect another. That outcome would imply that an individual was equally satisfied with more of both goods and less of both goods. We rule out such inconsistency.

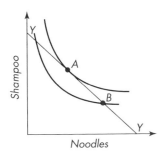

FIGURE 3.2 Consumer Choices Subject to a Budget Constraint

A consumer with income of YY will choose to buy the combination of goods at A, where the MRS (the slope of the indifference curve) equals the price ratio, P_n/P_s (the slope of the budget line).

---

1 The slope at a given point along the indifference curve, rather than over a discrete interval between two points along the curve, is represented as $-dS/dN = MU_n/MU_s$. The left-hand side of this expression is the slope of the indifference curve, where dS and dN represent infinitesimally small changes in the quantities of shampoo and noodles, respectively.

Representing the Preferences of Two Individuals

We are now ready to use the Edgeworth–Bowley box to represent the preferences of two individuals, Anne and Ben, and the allocation of goods between them. In the top panel of Figure 3.3, the set of indifference curves that represents Anne's preferences are measured from the origin O_A. Ben's preferences are measured from the origin O_B, as if we had taken his set of indifference curves derived as in Figure 3.1 and rotated them in a counterclockwise direction to the upper right corner of the box. The dimensions of the box are given by the total amount of noodles and shampoo that can be divided between Anne and Ben. Anne's welfare rises if she can move from A_1 to A_2 to A_3, while Ben's welfare falls if he moves from B_3 to B_2 to B_1.

Suppose Anne and Ben are each given half of the shampoo and half of the noodles at point E. In the case of identical preferences assumed in the top panel, no trade will take place. The reason is that both individuals are in equilibrium at E. Their two indifference curves, A_2 and B_2, are tangent to each other, an indication that their marginal rates of substitution of shampoo for noodles are the same. There is no basis for trade because they each place the same value on an extra box of noodles or bottle of shampoo. In fact, any initial distribution of noodles and shampoo that falls along the diagonal line $O_A - O_B$ appears to be characterized by this same condition; at the given price ratio shown by the tangency of their indifference curves, they choose to consume noodles and shampoo in the same proportions. Economists refer to the preferences in this case as **homothetic**: at unchanged prices an individual whose income doubles (halves) will double (halve) her consumption of both noodles and shampoo.

Identifying Potential Gains from Trade

In the middle panel of Figure 3.3 we retain the assumption of identical, homothetic tastes, but we alter the initial allocation of noodles and shampoo between Anne and Ben. At point E, Anne now has a larger share of the noodles and less of the shampoo. If we consider the slope of Anne's indifference curve through E, we see that its flatter slope is an indication of the lower value she places on the good along the horizontal axis, noodles. In contrast, the slope of Ben's indifference curve that passes through E is steeper, an indication that he places a high value on noodles. The difference in their marginal rates of substitution at E indicates a potential gain from trading. For allocations within the shaded area between indifference curves A_2 and B_1, both Anne and Ben can gain from trading. Later in this chapter we demonstrate how the equilibrium position from trade is determined based on the **offer curve** of each individual. We expect the new equilibrium to lie along the diagonal line, where the indifference curves of both individuals are tangent and both individuals place the same value on each good.

In the bottom panel of Figure 3.3, we consider an initial allocation of noodles and shampoo along the diagonal, just as in the top panel, but we no longer impose the assumption of identical, homothetic tastes. In the case drawn, Anne has a stronger preference for noodles than Ben, because her indifference curve through point E is much steeper than his. This difference in their valuation of the two goods creates a potential gain from trade, as shown by the shaded area between their indifference curves. The new equilibrium will be characterized by a point along the dotted curve where both individuals place the same value on the goods and their indifference curves are tangent.

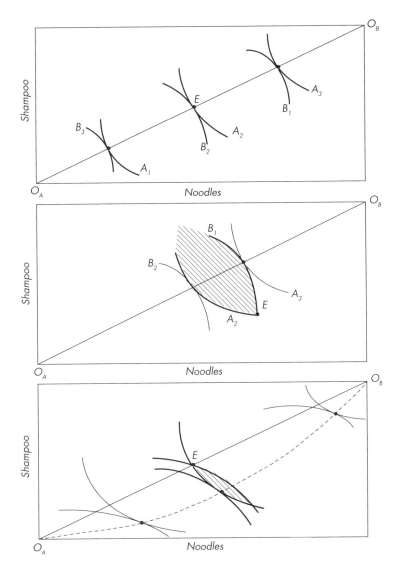

FIGURE 3.3 Potential Trade Between Two Individuals

When two individuals have the same MRS between goods, then at the initial allocation given by point E in the top panel, they do not become better off by trading. With a different allocation of goods, as in the middle panel, or with different tastes, as in the bottom panel, their marginal rates of substitution are not equal at the initial allocation, and they can gain by trading until their indifference curves are tangent.

In summary, these comparisons are intended to remind us there are two important sources of difference in prices that lead to trade: differences in preferences and differences in endowments or production capabilities. Before we develop those themes further in the context of international trade, however, we need to consider how easily we can shift from talking of the preferences of individual consumers to preferences of nations.

Indifference Curves for a Country

Only under very specific circumstances can we draw a set of indifference curves for a country that fulfills the conditions identified above for an individual. We can think of a **community indifference curve** as showing all the combinations of goods that will be necessary to leave two individuals just as well off as they are in a given pre-trade situation. If individuals do not have the same tastes, however, we will obtain a different community indifference curve for each distribution of income that we choose in the pre-trade equilibrium. Making any statement about a country's gains from trade on the basis of its opportunity to move to a higher indifference curve will be contingent on the initial distribution of income chosen.

This ambiguity arises because the different community indifference curves have different slopes. If individuals with a strong preference for clothing receive a larger share of income, for example, the community's marginal rate of substitution of food for clothing will be greater and society will demand more clothing than when a larger share of income is received by those who prefer food. An opportunity to trade that makes clothing available more cheaply may appear to raise community welfare if judged by the indifference curves generated from the first distribution of income but not from the second. To predict society's demand for a good we need to know how income is distributed in a society and how changing circumstances, such as a change in the international price ratio, may alter that income distribution.

If individuals have the same tastes and spend their incomes in the same proportions on the two goods (the situation labeled above as identical, homothetic tastes), we can predict total product demands in the economy in response to relative price changes without having to pay attention to changes in the income distribution. If we try to judge whether the price change makes society worse off, however, we confront another difficulty: the satisfaction or utility enjoyed by one individual cannot be compared with the utility enjoyed by another. Utility cannot be measured cardinally in units that are the same for all individuals.

If some individuals gain from trade while others lose, we have no way to make interpersonal comparisons of utility that would tell us how to weigh these separate effects. Therefore, economists typically talk of potential improvements in welfare, where gainers could compensate losers and still become better off as a result of trade.

One way to escape from these difficulties is to assume that every individual has exactly the same tastes and owns exactly the same amount of each factor of production. Then any price change leaves the distribution of income unchanged and everyone gains or loses to the same degree. In that situation, it is possible to conceive of community indifference curves just as we have described them for a single person. The reader may find it useful to apply that simplifying assumption to our subsequent discussion of the effects of trade. Alternatively, we may assume that the tastes of all individuals are appropriately characterized as identical and homothetic, which allows us to consistently project community demands irrespective of the distribution of income. In fact, we explicitly impose this assumption in the next chapter. Any claims about gains to the community, however, rest upon the convention of potential welfare improvements. These rationales may not be entirely persuasive, but we discuss them here to better appreciate how restrictive our assumptions must be to ignore issues that arise in the aggregation of individuals.

PRODUCTION CAPABILITIES AND THE GAINS FROM TRADE

Gains from trade exist under a much more general set of production conditions than assumed in Chapter 2, where we relied upon the labor theory of value. To demonstrate this claim, we consider several more formal economic models here and in the next two chapters. Rather than repeat all the qualifying assumptions each time we introduce a new model, it is useful to clarify at the outset which common set of circumstances is to apply in each trading nation. Recognizing which conditions are actually imposed should help us to appreciate how broadly our results may apply and to recognize when exceptions to our conclusions might arise. These assumptions and some of their implications are:

1. perfect competition in both commodity and factor markets: costs of production determine pre-trade prices, and flexibility of factor prices ensures that factors are fully employed;
2. fixed quantities of the factors of production: we do not consider capital formation or growth in the labor force;
3. factors of production are perfectly mobile between industries within each country but completely immobile between countries;
4. a given, unchanging level of technology;
5. zero transport costs and other barriers to trade: a good will have a single price internationally;
6. balanced trade, where the value of imports equals the value of exports;
7. identical, homothetic tastes: if income rises, purchases of all goods rise in the same proportion.

The Concept of Opportunity Cost

One way to avoid dependence on the labor theory of value is through the use of the now familiar concept of **opportunity cost**, which was introduced by Gottfried Haberler (1936). The opportunity cost of a unit of commodity A is the next best alternative given up in order to obtain it. In a two-good world, that is the amount of commodity B which is given up to obtain a unit of A. If just enough land, labor, and capital are withdrawn from B to permit the production of an extra unit of A, the opportunity cost of the additional (marginal) unit of A is the amount by which the output of B declines. A country has a comparative advantage in commodity A if it can produce an additional unit of A at a lower opportunity cost in terms of commodity B foregone than can another country.

The Production-Possibility Curve

This view of cost can be usefully represented by the concept of a production-possibility curve. Suppose that Germany can produce only two commodities: wheat and steel. If it puts all its productive resources into wheat, let us suppose that it can produce 100 million tons. Suppose further that German conditions of production are such that the opportunity cost of a ton of steel is 1 ton of wheat. Starting from an initial position in which Germany is fully specialized in wheat, as resources are shifted into steel the output of wheat will drop by 1 ton for each additional ton of steel produced.

When all German resources are devoted to steel production, its total output will be 100 million tons of steel and no wheat. Table 3.1 summarizes the alternative combinations of wheat and steel that Germany can produce.

This situation is shown in Figure 3.4. The straight line *AB* represents the production-possibility curve for the German economy. Points along the line *AB* represent alternative combinations of wheat and steel that Germany can produce at full employment. At *A*, it produces 100 million tons of wheat and no steel; at *B*, 100 million tons of steel and no wheat; at *P*, 60 million tons of wheat and 40 million tons of steel. The constant slope of *AB* represents the constant opportunity cost or internal ratio of exchange (one wheat for one steel). The line *AB*, therefore, represents the highest attainable combinations of wheat and steel that the German economy can produce at full employment. All points above and to the right of *AB*, such as *J*, represent combinations of wheat and steel that exceed current German productive capacity. Points to the left of *AB*, such as *K*, represent the existence of unemployment or the inefficient use of resources.

More can usefully be said about the slope of the production-possibility curve. Because Germany's economy is fully employed at both points *P* and *P'*, the additional cost from increasing the production of steel by *ΔS* (i.e. that change in quantity times the marginal cost of steel) must equal the cost saving from reducing the production of wheat by *−ΔW* (i.e. minus one times that change in quantity times

TABLE 3.1 German Production of Wheat and Steel (millions of tons)

Wheat	100	90	80	70	60	50	40	30	20	10	0
Steel	0	10	20	30	40	50	60	70	80	90	100

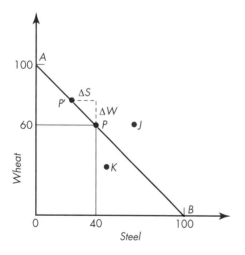

FIGURE 3.4 Germany's Production-Possibility Curve

This figure illustrates the combinations of wheat and steel that can be produced with a fixed available supply of labor. The slope of the line *AB* represents the ratio at which steel can be transformed into wheat.

the marginal cost of wheat), which can be expressed as $\Delta S \cdot MC_s = -\Delta W \cdot MC_w$. This formulation can also be written in terms of the absolute value of the slope of the production-possibility line, $\Delta W / \Delta S$, where we omit the minus sign in representing this slope as:

$$\Delta W / \Delta S = MC_s / MC_w \tag{3.2}$$

and note that it equals the ratio of the marginal cost of steel to the marginal cost of wheat. This ratio of marginal costs, which represents the rate at which the German economy can transform steel into wheat, is called the **marginal rate of transformation** (MRT).[2]

The fact that AB in Figure 3.4 is a straight line indicates that the relative costs of the two goods do not change as the economy shifts from all wheat to all steel, or anywhere in between. This case of constant costs, or a constant marginal rate of transformation, is most applicable when there is a single factor of production and when that factor is homogeneous within a country. Labor is the only input in Germany, for example, and all German workers have the same relative abilities to produce steel and wheat. Constant costs also may exist when more than one factor input is necessary to produce both goods, but the proportions in which the inputs are required must be identical in the two industries.

If a producer faces a relative price of steel, say 2 tons of wheat for 1 ton of steel, that is higher than the ratio of marginal costs identified above, 1 ton of wheat per 1 ton of steel, that situation serves as a signal to expand production of steel. As long as price exceeds marginal cost, the producer can increase profits by producing more steel. An important implication of a constant marginal cost ratio is that German producers will have an incentive to continue expanding the output of steel until the economy is completely specialized in steel production.

INTERNATIONAL TRADE WITH CONSTANT COSTS

We are now ready to bring supply and demand conditions together and to provide a more complete explanation of how and why trade takes place. Figure 3.5 shows the initial equilibrium in a closed economy, before trade. Community indifference curves for Germany are combined with its production-possibility curve from Figure 3.4. Under competitive conditions, the closed-economy or autarky equilibrium of the German economy will be at point P, where 60 million tons of wheat and

---

2 The production-possibility curve can be more formally represented by the expression $W = 100 - S$. The MRT, or slope of the PPC, $\Delta W / \Delta S$, is -1, determined by the ratio of the marginal cost of producing steel divided by the marginal cost of producing wheat. To produce 10 more tons of steel, 10 tons of wheat must be given up. This constant opportunity cost case can be related to the Ricardian example by noting that the endpoints of the PPC can be thought of as the available input bundle, L, divided by the input/output requirement in wheat and steel, a_{lw} and a_{ls}. Divide the endpoint for wheat by the endpoint for steel and the slope of the PPC is given by a_{ls} / a_{lw}. The more labor required in the production of steel, the higher the marginal cost of producing steel and the steeper the slope. The expression for the PPC in this formulation is $W = (L / a_{lw}) - (a_{ls} / a_{lw}) S$. If output of steel is reduced by one ton, that releases a_{ls} units of labor, and the extra wheat that can be produced is given by a_{ls} / a_{lw} which is equivalent to the ratio of the marginal costs of production as shown in the text.

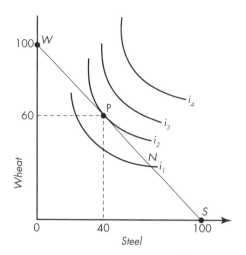

FIGURE 3.5 Constant Costs: Equilibrium in a Closed Economy

If *WS* is the production-possibility frontier, producing and consuming at point *P* results in the highest possible level of welfare for a closed economy that does not trade.

40 million tons of steel are produced. That is where Germany reaches the highest possible indifference curve (level of welfare) it can attain with its given productive resources. At the point of tangency *P* between the production-possibility curve *WS* and the community indifference curve i_2, the slopes of the two are equal, which means that the marginal rate of transformation is exactly equal to the community's marginal rate of substitution. At any other production point, it is possible to reallocate resources and move to a higher indifference curve. At *N*, for example, Germany is on i_1. By shifting resources from steel to wheat, it can move to *P* and thus reach a higher indifference curve, i_2.

Although we speak of Germany shifting resources from steel to wheat, in a competitive economy it is actually individual firms that are making these decisions and taking the necessary actions. Their motivation comes from price signals in the market. At *N*, the opportunity-cost ratio facing producers is not equal to the slope of the indifference curve that passes through *N*. Consumers are willing to swap, say, two tons of steel for one of wheat, whereas the opportunity cost in production is one ton of steel for one of wheat. When prices reflect this difference, producers are led to expand wheat production, and a move from *N* toward *P* occurs.

Trade from One Country's Perspective

Given the initial closed-economy equilibrium at *P*, now suppose that Germany has the opportunity to trade with the rest of the world (ROW) at an exchange ratio different from its domestic opportunity cost ratio (1*S*:1*W*). Specifically, suppose the exchange ratio in ROW is 1*S*:2*W*, and suppose that Germany is so small relative to ROW that German trade has no effect on world prices. Comparing Germany's domestic ratio to the international exchange ratio, we can see that Germany has a comparative advantage in steel. That is, its cost of steel (measured in foregone wheat) is less than the cost in ROW. Note that we do not need to know whether German labor is efficient or inefficient compared to labor in other countries. In fact, we do not need to know anything at all about the real cost in terms of labor hours, land area, or capital equipment. All that matters to Germany is that by transferring resources from wheat to steel, it can obtain more wheat through trade than through direct production at home. For every ton of wheat lost through curtailed production, Germany can obtain 2 tons through trade, a smaller cost in resources than it would incur at home. An opportunity for a gain from trade will exist provided the exchange ratio in ROW differs from Germany's domestic exchange ratio. That is, with a domestic ratio of $1S:1W$, Germany can benefit, provided it can get anything more than 1 ton of wheat for 1 ton of steel. If 1 ton of steel buys less than 1 ton of wheat in ROW, Germany will gain by trading wheat for steel. Only if the international exchange ratio is exactly equal to Germany's domestic ratio will there be no opportunity for gainful trade.

This example can be given a useful geometric interpretation, as in Figure 3.6, in which we add to Figure 3.5 the "consumption-possibility line" or barter line, SB, drawn with a slope equal to the autarky price ratio in ROW $(1S:2W)$. Once they have the opportunity to trade at the ROW ratio, German producers will shift from wheat to steel. With constant opportunity costs, they will continue to shift until they are fully specialized in steel (at S in Figure 3.6). German firms will have an incentive to trade steel for wheat, moving along the barter line to reach the highest possible level of welfare,

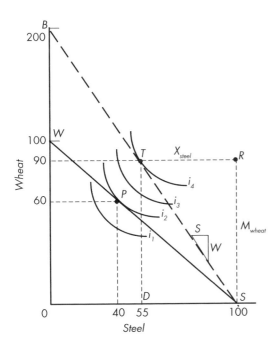

FIGURE 3.6 Germany Equilibrium Before and After Trade

If Germany is offered a barter ratio represented by the slope of line SB, firms choose to specialize in the production of steel at point S and trade out to point T. The country thereby consumes a combination of steel and wheat which is on indifference curve i_4. This combination is clearly superior to the initial consumption set at point P on indifference curve. i_2.

TABLE 3.2 German Production and Consumption (millions of tons)

	Before trade				
	Production (net national product)		=		Consumption
Wheat	60		=		60
Steel	40		=		40

	After trade							
	Production (NNP)	–	Exports	+	Imports	=	Consumption
Wheat	0	–	0	+	90	=	90
Steel	100	–	45	+	0	=	55

which will be found at the point of tangency between an indifference curve and the line *SB*. That is point *T* in Figure 3.6. At *T*, the price ratio is again equal to the marginal rate of substitution in consumption as represented by the slope of the indifference curve i_4 at that point.

In the final equilibrium position, Germany will produce at point *S* and consume at point *T*. It will produce *OS* of steel (100 million tons), keeping *OD* (55 million tons) for its own use and exporting *SD* of steel (45 million tons) in exchange for imports *DT* of wheat (90 million tons). We can identify the trade triangle, *TRS*, where *TR* = steel exports and *RS* = wheat imports, and the slope of the third side, *TS*, represents the relative price of steel.

Germany's gain from trade can clearly be seen in the final column of Table 3.2. Compare the amounts of wheat and steel that are available for domestic consumption before and after trade: 30 million more tons of wheat and 15 million more tons of steel are available after trade. Because population and resources employed remain the same, while more of both goods are available, Germany clearly can increase economic welfare in the sense of providing its population with more material goods than they had before trade began.

Another way of demonstrating that Germany gains from foreign trade is to note that it reaches a higher indifference curve: the movement from i_2 to i_4. This point is important because it may well be that a country will end up with more of one commodity and less of another as a result of trade. As we have seen, indifference curves enable us to determine whether or not welfare has increased in such cases.

Equilibrium Prices and Mutual Gains from Trade

Thus far we have focused on the position of one country and have assumed that it has the opportunity to trade at a fixed relative price of steel. We assumed that Germany's offer of steel on the world market did not affect the international exchange ratio. Now we consider how the international exchange ratio is determined when two countries of approximately equal size trade. In this situation, we again find that both countries can gain from international trade.

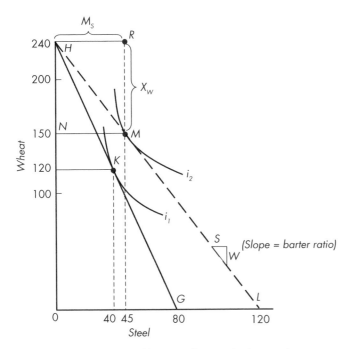

FIGURE 3.7 France Equilibrium Before and After Trade

At the barter price *HL* producers specialize in wheat at point *H*, and trade occurs along the barter line to point *M*. Welfare rises from indifference curve i_1 to i_2.

Let German supply and demand conditions remain the same as in Figure 3.6 and introduce France as a potential trade partner. We assume that France can produce 240 million tons of wheat or 80 million tons of steel if it specializes fully in one or the other. The French production-possibility curve, *HG*, drawn as a straight line to indicate a constant marginal rate of transformation of $1S:3W$, is shown in Figure 3.7, along with community indifference curves to represent French demand. In complete isolation, the French economy is in equilibrium at point *K*, where $120W$ and $40S$ are produced and consumed.

Before trade, the domestic exchange ratios differ in our two countries: in Germany $1S:1W$, in France $1S:3W$. The fact that these ratios are different is enough to show that comparative advantage exists. Steel is cheaper (in terms of foregone wheat) in Germany than it is in France; hence Germany has a comparative advantage in steel and France in wheat. Note that we need not compare the resources used in each country in order to determine comparative advantage; we need only to compare their opportunity–cost ratios. If these are different, a basis for trade exists.

Germany benefits if it can exchange $1S$ for anything more than $1W$, and France will benefit if it can obtain $1S$ for anything less than $3W$. Therefore, when trade begins between these two countries, the international exchange ratio may lie anywhere between the two domestic ratios: $1S:1W$ and $1S:3W$. Just where the international exchange ratio will settle depends on the willingness of each country to offer its export commodity and to purchase imports at various relative prices. To explain this process, we will first show the conditions that must prevail for an equilibrium to exist in our illustrative example, and then we will present a more general approach.

We have already determined Germany's demand for imports (90*W*) and its offer of exports (45*S*) at the intermediate exchange ratio 1*S*:2*W*. Those amounts are shown in Figure 3.6. How much wheat is France willing to export for how much steel at that exchange ratio? In Figure 3.7, we draw the line *HL* to represent France's barter line. It originates at *H* because France will specialize in wheat production. We see that by trading wheat for steel, France can barter along *HL* and attain a higher level of welfare than it can reach in isolation. At *M*, it reaches the highest possible indifference curve. At that point France will export 90*W* and import 45*S*, as indicated by its trade triangle, *HRM*.

Thus, it turns out that France is willing to export, at the exchange ratio 1*S*:2*W*, just the amount of wheat that Germany wants to import. And France wants to import just the amount of steel that Germany is willing to export. Geometrically, this equality can be seen by comparing the two trade triangles, *TRS* and *HRM* in Figures 3.6 and 3.7. They are identical, which means that we have hit upon the equilibrium terms-of-trade ratio. Note the conditions that are necessary for the exchange ratio 1*S*:2*W* to be an equilibrium ratio: each country must demand exactly the amount of its imported commodity that the other country is willing to supply.

We summarize the gains from trade for both France and Germany in Table 3.3. Although we know both countries are better off because they move to higher indifference curves, we can show the gains

TABLE 3.3 The Gain from Trade: Production and Consumption Before and After Trade

| | Wheat | | | | | Steel | | | | |
	P	− X	+ M	= C		P	− X	+ M	= C	
Situation before trade										
France	120				120	40				40
Germany	60				60	40				40
Total World	180				180	80				80
Situation after trade										
France	240	− 90	+ 0	=	150	0	− 0	+ 45	=	45
Germany	0	−	+ 90	=	90	100	− 45	+ 0	=	55
Total World	240				240	100				100
Gain from trade										
France			+ 30					+		5
Germany			+ 30					+		15
Total World			+ 60					+		20

Legend: P = Production, X = Exports, M = Imports, C = Consumption arithmetically for this particular case. Before trade, world outputs of wheat and steel were $180W$ and $80S$; post-trade outputs are $240W$ and $100S$. By what magic has world output of both commodities increased without the use of any additional resources? The answer is that specialization – the use of each nation's resources to produce the commodity in which it possesses a comparative advantage – has made possible a larger total output than can be achieved under self-sufficiency.

INTERNATIONAL TRADE WITH INCREASING COSTS

So far, we have assumed that opportunity costs in each country remain unchanged as resources shift from one industry to another. We now drop this assumption of constant costs and adopt the more realistic assumption of increasing costs. That is, we will now assume that as resources are shifted from, say, wheat production to cloth production, the opportunity cost of each additional unit of cloth increases. Such increasing costs could arise because factors of production vary in quality and in suitability for producing different commodities. Business firms, in their efforts to maximize profit, will be led through competition to use resources where they are best suited. Thus, when cloth production is increased, the resources (land, labor, and capital) drawn away from the wheat industry will be somewhat less well suited to cloth production than those already in the cloth industry. Hence, for a given increase in cloth output the cost in foregone wheat will be higher – that is, the marginal opportunity cost of cloth rises as its output increases. Also, if more than one factor of production exists, increasing opportunity costs arise when the two industries require the inputs in different proportions. That situation is examined more carefully in Chapter 4. For both reasons, it seems intuitively plausible to expect increasing costs to exist as a country moves toward greater specialization in a particular product.

Increasing costs give rise to a production-possibility curve that is bowed out (concave to the origin) as in Figure 3.8. At any point on the production-possibility curve, WC, the slope of the curve represents the opportunity–cost ratio (the marginal rate of transformation) at that point. For alternative production points along the curve from W toward C, the slope of the curve becomes steeper, which means that cloth costs more in terms of foregone wheat. In isolation, the country will seek to reach the highest possible indifference curve, which means that it will produce at point P in Figure 3.8. At P, the line RR is tangent to both the production-possibility curve, WC, and the indifference curve U_1. The slope of the tangent RR represents the domestic barter exchange ratio, which equals the marginal rate of transformation in production and the marginal rate of substitution in consumption. At P the country produces and consumes OC_1 of cloth and OW_1 of wheat, and the following condition holds:

$$\frac{P_c}{P_w} = \frac{MC_c}{MC_w} = \frac{MU_c}{MU_w} \tag{3.3}$$

Under this condition, the country is operating at maximum efficiency as a closed economy that does not trade.

Because this is a barter economy without money prices, we can only refer to a relative price ratio, or the price of cloth in terms of how many units of wheat are given up to obtain a unit of cloth. If the price line RR is steeper, the relative price of the good along the horizontal axis, cloth, is higher.

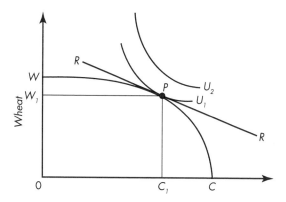

FIGURE 3.8 Increasing Costs: Equilibrium in a Closed Economy

With increasing costs of specialization, represented by the curvature of the production-possibility curve *WC*, this country maximizes welfare at point *P* as a closed economy.

Alternatively stated, we can think of P_w remaining constant at a value of one because all other prices are measured in terms of units of wheat. An increase in the ratio P_c/P_w then indicates that the price of cloth has risen. As *RR* becomes steeper, the point of tangency along the production-possibility curve will be further to the right, because a higher price for cloth justifies the higher cost of expanding cloth output.

As we apply this framework to a situation where trade is possible, most of the analysis developed in the case of constant costs also applies to the case of increasing costs. The major difference is that we must allow for the changing internal cost ratios in each country as trade begins to cause resources to shift toward employment in the comparative-advantage industry. Let us consider a two-country, two-commodity example as depicted in Figure 3.9.

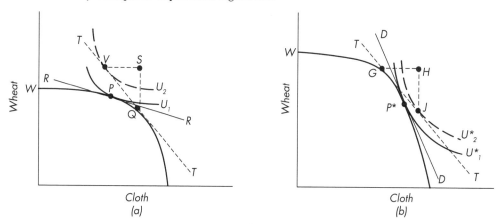

FIGURE 3.9 Equilibrium Trade in a Two-Country Case (Increasing Costs): (a) Country A (b) Country B

With trade, each country can consume a set of goods that is superior to that which occurred without trade. Country A shifts production from point *P* to *Q* and then trades to consume at point *V*, which is on a higher indifference curve. Country B produces at point *G* and trades to reach point *J*, which is also on a higher indifference curve.

The Pre-Trade Equilibrium

In Country A, the pre-trade or autarky equilibrium is at point *P* in Figure 3.9 (a) with production and consumption of cloth and wheat represented by the coordinates of point *P*. Country A's domestic exchange ratio is represented by the slope of *RR*, and its level of welfare by U_1. In Country B, the pre-trade equilibrium is at point *P** in Figure 3.9(b), with production and consumption of cloth and wheat represented by the coordinates of that point. B's domestic exchange ratio is represented by the slope of *DD*, and its level of welfare by U^*_1.

Because the slopes of the autarky price lines are different in Countries A and B, it is clear that a basis for mutually beneficial trade exists. In this case, cloth is relatively cheaper in A than in B, and wheat is relatively cheaper in B than in A. The difference in the slopes of the autarky price lines creates the following condition:

$$\frac{P^B_c}{P^B_w} = \frac{MC^B_c}{MC^B_w} = \frac{MU^B_c}{MU^B_w} > \frac{P^A_c}{P^A_w} = \frac{MC^A_c}{MC^A_w} = \frac{MU^A_c}{MU^A_w} \tag{3.4}$$

The equalities within each country mean that each closed economy is operating at maximum efficiency; it is the inequality in the middle that informs us that Country B has a comparative advantage in wheat, that Country A has a comparative advantage in cloth, and that mutually beneficial trade is therefore possible. If, by some chance, the two countries started out with the same domestic barter exchange ratios, and therefore with an equals sign in the middle of the above statement, there would be no comparative-advantage basis for trade.

The Post-Trade Equilibrium

When trade is opened up, producers in A will find it profitable to shift resources from wheat to cloth, moving along the production-possibility curve in Figure 3.9(a) from *P* toward Q, and exporting cloth to B for a higher price than they were getting at home, in isolation. How far this shift will go depends on the final international exchange ratio. Similarly, producers in B find it profitable to shift resources from cloth to wheat, moving from *P** toward G in Figure 3.9(b), and exporting wheat to A.

Trade will be in equilibrium at an exchange ratio at which the reciprocal demands are equal – that is, where A's exports of cloth precisely equal B's imports of cloth, and conversely for wheat. In Figure 3.9, the equilibrium–exchange ratio is shown as the slope of the line *TT*, common to both countries. At this ratio, the trade triangles *SVQ* and *HGJ* are identical. Thus A's cloth exports, *SV*, exactly equal B's cloth imports, *GH*; and A's wheat imports, *SQ*, exactly equal B's wheat exports, *HJ*. Country A produces at Q and consumes at *V*; Country B produces at G and consumes at *J*. Note that by trading both countries are able to reach higher indifference curves than in isolation.

Given the opportunity to trade, each country tends to specialize in the commodity in which it has a comparative advantage, but this tendency is checked by the presence of increasing costs. Country A does not fully specialize in cloth; instead, it continues to produce much of the wheat its population consumes. Similarly, B retains part of its cloth industry – the more efficient part, in fact.

The Effect of Trade

We pause to review and summarize the effects of trade. First, trade causes a reallocation of resources. Output expands in industries in which a country has a comparative advantage, pulling resources away from industries in which it has a comparative disadvantage. Graphically, we see this effect as a movement along the production-possibility curve – for example, the movement from P to Q in Country A in Figure 3.9(a). Under conditions of increasing costs, as resources move into the comparative-advantage industry, marginal opportunity cost increases in that industry and falls in the industry whose output is contracting. The shift in resources will stop when the domestic cost ratio becomes equal to the international exchange ratio, as at Q in Figure 3.9(a). Thus complete specialization normally will not occur. In the constant-cost case, however, where marginal costs do not change as resources move from one industry to another, complete specialization is likely.

This discussion of resource shifts throws into sharp relief the long-run nature of the theory we are discussing. Clearly, it will take much time for workers to be retrained and relocated and for capital to be converted into a form suitable for the new industry. The shift we show so easily as a movement from P to Q on a production-possibility curve may in fact involve a long and difficult transition period, with heavy human and social costs. These matters will be discussed more fully in later chapters; here we wish only to remind the reader to recognize the real-world aspects of the adjustment processes we are describing.

A second effect of trade is to equalize relative prices in the trading countries. (We again ignore transport costs.) Differences in relative pre-trade prices provide a basis for trade: they give traders an incentive to export one commodity and import the other. When trade occurs, it causes relative costs and prices to converge in both countries. In each country, the commodity that was relatively cheaper before trade tends to rise in price. Trade continues until the domestic exchange ratios become equal in the two countries, as at the international exchange ratio, TT, in Figure 3.9.

A third effect of trade is to improve economic welfare in both countries. Through trade, each country is able to obtain combinations of commodities that lie beyond its capacity to produce for itself. In the present analysis, the gain from trade is shown by the movement to a higher indifference curve.

In the final equilibrium, because the slope of TT is the same in both countries, the following condition holds:

$$\frac{P_c^B}{P_w^B} = \frac{MC_c^B}{MC_w^B} = \frac{MU_c^B}{MU_w^B} = \frac{P_c^A}{P_w^A} = \frac{MC_c^A}{MC_w^A} = \frac{MU_c^A}{MU_w^A} \tag{3.5}$$

The price ratios, the marginal rates of transformation, and the marginal rates of substitution are all equal across the two countries. When this condition holds, further trade will not create additional gains.

THE DIVISION OF THE GAINS FROM TRADE

The division of the gains from this exchange between Countries A and B depends on the ratio at which the two goods are exchanged, that is, on the international exchange ratio that causes the quantity that one country wants to export to just equal the quantity that the other wants to import. Of particular interest is what causes this international exchange ratio to be closer to the closed-economy exchange ratio that held in Country A or in Country B. We first utilize supply and demand curves to develop this point, because they may appear more familiar, and then introduce **offer curves**, which we can derive from the production-possibility curves and community indifference curves utilized thus far.

Figure 3.10 shows the domestic demand and supply curves of cloth for each country. It is similar to Figure 2.1, except here the supply curves look more familiar because we have assumed increasing opportunity costs hold. Such supply curves differ, however, from the supply curve economists use to represent a single industry that is too small to influence wages or the prices of other inputs. Here, in our two-good world, any additional inputs into cloth production must be bid away from wheat producers. The supply curve for cloth includes the adjustments that occur as inputs are reallocated and input prices change in the process. Economists refer to that outcome as a general equilibrium solution, in contrast to a partial equilibrium solution that ignores such adjustments outside the industry being considered.

As in Chapter 2, we can derive a residual export supply curve, which shows the quantity of cloth A is willing to export when price exceeds the autarky value P_A. At such a price, the corresponding quantity supplied to the export market equals the difference between the quantity produced domestically and the quantity consumed domestically. That export supply curve is shown in the center panel of Figure 3.10. Similarly, we can derive B's residual import demand curve, which shows the quantity of cloth B seeks to import when price is lower than its autarky value P_B. It represents the difference between the quantity demanded domestically and the quantity produced in B at a given price. The equilibrium price is given by the intersection of A's export supply curve and B's import demand curve. At that price (P_1), the volume of cloth that Country A wishes to export matches the volume that B wants to import.

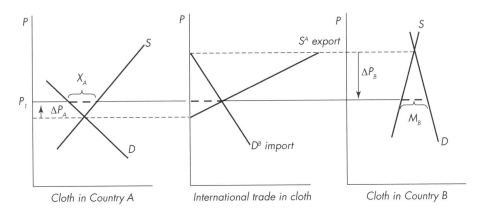

Cloth in Country A   International trade in cloth   Cloth in Country B

FIGURE 3.10 Equilibrium Price Determination

The equilibrium international price, P^1, is determined by the intersection of A's export supply curve with B's import demand curve where the quantity of cloth supplied by A exactly equals the quantity of cloth demanded by B. A's export supply is the residual or difference between its domestic quantity supplied and domestic quantity demanded. B's import demand is the residual or difference between its domestic quantity demanded and domestic quantity supplied.

Elasticities and the Terms of Trade

In this example, B gets most of the gains from trade, because the new equilibrium price for cloth internationally is much lower than the autarky price in B and only a little higher than the autarky price in A. B's import price falls much more than A's export price rises. Country B is able to purchase a great deal more cloth for a given amount of wheat, whereas Country A gains less, because a unit of cloth that it exports does not purchase a great deal more wheat than it could produce itself. Both countries still gain from trade, because the international price lies between the two autarky prices, but the gains are not distributed equally.

Why did this outcome favour B? We can observe that the supply and demand curves in B's market in the right panel are much less elastic than in A's market in the left panel.[3] When the price of cloth falls, B producers do not cut back their production much and B consumers do not increase their consumption much. Therefore, B's import demand curve shown in the center panel does not indicate much of a change in the quantity of imports demanded when the international price of cloth falls. In contrast, Country A's supply and demand functions are more elastic. As a consequence, its residual export supply curve in the center panel is quite elastic.

We can think of the role of these elasticities in the following way. Country B, whose import demand is less elastic, will not import much more cloth unless the price drops sharply. Country A is willing to export a large amount of cloth in response to only a modest price increase. As a result, the price of cloth must fall substantially in order that consumers in B choose to buy the additional cloth offered by producers in A. The general conclusion is that when trade becomes possible between two countries, most of the gains go to the country with the less elastic supply and demand functions.

Comparative Advantage and the Gains from Trade: Japan

A unique historical experiment occurred in Japan following the entry of Commodore Perry into Tokyo Harbor in 1853 to force Japan to abandon its policy that prohibited nearly all trade with the western world. As a new trade policy was implemented under the Meiji Restoration, a radical elimination of trade barriers resulted in a radical shift in relative prices. A study by Richard Huber (1971) showed the price changes summarized in Table 3.4; export products such as silk and tea could be sold at higher world prices, and imported iron and cotton textiles fell in price. The terms of trade, given by the price of exports divided by the price of imports, is a useful indicator of the change in what a unit of a country's exports can buy. After Japan's trade liberalization, its terms of trade improved by an amazing 240 percent.

---

3 When we assume the good being imported is identical to the good produced domestically, we know imports (M) equal domestic demand (D) minus domestic supply (S): $M = D - S$. For a small change in price, $dM/dP = dD/dP - dS/dP$. If we multiply both sides of the equation by P/M, we have the import elasticity of demand equals the domestic demand elasticity times (D/M) minus the domestic supply elasticity times (S/M). When the domestic demand and supply elasticities are larger in absolute value, the import demand elasticity will be larger in absolute value or more responsive to a change in price.

TABLE 3.4 Prices in Japan: Before and After Trade

	1846–55	1870–79
Price of Japanese Exports/World Prices	1.0	1.33
Price of Imported Goods /World Prices	1.0	0.39
Terms of Trade (Px/Pm)	1.0	3.4

If we relate this outcome to the situation shown in Figure 3.10, the opening of trade resulted in a major terms of trade improvement for Japan without much effect on the rest of the world. In the 1870s Japan accounted for less than 10 percent of world trade in silk and tea, and the elasticity of supply from competitors in China and India was high. Thus, demand for tea and silk produced in Japan was quite elastic. An expansion in Japanese output resulted primarily in a greater quantity sold by Japan, with little effect on world prices, because foreign consumers bought more tea at slightly lower prices and competing suppliers reduced their sales. As an importer, Japan accounted for an even smaller share of world markets, and consequently its opening to trade had an even smaller effect on world prices. Japan faced a very high elasticity of supply of the goods it imported, because producers could easily divert supply from other countries to sell to Japanese buyers. We can generalize this result to say that a small country is particularly likely to benefit from abandoning an autarky position of no trade.

How much difference does this extremely large terms of trade change make? Daniel Bernhofen and John Brown (2005) argue that Huber misinterprets the importance of these price changes. They ask the question how much more income would Japanese consumers have needed in 1850 with autarky prices to buy the bundle of goods they would have chosen if they could have bought at free trade prices. The answer they calculate is a 9 percent increase in income. The authors emphasize that this gain resulted from greater specialization, not from the later improvements in technology or the achievement of economies of scale. The reallocation of resources into sectors where Japan held a comparative advantage, with a doubling of silk output and the near extinction of the cotton textile industry, was what allowed this early increase in income.

Offer Curves

Offer curves, which are also known as "reciprocal demand curves," provide a more thorough means of illustrating how the equilibrium relative price ratio and the volume of trade in both commodities for our two countries are determined. An offer curve for one country illustrates the volume of trade (exports and imports) that it will choose to undertake at various terms of trade that it could be offered. By combining the offer curves for both countries and noting where they cross, we obtain an equilibrium price ratio and the volume of both goods traded.

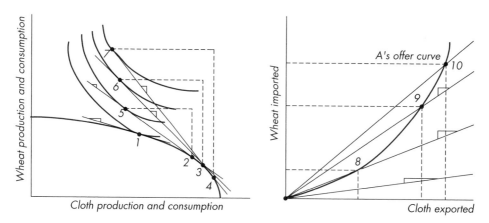

FIGURE 3.11 Derivation of Country A's Offer Curve.

As Country A's terms of trade improve in the left panel, A's willingness to trade increases, as shown by the three trade triangles. These trade triangles are then shown in the right panel as points *8*, *9*, and *10*, which represent Country A's willingness to export cloth and import wheat at the same three barter ratios shown in the left panel.

An offer curve can be derived in a number of ways. One of the more straightforward approaches is to begin with the earlier production-possibility curve and indifference curve set for Country A, shown in the left panel of Figure 3.11, and to note what happens to that country's trade triangles as its terms of trade improve. Starting from autarky at point *1*, as the price of cloth rises relative to the price of wheat, Country A shifts it production to point *2*, point *3*, and finally to point *4*. Consumption shifts from point *1* to *5*, *6*, and finally *7*. The three trade triangles, drawn with dotted lines, show how much Country A will choose to export and import at each of the three exchange ratios. In the right panel of Figure 3.11, the horizontal axis represents cloth exported by Country A, and the vertical axis is wheat imported. Exchange ratios are then shown as the slopes of rays from the origin; as the price of cloth increases, these rays become steeper. The flattest ray represents Country A's exchange ratio in autarky. As the price of cloth rises and the rays from the origin become steeper, Country A exports more cloth and imports more wheat.

The dimensions of the trade triangles in the left panel are then used to derive the volume of trade undertaken by Country A at each exchange ratio. Point *8* in the right panel represents the volume of trade that is based on production point *2* and consumption point *5* in the left panel; point *9* corresponds to A's offer at the improved terms of trade that result in production at point *3* and consumption at point *6*. A's offer of cloth for wheat is shown for each of the three prices represented in the left panel, and connecting those points in the right panel traces out A's offer curve. Country B's offer curve could be derived in the same manner. As shown in Figure 3.12, however, it curves in the opposite direction. At point *1* in Figure 3.12, where the offer curves cross, Countries A and B agree on the volumes of wheat and cloth to be exchanged, as well as on the exchange ratio for the two goods, which is shown as the slope of the ray from the origin. At any other exchange ratio, there would be no such agreement and the markets for the two goods would be out of equilibrium. If the barter line were steeper, for example, A would choose to import more wheat than B would be willing to export, while A would export more cloth than B would be willing to import. The excess demand

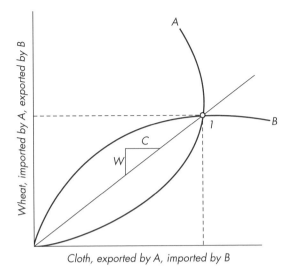

FIGURE 3.12 Offer Curves for Countries A and B, with the Equilibrium Barter Ratio and Trade Volumes

At point *1*, with a barter ratio represented by the slope of the ray from the origin, the two countries agree on the quantity of the two goods to be exchanged. There is no other barter ratio at which that is true, which means there is no other barter ratio at which the market for these goods can clear.

for wheat, which is an excess supply of cloth in a world of barter transactions, indicates that the price of wheat must rise relative to the price of cloth. The barter line becomes flatter. If the countries are out of equilibrium, the automatic adjustments of prices will bring them back.

Offer curves allow us to see explicitly how all the information in the production-possibility curves of the two countries and in the two sets of community indifference curves are relevant in determining the equilibrium volumes of trade and the international exchange ratio. The differing productive abilities of the two countries and the preferences of their consumers are all combined to determine the equilibrium point in Figure 3.12. Offer curves will also prove useful later to illustrate some important theoretical aspects of the impact of tariffs and the relationship between trade and economic growth.

Elasticities and the Terms of Trade with Offer Curves

In those later applications an important factor will be the elasticity of the offer curve. Therefore, before moving on, we consider how the offer curve is related to the more familiar import demand curve and the price elasticity of demand for imports. The left panel of Figure 3.13 shows an offer curve where the price of cloth has risen high enough that the amount of cloth A offers to trade for wheat actually declines. That is, when the price of cloth rises from *0a* to *0b*, A offers two more units of cloth in exchange for two more units of wheat, but when the price rises from *0b* to *0c*, A offers two fewer units of cloth in exchange for two more units of wheat. Is such behavior unusual or inconsistent?

The right panel of Figure 3.13, which shows A's demand for imports of wheat, is intended to remind us why a reduction in the quantity of cloth offered is not unexpected. Each point along the

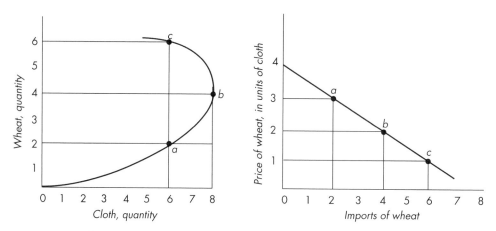

FIGURE 3.13 The Elasticity of Country A's Offer Curve

A's offer curve of cloth for wheat shown in the left panel is based on the same behavior as A's demand for imported wheat shown in the right panel. The maximum offer of cloth occurs when the elasticity of demand for imported wheat is unitary at point *b*.

import demand curve has the same label as the corresponding point along the offer curve. For example, at point *a* the import demand curve shows that A will demand two units of wheat from B when the price is three units of cloth per unit of wheat. A's total spending on wheat imports is six units of cloth, and along the offer curve we note that A offers six units of cloth for two units of wheat. At point *c*, A will demand six units of wheat from B at a price of one unit of cloth per unit of wheat. A's total spending on wheat imports again is six units of cloth, but along the offer curve this corresponds to A's offer of six units of cloth for six units of wheat.

As we move downward along A's import demand curve, the price elasticity of demand declines in absolute value.[4] You can also confirm that result, as well as the fact that A's maximum offer of cloth occurs at point *b*, where the elasticity is *–1.0*. At any price of wheat lower than at point *b*, demand is less elastic, and price will fall by a larger percentage than the quantity of wheat demanded increases. Consequently, total spending on imported wheat (A's offer of cloth) declines. At any price higher than at point *b*, demand is elastic. Price will rise by a smaller percentage than the quantity demanded falls, and total spending on imported wheat again declines. Therefore, as price rises or falls from point *b*, A offers less cloth for wheat.

---

4 The relevant elasticity, η, along a straight-line demand curve is given by the standard formula

$$\eta = \frac{\Delta Q \,/\, \Delta P}{Q \quad\;\; P} = \frac{\Delta Q}{\Delta P} \frac{P}{Q}$$

The second expression shows the inverse of the slope of the demand curve (–2) multiplied by price divided by quantity at any point chosen along the demand curve. By substituting the corresponding price and quantity values along the curve into the formula, you find that at point *a* the elasticity is *–3.0*, at point *b* it is *–1.0* and at point *c* it is *–0.33*.

Summary of Key Concepts

1. Individuals can gain from trade when their relative valuations of two goods initially differ.
2. Nations can experience potential gains from trade when their relative valuations of two goods initially differ, but actual gains in welfare depend upon whether individuals within the country who lose from trade are compensated by those who gain.
3. The opportunity cost of one good, say shampoo, is the amount of another good that must be given up to produce or acquire an additional bottle of shampoo. This concept is more general than the labor theory of value used by the classical economists.
4. A straight line production-possibility curve indicates a constant opportunity cost of obtaining additional output of a good, until the point of complete specialization in production is reached.
5. A country gains from trade when the international price ratio differs from the initial opportunity cost of production domestically or from its marginal rate of substitution in consumption.
6. When there are increasing opportunity costs of production, firms in an economy that trades will adjust their output so that the marginal rate of transformation in production just equals the international price ratio. The tendency to specialize in production is not as great as in the case of constant opportunity costs.
7. An equilibrium relative price ratio internationally is reached when the quantity of a good that one country wants to export just equals the quantity that the other country wants to import.
8. When countries become open to trade, their terms of trade (Px/Pm) are likely to improve the most when they face very elastic foreign demand and supply conditions, that is, a very elastic foreign offer curve.

CASE STUDY

Terms of Trade Changes and Australian Growth

Australia's experience over the period 2003–2006 provides an example of a favourable terms of trade change. During that period, its terms of trade improved by 30 percent and reached the highest level in the past 50 years. Strong commodity demand for coal and iron ore by its rapidly expanding Asian neighbors, especially China, contributed to this performance. The improvement in export prices was not the result of Australian attempts to reduce the quantity made available in world markets in order to drive up prices. In terms of the supply–demand framework in Figure 3.10 the price increase follows from the foreign import demand curve shifting up.

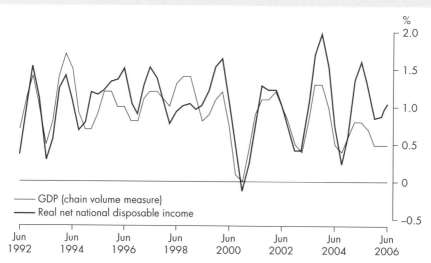

FIGURE 3.14 Two Measures of Australian Growth

Source: Australian Bureau of Statistics, *National Income, Expenditure and Product, Australian National Accounts*, September 2006, p.9. retrieved from http://www.abs.gov.aut

For 2003 to 2006, the quarterly growth rate for national income exceeds the rate for GDP due to an increase in the terms of trade.

Without more careful attention to other influences that operated over this period, we cannot determine the exact contribution of this terms of trade improvement to national welfare. Nevertheless, it is suggestive to note the difference between two measures of aggregate economic performance shown in Figure 3.14. Growth in Australian national income was especially strong over this period and exceeded 4.5 percent annually. This national income figure indicates the purchasing power of income earned from the production of goods and services in the country. Suppose incomes rise because producers of commodities receive higher prices for them. If most of that production is exported, then the higher prices result in more income received by Australians, but the price increase does not have much of an offsetting effect on what they can buy. By way of contrast, real gross domestic product measures the quantity of goods produced in a country. For these same years, the comparable growth rate in Australian GDP was less than 3 percent. If Australia produces the same number of tons of coal and sells them for a higher price in the export market, GDP is unchanged even though national income may rise. The difference between these two Australian figures represents a premium from rising terms of trade.

CASE STUDY QUESTIONS

1. For a country that is too small to influence world prices, we treat the foreign import demand curve as a horizontal straight line, which indicates an infinitely elastic demand for imports. How will an upward shift in such a foreign demand curve affect the small country's measures of real GDP and national income?

2. Suppose higher world prices of agricultural commodities result from a drought in Australia. That scenario implies Australia is large enough to affect world prices. What conditions with respect to world commodity demand and supply from alternative sources will result in the drought having a bigger effect on world prices? How would that situation complicate any explanation of the gains from improved terms of trade? How would that situation influence measures of real GDP and national income in Australia?

3. If productivity in the ocean transport of Australia's mineral wealth improves, how do you expect that to affect the quantity of iron ore demanded by domestic smelters and by foreign smelters? Demonstrate this result graphically in the supply–demand framework of Figure 3.10, paying special attention to the distinction between the price at which iron ore is supplied to the domestic market and to the international market when transportation costs must be included.

4. The World Bank reports the net barter terms of trade shown below for Australia, Germany (a major exporter of high-tech products), and Norway (a major petroleum exporter). Explain whether you expect the terms of trade bonus Australia experienced to be important for these additional countries.

Country	1995	1998	2001	2004
Norway	60.31	60.53	94.89	100.30
Germany	107.48	106.68	101.90	107.18
Australia	99.41	99.30	104.08	116.18

Questions for Study and Review

1. Suppose the marginal rate of substitution of wheat for cloth in a country equals 1.5 and the international exchange ratio is 1.0. Explain how this country will adjust its consumption of wheat and cloth if it can trade at international prices.

2. A country has the opportunity to export wheat in exchange for cloth. If engaging in trade redistributes income to individuals who have a stronger preference for cloth, how does the redistribution complicate any judgment that trade makes the nation better off?

3. In isolation, Country A produces 8 million tons of rice and 14 million tons of beans. One ton of rice exchanges for 2 tons of beans, and there are constant costs.

   a. Construct Country A's production-possibility curve, and label its endpoints.

   b. Suppose Country A now has the opportunity to trade with Country C at the exchange ratio 1R:1B. In equilibrium Country A consumes 16 million tons of beans.

      (i) What will Country A produce after trade?
      (ii) What will Country A consume after trade? Show its consumption point and its trade triangle.
      (iii) What is the gain from trade (in real terms) to Country A?

4. "Trade theory assumes that resources are fully employed both before and after trade and that technology remains unchanged. But if the same amounts of resources are actually used, both before and after trade, I don't see how any gain to the world as a whole can occur." Explain the basis for gains from trade to occur even when worker effort and technology remain the same.

5. Suppose Honduras can produce 120 million tons of bananas if it uses all of its productive resources in the banana industry, or 90 million square meters of cloth if it uses all of its resources in the cloth industry. Use a diagram to illustrate your answers to the following questions. Label the diagram and explain in words.

   a. Assuming constant opportunity costs, draw the Honduran production-possibility curve.

   b. With no trade, suppose Honduran consumers choose to consume 40 million tons of bananas. How much cloth will Honduras then be able to produce?

   c. What is the autarky price or barter exchange ratio in Honduras?

   d. Now suppose that Honduras has the opportunity to engage in foreign trade and that the world exchange ratio is 1B:1C. What will happen to the allocation of resources in Honduras? Explain why.

   e. If Honduras consumes 50 million tons of bananas after trade begins, how much cloth will it consume?

   f. What is the gain from trade to Honduras?

6. How do increasing-cost conditions affect the extent of international specialization and exchange? Why is a country less likely to become completely specialized in this situation compared to one of constant costs?

7. Suppose Countries A and B have identical production-possibility curves subject to increasing opportunity cost, but A consumers have a stronger preference for wheat relative to cloth than B consumers. What can you say about the autarky price in each country before trade takes place? How will the opportunity to trade affect A's production and consumption of wheat compared to the initial autarky condition?

8. What is meant by the terms of trade? Use the figures below to determine the extent of any improvement or worsening in Country A's terms of trade.

Prices	2000	2008
Exports	1.0	1.5
Imports	0.5	1.2

9. Consider the international trade framework shown in Figure 3.10. Suppose Country A, the exporter of cloth, finds that rising oil prices make it more expensive to transport goods to serve the export market.

   a. Explain in which of the three diagrams we should shift a supply or demand curve.

   b. Indicate what elasticity conditions make it more likely that Country B will face an increase in the price of cloth that is nearly as large as the additional cost of transporting the goods.

    c. Suggest how the price of cloth in Country A is affected by this change in the cost of serving the export market. Be sure to distinguish between the price paid by consumers in A's domestic market and the price paid by consumers in the world market.

10. Consider trade between Kenya and the E.U. in the offer curve framework.

    a. Draw an offer curve for Kenya that shows its willingness to trade tea for machinery. Include both an elastic and an inelastic range in Kenya's offer curve.

    b. Draw an offer curve for the E.U. that shows its willingness to trade machinery for tea. Show this E.U. curve intersecting the Kenyan offer curve in the inelastic range of the Kenyan curve. Note the equilibrium terms of trade established.

    c. Compare the equilibrium international price you found in question (b) to the autarky prices in Kenya and the E.U. (You can find a country's autarky price by drawing a line tangent to the offer curve at the origin.) Explain which country benefits the most from a more favorable movement in its terms of trade when it abandons its autarky position.

    d. "The Kenyan offer curve is likely to be less elastic than the E.U. offer curve." Justify this claim by explaining what factors determine the elasticity of an offer curve.

References and Suggestions for Further Reading

Contributions cited in this chapter include:

Bernhofen, Daniel and Brown, John (2005) "An Empirical Assessment of the Comparative Advantage Gains from Trade: Evidence from Japan," *American Economic Review* 95: 208–25.

Bowley, Arthur (1924) *The Mathematical Groundwork of Economics: An Introductory Treatise*. Reprinted New York: A.M. Kelly, 1965.

Edgeworth, Francis Y. (1881) *Mathematical Physics: An Essay on the Application of Mathematics to the Moral Sciences*. Reprinted New York: A.M. Kelly, 1967.

Haberler, Gottfried (1936) *The Theory of International Trade*, New York: Macmillan, ch. 12.

Huber, J. Richard (1971) "Effect on Prices of Japan's Entry into World Commerce after 1858," *Journal of Political Economy* 79: 614–28.

Additional sources that present analytical tools developed in this chapter are:

Ethier, Wilfred (2008) "The Greater the Differences, the Greater the Gains?" Penn Institute for Economic Research Working Paper 09–009.

Heller, H. Robert (1968) *International Trade, Theory and Empirical Evidence*, Englewood Cliffs, NJ: Prentice Hall, ch. 4.

Meade, James E. (1955) *Trade and Welfare*, London: Oxford University Press.

Samuelson, P.A. (1956) "Social Indifference Curves," *Quarterly Journal of Economics*, 70: 1–21.

Viner, Jacob (1937) *Studies in the Theory of International Trade*, New York: Harper.

APPENDIX: THE ROLE OF MONEY PRICES

In the modern world traders actually place their orders and strike bargains on the basis of money prices, not the barter exchange ratios that we have examined thus far. Traders buy a foreign good when its price is lower than it is at home. (For the sake of simplicity we are still ignoring transport costs, but traders must allow for them and for all other costs – tariffs, insurance, commissions, legal costs, and so on – in comparing domestic and foreign prices.) German wheat importers pay no attention to the barter exchange ratio between steel and wheat, and they may be oblivious to opportunity cost as we have used it earlier. Nevertheless, the basic principles on which trade is based will still apply when we bring in money prices. In this discussion, the determination of an equilibrium exchange rate between two currencies plays a key role, in a way very similar to the determination of relative wage rates across countries in the many-good model of comparative advantage. Because countries often find it more acceptable politically to talk of changing exchange rates rather than wage rates, and because exchange rates apply to all costs of production, not just wages, we develop the current explanation in terms of exchange rates.

A barter exchange ratio, such as the one we have used in our example of trade between France and Germany, implies a ratio of money prices. For example, if one apple exchanges for two oranges, the price of an apple is twice the price of an orange. (If an apple costs €0.50 and an orange costs €0.25, then one apple is equal in value to two oranges.) Therefore, if barter exchange ratios differ in two countries, relative money prices will also differ.

We can use the French–German constant-cost example to illustrate this point, but in discussing the money value of trade we shall use the separate national currencies that existed prior to the creation of the euro. Before trade, the domestic barter exchange ratios were:

France: 1 ton of steel for 3 tons of wheat
Germany: 1 ton of steel for 1 ton of wheat

The money price in France of 1 ton of steel is therefore equal to the money price of three tons of wheat. That is, 1 ton of steel costs 3 times as much as 1 ton of wheat. In Germany, the money price of 1 ton of steel is equal to the money price of 1 ton of wheat. We assume the following actual money prices in the two countries:

	France	Germany
Steel (per ton)	Fr 300	DM 400
Wheat (per ton)	Fr 100	DM 400
Ratio (P_s/P_w)	3:1	1:1

The ratios based on money prices mirror the differences in opportunity cost ratios in our barter example, and they tell us that an opportunity for gainful trade exists.

These are the money prices prevailing before trade begins. When trade opens up, how can traders compare prices? Will German buyers wish to buy French steel at Fr 300 per ton? Or will French buyers find German steel a bargain at DM 400 per ton? Since the currencies used are different, we must know the exchange rate between francs and marks before meaningful price comparisons can be made. The exchange rate is a price, a rate at which we can convert one currency into another. If the exchange rate is Fr 1 = DM 2, French buyers can compare German prices with their own: German steel will cost them Fr 200 per ton (Fr 200 = DM 400) compared to Fr 300 at home; German wheat will cost Fr 200 per ton compared to Fr 100 at home. French traders will therefore import steel and export wheat. At the same time, German traders will find French wheat cheaper (Fr 100 times DM 2/Fr = DM 200) than domestic wheat. Thus a two-way trade, profitable to both sides, will spring up: German steel will exchange for French wheat, although each trader is simply pursuing his or her own individual interest in buying at the cheapest possible price.

Although we examine in detail the determination of exchange rates in the second half of this book, here we consider the simple case where only merchandise trade between these two countries is possible. Therefore, we ask, will the money value of French imports of steel be equal to that of German imports of wheat? If so, we will have balanced trade; if not, the imbalance in trade will cause the exchange rate to shift. In the barter example summarized in Table 3.3, France imported 45 million tons of steel and exported 90 million tons of wheat. The money value of its trade, at the prices we have used above, would therefore be:

Wheat exports, 90 million tons @ Fr 100 = Fr 9 billion
Steel imports, 45 million tons @ Fr 200 = Fr 9 billion

Thus we have a position of balanced trade in money value, just as we did in barter terms.

If French exports did not equal imports in money value, the exchange rate would change. For example, if German traders wanted to buy 100 million tons of French wheat when the exchange rate was Fr 1 = DM 2, they would try to buy Fr 10 billion in the foreign exchange market, but French traders would be offering only Fr 9 billion for German steel. The excess demand for francs would drive up their price – that is, 1 franc would exchange for somewhat more than 2 marks, for example, Fr 1 = DM 2.5. If domestic money prices were kept unchanged in the two countries, the higher exchange value of the franc would make French wheat more expensive to German buyers, because one ton of wheat now costs DM 250 instead of DM 200. German steel would now be cheaper to French buyers, because one ton of steel now costs Fr 160 (400/2.5 = 160) instead of Fr 200. These price changes will tend to reduce German purchases of French wheat and increase French purchases of German steel. When exports become equal to imports in money value, the exchange rate will stop moving and equilibrium will exist. With fixed money prices in the two countries, the exchange rate thus plays the same role as the barter exchange ratio in our previous examples.

Are there any limits on the movement of the exchange rate? Profitable two-way trade can take place only at an exchange rate that makes wheat cheaper in France than in Germany. If *both* commodities were cheaper in Germany, trade would flow in only one direction: from Germany to France. The reader should consider the consequences of exchange rates such as Fr 1 = DM 5 (all goods cheaper in Germany), or Fr 1 = DM 1 (all goods cheaper in France) to see why the exchange rate must lie between the limits set by the money price ratios of steel (Fr 1 = DM 1.33) and wheat (Fr 1 = DM 4). These exchange rate limits are analogous to the limits on the barter terms of trade noted earlier. Again, if the ratio of the two money prices in the two countries is identical, then no basis for trade would exist.

Chapter 4

Trade and the Role of Factor Endowments

LEARNING OBJECTIVES

By the end of this chapter you should be able to explain:

- why differences in factor endowments across countries create a basis for trade

- why a higher international price of a country's export good will raise the return to the country's abundant factor throughout the economy

- what conditions must hold for trade to equalize wages in Britain and China

- how the effects of trade on the distribution of income differ in the short run, the intermediate run, and the long run

- why economists have obtained mixed, and sometimes paradoxical, results from their tests of the factor endowments theory's predictions of trade patterns

In the preceding two chapters we saw that if relative prices differ in two isolated countries, the introduction of trade between them will be mutually beneficial. Different relative prices of commodities indicate that relative opportunity costs differ in the two countries. In the simple two-good model, each country has a comparative advantage in one commodity and a comparative disadvantage in the other. Given the opportunity to trade, each country will increase production of the commodity in which it has a comparative advantage, exporting it in exchange for the commodity in which it has a comparative disadvantage.

Why do relative prices and costs differ in the first place? Classical theory did not ask this question: Ricardo simply took it for granted that labor cost ratios (and hence prices) differed in the two countries before trade. As noted in Chapter 2, Ricardo probably surprised his readers by giving an example where Portugal had an absolute advantage in the production of both wine and cloth. He never bothered to explain why the British were unable to figure out how the Portuguese achieved this superior performance. Apparently, technology could be transmitted extremely well within Portugal, but it could remain a secret inaccessible to the British. Such extreme assumptions may have seemed plausible in the case of Britain and Portugal, because here were two countries with different languages, different legal systems, and different religious and cultural traditions. Ricardo explicitly encouraged that interpretation by pointing to the "financial or real insecurity of capital" in operating abroad and "the natural disinclination which every man has to quit the country of his birth and connections."

Classical writers did envision technology and factors of production crossing borders, but Adam Smith included this possibility in his discussion of colonies. He noted that colonists carried with them "a knowledge of agriculture and other useful arts," as well as important understandings of commercial law and government structure. John Stuart Mill recognized that movements of capital to the colonies kept its return from declining in England.

The discussion in this chapter rests on yet another characterization of economies throughout the world, one where ideas and technology have diffused across countries to become equally accessible everywhere. Labor, capital, and other factors of production, however, are in fixed supply in each country. Differences across countries in these factor endowments provide a basis for explaining why opportunity cost ratios differ across countries. Thus, differences in factor endowments allow us to predict patterns of trade across countries.

FACTOR PROPORTIONS AS A DETERMINANT OF TRADE

The factor proportions theory of trade is attributed to two Swedish economists, Eli Heckscher and Bertil Ohlin. Their initial contributions appeared in Swedish and received little attention among English-speaking economists until the publication in 1933 of Ohlin's book *Interregional and International Trade.*

Let us begin with an example that draws on Ohlin's approach: why does Denmark export cheese to the United States and import wheat from the United States? The Heckscher–Ohlin model (hereafter referred to as the H–O model) that answers this question rests upon two key ideas that differ from the classical approach. First, rather than focus on the single input labor, the H–O model allows for additional inputs and recognizes that different goods require these inputs in different proportions. For example, both land and labor are necessary to produce either cheese or wheat, but cheese production requires relatively more labor and wheat production requires relatively more land. In fact, we assume that cheese is always the more labor-intensive good, regardless of what the relative costs of land and labor happen to be in a country. Second, differences across countries in technology are no longer assumed. The H–O model instead distinguishes countries by the availability of factors of production, that is, by their factor endowments. Although the United States has both more land and more labor than Denmark, it has relatively much more land than labor. Therefore, Ohlin reached the conclusion that the United States will have a comparative advantage in producing wheat, the good that requires relatively more land in production.

Broader Implications of the H–O Model

The classical model of two countries and two goods provides a simple but powerful analytical framework that also lends itself easily to subsequent diagrammatic representations. In a similar vein we will initially focus on how the basic H–O model explains the pattern of trade between two countries for two goods and two factor inputs (the $2 \times 2 \times 2$ case). We can then use this framework to investigate several related issues where the H–O model gives very provocative predictions. Two key examples are the implications of growth in factor endowments and the influence of trade on the distribution of income within a country.

In the classical model with a single factor input, growth in a country's endowment of labor could only lead to more exports, never fewer imports. Distributional issues were irrelevant: either all individuals gained from trade or all individuals lost, but there was no divergence of interests within the country. In the H–O model it is possible to consider the conflicting interests of different factors of production when prices change internationally. This approach does not predict that some factors gain a little and some gain a lot. Rather, the real income of some factors rises but for others it falls. Understanding the reasons for this outcome is quite relevant to our discussion in future chapters of the political economy of changing international trade policy.

Another modification of the H–O model we consider is what happens in the short run when not all factor inputs can be shifted immediately to their long-run desired uses. In many respects, such a model yields results that are less of a departure from a more simple partial equilibrium analysis of supply and demand conditions in a single market. Recognizing why results differ in the short run and the long run help to reinforce our understanding of the general equilibrium H–O model.

Just as we considered implications of the classical model in a many-good world as a way to understand how the theory might be tested in the real world, we follow the same procedure for the H–O model. The mixed results that economists have reported from various empirical tests suggest why the H–O model, useful as it is, does not reign as a comprehensive explanation of the observed patterns of international trade.

Building Blocks of the H–O Model

Our discussion of increasing opportunity cost in Chapter 3 suggested more than one plausible explanation. Two possibilities are especially relevant to the H–O theory: specialized inputs are more productive in one industry than another, or bundles of inputs are better suited to one industry than another. To distinguish the difference between these ideas, we formulate a model that retains the seven assumptions listed in Chapter 3 when we discussed the approach of neoclassical economists. That list was not exhaustive, however, and we must add to it here.

One possibility is to assume that specialized inputs are needed to produce different goods. In the extreme, that may mean an input is productive in one industry only and adds nothing to output in another industry if it is employed there. A less extreme situation exists when there are differences in the labor skills necessary to produce cheese from those needed to produce wheat. If firms have hired the most efficient workers in each industry initially, what happens as workers are transferred out of cheese production into wheat production? Those newly hired to grow wheat are likely to be progressively less productive than current employees who already have a practiced eye to know when to plant and harvest. Pasture land on mountainsides may sustain milk cows but yield very little additional output of wheat if it is transferred to that use. These various possibilities are elaborated later in the chapter when we discuss the **specific factors model**.

A second possibility is that differences among workers may not be so great when we allow enough time for retraining to occur, and land in the same climate zone and geographic location may be comparable in many uses. Nevertheless, homogeneous land and labor may be required in different proportions to produce different goods. We assume that the optimal land–labor ratio required in wheat production is greater than the land–labor ratio in cheese production. Reducing cheese output does not free up land and labor in the same proportions as they are currently being used in wheat production. Rather, too little land is available and too much labor. With this new, smaller ratio of land to labor being used in wheat production, output expands less than in the constant opportunity cost case. Because this new land–labor mix is less suited to producing wheat, less wheat is gained for a given amount of cheese foregone, and the opportunity cost of wheat rises. We demonstrate this situation with a more formal model.

Factor Endowments and the Production-Possibility Curve

Our goal is to demonstrate how a country's factor endowments influence the shape and position of its production-possibility curve. To do so, we first briefly review the diagrammatic tools economists use to represent the relationship between inputs of productive factors and the resulting output of a commodity. For example, wheat can be produced with many different combinations of land and labor. The same 160 metric tons of wheat might be produced with 80 hectares of land and 1 man-year of labor or with 8 hectares of land and 20 man-years of labor. Which is the best of the many possible combinations of land and labor that an agronomist might suggest will depend upon the relative cost of these inputs. We demonstrate these relationships using an isoquant for a representative wheat producer.

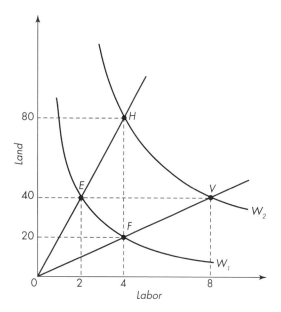

FIGURE 4.1 Isoquants for Wheat Production

W_1 shows all of the combinations of land and labor that are sufficient to produce a given amount of wheat. W_2 represents twice the output of wheat and requires twice the inputs of land and labor. The curvature of the isoquant results from the diminishing marginal rate of substitution of land for labor.

Isoquants for Wheat Producers

The isoquant W_1 in Figure 4.1 represents the various combinations of labor and land that can produce a constant output of wheat (160 metric tons). As we move down and to the right on W_1, for example from E to F, the proportion of land to labor decreases. The marginal rate of substitution of land for labor also declines, because progressively larger additions of labor are necessary to maintain output constant and offset the reduction of another hectare of land.

To show the input requirements for a larger output of wheat, above and to the right of W_1 we can draw another isoquant. W_2 shows the alternative combinations of land and labor required to produce 320 metric tons of wheat. The diagram incorporates constant returns to scale, because doubling the output of wheat requires doubling the input of both labor and land. A set of isoquants can be drawn to represent any other desired level of wheat production.

The H–O model assumes that the two countries have identical production functions, which means that this entire set of isoquants is the same for countries A and B. Note, however, that the two countries need not actually use the same combination of land and labor to produce wheat. Firms in different countries are likely to choose different points along the isoquant because the relative cost of labor and land is likely to differ in each country. For example, in India wheat is produced on tiny plots of land with highly labor-intensive methods, whereas in Australia a 500-hectare farm may be cultivated by a single farmer. Nevertheless, these facts are consistent with the assumption that production functions are everywhere the same. Producers in India have an incentive to choose more labor-intensive methods because relative wages are much lower in India.

Factor Prices and Production Decisions

In Figure 4.2 we show the firm's choice of the best combination of labor and land, given the ratio of factor prices. Let the firm's budget be given by the line *MN*, whose slope is determined by the wage rate relative to the rental rate for land. The budget is just sufficient to rent *OM* of land, *ON* of labor inputs, or any combination of land and labor inputs indicated by points lying on *MN*. Given this budget constraint, a wheat producer will maximize output by producing at point *E*, the point of tangency between *MN* and W_1. Wheat producers choose the land–labor ratio indicated by the vector *OE*. If they use any other input ratio, such as OB, they will find themselves on a lower isoquant, W_0, which means that they produce less wheat for the same expenditure.[1]

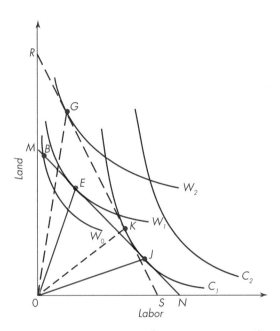

FIGURE 4.2 Comparison of Factor Intensity in Cheese and Wheat

The two sets of isoquants indicate that cheese is more labor-intensive than is wheat. With relative land and labor costs represented by the budget line *MN*, an amount of wheat represented by W_1 or an amount of cheese represented by C_1 can be produced. If land becomes cheaper, as represented by the line SR, the new expenditure level allows production of either C_1 or W_2; wheat production rises because land-intensive wheat benefits most from cheaper land.

---

1 Applying the same reasoning as in the consumer case, we recognize that the marginal rate of substitution in production will equal the marginal product of labor divided by the marginal product of land. At *B*, the *MRS* is greater than the wage–rental ratio. Because the gain to the producer from substituting labor for land exceeds the market price of labor, the firm gains by moving toward point *E*.

The assumptions of perfect competition and perfect mobility of factors within the economy additionally guarantee that producers of both wheat and cheese must pay the same wage rate and land rent. At the common factor–price ratio given by the slope of *MN*, firms choose factor proportions *OE* in wheat and *OJ* in cheese. If wages are higher, giving a common factor–price ratio as indicated by the slope of *RS*, firms choose to substitute land for labor and now use the factor proportions *OG* in wheat and *OK* in cheese.

Note that in both cases the ratio of land to labor is higher in wheat than in cheese. We impose the condition that within each country, for any given factor–price ratio, wheat will always be land-intensive relative to cheese. This assumption rules out a **factor intensity reversal**, where wheat production might become the relatively labor-intensive good at lower wage rates. That outcome potentially could occur if wheat producers were able to substitute labor for land much more easily in response to a fall in wages than cheese producers could, but we rule out such circumstances.

Derivation of the Production-Possibility Curve

Given production functions for wheat and cheese, once we know a country's resource endowment we can derive its production-possibility curve. To do so, we use the Edgeworth–Bowley box introduced in Chapter 3. Here, we apply it to show the allocation of land and labor in the production of cheese and wheat. The dimensions of the box are determined by the country's labor and land endowment. Output of cheese is measured from the O_{cheese} origin and wheat from the O_{wheat} origin.

We are interested in the **efficiency locus**, the collection of points at which the output of wheat is maximized, given the output of cheese. These efficient points are given by the points of tangency between wheat isoquants and cheese isoquants, such as points *P*, *Q*, and *R* in the upper section of Figure 4.3. The reason for this result can be seen as follows. Consider a point that is not on the efficiency locus, such as point *Z*. Cheese output is indicated by isoquant C_2, and wheat output by isoquant W_2. However, we can hold cheese output constant, move along isoquant C_2 to point *Q* (i.e. produce the same amount of cheese with less land and slightly more labor), and thereby release resources that make it possible to produce more wheat. At point *Q* we have the same output of cheese, but we have increased the output of wheat by moving from isoquant W_2 to W_3. At point *Q*, however, we have maximized wheat production keeping cheese output constant along C_2, and we cannot increase output of one good any further without decreasing output of the other. Point *Q* represents a combination of wheat and cheese outputs that lies on the production-possibility curve. *P*, *R*, and other points on the efficiency locus also correspond to points on the production-possibility curve.

Another way of seeing this point is to recall that firms in each industry have minimized costs to produce a given output when the factor–price ratio equals the slope of the production isoquant. But at *Z* the slopes of the isoquants are different in wheat and cheese; this condition implies that producers in the two sectors are responding to different wage–rental ratios. Unequal wage rental ratios indicate a disequilibrium situation in the market for productive factors, because under perfect competition factor prices will become the same in both industries. Only when the isoquants for wheat and cheese are tangent to each other will factor prices be the same in both industries. This equality ensures that no reallocation of land and labor can increase output of one good without decreasing output of the other.

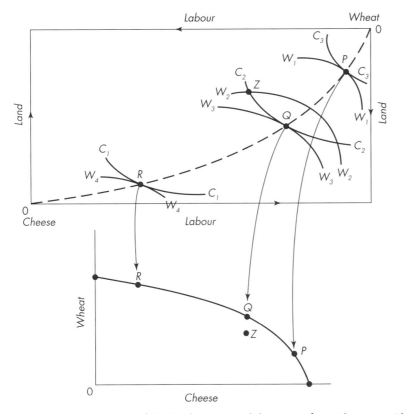

FIGURE 4.3 Derivation of the Production-Possibility Curve from Alternative Allocations of Land and Labor

In the box diagram Country A's endowment of labor is represented by the horizontal length of the box and its endowment of land represented by its vertical height. The country maximizes efficiency and therefore output at tangencies between C and W isoquants, where the marginal rate of substitution of labor for land is equal in both industries. Those tangencies generate a dashed efficiency locus. The combinations of wheat and cheese produced along that locus at points R, Q, and P in the box diagram then provide points R, Q and P along the production-possibility curve below. Point Z in the box diagram is not at a tangency and is therefore off the efficiency locus. It is inefficient, as shown by point Z inside the production-possibility curve.

Characteristics of the Production-Possibility Curve

The slope of the production-possibility curve depends upon differences in the factor intensities of wheat and cheese. If the two goods instead had identical intensities and used land and labor in the same proportions, then the efficiency locus in the Edgeworth–Bowley box would be a diagonal line from one origin to the other. The corresponding production-possibility curve would be a straight line indicating constant opportunity cost, because any expansion of cheese production could be achieved by maintaining the same factor proportions as at the original point. The factors the cheese industry needs to expand output at the same cost are exactly those released by the wheat industry.

When factor intensities in the two sectors differ, an expansion of cheese output, for example, causes its opportunity cost of production to rise; the contracting wheat industry releases less labor and more land than the cheese industry finds it efficient to use at initial prices, and the extra cheese produced per ton of wheat given up declines. The greater the difference in factor intensities, the more the contract curve in the box diagram will differ from the diagonal, and the greater the degree of increasing opportunity cost observed along the production-possibility curve.

Comparing the Production-Possibility Curves of Two Countries

We can also note how a country's resource endowment affects the dimensions of its Edgeworth–Bowley box and hence determines the shape and size of its production-possibility curve. The ratio of labor to land is higher in Denmark compared to the U.S., and we characterize Denmark as being relatively labor abundant. Its box diagram will be elongated along the horizontal labor axis. The U.S. has more land relative to labor compared to Denmark, and we can characterize the U.S. as relatively land abundant. Its box diagram will be elongated along the vertical land axis.

Figure 4.4 shows a box diagram for each country and the corresponding production-possibility curve. Because wheat requires a higher proportion of land to labor than does cheese, the U.S.'s relative

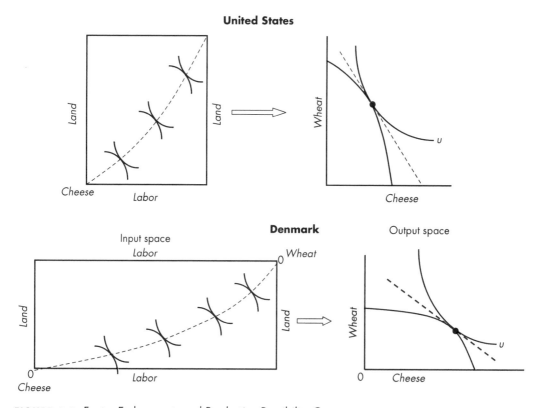

FIGURE 4.4 Factor Endowments and Production-Possibility Curves

The U.S. is relatively land abundant while Denmark is relatively labor abundant. Denmark's production-possibility curve shows a lower opportunity cost of producing cheese, based on the steeper slope of the U.S. curve at any common ratio in which the two goods are produced.

abundance of land causes its production-possibility curve to be elongated, or biased, along the wheat axis. Denmark's relative abundance of labor is similarly reflected in a greater relative capacity to produce cheese. Alternatively, we can compare the slopes of the two curves if both countries produce the two goods in the same proportion. Along a 45 degree line out of the origin, the slope of the Danish production-possibility curve will be flatter than the corresponding slope of the U.S. curve, because Denmark has a lower cost of producing cheese, the good along the horizontal axis.

We need to incorporate one more feature of the H–O model to derive its key result. Although we have demonstrated that Denmark will have a lower relative cost of producing cheese when the two countries produce both goods in the same proportion, we also must rule out demand preferences that otherwise may offset the Danish cost advantage. If Denmark has a particularly strong preference for cheese, it is possible that Danish consumers will demand so much cheese that its pre-trade price exceeds the price in the U.S. In that case Denmark will import cheese to satisfy this craving. We rule out such a possibility by imposing the condition that preferences in each country are identical and homothetic. Confront Danes and Americans with the same prices and give them the same income, and they will choose to buy the same bundle of goods. Furthermore, if income levels differ across the two countries, or income is distributed differently within the two countries, that does not affect the outcome because all individuals are assumed to spend their income on available goods in the same proportions, regardless of whether they are rich or poor. These strong demand assumptions guarantee an unambiguous result, although small deviations from these conditions are unlikely to be significant enough to overturn the importance of differences in supply conditions in determining autarky prices.

Given the production and demand conditions stated above, relative prices in the two countries will be different, and each country will have a comparative advantage in the commodity it produces more cheaply. What the H–O theory has added is an explanation of the cause of the relative price differences, a basic reason for the existence of comparative advantage. Based on this model of two

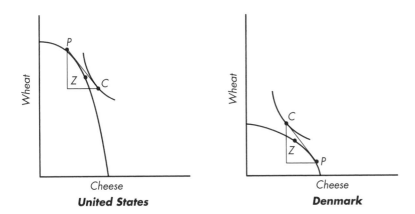

FIGURE 4.5 Patterns of Trade Given by the Factor Proportions Theory

Trade, according to the factor endowments theory, results in the relatively land-abundant country, shown in the left panel, exporting the land-intensive good (wheat) and importing the labor-intensive good (cheese) from the relatively labor-abundant country shown in the right panel. Trade causes each country to become more specialized in production at *P* than in the autarky equilibrium at *Z*. Both countries consume the two goods in the same proportion given by point *C* along an indifference curve that is higher than one drawn through *Z*.

countries, two goods, and two factors of production, we can now state the **Heckscher–Ohlin theorem**: *A country will export the good that uses intensively the factor in which it is relatively abundant.*

Trade in this situation is shown in Figure 4.5. Initial equilibrium positions at *Z* in each country demonstrate that the autarky price of cheese is lower in Denmark. When trade is possible, both countries become more specialized in production at point *P*, but more similar in consumption at point *C*. Even though Denmark and the U.S. are of unequal sizes, we can still find an equilibrium price that results in the U.S. import demand for cheese just equal to the Danish export supply of cheese.

How Different are Factor Endowments?

There are obvious differences in factor endowments across countries, but documenting them in a systematic way is difficult. Portions of a data set compiled by Daniel Trefler for 1992 provide the basis for the endowment shares reported in Table 4.1. Each entry shows a country's percentage share of the endowment of a given factor of production, where the calculation is based on the total endowment of the factor observed in a sample of 71 countries.

If there were just two factors, then simply comparing a country's usable land share to its labor share would show it was relatively land abundant if that ratio were greater than one. Because there

TABLE 4.1 Differences in Factor Endowments, Shown by Share of Total, by Country, 1992

	Capital	Not completed high school	Completed high school	Land	Energy	GNP share, PPP
Argentina	0.68	0.87	0.91	4.63	0.98	1.31
Bangladesh	0.13	2.98	0.92	0.24	0.44	0.52
Brazil	3.29	4.85	2.45	14.94	1.50	3.54
Canada	3.19	0.61	2.77	8.78	6.14	2.25
Germany	8.85	2.46	2.37	0.39	2.05	6.73
France	5.17	1.96	2.31	0.92	0.34	4.78
United Kingdom	3.27	2.06	2.78	0.41	1.45	4.56
Indonesia	2.83	6.40	2.47	2.94	3.49	1.67
India	3.69	30.14	13.51	5.03	5.20	5.63
Japan	17.12	5.18	9.44	0.62	0.43	11.37
Korea, Rep.	2.29	1.07	2.60	0.18	0.03	1.81
Mexico	2.08	2.48	1.38	2.87	10.29	2.46
Malaysia	0.84	0.62	0.47	0.50	2.94	0.42
Netherlands	1.13	0.43	0.72	0.05	2.59	1.33
Sweden	0.95	0.22	0.82	0.64	0.21	0.68

	Capital	Not completed high school	Completed high school	Land	Energy	GNP share, PPP
Turkey	0.99	2.19	1.07	1.14	0.37	1.24
United States	23.16	3.47	33.29	14.48	17.87	27.00
South Africa	0.60	1.25	0.22	4.15	2.45	1.19
Total	100	100	100	100	100	100

Source: Factor endowment data from Trefler (2002). Available at http://www.rotman.utoronto.ca/~dtrefler (accessed 2 September 2008). GNP data from World Bank (2007). All variables are expressed as shares of the 71-country total.

are many factors, however, other ratios might contradict this conclusion. A more appropriate comparison is to compare any endowment to the country's share of world income. The final column of the table gives that figure, where the measure of income has been adjusted to correct for differences in purchasing power across countries (a topic addressed in Part II of this book). The income share represents an approximation of domestic demand for the factor, given the H–O assumption that all countries spend their incomes in the same proportions. Therefore, if the country's endowment share for a factor exceeds the country's income share, the country is relatively abundant in that factor and will export goods that require it intensively.

Table 4.1 shows several countries are relatively abundant in unskilled or semi-skilled labor (individuals of working age who have not completed high school): Bangladesh, Brazil, Indonesia, India, Mexico, Malaysia, Turkey, and South Africa. The H–O model predicts that they will exports goods that use this less skilled labor intensively. That effect will be more pronounced when the difference between the domestic endowment (supply) and GNP (demand) is large.

Some industrial countries, such as the U.S., do not appear to be capital abundant. Rather, their comparative advantage appears to rest on the relative abundance of skilled labor. Some countries appear to be relatively scarce in all factors! In part, that may result from the consolidated measure of land and energy resources reported in the table. Trefler also breaks down those aggregates into different types of each resource, some of which these countries have in abundance. More importantly, the ability of some countries to generate high income from fewer inputs, the cause of the apparent scarcity, may indicate a more efficient economy. That situation contradicts the H–O assumption that the same technology is available everywhere. We discuss that possibility later in this chapter.

Implications of the H–O Theory

International trade economists have been particularly attracted to the H–O model because it yields several clear predictions that are testable. Two important examples are the consequences of changes in factor endowments and changes in the price of goods traded internationally. These changes are most straightforward to consider when they can be considered as exogenous, or independent of the amount of trade that occurs. An increase in the labor force due to a faster rate of population growth or a change in pension policy can plausibly be regarded as exogenous in the first case, and a country so small that its trade cannot influence prices internationally can treat price changes as exogenous. We consider this more restrictive setting in our initial applications of the model.

TRADE AND CHANGING FACTOR ENDOWMENTS

While the relationship of changing factor endowments to economic growth will be addressed more fully in Chapters 8 and 11, consider here the consequence of a one-time increase in the labor force of a country too small to affect world prices. As shown in Figure 4.6 the shift in the production-possibility curve is biased toward cheese, the labor-intensive good. In fact, at the same relative price of cheese (shown by the initial tangency of the international terms of trade line to the production-possibility curve at P) the point of tangency along the new curve occurs at P_1. Output of cheese has increased substantially, while the output of wheat has fallen. This effect, demonstrated by Thomas Rybczynski (1955), holds because at unchanged terms of trade and unchanged returns to land and labor, producers of cheese and wheat choose to use exactly the same factor proportions as at P.

How can the initial proportions of land to labor be maintained if there is no additional land available to the economy as a whole? Such an outcome is possible only if less of the land-intensive good, wheat, is produced. All of the extra labor is used to produce cheese. The same ratio of land to labor can be maintained in cheese production by reducing wheat output, which makes land (and some more labor) available to the expanding cheese sector. Without that reduction in wheat output, adding all the extra labor to the same amount of land in the cheese sector would drive up the return to land in that sector. A higher return in one sector than another represents a disequilibrium situation and a signal to shift land away from wheat production.

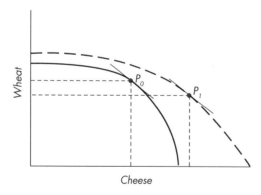

FIGURE 4.6 Growth in the Labor Force

When more labor becomes available, with constant output prices, the same factor proportions used in each industry at point P_0 will now be used at point P_1.

The Rybczynski Theorem Demonstrated in the Edgeworth–Bowley Box

We can use the Edgeworth–Bowley box diagram to show the reallocation of land and labor that occurs after an increase in the labor endowment. Consider the initial production point A, in Figure 4.7, where the cheese and wheat isoquants are tangent. If world prices remain constant, then the wage–rental ratio that corresponds to the equilibrium at A will be the same wage–rental ratio that applies when the country's labor force grows from L_0 to L_1. Correspondingly, the land–labor ratios chosen by cheese and wheat producers at A will be the same ratios chosen in the new equilibrium at B. At that new point, output of the labor-intensive good, cheese, has increased, and output of wheat has fallen.

We can make a stronger statement about the increase in cheese output: a given percentage increase in the labor force will result in a greater percentage increase in cheese production. Ronald Jones (1965) termed this result a magnification effect, and we present his algebraic demonstration of it in the appendix to this chapter. Not only is all of the additional labor in the economy allocated to cheese production, but labor and land are released by the contraction of wheat production necessary to maintain the land–labor ratio in cheese production. Therefore, the percentage increase in the amount of labor used in cheese production is greater than the percentage increase in the labor force. Both labor and land used in cheese production have grown by the same percentage when the economy moves from A to B, and because of the assumption of constant returns to scale, cheese production increases by that same percentage. Consequently, the percentage growth in cheese production exceeds the percentage growth in the labor force.

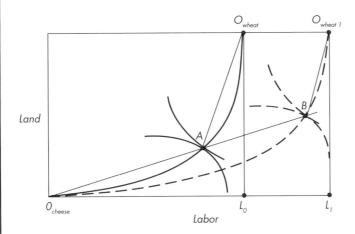

FIGURE 4.7 The Rybczynski Theorem

An increase in the labor force from L_0 to L_1 results in an expansion of cheese output from O_cA to O_cB, while wheat output falls from O_wA to $O_{w1}B$.

Changing Patterns of Factor Endowments and Comparative Advantage

A more general observation from the Denmark–U.S. example is that growth in the U.S. labor force makes the U.S. relative factor endowment more similar to Denmark's and consequently reduces the amount of trade predicted by the $2 \times 2 \times 2$ H–O model. Conversely, if factor endowments become less similar across countries, the H–O model predicts that more trade will occur. In accord with this theory, the choice of China and India to join the world trading system over the past 20 years will lead to an expansion of trade between industrialized and developing countries, because the addition of two very labor-abundant countries to the latter group has increased the disparity in relative factor endowments between the two groups.

In the H–O model a nation's comparative advantage position is not permanently fixed, but changes as factor supplies change both within the country and in its trading partners. For example, a nation's labor supply depends on its growth in population, and the proportion that is of working age. Labor-force participation rates among women and older workers also have changed substantially in many countries in recent decades. Distinctions between skilled and unskilled workers are often relevant, and creating a more skilled labor force depends on educational policy and other socioeconomic circumstances that can change through time. Capital can be accumulated through domestic saving.

Consider Taiwan's experience as an illustration of the influence of changing relative factor endowments. During the 1960s and 1970s it was a labor-abundant economy and exported inexpensive garments and shoes. Because of large expenditures on education and high rates of savings and investment, by the 1980s and 1990s a more highly skilled labor force and a larger physical capital stock allowed a shift in Taiwan's comparative advantage. Its exports included a larger share of products that required higher skills and more capital. By 2000, Taiwan was the fourth largest recipient of patents in the United States (Dean and Ulmonen, 2002), behind Japan and Germany. That progression indicates a further shift toward goods requiring more advanced technology, a topic we pursue in Chapter 5.

How Different are Factor Intensities?

The H–O theory requires that different goods use factor inputs in different proportions. Theoretically, this distinction is important, because the greater the differences in factor intensities, the greater the extent to which we will observe increasing opportunity costs of production and the more significant will factor endowments be in explaining autarky prices. Empirically, measuring these differences is not so straightforward.

One approach is to consider the value-added in an industry (the value of its output minus the value of intermediate inputs it buys from other industries) and to observe how it is divided among different factors. A useful category from national income accounts is compensation to employees. We attribute the rest of the value-added to factors such as land, tangible capital (plant and equipment), and intangible capital (patented ideas, trade secrets, brand image). The value-added generated by such factors represents a flow of factor services, not a stock of machines or ideas allocated to a particular industry. Not measuring the stock of capital avoids some problems, because machines and buildings are bought at different times at different prices and they wear out at different rates. Land varies tremendously in its fertility, and intangible ideas are even more difficult to measure. Looking at the income that factors receive avoids those problems, but introduces others. Profits may vary considerably over the business cycle, and some industries may be more sensitive to the business cycle than others. No single measure is ideal.

Column two of Table 4.2 gives labor's share of value-added in several U.S. manufacturing industries averaged over the 2000–2005 period. They are ordered by the relative importance of labor's

TABLE 4.2   Differences in Factor Input Requirements by Industry, 2000–2005

Industry	Employee compensation/ value-added	Employee compensation/ full-time equivalent worker
Computer and electronic products	0.976	88.840
Motor vehicles, bodies and trailers, and parts	0.805	76.451
Textile mills and textile mill products	0.766	38.160
Other transportation equipment	0.766	74.664
Furniture and related products	0.752	42.461
Machinery	0.743	61.556
Printing and related support activities	0.736	48.462
Apparel and leather and allied products	0.718	35.802
Primary metals	0.705	62.269
Construction	0.689	49.475
Fabricated metal products	0.683	50.131
Wood products	0.678	39.471
Paper products	0.665	64.609
Plastics and rubber products	0.611	46.767
Electrical equipment, appliances, and components	0.609	59.793
Miscellaneous manufacturing	0.597	54.506
Food and beverage and tobacco products	0.525	45.837
Chemical products	0.452	86.837
Mining	0.321	78.683
Petroleum and coal products	0.317	97.992
Agriculture, forestry, fishing, and hunting	0.311	28.624
Oil and gas extraction	0.190	126.027

Source: U.S. Department of Commerce (2007).

share. Note that industries such as textiles, apparel, and furniture are relatively labor-intensive, while chemicals and petroleum refining are not. When material inputs can be freely traded internationally, we expect relatively more of the labor-intensive activities to be located in more labor-abundant countries.

Not all labor inputs may be identical, however, and another important distinction is shown in column three, which gives the average compensation per employee in the industry. If labor is paid on the basis of its productivity, and if wage rates for labor of a given skill are equal in all industries, then we can infer that industries with higher average wages have higher skill requirements. In fact, economists find that there are systematic differences in wages across industries, and they cannot be explained by years of experience or education of the workers. Workers in some industries, such as motor vehicles, may receive a wage premium based on high profits earned historically in the industry. In the computer industry the higher average wage is more likely due to higher skill requirements, whereas apparel and textiles require less skill and pay lower wages. Countries relatively abundant in skilled labor are more likely to design and export products like computers, and countries relatively abundant in unskilled labor are more likely to produce and export products such as apparel.

TRADE, THE DISTRIBUTION OF INCOME, AND FACTOR PRICE CHANGES

The gains from trade identified by classical economists continue to exist in the H–O model, but now we can address an additional question: how are those gains from trade distributed across different factors of production? The application of the H–O framework to this issue by Wolfgang Stolper and Paul Samuelson (1941) results in remarkably strong predictions: a rise in the price of the good a country exports causes the real return of the relatively abundant factor to rise and the real return of the scarce factor to fall. The opportunity to trade does not simply let the abundant factor gain at a faster rate than the scarce factor; the latter becomes worse off.

To see why the strong Stolper–Samuelson result holds, consider the way producers of cheese and wheat respond to changes in factor prices. In Denmark, the opportunity to trade improves the Danish terms of trade and causes the price of cheese to increase. The increase in the price of cheese provides an incentive for cheese producers to expand output. As they try to hire more labor and rent more land, however, they must bid these inputs away from wheat production. Because wheat production is land-intensive, a cutback in wheat production releases more land relative to labor than cheese producers want to use at the current wage rate and rental rate for land. Too little labor is available and too much land, which causes the wage rate to rise relative to land's rental rate.

The same outcome arises if we think of this adjustment to greater trade resulting in greater competition for producers of the import-competing good, wheat. Again, a decline in wheat production results in a big reduction in demand for land that is not offset by the greater demand for land in the expanding cheese sector. Conversely, the reduction in demand for labor in wheat production is not great enough to satisfy the extra demand for labor in the cheese sector. Thus, wages must increase relative to land rental rates in order that both land and labor remain fully employed. The lower rental rate for land gives both cheese producers and wheat producers an incentive to substitute land for labor and to increase their demand for land enough to keep it fully utilized. Because producers in both sectors see this incentive to substitute land in place of labor, the land–labor ratio rises in both sectors.

At first glance, this result may seem curious. The total amounts of labor and land in the economy are fixed, yet we claim that the land–labor ratio rises in each sector. How is that possible? Consider a simple numerical example where initially wheat production accounts for 16 hectares of land and eight workers, while cheese production accounts for 8 hectares of land and 16 workers. Let the price of cheese rise in Denmark as a result of trade. Suppose we transfer one hectare of land and one worker out of wheat production into cheese production. In the new equilibrium 15 hectares of land and seven workers are utilized in wheat production, while 9 hectares of land and 17 workers produce cheese. The ratio of land to labor rises in each sector. The ratio can rise, even though total quantities of land and labor are fixed, because the labor-intensive cheese sector now accounts for a larger share of national output.

Implications of Changing Factor Proportions in Production

We dwell on the change in the land–labor ratio because the fact that it increases indicates that labor productivity rises in both sectors. As a consequence, labor's wage rises. This represents an increase in real income, because an hour's work now produces more kilograms of wheat, and also more kilograms of cheese, the good whose price has risen. Even if workers spend all of their income on cheese, they can buy more cheese than in the pre-trade equilibrium, because their output of cheese per hour has risen. At the same time, the return to land declines because the land—labor ratio rises in both sectors and production per hectare declines in both sectors. Rental rates for land decline, and Danish land-owners now are worse off than they were before trade. Even if the landowners spend all their income on wheat, the good whose price is held constant in this barter world, and avoid cheese entirely, they receive less wheat per hectare than they did previously.

We have now arrived at the **Stolper–Samuelson theorem**: *Liberalization of trade causes the abundant factor, which is used intensively in the export industry, to gain, and the scarce factor, which is used intensively in the import-competing industry, to lose.* We can also state this result in terms of the magnification effect identified by Jones: the return to the abundant factor will rise by a greater percentage than the increase in the export price. Consider the Danish case. Employers pay workers the value of their marginal product, which depends upon the price of cheese times the marginal product of labor in cheese production. Both of those have risen, not just the price of cheese. Therefore, the wage rate increases by a larger percentage than the price of cheese.

The Stolper–Samuelson Theorem Demonstrated in the Edgeworth–Bowley Box

We can give a clearer demonstration of the way land and labor are reallocated by referring to the Edgeworth–Bowley box in Figure 4.3. If we let the relative price of cheese rise, cheese production expands from point R to point Q, and the land–labor ratio in both sectors rises. We can confirm that by drawing a ray from each origin to points Q and R. The ray $O_{cheese}Q$ indicates a higher land–labor ratio than $O_{cheese}R$, just as $O_{wheat}Q$ indicates a higher land–labor ratio than $O_{wheat}R$. Because the land–labor ratio rises, labor is more productive and its wage rises. Conversely, because more labor is used with each hectare of land, the productivity of land falls and its return declines.

In the United States, trade liberalization causes the relative price of wheat to rise compared to its autarky level. As U.S. output of wheat rises, the land–labor ratio falls in each sector; the contracting cheese sector does not release enough land relative to labor to meet the rising demand created by land-intensive wheat production. A declining land–labor ratio means labor productivity falls, and as a result, U.S. wages fall. Land rents rise because more labor is available to work each hectare in both sectors. Again, the opportunity to trade has resulted in an increase in the real return to the abundant factor (land) used intensively in the production of the export good and a decline in the real return to the scarce factor (labor) used intensively in import-competing production.

Let us summarize these results from the two countries together. Originally, in the pre-trade situation, the United States had low returns to land and high wages, due to the relative scarcity of labor and abundance of land. Conversely, Denmark had high returns to land and low wages, due to the relative scarcity of land and abundance of labor. Trade creates more demand for each country's abundant factor and less demand for each country's scarce factor. In the United States land prices rise while in Denmark they fall. Wages fall in the United States and rise in Denmark. Thus, the pre-trade gap in factor returns declines as a result of trade.

Conditions for the Equalization of Factor Prices

Does the reduction in factor price differences across countries continue until they have been entirely eliminated and we reach a point of **factor-price equalization** across countries? The formal logic of the H–O model indicates that there will be the equilibrium outcome, as long as both Denmark and the United States continue to produce both wheat and cheese. Because wheat producers in each country, for example, face the same price of output, and have available the same technology to use in production, they will use exactly the same proportions of land to labor at a given ratio of wages and rental rates of land. A bigger share of the world's wheat production will be located in the United States than in Denmark, in comparison with their shares in cheese production, because the United States is relatively land-abundant. But, there will be no difference in the way wheat is produced in the two countries, nor in the way cheese is produced in the two countries. With producers of a given good in each country using factor inputs in exactly the same proportions, the productivity of those factors is the same in both countries, and consequently there will be no difference in factor rewards.

Formal Conditions for the Equalization of Factor Prices

The likelihood that factor prices will be equalized across countries can be better assessed in the graphical representation of Figure 4.8, introduced by Samuelson (1949). The left panel shows that over the range of prices where a country produces both goods, an increase in the relative price of wheat will increase the rental return to land and decrease the wage rate. This is just a graphical representation of the Stolper–Samuelson result. In the right panel of Figure 4.8 the two upward sloping lines labeled cheese and wheat show the best combinations of land and labor to use in producing those goods at a given wage–rental ratio. Each line simply summarizes the implication of a movement around an isoquant, from point Z to point Q in Figure 4.3, say. As the wage–rental ratio falls, a producer uses more labor relative to land. The wheat locus lies further to the right, because wheat is the more land-intensive good. The two lines do not intersect because of the assumption that no factor intensity reversal occurs; wheat always is the more land-intensive good regardless of the wage–rental ratio considered.

By representing a country's endowment of land relative to labor with a vertical line in the right panel, we can infer the mix of wheat and cheese that the country will produce. Choose any given price of wheat, determine the corresponding wage–rental ratio in the left panel, and extend a line horizontally into the right panel at that value. Note where this horizontal line intersects the vertical endowment line. When the price of wheat rises, that intersection will occur closer to the factor proportions line labeled wheat. The country will produce more wheat and less cheese. If the price of wheat continues to rise, eventually that will cause the country to specialize completely in producing wheat. Beyond that point, the wage–rental ratio will fall no further. No further decline in the land–labor ratio is possible. All land and labor are now used in producing wheat, and they both share the benefits of a higher price of wheat.

For the price ratio at A to be an equilibrium that results in factor price equalization in the two countries, the vertical endowment lines of the two countries must both lie between the range given

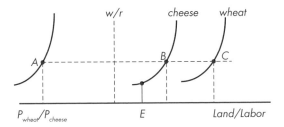

FIGURE 4.8 Factor Price Equalization

If a given world price of wheat relative to cheese represents an equilibrium where both countries will produce both goods, the same wage–rental ratio will be established in each country.

by points *B* and *C*. If Denmark's land–labor endowment were smaller, say at *E*, it would be completely specialized in cheese production, because that sector does not require much land. The downward sloping curve in the left panel would no longer apply in Denmark. Rather, for the relative price of wheat shown at *A*, there would be a lower wage–rental ratio in Denmark than in the United States. While the H–O prediction of the pattern of trade still holds even though Denmark is completely specialized, factor price equalization does not.

In the real world we do not observe that factor prices have actually equalized, but we can quickly recognize that the stringent assumptions of the H–O model often fail to hold. For example, trade is not free, and producers in all countries are not responding to the same prices of output. If the United States limits imports of cheese from Denmark, then Danish wages will not rise sufficiently to equal U.S. wages. Also, technology does not move costlessly from country to country, and consequently producers do not all have the same choices in how to produce. Our examples from the classical economists demonstrated that economies with more productive technologies could pay higher wages; that same principle applies in the more complicated H–O model, if the same quantities of labor and land inputs yield greater output in one country than another. Furthermore, our assumption that the two countries remain incompletely specialized is an important one. Once Denmark becomes completely specialized in cheese production, a higher price of cheese will no longer tend to benefit labor and harm landowners, which otherwise would raise Denmark's wage rental rate toward the U.S. level.

Other Implications of the Stolper–Samuelson Theorem

The basic insight from the Stolper–Samuelson theorem, that a rise in the price of exports will benefit the abundant factor and harm the scarce factor, is remarkably relevant in interpreting current controversies over the consequences of trade and closer integration of the world economy. Owners of the scarce factor (or factors) of production in any country tend to oppose free trade and to support protectionism. In the United States and Europe the relatively scarce factor is unskilled labor. Abundant factors in these countries are human capital (highly educated people) and physical capital. The losers from trade liberalization in those countries are unskilled or semi-skilled workers. Those who would gain from free trade are primarily people whose incomes are already above average, whereas the group being harmed consists overwhelmingly of those with below-average incomes. Free trade would increase total incomes in the United States and Europe but would make the distribution of income more unequal than it now is, according to the Stolper–Samuelson theorem.

The Widening Income Gap: Are Trade and Outsourcing to Blame?

Changes in the distribution of income in the United States and in Europe since 1980 have favored skilled labor and hurt unskilled labor. Can this be attributed to increased international trade? Some observers suspect that a major influence is the rapid ascent of China and India, countries that are abundant in unskilled labor, as they have turned away from policies of economic self-sufficiency and instead become important exporters of goods and services. That judgment remains controversial among trade and labor economists.

Many trade economists approach the topic by examining two important links in the Stolper–Samuelson line of reasoning: (1) have the relative prices of goods that require unskilled labor intensively actually fallen over this same period? and (2) has the expansion of output in industries that use skilled labor intensively caused the ratio of skilled labor to unskilled labor to decline in all sectors, as would be predicted for the United States and Europe? In the 1990s there was no convincing evidence that prices of unskilled labor-intensive goods declined relative to skilled labor-intensive goods. Furthermore, producers have not shifted to production techniques that require relatively more unskilled labor in response to the rising relative cost of skilled labor, a result we would predict if the incentives identified by the Stolper–Samuelson theorem were the major determinant of wage movements.

The most widely accepted alternative explanation for the decline in wages of unskilled labor is that changes in technology have played a dominant role, especially changes that have resulted in less demand for unskilled labor. This role of technology also seems relevant in explaining the experience of developing countries, where we would otherwise expect a rise in the price of goods that use unskilled labor intensively to result in higher relative wages for unskilled labor. Instead, in developing countries we also observe that demand for skilled labor is rising more rapidly than the demand for unskilled labor. Again, such a result appears attributable to significant changes in technology that reduce the demand for unskilled labor.

Others warn against too ready acceptance of this line of reasoning. Robert Feenstra (1998) notes that industries in developed countries have been able to increase their utilization of skilled labor relative to unskilled labor by breaking into separate steps their previously integrated production processes for goods and even services. They then outsource the most unskilled labor-intensive steps to low-wage countries. As this upgrading in the skill content of what is done domestically occurs within exporting and import-competing industries, relative prices of goods need not change as posited in the Stolper–Samuelson example. Yet, demand for skilled labor rises and demand for unskilled labor falls. As more business services (payroll accounting, customer service call centers) became tradable in the 1990s and an economic slowdown followed in the next decade, this outsourcing became a politically volatile issue, not just a concern restricted to low wage workers.

In developing countries, those same outsourced jobs may create demand for relatively more skilled workers, which is an additional force for divergence in wages within those countries, beyond the influence of any changes in technology. In the case of Mexico, Feenstra and Gordon Hanson

(1997) note that this increase in trade coincides with a greater capital inflow into Mexico. This additional capital is used to expand output in more capital-intensive industries. Daniel Trefler (2005) obtains a similar result for trade that occurs in a world of technology catch-up by developing countries, independent of any capital inflow. Developed countries cast off more labor-intensive technologies, which are adopted in developing countries where they are more skill intensive than the technologies already in use. Thus, the demand for physical and human capital may rise in developing countries.

Is North–South trade likely to expand in the future and create further downward pressure on unskilled wages? Even with the prospects of successfully completing a round of multilateral trade negotiations very uncertain (a topic addressed in Chapter 10), North–South trade has expanded sharply in the last decade, creating more competition for Northern producers of labor-intensive goods. Counteracting the potential negative effect on Northern wages is the possibility that Northern production of some unskilled labor-intensive goods may cease. Further declines in their prices no longer would create pressure for divergent shifts in skilled and unskilled wages, because the assumption of incomplete specialization in production no longer would be met. Instead, both skilled and unskilled labor would gain from the lower price of a good that neither of them produces. Peter Schott (2003) reports evidence in support of a stronger claim, that all OECD countries produce a different bundle of goods than low-income countries, which insulates workers in OECD countries from price declines of the most labor-intensive goods.

Consider the case of unskilled labor-abundant countries. When unskilled labor is relatively abundant, but available land, capital, and skilled labor are scarce, we predict unskilled labor will gain. Skilled workers and owners of capital and land will lose. In many cases, those potential losers are successful in maintaining a protectionist policy because politically they have special access to influence government trade policy. Unskilled workers may be too poorly organized to lobby effectively for a more open trade policy. Calls for workers of the world to unite in their opposition to more open trade appear to be consistent with the interests of labor in labor-scarce industrialized countries but are a disservice to those in most developing countries.

How are these theoretical predictions about income distribution borne out in practice? As Korea, Taiwan, and Singapore increased their labor-intensive exports of apparel and footwear products in the 1960s and 1970s, economists noted that the wages of unskilled workers rose relative to those of more skilled workers in those countries. That result is what we would predict on the basis of the Stolper–Samuelson theorem. When Latin American countries adopted more liberal trade policies in the 1980s, however, wage inequality increased in Colombia, Costa Rica, Mexico, and Uruguay.

What reasons might explain this different outcome in Latin America? Adrian Wood (1997) suggests one possibility: as Latin American countries reduced trade barriers, they faced greater import competition from even more labor-abundant countries, such as China, Indonesia, India, Bangladesh, and Pakistan, as well as more industrialized countries. This situation would imply that in Latin America the least skill-intensive and the most skill-intensive industries contracted, while those with intermediate skill requirements expanded. That result is consistent with the Stolper–Samuelson framework. An alternative possibility already raised in the case of industrialized countries is that technical change creates more demand for skilled workers and reduces demand for unskilled labor, which explains the fall in unskilled labor's wage.

RELAXING SOME ASSUMPTIONS OF THE H–O MODEL

The conclusion that the abundant factor of production gains from free trade and that the relatively scarce factor loses is based on the assumption that the adjustment to free trade is complete – that is, that both factors of production have moved from the import-competing to the export industry and that full employment has been re-established. Before this new equilibrium is reached, the results can be quite different. We consider two different time horizons, one when no factors of production are mobile, and one when only some factors of production are mobile. To better consider the role of adjustment over time, and the possibility that capital can move from one industry to another and in the long run be as productive in the new industry as capital already located there, we shift away from the wheat and cheese example to consider steel and apparel here.

Fixed Factors of Production in the Short Run

When neither capital nor labor can move, increased trade that causes contraction of the import-competing industry results in lower income for both capital and labor employed in that sector. Both factors in the expanding export sector become better off.

Consider a capital-abundant, labor-scarce country such as Canada. If free trade means that the labor-intensive apparel industry contracts while the capital-intensive steel industry expands, we do not immediately observe the Stolper–Samuelson result that all labor loses and all capital gains. While the apparel sector is shrinking, both capital and labor in that sector will suffer as jobs are lost and factories are shut down. In the expanding steel industry both labor and capital will benefit as sales, wages, and profits all grow. In fact, these short-run, industry-specific interests often dominate the political debate over trade policy, a topic we address in Chapter 7. The longer-run outcome, that a factor experiences the same change in income regardless of the industry where it is employed, only emerges gradually. As labor laid off in the apparel industry seeks employment in the steel industry, wages paid in the steel industry are driven down, too. Similarly, capital will leave the apparel industry until its return there is as high as can be earned in the steel industry.

Fixed Factors of Production in the Intermediate Run

The gradual adjustment of labor and capital cited above suggests the relevance of another model, the specific factors model. One application of this model corresponds to an intermediate run scenario when labor is mobile between two sectors but capital takes longer to adjust and still remains industry specific. In a two-good economy that produces apparel and steel, capital in the apparel industry is useful there but contributes nothing to productivity in the steel industry. Conversely, capital in the steel industry is of no use in the apparel industry. Figure 4.9 shows the allocation of labor between

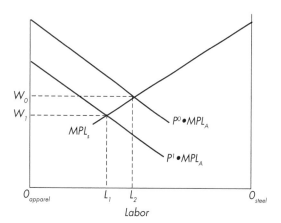

FIGURE 4.9 A Price Decline in the Specific Factors Model

A decline in the price of apparel results in losses to owners of apparel firms, gains to owners of steel firms, and an ambiguous effect on real wages.

the apparel and steel industries. The demand for labor in each industry depends upon the value of its marginal product, and the labor demand curves slope downward due to declining productivity as more labor is used with a fixed amount of capital. In the absence of labor unions, an equilibrium wage paid to all labor is reached at W_0, with the allocation of labor between the two industries given by L_0.

Now consider the consequences of trade liberalization that causes the price of the import-competing good, apparel, to fall. In Figure 4.9 the demand curve for labor in the apparel industry shifts downward. Because the wage firms pay equals the price of output times labor's marginal product ($w=P\cdot MPL$), and the price of apparel falls, employers offer a lower wage at a given level of employment. Apparel output falls and labor shifts out of the apparel industry into steel. That drives down the wage in the steel industry, as more labor is used with a fixed amount of capital.

Capital owners in the steel industry gain, because as output and exports rise, the wage paid to workers falls. Labor costs now account for a smaller share of revenue received by steel producers and more is left for capital owners. In the apparel industry just the opposite outcome occurs. A smaller labor force now works with the same amount of capital, and therefore the marginal product of labor rises. Labor accounts for a larger share of revenue received by apparel producers, and less is left for capital owners.

What happens to labor? The answer is ambiguous, because labor is paid the value of its marginal product. An hour of work will now buy less steel. An hour of work will buy more apparel, however, because the price of apparel has fallen (the magnitude shown by the downward shift in the demand curve) by more than the wage, when both are measured in terms of the numeraire good, steel. If a large enough share of labor's budget is spent on apparel, labor becomes better off. This ambiguous result suggests that labor may have less incentive to lobby for changes in trade policy than owners of industry-specific factors do.

Coca, Diamonds, Oil, and Timber: A Resource Curse?

Is a country unlucky if it discovers a large oil deposit in its territorial waters? For many developing countries, that judgment has seemed to be true. Natural resource riches have often attracted predatory politicians who seize as much of the return as possible and then spend or hoard this wealth abroad. Even without this extreme negative outcome, countries have experienced major reallocations of economic activity within their economies that have been politically painful. The experience of the Netherlands when it exploited a major natural gas find in the North Sea gave rise to the label "the **Dutch disease**." The specific factors model provides a useful framework to demonstrate this situation.

Consider two sectors, manufactures and natural gas, where capital is specific to manufacturing and natural gas deposits are a specific factor necessary for natural gas production. Assume labor is necessary for production in both sectors and is mobile between them. The initial allocation of labor is given by L_0 in Figure 4.10. If the country discovers more natural gas deposits, labor will become more productive in that sector and the demand for labor shifts outward. The equilibrium wage rises from w_0 to w_1 and L_0L_1 of labor is bid away from the manufacturing sector. Less labor is used with the same amount of capital in manufacturing, as labor's productivity must rise to warrant the higher wage it receives. Capitalists in the manufacturing sector see their return fall by the trapezoid b. Those falling profits mean capitalists will replace less of the capital currently used in manufacturing as it eventually wears out or becomes obsolete. The natural resource find leads to a decline in manufacturing. Some economists believe the manufacturing sector is characterized by **external economies of scale** that individual firms do not consider when deciding how much to produce, a topic addressed in Chapter 5. If this is a significant effect, the decline in manufacturing has a more negative effect than the labor adjustment identified above. If the resource extraction requires little labor, deindustrialization may still occur if the proceeds from natural resource production are spent on non-traded goods that do draw inputs away from manufacturing. The signal to shift away from

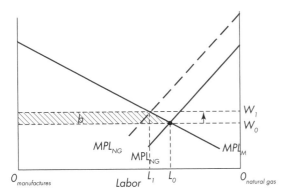

FIGURE 4.10 Consequences of More Natural Resources

The discovery of additional natural gas deposits results in a smaller manufacturing sector.

manufactures will be developed more fully in Part II of this text, where the effect of natural resource earnings on the country's exchange rate is shown to make the manufacturing sector less competitive internationally.

An example of the more ominous aspects of the resource curse is demonstrated by Joshua Angrist and Adriana Kugler (2007) in their analysis of the marked increase in coca production and processing in Colombia. That shift occurred after 1994 when the air bridge from traditional suppliers in Peru and Bolivia was effectively disrupted. As a result, there was an outward shift in the demand for Colombian coca production. Prices of coca base doubled, self-employed income rose and school enrolment of teenage boys declined relative to non-producing regions of the country. The authors note the large increase in the area under the coca demand curve, which represents a large increase in rents to those who control the coca trade. This payoff has been a magnet for various armed groups in Colombia, including the ELN (Ejército de Liberación Nacional), the FARC (Fuerzas Armadas Revolucionarias de Colombia), and paramilitaries. The greater the potential reward from effectively extorting these rents, the greater the escalation of violence in the producing areas. Angrist and Kugler show that violent deaths rose more rapidly in producing areas, even as other public health statistics improved. Any benefit to the producing regions appears to be quite limited, because the gains simply fuel more military activity.

While this pessimistic assessment of natural resource abundance is quite plausible, the historical success of the United States, Canada, and Australia, or the more recent exceptions such as Botswana and Norway suggest that other factors need to be considered before a curse can automatically be assumed to follow.

Trade: A Substitute for Factor Movements

Another important implication of factor proportions theory is that international trade can serve as a substitute for the movement of productive factors from one country to another, as demonstrated by Robert Mundell (1957). The actual distribution of productive factors among the nations of the world is obviously very unequal. One possible market response would be movements of labor and capital from countries where they are abundant and cheap to countries where they are scarce and more expensive, thus reducing the differences in factor rewards and making factor endowments more equal throughout the world.

The factor proportions theory suggests that international factor movements may not be necessary in any case, because the movement of goods in world trade can accomplish essentially the same purpose. Countries that have abundant labor can specialize in labor intensive goods and ship these goods to countries where labor is scarce. Labor is embodied in goods and redistributed through trade. The same point applies to capital, land, and other factors. The economic effects of international factor movements can be achieved without the factors themselves actually having to move.

The major economic effect of an international factor outflow is to alter the relative abundance or scarcity of that factor and thus to affect its price, that is, to raise the prices of abundant factors by making them less abundant relative to other factors. Thus, when Polish workers migrate to Germany, wage rates tend to rise in Poland because labor is made somewhat less abundant there, whereas wage rates in Germany tend to fall (or at least to rise less rapidly than they otherwise would) because the relative scarcity of labor is reduced. The same result is achieved when Germans buy Polish goods that are produced by relatively labor-intensive methods. More labor is demanded by Polish export industries, and Polish wage rates tend to rise. The fact that free trade and factor mobility are driven by parallel causes and have the same effects on the distribution of income has implications for the politics of immigration laws, which we examine in Chapter 8.

Trade and factor movements can be regarded as substitutes in the situation where trade barriers exist and factor flows occur in response to the differences in factor rewards created by those barriers. In other circumstances, however, trade and factor flows can be regarded as complements. For example, James Markusen (1983) presents a case where the H–O model is modified to rule out initial differences in factor endowments and to allow one country to have a technical advantage in producing the labor-intensive good. That country will have a comparative advantage in producing the labor-intensive good and will also pay a higher wage rate after trade occurs. Therefore, there is still an incentive for labor to immigrate to this country, and that will further reinforce its comparative advantage in producing the labor-intensive good. Trade and factor flows are complements in those circumstances.

EMPIRICAL VERIFICATION OF THE H–O MODEL

As in the case of the classical model, formulating an appropriate empirical test of the stylized $2 \times 2 \times 2$ model is difficult because actual data come from a world where there are many goods and many factors of production. Also, we cannot observe autarky or pre-trade costs, and therefore we must infer what they would be, based on characteristics such as factor endowments or factor intensities. Two basic approaches have been developed by past researchers: one attempts to predict trade in particular goods, as was the case for the classical model, and another predicts the factor content of trade. They both give useful insights into relationships implied by the H–O model, but they generally do not constitute complete tests of the theory, either. Because the second approach emerged first, and is more consistent with the full H–O model with factor price equalization, we now consider it.

The Leontief Paradox

Wassily Leontief framed the question by asking how much labor and capital were necessary to produce $1 million of U.S. exports and how much labor and capital would be required to produce domestically $1 million worth of imports. Leontief was uniquely positioned to make such a calculation because he had led the development of an input–output table that broke the U.S. economy into 200 different sectors and showed what any one sector bought from all the others. Besides showing demands for intermediate inputs, the table indicated how much of the primary factors, labor and capital, were employed in an industry. Therefore, Leontief could determine how much labor and capital were required, directly and indirectly through intermediate inputs, to produce a dollar's worth of output in any industry. To derive his final answer, he simply weighted each industry's input requirements by that industry's importance in total exports or total imports in 1947, although for imports he was forced to exclude goods such as tin and coffee that were not produced in the United States.

From all these calculations, Leontief ended up with four numbers: capital and labor inputs required to produce $1 million of exports, and capital and labor inputs required to produce $1 million of import-competing goods. It was generally believed (indeed, Leontief took it for granted) that the United States was a capital-rich country and that it had a greater abundance of capital relative to labor than did its trade partners. Consequently, the Heckscher–Ohlin theory predicted that U.S. exports would be more capital-intensive than its import-competing goods, that is, that:

[K/L] export goods > [K/L] import-competing goods.

To Leontief's great surprise, his results showed the opposite, namely that U.S. exports were more labor-intensive than its import-competing goods. Table 4.3 shows Leontief's actual figures on inputs required to produce $1 million of exports and $1 million of import-competing goods. The capital/labor ratio in export industries ($14,011) was lower than the capital/labor ratio in import-competing industries ($18,182).

This result, which contradicted the Heckscher–Ohlin thesis, came to be known as the **Leontief paradox**. It stimulated much further analysis of trade in other years and for other countries. Edward Leamer (1980) noted that the wrong standard was being applied to test the theory for a country whose trade was not balanced, and in fact no paradox exists in Leontief's data when the appropriate test is applied: U.S. production is capital-intensive relative to U.S. consumption. Aside from any resolution of Leontief's paradox, the substantial prior and subsequent effort to test the H–O theory has been instructive in demonstrating whether the theory is sensitive to changes in underlying assumptions and in developing more complete tests of the theory.

TABLE 4.3   Leontief's Analysis of U.S. Trade, 1947

	Exports	Imports
Labor years / $ million output	182	170
Capital in $ thousand /$ million output	2,551	3,091
Capital/Labor Ratio	14.0	18.1

Source: Leontief (1954)

Other Tests of the H–O Model

Several economists have suggested that considering only two productive factors, capital and labor, may give biased projections. With more than two factors, however, it becomes less straightforward to decide what we mean by factor abundance: is labor scarcity indicated by the capital–labor ratio or by some other ratio? Jaroslav Vanek (1968) suggests a useful framework to resolve that ambiguity, and we review that approach because it adds to our understanding of how to draw inferences from the H–O model in a many-good, many-factor model.

Additional Factors of Production

First, based on observed input requirements in each industry, determine what demand for a factor is created by the country's net trade position in each industry. That is, exports create more demand for a factor while imports reduce demand for it. Sum across all industries to obtain the net factor demand created by trade. According to the H–O theory, this net foreign demand for a factor should be equal to the endowment of the factor available in the country minus the amount of that factor used to satisfy demand by home consumers. For each factor considered, we expect the following:

$$
\begin{aligned}
\textit{Net factor demand from international trade} &= \textit{Factor endowment} \\
&- \textit{Factor demand from domestic expenditure}
\end{aligned}
\tag{4.1}
$$

We can be more precise about home demand, because of the H–O assumption that all individuals spend their income the same way, regardless of the level of income. What residents of a country consume is simply a bundle of goods that represents a claim on factor services equal to the country's share of world income. If a country accounts for 20 percent of the world's income, then its demand for goods represents a demand for 20 percent of the world's capital stock, 20 percent of the world's labor force, etc. Given that simplification, then, we can say that a country is relatively abundant in a factor when its share of the world endowment is greater than its share of world income. Thus, if a country accounts for 25 percent of the world's capital stock, and earns 20 percent of the world's income, it is relatively abundant in capital. Note that the relationship presented above applies to the balance of demand and supply of a single factor. How many factors to include in the analysis becomes another important issue, as well as the proper standard to apply in judging whether the observed patterns of trade do support the H–O–V theory.

Another strand of empirical literature paid particular attention to differences in labor skills and the importance of human capital. Baldwin (1971) and Stern and Maskus (1981) found that the United States tends to export goods that require skilled labor intensively and to import goods that require unskilled labor intensively. In the factor content equation above, the United States and many European countries are net exporters of skilled labor and net importers of unskilled labor. When a country's share of the world stock of skilled labor exceeds its share of world income, and that country's share of the world stock of unskilled labor is less than its share of world income, those observations support the H–O predictions that a country that is relatively abundant (scarce) in skilled labor (unskilled labor) will be a net exporter (importer) of skilled labor (unskilled labor).

A more comprehensive analysis of the factor content of trade for 12 different factors and 27 different countries by Bowen, Leamer, and Sveikauskas (1987) gives a less encouraging message regarding the generality of the H–O theory. The sign of the factor content of trade (surplus or deficit) is predicted correctly by relative factor abundance in merely half of the cases considered. Adrian Wood (1997) notes, however, that if we restrict attention to the nature of trade between industrialized and developing countries, the H–O theory explains such trade fairly well: developed countries export skilled labor-intensive goods to and import unskilled labor-intensive goods from developing countries.

Missing Trade and Other Mysteries

Another perspective that unearths additional complications is provided by the work of Daniel Trefler (1995). He pursues a line of reasoning suggested by Leontief: if U.S. labor is more productive than foreign labor, due to a U.S. technological advantage, then the United States will appear labor-abundant if it is possible to measure labor in units of comparable productivity everywhere. Trefler also points to the importance of differences in technology to explain observed patterns of trade. Based on his analysis of trade in 1982 for 33 countries and nine factors of production, he observes a basic problem that H–O predictions systematically perform poorly. Poor countries appear to be abundant in most factors, but export much too little, while rich countries appear to be scarce in most factors, but import much too little.

To account for this missing trade, Trefler allows for differences across countries in technology. Just as in Leontief's formulation, this changes the measure of relative factor abundance. Making that adjustment results in much less predicted trade than when technology is assumed to be the same everywhere. Subsequent work suggests the failure of factor prices to be equalized, even among industrialized countries, alters the measured factor content of production and trade. Adjusting for that effect reduces the extent of missing trade. In addition, taking into account the costliness of trade helps explain its observed factor content.

Another extension of Trefler's analysis by Patrick Conway (2002) suggests a further possibility: differences in technology across countries that are assumed to have the same effect on all factors of production may be less relevant in explaining the missing trade than differences that are specific to each factor but the same across countries. Conway proposes that differences in domestic factor mobility from contracting to expanding industries provide a better explanation of the missing trade. His measures of missing trade indicate a particularly large overprediction of trade for agricultural labor and sales labor, with much less effect on predictions for cropland, pastureland, and capital.

Trefler (2002) responds to this critique by agreeing that factor-specific explanations are important. Using a different categorization of labor, based on education rather than occupation, he reports that the missing trade generally plagues H–O–V explanations for unskilled labor. Skilled labor and capital are both more consistent with the H–O–V theory. These outcomes apply in 1972, 1992, and the change between those two years. The apparent complementarity of physical capital and human capital is relevant to two issues we encounter in this book, the distribution of income and the nature of technical change.

Can any conclusions be drawn regarding the overall validity of the H–O theory? In its unaltered form, the H–O model frequently does not perform well. While it appears to do well in predicting the direction of trade where a country's factor endowments differ most from the worldwide endowment pattern, as in trade between industrialized and developing countries, it does not give a very accurate prediction of the amount of trade that will occur. Explicitly recognizing the importance of differences in technology, the quality of factor inputs, or impediments to trade, all improve the model's predictive ability. Because the H–O model provides a coherent framework for addressing questions of trade patterns, income distribution, and economic growth, it will be an important building block for any hybrid approach that emerges.

Summary of Key Concepts

1. The two-good H–O model predicts that a country will have a lower autarky price and therefore export the good that uses intensively the factor in which it is relatively abundant.

2. If a country's endowment of its abundant factor increases, according to the Rybczynski theorem it will produce more of its export good and less of its import-competing good when it faces fixed prices internationally.

3. As a country becomes more similar to the rest of the world, it will trade less.

4. As trade equalizes prices of goods internationally, in the short run when all resources are immobile, those used in the country's export industry gain and those used in the import-competing industry lose.

5. According to the Stolper–Samuelson theorem, in the long run trade raises the real return of the abundant factor used intensively in producing the country's export good and reduces the real return of the scarce factor used intensively in producing the import-competing good.

6. If both countries continue to produce both goods in the $2 \times 2 \times 2$ H–O model, trade will result in identical factor returns in both countries.

7. In the specific factors model, an increase in a specific factor increases output of the good that uses it and reduces output of the other good, as in the case of the Dutch disease. An increase in the mobile factor increases output of both goods.

8. In the specific factors model, an increase in the price of a good increases the return to the specific factor it uses and reduces the return to the other specific factor. The effect on the return to the mobile factor depends upon how much of the higher-priced good it buys.

9. An early empirical test of the H–O model by Leontief found the unexpected result that U.S. exports were less capital intensive than its imports.

10. Later tests find that the H–O framework predicts much more trade than is actually observed, especially with respect to flows of goods that require unskilled labor.

CASE STUDY

Trade Liberalization and the Distribution of Income in Brazil

For Latin American countries such as Chile, Colombia, and Mexico, trade liberalization coincided with the distribution of income becoming more unequal. A recent study by Ferreira, Leite, and Wai-Poi (2007) suggests the opposite result occurred in Brazil. Over the period 1987–95 the average tax on imported goods, a tariff, fell from 43.4 percent to 13.9 percent. Imports as a share of consumption in the manufacturing sector rose from 15 percent to 31 percent. Wages for skilled labor relative to wages for unskilled labor fell by 14.3 percent, while total factor productivity rose by 6 percent.

A key distinction that the authors cite in the Brazilian case is that initially protection was highest in skill-intensive industries, and those were the industries where the largest tariff reductions occurred. Table 4.4 demonstrates this pattern.

To assess the effects of trade liberalization on the distribution of income, the authors first estimate

how an individual's wages are determined by individual and industry characteristics in each year between 1987 and 1995. Those estimates, based on a sample of more than 100,000 workers, indicate the benefits from an extra year of education or on-the-job experience, as well as the premium for being male, white or Asian, urban, or employed in a particular industry. Over time, they find that all of these premiums fell, except for the advantage of being white or Asian. The authors also estimate the

TABLE 4.4 Tariff Protection in Brazilian Industries

Industry	Nominal tariff	
	1988	1995
Agricultural products	17	7
Mining products	20	3
Oil and coal extraction	6	0
Non-metallic minerals	39	10
Steel and other metals	33	11
Machinery and tractors	47	19
Electrical and electronic equipment	50	21
Autos, trucks, and other vehicles	43	31
Wood products and furniture	30	11
Cellulose, paper and printing	32	10
Rubber products	49	13
Chemical products	66	15
Oil refining and petrochemicals	34	4
Pharmaceuticals	45	8
Plastic products	57	15
Textile products	57	15
Apparel	76	20
Footwear	41	18
Processing of vegetable products	42	12
Meat packing, dairy, and other food	63	20
Unclassified manufacturing	49	14
Simple average	44	17

Source: Kume, Piani, and de Souza (2000) presented in Ferreira, et al. (2007).

probability of an individual being employed in various occupations as a function of the individual's characteristics. They then consider how changes in the industry wage premium and occupational employment probabilities are related to changes in trade policy and other measures of the openness to trade.

They find the decline in inequality is not primarily due to a decline in the wage premium earned in high-skill industries, which the short-run model of adjustment would suggest when factors of production are immobile. Rather, the primary effect is attributable to an economy-wide reduction in the premium for more skilled workers, as the Stolper–Samuelson model predicts. A decline in the skilled wage rate also might be explained by an increase in the share of the work force that is skilled, from 20 percent to 24 percent. If that factor were the dominant influence, however, the H–O model would predict an expansion of output in skilled labor-intensive industries. Instead, there is a reallocation of production to unskilled labor-intensive industries, a pattern consistent with the influence of the Stolper–Samuelson adjustment process following trade liberalization.

CASE STUDY QUESTIONS

1. If the tariff rate on chemical products falls from 66 percent to 15 percent, what adjustment must be occurring to result in a much smaller decline in the wage rate for workers in the chemical industry? What do you assume about factor intensity in this industry relative to others?

2. Which industries would you expect to expand if the dominant change in the economy were an increase in the relative abundance of skilled labor?

3. If both skilled and unskilled labor are laid off in highly protected industries, why does skilled labor lose and unskilled labor gain?

4. With many prices changing as a result of Brazilian trade liberalization, how can we be confident that unskilled labor's real wage rises?

Questions for Study and Review

1. What does the factor proportions theory imply about the composition of a nation's exports and imports? Why?

2. Based on the $2 \times 2 \times 2$ factor proportions model, how will the opportunity to trade in a labor-abundant country affect output prices, returns to factors of production, and a firm's demand for capital relative to labor compared to a no-trade situation? Explain why.

3. "Alpha, a country with abundant capital and scarce labor, initially has completely free trade with the outside world. If Alpha imposes a tariff on imports, its ratio of wages to the return on capital will fall." Do you agree? Why or why not?

4. What role do factor intensities of production play in the factor proportions theory of trade? If there were no differences in the factor intensities of the goods produced, how could that affect the predicted pattern of trade?

5. Suppose that Argentina has abundant arable land and scarce labor compared with Bolivia. Assume that wheat is land-intensive relative to cloth and that the other Heckscher–Ohlin assumptions of the $2 \times 2 \times 2$ case apply.

   a. Show diagrammatically how the production-possibilities curves for the two countries differ, and explain how that creates the possibility for mutually beneficial trade between them. What is the sequence of changes that occurs as the two economies move from no trade to free trade?

   b. What groups in each country would you expect to support free trade based on the H–O model?

   c. If there are important transportation costs between these countries, what differences in the relative price of wheat and the ratio of wages to land rents will remain in Argentina compared to Bolivia?

   d. If Bolivia were completely specialized in cloth production, how would that situation affect the likelihood that the ratio of wages to rental rates would be equal in the two countries? Explain which country would have a higher wage–rental ratio.

6. Do you expect those opposing free trade in the short run to differ from those opposing it over a longer period? If labor and capital become mobile across industries in the long run, how does that transition affect the impact on a capitalist whose capital initially is used in an import-competing industry? How does your answer depend upon a country's relative factor endowments?

7. Debate how proposals to eliminate British trade barriers on imports of food in the nineteenth century put landowners in opposition to industrialists. Explain how the specific factors model helps to indicate the interests of landowners, industrialists, and labor. In what way are each of these factors tied to the import or export of output? If labor is the only factor that is mobile between industries, why is the effect of trade restrictions on labor ambiguous?

8. In which model, the specific factors model or the H–O model, is an increase in the labor force likely to cause the biggest change in output across sectors of the economy? What accounts for this difference?

9. If Angola discovers new oil deposits, how does the specific factors model suggest this development will affect local producers of sandals, an import-competing good? Suppose you have information about the elasticity of demand for labor in both the oil extraction sector and the sandal sector. What combination of elasticities will make contraction of sandal output more likely? Are those the same conditions that result in a very large increase in the wage rate?

10. In what way would more trade between the E.U. and Sub-Saharan Africa, due to fewer trade barriers or lower transport costs, reduce the gap in wages between them? How would that affect the incentive for residents of Sub-Saharan Africa to emigrate (legally or illegally) to Europe?

11. Suppose the E.U. accepts Ukraine as a member, and the Ukrainians benefit from the opportunity to trade goods and services freely with other members and to migrate to any other member state. If trade and factor flows are substitutes, what economic factors are likely to be relevant in predicting whether trade in goods or movements of people occurs? How is that distinction relevant in predicting the economic effects on current member states?

12. What exactly is paradoxical about the so-called Leontief paradox? What explanations have been offered to account for it or to resolve it?

13. You are given the following information about each country's share of the world endowment of a factor and about each country's share of world income (GNP). Explain how this information allows you to predict differences in the trade patterns of Japan and the United States. Indicate whether you expect much trade to occur between these countries according to the H–O theory.

Country	Physical capital	R&D scientists	Skilled labor	Semi-skilled labor	Unskilled labor	Arable land	GNP
U.S.	33.6%	50.7%	27.7%	19.1%	0.2%	29.3%	28.6%
Japan	15.5%	23.0%	8.7%	11.5%	0.3%	0.8%	11.2%

Entries represent the percentage of the world endowment of a factor accounted for by each country.

References and Suggestions for Further Reading

The classic articles that explain the formulation of the H–O model and draw out its basic implications for trade, income distribution, and growth are:

Heckscher, E. (1919) "The Effect of Foreign Trade on the Distribution of Income," translated and printed in H. Ellis and L. Metzler (eds) (1949) *Readings in the Theory of International Trade*, Philadelphia: Blakiston.
Ohlin, B. (1933) *Interregional and International Trade*, Cambridge, MA: Harvard University Press.
Rybczynski, T. M. (1955) "Factor Endowments and Relative Commodity Prices," *Economica* 22: 336–41; reprinted in R. Caves and H. Johnson (eds) (1968) *Readings in International Economics*, Homewood, IL: Irwin.
Samuelson, P.A. (1949) "International Factor-Price Equalization Once Again," *Economic Journal* 59: 181–97.
Stolper, W. and Samuelson, P.A. (1941) "Protection and Real Wages," *Review of Economic Studies* 9: 58–73.

A particularly useful algebraic presentation of the H–O model appears in:

Jones, R. (1965) "The Structure of Simple General Equilibrium Models," *Journal of Political Economy* 73: 557–72.

For other extensions of the basic H–O framework mentioned in the chapter, see:

Dean, J. and Ulmonen, T. (2002) "Long Adept at Copying Taiwan Takes to Patents," *Wall Street Journal*, January 11, p. A8.
Findlay, R., Jeung, L., and Lundhall, M. (eds) (2002) *Bertil Ohlin: A Centennial Celebration*, Cambridge, MA: MIT Press.
Markusen, J. (1983) "Factor Movements and Commodity Trade as Complements," *Journal of International Economics* 13: 341–56.
Mundell, R. (1957) "International Trade and Factor Mobility," *American Economic Review* 47: 321–35.
Savosnick, K. (1958) "The Box Diagram and the Production-Possibility Curve," *Ekonomisk Tidskrift* 60: 183–97.

For empirical tests of the H–O model and data issues, see:

Baldwin, R. (1971) "Determinants of the Commodity Structure of US Trade," *American Economic Review* 61: 126–46.

Bowen, H., Leamer, E., and Sveikauskas, L. (1987) "Multicountry, Multifactor Tests of the Factor Abundance Theory," *American Economic Review* 77: 791–801.

Conway, P. (2002) "The Case of the Missing Trade and Other Mysteries: Comment," *American Economic Review* 92: 394–404.

Davis, D. and Weinstein, D. (2001) "An Account of Global Factor Trade," *American Economic Review* 91: 1423–1453.

Deardorff, A. (1984) "Testing Trade Theories and Predicting Trade Flows," in R. Jones and P. Kenen (eds) *Handbook of International Economics, Vol. I*, Amsterdam: North-Holland.

Harrigan, J. (1997) "Technology, Factor Supplies, and International Specialization: Estimating the Neoclassical Model," *American Economic Review* 87: 475–94.

Leamer, E. (1980) "The Leontief Paradox Reconsidered," *Journal of Political Economy* 88: 495–503.

—— (1995) "The Heckscher–Ohlin Model in Theory and Practice," *Princeton Studies in International Finance*, no. 77.

Leamer, E. and Levinsohn, J. (1995) "International Trade Theory: The Evidence," in G. Grossman and K. Rogoff (eds), *Handbook of International Economics, Vol. III*, Amsterdam: North-Holland.

Leontief, W. (1954) "Domestic Production and Foreign Trade," *Economia Internazionale* 7: 3–32; reprinted in R. Caves and H.G. Johnson (eds) (1968) *Readings in International Economics*, Homewood, IL: Irwin.

Perdikis, N. and Kerr, W. (1998) *Trade Theories and Empirical Evidence*, Manchester: Manchester University Press.

Stern, R. and Maskus, K. (1981) "Determinants of the Structure of US Foreign Trade, 1958–76," *Journal of International Economics* XX: 207–24

Trefler, D. (1995) "The Case of the Missing Trade and Other Mysteries," *American Economic Review* 85: 1029–46.

—— (2002) "The Case of the Missing Trade and Other Mysteries: Reply," *American Economic Review* 92: 405–10.

U.S. Department of Commerce, Bureau of Economic Analysis (2007) "Interactive GDP by Industry Accounts," Available at http://www.bea.gov/national/nipaweb/Index.asp (accessed 24 April 2007).

Vanek, J. (1968) "The Factor Proportions Theory: The N-factor Case," *Kyklos* 21: 749–56.

World Bank (2007) *World Development Indicators*, Washington, D.C.: World Bank.

For the effects of trade and outsourcing on income distribution, see:

Bhagwati, J., Panagariya, A. and Srinivasan, T.N. (2004) "The Muddles over Outsourcing," *Journal of Economic Perspectives* 18: 93–114.

Feenstra, R. (1998) "Integration of Trade and Disintegration of Production in the Global Economy," *Journal of Economic Perspectives* 12: 31–50.

Feenstra, R., and Hanson, G. (1997) "Foreign Direct Investment and Relative Wages: Evidence from Mexico's Maquiladoras," *Journal of International Economics* 42: 371–93.

Ferreira, F., Leite, P., and Wai-Poi, M. (2007) "Trade Liberalization, Employment Flows and Wage Inequality in Brazil," World Bank Policy Research Working Paper 4108.

Goldberg, P. and Pavcnik, N. (2007) "Distributional Effects of Globalization in Developing Countries," *Journal of Economic Literature* 45: 39–82.

Gonzaga, G., Menezes-Filho, N. and Terra, C. (2006) "Trade Liberalization and the Evolution of Skill Earnings Differentials in Brazil," *Journal of International Economics* 68: 345–67.

Kume, H., Piani, G., and de Souza, C. (2000) "A politica brasileira de importacao no periodo: descricao e avaliacao," IPEA: Rio de Janeiro.

Krugman, P. and Lawrence, R. (1994) "Trade, Jobs and Wages," *Scientific American* 270: 44–9.

Schott, P. (2003) "One Size Fits All? Heckscher–Ohlin Specifications in Global Production," *American Economic Review* 93: 686–708.

Trefler, D. (2005) "Trade and Inequality in Developing Countries: a General Equilibrium Analysis," *Journal of International Economics* 65: 21–48.

Wood, A. (1997) "Openness and Wage Inequality in Developing Countries: the Latin American Challenge to East Asian Conventional Wisdom," *The World Bank Review* 11: 233–57.

For attention to the specific factors model, see:

Angrist, J. and Kugler, A. (2007) "Rural Windfall or a New Resource Curse? Coca, Income, and Civil Conflict in Colombia," IZA Discussion Paper No. 2790.
Jones, R. (1971) "A Three-Factor Model in Theory, Trade, and History," in J. Bhagwati (ed.) *Trade, the Balance of Payments and Growth*, Amsterdam: North Holland.

APPENDIX: MATHEMATICAL REPRESENTATIONS OF RELATIONSHIPS IN THE H–O MODEL

An algebraic representation of the Stolper–Samuelson theorem and the Rybczynski theorem contained in a classic paper by Ronald Jones (1965) provides a useful way to show more formally what determines the magnitudes of the diagrammatic results considered above. To derive the Stolper–Samuelson result, begin with the condition that factor payments to capital and labor just exhaust the revenue that producers receive, an outcome that holds in competitive markets and production under constant returns to scale:

$$a_{LC} \cdot w + a_{NC} \cdot r = p_C \qquad (a4.1)$$
$$a_{LG} \cdot w + a_{NG} \cdot r = p_G \qquad (a4.2)$$

where a_{LC} is the amount of labor used to produce a kilo of cheese, a_{NC} is the amount of land used to produce a kilo of cheese, w is the wage rate, r is the rental rate for land, and p_C is the price of cheese. Corresponding definitions hold for grain producers.

Totally differentiate each equation to show how changes in factor prices are related to changes in output prices. For cheese, this expression is:

$$a_{LC} \cdot dw + w \cdot d\,a_{LC} + a_{NC} \cdot dr + r \cdot d\,a_{NC} = dp_C \qquad (a4.3)$$

The terms $w \cdot d\,a_{LC} + r \cdot d\,a_{NC}$ sum to zero, because they represent a producer's cost-minimizing solution to adjust the amounts of labor and land used so that the ratio of the marginal products of the two factors equals the ratio of factor prices. We can express the remaining terms as percentage changes:

$$w \cdot a_{LC} \cdot dw/w + r \cdot a_{NC} \cdot dr/r = \theta_{LC} \cdot w^* + \theta_{NC} \cdot r^* = dp_C / p_C = p_C^* \qquad (a4.4)$$

where θ_{LC} is labor's share of the cost of producing cheese and similar notation applies to other inputs. The asterisk represents the percentage change in a variable.

The cheese and grain equations are:

$$\theta_{LC} \cdot w^* + \theta_{NC} \cdot r^* = p_C^* \qquad (a4.5)$$
$$\theta_{LG} \cdot w^* + \theta_{NG} \cdot r^* = p_G^* \qquad (a4.6)$$

Factor rewards can be solved in terms of product prices to show a magnification effect for the case of labor-intensive cheese production: $w^* > p_C^* > p_G^* > r^*$. To obtain that result, let the price of grain be the numeraire, so $p_G^* = 0$ and recognize $(\theta_{LC} - \theta_{LG}) > 0$. Substitute accordingly to find:

$$w^* / p_C^* = (1 - \theta_{LG}) / (\theta_{LC} - \theta_{LG}) > 1 \text{ and} \tag{a4.7}$$
$$r^* / p_C^* = -\theta_{LG} / (\theta_{LC} - \theta_{LG}) < 0 \tag{a4.8}$$

When a country produces both goods, a change in the relative price of those goods determines the change in factor rewards independent of the country's factor endowments.

Note that these expressions imply the *less* the difference in factor intensities between the two goods, the *greater* the magnification effect. That outcome may seem counter-intuitive, because a large increase in the land–labor ratio and the productivity of labor may seem most likely when factor intensities differ and lots of land is released from the grain sector. The counter-intuitive results holds, however, because a given price increase for cheese results in a much larger increase in the output of cheese when the factor intensities are similar. This large increase in cheese production indeed results in an increase in the land–labor ratio in both sectors.

The Rybczynski theorem can be derived from two equations that show both factors, labor (L) and land (N), are fully employed.

$$a_{LC} \cdot X_C + a_{LG} \cdot X_G = L \tag{a4.9}$$
$$a_{NC} \cdot X_C + a_{NG} \cdot X_G = N \tag{a4.10}$$

where X_C is the output of cheese and X_G the output of grain. As above, totally differentiate each equation. We show the labor equation as:

$$a_{LC} \cdot dX_C + X_C \cdot d\, a_{LC} + a_{NC} \cdot dX_G + X_G \cdot d\, a_{NC} = dL \tag{a4.11}$$

The terms showing changes in the input–output coefficients will be a weighted function of the ease of substituting labor for land in producing both goods. As we saw above, however, if the prices of output do not change, then the wage–rental ratio will be unchanged. In the diagrammatic treatment of the Rybczynski theorem we imposed that condition, which would apply to a small country, and we do so here, too. Therefore, the remaining terms can be written in percentage change form as:

$$\lambda_{LC} \cdot X_C^* + \lambda_{LG} \cdot X_G^* = L^* \tag{a4.12}$$
$$\lambda_{NC} \cdot X_C^* + \lambda_{NG} \cdot X_G^* = N^* \tag{a4.13}$$

where λ_{LC}, for example, is the share of the labor force employed in cheese production. For the case of labor-intensive cheese production these equations yield the magnification effect that $X_C^* > L^* > N^* > X_G^*$. To see this, let $N^* = 0$, recognize $(\lambda_{LC} - \lambda_{NC}) > 0$, and obtain the solutions:

$$X_C^* / L^* = (1 - \lambda_{NC}) / (\lambda_{LC} - \lambda_{NC}) > 1 \text{ and} \tag{a4.14}$$
$$X_G^* / L^* = -\lambda_{NC} / (\lambda_{LC} - \lambda_{NC}) < 0 \tag{a4.15}$$

Again consider the implication that when there is little difference in factor intensities across industries, the magnification effect is larger. When the labor force increases, not only is the additional labor allocated to cheese production, but any reduction in wheat production releases extra labor for each hectare of land that it makes available. Because labor used in cheese production (and consequently output of cheese) increases by a larger percentage than the labor force, $X_C^* > L^*$. To shift enough land into cheese production to maintain the original land–labor ratio requires a large reduction in wheat production.

In addition to Jones' demonstration of the Stolper–Samuelson and Rybczynski results, his paper also provides an excellent discussion of the general equilibrium supply curves used in Chapter 3.

Jones (1971) gives a similar presentation of the specific factors model, which we do not elaborate here. The existence of more factors than goods means that factor rewards no longer are determined by output prices alone. Even for a small country, we must pay additional attention to how easily one factor substitutes for another, because factor prices can change when output prices are constant.

Chapter 5

Scale, Competition, and Trade

LEARNING OBJECTIVES

By the end of this chapter you should be able to explain:

- how economies of scale create a basis for trade even in the absence of different autarky prices

- why trade in differentiated products provides an additional source of gains from trade

- how trade in industries where there are few competitors can alter the division of the gains from trade

- how collusion between producers internationally to form a cartel may drive up price at least temporarily

The role of factor endowments is particularly apparent when we observe trade between many industrialized and developing countries: the industrialized countries import goods that require unskilled labor and tropical land from less developed countries (LDCs), and export goods that require capital, skilled labor, and temperate-climate land-intensive goods to them. A far larger volume of trade occurs among industrialized countries, where differences in factor endowments are not as apparent.[1] While such trade may be consistent with the H–O framework, economists have paid particular attention to circumstances where trade may occur even when there is no apparent basis for comparative advantage. Based on the models developed in the past two chapters, that means no differences in factor endowments and no differences in technology, which might otherwise explain why their prices differ before trade. Instead, economists have focused on the nature of trade when there are economies of scale and markets are not perfectly competitive.

When economies of scale are possible, expanding output to serve a world market rather than a national market allows costs per unit to fall. Depending upon how prices are set in relation to costs, both countries can gain from trade in these circumstances. The actual pattern of trade, however, and the determination of what goods a country imports and what goods it exports, often reflect a created comparative advantage attributable to historical accident or government intervention.

Some economies of scale exist that are external to an individual firm. In this situation, a single firm continues to face rising marginal costs of production as it expands output, just as in the H–O world with perfectly competitive producers. If all firms in the industry expand output, however, costs for all of the firms as a group fall. Such economies may be particularly common if an industry is concentrated in a region. Examples of such concentrations are producers of semiconductors in Silicon Valley of California, international financial services in London, watches in Switzerland, and software in Bangalore, India. The potential of such economies can alter our conclusions about patterns of trade and gains from trade, as we show in the first section of this chapter even when we retain the assumption of perfectly competitive markets.

More often, economies of scale are internal to the firm. As an individual firm expands output, its cost per unit declines. As a result it may gain an advantage over other firms, both domestic and foreign, in producing a particular good or variety of good. Yet, economists have no single unified theory to predict how markets function between the extremes of perfect competition and monopoly. Therefore, theories of international trade that recognize the importance of internal economies of scale depend critically on what economists assume about a particular market. Are there many producers or only a few?

---

1 Donald Davis (1997) demonstrates that a large volume of north–north trade may occur even when factor endowments are similar if the factor requirements for different goods produced in the north also are similar. To be a net exporter of a country's relatively abundant factor may require that a country export a large volume of goods because it imports goods that use almost as much of the abundant factor that it exports.

To answer that question, it is often useful to know the importance of a firm's fixed costs, which must be borne even if the firm produces nothing at all, relative to its variable costs. When fixed costs are relatively unimportant, it is easier for new competitors to enter an industry when prices rise, and they are most likely to leave the industry when prices fall. In those circumstances, models of monopolistic competition and product differentiation provide important insights. For example, if Ireland imports Heineken beer from the Netherlands but exports Guinness beer to the Netherlands, this trade in similar products implies that the availability of different varieties of a product is important to consumers. Economists have developed increasingly more complete models to analyze trade under monopolistic competition.

In other markets, fixed costs may be large relative to variable costs, and a new firm may face major obstacles in entering an industry. Economists use the term "oligopoly market" to describe such a situation where few firms produce. Because of the high barriers to entry in such markets, such as aircraft production, firms may earn economic profits that are not competed away by others. Prices are not determined simply by costs of production but also by the producers' ability to charge more than the average cost of production. Cartels, such as OPEC, represent a related market structure, and we consider what conditions make their successful operations more likely.

EXTERNAL ECONOMIES OF SCALE

When several firms in the same industry expand output, they may all achieve lower costs of production. This situation characterizes external economies of scale and it is particularly likely to arise when the firms operate in the same region. Alfred Marshall identified several reasons for the success of the Lancashire cotton mills in the nineteenth century.[2] They could achieve lower costs due to the emergence of specialized input suppliers, benefits from a common pool of skilled workers, and the spillover of knowledge among firms, which allows new technologies to diffuse and develop more quickly. We consider these possibilities in turn.

Specialized Inputs

Specialized machinery to serve the needs of a specific industry can allow productivity to rise and costs of production to fall. However, a firm in that industry may find it quite time-consuming and inefficient to try to design and make such machinery itself. If the firm is part of an industry where several producers face similar production bottlenecks and limitations, they may all benefit if a new firm specializes in the task of developing more efficient equipment that all of them can buy. The gain will be even greater if there are enough producers of the final good to entice several new entrants into this specialization in input production, thereby resulting in more competition among them.

An example of this development is American agriculture as the country moved westward. A pioneer family had to be jacks-of-all trades, able to do all of the myriad tasks of clearing land, building

---

2 Stephen Broadberry (2002) notes Marshall's contributions and provides a broader discussion of additional sources of both static and dynamic economies of scale.

a house, planting and harvesting a crop, and tending livestock. Self-sufficiency was a more common goal than specialization. With the concentration of many farmers who needed a plow to break the sod on the prairie, it became viable for a blacksmith in Illinois named John Deere to specialize in manufacturing steel bottom plows rather than meet general needs for a smithy. Although Cyrus McCormick's invention of the reaper was initially greeted with skepticism, he moved to Chicago and continued to make a steady stream of improvements to it, fueled by the strong demand from farmers where land was abundant and labor was scarce.

A Common Pool of Skilled Labor

Not only may equipment become highly specialized to serve an industry, but labor skills specific to an industry are also likely to develop. To meet that need, one solution is for each firm to train the labor it requires. While that certainly may occur, proximity to other firms offers an additional advantage. Random good luck may cause the demand faced by one producer to rise, while random bad luck causes demand faced by another to contract. When the two firms are located in the same region, the expanding firm can hire the labor laid off by the contracting firm, without having to experience the cost and delay of training newcomers. Workers are less likely to be unemployed in such a locale, and therefore may be willing to accept a lower wage rate than if their hours of work were less predictable. Thus, production costs for the industry will be lower.

Spillovers of Knowledge

Spillovers of knowledge may spread new technology quickly among firms. When firms are geographically close to each other, that process occurs more easily and improvements are introduced at a faster pace. Of course, firms often have an incentive to keep new technology a secret. In the eighteenth and nineteenth centuries, immigrants to the United States arrived, not carrying a purloined set of blueprints for a machine, but having memorized how such a machine was built in Europe. What are the consequences of this transfer of technology? If firms reap no benefit from developing a new product or production process, their incentive to innovate is reduced. But, once an idea is developed, society benefits if it is shared widely. In Chapter 10 we consider the trade-off that exists between rigorous enforcement of the rights of the inventor and the social gains from others' gaining access to new technology. That issue has been particularly important in recent international negotiations over **intellectual property rights** and patents.

In industries where technology is changing very quickly, and one idea is quickly superseded by another, even innovating firms may benefit from rapid diffusion. The gain from access to new ideas offsets the loss from not being able to prevent spillovers to others. Under those circumstances, the innovator is less worried about competitors being free-riders on its research and development efforts.

Are external economies likely to be limited to a country or even some region within a country? Some barriers to diffusion are geographic because ideas spread more rapidly when those who work in the same industry move from company to company and socialize together. The spread of internet usage, however, may reduce the role of proximity or national boundaries in some industries.

Sometimes the barriers to diffusion are cultural. If American engineers do not read Japanese, they will not learn about the latest Japanese research and development in semiconductor design and production as rapidly. Sometimes the barriers to diffusion are legal. For example, legal scholars have attributed part of the success of the electronic revolution in California, and its retreat in Massachusetts, to different interpretations of what information an individual hopping from one firm to another can pass on without violating stipulations that they must not compete with their former employers (Gilson 1998). For the current discussion, we assume that there are settings where the potential sources of external economies within a country that we have mentioned here are significant.

Production with Decreasing Opportunity Cost

The existence of external economies affects the shape of the production-possibility curve. To demonstrate why that is true, we begin by restating the effect of these economies of scale in a slightly different form: an industry that doubles the inputs it hires will more than double the output it produces. Expansion of output by a greater proportion than inputs used in production is what allows costs per unit to fall.

The importance of this condition is shown in Figure 5.1, which represents an economy's ability to produce semiconductors and soybeans. To simplify our diagram, we assume there are no differences in factor intensities in the production of these two goods. If we imposed the assumption of constant returns to scale, we would be right back to the classical model of constant opportunity cost in Chapter

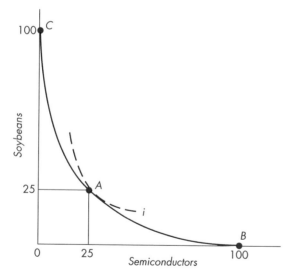

FIGURE 5.1 Equilibrium in a Closed Economy with Decreasing Opportunity Cost

External economies of scale allow industry output to expand by a greater proportion than the expansion of inputs used in production. Compare production at point *A* where half of the economy's resources are devoted to producing each good with points *B* and *C* where all resources are devoted to the production of a single good. Inputs double and output more than doubles.

3. In a more complete analysis, we could assess how differences in factor intensities create a tendency toward increasing opportunity costs, as demonstrated in Chapter 4, which in turn may be offset by increasing returns to scale and a tendency toward decreasing opportunity cost. Our more modest goal here is to show why increasing returns to scale result in decreasing opportunity cost.

The production-possibility curve is bowed inward (convex to the origin) in contrast to the curve that bowed outward (concave to the origin) in the case of increasing opportunity cost. Start at point *A*, which represents the case where just half of the country's resources are devoted to the production of each good. As drawn in Figure 5.1, that corresponds to being able to produce 25 units of each good. Suppose now that the economy allocates all resources to semiconductor production. Inputs into semiconductor production have just doubled. Due to economies of scale, however, output of semiconductors more than doubles to 100 units. A comparable result is shown if all resources are allocated to soybean production: doubling inputs leads to more than double the output.

We can interpret those changes in terms of opportunity cost, too. As the economy moves from point C to point *A*, it gives up 75 tons of soybeans in return for 25 semiconductors, which implies a relative cost of 3 tons of soybeans per semiconductor. Now move the economy from point *A* to point *B*. It has given up 25 tons of soybeans in return for 75 additional semiconductors, which implies a relative cost of 0.33 tons of soybeans per semiconductor. The marginal rate of transformation is declining as more semiconductors are produced, which also represents decreasing opportunity cost.

In a closed economy the equilibrium level of production of the two goods is again given by the tangency of the community indifference curve *i* with the production-possibility curve. All firms still act as price takers and each one expands its output of a good until its marginal cost of production equals the market price. Because that condition will not be met in the imperfectly competitive models that follow later in this chapter, we note it here. Thus far, the autarky solution for this economy appears no different from that in our previous models.

Trade with Decreasing Opportunity Cost

To evaluate trade patterns when there are decreasing opportunity costs, consider two economies that are identical in all respects. In autarky they both choose the same consumption point *A* along the production-possibility curve in Figure 5.1, and they both face the same relative prices at that point. By the principles of comparative advantage developed in the preceding two chapters, there would appear to be no basis for trade. Yet both economies could gain if one were to specialize in semiconductors and the other in soybeans. In Figure 5.2 we show the special case of symmetric demand and production conditions, where each economy can trade along the barter line *CDB*. One economy specializes in semiconductors. It produces at point *B*, consumes at point *D*, and trades *BE* of semiconductors for *ED* of soybeans. The other economy specializes in soybeans. It produces at point *C*, consumes at point *D*, and trades *CF* soybeans for *FD* semiconductors. The two trade triangles are identical at this equilibrium price. Also, both economies move to a higher indifference curve, from i_1 to i_2. Two countries can gain from trade by having each exhaust the available external economies in producing one good rather than each trying to be self-sufficient and unable to achieve those same economies.

The possibility of gains from trade is familiar, but we cannot rely upon differences in autarky prices to explain why this pattern of trade emerges. In this example of perfectly identical economies, the

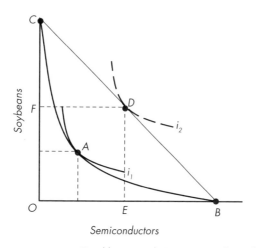

FIGURE 5.2 Equilibrium with Foreign Trade and Decreasing Opportunity Cost

This special case of trade under conditions of decreasing opportunity cost shows identical countries gaining equally from the opportunity to trade. One country specializes in semiconductors and trades *EB* semiconductors for *OF* soybeans. The other country specializes in soybean production and trades *CF* soybeans for *OE* semiconductors. Both countries move to the higher indifference curve i_2.

pattern of trade is indeterminate; it could be assigned by a master planner or settled by the flip of a coin but it would not matter, because both countries experience the same gains from trade. In a more realistic setting, the equilibrium price ratio is not likely to be one that results in both countries moving to the same higher indifference curve. For example, suppose consumers in both countries have a stronger preference for semiconductors than for soybeans. Let trade again result in the same specialized production pattern, but now observe that a higher price of semiconductors and a steeper barter line drawn from point *B* would allow the country that specializes in their production to reach a higher indifference curve. Correspondingly, the country that specializes in producing soybeans now finds that the barter line drawn from point *C* gives it a smaller gain in welfare than in the symmetric case of Figure 5.2. Although both countries start from identical circumstances, the pattern of production that emerges rewards one more than the other. Such an outcome fuels policy debates over the potential role of governments to pick successful industries that allow larger gains from trade and to avoid those that may even leave a country worse off. We return to this topic in Chapter 7.

Ambiguity over the actual pattern of trade also can arise when dynamic economies of scale exist. Such economies of scale may especially be attributable to the dynamic benefits of learning-by-doing benefits. One country may have greater potential to achieve low per-unit costs of production, perhaps due to a difference in endowments that favors the factor used intensively in producing the good where scale economies exist. The other country, however, may have a head-start in producing the good. Because of that head-start and higher cumulative volume of output, the producers in that country achieve economies of scale that allow them to sell at a lower price than the prospective competitor. We represent such a situation in Figure 5.3, which shows average cost curves that correspond to Chinese and Japanese production of automobiles. At any level of output, the Chinese industry's cost curve lies below the Japanese industry's curve. Yet, because of Japan's head-start, its industry

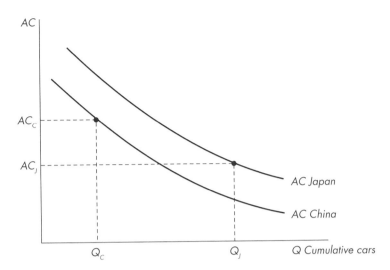

FIGURE 5.3 The Advantage of a Long-Established Industry where Scale Economies are Important

China has the potential to be a more efficient producer of this good than Japan, but the Japanese industry is already large, operating at Q_J, and therefore enjoys large-scale economies. The far smaller Chinese industry, operating at Q_C, cannot compete successfully against the Japanese industry because the Chinese lack the large-scale economies that Japan enjoys.

produces a much greater quantity of cars and achieves a lower average cost than China does based on its smaller volume of output and inability to expand immediately to a larger scale.

The existence of dynamic scale economies achieved from cumulative production can offset the importance of differences in factor intensities and relative factor abundance, which may otherwise account for China's projected cost advantage. Japan may export a labor-intensive good, even though labor is a scarce factor in Japan, because large external economies of scale exist in its production. If the Japanese industry expands aggressively, as its initial success and profitability allow it to do, it may maintain this advantage over China. The Chinese projected cost advantage is never observed in the market.

The Japanese advantage may rest not only on external economies of scale but also on economies of scale internal to the firm. To consider their role, however, we need to specify more fully what determines industry structure in each country and how firms set prices in relation to their costs. Those are topics we pursue later in this chapter.

INTERNAL ECONOMIES OF SCALE

When economies of scale are internal to a firm and not all firms share the same technology, the perfectly competitive markets assumed above are not appropriate. On the other hand, when new products and technologies are developed, the innovator is unlikely to gain a permanent monopoly position as the sole producer of such a product. Competitors may be able to enter the market and produce a close substitute. That possibility is particularly relevant when consumers value product variety. We turn to a progression of models that incorporate these perspectives.

The Product Cycle

Raymond Vernon (1966) observed that many new products pass through a series of stages in the course of their development. One country may have a comparative advantage at the stage of innovation, while another country may have a comparative advantage in mass producing it. The theory, often referred to as the "**Vernon product cycle**," applies best to trade in manufactured products.

Looking at the 1950s and 1960s, Vernon noted that many new products were initially developed in the United States. To some extent that was a function of U.S. scientific and innovative capacity, and indeed subsequent research has shown that U.S. exports used the skills of R&D scientists and engineers intensively. Yet some inventions that occurred outside the United States, such as television, were first commercialized in the United States. That aspect of the cycle was attributable to the U.S. position after World War II as a nation that did not have to use scarce resources to rebuild a war-torn economy. Rather, the United States could devote more of its resources to the production and consumption of new goods that were not simply essentials for survival but often luxuries that only those with more discretionary income could afford.

Thus, many new products were initially developed in the United States, with production and sales first occurring in the domestic market. Locating production close to buyers was important, so that problems identified by consumers could be communicated immediately to producers, and changes could be made without long delays or the build-up of a defective, unsatisfactory inventory. After a new product caught on in the United States, however, the U.S. producer might send a sales force abroad to cultivate foreign markets among consumers with similar preferences and income levels. Or, foreign merchants and trading companies attentive to developments in the United States might place orders for the product. Thus, the United States began to export the product.

As foreign demand grew, sales in some countries might eventually reach a threshold level large enough to tempt foreign firms to undertake production for themselves. Foreign firms might acquire the technology necessary to manufacture the product, or the U.S. producer might find it profitable to establish a subsidiary abroad to produce the good. In either case, a certain degree of standardization presumably had occurred with respect to the product's features and reliability, which meant that immediate contact between the producer and consumer was no longer so important. Production of the standardized good now relied upon assembly operations performed by less skilled workers. As production in other countries rose, U.S. exports to those markets fell, as well as to third-country markets.

Finally, as foreign firms mastered the production process and as their costs fell with the increased scale of production, they might begin to export the product to the United States itself. This sequence of events completed the cycle: the United States began as the exclusive exporter, then competed with foreign producers for export sales, and finally became a net importer of the new product. This scenario seems to fit very well the observed experience with a number of new products in recent decades, such as radio, television, synthetic fibers, transistors, and pocket calculators.

Because of changing circumstances internationally, the U.S. need not play a central role in current cycles. Many other countries also offer high income markets fertile for new product innovation. Differences in factor endowments are smaller and the distribution of scientists and engineers engaged in research and development is wider now than in the 1950s. Many countries now have higher wage costs and an incentive to develop labor-saving innovations. Therefore, we summarize the four stages of the product cycle more generically in Figure 5.4:

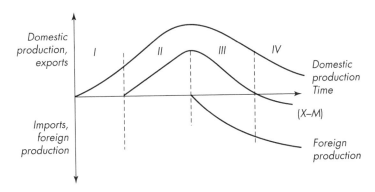

FIGURE 5.4 The Product Cycle

The innovator has a monopoly on the knowledge necessary to produce this good through stages I and II, and therefore has growing output and exports. At the beginning of stage III, production in other countries begins, pulling the original innovating country's output and exports down. At stage IV, this country imports the product that it had previously invented and exported.

  I Product development and sales in the home market.
  II Growth in exports as foreign demand is cultivated.
 III Decline in exports as production abroad begins to serve foreign markets.
 IV Home country becomes a net importer as foreign prices fall.

This theory is essentially short-run, and it is explicitly dynamic. The country with an innovating firm has a temporary comparative advantage in the latest product, but it steadily loses that advantage. It must continually develop other new products to replace those that are maturing and being lost to competitors. The country benefits from a favorable terms-of-trade shift and the monopoly power of its firms that introduce new products, but its terms of trade decline as competition from new producers and products occurs. Competitive cost conditions in the long run come to be determined by factor endowments.

The product cycle hypothesis provides important insights into the ways the process of new product innovation and production affects the mix of products a country trades internationally and the country's gains from that trade. As a predictive theory it is difficult to apply in a systematic way, though, because we are less able to claim where a product cycle will begin or how long it will last.

Preference Similarities and Intra-Industry Trade

Staffan Burenstam Linder (1961) formulated the **preference similarity hypothesis**. He starts with the proposition that as a rule a nation will export manufactured products for which it has a large and active domestic market. The reason is simply that production for the domestic market must be large enough to enable firms to achieve economies of scale and thus to reduce costs enough to break into foreign markets. Linder argues that the most promising and receptive markets for exports will be found in other countries whose income levels and tastes are generally comparable to those of the exporting country. This is why the term "preference similarity" is relevant. Linder contends that countries with similar income levels will have similar tastes. Each country will produce primarily for its home market, but part of the output will be exported to other countries where a receptive market exists.

Two key implications of this theory are that trade in manufactures will take place largely between countries with similar income levels, and that products entering into trade will be similar but in some way differentiated. These two implications accord well with current patterns: the great majority of international trade in manufactured goods takes place among the relatively high-income countries: the United States, Canada, Japan, and European countries. Furthermore, a great deal of this trade involves the exchange of similar products. Each country imports products that are very much like the products it exports. Germany exports BMWs to Italy while importing Fiats. France imports both car brands, and exports Peugeots and Renaults to Germany and Italy.

The Linder model does not explain why one country originates particular products or why particular firms enter the industry. These origins might be viewed as accidental. BMW happened to start producing cars in Bavaria, whereas Fiat began in Milan, and Peugeot entered the car business from Paris. Each local economy had to be large enough to support a firm that was big enough to gain economies of scale, thus making competitive exports possible. Otherwise, there is no particular explanation of why various types of cars are produced in each country.

This framework also depends on economies of scale and implies imperfectly competitive markets. If there were no economies of scale, intra-industry trade would be unlikely because each model or type of product could be efficiently produced in each country, thereby saving transport costs. BMW would have factories in France and Italy, while Fiat would produce in France and Germany. Sizable economies of scale in automobile assembly, however, would make it very inefficient for these companies to maintain factories in each country, and large savings would become available by concentrating production of each type of car in one factory and exporting cars to the two foreign markets.

Intra-Industry Trade: How General Is It?

Although intra-industry trade is important for a variety of high-income countries, this is not a universal pattern. Figures in Table 5.1 indicate a substantial discrepancy between the values observed for the United States and Europe on the one hand, and for Japan on the other hand.

Table 5.1 calculations are based on the following formula for intra-industry trade in industry i: $IIT_i = \{1 - [|X_i - M_i| / (X_i + M_i)]\} \cdot 100$. In the second term the numerator is the absolute value of the trade balance in that good. IIT ranges in value from zero to 100. A value of zero denotes no intra-industry trade and will occur when the product is either imported or exported, but exports and imports do not occur simultaneously. A value of 100 denotes exports equal to imports. The values for each industry are weighted by their share of trade to give a country average value. The 1970 entry for Japan of 32 represents much less intra-industry trade than the French value of 78 does.

Such calculations are always subject to imprecise interpretations because they may reflect two contrasting cases: (1) imported inputs of intermediate goods and exports of final goods categorized

TABLE 5.1 Average Intra-Industry Trade in Manufactured Products

Country	1970	1975	1980	1985
Japan	32	26	28	26
United States	57	62	62	61
France	78	78	82	82
West Germany	60	58	66	67
South Korea	19	36	40	49

Source: Lincoln (1990). Calculations based on three-digit SIC categories.

in the same industry, which may be quite consistent with the H–O model's explanation of trade when outsourcing of different stages of production is possible; and (2) trade in different varieties of final goods, which represents the type of trade predicted by Linder. Such calculations have fueled debate over the openness of the Japanese economy, the protective effect of private business practices, and the ease of distributing products within the current inefficient system. Critics claim the lack of intra-industry trade is clear evidence of a Japanese mercantilistic philosophy that tries to eliminate any reliance on foreign production for goods that can be produced domestically. Defenders of Japanese practice note that Japan's pattern of trade differs from that of other countries due to its much greater dependence on imports of raw materials and consequent need to export a larger volume of manufactured exports. As a result, imports of manufactures are unlikely to equal exports, and the measure of *IIT* will be smaller.

Such calculations have caused economists more recently to estimate whether a country's manufactured imports, or imports from a particular country, differ significantly from what we would predict after controlling for the country's domestic production or factor endowments. A study by James Harrigan (1996) calculates that Japan's ratio of imports to expenditure is only 28 percent of the U.S. value, and the U.S. value is much smaller than comparable European ratios, even when intra-E.U. trade is excluded.

An appeal to numbers alone is unlikely to resolve this debate. In years of depressed economic growth globally and large trade surpluses in many countries, the issue is certain to attract attention. Only the country names may differ in current controversies.

The examples of trade in cars demonstrate that consumers value product variety. Producers also gain from product variety, because specialized inputs enable firms to be more productive and produce at lower cost.[3] Steel alloys can differ in their tensile strength, corrosion resistance, and malleability, or semiconductors can differ in their performance at extreme temperatures or power requirements.

---

3 Wilfred Ethier (1982) formally develops these insights in a framework that allows for both internal and external economies of scale.

Different final uses require different specialized characteristics, and a single supplier will seldom find it efficient to produce all these different varieties.

Intra-industry trade can occur for a variety of reasons. To move beyond the anecdotal perceptions discussed thus far, we next examine product variety and imperfect competition more systematically.

ECONOMIES OF SCALE AND MONOPOLISTIC COMPETITION

The previous examples of individual firms specializing in different varieties of a product rest upon the existence of economies of scale internal to the firm: a firm's average cost of production falls as its own output rises. We begin by considering two possible sources of such economies of scale and the implication that a firm will find it efficient to specialize in particular products rather than produce an entire range of products itself. We then examine the sources of gains from trade in the case of monopolistic competition in two countries, where enough firms enter an expanding industry that any economic profits are eliminated.

One of the most common sources of economies of scale is fixed costs of production. To enter an industry, before it even starts to produce any output at all, a firm typically must buy equipment, set up a distribution network, engage in research and development, or launch an advertising campaign. These costs are then recovered through subsequent sales of the good it produces. The average fixed cost per unit declines the more units are sold, and the firm will be able to cover those costs at a lower price.

Fixed Costs That are Not Always Obvious

Simply setting up a production line to produce a different product can have a high opportunity cost, because production of one good must cease while machinery is recalibrated to produce another product. This down-time to produce very small quantities of a different good represents a fixed cost of production. Short production runs can only be justified if prices are sufficiently high to recover those fixed costs. Studies of the Canadian economy in the 1960s indicated the disadvantage of a policy to protect domestic producers and produce small amounts of a broad range of goods: few economies of scale were achieved in comparison with producers in the United States. Average costs of production were 20 percent higher for many household appliances (Daly, et al. 1968).

Economies of scale also exist when there are increasing returns to scale, and a doubling of variable inputs leads to more than a doubling of output. A set of industries where firms experience these economies of scale includes beer brewing, flour milling, oil refining, and chemical processing. Production in these industries often requires vats, tanks, silos, or warehouses where the material necessary to make the product depends upon their surface area, but the output obtained from them depends upon the volume they hold. Because the surface area of a sphere, for example, increases with the square of the radius, while the volume it holds is a function of the radius cubed, increasing returns to scale occur over an important range of output as the radius is increased.

Increasing returns to scale apply to cases such as the early automobile production lines of Henry Ford, who used much more capital equipment than the craft shops that initially dominated the auto industry. This much larger scale of plant allowed Ford to obtain a more than proportional increase in output. His ability to achieve these economies of scale as he produced large volumes of automobiles allowed his average cost per unit to fall below that of his competitors.

Further Reasons for Economies of Scale: The Learning Curve

Fixed costs and increasing returns to scale are not the only reasons why average costs of production fall as output rises. Another important factor in some industries has been the **learning curve**, which relates the firm's average cost of production to its cumulative output. An example of the way we might express such economies is that every time a company doubles its output, costs per unit fall by 25 percent. Such reductions in cost may occur due to better organization and scheduling of complex production processes, such as the assembly of aircraft. In the production of semiconductors they result from the ability to eliminate flaws in the production process. Initial production runs may yield as few as five usable chips out of 100 produced; after more experience is gained, the yield of usable chips may rise above 95 percent.

An important aspect of learning is whether it can be transferred from one plant to another within a company or whether it easily spills over to other firms in the same country or even to other countries, an example of the external economies of scale considered earlier. A steep learning curve where costs fall rapidly as output expands is likely to result in an industry with fewer firms, because learning represents a barrier to entry similar to fixed costs or increasing returns. Learning is less of a barrier to entry if it easily spills over to domestic competitors. If the learning of one firm spills over to another, and vice versa, then expansion of industry output allows all firms to produce more cheaply. Correspondingly, if learning spills over internationally to firms in other countries, then external economies do not create a competitive advantage for producers of just one nation.

A study by Douglas Irwin and Peter Klenow (1994) of the worldwide semiconductor industry provides empirical evidence on several of the points raised above. Based on analysis of seven successive generations of dynamic random-access memory chips (DRAMs) from 1972 to 1992, they report an average learning rate of 20 percent. This figure holds for both U.S. and Japanese firms. With respect to spillovers within the industry, they find that firms learn three times more from an additional unit of their own cumulative output than from another firm's cumulative output. Thus, firms appear able to appropriate a large share of the benefits from their learning. Because world output is far more than three times the output of any one firm, however, spillovers play a major role in allowing an individual firm's production costs to fall. Spillovers internationally are just as important as spillovers within a country, and therefore policies to promote national production end up providing a benefit to others. Also, spillovers across different generations of chips generally are not observed. Thus, fears that government measures can create successful firms in one generation and thereby develop a competitive advantage over other firms in subsequent generations do not appear well founded in this case.

Evidence from other industries yields contrary interpretations of the potential for national or international spillovers. Hiroshi Ohashi (2005) analyzes costs in the Japanese steel industry. He finds a steep learning curve for an individual firm but little spillover to other firms in the same industry. Lee Branstetter (2001) assesses the extent of spillovers from firm patent rates and R&D expenditures. He finds most spillovers are national, not international.

A firm's choice to expand output, however, is limited by the demand conditions it faces. It makes no sense for a firm to expand output if buyers are not willing to pay a price that at least covers the firm's additional costs of production. The model of monopolistic competition can be usefully applied to demonstrate a firm's best choice of price and output taking these circumstances into account.

Figure 5.5 shows a firm that faces a downward-sloping demand curve. The firm has market power to set prices, but it will not exercise that power arbitrarily. Rather, the firm will determine its optimal level of output where the extra revenue from producing another unit just equals the extra cost, that is, where marginal revenue equals marginal cost. The extra revenue from selling another unit of output no longer equals the price of that unit, as in a perfectly competitive market, because the firm must take into account the reduction in price necessary to attract more customers. Additional revenue is raised only when the gain from more units sold offsets the loss from offering existing customers a lower price. Marginal revenue will be positive only if demand for the product is elastic, and the positive quantity effect offsets the negative price effect. Based on the profit-maximizing rule that the firm produces where marginal revenue equals marginal cost, the firm chooses to produce at Q*.

The price that customers are willing to pay for this much output is P*. This price represents a mark-up above marginal cost, which will be larger when customers have fewer options and demand is less elastic. In spite of being able to charge a price greater than marginal cost, however, the firm

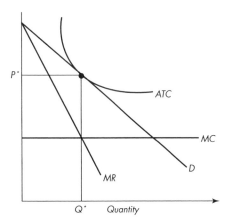

FIGURE 5.5 Production Under Monopolistic Competition

The firm produces at Q* where marginal revenue, MR, equals marginal cost, MC. The firm charges the price P*, which represents a mark-up above marginal cost, which will be greater the less elastic is demand. The firm makes an average rate of return, because P equals ATC.

only makes an average rate of return when other firms can freely enter or exit the industry. There are no economic or above-average returns. That result is shown by the tangency of the average total cost (ATC) curve to the demand curve at P^*, where ATC includes an average rate of return to capital used by the firm. If the ATC curve had been lower and positive economic profits had been earned, those profits would attract new entrants into the industry. The demand curve for the existing firm would shift inward and new entry would continue until this tangency condition was established.

Trade with Monopolistic Competition

When trade is possible between two countries that each have monopolistically competitive industries, what results can we predict regarding the pattern of trade and the gains from trade? If both countries have the same preferences and factor endowments, as well as the same technical capabilities, then firms have the same costs and prices initially, and we expect the same number of producers of a good to exist in autarky in each country.

Integration of the market still offers gains to both countries. One way in which gains can be achieved is through industry rationalization. With greater competition from extra firms in an integrated market, each individual firm will have less market power to mark up its price over marginal costs. If all firms adopt that strategy, they will not all be successful in covering their fixed costs of production. Some firms will be driven out of business as this process of industry rationalization occurs. We expect there will be fewer total firms in each country, but the average output of each one will be greater than before trade. Average costs of production fall as the demand curves for the remaining firms shift outward, as in Figure 5.5. The economy as a whole gains, because there is less duplication from separate firms meeting the fixed costs of entering this industry. If there are increasing returns to scale, which result in both average cost and marginal cost falling as each firm's output expands, the gain from rationalization is even easier to see.

These relationships between trade, price, and cost are shown in Figure 5.6, based on a framework suggested by Paul Krugman (1979). PP represents the relationship between the number of firms and the ability of competition to lower prices. The larger the number of firms, the more vigorous the competitive climate. CC shows that average costs per firm within a closed national economy vary with the number of firms. As the number of firms increases, the size of the typical firm declines and average costs rise. With a small number of firms, each enterprise will be larger. It will more fully exploit economies of scale, thereby driving down costs. With a closed national market, the equilibrium price is P_1. If the market is instead defined as the world, because imports and exports are allowed, the relationship between the number of firms and average costs shifts to CC′ because far more firms can exist without losing economies of scale in the much larger world market. Free trade then helps lower the equilibrium price to P_2, because the world market has both larger firms and more vigorous competition than were possible in an isolated national market.

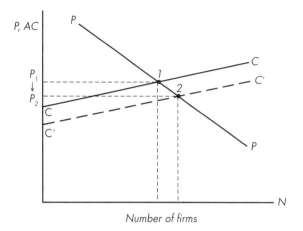

FIGURE 5.6 The Impact of Free Trade on Prices with Imperfect Competition: Increased Competitiveness and Economies of Scale

The *PP* line shows that as more firms enter the market, the more vigorous the competition and the lower the price charged. The *CC* line shows that average costs rise as the number of firms in the industry increases. For a given market size, more firms imply smaller firms that achieve fewer economies of scale. These firms must charge a higher price to cover their costs. If free trade exists, so that the relevant market includes foreign producers and markets, *CC* shifts to *C'C'* because there can be both more firms and bigger firms than would exist in a single domestic market. A combination of larger firms and more vigorous competition is therefore possible at point 2 than was true in a solely domestic market at point 1. Trade lowers prices internationally.

Where Are Scale Economies Especially Important?

As noted above, in the 1960s trade barriers to protect the Canadian manufacturing sector meant that economies of scale were not achieved in many industries. Long before a free trade agreement with the United States was negotiated, however, the two countries addressed that problem in the automobile sector with a special agreement. Before the 1965 U.S.–Canada auto pact, all of the major U.S. auto companies operated plants in Canada, but the market was so small that only a limited range of cars could be produced. Even with this limitation costs and prices were high. In the mid-1960s the United States and Canada signed an agreement to allow producers to freely trade cars and parts. The car companies and the Canadian government made side agreements guaranteeing the maintenance of Canadian production and employment. Through this arrangement all of the car models and types available in the United States became available in Canada. Moreover, the Canadian plants could sharply reduce costs by concentrating on the production of one or two models, with the vast majority of the output being shipped to the United States. Canadian car-buyers were able to choose from a far wider range of models and no longer had to pay the high prices that resulted when Canadian factories produced at a less-than-optimal scale.

Another gain that occurs with the opening of trade is the opportunity for consumers to buy a wider variety of goods. Even if industry rationalization and reductions in consumer prices do not occur, the extra variety represents a gain. The love-of-variety model proposed by Krugman (1980) rests on this rationale alone, and we present that framework in the appendix to this chapter. It yields the result that larger economies do not achieve greater economies of scale, but instead produce a greater variety of goods. Growth in a trading partner then conveys a benefit to the home country, because its consumers now gain from the availability of additional varieties of goods.

Gains from Variety?

During the heyday of the Cold War and explicit competition between Western capitalism and Soviet communism, rapid growth of the Soviet industrial machine left Western consumers consoling themselves that they at least had choice in the market place and were not forced to buy the single available variety produced by a government enterprise intent on exhausting all possible economies of scale. In the monopolistic competition framework considered here, choice and variety is the central metric for demonstrating the gains from trade in Krugman's love-of-variety model. Yet, how do economists put a monetary value on the benefits of choice?

Christian Broda and David Weinstein (2006) make such a calculation for the U.S. over the 1972–2001 period. A brief review of their analysis shows why such estimates are not very common. They consider the most disaggregated categories of goods tracked through the tariff schedule. They note that the number of distinct goods has more than doubled from less than 8,000 to over 16,000. The median number of countries from which a good is imported has doubled, from 6 to 12. Product differentiation appears to have exploded!

To assess what an economy gains, however, we need to know more than how many varieties exist. We need to know how easily a new variety substitutes for an existing one; if they are very close substitutes, then an additional variety does not create much of a benefit. One way of calculating that gain is by determining how much less a consumer needs to spend when more varieties are available in order to achieve the same level of utility possible with the initial set of goods. When the new variety is not a close substitute for what already exists, then the reduction in spending will be greater.

Broda and Weinstein estimate tens of thousands of elasticities of substitution, to verify how easily a variety from one country substitutes for the variety from another country. They estimate separate values for each good and they also make separate estimates for each year, to investigate whether product varieties are becoming less similar and less easily substitutable for each other. From those estimates they are able to say that an import price index that ignores the benefits of new varieties will overstate the price of imports by 1.2 percentage points each year. Over the 30-year period, they calculate that U.S. welfare is 2.6 percent higher due to the opportunity to acquire greater variety through trade.

The implications of this intra-industry trade for changes in the distribution of income differ from the H–O model, too. Because the basis for trade does not rest upon different factor intensities in production, there is no change in relative factor demands. While some firms may cease production when industry rationalization occurs, industry output nevertheless expands in the case of symmetric countries presented above. That expansion results from greater sales at the lower prices now charged. When trade is liberalized among countries that primarily produce differentiated manufactured goods with similar input requirements, workers laid off producing one good find jobs producing another differentiated good. In the love-of-variety model, domestic demand is just replaced by foreign demand. Such patterns of adjustment are likely to be much less contentious than the conflict between skilled labor and unskilled labor described in Chapter 4. Here, all factors of production can gain from trade because of the greater variety of products available.

Geography and Trade

When the role of transportation costs is recognized, the symmetric outcomes suggested above are less likely to occur, a possibility stressed by more recent contributions from the perspective of economic geography. Traditionally, economists have recognized that some countries have had bad luck in their geographic location. They may be far from major markets, they may be entirely landlocked, and they may be plagued by diseases or bad weather. Even without such bad luck, countries find that geography plays an important role in determining the location of production and trade. Models based on monopolistic competition have allowed economists to represent this situation more systematically. An influential paper by Paul Krugman (1991) and subsequent contributions by others give different answers to some of the questions raised in earlier chapters. For example, the expectation that wage rates will be equalized through free trade, a prediction from Chapter 4, is no longer guaranteed in economic geography models. The division of the gains from trade depends upon a different set of factors than those examined previously.

Consider two countries that produce an agricultural good under constant returns to scale and perfect competition, and manufactured goods where the sector is characterized by economies of scale and monopolistic competition. If transport costs are sufficiently high, the two economies will be self-sufficient and not trade. If transport costs fall from this extreme, then trade becomes profitable. If one country is larger, it benefits from more of the external economies identified earlier. It will also have a bigger market to be served by its manufacturing sector.

While such patterns of **agglomeration** have long been recognized by geographers, recent contributions consider more formally why such agglomeration occurs. They ask how an initial situation with equal-sized countries might evolve into a pattern with an industrial core and an agricultural periphery. From a symmetric starting point, consider the consequences of random luck such that one country attracts additional manufacturing firms. When some of those manufactured goods are used as intermediate inputs to produce final goods, the producers of those final goods benefit from the greater variety that now becomes available to them. Because they do not have to pay transportation costs to import such goods, their costs are lower than in the other country. They will sell more domestically and import less from the other country. The opportunity for firms to serve a larger market and to achieve lower costs of production offsets the disadvantage of having to compete against more firms.

Conversely, producers in the other country have fewer opportunities to achieve economies of scale and lower costs through the availability of intermediate goods. Through such a process the manufacturing core grows and the industrial sector in the periphery shrinks. If transport costs fall to zero, however, the core no longer has an advantage from better access to intermediate goods. Input costs are the same and any market can be served just as easily by a producer in the periphery as in the core.

The benefit of having a bigger market suggests that not all nations will converge to the same standard of living as more trade occurs. Rather, the big are likely to get bigger and richer, while the small, who can only access larger markets at some cost, are likely to deindustrialize. Wages do not converge with trade. Note the contrast to the H–O model, where transport costs could keep trade from causing wages to equalize, but trade would tend to reduce that gap. The economic geography model predicts that for a certain range of transport costs trade can increase the gap.

As we noted in Chapter 2, transport costs have fallen sharply in the past 100 years, and some commentators have characterized the new reality with the claim that "the world is flat." Others suggest that the big cost reduction for trade in goods has already occurred and that the costs of shipping and delivery will likely increase in the future. Some economists suggest that the falling cost of sharing knowledge reduces the incentive for agglomeration, and thus reduces the tendency for divergence noted above.

Transportation and the Gravity Model of Trade

As shown in Chapter 2, transportation costs influence trade patterns and result in some goods becoming nontraded goods. A more general way in which economists incorporate trade costs into their analysis has been with the **gravity model**. The name is borrowed from Sir Isaac Newton's observation that the force of gravity between two bodies is given by the product of their masses divided by the square root of the distance between them. The economic application of this concept implies that trade between two countries, T_{ij}, will be greater the larger the output or *GDP* of the countries and the smaller the distance between them:

$$T_{ij} = GDP_i^{g1} GDP_j^{g2} / Distance_{ij}^{g3} \qquad (5.1)$$

GDP_i in the exporting country represents the role of supply, GDP_j in the importing country represents the role of demand, and $Distance_{ij}$ is the distance between them. Further extensions of this framework allow for other forces of attraction (common cultural ties) or resistance (trade barriers).

Several authors have contributed to the economic rationale for such a functional form to hold. A comprehensive presentation by Jeffrey Bergstrand (1985) rests on the monopolistic competitive framework discussed above, and the two-way trade it implies. Elhanan Helpman (1987) notes that a testable proposition of the monopolistic competition framework is that as a group of countries becomes more similar in size, trade within the group should rise as a share of their GDPs. His estimates over a 26-year period for 14 industrialized countries, where we expect product differentiation to matter most, confirm this prediction.

A useful cautionary lesson is provided by subsequent analysis by David Hummels and James Levinsohn (1995). They estimate a similar relationship for a set of 14 primarily developing countries where we expect less of a role for product differentiation. They find that Helpman's result also holds for this second sample. They conclude that while the gravity equation fits trade data well, that framework does not appear to let us distinguish among competing theories of why trade occurs. In fact, Alan Deardorff (1998) suggests that the gravity equation can be derived under a variety of economic circumstances, including a model with perfect competition but the production of country-specific goods.

In any event this model has been quite successful in describing trade patterns at an aggregate level and also for particular industries. Consensus estimates find that $g1$ and $g2$ are close to 1.0 and $g3$ is about 0.7. That is, if either the exporting or importing country were 10 percent larger, there would be 10 percent more trade between them. If they were 10 percent further apart than a comparably sized pair of countries, the trade between them would be 7 percent less. The advantage of a location close to a large neighbour that provides a large market is clearly indicated by these estimates. The framework does not, however, provide a clear basis for policy makers to design appropriate steps to overcome any disadvantages from being far from a major market.

TRADE WITH OTHER FORMS OF IMPERFECT COMPETITION

Our analysis in the preceding section was simplified by the assumption that entry of new firms into the industry allowed any above-average profits to be competed away. The smaller are fixed costs relative to variable costs, the smaller are the barriers to entry in the industry. A surge in demand and the resulting higher profits attract new entrants into the industry. On the other hand, some industries are not well described by those conditions. Barriers to entry are significant enough that some firms can earn above-average profits and no new entrant competes them away. If cost-saving innovations occur, it is less clear what portion is passed on to consumers in the form of lower prices. A further contrast to models of monopolistic competition is that there are few enough firms in the industry that the action of one will not be ignored by the others.

Economists have proposed several different models to represent the effects of trade when only a few firms operate. One extreme is the case where a single domestic producer would not find it attractive to produce for the domestic market alone, but the opportunity to trade and serve the larger world market would warrant the entry of one firm. High research and development costs to develop a drug that very few people in any one country ever require represents such a case. In the absence of trade, the drug simply would not exist, a clear loss to world welfare. Similarly, the high cost of developing a wide-bodied long-range aircraft to seat 600 passengers would never be warranted if sales were limited to airlines based in a single-country market, and even with access to the world market, no more than one producer appears likely to produce such a plane.

Trade under a Duopoly

Consider a less extreme case where two firms producing an identical product do exist to serve the world market. We begin by applying a duopoly model that shows how one firm alters its output in response to output decisions of the other firm. Such a model, developed by Augustin Cournot (1838), can be summarized in two reaction curves as shown in Figure 5.7. Let the two curves correspond to a Dutch firm and to an English firm who serve an integrated European market. If the Dutch firm held a monopoly it would produce at point D_M along the vertical axis; if the English firm held a monopoly it would produce at point E_M along the horizontal axis. The English firm's reaction function shows that as Dutch output rises, English production will fall. Because two firms find it profitable to operate in this industry, the English firm will not be able to operate as a monopolist at point E_M. If English output initially were at that level, the Dutch response would be to produce at D_1, as given by the Dutch reaction function. At that level of output, the English firm would then choose to produce E_1. In turn, the Dutch firm would respond by producing D_2. This process converges to the equilibrium shown at Z where the two reaction curves intersect. Point Z does not lie along a straight line connecting D_M and E_M, and therefore this solution shows that more total output will be produced than when a monopoly controls the market. Because more output is sold, a lower price must be charged. Thus, gains from competition are possible in a duopoly setting.

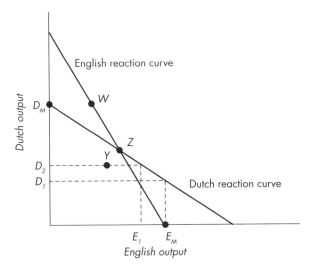

FIGURE 5.7 Reaction Curves and Duopoly Trade

An English monopolist chooses to produce E_M. If a Dutch firm enters the market, it offers the quantity D_1 as indicated by its reaction curve. The English firm reacts by producing E_1, as indicated by its reaction curve, which results in a further Dutch response to offer D_2. This sequential adjustment leads to equilibrium at point Z.

Oligopolistic Rivalry in History

Douglas Irwin (1991) applied this duopoly framework to explain the rivalry between the English East India Company and the Dutch United East India Company for the spice trade with Southeast Asia from 1600 to 1630. Because land transportation was such an expensive alternative, competition between sea-faring traders provided the main check on the market power of any one firm. Furthermore, Queen Elizabeth I granted a 15-year exclusive monopoly to the English East India Company, and the Dutch similarly granted the Dutch United East India Company monopoly rights to trade with Asia. No other country had comparable maritime power, and thus, a duopoly setting describes this trading situation quite accurately.

Each trading company determined the number of ships to send to Asia and then auctioned off the pepper brought back to Europe. They both had access to the Asian markets to acquire pepper, and they had comparable costs to transport it back to Europe. Under the symmetric setting of Figure 5.7 appropriate to these circumstances, we expect each firm to gain half of the market.

A symmetric outcome in the pepper trade, however, did not emerge. The Dutch accounted for nearly 60 percent of the market. Irwin suggests that the Dutch East India Company followed a strategy that differed from the Cournot model. Stockholders could not check the actions of company agents in the field, whose remuneration depended upon total turnover and growth. Such agents had no incentive to cut back their efforts when British sales expanded, and the Dutch produced more than called for by the Cournot model. Nevertheless, this strategy was beneficial to the Dutch, giving them 20 percent higher profits than in the Cournot case, because it in effect implemented a leadership strategy later identified by Heinrich von Stackelberg (1934). The success of the strategy arose due to the reduction in the competitor's (British) output, given the leader's (Dutch) decision to expand so much. The outcome is comparable to Dutch maximization of profits assuming it could count on a subsequent British reduction in output. In terms of Figure 5.7, the strategy represents a point such as W, where total industry output (British plus Dutch) is greater than at Z, and prices are lower. Dutch profits are greater due to their larger share of this expanded market.

If the two firms could have reached an agreement not to compete against each other, Irwin calculates their combined profits would have been 12 percent greater than in the Cournot solution. With collusion, both firms produce half the amount that a monopolist would choose, at point Y in Figure 5.7. As long as this market-sharing arrangement can be enforced, the two firms can each earn higher profits and gain at the expense of the world's consumers.

As a variant of this framework, consider the case of two identical countries that initially are each served by a domestic monopoly. If trade becomes possible and the two firms compete as Cournot oligopolists, with the same cost of serving either market, the solution in Figure 5.7 applies to any one country's market. The English producer, for example, no longer holds a monopoly in the English market. Competition with the Dutch firm leads to the solution at point Z, where more of the product is sold to consumers at a lower price. In the Dutch market, the Dutch monopolist likewise must compete with the English firm, which results in a greater quantity and a lower price being charged.

The possibility of trade has a pro-competitive effect that benefits each country, because the market price comes closer to marginal cost, the optimal condition from a competitive market. Although monopoly profits fall, that represents a benefit to consumers, and in the symmetric case assumed here, any loss in English (Dutch) profits is more than offset by gains to English (Dutch) consumers.

Other Outcomes in Duopoly Trade

The Cournot assumptions represent just one of several strategies that a duopolist might follow. The duopolist may not assume that its competitor will leave output unchanged, and it instead may try to anticipate the competitor's response. Or, in some industries, it may be more appropriate to assume that a firm sets its price, rather than its output, assuming its competitor will leave its price unchanged. In Chapter 7 we return to this topic because oligopoly behaviour is quite applicable in debates over **strategic trade policy**. Because of the variety of plausible responses suggested here, we can see why many results may be specific to the model chosen. Nevertheless, the presumption of a pro-competitive effect from trade is a common element.

Cartels

Real-world examples of cartels generally do not exhibit the symmetries assumed in the pepper trade example. It is worth examining more realistic cases to understand why collusion and cartel agreements are often fragile. The most significant example of the past four decades has been the Organization of Petroleum Exporting Countries (OPEC). Its success in the 1970s appeared to be a role model for exporters of other primary products, who envisioned a new world order emerging. The requirements for creating a successful cartel are rather stringent, however, and cartels have a tendency to weaken the longer they are in operation. For a cartel to be successful in raising prices well above marginal costs, the following conditions must exist:

1. The price elasticity of demand for the product must be low, which means that it has no close substitutes. Otherwise the volume sold will shrink dramatically when prices are raised.
2. The elasticity of supply for the product from outside the cartel membership must be low, which means that new firms or countries are not able to enter the market easily in response to the higher price. If this condition does not hold, the cartel will discover that higher prices result in a large reduction in its sales as new entrants crowd into the business.
3. At least a few members of the cartel must be willing to reduce production and sales to hold the price up. If all members insist on producing at previous levels despite the higher price, there will almost certainly be an excess supply of the product, resulting in a price decline. Such increases in production often follow secret price cuts by members competing for sales despite promises not to do so. Production and sales cutbacks are easier to maintain if a product is durable and can be stored. Failure to sell perishable crops results in large losses.
4. The membership of the cartel must be congenial and small enough to allow successful negotiations over prices, production quotas, and a variety of other matters. Cartels are more difficult to maintain as the number of members rises, particularly if some of them are historic adversaries.

From this list of conditions a reader can see why OPEC's success has been so rare in other markets. Most products do have substitutes and/or can be produced by new firms or countries if prices are increased sharply. Cartels and commodity agreements have frequently failed when the market available to the members shrank, but none of them was willing to cut production sufficiently to support the price. Cheating in the form of secret price cuts to gain new customers followed, and the intended monopoly collapsed.

OPEC was successful in the 1970s because all four of the above conditions held for oil, but the longer high prices remained in effect, the weaker OPEC became. Efforts to conserve energy and the increased use of alternative energy sources reduced the demand for oil. Non-OPEC countries, such as Mexico and the United Kingdom, increased production sharply in the late 1970s. The result was a reduction in the volume of oil that OPEC members could sell. When Saudi Arabia became unwilling to be the primary producer to make major cutbacks in production, a sharp price drop occurred in 1986, as can be seen in Figure 5.8.

Subsequent developments demonstrate the importance of demand factors. The Asian financial crisis of the late 1990s led to a period of slow growth and less demand for oil; at the same time economically distressed oil-producing countries were unwilling to reduce output. The terms of trade of oil producers in 1998 fell to a level nearly as low as before OPEC's formation. That situation was reversed rather quickly. During the 2001–2002 downturn OPEC reduced output while non-OPEC

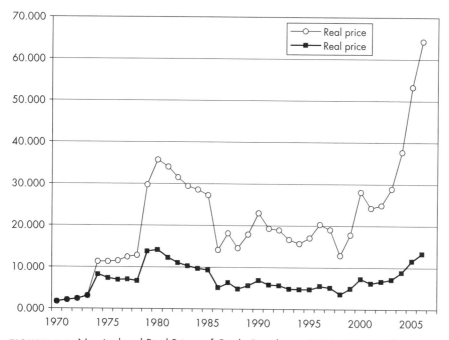

FIGURE 5.8 Nominal and Real Prices of Crude Petroleum, 1970–2006 (Dollars per Barrel)

Source: IMF, *International Financial Statistics.* The real price is based on the average price of crude oil divided by the export unit value index for industrial countries, which was set equal to 1.0 for 1973.

The real price of oil was not much higher in the 1990s than prior to OPEC. Price increases in the twenty-first century demonstrate renewed market power due to rapid growth in demand.

TABLE 5.2 World Oil Production, Peak Years, and Recent Detail (millions of barrels per day)

	OPEC	Non-OPEC	World
1970	23.7	25.3	49.0
1979	31.5	35.5	67.0
1990	24.9	41.5	66.4
2000	32.3	45.5	77.8
2002	29.9	47.1	77.0
2006	35.8	48.7	84.5

Source: U.S. Department of Energy, Energy Information Administration (2008).

production rose. In the subsequent recovery, the surge in oil production was led by OPEC producers, who expanded more rapidly than non-OPEC producers. Strong demand drove higher prices that let OPEC avoid the allocation of production cuts among its members.

Further Aspects of Trade with Imperfect Competition

Another element of trade with imperfect competition that warrants attention is the effect of trade when we no longer start from symmetric situations in the two countries. Previously, we considered the potential gains from trade when an equal number of identical, monopolistically competitive firms operate in each country in autarky, or when two monopolists in separate home markets become a duopoly in an integrated world market. What if the symmetric expansion of production and consumption does not hold?

First consider the production choice that a monopolist producer of cars makes, as shown in Figure 5.9. The autarky production and consumption point is *A*. At that point, the slope of the production-possibility curve, which gives the relative marginal costs of producing the two goods, is not the same as the slope of the community indifference curve, which corresponds to the price at which consumers substitute one good for another. The steeper slope of the indifference curve indicates that the relative price of cars is greater than the relative cost of producing cars. The gap between those two lines represents the mark-up of the domestic monopolist in car production. Indeed, the existence of the monopoly leaves the country worse off than it would be at point *B* with competitive markets, where more cars would be produced and sold at a lower price.

Now introduce trade into this situation. The new equilibrium will depend upon whether the monopolist competes with just one other firm or with several additional firms. The most straight-forward case occurs if the monopolist is forced to operate as a perfect competitor. In the new equilibrium, price must equal marginal cost, the international price line is tangent to the production-possibility curve, and the country gains from trade. Not only does the country benefit from importing a product where it has a comparative disadvantage, but it also benefits because the monopoly distortion has been eliminated.

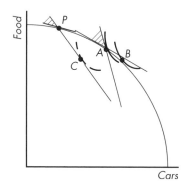

FIGURE 5.9 A Possible Decline in Welfare from Trade with Imperfect Competition

In autarky the economy produces and consumes at point *A*. The monopoly producer of cars chooses a price (given by the line tangent to the indifference curve at *A*) that is steeper than the marginal cost of production (given by the line tangent to the production-possibility curve). Under duopoly trade, the firm's market power declines, and the gap between price and marginal cost falls, as shown at production point *P*. Because price still exceeds marginal cost and output of cars falls, it is possible that the new equilibrium lies on a lower indifference at point *C*.

Figure 5.9 represents a different trading situation. Suppose two monopolists in autarky now compete against each other. The monopolist in country A has a much higher marginal cost of producing cars than its competitor in B, and in the new Cournot equilibrium country A imports cars. World output of cars rises compared to the autarky situation, but if we distinguish by country, output in B rises while output in A falls. Additional competition has reduced the gap between price and marginal cost, a benefit to A. But, A's production of cars has fallen, and because price still exceeds marginal cost, that represents a loss. The country may become worse off, shown by the movement to a lower indifference curve. More generally, if trade results in greater output of goods for which price exceeds marginal cost, the economy unambiguously benefits.

This outcome contrasts with the earlier symmetric case, where the domestic monopoly became an exporter and increased its sales in the foreign market at the same time as it was subject to more competition at home. If there is little or no potential to increase sales abroad, a large country with a high-cost producer may lose from this shift in monopoly output to foreign producers. We return to this topic in Chapter 7 where alternative trade policies and potential profit-shifting strategies are evaluated.

Summary of Key Concepts

1. External economies of scale allow average costs in an industry to fall as the output of individual firms rises.
2. Countries can gain from specialization and trade, even when there are no differences in autarky prices. How countries specialize is indeterminate theoretically, and the actual pattern may be the result of historical accident or government intervention.
3. Internal economies of scale allow average costs of a firm to fall as its output expands. When these economies of scale are not so great that they create a major barrier to entry in an industry, there are likely to be many producers of differentiated products in the industry under monopolistic competition.
4. Two-way intra-industry trade is likely under monopolistic competition. The gains from trade come from industry rationalization, as prices fall and a smaller number of producers

within a country exhaust more economies of scale, and from a greater variety of products becoming available in an open world market.

5. Internal economies of scale may be so great that only a few firms produce in an industry. Predicting trade in oligopoly industries requires predicting how a firm responds to the output or price decisions of another firm.

6. Gains from trade include greater competition and lower prices, but the opportunity to shift oligopoly profits from one country to another makes net benefits less certain.

7. Oligopolistic firms may collude by forming cartels to reduce competition among themselves. Cartels are difficult to maintain, because new entrants may be attracted by the higher profits, and members of the cartel have an incentive to cheat by increasing output above agreed levels.

CASE STUDY

A Further Case of Intra-Industry Trade: Carrying Coals to Newcastle?

Recall that intra-industry trade can be simply a statistical artifact from dissimilar products being lumped together into the same reporting category. Or, it can reflect product differentiation suggested by the model of monopolistic competition. What about two-way trade in products that are identical?

In a perfectly competitive model, we do not expect two-way trade of identical goods to occur. When markets are characterized by large barriers to entry, however, oligopoly results, and firms have the chance to earn economic profits. When there are not substantial trade barriers or transport costs, a firm has an incentive to sell not only in the domestic market but also in the foreign market. Two-way trade in identical products can result, as the oligopolist tries to gain some of the profits earned by the foreign firm. That possibility is related to an outcome that economists label **reciprocal dumping**, a topic that we discuss more fully in Chapter 7.

Daniel Bernhofen (1999) applies that framework to develop a model for predicting when intra-industry trade will occur. He starts from the symmetric case considered in the text, where two countries are the same size, all producers of a good have identical costs, and the number of firms in each country is identical. For a Cournot model where each firm sets its quantity of output assuming its competitor will keep its output constant, he demonstrates that in equilibrium the index of intra-industry trade (IIT) will equal 100. Bernhofen varies those conditions in three ways: (a) let one country have a more concentrated market with fewer firms; (b) let one country have much lower marginal costs of production; and (c) let one country have a much larger market than the other. He predicts that for each of these changes, there will be less intra-industry trade and the value of the IIT index will be lower.

To test empirically whether actual trade patterns confirm these theoretical insights, Bernhofen examines German–U.S. trade in petrochemicals. He considers 28 different chemical products at such a fine level of disaggregation that they can be considered identical, homogeneous goods. He uses German–U.S. bilateral trade for the 1988–1992 period. Because these products are not commonly recognized house-

TABLE 5.3 Intra-Industry Trade in Petrochemicals, Germany and the United States

Product	Average IIT value, 1988–1992
Plastics	
High-density polyethylene	11
Polypropylene	93
Polyvinylchloride	53
Polycarbonate	74
Melamine resin	37
Synthetic rubbers	
Polybutadiene	92
Basic Petrochemicals	
Carbon black	8
Benzene	0
Industrial Chemicals	
Styrene	14
Ethylbenzene	0
Ethyl glycol	19
Acetone	67

Source: Bernhofen (1999).

hold goods, Table 5.3 provides some sample categories and the corresponding IIT value observed.

Bernhofen's study is unique, because he has access to engineering data for the costs of different production processes in both countries. This source also confirms that the marginal cost of production does not vary as the output of the firm is higher or lower. Thus, he can determine the relative production costs of a representative firm in each country, and he can compare the number of firms producing each product and the total sales in the U.S. and German markets. He finds that a lower IIT value results when there is a greater difference between countries with respect to the size of their markets, the industry concentration of producers, and the marginal cost of production.

Economists refer to these findings with respect to the pattern of trade as positive, as opposed to normative, results. The former refer to what "is" versus the focus of the latter on what "should be," for example, to maximize a country's welfare. Chapters 6 and 7 consider this latter perspective.

CASE STUDY QUESTIONS

1. If marginal costs of production in Germany and the U.S. are the same, why will differences in the size of their two markets influence the amount of intra-industry trade?

2. Why would a country whose firms have lower marginal costs of production in a product be less likely to engage in intra-industry trade? How would its exports and imports of that product be affected?

3. If the German and U.S. markets are the same size but there are fewer producers in Germany, what does that imply about the extra competition that U.S. producers will face in the U.S. market when trade is possible? How does that imply less intra-industry trade?

4. The monopoly markup of price as a multiple of marginal cost is $\eta/(\eta-1)$ where η is the absolute value of the elasticity of demand. In the oligopoly model applied by Bernhofen, the markup is $\eta/(\eta-s)$, where s is the firm's share of the market. Explain the difference between the markup you calculate for the monopoly case and the symmetric duopoly case ($s = 1$ and $s = \frac{1}{2}$) when $\eta = 2$.

Questions for Study and Review

1. If the production of athletic shoes is an industry where external economies of scale are important determinants of costs of production, how would that make it more difficult for China to replace Korea as the world's leading producer? If China nevertheless were able to become the top producer, would you expect all production to take place in a single province? What role does proximity among producers play in determining whether external economies of scale are achieved?

2. What assumptions of the factor proportions model does the product cycle model relax or violate? To what extent are predictions of the product cycle model consistent with the factor proportions model? Does the product cycle model help explain the Leontief paradox?

3. Why does Linder's theory of trade in manufactured products predict that more trade will take place between similar countries? Trade in services is becoming increasingly important to the United States; would you predict that this U.S. trade is more likely to be conducted with similar countries or with dissimilar countries?

4. Explain what the index of intra-industry trade shows, and suggest why the values of this index for Japan and Germany are so different.

5. Trade patterns of countries Y and Z are given in the table below:

	Country Y		Country Z	
	Exports	Imports	Exports	Imports
Industry A	80	20	100	0
Industry B	20	80	60	40
Industry C	50	50	40	60
Industry D	70	30	0	100

■ Apply the formula in the Box on page 116 to calculate the index of Intra-Industry Trade for each country. Note that the amount of trade in each industry is equal, so that you need not calculate separate weights for each industry in calculating a country average.

■ For the country with the higher average IIT value, explain what industry patterns above contribute to that ranking.

■ In what sense is the trade of the country with the lower IIT value more likely to be determined by the factor endowments theory?

6. Assume the fashion industry represents a monopolistically competitive industry, and explain what types of economies of scale exist that keep it from being a perfectly competitive industry. How is the opportunity to trade likely to change the structure of the fashion industry and the output of each designer in the industry?

7. Why may trade liberalization in monopolistically competitive industries have less effect on the distribution of income than trade liberalization in the H–O framework? What sort of adjustments in output per firm do you expect in the case of monopolistic competition?

8. If significant external economies from production in industry A occur, how does that contribute to agglomeration benefits that allow a country to have a higher standard of living than its smaller neighbour that has the same relative factor endowments?

9. You have the following information about GDP for countries A, B, and C. Assume that the distance between each country pair is identical and that the coefficients of the two GDP terms in the gravity equation equal one.

	Country A	Country B	Country C
GDP	100	75	50

■ If A exports to B equal 40, by the gravity model, what will B's exports to C be?

■ What are C's exports to A?

■ If the distance from A and B to C is twice as far as between A and B, we expect fewer exports from C to B. If the coefficient of the distance variable in the gravity model is –.7, calculate how much smaller the trade between B and C is compared to your previous answer.

10. Suppose two firms serve an integrated world market, and their reaction curves are given by:

$$q_1 = 30 - 0.5 \, q_2$$
$$q_2 = 30 - 0.5 \, q_1$$

where q_1 is the output of firm 1 and q_2 is the output of firm 2. If firm 1 were guaranteed a monopoly in this market, what would it choose to produce? What will each duopolist produce in the equilibrium given by the intersection of these curves? Comparing the duopoly solution to the monopoly solution, how has total output changed? If these two firms were to collude, what would they produce instead?

11. Trade increases competition in previously closed markets. What economic conditions discussed in this chapter suggest such competition nevertheless can leave a country worse off?

References and Suggestions for Further Reading

For greater attention to the case of external economies of scale and spillovers, see:

Broadberry, S. (2002) "External Economies of Scale in the Lancashire Cotton Industry," *Economic History Review* 55: 51–77.
Gilson, R. (1998) "The Legal Infrastructure of High Technology Industrial Districts: Silicon Valley, Route 128, and Covenants Not to Compete," unpublished paper, Columbia University.
Kemp, M. (1964) *The Pure Theory of International Trade*, Englewood Cliffs, NJ: Prentice Hall, Chapter 8.

For attention to product innovation, demand and trade, see:

Baldwin, R. (1971) "Determinants of the Commodity Structure of US Trade," *American Economic Review* 61: 126–46.
Gruber, W., Mehta, D., and Vernon, R. (1967) "The R and D Factor in International Trade and Investment of United States Industries," *Journal of Political Economy* 75: 20–37.
Linder, S. (1961) *An Essay on Trade and Transformation*, New York: Wiley.
Perdikis, N. and Kerr, W. (1998) *Trade Theories and Empirical Evidence*, Manchester: Manchester University Press.
Vernon, R. (1966) "International Investment and International Trade in the Product Cycle," *Quarterly Journal of Economics* 80:190–207.

For insight into formal models of trade with product variety see:

Broda, C. and Weinstein, D. (2006) "Globalization and the Gains from Variety," *Quarterly Journal of Economics* 121: pp. 541–85.
Deardorff, A. (1998) "Determinants of Bilateral Trade: Does Gravity Work in a Neoclassical Model?" in T. Ito and A. Krueger (eds.) *Regionalization in the World Economy*, Chicago: University of Chicago Press.
Ethier, W. (1982) "National and International Returns to Scale in the Modern Theory of International Trade," *American Economic Review* 72: 389–405.
Helpman, E. (1984) "Increasing Returns, Imperfect Markets, and Trade Theory," in R. Jones and P. Kenen (eds) *Handbook of International Economics, Vol. I*, Amsterdam: North-Holland, pp. 325–65.
Helpman, E. and Krugman, P. (1985) *Market Structure and Foreign Trade*, Cambridge, MA: MIT Press.
Jones, R. and Neary, P. (1984) "The Positive Theory of International Trade," in R. Jones and P. Kenen (eds) *Handbook of International Economics, Vol. I*, Amsterdam: North-Holland, pp. 48–53.
Krugman, P. (1979) "Increasing Returns, Monopolistic Competition, and International Trade," *Journal of International Economics* 9: 469–79.
—— (1980) "Scale Economies, Product Differentiation, and the Pattern of Trade," *American Economic Review* 70: 950–9.
—— (1981) "Intraindustry Specialization and the Gains from Trade," *Journal of Political Economy* 89: 959–73.
Van Merrewijk, C. (2007) *International Economics*, Oxford: Oxford University Press.

For empirical contributions that investigate aspects of trade under monopolistic competition, see:

Bergstrand, J. (1985) "The Gravity Equation in International Trade: Some Microeconomic Foundations and Empirical Evidence," *Review of Economics and Statistics* 67: 474–81.

Branstetter, L. (2001) "Are Knowledge Spillovers International or Intranational in Scope? Microeconometric Evidence from the United States and Japan," *Journal of International Economics* 53: 53–79.

Daly, D.J., Keys, B.A., and Spence, E.J. (1968) *Scale and Specialization in Canadian Manufacturing*, Economic Council of Canada, Staff Study No. 21. Ottawa: Queen's Printer.

Grubel, H. and Lloyd, P. (1975) *Intra-Industry Trade: The Theory and Measurement of International Trade in Differentiated Products*, New York: Wiley.

Harrigan, J. (1996) "Openness to Trade in Manufactures in the OECD," *Journal of International Economics* 40: 23–39.

Helpman, E. (1987) "Imperfect Competition and International Trade: Evidence from Fourteen Industrial Countries," *Journal of the Japanese and International Economies* 1: 62–81.

Hummels, D. and Levinsohn, J. (1995) "Monopolistic Competition and International Trade: Reconsidering the Evidence," *Quarterly Journal of Economics* 110: 799–836.

Irwin, D. and Klenow, P. (1994) "Learning-by-Doing Spillovers in the Semiconductor Industry," *Journal of Political Economy* 102: 1200–1227.

Lincoln, E. (1990) *Japan's Unequal Trade*, Washington, DC: Brookings Institution.

Ohashi, H. (2005) "Learning by doing, export subsidies, and industry growth: Japanese steel in the 1950s and 1960s," *Journal of International Economics* 66: 297–323.

For useful insights in the new economic geography literature, see:

Anderson, J. and van Wincoop, E. (2004) "Trade Costs," *Journal of Economic Literature*, 42: 691–751.

Baldwin, R., Forslid, R., Martin, P., Ottaviano, G., and Robert-Nicoud, F. (2003) *Economic Geography and Public Policy*, Princeton: Princeton University Press.

Gallup, J.L., Sachs, J. with Mellinger, A., "Geography and Economic Growth," paper prepared for the Annual Bank Conference on Development Economics, Washington, D.C., April 20–21, 1998.

Krugman, P. (1991) "Increasing Returns and Economic Geography," *Journal of Political Economy* 99: 483–99

Krugman, P. and Venables, A. (1995) "Globalization and the Inequality of Nations," *Quarterly Journal of Economics* 110: 857–80

Neary, J. P. (2001) "Of Hype and Hyperbolas: Introducing the New Economic Geography," *Journal of Economic Literature* 39: 536–60.

Puga, D. (1999) "The Rise and Fall of Regional Inequalities," *European Economic Review* 43: 303–34.

For contributions that present, explain, or apply oligopoly and monopoly theory, see:

Bernhofen, D. (1999) "Intra-industry trade and strategic interaction: Theory and evidence," *Journal of International Economics* 47 (1999) pp. 225–44.

Cournot, A. (1838) *Researches into the Mathematical Principles of the Theory of Wealth*, New York: Macmillan.

Irwin, D. (1991) "Mercantilism as Strategic Trade Policy: The Anglo–Dutch Rivalry for the East India Trade," *Journal of Political Economy* 99: 1296–1314.

Markusen, J., Melvin, J., Kaempfer, W., and Maskus, K. (1995) *International Trade Theory and Evidence*, New York: McGraw Hill.

Melvin, J. and Warne, R. (1973) "Monopoly and the Theory of International Trade," *Journal of International Economics* 3: 17–34.

von Stackelberg, H. (1934) *Marktform und Gleichgewicht*, Vienna and Berlin: J. Springer.

Varian, Hal (1987) *Intermediate Microeconomics*, New York: W.W. Norton.

For a more detailed discussion of cartels in oil and agricultural markets see:

Vernon, R. (ed.) (1976) *The Oil Crisis*, New York: W.W. Norton.

U.S. Department of Energy, Energy Information Administration (2008) *International Petroleum Monthly*, available at http://www.eia.doe.gov/emeu/international/oilproduction.html (accessed 4 September 2008).

World Bank (1986) *World Development Report*, Washington, DC: World Bank.

For other material cited in this chapter:

Davis, D. (1997) "Critical Evidence on Comparative Advantage? North–North Trade in a Multilateral World," *Journal of Political Economy* 105: 1051–1060.

Friedman, T. (2006) *The World is Flat*, New York: Farrar, Strauss and Girou.

APPENDIX A: MONOPOLISTIC COMPETITION AND TRADE

A simplified model of trade with monopolistic competition, slightly different from the one discussed in the chapter, is the love-of-variety model of Krugman (1980). The name of the model comes from the specific utility function assumed:

$$U = [\sum_{i=1}^{N} c_i^{(e-1)/e}]^{e/(e-1)}$$

where c_i is consumption of variety i and e is the elasticity of substitution among varieties. If consumers buy equal amounts of each of the N available varieties, utility simplifies to $U = N^{e/(e-1)}c$. To represent a given level of expenditure, Nc, regroup these terms to give $U = N^{1/(e-1)}Nc$. As the number of varieties increases, even though total expenditure remains constant, utility increases.

The determination of equilibrium prices and output in this model can be summarized very concisely. Production of the differentiated manufactured goods is characterized by the following condition:

$$L_i = \alpha + \beta x_i \qquad (a5.1)$$

where α is a fixed amount of labor required to establish a firm and initiate production, and β is the additional amount of labor necessary to increase production of x by one unit. Each firm attempts to maximize its profits, given by

$$\Pi = px - (\alpha + \beta x_i)\, w \qquad (a5.2)$$

where p is the price and w the wage rate. Because of the large number of competitors, assume each firm ignores the pricing strategy of other firms, and given the utility function presented above, regards the demand it faces as

$$x = \gamma p^{-e} \qquad (a5.3)$$

where e is constant and assumed to be greater than one, and γ represents other determinants of demand. Note that this assumption differs from the earlier Krugman (1979) model discussed in the chapter, where the elasticity of demand the firm faces depends upon the number of competitors in the market. Here, the elasticity of demand is constant and the profit maximizing price is:

$$p = [e/(e-1)] \; w \; \beta \tag{a5.4}$$

The firm will set a higher markup the less elastic is demand. Higher wages and labor requirements result in a higher price.

In a monopolistically competitive market, the equilibrium condition that sufficient entry of firms will occur to eliminate any economic profits means that price equals average fixed cost plus average variable cost:

$$p = [e/(e-1)] \; w \; \beta = \alpha \, w \, / \, x + w \, \beta, \; or \tag{a5.5}$$
$$x = [\alpha/\beta](e-1) \tag{a5.6}$$

The optimal level of output of a firm will be larger the greater are fixed costs relative to variable costs and the greater the elasticity of demand.

The number of firms, N, that produce in a country can be determined from the endowment of labor in the economy:

$$N = L/(\alpha + \beta \, x) = L/\{\alpha + \beta \, [\alpha/\beta](e-1)\} = L/\alpha e \tag{a5.7}$$

More firms will produce in a country with a larger labor force, and when output of the typical firm is smaller (fixed costs are smaller, and the elasticity of substitution in demand is small, because a new variety is not a good substitute for an existing variety).

In a closed economy, it will be the case that labor earnings, wL, equal total spending on the goods produced, Npx. If trade is possible, consumers in a country will have more varieties from which to choose. Although consumers in A will now spend less of their income on home varieties, consumers in B will now buy the additional varieties available from A. In the absence of transport costs, prices and wages are equal in the two countries, and the share of income that Country A spends on B's goods is $N_b L_a/(N_a + N_b)$, while the amount of income that B's consumers spend on A's goods is $N_a L_b/(N_a + N_b)$. Trade is balanced because the ratio of the number of firms in each country equals the ratio of the labor forces in the two countries.

Trade does not result in a change in the number of firms that produce, so no industry rationalization occurs. The price of goods produced does not change. Consumers still are better off with trade because of the additional variety they enjoy, given their access to foreign goods. Also, if Country B grows and produces more varieties, then consumers in A benefit from that development because they now have more choice.

APPENDIX B: OLIGOPOLY, THE COURNOT MODEL, AND TRADE

We present diagrammatic and algebraic derivations of duopolist reaction curves based on the Cournot model of behaviour. Begin by assuming that we can determine the profits of the English producer at all possible combinations of English and Dutch output. If we connect all points that represent the same level of profit (an isoprofit curve) we obtain the sort of curves shown in Figure 5.10. For English output of a_1, a_2, or a_3, English profits are the same.

We already know that E_M represents the English monopoly solution, and we recognize that producing a smaller amount at a_1 or a larger amount at a_3 implies a lower level of profits. That level of profits is also what the English firm earns at a_2, where it is no longer a monopolist. In fact, if Dutch output is given by D_1, then a_2 represents the English firm's best output choice. Any other level of English output, such as at point b_1 or point b_3, lies on a lower isoprofit curve further away from the maximum attained at E_M. Other points along the English reaction curve are derived by this same process of determining the highest isoprofit curve that can be attained for a given level of Dutch output. If the English firm expects Dutch output to remain constant irrespective of its own choice of output, its profit-maximizing output choice will be given by a point along its reaction curve.

As Dutch output rises, the English firm does not reduce output by a comparable amount to restore the initial price. That response would not maximize the firm's own profits because it would not be the sole beneficiary of a price increase. The Dutch firm also would reap part of the benefit from a higher price. Therefore, any rise in Dutch output exceeds the reduction in English output, as indicated by the steeper slope of the English reaction curve and the smaller English response. Consequently, total output of the duopolists exceeds the output of a monopolist.

To derive the reaction curves mathematically, begin with the assumptions that two firms produce an identical product and each takes the other's output as given when considering a change in its own output. Let the market demand curve, Q, be given by:

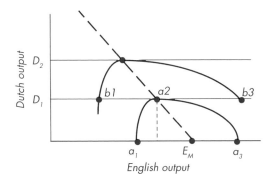

FIGURE 5.10 Isoprofit Curves and the Derivation of a Reaction Curve

An isoprofit curve for England connects all combinations of Dutch and English output that yield the same level of English profit. If Dutch output is given at D_1, English profits are higher at a_2 than at b_1 or b_3, and therefore a_2 is the English firm's profit-maximizing level of output. The English reaction curve is given by finding the English profit-maximizing output, which occurs at the peak of an isoprofit curve, for each level of Dutch output.

$$Q = q_1 + q_2 = A - P \tag{a5.8}$$

where q_1 and q_2 are the outputs of each firm, A is a constant that depends upon the price. Each firm's total costs are a function of fixed costs, b, and its constant marginal cost, c, multiplied by its output. Profits for firm 1, π_1, will be:

$$\pi_1 = q_1 P - b - cq_1 = Aq_1 - q_1^2 - q_1 q_2 - b - cq_1 \tag{a5.9}$$

using the demand curve to substitute for P. Differentiating this equation with respect to q_1 and setting that expression equal to zero gives firm 1's reaction curve as:

$$q_1 = .5 \, [(A - c - q_2) \tag{a5.10}$$

Note that the coefficient of 0.5 on the q_2 term is less than one as explained above. The reaction curve for firm 2 will be $q_2 = .5 \, [A - c - q_1]$, and the intersection of these two curves will occur where

$$q_1 = q_2 = (A - c)/3 \tag{a5.11}$$

The price will be $P = (1/3) \, A + (2/3) \, c$. We assume each firm is able to cover its fixed costs of production; its profits will be $[(A - c)/3]^2 - b$. To check your understanding of this derivation, derive the comparable expression when marginal costs of production of the two firms are not equal.

Chapter 6

The Theory of Protection

Tariffs and Other Barriers to Trade

LEARNING OBJECTIVES

By the end of this chapter you should be able to demonstrate:

- how tariffs reduce economic efficiency

- why quotas can result in larger efficiency losses than tariffs

- why greater domestic production can be achieved more efficiently through subsidies than trade barriers

- how a large economy may gain at the expense of others when it imposes a tariff

- how the nominal tariff rate may understate the protection provided to an industry

- why export taxes have effects comparable to import tariffs

In our exposition of the theory of international trade, we started with countries that were initially operating as closed economies. We allowed these isolated economies to trade freely with each other, and then we analyzed the economic effects of trade. An important conclusion we drew was that economies, if not all individuals in the economy, generally gain from trade. When each country specializes in products in which it has a comparative advantage, exporting them in exchange for imports of other products in which it has a comparative disadvantage, the result is a gain in economic welfare. Even when comparative advantage and autarky differences in costs of production do not provide a basis for trade, gains are possible as economies of scale are attained and competition results in greater production, lower prices, and additional variety.

That countries gain from free trade has long been a major tenet of trade theory. One of Adam Smith's principal objectives in his *Wealth of Nations* was to overturn and destroy the mass of mercantilist regulations that limited international trade. He argued that elimination of artificial barriers to trade and specialization would lead to an increase in real national income. David Ricardo shared this belief, as have most economists in subsequent generations.

Hardly any country maintains a policy of complete self-sufficiency, and instead most end up somewhere between the extremes of free trade and no trade. To assess the consequences of such intermediate positions, we start from a position of completely free trade, and ask what is the effect of introducing a restriction on trade? Can a nation's welfare be improved by imposing tariffs or other barriers to trade, not necessarily to eliminate trade but at least to reduce it below the free-trade level?

Administrative Issues in Restricting Trade

In the nineteenth century through the mid-twentieth century, tariffs (taxes on imports) were the dominant form of government regulation of trade. For most industrialized countries that has changed. Average tariff levels have fallen, in part due to the successful completion of several rounds of multilateral negotiations. Governments, however, have sought ways to restrict trade without violating commitments to lower tariffs. As a result, **nontariff trade barriers**, widely known as NTBs, have proliferated and have become the most active means of interference with trade. A nontariff trade barrier is any government policy, other than a tariff, which reduces imports but does not similarly restrict domestic production of import substitutes. Quotas and related quantitative restrictions, which are limits on the physical volume of a product that may be imported during a period of time, are the most straightforward NTB to consider. Other important examples that have consequences similar to tariffs and quotas in favoring domestic producers are government procurement policies and product safety, health, and technical regulations. This chapter does not try to cover all possible policy instruments, but deals first with tariffs, and then with quotas, tariff-rate quotas, and subsidies.

Import tariffs may be *ad valorem* (a percentage of the value of the imported article), specific (a given amount of money per unit, such as $0.50 per yard of cloth), or compound (a combination of *ad valorem* and specific, such as 10 percent *ad valorem* plus €0.20 per square meter of cloth). ***Ad valorem* tariffs** have the administrative advantage of rising automatically with inflation and of taxing different qualities of products at the same percentage rate. A tariff of 10 percent on wine produces proportionally more revenue as the price and quality of imported wine rise. A **specific tariff** will not have this effect. Its protective effect will decline in periods of inflation. The very high level of protection of U.S. agricultural output established in the 1930s has subsequently fallen a great deal, not due to multilateral trade negotiations, but rather to a rising price level that reduces the protective effect of specific tariffs. A specific tariff will also severely restrict imports of lower priced items within a product category while having little effect on expensive items. A tariff of $2 per bottle on wine would be prohibitive for inexpensive wines, but would have very little impact on imports of high-priced wines. Such a tariff gives foreign producers an incentive to upgrade their production.

A disadvantage of an *ad valorem* tariff is that it creates opportunities for cheating through false invoicing. If a misleading low price is shown on the shipping invoice, part of the tariff can be avoided. A 10 percent tariff on cars, for example, might encourage both car exporters and their customers to invoice the cars $1000 below their true value, thus saving $100, with a fictitious transaction being used to move the $1000 as well as part of the $100 back to the exporter. A specific tariff of $500 per car would avoid this problem, because the customs official would simply collect $500 times the number of cars driven off the ship and have no interest in the value of each car.

Tariff Administration and a Helping Hand

In many countries, getting a job as a customs official promises an opportunity to amass a fortune quickly and retire early. The official is in a position to accept bribes to impose a tariff at a much lower rate than called for under the country's tariff schedule. Both the importer and the official gain from this arrangement. Perhaps even the country as a whole gains from this unofficial reduction in its tariff barriers. Government tariff receipts fall, however, and in some countries that still may be an important source of revenue for the public sector.

For countries that try to reduce such corruption, an option is to outsource their customs collections to the Swiss company SGS. The company can verify the prices of goods sold on world markets and challenge unrealistically low valuations declared in a given client country, when importers want to avoid high tariffs, or unrealistically high valuations when importers want to receive foreign currency at a preferential rate from the Central Bank (a topic addressed in Part II of this book).

PARTIAL EQUILIBRIUM ANALYSIS OF TRADE BARRIERS

Begin by considering the effects of a tariff imposed on a single good. Assume that the industry involved is a very small part of the total economy. It is so small, in fact, that changes in this industry have negligible effects on the rest of the economy, and these effects can be ignored. We call this framework partial equilibrium analysis. Also, we consider the case of a competitive market, where an industry supply curve represents the aggregate response of many individual firms to the market price. No single firm is big enough to affect the market price by its own decision to increase or decrease output. In Chapter 7 we consider situations where there are fewer firms in an industry and each one has some power to influence the market price.

Tariffs in the Small-Country Case

In Figure 6.1 we represent the market for shoes in the E.U., where we assume that domestic and foreign shoes are identical and sell at the same price. In the left panel, we show the E.U.'s domestic demand (D) and supply (S) curves for shoes. If trade is free, shoes will be imported into the E.U. at the prevailing world price, P_w of €18. At that price, the E.U.'s total consumption will be 720 million pairs of shoes, its production will be 130 million, and imports will make up the difference, 590 million. Total supply (130 of domestic output plus 590 of imports) equals total demand (720) at that price. Alternatively, we can show this same situation in the right panel of Figure 6.1, where we use the residual import demand curve first presented in Chapters 2 and 3. Note that there is no demand for imports at a price of shoes greater than the autarky price, P_A. At a price lower than P_R, where the domestic supply curve cuts the vertical axis and the quantity supplied equals zero, then the import demand curve is the same as the market demand curve. At prices between P_A and P_R the quantity of imports demanded is simply the difference between the quantity demanded and the quantity supplied domestically. At the world price P_w the import quantity is 590 million.

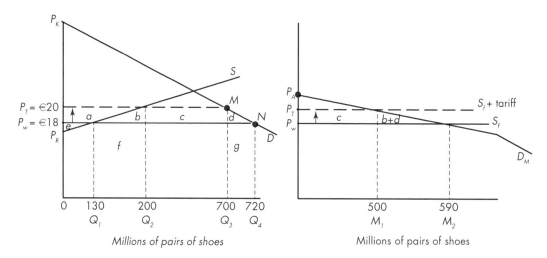

FIGURE 6.1 The Effects of a Tariff: Partial Equilibrium, Small-Country Case

The imposition of a €2 per pair tariff shifts the world supply price from P_w at €18 to P_T at €20, and reduces the quantity of imports from 590 million pairs to 500 million pairs. The lost consumers' surplus, $a + b + c + d$, is divided between the government, which collects tariff revenue of area c, and the domestic industry, which receives additional producers' surplus of area a. Triangles b and d are deadweight losses.

Now suppose that the E.U. imposes a tariff, equal to T or €2 per pair of imported shoes. The immediate result of the tariff is that the price of shoes in the E.U. will rise by the amount of the tariff to P_T. In this section of the chapter we assume that the world price of shoes remains unchanged when the E.U. imposes its tariff. That is, we assume that the E.U. is a small country whose actions will not affect the world market. The increase in price has a number of effects that can conveniently be examined in Figure 6.1. The first effect is that the consumption of shoes is reduced from 720 to 700. The second effect is that domestic output rises from 130 to 200. Domestic producers do not pay the import tariff, and the higher domestic price gives them an incentive to increase their output, as indicated by a movement along the supply curve. The third effect is that imports fall from 590 to 500. Both the fall in consumption and the rise in production cut into the previous level of imports of shoes. Note that if the tariff were large enough to raise the price to P_A imports would fall to zero. Domestic producers would supply the entire demand. This would be a prohibitive tariff.

Winners, Losers, and Welfare Measures

We can also use Figure 6.1 to show the welfare gains and losses that result from the tariff. To show these gains and losses, we use the concepts of **consumers' surplus** and **producers' surplus**. First, we recognize that the area under the demand curve shows what consumers are willing to pay for a product. Consumers are willing to pay a lot for the first pair of shoes that protects their feet, but because consumers value each succeeding pair less they offer a progressively lower price as we move downward along the demand curve. Another way of interpreting this downward slope is that many consumers are likely to require a reduction in price to convince them to buy shoes as a fashion accessory rather than a belt, scarf, or purse. When consumers pay the market price for all of the shoes purchased, they receive a benefit given by the difference between the price they are willing to pay and the price they actually have to pay for each pair of shoes bought. At the world price P_W this measure of consumers' surplus is the triangle $P_K N P_W$, which is the total area under the demand curve, $P_K N Q_4 O$, less the amount spent on shoes, $P_W N Q_4 O$. Imposition of the tariff reduces the consumers' surplus to $P_K M P_T$, and the change equals the area of the trapezoid $P_W P_T M N$. That trapezoid includes the separate areas a, b, c, and d. For those who like to confirm such calculations numerically, the area is €1,420 million for the values show in the diagram.

Although consumers lose from the imposition of the tariff, domestic producers gain. They are now able to charge a higher price and sell a larger quantity, which causes their revenues to rise by areas a, b, and f. Not all of that additional revenue represents higher profits, though, because domestic costs of production rise too. In a competitive industry where the supply curve is based upon the marginal cost of output of the firms in the industry, the extra cost of producing $Q_1 Q_2$ of output is areas $b + f$. Therefore, the change in producers' surplus is the change in revenue minus the change in cost, area a, which equals €330 million for the numerical values shown. Alternatively, area a can be interpreted as a windfall gain to domestic producers. Previously, they were willing to sell Q_1 of output at P_W, and now they receive P_T, a gain of €2 per pair of shoes. Also, as they expand output from Q_1 to Q_2, P_T exceeds the extra cost of producing that output for all shoes except the very last one at Q_2. The gain on existing output plus additional output motivated by the tariff is represented by area a. A final way to think of this change in producers' surplus is to calculate the value of producers' surplus before the tariff is imposed and then calculate it after the tariff is imposed. We define producers' surplus as the difference between the price that a supplier is willing to accept compared to the price actually received in the market. Because the price a firm is willing to accept is given by the supply curve, area e represents the initial value of producers' surplus. When price rises to P_T, then the producers' surplus triangle becomes $e + a$, and the change in producers' surplus is represented by the trapezoid a.

Not only do domestic producers gain, but the government also gains tariff revenue equal to area c. The tariff revenue is equal to the tariff, T, times the imports on which the tariff is collected, Q_2Q_3, which equals €1,000 million for the numerical values shown. It is a transfer from consumers to the government.

Net Welfare Effects and Economic Efficiency

From a national point of view, areas a and c are not net losses. Rather, they are transfers from consumers to producers and to the government, respectively. But the situation is different for the remaining pieces of the decreased consumer surplus. Areas b and d are lost to consumers, but they are not gained by any other sector. These areas therefore represent the net welfare loss resulting from the tariff, sometimes called the **deadweight loss**. Area b can be thought of as a loss resulting from inefficiency in production, as resources are drawn into shoe production and paid more than would be needed to buy imported shoes through free trade. Similarly, area d is a loss from a less favorable consumption choice. Consumers are willing to pay areas $d + g$ for Q_3Q_4 of shoes, but when the tariff causes them to buy other products they only get satisfaction equivalent to g and lose area d. The numerical values of areas b and d are €70 million and €20 million, respectively, giving a total deadweight loss of €90 million.

The net effects of a tariff that we have identified in the left panel of Figure 6.1 can also be derived in the right panel. The apparent loss in consumers' surplus that we infer from the import demand curve is given by areas $c + b + d$. Because this is a residual demand curve, however, it represents the loss to consumers net of the gain to producers. Thus, area a does not appear, and looking at the import market alone misses important distributional effects within the country that imposes the tariff. Nevertheless, we can observe the same gain in tariff revenue, given by T times the quantity of imports, or area c. The same deadweight loss, areas $b + d$, arises as the quantity of imports falls. We know the single deadweight loss triangle in the import market must equal the two deadweight loss triangles in the domestic market; the change in price is identical and the two quantities that serve as the bases of triangles b and d (the change in domestic production and the change in consumption) are exactly equal to the change in the quantity of imports that serves as the base of the triangle in the import market. For the numerical values shown in Figure 6.1, the deadweight loss triangle shown in the import market is €90 million, which is identical to what we reported earlier based on the left panel of the figure. The import market representation is particularly useful when we consider other policies and relax the small country assumption of a horizontal foreign supply curve, and therefore we introduce it here.

How Do Economists Measure Welfare Changes?

Economists often predict the size of the deadweight loss for a proposed tariff, but they usually are not given a diagram like Figure 6.1. Instead, they know how much is spent on the imported good, PM. An econometrician may have estimated the elasticity of demand for imports, which tells how large a percentage reduction in the quantity of imports will result from a 1 percent increase in the price of imports. How can we use those two pieces of information? First, we recognize that when demand and supply curves are approximately straight lines in the relevant range, then the deadweight loss triangle is equal to one-half times the reduction in imports times the increase in price, which, for a small country, is the tariff, T. Economists project the percentage reduction in imports, $(\Delta M/M)$, on the basis of the estimated value of the elasticity of demand for imports, η, and the predicted percentage change in price, $\Delta P/P$:

$$(\Delta M/M) = \eta \ (\Delta P/P) = \eta \ (T/P) \qquad (6.1)$$

where the percentage change in price equals (T/P), assuming that the foreign supply curve is horizontal. The deadweight loss to the economy is:

$$Welfare \ loss = 0.5\Delta M\Delta P = 0.5 \ (\Delta M/M) \ (T/P) \ PM = 0.5 \ \eta \ (T/P)^2 \ PM. \qquad (6.2)$$

The equation shows that the welfare loss will be larger when the import elasticity of demand is larger in absolute value, when the tariff is larger, and when initial spending on imports is larger. A larger elasticity of demand means that a bigger change in imports will occur, which represents a bigger distortion of consumer choices and production patterns. Note that the tariff term is squared, which indicates that high tariff rates are particularly costly to an economy; in an economy with a 100 percent tariff compared to an economy with a 5 percent tariff, all else equal, the welfare loss will be 400 times as great. For that reason the World Bank often recommends in its structural adjustment programs that countries reduce high tariff rates; further reasoning in support of this policy approach is provided by Harberger (1990) and Panagariya and Rodrik (1993). Note that the loss in efficiency is so large because a progressively higher tariff rate not only distorts consumer choices but also leads to a loss in tariff revenue that would be collected at lower rates.

Calculations of deadweight losses from tariffs often turn out to be quite small when expressed as a share of GDP, which causes some critics to say there is no reason to worry about the loss in efficiency from current tariffs. Nevertheless, that is not the most appropriate comparison. If the goal of tariff policy is to preserve output, profits or jobs in the domestic sector, then the change in one of those variables is a more appropriate denominator by which to judge the tariff's effectiveness.

In fact, the political debate is more likely to revolve around the costs imposed on consumers or users of a product from a tariff that generates higher profits for producers. Those distributional effects typically are much larger than the deadweight losses. Some analysts pay less attention to the losses to capital from a change in trade policy, because capitalists can diversify their holdings across expanding and contracting industries. Workers do not have that same opportunity. Estimates of consumer losses per job saved in trade-impacted industries, however, have far exceeded what a worker would earn in the industry – values as high as $200,000 to $300,000 per worker are not uncommon. In otherwords, consumers could cover the loss in income of displaced workers and still be much better off if they could avoid trade restrictions.

World Steel Trade – What Form of Intervention?

President Bush's intervention to protect the U.S. steel industry in 2002 raised severe doubts about U.S. leadership of any movement toward a more open trading system, a policy U.S. officials advocated for other countries. Yet, government intervention in the steel market has a long history. Unfair trade cases filed in the United States in 1968, and the subsequent adoption of voluntary export restraints, represented a pattern that was repeated several times over the following decades.

The significant government role arises for several reasons. Large integrated steel producers have very high fixed costs of plant and equipment. In many countries worker layoffs are unacceptable, and labor costs become fixed regardless of the amount of steel produced. Even in the United States, where layoffs are more common, health and pension benefits to retired union workers represent a significant fixed cost that must be met regardless of actual output. Under such cost conditions, firms are likely to continue producing even when prices fall substantially, a sign of inelastic supply. Falling profits create a strong incentive to lobby for government intervention.

For many countries, a successful steel industry has been seen as a necessary step for economic development and the expansion of the manufacturing sector. In some cases governments established state-owned enterprises with little consideration of their economic profitability, while in others they provided favorable financing and adopted other policies to promote a national champion. Those policies contributed to a major expansion in world steel capacity, and even when state-owned enterprises were subsequently privatized, that additional capacity remained in production.

The issue of firms selling at prices below costs of production has led to a plethora of antidumping cases (a topic addressed in Chapter 7). Similarly, producers have brought countervailing duty cases to offset government subsidies. As noted by Hufbauer and Goodrich (2001), the fundamental problem is that demand for steel has not grown nearly as rapidly as the world economy as a whole in this electronic age. Rising labor productivity has reduced the demand for steel workers worldwide, as shown in Table 6.1.

The U.S. industry has further changed with the growth of mini-mills that employ non-union workers and use scrap steel inputs to produce in electrical furnaces. These producers have much lower fixed costs but higher variable costs. They actually expanded capacity from 1995 to 2000. Thus, the industry does not speak with a single voice on the appropriate solution to the challenges it faces.

The Asian financial crises of 1997–8 resulted in an economic recession in that part of the world and the diversion of steel to the U.S. market. This surge of imports, shown in Table 6.2, led to trade

TABLE 6.1 Employment in the Steel Industry

Country	1974	1990	1999
E.U.	998	434	280
Brazil	118	115	59
Japan	459	305	208
U.S.	521	204	153

Source: International Iron and Steel Institute, cited in Hufbauer and Goodrich (2001).

TABLE 6.2 The U.S. Market for Steel Mill Products

	1997	1998	1999	2000	2001
U.S. imports	13,617	16,434	12,749	15,026	11,630
U.S. domestic shipments	68,700	65,500	59,200	60,30	51,074
Imports/Consumption	17.6	21.3	18.8	21.3	20.1
Producer price index, steel	112.0	110.0	102.3	104.4	98.4

Source: U.S. International Trade Commission (2002).

restrictions being imposed on steel wire rod under President Clinton, and a broader set of restrictions under President Bush. Tariffs up to 30 percent were imposed on 13 million tons of imported steel. The relief was temporary, for a 3-year period, and theoretically contingent on the industry developing a plan to become economically viable by the end of this protection.

What economic and political consequences followed? From the U.S. perspective, Hufbauer and Goodrich predicted quite negative downstream effects on users of steel, who would face lower sales and reduced profits as they tried to pass on higher costs of production. Due to those losses, they project the cost of every job saved in the steel industry to be $360,000 per year. As an indication of the cost disadvantage U.S. steel users faced, in October of 2002 the U.S. price of hot rolled steel was $350 per ton, while in the E.U. it was $270 per ton (Matthews 2002).

Subsequent events demonstrate a mixed picture. In December of 2003, the U.S. removed the temporary tariffs on steel. President Bush declared that economic circumstances had changed and the restrictions had served their purpose (Alden 2003). His decision was prompted by a WTO ruling that U.S. action was not warranted under the safeguard provisions that allow countries to restrict imports when they cause serious injury to domestic producers. The E.U. had threatened retaliatory tariffs affecting $2.2 billion in trade. Not all U.S. restrictions on trade in steel have been removed, however. By way of contrast, when U.S. anti-dumping duties on hot rolled steel from Brazil, Russia, and Japan came up for review in April 2005, the United States International Trade Commission voted to maintain them (Alden 2005). At that time, the price of hot rolled steel had fallen from a peak of $750 in September of 2004 to $622 in February 2005. Auto producers such as Ford noted their disappointment with the USITC decision.

Quotas and Other Nontariff Trade Barriers

As was noted earlier, barriers to trade other than tariffs have become far more important in recent years as governments have looked for ways to restrict imports without raising tariffs. Quotas, which are limits on the physical volume of a product that may be imported per period of time, are the most transparent NTB, but there are many others. The mere fact that a policy reduces imports does not make it a trade barrier, however; it must discriminate against imports relative to domestic alternatives. Higher gasoline taxes would reduce imports of gasoline, but would equally discourage consumption of domestic gasoline and would therefore not be a trade barrier.

Most NTBs are decidedly intentional, but they are sometimes disguised to look like a policy directed at another goal. Product quality standards are a particularly common way to keep foreign products out while appearing to have another purpose. Such standards are often written by domestic producer groups, and they often focus on aspects of product design that only local producers meet, in contrast to standards of performance attained regardless of design. For years foreign producers were frustrated by Japanese product standards that found U.S. baseball bats, European skis and Canadian lumber unacceptable. While the European ban on approving the sale of genetically modified foods in the late 1900s raised important scientific issues over what constituted convincing evidence of food safety, the policy had a substantial protective effect as well.

Countries sometimes use administrative procedures to slow the passage of goods through customs. France, for example, unhappy about the volume of Japanese VCRs coming into its market, simply required that they all pass through a single customs post, which was located far from any airport or seaport and was open for only part of the week. The extra cost of shipping the VCRs to this customs post and the delay in clearing the machines into France effectively kept the Japanese products out of France for a number of months until GATT ruled against the French procedures. When the products being imported are perishable or directed at a seasonal market, delays in clearing customs can be very effective in keeping foreign products out of a national market.

Governmental procurement rules are probably the most important NTB other than quotas. Such rules usually require that whenever government money is being spent domestic products must be purchased even if they are more expensive or less useful than imported alternatives. Many governments have such rules, although Europeans hope to eliminate them within the European Union, which would mean that a French firm would be able to compete equally with German firms in bidding on German government contracts.

Quantitative Restrictions on Imports

Quotas or limits on the quantity of allowable imports have some effects that are similar to a tariff but others that are quite different. Agricultural products are often protected by quotas, in many cases seasonal ones, although a major accomplishment of the Uruguay Round of trade negotiations concluded in 1995 was to require the conversion of these quotas into tariffs. Much of the world trade in textile and apparel products was governed by quotas from the 1960s onward, but these protectionist regimes were eliminated in 2005 under Uruguay Round agreements. Another form of quantitative restrictions to limit trade in manufactured goods became quite prevalent during the 1970s and 1980s, an **orderly marketing agreement** (OMA) or a **voluntary export restraint** (VER). While the importing country did not restrict the quantity imported by some regulation or statute, the exporting country agreed to limit the volume being exported. These, too, were prohibited by the Uruguay Round agreements.

The effects of an import quota are shown in Figure 6.2. If 500 million pairs of imported shoes are allowed into the E.U., the sum of domestic plus imported shoes will be given by the dashed supply curve that is drawn parallel to the domestic supply curve. The reduction in available supply in the E.U. results in the price rising from €18 to €20, just as in Figure 6.1. Producers gain area *a* in producers' surplus, but consumers lose areas *a* + *b* + *c* + *d* in consumers' surplus. Areas *b* and *d* again are deadweight losses.

Area *c*, however, is different. If a tariff is maintained, that area is government revenue that can be used to make public expenditures or to allow a reduction of other taxes. Under a quota, however, this tariff-equivalent revenue goes to whoever is fortunate enough to have the right to ship the product from the exporting to the importing country. If quota rights are allocated to importers, they receive the windfall profit. If the E.U. importers are able to buy foreign goods at a world price that does not rise as a result of the restrictions, they buy shoes at the world price of €18, but then are able

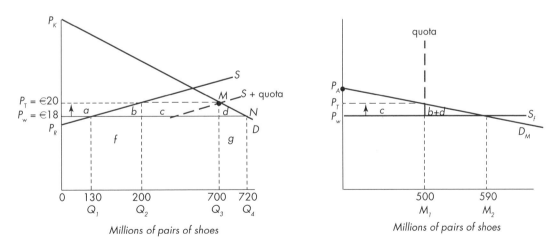

FIGURE 6.2 The Effects of an Import Quota

If an import quota of 500 million pairs of shoes is imposed, the domestic price rises to P_T as imports fall by 90 million; the same price effect occurs as in Figure 6.1. Consumers lose areas *a* + *b* + *c* + *d*, domestic producers gain area *a*, and areas *b* + *d* are deadweight losses. Who receives the tariff-equivalent revenue created by the quota, area *c*?

to sell this limited quantity for €20 per pair. This outcome is particularly likely when there are many foreign producers who are not organized in any way to take advantage of the scarcity of the product in the import market. E.U. importers can seek competitive bids to fill the available quota of goods that can be imported, and they gain area c as a result.

The outcome may be different if foreigners organize themselves or government action accomplishes the same effect. In the case of apparel trade, exporting nations such as Hong Kong established a system of export quota tickets that had to be acquired for goods to leave the country. These tickets were freely bought and sold among apparel producers, and their value increased when foreign demand for apparel items rose. Even though there were many producers who could not easily be organized into a group to bargain with American or European buyers, the trade in quota tickets ensured that part of area c was captured by Hong Kong producers who would no longer be willing to sell at the world price P_W.

In the case of a VER, the exporting country explicitly limits the volume shipped, and it can allocate the quota rights and determine who gets the windfall profits. In this case the bonanza goes to exporting firms rather than to importers. As a result, exporting countries often accept VERs. The VER on Japanese cars that limited sales in the United States to 1.85 million cars per year during the early 1980s had the effect of raising U.S. car prices by almost $1,000 per car (Crandall 1984). That meant an additional profit of about $1.85 billion per year for the Japanese car companies. They were forced to reduce sales but were compensated through a gift of almost $2 billion per year. Because the Japanese government told each firm how much it would export, there was no reason for Japanese producers to compete against each other to try to win a bigger share of the restricted U.S. market. An implication of this large windfall for Japanese producers was that the competitive position of U.S. producers may not have improved much as a result of the VER. While a VER allows domestic profits to rise and provides a source of finance for retooling efforts, the foreign producer may receive an even larger boost in profits and be better positioned to introduce new products.

If the U.S. government had auctioned the quota rights to the highest bidder, the Treasury would have recaptured the monopoly rents through the auction revenues. If there was a competitive market to distribute cars and therefore the auction was competitive, dealers would bid approximately the area of the windfall profit rectangle for the right to bring cars into this market. Such an outcome was observed in Australia, which auctioned a portion of its quota rights to importers of apparel and footwear. Of course, foreign producers are less likely to accept such a system, because they no longer capture area c. Rather than voluntarily agree to a cutback in their exports under a VER, they are more likely to demand compensation under GATT provisions ruling out actions that impair the value of prior concessions those countries have made.

It is much more common for governments to allocate quota rights arbitrarily, which creates obvious opportunities for graft and corruption. The allocation of quotas can be a source of bribery if importers offer money to the government officials in charge of deciding who gets the rights. In the case of VERs the executive branch of government may readily accept the loss of a potential source of revenue from a tariff or quota auction because it gains flexibility in administering trade policy. Specific markets can be protected without having to pass legislation that would quickly attract protectionist interests from many more industries. VERs can be negotiated country-by-country, rather than applied across the board to all suppliers, which allows allies to receive more favorable treatment or exploits the weak bargaining position of countries with access to few alternative markets.

The variations discussed above, which determine whether the importer, the foreign exporter, or the government gains the tariff-equivalent of the quota, are important from the perspective of economic efficiency. The cost that quantitative restrictions imposes on the importing country obviously is greater if it loses not only the deadweight loss triangles $b + d$ but also area c.

Reasons Domestic Producers Prefer Quantitative Restrictions

Domestic producers enjoy the stability created by a quota. If a foreign innovation allows foreign producers to supply goods at a much lower cost, domestic producers are insulated from the competitive advantage that foreigners would otherwise gain. The foreign supply curve may shift downward, but foreigners cannot gain a larger share of the market by selling at a lower price. Similarly, in a world with volatile exchange rates, if the home currency rises in value internationally, foreigners can charge a lower price in the currency of the importing country and still cover their costs of production. In the first half of the 1980s when the U.S. dollar rose sharply in value, the enhanced competitive position of foreign producers was blunted by VERs negotiated to protect U.S. producers from what many saw as an unpredictable and unexpected change in market conditions. The **U.S. Trade Representative (USTR)** often negotiated VERs with exporting countries under the perceived threat that the U.S. Congress might enact even more severe measures.

Domestic producers also gain from a quota when market demand is expanding. From Figure 6.2 note the outcome of an outward shift in the demand curve when the quantity of imports is fixed. Prices rise and the tariff-equivalent effect of the quantitative restrictions rises. Without a separate legislative vote or executive review, the protective effect of the quantity restriction rises over time.

A further distinction between a tariff and a quota arises if the domestic industry is not perfectly competitive, and producers have market power. Think of the extreme case where demand can be met by imports or by a domestic monopoly. A tariff, unless it is extremely high, provides only limited protection for the local monopoly because the maximum price it can charge is the world price plus the tariff. Any attempt to charge more than that will result in a flood of imports that will decimate its sales volume. A quota, however, offers much more protection for the monopolist. Once the quota amount has been imported, the monopolist has nothing more to fear from foreign suppliers. The monopolist sells less than it would in autarky by the amount of the quota, but once that volume has arrived from abroad, it has an incentive to restrict output to the level at which marginal cost equals marginal revenue and still to charge more than a competitive price. With the same level of imports, a quota will allow higher prices and monopoly profits than will a tariff. Tariffs are clearly preferable to quotas, then, if elements of monopoly exist in the domestic import-competing industry.

Foreigners may respond to quantitative restrictions by upgrading the product exported to the protected market. Recall the earlier distinction between an *ad valorem* tariff and a specific tariff; the specific tariff has a bigger effect in deterring imports of low-cost goods than high-cost goods. Quantitative restrictions have this same effect, comparable to a quota ticket price of a fixed amount per unit imported. The consequent percentage increase in the price of low-cost goods is much greater than the percentage increase in the price of high-cost goods. During the period in which Japanese firms were limited to selling 1.85 million cars per year in the United States, virtually all of the cars exported to the United States were top-of-the-line models and had a variety of expensive options. Japanese producers moved beyond their market niche for small fuel-efficient cars and began to compete in the market for larger sedans, where U.S. producers previously held a more dominant market share. The deadweight loss to the economy is also larger, because of the disproportionately large price increase for low-end goods; recall our earlier demonstration that the loss in efficiency rises as a function of the price increase squared.

Peaks in Protection in the E.U.

Measuring the extent of protection that imposes high costs on consumers is not straightforward, especially when most of the protection is provided by measures other than *ad valorem* tariffs. The Institute for International Economics sponsored studies of U.S., Japanese, and E.U. policies to demonstrate which industries benefited from particularly high trade restrictions. The E.U. study by Patrick Messerlin (2001) identified the industries shown in Table 6.3 based on tariffs, NTBs, and antidumping duties. The values shown are based on 1990 trade to facilitate comparison with the other two studies, although Messerlin emphasizes that the extent of protection provided for these particular industries changed little over the 1990s, in spite of other concessions made in the Uruguay Round trade agreement. Tariff peaks have been particularly resistant to change in all three countries.

Messerlin had to make several specific decisions regarding the best way to represent restrictions. For tariffs, if he simply took the tariff duty collected and divided by the value of imports, he would understate the extent of protection for two reasons. Categories with high tariffs but few imports would collect little tariff revenue and therefore be underweighted by such a measure. If the E.U. imported goods from some countries on a preferential basis and did not impose any tariff on those imports, the implied absence of restrictions would ignore the fact that those favored countries could sell their goods at the high E.U. internal price made possible by restrictions on other exporters.

To compare these E.U. results with those for other countries, Messerlin based his calculation on an assumed setting of perfect competition, where there were so many competitors that they could not collude with each other. He also noted, however, that many of the peaks in E.U. protection occur in industries where there are few competitors, and those firms have some ability to cooperate in reducing output and driving up price if protection is granted. Therefore, Table 6.3 includes his estimates for both of those cases.

The relative size of these industries is indicated by the value of imports and by the number of workers in the domestic industry. These industries account for 15 percent of workers in manufacturing and 29 percent of workers in agriculture. Costs of restrictions in agriculture and manufacturing account for 6 percent of E.U. GDP generated in these sectors, a sign that industries subject to restrictions represent an important share of output in these two sectors. The final two columns of the table give another perspective by showing the cost to consumers of protecting a job through trade restrictions versus the average wage in the industry. Liberalization results in a gain in consumers' surplus per job lost in the protected industry that far exceeds the annual wage, and is reported in excess of €3 million per job in the dairy industry and photocopier production. Messerlin concludes that trade protection is a very expensive way for consumers to pay for the preservation of jobs in a domestic industry.

TABLE 6.3 The Industry Effects of E.U. Trade Liberalization

Industry	Overall ad valorem equiv. tariff	Value imports	Number workers	Consumer gain, perfect comp.	Consumer gain, imperfect comp.	CS gain/ job lost, €1,000	Average annual wage, €1,000
Cement	228	291	58.0	674	78	857	23.5
Fertilizer	327	1938	28.0	716	642	183	34.4
LD Polyethylene	125	1407	34.0	618	300	280	34.4
Polyvinyl chloride	125	598	18.0	341	132	53	34.4
Hardboard	250	2636	71.0	974	739	611	15.0
Newsprint	70	2437	14.0	276	192	800	25.0
Chemical fibers	229	1942	71.8	1020	580	526	34.4
Videocassette recorders	302	711	16.0	363	313	420	27.5
Integrated circuits	476	4606	41.6	2240	2187	366	25.5
Photocopiers	337	962	24.0	363	314	3483	23.9
Steel	219	4994	379.4	4403	1626	316	26.1
Passenger cars	171	10567	1229.0	5418	2101	569	28.4
Textiles	214	21353	1636.5	7096	7096	180	15.5
Clothing	313	18096	1234.6	7103	7102	214	12.2
Cereals	630	1382	1134.0	3212	3212	69	13.7
Meat	950	2767	946.1	4108	4108	117	16.1
Dairy	1040	1462	36.9	2717	2717	3246	18.8
Sugar	1170	1789	275.1	4268	4268	147	13.7
Bananas	819	1188	25.0	825	825	197	7.0

Source: Messerlin (2001), pp. 43, 46, 54, 59.

He also calculates the economic efficiency effects of these restrictions, where the loss is not just the deadweight loss triangles shown in Figures 6.1 and 6.2, but also the loss of economic rents to foreigners from voluntary export restraints and quotas, as well as the waste of resources that domestic firms pour into lobbying for more favorable treatment. Although those costs are not reported here, they are substantial, too.

Tariff Rate Quotas

Many agricultural products are subject to tariff rate quotas, primarily the result of trade commitments made by countries in the Uruguay Round to convert quota restrictions into tariffs. Figure 6.3 shows the situation where a country allows tariff-free access of a certain quantity of the good, but any imports beyond the level, Q, are subject to a tariff. The effect of this policy depends upon actual demand conditions, as represented by D_0, D_1, or D_2. If D_1 represents the relevant demand curve, the tariff is prohibitively high and no imports occur beyond the quota level. Potential quota rents are earned by foreign exporters who receive the difference between the foreign price at which they would be willing to sell and the price at which the restricted amount of imports can be sold.

Consider how this situation applies to two different commodities imported into the United States. In 2002 within-quota imports of raw sugar were subject to a tariff of 0.625 cents per pound, but over-quota imports faced a tariff of 15.36 cents per pound. The over-quota tariff was prohibitive, and only the quota amount was imported. In the case of butter, again there was a substantial difference between the in-quota tariff of 12.3 cents per kilo and the over-quota tariff of $1.54 cents per kilo. The latter tariff was not prohibitive, however, and 772 metric tons of over-quota butter were imported. The landed, duty-paid price of butter for the in-quota category was $1.87 per kilo, and the

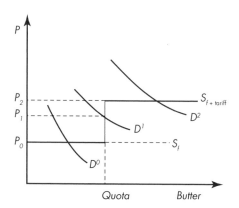

FIGURE 6.3 The Effect of a Tariff Rate Quota

The demand for imports relative to the quantity allowed under the quota determines whether the price will be P_0 when the quota is not binding, between P_0 and P_2 when the quota is binding, or P_2 when over-quota imports occur.

corresponding price for over-quota imports was $3.56 per kilo. That price differential suggests that U.S. importers gained the tariff equivalent revenue created by the quota.

Production Subsidies

If a government objective is to increase output in a particular industry, economists claim that a first-best solution is to provide a subsidy to producers rather than to impose a tariff. Figure 6.4 shows this case, based on exactly the same initial situation as in Figure 6.1. If a subsidy equal to s (per unit) is paid to E.U. producers, their supply curve shifts from S to S' because the subsidy reduces average and marginal costs of production. They will expand output to OQ_2. Because the price of shoes to E.U. consumers remains at P_{wt} they continue to purchase OQ_4, and imports are Q_2Q_4. The loss of consumers' surplus does not occur. The subsidy to domestic producers must be included in government expenditures, however, and represents a transfer payment to producers from the rest of the economy. The amount of the subsidy appears in Figure 6.4 as area a plus area b. Taxes in that amount must be levied to pay it. Area a is a pure transfer from taxpayers to producers, but area b involves the same inefficiency in resource use as before and can therefore be regarded as a deadweight loss. Since the subsidy does not reduce consumption, however, we avoid the other part of deadweight loss (area d in Figure 6.1). The conclusion is that a production subsidy is preferable to a tariff on welfare grounds: It has a smaller deadweight loss, and it leaves consumption unchanged.[1]

Although subsidies are a less inefficient means of increasing domestic output, they are relatively uncommon because they are politically unpopular. A tariff raises money for the government, and a

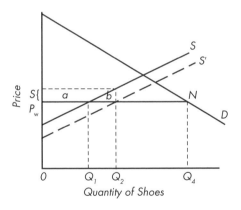

FIGURE 6.4 The Effect of a Subsidy: Partial Equilibrium, Small-Country Case

The domestic supply function shifts down by the amount of the subsidy s, that is, from S to S'. Domestic production rises by Q_1Q_2. The cost of the subsidy to the government is the rectangle consisting of areas a and b. Area a is increased producers' surplus for the domestic industry, and triangle b is a deadweight loss due to less efficient production.

---

1 This judgment assumes that tax revenues can be raised without imposing some deadweight loss on the economy. Public finance economists typically challenge this assumption and in the United States suggest that for every dollar of tax revenue raised, the cost to the economy is $1.23 (Ballard, Fullerton, Shoven, and Whalley 1985).

quota appears to be costless, but the taxpayers have to provide the funds for a subsidy. The domestic industry does not want to be seen as the recipient of a public handout, which must be approved annually in government budget deliberations. Instead, it prefers a tariff or quota (particularly if it is allocated the import rights), which is a more indirect and less obvious form of public support. Subsidies are common in the case of agricultural production, however, and the attempt to limit them more strictly in international trade negotiations has frequently stymied progress in such negotiations, as discussed in Chapter 10.

Tariffs in the Large-Country Case

Returning to the analysis of tariffs, we can extend the earlier partial equilibrium analysis to deal with the case in which the E.U. is large enough to influence the world price when it changes the quantity imported. We continue to ignore the effects of any changes outside of the shoe industry.

In Figure 6.5 we simply modify the right panel depicting the import market to show that the foreign supply curve is no longer horizontal at the free trade world price, P_{w0}. If a country imposes a specific tariff of T on imports of shoes, the new foreign supply curve shifts up parallel to the original foreign supply curve by the amount of the tariff. The new equilibrium price faced by consumers, P_1, however, does not rise by the amount of the tariff, because at that price consumers are unwilling to buy the quantity M_0 of imports. At P_1, we can subtract the tariff T to see the price net of the tariff that foreign producers receive, P_{w1}. Because the price falls from P_{w0} to P_{w1}, foreigners supply a smaller quantity of imports. Because the price consumers face rises from P_0 to P_1, they only wish to demand this smaller quantity of imports.

What determines whether the tariff is reflected primarily by a rise in price seen by consumers or a fall in price seen by foreign producers? The size of the elasticity of foreign export supply, ε, and the elasticity of demand for imports, η, determine this outcome. As shown in the footnote, the percentage increase in price to consumers is:

$$\frac{\Delta P}{P} = \frac{\varepsilon}{\varepsilon - \eta} \cdot \frac{T}{P} \qquad (6.3)$$

which indicates that a larger elasticity of foreign export supply and a smaller import elasticity of demand (in absolute value) cause a bigger price increase.[2] For example, if ε equals 4 and η equals -2, then the fraction $\varepsilon / (\varepsilon - \eta)$ equals two-thirds, and two-thirds of the tariff is passed forward to consumers and one-third is passed backward to foreign suppliers.

What causes the elasticity of foreign export supply to be larger? In our discussion of the small country case, where ε is so large that the supply curve is a horizontal line, we noted that foreign

---

2 The expression for the change in price that results from the imposition of the tariff can be derived from a linear demand curve, $m - nP$, and a linear supply curve, $u + vP$. Setting quantity demanded equal to quantity supplied gives the initial equilibrium price as $P_0 = (m - u) / (v + n)$. When the tariff is imposed the supply curve becomes $u + v(P - T)$ and the new price faced by consumers is $P_1 = (m - u) / (v + n) + Tv / (v + n)$. The change in price, ΔP, equals $Tv / (v + n)$, or in percentage terms $\Delta P / P = [v / (v + n)] \, T / P$. The expression $v / (v + n)$ is written in terms of the slopes of the supply and demand curves, but if the numerator and denominator of the fraction are each multiplied by P / Q, then $Pv / Q = \varepsilon$, the elasticity of supply and $Pn / Q = \eta$, the elasticity of demand, and $\Delta P / P = [\varepsilon / (\varepsilon - \eta)] \, T / P$.

producers have many good options or alternative markets where they can sell this product. If the net-of-tariff price offered by the E.U. falls, foreign suppliers divert their sales to other markets. A high foreign export supply elasticity also may indicate that a small drop in price will lead to a large increase in sales by foreigners in their domestic market. Or, the inputs used in producing this good may easily be transferred to other uses; producers of shoes may make luggage instead, using much of the same cutting and stitching equipment.

Why may the demand for imports be less elastic? E.U. consumers may not feel there are good substitutes available when the price of shoes rises, and E.U. producers may not be able to expand output of shoes very easily without their costs rising substantially. In that case, E.U. consumers have few alternatives other than buying from the foreign supplier.

The extent to which the tariff drives up the price faced in the E.U. is important in determining who within the E.U. benefits and who loses from the tariff and whether the country as a whole may benefit. As shown in the left panel of Figure 6.5, the rise in price causes consumers to lose areas $a + b + c + d$, and producers to gain area a. The tariff revenue gained by the government is no longer just equal to area c. Rather, in the right panel of Figure 6.5 we can see tariff revenue collected is $c + h$. Adding these three effects together shows that the net economic efficiency effect on the E.U. is $h - b - d$. Areas b and d still represent deadweight losses from less efficient production and consumption choices, but the E.U. now gains area h at the expense of producers in the rest of the world. We can refer to area h as a terms-of-trade gain, because the E.U. is now able to pay foreigners a lower net-of-tariff price for the goods that it imports. For a given import demand elasticity, this terms-of-trade gain is likely to be greater the less elastic is the foreign export supply curve, that is, the more dependent foreigners are on sales to the E.U.

Whether a country gains from imposing a tariff depends upon whether its trading partners retaliate and impose tariffs of their own. While a trade war may leave all countries worse off, the economic

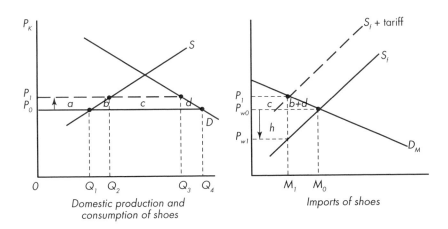

FIGURE 6.5 The Effect of a Tariff: Partial Equilibrium, Large-Country Case

When a large country imposes a tariff, a portion of it results in higher domestic prices, which cause a loss to consumers of $a + b + c + d$ and a gain to domestic producers of a. Some portion of the tariff is borne by foreign producers who now receive a lower price, P_{w1}, for their exports. The government gains tariff revenue of $c + h$. The net efficiency effect is $h - b - d$.

power of individual countries is not symmetric. Some may be able to gain at the expense of others. The world as a whole loses, though, and that is one of the key motivations for establishing international rules that limit the ability of individual countries to exploit that power.

GENERAL EQUILIBRIUM ANALYSIS OF TRADE BARRIERS

The foregoing analysis establishes many useful conclusions about the effects of tariffs, and it is quite relevant in evaluating the effects of policy in narrowly defined industries that account for small shares of national output. The approach ignores repercussions that in some cases may be quite significant, however. For example, when a tariff causes the output of a particular commodity to rise in the importing country, resources must be drawn into that industry. Yet, we do not explicitly consider what happens in other industries from which those resources must be taken. Assuming full employment, output of other commodities must fall. Similarly, when one country's imports decline, other countries will have less money to spend on their imports; therefore the country that levies a tariff will see its exports decline. Import tariffs have many such effects that reverberate through the economy. To deal with these in a comprehensive way we must utilize a form of general equilibrium analysis.

One approach is to use the tools of analysis that we developed in Chapter 3, the production-possibility curve and community indifference map. These tools bring us back to the abstract world of two countries, two commodities, two factors, and perfect competition. Also, assume that the tariff revenue is redistributed to consumers, which means we do not need to introduce a separate set of preferences for the government.

The Small-Country Case

It is convenient to start with a small country, where the world terms of trade remain unchanged. Recall that in the two-good model of Chapter 3 we concluded that in free-trade equilibrium, Country A will maximize its welfare by producing at the point where its domestic ratio of marginal costs equals the world exchange ratio, and then by engaging in trade in order to reach the highest possible indifference curve. Such a free-trade equilibrium is shown in Figure 6.6, with the world price ratio shown by the slope of TT, production at point P_1, and consumption at point C_1, where TT is tangent to the indifference curve i_2. Country A exports cloth and imports food.

Now if Country A imposes a tariff on its imports of food, that policy will increase the domestic price of food. The domestic exchange ratio will diverge from the world exchange ratio. We show this effect in Figure 6.6; the domestic exchange ratio becomes equal to the slope of DD, which is flatter than TT, indicating a higher relative price of food. The tariff drives a wedge between the domestic and external price ratios. Geometrically, that wedge can be seen as the angle between the two price lines. The higher price of food induces firms to expand food production and to reduce cloth production. The production point moves to P_2, where the domestic price line (DD) is tangent to the production-possibility curve.

Because we are assuming that the world price ratio remains unchanged, international trade takes place along the line $P_2 C_2$ (parallel to TT). A new equilibrium in consumption is reached when two

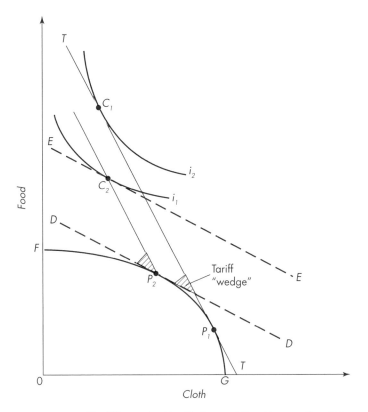

FIGURE 6.6 The Effects of a Tariff: General Equilibrium, Small-Country Case

With free trade this country produces at P_1 and consumes at C_1. The slope of TT is the price ratio between the two goods. The tariff shifts the internal price ratio to the slope of DD and EE, while the world price ratio remains the slope of TT and the line parallel to it on the left. This country now produces at P_2 and consumes at C_2, the volume of trade being sharply reduced by the tariff. The tariff "wedge" refers to the difference between the two price ratios, represented by the differences between the slopes of the lines where the wedge appears.

conditions are satisfied: (1) a domestic price line, EE, whose slope is equal to the tariff-distorted domestic price ratio, is tangent to a community indifference curve; and (2) the world price line, P_2 C_2, intersects the community indifference curve at its point of tangency with the domestic price line, EE. These two conditions are both satisfied at the point C_2 in Figure 6.6. Technically, the first condition guarantees that the marginal rate of substitution in consumption equals the domestic price ratio facing consumers; the second condition satisfies the requirement that the domestic price ratio diverges from the world price ratio exactly in proportion to the tariff.

In the new equilibrium, Country A continues to export cloth and import food but in smaller quantities than before. The tariff has stimulated domestic production of food, reducing Country A's dependence on food imports. It has also reduced domestic output and exports of cloth and reduced welfare, as indicated by the movement to the lower indifference curve, from i_2 to i_1. Thus we reach the same conclusion in both general and partial equilibrium analysis: in the small-country case a tariff reduces national welfare.

The Large-Country Case

When the country imposing a tariff is large enough to influence world prices, we must consider what effect a tariff will have on the world price ratio. To continue the same example, when Country A levies a tariff on food, the result may be that the world price of food falls relative to the price of cloth. For a given *ad valorem* tariff, the domestic price of food will not rise as much as before. Thus, the shift in production will be somewhat smaller. We illustrate this outcome in Figure 6.7, where conditions are the same as in the case just described except that the tariff now causes the world price ratio to change from the slope of the line TT to the slope of the line $P_1 C_1$. Production takes place at P_1. (Note that the tariff is the same proportion as before, as measured by the size of the wedge.)

International trade now takes place at the world price ratio (i.e. along the line $P_1 C_3$). A new equilibrium in consumption is reached at point C_1, where the tariff-distorted domestic price line is tangent to a community indifference curve, and the world price line also passes through this point of tangency. As drawn in Figure 6.7, Country A reaches a higher indifference curve as a result of the tariff. This result is not inevitable, however. It depends on the magnitude of the change in the world exchange ratio. Intuitively, one can see that country A benefits from the tariff when its gain from the improved terms of trade outweighs its loss from a less efficient use of domestic resources. How much its terms of trade will improve depends in turn on domestic and foreign elasticities of demand and supply.

Any gain, however, is at the expense of the rest of the world. If other countries act in concert, they can retaliate by imposing tariffs of their own, thus causing the terms of trade to shift back the other

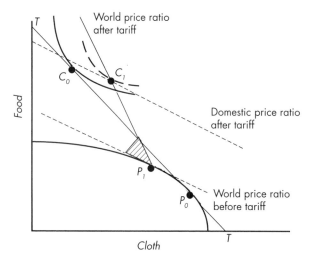

FIGURE 6.7 The Effects of a Tariff: General Equilibrium, Large-Country Case

This graph differs from the previous figure because this country is large enough that its tariff will cause worsened terms of trade in the rest of the world. The country imposing the tariff enjoys improved terms of trade, as the slope of the world trading line changes from that of TT to that of $P_1 C_1$, a higher relative price of cloth, the large country's export good. This country produces at P_1 and consumes at C_1, which is a slight welfare improvement from the free-trade outcome, because of the terms-of-trade improvement.

way. The terms of trade may return to the free-trade ratio (not a necessary result), but world trade is greatly reduced and so is world welfare. A trade agreement for the mutual, reciprocal reduction of tariffs is likely to benefit both countries, a case we consider in Chapter 10.

THE EFFECTIVE RATE OF PROTECTION

Thus far we have assumed that a given commodity is wholly produced in one country. For example, a yard of cloth is the output that results from using a certain combination of inputs of primary factors of production (land, labor, capital) in that country. We have ignored the case in which some of the inputs are imported. Thus we have ignored the large and important trade in intermediate products.

For many purposes, this omission is harmless. For analyzing the protective effect of tariffs, the treatment of intermediate products makes a great deal of difference. The key point is that when a producer has the option of importing some of the material inputs required for the production of a given product, the *ad valorem* tariff on that product may not accurately indicate the protection being provided to the producer. A distinction needs to be drawn between the nominal tariff rate, which is just the usual *ad valorem* tariff or its equivalent, and the effective rate of protection (ERP).

The ERP refers to the level of protection being provided to a particular process of production by the given nominal tariffs on a product and on material inputs used in its production. We are particularly interested in how a set of tariffs affects the firm's value-added or what is available to cover primary factor costs, such as payments for the services of labor and capital, and also the net profit of the firm. We define the ERP as the percentage increase in an industry's value-added per unit of output that results from a country's tariff structure. The standard of comparison is value-added under free trade.

Tariff Escalation

The tendency for countries to levy higher tariffs on fully processed goods than on raw materials is a fairly general characteristic of current trade policy. The WTO provides the following summary of tariff escalation in several countries for the textile and leather sector.

Such escalation can be expected to yield high effective rates of protection in fully processed goods, in this case apparel and footwear in contrast to fabric and yarn. Consider the ERP that results for apparel products (3rd column) that require inputs of cloth (2nd column), or fabric producers that require yarn (1st column). If value-added in apparel is 40 percent of the value of production, and material inputs 60 percent, then for apparel production in Mexico:

$$ERP = [31.4 - (.6)*17.9]/ [1 - .6] = 52 \tag{6.4}$$

Costs of apparel assembly in Mexico can be 52 percent higher than under free trade. To determine whether Mexican apparel output rises as a result, however, we need to know what protection is

TABLE 6.4 Tariff Escalation in the Textile and Leather Sector

	Initial Processing	Semi-processed	Fully processed
E.U.	0.8	7.2	9.4
USA	2.4	8.5	9.5
Japan	24.3	6.5	11.4
Argentina	11.4	18.8	22.4
Brazil	8.3	15.6	19.1
Mexico	12.7	17.9	31.4
Korea	5.2	8.8	11.4
India	17.4	15.0	15.1
South Africa	4.7	22.0	32.3
China	11.9	9.0	14.6

Source: WTO (2006), pp. 14–15.

provided to other sectors. The difference between protection in apparel and fabric is not so great for the E.U., but consider the protection provided to fabric producers in the E.U., when material inputs account for 70 percent of production costs:

$$ERP = [7.2 - .7*(0.8)]/[1 - 0.7] = 22 \tag{6.5}$$

E.U. costs in producing fabric can exceed free trade costs by 22 percent, not the nominal rate of 7 percent.

When tariff escalation is pronounced in developed countries, this is likely to have a particularly negative effect on labor-abundant countries that are otherwise competitive in the labor-intensive production of apparel and footwear. This pattern also appears in the processing of primary products. Raw materials are subject to a low tariff, but semi-processed and final goods that require more manufacturing are subject to progressively higher tariffs. This pattern discourages efforts of primary producers in developing countries to industrialize. Their competitors in richer, developed countries benefit from high effective rates of protection, which allow their costs in assembly and processing to be much higher than producers elsewhere in the world. Note, however, that the tariff structures of many developing countries are also characterized by escalation. They provide more protection for the labor-intensive final assembly of fully processed goods where a casual observer might predict they have a comparative advantage. Differences among developing countries are an important distinction that you are to explore in the chapter case study of the apparel and textile trade.

An example will help to explain the meaning of this definition. Suppose the world price of shoes is $20 and that it takes $12 worth of leather at the free-trade world price to make a pair of shoes. In the manufacture of shoes, then, value-added at world prices is $8. Now suppose Country A levies a nominal tariff of 30 percent on shoe imports but allows leather to be imported duty free. The price of shoes in Country A would rise to $26 (i.e. the world price plus the tariff), and consequently the value-added of domestic shoe producers would become $14. In other words, they could incur factor costs of $14 and still be competitive with a foreign firm whose factor costs were $8. Value-added in Country A can be 75 percent larger than value-added at the free-trade price [($14 – $8)/$8 = 75 percent]. Thus the ERP is 75 percent, while the nominal tariff is only 30 percent. Compare a shoe-producing firm in Country A and its free-trade competitor:

	Firm in Country A	Free-trade competitor
Shoe price	$26	$20
Leather input	$12	$12
Value-added	$14	$8

We expect that high effective rates of protection will attract resources into industries where a country has production costs much higher than abroad, i.e. where it has a comparative disadvantage. As a result, the country's economic efficiency falls.

Note that a tariff on leather would reduce the effective rate of protection for shoes. The reason is obvious: a tariff on leather increases the price of leather in Country A and raises A firms' costs of production, which means value-added must be smaller for A firms to continue selling shoes at $26. In our example, a 20 percent nominal tariff on leather would lead to the following result:

	Firm in Country A	Free-trade competitor
Shoe price	$26.00	$20.00
Leather input	$14.40	$12.00
Value-added	$11.60	$8.00

The **effective tariff** rate on shoes has fallen from 75 percent to 45 percent [($11.60 – $8) / $8 = 45 percent] as a result of the tariff on leather. Shoe producers in Country A will tend to favor tariffs on shoes but oppose tariffs on leather.

A formula for calculating the effective tariff rate follows from the above discussion:

$$e_j = \frac{t_j - \sum_i a_{ij} \cdot t_i}{1 - \sum_i a_{ij}}$$

(6.6)

where we define the terms above and apply them to the shoe example:

e_j = the effective rate of protection in industry j, shoe production

t_j = the nominal tariff rate in industry j = 30 percent tariff on shoes

t_i = the nominal tariff rate in industry i = 20 percent tariff on leather

a_{ij} = the share of inputs from industry i in the value of output of industry j at free-trade prices = ($\$12/20$) = 0.60

and the sigma term, Σ, represents summation over all the necessary intermediate inputs i. Therefore the effective rate of protection for shoes is

$$e_j = \frac{30\% - 0.60(20\%)}{1 - 0.60} = \frac{18\%}{0.40} = \frac{0.18}{0.40} = 45\% \qquad (6.7)$$

In this example we had only a single intermediate input, leather. In actual practice, a given product has many intermediate inputs, each with its own nominal tariff rate. The formula uses the share of each such input (a_{ij}) to weight the nominal tariff rates in forming the sum ($\Sigma a_{ij}t_i$).

The tariff structures of many countries show a systematic pattern in which nominal tariff rates increase as the stage of production advances – that is, tariff rates are low (or zero) on raw materials, higher on semi-finished products, and highest on finished manufactures. Such a pattern in nominal tariff rates produces an even greater escalation in effective tariff rates, with very high protection being accorded the higher stages of manufacture. Industrial countries have been accused of using such a tariff structure to preserve their lead in manufacturing and to keep the less-developed countries from developing exports of finished manufactures.

Although ERPs are higher than nominal rates in the examples above, they can also be lower and may even be negative. In our shoe industry example, if the nominal rate on leather were increased to 60 percent, then the ERP for shoes would be –15 percent. The economic meaning of such a rate is that a firm must pay such high nominal tariffs on its imported inputs that it is actually at a disadvantage in comparison to its free-trade competitors in the outside world. That is, its value-added margin must be less than that of a free-trade competitor. The disadvantage of the domestic firm is shown in the following comparison:

	Firm in Country A	Free-trade competitor
Shoe price	$26.00	$20.00
Leather input	$19.20	$12.00
Value-added	$6.80	$8.00

To compete with a foreign firm whose factor costs are $8.00, the firm in Country A must hold its factor costs to $6.80.

Negative effective tariff rates often turn up among a nation's export products. The nominal tariff applicable for an export product is zero because it is being sold in foreign countries at the world market price. Therefore, if firms producing the export item use any imported inputs at all that are subject to tariffs, their effective tariff rate is negative, which means that there is an implicit tax on exports. Suppose, for example, that Thailand exports rice at the world market price, whereas rice production uses imported inputs such as fertilizer, water pumps, and tractors, on which nominal tariffs are levied. The result is that the value-added margin of Thai rice producers is lower, because of the nation's tariff structure, than it would be under full free trade. The effective tariff on rice is negative.

Effective Rates of Protection and the Indonesian Bicycle Boom

In the late 1980s and early 1990s, Indonesian bicycle exports grew rapidly, fostered by special tariff preferences on sales in the European market. This expansion occurred without major promotional efforts by the government, and it certainly raised hopes that Indonesian sales to the U.S. market might take off. In that market, however, Indonesian bicycles were granted no special preferences in competition with Chinese bicycles. What factors might affect the competitive positions of these two producers?

The concept of effective rate of protection provides important insights. The cost of an $80 bicycle is accounted for by $25 of imported parts (gears, chain wheels, and hubs), $40 of domestically produced parts (tubing for frame), and $15 of value-added in the bicycle sector. Indonesia imposes a tariff of 40 percent on bicycles and 30 percent on bicycle parts. Also, domestically produced parts are $4 higher than free-trade prices due to protection provided to the domestic monopoly producer of steel.

We can organize this information to reflect three situations: production when no tariffs are imposed, traditional production for a protected home market, and modern production for the European export market.

The traditional producer serving a protected home market can have costs 108 percent greater than European producers [($39.50/$19.00) – 1]*100, a high effective rate of protection that results from an escalating tariff structure. If Indonesian export producers (often with Japanese or Taiwanese partners) are unable to receive a rebate for the $7.50 tariff paid on imported parts, the effective

TABLE 6.5 The Economics of Indonesian Bicycle Assembly

	No tariffs	Home market	Exporter
Price of bicycle	$80.00	$80 + 40% tariff = $112	$80.00
Price of imported parts	$25.00	$25 + 30% tariff = $32.50	$32.50
Price of domestic parts	$36.00	$36 + $4* = $40.00	$40.00
Value-added	$19.00	$39.50	$7.50
Effective rate of protection		108%	–60%

* Protection of the domestic steel industry causes the price of domestic parts to rise by $4.

rate of protection for exporters is –60 percent. Their costs must be only 40 percent of European producers' costs. If Indonesian exporters do receive prompt payment of such a rebate for bicycles that are exported, or if they operate in export processing zones where they are exempt from the tariff on foreign parts, their value-added can rise to $15 and the effective rate of protection is –21 percent. The higher cost of parts made with domestic steel still imposes a significant penalty on Indonesian bicycle exports (Morgan and Wahjudi 1992).

Many developing countries have strong comparative advantages in final products which nevertheless are not exported, because they impose a tariff or otherwise restrict imports of inputs where they have a comparative disadvantage. A partial response to this problem is the establishment of free trade zones, which allow producers to claim a rebate for duties paid on imported inputs if the producers export their final output.

A potential problem in calculating ERPs is the assumption, made in all input–output analyses, that the input coefficients are fixed constants, unaffected by changes in prices. We know that international trade causes changes in relative prices and shifts in the allocation of resources. It seems likely that these changes will also affect the amounts of various inputs used to produce a particular product, but ERP calculations do not allow for this influence.

INTERVENTION IN EXPORT MARKETS

The issues presented thus far suggest that government regulation of international trade is intended solely to restrict imports. Although that remains the dominant form of intervention, governments sometimes attempt to encourage exports through subsidies. This may occur because of a desire to improve a country's trade account, aid a politically powerful industry, or help a depressed region in which an export industry is located. The subsidy may be a simple cash payment to exporters, but is frequently more indirect or subtle. Research and development grants, favorable financing or tax treatment, or a variety of other government benefits may be provided to encourage exports. In order to simplify this discussion, however, assume that the subsidy takes the form of a fixed cash payment for each unit of a product which is exported.

Figure 6.8 illustrates the effects of an export subsidy in a competitive market, where we allow the country to be large enough to affect the world price of the good. Just as we derived the import demand curve as a residual from domestic demand less domestic supply, here we show the export supply curve in the right panel, a residual from domestic supply less domestic demand. The free-trade world price P_0 is given by the intersection of country A's export supply curve with the demand curve for the rest of the world. Exports are equal to domestic production of Q_3 minus consumption of Q_2.

We show the effect of the export subsidy by a downward shift in the export supply curve; exporters will accept a lower price in foreign markets than they do in the domestic market, because the difference is made up by the government payment. The result of the subsidy is that the quantity of exports rises, as foreign consumers respond to the drop in price from P_0 to P_{w1}. In the domestic

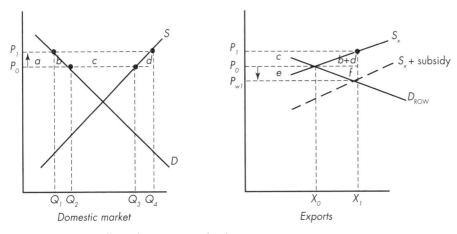

FIGURE 6.8 The Effect of an Export Subsidy

Introducing an export subsidy results in producers expanding output from Q_3 to Q_4 and diverting sales from the domestic market to the foreign market, Q_2 minus Q_1. Foreign buyers benefit from a lower world price, P_{w1}, but domestic consumers face a higher price, P_1, as exports rise from X_0 to X_1.

market, however, the price rises to P_1, assuming that goods sold more cheaply abroad cannot be re-imported. The higher price discourages domestic consumption, which falls from Q_2 to Q_1, and encourages domestic production, which rises from Q_3 to Q_4. These changes in domestic production and consumption are what make more of the good available for export.

The distributional effects of the subsidy within the exporting country are that domestic consumers lose areas $a + b$, while domestic producers gain areas $a + b + c$. In addition, the cost of the subsidy to the government is $c + b + d + e + f$, shown in the right panel. A key effect of the subsidy is to drive down the price received in foreign markets, and areas $e + f$ represent this terms-of-trade loss to the exporting country. Furthermore, the higher domestic price results in higher domestic profits, but two deadweight losses: area d represents a loss in the efficiency of production, because marginal cost rises above the initial world price, and area b represents a loss in the efficiency of consumption, because consumers buy less of the good they would prefer at the initial world price. The net effect is that the country loses $e + f + b + d$. The drop in price internationally provides an obvious benefit to customers in the rest of the world, but producers in the rest of the world will be worse off. Direct government subsidies of manufactured products are regarded as an unfair trade practice under international trade rules of the WTO. **Countervailing duties** can be imposed on subsidized exports if producers in the importing country are injured, and third country exporters who are negatively affected can challenge such subsidies in the WTO.

Determining what government assistance constitutes an unfair subsidy has proven quite contentious in practice. Typically, those who lodge a complaint must distinguish between practices that provide a benefit to a specific industry, in contrast to practices that are available to all industries. For example, a lower corporate tax rate or a lower interest rate that benefits all industries does not represent a countervailable subsidy. Favorable government financing for particular companies, such as state-owned steel companies in Europe or memory chip producers in Korea, has been the subject of international complaints.

Another key issue to be negotiated multilaterally is any limitation on the favorable financing provided on export sales. Such financing is especially important in the sale of large capital goods, such as airplanes or power plants. An agreement among OECD countries sets conditions on the maximum length and minimum interest rates on commercial terms for such loans.

E.U. Sugar Subsidies as Barriers to Development

An important example of the effects of export subsidies is provided by the E.U. sugar provisions under the Common Agricultural Policy (CAP). High E.U. target or intervention prices domestically mean that producers have an incentive to produce more than they would at world prices. For given national quotas the E.U. is obligated to purchase sugar. To reduce the need for such purchases, imports (aside from preferential trade agreements) are eliminated by a tariff on foreign sugar, which makes it noncompetitive. This complex scheme allows the domestic price to be three to four times the world price. For example, in 2004 the world price was €157 per ton while the intervention price was €631 and the minimum import price was €716. Furthermore, because of extra domestic production, the E.U. no longer is a net importer of sugar. Rather, it now is the second largest exporter of sugar in the world, accounting for 20 percent of all exports, which it accomplishes through subsidies.

This situation led Australia, Brazil, and Thailand to challenge E.U. subsidy practices before the WTO. The Appellate Board ruling adopted in May 2005 rejected two key E.U. arguments. First, if the E.U. chooses to import raw sugar from former colonies and lets them benefit from the high internal price within the E.U., its practice of then subsidizing the re-export of that refined sugar must be counted against the E.U. commitment to hold its sugar export subsidies under a specified limit. Such an expenditure cannot be excluded on the grounds that it is development aid. Second, the E.U. system of guaranteeing high prices for sugar within a given domestic quota and then requiring that any excess production must be exported without the benefit of public funds does not mean that those latter export sales are consistent with the E.U.'s WTO obligations. Rather, the WTO found that the high prices for domestic in-quota sugar amounted to a cross-subsidy to export over-quota sugar. The high price for the in-quota sales allowed farmers to cover all of their fixed costs of production, and then to sell over-quota sugar at a price that covered the marginal cost of producing it. Such a strategy of price discrimination, or dumping, is viable only because of the high returns earned in the protected domestic market.

Why does such a policy attract world attention? Many developing countries with a comparative advantage in sugar production are highly dependent on sugar exports as a source of foreign exchange. Because the price elasticities of supply and demand in world markets are low, the large increase in quantity supplied by the E.U. has a severe depressing effect on the world price. Economists estimate that eliminating the subsidies would allow world sugar prices to rise by 20 percent, a major boon to developing countries. Annual losses to the largest exporters as a result of E.U. policy were Brazil ($494 million), Thailand ($151 million), South Africa and India ($60 million).

Subsequent reform of E.U. sugar policy calls for a reduction in the domestic price from €632 to €441. That outcome has worried producers in the E.U. and also those countries that have preferential access to the E.U. market.

A long-running conflict between Canada and the United States demonstrates other difficulties that exist in interpreting subsidy provisions. In the case of softwood lumber production, British Columbia allows local firms to harvest lumber on provincially owned land in exchange for stumpage fees which are considerably lower than those prevailing in the United States. Canadians argue that such a benefit is a windfall gain that does not alter the marginal cost of production or optimal level of output. The U.S. lumber industry, however, views the lower Canadian stumpage fees as an unfair cost advantage for British Columbia that promotes greater production. A series of cases dating from the 1980s have resulted in frequent government intervention, either in the form of U.S. import duties or Canadian export taxes. The solution negotiated in 2006 does not restore a free market, and instead calls for export taxes or quotas in periods of depressed demand.

Subsidies are also viewed as an important tool of strategic trade policy in industries where economies of scale exist. We return to that topic in the following chapter.

Export Tariffs

Although governments usually design trade policies to reduce imports or encourage exports, some countries have applied tariffs to exports.[3] Less developed countries sometimes do so in order to raise revenues. Export taxes may be less costly to collect than other taxes, and they are often perceived as falling on wealthy landowners in the case of agricultural exports. **Export tariffs** may also be used to protect consumers from increases in world prices of an export commodity. In the early 1970s, President Nixon imposed an **embargo** on U.S. soybean exports to keep U.S. food prices low. In the late 1970s, and again in the 1980s, India used an export tax on tea to hold down prices to domestic consumers when world tea prices increased sharply. Argentina banned beef exports during parts of 2006 to satisfy local consumers, whose domestic consumption per capita tops all other countries, and in 2008 several countries restricted rice exports. Sometimes the favored domestic purchasers are processors, who are being encouraged to create more value-added at home rather than export raw materials. For example, an Argentine tax on the export of soybeans was intended to keep prices of beans low for crushers of soybean oil and meal, and an Indonesian ban on rattan exports promoted production of furniture domestically.

Some of these effects of an export tax can be shown in Figure 6.9. In contrast to the case of an export subsidy, now the export supply curve shifts upward by the amount of the tax. As shown in the right panel, exports fall from X_0 to X_1 as world price rises from P_0 to P_W, and the domestic price falls to P_1. In the left panel this price decline causes consumers to expand purchases from Q_1 to Q_2 and to gain area a. Producers reduce output from Q_4 to Q_3 and lose areas $a + b + c + d$. The government collects tax revenue of $c + e$, as shown in the right panel. Area e represents a terms of trade gain, and if demand in the rest of the world is less elastic relative to export supply, this gain will be larger. Areas b and d are deadweight losses: lower domestic production releases resources that produce a lower value of output elsewhere in the economy, area d, and greater domestic consumption shifts output to those who value it less than it is worth in foreign markets, area b. The net effect on Country A is $e - b - d$.

---

3 Section 9 of Article I of the U.S. Constitution prohibits taxes on exports. This provision was included at the insistence of southern states which feared that northern states would attempt to tax their exports of agricultural commodities.

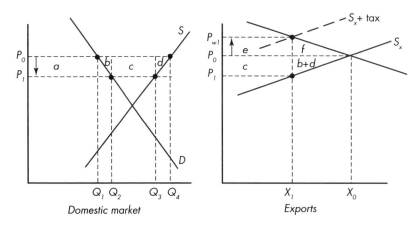

FIGURE 6.9 The Effect of an Export Tax

Introducing an export tax results in producers contracting output from Q_4 to Q_3 and domestic consumers purchasing Q_2 rather than Q_1. Exports fall from X_0 to X_1 as domestic producers respond to the lower domestic price P_1 and foreign purchasers to the higher world price P_{w1}.

This outcome appears remarkably symmetric to the situation reported for a tariff levied by a large country: trade is restricted, the country's terms of trade improve, but deadweight losses in efficiency are created. Such symmetry was formally demonstrated by Abba Lerner (1936).

An export tax allows a country to exploit its dominant position in an export market. Because the tax applies to all of the country's exporters, the terms of trade improvement can be achieved without forming a cartel among all producers. The distributional effects differ from those of a successful cartel, though, because with an export tax the government gains while producers lose. As in the case of a tariff, the gain comes at the expense of other countries, and the world as a whole is less efficient, by areas $b + d + f$.

Summary of Key Concepts

1. For a small country that cannot affect international prices, levying a tariff reduces its national income by encouraging too much domestic production and discouraging domestic consumption.

2. Tariffs can significantly redistribute income within a country. Producers' profits and government tariff revenue rise, but the loss to consumers from higher domestic prices is even greater.

3. A quota limits the amount of goods that can be imported. Imposing a quota results in a larger net loss to the economy, compared to a tariff that yields the same reduction in imports, if foreigners gain the tariff-equivalent revenue created by the quota.

4. The same expansion in domestic production achieved by a tariff or a quota can be accomplished at lower cost with a production subsidy that does not distort consumption choices.

5. A country large enough to affect international prices may improve its terms of trade by levying a tariff. The price it pays to foreigners will fall more when the elasticity of demand for imports is large relative to the foreign export elasticity of supply.
6. The effective rate of protection indicates how much higher value-added in an industry can be compared to free trade. The ERP often exceeds the nominal rate of protection for many finished manufactured goods, but it is likely to be negative for export goods.
7. Export subsidies hurt domestic consumers and help domestic producers. In a competitive industry, the export subsidy reduces national welfare.
8. Export taxes help domestic consumers and hurt domestic producers. Their effect on foreigners is similar to a tariff: domestic welfare may increase at the expense of foreigners.

CASE STUDY

The Elimination of the MFA

One of the noteworthy agreements of the Uruguay Round of multilateral trade negotiations concluded in 1993 was the termination of the Multifibre Agreement (MFA). For the previous three decades industrialized countries had imposed country-specific quotas on textile and apparel imports from developing countries. Although the termination was to be achieved through a phased reduction of existing barriers, many importing countries made minimal reductions before the January 1, 2005 deadline. The change in policy that occurred at that time was quite substantial.

Not surprisingly, many producers in developed countries lobbied against this liberalization. Many exporters lobbied against this change, too. They feared that without the country-specific quotas that let them benefit from high prices in the developed country markets, they would lose their market share to more efficient producers. Similarly, countries that had signed preferential trade agreements with the E.U. and the U.S. expected that their special access would no longer offer much benefit. The most feared competitor was China.

How did market shares change as a result of this policy change? Table 6.6 shows U.S. imports in 2004 and 2005 from several key suppliers, where some of the largest shifts occurred. Some key conclusions can be drawn from these changes:

1. China did expand its sales impressively by 57 percent for the two key apparel sectors (HTS 61 and 62 under the Harmonizes Tariff System used to report international trade statistics on a comparable basis across countries).
2. Some other Asian producers did well, too, including India, Bangladesh, and Indonesia. Their level of sales and growth rates, however, were both substantially lower than the figures for China.
3. High income Asian suppliers like Korea and Taiwan saw major reductions in their sales, as their historical role as suppliers of labor-intensive goods no longer was consistent with their current factor endowments, wage rates, and comparative advantage.
4. Supplier in Africa and Latin America, who benefit from special trade preferences under the African Growth Opportunity Act (AGOA),

TABLE 6.6 U.S. Apparel Imports

Country	2004, $ billions	2005, $ billions	Apparel/ All imports from country	% increase, 2004–5
Asia				
China	10.7	16.8	6.9	57
Hong Kong	3.9	3.5	39.5	–9
India	2.3	3.1	16.4	36
Indonesia	2.4	2.9	24.0	20
Vietnam	2.5	2.7	40.8	6
Bangladesh	1.9	2.3	84.2	21
Korea	1.8	1.2	2.7	–35
Taiwan	1.5	1.1	3.1	–26
Latin America				
Mexico	6.8	6.2	3.7	–9
Honduras	2.7	2.7	71.4	–2
Dominican Republic	2.0	1.8	39.8	–10
Guatemala	2.0	1.8	58.2	–7
Africa (millions)				
Lesotho	456	391	96.8	–14
Madagascar	323	277	85.5	–14
Kenya	277	270	77.7	–3
Mauritius	226	167	75.0	–26

Source: United States International Trade Commission (2008).

the North American Free Trade Agreement (NAFTA), and the Caribbean Basin Trade Partners Act (CBTPA), found that the benefits of those preferences eroded. The quantities of Chinese exports were no longer restricted, although Chinese goods were still subject to tariffs from which favored partners were exempt.

In addition to these changes in shares of the import market, the share of U.S. producers in their domestic market declined. From 2002 to 2005 the import share of the U.S. market rose from 57.5 percent to 67.5 percent, and the nominal value of U.S. shipments fell by 22 percent. Employment fell from 360,000 workers to 260,000 workers, a decline of 28 percent.

The annual figures mask even more challenging adjustments that occurred in 2005. During the first six months of the year, the rate of increase of U.S. imports from China was 82 percent, compared to the same period the previous year. Similar import surges in Europe led the E.U. to negotiate quantitative restrictions with China to limit imports for the years 2005–2007. The U.S. followed suit with restrictions to applying over the years 2006–2008.

To predict what might happen when those restrictions are removed, we might note which producers were most successful during the first six months when imports from China rose 82 percent. On the other hand, three years of additional devel-opment in China may alter its status as a low-cost provider with a comparative advantage in unskilled-labor-intensive goods, and additional countries may become successful in the world apparel trade.

CASE STUDY QUESTIONS

1. How do country-specific quotas have a different effect on the U.S. and on exporting countries than would a first-come, first-served quota?

2. When quotas were reimposed on China, what likely happened to the average price of Chinese goods sent to the U.S.? Would Chinese costs of production have fallen if less were produced, or would Chinese producers have an incentive to upgrade what they exported? Interpret the following average unit prices of U.S. imports of men's trousers from China: 2004 – $94/dozen; 2005 – $60/dozen; and 2006 – $78/dozen.

3. The allowable annual growth rate for the quantity of Chinese goods sent to the U.S. was 10 to 12 percent, depending upon the item. What does this growth rate imply about the protective effect of the quota over time?

4. Table 6.6 shows that some countries are quite dependent upon apparel trade as a share of their total exports to the U.S. If those countries have few alternative export activities into which resources can be reallocated, what might that imply about the elasticity of supply of exports from them?

5. Assess E.U. textile and apparel import information provided at the following link http://ec.europa.eu/trade/issues/sectoral/industry/textile/pr281105_en.htm. In what ways is the E.U. situation comparable to the U.S. situation, and in what ways is it different?

Questions for Study and Review

1. Explain how import restrictions affect domestic producers and consumers. How are the concepts of producers' surplus and consumers' surplus useful in demonstrating these effects?

2. You are given the following information about copper in the European Union:

	Situation with tariff	Situation without tariff
World price	€1.50 per kg	€1.50 per kg
Tariff (specific)	€0.15 per kg	0
E.U. domestic price	€1.65 per kg	€1.50 per kg
E.U. consumption	200 million kg	230 million kg
E.U. production	160 million kg	100 million kg

Draw a supply–demand diagram on the basis of these data and indicate imports with and without the tariff. Calculate:

a. The gain to E.U. consumers from removing the tariff.

b. The loss to E.U. producers from removing the tariff.

c. The loss of tariff revenue to government when the tariff is removed.

d. The net gain or loss to the E.U. economy as a whole.

Explain briefly the meaning of each calculation. In the case of (d), what implicit assumptions do you make in reporting a net result?

3. Problem 2 assumes that the E.U. acts as a small country in the world copper market, because the world price remains constant at 1.50 euros per kilo. Assume instead that with the €0.15 tariff the world price becomes €1.45 per kilo, E.U. consumption falls to 210 million kilos and E.U. production rises to 140 million kilos. Show that new situation diagrammatically and calculate the effect of the tariff on E.U. consumers, E.U. producers, government, and the economy as a whole.

4. Suppose the domestic steel industry faces severe competition from a country that is not a member of the WTO. The industry asks you to prepare a position paper its lobbyist can use to seek government assistance. Contrast the consequences of imposing a quota, negotiating a VER, and providing a production subsidy.

5. At free-trade prices, half of the value of leather shoes is accounted for by leather, and all other intermediate inputs account for 20 percent of the value. The tariff rates on shoes, leather, and other intermediate inputs are 18 percent, 10 percent, and 5 percent, respectively.

a. Calculate the effective rate of protection for leather shoes.

b. For shoes sold in the protected domestic market, what does this ERP value imply about payments to labor and capital in shoe production in this country compared to those payments when production occurs at world prices?

c. The tariff structure above implies tariff escalation. Explain some of the consequences of such escalation on the effective rate of protection received by the shoe industry.

6. A country imposes a tariff rate quota (TRQ) on imports of tuna fish. Suppose that for imports up to 3,000 tons the tariff is $0, and for imports greater than 3,000 tons the tariff is $175 per ton.

a. If the demand for imports of tuna is $Q = 5,000 − 4P$, and the supply of imported tuna is $Q = 200 + 8P$, what is the price paid by consumers? Compare this solution to the free trade equilibrium. Be sure to comment on the role of the TRQ.

b. If the demand curve becomes $Q = 6,000 − 4P$, due to the alleged benefits of tuna consumption to ensure long life and improved intellectual acuity, what influence does that have on the price and quantity of imports? Again, comment on the role of the TRQ. (Hint: if P represents the price paid by consumers, then the foreign supplier now receives P − $175.)

c. If foreign productivity in tuna fish production rises so that the new foreign supply curve is $Q = 1,000 + 8P$, how does productivity improvement get shared between producers and consumers, compared to the solution you found in part (b)? Again, comment on the role of the TRQ.

7. You observe the following information reported by the USITC regarding imports of butter: the within-quota landed, duty-paid price of butter is $2.798 per kilogram, and the comparable over-quota price is $3.299. The within-quota tariff is 13.3 cents per kilogram, and the over-quota tariff is 154.1 cents per kilogram. What do these numbers suggest about the portion of the tariff equivalent of the quota that is captured by foreign suppliers?

8. Given your understanding of the different effects of tariffs and quotas, what benefit would you expect from the World Trade Organization's success in converting quotas and other quantitative restrictions into tariffs?

9. Who gains and who loses from the imposition of an export tax? For countries that have constitutional prohibitions against imposing export taxes, have they lost an effective trade policy tool? Explain. If a country bans the export of a product, why does that not make effective use of its market power internationally?

10. Why does a small country lose less from an export subsidy than a large country? Can a country gain from an export subsidy in a perfectly competitive industry?

References and Suggestions for Further Reading

For tariff schedules of the E.U. and the U.S. use the following links:

http://www.usitc.gov/tata/hts/
http://ec.europa.eu/taxation_customs/common/databases/index_en.htm
http://www.export.gov/static/E.U._tariff_schedule.pdf

For examples of partial equilibrium studies of the effects of trade barriers:

Crandall, R. (1984) "Import Quotas and the Automobile Industry: The Cost of Protectionism," *Brookings Review*, Summer.

François, J. and Hall, K. (1997) "Partial Equilibrium Modeling," in J. François and K. Reinert (eds) *Applied Methods for Trade Policy Analysis*, New York: Cambridge University Press.

Hufbauer, G., and Elliott, K. (1994) *Measuring the Costs of Protection in the United States*, Washington, DC: Institute for International Economics.

Messerlin, P. (2001) *Measuring the Cost of Protection in Europe*, Washington, DC: Institute for International Economics.

Mutti, J. (1978) "Aspects of Unilateral Trade Policy and Factor Adjustment Costs," *Review of Economics and Statistics*, 60: 102–10.

Sazanami, Y., Urata, S., and Kawai, H. (1995) *Measuring the Costs of Protection in Japan*, Washington, DC: Institute for International Economics.

Tarr, D. and Morkre, M. (1984) *Aggregate Costs to the United States of Tariffs and Quotas on Imports*, Washington, DC: Federal Trade Commission.

The following government reports that you can access through the internet include many case studies and general assessments of the effects of trade barriers:

U.S. International Trade Commission (2007) *The Economic Effects of Significant U.S. Import Restraints: Fifth Update*, Investigation No. 332–325, Publication 3906. <http://www.usitc.gov/publications/abstract_3906.htm>
World Trade Organization (2005) *Managing the Challenges of WTO Participation – 45 Case Studies*, P. Gallagher, P. Low, and A. L. Stoler (eds) <http://www.wto.org/english/res_e/booksp_e/casestudies_e/casestudies_e.htm>

E.U. trade directorate general, external trade, sectoral issues http://ec.europa.eu/trade/issues/sectoral/index_en.htm
for example http://ec.europa.eu/trade/issues/sectoral/industry/textile/trade_text_en.htm
http://www.eurunion.org/policyareas/trade.htm

Events reported regarding steel industry policy:

Alden, E. (2003) "Bush backs down by lifting tariffs on steel imports," *Financial Times*, December 5, p. 1.
—— (2005) "US to keep tariffs on imports of steel," *Financial Times*, April 15, p.4.
Hufbauer, G., and Goodrich, B. (2001) "Steel: Big Problems, Better Solutions," Institute for International Economics, Policy Brief PB01–9, July.
Matthews, R. (2002) "Foreign Steelmakers' Prices Rise," *The Wall Street Journal*, October 8, 2002, p. A8.
U.S. International Trade Commission (2002) "Profiles of US Industry and Market, by Industry/Commodity Groups and Subgroups, 1997–2001," Available at http://hotdocs.usitc.gov/docs/pubs/332/pub3525A.pdf (accessed 4 September 2008).

Analysis and events reported regarding subsidies and E.U. trade in sugar:

Hufbauer, G. and Erb, J. (1984) *Subsidies in International Trade*, Washington, DC: Institute for International Economics.
Netherlands Economic Institute (2000) *Evaluation of the Common Organization of the Markets in the Sugar Sector*, September.
Oxfam (2004) "Dumping on the World: How EU Sugar Policies Hurt Poor Countries," Briefing Paper 61, March.
WTO (2006) *WTO Dispute Settlement: One-page Case Summaries, 1995–September 2006*, p. 97

For further treatment of effective rates of protection see:

Balassa, B. (1971) *The Structure of Protection in Developing Countries*, Baltimore: Johns Hopkins Press.
Corden, M. (1966) "The Structure of a Tariff System and the Effective Rate of Protection," *Journal of Political Economy* 74: 221–37.
Deardorff, A. and Stern, R. (1984) "The Effects of the Tokyo Round on the Structure of Protection," in R. Baldwin and A. Krueger (eds), *The Structure and Evolution of Recent U.S. Trade Policy*, Chicago: University of Chicago Press, pp. 370–5.
Morgan, W. and Wahjudi, B. (1992) "The Indonesian Bicycle Industry: A Boom Export Sector," University of Wyoming Working Paper.

Other sources cited in this chapter:

Ballard, C., Fullerton, D., Shoven, J., and Whalley, J. (1985) *A General Equilibrium Model for Tax Policy Evaluation*, Chicago: University of Chicago Press.
Harberger, A. (1990) "Reflections on Uniform Taxation," in R. Jones and A. Krueger (eds) *The Political Economy of International Trade, Essays in Honour of Robert E. Baldwin*, Oxford: Basil Blackwell, pp. 75–89.
Lerner, A. (1936) "The Symmetry between Import and Export Taxes," *Economica* 3: 306–13.

Panagariya, A. and Rodrik, D. (1993) "Political-Economy Arguments for a Uniform Tariff," *International Economic Review* 34: 685–703.

United States International Trade Commission (2008) Dataweb, available at http://dataweb.usitc.gov (accessed 9 September 2008).

WTO (2006) *Overview of Developments in the International Trade Environment*, Annual Report by the Director General, WT/TPR/OV/11, February.

Chapter 7

Arguments for Protection

and the Political Economy of Trade Policy

LEARNING OBJECTIVES

By the end of this chapter you should be able to explain:

■ why tariffs are an inefficient way to address macroeconomic goals regarding employment or the balance of trade

■ the rationale for scarce factors of production to seek protection

■ how a large country may gain at the expense of others by levying a tariff

■ what conditions allow an economy to gain from targeting particular industries

■ how antidumping laws have become popular measures to grant protection

■ why democratically elected governments may choose protectionist policies

Although the basic assumption that countries gain from trade is accepted by most economists, this has not consistently translated into comparable political support for an open trading system. As you found in Chapter 6, a wide variety of trade barriers exist in practice. Corporations, industry associations, and labor unions adversely affected by foreign competition frequently lobby for protection, often going to great lengths to demonstrate why they represent a special case or national interest that warrants government intervention. They appear to be quite successful!

Some industries argue that protection is necessary to maintain a way of life. Farm groups in Europe and the United States frequently make this claim, as do those in developing countries who appeal for the preservation of indigenous cultures and a halt to the inroads of modernization. Or, domestic production may be defended as vital to national security and a nation's ability to feed, clothe, and defend its people, as in the case of Japanese and Korean bans on imported rice or U.S. restrictions on coastal shipping. Fear of dependence on outside suppliers may be an argument raised not only in the case of food and energy, but also in the case of innovations at the forefront of technological advance. Governments may intervene to promote national champions in high-technology industries, as the French have done in the computer industry or a group of European countries did to launch Airbus. Producers in developing countries often claim that protection is necessary because free trade will leave them producing primary products with limited opportunities to develop their own industrial capability.

The way a group frames its arguments for government intervention and whether granting protection will raise national welfare may be less important than the underlying economic incentive for a group to seek the economic rents created by trade barriers. Large potential payoffs warrant substantial effort to organize and to influence government policy. How government officials or politicians respond to these efforts determines the trade policy that emerges. Therefore, economists are interested in the process that translates individual interests into group action, and the role of politicians and government officials who may have other priorities besides the maximization of national welfare.

We may ask why any country ends up with the trade policy it has. Have economists simply ignored those adversely affected by import competition and failed to respond to weak or self-serving arguments against freer trade? Are there more sophisticated economic arguments in favor of government intervention that we have not addressed thus far? Does the political process mean that net economic efficiency and aggregate gains to the economy as a whole – a standard we applied in the previous chapter – provide a poor basis by which to judge the attractiveness of a policy? If trade policy is simply an exercise in redistributing income within a country, can interest groups find a more efficient way to accomplish that goal? While claims for protection seem to dominate policy debate in many countries, what accounts for the choice of other countries to pursue liberalization strategies unilaterally? This chapter addresses such questions.

ARGUMENTS FOR RESTRICTING IMPORTS

Here is a roadmap to the way various arguments for protection are addressed in this section of the chapter. Claims for government intervention are often voiced most loudly when the macroeconomy is performing poorly and unemployment is high. Workers laid off in one industry are unlikely to find jobs quickly elsewhere in the economy. We consider government policies to deal with macroeconomic downturns in Part II of this book, and merely note here that permanent protection builds in permanent inefficiency that reduces economic output long after a temporary decline in demand or increase in the trade deficit has been reversed. We begin by briefly discussing claims related to these macroeconomic problems.

Even when the economy is operating at full employment, however, changing patterns of trade can have important effects on the distribution of income. Whether governments have alternative policies available to respond to those who lose from such changes is another key aspect of public debate about trade. That topic has been most relevant in countries without broad social safety nets.

We next consider the generality of claims that economists have made for over 200 years to justify trade barriers that protect national security or that exploit an economy's market power internationally. Similarly, economists have long debated the case for temporarily protecting infant industries. In the past 30 years, economists have paid more attention to potential gains from strategic trade intervention and industry targeting. In this chapter, we consider aspects of this controversy that are most applicable to industrialized countries, and in Chapter 11 we treat issues of most relevance to developing countries.

Actual implementation of trade policy often does not occur as the result of public debate and legislative action or through treaty negotiations. Rather, administrative procedures to deal with allegations of unfair trade have assumed a major role. We pay special attention to the practice of dumping and government responses to it as an avenue for trade restrictions.

Save Jobs at Home

It is often argued that protectionism is a desirable way of increasing output, incomes, and employment because it shifts demand to domestically produced goods and away from imports. Protection for one industry may temporarily save local jobs, but that proves to be a poor guide to policy.

First, domestic output of import-competing goods does not increase by the amount that imports decline. In our graphical representations of tariffs and quotas presented in Chapter 6, such protectionism produced only a partial increase of output in competing domestic industries; the remainder of the import decline was caused by reduced consumption. If imports decline by €10 billion, domestic production in the favored industry may only rise by €5 billion, as consumption falls by the other €5 billion.

If output of domestic substitutes rises, even a little, advocates note that this extra demand may be a stimulus to further economic expansion, as rising income leads to rising consumption. In a business downturn this might be temporarily true, but few advocates of tariffs seek their imposition for only a short-run time frame, until the cyclical demand for investment goods and consumer durables recovers. Politically, tariffs are extremely difficult to remove once they are imposed, and therefore they are poorly suited to deal with temporary macroeconomic problems.

In addition, this argument assumes no retaliation by countries that lose export sales and output. Protectionism does not increase employment worldwide; rather, it merely shifts it from one country to another, and the country on the losing end of the process is very likely to respond by reclaiming the output and employment with protection of its own. The passage in the U.S. of the Smoot–Hawley Tariff Act of 1930 set in motion a particularly destructive cycle of retaliation that reduced output and employment worldwide during the Great Depression.

This argument for protection ignores the availability of alternative policies to increase output and employment in a cyclical downturn. If a country's level of aggregate demand is insufficient to support acceptable levels of output and employment, expansionary fiscal and/or monetary policies provide a better remedy, a topic addressed in Part II of this book. For a country that does impose trade barriers, recall the examples cited in Chapter 6 of the very high cost to consumers of each job saved.

Close a Trade Deficit

Countries with large balance-of-payments deficits sometimes view import restraints as a means of reducing or eliminating such problems. The causes and possible solutions for balance-of-trade problems will also be discussed in Part II, but for now it is sufficient to note that such deficits are normally macroeconomic in cause, the result of less domestic saving than domestic investment. Solutions are typically to be found in exchange rate changes and other macroeconomic policies. When a deficit is large enough to threaten a country's ability to maintain a target value for its exchange rate, however, governments often seek any short-term policy available, and limits on nonessential imports are sometimes adopted as a stopgap measure.

The consequences of a policy to impose a tariff on imports from a single country, such as China, are likely to disappoint its advocates. The importer's voracious demand for foreign goods remains high and is met by goods produced in other countries. Restricting all imports, in the absence of resources to produce more goods domestically, simply leaves a less efficient economy with a lower standard of living.

Do Not Reward Sweatshop Labor

One of the oldest arguments against free trade is based on a simple comparison between foreign wages and those prevailing in the home country. Employers in industrialized countries argue that it is impossible for their employees to compete against the pauper labor (i.e. low-wage labor) available abroad. A modern variant of this complaint is that foreign producers exploit their employees by forcing them to work in sweatshop conditions at less than a living wage. Employers in industrialized countries often object that minimum wage laws make it illegal for domestic firms to pay wages that would match those that prevail in developing countries from which competing products are imported. If apparel manufacturers in developed countries must pay wages that are ten times as high as in India or China, not surprisingly those firms feel that they are at an unreasonable competitive disadvantage. They are likely to argue for tariffs that offset these cost differences, thus putting them on a level playing field in competing with imports.

Imports and Moral Imperatives

In the late eighteenth century, a British movement to boycott West Indian sugar was led by activists who hoped to raise the social conscience of British society. Their point was that slave labor made this product available, and a British addiction to sweetness raised the profits of sugar planters. By reducing British demand, abolitionists hoped to reduce the profit motive behind the slave trade.

Britain did ban slavery throughout the empire in 1807, and the boycott lost some its force. In the 1820s, however, another effort was made to boycott sugar, this time by some who viewed with disapproval the tax on sugar that served as a ready source of finance for British military adventures. A ringing proclamation that Thomas Love Peacock included in one of his novels framed the issue in these terms: "the use of sugar is economically superfluous, physically pernicious, morally atrocious, and politically abominable."[1]

In any age, changing consumer tastes is not an easy task. In recent years activists have made consumers aware that child labor is used to produce rugs and soccer balls and that the availability of cheap lumber and paper is the result of destruction of the rainforest. In the case of sweatshop labor used to produce shoes and clothing, activists have pushed consumers to demand certification of acceptable working conditions in foreign factories. If workers in a single plant were to organize and demand higher wages and better working conditions, producers might simply close factories in that location and set up shop elsewhere. Importers might receive lower bids from producers in countries where wage rates were even lower and labor had less ability to organize.

Even if workers in all locations could be organized, and the cost of higher wages could be passed forward to consumers, the success of the policy depends upon demand for such products being inelastic. Otherwise, the increased costs will result in a larger percentage decline in output. In some industries, firms may earn above-average profits from successful brand images, such as Adidas or Nike, and in those cases workers might gain a large enough share of those profits to offset the reduction in output. More generally, changing consumer tastes and creating a willingness to pay for better conditions abroad will be necessary if activists are not to leave many sweatshop workers unemployed and worse off than before the undesirable jobs existed.

Despite its initial attractions, this argument ignores a couple of the important concepts we encountered in Chapters 2 and 3. First, it implicitly assumes that labor is the only cost of production. Capital, raw materials, and a variety of other inputs may be cheaper in the industrialized country, largely offsetting the differences in wage costs. We especially expect that to be true for goods that are capital or resource intensive.

Second, recall from Chapter 2 that Country A can pay higher wages because labor is more productive on average than in Country B. Country A will have some industries where its productivity

---

1 As cited in *The Economist* (2006). See also "British History: Abolition of the Slave Trade 1807," at http://www. bbc.co.uk/history/british/abolition.

advantage more than offsets its higher wage rate, and it will export those goods. In other industries, its productivity advantage will not be sufficient to offset the higher wage that it must pay. As a result it will import those goods. The suggestion that the high-wage country should only trade with countries whose wage rates are comparable ignores productivity differences across countries. If Austria were to refuse to trade with Bulgaria because of its lower wages, the result would be higher unemployment in Bulgaria and a higher cost of living in Austria. Correspondingly, when East and West Germany were unified in 1990, imposing the same wage agreements in both sectors contributed to widescale unemployment in the East. The productivity of workers in the East was not high enough to allow firms producing there to be competitive with firms producing in the West.

Avoid Adverse Effects on Income Distribution

For trade based on the factor endowments theory, relatively scarce factors of production are likely to favor the imposition of trade barriers. Factors used only in import-competing industries are likely to share that view. For unskilled and semi-skilled workers in industrialized countries, the fact that free trade would increase total national income is irrelevant, because they end up worse off. In Europe, reductions in existing trade barriers would likely add to the already high unemployment rate of unskilled workers, while in the United States such a policy would likely reduce the real wage rate of unskilled workers. Labor unions and others representing the interests of labor understandably try to restrict imports of labor-intensive products in order to preclude the effects of the factor-price equalization process.

   Could a policy of taxes and transfer payments to compensate unskilled workers for their losses effectively shift part of the gains from trade experienced by skilled labor, capital and land in industrial countries? In that way a country could enjoy the benefits of freer trade without having to accept a politically undesired shift in the distribution of income. How such compensation might be provided is not a straightforward question, however. **Trade Adjustment Assistance** (TAA) is a U.S. program intended to provide cash payments, retraining, and relocation assistance to individuals who lose their jobs as a result of trade. It was initially created in 1962 with the proviso that assistance be provided to those who could demonstrate that they lost their jobs because of a change in trade policy agreed to under the Kennedy Round negotiations. So few workers qualified under that standard that the link between greater imports and a change in trade policy was dropped in 1974. Primary recipients of assistance in the 1970s turned out to be auto workers affected by imports of fuel-efficient cars; little adjustment in helping those workers move to other industries occurred, because their high wages in the auto industry made it more logical for them to await recall in that industry.[2] If TAA did not promote adjustment, at least the payments did represent a form of compensation. However, the long-run Stolper–Samuelson result, that all unskilled workers will be adversely affected throughout the economy, means that only a small proportion of those who lose from greater trade actually receive any compensation.

---

2 The number of TAA recipients reached a peak in 1980 at nearly 600,000; the number in the 1990s varied between 60,000 and 90,000 workers. For a summary of the program's operation, see: http://aspe.os.dhhs.gov/96gb/07TAA.TXT.

Retraining and relocation programs are of less benefit to older workers. An early sample of workers who received TAA benefits showed that 40 percent never found another job (Bale 1974). Over the 1979–99 period, the experience of import-impacted workers continued to quite mixed: 63 percent did become re-employed, but among those workers 36 percent reported the same or higher wages, while 25 percent reported a drop of 30 percent or more in their wages (Kletzer 2001). An outgrowth of that analysis is a new feature of the TAA program adopted in 2002, which provides wage insurance to encourage workers to find another job quickly, even if they have to accept lower wages. This provision is limited to workers older than 50, although workers who supply trade-impacted industries also can claim benefits.

U.S. trade economists and politicians generally view TAA as a useful and necessary step to support a more open trade policy. Labor economists, on the other hand, have been perplexed by the attention given to just one group of workers. They point out that a better adjustment program for all the unemployed would be desirable. How to strike the appropriate balance between compensation and adjustment, however, is a point of debate that not all European countries answer the same way in establishing social safety nets.

National Defense and National Security

A particular industry may be considered essential to maintain a nation's military strength. The footwear industry, for example, notes that no army has ever marched into war without boots. In order to preserve some capacity to produce in this industry, the nation may choose to protect it. Economists have always recognized this exception to the case for free trade, and even Adam Smith observed that "defense is more important than opulence." However, it is quite difficult to prove how much the gains from domestic production contribute to national defense.

The real issue concerning national security is maintenance of a domestic capacity to produce certain essential items, if trade, even with allies, will be interrupted in a time of war. If that capacity is not maintained, skills and technological expertise may be lost, and the nation becomes dependent on foreign sources of supply. Trade increases specialization, and the other side of that coin is interdependence. The only real escape is to become self-sufficient, but self-sufficiency is extremely inefficient. Pursuing that goal could weaken the nation by impoverishing it. Consequently, any serious use of the national defense argument for protection requires a careful calculation of the trade-off between efficiency and defense essentiality.

Countries contemplating energy independence policies face such trade-offs, as they attempt to reduce their reliance on imported oil or natural gas. Measures to alter patterns of demand may be just as important as efforts to promote production of more energy domestically. More production of non-renewable resources, and exhausting them more quickly, shifts to the future the potential vulnerability of the economy. A U.S. post-World War II policy to limit oil imports in order to pump more U.S. oil was wisely replaced in the 1980s by a Strategic Petroleum Reserve, which better serves the purpose of guaranteeing a supply of oil in an emergency.

Take Advantage of a Country's Market Power

As we found in Chapter 6, by imposing a tariff a large country may be able to turn the terms of trade in its favor. This gain may be large enough to outweigh the loss from a reduced volume of trade. So runs the terms-of-trade argument, which is also known as the "**optimum tariff**" case, although it is optimal only for the country imposing the tariff and not for the world.

In the left-hand panel of Figure 7.1 we show that a tariff causes the price of domestic purchases to rise to P_c but the price received by foreign suppliers falls to P_f. A portion of the tariff revenue raised is not simply a transfer from domestic purchasers, but comes from foreign producers, as shown by the area m. When imports decline from M_0 to M_1, however, economic efficiency declines by area n, which represents the combined effect of less efficient domestic producers expanding their output and of domestic consumers shifting to less desirable substitutes. The tariff that results in the largest value of area m minus area n is the optimum tariff. An appendix to this chapter elaborates this point.

We show a comparable effect from imposing an export tax in the right-hand panel of Figure 7.1. In that situation, the tax results in foreign buyers paying a higher price for the export good, P_f, but domestic consumers now pay P_d. The exporting country gains part of the export tax revenue at the expense of foreign buyers, which is shown by area m. That gain may offset the efficiency loss, shown by area n, which results from less production of a good where the country has a comparative advantage and from greater domestic consumption of it. The optimal export tax maximizes the difference between area m and area n.

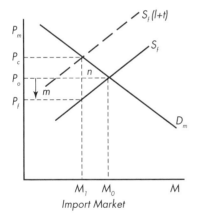 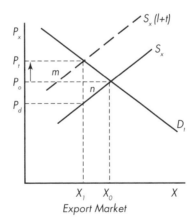

Import Market Export Market

FIGURE 7.1 An Optimum Tariff in a Partial Equilibrium Model

In the import market, an optimum tariff maximizes the difference between the terms-of-trade gain at the expense of foreign suppliers, area m, and the loss in economic efficiency from reducing the quantity of imports, area n. In the export market, the optimum export tax maximizes the difference between the terms-of-trade gain at the expense of foreign buyers, area m, and the loss in economic efficiency from reducing the quantity of exports, area n.

Optimum Tariffs: Did Britain Give a Gift to the World?

During the Napoleonic Wars, British trade with the continent was limited, and landowners benefited from high grain prices. To maintain this favourable position, in 1815 landowners were able to gain passage of a law that prohibited imports of grain unless the domestic price exceeded a generous minimum level. In the following decades, industrialists argued for the repeal of these Corn Laws. Among other negative consequences, they noted that the high cost of food left workers with little income to spend on manufactures, made labor more expensive, and ate into the profits that could finance further industrialization. The rising power of the middle class increased the potency of these arguments in the political arena, and the Irish potato blight of 1845 generated further pressure for repeal, which occurred in 1846.

The debate over repeal, however, was not simply a controversy between landowners and industrialists about the division of national income. Robert Torrens was the most outspoken of classical economists who claimed that the net effect on the country as a whole from unilateral removal of tariffs would be negative. The loss would occur due to an adverse shift in the terms of trade, a point we encountered in Chapter 6. British terms-of-trade would fall, but to determine whether that decline would be large enough to offset other efficiency gains from tariff removal requires that we calculate the relative size of these effects.

The likelihood that Britain could lose from unilaterally reducing its trade barriers exists because it certainly was not a small country in the sense that it faced a fixed world price for its imports and exports. As the birthplace of the Industrial Revolution, it was the primary source of manufactured goods on world markets. A tariff on food diverted resources away from the production of manufactured goods, and the consequent reduction in the quantity of British exports supplied resulted in improved British terms-of-trade. By repealing the Corn Laws did Britain give up some of its monopoly gains?

Douglas Irwin (1988) estimates relevant demand and supply elasticities for Britain in that era, and he applies them in assessing the effect of a reduction in the average British tariff rate from 35 percent to 31 percent. He finds that British terms of trade would worsen by 3.5 percent and result in a loss in national income of 0.4 percent. Although Irwin does not calculate whether 35 percent represents an optimum British tariff, his result indicates that Britain was moving away from an optimum tariff, because its welfare fell.

How should we judge the actual repeal of the Corn Laws? Irwin notes that Britain probably did not lose from this policy because other European nations happened to reduce trade barriers shortly after the British action. Furthermore, as Britain's share of world industrial production declined and more alternatives to British goods became available, its optimum tariff would have been lower, even in the absence of tariff reductions by others.

Regardless of whether Country A levies an import tariff or export tax, its gain comes at the expense of the rest of the world. Because the tariff reduces the degree of specialization in the world economy, world welfare is reduced. This effect matches what we observed in the case of cartels in Chapter 5; the world as a whole loses, but the export tax considered here ensures that all firms will raise the price at which they sell. The terms-of-trade argument takes a national perspective: it suggests that a nation may be able to use a tariff to capture a larger share of the gains from trade, thereby improving its welfare. This argument is logically correct, but it is not relevant for nations that have little influence on world prices.

Even for large countries, the benefit obtained through improved terms of trade may be lost if other countries retaliate by imposing tariffs of their own. Any benefits may also erode if the higher relative price of Country A's export good attracts greater entry and competition from producers in other countries. The country's market power and optimum tariff will decline over time.

King Cotton and the Market Power of Exporters

Another nineteenth-century example of a country that might have gained by imposing trade barriers to exploit its market power was the U.S. The potential gain arose from the dominant U.S. position as a supplier of cotton on world markets; the U.S. accounted for 80 percent of world production. In the absence of a way to organize U.S. producers, an export tax would have resulted in a decline in the price received by U.S. producers, a decline in U.S. production and the quantity of exports, a higher world price and a potential gain to the U.S. as a whole due to this improvement in its terms of trade.

To determine the tax rate that would maximize U.S. welfare, we must know how responsive foreign demand for cotton was, by how much a tax would affect U.S. output, how easily other suppliers of cotton could expand output, and how closely those varieties of cotton could substitute for U.S. varieties. Douglas Irwin (2003) estimates several of these parameters, and he combines them with the work of others to come up with a composite effect that the elasticity of demand for U.S. exports was −1.7 and the U.S. elasticity of supply of exports of cotton was 1.6. Irwin calculates that an export tax of 50 percent would have reduced cotton exports by about 32 percent and raised the world price of cotton by about 16 percent. This policy would have raised welfare in the South (if it had been a separate country) by about one percent.

The U.S. constitution prohibits export taxes, and efforts to change the constitution after the Civil War were not successful, in spite of attempts by those who wanted to punish the South. During the war, the Confederate government imposed an export tax, but was not very successful in actually collecting it. After the war, the U.S. did levy an excise tax on cotton producers, a measure that would hurt not only U.S. cotton producers, but also Northern textile producers.

Market Power Using Offer Curve Analysis

The opportunity for a country to improve its terms of trade by levying a tariff can also be shown with offer curves. If Country A imposes a tariff on imports of food, for example, that will shift its offer curve inward from OA to OA^1, and A's terms of trade improve as the relative price of cloth rises from OE to OE^1. The potential for Country A to gain depends importantly upon the elasticity of the foreign offer curve. In Figure 7.2, the initial equilibrium occurs along the inelastic range of Country

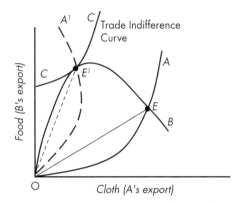

FIGURE 7.2 An Optimum Tariff with Offer Curves

The imposition of a tariff by Country A shifts its offer curve from *OA* to *OA′*, producing a large improvement in A's terms of trade, from *OE* to *OE′*, if no retaliation occurs. This choice allows Country A to reach its highest possible trade indifference curve, *CC*.

B's offer curve. Just as a monopolist in a domestic market wants to restrict output to find an optimal solution along the elastic portion of the industry demand curve, a country seeking to impose an optimal tariff will want to reach a solution along the elastic range of Country B's offer curve. At the equilibrium shown at point E^1, Country A offers much less cloth in return for a greater amount of food than it received in the initial equilibrium. Assuming that no retaliation will occur, Country A's choice of an optimal tariff maximizes its welfare by allowing it to reach the highest possible community indifference curve.

How do we know that the equilibrium at E^1 represents the best possible outcome for Country A? We make use of a concept developed by James Meade (1952), a trade indifference curve. Figure 7.2 shows a trade indifference curve for Country A, which gives all of the combinations of cloth exports and food imports that leave the country equally as well off. The curve is traced out by the origin of A's production-possibility curve as it slides along a given community indifference curve. For the autarky level of welfare, the trade indifference curve would start from the origin O; the curve CC represents a higher level of welfare.[3] Not surprisingly, its slope shows that for Country A to export an extra bolt of cloth, progressively more units of imported food are necessary to maintain the same level of welfare. Meade demonstrated that Country A should set the tariff that allows it to reach the point where the highest possible trade indifference curve is tangent to Country B's offer curve.

3 This explanation can best be understood in terms of a four-quadrant diagram, with the production-possibility curve and the community indifference curve represented in the northwest or second quadrant. As the PPC moves along the community indifference curve, the origin of that diagram will trace out an upward sloping trade indifference curve in the northeast or first quadrant for the country's exports of the good shown on the horizontal axis.

Promote an Infant Industry

When production of a commodity first begins in a country, the firms producing it are often small, inexperienced, and unfamiliar with the technology they are using. Workers are also inexperienced and less efficient than they will become in time. During this breaking-in stage, costs are higher than they will be later on, and infant firms in the new industry may need temporary protection from older, established firms in other countries. So runs the infant-industry argument for tariff protection.

Thus stated, the infant-industry argument is analytically persuasive. It does not conflict with the principle of comparative advantage. In terms of our earlier analysis of trade, the argument is that the country's present production-possibility curve does not reflect its true potential. Given time to develop an industry that is now in its infancy, the production-possibility curve will shift and a potential comparative advantage will be realized. Also, note that the infant-industry argument takes a global perspective: in the long run, world economic welfare is improved because tariff protection enables a potential comparative advantage to be realized and a more efficient utilization of resources to be achieved. Thus world output is increased.

This argument has great appeal for countries in an early stage of industrialization that are eager to develop a modern industrial sector. They fear that their attempts to develop new industries will be defeated by vigorous price competition from already established firms in advanced industrial countries such as the United States, Germany, and Japan. Early in American history Alexander Hamilton (1791) forcefully advocated the infant-industry argument in his *Report on Manufactures*. His reasoning provided a rationale for the protective tariffs imposed in 1815 after Britain lifted its war-time blockade of the United States. U.S. industries that had sprung up during the War of 1812 feared the ravages of competition with the more advanced industries of Europe. Friedrich List made similar arguments in favor of a protective tariff in the United States and in Germany; later in the century, as Bismarck unified the separate German states and sought to expand their industrial capacity, he granted protection to the iron, steel, coal, and textile industries.

Despite its analytical validity and its appeal to common sense, **infant-industry protection** encounters severe difficulties in actual practice (Baldwin 1969). A country may easily end up protecting an industry where it has no long-run comparative advantage, and any scale economies or learning opportunities are not sufficient to offset other cost disadvantages. Recall from Chapter 6 the example of high-priced, capital-intensive Indonesian steel, which resulted in labor-intensive, steel-using industries such as bicyles, tools, and hardware becoming non-competitive. The steel producer can expand capacity under protection, but costs per unit still remain high. Permanent protection becomes necessary for its survival. Similarly, the 1984 Brazilian informatics law that prohibited the importation of electronic products that could be produced domestically had the result of saddling domestic industries reliant on computing power with an expensive, outmoded technology. Wrong choices result in higher prices than would be necessary with free trade.

The record of infant-industry protection is mixed, but infant industries have shown a distressing tendency to remain dependent on protection. Owners and workers in the new industry have a vested interest in it, and they will fight to preserve it. This negative effect is compounded when the protected home market is so small that it can support only a few modern plants, and consequently there is little competitive pressure for such firms to produce efficiently behind a tariff wall.

Some economists argue that a country should let the market decide which industries have the greatest potential to perform well. They doubt that government officials, no matter how dedicated, honest, and intelligent, can have the foresight to pick out, in advance, exactly those industries in which a potential comparative advantage exists. If an industry is potentially profitable, private entrepreneurs will discover it, and they will bear the cost of its learning stage just as they bear the cost of construction, capital equipment, and training labor in any new venture. If the fundamental problem is an inefficient capital market that limits the ability of an individual with a bright idea to finance those early stages of production, these economists regard direct steps to improve the functioning of the capital market as a more useful step.

Some of the distortions that an infant industry must overcome are related to externalities we considered in Chapter 5. For example, a firm may develop a more efficient method of production that can then be copied by others or it may train workers who are then hired away by competitors. A direct subsidy to that firm encourages the activity that otherwise goes unrewarded in the market and will be underproduced. In contrast, a tariff encourages firms that copy a good idea or lure away trained workers just as much as it favors the firm that is the initial innovator or trainer.

A more favourable verdict emerges if production by any firm in the industry creates a positive spillover of knowledge that benefits others. While each firm views its marginal costs as rising when it expands output, that perception ignores the positive effect on other firms that are now able to achieve lower costs. In Figure 7.3 we draw a short-run industry supply curve that shifts outward, with a lag, when cumulative industry output rises. We can think of the long-run industry supply curve sloping downward, at least until some threshold level of output is reached and the spillover benefits are exhausted. (If the spillover never attenuated, the infant industry would never catch up with producers in the industrialized world who also continued to benefit from such spillovers.) The effect

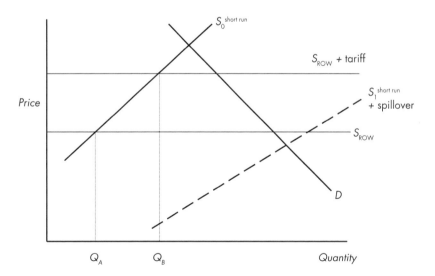

FIGURE 7.3 Infant-Industry Protection

Protection allows industry output to rise. If the increase in cumulative output allows lower costs to be achieved, the short-run industry supply curve shifts outward. For a large enough shift, the country may become a net exporter of the product.

of protection in this setting depends upon how large this spillover effect is. The impact effect is for output to rise from Q_A to Q_B along the short-run supply curve S_0. If the spillover benefit is large enough to shift the new short-run supply curve to S_1, infant industry protection has successfully launched a viable export industry. Again, the challenge is to identify industries where these conditions are relevant.

Industrial Policy and Strategic Trade

Industrial targeting may appear to be an attractive policy when one country attempts to catch up with others and follows their blueprint for development. Such a plan may provide infant-industry protection to create a competitive advantage for successively more complex industries. We address those possibilities in Chapter 11, where we consider trade and the growth prospects of developing countries. For countries that are not playing catch up, we consider two different situations where industrial targeting and strategic trade policy may allow national welfare to rise: (i) government action may shift economic profits to its own firms rather than let them be captured by other producers; and (ii) protection may allow firms to reduce their costs of production or otherwise benefit from spillovers that occur if more of the production takes place within the country's borders rather than somewhere else in the world.

Economists paid particular attention to these possibilities in the 1980s when some commentators faulted the U.S. government for its failure to pursue a more active trade policy to keep American industry from falling behind Japanese producers of high-technology products. This critique predicted that without government intervention to ensure that producers could achieve economies of scale at home, U.S. producers would be ill-prepared to compete internationally. It claimed that Japanese firms had been able to earn high profits in a closed domestic market, which allowed them to make additional sales at lower prices in foreign markets where demand was more elastic. By this line of reasoning, free trade was an outmoded policy that was no longer relevant in a world of imperfect competition (Krugman 1987).

Targeting Industries Where Profit Shifting is Possible

The opportunity to shift profits is particularly relevant in oligopolistic industries. Because significant barriers to entry exist, a firm can permanently earn economic profits without their being competed away by new entrants into the industry. Based on the Chapter 5 model of oligopoly competition, we can demonstrate how government action to ensure that its own firms earn those profits may create a gain for the country as a whole.

Consider the potential market for space age travel away from planet earth, a concept pioneered by Virgin Galactic under the leadership of Sir Richard Branson. As reported in *The Economist* (2008) hundreds of customers have put down deposits for a $200,000 ticket to reserve a seat on a future flight. The size of this market is not known with much precision, given that potential customers not only need to be wealthy but also to be sufficiently healthy to endure the rigors of space travel. Nevertheless, the prospects of economic viability are rumored to have attracted the interest of others, including Jeff Bezos, the founder of Amazon.com, through his company Blue Origin.

In terms of potential profits, Virgin Galactic is likely to have greater sales and profits if Blue Origin does not enter the market. If either company, or its government, could somehow discourage the other company from undertaking the research to develop such a spacecraft, a single monopoly producer would receive larger profits. The "payoff matrix" facing the two firms might be as shown in the matrix below.

In this matrix, p stands for Virgin Galactic producing and n stands for it not producing. P stands for Blue Origin producing, and N stands for it not producing. In each box, the number at the lower left is Blue Origin's profit and the number to the upper right is Virgin Galactic's profit. If both produce, and the market is limited to a small niche of travellers, each company absorbs a loss of $100 million. Each firm has a relatively low customer base across which to spread its large research costs. If only one firm produces, it earns $500 million because it can charge a higher price and serve more customers than when it must share the market with a competitor. If both firms view the potential market in these terms, and one firm achieves a substantial head start in developing its spacecraft, the other firm is not likely to enter, because it expects a loss if both firms end up producing.

Virgin Galactic

		p	n
		−100	0
P	−100		+500
Blue Origin			
		+500	0
N	0		0

A government might adopt a policy to shift the payoff matrix in favour of its national champion. For example, if Blue Origin receives a government subsidy of $200 million, that will ensure Blue Origin makes a profit even if Virgin Galactic enters the market. The payoff matrix shifts as follows:

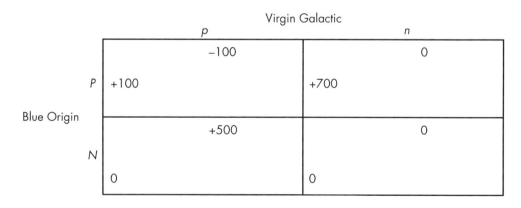

Virgin Galactic

		p	n
		−100	0
P	+100		+700
Blue Origin			
		+500	0
N	0		0

The subsidy means that if both firms enter the market, Virgin Galactic will lose $100 million, whereas Blue Origin will report profits of $100 million. Consequently, Blue Origin will enter the market without regard to what Virgin Galactic decides. But under those circumstances, Virgin Galactic will be strongly discouraged from proceeding because it faces certain losses of $100 million. Without competition from Virgin Galactic, Blue Origin earns profits of $700 million, some part of which accrues to the subsidizing government in the form of income taxes.

A less extreme outcome can be represented with the reaction curve framework from Chapter 5, as is presented in Figure 7.4. If the U.S. government offers a subsidy per trip to Blue Origin, its reaction curve shifts to the right. Blue Origin's equilibrium production is greater at W than at Z. The benefit from extra production is particularly large if the firm's marginal cost of production falls as output rises, which occurs with increasing returns to scale. Even without that gain, the United States benefits from the expansion of sales at a lower price, something that did not hold true in the case of an export subsidy under perfect competition, which was shown in Figure 6.8. The difference here is that for these extra sales marginal revenue exceeds marginal cost, and monopoly profits are transferred to the country that offers the subsidy. The situation in Figure 7.4 also suggests a gain even if the competitor is not driven out of the market. In the absence of a subsidy, Blue Origin would not expand its capacity to such an extent, if it knew Virgin Galactic's capacity would remain at the same level given at Z. The government subsidy, however, reduces the market price and makes Virgin Galactic's trips less profitable. Thus, Virgin Galactic reduces its capacity. Government intervention has assisted Blue Origin in pursuing the leadership strategy discussed in Chapter 5, where expansion of the Dutch United East India Company came at the expense of the British East India Company.

A less futuristic perspective on strategic targeting is the early analysis by Baldwin and Krugman (1988) of the competition between Airbus and Boeing in the market for medium-range, wide-bodied jet aircraft. In that case Airbus subsidized the entry of the A300 but did not deter Boeing from producing the 767 too. Baldwin and Krugman found that European subsidies clearly benefited consumers of aircraft everywhere, as more competition reduced prices faced by airlines. Also, those

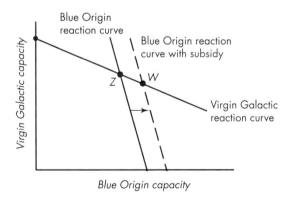

FIGURE 7.4 Subsidization of a Cournot Oligopoly Producer

A subsidy to Blue Origin shifts its reaction curve to the right and results in greater industry capacity and a lower price. Because the lower price results in a decline in Virgin Galactic's capacity, Blue Origin gains even if it must repay the subsidy.

subsidies adversely affected the profitability of Boeing, because it could not charge a monopoly price for the 767. In addition, because Boeing sold fewer airplanes, its cost of production per plane rose as it learned less from its smaller cumulative output. Although U.S. consumers benefited, the United States is a net exporter of aircraft, and therefore Boeing's losses more than offset those consumer gains.

With respect to Europe itself, the outcome is more ambiguous. Consumers gained but taxpayers had to provide the subsidy that allowed Airbus to enter the market. Baldwin and Krugman found that Europe either had a small gain or a small loss as a result of its intervention, depending upon the way future consumer gains were calculated. Similarly, for the world as a whole, the gain from E.C. intervention is ambiguous. Entry reduces the distortion caused by Boeing's monopoly pricing, but entry requires the additional outlay for research and development and other fixed costs of a second competitor. The Baldwin–Krugman calculation indicates the world as a whole lost from European intervention, although by looking at a single generation of products, they ignore potential gains from the more rapid introduction of innovations that is likely to occur under a duopoly in comparison with a monopoly.

Other Aspects of Strategic Targeting

Even the ambiguous answers that emerge in the examples above must be qualified on two additional grounds. One depends upon the nature of competition within the targeted industry, and the other on circumstances outside the industry.

If barriers to entry are not substantial, the higher profits possible with government assistance may attract new entrants into the industry. With more firms producing, more resources must be devoted to duplicate the fixed costs of production, and fewer economies of scale will be achieved by each firm. More competition lowers prices and may eliminate the economic profits that the government hoped to shift to its own producers.

Additionally, behaviour under the Cournot model assumes that each firm sets its capacity or output depending upon the output choice of the other. If firms instead compete by setting prices, as assumed under the Bertrand model of competition, different implications follow. If the firms produce an identical product, they will be driven to marginal cost pricing in equilibrium. If they produce differentiated products and retain some market power, in equilibrium their production is higher than under Cournot competition.[4] Of particular importance from the standpoint of strategic trade policy is the demonstration by Eaton and Grossman (1986) that optimal policy in this case calls for an export tax, not an export subsidy.

The discussion thus far considers industry targeting in a partial equilibrium setting, but there also are general equilibrium implications in the rest of the economy. If the industry requires an input that cannot easily be attracted away from other industries, promoting that industry may simply result in a large increase in returns to owners of that input without achieving much of an increase in production. Conversely, if promoting aerospace ventures allows firms in that industry to attract engineers away from other industries, such as the design of environmental control devices, the net gain to the nation depends upon monopoly profits being greater in the former industry than the latter industry.

---

4 That difference arises because when firm A lowers its price, it assumes that firm B will reduce its output as necessary to keep its own price constant. Firm B instead responds to A's lower price by reducing its own price, and the total quantity supplied to the market increases. See Markusen, et al. (1995).

Targeting Industries where Positive Externalities Are Important

In addition to profit shifting, a second reason for intervention may exist if production at home generates positive externalities or spillovers. If additional output by one firm, and the learning it acquires, spills over to other firms, the analysis is similar to our discussion of infant industries above. Again, the source of any external economies must be considered carefully in claiming that large gains will result from government intervention.

Spillovers may exist between industries. Advances in one industry may benefit another industry. For example, new semiconductors may allow more efficient computers to be designed and produced. If the new semiconductor becomes available to all producers at the same time, then computer producers everywhere benefit. If the new semiconductor is only available in the country where it is developed, and at least in the initial stages of production is a nontraded good, then computer producers in that country with access to the new semiconductor will have an advantage over producers elsewhere. During the 1980s U.S. producers of supercomputers were worried about their access to fast chips produced by their Japanese competitor, Fujitsu. Fujitsu would grab the lead in designing, testing, and delivering a new generation of supercomputers if its own scientists and engineers could work with the new chips before they became available to U.S. competitors. While the advantage in that case may be only temporary, it can be quite significant in an industry where product life is short. If this spillover is particularly important, we might expect a semiconductor producer and a computer producer to merge, irrespective of trade policy.

Semiconductors and Strategic Trade Policy

What effects are important in evaluating policies that restrict access to the domestic market and rely upon import protection as a form of export promotion? As suggested in general terms above, such a strategy may be successful as a result of allowing domestic producers to achieve economies of scale or reduce costs through learning by doing. The profits that can be earned in a protected home market may allow domestic producers to expand capacity and deter competitors from expanding. Because the significance of these factors cannot be demonstrated in the abstract, we again turn to a numerical calculation that takes into account these various effects.

In another early example of such analysis, Baldwin and Krugman (1988b) present a simulation model to assess whether closure of the Japanese semiconductor market to U.S. competitors was a critical step in allowing their ascendancy in the industry. In contrast to the previous examples of an integrated world market, here segmented markets are central to the analysis. Baldwin and Krugman ignore the extent to which the learning from output by one firm spills over to benefit other firms, and therefore they may overstate the benefits from a closed market if the international spillovers subsequently reported by Irwin and Klenow (1994) are recognized. In any event, Baldwin and Krugman conclude that restricted entry into the Japanese market for 16K Dynamic Random Access Memory chips (DRAMs) was critical to the success of Japanese producers in achieving sufficient economies of scale to be competitive with U.S. producers.

They project that Japanese entry, however, resulted in higher prices both in the United States and in Japan than would have occurred under a policy of free trade, because the market would not have been split among as many firms. Potential gains from protection are dissipated by the entry of more firms, which duplicates fixed costs of entry and results in less output and learning by each firm. If the United States had reacted by closing its market, and no trade were possible, Japan would have become even worse off by being confined to its own limited market. The United States would have become worse off, too, because its firms would have become smaller, benefited from less learning, and had higher marginal costs. A trade war becomes more expensive to both countries than in the case of constant costs of production because both countries lose economies of scale.

Any verdict on actual trade policy has been even more complicated than the simulation models described above. Restrictions in the semiconductor market negotiated in 1986 by Japan and the United States demonstrate some of the complexities. Japanese producers were forced to raise prices to avoid charges of dumping. The higher price resulted in a major transfer of profits to Japanese firms, because they already controlled over 80 percent of the U.S. market for DRAMs. That benefit left them even better prepared to finance production of the next generation of memory chips. Their continued domination of this segment of the market would have been even more likely, if not for the entry of Korean producers who may have benefited from their own government's targeting strategy. In the case of another type of memory chips, EPROMs, Japanese producers accounted for less than 40 percent of the market. U.S. producers had sufficient capacity to meet additional demand generated by the agreement, and Japanese firms had less incentive to act collusively when demand recovered (Tyson 1992).

Although plausible cases may exist for trade intervention in some industries, who is going to pick the "winners" and distinguish them from the "losers" who should not be protected? If this task falls to an elected legislature, politics and the desire of powerful elected officials to protect their constituents are likely to dominate the outcome. There is no reason to believe that the executive branch of the government would be any better than the legislature in picking winners. Casual observers assumed that Tokyo had this problem solved, and that all of its choices had paid off. A closer look at Japan's experience, however, suggests this presumption of uniform success is unwarranted. As noted by Noland and Pack (2003), over 80 percent of Japanese budget subsidies in the 1955–80 period were provided to agriculture. With respect to the performance of the specific manufacturing industries that were favored, researchers have not detected any systematic increase in their returns to scale, capital accumulation, or factor productivity (Beason and Weinstein 1996). While any conclusive judgment is not possible, because economists cannot say how the Japanese economy would have performed in the absence of its industrial policy, many regard its impressive growth record as primarily driven by a very high savings and investment rate and the development of a huge stock of human capital.

DUMPING

An increasingly common way that industries worldwide have received protection is by alleging that imported goods benefit from unfair trade practices. Two such situations arise if imported products are dumped at unfairly low prices or if they receive government subsidies. In fact, the rules of the World Trade Organization allow governments to take actions that offset the unfair practices. Complaints about dumping are far more prevalent than complaints about subsidies. From January 1995 to June 2005, the WTO reports that 2,743 antidumping cases were initiated worldwide, compared to 178 countervailing duty cases to address foreign subsidies (WTO 2006). Therefore, we focus on dumping.

Because transport costs and border regulations do separate national markets, firms may choose to discriminate across markets and charge different prices in different countries. When the firm chooses to charge a higher price in the home market and a lower price in the foreign market, economists refer to the practice as dumping. We first demonstrate how dumping represents a profit-maximizing strategy for the firm and then consider the effects of dumping on the importing country.

The firm will distinguish between markets because the elasticity of demand is not the same in each market. The firm often benefits from protection in the home market, due either to high transport costs or various tariff and nontariff barriers that keep out foreign competitors. Because foreign substitutes are not available, demand is less elastic than in foreign markets where the firm's product must compete with producers from many other countries.

Figure 7.5 presents an extreme example of this rationale for dumping. The firm faces a downward sloping demand curve, denoted D, in the home market but must act as a perfectly competitive firm in the foreign market, where it faces a horizontal demand curve, denoted D'. If there is no foreign trade, the firm will produce Q_1 of output and charge the price P_1. Now suppose the firm has the

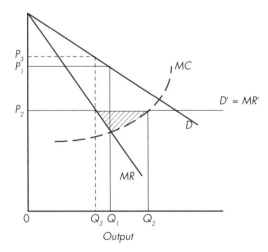

FIGURE 7.5 Dumping as an Example of Price Discrimination

This firm charges a price of P_3 and sells a volume Q_3 in the home market. It then exports volume $Q_2 - Q_3$ at a price of P_2, thereby maximizing total profits earned in the two separate markets.

opportunity to export its output at the fixed world price P_2. If it can prevent the exported output from being brought back into the domestic market, to maximize its profit the firm will now raise its domestic price to P_3 and reduce its domestic sales to Q_3 and export the quantity Q_2–Q_3 at the world price P_2.

At first glance it may seem counter-intuitive that the firm reduces its sales in the higher-priced market, but on closer examination the firm is simply following the general rule of profit maximization: it equates marginal revenue and marginal cost, and does so in each market. The marginal revenue curve for sales in the domestic market is downward-sloping, but it becomes horizontal at P_2 for export sales at $D' = MR'$. Therefore, no output will be sold in the home market that yields a marginal revenue less than P_2. On the other hand, exports are profitable out to the point at which $MR = MC$. The opportunity to sell in foreign markets at the lower world price increases the firm's profits by the amounts indicated by the shaded areas in Figure 7.5 – the difference between MR' and MC for the output that is exported. Again, this whole argument depends on the assumption that the two markets can be kept separated: the exported output cannot be returned to the home market. If it could be returned, the domestic price would fall to P_2 and the country would become a net importer.

This result is a special case of a general proposition about price discrimination. A firm that sells its output in two or more separate markets will maximize its profits by equating MR and MC in each market. For given MC conditions, the price will be higher the smaller the elasticity of demand in that market. This same reasoning explains why students in many countries benefit from lower airfares than business travellers. Airlines need not believe that students are more deserving, only that their demand is more elastic.

Government Responses to Dumping

The WTO recognizes dumping as an unfair trade practice. If dumping is found to exist, and the domestic industry is injured by the dumping, then an antidumping duty can be imposed.

Governments do have a valid economic interest in preventing **predatory dumping**, but the conditions for it to occur are rarely observed. Predatory dumping implies that foreign firms cut prices temporarily in order to drive domestic firms out of business, after which they will raise prices to exploit a monopoly advantage. It is more likely in industries in which start-up costs are high or in which other barriers prevent the entry of new firms. Although national antitrust or competition laws are intended to address such practices, enforcing them against foreign firms may not always be feasible. That is one justification for international agreements against dumping. In the vast majority of dumping cases, however, offending foreign producers account for small shares of the relevant market, which makes the predatory outcome unlikely. Foreign firms have little likelihood of driving domestic competitors out of the market.

Even when they cannot drive a competitor out of the market, firms find dumping to be a profit-maximizing strategy. Within a given country, a domestic firm cannot be restricted from charging a lower price to enter a new market. Firms that compete internationally cannot apply this same strategy, however, or they will be subject to dumping complaints. If firms in each country were to pursue a dumping strategy, would that be desirable from the standpoint of world welfare? In Chapter 5 we encountered the example of reciprocal dumping in the U.S. and German chemical industries, but at that point we did not examine whether U.S. or German welfare rose as a result. Consumers in both countries gain from greater competition and lower prices. Yet, the expense of transporting identical goods into and out of the country is a waste of resources. While no general rule can be derived, the case of reciprocal dumping of mineral water in the Swedish market reported in the following box suggests that the gains from import competition are likely to dominate. Nevertheless, if Country A's market is open and its producers must compete against goods dumped by its competitors from B, but B's market is closed, producers in A are likely to complain of an uneven playing field.

Discriminating Tastes in the Swedish Market for Water

Is a country likely to gain from importing the same commodity that it exports, especially when transports costs are high relative to the value of production, there are few technological economies of scale in production to be achieved, and the two products are nearly identical? Economic theory suggests that trade under these circumstances, which results from reciprocal dumping, is more likely to result in a loss due to the waste of resources in hauling the goods back and forth.

Richard Friberg and Mattias Ganslandt show that Sweden's two-way trade in mineral water conforms to these conditions, but even here world welfare would fall if such trade were banned (2006). Although there are barriers to entry in establishing a brand name in this market, there are several brands available. In the less popular still water segment, consumers can choose among the Norwegian brand Imsdal, the French brands Evian and Vittel, and the Swedish brand Blåvitt, with imports accounting for over 60 percent of the market. In the sparkling water segment, Swedish brands account for over 97 percent of the market, but even here sales of Perrier (France), Verdiana and Vittoria (Italy), and Rogaska (Slovenia) occur, among a list of 17 imports.

The authors' econometric analysis shows that one brand of water is a pretty close substitute for any other brand, and companies are only able to mark up prices above marginal costs by 20 percent. If imports are banned, consumers lose from less variety and higher prices set by domestic firms, but the loss is limited due to the relatively small differences among varieties and the low markups charged. Profits rise for domestic firms and fall for foreign firms. The net effect is a small decline in world welfare. Sweden, however, would gain due to the higher profits earned by its domestic firms. Transport costs are an important part of this story, because they allow domestic firms to serve the market more profitably than foreign firms. The fact that one of the main Swedish producers, Blåvitt, is located in the far north of the country results in the potential gain from lower domestic transport costs being too small to offset the consumer loss if imported water is not available.

Other Issues in Implementing Antidumping Laws

A further controversial aspect of antidumping laws is that in many countries they prohibit sales below the average cost of production. As a result foreign firms can be found guilty of dumping even when they charge the same price in all markets. Because the average cost of production is interpreted to include an average rate of return to capital, this rules out sales below a full-cost price, which commonly take place during business downturns. The domestic practice of holding a sale to clear out overstocked merchandise is not legal by this standard. This form of dumping can be observed in competitive markets where individual firms have no power to set prices and discriminate against some buyers and favor others. Both foreign and domestic firms sell at a lower price, which still covers their variable costs of production, and they hope for more favorable conditions in the future that will allow them to earn an average rate of return. Yet, the dumping law says this strategy is legal for the domestic firm and illegal for the foreign firm.

The actual practice of calculating dumping margins raises further concerns. Foreign firms are required to provide enormous amounts of accounting data in computer-readable form to defend themselves against such charges. If they cannot do so within a brief period of time, administrators use the "best information available," which often means figures submitted by those who bring the complaint, to determine the margin of dumping. Given those circumstances, unsuccessful dumping cases in the United States typically do not fail because the Department of Commerce rules that no dumping occurs, but instead because the U.S. International Trade Commission finds that the alleged dumping does not cause material injury to the U.S. industry.

Even when cases do not result in the imposition of antidumping duties, the firm accused of dumping must cover the high legal costs of a defense, which may deter it or other firms from competing aggressively in the foreign market. Thomas Prusa (1992) cites U.S. evidence from the early 1980s that suggests when cases are withdrawn (roughly one third), industries do roughly as well as when they win. Apparently dumping actions serve as a signal to foreign competitors to collude and negotiate a settlement that approximates the monopoly cartel solution identified above. Christopher Taylor (2004) does not find evidence of this pattern in U.S. cases over the 1990–97 period. In contrast, for new cases brought in the E.U. during the 1996–2004 period, Aleksander Rutkowski (2007) observes that prices rise and imports fall more in cases that are withdrawn compared to those terminated for other reasons. A further expected result obtained by Konings and Vandenbussche (2005) is that the profit margins of E.U. firms rise when AD duties are imposed, a clear payoff to those who bring successful cases.

Trade in Shrimp: Has Trade Converted a Delicacy into Standard Fare?

In most of the developed world, the price of shrimp has fallen over the past decade, as shrimp farming in warmer countries has greatly expanded the available supply. That expansion has transformed what was once a luxury product of the elite into one that has become increasingly popular at parties and holiday celebrations.

Not surprisingly, as imports have risen, shrimp have been the subject of several international trade disputes. In September 2001 the E.U. established regulations that required all imports of shrimp to be free of chloramphenicol, an antibiotic used by producers to combat salmonella. The E.U. initiated more stringent testing of shrimp imported from various Asian countries. It halted imports from China in January 2002 and applied a 100 percent testing regime to imports from Thailand. E.U. consumers shifted their purchases to shrimp caught in northern waters. Japan also drastically reduced its imports due to similar concerns over contamination.

Did changing trade patterns and falling prices mean that products that could no longer be sold in the E.U. or Japan were being dumped in other markets? In December 2003 the U.S. brought antidumping cases against producers in Brazil, China, Ecuador, India, Thailand, and Vietnam, and in February 2005 imposed final antidumping duties on them. As shown in Table 7.1, the U.S. market expanded by over 20 percent between 2001 and 2003, but U.S. producers' share of the market fell from 15.4 percent to 12.0 percent. Essentially, all of the market growth was captured by the six countries named in the AD actions, as the market share for imports from other countries also fell.

While U.S. production was similar in both years, the price received fell by more than 20 percent. As a result, net income as a share of sales fell from a small profit of 0.2 percent to a loss of 8.0 percent. Daily wages, which are based on the value of the catch, fell from $26.17 to $24.25. Given these circumstances, U.S. supply would appear to be relatively inelastic.

Was the plight of U.S. fishermen due to dumping from abroad, or were foreign producers simply able to produce more cheaply? U.S. shrimp were caught in the wild over a season limited to May–December, while foreign shrimp were farmed year round in warmer waters in countries with lower wage rates. Foreigners shifted from producing black tiger shrimp to producing white shrimp, because a greater density per acre could be achieved.

TABLE 7.1 The U.S. Shrimp Market, 2001–2003, millions of pounds

	2001	2003	AD duty
U.S. consumption	1,007	1,217	
U.S. production	182	183	
U.S. shipments	154	146	
U.S. imports	853	1,066	
Brazil	21.6	48.0	4.97–67.80
China	*	*	0.07–112.81
Ecuador	55.6	73.1	1.97–4.42
India	71.8	99.2	4.94–15.36
Thailand	296.4	281.0	5.29–6.82
Vietnam	72.8	124.5	4.30–25.76
All other	274	271	

Source: United States International Trade Commission (2005).

* denotes figures not reported to the public, in order to maintain the confidentiality of Chinese producers subject to the complaint and those who were not.

The strength of any incentive to dump in the U.S. market would likely depend upon how significant the shift away from foreign markets was. Thai and Chinese exports to the E.U. fell by 50 percent and to Japan by 11 percent between 2002 and 2003, while U.S. imports from the two countries rose by 24 percent. Such a pattern suggests output was diverted to the U.S. market. However, sales by India, Ecuador, and Brazil to the E.U. were 8 times greater than the Thai–Chinese figure, and sales to the E.U. by the former group rose by 48 percent between 2003 and 2004.[5]

The Department of Commerce (DOC) determined that shrimp from these countries were dumped.[6] Under U.S. antidumping procedures, no attention is paid to consumer interests, and the very small domestic share of the market is not relevant in balancing consumer costs and producer gains from any duties levied. Likewise, no foreign policy interests are considered and no review by the President occurs, as would be the case if the industry had instead asked for protection from imports of shrimp that were fairly traded, the trade policy provision relevant in the steel case presented in Chapter 6. Once the U.S. International Trade Commission (USITC) determines that the dumped imports have materially injured the domestic industry, the duties determined by the DOC are imposed.

The U.S. action was not the end of judicial activity in this case. Ecuador challenged the U.S. determination of AD duties in a dispute settlement case brought to the WTO in November 2005. In January 2007 the Dispute Settlement Body (DSB) ruled in favor of Ecuador, that the U.S. practice of ignoring sales at prices higher than normal value created an upward bias in the duties levied.

Who Uses Antidumping Laws?

During the 1980s, Australia, Canada, the European Union, and the United States accounted for 96 percent of all dumping cases filed. That pattern is not surprising, because the larger the country, the more likely that measures to prevent dumping will benefit domestic producers rather than other foreign producers. Dumping margins found in these cases far exceed the average tariffs imposed on manufactured goods, another sign that seeking protection through AD laws is an attractive strategy.

The popularity of this policy tool is spreading. In the 1990s, many more countries came to rely on antidumping duties to protect domestic industries. As shown in Table 7.2, from 1995 through June, 2005 the largest initiators of antidumping cases were India, the U.S., and the E.U. (WTO 2006). The countries most often named in such complaints were China, E.U. members, and Korea. Within this period, the number of cases brought peaked in 2001, a year of depressed economic activity in many parts of the world. Base metals and chemicals accounted for half of the cases brought, a pattern quite

---

5 These comparisons are based on figures retrieved from the United Nations Commodity Trade Statistics database at http://comtrade.un.org.

6 Because two of the cited countries were regarded as non-market economies, the DOC used prices of inputs from surrogate countries to establish a normal value for shrimp produced in China and Vietnam. The surrogate for China was India, and for Vietnam was Bangladesh. Note the treatment of non-market economies in the E.U. shoe case presented as a Case Study in this chapter.

TABLE 7.2 Summary Statistics for Anti-Dumping Cases, 1995–2005 (Leading Participants)

Initiating country	Cases brought	Measures adopted	Country targeted	Cases to defend	Measures imposed
India	412	309	China	434	317
U.S.	358	229	E.U.	403	231
E.U.	318	200	Korea		123
WTO Total	2,743	1,728			

Source: World Trade Organization (2006).

similar to the preceding decade when a different set of countries was involved. Across all countries, 63 percent of cases resulted in antidumping measures being applied, with complainants having above-average success in India.

Figure 7.6 shows the main targets of E.U. anti-dumping actions by a somewhat different metric, the number of anti-dumping measures in place at the end of 2006. Anti-dumping measures are periodically reviewed and allowed to lapse if dumping, or the threat of dumping, is no longer a cause of injury to the domestic industry. The significant role of China in international trade is suggested by its number one ranking. The case study at the end of the chapter suggests some of the special factors that arise in cases involving China. The pattern is also suggestive of one that Blonigen and Bown

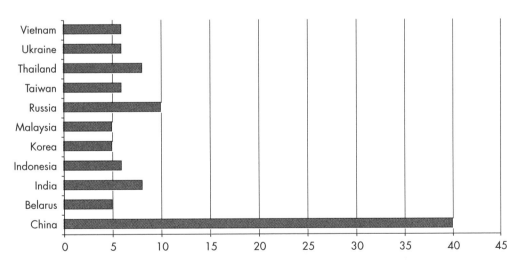

FIGURE 7.6 E.U. Anti-dumping Measures in Force

Source: the European Commission at http://europa.eu.int/comm/trade/issues/respectrules/anti_dumping/stats.htm

This figure shows the most common countries of origin of imports subject to anti-dumping measures in force as of Dec 31 2006.

(2003) find for the United States. They ask the following question: if antidumping cases have such a high rate of success, why do we not see even more of them? They demonstrate that industries are much less likely to bring cases against producers in countries that can effectively retaliate, and they find positive rulings are less likely in those circumstances, too.

Some commentators regard dumping cases as a substitute for tariffs and other trade barriers now constrained by the WTO. Others consider a country's reliance on dumping actions as part of a broader approach to trade and competition policy. Some countries may not rely on dumping actions because domestic firms can effectively limit imports through collusive business practices rather than resort to dumping laws. Any attempt to negotiate tighter limits on the way antidumping restrictions are used is likely to require simultaneous attention to other uncompetitive practices.

THE POLITICAL ECONOMY OF TRADE POLICY

Economists are on firmest ground in predicting who will win or lose if a trade restriction is adopted. *Why* a government chooses that particular policy poses a much more difficult question. Under what circumstances will individual winners or losers form an effective group to influence policy? Institutionally, who should they attempt to influence? Presidents and the executive branch of government, elected legislators, or bureaucrats who write and administer rules and regulations? What factors will improve a group's chances of success in having its preferred policy implemented? The field of political economy addresses these sorts of questions.

The Median Voter Model

Economists have addressed the complicated set of questions above in piecemeal fashion. One starting point is the median voter model, which assumes a world of direct democracy: every issue is submitted to the voters in a referendum. If voters were ordered by their preference on a given issue, such as the appropriate tariff to levy on imported cars, then the median voter would play a key role: half of the group would desire a higher tariff, and half would desire a lower tariff. The preference of the median voter would determine the outcome of a referendum in which everyone voted, because any lower value could be defeated by a majority of voters and similarly any higher value could be defeated by a majority of voters.

In the case of the factor endowments model from Chapter 4, this approach yields the prediction that in a labor-scarce country, labor will vote to impose trade restrictions on labor-intensive goods. If the median voter is a worker with little capital, this outcome follows. Figure 7.7 shows the extreme case that results when all workers are identical and none own any capital. There is no smooth continuum of individual preferences favoring a progressively higher tariff. Rather, all workers favour a prohibitive tariff that eliminates the competition they face in producing labor-intensive goods. Conversely, for a labor-abundant country, we expect labor to favor subsidies to labor-intensive exports (Mayer 1984).

The median voter predictions may be misleading because most governments are far from direct democracies. If voters consider more than one issue at a time or if not everyone votes, the role of the

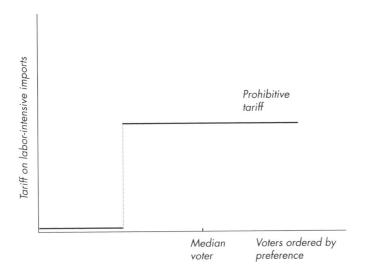

FIGURE 7.7 The Median Voter Model and the Heckscher–Ohlin World

In a labor-scarce country where workers own no capital and capital income is received by a few individuals, the median voter will be a worker who prefers a prohibitive tariff on labor-intensive imports.

median voter is less central. Also, the factor endowments model assumes long-run adjustments, and individuals may not recognize what consequences emerge in the long run. For example, in a labor-abundant country restaurant workers may not expect any gain from a subsidy to apparel exports. Nevertheless, Dutt and Mitra (2002) do observe results that give some importance to income distribution and the position of the median voter: for a given increase in inequality in an economy, protection will rise in countries with higher capital/labor endowments, whereas in countries with low capital/labor endowments, the increase in inequality leads to lower tariffs.

The median voter model pays no attention to the intensity of voter preferences. Capitalists with a very strong interest in free trade due to the gains they receive have no way to make their preference felt. If other votes can be considered at the same time, however, logrolling or trading of votes may occur. Capitalists may be willing to vote for training programs, regional development programs, urban renewal, or any other issue that labor regards as important enough to modify its vote on trade policy.

Protection for Sale

Gene Grossman and Elhanan Helpman (1994) formulate a more comprehensive model to predict trade policy, termed "protection for sale." They posit that politicians do attach some importance to consumer welfare and the price of imports, but also to the monetary contributions of lobbyists. In other words, monetary contributions cause politicians to attach more weight to the interests of those who can effectively organize and lobby. Their framework suggests that when demand for imports is more elastic and the import share is greater, governments are less likely to impose trade barriers, because the deadweight efficiency loss is greater. If the industry is organized to lobby, however, then a larger import share means that there are fewer domestic producers who will gain from the trade restrictions and make political contributions. Alternatively, if the domestic industry is very large, it will gain a lot from trade restrictions. The government will receive more political contributions when the import share is low, and it will set a higher tariff in those circumstances. That prediction contradicts the conventional wisdom that the sunset industries lobby is most successful in gaining protection.

Testing these predictions is not straightforward, because the relevant policy setting is one where a government acts unilaterally, not as the result of international negotiations with other countries where additional interests and compromises enter. Several authors have used the set of U.S. non-tariff barriers imposed in 1983 to estimate the "protection for sale" model, and their results provide strong support for its predictions. From those estimates, we also can infer the relative importance politicians assign to consumer interests versus lobbying activity. One study finds that consumer interests are 25 to 50 times more important!

Other Issues of Collective Action

The importance of short-run interests is consistent with the specific factors model of Chapter 4, and that approach suggests a different interpretation than the long-run consequences cited above. Stephen Magee (1980) suggests that such a long-run view, where all labor perceives its interests to be the same and all capital likewise votes as a bloc, does not describe the U.S. political process well. He noted whether Congressional testimony on the 1974 Trade Act by unions and manufacturers' associations within the same industry advocated the same position, as we would expect from a short-run, specific-factors model of trade, or whether their testimony supported different positions, as we would expect from the long-run Stolper–Samuelson theorem. Magee reports that in 19 of 21 industries, labor and capital took the same position, a result that supports a short-run interpretation of interest-group participation.[7] The specific factors model seems all the more relevant, because the prospect of protection slows down any shift of workers and owners out of industries that face more import competition.

The specific factors model also provides a ready identification of impact effects when a decision in a single industry is under consideration. For labor and capital outside the industry, their primary role is as consumers, who often feel only minor effects of any policy. For example, the E.U.'s highly restrictive sugar policy that resulted in a domestic price four times the world price cost the typical E.U. family €64 annually (Oxfam 2004). The relatively small effect may result in many individuals not being concerned enough to voice any opposition to the policy. Voters may remain rationally ignorant on many issues, because the time and effort necessary to become informed exceeds any loss from an unfavorable policy.

Even when the cost of protection is more substantial, individuals often do not organize to change policy. For example, when the Japanese auto VER cost U.S. consumers over $1,000 per car in the

---

7 The only two exceptions were petroleum (a net import industry) where only labor favored restrictions, and tobacco (a net export industry) where only labor favored free trade.

1980s, no consumer interest groups successfully raised money to lobby for the policy to be reversed. Presumably, any one person feels his or her contribution is unlikely to influence the outcome. Rather, each individual expects to free-ride on the efforts of others. That calculus often results in no action at all. When benefits from trade restrictions are more highly concentrated than costs, the expected return to special-interest voters is greater. Because there are fewer beneficiaries to organize into a lobby that favors trade restrictions, free-riding will be less common. When the protected industry produces an input used by others, as in the case of steel used in car and machinery production recounted in Chapter 6, we might expect that the balance between those seeking protection and those opposed to it would be more even. Yet, claims for protection in the steel industry have been quite successful.

Although trade barriers are not as economically efficient as direct cash payments to reward a particular sector, they appear politically to represent a more credible commitment of assistance than alternative policies. Why they retain this preferred position is a question that economists and political scientists cannot answer very convincingly.

Summary of Key Concepts

1. Claims that protection will raise domestic employment or eliminate a trade deficit ignore important macroeconomic relationships in the economy.
2. A refusal by high-wage countries to trade with low-wage countries ignores the fact that high-wage countries are more productive. In some industries, the productivity advantage will be so great that firms can export in spite of high wages, while in other industries, where the productivity advantage is not as great, the country will be a net importer.
3. Trade barriers raise the real income of scarce factors, which gives them a big incentive to lobby for protection.
4. A country large enough to affect international prices can improve its terms of trade by imposing a tariff or an export tax. Retaliation by trading partners may leave all countries worse off.
5. Protection for an infant industry may allow it to cover fixed costs of entry and learn enough to become competitive eventually.
6. Strategic trade policy to subsidize exports may allow a country to shift monopoly profits to its own producers, or to benefit from lower costs and greater productivity with higher domestic production. How easily a government can identify appropriate industries and design effective policies remains controversial.
7. A firm with market power can maximize its profits by charging a lower price in the export market than it does at home. International trading rules allow governments to offset such dumping when it hurts domestic producers.
8. Governments are more likely to grant protection to industries where the benefits are more concentrated than the costs imposed on others.

CASE STUDY

Are Chinese and Vietnamese Shoes Dumped in the E.U. Market?

In October 2006 the E.U. imposed antidumping duties on leather footwear imported from China (PRC) at the rate of 16.5 percent and from Vietnam at a rate of 10 percent. Is this a case of careful economic analysis to restrict unfair trade or a tool of old-fashioned protectionism? Is this a case where predation is likely to result in an Asian monopoly over the E.U. footwear market?

The E.U. first had to determine the extent of Asian dumping. The E.U. did not recognize either the PRC or Vietnam as a market economy. The E.U. further considered whether individual producers warranted market treatment based on several factors: Was the firm subject to government controls on what they produced and sold? Did it respond to market conditions in making business decisions? Did it keep accounting records in accord with international standards? Had it benefited from favorable transfers of state assets? And could it exchange currency at non-market rates? Only one Chinese firm was regarded as sufficiently independent of government support and influence to warrant market economy treatment, but that firm did not have any domestic sales during the investigation period to allow the determination of normal value in the domestic market. Therefore, the E.U. relied upon a surrogate value from a country whose firms produced similar goods and had enough domestic sales to establish an appropriate normal value. The E.U. chose Brazil as the appropriate surrogate country, given inadequate cooperation by producers in other countries to ensure a representative price of comparable products from them.

The responding countries objected that Brazil had a much higher standard of living than they did, and that the domestic price in that country was not representative of their costs of production. For example, based on purchasing power parity measures of GDP per capita, Brazil's $8,300 exceeds

the PRC at $6,800 and Vietnam at $2,800. Nevertheless, based on a comparison of the export prices of the PRC and Vietnam with this normal value, the E.U. found country-wide dumping margins of 28.9 percent for the PRC and 70.1 percent for Vietnam.

The E.U. further considered whether this dumping resulted in injury to the domestic industry, and what antidumping duty would be necessary to eliminate this injury. Table 7.3 reports the values for important economic variables observed over the period to determine injury (2001–2004) as well as the investigation period when imports surged (April 2004 to March 2005).

European consumption was rather stagnant over this period, while there was a four-fold increase in imports from China, and imports from Vietnam more than doubled. The market share of these latter two countries rose from 9 percent to 23 percent, while the domestic E.U. share fell from 27 percent to 18 percent. Some of the import expansion of these two countries came at the expense of other foreign countries, but more came at the expense of E.U. producers. The E.U. considered whether any other factors could have contributed to the decline in price and the reduction in orders for E.U. production. They rejected possibilities such as declining E.U. export sales, changes in consumer tastes, appreciation of the euro, or increased E.U. production costs.

The E.U. also assessed whether there were any other domestic interest that ought to be considered. They concluded that the effect on consumer prices would be small because of the availability of goods from other sources. Based on an additional calculation of the extent of underselling by foreign producers, the E.U. determined that the appropriate duties to eliminate injury from the dumped imports were the 16.5 percent and 10 percent rates cited above, to be applied for a duration of two years, not the more standard five years.

TABLE 7.3 E.U. Footwear Imports and the Competitive Pressures (millions of pairs of shoes, thousands of employees)

	2001	2004	Investigation Prd
E.U. consumption	781.2	699.6	714.2
Chinese exports to E.U.	15.6	30.7	63.0
Vietnamese exports to E.U.	51.4	103.2	102.6
Domestic sales	190.1	133.1	126.6
Price of domestic goods	€19.7	€18.6	€18.2
Price of investigated imports	€11.8	€8.8	€8.5
Domestic employment	84.7	61.6	57.0

Source: Council Regulation (EC) No. 1472 (2006).

CASE STUDY QUESTIONS

1. Why does the E.U. distinguish between market economies and non-market economies in evaluating cases of dumping? What evidence would you consider to determine whether Brazil was a good surrogate country for Vietnam?

2. What demand conditions would warrant a policy of price discrimination by Chinese and Vietnamese producers to charge a lower price in the E.U. market?

3. If anti-dumping duties are unlikely to have a negative effect on E.U. consumers, are they likely to have a positive effect on E.U. producers? What factors determine the price change that will occur when anti-dumping duties are imposed?

Questions for Study and Review

1. If a country experiences a recession and the demand for steel falls, why are economists skeptical of a strategy to impose tariffs on imports of steel in order to preserve jobs in the steel industry? How are job prospects in other industries affected by the imposition of tariffs on steel? When the economy recovers and demand for steel rises, what political problems arise in subsequently adjusting tariffs?

2. "To show solidarity with underpaid workers in poor countries who are exploited in sweatshops and made to work in unsatisfactory conditions, the European Union should restrict imports from countries where such conditions are allowed to exist." How would E.U. restrictions affect both domestic and foreign workers, and the amount of trade that occurs?

3. High tariffs are often imposed in the E.U. and the U.S. on imports of labor-intensive goods such as apparel and footwear. How do those tariffs affect the distribution of income, according to the Stolper–Samuelson theorem? Why will eliminating a tariff on clothing have a different effect on income distribution than eliminating a tariff on airplanes?

4. a. Consider the import market shown below. Confirm that the initial equilibrium price is €45 and the quantity is 55.

$$M_d = 100 - P \text{ and } M_s = -80 + 3P \qquad (7.1)$$

    b. Now determine the consequences of imposing a tariff of €20 per unit. Calculate the gain in the terms of trade, the loss in economic efficiency from the decline in imports, and the net effect on the importing country. Also, calculate the loss for the world as a whole (including both the importer and the exporter) from this policy.

    c. If the demand curve were to shift inward and become $M_d = 50 - P$, determine the new equilibrium price and quantity and then impose the same tariff. Explain why the consequences of the tariff for national efficiency change, while the impact on world efficiency remains the same.

5. A business projects that its costs from initiating production of a new toy in Country B will be $120 in the first year, $100 in the second year, and $80 in the third year, after which the toy will become obsolete. It will face competition from producers in country A, whose costs will remain $100 for all three years. How does this situation represent issues that arise in promoting an infant industry, and when is the case for government intervention most convincing? How should the decision-maker account for the fact that a dollar earned in three years is worth less than a dollar spent today?

6. India argues that infant-industry protection of its automobile industry is necessary. What factors support this claim? How would you assess the benefits and the costs from targeting this industry versus the toy industry?

7. "Russian wages are so low that European producers will require additional protection to maintain current wages and generous welfare state benefits." Evaluate the economic basis for this statement.

8. How can subsidizing exports and accepting a decline in a country's terms of trade make a country better off?

9. Suppose two firms, one U.S. and the other French, compete in the satellite launching market as Cournot duopolists who take the output of their competitor as given in determining their own capacity. Their profit-maximizing strategies can be represented by the following reaction functions:

$$Q_{us} = .5(A - MC_{us}) - .5\, Q_f \qquad (7.2)$$

$$Q_f = .5(A - MC_f) - .5\, Q_{us} \qquad (7.3)$$

a. Assume that $A = 42$ represents the non-price determinants of market demand and marginal costs are $MC_{us} = 9$, and $MC_f = 6$. Solve for the output of each firm in the absence of government intervention. If market demand is given by $Q = Q_{us} + Q_f = A - P$, what price will be set?

b. Consider the effect of a U.S. subsidy of 3 per launch. (Hint: represent this as a lower U.S. marginal cost.) Solve for the effect on the distribution of launches and the equilibrium price. Determine how U.S. government expenditures, U.S. profits, and French profits are affected, and explain what principle underlies these results.

10. Two firms, home and foreign, compete in the export market as Bertrand duopolists, where each sets its price assuming that the price of the competitor will remain unchanged. Because the goods they produce are imperfect substitutes, they need not sell at the same price. Based on the two inverse demand functions,

$$P_h = a - bX_h - c\,X_f \tag{7.4}$$

and

$$P_f = a - bX_f - c\,X_{h,} \tag{7.5}$$

the corresponding reaction functions are:

$$P_h = (ab - ac + b\,MC_h)/2b + (c/2b)\,P_f \tag{7.6}$$

$$P_f = (ab - ac + b\,MC_f)/2b + (c/2b)\,P_h \tag{7.7}$$

a. For marginal costs, MC, equal to 12 for both firms, and $a = 60$, $b = 5$, and $c = 4$, find the equilibrium price each firm will set, and determine the output of each firm. (Hint: the inverse demand functions can be solved to show:

$$X_h = [(ab-ac) - bP_h + cP_f]/(b^2 - c^2).) \tag{7.8}$$

b. If the home government were to impose a per unit export tax of 3.36, the home firm's sales fall, but its profits plus the government's tax revenue rise. For the values shown above, calculate how large this effect is and explain why a tax is desirable in this situation.

11. "Dumping will be observed most often in imperfectly competitive markets where above-average profits can be earned." Explain whether you agree or disagree with this statement. How does the imposition of anti-dumping duties affect producers in the importing country? Why may your answer depend upon their market share?

12. Why do you expect a country's trade policy to be different in a country depending upon how wealth is distributed in the country? For a labor-scarce country with a very unequal distribution of income, what is most likely to be in the interest of the median voter?

13. If large financial contributions by political action committees and other special-interest groups account for most of a candidate's campaign financing, what keeps a country's trade policy from being highly protectionistic? Why do we not observe a political action committee representing consumers of cars? Where do you expect the highest trade barriers to be imposed?

References and Suggestions for Further Reading

For material on optimal tariff policy see:

Irwin, D. (1988) "Welfare Effects of British Free Trade: Debate and Evidence from the 1840s," *Journal of Political Economy* 96: 1142–1164.
—— (2003) "The optimal tax on antebellum US cotton exports," *Journal of International Economics* 60: 275–91.
Meade, J. (1952) *A Geometry of International Trade*, London: George Allen and Unwin.

For contributions on infant-industry protection, industry targeting, and strategic trade policy, see:

Baldwin, R. (1969) "The Case Against Infant-Industry Protection," *Journal of Political Economy* 77: 285–305.
Baldwin, R. and Krugman, P. (1988a) "Market Access and Competition: A Simulation Study of 16K Random Access Memories," in R. Feenstra (ed.) *Empirical Research in Industrial Trade*, Cambridge, MA: MIT Press.
—— (1988b) "Industrial Political and International Competition in Wide-bodied Jet Aircraft," in R. Baldwin, (ed.) *Trade Policy Issues and Empirical Analysis*, Chicago: University of Chicago Press, pp. 45–71.
Bardhan, P. (1971) "On Optimum Subsidy to a Learning Industry: An Aspect of the Theory of Infant Industry Protection," *International Economic Review* 12: 54–70.
Beason, R. and Weinstein, D. (1996) "Growth, Economies of Scale, and Targeting in Japan," *Review of Economics and Statistics* 78: 286–95.
Brander, J. and Spencer, B. (1985) "Export Subsidies and International Market Share Rivalry," *Journal of International Economics* 16: 83–100.
Eaton, J. and Grossman, G. (1986) "Optimal Trade and Industrial Policy under Oligopoly," *Quarterly Journal of Economics* 101: 383–406.
Feenstra, R. (ed.) (1989) *Trade Policies for International Competitiveness*, Chicago: University of Chicago Press.
Hamilton, A. (1791) *Report on Manufactures*. Available at http://www.union.edu/PUBLIC/ECODEPT/kleind/eco024/documents/hamilton/mfg_text.doc.
Irwin, D. and Klenow, P. (1994) "Learning-by-Doing Spillovers in the Semiconductor Industry," *Journal of Political Economy* 102: 1200–1227.
Krugman, P. (1984) "Import Protection as Export Promotion: International Competition in the Presence of Oligopoly and Economies of Scale," in H. Kierzkowski (ed.) *Monopolistic Competition in International Trade*, Oxford: Oxford University Press, pp. 180–93.
—— (ed.) (1986) *Strategic Trade Policy and the New International Economics*, Cambridge, MA: MIT Press.
—— (1987) "Is Free Trade Passé?," *Journal of Economic Perspectives* 1: 131–41.
Krugman, P. and Smith, A. (eds) (1994) *Empirical Studies of Strategic Trade Policy*, Chicago: University of Chicago Press.
Markusen, J., Melvin, J., Kaempfer, W., and Maskus, K. (1995) *International Trade Theory and Evidence*, New York: McGraw Hill, pp. 293–300.
Noland, M. and Pack, H. (2003) *Industrial Policy in an Era of Globalization: Lessons from Asia*, Washington, DC: Institute for International Economics.

Pack, H. and Saggi, K. (2006) "The case for industrial policy: a critical survey," World Bank Policy Research Working Paper 3839, February.

Stern, R. (ed.) (1987) *US Trade Policies in a Changing World Economy*, Cambridge, MA: MIT Press.

Tyson, L. (1992) *Who's Bashing Whom: Trade Conflict in High Technology Industries*, Washington DC: Institute for International Economics.

For contributions to the literature on dumping see:

Blonigen, B. and Bown, C. (2003) "Antidumping and Retaliation Threats," *Journal of International Economics* 60: 249–73.

Brander, J.(1981) "Intra-industry trade in identical products," *Journal of International Economics* 11: 1–11.

Friberg, R. and Ganslandt, M. (2006) "An empirical assessment of the welfare effects of reciprocal dumping," *Journal of International Economics* 70: 1–24.

Konings, J. and Vandenbussche, H. (2005) "Antidumping protection and markups of domestic firms," *Journal of International Economics* 65: 151–65.

Prusa, T. (1992) "Why Are so Many Antidumping Petitions Withdrawn?," *Journal of International Economics* 33: 1–20.

Rutkowski, A. (2007) "Withdrawals of Anti-dumping Complaints in the EU: A Sign of Collusion," *World Economy* 30: 470–503.

Taylor, C. (2004) "The Economic Effects of Withdrawn Antidumping Investigations: Is There Evidence of Collusive Settlements?," *Journal of International Economics* 62: 295–312.

World Trade Organization (2006) *Overview of Developments in the International Trading Environment*, Annual Report by the Director General (WT/TPR/OV/11).

For contributions to the political economy literature see:

Dutt, P. and Mitra, D. (2002) "Endogenous Trade Policy through Majority Voting," *Journal of International Economics* 58: 107–34.

Eicher, T. and Osang, T. (2002) "Protection for Sale: An Empirical Investigation: Comment," *American Economic Review* 92: 1702–1710.

Gawande, K. and Bandyopadhay, H. (2000) "Is Protection for Sale? Evidence on the Grossman–Helpman Theory of Endogenous Protection," *Review of Economics and Statistics* 82: 139–52.

Goldberg, P. and Maggi, G. (1999) "Protection for Sale: An Empirical Investigation," *American Economic Review* 89: 1135–1155.

Grossman, G. and Helpman, E. (1994) "Protection for Sale," *American Economics Review* 84: 833–50.

Grossman, G. and Helpman, E. (1996) "Electoral Competition and Special Interest Politics," *Review of Economic Studies* 63: 265–86.

Magee, S. (1980) "Three Simple Tests of the Stolper–Samuelson Theorem," in P. Oppenheimer (ed.) *Issues in International Economics*, London: Oriel Press, pp. 138–53.

Mayer, W. (1984) "Endogenous Tariff Formation," *American Economic Review* 74: 970–85.

Rodrik, D.(1995) "Political Economy of Trade Policy," in G. Grossman and K. Rogoff (eds) *Handbook of International Economics, Vol. III*, New York: Elsevier Science B.V., pp. 1457–1494.

For other works cited in this chapter:

Bale, M. (1974) "Adjustment Assistance under the Trade Expansion Act of 1962," *Journal of International Law and Economics* 4: 49.

Council Regulation (EC) No. 1472 (2006) *Official Journal of the European Union*, 5 October.

The Economist (2006) "Sugar boycott," December 23, p. 94.

—— (2008) "Starship Enterprise: The Next Generation," January 24.

Kletzer, L. (2001) *Job Loss from Imports: Measuring the Costs'* Washington, DC: Institute for International Economics.

Oxfam (2004) *Dumping on the World, How EU Sugar Policies Hurt Poor Countries*, Oxfam Briefing Paper 61.

Srinivasan, T.N. (1987) "The National Defense Argument for Intervention in Foreign Trade," in R. Stern, (ed.) *U.S. Trade Policy in a Changing World Economy*, Cambridge, MA: MIT Press, pp. 337–76.

United States International Trade Commission (2005) "Certain Frozen or Canned Warmwater Shrimp and Prawns from Brazil, China, Ecuador, India, Thailand, and Vietnam," Publication 3748, Washington, DC: USITC.

APPENDIX: OPTIMUM TARIFFS: A PARTIAL EQUILIBRIUM PERSPECTIVE

In Chapters 6 and 7, we identify the potential gain to a country with market power from levying a tariff on imports or a tax on exports, as long as foreigners do not retaliate. In the partial equilibrium framework for a tariff, there is a clear trade off between a country's terms of trade gain at the expense of foreigners and its loss in economic efficiency from producing more of a good where it has a comparative disadvantage and the loss from consuming less of a good that it prefers. In Figure 7.1 those two effects are labeled m and n, respectively. The net effect, $m - n$, is given by:

$$(1) \qquad \Delta Welfare = M_1(P_0 - P_1) - \tfrac{1}{2}(M_0 - M_1)(P_1 + T - P_0). \qquad (a7.1)$$

Consider the following linear import demand and supply curves:

$$Md = a - bP \qquad (a7.2)$$

$$Ms = -c + eP \qquad (a7.3)$$

These two curves result in an equilibrium price, $P_0 = (a+c)/(b+e)$. For our answer to be economically meaningful, we need to verify that this intersection of the import demand and supply curves occurs for a positive value of imports. Otherwise, we would be looking at an export product, not an import. Substituting the price solution into the demand equation gives $M_0 = a + [b/(b+e)][a + c]$.

If the importing country imposes a specific tariff, T, then the price received by the foreign supplier is:

$$P_1 = (a+c)/(b+e) - [b/(b+e)]T \qquad (a7.4)$$

Clearly, P_1 is less than P_0, because some portion of the tariff is born by the supplier. This terms of trade gain will be larger when $b/(b-e)$ is larger. This fraction is related to the elasticity condition considered in Chapter 6, although here we are solving for the price received by the foreign supplier, not the price paid by the domestic consumer. When e is a small number, which results when the exporting country has few alternative markets in which to sell, most of the tariff is borne by the foreign exporter. When e is a larger number, as in the case of a small country, P_1 will be nearly identical to P_0, and any terms of trade gain will be slight.

Another way of stating that result is that for a small country that faces a large foreign supply elasticity, the optimal tariff will be very small. We can demonstrate that by substituting the relevant terms into the net welfare expression above and observing where it reaches a maximum. As a preliminary step, solve for the post-tariff import quantity:

$$M_1 = a + b(P_1 + T) = a - [b/(b+e)] [a+c] - [be/(b+e)] T \tag{a7.5}$$

Substituting into the change in net welfare equation (1) given above yields the expression:

$$\Delta Welfare = \{a - [b/(b+e)] [a+c] - [be/(b+e)]T\}\{[b/(b+e)]T\} - \tfrac{1}{2}\{[be/(b+e)]T\}\{[e/(b+e)]T\} \tag{a7.6}$$

If we differentiate this expression with respect to T and set that condition equal to zero, we can find the value of T that maximizes net welfare. The solution that we obtain is:

$$T = [a(b+e) - b(a+c)]/2[be + \tfrac{1}{2} e^2] \tag{a7.7}$$

We can see that as e become larger, T becomes smaller, while if b becomes larger, then T becomes larger.

If we let $Md = 100-10P$ and $Ms = -110+20P$, the initial equilibrium is $P_0 = 7$ and $M_0 = 30$. Using the formula for T above, the optimal tariff is 1.125, and $P_1 = 6.625$ and $M_1 = 22.5$. The net welfare 5.625, based on a terms of trade gain of 8.4375 and an efficiency loss of 2.8125. bstitute other values for the specific tariff, T, to convince yourself that net welfare er for any other choice. Also, you can substitute different values for b and e to verify above about the effect of a country's market power on its optimal tariff.

Chapter 8

International Mobility of Labor and Capital

LEARNING OBJECTIVES

By the end of this chapter you should be able to demonstrate why:

- international capital flows reduce differences in returns across countries and raise world output

- international flows of labor reduce differences in wages across countries but may reduce per capita income in the host country

- a firm may operate in more than one country (as a multinational corporation), either to serve the local market rather than export (horizontal integration) or to source inputs more efficiently (vertical integration)

The previous chapters assume that goods can be traded internationally but that factors of production are not mobile. The basis of Heckscher–Ohlin trade is precisely that large differences in relative factor endowments result in differences in factor prices and relative output price, which makes trade based on comparative advantage possible. A country with a relative abundance of labor, for example, will have low wages, which will give it a comparative advantage in labor-intensive goods such as apparel and shoes. Differences in factor prices exist prior to trade because labor and capital cannot move freely from one country to another. Otherwise, labor and capital would relocate to eliminate these differences.

Daily news reports regularly warn of the challenges posed by immigration or debate the desirability of allowing foreign investment. Consequently, we must admit that the assumption of completely immobile factors of production conflicts with reality. At least some labor and capital movement occurs between countries, as we document below. Labor migrates, legally or otherwise, from low- to higher-wage countries. Capital flows internationally in response to differences in rates of return. Of course, labor mobility is limited by immigration laws, transportation costs, lack of information about job opportunities, and language differences. International investors are deterred by different legal and regulatory environments, discriminatory taxes, potential expropriation, incomplete information, and various other risks. Nevertheless, concerns over globalization rest as much on the rapid increases in labor and capital mobility internationally as on the increase in international trade.

In Chapter 4 we found that trade between countries with different factor endowments can lead to a reduction in wages in labor-scarce countries. Greater immigration into labor-scarce countries can result in lower wages, too. From a political perspective, labor is likely to oppose freer trade in a labor-scarce country. It also is likely to advocate stricter immigration policies and fewer incentives for capitalists to invest abroad. This chapter elaborates the rationale for such positions.

With respect to capital mobility we address the seemingly straightforward issues that arise in moving capital from a country where its return is low to one where it is high. Even in that case, international tax practices can alter the standard prediction that both parties gain from greater capital mobility. We also consider the more complicated situation posed by a company that becomes a multinational corporation (MNC) by establishing operations in more than one country. That choice typically has less to do with a scarcity of capital in the host country and more to do with the way a company can exploit its unique technology and ideas internationally. How both the parent and the host country share in these gains remains a controversial issue.

Alternative Measures of Labor Mobility

We may be tempted to view current increased flows of labor and capital as unprecedented, a sign that the world is changing at an ever faster pace. Some historical perspective, therefore, is useful at the outset. But, measuring labor and capital flows is not that straightforward. For example, in the case of labor we might look at the annual flow of immigrants into a country or at the accumulated total of foreign-born workers that live in a country. Jeffrey Williamson (2004) summarizes U.S. experience in these two dimensions in the following terms:

> The US annual immigration rate fell from 11.6 immigrants per thousand in the 1900s to 0.4 immigrants per thousand in the 1940s, before rising again to 4 immigrants per thousand in the 1990s. The proportion of the US population foreign born had fallen from a 1910 peak of 15 percent to an all-century low of 4.7 percent in 1970. The postwar immigration boom increased the foreign-born share to more than 8 percent in 1990 and more than 10 percent in 2000. Thus, the US has come two-thirds of the way back to reclaiming the title "a nation of immigrants" after a half-century retreat. While the immigration *rate* is now only a third of that achieved at its peak in the first decade of the 20th century, the contribution of immigration to population and labor force *growth* is similar because the rate of natural increase has also declined.

Within Europe, Germany experienced immigration rates greater than 1.0 percent in the early 1990s due to the opening up of Eastern Europe. Table 8.1 reports the share of the immigrant population in

TABLE 8.1 Foreign-born Population as a Percentage of the Total Population

Country	1982	1993	1999	2001	2004
Australia	20.6	22.9	23.1	23.1	23.6
Austria	4.0	6.8	10.9	11.1	13.0
Belgium	9.0	9.2	10.2	10.8	—
Canada	16.1	15.6	17.2	17.5	18.0
Denmark	2.0	3.3	5.6	6.0	6.3
Finland			2.5	2.7	3.2
France	6.8		10.0	—	—
Germany	7.6	7.3	12.4	12.6	—
Greece			—	10.3	—
Hungary			2.9	3.0	3.2
Ireland			8.2	9.3	11.0
Italy			—	2.5	—
Luxembourg	26.2	30.2	32.8	32.8	33.1
Netherlands	3.8	4.8	9.8	10.4	10.6
New Zealand			16.8	18.0	18.8
Norway			6.5	6.9	7.8
Portugal			5.1	6.3	6.7
Spain	0.5	0.9	—	5.3	—
Sweden	4.9	5.7	11.8	11.5	12.2
Switzerland	14.4	17.1	21.6	22.3	23.5
United Kingdom	2.8	3.1	7.6	8.2	9.3
United States	4.7	7.9	10.6	11.3	12.8

Source: Adapted from Organization for Economic Cooperation and Development (1995, 2001, 2007).

several OECD countries, a figure that can be measured more accurately from census data than most annual flow calculations are. They show that in most of Europe and in the United States, there has been a noticeable increase in the immigrant share of the population. The rising ratio can be explained by the large role that immigration plays in overall population growth for these countries. For example, between 1999 and 2004 the U.K. population rose by a little over 1 million people, and the number of immigrants living in the U.K. rose by a little over 1 million people. Not surprisingly, the immigrant share of the total population rose from 7.6 percent to 9.3 percent.

An Important Measure of Capital Mobility

Capital flows are treated in greater detail in Part II of this book, although we examine some of their implications for income distribution and economic efficiency here. An important component of those capital flows is the investment by multinational corporations (MNC)s. The last four columns of Table 8.2 show the cumulative stock of MNC investment as a share of GDP. For most countries, both industrialized and developing, that figure has risen over the past 25 years. Those increases are not always smooth and predictable, however, and not all countries within the groupings shown fare as well as the average reported. The growing importance of both inward and outward investment is a sign that economies are becoming more interdependent. Also, the generalization that MNCs must be from rich countries is unwarranted.

TABLE 8.2 Measures of Investment Internationally

Region/economy	Current year MNC inward investment as share of host gross fixed capital formation 2005	Cumulative stock of MNC investment as a share of Gross Domestic Product, (Inward on top line, outward on bottom line)			
		1980	1990	2000	2005
Europe	15.7	6.8	11.0	26.4	33.5
		6.4	12.0	41.8	44.2
United States	4.0	3.0	6.9	12.9	13.0
		7.8	7.5	13.5	16.4
Japan	0.3	0.3	0.3	1.1	2.2
		1.8	6.6	5.9	8.5
Developing economies	12.8	5.4	9.8	26.3	27.0
		3.7	4.1	13.0	12.5
Africa	19.1	9.1	12.2	26.0	28.2
		1.9	4.3	7.7	5.8
Latin America and the Caribbean	16.8	5.0	10.3	25.8	36.7
		6.3	5.4	10.2	13.5

TABLE 8.2 continued

Region/economy	Current year MNC inward investment as share of host gross fixed capital formation 2005	Cumulative stock of MNC investment as a share of Gross Domestic Product, (Inward on top line, outward on bottom line)			
		1980	1990	2000	2005
Asia and Oceania	11.1	4.5	9.0	26.5	23.2
		2.1	3.3	15.3	13.0
Developing excl China	14.5	5.1	4.4	8.4	12.7
			2.2	12.7	10.9

Source: Adapted from United Nations Conference on Trade and Development (2006).

Another measure of the importance of MNC investment is given by expressing the amount that occurs in a single year relative to total investment in the host economy, as shown in the first column of Table 8.2. For smaller developing countries, MNCs account for an important share of the total. Because total investment includes housing construction and government capital formation, where the role of MNCs is minimal, the figures reported here imply that MNCs are a particularly significant source of business investment.

A BASIC MODEL OF CAPITAL MOBILITY

To indicate the consequences of factor movements, consider a framework similar to the specific factors model introduced in Chapter 4. Figure 8.1 shows the utilization of capital in two economies that produce the same good. Therefore, we cannot use this framework to show how trade is affected by factor flows. The approach is quite useful, however, to show how factor mobility increases efficiency and total output, which occurs because scarce productive assets move from less productive to more productive locations and uses. Rates of return, and therefore marginal products, are equated by the reallocation of capital. The marginal product of capital (MPK in the figure) is the increase in total output that results from adding one unit of capital while holding inputs of other factors unchanged. The marginal product lines slope down because of the law of diminishing returns. That is, adding more capital to unchanged amounts of labor and land reduces the marginal product of capital.

One way of thinking of capital mobility is in terms of an individual who owns a stock of machines and chooses to lease them to firms that will use them in production. Airplanes, railroad cars, and trucks are often leased in this way. When capital is mobile internationally, the equipment can be leased to operators on either side of the border, but with immobile capital, owners can only lease to operators on their own side of the border. Thus, in labeling the vertical axis of Figure 8.1, we can

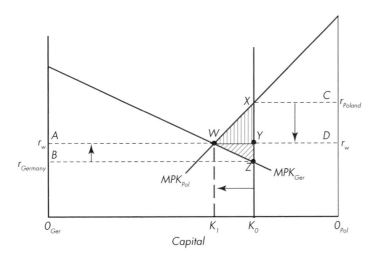

FIGURE 8.1 Effects of German Capital Flows to Poland

At the initial allocation of capital, K_0, the rate of return in Poland is higher than the German rate of return. If capital can move to where the rate of return is higher, K_0K_1 of capital moves from Germany to Poland and a common rate of return, r_w, is earned. Poland gains the top triangle WYX, and Germany gains the lower triangle WYZ.

think of the price showing the rental rate received for the leased machines. Or, we can express this return in percentage form as a share of the value of the machine. That form may seem more familiar when we think of financial flows across borders, which then allow borrowers to make investments in plant and equipment. The model applies to both situations.

Suppose capital flows initially are prohibited, and the allocation of capital is given by K_0 where the return in Poland is r_{Pol} and the return in Germany is r_{Ger}. If those prohibitions are eliminated, the higher return in Poland than in Germany attracts an inflow of capital, K_1K_0, which equalizes rates of return in both countries at r_w. The extra output in Poland is given by the area under the MPK_{Pol} curve, the trapezoid WXK_0K_1, but German capital owners only need be paid the rectangle WYK_0K_1. That results in a gain to the Polish economy of the cross-hatched triangle WXY. In Germany, output falls by the area under the MPK_{Ger} curve, the trapezoid WZK_0K_1. Because German capital owners gain the rectangle WYK_0K_1, the German economy as a whole gains the vertically-hatched triangle WYZ. Capital moves from less to more efficient uses, interest rates are arbitraged together, and total income in both countries increases.

Sizable income redistribution effects exist, however. Capitalists in Poland previously earned the rectangle $XCO_{Pol}K_0$, but now only receive $YDO_{Pol}K_0$, a loss of $XCDY$. If labor is the other factor used in production and it is fixed in supply, labor gains this rectangle as well as the triangle WXY, a benefit from the inflow of capital that makes labor more productive. In Poland capital loses and labor gains. The redistribution in Germany is in just the opposite direction. German capital owners previously earned the rectangle BZK_0O_{Ger}, but now earn AWK_1O_{Ger} from the portion of their capital that remains in Germany and WYK_0K_1 from the portion now utilized in Poland. In total, German capitalists gain the rectangle $AYZB$. German labor now has less capital with which to work, and the income it receives falls by the trapezoid $AWZB$. German capital gains and German labor loses.

International factor mobility produces the same dilemmas as does free trade. Total output and incomes clearly rise, but income is redistributed in ways that may be painful and politically controversial. From the perspective of Polish labor and German capital, the process described here should be encouraged, but German workers and Polish owners of capital will have the opposite view. Political conflicts over immigration laws and policies affecting international capital movements are likely to reflect these differing interests.

Tax Competition and the Taxation of Capital Income

Taxes can affect the conclusion that total incomes in both countries rise as a result of these factor movements. The situation in Figure 8.1 assumes that German capitalists lease capital to Polish producers, and that rental income is not subject to any Polish tax. If instead a Polish tax is imposed, and as a result the Polish government rather than the German government taxes this income, Germany as a whole may lose from the capital outflow.

Consider a situation where both countries impose a 40 percent income tax. If a German firm invests domestically, let the pre-tax return be 10 percent. The net return to its investors is only 6 percent, but the German Treasury gets 4 percent, which can be used for public purposes. Suppose the pre-tax return in Poland is 12 percent. The after-tax return to a German investor in Poland is 7.2 percent, but the German Treasury gets nothing, if the German government exempts this income from taxation or any tax liability is offset by a credit for the Polish tax paid. The total return to Germany is 7.2 percent rather than 10 percent if the capital had stayed home, meaning a loss of 2.8 percent. World output rises by the 2 percent difference in gross yields, and the Polish government and German private investors certainly gain. However, the German government loses 4 percent of the investment income per year, and the German economy as a whole loses 2.8 percent. International capital flows do increase efficiency, as does a system of granting foreign tax credits, but the flows may not benefit both the investing and the host country.

The implication that host countries will choose to tax foreign capital to capture such gains in public revenue conflicts with headlines of tax competition and a "race to the bottom" regarding tax rates levied by potential host countries.[1] To evaluate that rationale, extend the model above to consider a world with many potential investment sites and the possibility that a higher rate of return can result in a larger capital stock in a country through greater domestic saving. Figure 8.2 shows the effect of a tax levied by a country too small to affect the rate of return internationally. The supply of capital to it from the rest of the world is horizontal at the world rate of return, r_w. If the tax revenue is not used in a way that benefits capital owners, a country that levies a higher tax on capital than its competitors will experience a capital outflow. Capital will flow out of the country until the before-tax return is high enough to yield the same after-tax return available elsewhere in the world. In this case, the economy loses K_1K_0 of capital. Note that the domestically provided capital, K_d, has remained unchanged, while all the loss is accounted for by a smaller inflow from the rest of the world.

---

1 For the likelihood that the equilibrium tax rate on capital income will fall to zero, see Roger Gordon (1986).

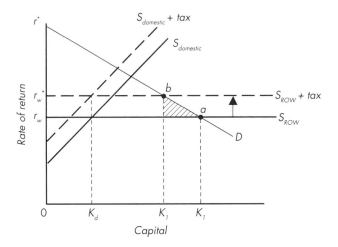

FIGURE 8.2 A Tax on Capital in a Small Country

A tax on capital in Country A results in a decline in its capital stock from K_0 to K_1, which causes the return on capital to rise by the amount of tax. The return to immobile land and labor falls by the amount of the tax revenue collected and also by the loss in efficiency given by the cross-hatched triangle.

Again, we can use this diagram to demonstrate distributional effects of the tax on capital used in the country. The demand curve for capital is based upon the extra output produced by an additional unit of capital. The output of the economy for the capital stock of K_0 is given by the area under the demand curve, r^*aK_0. Total payments to capital are represented by the rectangle given by r_w times K_0. The portion left over for immobile labor is the triangle given by r^*ar_w. Now note what happens to this area when the tax is levied. Because the before-tax return to capital rises, the triangle representing the return to labor and land declines to $r^*br_w^*$. The burden of the tax on capital has been shifted entirely to the immobile factors of production, labor and land.[2] In fact, the loss to them is greater than the gain to the government due to the loss of the cross-hatched triangle in Figure 8.2. The less efficient allocation of resources leaves less capital to work with labor and land. For a country that is too small to affect prices of goods or returns to mobile capital internationally, taxing **portfolio capital** (investment that entails no management control) reduces national income and is less desirable than taxing land and labor directly.

Perhaps in recognition of this principle, most developed countries do not levy a high withholding tax on interest income earned by foreign lenders, and many, such as France, Germany, the United Kingdom, and the United States, impose no tax at all. Many developing countries, however, impose withholding rates of 10 to 15 percent, and cite the principle that the source of the income should be where it is taxed. In spite of the outcome that land and labor bear the burden of the tax on capital, developing countries may choose this policy because of the difficulty of directly taxing fixed factors such as labor and land.

---

2 In a model where more than one good is produced, economists have noted further reasons why the burden shifted to labor may be even greater than the tax revenue collected. See Harberger (1983) and Mutti and Grubert (1985).

The Role of Risk and Other Factors

The model above also has the implication that the flow of capital is in just one direction, from a capital-abundant to a capital-scarce country. In reality, we often observe two-way capital flows. When savers in one country choose to lend to borrowers in another country, as when they buy a government or corporate bond, they clearly do respond to differences in real rates of return across countries, all else being equal. They are most interested, however, in the way a purchase of a bond in another country will affect the return to their total savings or portfolio. Buying a bond that offers a lower rate of return can still make sense when it reduces the riskiness of the portfolio, or the volatility of all returns received. If returns in Japan rise exactly when returns in the United States fall, and vice versa, a Japanese saver's portfolio can yield the same return at a lower level of risk if it is diversified and includes U.S. bonds. Even though both the United States and Japan are capital-abundant countries, capital may flow from Japan to the United States, and vice versa, as a result of these gains from diversification. That topic is covered in Part II. The model assumed in Figure 8.1 best applies to net flows of capital.

Our capital flow model abstracts from another aspect of capital mobility that was a feature of the 1990s: financial instability. If lenders reassess the attractiveness of providing capital to foreigners, the adjustment in the case of financial flows is not as simple as a leasing company bringing its equipment home. Rather, the desire of lenders to withdraw funds may require borrowers to sell assets that have few alternative uses. Over-reliance on short-term borrowing to finance long-lived assets results in the borrower becoming particularly vulnerable to unexpected bad news. Determining a firm's appropriate financial strategy to avoid such problems is another important topic in international finance.

ADDITIONAL ISSUES RAISED BY LABOR MOBILITY

The one-good model with capital flows represented in Figure 8.1 can be applied to the case of labor mobility, too, if we assume that labor moves while capital remains fixed. The implications are straightforward: immigration will cause the wage to fall in the country that initially has the higher wage and to rise in the country that initially has the lower wage. Capital and other fixed factors gain in the former country and lose in the latter country. Income for each country rises.

Are those predictions born out in empirical studies? We consider below some of the potentially offsetting factors that make it surprisingly difficult to demonstrate such outcomes. When the amount of labor that comes into a country is large relative to any other changes that may be occurring at the same time, however, those predicted wage effects can be observed. Striking historical evidence comes from the four decades before 1913: in Australia the wage rental ratio fell by 75 percent, in Argentina by 80 percent, and in the U.S. by more than 50 percent, while it rose by a factor of 2.7 in Britain and 2.3 in Denmark and Sweden (O'Rourke, et al. 1996). A more recent example is the influx of Soviet Jews into Israel in the 1990s, which resulted in a 20 percent increase in the labor force and a 10 percent fall in wages below their trend value.

If wages in the high-wage country fall, the median voter model discussed in Chapter 6 suggests that high-wage countries may consider more restrictive immigration policies in spite of the rise in national income. Additionally, such immigration does not necessarily increase per capita income, because the receiving country's population grows. If the immigrants are unskilled, bring little or no capital with them, and are less likely to become part of the labor force, they are likely to lower European or U.S. per capita output. This outcome can be demonstrated as follows:

$$Y = F\,(K,\,LB,\,LN) \tag{8.1}$$

where Y is gross domestic product, K is capital stock, LB is labor force, and LN is the stock of land. This equation states that potential output is a positive function of the size of the capital stock, the labor force, and the availability of land. Technology determines the nature of this function. Capital is defined as including education and training, which is often referred to as "human capital."

If the labor force is a constant proportion, a, of the population, then output per capita, Y/c, can be expressed as:

$$Y/c = aF(K\,/\,LB,\,LN\,/\,LB) \tag{8.2}$$

where we have assumed constant returns to scale in production. In fact, a is not constant, and policy makers in the E.U. and the U.S. are concerned that in the case of legal immigrants, their labor force participation is lower than for the existing population. Even when a is constant, this equation points to another issue. Output per capita is positively related to the capital-to-labor ratio and the land-to-labor ratio. Output per capita will grow if the amount of capital per worker rises or if the amount of land per worker increases. Improvements in technology also allow output per capita to rise. Increases in the population of a country, without corresponding increases in the stocks of capital and land, will cause GDP per capita to fall.

Furthermore, an influx of immigrants can affect welfare in the host country when it leads to congestion in the use of public goods and services, such as roads, parks, and schools, or greater demand for transfer payments to cover expenses of housing, food, and medical care. The net fiscal balance from immigration depends upon taxes paid versus the extra demands for services and transfers created. Current debates over immigration policy are not limited to these economic costs and benefits, however, but also extend to social concerns over the assimilation of immigrants. While some observers celebrate diversity and point to immigration as an antidote to the problems of aging Western societies, others worry about the creation of a separate underclass that practices a different religion, speaks a different language, and values different traditions.

The situation summarized above suggests why industrialized countries may not find it in their interest to allow unlimited immigration. While total output would rise in the industrialized countries, output per capita would not. Conversely, labor-abundant developing countries may view emigration as a vital safety valve that raises national income. The World Bank (2005) estimates that allowing sufficient immigration to increase labor forces in high-income countries by 3 percent would raise world income by 0.6 percent, with developing countries receiving over 80 percent of that benefit. Yet, attention should not be restricted to high-income countries alone, because World Bank economists estimate that 40 percent of immigrants have moved to another developing country. Indonesians migrate to Malaysia, Guatemalans to Mexico, and Mozambicans to South Africa. Negotiations to allow freer movements of labor internationally have made little progress, in part due to many opposing and conflicting interests.

Mitigating Factors

The scenario sketched above is not the only possible outcome. Some of the factors held constant in that analysis may in fact change. A concentrated impact within the host country is often not observed where immigrants settle, because there is offsetting movement of the native population away from those regions. The Mariel boatlift of emigrants from the jails of Cuba to Miami is one example of this effect, where no measurable negative effect on wages in Miami occurred. The migration out by previous residents results in a pattern of adjustment that spreads any downward pressure on wages over a larger labor market. Any change in wages is less visible. Furthermore, there may not be a reduction in wages if not only labor moves, but also capital. Any tendency for labor to drive down wages and costs of production in that location and to raise the return to capital may attract a capital inflow. If both capital and labor increase by the same proportion, the ratio does not decline, and labor productivity does not fall as assumed above.

The assumption that only one good is produced also affects the outcome. In the H–O model with two produced goods, an influx of unskilled labor leads to a shift in output toward goods that require unskilled labor intensively, such as apparel. At unchanged prices, there is no reason for wages to fall. Capital can be attracted out of capital-intensive sectors, whose output will fall, to be reallocated to the expanding labor-intensive sector. With no decline in the capital-to-labor ratio, wages are not driven down. That is the Rybczinski result encountered in Chapter 4.

A related insight was presented by Robert Mundell (1957) in a classic article that demonstrates the consequences of tariff protection when factors of production are mobile. A tariff to protect a labor-intensive good such as apparel has the initial effect of raising wages, but that attracts a labor inflow. The inflow will continue until the wage is driven down and the basis for trade is eliminated. The country that levies the protective tariff simply attracts a larger labor force that now produces domestically the good that it used to import, but the wage rate does not rise from its pre-tariff level.

When labor is more productive in industrialized countries, however, the increase in their output of apparel will exceed the decline in apparel output in the country the immigrants have left. Total apparel output will rise and therefore we expect its price to decline. The wages of unskilled workers will fall, just as we observed in the one-good model, because the value of their output declines. But, as net importers of apparel, the industrialized countries will benefit from a decline in the price of apparel. The effect on income per capita cannot be determined as easily as equation (8.2) implies.

Germany: A Country of Immigrants?

Australia, Canada, and the U.S. are countries with a long history of immigration. Should Germany be regarded as a country of immigrants, too? Four German economists, to whom we refer as the IZA authors, argue that it should see itself in that light, but in a targeted way that calls for greater attention to Germany's economic interests (Zimmerman, et al. 2007).

Over the past 60 years, Germany has experienced three waves of immigration: one right after World War II up until the erection of the Berlin Wall in 1961, a time span when many ethnic

Germans emigrated from Eastern European countries; a second wave from 1961–1973 when guest workers were recruited from Southern European countries at a time of rapid German economic expansion; and a third wave following the fall of the Berlin Wall in 1989, when a large influx of ethnic Germans and asylum seekers arrived. Net immigration relative to the population peaked in 1992 at one percent. Subsequent changes in German law reduced the numbers of asylum seekers, selection procedures were applied to ethnic German immigrants, and Germany maintained interim restrictions to limit free movement of individuals from new E.U. members.

The IZA economists argue for a further change in policy, and the national psyche, to replace a general skepticism against immigration with a recognition that the German system discourages the "best and the brightest" potential immigrants from choosing Germany. Merely continuing current policy ignores a growing shortage of skilled technical workers necessary for a knowledge-based economy. The authors advocate the establishment of a point system that pays attention to the education, age, work experience, and health of potential immigrants, an approach that draws on the experience of Canada, Australia, and New Zealand.

The immigration systems of those three countries are based on the goal that 60 percent of immigrants be accounted for by the economically based point system, with family reunification accounting for 25–30 percent, and refugees and asylum seekers 10–15 percent. Table 8.3 reports the actual immigration breakdown for these countries, which geographically are well placed to monitor the entry and exit of people better than most countries. Also, the table includes legal immigration into the United States, to give the record of a country that puts much less emphasis on economic criteria. Indeed, U.S. figures show less than 20 percent of immigrants enter under employment-based provisions and over 60 percent are family related.

For Germany to shift toward a more economically motivated policy, the IZA authors recommend a two-pronged strategy, one to deal with permanent immigration to address the shortage of highly skilled individuals and another to deal with temporary immigration to meet short-run fluctuations in the demand for skilled workers. In the latter case, the authors recommend auctioning immigration certificates to prospective employers, an approach that overcomes the difficulty of determining

TABLE 8.3 Immigration and the Role of National Policy, 2004

| Country | % distribution of immigrants by category | | | |
	Family related	Employment	Refugee/Asylum	Other
Australia	33	56	11	—
Canada	26	57	14	—
New Zealand	35	53	13	—
United States	66	16	8	10

Source: Zimmerman, et al. (2007) pp. 122, 140.

exactly which industries need what number of workers. In the former case, however, they believe Germany faces such competition internationally for highly trained individuals that charging fees would be counterproductive.

With the British adoption of a five-tiered point system in 2008, the experience of another European country may demonstrate how easily this attempt to alter the composition of immigrant flows can be implemented in the E.U. Because of the eventual provision for free movement of workers within the E.U., the proposed point systems faced by non-members of the E.U. will likely apply to less than half of the immigration E.U. member countries' experience.

Different Types of Immigrants

The model based on Figure 8.1 implies that all workers are identical. From Chapter 4 we know that the distinction between skilled and unskilled labor is an important one to make with respect to comparative advantage and trade, and it is important in the case of immigration, too. Which groups of workers are most likely to immigrate, and how do the consequences differ? Economists have found that the poorest workers are not necessarily the most likely to emigrate, even though their wage gap may be the greatest, because the economic and psychic costs of emigration exceed their ability and willingness to pay. The greater the distance to travel, the higher will be the proportion of skilled immigrants.

Host countries often encourage the most educated to immigrate, because the human capital they bring means the capital/labor ratio can rise and output per capita can increase. Also, skilled immigrants will pay more in taxes than they demand in public services. A study by the National Research Council calculates for the U.S. that an immigrant with less than a high-school education will cause a fiscal drain, while an immigrant with a high-school education or more will be a net fiscal contributor (Smith and Edmonston 1997). With respect to who actually migrates, Docquier and Marfouk (2004) compile data for OECD countries over the 1990–2000 period, and they report that immigration of the highly skilled has exceeded that of the low skilled. Nevertheless, bimodal patterns can result, as in the U.S. where high demand in agriculture and construction creates an incentive for the immigration of less skilled workers, primarily from Mexico.

Brain Drain and Brain Gain Concerns

The United States benefited enormously from the arrival of large numbers of scientists and engineers fleeing Europe before World War II, as it is benefiting today from the talented people migrating from a variety of developing countries. Scientists from East and South Asia have become a major force in U.S. high-technology industries. The European Commission Green Paper on immigration policy (2005) notes the advantage of greater harmonization of national immigration policies by its member states, which would avoid "potentially harmful competition between Member States in the recruitment of certain categories of workers." The prime category implied by this statement is the high-skilled worker group.

Conversely, source nations that lose their skilled workers to others worry about a **brain drain**. Just as Germany lost tax revenue in the case of capital mobility treated above, source nations face a loss when skilled workers emigrate, even if world welfare rises. The problem is compounded because much of the education of these individuals is paid for with public funds. The benefits of providing more education simply spill over to the rest of the world. Although some countries have imposed exit taxes on those emigrating, some commentators instead call for payments by the wealthy host countries to compensate for this loss of revenue.

More recently, economists have explored the potential gains, even to a source country, that may arise from skilled emigration. The H–O model would predict that a scarce factor such as skilled labor should earn high returns within a source country that is relatively abundant in unskilled labor, and therefore it should have little incentive to migrate. Nevertheless, skilled individuals in developing countries may find that they are much more productive if they are able to work in an industrialized country with better technology and other skilled individuals. The source country sees some gain in that situation from the remittances that its residents receive from abroad. The source country also may benefit from the possible return of those skilled individuals at some future time, when they serve as a conduit for new ideas and technologies to be brought back to the home country. The ascent of the information technology sector of India and the science parks of China demonstrate that this outcome is not just wishful thinking. Additionally, the attraction of a high-paying foreign job may encourage more individuals to acquire additional education in the source country, and if not all of those individuals are actually successful in winning the lottery for a visa abroad, the pool of trained workers in the source country may rise. That possibility is particularly relevant when individuals can finance the investment in additional education.

For some source countries, a gain may be possible, but for many, the actual amount of emigration is far beyond that point. Table 8.4 shows the extent to which skilled workers are a much bigger share of those who migrate than of the general population. The grouped results indicate the particularly extreme positions of low income and least developed countries. Analysis of individual countries shows that the loss of skilled labor is large for small countries and those that have not experienced rapid growth at home, a pattern that confirms an earlier observation that nearly one-third of skilled Africans

TABLE 8.4 Skilled Emigration, 2000

Countries by income group	Skilled workers as share of group	
	Residents	Emigrants
High income countries	30.7	38.3
Upper–middle income countries	13.0	25.2
Lower–middle income countries	14.2	35.4
Low income countries	3.5	45.1
UN least developed countries	2.5	34.0

Source: Docquier and Marfouk (2004).

had moved to Europe as of 1987 (Docquier and Rapaport 2007). In those cases no brain gain occurs. For larger countries, such as China, India, Brazil, and Indonesia, the balance appears more favourable.

MULTINATIONAL CORPORATIONS

A multinational corporation is a firm that operates outside the home country in one or more branches or subsidiaries that it effectively controls. MNCs are not equally likely to be observed in all industries, and not necessarily in capital-intensive sectors. They are likely to be in industries where superior technology or unique products provide an important competitive advantage to the firm.

The shrill rhetoric directed at U.S. MNCs and U.S. imperialism in the 1960s and 1970s has declined, at least by potential host country governments. Direct investment has become characterized by two-way flows, primarily between industrialized countries but increasingly involving developing countries as both source and host countries. While not many MNCs headquartered in developing countries have yet become household names in industrialized countries, they account for 14 percent of the stock of assets held abroad. Countries everywhere recognize the advantages of gaining access to the production and marketing networks of MNCs; roughly one-third of manufactured goods traded internationally are accounted for by MNC sales, particularly sales from one affiliate to another as intra-company shipments. MNCs have played a significant role in integrating the world economy.

With respect to individual companies, their international focus can be characterized in several different ways. Table 8.5 presents a categorization used by the United Nations, based on the assets that an MNC holds outside of its home country. A variety of industries is represented. One feature

TABLE 8.5 Major Non-financial MNCs (billions of dollars and thousands of employees)

Ranking by:				Assets		Employment	
Foreign assets	Corporation	Home economy	Industry	Foreign	Total	Foreign	Total
1	General Electric	U.S.	Electrical and electronic	449	751	142	307
2	Vodafone Group	U.K.	Telecom	248	259	46	57
3	Ford Motor	U.S.	Motor vehicles	180	305	103	226
4	General Motors	U.S.	Motor vehicles	174	480	115	324
5	British Petroleum	U.K.	Petroleum expl./ ref./distr.	155	193	86	103
6	ExxonMobil	U.S.	Petroleum expl./ ref./distr.	135	195	53	105

TABLE 8.5 continued

Ranking by:				Assets		Employment	
Foreign assets	Corporation	Home economy	Industry	Foreign	Total	Foreign	Total
7	Royal Dutch Shell	U.K./Neth.	Petroleum expl./ ref./distr.	130	193	96	114
8	Toyota Motor	Japan	Motor vehicles	123	234	95	266
9	Total	France	Petroleum expl./ ref./distr.	99	115	62	111
10	France Télécom	France	Telecom	86	131	82	207
11	Volkswagen	Germany	Motor vehicles	84	173	165	343
12	Sanofi-Aventis	France	Pharmaceuticals	83	105	69	96
13	Deutsche Telekom AG	Germany	Telecom	80	147	74	245
14	RWE Group	Germany	Electricity, gas and water	79	127	42	98
15	Suez	France	Electricity, gas and water	74	86	100	161
16	E.on	Germany	Electricity, gas and water	73	155	33	72
17	Hutchison Whampoa	Hong Kong, China	Diversified	68	84	151	180
18	Siemens AG	Germany	Electrical and electronic	66	108	266	430
19	Nestlé SA	Switz.	Food and beverages	65	77	240	247
20	Electricité de France	France	Electricity, gas and water	65	200	51	156
21	Honda Motor	Japan	Motor vehicles	65	89	77	138
22	Vivendi Universal	France	Diversified	58	94	23	38
23	ChevronTexaco	U.S.	Motor vehicles	57	93	31	56
24	BMW AG	Germany	Motor vehicles	56	92	71	106

Source: Adapted from United Nations Conference on Trade and Development (2006).

to note is that many of the largest industrial corporations operate in mature industries, such as automobiles, petroleum, and utilities. Newly emerging industries where technological breakthroughs are most critical to success are less likely to have grown large enough to make this list. Some industries are more capital intensive, so firms in those industries rank much higher by assets than they do by employment. Actual rankings across years are likely to show further variation, because competition within an industry, or the decline of an entire industry, contributes to changes in this list. While a conglomerate that operated in every industry and in every country would be more immune to such variation, such conglomerates do not tend to be the most successful MNCs.

Given that there are many disadvantages of operating in a foreign country where local firms have the advantage of a better understanding of local culture, customs, and contacts, why does a firm become an MNC? J.H. Dunning (1974) provides a useful framework to answer that question. He considers three factors: ownership, location, and internalization. We shall define these terms and show how they help determine a firm's decision to become an MNC. We then consider how both the host and the home country are affected by the operations of MNCs and how they try to influence those operations.

Ownership

An MNC typically has some special expertise that it has developed and now hopes to exploit in a larger market. Such expertise may include technological know-how that it has acquired through research and development or learned from its past experience. This may include a particular new product innovation or a process to produce a product. Advertising that creates a brand image and an organizational strategy that coordinates complex production and distribution systems also qualify as ownership advantages. A common characteristic of many of these items is that they represent intangible knowledge that can be provided to one operation without leaving less for others to use. The firm that owns these intangible assets can spread the costs of developing this knowledge over more customers by selling in foreign as well as domestic markets. Yet we have not demonstrated why such sales could not simply occur as exports from the innovating country. Therefore, we need to consider the other categories proposed by Dunning.

Location

Location includes a variety of factors that make production abroad, rather than in the MNC's home country, attractive. In many service industries, the MNC must be located in the same country as the customer in order to provide the service. McDonald's can satisfy Muscovite demand for a Big Mac only by locating in Moscow. In other industries high transportation costs may preclude exports from one country to another. A French firm such as LaFarge that has special expertise in producing cement nevertheless will not find it economical to export cement to the United States. Instead the firm will produce cement in the United States, where it can serve U.S. customers without incurring high transport costs. Location becomes an especially important factor to MNCs when trade barriers are imposed or threatened, and MNCs find that the protected markets can best be served by producing within a country rather than exporting to it. For example, the common external tariff of the European Economic Community was a major stimulus to the large direct investments made by U.S. firms in Europe during the 1960s. U.S. and European restrictions on imports of Japanese automobiles in the 1980s gave Japanese firms an incentive to locate assembly plants in those countries.

The examples above are particularly relevant in identifying likely differences in the marginal cost of serving a market from different locations. MNCs, however, are concerned about fixed costs as well. A particularly useful way of recognizing the role of fixed costs is to distinguish those that are specific to a plant and those that are specific to the firm as a whole (Horstman and Markusen 1992). A firm's research and development which generates ideas applicable in all locations is a fixed cost specific to the firm as a whole, while the fixed cost of building a factory and installing machinery is specific to a plant. The existence of high firm-specific fixed costs makes it more likely the firm will try to serve foreign markets to exploit its unique knowledge, but high plant-specific costs make it more likely the firm will do so by exporting rather than by producing abroad. Separate plants in many separate locations result in the duplication of expenditures for plant-specific costs and raise the average total cost of serving the market that way. Conversely, when plant-specific fixed costs are low but transportation costs and trade barriers are high and the host country's factor endowments are well matched to the inputs necessary to produce the good, the MNC is more likely to locate a plant abroad.

These trade-offs are summarized in Figure 8.3, which shows the demand and marginal revenue conditions that a firm faces in the foreign country. Marginal costs of serving that market may be lower than exporting from home, due to factors such as lower labor costs, high transportation costs, or trade barriers, which all contribute to MC_H lying above MC_F. Note that lower labor costs need not imply lower wages, because MNCs tend to require more skilled workers, whose higher productivity offsets the higher wages they receive. In the case of exports, however, assume MC_H equals ATC_H, due to the large scale of output achieved in the home country market. In the foreign country, however, the MNC must meet the additional fixed costs of setting up a plant. Given the scale of the host market shown, ATC may still lie well above MC because those fixed costs cannot be spread across very many

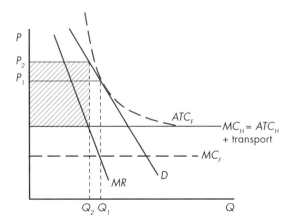

FIGURE 8.3 Potential Horizontal Integration by an MNC

In spite of lower marginal costs in the foreign country, an MNC will not establish an affiliate there, because local demand is insufficient to make local production more profitable than exports from the home country.

sales. In this example, if the MNC were to produce abroad, it would produce Q_1 and set the price at P_1, which just enables it to cover its total costs. If it were to export from the home country, it would sell Q_2 at a price P_2, which would allow it to earn economic profits shown by the shaded box. In this situation, the firm would not choose to produce in the foreign market, as exports are a substitute for production abroad. A larger host country market attracts more of this form of investment.

Determinants of Vertical Integration

Not all MNC activity need follow this model of horizontal integration, where the firm produces comparable products in each location. An MNC instead might break its production process into separate stages, and complete some of them in one location and others in a different location. That pattern is labeled vertical integration. As an example, a shoe that is designed by Adidas in Germany but produced in Indonesia takes advantage of differences in factor endowments in the two locations according to their requirements in two different stages of the production process. The skills necessary to carry out the design stage differ from those necessary to produce a standardized, labor-intensive product. In this case, the size of the host market no longer plays the same critical role, and high tariffs and transport costs discourage MNC production in the host country.

MNC investment to extract natural resources is certainly driven by location, and that situation typically represents vertical integration, because further processing of those natural resources often occurs in other countries. The bargaining position of the host government is stronger when there are few alternative locations where production is economically viable. The large fixed-capital outlays necessary to carry out production further lock the MNC into production in a given location. Host governments may renegotiate contracts and impose additional taxes, as Venezuela, Russia, and other oil exporters have in the first decade of the twenty-first century. When MNCs are uncertain about future policies that will leave them with less than a normal return, they are less likely to invest even though recoverable reserves clearly exist.

Internalization

If the MNC has decided that production abroad or sourcing inputs abroad is more efficient than exporting or producing all of the product at home, we still must consider the final criterion mentioned above, internalization. Why does the MNC choose to operate its own plant rather than license someone else to produce the good or input abroad? An advantage of licensing is that the firm need not raise capital itself or tie up its own management resources in learning how to produce in a foreign setting. Yet, by licensing technology to others, the innovator takes the risk that this information may leak out to others or be used to compete directly with it. Production abroad also raises the possibility that employees will defect and start their own competing firm. In the latter case, the MNC can at least control that process better through the incentives and wages it pays its employees.

When the pace of technological change is rapid in an industry, the firm may find licensing is the best way to earn an additional return on its innovation before that product is superceded by another. In the semiconductor industry, for example, companies have chosen to use licensing agreements to exploit their technological advances quickly. Licensees are more likely to become competitors when a high tariff creates high profit potential and when plant-specific costs are low and entry of new firms is easy (Ethier and Markusen 1996).

Licensing may not be feasible if the innovator and prospective foreign producer cannot agree on an acceptable royalty rate and means of enforcing the contract. Such agreements will be easier to reach when both parties have a good basis for judging the success of the technology being transferred. If those conditions hold, we expect to observe large royalty payments between unrelated parties. For the United States, that outcome is not common: over three-quarters of royalties received by U.S. companies from abroad come from related affiliates. Reaching and enforcing international agreements to transfer technology is far from straightforward.

How to Enter a New Market? Mergers and Acquisitions

Foreign direct investment has risen sharply, but over three-quarters of that investment is accounted for by one firm acquiring another firm, not by one firm establishing a new business enterprise in the host country. This strategy raises the question why a foreign owner would be willing to pay more than any other bidder, domestic or foreign, to acquire the target firm. One useful way of thinking about the potential value of the target firm is to consider the stream of profits that it will generate into the future, and the relevant interest rate that determines the cost of raising funds to make the acquisition. In the simplified case where the same income stream can be earned forever, the following expression summarizes this relationship:

$$Value = Income/interest\ rate$$

The acquiring firm may make a higher bid, because it anticipates it can earn higher income from the same assets, or it can finance the acquisition more cheaply than a competitor. Higher income may be possible because the acquiring firm will be able to reduce costs, by eliminating duplication of some of its head office expenses or by purchasing inputs more cheaply because of its greater volume of business. Popular press reports often refer to these savings as cost synergies. Higher income may also be possible because the acquiring firm gains access to a new market and does not have to face competition from the target firm. This market-seeking motivation suggests that the firm can earn a higher return and impose a higher markup under the acquisition strategy. Finally, a firm that is financially healthy with favorable prospects for the future may be able to raise funds for an acquisition more easily.

What pattern of acquisitions can be observed internationally? Brakman, Garretsen, and Van Marrewijk (2006) present an insightful summary of mergers and acquisitions worldwide over the period 1986–2005. Among their principal findings are the following:

- Acquiring firms in most cases acquire majority control;
- Acquiring firms in almost all cases pay cash;
- Horizontal acquisitions within the same industry have remained remarkably steady at roughly half of the total;

TABLE 8.6 The Ten Largest Acquiring and Target Merger and Acquisition Countries, 1986–2005 (constant 2005 $ billion)

Country	Av. annual acquiring flows	Av. annual target flows
United States	85.9	117.3
United Kingdom	85.3	66.2
France	37.7	18.4
Germany	29.3	33.9
Netherlands	21.2	14.7
Canada	18.7	19.5
Switzerland	14.7	—
Spain	14.1	7.8
Australia	11.9	11.0
Japan	10.6	—
Italy	—	10.5
Sweden	—	10.2

Source: Brakman, Garretsen, and van Marrewijk (2006)

■ Western Europe (55%) and North America (30%) account for most of the acquiring firms, as well as 44% and 38%, respectively, of target firms;
■ The importance of large deals as a share of the total has risen over time.

Table 8.6 provides some of their summary measures for individual countries.

Because mergers tend to occur in waves, economists have yet to explain what sets off a new wave of acquisitions. Also, economists must explain why horizontal acquisitions continue to play such an important role in spite of falling transportation and trade costs that instead would favour parent exports or vertical integration.

Effects of MNC Operations in the Home Country

The discussion thus far indicates how an MNC determines the most profitable way to exploit its specialized expertise and expand into foreign markets. By making location choices that allow it to produce more output at lower cost, and by transferring technology to and mobilizing productive resources in locations where they were scarce, the MNC generally contributes toward a more efficient world pattern of production. Whether the home country and the host country both share in those benefits is an issue that has proven to be the source of contentious debate. Home countries often worry about negative effects from less availability of capital domestically, a reduction in parent exports and output, and a loss in parent tax revenue.

Early treatments of MNC investment focused on flows of capital from the home country to the host country. With a smaller capital stock at home, labor receives a lower wage. More consistent with the rationale for MNCs discussed above, however, is the situation where the MNC does not bring capital from the home country, but instead raises capital in the host country by borrowing locally, or otherwise raises funds in third-country markets. In the latter situation, a negative distributional effect in the home country does not arise due to a falling capital-to-labor ratio.

The shift in production to the host country may displace previous exports from the home country and thereby reduce demand for factors used intensively in their production. U.S. evidence suggests that the majority of MNC investment is intended to serve the host-country market, and that the ratio of affiliate sales to parent-company exports is higher in markets where transport costs and trade barriers are high. On the other hand, many economists find that firms that produce more abroad also export more. The apparent complementary relationship may arise due to investment abroad in distribution, sales, and service networks that benefit sales of goods produced in the host country but also other goods in a firm's product line that are produced in the home country.

This potential relationship is relevant to the debate over outsourcing. The MNC reduces demand for certain jobs in the home country. However, if the lower costs of production and lower prices that result from outsourcing also create greater demand for the stages of production that the MNC retains in the home country, MNC activity in the home country may rise. Successful MNCs create more demand for headquarters services and demand for skilled labor in the home country. Whether the choice of an MNC to produce abroad necessarily reduces output at home remains a question that has yet to be resolved by the available evidence.

Higher MNC profits are a benefit to owners of the firm, and they may result in a general benefit to the home-country government if it shares in this gain through higher tax revenue. For countries that tax the worldwide income of their residents and corporations, as do Japan, the United Kingdom, and the United States, a gain in tax revenue is possible. As we noted in the case of portfolio capital, though, these countries grant a credit for foreign income tax paid, up to the tax liability due in the home country. The host country gets the first opportunity to tax this income, and the home country collects a residual tax. In reality most of the tax revenue from active business income of affiliates is collected by the host-country government. That is automatically true in the case of MNC investment from countries such as Canada, France, Germany, and the Netherlands that entirely exempt from tax the active foreign income earned by affiliates of their MNCs. Such a territorial system of taxation benefits the MNCs headquartered in those countries, but as shown earlier in the chapter it can result in investment being allocated to countries where the before-tax return is lower.

Effects of MNC Operations in the Host Country

Host countries may gain from the introduction of new technology and management, training of labor, and access to capital markets and sales networks that MNCs bring. More productive use of resources in the country causes income to rise. There may be spillovers from the activity of MNCs to the rest of the economy, much as we outlined in Chapter 5 regarding external economies of scale, due to its creation of a pool of trained labor and the spread of ideas from the MNC to suppliers of inputs and to potential competitors.

On the other hand, local producers may not benefit from many spillovers unless the level of skills in the host country reaches some threshold level. The entry of MNCs may bring new ideas, but it may also create more competition that reduces the economies of scale achieved by domestic producers. When MNCs raise capital locally, rather than bring additional funds into countries with limited savings and few links to world capital markets, the resulting competition for funds with local producers displaces the latter and reduces the base of local entrepreneurs. The argument is particularly relevant if the domestic industry initially earns monopoly profits in a protected market, and the entry of an MNC transfers those profits from domestic producers to foreign owners. At a more basic level, host countries often fear greater concentration of both market power and political power in the hands of MNCs.

What evidence have economists found in favor of either of these perspectives? Very mixed results have emerged thus far. The most convincing studies have attempted to measure how the productivity of individual domestic firms changes in response to a greater MNC presence in that country and industry. Studies that control for the many unmeasured factors that influence the performance of a given firm over time generally find limited spillover effects.

We elaborate some distinctions that appear important in the case of industrialized countries here, and consider applications to developing countries in Chapter 11. A study of Lithuanian firms observed spillovers from **Foreign Direct Investment** (FDI), but in supplying industries and not in industries where firms compete directly with MNCs (Javorcik 2004). Barrios, Görg, and Strobel (2005) report a U-shaped relationship with respect to the presence of MNCs in the Irish economy and the net entry of domestic manufacturing firms in that industry. At low levels of MNC penetration, the negative effect of greater competition created by the MNC dominates, but for a higher presence, a positive spillover effect dominates. In Britain, research shows that FDI leads to convergence of productivity among domestic firms by improving the performance of low-productivity firms (Griffith, et al., 2002). For the United States, Keller and Yeaple (2005) calculate a particularly large effect: increased FDI accounts for 10 percent of the improvement in manufacturing productivity that occurred from 1987–1996. An implication of the mixed results to date is that not all FDI is likely to have the same effect. Greater attention must be paid to what activities the MNC carries out in the host country and to the actual channels that allow positive productivity spillovers to occur. Note, too, that most studies apply to the manufacturing sector of the economy, but much FDI occurs outside that sector.

Taxation and Profit Shifting

Host countries have the opportunity to tax MNC income first, and for many developing countries there is a benefit from being able to impose a corporate tax on enterprises that keep books and are subject to financial audits, conditions that may not hold for domestic enterprises. If the MNC primarily serves a protected host-country market, then the host country is less likely to be forced by tax competition to offer a zero tax rate to attract investment. Those who buy what the MNC produces must pay a higher price to cover the MNC's higher cost of capital. But, if the MNC is making monopoly profits, then the host country can gain some share of those profits. If an MNC hopes to export, however, a higher host-country tax that raises the cost of capital to the firm is more likely to deter investment in the country. The MNC will consider alternative locations that let it serve the same export market without being subject to a high tax. Some economists have found that host-country tax rates have significant effects on the location of investment and production, especially so when a country pursues an open trade policy (Mutti and Grubert 2004).

Even when host countries are in a position to tax monopoly profits, they often complain that MNCs can all too easily shift income out of their jurisdiction to avoid taxation there. Two common ways to accomplish this income shifting are through debt finance and through transfer pricing. For example, if an affiliate in the host country borrows from a related affiliate in the Cayman Islands to finance its operations, it deducts the interest payments from its income to be taxed in the host country. The interest payment is received in a tax-haven country where that subsidiary pays no tax, and in some circumstances the parent MNC may even avoid paying a residual tax to its home government. Neither the home country nor the host country gains a share of the MNC profits. The loss of tax revenue to the host country is one reason why it may not recognize interest paid on loans from a related party as a deductible cost of doing business.

Transfer-pricing occurs when MNCs operating in high-tax countries pay higher prices for goods they buy from related parties and charge lower prices for goods they sell to related parties. The affiliate will have less income to declare in the high-tax jurisdiction. Even though the MNC still has a factory in the high-tax location, the tax base can be shifted out of the country more easily than the plant and equipment. A study of income-shifting by U.S. MNCs suggests that in a host country with a tax rate of 40 percent they will declare a before-tax return on sales of 9.3 percent but in a host country with a tax rate of 20 percent this margin rises to 15.8 percent.

How the gains from transferring technology to the host country are shared depend upon some of these same factors. Royalties paid to the parent represent one way the home country benefits, but that payment reduces the MNC's taxable income in the host country. Some host countries remain suspicious of royalty payments that transfer taxable income out of their jurisdiction, and they impose high withholding taxes on those payments. This is another example of the natural conflict between home and host countries in determining how the rents from new technology are to be divided.

Political Perspectives on MNC activities

Regulating MNC operations raises several quasi-political issues that touch on sovereignty, political control, legal jurisdictions, and the fairness of contracts. Since direct investment implies managerial control by the parent company over the foreign affiliate, there is ample scope for jurisdictional conflicts between the source country, whose laws govern the parent company, and the host country, whose laws govern the affiliate.

One such jurisdictional conflict has involved the U.S. insistence that foreign subsidiaries of U.S. firms are subject to certain U.S. laws and regulations. These laws may run into conflict with the laws of the host country. For example, in the 1970s the United States required Canadian subsidiaries of U.S. firms to abide by a U.S. ban on exports to Cuba. Canada had no such ban, and Canadians were incensed about the infringement on their sovereignty when this U.S. law was applied to firms incorporated in Canada.

These conflicts are difficult to resolve. From the U.S. point of view, its laws would be made ineffective if U.S. firms could evade them simply by setting up a foreign subsidiary. But from the host-country point of view, the extension of U.S. laws into its geographical domain is an unacceptable violation of national sovereignty. The word "extraterritoriality" is often applied to this issue because it involves attempts by the United States to enforce its laws outside its territory.

Attitudes toward MNCs in developing countries appear to have gone through a full cycle. During the 1950s and early 1960s, they were viewed as engines of development and therefore as highly desirable. During the latter half of the 1960s and throughout the 1970s, they were widely viewed as agents of imperialism, who operated as uncontrolled monopolists that would exploit domestic consumers or workers and destroy local cultures. During the 1980s, however, opinions appeared to have come back to the center. Most leaders in developing countries now view MNCs as desirable elements in their economies but want to bargain over how the benefits of their activities will be divided. MNC investments are actively sought, but governments want promises that the firms will export guaranteed proportions of their output, employ and train local workers, pay taxes in reasonable proportion to the local business they do, and so on. Host countries appear to be in a stronger bargaining position now than in the past, because of the great expansion in the number of MNCs, which compete against each other to win contracts, make sales, or locate plants abroad. On the other hand, there are many more potential locations from which to choose, because many countries are more receptive to MNCs and have chosen to participate in an integrated world economy.

Summary of Key Concepts

1. Mobility of labor and capital internationally reduces differences in wages and rates of return across countries.
2. Factor flows redistribute income within countries. For example, an inflow of capital into a capital-scarce country raises labor productivity and wage rates, while returns to capital decline.
3. An inflow of labor may raise national income but reduce income per capita in the host country if immigrants bring little human capital and attract little financial capital.
4. A primary motive for firms to become multinational corporations is the opportunity to exploit their special expertise through expanding production and sales internationally.
5. Much MNC investment is horizontal, intended to serve a local market. This strategy is more attractive when the costs of establishing a plant in a new location are a small share of total costs and when transport costs and trade barriers are high. A large host country market attracts more horizontal investment.
6. Vertically integrated MNCs break a production process into stages and choose the lowest-cost location for each stage. The size of the host country market is not so relevant, but high transport costs and trade barriers discourage this form of investment.
7. MNC operations generally increase world production by introducing technology and managerial expertise that allow greater output from the same inputs. Economists have had limited success in measuring when and how much domestic firms benefit from greater MNC operations.

CASE STUDY

The Daimler Chrysler Marriage and Divorce

In May 1998 Daimler-Benz of Germany and Chrysler of the United States announced a merger of equals, creating a company with revenues of $130 billion and 420,000 employees that produced 4 million vehicles annually. The complicated transaction called for the company to have two headquarters, one in Stuttgart and one in Auburn Hills, Michigan, and both companies to have an equal number of seats on the new board. English became the official internal language of the new company. The new company was incorporated in Germany, and Chrysler became a subsidiary of it. Daimler-Benz, whose initial value was about $55 billion, was the bigger company, and its shareholders were to control 53 percent of the new company. Chrysler stockholders received 0.547 shares in the new company for each share of Chrysler stock, which represented an aggregate value of about $38 billion.

In many mergers companies anticipate savings through eliminating the duplication of costs, but in this case the two product lines were quite distinct, with Chrysler's strengths in Jeeps, light trucks, and minivans, while Daimler-Benz was noted for luxury cars and heavy trucks. The new company still projected that it could be more successful than the two companies separately. It anticipated achieving economies in purchasing inputs through using common parts, improving the distribution of existing products, and saving costs in new product development. Over the longer run it expected additional revenue from introducing new products, such as a mass-market auto for the European market to compete with Opel (GM), Ford, and Volkswagen. This was just one step in establishing a worldwide alliance under the vision of chief executive Jürgen Schrempp, which came to include Hyundai of South Korea and Mitsubishi Motors of Japan. Those latter positions were terminated earlier, with the sale of the Hyundai stake in 2004 and the Mitsubishi shares in 2005.

In the case of the Chrysler division, the year after the merger represented its peak performance, followed by several rocky years. Although it recovered somewhat by 2004 and 2005, its losses mounted in 2006 again, as gasoline prices rose and consumers became less interested in trucks and SUVs.

In May, 2007, CEO Dieter Zetsche announced that Daimler Chrysler would sell 80.1 percent of the Chrysler division to Cerberus Capital Management, a private equity fund. Although most sales occur to other public companies, the interest of Cerberus was consistent with its prior purchase of a 51 percent interest in General Motors Acceptance Corporation and its ongoing effort to buy shares of Delphi, the auto parts subsidiary spun off by GM. Although the purchase price was announced as $7.4 billion, most of that figure represented funds that Cerberus was to invest in the new company, Chrysler Holdings. In addition, Daimler was responsible for Chrysler's outstanding debt and the losses it incurred until the deal closed. The advantage to Daimler was that it freed itself from the liability for future health care costs of Chrysler employees and retirees, estimated to be $18 billion. Although the United Auto Workers did accept the agreement, with the proviso that Daimler retain an interest in the new company, many members feared the likely cost-cutting steps that Cerberus would take.

Sources: "Companies – Chrysler Sale," *The Financial Times*, May 15, 2007, p. 20, "The Daimler-Chrysler Emulsion," *The Economist*, July 29, 2000, p. 67, "Divorced," *The Economist*, May 17, 2007, and Wikipedia, "Chrysler," accessed September 28, 2007.

CASE STUDY QUESTIONS

1. What justification for the original merger proved to be inaccurate?

2. Why may Cerberus be more successful than Daimler in managing the Chrysler division?

3. Chrysler primarily sells vehicles in the North American market. In what ways does that represent a disadvantage for it?

Questions for Study and Review

1. In what ways does an increase in factor mobility substitute for merchandise trade? At the end of the nineteenth century when the world experienced more trade and more factor mobility, explain what the effects were on the distribution of income internationally.

2. How does a country gain from allowing an outflow of capital? Who gains and who loses from that opportunity? How does tax policy in the host country affect your answer?

3. Canada pursues a policy that encourages the immigration of skilled workers. What circumstances explain the economic and political benefits from this approach?

4. Many industrialized countries have become concerned about a large inflow of illegal immigrants. If those countries were successfully to impose a tax on the employers of these immigrants, explain who would bear the burden of this tax, the employer or the immigrant.

5. Under some conditions, a developing country can gain from allowing an outflow of its educated citizens. Consider figures reported by Docquier and Marfouk for the emigration rate of high-skilled workers from the following countries: Haiti 74%, Sierra Leone 48%, Kenya 33%, Vietnam 15%, and Poland 11%. Explain whether any of these countries is likely to experience a brain gain rather than a brain drain.

6. Given the model of horizontal integration presented in this chapter, how do you expect the high transport costs and high trade barriers faced by U.S. businesses seeking to sell in Australia to affect foreign direct investment in that country? If New Zealand pursued the same policies as Australia, why would you expect the FDI response to be different?

7. What kind of FDI do you expect a small island economy such as Mauritius to attract successfully?

8. Host countries often have difficulty taxing MNCs. What strategies must they be concerned about? What is an appropriate government response?

9. Latin American countries long preferred portfolio inflows of capital rather than FDI, because it avoided foreign control over productive resources. Why has that attitude changed in more recent years?

10. What advantages are gained by a home country when its MNCs claim a bigger share of world markets? Are there groups in the home country that nevertheless would be adversely affected? What happens to domestic employment and wages?

References and Suggestions for Further Reading

For an overview of immigration issues and data sources see:

Borjas, G. (1994) "The Economics of Immigration," *Journal of Economic Literature* 32: 1667–1717.
—— (1995) "The Economic Benefits from Immigration," *Journal of Economic Perspectives* 9: 3–22.
Commmission of the European Communities (2005) *Green Paper on an EU Approach to Managing Economic Migration*, Brussels.
Docquier, F. and Marfouk, A. (2004) "Measuring international migration by educational attainment, 1990–2000," in C. Ozden and M. Schiff (eds) *International Migration, Remittances and the Brain Drain*, New York: McMillan and Palgrave, pp. 151–99.
Docquier, F. and Rapaport, H. (2007) "Skilled Migration: The Perspective of Developing Countries," World Bank Policy Research Paper No. 3382.
Mundell, R. (1957) "International Trade and Factor Mobility," *American Economic Review* 47: 321–35.
Organization for Economic Cooperation and Development (1995) *OECD Observer*, 192 (February/March). Paris: OECD.
—— (2001) *Trends in International Migration*, Paris: OECD.
—— (2007) *International Migration Outlook*, Paris: OECD.
O'Rourke, K., Taylor, A., and Williamson, J. (1996) "Factor Price Convergence in the Late Nineteenth Century," *International Economic Review* 37: 499–530.
Smith, J. and Edmonston, B. (1997) *The New Americans: Economic, Demographic, and Fiscal Effects of Immigration*, Washington, D.C.: National Academy Press.
Williamson, J. (2004) "The Political Economy of World Mass Migration: Comparing Two Global Centuries," American Enterprise Institute, The Wendt Distinguished Lecture.
World Bank (2005) *Global Economic Prospects 2006: Economic Implications of Remittances and Migration*, Washington, DC.
Zimmerman, K., Bonin, H., Fahr, R., and Hinte, H. (2007) *Immigration Policy and the Labor Market, the German Experience and Lessons for Europe*, New York: Springer.

For issues of the incidence of capital taxation see:

Gordon, R. (1986) "Taxation of Investment and Savings in a World Economy," *American Economic Review* 76: 1086–1102.
Harberger, A. (1983) "Corporate Tax Incidence in Closed and Open Economies," paper presented to NBER summer institute in taxation.
Mutti, J. and Grubert, H. (1985) "The Taxation of Capital Income in an Open Economy: The importance of Resident–Nonresident Tax Treatment," *Journal of Public Economics*, 27: 291–309.
—— (2004) "Empirical Asymmetries in Foreign Direct Investment and Taxation," *Journal of International Economics* 62: 337–58.

For a broader discussion of MNC operations, and its changing focus over several decades, see:

Barnet, R. and Muller, R. (1974) *Global Reach*, New York: Simon and Schuster.
Barrios, S., Görg, H., and Strobl, E. (2005) "Foreign Direct Investment, Competition, and Industrial Development in the Host Country," *European Economic Review* 49: 1761–1784.
Bergsten, C.F., Horst, T., and Moran, T. (1978) *American Multinationals and American Interests*, Washington, DC: Brookings, 1978.
Bernard, A., Jensen, B., Redding, S., and Schott, P. (2007) "Firms in International Trade," *Journal of Economic Perspectives* 21: 105–30.

Bhagwati, J. and Brecher, R. (1980) "National Welfare in an Open Economy in the Presence of Foreign-owned Factors of Production," *Journal of International Economics* 10: 103–15.

Brainard, L. (1997) "An Empirical Assessment of the Proximity–Concentration Tradeoff between Multinational Sales and Trade," *American Economic Review* 87: 520–44.

Brakman, S., Garretsen, H., and van Marrewijk, C. (2006) "Cross-Border Mergers and Acquisitions: The Facts as a Guide for International Economics," CESifo Working Paper No. 1823.

Caves, R. (1996) *Multinational Enterprises and Economic Analysis*, 2nd ed., London: Cambridge University Press.

Dunning, J. (1974) *Economic Analysis and the Multinational Enterprise*, London: Allen and Unwin.

Dunning, J. and Hamdani, K. (eds) (1997) *The New Globalism and the Developing Countries*, New York: United Nations University Press.

Ethier, W. and Markusen, J. (1996) "Multinational Firms, Technology Diffusion and Trade," *Journal of International Economics* 41: 1–28.

Graham, E. and Krugman, P. (1995) *Foreign Direct Investment in the United States*, 3rd edn, Washington, DC: Institute for International Economics.

Griffith, R., Redding, S., and Simpson, H. (2002) "Productivity Convergence and Foreign Ownership at the Establishment Level," Institute for Fiscal Studies Working Paper, w02/22.

Grubert, H. and Mutti, J. (1991) "Taxes, Tariffs and Transfer Pricing in Multinational Corporate Decision Making," *Review of Economics and Statistics* 73: 285–93.

Horstman, I. and Markusen, J. (1992) "Endogenous Market Structures in International Trade," *Journal of International Economics* 32: 109–29.

Javorcik, B. (2004) "Does Foreign Direct Investment Increase the Productivity of Domestic Firms? In search of Spillovers through Backward Linkages," *American Economic Review* 94: 605–627.

Keller, W. and Yeaple, S. (2005) "Multinational Enterprises, International Trade, and Productivity Growth: Firm-Level Evidence from the United States," Deutsche Bundesbank Discussion Paper Series 1.

Lipsey, R. and Weiss, M. (1984) "Foreign Production and Exports of Individual Firms," *Review of Economics and Statistics* 66: 304–8.

Markusen, J. (2002) *Multinational Firms and the Theory of International Trade*, Cambridge, MA: MIT Press.

Mutti, J. and Grubert, H. (2004) "Empirical Asymmetries in Foreign Direct Investment and Taxation," *Journal of International Economics* 62: 337–58.

Servan-Schreiber, J. (1968) *The American Challenge*, New York: Athenaeum.

United Nations Conference on Trade and Development (2006) *World Investment Report*, New York: United Nations.

Vernon, R. (1971) *Sovereignty at Bay*, New York: Basic Books.

Chapter 9

Regional Blocs

Preferential Trade Liberalization

LEARNING OBJECTIVES

By the end of this chapter you should be able to understand:

- why various degrees of economic integration within preferential trade blocs exist

- how trade blocs may affect members and non-members, through trade creation and trade diversion, as well as potential gains from economies of scale and greater capital formation

- how economists assess the consequences of particular trade blocs such as the European Union and NAFTA

To this point we have assumed that restrictions on imports are nondiscriminatory; that is, all trading partners are treated equally in terms of market access. Such nondiscriminatory trade is a major goal of the GATT/WTO system, which we examine in Chapter 10, but it is far from universal. Most countries have different levels of protection, maintaining the lowest level for partners in trade blocs or friends, and less favorable circumstances for others. The GATT articles of agreement allow such trading blocs when their preferential treatment applies to substantially all trade among the partners. The WTO reports that in October 2007 there were 194 active agreements, and by 2010 it anticipates there will be 400.[1]

The European Union (E.U.) is the most ambitious trade bloc with regard to its size and the extent of economic integration it has fostered among its members, and we pay primary attention to it in this chapter. We also consider the North American Free Trade Agreement (NAFTA), a more recent and less comprehensive agreement which nevertheless creates an internal market nearly as large as the E.U. market.

In whichever case we consider, several key questions arise: Who benefits from preferential trade agreements (PTAs) – just some members, all members, or the world as a whole? If members gain at the expense of non-member countries, does this GATT exception make sense, or do PTAs represent an important step toward a more liberal trading order that ought to be encouraged? Should PTAs be regarded as stumbling blocks or building blocks? We begin this chapter by considering alternative structures for preferential trade areas. We then consider what factors are especially relevant in assessing the gains and losses from their establishment, before addressing the experience of the E.U. and NAFTA.

ALTERNATIVE FORMS OF PREFERENTIAL TRADE AGREEMENTS

Preferential trade agreements can be categorized according to how extensive the integration of national economies becomes. The first and easiest to negotiate is a **free-trade area**, under which tariffs and other barriers to trade among the members are removed (sometimes only for manufactured goods, due to differing agricultural support programs). To the extent that each country retains its own antidumping procedures, national restrictions can still influence trade among members. Also, each country maintains its own tariff schedule and other commercial policies with regard to goods coming from non-member countries. Such arrangements encourage the importation of goods into

---

1 See the WTO website for a complete listing of these notifications at http://www.wto.org/english/tratop_e/ region_e/regfac_e.htm. (Accessed October 4, 2007.)

whichever member has the lowest tariffs and their subsequent reshipment to member countries with higher external tariffs. Certificates of origin are supposed to guarantee that products coming tariff-free from a member country really were produced there, but enforcing such a system effectively to prohibit transshipments is far from automatic.

This problem can be avoided with the adoption of a **customs union** arrangement. A customs union is a free-trade area in which external tariffs and other barriers to imports coming from non-members are unified; that is, all member countries maintain the same restrictions on imports from non-members. A **common market**, the next step in regional integration, is a customs union that allows the free mobility of capital and labor among the member countries. A final step is **economic union**, a customs union where countries have agreed to common tax and expenditure policies and a jointly managed monetary policy. The European Economic Community (EEC), established by the Treaty of Rome in 1957, led to a unified customs union by 1968. Subsequent progress in removing other barriers to the free movement of goods, services, labor, and capital in a single market and in achieving greater coordination of economic and social policies was reflected in the establishment of the European Union in 1993.

EFFICIENCY GAINS AND LOSSES FROM PREFERENTIAL TRADE AGREEMENTS

The creation of a regional bloc or other form of PTA would appear to be a movement toward free trade and therefore toward greater economic efficiency. Because some barriers to trade are being eliminated and others are being left in place, the average tariff level for the world declines. This appearance of liberalization and of greater efficiency can be deceptive, however. Some regional blocs do increase efficiency, but others can represent a movement away from the allocation of resources that would occur under free trade and can therefore reduce world efficiency. The fact that the tariff cutting is discriminatory creates this possibility. In the absence of compensatory taxes and subsidies or any effort to maintain trade with the rest of the world, there is no general rule to establish whether PTAs increase or decrease efficiency; instead, each must be evaluated separately.

Trade Creation and Trade Diversion

To evaluate the consequences of a PTA, Jacob Viner (1953) introduced the concepts of trade creation and trade diversion. Because these terms still are commonly used, we start by explaining them:

■ *Trade creation.* This is the beneficial effect of a preferential trading arrangement on its member countries. When a tariff is eliminated on a good produced in a partner country, the price seen by domestic producers and consumers falls. Consumers buy more of the good and imports rise. Part of the increase in imports is accounted for by a reduction in inefficient domestic production, which is replaced by more efficient production in the partner country. For example, if the E.U. reduces its tariff on bananas from African and Caribbean countries, its imports of bananas from those countries rise.

■ *Trade diversion.* This is the undesirable or efficiency-reducing effect of such a bloc. It occurs when a member country was previously importing a product from a country that does not become a member of the bloc. When the discriminatory tariff-cutting occurs, a member country's export sales rise, but those of the non-member fall. Under those circumstances, world efficiency falls because trade is diverted from low-cost to higher-cost sources. For example, the E.U. tariff reduction on African and Caribbean bananas reduces E.U. imports of bananas from more efficient South American producers such as Ecuador.

A simple modification to the Chapter 5 treatment of a tariff in a small country can show these two measures. Consider French production and imports of bicycles from two potential sources, Germany and Japan. If the French supply curve is upward-sloping, while supply curves for Germany and Japan remain horizontal, it is possible to show both trade creation and trade diversion in the same market. This situation can be seen in Figure 9.1. Prior to the creation of the customs union, France maintains a uniform tariff, which is shown as the vertical distance between S_J and $S_J + T$. German costs are

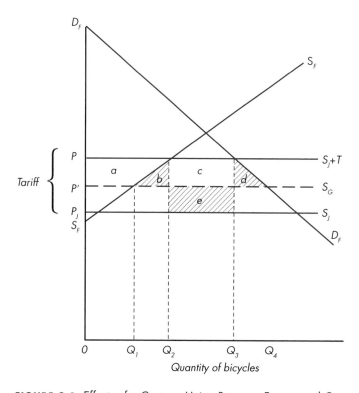

FIGURE 9.1 Effects of a Customs Union Between France and Germany

Before the customs union is formed, Japan, which is the lowest-cost producer, exports a volume of Q_2Q_3 to France. Germany, with higher costs and no preferential advantage, has no sales in France. The customs union, however, gives Germany a discriminatory advantage, and its supply curve to France becomes S_G, while the Japanese supply curve remains at $S_J + T$. All French imports now shift to German sources, and imports rise to Q_1Q_4. The trade creation gains are triangles b and d, but the trade distortion loss is rectangle e. The French government loses tariff revenues of rectangles c plus e.

higher, as shown by S_G, so with the uniform tariff, Germany sells no bicycles in France. The elimination of the French tariff on German bikes makes S_G the relevant import supply function. Japan loses export sales of Q_3Q_2, with a resulting efficiency loss of rectangle e, which represents the difference between German and Japanese costs times the number of bicycles whose production is diverted. Since the French price of bicycles declines from P to P', however, consumption expands from Q_3 to Q_4 and French production declines from Q_2 to Q_1, thus increasing total imports from Q_3Q_2 to Q_4Q_1. The efficiency gains from this expansion of trade consist of the areas of triangles b and d. Whether efficiency increases or declines in this market depends on the relationship between the area of rectangle e (loss) and the sum of triangles b and d (gain). This net effect can be derived from the increase in consumers' surplus of area $a + b + c + d$, while French manufacturers lose producers' surplus of area a and the French government loses tariff revenue of areas $c + e$.

Although the government loses revenues and manufacturers lose profits, French consumers gain a large amount of consumer surplus, and German firms gain sales. Correspondingly, similar effects can be identified for other goods where French exports to Germany rise at the expense of Japanese exports. Japan appears to be a clear loser: it loses export revenues, and its firms lose sales to firms that are less efficient. Except for potentially unbalanced impacts on government revenues, regional blocs are generally beneficial to the members, but they can be decidedly harmful to non-members. If a member of a free-trade area found that it did not gain because its losses from trade diversion exceeded its gains from trade creation, it could simply reduce its tariff sufficiently to eliminate the loss from diversion. A member of a customs union with a common external tariff, however, does not have this same opportunity.

A loss to Japan can be demonstrated more clearly if we add another possible effect to the situation shown in Figure 9.1. If the foreign supply curves are not horizontal, the price the French pay for Japanese goods will fall. Preferential treatment of imports from Germany is less likely to displace Japanese exports completely. Rather, if Japanese exporters cannot easily shift these goods to other markets, they are willing to accept a decline in the before-tariff price they receive. This price reduction represents a gain to France and a loss to Japan.[2] We discussed a similar effect in Chapter 6 regarding the optimum tariff a large country might levy. As countries join together in regional trading blocs, their market power and potential to shift the terms of trade in their favor increases.

Arvind Panagariya (1999) suggests another modification shown in Figure 9.2. Suppose France produces none of the imported product, and the upward sloping supply curve instead represents German production. An initial tariff on imports from Germany would shift that supply curve to the left, implying a smaller German share of the market and a larger Japanese share. Removing the tariff on German goods only does not affect the price seen by consumers, which is determined by the tariff-laden Japanese goods, but German production expands while French imports from Japan fall. Thus, France gets no benefit from trade creation, but experiences a big trade diversion loss captured by Germany. Panagariya suggests such asymmetric outcomes are likely when a high-tariff, small developing country

---

2 In this example, France's terms of trade with Germany may worsen, as greater French demand for German bicycles drives up their price. If German gains turned out to be greater than comparable French terms-of-trade gains on items exported to Germany, further negotiation within the union might be necessary to ensure that all members gain. The division of gains became a significant issue in the case of British entry into the European Economic Community.

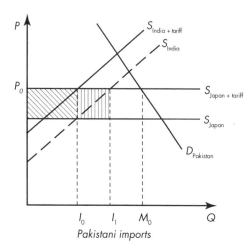

FIGURE 9.2   Significant Revenue Effects of a Customs Union

Before the formation of a customs union between India and Pakistan, total imports are M_0, with I_0 originating in India and the rest from Japan. If Pakistan eliminates its tariff only on Indian imports, they rise to I_1. Total imports are unchanged and there is no trade creation. Pakistan loses all of the tariff revenue previously collected on imports from India and on the Japanese imports displaced by greater imports from India, shown by the two shaded rectangles.

joins with a low-tariff, more developed country, such as Mexico and the United States in NAFTA, or the E.U. in its southern expansion to include Greece, Spain, and Portugal in the 1980s.

Broader Considerations in Evaluating Preferential Arrangements

Economists recognize that the trade creation/trade diversion framework leaves out additional relevant effects. An alternative approach that can be applied to demonstrate the effect on members and non-members is based on deconstructing a country's change in welfare into terms of trade and volume of trade effects:

$$dWelfare = -M \, dp_e + (p - p_e) \, dM \tag{9.1}$$

where M is the country's quantity of imports, p_e is the price paid to foreigners exclusive of the tariff, p is the domestic price of the good, and dp_e and dM denote small changes in those variables. The first term is the terms-of-trade effect, and the second term represents a gain from importing more of those goods where domestic price exceeds the foreign price. For any country, sum these terms for all goods and trade partners where net imports or exports occur.

In contrast to Figure 9.1, this approach includes all trade, not just markets where goods are imported from member countries. It also allows for the potential effect of rising income increasing imports from members and non-members, in which case trade diversion is not observed and both groups may gain from the formation of the bloc. Another implication from this framework is that two partners are most likely to gain if both start from a near autarky position, where $M\,dp_e$ is quite small. In that case, neither country is likely to improve its terms of trade at the expense of its partner.

The Additional Role of Economies of Scale

This approach can be further modified to take into account situations where economies of scale and imperfect competition exist. Scale effects have been found to be a significant source of additional gain. Recall that internal economies of scale depend upon a firm's output, not the industry's output. Therefore, an important determinant of these potential gains is what happens to the number of firms in an industry. If the formation of a European customs union results in greater competition between previously protected French and German producers, they each perceive a more elastic demand for their output, and the profit margins they charge will be reduced. Output per firm rises, which results in lower average costs of production. This benefit from greater competition will be greater among countries that have overlapping industry structures.

Based on the reasoning developed in Chapter 5, we expect the total number of producers in France and Germany to fall, which means fewer resources need be devoted to the fixed costs of a firm entering the industry. The remaining firms producing this particular product achieve greater economies of scale. When producers who do cease production of this product can easily shift inputs into producing other products, say a shift from large refrigerators to small refrigerators, the economic and social costs of adjustment are likely to be much smaller than in the case of trade motivated by differences in factor endowments, such as labor-intensive clothing versus capital-intensive chemicals.

An alternative reason for scale economies to be observed is the decline in average costs of production possible when external economies of scale exist. Concentration of output in one country might lower costs of production by promoting the introduction of specialized intermediate-input suppliers, by creating a pool of trained labor, and by encouraging the spread of information about new technologies. A larger market created within the preferential trade bloc may make it more likely that these externalities or benefits from agglomeration are realized.

A major concern *within* trading blocs has been where these more efficient producers will tend to be located. As suggested by the economic geography model introduced in Chapter 5, footloose manufacturing activity that benefits from agglomeration is likely to be concentrated in the center or core of the market, with peripheral areas left producing agricultural commodities or other goods where agglomeration benefits are not important. If labor is perfectly mobile within the bloc, these effects are accentuated by labor moving to the core. When labor is not so mobile, then labor in the periphery may be left earning a lower wage.[3] However, in this latter case, the agglomeration outcome may not be a permanent result, but instead will depend upon whether the cost of trade continues to decline within the union. We return to this topic in considering the specific E.U. situation.

---

3 See Diego Puga (1999) for a two-region model where initial declines in trade costs result in greater agglomeration but subsequent reductions result in the dispersion of footloose activity.

Other Potential Gains from PTAs

Economists also point to dynamic gains from economic integration. Not only may joining a trade bloc attract an inflow of capital, but a country's increase in output and income also may allow greater saving to occur. Either of those effects can result in a larger national capital stock and greater productive capacity in the country, which creates an extra benefit from joining the trade bloc.

Finally, the conceptual framework discussed thus far assumes that prior to the formation of the preferential trading bloc, firms are operating efficiently given the limited national markets they face and the market power they possess. A more fundamental possibility is that firms have grown complacent in sheltered national markets. Competition from rivals in other member countries is a powerful stimulus to managerial efficiency. Firms become acutely cost-conscious and much more receptive to technological improvements. The European Commission identified this as an expected source of gain from the 1992 single market program.

MEASURING THE ECONOMIC EFFECTS OF A PREFERENTIAL TRADE AGREEMENT

Can any of these economic effects from the formation of a PTA be accurately measured? Economists have addressed this issue in two different ways. *Ex ante* studies before the implementation of an agreement have relied upon computable general equilibrium (CGE) models to predict how prices and output will change once trade barriers that apply to trade between members are reduced. *Ex post* studies assess how much trade actually did change. They must control for how the economy would have performed in the absence of the agreement. Economists have used the gravity model of trade introduced in Chapter 5 to draw such inferences.

Projected Effects from Computable General Equilibrium Models

CGE models consist of a set of demand and supply equations for output and input markets, and market equilibrium conditions. Which products to represent in greatest detail will depend upon the countries to be considered and their economic structure. In this chapter we refer to specific models that have been used in analyzing various aspects of the E.U. and NAFTA. As stated above, however, there are no generally accepted propositions about the way members and non-members will be affected by a preferential trade agreement.

A suggestive approach by Abrego, Reizman, and Whalley (2006) represents one way of thinking about probable outcomes. They start from a simple model with three countries that trade three different goods, and then consider the outcome from two of the countries forming a customs union. On the basis of random draws for different country endowments of the goods and consumer preferences for the goods, they report several general tendencies. Three of them are quite consistent with the rapid rise of PTAs, although they do not appear to be a good omen for establishing a multilateral trading system based on comparable treatment of all countries, a topic we address in Chapter 10.

■ First, in about half of the cases, two countries find that a customs union makes them better off than if they had each followed the policy of levying their own optimal tariffs. Thus, there is likely to be a gain in economic efficiency from jointly reducing trade barriers within a region.

■ Second, for the pair of countries that do gain from the customs union, less than 3 percent will find it desirable to go ahead and pursue free trade among all countries. Thus, customs unions do not appear to be very promising stepping stones for moving to a free trade solution.

■ Third, if economists could somehow wave a magic wand and create a free trade equilibrium, in 23 percent of the cases two countries would have an incentive to back out of such an agreement and form a customs union.

Of course, these simulations apply to a simplistic setting where countries produce nothing and merely trade given endowments of goods. Nevertheless, economists who examine countries' actual behaviour observe such tendencies for PTAs to make multilateral trade liberalization less likely. Nuno Limão (2006) assesses the tariff concessions for specific goods that the U.S. made in the Uruguay Round of multilateral trade negotiations. He finds that the U.S. made smaller concessions for those goods where preferential trade partners particularly benefited from their special access to the U.S. market. Karacaovali and Limão (2008) report similar evidence for the E.U., except in the case of trade between countries that actually joined the E.U.

Estimated Effects from Gravity Models

After the fact, economists can observe the trade that occurs when a PTA is created, but they must be able to contrast that to what would have happened in the absence of the PTA. Because that counterfactual situation cannot be observed directly, economists use the gravity model of bilateral trade between countries i and j to control on important factors such as their incomes and the distance between them. A simplified version is shown in equation (9.2).

$$ln\ X_{ij} = \alpha_0 + \alpha_1\ ln\ GDP_i + \alpha_2\ ln\ GDP_j - \alpha_3\ ln\ Distance_{ij} + \alpha_4\ PTA \qquad (9.2)$$

To assess the importance of a PTA, economists include a dummy variable whose value equals one when a formal trade agreement exists between two countries that trade. Otherwise, the dummy variable equals zero. A positive coefficient for that variable indicates that two member countries trade more than would be expected just on the basis of their incomes or location. Such an approach avoids any need to measure the actual extent of trade policy preferences granted by the agreement. The estimates are usually made for measures of total trade, without attention to individual products.

Studies that followed this approach initially were based on a cross-section of trade in a given year. Such estimates were often quite sensitive to the year chosen, the countries included, and the econometric approach applied. For many agreements they appeared to give estimates that were biased downward. Baier and Bergstrand (2007) identify two reasons for those outcomes. First, more complete derivations of the economic basis for the gravity model show that a researcher should be considering not only the price of the good being traded bilaterally, but also the prices of goods in other potential trade partners. Second, the formation of a trade bloc should not be treated as something determined, independent from the amount of trade that occurs. Rather, the choice to negotiate an agreement may depend upon the initial amount of trade and the expected increase in trade.[4] When the authors adopt appropriate estimating strategies to deal with those problems in data sets that include many years, they find that a trade agreement is likely to result in a doubling of trade between members within ten years. We comment on estimates for a few specific agreements after describing their key features.

THE EUROPEAN UNION

European political and economic cooperation over the past 60 years demonstrates remarkable progress in achieving deeper economic integration and in expanding to include more countries. Figure 9.3 summarizes this process of expansion from the six founding members of the European Economic Community (EEC) in 1958 to the 27 members of the European Union (E.U.) in 2007. The sequential steps by which this expansion has occurred should serve as a warning that to achieve similar success in PTAs elsewhere in the world may take considerable time. A noteworthy economic initiative undertaken in 1987 was the commitment to establish a single European market by 1992. Another was the Maastricht Treaty, signed in 1991, that created the European Union and promoted closer coordination of national economic policies. It also established a plan to introduce a common currency, the euro, in 1999; the latter topic is addressed in Chapter 22.

E.U. expansion in 2004 to include several former members of the Soviet bloc was a major force in promoting economic reforms and democratic governments in those countries. These accessions have important implications for the future governance of the E.U., as well as its major expenditure programs. Deliberations to write a constitutional treaty began in 2002, but the final document agreed in 2004 was subsequently rejected in referendums held in France and the Netherlands in 2005. A reform treaty proposed in 2007 was rejected in an Irish referendum in 2008, and final acceptance had not occurred before the publication of this book. The treaty deals with serious political and administrative issues that warrant careful deliberation, but the following discussion focuses instead on some of the economic issues and challenges that ever closer union has raised.

Empirical Assessments and Interpretations

With respect to the initial formation of the EEC, the most systematic analyses have addressed trade in manufactured goods. For example, between 1958 and 1970, Bela Balassa (1975) reported that imports from members as a share of domestic consumption rose from 4.8 percent to 12.4 percent, while the comparable figure for imports from non-members rose from 6.4 percent to 8.7 percent. He controlled for the way these shares would have changed in the absence of the EEC by examining the

---

4 Baier and Bergstrand suggest that countries are more likely to form an agreement with the hope of closer economic integration when there are substantial regulatory barriers that reduce trade between them. The unmeasured regulatory climate is an omitted variable that biases downward the estimated influence of the PTA.

1948 Belgium, Luxembourg, and the Netherlands form the Benelux Customs Union

1951 France, Germany, Italy, and the Benelux countries form the European Coal and Steel Community (ECSC)

1958 The European Economic Community (EEC) is created by implementation of the Treaty of Rome, signed by the six members of the ECSC.

1967 The EEC joins with the ECSC and Euratom to form the European Community

1968 The EEC becomes a customs union with a common external tariff

1971 Denmark, Ireland, and the United Kingdom join the EEC

1981 Greece joins the EEC

1986 Portugal and Spain join the EEC

The Single European Act commits members to create a single E.U. market for goods, services, capital, and labor

1993 The European Union (E.U.) is created by implementation of the Maastricht Treaty

1995 Austria, Finland, and Sweden join the E.U.

2004 Cyprus, the Czech Republic, Estonia, Hungary, Latvia, Lithuania, Malta, Poland, the Slovak Republic, and Slovenia join the E.U.

2007 Bulgaria and Romania join the E.U.

FIGURE 9.3 The Progression of Economic Integration Within Europe

way growth in income affected imports from both sources in the 1953–9 base period, an approach that predates the more formal application of the gravity model. He concluded that trade creation exceeded trade diversion by $11.4 billion. In terms of the welfare triangles shown in Figure 9.1, he calculated that the gain from this trade creation represents 0.15 percent of GNP. In the case of agricultural trade, he reported a loss from trade diversion equal to half that amount. He further applied a very general procedure to project that gains from economies of scale equal 0.5 percent of GNP. Because much of the EEC expansion in trade was intra-industry, the social tensions involved in the adjustment process were much lower than if large industry contractions had been necessary.

Although the United Kingdom had originally chosen to remain outside of the EEC, and its attempts to enter in the 1960s were unsuccessful, it did negotiate an accession agreement by 1971. A significant economic and political factor was the projected higher cost of food and the transfer of tariff revenue from the U.K. to the EC. Because higher food prices have the greatest impact on low-income families, the Labour Party opposed British membership, and as late as 1983 it waged an unsuccessful general election campaign to withdraw from the EEC. A more complete overview of the potential economic effects was provided by the CGE model of Miller and Spencer (1977), one of the first such applications to evaluate a preferential trade agreement. Those authors found that British acceptance of import restrictions under the Common Agricultural Policy, the loss of the previous subsidy benefit on food imports from the EC, and the required transfer of 90 percent of tariff revenue to the Community were projected to result in a loss of 1.9 percent of GDP. This effect more than offset gains of 0.13 percent of GDP from trade creation/diversion effects on manufactured trade.

The issue of British support of the EC budget was a point of contention from the outset (Winters 1985). For example, in 1979 the United Kingdom contributed over 21 percent of the budget but received less than 13 percent of expenditures. On an ability-to-pay principle such a financial burden would not seem warranted because the U.K. was far from the highest-income country within the Community. In 1984 the U.K. was able to renegotiate those terms, but still remained a net contributor because its small agricultural sector benefited less from the high internal commodity prices that were advocated by the French, Danes, and Irish, and financed by the EC budget.

The single market program begun in 1987 was not completed by 1992, but that date has provided a focal point for other economic analyses. Tariffs had long since been removed on intra-EC trade, but several other barriers kept national markets segmented rather than unified. These included differing industrial product standards, government procurement policies that favor national producers, professional licensing requirements that limit labor mobility, capital controls, border regulations, and restrictions on trade in services such as banking, insurance, and transportation. To achieve the goals of free movement of people, capital, goods, and services requires changes in thousands of national laws, regulations, and procedures. The positive economic implications were projected by the European Commission to be quite large. Reasons for its strong advocacy are summarized in Table 9.1 from initial estimates in the Cecchini Report (1988), which projects that forming a single market will raise GDP by 4 to 6 percent.

Subsequent analysis by economists using more comprehensive analytical models, which at the same time do not purport to measure as many separate influences, put this gain in a smaller range. A survey by Baldwin and Venables (1995) of five different studies breaks their effects into the three sources of gain identified earlier: general trade-creation effects raise GDP by 0.5 percent including economies of scale raises that figure to 0.40–1.18 percent of GDP; and adding effects of capital accumulation raises it to 0.8–2.60 percent. Attention to factors beyond trade creation and trade diversion is clearly important.

TABLE 9.1 The Gains from Establishing a Single Market

	% of GDP
Gain from removal of trade barriers	0.2–0.3
Gain from removal of barriers affecting overall production	2.0–2.4
Gains from exploiting economies of scale more fully	2.1
Gains from intensified competition reducing business efficiencies and monopoly profits	1.6
Total	4.3–6.2

Source: Commission of EC, Study of Directorate-General for Economic and Financial Affairs, in Cecchini Report (1988), Table 9.2.

Implications of Trade and Mobility within the E.U.

As suggested above, a customs union is likely to improve the welfare of its members, but that outcome is not automatically guaranteed. Some system of transfers or subsidies may be necessary to achieve this result. The E.U. devotes an important part of its budget to structural adjustment programs that promote convergence in economic performance within the union. Are such expenditures likely to be necessary many decades into the future? The answer to that question is more likely to be yes if the benefits from agglomeration of production in core locations are strong enough to offset the competitive advantage from lower wages in poorer regions.

A study by Brakman, Garretsen, and Schramm (2005) provides useful insight on the strength of any tendencies toward agglomeration within Europe. These authors note that one implication of the new economic geography models is that as trade becomes less costly, more agglomeration of activity in a core location will occur, because producers there can obtain intermediate inputs more cheaply and sell to a larger home market. Wages in core areas will be higher than in the periphery. But, as trade costs fall further, the economy may reach a point where the benefits from agglomeration in the core no longer offset higher wages. Greater dispersion of activity again occurs. A key question becomes: Is the E.U. currently in a position where the benefits from agglomeration are rising or falling?

Based on this theory, the authors estimate a wage relationship for the 214 NUTS II (Nomenclature of Territorial Units for Statistics) regions in Europe. In their short-run framework, they take the distribution of firms and workers as given, control for differences in the physical geography of their regions, and estimate how wages vary with distance from other regions. Their estimates demonstrate that wages are higher where there are benefits of agglomeration. They can also infer values for the way transport costs vary with distance and for the degree of substitutability between goods produced in different regions. In the **economic geography** framework, those two terms determine the attractiveness or ease of trade. Somewhat surprisingly, their estimates over the 1992–2000 period show no change in the ease of trade within the E.U., in spite of the ambitious program to establish a single market.

In the long run labor can move. Nevertheless, the authors conclude that the forces for agglomeration are largely local. For distances greater than 200 kilometres, they find no agglomeration effect. For specific industries, they report that agglomeration is most important in the case of plastics and drugs, ferrous metals, and vehicles.

Important Challenges

The accession of twelve new members has important implications for the two major expenditure categories of the E.U. budget: agriculture and structural measures. Under the 2007–2013 Financial Framework agreed in 2006, the Common Agricultural Policy and rural development still account for 43 percent of the total, and structural funds another 36 percent.[5] Because total spending

---

5 See the Interinstitutional Agreement and Financial Framework, 2007–2013 available at http://europa.eu/scadplus/leg/en/lvb/l34020.htm and O. Schneider (2007).

commitments are fixed at 1.24 percent of E.U. income, these amounts are much smaller than national budgets, but as shown in Table 9.2 they still account for significant shares of member country's incomes. The three budget items shown separately there do not sum to the figure given in the total column, because the latter includes administrative expenditures, especially important in Belgium and Luxembourg, and compensation payments to new accession countries. Because the latter payments are scheduled to decline, the first three items can be thought of as showing more permanent influences on the member countries.

TABLE 9.2 Spending from the E.U. Budget 2006, selected categories (% of Gross National Income in Recipient Country)

	Agriculture	Structural actions	Internal policies	Total
Belgium	0.30	0.10	0.25	1.78
Bulgaria	0.00	0.00	0.04	1.43
Czech Rep.	0.46	0.43	0.05	1.24
Denmark	0.52	0.06	0.07	0.67
Germany	0.28	0.19	0.05	0.53
Estonia	0.60	1.13	0.40	2.39
Greece	1.62	1.89	0.08	3.59
Spain	0.70	0.60	0.04	1.34
France	0.56	0.12	0.04	0.75
Ireland	1.15	0.31	0.14	1.63
Italy	0.37	0.31	0.05	0.74
Cyprus	0.37	0.10	0.16	1.71
Latvia	0.87	0.89	0.39	2.56
Lithuania	1.33	0.83	0.98	3.45
Luxembourg	0.17	0.08	0.40	4.34
Hungary	1.02	8.83	0.15	2.22
Malta	0.19	0.34	0.22	3.25
Netherlands	0.22	0.08	0.08	0.40
Austria	0.50	0.12	0.09	0.72
Poland	0.83	0.75	0.11	2.05
Portugal	0.64	1.70	0.09	2.44
Romania	0.00	0.00	0.01	0.74
Slovenia	0.54	0.31	0.27	1.38
Slovakia	0.65	0.63	0.14	1.63
Finland	0.49	0.19	0.07	0.76
Sweden	0.30	0.10	0.10	0.51
U.K.	0.22	0.16	0.04	0.43
E.U.	0.44	0.28	0.07	0.85

Source: European Commission (2006).

The Common Agricultural Policy

The Common Agricultural Policy (CAP) raises farm incomes. The E.U. stands ready to buy surplus production of several commodities because domestic output at target prices exceeds domestic demand. Until 1995 imports of agricultural commodities were limited by a variable levy that raised the price of foreign commodities above the European target price level. The tariff-rate quotas subsequently imposed still severely restrict access to the E.U. market. To avoid buying and storing surplus production the E.U. subsidizes export sales. As noted in Chapter 6, that has resulted in lower food prices in international markets, a benefit to non-members who are net importers of food and a loss to other net exporters.

Within the E.U., an initial effect of the CAP was to redistribute income from Germany to France. The accession of Greece, Spain, and Portugal added other net recipients of funds. The enlargement of the E.U. brings in other countries with large agricultural sectors. A key point of the eastern accession agreements rested on newcomers initially receiving less than half of the direct subsidy rate available to current farmers, although new members were given the right to provide additional assistance from national funds. A 10-year phase-in period before full benefits became available was intended to allow time for the restructuring of their agricultural sectors. Whether the national responsibility of new members to top up the assistance to its own farmers becomes a pattern for all members to follow will undoubtedly be debated in the future. As a larger share of CAP expenditures are accounted for by direct payment to farmers, not related to their current production or market prices, the rationale for redistributing income across the union in this way is likely to face greater scrutiny. The 2007–2013 CAP expenditures were fixed by the European Council in 2002, thereby removing that item from consideration in the subsequent discussions over the rest of the budget.

Regional Assistance and Social Programs

Regional assistance represents a second important issue. The potential concentration of economic activity in core countries with better infrastructure and higher levels of education, leaving peripheral countries with fewer prospects for growth, required E.U. attention even before enlargement. The largest share of the funds is distributed under the convergence criteria to regions with income per capita less than 75 percent of the E.U. average. The admission of new members with below average incomes resulted in the E.U. average declining, and therefore some previously eligible regions no longer met this standard. The Commission proposed allowing the group of transitional regions to qualify for structural funds, and the E.U.-15 members still accounted for over half of these expenditures in 2005.

A further issue of importance within the E.U. is the goal of harmonization of government policies, such as social programs, taxes, and environmental standards. In a market where there are fewer barriers to the movement of goods, services, people, and capital, the influence of government programs that address national problems or preferences now accounts for more of the difference in relative prices across suppliers in different countries. Previously those price differences had less impact, because other prohibitions and regulations limited the entry of outsiders. Now capital can move more freely within the E.U. to whatever location offers a higher return. Some observers fear a race to the bottom in providing social services, if economic activity and the tax bases of more generous states are eroded by these new freedoms.

NAFTA

A precursor to NAFTA was the Canada–U.S. Free Trade Agreement, established in 1989. The trade flow between the two countries was already the largest bilateral flow in the world (about $220 billion per year). Given this large amount of trade initially, and the prospect of gains in efficiency from greater competition among overlapping industries, the agreement appeared to be overwhelmingly trade creating. From the perspective of trade policy, the United States viewed this agreement, and later NAFTA, as a demonstration that like-minded countries could reach more comprehensive agreements than was possible multilaterally. Indeed, the many obstacles to progress in the multilateral Uruguay Round negotiations from 1986 to 1993 fed this perception. Because the Canadian market was only one-tenth the size of the U.S. market and similar wages were paid in both countries, much of U.S. industry anticipated neither major gains nor losses from the agreement.

Canadian Perspectives

Within Canada the agreement was controversial. The western provinces specialized in natural-resource-based products exported to the United States, such as lumber, metals, oil, and gas, and they stood to benefit from cheaper imports. Ontario had a large manufacturing sector, much of which was of relatively small scale and high cost. Many Ontario residents, fearing that their manufacturing jobs would be lost as U.S. products arrived on a free-trade basis, strongly opposed the pact. However, David Cox and Richard Harris (1995) projected that Canadian producers could realize substantial economies of scale by exporting to the much larger U.S. market, and their CGE analysis pioneered academic efforts to include scale economies in such models. On that account they indicated there were significant gains to Canada from approving the free-trade agreement.

Canadians as Hewers of Wood and Drawers of Water?

While the Canada–U.S. Free Trade Agreement that took effect in 1989 hardly caused a stir politically in the United States, in Canada it was the key issue in a national election that highlighted concerns over cultural and political sovereignty. Brian Mulroney's Progressive Conservative party, which won the 1988 election, received only 43 percent of the votes cast, in no small part due to the fear that Canadian manufacturing capacity would wither under greater competition from U.S. firms, and Canada would be relegated to produce natural resource products.

Were the effects so drastic? Past research suggested small effects, although some analysts did note that the average Canadian tariff rate of 8.1 percent was greater than the U.S. tariff rate of 4.0 percent, a signal of a possible trade diversion loss for Canada. A recent study by Daniel Trefler (2004) allows a more nuanced assessment of the outcome. He expected potentially significant effects because one in four Canadian industries was protected by a tariff that exceeded 10 percent, and even the average 8.1 percent nominal rate implied an effective rate of protection equal to 16 percent. A key to his analysis was that he used much more precisely defined industries than previous researchers – 213 separate industries (at the 4-digit SIC level). He considered how Canadian employment, labor productivity, trade, and prices were affected by the FTA. His approach was to look at how values of these variables changed over the period 1988–1996 compared to changes in the pre-agreement period 1980–1986. He explained these differences, measured within an industry or even within a plant, as a result of the tariff changes made by Canada and the U.S. in each period, as well as the change in U.S. output and a measure of business cycle conditions in Canada.

Here are some of the key results he found:

- The FTA reduced Canadian manufacturing employment by 5 percent, and in the most import-impacted industries the decline was 12 percent. Trefler characterized these losses as short-run effects, because ten years later Canadian manufacturing employment had increased even though U.S. manufacturing employment fell over that same period.
- The FTA raised labor productivity in manufacturing by 7.4 percent, with figures double that rate for the most import-impacted and the most export-oriented industries.
- Trade creation exceeded trade diversion.
- Relative import prices from the U.S. did not rise.
- There was no effect on the wages of production workers versus non-production workers, a common measure of income inequality effects.

Trefler concludes that the FTA did have quite visible effects on the Canadian economy. Although much of the bilateral trade was duty free initially, the pockets of high protection did result in significant short-run adjustments. But, Canada did not de-industrialize and become exclusively dependent on natural resource exports.

Another important gain to Canada, in spite of low U.S. tariffs prior to the agreement, was a binational dispute resolution mechanism that provided a check on the arbitrary application of U.S. antidumping and countervailing duty laws against Canadian exporters. These panels gave producers in either country the opportunity to appeal decisions where they felt the local law was misapplied, a major innovation relative to weak dispute resolution procedures available multilaterally at that time.

Mexico–U.S. Issues

Debate in the United States over the North American Free Trade Agreement, which extended the free-trade area to include Mexico, was much more contentious than for the Canada–U.S. agreement. It was negotiated and signed in 1992, approved by Congress in late 1993, and began operation in 1994. To gain Congressional approval, however, the Clinton administration added side-agreements to address fears that U.S. firms would shift production to Mexico to take advantage of lax enforcement of pollution control laws and guarantees of workers' rights. Although a 10-year phase-in period was specified for the movement to free trade, many tariffs were reduced more quickly. The treaty liberalized investment rules in Mexico, although a few sectors such as petroleum were excluded.

The dominant reason for the controversy over NAFTA was the fear that relatively abundant low-wage labor in Mexico would threaten unskilled workers in the United States and Canada. Owners of firms that produced labor-intensive goods also opposed the agreement. Although most U.S. farmers supported NAFTA, those in California and Florida who produced fruit and vegetables that are grown in Mexico opposed it. The strongest U.S. support for NAFTA came from the management of firms such as IBM, Kodak, and others in high-tech or capital-intensive industries. Because human and physical capital are more abundant in the United States than in Mexico, firms that produced items that use those factors intensively expected expanding sales in Mexico.

A major U.S. motive in negotiating NAFTA was to encourage rapid economic growth in Mexico and to promote the continuation of policy reforms initiated in the late 1980s. The formal treaty structure of NAFTA gives prospective foreign investors more confidence that Mexican policy will not revert to the more restrictive environment pursued during Mexico's years of inward-oriented development policies. More rapid job creation in Mexico was also projected to reduce the incentive for immigration into the United States, although Mexican agricultural reforms carried out at the same time probably contributed to the opposite effect.

Baldwin and Venables' summary of *ex ante* predictions of NAFTA's effects were as follows: general trade-creation effects would increase GDP in Mexico by 0.3 percent; including economies of scale raised that figure to 1.6–3.4 percent; and adding the effect of capital accumulation raised it further to 4.6–5.0 percent. The gain to the United States was roughly 0.1 percent of GDP, an indication of the relatively small size of the Mexican market and the more limited change in U.S. trade policy.

Because the Mexican economy was one-twentieth the size of the U.S. economy, both positive and negative trade effects were likely to be small. Nevertheless, if these marginal effects added to an already difficult process of adjustment for U.S. industries, the demands for government intervention would be magnified. That situation was particularly relevant in the U.S. apparel industry where employment fell 23 percent between 1993 and 1998, even as U.S. consumption rose by 20 percent. Apparel imports from all sources rose to 45 percent of domestic consumption, and the Mexican share of those imports doubled from 6.6 percent to 13.4 percent, a sign of trade diversion. Most U.S. industries were not confronted with such extreme forces for contraction. In spite of the Mexican peso crisis in 1994–5, which slowed growth in U.S. exports, the phase-in of NAFTA occurred during a major U.S. economic expansion, a favourable macroeconomic position to reduce adjustment pressures in other industries.

Other Regional Groups

Many other PTAs have been formed, several among developing countries. Economists initially thought that developing countries would be especially likely to benefit from regional economic integration, because they could then overcome limitations imposed by the small size of national markets. The wave of recent agreements suggests that the participants expect economic or political benefits. Skeptics point to some drawbacks however. When member countries export primary products such as coffee or cocoa, their major markets are in the industrial countries, and regional integration does nothing to expand the market. If a new industry does become viable, the same concerns over the location of that production arise as in the E.U.'s attention to the core versus the periphery. For example, do Tanzania and Uganda fear that they will pay higher prices for goods that fuel Kenyan industrialization?

We limit discussion here to MERCOSUR, an example of a trade bloc among developing countries that has the potential to create a large integrated market. It was formed in 1991 and consists of Brazil, Argentina, Paraguay, and Uruguay; Bolivia, Chile, Colombia, Ecuador, and Peru have associate status, and Venezuela has applied for full membership. Because the four members are geographic neighbors and rather distant from other trade partners, significant economic gains from removing high initial trade barriers are quite plausible.

Trade among members expanded much more rapidly than would be predicted on the basis of geographic proximity and the size of their economies. Over the 1990–6 period MERCOSUR imports from members rose 314 percent to $17.1 billion, imports from non-members rose 185 percent to $66.7 billion, and exports to non-members rose 37 percent to $57.9 billion (USITC 1997). Did this rapid pace of intra-regional integration result from trade diversion? Based on early trade patterns through 1994, Alexander Yeats (1998) noted that the product items where the exports of MERCOSUR members to each other grew most rapidly were those where trade barriers against non-member producers were the greatest, such as motor vehicles. In addition, these industries tended to be capital-intensive and were not industries where members had a revealed comparative advantage, a further sign of trade diversion.[6] An additional effect reported by Chang and Winters (2001) was that MERCOSUR improved its terms of trade relative to non-members, evidence that the goal of increasing the group's market power was achieved.

MERCOSUR intends to establish a common external tariff, although a Brazilian currency depreciation in 1998 and a subsequent Argentine financial crisis in 2002 coincided with the Argentine decision to unilaterally impose trade restrictions. A further goal of the members is to allow the free movement of goods, services, people, and capital, but that step will require much more consensus over national economic policies.

Gravity Model Estimates of PTA Effects

As indicated above, an advantage of estimating the effect of PTAs based on the gravity model is that the actual tariff concessions on thousands of different products need not be examined. From one large data base of actual bilateral trade, the influence of many different PTAs can be assessed. Past work gives a mixed assessment of the success of the three PTAs discussed in this chapter. Without implying that there is a consensus position among economists, we cite two recent studies that find large positive effects from PTAs.

Baier, Bergstrand, and Vidal (2007) propose a framework that rules out the ability to examine the role of other factors in the gravity equation but which does give an unbiased estimate of the amount

---

6 Revealed comparative advantage is calculated by considering how important a member's exports are in the shoe industry, say, relative to its total exports, compared to the importance of world trade in shoes relative to world trade in all goods. If Brazil's exports of shoes account for 5 percent of its total exports, while shoes as a group account for 3 percent of world trade, then Brazil has a revealed comparative advantage in shoes.

of trade between two countries due to various PTAs being in place. Their data are drawn at five-year intervals between 1960 and 2000 for 96 potential trading partners. For MERCOSUR members, they report that by the year 2000 trade among members had increased 116 percent above what it would otherwise have been. They estimate nearly as large an effect for the Central American Common Market (El Salvador, Guatemala, Honduras, Nicaragua, and Costa Rica) when it was re-established in 1990, with a projected boost to their trade of 84 percent by 2000. In the case of NAFTA their estimate implies a similar annual rate of increase of slightly over 6 percent, but it is not statistically significant. For most bilateral agreements, they detect no effect. Their general conclusion is that regional integration agreements in the Americas have been successful, not just in terms of anecdotes about greater trade opportunities but in terms of comprehensive measures of trade.

Eicher, Henn, and Papageorgiou (2008) base their analysis on a data set for 186 countries over the five year intervals from 1970–1995. Of particular interest is their finding for the E.U. Their formulation gives an estimate of trade creation and trade diversion effects. They find that the E.U. resulted in a 93 percent increase in trade among members, with a decline in trade with NAFTA but an increase in trade with Asian and other European countries.

Because many PTAs are recent and the consequent changes in trade policy are not immediate, we cannot yet project how well the patterns observed for existing agreements might apply to newer ones. Many PTAs have not addressed thorny issues such as trade in agriculture, as members have preferred to negotiate such policy changes multilaterally. The role for multilateral trade policy is addressed in the next chapter.

Summary of Key Concepts

1. Preferential trade liberalization may or may not increase the welfare of all members of the group or the efficiency of the world trading system.
2. Trade creation arises when prices of imports fall and consumption of the protected good increases. It benefits both the importing country and world efficiency. Trade diversion arises when imports from more efficient non-members decline. World efficiency falls and the importing country loses tariff revenue.
3. Preferential trade blocs may alter the terms of trade in their favor, a benefit that comes at the expense of non-members and therefore does not improve world efficiency.
4. Achieving economies of scale in larger, more competitive markets may benefit members. Projections of these effects from simulation models indicate that for small countries they are quite large relative to trade-creation gains.
5. The European Union, composed of 27 countries, imposes a common external tariff and promotes the free movement of goods, services, capital, and people among its members.
6. NAFTA is a free-trade agreement between Canada, Mexico, and the United States that also promotes free investment flows. Because more trade with Mexico is based on differences in factor endowments, potential effects on U.S. income distribution have been more prominent than in E.U. debates over expansion.

CASE STUDY

A Russia–E.U. Free Trade Agreement?

The expansion of the E.U. eastward and the potential entry of Russia into the World Trade Organization (a process considered in Chapter 10) raised the expectation that an FTA between the E.U. and Russia might be concluded. This case study considers alternative projections of the potential benefits and costs of such an arrangement. Assessing these effects is complicated by the future order of events, however. If Russia is first presumed to join the WTO, are there additional benefits from a further agreement with the E.U.? How important is the first step relative to the second step, and how have changing political and economic stances within Russia affected the likelihood of either event occurring?

Although the working party on Russian accession to the WTO was formed in 1993, little progress was made until Russian President Putin made it a top priority in his first term in office from 2000. From an economic perspective, a World Bank study by Jensen, Rutherford, and Tarr (2004) projected large gains from Russian entry, up to 3.3 percent of GDP in the medium term and 11.0 percent in the long run. The authors allowed for several possible effects discussed in previous chapters. One was better market access due to the right to challenge antidumping rulings within the WTO. Another was greater productivity from the availability of more specialized intermediate inputs in industrial sectors with increasing returns to scale. The major effect that accounted for 70 percent of the Russian gain, however, resulted from reduced barriers to foreign direct investment in several service industries. Based on specially commissioned survey results, the authors treated the initial barriers to investment in service industries such as telecommunications and financial and business services as equivalent to a 33 percent *ad valorem* tariff. In maritime and air transportation sectors the effect was comparable to at least a 90 percent tariff. Ambitious progress in reducing those barriers would allow a significant increase in Russian productivity, a result of additional foreign investment in those sectors given the necessity of a local presence to provide service. The larger long-run gains came from a projected increase in the return to capital and an increase in the capital stock of 14.4 percent.

Applying a different computable general equilibrium model without attention to economies of scale or the foreign direct investment issues highlighted above, Miriam Manchin (2004) focused on how extensive any FTA agreement might be. Additionally, she demonstrated the importance of Russia's bilateral negotiations with each existing WTO member, a necessary step for WTO accession to move forward. In particular, the E.U. agreement with Russia reached in March, 2004, called for a doubling of domestic natural gas prices, which Manchin found would have a marked effect in promoting output of Russia's non-energy intensive industries compared to the World Bank study. If the E.U.-Russian negotiations were limited to tariff reductions on manufactured goods alone, she reported that Russia would lose from an FTA with the E.U. That outcome followed because E.U. tariffs on industrial products already were fairly low, about 2.0 percent. Russia had good access to most E.U. markets, especially for its existing resource-intensive exports. Russian tariffs, though, were higher and averaged about 8.4 percent. Thus, the terms of trade loss to Russia from trade diversion would offset possible gains from trade creation. Only if the FTA were extended to areas of agriculture and services would Russia gain. For that broader FTA, Manchin reports an annual gain of over $5 billion to Russia, measured with 2001 as the base year.

Given the substantial increase in energy prices that occurred since the trough of 1998, the Russian attitude toward WTO admission changed substantially in President Putin's second term. With respect to the bilateral negotiations cited above, progress was irregular and halting. Russia reached agreement with the U.S. in November, 2006, after granting additional access to U.S. meat exports. Because of Russia's embargoes on imports from Georgia and Moldova, however, its ability to gain the unanimous consent necessary for admission to the WTO appeared to have hit a road block more for political reasons than for economic reasons. With Russia no longer making a major push to diversify the economy away from its dependence on natural resource exports, the prospects for quick agreement between Russia and the E.U. appear small.

CASE STUDY QUESTIONS

1. The trade-weighted average tariff imposed by Russia was 8.4 percent, while the simple average tariff was 9.6 percent. What causes those two figures to differ?

2. Why does a higher Russian tariff make losses from trade diversion more likely? If both the E.U. and the U.S. export machinery to Russia, how will a Russia–E.U. FTA affect such trade?

3. Progress in reducing barriers to trade and investment in services has been slow, even among existing WTO members. What additional political factors make such negotiations more complicated than those over industrial tariffs?

4. If Russia has particularly high barriers to investment in service sectors, which account for most of its gains in the World Bank study, what case can you make for Russia to unilaterally reduce those barriers?

5. Consult the UNCTAD/WTO tariff profile for the Russian Federation, available at http://www.intracen.org/ eshop/world_tariff/. What industries receive particularly high protection within Russia? What sort of political economy reasons may explain peaks in the Russian tariff schedule? Do these peaks occur where you expect a large E.U. comparative advantage?

Questions for Study and Review

1. Country A's elasticity of demand for imported manufactures is quite small, because its own elasticity of supply of manufactures is quite small. How do those circumstances affect its likely gains from trade creation if it joins a preferential trade agreement?

2. Country B joins a customs union and for trade with other members it eliminates its 50 percent tariff on imported automobiles. Explain how Country B is affected by the choice of the common external tariff, based on the framework assumed in Figure 9.1. Do you expect other effects that are not well represented in that framework?

3. Consider the import market for Country C, where import demand is given by the difference between total demand for the product and its domestic supply:

$$M_D = Q_D - Q_S \text{ with } Q_D = 140 - P \text{ and } Q_S = -100 + 2P$$

a. If Country C trades with both Countries A and B, but imposes a specific tariff of 20 on imported goods, solve for the equilibrium price and quantity in the import market if the constant foreign prices exclusive of the tariff are $P_A = 50$ and $P_B = 40$.

b. If Country C forms a PTA with Country A and eliminates this tariff on imports from A while maintaining it on imports from B, what is the new equilibrium in the import market? Calculate the gains from trade creation and the losses from trade diversion. How much better off are consumers in C? By how much do profits in the import-competing industries fall?

4. Terms of trade effects are often the dominant outcome from customs union formation. What conditions make it more likely that a country will improve its terms of trade at the expense of other members? . . . at the expense of non-members?

5. Country C's demand for imports is $M_D = 240 - 3P$, and it faces supplies from economies A and B as follows:

$$M_{SA} = -40 + 2P$$
$$M_{SB} = -120 + 3P$$

a. Assume Country C imposes a tariff of 8 initially on all imports and solve for the equilibrium price and quantity in this market. Also, calculate the quantity supplied by both foreign suppliers.

b. Country C is considering forming a customs union with either A or B. One group of advisers recommends choosing Country A because historically it has traded more with C. Another group of advisers recommends Country B, because B appears able to expand output more easily. Determine the consequences of C removing the tariff on imports from A while maintaining it on B, and calculate the net terms of trade gain or loss C will experience from its trade with A and B.

c. Remove the tariff on Country B while maintaining it on A, and make the same calculation of the net terms of trade gain. In which case is there a larger increase in imports? Which situation appears more favorable for Country C? Which group of advisers would your analysis support?

6. Trade between Argentine and Brazil rose after the formation of MERCOSUR. How do economists distinguish whether this extra trade would have occurred anyway in the absence of MERCOSUR?

7. You are asked to interpret the following estimate of the effect of a PTA on bilateral trade between countries i and j:

$$\ln X_{ij} = 1.0 \ln GDP_i + 1.0 \ln GDP_j - 0.7 \ln Distance_{ij} + 0.3\, PTA$$

If GDP in both countries doubles over the same time that the PTA is implemented, by how much do you expect the bilateral trade of its members to rise? [Hint: You can also think of this relationship as:

$$X_{ij} = GDP_i GDP_j Distance_{ij}^{-0.7} e^{0.3PAT}$$ where PTA equals 0 initially and equals 1 in the new equilibrium where the PTA exists.]

8. If the E.U. adds more members that are distant from the industrial core, what conditions make it more likely that these members will lag behind the growth of the existing members? What difference does it make to your answer if labor is quite mobile within Europe? . . . if capital is quite mobile within Europe?

9. If Canadian tariffs were twice as high as U.S. tariffs on manufactured goods before the Canada–United States Free Trade Agreement was formed, why did that signal a possible trade diversion loss for Canada? What was the basis for others to predict an increase in Canadian productivity? If rising productivity in an industry means fewer workers are needed to produce the same output, what must economists be assuming about the workers no longer needed in the industry with rising productivity?

10. The NAFTA agreement was approved over substantial opposition by the Democratic party in 1993. What were the sources of opposition to that agreement? Would you expect opposition for the same reasons to an agreement with Korea in 2007?

References and Suggestions for Further Reading

For theoretical aspects of preferential trade agreements, see:

Abrego, L., Riezman, R., and Whalley, J. (2006) "How Often are Propositions on the Effects of Regional Trade Agreements Theoretical Curiosa?" *Journal of International Economics* 68: 59–78.

Baldwin, R. (1989) "The Growth Effects of 1992," *Economic Policy: A European Forum* 9: 247–81.

Baldwin, R. and Venables, A. (1995) "Regional Economic Integration," in G. Grossman and K. Rogof (eds) *Handbook of International Economics, Vol. III*, Amsterdam: Elsevier Science, pp. 1598–1640.

Davis, D. (1998) "The Home Market, Trade, and Industrial Structure," *American Economic Review* 88: 1264–1276.

Helpman, E. and Krugman, P. (1985) *Market Structure and Foreign Trade*, Cambridge, MA: MIT Press.

Krugman, P. (1991a) "Is Bilateralism Bad," in E. Helpman and A. Razin (eds) *International Trade and Trade Policy*, Cambridge, MA: MIT Press.

—— (1991b) "The Move Toward Free Trade Zones," in *Policy Implications of Trade and Currency Zones*, Federal Reserve Bank of Kansas City, pp. 7–41.

Lipsey, R.G. (1960) "The Theory of Customs Unions: A General Survey," *Economic Journal* 70: 496–513.

Panagariya, A. (1999) "The Regionalism Debate: An Overview," *The World Economy* 22: 477–511.

Panagariya, A. and Bhagwati, J. (eds) (1996) *Free Trade Area or Free Trade? The Economics of Preferential Trade Agreements*, Washington, DC: American Enterprise Institute.

Kowalczyk, C. (2000) "Welfare and Integration," *International Economic Review* 41: 483–94.

Viner, J. (1953) *The Customs Union Issue*, New York: Carnegie Endowment for International Peace.

For empirical assessments of preferential trade agreements and commentaries on particular trade blocs see:

Aslund, A. (2006) Testimony at the Hearing on EU Economic and Trade Relations with Russia, Committee on International Trade, European Parliament, Brussels, November 21, accessed at http://www.iie.com.

Baier, S. and Bergstrand, J. (2007) "Do Free Trade Agreements Actually Increase Member's International Trade?" *Journal of International Economics* 71: 72–95.

Baier, S., Bergstrand, J., and Vidal, E. (2007) "Free Trade Agreements in the Americas: Are the Trade Effects Larger than Anticipated?" *World Economy* 30: 1347–1377.

Balassa, B. (1975) "Trade Creation and Diversion in the European Common Market," *European Economic Integration*. Amsterdam: North-Holland.

Brakman, S., Garretsen, H., and Schramm, M. (2005) "Putting New Economic Geography to the Test: Free-ness of Trade and Agglomeration in the EU Regions," CESifo working paper No. 1566.

Brown, D. and Stern, R. (1987) "A Modeling Perspective," in R. Stern, P. Trezise, and J. Whally (eds) *Perspectives on a U.S.–Canadian Free Trade Agreement*, Washington, D.C.: The Brookings Institution, pp. 155–87.

Brown, A., Deardorff, A., and Stern, R. (1992) "North American Integration," *Economic Journal* 102: 1507–1518.

Cecchini Report (1988) *The European Challenge* 1992, Aldershot, U.K.: Wildwood House.

Chang, W. and Winters, A. (2001) "Preferential Trading Arrangements and Excluded Countries: Ex Poste Estimates of the Effects on Prices," *World Economy* 24: 797–807.

Cox, D. and Harris, R. (1995) "Trade Liberalization and Industrial Organization: Some Estimates for Canada," *Journal of Political Economy*, pp. 115–45.

Eicher, T., Henn, C., and Papageorgiou, C. (2008) "Trade Creation and Diversion Revisited: Accounting for Model Uncertainty and Natural Trading Partner Effects," IMF Working Paper WP/08/66.

European Commission (2006) *E.U. Budget 2006 Financial Report*, Available at at http://ec.europa.eu/budget/library/publications/fin_reports/fin_report_06_en.pdf (accessed 15 October 2007).

Frankel, J.(1997) *Regional Trading Blocs in the World Economic System*, Washington, DC: Institute for International Economics.

Head, J. and Mayer, T. (2004) "The Empirics of Agglomeration and Trade," in J.V. Henderson and J-F. Thisse (eds) *Handbook of Regional and Urban Economics*, Amsterdam: Elsevier, pp. 2609–2665.

Hufbauer, G. and Schott, J. (1993) *NAFTA: An Assessment*, Washington, DC: Institute for International Economics.

Jensen, J., Rutherford, T., and Tarr, D. (2004) "The Impact of Liberalizing Barriers to Foreign Direct Investment in Services: The Case of Russian Accession to the World Trade Organization," World Bank Working Paper 3391.

Karacaovali, B. and Limão, N. (2008) "The Clash of Liberalizations: Preferential vs. Multilateral Trade Liberalization in the European Union," *Journal of International Economics* 74: 299–327.

Limão, N. (2006) "Preferential Trade Agreements as Stumbling Blocks for Multilateral Trade Liberalization: Evidence for the United States," *American Economic Review* 96: 896–914.

Manchin, M. (2004) "The Economic Effects of a Russia–EU FTA," Tinbergen Institute Discussion Paper 131/2.

Miller, M. and Spencer, J. (1977) "The Static Economic Effects of the UK Joining the EEC: A General Equilibrium Approach," *Review of Economic Studies* 44: 71–93.

Morici, P. (ed.) (1990) *Making Free Trade Work: The Canada–US Agreement*, New York: Council on Foreign Relations Press.

Mutti, J. (2001) *NAFTA: The Economic Consequences for Mexico and the United States*, Washington, DC: Economic Strategy Institute.

Puga, D. (1999) "The Rise and Fall of Regional Inequalities," *European Economic Review* 43: 303–34.

Schneider, O. (2007) "The EU Budget Dispute – A Blessing in Disguise?" CESifo Working Paper No. 1986.

Schott, J. and Smith, M. (eds) (1988) *The Canada–United States Free Trade Agreement: The Global Impact*, Washington, DC: Institute for International Economics.

Trefler, D. (2004) "The Long and the Short of the Canada–US Free Trade Agreement," *American Economic Review* 94: 870–95.

US International Trade Commission (1997) *Market Developments in Mercosur Countries Affecting Leading US Exporter*, Washington, DC: USITC.

Winters, A. (1985) *International Economics*, London: George Allen and Unwin, pp. 124–31.

—— (1987) "Britain in Europe: A Survey of Quantitative Trade Studies," *Journal of Common Market Studies* 25: 315–53.

Yeats, A. (1998) "Does Mercosur's Trade Performance Raise Concerns about the Effects of Regional Trade Arrangements?" *World Bank Economic Review* 12: 1–28.

Chapter 10

Commercial Policy and the WTO

LEARNING OBJECTIVES

By the end of this chapter you should be able to explain:

- why countries are more likely to reduce trade restrictions multilaterally rather than unilaterally

- why non-discrimination and reciprocity are key principles of the General Agreement on Tariffs and Trade (GATT)

- how successive rounds of multilateral trade negotiations have contributed to substantial reductions in tariffs from the high levels imposed in the 1930s

- what mechanism to resolve trade disputes has been established within the World Trade Organization (WTO)

- why extending the WTO authority over policies with a primarily domestic focus has been particularly controversial

- how the interests of developing countries have been addressed or ignored within the WTO

In Chapters 6 and 7 we examined the consequences of unilateral trade policy choices by a single country. We recognized plausible exceptions to the claim that free trade always improves a country's economic efficiency, but those gains often come at the expense of foreign countries. Nationalistic policies of protectionism and the breakdown of international commerce during the worldwide depression of the 1930s provided special impetus for subsequent efforts to restore a more open trading system. Economists debate how much regional trade agreements, such as those surveyed in Chapter 9, have contributed to this process, in comparison with multilateral agreements. In this chapter we consider the changing nature of national commercial policies, and we particularly focus on multilateral cooperation through the GATT and the WTO.

THE RATIONALE FOR MULTILATERAL TRADE LIBERALIZATION

The prisoners' dilemma introduced in Chapter 6 captures a key strategic consideration faced by individual countries as they select their trade policies. In the Ricardian paradigm, all countries gain from trade if none of them imposes restrictions. But, if one limits access to its own market while all others provide free access to their markets, the country that imposes restrictions may gain even more. The gain occurs in the form of better terms of trade, as the country receives a higher price for the exports its producers sell compared to what foreigners receive for the goods that are imported.

Conversely, if both countries start from a position where they unilaterally impose trade restrictions to attempt to gain this advantage, then they restrict trade too much and there are potential gains from cooperation. That situation is shown in Figure 10.1 where the equilibrium in the absence of trade restrictions is given by the terms of trade line OE_0. The welfare each country enjoys is given by the trade indifference curves U_{A0} and U_{B0}. If each country levies an optimal tariff, where its trade indifference curve is tangent to the tariff-distorted offer curve of the other country, the new terms of trade become OE_1. Note that Country B has moved to a higher trade indifference curve, U_{B1}, but Country A's best response still leaves it on a lower indifference curve, U_{A1}. In otherwords, Country B has more market power than Country A and emerges a winner from a tariff war. Nevertheless, some form of cooperative agreement to reduce those optimal tariffs could let both A and B become better off and reach a higher trade indifference curve within the area traced out by U_{A1} and U_{B1}.

Kyle Bagwell and Robert Staiger (2002) suggest norms for successful multilateral cooperation. They present two key principles, reciprocity and non-discrimination. Reciprocity means that if Country B agrees to reduce its tariff by a given amount, it expects Country A to make some tariff reduction, too. With a balance of concessions, each country can avoid a decline in its terms of trade and will benefit from a greater volume of trade. From a political economy perspective reciprocity can be important because exporters have an additional incentive to lobby for trade liberalization, which

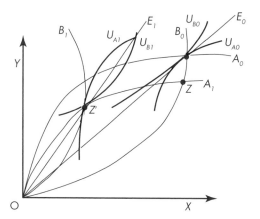

FIGURE 10.1 Gains from Multilateral Tariff Reduction

If each country levies its optimum tariff, the international price ratio changes from OE_0 to OE_1. Country B moves to a higher trade indifference curve and Country A moves to a lower trade indifference curve at Z', an outcome that suggests B can win a tariff war. Note, however, that both A and B can move to a higher trade indifference curve within the lens space formed by U_{B1} and U_{A1}, an outcome that can be achieved through a multilateral agreement.

would not exist with unilateral liberalization. Bagwell and Staiger combine those perspectives by extending the "protection for sale model" of Chapter 7 to recognize that for any agreement to be adopted, the government must garner political support from various interest groups, which includes exporters. This attention to political factors represents another explanatory factor to add to the framework in Figure 10.1. If the political power of exporters is strong enough, a country may even be willing to subsidize its exports and accept less favourable terms of trade.

Non-discrimination through the **most-favored-nation** (MFN) clause ensures that any tariff reduction offered to one country also applies to all others. Suppose Country B agrees to reduce the tariff on imported shoes from Country A to 10 percent, but B later negotiates an agreement with Country C to reduce the tariff it imposes on shoes from C to 5 percent. A MFN clause in B's agreement with A means that shoes from A will only be subject to a 5 percent tariff, too. This provision rules out discriminatory tariff regimes and any potential inefficiencies they may create, but it allows for countries to free-ride on the concessions of others. Reciprocity is necessary to avoid the situation where a country does not reduce its tariffs at all and simply benefits from its improved terms of trade when other countries reduce their tariffs.

PRECURSORS TO MULTILATERAL TRADE LIBERALIZATION

In the middle of the nineteenth century, Great Britain was unmistakably the leader in the movement to reduce trade barriers. Chapter 7 recounted the repeal of the Corn Laws (which placed restrictions on grain imports) in 1846. By 1850 virtually all British tariffs and other restrictions on imports had been swept away. Great Britain unilaterally adopted a policy of free trade without waiting for some comprehensive international agreement. Because other European nations were influenced by the

British example and reduced their trade barriers, however, Britain did not suffer as large a terms-of-trade decline as would otherwise be predicted for a country large enough to affect international prices. The pattern of simultaneous trade liberalization by several countries meant that the volume of trade expanded more rapidly and relative prices internationally changed less than if Britain alone had changed policy.

When tariff reductions occurred through commercial treaties, Britain typically included a clause requiring most-favored-nation status: the signatory countries agreed to extend to each other, automatically, the lowest tariff rates that might be granted to any third country in the future. That clause meant that the expected value from any concession granted to Britain would not be eroded by a subsequently more favorable agreement the partner signed with another country. The resulting network of commercial treaties accomplished a substantial reduction in the level of protection in European trade.

The free-trade tide reached its peak in about 1870 but then began to ebb. In Germany, France, Italy, and other European countries, emerging industries called for protection against the established industries in the U.K. The rapid expansion of American grain exports after 1870 led European agrarian interests to join with the industrialists in support of higher tariffs. Tariff increases were frequent in the last quarter of the nineteenth century. Of the major trading nations, only Britain and Holland clung to free trade.

The United States did not participate in the free-trade movement during the nineteenth century. From 1789 to 1934, tariff rates were set by acts of Congress, and the levels set in successive tariff acts reflected Congressional preoccupation with domestic political and economic concerns. Rates rose and fell several times, sometimes sharply, between 1820 and 1930, but for most of the period, tariffs were quite high. By the end of this period U.S. actions had a significant impact on other countries. **The Smoot–Hawley Tariff** Act of 1930 imposed an average rate exceeding 50 percent, which represented a higher level than existed at the previous peak in 1828. The United States, however, had emerged from World War I as a major market. Other countries had borrowed heavily from it both during and after the war. To pay their debts, other nations had to sell the United States their goods and services, but the Smoot–Hawley Tariff seriously limited their ability to do so.

Other countries soon retaliated with increases in their tariffs, and world trade steadily shrank as the world sank into depression. No one can say exactly how much the Smoot–Hawley Tariff Act was responsible for the economic woes of the 1930s, but it seems clear that it had a substantial effect. U.S. trade dropped 70 percent in value (50 percent in volume) from 1929 to 1932, and declining world trade contributed to the spread of depression throughout the world. It was under those circumstances that another swing toward free trade got under way.

Steps to Recover from the 1930s' Contraction of Trade

In 1934 the U.S. Congress passed the Reciprocal Trade Agreements Act, which authorized the president to reduce existing tariff rates by up to 50 percent. One of the remarkable features of this legislation was that Congress delegated to the President the power to set tax rates (i.e. tariffs), perhaps its most jealously guarded prerogative. Congress could rescind the delegation any time it chose, but the fact is that since 1934 U.S. tariff rates in effect have been determined by the President.

From 1934 to 1947, the United States negotiated bilateral trade agreements with 29 nations. These agreements provided for tariff concessions on 69 percent of all dutiable imports into the United States and reduced the average tariff by about one-third (U.S. Tariff Commission 1974). Two aspects of the agreements are noteworthy. First, they included unconditional MFN clauses, which kept U.S. tariff rates uniform and equal for all signatory countries. Second, the U.S. sought to bargain with the chief supplier of a given imported commodity. When the United States offered a tariff reduction on leather footwear, say, it obtained in return a tariff reduction on automobiles. This procedure achieved reciprocity, and it had the effect of reducing the benefits gained by third countries that offered no additional concessions. On the other hand, small countries that were not chief suppliers of products had little power to ensure that items of interest to them became the subject of negotiations.

MULTILATERAL TRADE LIBERALIZATION UNDER THE GATT

During and after World War II, plans were drawn up for an International Trade Organization through which nations could regulate and coordinate their commercial policies. In 1945 the United States presented a draft charter for such an organization that would serve as a counterpart, in the field of trade and commercial policy, to the International Monetary Fund in the monetary field. However, this proposed charter ran into heavy opposition. When the U.S. Congress declined to approve it, it was quietly dropped.

Under the authority contained in the Reciprocal Trade Agreements Act, the United States invited other nations to participate in multilateral negotiations for the reduction of trade barriers. At a conference held in 1947, a General Agreement on Tariffs and Trade was adopted. From this unlikely beginning an international organization by that name, which is frequently known by its acronym, GATT, also emerged. In 1995 the newly created World Trade Organization replaced the GATT organization and established a more comprehensive multilateral decision-making structure.

GATT Principles

The 1947 GATT articles of agreement constitute a code of conduct for international trade and a basis for multilateral negotiation of trade agreements. They seek to place all countries on an equal legal footing in their trade relationships and to reduce tariffs and other barriers to trade. The article headings are shown in Table 10.1. Article I incorporates the unconditional most-favored-nation clause explained earlier. There are two important exceptions to Article I, however. First, when a group of countries forms a customs union or free-trade area, they may eliminate tariffs among themselves but retain tariffs against other GATT members (Article XXIV). Second, countries may apply lower tariff rates to imports coming from developing countries than they apply to imports from other countries. That exception was adopted in 1971 in response to the demands of developing countries to encourage their export industries.

Article III is another central principle of the agreement. It calls for national treatment of foreign and domestic goods. Once foreign goods enter a country and clear customs, they must be treated

TABLE 10.1 Articles of the General Agreement on Tariffs and Trade

Article	Title
Article I	General most-favored-nation treatment
Article II	Schedules of concessions
Article III	National treatment on internal taxation and regulation
Article IV	Special provisions relating to cinematograph films
Article V	Freedom of transit
Article VI	Anti-dumping and countervailing duties
Article VII	Valuation for customs purposes
Article VIII	Fees and formalities connected with importation and exportation
Article IX	Marks of origin
Article X	Publication and administration of trade regulations
Article XI	General elimination of quantitative restrictions
Article XII	Restrictions to safeguard the balance of payments
Article XIII	Non-discriminatory administration of quantitative restrictions
Article XIV	Exceptions to the rule of non-discrimination
Article XV	Exchange arrangements
Article XVI	Subsidies
Article XVII	State trading enterprises
Article XVIII	Governmental assistance to economic development
Article XIX	Emergency action on imports of particular products
Article XX	General exceptions
Article XXI	Security exceptions
Article XXII	Consultation
Article XXIII	Nullification or impairment
Article XXIV	Territorial application, frontier traffic, customs unions and free-trade areas
Article XXV	Joint action by the contracting parties
Article XXVI	Acceptance. Entry into force and registration
Article XXVII	Withholding or withdrawal of concessions
Article XXVIII	Modification of schedules
Article XXVIII (bis)	Tariff negotiations
Article XXIX	The relation of this agreement to the Havana Charter
Article XXX	Amendments
Article XXXI	Withdrawal
Article XXXII	Contracting parties
Article XXXIII	Accession
Article XXXIV	Annexes
Article XXXV	Non-application of the agreement between particular contracting parties

no less favorably than domestically produced goods. An explicit intent of this provision is to keep discriminatory domestic taxes and regulations from protecting domestic producers, because those measures could otherwise be used to offset the effect of tariff concessions.

The agreement also opposes quantitative restrictions (quotas) on trade. The general position is that if trade barriers are to exist, they should take the form of explicit tariffs so that everyone can judge their severity and determine that they are being applied in a nondiscriminatory manner. One rather open-ended exception provides that quantitative restrictions can be applied by a country in order to safeguard its balance of payments. Another exception allows such restrictions if they are needed because of a country's economic development policies. Such provisions do not set any standard to judge when a country's balance of payments again is satisfactory or whether a country has graduated from the need to impose barriers for development purposes. Only the GATT's consultative machinery enabled these loosely worded exceptions to remain manageable.

When countries agree to reduce tariffs, they cannot foresee the outcomes that may result in the future. As Ethier (2001) notes, when the U.S. and EEC negotiated tariff reduction on automobiles in the 1960s, they could not foresee the rise of Japan as a major automobile exporter in the 1980s. Because of such uncertainty over the consequences of any tariff change, countries are more likely to negotiate reductions if they are allowed to retain an **escape clause**: a provision to allow the country to assist an industry injured by tariff reductions (Article XIX). No allegation of unfair trade is made in escape clause actions. The petitioner simply claims that some period of relief from import competition is necessary to allow retooling, retraining, or implementing some other strategy to adjust. The U.S. steel industry examined in Chapter 6 relied upon this form of relief in 2002, but the provision requires a high burden of proof that the industry's problems are due to trade, not some other cause.[1] A lower injury threshold applies to unfair trade practices such as dumping and subsidization (Articles VI and XVI), and the example of the E.U. footwear industry considered in Chapter 6 demonstrated some of the issues that arise in allowing that form of intervention.

Tariff Reductions under the GATT

The GATT organization's most important activity was its sponsorship of a series of negotiations in which member countries bargained to reduce their tariffs and other trade barriers. In the initial negotiations, each country prepared lists of the concessions it was willing to offer and of concessions it wanted to obtain from other countries. Although these offers and requests were initially bilateral,

---

1 Under U.S. procedures to invoke the escape clause, the industry files a petition with the U.S. International Trade Commission. The USITC investigates and reports its findings to the President, who then weighs foreign policy interests and consumer impacts in determining an appropriate response. By way of contrast, if unfair trade practices are found in antidumping or countervailing duty cases, and they are ruled to be an important cause of injury to the domestic industry, offsetting duties are applied automatically, without presidential review. Economists have noted that large industries with a high political profile are more likely to be successful in gaining protection from escape-clause relief actions, whereas smaller, less politically powerful industries are more likely to rely upon unfair trade laws. For example, see J.M. Finger, H. Keith Hall, and D. Nelson, "The Political Economy of Administered Protection," *American Economic Review* 72, 1982, pp. 452–66.

they acquired a multilateral aspect because they were circulated to all other participating countries. By having all countries negotiating simultaneously, each country could evaluate the benefits it might obtain because of concessions made between any two other countries, given the most-favored-nation clause.

This negotiating process is complicated, cumbersome, and lengthy. As summarized in Table 10.2, five rounds of multilateral negotiations took place between 1947 and 1961. They varied in scope and in the size of the tariff reductions accomplished, but their cumulative effect was a substantial reduction in tariff levels for manufactured goods levied by industrial countries. The average U.S. tariff on dutiable goods declined from 53 percent in 1933 (the peak level reached after the Smoot–Hawley Tariff Act) to about 10 percent in the 1960s. A substantial part of that decline, however, appears to be due to inflation in the 1940s which eroded the protective effect of specific tariffs, and therefore we should not overstate the role of negotiations (Irwin 1998). Furthermore, tariff averages conceal large disparities in tariff rates on individual items and much room remained for further moves toward trade liberalization. We describe some key aspects of the three subsequent GATT rounds cited in Table 10.2.

TABLE 10.2 Tariff Reductions Under the GATT/WTO

Implementation Period	Round covered (dates of negotiations and number of countries)	Weighted tariff reduction
1948	Geneva (1947 : 23 countries)	−26
1950	Annecy (1949 : 33 countries)	−3
1952	Torquay (1950–1 : 34 countries)	−4
1956–8	Geneva (1955–6 : 22 countries)	−3
1962–4	Dillon Round (1961–2 : 45 countries)	−4
1968–72	Kennedy Round (1964–7 : 48 countries)	−38
1980–7	Tokyo Round (1973–9 : 99 countries)	−33
1995–9	Uruguay Round (1986–94 : 117 countries)	−38

Source: Adapted from *World Trade Organization (2007) Tables 4 and 5.*

Note: MFN tariff reductions by industrial countries for industrial products, excluding petroleum. Tariff reductions for the first five rounds refer to the United States only. The calculation of average rates of reductions are weighted by MFN import values.

Tariff Bindings and Applied Tariffs

Agreements to reduce tariff rates multilaterally have been central to GATT negotiations since 1947. Also important has been the effort to encourage each country to bind its existing tariffs at maximum rates that cannot be exceeded without consulting with its trading partners, should a country choose to alter its trade policy in the future. Binding creates predictability in the world trading system, and that extra certainty warrants greater investment to serve the world market. In the Uruguay Round developing countries in particular increased the extent to which they bound their tariffs.

The figures shown in Table 10.3 are somewhat imprecise, because they do not include some specific duties for which *ad valorem* equivalents are not available. In general, they demonstrate that tariffs in industrialized countries are much lower than in developing countries for manufactured products. Distinctions over agricultural protection in developed versus developing countries are less apparent. Many developing countries have accepted the rationale for making tariff bindings, but as is the case for three of the countries shown here, they have bound rates at levels much higher than they actually apply. That situation does provide some ability for them to raise rates in the future. The applied rates for India in 2005, however, were roughly half of what they were in 1997, a sign of continued liberalization. China's tariff bindings have already increased under the terms of its WTO accession in 2001, but for the other countries further changes in bound rates likely await the successful completion of another round of multilateral trade negotiations.

TABLE 10.3 Tariff Bindings and Applied Tariffs

Country	% Bound lines	Simple Average Bound Rates		Simple Average Applied Rates	
		agriculture	industry	agriculture	industry
E.U.	100.0	16.7	3.9	16.6	3.7
Japan	98.9	16.8	3.9	16.1	3.8
U.S.	100.0	8.1	4.0	9.5	4.0
South Africa	96.2	46.8	18.1	11.5	11.4
Brazil	100.0	35.8	29.5	10.4	10.4
China	100.0	14.7	9.1	14.6	8.9
India	74.0	115.4	35.7	42.8	15.4

Source: World Trade Organization (2006), p. 5–6.

Tariff Cutting Formulas

Under the Kennedy Round agreement reached in 1967, most tariff reductions occurred across the board, a contrast to the pattern from earlier rounds. Many exceptions were made, as each country had its list of sensitive items requiring special treatment, but for the great majority of tariff lines, existing tariffs were reduced by a uniform percentage. The average tariff reduction by industrial countries was 35 percent.

One point of tension arose because the European Economic Community had just agreed on a common external tariff schedule for its six member nations and had achieved much more uniformity in its tariff schedule than was true for the U.K. or the U.S. The EEC wanted greater cuts made in higher tariffs, which would affect it less. In contrast, the U.S. proposed a simple linear reduction of all tariffs by 50 percent.

In the Tokyo Round concluded in 1979, negotiators agreed upon a formula for tariff reductions that addressed the concern over high tariffs:

$$Tariff\ reduction = 100 \cdot t / (t + 0.14) \tag{10.1}$$

where t is the current *ad valorem* tariff rate. The formula has the effect of reducing high tariff rates more than low ones, thus tending to harmonize tariff levels around the world.[2] Because tariff cuts on finished goods were deeper than those on raw materials, this approach reduced the tendency for tariffs to escalate as more processing took place. This outcome lowered the effective rate of protection on finished goods. Variants of this approach have played a role in subsequent negotiations.

The Creation of a Single Package

The success of the GATT in reducing tariffs has led to comparable efforts to address non-tariff barriers (NTBs). Achieving such reductions is difficult, however, because they often involve elements of domestic policy that national legislatures have typically controlled. The Tokyo Round addressed NTBs through separate codes and agreements in several areas: subsidies; technical barriers to trade; import licensing procedures; government procurement; customs valuation; and dumping. Not all countries signed these codes, and they were not automatically administered through the same dispute resolution mechanism as the tariff agreement. The reliance on codes and their potentially limited applicability across countries raised the fear of a GATT à la carte, where countries could pick and choose what provisions to accept.

The subsequent Uruguay Round sought to avoid that outcome. It treated the various agreements reached as a single package. Countries did not have the opportunity to pick and choose what sections to accept. Because countries did not expect a favorable balance of concessions in every group, gains in one area could offset losses in another, so a much more ambitious agreement was reached. Too ambitious an agenda, however, runs the risk of causing at least one country to reject the agreement, and under the GATT's consensus decision-making procedure, that will result in the progress on other items being lost.

---

2 For example, a 40 percent existing tariff would be cut by $100 \cdot 0.40/(0.40 + 0.14) = 74$ percent, whereas a 10 percent existing tariff would be cut by $0.10/(0.10 + 0.14) = 42$ percent.

Issues in Ratification

A difficulty that arose in the Kennedy Round negotiations was the U.S. practice of imposing a variable levy on certain chemical and footwear products. Because the U.S. needed separate Congressional approval to address those issues, they were handled in a separate protocol agreement, with concessions by other countries contingent on their adoption. When the U.S. Congress failed to approve that side-agreement, one portion of the negotiations was simply lost (Jackson 1997).

More generally, countries are unlikely to devote the effort to negotiating the best possible mutual agreement among them, only to have national legislatures then pick apart and alter the agreement item by item during the ratification process. To avoid that problem in the U.S., Congress has granted the President the authority to negotiate an agreement the Congress will then vote to accept or reject in its entirety. For the implementation of the Tokyo Round agreement, the Congress specified that a bill to approve agreements on nontariff measures could not be amended once introduced, it must be reported out of committee within a specified time limit, and floor debate on it would be limited. Because Congress grants such fast-track authority (subsequently renamed trade promotion authority) for a specific time period, that deadline has often served as a motivation to complete multilateral negotiations. Because of the many side deals Presidents have had to make to garner enough votes in favour of trade promotion authority, the U.S. is more likely to support ambitious liberalization agendas rather than small, incremental changes in the status quo.

THE ESTABLISHMENT OF THE WTO

The Uruguay Round, which took over 7 years to complete, was by far the most difficult GATT negotiation to conclude. It almost failed. Negotiations began in 1986, were suspended in 1990 and 1992 due to an impasse over agricultural provisions, and finally were completed on the day that the U.S. fast-track negotiating authority expired.

Aside from the Uruguay Round's success in reducing the tariffs on the manufactured goods of industrialized countries by one third, important areas that had escaped much GATT discipline in the past were addressed. New areas were added, and a stronger organization, the World Trade Organization, was created to oversee the world trading system. The GATT agreement became just one of several agreements under the WTO umbrella. We summarize key aspects of those developments below.

Agriculture

The chapter case study (p. 296) recounts the way agricultural trade has avoided much GATT discipline over national policies. The Uruguay Round altered that standard. Export subsidies and import barriers were to be reduced. Domestic farm supports, which generate the surpluses that then are exported, were to be cut by 20 percent. Subsidized exports were to fall by 36 percent in value. The inconsistencies of E.U. sugar policy with these goals have been discussed in Chapter 6, and the case study at the end of this chapter recounts how U.S. cotton subsidies violated these commitments. With respect to import barriers, countries converted their quantitative restrictions to bound tariffs and were to cut them by 36 percent. Also, countries committed to allowing minimum import access equal to 3 percent of domestic production initially, a figure that was to grow to 5 percent. Those steps gave rise to the tariff rate quotas discussed in Chapter 6. Implications of the agreement were that Japan and Korea opened their previously closed rice markets a little, and the E.U. gave up its variable levy.

Textiles and Clothing

International trade in textiles and clothing, an item of particular interest to labor-abundant developing countries such as Bangladesh and India, had long been subject to country-specific quotas, a clear contrast to normal GATT commitments. Those quotas were to be phased out over ten years, as explained in the case study of Chapter 6, p. 175.

Trade-Related Investment Measures (TRIMs)

Although some countries sought a comprehensive set of rules to govern foreign direct investment within the WTO, with provisions against technology transfer requirements or minimum export requirements, the TRIMs agreement is more limited in scope. It prohibits two practices governing investment that restrict trade. One is a domestic content requirement, which requires some specified share of production in the host country and restricts the ability of companies to use imported parts in their production. Another is a trade balance or foreign exchange balance requirement, which requires a company to export goods in some proportion to the amount it imports. Because these provisions apply to both domestic and foreign firms, they do not directly address foreign direct investment, although foreign firms most often complain of being subject to such requirements.

Countries interested in addressing a wider set of investment issues attempted to do so in subsequent negotiations under the auspices of the Organization for Economic Cooperation and Development. Those negotiations broke down in 1998, however, due to objections raised over potential infringement of an individual country's ability to deal with environmental degradation, food safety, cultural diversity, and social cohesion (Graham 2000).

General Agreement on Trade in Services (GATS)

The General Agreement on Trade in Services was established as part of the WTO, a step of particular interest to the U.S., a major service exporter. The GATS did not create conditions immediately comparable to the GATT with respect to trade of goods. There was no presumption that foreigners would receive the same treatment as domestic providers, unless a country chose to make that commitment. A country could exempt certain sectors from MFN treatment for a ten-year period. Under the agreed framework, a country needed to designate sectors in which it made any commitment on market access. The range of sectors over which distinctions could be made was quite broad; examples include advertising, architecture, business management, education, engineering, information processing, legal, medical, tourist, or transport services.

Furthermore, a country's submission to the GATS Council distinguished any limitations it imposed regarding four different modes in which trade in services might occur: cross-border supply, consumption abroad, commercial presence, or the presence of natural persons. As a more concrete example of what this GATS language implies, developing countries likely have greater interest in their residents being able to move abroad to provide construction services (mode 4), while high-income countries may be more interested in establishing an affiliate abroad to provide banking services (mode 3). The scope for negotiations is quite broad! The Uruguay Round essentially created a standstill with respect to current restrictions, because most countries agree not to impose any new restrictions on foreign-service providers. Any liberalization, however, required further negotiation.

Two areas in which little progress occurred were financial services and telecommunications. In 1997, however, agreements were reached in these two areas. That result is somewhat surprising, because any potential disadvantages arising from these concessions were not balanced by favorable benefits in some other agreement, as under the Single Package approach. Perhaps the important role played by an adequate financial and communications infrastructure in producing other goods provided enough incentive for progress to be made.

Trade-Related Aspects of Intellectual Property Rights (TRIPs)

The Agreement on Trade-Related Aspects of Intellectual Property Rights was established as part of the WTO. The agreement stipulated that patents for products and processes are to be provided for 20 years from the filing of an application. Copyright protection of music, literature, computer programs, and computer chip designs, among other items, is to be provided. Even geographic indications are protected: thus, if a cheese or wine carries the name of a French region, it must come from that region of France. A major implication was that developing countries agreed to much stricter protection for intellectual property.

The treatment of intellectual property rights under the WTO has proven particularly contentious. In contrast to multilateral tariff reductions, where both parties are likely to gain, the adoption of common intellectual property standards may leave developing countries worse off. Big budget movies from Hollywood, music recordings by U2 or the Beatles, software written by Microsoft or SAP, or textbooks published by Routledge may be copied in China and sold without payment of royalties to the copyright holder. An agreement that prohibits such unauthorized copying hurts those who buy the bootleg copies and reduces the profits of the successful copiers.

More generally, developed countries have a comparative advantage in research-and-development-intensive industries, and they benefit from the monopoly profits earned before their technology becomes widely available in other countries. As a consequence, developed countries were strong advocates of the TRIPs agreement, while developing countries were reluctant to see this item added to the WTO agenda.

The loss of profits to firms that innovate makes the issue of copying an existing product or process appear to be primarily a matter of transferring funds from the North to the South. Yet, the world as a whole has a wider interest in ensuring that innovation continues to occur in the future. Stricter enforcement of patents and copyrights allows higher returns to be earned by the creators of existing literary and musical innovative works, new products, and more efficient production processes. Those profits also provide an incentive for future innovation and result in greater willingness to finance current research and creative activity. Thus, intellectual property protection affects the speed at which science and technology advance.

Pharmaceutical Flip Flops and the TRIPS Agreement

The Uruguay Round TRIPs Agreement stipulates that members provide patent protection for pharmaceutical products, among its various provisions. While copyrights and patents for other products are important, the economic value of pharmaceutical patents is particularly high. At the same time, poor countries reliant on foreign technology are concerned that their failure to gain access to patented medicines at low prices will cost human lives. The tension between these two points of view explains some ambiguities in the agreement over the flexibility of countries to take measures to protect public health.

Just as the textile agreement was phased in slowly over time, developing and transition economies were given 5 years, and least developed countries 11 years, to fulfill this commitment. Over that time frame, however, discussion changed substantially due to the AIDS epidemic and high rates of HIV infection in many developing countries, which could not afford to pay the high price of treatment in industrialized countries. Protests in favor of compulsory licensing for HIV drugs occurred in Thailand and South Africa. An Indian generic drug producer offered to sell HIV drugs at a 90 percent discount from prices in industrialized countries. Brazil produced its own copies of several of these drugs, and its expenditures per AIDS patient were roughly one-third of the annual expense in the United States. As Brazil succeeded in containing the spread of the virus and cutting its AIDS-related deaths by 50 percent, its program was viewed as a model for other middle-income countries to follow (Jordan 2001). For countries that had no indigenous generic producers, that raised a further trade issue regarding the rights of such countries to import drugs from producers that had no assent from the patent holders.

Yet, if pharmaceuticals can be freely exported and imported by any country, including the United States, what happens to the ability of drug firms to price discriminate and charge high prices in the U.S. market where there is a higher ability and willingness to pay? Without these high-priced sales, the return on innovation of new drugs will be much lower. Unless an alternative method of financing drug research is adopted, fewer life-saving remedies will be developed.

Discourse on this topic further changed with terrorist attacks on the United States and a subsequent scare over an anthrax epidemic in 2001. The U.S. Secretary for Health and Human Services demanded a lower price from the makers of Cipro, a powerful antibiotic, to be able to address this emergency. Many developing countries noted that AIDS, tuberculosis, and malaria constituted public health emergencies in their countries, and their demands for lower prices or compulsory licensing agreements were comparable.

> The ability to address public health crises by requiring that licenses be issued to domestic producers became a major element of the Doha Development Agenda, which was established at the November 2001 ministerial meeting that launched a new round of trade talks. Least developed countries were exempt from the requirement to grant pharmaceutical patents until 2016. In August of 2003 an agreement was reached regarding the right of countries without any domestic manufacturing capacity to import pharmaceuticals, from producers that were not licensed by the patent holder, as necessary to deal with the emergency a country faced. Developing countries were to notify the TRIPs Council of the amounts of drugs they imported under this clause. Twenty-three developed countries committed not to use this flexibility, and that number expanded by ten when the E.U. membership grew in 2004. Although these provisions are to be adopted as an amendment to the TRIPs agreement, other contentious issues, such as the patenting of genetic material, remain to be addressed in the Doha Round (WTO 2006).

Developing countries often have weak regimes to protect intellectual property, because that effort drains funds and skilled personnel away from alternative uses that would directly benefit their residents rather than foreign copyright and patent holders. Charles Dickens complained of weak U.S. copyright protection in the nineteenth century, and in a similar vein developing countries see little direct benefit from stricter enforcement today. Rather, they expect to gain as **free riders** on the efforts of others to promote innovation. That strategy likely means that fewer products are developed that primarily benefit developing countries. In the case of products aimed at a worldwide market, however, developing countries are rightly skeptical that their payment of monopoly prices for existing products will have much effect on the likelihood that a whole new generation of products will be developed.

What is the effect on world welfare of enforcing rules to extract greater payments for innovators of new products? To answer that question economists need to know whether too little research is carried on presently, a likely outcome when much of the benefit from an innovation spills over to others. They also must judge whether granting monopoly power to an innovator for a 20-year period, the patent life agreed to in the Uruguay Round, is a reasonable rule of thumb. Does it appropriately balance the payoff from future innovation against the welfare loss that comes from charging monopoly prices that far exceed marginal costs of production? In turn, that requires assessing how productive is more money spent on research in generating new ideas, and how great will the incentive be for a monopolist to introduce a new product that undercuts demand for one of its existing products.

RESOLVING TRADE DISPUTES IN THE WTO

The World Trade Organization was established as the successor to the GATT, and a much more rigorous, rules-oriented basis for dispute resolution procedures was created. If one country believes that the actions of another country are not consistent with its WTO obligations, a first step is to request consultations with that country. If no satisfactory resolution is reached, the country with a complaint can request that a panel be formed to hear the case. The panel evaluates the evidence submitted to it, and it must deliver a decision within one year for a normal case. Panel reports are automatically approved unless appealed to a newly created Appellate Body. The Appellate Body's findings are adopted automatically unless there is consensus not to do so. This contrasts with the prior GATT procedure, where adoption of a panel report required unanimous consent. A guilty party could simply block the adoption of a report unfavorable to it.

There has been considerable use of the WTO dispute resolution procedures. As of October 2005 the number of requests for consultation was 333. The major complainants were the U.S. (80) and the E.U. (70), although developing countries brought 126 complaints. Early examples of panel rulings favorable to developing countries, as were made in the case of U.S. restrictions on underwear imports from Costa Rica, wool shirts from India, and reformulated gasoline from Brazil and Venezuela, demonstrate the advantages of a rule-based system to smaller countries.

The goal of dispute resolution is that countries bring their practices into conformity with WTO obligations. Offending countries cannot be forced by the WTO to bring their practices into compliance, however, and they may not be willing to offer satisfactory compensation to those who brought the complaint. In that case an arbitration panel may grant the complaining country the right to retaliate to "restore the prior balance of concessions." Few cases reach that latter stage. Retaliation was authorized in the case of the E.U. ban on hormone-treated beef imports, the E.U. banana import regime, Brazilian export financing of aircraft, U.S. export subsidies provided through the tax code, Canadian export credits for aircraft, an early U.S. anti-dumping law, and U.S. disbursal of anti-dumping and countervailing duties to domestic producers (WTO 2006).

Because small countries may gain little benefit or leverage by retaliating against a large country, proposals have been made instead to impose fines or to allow retaliation rights to be auctioned off to other countries. Table 10.4 lists dispute settlement cases initiated from September 2006 through September 2007 to indicate the breadth of complaints brought to the WTO.

How does a country know if competitive problems faced by its producers are the result of WTO-illegal actions by another country? Aside from complaints by its own producers, another important source of information is the WTO Trade Policy Review Body. This group examines and evaluates trade policies of member countries on a regular schedule. The process calls for a statement of policy by the country being examined and a report by the WTO secretariat. Other members have the chance to ask questions about the practices notified in the report. These reports are available on the WTO web page.

The success of the dispute resolution mechanism will depend upon the way individual countries use the WTO procedures and implement their commitments. If member countries treat WTO procedures as a forum to handle minor disputes, but rely on bilateral negotiations to deal with major issues, the tension between rule of law and rule of negotiating power will remain. If large countries ignore rulings against their practices, they should not be surprised that small countries will see little reason to implement panel rulings.

TABLE 10.4 Dispute Settlement Cases before the WTO, Sept. 2006–Sept. 2007

Respondent	Issue	Complainant
E.U.	Importation and marketing of seal products	Canada
United States	Preliminary antidumping and countervailing duty determinations on coated free sheet paper	China
Australia	Importation of apples	New Zealand
Colombia	Indicative prices and restrictions on ports of entry	Panama
United States	Domestic support and export credit guarantees for agricultural products	Brazil
E.U.	Regime for the importation of bananas	Panama
China	Trading rights and distribution of certain publications and audiovisual entertainment products	United States
China	Protection and enforcement of intellectual property rights	United States
E.U.	Regime for the importation of bananas	Colombia
India	Additional and extra-additional duties on imports	United States
China	Refunds, reductions or exemptions from taxes	Mexico
China	Refunds, reductions or exemptions from taxes	United States
United States	Subsidies and other domestic support for corn	Canada
Chile	Definitive safeguard measures on milk products	Argentina
Brazil	Antidumping measures on imports of resins	Argentina
Canada	Tax exemptions and reductions for wine and beer	E.U.
United States	Trade in large civil aircraft	E.U.
India	Importation and sale of wines and spirits	E.U.
Chile	Provisional safeguard measure on milk products	Argentina
United States	Continued application of zeroing methodology	E.U.
E.U.	Tariff quota for fresh or chilled garlic	Argentina

Source: World Trade Organization (2007)

WTO Dispute Resolution and the Long-standing Banana Controversy

In 1999 the European Union and the United States had severe disagreements over several trade issues, including bananas, beef, and biotechnology. The value of trade involved did not seem to explain very well the intensity of the rhetoric from each side, and the difficulty in resolving the least significant one, the banana dispute, was not a good omen for the future operation of the dispute resolution mechanism.

The E.U. banana regime, adopted in 1993, extended to the E.U. market prior British and French preferences for bananas from former colonies in Africa, the Caribbean, and the Pacific. Those sources were to be guaranteed 30 percent of the E.U. market. Europeans were reluctant to reopen this issue, which effectively passed the cost of supporting high banana prices on to other E.U. partners. The change in policy harmed more efficient Latin American producers who previously supplied the E.U. market, as well as U.S. distributors who handled those bananas. The World Bank judged the policy to be a highly inefficient way of aiding the Caribbean states and recommended a more generous development program.

In May 1993 a GATT panel ruled against the EC banana regime, but under GATT rules that required panel reports to be adopted by consensus, the EC was able to block adoption of the report. The EC issued new regulations in July, which it claimed met its GATT obligations. In January 1994 a GATT panel ruled against this regime as well, and the EC again blocked the adoption of the report by the GATT council. With the formation of the WTO, panel reports could no longer be blocked by the offending party. A 1997 panel found that the E.U. banana regime violated both the GATT and the GATS. The E.U. appealed against these findings to the WTO Appellate Body, which upheld the panel ruling. Efforts to negotiate a settlement were not fruitful, and in 1998 the E.U. announced modifications to the banana regime that it claimed were WTO-consistent. The E.U. blocked reconvening the WTO panel in the fall of 1998 and the U.S. announced retaliatory steps. Eventually, the panel was reconvened, and yet again it ruled against the E.U. program.

In April 1999 WTO arbitrators ruled that the U.S. could impose retaliatory trade measures that affected $191 million of imports from the E.U. Items selected by the U.S. included handbags, paper, bed linen, and coffee makers, although some lawmakers favored a rotating retaliation list, to create maximum political pressure for a settlement.

In fact, a successful compromise between the U.S. and the E.U. was reached in April 2001 to resolve this dispute. Latin-American banana exporters conditioned their acceptance of a WTO waiver for an E.U.–Africa, Caribbean and Pacific (ACP) Economic Partnership upon good faith implementation of the banana accord.

In 2004 the E.U. submitted a proposal to establish a unified banana regime by 2006 with the imposition of a €230 per ton tariff on all MFN bananas (non-ACP countries). The Latin American producers requested arbitration to determine whether this proposal would maintain their access to the E.U. market, and in 2005 the arbitrators ruled that this rebinding of the tariff would not fulfill this condition. A subsequent E.U. proposal with a €187 tariff and a duty-free quota of 775,000 tons of

> ACP bananas was also rejected by the Latin American producers, and arbitrators again ruled against the E.U. proposal. In November 2005 the E.U. adopted a tariff to €176 on MFN bananas. As shown in list of dispute resolution cases in 2006–2007 of Table 10.4, the banana controversy is back before the WTO yet again.

DEVELOPING COUNTRIES AND THE WTO

Whether the GATT/WTO trading order benefits or penalizes developing countries was a point of controversy from the outset and remains so today. While many developing countries elected not to join the GATT initially, that stance has changed. Most developing countries are now included among the WTO's 150 plus members. Nevertheless, while accession to the WTO implies that the benefits outweigh the costs of membership, it does not signify satisfaction with all WTO obligations and procedures.

The GATT articles cited in Table 10.1 are not particularly focused on the issue of developing versus industrialized countries. Some articles provide benefits that have been particularly relevant to developing countries, however. The provision of MFN treatment to all members, regardless of whether they make reciprocal concessions, allows developing countries access to industrial markets without forcing any liberalization of their own trade policies. In addition, Article XII provides a balance of payments justification to impose import quotas in order to avoid a serious loss of foreign exchange reserves. Article XVIII regarding government assistance to economic development allows measures that promote the establishment of a particular industry.

The combined effect of these GATT provisions is to allow developing countries the freedom to pursue just about any trade policy they might choose (Jackson 1997). Indeed, studies of the trade policies and trade patterns of otherwise comparable members and non-members often find little difference results from GATT membership (Rose 2004). Not surprisingly, however, subjects of greatest interest to developing countries may not receive much attention within the GATT.

Differential and More Favourable Treatment?

Explicitly different treatment for developing countries was provided in 1971 by a waiver from the MFN clause that allows members to treat imports from developing countries more favorably. Industrialized countries are free to establish a **Generalized System of Preferences** (GSP). The E.U. and the U.S. have their own lists of goods and countries that qualify for duty-free entry of imports. Commodities that threaten to injure domestic producers are generally excluded, and countries that already account for a major market share typically are graduated from eligibility. Trade under these provisions has accounted for less than 5 percent of E.U. and U.S. trade.

The E.U. program that will apply for the 2006–2015 period includes three different categories of beneficiaries: (1) a general arrangement for all beneficiary countries; (2) special incentives for countries that implement international standards in human and labor rights, environmental protection, the fight against drugs, and good governance; and (3) an "everything but arms" initiative to grant duty-free and quota-free access for imports from the 49 **least developed countries** identified by the United Nations.[3] The most generous provisions are provided for countries that pose the smallest competitive threat.

Because the E.U. and the U.S. can alter the conditions of their GSP programs at their own discretion, many developing countries have concluded that a more stable arrangement is to negotiate treaty commitments instead. The U.S.–Central American Free Trade Agreement of 2006 represents a treaty with reciprocal concessions, in contrast to the Caribbean Basin Initiative of unilateral preferences provided by the U.S. The Cotonou Agreement between the E.U. and the African, Caribbean, and Pacific group of countries calls for economic partnership agreements to become effective in 2008. These agreements will result in tariff-free trade for E.U. exports to countries that are not in the least developed category, not just tariff-free entry of ACP products into the E.U.

The Doha Development Agenda

Although the Uruguay Round broke ground in many new areas, it merely marked the status quo in some of them. Most countries anticipated a subsequent round of negotiations to address this unfinished business. The Uruguay Round mandated that negotiations start no later than 2000 to ensure that improved agricultural market access was accomplished.

The expectations of initiating another round were not met at the ministerial meeting held in Seattle in November 1999. Prior to the meeting wide gaps in country positions still existed, and the protests of labor unions, environmental activists, and other antiglobalization forces created further pressures. Complaints were raised over secrecy and the decision-making processes within the WTO. U.S. and E.U. representatives talked of the need to incorporate labor rights and environmental protection into the WTO, while many developing countries saw these as code words to limit their potential exports.

A new round of multilateral trade negotiations was initiated at the WTO's fourth ministerial conference in Doha, Qatar, in November 2001. Developing countries were skeptical of participating in such a round, because they claimed that few concrete benefits to them had emerged from the Uruguay Round. Therefore, industrialized nations made an effort to ensure that the concerns of developing countries would be addressed more directly through the Doha Development Agenda. Most negotiating items made specific reference to "special and differential treatment" for developing and least developed countries, which were not expected to make as extensive concessions as the industrialized countries and were allowed more time to implement any agreements.

The interests of the developing countries were not all identical in areas such as agriculture, where some countries were net importers and some were net exporters. Even with respect to the goal of reducing high industrialized tariffs on items where many developing countries had a competitive advantage, the developing countries that already had preferential access to industrial markets wanted

---

3 Accessed from http://ec.europa.eu/trade/issues/global/gsp/index_en.htm on December 21 2007. The "everything but arms" program excluded bananas, rice, and sugar from immediate benefits.

compensation for losing this advantage. Most developing countries were in agreement in pushing for greater flexibility to address public health concerns under the TRIPs agreement and taking a wider focus in GATS negotiations to liberalize the mode 4 movement of people.

In spite of the general optimism generated at Doha, differences between industrialized and developing countries, and even within each group, could not be overcome at the 2003 ministerial meeting in Cancún, Mexico, and the 2005 ministerial meeting in Hong Kong. WTO members were unable to agree upon a basic format or text to initiate negotiations in each area (the modalities of the negotiations) before the U.S. fast-track negotiating authority expired in 2007. Subsequent efforts in 2008 again foundered over divergent positions on agricultural trade.

Who's Afraid of China?

After a lengthy process of negotiating to join the World Trade Organization, China became a member on December 1 2001. Although all countries had to approve China's membership, some of the most contentious bilateral talks occurred with the E.U. and with the U.S. In addition to the access they sought to Chinese markets for goods and services, both were concerned about a potential flood of products from China. In particular, worries abounded that in sectors where state-owned enterprises still dominated production, trade would be determined by government preferences and priorities, not by comparative advantage or market forces. Organized labor in the United States vehemently opposed Chinese entry, as it feared that competition with such a labor-abundant country would drive down U.S. wages.

Developing countries, on the one hand, expected some benefit from having the strong voice of a powerful developing country in the WTO. On the other hand, developing countries were worried because they saw themselves competing much more directly with Chinese goods. Other Asian countries feared China as an alternative site for foreign direct investment in export-oriented industries. As country-specific quotas on textiles and apparel were removed, would countries such as Bangladesh be able to export as much clothing as in 2000?

Even a country as seemingly removed from the scene as Mexico was affected, and in fact Mexico was the last country to assent to Chinese entry into the WTO. Was such concern warranted? The rapid growth of the assembly industry in Mexico under NAFTA was adversely affected by the U.S. economic slowdown in 2001, as was U.S. trade with China. In 2002, however, after China's accession to the WTO, U.S. imports from China rose by $20 billion or 20 percent, while imports from Mexico only rose 2 percent. The two countries do not compete head to head in all categories, but Chinese expansion and Mexican contraction in several key assembly operations are evident. In the three tariff categories for computers, office machinery, and calculators, Chinese sales rose by $3.8 billion, or 40 percent, while Mexican sales fell by $1.4 billion or 15 percent. A less dramatic pattern shows up in apparel, where Chinese sales rose by $0.5 billion or 7 percent, while Mexican sales fell $0.5 billion or 6 percent. Although this record also may reflect minor influences from exchange rate changes, the Mexican forecast of trouble ahead appears to be accurate.

Furthermore, the difference in performance across different industry categories does not seem to be related to variation in the level of U.S. tariff protection. The attraction of Chinese-based assembly seems to have risen due to the greater perceived predictability and consistency of Chinese policy, now that it is a WTO member.

Expanding the World Trade Organization

Vietnam became the 150th member of the WTO on 1 January 2007. As noted in the discussion of China's accession, successfully negotiating entry requires the assent of all existing members. For non-market economies the process is especially likely to require major changes in domestic policy to establish a commercial legal system that can fulfill the standards of national treatment mentioned in Article III. An expected benefit is that the member will now automatically be eligible for most-favored-nation treatment of its exports to other members, and it can use the WTO dispute settlement procedure when it believes that the foreign treatment of its exports is not consistent with GATT standards. By signing such an agreement, the prospective member also provides more assurance about the consistency of its future policy, often an important step in promoting more trade and investment.

As noted in Chapter 9, important countries such as Russia remain outside of the WTO and currently do not appear to place a high priority upon entry. Russia may feel little need to make its natural resource exports more attractive, and it may be unwilling to accept restrictions on its domestic energy pricing policies and financial regulation that concern current WTO members. China's entry was framed with many transition rules and safeguards because of concern over the way prices and costs are determined in non-market economies and the way business decisions are made by state enterprises. Because Russia is also a large economy that can potentially affect prices in many international markets, both WTO members and Russia are likely to be cautious in pursuing this possible accession.

Summary of Key Concepts

1. Compared to unilateral tariff reductions, countries generally find multilateral reductions more attractive, because terms-of-trade declines are smaller and political support of exporters can be mobilized.
2. During the nineteenth century, Great Britain unilaterally adopted a policy of free trade, which many other countries subsequently followed.
3. High tariffs adopted by the United States and other countries in the 1930s contributed to a major reduction in trade and production worldwide.
4. The General Agreement on Tariffs and Trade, founded in 1948, established a set of rules for international trade. It encouraged negotiations to reduce trade barriers on a nondiscriminatory basis.

5. The Uruguay Round, completed in 1994, reduced tariffs but also addressed important items that had escaped GATT discipline (agriculture and textiles) and reached agreements in several new areas (services, intellectual property, and investment requirements).

6. The Uruguay Round also established the World Trade Organization as a successor to the GATT. An important feature of the WTO was a more rigorous dispute resolution mechanism.

7. Whether GATT membership benefits developing countries remains controversial.

CASE STUDY

Discipline Over Agricultural Policies? The Case of U.S. Cotton Subsidies

For most of the post-World War II period, domestic agricultural policies and trade restrictions were largely exempt from any internationally imposed limitations. In 1955 the U.S. claimed a waiver from its obligations under the GATT with respect to its restrictions on agricultural imports, which were designed to allow higher domestic prices. Others, such as the E.U. and Japan, subsequently claimed similar privileges (Jackson 1997). The Uruguay Round concluded in 1994 broke that pattern. One key aspect of that agreement was that countries would reduce domestic production subsidies by 20 percent, although from values observed in an earlier peak period. That choice limited any immediate cuts. As commodity prices fell later in the decade, U.S. payments to cotton farmers rose so much that they exceeded the 1992 limit that countries had accepted as part of a Peace Clause to forestall WTO challenges. U.S. cotton subsidies in 1992 were $1.62 billion, but in both 1999 and 2001 they exceeded $2 billion. The U.S. share of world cotton exports rose from 20 percent to 40 percent, although the U.S. is not a low-cost supplier in the absence of subsidies. The increase in exports was not the result of greater U.S. output, however, but reduced U.S. domestic demand.

Brazil filed a complaint in the WTO, and in 2003 a panel was formed. The panel found that several domestic policies, such as marketing loan payments, counter-cyclical payments, and market loss assistance payments had resulted in extra production. In the language of the WTO, that caused significant price suppression, and lower prices caused serious prejudice to Brazil's interests. The panel additionally concluded that export credit guarantees and payments to users of U.S. cotton were export subsidies that should be withdrawn without delay. The Appellate Body upheld these positions in its 2005 ruling.

Brazil claimed that without the illegal subsidies, U.S. output would fall 29 percent and world prices would rise 12.6 percent. While Brazil calculated its losses at over $500 million annually, four small African nations felt a negative effect as large as 1 to 2 percent of GDP. Their objections contributed to the unsuccessful conclusion of the Ministerial Meeting in Cancún, Mexico in September, 2003.

An important issue that arose in this case was the treatment of direct payments to cotton producers, which the U.S. claimed were unrelated to output. This decoupling meant that they did not create a distortion in world cotton markets and were consistent with a country's WTO obligations. The panel ruled, however, that the payments had not been effectively decoupled from production. U.S. rules limited what cotton farmers could grow on their land if they accepted these payments. Also, eligibility to receive these payments depended upon output in a base period, and that base period was updated in 2002. If producers can expect such adjustments in the future, that creates an incentive to plant more cotton today. That ruling demonstrated the difficulty countries will face in claiming that their subsidies to farmers do not in fact create the incentive to increase production.

Bagwell and Staiger (2002) raise an alternative view of the WTO subsidy provisions. Because the subsidies raise the total amount of trade, those economists see little reason to control such payments. The subsidizing country presumably believes it is better off, and the gain to consumers throughout the world exceeds the loss to competing producers. Their perspective questions the desirability of this GATT provision.

CASE STUDY QUESTIONS

1. WTO rules distinguish between an export subsidy, which is prohibited, and a production subsidy, which may be subject to complaint if it adversely affects producers in other member countries. What case can you make to support this distinction?

2. The U.S. share of the world cotton market rose even though U.S. production did not rise. Explain how those two facts are consistent and suggest what may have affected U.S. demand for cotton.

3. What supply and demand conditions in world markets would make it more likely that Brazil's claim of significant price suppression was correct? In particular, what role is played by the U.S. export elasticity of supply and the world import elasticity of demand?

4. If a small African producer also subsidized its cotton producers, why would the consequent price suppression be slight?

5. If direct payments by the government are made to cotton producers regardless of how much cotton or any other commodity they produce, why does economic theory support the claim that such payments will not lead to over-production of cotton in the subsidizing country?

Questions for study and review

1. Does the chance for countries to free-ride on the concessions of others make the principle of most-favored-nation status a weakness of the WTO? Do regional agreements represent an effective way to exclude free riders?

2. Does the growth of regional trading blocs warrant WTO encouragement? If regional groups had an open membership policy to accept all who applied, would that be more desirable from a world standpoint?

3. Large countries are likely to have an advantage in any trade war. Why are those countries still willing to join the WTO, which limits their ability to exploit their market power?

4. The Swiss tariff-cutting formula proposed in the Doha Round negotiations was the following: $t_1 = a t_0 / (a + t_0)$, where t_0 is the initial tariff expressed in percentage form, t_1 is the new tariff,

and *a* is a parameter that must be agreed by the negotiators. One proposal called for *a* = 5 for industrialized countries and *a* = 30 for developing countries. Calculate what difference this treatment would imply for a tariff of 2 percent versus a tariff of 60 percent. What benefit does this approach provide for developing countries?

5. Do international negotiations where countries count their gains in terms of greater access to foreign markets represent misplaced attention to exports alone? Regardless of the motive for such negotiations, in what ways do countries gain from cooperating multilaterally?

6. Why does the WTO regard quantitative restrictions as less desirable policy instruments than *ad valorem* tariffs? How is the current existence of tariff-rate quotas consistent with this preference?

7. The WTO reports the following differences in average tariff rates on agricultural products for those subject to *ad valorem* tariffs versus the *ad valorem* equivalent for those subject to other tariffs:

Country	Average ad valorem *rate*	Average ad valorem equivalent rate	% of tariff lines subject to non ad valorem *rate*
Canada	4.3	81.5	22.3
EC	7.7	30.4	46.3
Japan	9.8	65.6	17.2
U.S.	8.1	11.8	43.2

How do you expect these differences to affect the bargaining positions of these countries in the Doha Round regarding the extent of exceptions for sensitive products and the treatment of tariff peaks? Why may specific tariffs have a particularly adverse effect on exports from developing countries?

8. When disputes over unfair trade practices arise, what standards should be applied to non-market economies, and how different from those applied to firms in market economies must they be to provide comparable treatment?

9. If there were no dispute settlement mechanism within the WTO, how would that weaken the credibility of any multilateral agreements reached? If individual members regard some issues as too important to be addressed by dispute resolution within the WTO, what alternative do they have in responding to WTO panel rulings?

10. "When a small country reduces its tariffs as part of a WTO agreement, that is likely to reduce inefficiencies in the country and make it better off, but if the country must increase its payments to others for the right to use their intellectual property, that is likely to make the country worse off." Evaluate this claim by advocates from developing countries who feel the Uruguay Round agreements were against their interests.

References and Suggestions for Further Reading

For theoretical perspectives on multilateral trade agreements, see:

Bagwell, K. and Staiger, R. (2002) *The Economics of the World Trading System*, Cambridge, MA: MIT Press.
Ethier, Wilfred (2001) "Theoretical Problems in Negotiating Trade Liberalization," *European Journal of Political Economy* 17: 209–32.
Johnson, Harry (1953) "Optimum Tariffs and Retaliation," *Review of Economic Studies* 21: 142–53.
Staiger, Robert (1995) "International Rules and Institutions for Trade Policy," in G. Grossman and K. Rogoff (eds) *Handbook of International Economics, Vol. III*, Amsterdam: Elsevier Science, pp. 1495–1551.

For general overviews of GATT/WTO policy or negotiating rounds, see:

Cline, William (1977) *Trade Negotiations in the Tokyo Round: A Quantitative Assessment*, Washington, D.C.: Brookings Institution.
Hoekman, B., Mattoo, A., and English, P. (eds) (2002) *Development, Trade and the World Trade Organization: A Handbook*, Washington, D.C.: World Bank.
Jackson, John (1997) *The World Trading System, Law and Policy of International Economic Relations*, 2nd edn, Cambridge, MA: MIT Press.
Preeg, Ernest (1970) *Traders and Diplomats: An Analysis of the Kennedy Round Negotiations under the General Agreement on Tariffs and Trade*, Washington, D.C.: Brookings Institution.
Rose, Andrew (2004) "Do WTO Members Have More Liberal Trade Policy?" *Journal of International Economics* 63: 209–35.
—— (2004) "Do We Really Know that the WTO Increases Trade?" *American Economic Review* 94: 98–114,
Schott, Jeffrey (1994) *The Uruguay Round: An Assessment*, Washington, D.C.: Institute for International Economics.
U.S. Tariff Commission (1974) *Trade Barriers, Vol. 3*, Washington, D.C.: USTC, Chapter 5.
World Trade Organization (2007) *The World Trade Report 2007*, Switzerland: WTO, Chapter II.

For discussions of specific trade policies and other issues, see:

Arias, P., Hallam, D., Hubbard, L., and Liu, P. (2006) "The elusive tariff equivalent for the EU banana market," *Commodity Market Review 2005–2006*, Rome: Food and Agricultural Organization of the United Nations, pp. 107–24.
"At Daggers Drawn," (1999) *The Economist*, May 8, pp. 17–19.
Finger, J.M., Hall, K., and Nelson, D. (1982) "The Political Economy of Administered Protection," *American Economic Review* 72: 452–66.
Graham, E. (2000) *Fighting the Wrong Enemy*, Washington, D.C.: Institute for International Economics.
Irwin, Douglas (1998) "Changes in US Tariffs: The Role of Import Prices and Commercial Policies," *American Economic Review* 88: 1015–1026.
de Jonquières, Guy (1997) "WTO Puts Skids under Banana Regime," *The Financial Times*, March 20, p. 7.
—— (1999) "Trade Goes Bananas," *The Financial Times*, January 26, p. 15.
Jordan, Miriam (2001) "Brazil May Flout Trade Laws to keep AIDS Drugs Free for Patients," *Wall Street Journal*, February 12, p. B1.
Oxfam (2004) "Cultivating Poverty: The Impact of US Cotton Subsidies on Africa," Briefing Paper 30.
United Nations (2002) *Human Development Report 2002*, New York: UN, p. 106.
"Unpicking Cotton Subsidies," (2004) *The Economist*, April 30.
WTO (2005) *US Subsidies on Upland Cotton*, WT/DS267/AB/R.
WTO (2006) *Overview of Developments in the International Trading Environment*, WT/TPR/OV/11.
WTO (2007) "Overview of the State-of-Play of WTO Disputes," available http://www.wto.org/english/tratop_e/dispu_e/dispu_status_e.htm, (accessed October 9 2007).

Chapter 11

Trade and Growth

LEARNING OBJECTIVES

By the end of this chapter you should be able to demonstrate:

- how increases in factor endowments, improvements in technology and choices of how to spend rising incomes all affect trade

- why developing countries that rely upon primary product exports have been vulnerable to volatile export earnings and declining terms of trade

- how import substitution policies attempt to avoid such terms-of-trade declines but risk creating permanent inefficiencies

- why more open trade policies have been an important part of the success of economies that have grown more rapidly

- how growth may cause a negative externality such as pollution, and government regulations to reduce pollution may affect the location of production and pattern of trade

Growth offers the hope of rising standards of living. Faster growth in developing countries may allow them to close the gap between the higher levels of income per capita in industrial countries and their own level. Although international organizations such as the World Bank and the United Nations seek to promote growth in the developing world, many countries are not sanguine about all aspects of that outcome. Europeans and Americans worry that the impressive growth of China and India over the past decade poses a threat to them, anticipating ever greater competition internationally. That concern might be alternatively phrased: as countries become more similar, does that reduce the gains from trading for some? On the other hand, some developing countries do not see themselves competing with the E.U. or the U.S. Instead, they worry that expansion of their export sectors may result in little benefit to them because of the adverse effect on prices in international markets. Whether either of these concerns is relevant depends upon the sources of growth, not just the fact that GDP per capita has risen. One goal of this chapter is to demonstrate when circumstances warrant these worries and when a more optimistic outlook is appropriate.

Not only is growth likely to affect trade, but economists and politicians have long debated how trade will affect a country's growth prospects. In the second part of this chapter, we address this issue with special attention to developing countries. In the 1950s and 1960s many of the latter rejected the view that there are mutual gains from trade. Instead, they viewed the international trading system as likely to impoverish developing countries further. Newly independent countries such as India, Indonesia, Ghana, and Tanzania wanted to reject links to their colonial past and the market system. Instead, they aimed for less dependency on the outside world and more self-sufficiency.

In the 1970s, many developing countries argued for a radical transformation of the trading system. The **United Nations Conference on Trade and Development (UNCTAD)** was the primary forum to formulate and promote these ideas. This agenda called for higher and more stable prices for agricultural commodities, basic minerals and fuels, special trade preferences for developing countries, and greater foreign aid.

Little of this agenda was adopted in the 1980s due to a change in perceptions. The view that growth was not possible under existing market mechanisms was less persuasive. Countries such as the four Asian Tigers (Hong Kong, Korea, Singapore, and Taiwan) had achieved rapid economic growth within the existing order. Crises emerged under inward-looking policies of **import substitution industrialization**. The World Bank advocated adjustment policies that included greater openness to trade and **export-led growth**, a strategy that it attributed to the successful experience of **newly industrialized countries** (NICs) in Asia. In this chapter we assess the elements of that new prescription and the ongoing controversy as to whether the star performers in the developing world actually followed its precepts.

Finally, we consider another aspect of economic growth, a possible negative **externality** that results from greater pollution and damage to the environment. How countries choose to deal with these negative environmental effects of their increased production can affect patterns of international trade, too. Some observers worry that a quest for growth at any cost will result in a race to the bottom in terms of environmental standards and a shift of the dirtiest industries to the poorest countries. Not all negative externalities are confined within the borders of producing countries, as the international debate over global warming forces us to recognize. How countries move beyond the Kyoto Protocol to the Climate Change Convention, which expires in 2012, again has important implications for the pattern of international production and trade.

BUILDING BLOCKS TO DETERMINE THE EFFECTS OF ECONOMIC GROWTH ON TRADE

Countries' patterns of trade clearly change over time. In the eighteenth and nineteenth centuries, the United States primarily exported tobacco, then cotton, and later foodstuffs. By the twentieth century it became a major exporter of manufactured goods, but in the first decade of the twenty-first century, it is instead a net exporter of services. For an even more rapid transformation in the post-war period, consider Korea's shift from initially being an exporter of primary materials, next becoming a dominant provider of apparel and footwear, and most recently excelling in steel, electronics, and semiconductors.

Our previous chapters have presented more than one explanation for the pattern of trade we might observe, and those alternative perspectives again are relevant here. We begin our analysis by reviewing the effect of changing factor endowments and changing technology in a world with perfectly competitive firms. We also address the role of domestic demand conditions. We first consider the implications for the volume of trade of a small country that cannot affect prices internationally, and then allow for additional issues that arise when prices do change.

The Neutral Case of Proportional Growth and Demand

If all factor inputs increase by the same proportion and constant returns to scale hold, then a country's production-possibility curve uniformly shifts out by that same proportion along any ray from the origin. That situation is shown in Figure 11.1, where the proportional increase from C_1 to C_2 is the same as the proportional increase from F_1 to F_2 or P to P'. Alternatively, such a shift in the production-possibility curve can result from an increase in the productivity of all factor inputs in all sectors by the same percentage; more output can be obtained from the same inputs. For developing countries, the World Bank notes that increases in the availability of factor inputs have been the primary source of their growth.

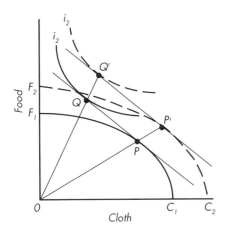

FIGURE 11.1 Neutral Growth in a Small Country

With proportional growth in its ability to produce both goods and with no change in its terms of trade, Country A shifts its consumption point from Q to Q', and its trade grows by the same proportion as its output.

Sustaining Growth and Economic Miracles

The East Asian Miracle. This is the title of a 1993 World Bank book that recognized the remarkable record of eight East Asian economies that had grown significantly faster than any other region of the world over the 1965–1990 period and simultaneously achieved greater income equality. The study suggested why these economies were unusually successful and drew general policy lessons for other countries that aspired to match their progress.

Traditionally, economists focused on increases in the capital stock, made possible by greater saving and investment within an economy or by foreign investment or foreign aid from outside the economy, as a key to economic growth. The East Asian experience also exemplified the importance of human capital, which creates the opportunity to raise worker productivity by education and training and to adjust more effectively to changing technology. As suggested in Chapter 8, the ability to increase factor inputs other than unskilled labor is an important determinant of rising standards of living.

To what extent is economic growth determined by the greater availability of factor inputs? For the East Asian economies, the World Bank judged that the contribution of high saving and investment, increases in schooling, and an increase in the share of the population in the work force accounted for about two thirds of their growth. The increase in these inputs meant these economies sacrificed considerable current consumption in order to build up their productive capacity, and their successful growth shows that the resources were allocated efficiently. That outcome alone can be regarded as miraculous in many respects, because in other high-saving economies, such as the USSR, merely accumulating capital did not guarantee sustained growth. With respect to East Asian trade patterns, the success of these economies in exporting goods that use physical and human capital more intensively is quite consistent with this change in their factor endowments.

How much of a country's growth occurs for reasons above and beyond the increase in available inputs, and is due instead to rising productivity? When that latter element is larger, we might regard the country's growth record as even more miraculous. A provocative study of Singapore's experience by Alwyn Young (1995) found that the contribution of additional inputs accounted for all of its growth, and no increase in productivity occurred. For the East Asian countries as a group, the Bank reports that additional inputs were not the whole story, and rising productivity accounted for a third of their growth. In part, this effect can be viewed as the success of these countries in catching up to industrial countries by applying better technologies. Their ability to become competitive in new industries further affected the patterns of trade we observe for them.

Trade appears to lead to higher growth rates. Possible explanations are that it provides access to more productive imported machinery, more specialized intermediate inputs, or the transmission of ideas. If the gap between best-practice techniques and those actually used can be reduced and thereby allow faster growth, trade may contribute to that process. We consider other unresolved aspects of this relationship later in this chapter.

At unchanged terms of trade, Country A will continue to produce the two commodities in the same proportions as in the initial equilibrium, as indicated by the points P and P' on the vector OP'. The effects on Country A's consumption and its volume of trade depend on its pattern of demand, as shown by its community indifference curves. If Country A chooses to consume food and cloth in the same proportions as before, both its imports of food and its exports of cloth will rise in proportion to the increase in output. In this case, Country A's income elasticity of demand for both goods is unity, and its consumption points (Q and Q') will lie on the vector OQ'. Consumption of both goods increases in proportion to economic growth.

The Effect of a Bias in Demand

Figure 11.2 summarizes possible outcomes for the case of proportional growth in factor supplies but a biased demand response to growth. Initially, production occurs at P, consumption at Q, and the trade triangle SPQ represents cloth exports, SP, and food imports, SQ. At unchanged international prices, growth results in the new production point Q'. Various effects on trade are possible, depending upon demand conditions. The neutral expansion path, with income elasticity of unity for both goods, is along the vector OQ': consumption of both goods rises in proportion to income growth.

If the demand for food rises more than in proportion to income (income elasticity of demand for food is greater than one), then the expansion path will be steeper than QQ', falling in the angle GQQ', and exports will increase by a greater proportion than output. Growth is then biased toward trade. If the demand for food rises less than in proportion to income (income elasticity less than one), then the expansion path will be less steep than QQ', falling in the angle $Q'QH$, and exports will

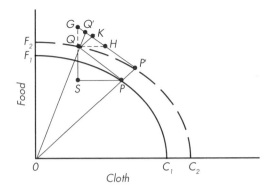

FIGURE 11.2 Effect of Demand Conditions on the Volume of Trade

With unbiased growth and unchanged terms of trade, Country A shifts its production from point P to P'. If we rule out inferior goods, A can consume anywhere between points H and G on the barter line P'G. If the income elasticity of demand for food exceeds one, A will consume between points Q' and G, while a low-income elasticity of demand for food results in points between Q' and H.

increase by a smaller proportion than output, or they may even decline. The latter case results if the new demand for food is below point K along the barter line $P'G$, where K is determined from drawing QK parallel to PP'. Growth is biased against trade in that case. The greater the income elasticity of demand for the export good, the more likely the bias against trade.

The Effect of a Bias in Supply

From Chapter 4 recall the Rybczynski Theorem: an increase in the labor force results in greater output of the labor-intensive good and a reduction in the output of the capital-intensive good at unchanged prices of output. If the country initially is labor-abundant, then the increase in the labor force results in a particularly large increase in exports. Conversely, if that country's capital stock grows, the country becomes more similar to the rest of the world. Its production in the import-competing, capital-intensive sector expands, and it produces less of its labor-intensive export good. If a labor-abundant country experiences a large enough expansion of its capital stock, it can become a capital-abundant country, and its comparative advantage will shift from labor-intensive goods to capital-intensive goods.

Evolving Trade Patterns of Asian Tigers

The remarkable growth of Asian economies in the past several decades is reflected in the changing composition of the products these countries trade. Here we consider two countries, Malaysia and China, which represent this process in different decades.

Malaysia grew so rapidly in the 1970s and 1980s that it qualifies as part of the second wave of Asian Tigers or Newly Industrialized Countries (NICs), after the first wave of Hong Kong, Korea, Singapore, and Taiwan. Table 11.1 shows how Malaysia's trade patterns differed in 1965 and 1995. Initially its exports primarily reflected its bountiful endowment of natural resources:

TABLE 11.1 Leading Malaysian Exports, 1965 and 1995 (U.S.$ million)

1965			**1995**		
SITC code	Commodity	Value	SITC code	Commodity	Value
231.1	Rubber	477.7	776	Transistors, valves, etc.	13240.0
687.1	Tin and alloys unwrought	282.4	759	Office, ADP machinery parts	4767.8
242.3	Saw logs and veneer logs	85.5	42.4	Fixed veg. oil, nonsoft	3833.6
281.3	Iron ore and concentrates	52.7	764	Telecom equipment and parts	3784.4
332.0	Petroleum products	52.4	762	Radio broadcast receivers	3485.1
422.2	Fixed vegetable oil	39.5	763	Sound recorders, phonographs	2792.0
243.3	Lumber (non-conifer)	31.6	333	Crude petroleum	2684.6
75.1	Pepper and pimiento	13.6	761	Television receivers	2239.1
53.0	Fruit, prepared or preserved	13.4	752	Automatic data proc. equip.	2185.1
			248	Wood shaped sleepers	1833.2
			634	Veneers, plywood, etc.	1687.3
			232	Natural rubber gums	1612.9
Items shown as a percent of total exports		28%			24%

Source: United Nations (1965, 1995)

rubber, tin, lumber, iron ore, petroleum, and food products. By 1995 those natural resources were still important, but even more of Malaysia's export earnings came from a variety of electronic products. Its exports became much more diversified. A well-trained, English-speaking labor force has been an attraction for multinational corporations who in turn have added to the available capital stock and technology base. A combination of changes in factor supplies, factor productivity, and available technology appears important in explaining Malaysia's changing pattern of trade.

Other observers point to Malaysia's progression within a flying geese formation, a metaphor popularized by Akamatsu (1961), led by Japan and then the initial Four Tigers. As the leaders produce successively more advanced products, and lose their comparative advantage in more standardized products, new opportunities become available to Malaysia, provided that it keeps up with the leaders by increasing its capital stock and the education of its work force.

Table 11.2 represents the Chinese situation from a slightly different perspective, with less focus on specific product lines. Nevertheless, as the Chinese policy of liberalizing its economy progressed, a transition away from natural resources in agriculture and mining also appears in these figures. The growth of manufacturing is striking, although with these figures for export values it is not possible to distinguish what portion of the value was added within China. The high rate of saving and capital accumulation clearly allowed expansion in categories that were not the most labor-intensive, although the electronic assembly and apparel production that shifted away from countries such as Mexico do show up as an important part of China's well diversified export bundle. UN data on the role of imported parts in the machinery sector show a sharp increase from 5.7 percent of total imports in 1994 to 25.7 percent in 2004, further evidence of rapid changes in China's links to the outside world.

TABLE 11.2 Chinese Exports by Product Category

Category	1986	1994	2004
Agriculture (SITC 0–1)	18.5	9.2	3.2
Crude Materials and Fuel (SITC 2–3)	26.2	6.8	3.4
Manufacturing (SITC 5–8)	55.3	84.1	93.4
Chemicals (SITC 5)	7.1	5.1	4.5
Primarily by materials (SITC 6)	23.8	19.8	17.0
Textiles (SITC 65)	17.0	9.9	5.7
Steel (SITC 67)	0.7	1.6	2.3
Machinery and Transport (SITC 7)	4.5	18.2	45.4
Office Machinery (SITC 75)	0.2	2.2	14.7
Telecommunication (SITC 77)	1.0	5.6	11.6
Miscellaneous (SITC 8)	20.0	40.9	26.5
Clothing (SITC 84)	11.8	19.8	10.5

Source: United Nations (1989, 1994, 2004).

For industrialized countries, increases in factor productivity have been more important sources of rising output than increases in factor supplies. Changes in factor productivity are more complicated to analyze, however, because wages and returns to capital can change even though prices of goods remain unchanged. As a very basic case, consider an increase in labor productivity by the same proportion in all sectors. The consequences are very similar to what we just demonstrated for the Rybczynski Theorem: output of the labor-intensive good will rise and output of the capital intensive good will fall at unchanged prices. One exception, however, is that more productive labor can now be paid a higher wage.

In the appendix to this chapter we present a more complete framework for analyzing a broader set of productivity changes. In particular, we can use it to assess the implications for changes in output and the wages of skilled versus unskilled labor when new technologies require more skilled labor and less unskilled labor.

LARGE COUNTRIES AND CHANGES IN THE TERMS OF TRADE

If growth leads to a decrease in the quantity of exports a country supplies at the initial price ratio, and the country is large enough to affect prices internationally, it benefits from an improvement in its terms of trade. Conversely, if growth causes an increase in the quantity of exports supplied, the country's producers must accept a lower price in order to sell these additional exports. Such a decline in its terms of trade reduces the benefits derived from economic growth. Also, if countries such as China and India effectively catch up with industrial countries and have less need to import capital-intensive, high-tech goods, the terms of trade of industrial countries that export those goods will decline.

Differentiated Products and Other Aspects of Growth

The terms-of-trade predictions above follow from the two-good model presented in Chapters 3 and 4, where growth occurs due to an increase in the output of the two existing goods. If we consider Krugman's love of variety model from Chapter 5, however, growth comes from the production of more varieties by monopolistically competitive firms. New firms in that economy simply produce additional varieties of goods at the same price as those that already exist. No decline in the terms of trade occurs.

Economists have examined the contrasting role of growth on the intensive margin (more exports of the same product) versus the extensive margin (exports of more varieties of goods) to assess which characterization is more relevant. David Hummels and Peter Klenow (2005) carry out such an analysis and make a further distinction to consider changes in the quality of existing goods. From 1995 trade data they conclude that larger countries export more than smaller countries, with 62 percent of this difference due to the extensive margin and 38 percent to the intensive margin. The increase in varieties is not as great as the Krugman model predicts, but still considerable. The authors also find that large, high-income countries do not rely upon lower prices to sell additional varieties. Rather, high-income countries tend to export higher priced (higher quality) goods within a product category.

Insights from Models of Endogenous Growth

The discussions above, based on increasing factor endowments or improved technologies, rely upon static models. Once the economy has shifted to the new equilibrium consistent with a larger labor force or an improved technology, no further change occurs. A more complicated set of answers follows when economists address the process of technical change and do not regard it as a lucky gift from heaven. Endogenous growth models suggest why an economy can continue to grow, but also why countries may not converge at the same growth rate.[1]

Without developing those models more formally, we can arrive at some of the same insights and face the same policy dilemmas by using the model of dynamic economies of scale presented in Chapter 5. Alwyn Young (1991) proposes a learning-by-doing framework slightly different from the learning curve we discussed in the semiconductor industry. In that latter case, where learning allows costs to fall at a constant rate as cumulative output rises, the initial innovator of a product has a tremendous advantage. A late-comer will never catch up, unless it somehow benefits from a steeper learning curve and a faster reduction in costs.

That situation leaves no room for the infant industry analysis we encountered in Chapter 7. The modification proposed by Young is to limit the range of learning. Firms eventually exhaust all the opportunities to cut costs. R&D effort is necessary to introduce new goods, where opportunities for learning in production will be possible. Within a country, knowledge of better production techniques spills over to other firms, so that no monopoly profits are earned. If we think of countries producing a continuum of goods with increasing technical sophistication, suppose one large country produces only goods where learning occurs and one small country produces only those goods where learning has been exhausted. This pattern of trade between countries will be maintained into the future and the technological gap between them will grow, although both countries will benefit from new products being introduced.

Suppose, however, that the initial difference in technical sophistication between the countries is not as large. Trade may now put the least sophisticated goods in the advanced country in competition with the most sophisticated goods in the small country. That additional competition results in less learning in the small country and a slower rate of growth than it could achieve without trade. Or, suppose that the less advanced country is larger and thereby able to consume a wider range of goods and achieve a faster rate of technical progress. If it is not too far behind the advanced country, it may surpass it and become the advanced country. Thus, multiple outcomes are possible, and no single policy prescription emerges.

---

1 For example, Robert Feenstra (2004) provides a useful overview of models where productivity and the rate of growth depend upon the variety of intermediate inputs available. An implication from such models is that free trade may result in smaller countries growing at a slower rate than larger countries, an outcome that is more likely the smaller are any spillovers of technology from large countries to small countries.

The Terms-of-Trade Effects of Growth: Offer Curve Analysis

Analysis of change in the terms of trade can usefully be put in terms of the offer curves described in Chapter 3. Suppose Country A's original offer curve is OA, as in Figure 11.3. At the initial equilibrium, with terms of trade OT, Country A exports OC_1 of cloth and imports OF_1 of food. Then, as a result of growth in its labor force, Country A's offer curve shifts from OA to OA^1, indicating its willingness to export a larger quantity of cloth at each terms of trade. This is export-biased growth.

How are Country A's terms of trade affected? In Figure 11.3 we show three possible outcomes:

1. If Country A is a small country, too small to affect the world price, then the offer curve for the rest of the world (ROW) will be the straight line OT and the new equilibrium will be at E_2, where Country A exports OC_2 of cloth and imports OF_2 of food.

2. If Country A is large enough to influence the world price and the ROW offer curve is elastic, as indicated by the offer curve labeled ROW in Figure 11.3, the shift in Country A's offer curve will now cause a fall in the price of cloth relative to the price of food. The new equilibrium is at E_3, where A's offer of cloth has increased by a bigger proportion (from OC_1 to OC_3) than has the amount of food it receives in return (from OF_1 to OF_3). Country A's terms of trade have fallen, because a unit of cloth now buys less food, shown by the flatter terms-of-trade line OT^1.

3. If the initial equilibrium occurs on the inelastic range of the ROW offer curve, as shown by the offer curve ROW*, the new equilibrium will be at E_4. Country A offers more of its export good, OC_4, as a result of growth, but it receives back less of the good it imports, OF^4, compared to the original solution at E^1. An inelastic foreign demand, which contributes to a large terms-of-trade deterioration, is one of the conditions that results in immiserizing growth.

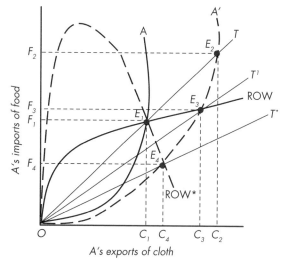

FIGURE 11.3 Effect of Growth on the Terms of Trade

Rapid expansion in Country A's export capacity results in its offer curve shifting from OA to OA^1. The effect on Country A's terms of trade depends upon the elasticity of demand in the rest of the world: when foreign demand is infinitely elastic, the relative price of cloth remains OT; when foreign demand is elastic, the relative price of cloth falls to OT^1; and when foreign demand is inelastic, the relative price of cloth falls to $OT*$.

Immiserizing Growth

We consider here a more traditional concern in the two-good model for a country that experiences growth in its export good. Is it possible that the loss from an adverse change in the terms of trade will exceed the gain from increased capacity? If so, the country becomes worse off than before it grew. This rather extreme case, called "immiserizing growth," has attracted much attention, especially in connection with complaints of developing countries over their unfavorable prospects in world trade. For example, in the 1950s Brazil and Colombia dominated the world coffee market, and India and Sri Lanka dominated the world tea market. The exports of these countries were highly concentrated in these categories. If these countries produced more coffee or tea, they feared that prices would fall so much that they would indeed become worse off.

To demonstrate more explicitly when such a case might arise, let production and consumption for Country A change as shown in Figure 11.4. Initially, A is producing at P_0 and exporting primary products in exchange for manufactures at the terms-of-trade ratio indicated by the slope of P_0 C_0. Through trade it can reach the welfare level represented by indifference curve i_0. Consumption is at C_0.

As a result of growth in the supply of factors used in the production of primary products, A's production-possibility curve shifts to the right, from AB to HK. It now offers larger quantities of exports, and its terms of trade decline as shown by the flatter slope of P_1C_1. At this exchange ratio, A continues to export primary products, but it can only reach the lower indifference curve, i_1. Thus, growth in capacity has reduced economic welfare. This outcome is more pronounced when an export-biased production effect is combined with a strong preference in Country A to spend additional income on manufactured goods. Growth results in a large increase in the quantity of exports supplied, and if import demand in the rest of the world is inelastic, there is a substantial decline in the relative

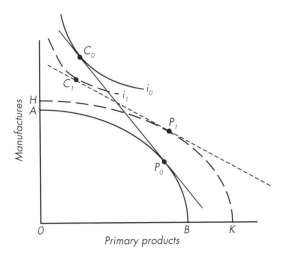

FIGURE 11.4 The Case of Immiserizing Growth

Economic growth has left this country worse off because of a terms-of-trade deterioration. It was producing P_0 and consuming at C_0. Now it produces at P_1 and consumes at C_1 which is on a lower indifference curve.

price of primary goods. Country A receives a smaller quantity of manufactured goods in exchange for a larger quantity of primary-product exports.

Although the theoretical possibility clearly exists, actual cases of immiserizing growth are especially hard to prove. It requires a country large enough to have a significant effect on the world price of its export, and one whose growth is strongly biased toward exports. For example, the demand for imports of sugar may be inelastic, but the import demand for sugar from Mexico is likely to be elastic. Mexican sugar is a very good substitute for sugar from other countries, and because Mexico accounts for a small share of the market it can attract customers away from other suppliers. Some economists believe that groups of developing countries have sometimes suffered losses as a result of their joint expansion of capacity to produce certain export commodities. In that case, a single country no longer increases its market share at the expense of others, and all face a lower price. Although this outcome is just a possibility, countries have adopted policies motivated by the worry that it will occur, which leads us to consider alternative trade policies.

DEVELOPING-COUNTRY PERSPECTIVES AND THE EFFECTS OF TRADE ON GROWTH

Developing countries do not speak with a single voice on the way the world trading system might change in order to be a more positive factor in achieving their goals with respect to economic growth. Therefore, treating them as a group in Table 11.3 is a useful starting point, but it provides an admittedly incomplete overview. Similarly, a comparison of terms-of-trade movements over the 1965–2006 period, given in Figure 11.5 for some major country groupings, shows that important distinctions must be made among developing countries. The experience of oil exporters is quite different from developing non-oil exporters. The latter group has experienced a decline in its terms of trade since 1980, as have industrial countries, but for the developing non-oil exporters both the downward trend and volatility around that trend are greater. The record for oil exporters is quite volatile, but not closely matched to producers of other primary products.

To evaluate these patterns more carefully, we begin by considering those countries that are reliant upon primary product exports. We then examine the experience of countries that have come to rely more upon manufactured exports and pay special attention to the policy debate over the best way to accomplish this shift.

An Overview of Developing-Country Trade

Table 11.3 shows the pattern of developing country exports for 40 years, starting in 1965, when much of the developing world was just gaining independence from the colonial powers, up to 2005, when the giant Asian economies of China and India were becoming more closely integrated into the international trading order. Given the focus on "trade, not aid" in the new millennium, the figures give some indication of where the opportunity to trade has risen. Because the figures reported are in nominal dollars, they do not provide a good basis for demonstrating how rapidly trade volumes have grown. They are useful, however, in showing the extent to which patterns of trade have changed, even though the destination of some trade could not always be determined. For the exports of developing countries, here are key points to note:

- Exports to industrial countries accounted for 69 percent of their total exports in 1965, and that figure was no smaller by 1980. The period up to 1995, however, showed a very sharp decline in their role to 54 percent, which continued at a much slower pace to 52 percent through 2005. For the early years in the period, developing countries experienced an improvement in their terms of trade, which probably contributed to the continued large role played by exports to industrial countries.
- Conversely, a big increase in the share of trade with other developing countries occurred between 1980 and 1995, a jump from 28 percent to 43 percent. A further increase to 46 percent followed through 2005. These figures suggest that establishing production chains across many countries to accomplish each step where it could occur most efficiently had already occurred in the case of merchandise trade, long before the public focus on outsourcing of services in 2004.
- Among developing country destinations, the biggest increase occurred for Asia. One reason is that the export value figures include imported intermediate inputs as well as domestic value added in the production and assembly of electronic components into final goods. As in the case

TABLE 11.3 Trade of Developing Countries Across Foreign Markets

Exports to: (given in percentages)	1965	1980	1995	2005
Industrialized economies	69.0	70.2	54.4	51.8
Europe	39.3	32.5	21.4	25.2
U.S.	18.3	20.9	19.9	18.9
Japan	7.2	14.0	10.0	7.2
Developing economies	27.9	28.5	43.3	46.4
Africa	2.9	2.4	1.9	2.1
Asia	10.3	11.2	27.4	28.9
Europe	5.3	2.9	6.6	7.3
Middle East	2.4	4.1	2.9	3.8
Western Hemisphere	6.6	7.9	4.6	4.2
Other	3.1	1.3	2.3	1.8
Total (U.S.$ billion)	**37.7**	**557.7**	**1,646.0**	**4,415.2**

Source: United Nations (1982, 1984), Special Table B, and IMF (1998, 2007).

of the Apple iPod discussed in Chapter 1, a disc drive shipped from the Philippines for assembly into an iPod in China that will be sold in India contributes more transactions than would be the case for an iPod produced completely by China. The more rapid expansion of that Asian trade results in smaller shares for Africa and the Western Hemisphere.

■ Among industrial countries, Europeans did not hold onto the commanding post-colonial position with which they started the period, but subsequent variations reflect no pronounced trends. Rather, they are largely due to differences in exchange rates and rates of growth. For example, due to slow growth in the post-1990 period, the Japanese share has declined in importance as a destination for developing country exports.

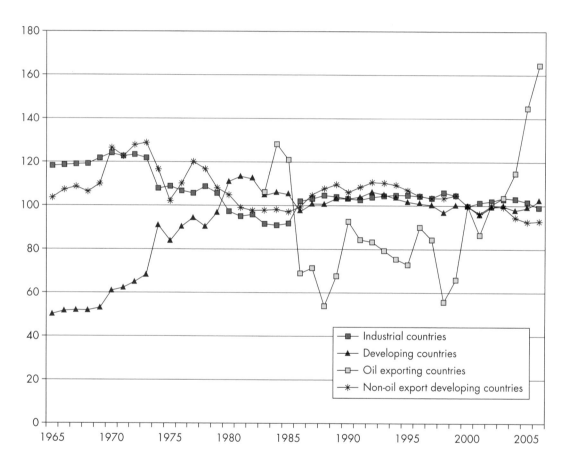

FIGURE 11.5 Terms of Trade Comparison, 1965–2006

Source: Calculated from export and import unit value series, International Monetary Fund, *International Financial Statistics*.

Industrial countries have seen far smaller changes in their terms of trade than oil exporters or non-oil exporting developing countries.

Primary Product Exporters and Price Volatility

Many of the poorest developing countries typically export large amounts of a small number of products, often primary products, which has made their export revenues quite volatile. Many OPEC members derive more than 80 percent of their export revenues from oil and gas. Consequently those countries faced severe declines in their export receipts in the 1980s and 1990s, and then a bonanza of revenue in the following ten years. A country with highly concentrated exports is analogous to a family with all of its net worth invested in the common stocks of one or two companies in a single industry: the family's investment income is likely to be very unstable. For a sample of the least developed countries, Table 11.4 reports the large role played by their top three exports, and their consequent vulnerability to volatility and declines in those prices. Various World Bank and UNCTAD studies document greater volatility of primary product prices than prices of manufactures.

What explains this greater volatility? One reason may be that the prices of many primary products are determined in highly competitive auction markets, such as the London Metal Exchange, whereas manufactured goods prices are determined in more oligopolistic markets. Highly competitive markets are known to have more price variability than do oligopolistic markets. Another explanation is that elasticities of supply and demand are lower for primary products than for manufactured goods. A

TABLE 11.4 Concentration of Merchandise Exports for Least Developed Countries

Country	Products	Share (three leading exports)/(total merchandise exports)	
		1981–3	*1997–9*
Afghanistan	Grapes, furs and skins, wool carpets	67.7	43.5
Angola	Petroleum and diamonds	96.5	97.6
Bangladesh	Men's and women's clothing	60.3	53.2
Cambodia	Garments, footwear, wood	64.4	61.3
Ethiopia	Coffee, sesame seed, leather	80.2	81.1
Liberia	Diamonds, rubber, timber	84.6	92.2
Madagascar	Garments, shellfish, coffee	70.7	40.5
Malawi	Tobacco, sugar, tea/coffee	82.9	78.8
Nepal	Carpets, garments	39.6	61.7
Tanzania	Coffee, cashew nuts	54.9	51.3
Uganda	Coffee, fish	97.5	69.9
Zambia	Copper, cobalt	93.8	89.3
Weighted average, LDCs		78.2	76.0

Source: UNCTAD (2002), p. 110.

developing country that has grown a certain amount of a perishable commodity is willing to sell it for whatever price is available, because in the short run it has few alternatives; its supply is very inelastic. If the price elasticity of demand for these products is also very low, because they have relatively few substitutes, the likelihood of large price swings is greater. A shift of either the supply or the demand curve causes a far larger price change than will occur when the demand and supply curves are more elastic.

International commodity-price stabilization programs are often suggested as a solution to this problem of price volatility. If both importers and exporters agree on a target or "normal" price and if the industrialized consuming countries are willing to provide initial financing, the stabilization fund purchases and stores the commodity whenever the market price falls below the target, thereby pushing it back up. When market prices rise above the target, the program sells the commodity from previously accumulated stocks, pushing the price back down.

This approach sounds attractive, but such programs have a poor track record. Consumers and producers seldom agree on the target price, and when such prices have been set, they are almost always too high. The fund has to continually purchase the commodity and soon runs out of money. Production quotas are frequently proposed as a way to support prices without continual commodity purchases by the fund, but every exporting country wants a large quota. If quotas are agreed upon, countries frequently cheat by producing above their quotas and trying to sell this output secretly. Programs in coffee, coca, tin, and sugar have proved unsuccessful.

Furthermore, stabilizing commodity prices is not synonymous with stabilizing export revenues. If price shocks primarily originate on the demand side, the two goals may coincide, but if supply shocks (weather, crop diseases) are more typical, stabilizing prices with a buffer stock program such as that described above is actually likely to destabilize export incomes. In years of small harvests, an offsetting rise in prices is not allowed, while in years of large harvests, a high price is paid anyway.

Volatility of export earnings is problematic for several reasons. The ability of countries to maintain their standard of living suffers when earnings fall. Countries are likely to reduce their investment as incomes and foreign exchange earnings decline, which adversely affects their long-run growth. The high earnings in boom-years may attract opportunistic politicians, who gain considerable personal wealth rather than use the funds effectively to cushion periods of price decline. As suggested in the Chapter 4 discussion of a possible resource curse, democratic succession becomes less likely and armed conflict more likely as well.

A long-term answer to the problem of revenue volatility is product diversification. Countries that develop new or non-traditional export markets benefit from the fact that prices in these markets are not likely to change in the same direction all the time and the elasticity of demand for the individual goods is likely to be larger for a new entrant who accounts for a small share of the market.

Primary Product Producers and Deteriorating Terms of Trade

Over the past few decades, the larger problem for primary product exporters has been not price volatility, but prolonged price declines. Over the 1980s and 1990s, prices of non-fuel commodities relative to manufactured goods exported by developed countries fell by 45 percent.

Such a negative relationship was predicted by Raul Prebisch (1950) and by Hans Singer (1950). The **Prebisch–Singer hypothesis** followed from these authors' observation of the change in Britain's terms of trade over the period from 1876 to 1947. They noted that technical progress in manufacturing did not create an expected benefit for primary product producers in the form of improved terms of trade. Rather, the opposite occurred, as the prices of manufactures rose relative to the prices of primary products.

A further concern was that demand for primary commodities did not rise much when world income rose. Foods and beverage markets have always operated under the cloud of Engel's law: the income elasticity of demand for such products is less than one. This idea is named after Ernst Engel, a nineteenth-century economist who found that poor people spend a high percentage of their incomes on food, but this percentage steadily declines as incomes rise. Consequently, markets for food and beverage items do not expand as rapidly as the world economy unless the distribution of income shifts to lower-income groups.

Technical progress in manufacturing has also tended to reduce demand for raw materials. That scenario is particularly relevant in explaining the experience in the 1980s. Prices of metals, fuels, and fibers declined in the early 1980s when virtually all of the industrialized world was in a recession, which sharply reduced the demand for these products. The lack of price increases during the strong macroeconomic recovery of the mid- and late 1980s, however, came as something of a surprise. Technical breakthroughs, which produced substitutes for some primary products, were one cause of this outcome. Fiber optics replaced copper in the telephone industry. Steel was replaced by plastic, aluminum, and other products in various uses. Natural fibers were supplanted by artificial fibers, and technical changes reduced the amount of oil consumed in many industries.

Over the longer run, the situation is more difficult to characterize. Economists have progressively assembled better data to carry out such analysis. Also, they have more carefully tested whether the pattern of prices represents random variation without a clear trend and whether there have been clear breaks in any trend. A tentative summary of the evidence for the twentieth century is that no clear trend exists, and a break in the series likely occurred in 1921.

Trade Policy and Government Revenue

Our primary emphasis in this chapter is on the way trade policy alters prices and the pattern of production within a country. Regardless of the trade policy a country chooses, however, another important constraint on the way tariffs are set is their importance as a source of government revenue. Too high a tariff eliminates trade and any ability to collect tariff revenue, while immediate abolition of a tariff forces a country to reduce spending or to rely on other taxes that may be quite difficult to collect. For many developing countries tariffs are a major source of government revenue, as shown in Table 11.5.

Tariffs on necessities that cannot be produced domestically can raise large sums of money without creating large distortions in the economy. In the late nineteenth century, the British tariff structure was designed exclusively to collect revenue from imports of tobacco, tea, spirits, and wine, goods which either were not produced at home or were subject to a comparable excise tax. Thus, the tariff did not create a deadweight loss by attracting resources into domestic production. In the United States

TABLE 11.5 Taxes on International Trade/Total Tax Revenue (reported as percentages)

Country Name	2002	2003	2004
Côte d'Ivoire	43.0	46.0	—
Madagascar	36.0	33.2	26.9
Namibia	25.1	31.8	—
Bangladesh	29.9	25.1	32.6
Philippines	17.0	17.0	17.5
Argentina	13.6	16.5	15.8
Uganda	15.2	15.9	—
India	15.4	14.8	13.8
Guatemala	10.9	11.0	10.4
Jordan	13.2	10.5	11.3
Sri Lanka	11.9	—	—
Thailand	—	9.7	8.4
Pakistan	6.7	9.2	10.9
Colombia	6.3	5.3	5.2
Bolivia	3.9	3.2	3.1
Indonesia	3.3	3.2	3.0
South Africa	2.7	2.1	3.1

Source: World Bank (2007).

tariffs accounted for 95 percent of federal government receipts at the onset of the Civil War in 1860, and even after subsequent growth in alcohol and tobacco taxes, tariffs still accounted for nearly half of federal government receipts in 1913. U.S. tariffs, however, were not designed to avoid an expansion of output by competing domestic producers. Much of the developing world has followed the U.S. pattern.

Tariffs and export taxes are attractive sources of revenue for a developing country because of the lack of alternative ways to tax efficiently. If much of an economy is subsistence farming or is based on barter, domestic taxes are difficult to impose. Even in that part of the economy that is monetized, most transactions may be made with paper currency rather than checks; therefore accurate records of transactions may be unavailable, making consistent taxation impossible. International trade may be the only large sector of the economy for which good records of transactions are available, so it becomes an obvious target for taxation. Goods entering through a single port or a few border checkpoints can be monitored relatively easily. If tariffs on imports (or exports) are high, however, smuggling becomes an attractive route for tax avoidance and revenues decline.

Table 11.5 gives the importance of taxes on trade as a share of total tax revenues raised by the central government for a group of countries for which data are available from the World Bank. There has been some decline over time in the importance of such taxes, as developing countries have successfully implemented other more efficient methods of raising revenue, for example through value added taxes. Nevertheless, this is a slow process, and it is not surprising that many governments resist cutting tariffs, because they are an important source of operating revenues. Whether the revenues are spent on infrastructure and other categories that raise the economy's productive capacity is an important determinant of how a country's growth prospects are affected.

ALTERNATIVE TRADE POLICIES AND THE TRANSITION TO GREATER MANUFACTURED OUTPUT

The governments of many developing countries concluded some time ago that reliance on expanding output and exports of their traditional primary products was not a promising development strategy. This realization led to a search for alternatives. Two broad policy trends that have emerged are commonly referred to as import substitution industrialization and export-led growth.

Import Substitution Industrialization (ISI)

During the 1950–70 period, the governments of many developing countries adopted policies to minimize their reliance on trade. Instead of promoting more output of primary export commodities, they imposed tariffs and provided other assistance to encourage the growth of local industries, which could produce substitutes for products that they imported. This inward-looking strategy meant that declining primary product prices would be less threatening, because large export revenues were no longer needed to pay for imports. The export sector could be ignored or even taxed, a strategy that promoted the shift of resources out of primary production. This policy orientation meant that developing countries had little interest in participating in GATT, as noted in Chapter 10.

ISI policies involved major government intervention in the economy on the grounds that there were major coordination failures that could not be overcome by market incentives alone. For example, the success of a shipbuilding industry may require the ready availability of steel, but if the country's transportation infrastructure is inadequate to allow steel to be imported, the downstream industries will never develop.

The models presented in Chapters 3 and 4 of this book suggest that this retreat from trade may result in large efficiency losses to the economy. Scarce resources are invested precisely where they will be used less efficiently. Labor-abundant countries like India, with very limited investment budgets, allocate large amounts of money to capital-intensive industries such as chemicals that provide very little employment. The factor endowments theory suggests they should be doing just the opposite: spread their limited capital stocks thinly across labor-intensive industries, where comparative advantages exist. That choice results in higher wages or greater employment opportunities for an abundant labor force and generates export revenues. The extremes of the ISI policy are demonstrated in the effective rate of protection for consumer durables in several developing countries during the early 1960s as calculated by Bela Balassa (1971): Brazil 285 percent, Chile 123 percent, Mexico 85 percent, Malaysia –5 percent, Pakistan 510 percent, and the Philippines 81 percent.

Limitations of ISI

This policy orientation fell from favour when financial crises severely limited the ability of countries to borrow the funds necessary to expand capital-intensive industries and pay for oil imports. Also, policy makers could not ignore the success of more open economies. Although most economists reject the view that protection is a good recipe for economic growth, the historical record indicates that this approach can succeed if it is pursued for a limited period of time in carefully chosen sectors. The World Bank studies of the East Asian miracle note that some countries did intervene in the market, but they were successful in "pulling the plug" on those industries that were unsuccessful, such as chemicals in Korea and heavy industry in Malaysia. Developing some system of accountability and providing protection for only a limited time avoids the danger of perpetuating mistakes if the infant industry never matures. Success was most likely initially when the industries for which protection was provided were relatively labor-intensive. Both Korea and Taiwan used this approach, but as the favored industries became exporters, protection was not the key to their expansion.

Import substitution was an expensive failure in countries such as India that relied upon it for decades and extended it to highly capital-intensive industries. This policy is particularly disastrous if applied to industries whose products are inputs for sectors that should export. As a consequence, effective rates of protection in the export sector become negative. A country may have a comparative advantage, for example in textiles, but a comparative disadvantage in dyestuffs and textile machinery. If such a country protects inefficient manufacturers of dyestuffs and textile machinery, it will destroy its export potential in cloth. The prices of dyestuffs and machinery will be so high that the country cannot compete in world textile markets, despite an abundance of inexpensive labor. Many developing countries protect inefficient steel industries, and thereby lose the opportunity to export products that use steel; recall the example of the Indonesian bicycle industry in Chapter 6. For many years Brazil was determined to develop a local computer industry and therefore prohibited the importation of foreign computers. Because the local computers that were available in Brazil were expensive and outdated, that policy harmed every export industry that relied upon computers.

Free-Trade Zones and Duty Drawbacks

Even if policy makers decide to abandon a policy of import substitution, such a move may be difficult to accomplish politically, given powerful established interests in protected industries. A piecemeal strategy that many developing countries have pursued is to establish a special enterprise zone or free-trade zone, which may allow a country to develop export industries that require inputs that the country protects and produces inefficiently. This protection is eliminated for firms who produce in the zone, where they can import the necessary inputs at world prices, as long as they sell their output in foreign markets. If the finished goods are sold locally, tariffs apply. Locating the zone at a seaport or airport often is most economically efficient and administratively feasible, to reduce transport costs for inputs and exports and to prevent the diversion of assembled goods into the domestic market.

An additional benefit from this strategy can be realized if the final export market treats the output more favourably by imposing an import tariff only on the value added in the zone, not on the value of the intermediate inputs used in its assembly. Such a relationship between Mexico and the U.S. was one of the motives for the establishment of the **maquiladora** assembly industry along the northern border of Mexico in the 1960s. The intermediate inputs had to come from the U.S., however, to receive this treatment. U.S. trade provisions under the African Growth and Oppportunity Act of 2000 did not impose the requirement that U.S. cloth be used to stitch garments to be sold in the U.S., and as a result Lesotho's apparel exports to the U.S. took off.

Similar benefits are available under programs that allow imports to come into the country under a bond, which will be returned once the producer shows proof that the imports have been used in goods that have been exported. Alternatively, some countries operate duty drawback schemes that allow producers to claim a refund for any tariffs paid on inputs, once they demonstrate that those imports have been used in assembled exports. Administering any of these programs can become complicated, but they do represent an intermediate step between a policy of free trade and protection of the home market

Export-Led growth

The World Bank book *East Asian Miracle* states the 1990's consensus position that an export-led growth approach to trade policy is more promising than import substitution.[2] As early as the 1970s, studies were published showing that developing countries that pursued an export-led approach experienced far more rapid economic growth than did countries with protectionist policies.[3] The original Four Tigers (Hong Kong, Taiwan, Singapore, and South Korea) were the subject of most of this early research, but the second wave of Asian NICs (Indonesia, Thailand, Malaysia, and China) has also been very successful in pursuing export markets. India, Mexico, and Brazil could be added as recent converts to important aspects of this approach. These countries have been successful exporting labor-intensive manufactured goods, as Heckscher–Ohlin would predict, but more capital- and skill-intensive industries are beginning to prosper in these markets. Better education has proven to be an important prerequisite to benefit from the spillovers of technology from more advanced countries. Outsourcing of services to India has drawn much attention, because it, too, has been characterized by progressively more advanced processes being shifted there.

Note that this export promotion strategy rests upon diversification and expansion of non-traditional exports. Countries blessed with fertile land do not automatically exit from all agricultural industries, but they consider alternatives to the narrow set of traditional commodities produced. For example, Malaysia successfully reduced its dependence on rubber production by shifting to palm-oil production. Tapping foreign markets for non-traditional export goods, where demand is quite elastic,

---

2 The term "Washington consensus" was coined by John Williamson (2004) to refer to the apparent consensus among the IMF, the World Bank, and the U.S. Treasury Department, all located in Washington, D.C., over the appropriate policies to promote stability and growth in developing countries. Other indications of support for this interpretation are P. Chow (1987) and S. Edwards (1993).

3 In addition to numerous country studies, there are three volumes that synthesize and summarize the overall results of this research: I. Little, T. Scitovsky, and M. Scott (1970), Jagdish Bhagwati (1976), and Anne Krueger (1976). A later survey of the literature on trade policy and development can be found in Oli Havrylyshyn (1990).

is particularly important for the expansion of industries where economies of scale are important and cannot be realized in a small economy.

The governments of some of the Asian Tigers actively intervened in the market by providing favourable financing and direct export subsidies, policies that today would draw greater scrutiny under the WTO. Even in the absence of those measures, an export-led policy does not imply no role for the government. Governments need to promote physical infrastructure, such as ports, roads, electricity and telephone service. Basic health and education ensure a more capable labor force. A clear set of legal rights and its consistent application and enforcement encourage long-term investments. The Chapter 6 discussion of effective rates of protection demonstrates why high tariffs on intermediate inputs are counterproductive. They raise the cost of production for export sectors that receive no offsetting benefit, which results in negative effective protection. In spite of trade liberalization during the 1980s and 1990s, the World Bank (2004) calculates that agricultural processing, labor-intensive manufacturing, and capital-intensive manufacturing in Brazil, China, and India all receive negative effective rates of protection, with rates that ranged from –17 percent to –54 percent.

For countries whose major comparative advantage still rests on cheap unskilled labor, a significant problem for those hoping to export goods that require unskilled labor intensively is that industrialized countries continue to maintain peak protection in such industries. To the extent that earlier waves of NICs have successfully penetrated such markets and account for a large share of sales, then expansion by newcomers may come at the expense of the earlier exporters. For example, Chinese, Vietnamese, and Indonesian shoe production has largely displaced Korean and Taiwanese exports. In the apparel and textile sector, however, industrial countries still have substantial domestic production, which will face further competitive pressure as more developing countries become integrated into the world trading system.

Export-Led Growth: Strong Reasons to Expect Success?

One of the key elements of the World Bank's analysis of the East Asian Miracle was the benefit of a more open or outward-looking trade policy. Do economic models suggest why greater exports lead to faster economic growth? Growth based on exogenous technical progress does not offer much basis for this claim, because what generates growth is treated like a black box – no role for policy is very apparent. Measures that improve the efficiency of an economy allow it to achieve a higher standard of living, but such one-time increases in income are different from continued growth year after year. An increase in income may allow greater saving, an increase in investment, and expansion of an economy's productive capacity, but the success of that strategy depends upon many factors other than an economy's openness to the outside world.

The endogenous growth models discussed above typically yield many possible outcomes, but one frequent implication is that developing countries may face an ambiguous outcome from allowing free trade: the static gains from trade highlighted in Chapter 6 may be achieved, but the rate of growth of the developing economy may be pushed below what it could attain under a less open policy. The net result is unclear. In Young's model, for example, a developing country may find that its most technically advanced industries face greater competition from industrialized countries, and more of its production will end up in industries where there are few opportunities for learning by doing and accelerating economic growth. That model also implies that not all developing countries may advance at a symmetric pace of industrialization, either. Rather, waves of industrial activity are more likely to occur, with production of more advanced goods concentrated in just a few of them. NICs benefit from the agglomeration of activity in them, while countries with fewer technical capabilities end up waiting until the NICs abandon production of less sophisticated goods.

Just as we found in the case of strategic trade policy when the gains occurred in a static world, a more dynamic setting still poses the same basic question: how easily can a government pick a winning policy and avoid being captured by special interests that leave the economy worse off?

Foreign Direct Investment

The advantage of gaining access to foreign markets through the supply chains of MNCs has been an important reason for many developing countries to rethink their reluctance to let foreigners gain control over important sectors of their economies. As we found in Chapter 9, economists have turned greater attention to measuring the potential spillover benefits to domestic producers from a country being a host to MNC operations. Potential ways for domestic producers to receive benefits that the MNC does not capture are an increase in the pool of labor skills, the transfer of ideas and technology that leak out to others, or improvement in the efficiency of local suppliers who can use that knowledge in selling to others.

In the case of developing countries, economists have found that such gains are more likely when the MNC produces for the export market, and both trade and foreign direct investment expand together. MNC production in a protected import market does not offer the same benefits, and may well reduce host country welfare if it drives domestic firms out of business, reduces competition in the market, and raises the profits of foreigners. These outcomes are not universal, however, and depend importantly on the characteristics of the host country. What human resources are available, how competitive are its markets, and what are the technological capabilities of domestic producers? Even when externalities do exist, offering subsidies to MNCs that generate them is problematic, because of the imprecise estimates of the size of these externalities.

Additional Perspectives

The World Bank's 2005 book, *Economic Growth in the 1990s: Learning from a Decade of Reform*, does not prescribe such a precise set of policies as was the case a decade earlier. Even though the goals of stable macroeconomic conditions, market-oriented incentives, and an outward orientation are still recognized as highly desirable, the authors do not maintain that there is a single way to move toward achieving them. Also, it advocates a focus on what are the binding constraints on growth, rather than pushing governments to dissipate political capital and administrative capability on achieving best practice across the board. This more modest agenda also recognizes that precisely how and how much more exports contribute to faster growth remains an active area of research that is less definitive than the earlier consensus suggested.

With respect to the goal of a more open economy, Dani Rodrik (2006b) gives an example of this more flexible approach: best practice may call for reducing import tariffs, but if there is no alternative source of tax revenue to finance government expenditure, then a more realistic step toward openness would be to establish an export processing zone. To implement this more incremental strategy, Rodrik suggests a diagnostic approach to determine what constraints are binding, which in some cases may call for priority attention to trade policy but in other cases not. The chapter case study contains other insights regarding the nature of growth in China and the reasons for its success.

Other Views of the Asian Miracle

Not all economists assign a high priority to exports as a secret to successful growth. Dani Rodrik (2006a) looks at the experience of Korea and Taiwan, and he suggests that exports are too small a share of national output to explain these economies' strong growth. Instead, he assigns a central role to investment. Further he argues that government played a key role in directing investment into productive uses. Rodrik believes that Korea and Taiwan escaped the problem of a self-serving elite dictating policy, because compared to other countries, they emerged from World War II with relatively equal distributions of income. In those circumstances they avoided the counterproductive populist policies promised by Latin American governments, such as Peron's Argentina.

Is it sufficient to observe that the high saving rates in these two Asian countries provide a cushion that can finance a high level of investment? Or, are there coordination failures in the market place that only the government can effectively overcome? The challenge for economists is to document the scale and scope of the specific policies pursued by the Asian governments, and to demonstrate the consequent response by companies to these incentives.

GROWTH AND ENVIRONMENTAL EXTERNALITIES

Just as economists treat natural resources as a source of growth, even when such resources are exhaustible, environmental quality may be treated in this same way. Countries may choose to degrade their environmental quality in order to achieve additional economic output or growth. Those who must live and work in a more polluted environment bear additional costs, due to poorer health, less productivity on the job, or less enjoyment of their surroundings, for example. These are negative externalities that producing firms need not consider in the absence of government action or an organized coalition of those affected. Countries are likely to differ in the way they deal with such externalities, and few are likely to choose no pollution at all as the optimal policy. Economists consider the efficient level of pollution as one where the extra benefit of being free of another unit of pollution just equals the extra cost from cleaning up that unit of pollution. That situation is shown in Figure 11.6, where the marginal benefit curve and the marginal cost curve intersect.

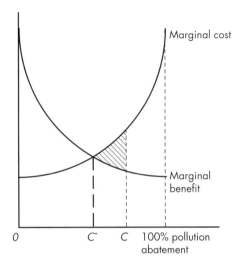

FIGURE 11.6 Marginal Benefits and Marginal Costs of Pollution Abatement

The optimal amount of environmental clean-up is given at C^* where the marginal benefits of clean-up just equal the marginal costs. Imposing a more stringent standard at C, say, results in additional costs greater than additional benefits and a loss in economic efficiency given by the cross-hatched triangle.

If all countries placed the same value on a cleaner environment and faced the same cleanup costs, which would be shown by identical marginal benefit and marginal cost curves for all countries, then unilateral action by each country would result in the same cleanup standards everywhere. In that situation, there would be no tendency for runaway plants to leave a country that imposed its own optimal pollution control standard, because the plant would be subject to the same controls in any alternative location. The existence of the externality, and the government's effort to make the offending plant recognize the cost it imposes on others, would not alter trade patterns, because relative costs of production would be affected identically in all countries.

Explaining Differences across Countries in Pollution

More typically, there are differences in the way countries value a cleaner environment, or there are differences in the cleanup costs they face. The marginal benefit and marginal cost curves will not be identical in each country, and on economic grounds it is then in the interest of countries to choose different pollution control standards. The value that countries place on environmental cleanup is especially likely to diverge when one of the countries is an industrialized country and the other is a developing country. Environmental quality tends to be a luxury good; as income rises, demand for environmental quality rises to a greater extent. Based on this relationship we predict that richer countries will impose stricter standards and enforce them more stringently.

Growth in richer countries may be due to increases in human capital, which is used intensively in clean rather than dirty industries, whereas growth in poor countries may be due to increases in physical capital, which is used intensively in dirty industries. In spite of the changing composition of output in both groups, however, production per person is much greater in high-income countries. Therefore, it is not clear whether richer or poorer countries suffer from more pollution. Initial research in this area asked the following question: as a country's income rises, does its environmental quality rise?

Environmental Kuznets Curves

Grossman and Krueger (1992) spawned a new research area by examining how several measures of pollution varied with income. Based on a cross section of 42 countries, they found an inverted U-shaped relationship: pollution rises as output rises up to a certain threshold, and then declines. This relationship has been called the Environmental Kuznets Curve (EKC), because it is similar to what Simon Kuznets conjectured for inequality in the distribution of income as countries became richer. Subsequent research has refined this analysis, examining changes over time within a country, not simply differences across countries. In many respects the EKC is a black box that presumably depends upon the sources of growth in a country, the strength of consumer preferences for environmental quality at different levels of income, and the technology available to abate pollution. For policy purposes, a more complete treatment needs to recognize that the measures of some current flows of pollution (carbon dioxide or chlorofluorocarbons) need to be related to the accumulated stock of those pollutants. While pursuing those extensions clearly is warranted, one clear implication of the EKC is that countries will choose different standards of environmental quality.

Do these different policy choices, and the opportunity to pollute more in developing countries, mean that there is a significant cost incentive to locate more dirty industries in the developing world? Casual empiricists might point to the change between 1965 and 1988 in the share of exports accounted for by dirty industries (steel, nonferrous metals, industrial chemicals, petroleum refining, and non-metallic mining): it declined from 20 percent to 16 percent for OECD countries but increased in Eastern Europe and Latin America (Low and Yeats 1992). Over that same time period the stringency of OECD regulations to reduce pollution rose. At first glance those two trends seem to support the concern that developing countries will become a dumping ground for dirty activity. On further reflection, however, analysts need also to consider what other factors changed over this same interval that may explain changing export patterns. Copeland and Taylor (2004) suggest that changes in factor endowments are one plausible alternative, which is especially relevant if the relative endowments of capital, used intensively in dirty industries, grew rapidly in developing countries. In addition, more capital in developing countries would contribute to a reduction in the relative price of dirty goods, whereas more stringent pollution controls in the OECD would raise the price of dirty goods. No clear trend in the relative prices of dirty goods occurs over this period, a signal that we should not restrict our attention to environmental regulations in explaining the shift in production that occurred.

Early studies did not find that more stringent environmental policy led countries to import more dirty goods, a result that implied a rejection of the pollution haven effect. Those studies assumed that environmental policies were chosen irrespective of the level of imports, however. If governments set policies taking into account the level of imports, with more imports resulting in weaker domestic policies, then the estimated effect of policy will be understated. Studies on industrial location within the U.S. find a major response to clean air regulations, but comparable international evidence is severely limited by the lack of data for many developing countries.

The Tragedy of the Commons and Global Warming

The environmental externalities considered thus far are assumed to have a negative effect strictly in the country where production occurs. That framework ignores production and consumption that can alter conditions across borders and even globally. Global warming is one such example. Addressing that problem is particularly difficult, because no single country can expect benefits large enough to warrant unilateral action. Global climate conditions can be regarded as a **common property resource**, and countries that choose not to take action to stabilize global temperatures cannot be excluded from the benefits of any successful stabilization efforts. The disincentive for an individual country to take action that would avoid global warming results in a tragedy of the commons.

In spite of that pessimistic prediction, the E.U. has taken a leadership role in advocating action to curb emissions of greenhouse gases under the precautionary principle: although all the scientific relationships that explain global warming are still not clearly understood, to fail to take action now would be imprudent and likely cause even higher costs of environmental cleanup or adaptation in the future. The Kyoto Protocol to the Climate Change Convention agreed to in December 1997 called for industrialized countries to reduce greenhouse gas emissions from their 1990 levels by the year 2012.[4] Reductions were to be 8 percent in Europe, 7 percent in the United States, and 6 percent in Japan and Canada, while Russia was to stabilize its emissions. The ratification of the agreement by Russia in 2004 satisfied the trigger condition (developed countries representing at least 55 percent of the group's carbon dioxide emissions in 1990 must join) for the agreement to come into effect in February, 2005. Australia ratified the agreement in 2008, leaving the United States as the sole industrial country that did not agree to participate. Because the agreement will expire in 2012, much debate now centers on what type of successor agreement can be reached.

The Stern Review

Three key questions underlying this debate are how much cleanup is warranted, how quickly should it occur and who should do the cleaning up. The **Stern Review** of the economics of climate change, prepared by Sir Nicholas Stern for Britain's Chancellor of the Exchequer in October 2006, projects that maintaining the current rate of greenhouse gas emissions will likely result in an increase in average temperature of 2° Celsius by 2050. More severe impacts in the future will occur if there are irreversible changes in climate conditions, such as the melting of the Greenland ice sheet, the drying up of the Amazon Rainforest, or a shift of the Atlantic Gulf Stream. To avoid a reduction of per capita consumption of 5 to 20 percent, the report advocates immediate efforts to reduce emissions so that the 2° increase in temperature will not be exceeded.

---

4 For more complete information on the UN Framework Convention on Climate Change and its Kyoto Protocol, as well as further analysis by the Intergovernmental Panel on Climate Change, see updates from http://unfccc.int.

Critics such as William Nordhaus (2007) note that this case rests on the choice of a very low discount rate, 0.1 percent, which gives great weight to events happening in the next century. Those individuals advocate a more gradual increase in the stringency of any emission reductions. Others argue that the Stern review may be right for the wrong reasons: uncertainty over the occurrence of drastic changes warrants action now as an insurance policy (Weitzman 2007).

While this aspect of the situation is unresolved, the gainers and losers from global warming are less uncertain. Losers will be tropical countries dependent on agriculture, forestry, and economic activity in coastal plains. Small countries with only a single climate zone are particularly vulnerable, as are islands with little elevation above sea level. Table 11.6 gives a summary of these effects for larger groups of countries. Russia and other northern countries may gain from global warming that unlocks frozen northlands and opens new navigation routes, and over the next few decades world agricultural output may even rise if higher concentrations of CO_2 have a positive fertilizing effect.

With respect to who should pay for the cleanup, the Kyoto agreement requires no reductions in greenhouse gas emissions from developing countries. Industrial countries can meet a portion of their commitment by jointly implementing projects with former communist transition economies and by carrying out clean development projects in developing countries. Developing countries regard the buildup of greenhouse gases in the atmosphere as the responsibility of industrial countries that accounted for much of that accumulation through their progressively higher energy usage over the past two centuries. Developing countries reject any agreement that denies their opportunity to industrialize, simply because environmental awareness has risen.

Designers of a new agreement are particularly constrained by the self-interest of two of the countries shown in Table 11.6, the United States and China. Because the U.S. accounted for 23.4 percent of greenhouse gas emissions in 1990 and China is projected to account for 24.5 percent in 2030, the largest current and future emitters are both likely to face large net costs, from the standpoint of national self-interest, if they make binding commitments to reduce emissions. Perhaps public perceptions are changing sufficiently to overcome this arithmetic.

TABLE 11.6 Damage from a 2.5° Warming (expressed as % of GDP)

India	4.93
Africa	3.91
OECD Europe	2.83
Eastern Europe	0.71
Japan	0.50
U.S.	0.45
China	0.22
Russia	−0.65

Source: Nordhaus and Boyer (2000), cited in C. Sundstein (2006)

Summary of Key Concepts

1. If growth at constant prices results in a disproportionately large increase in output of the export good, but consumers wish to spend their extra income on the import good, then the increase in the country's export supply will be especially large.
2. If a country is large enough to affect world prices, growth that results in a large increase in the supply of exports may result in a sufficiently large decline in the relative price of the export good to leave the country worse off.
3. Growth likely causes smaller changes in the terms of trade when it results from the introduction of new varieties of goods.
4. Developing countries that depend on the exportation of primary products are hurt by the volatility of those prices and by long periods of decline in those prices.
5. Import-substitution industrialization reduced the reliance of developing countries on primary exports, but it became quite costly when countries chose to permanently protect capital-intensive industries.
6. Export-led growth has been a successful strategy for countries that exported labor-intensive goods initially, but later shifted to more technologically advanced goods as they acquired more physical and human capital.
7. Industrialized countries have chosen to impose more stringent environmental standards than developing countries, but the expansion of dirty industries in the developing countries has more to do with their accumulation of capital.

CASE STUDY

China's Trade: Lessons to be Learned?

Chinese growth and the export performance of the Chinese economy over the past three decades has been impressive, with GDP per capita rising over 8 percent per year and exports rising as a share of GDP from less than 10 percent to over 34 percent. Not surprisingly, economists have attempted to extract some of the reasons for this success. Although we pointed to changes in factor endowments and technology as reasons behind China's changing composition of exports in Table 11.2, that level of aggregation of products into broader industries may hide some of the changes that have occurred. We summarize here some of the additional insights economists have found by looking at finer product categories.

The logic of the factor endowments model, that China is a labor-abundant country that will export labor-intensive goods, does not provide us with clear guidance in a world with thousands of different goods. The snapshot characterization that China must export toys and clothes is increasingly a smaller part of the story. Although Chinese liberalization began in 1979, by 1994 a striking feature of Chinese exports is that they occur in a large number of industries. With the segmentation of production that has occurred in globalized supply chains, it is possible that China was just carrying out the most labor-intensive steps of what needed to be done in assembling lots of different products. At a very aggregate level, one indication of the steady rise of assembly operations is the increase in imports of parts, from 15 percent to 31 percent of total Chinese imports between 1992 and 2004. Another is the increased role of computer and electronic equipment exports.

With respect to the sophistication of these exports, Dani Rodrik (2005) suggests a useful approach. He categorizes exports at the 6-digit SITC level (an indication of pretty specific goods) on the basis of the average income level of countries that have a revealed comparative advantage in that good. Aircraft, for example, are characterized by a high average income. He presumes that goods exported by high-income countries are more technologically advanced, and he finds that China has a much higher proportion of advanced or sophisticated exports than would be predicted on the basis of its stage of development. Rather, China is more comparable to Mexico and middle-income Asian countries. Potentially consistent with these observations is the analysis of other economists who note that growth results in more production of existing exports, but also the production of new varieties and higher quality. Mary Amiti and Caroline Freund (2007), however, find that outside of China's assembly operations, the skill level of its exports has not risen from 1992 to 2005, while the skill level of its imported inputs for assembly appears to account for the increase in the sophistication of the assembled exports.

How do producers in a country determine that it is profitable to begin production of a different good? Rodrik points to the very idiosyncratic nature of country exports, even among similar countries. Taiwan exports bicycles and no microwave ovens, while Korea exports microwave ovens but no bicycles. In some cases, multinational corporations may be a source of such information. Rodrik refers to a discovery process, in which an entrepreneur finds out that a new idea is indeed profitable, but after which many competitors enter the industry and drive down the return on this special knowledge. Thus, he believes there is a role for government in encouraging the process of discovery. Possible policy tools may include an undervalued exchange rate (a concept presented in Chapter 13), tax credits, favorable finance, production subsidies, or tariff protection. But, to avoid the pitfalls of previous ISI strategies, governments must be able to withdraw such incentives when the infant industry does not grow up. In other words, the government must not be so intent on picking winners that they fail discarding losers.

One result of China's successful track record is that it no longer competes directly with most low-income developing countries. David Dollar (2007) compares manufacturing wages across several countries, and notes that Chinese wages are at least 50 percent higher than in other Asian countries such as India, Vietnam, Pakistan, or Bangladesh. The gap is even greater if it is based on the coastal areas of China. He further notes that those coastal cities have created a more favorable business environment, and have much lower losses due to electricity interruptions or days spent on customs clearances. He even finds that these locations with favorable business environments and higher wages also have better environmental indicators in terms of clean air and proper treatment of industrial waste. Given restrictions on labor mobility within China, there is not a national wage rate, and interior regions of China are likely to be involved in trade in a very different way.

CASE STUDY QUESTIONS

1. In comparing the role of exports as a share of national output in China versus India, say, why may the much more important role of assembly operations in China require extra caution in any interpretation of how X/GDP has changed for each country over time?

2. Based on the factor endowments model, economists would question the wisdom of a strategy that allocates scarce physical and human capital in developing countries to increase the production of highly sophisticated goods. Explain that line of reasoning and indicate why Rodrik rejects that perspective.

3. What do rising wages in China suggest about the changing composition of its exports compared to those of other developing countries? What would you predict about the trading relationships of interior regions of China?

4. Recall from Chapter 5 that producing new varieties of intermediate inputs may allow a country to increase its productivity in producing final goods and expand its exports of the latter. If Chinese growth were primarily characterized by diversification into producing additional varieties of goods, would that be less threatening to middle-income countries?

Questions for study and review

1. A capital abundant country increases its capital stock by 5 percent, all else constant. How does that change affect its production and volume of trade? Do its terms of trade change in a way that creates a further benefit for the country?

2. A labor-abundant country increases its capital stock by 5 percent, all else constant. How does that change affect its production and volume of trade? Do its terms of trade change in a way that creates a further benefit for the country?

3. If a large economy grows at the same rate as the rest of the world, why are its demand preferences important in predicting whether its terms of trade will improve or not?

4. Use the Lerner diagram to demonstrate the expected shift in the production-possibility curve of a country that experiences labor-using technical progress in its capital-intensive sector. How is the capital–labor ratio in each industry affected? If the country is large and labor-abundant, how will its terms of trade be affected?

5. Why may a price stabilization pact not be successful in reducing the volatility of the export earnings of primary product producers, even when it successfully stabilizes prices? What challenges do pacts face in successfully stabilizing prices?

6. Falling computer prices do not seem to be a source of hardship in industrial countries that exported them in the 1980s and 1990s. Why are the falling prices of primary commodities in LDCs a serious problem?

7. Vietnam increased its share of the world coffee market from 1 percent to 15 percent over a 10-year period. Was this expansion of a primary product export likely to result in immiserizing growth for Vietnam? When is that concern most relevant?

8. When many countries pursued policies of import substitution, their growth rates were high in the 1960s and 1970s but fell in the 1980s. Is that evidence of the success of these policies or the limits of these policies?

9. "LDC tariffs intended to promote an industry may in fact inhibit development of the LDCs' most efficient industries." Explain how this could happen.

10. Why is it difficult for a country to pursue import substitution and export promotion at the same time? What policies are called for under each strategy?

11. Is there an economic rationale for countries to adopt different pollution control standards? Under what circumstances will their choices have little influence on the location of production and trade internationally?

12. The E.U. established an Emission Trading Scheme in 2005 that applied to large installations like power plants. The price of being allowed to emit a ton of CO_2 fell in 2006 and 2007 because national governments distributed so many allowances that little cleanup was required. If those allowances are reduced in the future, how do you expect that to affect E.U. production and trade?

References and Suggestions for Further Reading

For various perspectives on growth, development, and trade, as well as relevant data, see:

Akamatsu, K. (1961) "A Historical Pattern of Economic Growth in Developing Countries," *The Developing Economies*, preliminary issue, 1–23.

Amiti, M. and Freund, C. (2007) "An Anatomy of China's Export Growth," Paper prepared for Global Implications of China's Trade, Investment and Growth Conference, IMF Research Department.

Amsden, A. (2001) *The Rise of "the Rest,"* New York: Oxford University Press.

Balassa, B. (1971) *The Structure of Protection in Developing Countries*, Baltimore: Johns Hopkins University Press.

Batra, R. (1973) *Studies in the Pure Theory of International Trade*, New York: St. Martin's Press.

Behrman, J. (1978) *Development, the International Economic Order, and Commodity Agreements*, Reading, MA: Addison-Wesley.

Bhagwati, J. (1976) *Foreign Trade Regimes and Economic Development: Anatomy and Consequences of Exchange Control Regimes*, New York: Columbia University Press.

Chang, H. (2002) "Kicking Away the Ladder – Tariffs and Economic Development," *Challenge* 45: 63–97.

Chow, P. (1987) "Causality between Export Growth and Industrial Development: Empirical Evidence for the NICs," *Journal of Development Economics* 26: 55–63.

Cuddington, J., Ludema, R., and Jayasuriya, S. (2002) "Prebisch–Singer Redux," U.S. International Trade Commission, Working Paper.

Dollar, D. (2007) "Asian Century or Multi-polar Century?" World Bank Policy Research Working Paper 4174.

Edwards, S. (1993) "Openness, Trade Liberalization, and Growth in Developing Countries," *Journal of Economic Literature*, September 1993, pp. 1358–1393.

Feenstra, R. (2004) *Advanced International Trade, Theory and Evidence*, Princeton, NJ: Princeton University Press, Chapter 10.

Findlay, R. and Grubert, H. (1959) "Factor Intensities, Technological Progress, and the Terms of Trade," *Oxford Economic Papers*, New Series, 11:111–21.

Grossman, G. and Helpman, E. (1991) *Innovation and Growth in the Global Economy*, Cambridge, Mass: MIT Press.

Havrylyshyn, O. (1990) "Trade Policy and Productivity Gains in Developing Countries," *World Bank Research Observer*, 1–24.

Hummels, D. and Klenow, P. (2005) "The Variety and Quality of a Nation's Exports," *American Economic Review 95*: 704–23.

International Monetary Fund (1998) *Direction of Trade Statistics*, Washington, D.C.: IMF.

—— (2007) *Direction of Trade Statistics*, Washington, D.C.: IMF.

Irwin, D. (2001) "Tariffs and Growth in Late Nineteenth Century America," *The World Economy* 24: 15–30.

Krueger, A. (1976) *Foreign Trade Regimes and Economic Development: Liberalization Attempts and Consequences*, New York: Columbia University Press.

—— (1984) "Trade Policies in Developing Countries," in R. Jones and P. Kenen (eds) *Handbook of International Economics, Volume I*, Amsterdam: Elsevier Science Publishers, 519–69.

Lerner, A. (1952) "Factor Prices and International Trade," *Economica* (new series) 19: 1–15.

Little, I., Scitovsky, T., and Scott, M. (1970) *Industry and Trade in Some Developing Countries: A Comparative Study*, Oxford: Oxford University Press.

Prebisch, R. (1950) "The Economic Development of Latin America and its Principal Problems," *Economic Bulletin for Latin America*, 7: 1–22.

Puga, D. and Venables, A. (1999) "Agglomeration and Economic Development: Import Substitution vs. Trade Liberalization," *Economic Journal* 109: 292–311.

Rodrik, D. (2005) "Policies for economic diversification," *CEPAL Review* 87: 7–23.

—— (2006a) "Getting Interventions Right: How South Korea and Taiwan Grew Rich," *Economic Policy* 10: 55–107.

—— (2006b) "Goodbye Washington Consensus, Hello Washington Confusion? A Review of the World Bank's Economic Growth in the 1990s: Learning from a Decade of Reform," *Journal of Economic Literature* 64: 973–87.

Singer, H. (1950) "The Distribution of Gains between Investing and Borrowing Countries," *American Economic Review* 40: 473–85.

United Nations (1982) *Yearbook of International Trade Statistics*, New York: UN.

—— (1984) *Yearbook of International Trade Statistics*, New York: UN.

UNCTAD (2002) *Least Developed Countries Report 2002*, New York: United Nations, p. 142.

Wade, R. (1990) *Governing the Market: Economic Theory and the Role of the Government in East Asian Industrialization*, Princeton, NJ: Princeton University Press.

Williamson, J. (2004) "A Short History of the Washington Consensus," available at http://www.iie.com/publications/papers/williamson0904-2.pdf. (accessed 9 September 2008).

World Bank (1993) *The East Asian Miracle, Economic Growth and Public Policy*, New York: Oxford University Press.

—— (1994) *Global Economic Prospects and the Developing Countries*, Washington, D.C.: World Bank, p. 52.

—— (2004) *Global Economic Prospects*, Washington, D.C.: World Bank, p. 77.

—— (2005) *Economic Growth in the 1990s: Learning from a Decade of Reform*, New York: Oxford University Press.

—— (2007) *World Development Indicators*, Washington, D.C.: World Bank.

Young, A. (1991) "Learning by Doing and the Dynamic Effects of International Trade," *Quarterly Journal of Economics* 106: 369–405.

—— (1995) "The Tyranny of Numbers: Confronting the Statistical Realities of the East Asian Growth Experience," *Quarterly Journal of Economics* 110: 641–80.

For discussion of environmental externalities and policies adopted to deal with them see:

Copeland, B. and Taylor, S. (2004) "Trade, Growth, and the Environment," *Journal of Economic Literature* 62: 7–71.

Dasgupta, S., Laplante, Wang, H., and Wheeler, D. (2002) "Confronting the Environmental Kuznets Curve," *Journal of Economic Perspectives*, 16: 147–68.

Grossman, G. and Krueger, A. (1992) "Environmental Impacts of a North American Free Trade Agreement," in P. Garber (ed.) *The Mexico–U.S. Free Trade Agreement*, Cambridge, MA: MIT Press, 13–56.

—— (1995) "Economic Growth and the Environment," *Quarterly Journal of Economics* 110: 353–77.

Low, P. and Yeats, A. (1992) "Do Dirty Industries Migrate?" in P. Low (ed.) *International Trade and the Environment*, Washington, D.C.: World Bank, 89–104.

Nordhaus, W. (2007) "A Review of the Stern Review on the Economics of Climate Change," *Journal of Economic Literature* 45: 686–702.

Sandler, T. (1997) *Global Challenges: An Approach to Environmental, Political and Economic Problems*, Cambridge: Cambridge University Press.

Stern, N. (2007) *The Economics of Global Climate Change: The Stern Review*, Cambridge: Cambridge University Press.

Sundstein, C. (2006) "Montreal versus Kyoto: A Tale of Two Protocols," AEI-Brookings Joint Center for Regulatory Studies, Working Paper 06–17.

Weitzman, M. (2007) "A Review of the Stern Review on the Economics of Climate Change," *Journal of Economic Literature* 45: 703–724.

APPENDIX: DEMONSTRATING THE EFFECTS OF EXOGENOUS TECHNICAL CHANGE

To demonstrate how changes in technology affect output and factor rewards, Findlay and Grubert (1959) present a framework based on the Lerner diagram shown in Figure 11.7.[5] Isoquants for steel and textiles are shown which represent one euro of output. At the wage–rental ratio represented by the budget constraint $C_0 C_0$, steel producers will choose to use the capital–labor ratio given along the ray OS_0, while textile producers will choose the capital–labor ratio given along the ray OT_0. Because both isoquants are tangent to the same budget constraint, that means that costs and prices of the two goods are identical.

How much of each good will be produced? That depends upon the country's factor endowment. Instead of using the Edgeworth box to represent that situation, here we take an alternative approach. Point E represents the economy's endowment of capital and labor. Draw rays from E that are parallel to OS_0 and OT_0. EB intersects OT_0 at B and EA intersects OS_0 at A. The economy produces OA of steel and OB of textiles when both factors are fully employed at the given wage–rental ratio. The parallelogram $OAEB$ depends upon the country's factor endowment and the equilibrium wage–rental ratio.

Now consider the effect of a change in factor productivity in this diagram. If capital and labor requirements fall by the same proportion in the textile sector only, this saving of inputs allows the unit isoquant for textiles to shift inward. Because the percentage effects on capital and labor in the textile industry are the same, the new isoquant has the same slope along the ray OT_0 as was observed initially. The lower cost of producing textiles, however, gives firms an incentive to expand output. As output of the labor-intensive good rises, the wage rate increases relative to the rental return to capital. The new budget line that again represents one euro of output in each industry, $C_1 C_1$, is tangent to the new textile isoquant and the initial steel isoquant at T_1 and S_1, respectively. The higher wage–rental ratio gives producers in both sectors an incentive to use a higher ratio of capital to labor.

---

5 The theoretical framework assumes constant returns to scale and no factor intensity reversal (textiles are labor intensive at all wage–rental ratios), conditions that were imposed in the analysis of Chapter 3.

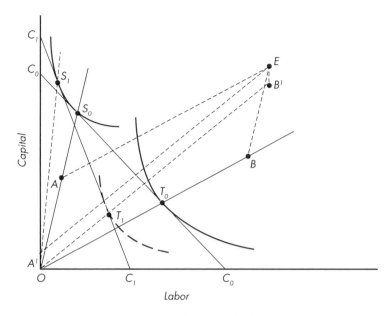

FIGURE 11.7 Inputs, Output, and Technical Change

Neutral technical progress in textile production results in higher capital–labor ratios in both sectors and a higher wage–rental ratio. Output of textiles rises and output of steel falls at unchanged output prices.

We now have two new rays indicating the best capital–labor ratios to use in production after the technical change occurs, and we can again complete the parallelogram from point E to determine how output changes. That new solution is shown by the dotted blue lines that form the parallelogram OA^1EB^1. That outcome shows a large increase in textile production and a reduction in steel output. In this case, the shift in the production-possibility curve is quite similar to what we found above for an increase in the factor endowment. A biased trade effect occurs, with more trade occurring if the country is labor-abundant but less trade occurring if the country is capital abundant.

If we re-label the two factor axes as skilled labor and unskilled labor, draw two new unit isoquants that demonstrate skilled-labor-using technical change, the ratio of skilled labor to unskilled labor rises in both industries and the relative wage of skilled labor increases. Because both sectors use less unskilled labor per unit of output; a key implication of that case is that the unskilled-labor-intensive industry must expand to maintain full employment at constant prices.

Part II

International Finance and Open Economy Macroeconomics

The first part of the book covers trade theory and policy. The models developed there are based on microeconomics. We used tools from the theory of the producers (e.g. production-possibility frontiers) and the theory of the consumers (e.g. indifference curves). We dealt overwhelmingly with aspects of the international economy that are "real" and "microeconomic" in nature. Monetary or financial issues, "macroeconomic" in nature seldom intruded. Now this all changes: in the second half of the book, we discuss the macroeconomic aspects of international economics and investigate extensively monetary and financial matters.

This half of the book is organized around three major subjects. First we present two fundamental concepts of the open economy – the balance of payments and the exchange rate – allowing us to understand the functioning of an economy that interacts with the rest of the world. Then we construct models of the open economy using the framework lent by the balance of payments and the exchange rate. These models become more complex as we investigate more general cases. We use these models to analyse the impact of various government policies or shocks to the economy. Finally, we move from the models to the real world and study the international monetary developments over the years and around the globe. From the gold standard to Bretton Woods, from the European efforts toward monetary integration to the various currency crises affecting the world from time to time.

Balance of Payments and Foreign Exchange Markets Basics

Chapter 12 introduces the basic accounting device that records all the transactions between a nation and the rest of the world, the balance of payments. The significance of the balance of payments goes well beyond just recording transactions; it defines the main variables examined in the second part of the course and outlines their *ex post* relations. As a start, the balance of payments measures the movements of goods and services across borders as well as the capital flows in and out of the country. The balance of payments thus sets up the framework for the models developed in the following chapters. This chapter underlines another basic fact: most sovereign countries use their own unit of account, their own currency. To compare any international monetary variables, we need a common denominator in order to convert the currency in which they are quoted into another currency, we need an exchange rate. There is more than one way to construct this measure, and we present various forms of exchange rates.

In Chapter 13, we discuss how exchange rates are determined. Since exchange rates are prices (the relative price of two currencies), anyone versed in economics will understand that they can be determined by the basic market forces of supply of and demand for foreign exchange. Some countries might be happy to let market forces operate freely, but, for various reasons, others may not. This raises an important policy issue as nations can choose their exchange rate regime: either allowing market forces to determine it (a flexible or floating regime) or setting an exchange rate and intervening constantly in the market to uphold it (a fixed and pegged exchange rate). Clearly these are two polar cases, but a number of hybrid forms also exist in the real world. Further basic concepts that are relevant to the operation of a fixed exchange rate regime, such as exchange market intervention, sterilization, and devaluation, are introduced in this chapter to steer us towards the following modeling and policy chapters.

The Open Macroeconomics Models and Their Policy Implications

Returning to the framework provided by the balance of payments, we note that, although it comprises both the balance of trade and international movements of capital, the importance of the second element depends on the policy chosen. If a country restricts these movements with strict capital controls, the role of the balance of trade becomes central. So we proceed by first considering models of the open economy that ignore autonomous movements of capital.

Chapters 14 and 15 expand the basic Keynesian model of the goods market to the open economy, by taking into account foreign demand for (exports) and foreign supply of (imports) goods and services. In Chapter 14, the short-run model is developed in the framework of either flexible or fixed exchange rates. We use the model to show how balance-of-trade deficits or surpluses are linked to more fundamental macroeconomic imbalances and may not be caused solely by the exchange rate. Then we consider the impact of policy, mainly fiscal and exchange rate policy (devaluation/revaluation).

In Chapter 15, the simple model is extended into a longer time frame where an adjustment mechanism takes place through changes in the money supply; the implications of the policy option to sterilize (to neutralize these effects) or not to sterilize is thoroughly discussed. The feasibility of using several policy instruments to achieve several goals is also investigated. Finally, we consider the possibility of foreign repercussions resulting from the use of policy in one country. Up to now, we have assumed that the economy considered is too small for its policy to have any impact on its trade partners' economies. Dropping the small country assumption, this last extension discusses the channels through which, in a two-country model, policy choices in one country have eventual ramifications on both countries.

We next leave this simplistic world without capital mobility. First we analyze the international capital markets and then we integrate them into a more sophisticated model. Chapter 16 illustrates the phenomenal expansion of the international capital markets in the last 20 years. It discusses the various foreign exchange markets (e.g. spot, forward, swap) and describes traditional motivations to carry out transactions in these markets (e.g. hedging, speculation) as well as newer opportunities available (e.g. futures, options). As an example of short-run determinants of prices in these markets, we describe the practice of technical analysis for day trading.

Chapter 17 takes us back to macroeconomic modeling. The challenge is to find a way to integrate the international financial markets into the original model of Chapter 15, thus expanding it into a model of the balance of payments (and not just the balance of trade). To do so, we need a macro-economic variable that can act as a link between them: interest arbitrage, a basic operation performed on the foreign exchange markets, provides that link. This allows us to develop a relation explaining international capital flows as a function of the interest differential between countries, among other things. We need only to include the balance of trade to get a specification for the balance of payments.

In Chapter 18, we combine this new relation with the IS–LM model to construct the Mundell–Fleming model. We now have a more extensive model integrating the goods and the money markets with the balance of payments. Chapters 18 and 19 focus on monetary and fiscal policies under fixed and under flexible exchange rates, respectively. We show how different policies perform, under different degrees of capital mobility. With a more elaborate model, we consider the same issues as in Chapters 14 and 15: the impact of sterilization versus non-sterilization, and the policy mix. The extensions of this model include adding a second country, which raises the possibility of conflicting national policies, and addressing the long-run adjustment to prices changes within the Mundell–Fleming model.

Except for this last section, adjustments to any international imbalance have taken place through change in variables other than the price level. In Chapter 20, we introduce the concept of perfectly flexible prices and the monetary approach to the exchange rate. Assuming perfect international arbitrage, the prices of goods in all the countries should be equalized and the exchange rate is just the ratio of these prices, as they are quoted in different currencies. How realistic is this assumption? Although it is controversial, an important application based on this idea, purchasing power parity, allows international agencies to make more realistic standard-of-living comparisons across countries. Finally, the model of exchange rate overshooting, relying on dynamics, attempts to explain the high volatility of flexible exchange rates. With all the knowledge acquired from the various models, we now look at the international monetary experience.

International Monetary Developments: from the Gold Standard to the Asian Crises

In Chapter 21, we present a brief history of the international monetary system. Benefiting from a long period of stability and peace at the end of the nineteenth century until the onset of World War I, the gold standard era is remembered as an exceptional age. Unfortunately, the post-war circumstances were very different. The economic upheavals that originated from this destructive conflict devastated the harmonious framework nurturing the gold standard. It was not until the end of World War II that a new international monetary order could be reinstated, which occurred as a result of the Bretton Woods negotiations in 1944. This new order was a gold exchange standard, maybe a second best to the earlier arrangement. At first, it had a substantial impact on the reconstruction of the war-torn economies, but, due to inherent weaknesses, the system collapsed in the early seventies. Most countries then moved to a floating exchange rate regime.

In Chapter 22, we note that the Western European countries, keen on fixed exchange rate systems, decided to set up their own Bretton Woods-like arrangement (the European Monetary System). These countries were already cooperating in establishing a common market, but they had more ambitious objectives at the macroeconomic level. They were aiming for a currency union, implying a common currency and a common central bank to carry out the common monetary policy. The road toward achieving these goals was rocky, with currency crises in the early nineties that caused countries to drop out of the great plan. Since 1999 the European Monetary Union, with the euro as its common currency, has been a strong player in world international finance. Through 2008, the original 11 members have been joined by 4 additional members. A fundamental question remains, however: is it an optimum currency area?

The last chapter describes the challenges faced by the emerging economies. These economies have made amazing strides in becoming important players in international markets. Their rapid growth has not been constant, with setbacks in the form of currency crises in the 1980s and the 1990s. In this chapter, we show how currency crises unfold and discuss how international organizations may have a counter-productive effect of nurturing the risk of moral hazard. The Asian economies have now recovered from these predicaments. In the process, they have moved from being reckless to being over-cautious: to ensure they can now fend off any speculative attack, they have accumulated huge dollar reserves that might shift the risk onto the U.S. economy.

Chapter 12

The Balance of Payments and the Exchange Rate

LEARNING OBJECTIVES

By the end of this chapter you should be able to understand:

- the balance of payments as an accounting device recording the nation's– international transactions with the rest of the world

- the balance of payments double-entry system ensuring that it always balances, and the distinction between transactions that correspond to debit entries or credit entries

- the difference between the goods (merchandises) balance, the balance of trade, and the current account

- the link with chronic trade deficits and foreigners acquiring domestic assets, i.e. capital inflows

- the link between the balance of payments and the international investment position of a country

- the concept of exchange rate as the relative price of a foreign currency

- the importance and applications of the real exchange rate and the effective exchange rate

In today's global economy, the phenomenon of the "closed economy" – one that is unaffected by international trade and capital flows – is little more than an abstract textbook concept. The notion of a closed economy is nevertheless quite useful in intermediate macroeconomics, as it allows for the analysis of the fundamental aspects of the economy (e.g. the impact of monetary and fiscal policy) without considering the complicating effects of globalization. With the fundamentals well understood, however, we can now provide more realism by looking at the "open economy" that is directly affected by the global marketplace. We are now focusing on the macroeconomic linkages between the world economies and to do so, we need to extend the information we gather in the national accounts to take these linkages into account.

Considering an economy as part of the global marketplace adds complexity to our model. The first bit of complexity comes in form of new terminology and concepts. We shall start by introducing the two fundamental concepts of the open economy: the **balance of payments** (BoP) and the **exchange rate**. These two notions are both elementary and extraordinarily powerful in providing rich insights into the workings of an international economy. The balance of payments is usually compiled by each country's central bank or finance ministry. In the U.S., the Bureau of Economic Analysis (U.S. Department of Commerce) compiles the balance of payments under the heading **International Transactions Accounts**.[1] In the U.K., the information is recorded in the Pink Book. In addition to the balance of payments, tracking the international flows of goods or capital, we will also consider the **international investment position** of a country, tracking the stock of investments a country owns abroad and the stock of investments owned by foreigners in the domestic economy.

THE BALANCE OF PAYMENTS: INTERNATIONAL TRANSACTIONS ACCOUNTS

The balance of payments (BoP) records all international transactions in goods, services, and assets over a year. The BoP is a simple double-entry accounting tool akin to a firm's income statement. After we have studied all the components of the BoP, we will find that it serves as the most important source of information in the open economy since it summarizes exactly how the domestic economy interacts with the rest of the world.

---

1 See http://www.bea.gov/bea/di/home/bop.htm for the U.S. balance of payments.
  The U.K. balance of payments can be downloaded from: http://www.statistics.gov.uk/StatBase/Product.asp?vlnk= 1140

Key Components of the Balance of Payments

The BoP is broken down into three important sub-components: the **current account balance** (CA), the **capital account balance** (KA), and the **financial account balance** (FA):

$$BoP = CA + KA + FA \qquad (12.1)$$

Table 12.1 shows the entire BoP with all its sub-components for the U.S. in 2006. We will discuss each of the major sub-component in detail below, but for now we want to keep in mind that the current account basically represents trade in goods and services and the financial account collects information on financial transactions such as international stock and bond purchases or sales. Finally, the capital account keeps track of the flow of all non-financial assets, such as the transfer of intellectual property rights. Changes in each sub-component will have a different impact on the domestic economy.

TABLE 12.1 Main Categories in the U.S. Balance of Payments, 2006 (in millions of dollars) Credit (+); Debits (−)

Current account:		
Exports		
(1) Goods		1,023,689
(2) Services		413,127
(3) Income receipts		622,020
Imports		
(4) Goods		−1,859,655
(5) Services		−342,428
(6) Income payments		−629,286
(7) Unilateral current transfers (IT), net		−84,122
(8) Capital account:		−3,914
Financial account:		
(9) U.S.-owned assets abroad, net (increase/financial outflow (−))		−1,045,760
U.S. official reserve assets (ORT), net		2,374
Other U.S. assets, net		−1,048,134
Other government assets	5,219	
Direct investments (FDI)	−248,856	
Foreign securities (PI)	−277,691	
Other	−526,806	

TABLE 12.1 continued

(10) Foreign-owned assets in the U.S., net (increase/financial inflow (+))			1,764,909
Foreign official assets in the U.S., net		300,510	
Other foreign assets, net		1,464,399	
Direct investments (FDI)	183,571		
U.S. securities (PI)	650,571		
Other	630,257		
(11) Statistical discrepancy (SD)			
– {(1) through (10)}			141,419
Goods balance (GB) (1) + (4)			–835,966
Services balance (SB) (2) + (5)			70,699
Net income receipts (NIR) (3) + (6)			–7,266
Trade balance (TB) (1) + (2) + (4) + (5)			–765,267
Current account balance (CA) (1) + (2) + (3) + (4) + (5) + (6) + (7)			–856,655
Financial account balance (FA) (9) + (10)			719,149

Source: adapted from U.S. International Transaction Accounts, Bureau of Economic Analysis (http://www.bea.gov/bea/di/home/bop.htm).

The BoP is recorded using double-entry accounting. Double-entry accounting means that every transaction enters the BoP twice, once as a credit (+), for example the export of a car to a non-resident, and once as a debit (–), the payment by the non-resident for the car. Therefore the BoP is actually an identity:

$$BoP = CA + KA + FA \equiv 0 \qquad (12.2)$$

The sum of all the entries in the three sub accounts (CA, KA, FA) must be equal to zero since every entry has a counterpart with the opposite sign in some other section of the BoP.

The Current Account

The current account includes the **goods balance** (GB), the **services balance** (SB), **net income receipts** (NIR), and **net international transfers** (IT).

$$CA = GB + SB + NIR + IT \qquad (12.3)$$

We will explain each component of the current account separately below. Starting with the goods balance, it is important to remember that trade in goods refers only to physical goods that cross a border. In this sense, the trade balance in physical goods is equivalent to a net flow of goods. When more goods flow out of a country (are exported) than flow in (are imported), the GB will be in surplus. To avoid confusion, it is crucial to introduce the definition of BoP **credit** and **debit**.

A BoP credit is a positive entry into the BoP; it represents international transactions that generate receipts for the domestic economy, for example, via an export, or an interest payment on a foreign bond. In contrast, a debit is a negative entry into the BoP; it represents international transactions that give rise to a payment from the domestic economy to foreigners, for example through an import, or a dividend for domestic stocks held by foreigners. Indeed, exporting involves shipments of merchandise from the domestic economy to a foreign country in return for payments by the foreigners, so exports are reported as a credit. Importing involves shipments of merchandise from foreign countries into the domestic economy, resulting in payments by the domestic economy, so they are reported as a debit. If merchandise exports are greater than imports, the exporting country finds itself with a positive GB.

The Goods Balance, the Services Balance, and the Trade Balance

Where does the U.S. stand as far as the goods balance goes? For a number of years, the U.S. has posted the world's largest goods balance deficits. In 2006, the U.S. exported about one trillion dollars of goods and imported $1.8 trillion to generate a massive $800 billion dollar deficit. Figure 12.1 shows the evolution of the U.S. goods balance and its components since 1980. It shows that imports are outpacing exports of goods in the U.S. at an increasing rate. In open economy macroeconomics, we study the impact of such a massive goods balance deficit on the domestic economy.

The services balance refers to travel and transportation services as well as financial, accounting, legal, and other services that are tradable across countries. Conceptually, exports and imports of services are analogous to exports and imports of goods. The exact sub-components of the account can be found on Table A12.1 at the end of the chapter. A service is entered as a credit when a nation contracts out ("exports") its domestic labor to provide, say, legal services to a company in a foreign country. Conversely, a service is recorded as a debit when a nation contracts for ("imports") foreign labor to provide, say, financial services to the domestic economy. As with the goods balance, the services balance is equal to exports minus imports of services.

In contrast to the deficit in its goods balance, the U.S., like many developed nations, exhibits a surplus in its services balance. Most industrialized nations have developed an extensive service sector, to the point where manufacturing constitutes less than 50 percent of the economic activity. The fact that the U.S. is at the forefront of the technological advances fostering a highly developed and competitive services sector explains why the U.S. is running a substantial services balance surplus. However, the magnitude of the services balance surplus (about $70 billion) is dwarfed by the goods balance deficit.

The sum of the goods balance and services balance is called the **trade balance** (TB), which is also the sub-component of the BoP most often quoted by the press and by politicians. On a quarterly and

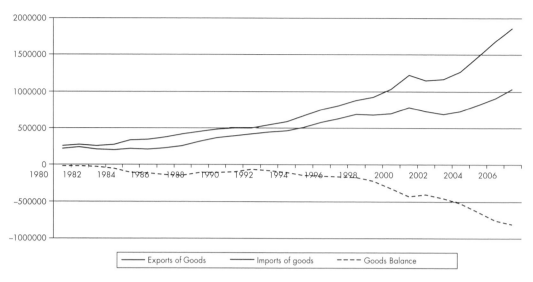

FIGURE 12.1 U.S. Goods Balance, 1980–2007 (in millions of dollars)

Source: adapted from U.S. Department of Commerce, Bureau of Economic Analysis, www.bea.gov/bea/international/bp_web/

even monthly basis, news agencies eagerly await the release of the latest trade balance data as it provides a quick look at the international competitiveness of the country.

$$TB = GB + SB \qquad (12.4)$$

The trade balance is calculated by subtracting all imports of goods and services (M) from the exports of goods and services (X). If a country's imports exceed its exports (*X–M<0*), it is said to be running a trade **deficit**. Conversely, if net exports are positive (*X–M>0*), the country is running a trade **surplus**, meaning that the quantity of goods and services sold to the world market exceeds the quantity of goods and services bought from the world market.

Net Income Receipts and Unilateral Transfers

Two additional components round out our discussion of the current account: **net income receipts** (i.e. receipts less payments) and **unilateral transfers**. Net income receipts are an important subcomponent of the BoP as they represent the sum of income receipts from U.S.-owned assets abroad (credit +) and income payments on foreign-owned assets in the United States (debit –). The exact sub-components of income receipts are presented in Table A12.1 at the end of the chapter. Net income receipts enter positively in the current account when income receipts from financial investments abroad (profits, dividends, capital gains, and interest on bonds) exceed the income payments sent abroad by the home country. The balance on income receipts has been consistently positive for the U.S., but, in 2006, it turned negative for the first time. Some argue that this may be an artifact of imprecise measurement of income receipts, see for example, Case Study II on "Dark Matter" at the end of the chapter.

Unilateral transfers comprise all private transfers (e.g. wages earned by immigrants forwarded to families in foreign countries) and public transfers (e.g. government aid). This component of the current account is positive when transfers received from foreign entities are larger than transfers sent to foreign entities. The BoP category for unilateral transfers was created since the BoP's double-entry system cannot deal with gifts. So unilateral transfers account for the fact that some international exchanges are not transactions, i.e. they are one-sided affairs since there is no payment involved (a thank you note is not a payment!). For instance, if your French cousin sends you a case of Bordeaux for your birthday (lucky you!), the wine will be reported as an import (a debit, i.e. a negative entry) when it reaches the U.S. border, but there is no payment involved since it is a gift. So we need to create a credit entry, unilateral transfer or gift, to balance the accounts.

As one would expect from an advanced country, net unilateral current transfers are negative in the U.S.: more grants and gifts are bestowed than received. This item adds to the U.S. current account deficit. Note also that the largest component consists of remittances, which are usually cash gifts based on immigrants' U.S. wage incomes to their families in their home countries. Given the huge size of the U.S. trade deficit, the income and unilateral accounts balances do not significantly impact the balance of payments. All in all, the U.S. trade deficit is driving its massive current account deficits.

The Capital Account

The capital account is a minor portion of the BoP that was redefined by the Bureau of Economic Analysis (BEA) in 1999 in order to bring U.S. national accounting closer in line with international standards.[2] It is a small subset of the transactions formerly recorded in the transfer portion of the current account. It records capital transfers and the buying and selling of non-produced and non-financial assets. The major components of the capital transfers subcomponent of the BoP are migrant transfers and debt forgiveness. Migrant transfers are transfers of ownership such as title of U.S. land and business deeds, from foreigners residing in the U.S. to foreigners living abroad. These transfers must be distinguished from transfers of income earned in the U.S. by foreigners or abroad by American residents that are included in the current account under compensation of employees. The major components of non-produced and non-financial assets are the transfer of ownership in natural resources, intellectual property rights, franchises, and leases. Compared to the current and financial accounts, the capital account is negligible in size.

---

2 Another example is the shift from Gross National Product (GNP) to Gross Domestic Product (GDP).

"Financial Investment" versus "Capital Investment"

Financial investment and capital investment are two very different types of investments that can confuse students. However, an important difference exists between the two. Financial investment means buying a financial asset. But when you buy a financial asset, like a U.S. treasury bill, no good is produced. In addition, investors expect a return on their financial investment usually in the form of the interest rate. So when the interest on a U.S. treasury bill rises, it becomes relatively more attractive as compared to, say, a German government bond. Therefore financial investment in the U.S. increases as the interest rate rises.

Capital investment, on the other hand, is investment in physical capital that represents purchases of actual goods or services such as capital equipment that increase the economy's future ability to produce. Capital investment is included in the Investment/Savings (IS) relationship that captures the goods market equilibrium in the IS/LM model. When an American airline buys a Boeing 777 aircraft, we have an example of capital investment – the purchase of a good produced by Boeing, an American aircraft manufacturer, and used by an airline to transport passengers. Capital investment decreases as the interest rate rises, since the cost of amortizing the loan to purchase the asset increases.

The Financial Account

Broadly speaking, the financial account tracks financial flows coming in and going out of the economy. The importance of financial flows has grown significantly in the past half-century, from being a relatively unimportant consideration in the 1960s to becoming a major component of the BoP. The three major categories included in the financial account are **foreign direct investment** (FDI), **portfolio investment** (PI), and **official reserve transactions** (ORT).

Foreign Direct Investment Flows

Foreign direct investment consists in long-term financial investment abroad, characterized by large ownership stakes (over 10 percent) in foreign firms. The 10 percent rule is somehow arbitrary, but economists think of foreign investment as highly illiquid. While one can easily sell a foreign bond, large stakes in foreign enterprises are thought to represent ownership interests that cannot be liquidated readily.

For example, Samsung Corporation of South Korea might see a potentially profitable financial investment opportunity in a Japanese startup, and thus acquires more than 10 percent of the startup's stock. This transaction is recorded as a debit on South Korea's BoP, since it is a purchase of foreign assets (by analogy the purchase of foreign goods, an import, is also a debit). The purchase of financial assets is accompanied by some payment – with double-entry accounting – and this payment corresponds to a flow of financial capital from Korea to Japan. It is thus clear that a purchase of assets abroad will trigger a capital outflow – Korean financial capital is put to work abroad. Since goods exports are recorded as a credit on the Korean BoP, one might mistakenly think that South Korea's capital "exports" should also be recorded in the same manner. However, from the point of view of South Korea, Samsung is purchasing Japanese assets, and all purchases are recorded as debits (just like imports, the purchase of foreign goods). By the same reasoning, a sale of assets to foreigners – recorded as a credit in the financial account triggers a capital inflow – foreign capital is put to work in the domestic economy.

Portfolio Investment Flows

The next subcategory of the financial account, portfolio investment, is composed of more liquid financial investments, generally undertaken in the form of stocks, bonds, and bank balances. In the BoP in Table 12.1, portfolio investment is given by the categories that refer to "securities." The accounting for this category works in the same way as for FDI. If the country is buying foreign assets (investing abroad), capital is flowing out of the country (capital outflow); the purchase of the foreign assets is recorded as a negative in the financial account for that country. If the foreigners are buying assets in the domestic economy (investing in the domestic economy), financial capital is flowing into the country (capital inflows): the sale of domestic assets to foreigners is recorded as a positive in the financial account. For example, if Russian businessmen want to invest in the British stock market, their investment in the British economy is counted negatively on the portfolio investment subsection of Russia's financial account balance. Conversely, the Russian investment in the British economy is entered positively on Britain's financial account balance. It is a capital outflow for Russia and a capital inflow for Britain. In the past 30 years, net portfolio investment flows into the U.S. have outpaced net foreign direct investment in the U.S., as shown in Figure 12.2.

Figure 12.2 shows the portfolio balance in the U.S., consisting of foreign purchases of U.S. securities less U.S. purchases of foreign securities abroad. A positive value indicates net portfolio capital inflows into the U.S.: the spike in the late nineties clearly indicates the appeal of high stock returns in the U.S. at the time; the subsequent market correction in early 2000 is unmistakable. The FDI balance represents foreign-owned direct investment flows in the U.S. minus U.S.-owned private direct investment flows abroad. The balance is negative when the U.S. purchase more FDI abroad than foreigners purchase in the U.S. over the period considered. A comparison of Figures 12.1 and 12.2 highlights the fact that financial flows are much more volatile than goods flows. This volatility will be the topic of much discussion in our analysis of the open economy.

Categorizing changes in bank balances as credits or debits is more difficult to conceptualize. There are several ways to explain it. If an American draws on his Barclays Bank balance in London to make a payment for a British good, he is lowering his claims on Britain as he is relinquishing (selling) some of his assets (the British pounds in this London account): all this points to a credit (a sale). A more simplistic approach would be to assert that, since he purchased a British good (a negative entry), the other side of the transaction, the payment for the good, has to be a positive entry in the scope of a double-entry accounting system.

These changes in bank balances allow us to suggest another way to categorize the financial accounts: the **autonomous accounts** and the **settlement accounts**. The autonomous accounts correspond to the initial deal (e.g. buying bonds) while the settlement accounts correspond to the resulting payment for the deal, a change in bank balance or in currency holding.

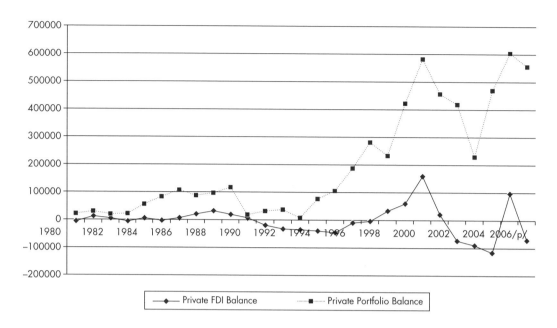

FIGURE 12.2 U.S. Foreign Portfolio Investment Balance and Foreign Direct Investment Balance, 1980–2007 (in millions of dollars)

Source: adapted from U.S. Department of Commerce, Bureau of Economic Analysis, www.bea.gov/bea/international/bp_web/

Foreign direct investments and portfolio investments are undertaken by private citizens mostly. In addition, the government might also acquire foreign investments: for instance, the government could build a university or an air base in a foreign country or invest in foreign companies. However, the financial account makes a strict distinction between international financial transactions carried out by the government and those carried out by the central bank so-called official reserve transactions. The changes in the account involved (the official reserve transactions) directly affect the level of assets in the central bank balance sheet and, in the process, contain some monetary implications. Moreover, we will see later on that the importance of these changes depends on the exchange rate regime adopted.

The Official Reserve Transactions

The final component of the financial account consists of official reserve transactions (ORT). The ORT subsection of the financial account tracks the international currency dealings of a country's central bank. The central bank interacts not only in the domestic bond and money markets, but also in international currency markets; the central bank also cooperates with foreign central banks and international institutions like the International Monetary Fund and the World Bank.

It is important to remember that the central bank is an independent branch of government. The central bank does not issue government debt, such as U.S. treasury bills – that is the role of the treasury department. The central bank has no ties to the fiscal authorities, and central bank charters clearly indicate that their sole task is to conduct monetary policy. All the other non-central bank international transactions carried out by the government are recorded under government assets, in the category called other than "Official reserve assets."

Any time a central bank buys foreign currency on the international currency markets, the transaction is recorded as a debit in the BoP because it is equivalent to a purchase of foreign assets. In terms of double-entry accounting, such a purchase is at the same time a sale of domestic currency to the foreigners. So a sale of domestic currency on the international currency markets is a debit in the financial accounts. As part of its task of conducting monetary policy at the national level, the central bank may hold a diversified international portfolio that includes international currency reserves and foreign government bonds.

The Statistical Discrepancy

The **statistical discrepancy** (SD) is defined as the sum of all the BoP items with their signs reversed, i.e.

$$SD = -(CA+KA+FA) \tag{12.5}$$

In trillion dollar economies, it is difficult to keep track of every transaction. Not all the sources of information are reliable, for instance, multinational corporations are often in a position to report their profits in the country that will impose the lowest rates of corporate taxes: this may not be the country where the profit was actually generated. Another example might be the payments for services that can be easily adjusted to suit clients' tax purposes. Finally, the existence of illegal international transactions such as smuggling, drugs trade, etc. will throw off the neat double-entry accounting. Several industrialized countries have a positive statistical discrepancy – business or citizens underreporting their income abroad.

Are Statistical Discrepancies Random?

When observing the statistical discrepancy in the U.S. since 1960, we see a negative bias until 1975 and then a positive bias until 1987. Afterward it seems to switch haphazardly from positive to negative and vice versa. If the statistical discrepancy is due to some transaction reported in the wrong balance of payments (for tax avoidance or other reasons), one would think that the sum of all the statistical discrepancies of all the countries should add up to zero. The International Monetary Fund (IMF) tracks these data and it is clear that this is not the case. In 2004, the global statistical discrepancy on the current accounts amounted to $-27 billion or 0.1 percent of the total transactions, while the global statistical discrepancy on the financial accounts amounted to $-95 billion. Within the financial account, the largest discrepancy can be found in the portfolio investment accounts. In the nineties, the discrepancy used to be negative, implying missing credit transactions. Although it became positive later on, it turned negative again in 2004. The causes for these swings are hard to pinpoint and the volatility is even greater when considering the sub-accounts. Within the financial account, a tightening of the definition of the various transactions could correct the extent of the discrepancy.

This discussion of the statistical discrepancy of the BoP exhausts our description of all major subcomponents. Each subsection discussed above is again divided into further sub-subsections in the full BoP that we present in the Appendix. Above we chose to keep the level of detail to a minimum and explored only the main components that are the key drivers of the BoP.

THE INTERNATIONAL INVESTMENT POSITION

The balance of payments measures the international flows of goods, services, and capital over the period of one calendar year. It is also important, however, to measure the stock of international assets held by U.S. residents and the stock of American assets owned by foreigners at the end of the year. In this context, the term "stock" corresponds to a variable that can be expressed as a quantity at a specific point of time in contrast to a flow, a variable that is expressed as a quantity per unit of time. Here, the term "stock" does not refer to a share of ownership in a corporation.

The financial accounts measure changes in assets ownership taking place over the year. By summing up all the changes over the years, we can measure the stock of assets held by a country at a specific point of time. This is what the international investment position measures. In the U.S., this information is again tracked by the Commerce Department's Bureau of Economic Analysis. Not all countries report this account since it is difficult to keep track of capital stocks over time. The most consistent international source for this data is provided by the International Monetary Funds *Balance of Payments and International Investment Position Statistics* (http://www.imf.org/external/np/sta/bop/bop.htm).

Since the BoP tracks the changes over a year in ownership of international assets, the BoP and the account of the International Investment Position are closely related. As we have seen in Figure 12.1, the U.S. has been running a chronic deficit in its current account. From our understanding of the double-entry bookkeeping method used to compile the BoP, current account deficits have to be reflected in equivalent capital and financial account surpluses (see equation 1.2). Somehow a country has to finance its current account (mainly trade) deficits. This financing of these deficits will, by our method of double-entry bookkeeping, be reflected in the financial account transactions (since the capital account is negligible, we ignore it here).

Surpluses in the U.S. financial account occur when foreigners buy more U.S. assets than U.S. residents buy foreign assets. In other words, the U.S. economy is selling more assets to the rest of the world than acquiring foreign assets. The balance of payments records these flows of assets exchanged during the year. However it is clear that over the years, foreigners' total holdings of U.S. assets will grow at a faster rate than the U.S. holdings of foreign assets. So eventually the stocks of foreign assets held by the U.S. will be smaller than the stocks of U.S. assets held by the rest of the world. This is precisely what the Table A12.3 illustrates.

After World War II, the U.S. financed a large part of global post-war reconstruction and U.S.-owned capital was invested all around the world economies. These capital outflows from the U.S. (or net increase in U.S.-owned assets abroad) were substantially larger than any increases in foreign-owned assets in the U.S. at the time. This made the U.S. a net creditor (owning more assets abroad than the foreigners in the U.S.). However, once the U.S. started to exhibit increasingly large current account deficits financed by large financial account surpluses, the U.S. position switched in the 1980s from being a net creditor to becoming a net debtor.

Plainly speaking, foreigners own more assets in the U.S. than U.S. residents own assets in the rest of the world. As the U.S. is a net borrower, the U.S. is expected to pay more interest, dividends, etc. than to receive income. The various forms of income from these assets are recorded in the current account under income receipts and income payments. Amazingly the income balance has been positive over the years: receipts have been greater than payments! How can we explain such an anomaly? Economists do not agree on how to interpret it and further discussion is presented in Case Studies at the end of the chapter.

THE EXCHANGE RATE

When the BoP registers a purchase of a foreign asset or the sale of a domestic commodity abroad, this may implicitly indicate a change in the demand for or in the supply of the foreign currency. To complete the international transaction, one of the parties to the transaction, either the buyer or the seller, may have to exchange his/her domestic currency for foreign currency. Therefore changes in the components of the BoP affect the supply of and demand for foreign currency.

The key variable that allows the supply of and demand for foreign currency to be equilibrated is the exchange rate. In the first part of this book, we considered real variables mainly; the first example discussed trade in wine and cloth between Portugal and England. There was no need for the exchange rate to explain comparative advantage. Now that we look at aggregates, we have to use domestic currency to construct these aggregates. Then the exchange rate becomes an essential tool to convert all the currencies into each other.

The **exchange rate** (E) is defined as the relative price of the foreign currency in terms of the domestic currency. So if a domestic resident wants to buy the currency of another country, the exchange rate states the price for one unit of foreign currency, i.e. how many units of domestic currency are needed to buy one unit of foreign currency. For example, if we assume for the moment that the dollar is the domestic currency, the exchange rate between the dollar ($\$$) and the British pound sterling ($\pounds$) is:

$$E = \$/\pounds \qquad (12.6)$$

One complication is that the definition of the exchange rate is ambiguous, depending on the reference of location. With this definition, Americans will identify the pound as the foreign currency, while the British identify the dollar as the foreign currency. This means there are two versions of the exchange rate, one based on dollars per pound (U.S.) and the other based on pounds per dollar (U.K.). As a result, most sources quote both versions of the exchange rate: "U.S.\$ equivalence" and "Currency per U.S.\$" in their statistics. For example, from the point of view of the U.K., the exchange rate between the two currencies is $E^* = £/\$$. That is, for British residents the exchange rate indicates how many pounds they have to pay to buy one U.S. dollar. Consequently if $E = \$1.5$ then $E^* = 1/E = £0.66$. Table 12.2 shows the cross-rates between various currencies.

We now consider the exchange rate from the U.S. point of view. If an American wants to plan her next vacation abroad and estimate the dollar price of a rental car in the U.K., she would simply have to multiply the British pound price (P^*) by the exchange rate (E, the number of $\$$ in one £) to find the dollar price as EP^*. We can take this notion a bit further and find the dollar value of all our imports by multiplying the quantity of imports (M), by the exchange rate times the foreign price of imports (EP^*). So EP^*M is the total value of all imported goods in terms of domestic currency.

Changes in the exchange rate have their own terminology. If the U.S.\$/British£ rate increases from 1.5 to 3 (E *increases*), you would now have to pay 3 dollars per British pound. The price of U.K. currency has increased, or your dollars are worth less. Economists speak of a **depreciation** of the dollar relative to the British pound. It is a common mistake to think that a depreciation of the domestic currency results in a decrease in the exchange rate. A quick check of our definition of the exchange rate shows that E actually increases as the dollar depreciates. This is because E is the price of foreign currency and this price increases as the dollar loses value. If the exchange rate declines from 1.5 to 1, then the price of foreign currency has fallen. Fewer dollars are needed to purchase 1 pound, implying

TABLE 12.2 Cross-Rates Between Various Currencies (April 4, 2008)

	Currency	Can\$	DKr	€	¥	NKr	SKr	SFr	£	\$
Canada	Can\$	1	4.698	0.63	100.7	5.024	5.908	0.995	0.497	0.992
Denmark	DKr	2.129	10	1.341	214.4	10.7	12.58	2.117	1.058	2.111
Euro area	€	1.588	7.459	1	159.9	7.977	9.38	1.579	0.789	1.574
Japan	¥	0.993	4.664	0.625	100	4.989	5.866	0.988	0.494	0.984
Norway	NKr	1.99	9.35	1.254	200.4	10	11.76	1.98	0.989	1.973
Sweden	SKr	1.693	7.951	1.066	170.5	8.504	10	1.683	0.841	1.678
Switzerland	SFr	1.005	4.723	0.633	101.3	5.052	5.92	1	0.5	0.997
U.K.	£	2.012	9.45	1.267	203.6	10.11	11.88	2.001	1	1.994
U.S.	\$	1.009	4.738	0.635	101.6	5.067	5.959	1.003	0.501	1

¥ per 100 – DKr, NKr, and SKr per 10

Note that the numbers in the upper triangle are the inverse of those in the lower triangle with the appropriate correcting factors listed immediately under the table.

that the dollar has become stronger, or as economists say, has appreciated relatively to the pound. We must also note that since exchange rates are relative prices, if one needs more dollars to buy one pound (a depreciation of the dollar), this is equivalent to saying that one needs fewer pounds to buy one dollar or that the pound has appreciated with respect to the dollar. Conversely, an **appreciation** of the dollar is equivalent to a depreciation of the pound. It is thus imperative to always specify which currency appreciates or depreciates.

Since the exchange rate is *the price* of foreign currency, it equilibrates the supply and demand of foreign currency, just like the price for milk equilibrates the supply of and demand for milk. Identically to the market for milk, where fluctuations in the supply of and demand for milk alter the price of milk, fluctuations in the supply of and demand for foreign currency set off appreciations and depreciations of the exchange rate. While the supply of and demand for milk comes from cows and cheese lovers respectively, the supply of and demand for foreign currency is triggered by the actions of the various agents involved in the BoP transactions. We can now consider the BoP in a new light and appreciate its role summarizing all international transactions and immediately informing us whether the supply of and demand for foreign currency has been altered.

Understanding the relevance of the balance of payments and the exchange rate is the key to grasping most concepts of the open economy. The BoP not only represents a statistical account of a country's international transactions. The fundamental insight is that changes in the BoP set off, by definition, changes in the market for foreign currency. Therefore we have reached our first important conclusion: one aspect of international macroeconomics is the study of how changes in the exchange rate affect the economy – often with new and dramatic ramifications that we did not consider in the closed economy. It is absolutely crucial that we recall throughout our study of the open economy that changes in the exchange rate are fundamentally driven by changes in the balance of payments.

The Need for Exchange Rates is Relatively Recent

When international transactions were settled with gold or silver coins, there was no such need. All that counted was the weight of the coin. People were indifferent as to whether it was a gold coin embossed with the face of the king of France, a Louis d'or, or a coin with the face of the Emperor of Austria, a gold ducat. Gold was gold, so people did not need to exchange these coins according to an exchange rate but only according to the amount of gold in the coin. Then countries introduced paper currency and switched to a gold standard. Originally the paper currency was fully backed by gold, so the exchange rate was fixed and still not that important. It was only when countries had to give up backing their currency by gold that exchange rates became of paramount importance for international trade.

Real and Nominal Exchange Rates

The exchange rates are reported daily in the major newspapers and minute-to-minute quotes of the prices of foreign currencies can be obtained on the internet. These quoted prices represent the nominal exchange rate (it is also called the spot exchange rate as it is quoted on the **spot market**). As economists, we are interested in digging a bit deeper to make a distinction between real and nominal variables, specifically real and nominal exchange rates. Real variables are always adjusted for inflation, thus the **real exchange rate** describes the fluctuations in the price of foreign currency after we have taken into account domestic and foreign rates of inflation. In Chapter 20, we will discuss an alternative definition of the real exchange rate based on specific economic theory.

While the nominal exchange rate, $E_{\$/£} = \$/£$, is simply the number of dollars you have to pay to get one British pound, £, the real exchange rate, $e_{\$/£}$, accounts for inflation in both countries.

$$e_{\$/£} = \frac{\$/P_\$}{£/P_£} = \frac{\$}{£} \frac{P_£}{P_\$} = E_{\$/£} \frac{P_£}{P_\$} \tag{12.7}$$

In the equation above, $P_\$$ and $P_£$ are the respective price levels in the U.S. and Britain. To obtain the real exchange rate, we first divide the amount of dollars we have to pay by the U.S. price level and the amount of British pounds we receive (£1) by the U.K. price level. Basically we are now looking at "real" dollar and "real" pounds, i.e. real in terms of their domestic purchasing power. Now assume that the U.S. price level increases by 5 percent while the U.K. price level does not change. This means that, in terms of its purchasing power, the dollar buys 5 percent fewer domestic goods, or the value of the real dollar $\$/P_\$$ has dropped by 5 percent while the value of the real pound $£/P_£$ has not changed. However the nominal exchange rate E has remained constant: one U.S. dollar can still buy exactly the same amount of pounds. So now one U.S. dollar can buy more British goods than American goods since the prices of the British goods have not changed while the prices of the American goods have increased. This phenomenon is identified as a real appreciation of the dollar. Of course if, at the same time, the dollar underwent a nominal depreciation equal to 5 percent, nothing would change as the real exchange rate will not have changed. The U.S. citizen will not feel richer: the British goods would be relatively cheaper, but the pound would be more expensive, so one would not be able to buy any more British goods. That is why we divide the quantities of currencies in (12.7) by their respective price levels in the domestic and foreign economies.

When we consider equation (12.7), it is clear that the real exchange rate can be broken down into two parts. First the nominal exchange rate, $E_{\$/£}$, and second the relative price level, $P_£/P_\$$. The real exchange rate is thus simply the nominal exchange rate multiplied by an adjustment for the relative prices abroad and at home. The difference between real and nominal rates becomes crucially important when we compare their respective changes over time. To see this, consider the definitional relationship $e = EP^*/P$ where e is the real exchange rate, E the nominal exchange rate, P the domestic price level (or the consumer price index, CPI), and P^* the foreign price level (or foreign CPI). Taking percentage changes (denoted by ^), we obtain the following approximation

$$\hat{e} = \hat{E} + \hat{P}^* - \hat{P} \tag{12.8}$$

where, for any variable x, $\hat{x} \equiv dx / x$.[3] The changes per unit time are then obtained by dividing both sides of (12.8) by the time unit, dt.

Examining changes in the real exchange rate over time underscores that any percentage change in the real price of the foreign currency is a composite of three separate terms: (a) the percentage change in the nominal price of the foreign currency, (b) the percentage change in the foreign price level, and (c) the percentage change in the domestic price level.

Simply said, if the nominal exchange rate increases by 2 percent over a one-year period, foreigners find it 2 percent cheaper to buy U.S. dollars. This renders all U.S. goods 2 percent cheaper *in nominal terms*. However, if U.S. inflation was 4 percent and foreign inflation was 2 percent over the past year, foreigners find it just as attractive in *real terms* to buy U.S. goods as they did last year (as $\hat{e} = 2 + 2 - 4 = 0$). This example highlights that, while the nominal exchange rate may have changed, the real exchange rate may well remain constant when we account for inflation.

In conclusion, the real exchange rate is a measure of the international competitiveness of a country: we saw above that changes in international competitiveness depend not only on changes in the nominal exchange rate, but also on changes in the relative price level in the two countries. A real depreciation that can be caused either by a nominal depreciation or a decrease in the domestic price level or an increase in the foreign price level (or some combination of these) will enhance a country's international competitiveness while a real appreciation will have the opposite impact.

Real Exchange Rates and Terms of Trade

In the first part of this book, everything was in real terms. Since we were studying trade, we needed to set up some exchange ratio to find out how many units of a good one country could obtain from its trade partner for each unit of the good it gives up. This was the terms of trade: how many units of imports a country can acquire for each unit of exports. In addition, an increase was considered as an improvement in the terms of trade. It would seem that the concept of real exchange rate has similarities with the terms of trade since it is real too. However the models in the first part of the book assumed balanced trade at all time, so an increase in the terms of trade did not affect this assumption. In the second part, macroeconomists acknowledge the fact that trade is not necessarily balanced and changes in the real exchange rate affect the balance of trade. The equivalent of an increase in the terms of trade is a real appreciation; by worsening the balance of trade, it is not considered a welcome improvement.

Since economists are keenly interested in real variables, the open economy models presented later on in this text will take real exchange rate into account. However in the next few chapters, we start with models that assume fixed prices. In this case the nominal and real exchange rates coincide.

---

3 More formally, this relationship is obtained by first taking logarithms of the definitional relationship and then taking the differential.

The Effective Exchange Rate

The nominal and real exchange rates presented above are *bilateral* exchange rates. The usefulness of bilateral exchange rates is limited as it helps us identify the relative strength of the domestic currency relatively to *one* other currency only. For example, is the euro appreciating or depreciating against the British pound? If the value of the euro depreciates against the pound, we know that euro area goods become relatively cheaper in the U.K. (in other words, more competitive in the British markets). But this does not give us a broad picture of how euro area goods fare in the world markets.

While bilateral competitiveness is of great interest, economists are even more interested in a country's competitiveness vis-à-vis all of its trading partners. To measure a country's *overall* export competitiveness, we need a more general measure of the exchange rate, one that extends our bilateral measure into a *multilateral* measure. This multilateral measure accounts for the fact that we trade with many countries. For example, it is not hard to imagine a situation where the Japanese yen *depreciates* against the dollar, but *appreciates* against the euro over a given time period. Do Japanese products then become more or less attractive to the rest of the world overall? Does the Japanese trade balance improve or deteriorate? We can certainly say that Japanese exports' competitiveness improved relative to the U.S. and deteriorated against European goods. However, can we determine whether Japanese exports became more or less competitive *overall*? To answer this question we need to develop a new measure of the exchange rate.

The most comprehensive measure of overall export competitiveness compares the value of the domestic currency to the value of the currencies of all the trade partners. This measure is called the **effective exchange rate** and is defined as

$$E_{Effective} = \sum_{j=1}^{N} q_j E_j \qquad with \sum_{j=1}^{N} q_j = 1 \qquad (12.9)$$

The effective exchange rate is therefore the weighted sum of all bilateral exchange rates. The weight, q_j, for a bilateral exchange rate, E_j, is simply the fraction of total trade that the domestic economy conducts with country j.[4] Note that there are $j = 1, 2, \ldots, N$ countries in this index, corresponding to the home country's N trading partners. The effective exchange rate is also referred to as the *multilateral*, or *trade-weighted exchange rate*. An example of the effective exchange rate is given in Figure 12.3.

Figure 12.3 shows that the yen appreciated against the dollar between 1973 and 1995 as the yen-dollar exchange rate dropped over the period. After 1995, the yen became weaker: at that time, the U.S. criticized Japan for manipulating its exchange rate and keeping the yen artificially weak; obviously Japan was trying to keep its exports competitive on the U.S. markets. With the exception of a few short fluctuations, the trade-weighted dollar (1997 = 100) chart shows an overall *appreciation* of the dollar against all its trading partners until 2002. Afterward, a persistent depreciation of the dollar started its course.

---

4 Since each bilateral exchange rate is expressed in different units (the respective foreign country's currency) one cannot simply add up all exchange rates; they must first be converted into indices with 100 for the base year. These indices can then be summed as indicated in equation 12.9.

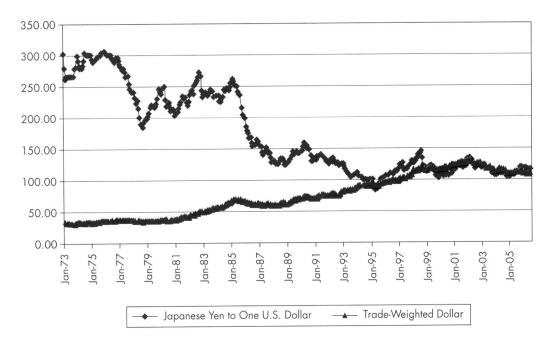

FIGURE 12.3 Bilateral (yen/dollar) Exchange Rate and Trade-Weighted Exchange Rate for the Dollar

Source: adapted from Federal Reserve Bank of St. Louis, Trade Weighted Exchange Rate (broad) – http://research. stlouisfed.org/fred2/categories/105 and Japan/U.S. Foreign Exchange Rate – http://research.stlouisfed.org/fred2/ categories/275

The vertical axis measures both the bilateral exchange rate as number of yens per dollar and the U.S. trade-weighted exchange rate with Jan 1997 = 100.

The effective exchange rate can also be adjusted when we are interested in real rather than nominal variables. All we have to do is to sum over all real exchange rates (in index form) rather than the nominal exchange rates given in equation (12.9) to obtain the real **effective exchange rate**.

$$e_{Effective} = \sum_{j=1}^{N} q_j e_j \qquad with \sum_{j=1}^{N} q_j = 1 \qquad (12.10)$$

This index can be calculated using the IMF's *International Financial Statistics* data on exchange rates and consumer price indices (http://ifs.apdi.net/imf), and the IMF's *Direction of Trade* data for trade weights. Most central banks provide data on nominal and real bilateral exchange rates, as well as the nominal and real effective exchange rates on their web site.

In this chapter, we have introduced an accounting device, the balance of payments, that will provide a framework for the analysis of the macroeconomic models of the open economy. We have also derived four working definitions of the exchange rate: the nominal and real bilateral exchange rates and the nominal and real effective exchange rate. We now understand that the real (or real effective) exchange rate gives us a more accurate picture of a country's international competitiveness. The next task is to figure out how the exchange rate is determined. Realizing that the supply of and the demand for foreign currency crucially influence its price (i.e. the exchange rate), we need to dig deeper and find out what influences the supply of and demand for foreign currency. The next chapter will focus on the determination of the nominal exchange rate.

Summary of Key Concepts

1. The balance of payments keeps track of all the transactions between a country and the rest of the world during a year.
2. In the BoP, sales of goods and services are credits and purchases are debits. Therefore exports are credits (+) and imports are debits (−).
3. Financial account sales are increases in foreign-owned assets in the U.S. (i.e. sales of U.S. assets to the rest of the world resulting in *financial inflows*). By analogy to current account sales (exports thus credit), increases in foreign-owned assets in the U.S. are credit (+) entries.
4. Financial account purchases are increases in U.S.-owned assets abroad (i.e. U.S. purchases of foreign assets resulting in *financial outflows*). By analogy to current account purchases (imports thus debit), increases in U.S.-owned assets abroad are debit (−) entries.
5. In the balance of payments, the financial accounts refer to financial flows (in or out) over-time, i.e. to change in stocks of assets. At the end of the year the new level of the stocks of assets owned by the U.S. overseas and the stocks of assets owned by foreigners in the U.S. are recorded in a table entitled the "International Investment Position of the U.S". published by the Bureau of Economic Analysis.
6. The exchange rate is the relative price of two currencies; it can always be quoted by one number or by its inverse.
7. The standard approach is to quote the exchange rate from the point of view of the domestic economy as the price of one unit of foreign currency.
8. When we mention appreciation or depreciation, we must always specify the currencies involved, since the appreciation of one currency must necessarily correspond to the depreciation of the other currency.
9. In the short run with fixed prices, nominal and real exchange rates are equivalent.
10. With bilateral exchange rates, a depreciation of the domestic currency is an increase in the exchange rate (more units of domestic currency needed to buy one unit of foreign currency). With multilateral exchange rates, a depreciation is a decrease in the index measuring the overall exchange rate of the domestic currency with respect to its trade partners' currencies.

CASE STUDY I

CSI: Trade Deficit
By Paul Krugman
New York Times, April 24, 2006

Forensics are in. If you turn on the TV during prime time, you're likely to find yourself watching people sorting through clues from a crime scene, trying to figure out what really happened.

That's more or less what's going on right now among international finance experts. The crime in question is the U.S. trade deficit, which according to the broadest measure reached an amazing $805 billion last year. The mystery is how we've been able to run huge deficits, year after year, with so few visible adverse consequences. And the future of the U.S. economy depends on which of two proposed solutions to the mystery is right.

Here's the puzzle: the trade deficit means that America is living beyond its means, spending far more than it earns. (In 2005, the United States exported only 53 cents' worth of goods for every dollar it spent on imports.) To pay for the excess of imports over exports, the United States has to sell stocks, bonds and businesses to foreigners. In fact, we've borrowed more than $3 trillion just since 1999.

By rights, then, the investment income – interest payments, stock dividends and so on – that Americans pay to foreigners should be a lot larger than the investment income foreigners pay to Americans. But according to official statistics, the United States still has a slightly positive balance on investment income.

How is this possible? The answer, almost certainly, is that there's something wrong with the numbers. (Laypeople tend to treat official statistics as gospel; professional economists know that putting these numbers together involves a lot of educated guesswork – and sometimes the guesses are wrong.) But depending on exactly what's wrong, the U.S. economy either has hidden strengths, or it's in even worse shape than it seems.

In one corner are economists who think the official statistics miss invisible U.S. exports – exports not of goods and services, but of intangibles like knowledge and brand-name recognition, which allow U.S. companies to earn high rates of return on their foreign investments. Proponents of this view claim that if we counted these invisible exports, which they call "dark matter," much of the U.S. trade deficit would disappear.

The dark matter hypothesis has been eagerly taken up by some journalists, who like its upbeat message. It seems to say that the U.S. economy is, as a cover article in *Business Week* put it, "much stronger than you think."

But there's a problem: U.S. companies operating abroad don't, in fact, seem to earn especially high rates of return. Why, then, doesn't the United States seem to be paying a price for all its borrowing? Because, according to the official data, foreign companies operating in the United States are remarkably unprofitable, earning an average return of only 2.2 percent a year.

There's something wrong with this picture. As Daniel Gros of the Center for European Policy Studies puts it, it's hard to believe that foreigners would continue investing in the United States "if they were really being constantly taken to the cleaners."

In a new paper, Mr. Gros argues – compellingly, in my view – that what's really happening is that foreign companies are understating the profits of their U.S. subsidiaries, probably to avoid taxes, and that official data are, in particular, failing to pick up foreign profits that are reinvested in U.S. operations.

If Mr. Gros is right, the true position of the U.S. economy isn't as bad as you think – it's worse. The true trade deficit, including unreported profits that accrue to foreign companies, isn't $800 billion – it's more than $900 billion. And America's foreign debt, including the value of foreign-owned businesses, is at least $1 trillion bigger than the official numbers say.

Of course, optimists have a comeback: if things are really that bad, why are so many foreign investors still buying U.S. bonds? And they point out that those predicting problems from the trade deficit have been wrong so far. But I have two words for those who place their faith in the judgment of investors, and believe that a few good years are enough to prove the skeptics wrong: Nasdaq[5] 5,000.

Right now, forensic analysis seems to say that the U.S. trade position is worse, not better, than it looks. And the answer to the question, "Why haven't we paid a price for our trade deficit?" is, just you wait.

Source: From the *New York Times* April 24, 2006 © 2006 the New York Times.

CASE STUDY QUESTIONS

1. What is the anomaly observed by all the economists?

2. It seems that economists have different interpretations for it. What is the cause of the anomaly according to the optimists? What would be the impact on the current account?

3. Why doesn't the optimists' explanation hold?

4. What is the cause of the anomaly according to Gros/Krugman?

5. What is the consequence of Gros/Krugman explanations on the current account and on the investment position of the U.S.?

CASE STUDY II

"Dark Matter" Makes the U.S. Deficit Disappear
By Ricardo Hausmann and Federico Sturzenegger
Financial Times, December 7, 2005

In 2005 the U.S. current account deficit is expected to top $700 bn (£404 bn). It comes after 27 years of unbroken deficits that have totaled more than $5,000 bn, leading to concerns of an impending global crisis. Once the massive financing required to keep on paying for such a widening gap dries up, there will be an ugly adjustment in the world economy. The dollar will collapse, triggering a stampede away from U.S. debt, interest rates will shoot up and a sharp global recession will ensue.

But wait a minute. If this is such an open and shut case, why have markets not precipitated the crisis already?

Maybe it is because there is something wrong with the diagnosis. Let us look at some facts. The Bureau of Economic Analysis indicates that in 1980 the U.S. had about $365 bn of net foreign assets that rendered a net return of about $30 bn. Between 1980 and 2004, the U.S. accumulated a current account deficit of $4,500 bn. You would expect the net foreign assets of the U.S. to have fallen by that amount to, say, minus $4,100 bn. If it paid 5 per cent on that debt, the net return on its financial position should have moved from an income of $30 bn in 1982 to an expenditure of $210 bn a year in 2004. Right? After all, debtors need to service their debt.

---

5 A stockmarket index including the largest U.S. and international securities.

But the 2004 number was, still, an income of $30 bn, as in 1980. The U.S. has spent $4,500 bn more than it has earned (which is what the cumulative current account deficit implies) for free.

How could this be? Here the official story becomes murky. Part of the answer is that the U.S. benefited from about $1,600 bn of net capital gains (which, at best, cuts the puzzle in half). The other part of the official answer is that the U.S. earns a higher return on its holdings of foreign assets than it pays to foreigners on its liabilities. But where did those large capital gains come from? Or, why are U.S. investors abroad so much smarter than foreign investors in the U.S.? We propose a different way of describing the facts. We measure the assets according to how much they earn and the current account by how much these assets change over time. This is just like valuing a company by calculating its earnings and multiplying by a price earnings ratio. Of course this opens up methodological questions, but the discrepancies with official numbers are so big that the details do not matter. To keep things simple in what follows we just take an arbitrary 5 per cent rate of return, which implies a price-earnings ratio of 20.

Let's get to work. We know that the U.S. net income on its financial portfolio is $30 bn. This is a 5 percent return on an asset of $600 bn. So the U.S. is a $600 bn net creditor, not a $4,100 bn net debtor. Since the assets have remained stable then on average the U.S. has not had a current account deficit at all over the past 25 years. That is why it is still a net creditor.

We call the $4,700 bn difference between our measure of U.S. net assets and the standard numbers "dark matter," because it corresponds to assets that generate revenue but cannot be seen. The name is taken from a term used in physics to account for the fact that the world is more stable than you would think if it were held together only by gravity emanating from visible matter.

There are several reasons why dark matter exists. The most obvious is superior returns on U.S. foreign direct investment. Why do U.S. assets earn such returns? Because that investment comes with a substantial amount of know-how that increases its earning potential. It explains why the U.S. can earn more on its assets than it pays on its liabilities and why foreigners cannot do the same. In measuring FDI, the value of the know-how is poorly accounted for. There are other sources of dark matter, but FDI is where the big bucks are. Once dark matter is considered, the world is surprisingly balanced. The U.S. and European Union essentially cover their apparent imbalance with the export of dark matter, emerging markets use their surplus to import dark matter and Japan finances the rest of the world. Net asset positions of all big regions are fairly small.

Is U.S. dark matter a stable asset? We find that it is. It now stands at more than 40 per cent of gross domestic product and has fallen in only six of the last 25 years, never by more than 1.9 per cent of GDP. In a nutshell our story is simple. Once assets are valued according to the income they generate, there has not been a big U.S. external imbalance and there are no serious global imbalances.

Financial Times December 7, 2005

CASE STUDY QUESTIONS

1. If the dark matter is true, would you expect other countries to have dark matter, too?

2. What might be the source of the dark matter?

3. Does the existence of dark matter imply that a country need not worry about its current account deficit?

Questions for Study and Review

In your answers for questions 1–4 below, please identify the primary BoP account affected and ignore the settlement side that is part of the BoP's double-entry accounting.

1. On August 8 2002, Brazil received a 30-billion dollar loan from the IMF. When the first $1 billion wire was received by the Brazilian government's treasury department, exactly which part of the Brazilian balance of payments was affected positively or negatively?

2. The Wall Street Journal reported on August 4 2002 that "Washington agreed to provide a $1.5 billion short-term loan to the Uruguayan government" to provide funding that the International Monetary Fund and the World Bank were unwilling to provide. When the $1.5 billion wire arrived in Uruguay, *exactly* which part of the Uruguayan balance of payments was affected positively or negatively?

3. In 2003, the largest category of the Mexican current account was the funds wired from Mexican workers in the U.S. to relatives in Mexico. Exactly which aspect of the Mexican balance of payments is affected positively or negatively by such payments?

4. Balance of payments accounts.

   a. Which part of the U.S. balance of payments is affected (positively or negatively) if U.S.-based currency traders sell the dollar and buy foreign bonds?

   b. The interest income on these foreign bonds will post (as a debit or credit?) next year as part of which category of the balance of payments?

5. Assuming zero inflation in all countries and deflation in Japan over the year, assume also that the yen has depreciated over the year against all the other currencies.

   a. Compare the relative movements of Japan's nominal and real exchange rates with the U.S.

   b. What can you say about Japan's real effective exchange rates with the rest of the world including the U.S.?

   c. What can you say about Japan's international competitiveness?

6. Let P_{UK} be the GDP deflator in Great Britain (U.K.) and P_S the GDP deflator in Switzerland. Suppose $P_{UK} = 2.5$ and $P_S = 1.5$

   a. Calculate the real exchange rate (RER Switzerland/U.K. – Switzerland is the domestic economy) corresponding to each of the following $SF/£$ nominal exchange rates (E): the exchange rate quoted in Switzerland on April 12, 2007 is $E_{SF/£} = 2.4085$ and on May 12, 2007 it is $E_{SF/£} = 2.415$

   b. As E increases, i. What happens to the Swiss *real* exchange rate above? ii. What happens to the price of Swiss goods in terms of British goods?

   c. If the price level in Great Britain increases faster than the price level in Switzerland, i. What happens to the *real* exchange rate above? (assume no change in the nominal exchange rate). ii. What happens to Swiss international competitiveness?

   d. Compare your results in (b) and (c).

7. Use the bilateral exchange rate data between the euro and the British pound and between the euro and the dollar in 2 consecutive years (5/9/2006 and 5/9/2007) to calculate the trade weighted or multilateral exchange rate (TWI) for the euro over the period. Set the first year as the base year, i.e. set the multilateral exchange rate for this year as 100. Assume that, in this period, the U.K. and the U.S. are the Euro area's only trade partners: the share of trade of the Euro area with the U.K. – 40 percent – remains the same over the two years considered. Fill in the table below to show how you construct the trade-weighted index.

ER	E_0	Index	Weight	Weighted index	E_1	Index	Weight	Weighted index
£/€	0.69	100	.40	40	0.68	98.55	.40	39.42
$/€	1.28	100	.60	60	1.35	105.47	.60	63.28
TWI	XX	XXX	XXX	100	XX	XXX	XXX	102.7

Data: over the period, the €/£ exchange rate increases from $E_0 = 1.44$ to $E_1 = 1.48$ and the €/$ decreases from $E_0 = 0.78$ to $E_1 = 0.74$. Over this period, has the euro appreciated or depreciated with respect to the dollar, the pound, or overall?

References and Suggestions for Further Reading

Bureau of Economic Analysis (1990) "Balance of Payments (the) of the United States, Concepts, Data Sources, and Estimating Procedures," by R. A. Mosbacher and M. R. Darby, Under Secretary for Economics Affairs.

Bureau of Economic Analysis (2006) "How BEA Aligns and Augments Source Data From the US Treasury Department for Inclusion in the International Transactions Accounts," *Survey of Current Business*, July.

Bureau of Economic Analysis, "International Transaction Accounts, various years (http://www.bea.gov/bea/di/home/bop.htm)

Hausmann, R., and Sturzenegger, F. (2005) " 'Dark Matter' Makes the US Deficit Disappear," *Financial Times*, December 7.

International Economic Accounts, Bureau of Economic Analysis, US Department of Commerce (http://www.bea.gov/international/index.htm#bop)

International Monetary Fund, *Balance of Payments Yearbook*, Washington D.C.: IMF annual.

International Monetary Fund, *International Financial Statistics*, Washington D.C.: IMF monthly (http://ifs.apdi.net/imf).

International Monetary Fund, *Balance of Payments Manual*, Washington D.C. (http://www.imf.org/external/np/stat/bop/BOPman.pdf)

Krugman, P. (2006) "CSI: Trade Deficit," *New York Times*, April 24.

Office for National Statistics, *United Kingdom Balance of Payments – The Pink Book*, Annual. (http://www.statistics.gov.uk/StatBase/Product.asp?vlnk=1140)

APPENDIX

TABLE A12.1 U.S. International Transactions Accounts, 2006 and 2007 [millions of dollars]

		2006	2007/p/
	Current account		
1	**Exports of goods and services and income receipts**	**2096165**	**2410587**
2	Exports of goods and services	1445703	1628358
3	Goods, balance of payments basis	1023109	1149208
4	Services	422594	479150
5	Transfers under U.S. military agency sales contracts	17112	15706
6	Travel	85694	97097
7	Passenger fares	22187	25329
8	Other transportation	46297	51854
9	Royalties and license fees	62378	71345
10	Other private services	187771	216609
11	U.S. Government miscellaneous services	1155	1210
12	Income receipts	650462	782229
13	Income receipts on U.S.-owned assets abroad	647582	779267
14	Direct investment receipts	310224	352636
15	Other private receipts	334958	424433
16	U.S. Government receipts	2400	2198
17	Compensation of employees	2880	2962
18	**Imports of goods and services and income payments**	**–2818047**	**–3044786**
19	Imports of goods and services	–2204225	–2336873
20	Goods, balance of payments basis	–1861380	–1964577
21	Services	–342845	–372296
22	Direct defense expenditures	–31054	–32811
23	Travel	–72029	–76426
24	Passenger fares	–27503	–28574
25	Other transportation	–65282	–67094
26	Royalties and license fees	–26432	–27924
27	Other private services	–116524	–135285
28	U.S. Government miscellaneous services	–4021	–4182
29	Income payments	–613823	–707913
30	Income payments on foreign-owned assets in the U.S.	–604410	–698202
31	Direct investment payments	–136010	–129034
32	Other private payments	–334645	–411924
33	U.S. Government payments	–133755	–157244
34	Compensation of employees	–9412	–9711

		2006	2007/p/
35	**Unilateral current transfers, net**	**–89595**	**–104438**
36	U.S. Government grants	–27142	–32699
37	U.S. Government pensions and other transfers	–6508	–6835
38	Private remittances and other transfers	–55945	–64904
	Capital account		
39	Capital account transactions, net	–3913	–2317
	Financial account		
40	**U.S.-owned assets abroad (increase/financial outflow (–))**	**–1055176**	**–1206332**
41	U.S. official reserve assets	2374	–122
42	Gold	0	0
43	Special drawing rights	–223	–154
44	Reserve position in the International Monetary Fund	3331	1021
45	Foreign currencies	–734	–989
46	U.S. Government assets, other than official reserve assets	5346	–22931
47	U.S. credits and other long-term assets	–2992	–2441
48	Repayments on U.S. credits and other long-term assets	8329	3450
49	U.S. foreign currency holdings and U.S. short-term assets	9	–23940
50	U.S. private assets	–1062896	–1183278
51	Direct investment	–235358	–335415
52	Foreign securities	–289422	–273851
53	U.S. claims on unaffiliated foreigners reported by U.S. nonbanking concerns	–83531	15819
54	U.S. claims reported by U.S. banks, not included elsewhere	–454585	–589831
55	**Foreign-owned assets in the U.S. (increase/financial inflow (+))**	**1859597**	**1863697**
56	Foreign official assets in the United States	440264	412698
57	U.S. Government securities	380734	231852
58	U.S. Treasury securities	189181	49900
59	Other	191553	181952
60	Other U.S. Government liabilities	3133	5673
61	U.S. liabilities reported by U.S. banks, not included elsewhere	22040	108456
62	Other foreign official assets	34357	66717
63	Other foreign assets in the United States	1419333	1450999
64	Direct investment	180580	204414
65	U.S. Treasury securities	–35931	166301
66	U.S. securities other than U.S. Treasury securities	591951	391884
67	U.S. currency	12571	10937
68	U.S. liabilities to unaffiliated foreigners reported by U.S. nonbanking concerns	235769	166579

TABLE A12.1 continued

		2006	2007/p/
69	U.S. liabilities reported by U.S. banks, not included elsewhere	434393	510884
70	Financial derivatives, net	28762	n.a.
71	**Statistical discrepancy (sum of above items with sign reversed)**	**−17794**	**83590**
71a	Of which: Seasonal adjustment discrepancy	. . . . .	. . . . .
	Memoranda:		
72	Balance on goods (lines 3 and 20)	−838271	−815370
73	Balance on services (lines 4 and 21)	79749	106854
74	Balance on goods and services (lines 2 and 19)	−758522	−708515
75	Balance on income (lines 12 and 29)	36640	74316
76	Unilateral current transfers, net (line 35)	−89595	−104438
77	Balance on current account (lines 1, 18, and 35 or lines 74, 75, and 76)	−811477	−738638

Line (Credits +; debits −)

Source: U.S. Department of Commerce, Bureau of Economic Analysis, (http://www.bea.gov/bea/di/home/bop.htm)

TABLE A12.2 U.K. Balance of Payments, 2006

	£ million	
	Credits	Debits
1. Current account		
A. Goods and services	369 691	424 128
1. Goods	345 105	328 736
2. Services	124 586	95 392
2.1. Transportation	16 704	19 426
2.2. Travel	18 313	34 291
2.3. Communications	4 259	3 969
2.4. Construction	658	529
2.5. Insurance	3 525	960
2.6. Financial	28 420	5 845
2.7. Computer and Information	6 489	2 658

	Credits	£ million Debits
2.8. Royalties and Licence Fees	7 381	5 407
2.9. Other business	34 733	18 884
2.10. Personal, cultural and recreational	2 031	746
2.11. Government	2 073	2 677
B. Income	341 350	222 795
1. Compensation of employees	1 047	1 785
2. Investment income	240 303	221 010
2.1 Direct investment	90 502	47 377
2.2 Portfolio investment	54 479	57 013
2.3 Other investment (including earnings on reserve assets)	95 322	116 620
C. Current transfers	16 165	28 064
1. Central government	4 245	13 828
2. Other sectors	11 920	14 236
Total current account	627 206	674 987
2. Capital and financial accounts		
A. Capital account	3 818	2 988
1. Capital transfers	3 393	2 358
2. Acquisition disposal of non-produced, non-financial assets	425	630
B. Financial account	687 387	654 582
1. Direct investment	76 891	69 496
Abroad		69 496
1.1. Equity capital		16 047
1.2. Reinvested earnings		52 372
1.3. Other capital[1]		1 077
In United Kingdom	76 891	
1.1. Equity capital	56 000	
1.2. Reinvested earnings	23 073	
1.3. Other capital[2]	-2 182	
2. Portfolio Investment	155 631	199 118
Assets		199 118
2.1. Equity securities		19 718
2.2. Debt securities		179 400

TABLE A12.2 continued

	£ million	
	Credits	Debits
Liabilities	155 631	
2.1. Equity securities	–5 069	
2.2. Debt securities	160 700	
3. Financial derivatives (net)		–7 449
4. Other investment	454 865	393 843
Assets		393 843
4.1. Trade credit		36
4.2. Loans		117 376
4.3. Currency and deposits		276 513
4.4. Other assets		–82
Liabilities	454 865	
4.1. Trade credits	–	
4.2. Loans	121 012	
4.3. Currency and deposits	333 272	
4.4. Other liabilities	581	
5. Reserve assets		–426
5.1. Monetary gold		–4
5.2. Special drawing rights		51
5.3. Reserve position in the IMF		–225
5.4. Foreign exchange		62
Total capital and financial accounts	691 205	657 570
Total current, capital and financial accounts	1 318 411	1 332 557
Net errors and omissions	14 146	

1 Other capital transactions on direct investment abroad represent claims on affiliated enterprises less liabilities to affiliated enterprises
2 Other capital transactions on direct investment in the United Kingdom represent liabilities to direct investors less claims on direct investors

Source: http://www.statistics.gov.uk/StatBase/Product.asp?vlnk = 1140

TABLE A12.3 International Investment Position of U.S., Selected Years (in millions of dollars)

Line	Type of Investment	1976	1981	1986	1991	1996	2001	2006p
1	**Net international investment position of the United States (lines 2+3)**	**164,832**	**339,767**	**−36,209**	**−309,259**	**−495,055**	**−1,919,430**	**−2,539,629**
2	Financial derivatives, net (line 5 less line 25)							58,935
3	Net international investment position, excluding financial derivatives (line 6 less line 26)	164,832	339,767	−36,209	−309,259	−495,055	−1,919,430	−2,598,564
4	**U.S.-owned assets abroad (lines 5+6)**	**456,964**	**1,001,667**	**1,469,396**	**2,286,456**	**4,032,307**	**6,308,681**	**13,754,990**
5	Financial derivatives, gross positive fair value							1,237,564
6	U.S.-owned assets abroad, excluding financial derivatives (lines 7+12+17)	456,964	1,001,667	1,469,396	2,286,456	4,032,307	6,308,681	12,517,426
7	U.S. official reserve assets	44,094	124,568	139,875	159,223	160,739	129,961	219,853
8	Gold	36,944	105,644	102,428	92,561	96,698	72,328	165,267
9	Special drawing rights	2,395	4,096	8,395	11,240	10,312	10,783	8,870
10	Reserve position in the International Monetary Fund	4,434	5,054	11,730	9,488	15,435	17,869	5,040
11	Foreign currencies	321	9,774	17,322	45,934	38,294	28,981	40,676
12	U.S. Government assets, other than official reserve assets	44,978	70,893	91,850	81,422	86,123	85,654	72,189
13	U.S. credits and other long-term assets	44,124	69,320	90,923	79,776	83,999	83,132	71,635

TABLE A12.3 continued

14	Repayable in dollars	41,309	66,591	89,271	78,814	83,606	82,854	71,362
15	Other	2,815	2,729	1,652	962	393	278	273
16	U.S. foreign currency holdings and U.S. short-term assets	854	1,573	927	1,646	2,124	2,522	554
17	U.S. private assets	367,892	806,206	1,237,671	2,045,811	3,785,445	6,093,066	12,225,384
18	Direct investment at current cost	222,283	407,804	404,818	643,364	989,810	1,693,131	2,855,619
19	Foreign securities	44,157	62,142	158,123	455,750	1,487,546	2,169,735	5,432,264
20	Bonds	34,704	45,675	85,724	176,774	481,411	557,062	1,180,758
21	Corporate stocks	9,453	16,467	72,399	278,976	1,006,135	1,612,673	4,251,506
22	U.S. claims on unafflicted foreigners reported by U.S. non banking concerns	20,317	42,752	167,392	256,295	450,578	839,303	848,464
23	U.S. claims reported by U.S. banks, not included elsewhere	81,135	293,508	507,338	690,402	857,511	1,390,897	3,089,037
24	**Foreign-owned assets in the United States (lines 25+26)**	**292,132**	**661,900**	**1,505,605**	**2,595,715**	**4,527,362**	**8,228,111**	**16,294,619**
25	Financial derivatives, gross negative fair value						1,178,629	
26	Foreign-owned assets in the United States, excluding financial derivatives (lines 27+34)	292,132	661,900	1,505,605	2,595,715	4,527,362	8,228,111	15,115,990
27	Foreign official assets in the United States	104,445	180,425	241,226	398,538	820,823	1,109,072	2,770,165
28	U.S. Government securities	72,572	125,130	178,916	311,199	631,088	847,005	2,104,696
29	U.S. Treasury securities	70,555	117,004	173,310	305,994	606,427	720,149	1,520,768

TABLE A12.3 continued

30	Other	2,017	8,126	5,606	5,205	24,661	126,856	583,928
31	Other U.S. Government liabilities	8,860	13,029	17,993	18,610	22,592	17,007	18,999
32	U.S. liabilities reported by U.S. banks, not included elsewhere	17,231	26,737	27,920	38,396	113,098	134,655	296,687
33	Other foreign official assets	5,782	15,529	16,397	30,333	54,045	110,405	349,783
34	Other foreign assets	187,687	481,475	1,264,379	2,197,177	3,706,539	7,119,039	12,345,825
35	Direct investment at current cost	47,528	164,623	284,701	533,404	745,619	1,518,473	2,099,426
36	U.S. Treasury securities	7,028	18,505	96,078	170,295	433,903	375,059	594,243
37	U.S. securities other than U.S. Treasury securities	54,913	75,085	309,803	546,008	1,165,113	2,821,372	5,228,536
38	Corporate and other bonds	11,964	10,694	140,863	274,136	539,308	1,343,071	2,689,816
39	Corporate stocks	42,949	64,391	168,940	271,872	625,805	1,478,301	2,538,720
40	U.S. currency	11,792	27,295	50,122	101,317	186,846	279,755	364,277
41	U.S. liabilities to unaffiliated foreigners reported by U.S. nonbanking concerns	12,961	30,606	90,703	208,908	346,810	798,314	740,365
42	U.S. liabilities reported by U.S. banks, not included elsewhere	53,465	165,361	432,972	637,245	828,248	1,326,066	3,318,978
Memoranda:								
43	Direct investment abroad at market value			530,074	827,537	1,608,340	2,314,934	4,377,830
44	Direct investment in the United States at market value			272,966	669,137	1,229,118	2,560,294	3,222,479

p Preliminary.
r Revised.

Source: adapted from U.S. Department of Commerce, Bureau of Economic Analysis, International Investment Position of the U.S. – www.bea.gov/bea/international/bp_web/

Chapter 13

Fundamentals of Exchange Rate Systems

LEARNING OBJECTIVES

By the end of this chapter you should be able to understand:

- that the mechanism of supply and demand for foreign currency works the same way as supply and demand for any other commodity

- the difference between flexible and fixed exchange rates, i.e. the difference between a free market for foreign exchange and a regulated market

- that a fixed exchange rate does not happen naturally and requires continuous attention on the part of countries' central banks

- how the exchange rate regime, directly or indirectly, affects the domestic economy

- the specific circumstances under which changes in the price of foreign currency may improve or worsen the balance of trade

- why foreign trade may adjust sluggishly to changes in the exchange rate

The basic tenet of Chapter 12 rests on the idea that the BoP is a double-entry accounting device so it will always balance, i.e. BoP = 0 at all time. But we also hear about "imbalances" in the balance of payments, and this chapter clarifies what such imbalances may be. For instance, we hear about chronic trade deficits and there seems to be a popular notion that such deficits cannot be sustained indefinitely. These imbalances refer directly to subcomponents of the BoP – imbalances related to trade, to capital flows, and to central bank interventions.

Our discussion now switches from describing the BoP as an accounting device, to studying the economic forces underlying and affecting the various subcomponents of the BoP: some BoP components may be causing imbalances, others can be triggering an adjustment. Formally, from now on, we are switching from the "ex post" approach in Chapter 12 (where we simply reconciled transactions that had taken place in a balance sheet) to an "ex ante" approach where we are looking for relations between the BoP components that allow us to predict how they behave together.[1] Our goal now is to formulate models or frameworks that help us understand the effects of such imbalances. The BoP happens to be a remarkable instrument that highlights all imbalances at once; it helps us study the effect of each component on the economy.

In this chapter, we focus on the exchange rate. Chapter 12 introduced a number of different exchange rate concepts, from the nominal exchange rate to the real effective exchange rate. Here we focus on the *nominal bilateral exchange rate, E*. First, we develop an economic model to show how the exchange rate is determined. Second, we explain the various adjustment mechanisms that determine the level of the exchange rate. We can then observe how the exchange rate tends to alleviate imbalance in BoP subcomponents. It is crucial to note that the specific way the exchange rate can influence the adjustment mechanism depends on a country's specific exchange rate regime.

Basic Foreign Exchange Regimes

There are two polar arrangements when it comes to exchange rate regimes, one is called a **flexible** (or floating) **exchange rate** regime, and the other is a **fixed** (or pegged) **exchange rate** regime. A flexible arrangement implies a purely laissez–faire environment where market forces alone determine the exchange rate. There exists no official intervention whatsoever to influence the value of the exchange rate. At the other end of the spectrum is the fixed exchange rate regime, implying that the central bank constantly intervenes to keep the price of foreign currency always constant. The strongest form of a fixed exchange rate is a **currency board**. Under a currency board, a country actually passes a law stipulating a fixed exchange rate between the domestic currency and a specific foreign currency. In addition, the law forces the central bank to print domestic currency only if it can back it with **foreign exchange reserves**.

There are many variants on the fixed or flexible regimes that represent hybrids of the two. A frequently used hybrid is called a **managed float** (or **dirty float**) **exchange rate** regime. Under a managed float, the currency is allowed to float freely up to a certain extent. If a country finds that its currency is appreciating or depreciating excessively, the central bank intervenes to stabilize the

---

1 *Ex post* and *ex ante* are Latin terms used by economists meaning respectively "after the fact" and "beforehand."

currency. This exchange rate regime has the advantage that the exchange rate is largely determined by market forces, but at the same time everyone is assured that there will not be any wild swings in the exchange rate.

A compromise between fixed and flexible exchange rate regimes is called a **currency band** exchange rate system. The currency band takes the guess work out of a managed float, as it implies that the central bank announces how much it will allow the exchange rate to fluctuate before it intervenes. The most prominent example of the currency band is the exchange rate of the Chinese renminbi (also named the Chinese yuan) pegged at about 8.11 renminbi per U.S. dollar; the Chinese central bank allows fluctuations, or "band" above and below that price of ±0.5 percent. When the price of the currency hits the upper or lower band, the central bank intervenes to insure the price lies within the bands. How flexible or how fixed the exchange rate is depends on the width of the bands. For instance in the nineties, after weathering various currency crises with their pegged system, a number of European countries widened their band to ±15.0 percent making it closer to a floating regime.[2]

If we classify the various regimes on a scale from fully flexible to fully fixed, managed or dirty floats are slightly altered forms of floating exchange rates. On the other hand the next two regimes, the **crawling peg** and the **joint float**, are closer to fixed exchange rate regimes; but they involve some flexibility in terms of being able to change the peg or in terms of the number of countries involved. A crawling peg is a fixed exchange rate regime where the central bank changes the peg frequently to respond to changes in the real exchange rate. The joint float corresponds to a system where a group of currencies are tied together through a fixed exchange rate system, but float freely against currencies from other countries.

Exchange Rate Regime – Scale from Fixed to Flexible

FIXED (pegged)/currency board ⇒ crawling peg ⇔ joint float

⇒ managed float (dirty float) ⇒ FLEXIBLE (floating)

Depending on the width of the band, a currency band regime could lie anywhere in this spectrum.

There also exist countries that do not have an exchange rate. This is simply because the country's monetary authority has given up its control over domestic monetary policy by adopting another country's currency. For example, a number of countries have dollarized their economies by simply adopting the U.S. dollar as legal tender. The IMF keeps a record of all the various arrangements followed by its members (see Table 13.1).

The simple description of some of the most common exchange rate regimes foretells that the prices of foreign currencies are likely to behave very differently depending on the type of regime a country

---

2 These developments are described in Chapter 22 on European Monetary Integration.

TABLE 13.1 De Facto Exchange Rate Arrangements, 2006

Exchange rate regime (number of countries)	Exchange rate anchor		
Exchange regimes with no separate legal tender[1] (44)[2]	Another currency as legal tender (9)	ECCU (6)[3]	Franc Zone (14)
	Ecuador, El Salvador,[4] Kiribati, Marshall Islands, Micronesia, Fed. States of Palau, Panama, San Marino, Dem. Rep. of Timor-Leste	Antigua and Barbuda, Dominica, Grenada, St. Kitts and Nevis, St. Lucia, St. Vincent and the Grenadines	Benin, Burkina Faso, Côte d'Ivoire, Guinea-Bissau, Mali, Niger, Senegal, Togo, Cameroon Central African Rep., Chad, Congo, Rep. of Equatorial Guinea Gabon
Currency board (7)	Bosnia and Herzegovina, Brunei Darussalam, Bulgaria, Hong Kong, Djibouti, Estonia,[5] Lithuania[5]		
Other conventional fixed peg arrangements (51)	*Against a single currency (47):* Aruba, Bahamas,[9] Bahrain, Barbados, Belarus,[7] Belize, Bhutan, Bolivia,[7, 10] Cape Verde, Comoros,[11] Egypt,[7] Eritrea, Ethiopia,[7] Guyana,[7, 8] Honduras,[7] Iraq,[7] Jordan,[7] Kuwait, Latvia,[5] Lebanon,[7] Lesotho, Macedonia, FYR,[7] Maldives, Malta,[5] Mauritania,[7] Namibia, Nepal, Netherlands Antilles, Oman, Pakistan,[7] Qatar, Rwanda, Saudi Arabia, Seychelles,[7] Sierra Leone,[7] Solomon Islands,[7] Suriname,[7, 9] Swaziland, Syrian Arab Rep.,[9] Trinidad and Tobago,[7] Turkmenistan,[7] Ukraine,[7] United Arab Emirates, Venezuela, Vietnam,[7] Zimbabwe[9] *Against a composite (basket of) currencies (5),* Fiji, Libyan Arab Jamahiriya, Morocco, Samoa, Vanuatu		
Currency bands (7)[12]	*Within a cooperative arrangement (4)* China, Cyprus,[5] Denmark,[5] Slovak Rep.,[5] Slovenia[5] *Other band arrangements (2)* Hungary, Tonga		
Crawling pegs (5)	Azerbaijan,[7] Botswana,[9] Costa Rica, Iran,[7, 13] Nicaragua		
Managed floating with no pre-determined path for the exchange rate (51)	Argentina, Bangladesh, Cambodia, Gambia,[7] Ghana,[7] Haiti,[7] Jamaica,[7] Lao P.D.R.,[9] Madagascar,[7] Malawi, Mauritius, Moldova, Mongolia, Sri Lanka,[7] Sudan, Tajikistan, Tunisia, Uruguay, Rep of Yemen,[7] Zambia, Colombia, Czech Rep., Guatemala,[7] Peru, Romania, Serbia,[14] Thailand, Afghanistan, Armenia,[7] Georgia, Kenya, Kyrgyz		

TABLE 13.1 continued

	Rep., Mozambique,[7] Algeria , Angola, Burundi, Croatia, Dominican Rep., Guinea,[7] India, Kazakhstan, Liberia,[7] Malaysia, Myanmar, Nigeria,[7] Papua, New Guinea,[7] Paraguay, Russian Federation, São Tomé and Príncipe, Singapore, Uzbekistan
Independently floating (25)	Albania, Congo, Indonesia, Uganda, Australia, Brazil, Canada, Chile, Iceland, Israel, Korea, Mexico, New Zealand, Norway, Philippines, Poland, South Africa, Sweden, Turkey, United Kingdom, Tanzania,[7] Japan, Somalia,[9, 15] Switzerland, United States

Source: adapted from IMF (http://www.imf.org/external/np/mfd/er/2006/eng/0706.htm).

1 The sole legal tender is another country's currency, or the countries are members of a currency union with one common legal tender.
2 The 15 countries forming the European Economic and Monetary Union belong in this category. Their common legal tender is the euro. They are Austria, Belgium, Cyprus, Finland, France, Germany, Greece, Ireland, Italy, Luxembourg, Malta, Netherlands, Portugal, Slovenia, Spain.
3 The Eastern Caribbean Currency Union has a currency board arrangement.
4 The printing of new colónes, the domestic currency, is prohibited, but the existing stock of colónes will continue to circulate along with the U.S. dollar as legal tender until all colón notes wear out physically.
5 The member participates in the ERM II.
7 The regime operating de facto in the country is different from its *de jure* regime.
8 There is no evidence of direct intervention by the authorities in the foreign exchange market.
9 The member maintains an exchange arrangement involving more than one foreign exchange market. The arrangement shown is that maintained in the major market.
10 This is a de facto classification. The Bolivian authorities consider their regime as a crawling peg and have not committed to the current level of the exchange rate.
11 Comoros has the same arrangement with the French Treasury as the CFA franc zone countries.
12 The bands for these countries are as follows: Cyprus ±15%, Denmark ±2.25%, Hungary ±15%, Slovak Republic ±15%, Slovenia (undisclosed), and Tonga ±5%, China ±0.5%.
13 The rial crawls vis-à-vis an unannounced basket of currencies.
14 While the current monetary framework is anchored by the announcement of core inflation objectives, the National Bank of Serbia is preparing the transition to full-fledged inflation targeting.
15 Insufficient information on the country is available to confirm this classification, and so the classification of the last official consultation is used.

adopts. Clearly this must have important repercussions on the domestic economy. The study of these repercussions is at the heart of international macroeconomics. For simplicity, we will focus on the two polar cases, flexible exchange rate and fixed exchange rate.

FLEXIBLE EXCHANGE RATES: ADJUSTMENT THROUGH MARKET FORCES

In the absence of government or central bank controlling the market, the only factors influencing the price of the foreign currency are the supply and the demand, just like in the market for milk. We can easily depict this situation graphically (Figure 13.1).

Just as supply of and demand for milk jointly determine the price of milk in the milk market, supply of and demand for the British pound determine the exchange rate between the dollar and the pound in the U.S. foreign exchange market. In Figure 13.1 (right panel), the price of foreign currency is on the vertical axis (a.k.a. exchange rate = how many dollars we need to pay to purchase one British pound) and the quantity of pounds or foreign exchange traded is on the horizontal axis. Notice that this graph is absolutely identical to our basic supply/demand graph corresponding to any other market, for instance milk (left panel). The only difference is that the labels on the axes are different.

While the supply of milk comes from cows on the pasture and the demand for milk comes (among many others) from millions of latte-drinking Starbucks customers, the sources of the supply of and demand for foreign currency can be found by looking at the various categories of the BoP. After all, the BoP is the statistical account of all transactions with the rest of the world, so it records, for example, all transactions that require foreign currency on the part of domestic citizens. In the next section, we highlight the sources of the demand for and the supply of foreign exchange.

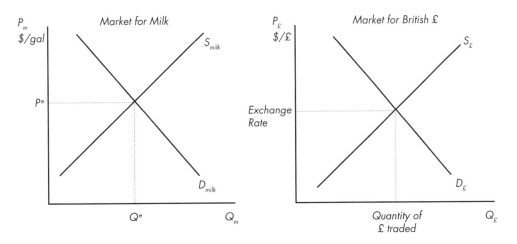

FIGURE 13.1 The Milk Market and the Foreign Exchange Market

Both the market for milk and the market for British £ (the foreign exchange market) have an upward-sloping supply curve and a downward-sloping demand curve. The intersection of these two curves determines simultaneously the equilibrium price and the quantity traded. In the foreign exchange market, the equilibrium price of foreign exchange, in this case the £, is no other than the exchange rate between the $ and the £ or the number of $ needed to buy one £.

The Demand for Foreign Exchange

To understand the nature and mechanism of the demand for foreign exchange, we need to identify the economic agents who require foreign exchange. To do so, we only have to scrutinize the BoP, since it captures all the transactions where foreign exchange is needed for payments.[3] Within the BoP, we focus on the debit accounts: imports of goods and services, income payments, and purchases of foreign assets (FDI or portfolio investment). The demand for foreign exchange thus originates with importers, interest arbitrageurs, and investors, whose primary demand is for foreign goods and services or for foreign bonds and stocks. However to acquire these foreign goods/assets, they first need to acquire foreign currency. So the demand for foreign exchange is a *derived demand* as it results from the demand for foreign goods and services and foreign bonds and stocks.

In any functioning market, as the price of a good falls, the quantity demanded rises. The mechanism is slightly more complicated with a derived demand. For an importer who has to pay in terms of foreign currency, the price of a foreign good is equal to the price quoted in foreign currency multiplied by the exchange rate in order to convert this price into the domestic currency. As the price of a foreign currency (exchange rate) falls, foreign goods quoted in domestic currency become relatively cheaper; this raises the demand for foreign goods, resulting in an increase in the demand for foreign currency (to purchase these goods).

We can illustrate this process with a specific example. If the price of the Japanese currency (the yen) falls from 0.008 dollar per yen to 0.007 dollar per yen, it will be cheaper for an American consumer to purchase a Japanese computer priced 100,000 yens as he will only need 100,000*0.007 or 700 dollars to buy the necessary yens instead of 100,000*0.008 or 800 dollars. The price of the Japanese computer converted into dollars drops from $800 to $700: this will trigger an increase in the demand for Japanese computers. The rush to buy Japanese computers and other Japanese products will drive upwards the quantity of yens demanded by American consumers. A fall in the exchange rate $/yen (more precisely an appreciation of the dollar) results in an increase in the demand for foreign currency (the yen). The demand curve for foreign currency and the demand curve for milk are both downward-sloping for the same basic reasons.

The demand for milk depends on more than just the price of milk: among other things, it also depends on the level of income, the taste of potential consumers, and the price of the substitutes or complements. Similarly, the foreign exchange market is subject to changes in these variables, resulting in a shift of the demand curve, as opposed to changes in the price resulting in a movement along the curve. For instance, if the American consumers become conscious that gas-guzzling American SUVs are bad for the environment, they may decide to buy more Japanese hybrids instead. As the demand for Japanese cars increases (their demand curve shifts out), the demand for yen also increases proportionately at each exchange rate. In sum, given any exchange rate, the quantity of foreign goods demanded and consequently the demand for foreign currency will be higher than before. Thus, the demand curve shifts outwards from D to D' (Figure 13.2).

---

3 Payments can take place either in the foreign or domestic currency.

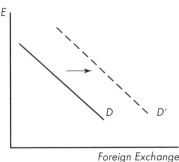

FIGURE 13.2 An Increase in Demand for Foreign Exchange

In the example above, *D* is the downward-sloping demand for yen, *E* on the vertical axis corresponds to the exchange rate, or the number of dollars per yen, and foreign exchange on the horizontal axis is the quantity of yen traded. A switch in U.S. demand from American SUVs to Japanese hybrids results in a rightward shift of the demand curve for yen from *D* to *D'*.

The Supply of Foreign Exchange

In a similar fashion, we can trace the determinants of the supply of foreign currency to the BoP: all the credit accounts such as exports of goods and services, income receipts, sales of assets to the foreigners, for example, generate foreign currency receipts in the domestic economy.[4] To generate these credits, however, foreigners must wish to trade with the domestic economy. So the root of the supply of foreign exchange in the domestic economy is the foreigners' demand for domestic goods and services or domestic assets.

What is the relation between the exchange rate and the quantity of foreign exchange supplied? Indeed, the foreign demand for domestic goods is going to be affected by the exchange rate. A depreciation of the domestic currency (an increase in the exchange rate) renders domestic goods cheaper to the foreigners, so their demand for domestic goods increases (assume for now that foreign demand is elastic; we will discuss other cases later). In this case, the quantity of foreign currency supplied also increases.

We have used an example to construct the demand for yen, so now we need an illustration for the supply of yen to complete the market for yens. The Japanese are quite fond of acquiring Apple iPods. The U.S. list price is $250. When the exchange rate is $0.008 per yen, this translates into 250/0.008 or 31,250 yen per iPod. When the dollar depreciates to $0.0081 per yen, the price in Japan drops to 250/0.0081 or 30,864 yen per iPod. The drop in the yen price of iPods will clearly result in an increase in the quantity of iPods demanded by Japanese consumers. We must now assume that the Japanese demand for iPods is elastic.[5] This would imply that the percentage increase

---

4 We assume again that payments to the domestic economy are denominated in foreign currency.

5 If this condition does not hold, the resulting demand for the dollar would drop rather than increase, leading to a backward-bending supply curve. This issue will be discussed later in the chapter under the heading Marshall–Lerner conditions.

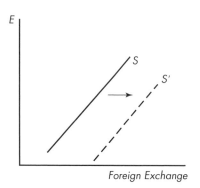

FIGURE 13.3 An Increase in Supply of Foreign Exchange

In the example above, S is the upward-sloping supply of yen, E on the vertical axis corresponds to the exchange rate, or the number of dollars per yen, and foreign exchange on the horizontal axis is the quantity of yen traded. A tax break in Japan would allow Japanese to buy more iPods. To do so they would need more dollars than they acquire by selling yen. So the supply of yen increases – a shift from S to S'.

in the quantity demanded is greater than the percentage drop in price. In this case, there will be an increase in the Japanese demand for dollars, or equivalently, an increase in the supply of yen to U.S. exporters. In sum, a depreciation of the dollar results in an increase in the quantity of yen supplied, and therefore the yen supply curve, S, is upward sloping in Figure 13.3 (assuming an elastic foreign demand).

Finally, again just like the supply of milk, the supply of foreign exchange depends on other economic factors beside the exchange rate. A change in any of these factors results in a shift of the supply curve. Specifically, these factors are: change in foreign income, change in foreign taste, change in the price of substitutes or complements in the foreign country.

A tangible real world example highlights how these factors affect the supply of foreign currency. Let us take the example of the U.S. government, which has complained bitterly in the last decade that the Japanese save too much (or spend too little). What would happen if the Japanese government decided to institute tax breaks for its citizens to increase consumption demand. With higher after tax income, the Japanese can buy more American products. If the Japanese demand for American products increases, their demand for dollars, or equivalently the supply of yen to the U.S., also increases. This shifts the supply curve in Figure 13.3 to the right from S to S'.

Equilibrium in the Foreign Exchange Market

In the foreign exchange market, just as in any other commodity market, the interaction between supply and demand determines the price. That price happens to be called the exchange rate in the foreign exchange market. Allowing the price to equilibrate quantity supplied and quantity demanded assumes no government interference whatsoever in the foreign exchange market, i.e. the existence of a fully *flexible exchange rate* regime. This market equilibrium is illustrated in Figure 13.4 where the

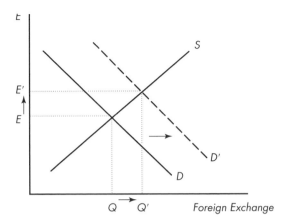

FIGURE 13.4 Foreign Exchange Market Equilibrium

Just as in Figure 13.1, the intersection of the supply and the demand determines simultaneously E, the equilibrium exchange rate (the number of $ per yen in the example), and Q, the corresponding quantity of yen traded on the foreign exchange market. An increase in the U.S. demand for Japanese Prius hybrids (due to an increase in the price of oil) causes an increase in the U.S. demand for Japanese yen and D shifts out to D'. This results in an increase in the price of yen in terms of dollars (an appreciation of the yen or equivalently a depreciation of the dollar) and an increase in the quantity of yen traded on the foreign exchange market.

initial supply, S, and demand, D, determine simultaneously the equilibrium price of the foreign currency E and the quantity traded Q.

A sudden jump in U.S. demand for foreign goods, say for Japanese Prius as oil prices rise, would increase the demand for foreign currency. This shifts the demand curve in Figure 13.4 from D to D', leading to a new equilibrium exchange rate E'. Under flexible exchange rates, the increase in demand for foreign goods thus leads to a depreciation of the domestic currency and an increase in the quantity traded Q to Q'.

Similarly, an increase in the foreign demand for domestic products shifts the supply of foreign currency to the right causing an appreciation of the dollar. In sum, under *flexible exchange rates*, the market determines the exchange rate and nothing inhibits it from adjusting to equilibrate foreign currency demand with supply.

FIXED EXCHANGE RATES: ADJUSTMENT THROUGH CENTRAL BANK INTERVENTION

In contrast with the situation where the market determines the exchange rate, a country could fix the price of foreign currency at some arbitrary level. In a fixed exchange rate regime, a central bank announces that it will keep the exchange rate constant for an indefinite period of time. Throughout the book, we will discuss the merits of such a policy that seems like heavy-handed meddling in the currency market on the part of the central bank. The operations carried out by the central bank to uphold a fixed exchange rate are called **intervention**.[6]

Why do we care whether the central bank intervenes in the foreign exchange market? It turns out that it makes a big difference whether domestic residents can always count on a constant price of foreign exchange or not. International trade is hampered when the exchange rate fluctuates dramatically; changes in the exchange rate may well wipe out importers' and exporters' profits overnight. Of course, exchange rates are not held fixed by central banks by simply waving a wand and declaring them so. Indeed, holding the exchange rate constant at every point in time requires assiduous diligence on the part of the central bank: it must constantly intervene in the currency market to ensure that the exchange rate never changes. Let us have a closer look at the mechanics of this intervention.

Every time there is excess demand for (supply of) foreign currency in the market, the central bank must intervene by selling (buying) foreign currency to keep its price steady. Figure 13.5 shows an increased demand for foreign currency as the demand curve shifts from D to D', perhaps because domestic residents have all of a sudden decided to shift their preferences towards imports. With a flexible exchange rate regime, this would increase the price of the foreign currency E, causing a depreciation of the domestic currency. In order for the central bank to keep its promise of a constant

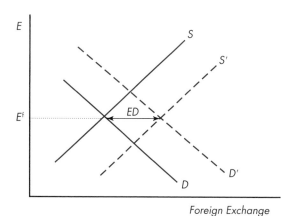

Foreign Exchange

FIGURE 13.5 An Increase in Demand for Foreign Currency and the Required Central Bank Intervention to Maintain a Fixed Exchange Rate

With flexible exchange rates, an increase in the demand for foreign exchange from D to D' would result in a depreciation of the dollar (or equivalently an appreciation of the foreign currency). However, with fixed exchange rates, this is not permissible. The central bank must intervene by providing any amount of foreign exchange needed to prevent the dollar from depreciating (or equivalently to prevent the foreign currency from appreciating). The central bank adds to the market supply S its own supply of foreign exchange until the new total supply S' intersects with the new demand D' at the fixed exchange rate E^f. The exact amount that the central bank has to supply is equal to ED, the excess demand for foreign exchange at exchange rate E^f.

---

6 A more general definition would designate as intervention any central bank operation on the foreign exchange market meant to affect the exchange rate (cf. managed floating).

exchange rate and stop the depreciation from happening, it must now intervene in the market by supplying foreign currency at the fixed, agreed upon exchange rate. However at the fixed exchange rate E^f, there is an excess demand for the foreign currency measured by the line segment ED in Figure 13.5.

The central bank must supply the quantity of foreign exchange equal to ED at the fixed exchange rate. This is illustrated by a shift of the supply curve from S to S'. The new supply curve S' corresponds to the central bank's supply added to the original supply S. The intervention is illustrated in Figure 13.5 as the shift from S to S' as the central bank intervenes so that the new supply and demand curves intersect at the original equilibrium price E^f. Applying this to our previous example, the increase in the U.S. demand for Prius hybrids puts pressures on the dollar to depreciate; if the dollar and the yen are on a fixed exchange rate regime, the Federal Reserve cannot allow this to happen and must sell yen on the foreign exchange market at the fixed exchange rate to support the dollar (and weaken the yen).

The two different adjustment mechanisms under flexible and under fixed exchange rates can be summarized and compared on a single graph. Figure 13.6 illustrates these differences in adjustments. In both cases, we start with an increase in the demand for foreign exchange (resulting from an increase in the demand for foreign goods). Under a fixed exchange rate regime, the pressure of the domestic currency to depreciate requires the central bank to intervene in the foreign currency market to keep the price of foreign currency fixed. Under flexible exchange rates, any pressure on the exchange rate is reflected in the change in the price of the foreign currency as the market equates demand and supply for foreign currency. This adjustment then represents either an appreciation or in the case of Figure 13.6, a depreciation.

When exchange rates are flexible, the adjustment occurs via a change in the price of the foreign currency from E_0 to E_1. In contrast, under fixed exchange rates the adjustment is generated by a

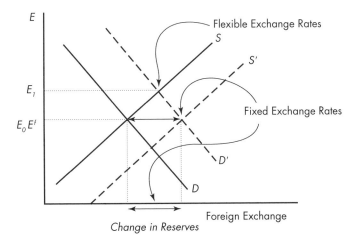

FIGURE 13.6 Fixed Versus Flexible Exchange Rates

With fixed exchange rates, the central bank, through intervention, adds its own supply to the market supply to prevent the domestic currency from depreciating. With flexible exchange rates, the free forces of the market are allowed to work: the price of the foreign currency is allowed to rise to clear the market, i.e. the domestic currency is allowed to depreciate.

carefully timed change in the supply of foreign currency on the part of the central bank. Note that the central bank must hold sufficient foreign currency reserves to satisfy the excess demand for foreign exchange at the fixed exchange rate E^f. Any increase in demand is thus reflected by an equivalent reduction in the central bank's foreign currency reserves. The intervention of the central bank under fixed exchange rates has important implications for the domestic economy. We will investigate these repercussions in the next section.

Intervention and the Central Bank

The foreign currency that the central bank injects into the market does not appear out of nowhere. To insure that it can always meet excess demand in the market, the central bank must keep a stash of foreign currency reserves, or **reserves** for short. If the central bank does not possess sufficient reserves to satisfy the excess demand for foreign currency, it will not be able to keep its promise to hold the exchange rate constant. If the central bank runs out of foreign currency, the fixed exchange rate regime will collapse, freeing the exchange rate to float to its market-determined level.

A recent case in point is Argentina: throughout much of the 1990s Argentina maintained a fixed one-for-one exchange rate between the Argentinian peso and the U.S. dollar, despite a relentlessly increasing domestic demand for dollars and a reduction in the supply of foreign currency. Finally, in 2001, Argentinean foreign currency reserves were depleted, and the central bank could no longer prop up the exchange rate. As a result the central bank had no choice but to abandon the fixed exchange rate regime and devalue the peso.

Devaluation and Revaluation under Fixed Exchange Rates

With flexible exchange rates, we used the terms depreciation and appreciation to identify changes in the price of foreign currency. The terms **devaluation** and depreciation both refer to a weakening of the currency, but in the first case it happens as a result of a policy change while in the second case, it happens automatically through the forces of the markets. The same distinction applies to **revaluation** versus appreciation.

If the fixed exchange rate is set too low (making the purchase of foreign currency cheap), the currency becomes artificially strong. While, at times, politicians (who may not have taken an international macroeconomics class) seem to value strong currencies, such an overvalued domestic currency implies the country is sure to suffer from chronic balance-of-trade deficits. This is because the overvalued exchange rate discourages foreigners from buying the country's goods while imports seem artificially cheap to domestic residents. Since the country cannot lose its foreign reserves indefinitely through intervention, the only solution is to redefine the peg at a more realistic level, i.e. at a level where its current account is balanced. Such a one-time change in the price of foreign currency is called a devaluation.

> The opposite situation can, of course, also occur. If a country experiences chronic surpluses because its peg is too weak, it might decide on *revaluing* its currency. Germany, for example, revalued the Deutsche Mark relative to the dollar several times in the 1960s.

We must point out that intervention is not always a lone affair where one central bank buys or sells foreign currency to weaken or strengthen its exchange rate. There have been many instances where two or more countries agreed on coordinated exchange rate interventions. For example, when the dollar became too strong in the mid 1980s, the central banks of each of the G-5 countries carried out concerted interventions, agreed upon in the Plaza Accord in 1985, to remedy the problem (by selling/weakening the dollar). A few years later, as a result of an unexpected weakening of the dollar, the same group of countries decided to rescue the dollar with concerted interventions known as the Louvre Accord of 1987 (these will be discussed in greater details in Chapter 21).

An alternative approach to examining the effects of central bank interventions is to focus on the central bank's balance sheet. Central bank assets can be broken down into **domestic credit** (DC) and **foreign currency reserves** (RES). Domestic credit consists in the central bank's claims against its own citizens and government, for example the government bonds that the central bank purchased last year. Foreign reserves are holdings of foreign currency and foreign government bonds[7] by the central bank. Reserves are expressed in units of domestic currency, which means that RES are multiplied by the exchange rate to obtain their domestic currency value. The liabilities of the central bank correspond to the currency in circulation (CU) and the reserves of the commercial banks (CBRE). The sum of these two forms of liabilities is the **monetary base** (MB), also called high-powered money. A summary representation of the central bank balance sheet highlighting the relevant accounts is presented in Figure 13.7.

Assets	Liabilities	
Domestic Crecit (*DC*)	Currency (*CU*)	
Foreign Reserves (*RES*) ($\Downarrow$)	Commercial Banks Reserves (*CBRE*)	*MB* ($\Downarrow$)

FIGURE 13.7 Central Bank Balance Sheet and Intervention

This is a summary of the central bank balance sheet, mainly focusing on the accounts involved in the intervention mechanisms. The arrows illustrate the fact that intervention to support the domestic currency reduces the foreign reserves (*RES*); consequently the monetary base (*MB*) is also reduced by exactly the same amount. When the central bank sells foreign exchange to the public, it receives domestic currency as payment and its liabilities (*MB*) are reduced.

---

7 The account also includes gold and SDR (Special Drawing Rights, an IMF basket of currencies).

When the central bank provides foreign currency to importers, its foreign reserves assets decrease and the monetary base (the central bank's liabilities) drops as the public pays the central bank with domestic currency or commercial bank checks (a decrease in the central bank liabilities). This illustrates the formal process of a central bank intervention.

Since commercial banks create money in the economy, the money supply (MS) is a multiple of the monetary base: this multiple is called the *money multiplier*, μ. Since the sum over all assets must be identical to the sum over all liabilities, we can state that the money supply is equal to the sum of domestic credit and foreign reserves multiplied by μ.

$$M^S = \mu(DC + RES) \tag{13.1}$$

The central bank balance sheet highlights a basic tenet of fixed exchange rate regimes. In the absence of further central bank action, the domestic money supply, often considered as a purely internal economic variable, and the amount of foreign reserves, a variable intrinsically affected by external factors, are automatically linked in fixed exchange rate regimes.

Central bank intervention to stabilize the price of foreign exchange sparks off an immediate macroeconomic side effect. In the case of excess demand for foreign currency, the central bank supplies the foreign currency and, in exchange, the buyers of foreign exchange deliver U.S. dollars to the central bank. In the process of providing the extra foreign exchange, the central bank therefore *reduces* the amount of U.S. dollars in circulation. An equivalent problem may appear in the case of excess supply of foreign currency. In the process of soaking out the extra foreign exchange from the hands of the public, the central bank builds up its reserves *increasing* the amount of U.S. dollars in circulation. As a result, central bank interventions aimed at stabilizing the price of the foreign currency have the side effect of also altering the size of the domestic money supply.

Intermediate macroeconomics clearly outline that any change in the money supply leads to a change in domestic interest rates thus affecting capital investment activity. Therefore the simple act of supporting the price of domestic currency affects the domestic economy both ways. If the domestic currency is too weak (excess demand for foreign currency), the reduction in the money supply could raise the interest rate and reduce the level of investment. If the domestic currency is too strong (excess supply of foreign currency), it could trigger inflationary pressures. Interventions that deplete the reserves could easily induce a capital investment slump and even lead to recession! Alternatively, if the economy happens to be at full-employment, it could get overheated. Here then is a further example of the drastic impact foreign transactions have on the domestic economy. In the next section, we examine the options available to central banks to circumvent the negative impact of foreign exchange intervention.

Sterilization and the Central Bank

Since the necessary intervention could have undesirable effects on the economy, how can a central bank avoid rising interest rates and investment slumps as it attempts to keep the value of its currency from falling or alternatively how can the central bank put a break on an overheated economy caused by a currency that is too strong? One avenue open to central banks is to neutralize, or sterilize, the effect of its foreign currency transactions through open market operations. **Sterilization** is a specific term that implies that the central bank undertakes actions to keep the money supply constant, despite any intervention in the foreign exchange market. As we can immediately see from equation 13.1 above, in order to sterilize the impact of a change in foreign reserves, the central bank must undertake an exactly opposite change in its domestic credit account.

$$\text{Sterilization: } \Delta M^S = 0 \rightarrow \Delta RES = -\Delta DC \qquad (13.2)$$

The central bank can thus sterilize the effect of its foreign exchange market intervention by changing the level of its domestic credit assets. The changes in domestic credit are undertaken by performing open market operations. For instance, the central bank can sterilize the impact of a foreign currency sale to support the domestic currency (*RES* drop) by buying bonds from the public, (an open market purchase, *DC* increases). This is illustrated in Figure 13.8 below:

Assets	Liabilities	
Domestic Crecit (*DC*) (⇑)	Currency (*CU*)	
Foreign Reserves (*RES*) (⇓)	Commercial Banks Reserves (*CBRE*)	*MB* (⇔) (no change)

FIGURE 13.8 Central Bank Balance Sheet and Sterilization

This figure illustrates two actions by the central bank: first the intervention to keep the exchange rate fixed and second the sterilization to keep the money supply fixed, i.e. to isolate the money supply from the consequences of the intervention. First, the central bank sells reserves (*RES* falls) to support the domestic currency. Second, to offset the resulting monetary contraction, the central bank carries out an open market purchase of exactly the same extent (*DC* increases). The sales of reserves decrease the central bank liabilities and the purchase of bonds from the public increases the central bank liabilities by exactly the same amount. As a result, the monetary base (*MB*) does not change.

Sterilization versus Non-Sterilization

The central bank's alternative to sterilization is to allow its interventions in the currency markets to affect the money supply directly. Such a policy stance is called **non-sterilization**. Under non-sterilization, equation (13.1) shows that any changes in foreign reserves generate proportional fluctuations in the money supply. Non-sterilization thus allows the full force of the changes in supply and demand for foreign currency to be translated into direct effects on the economy.

To illustrate the mechanics of intervention and its impact on the money supply, let us consider the case of the U.S. and China. The Chinese central bank maintains a fixed exchange rate with the dollar. In the past decade, the Chinese economy has transformed itself to become a major supplier of U.S. consumer goods. Nevertheless the exchange rate has remained constant. The increased demand from the U.S. for Chinese consumer goods has translated into an increased demand for the Chinese currency, the renminbi. This has created upward pressures on the price of the renminbi. In the absence of intervention, the price of the renminbi would rise and the dollar would depreciate as the renminbi appreciates. China has, however, chosen to stem any appreciation of the renminbi by resorting to a fixed peg with the U.S. dollar. As a result, the Chinese central bank has to intervene constantly.[8]

To maintain its fixed exchange rate regime, the Chinese central bank buys U.S. dollars (and sells renminbi to the public) as demand for the renminbi exceeds supply. At this point, the central bank can choose the non-sterilization path or sterilization. With non-sterilization, the Chinese central bank floods the Chinese market with renminbi; this could put upward pressures on price. Alternatively, to rein in the threat of inflation on its economy, China can choose to sterilize with open-market sale operations; this would cause a decrease in the money supply compensating for the increase due to intervention so that the money supply remains stable.

We now understand the adjustment mechanism under both flexible and fixed exchange rates. The rest of the chapter is devoted to three important issues concerning the impact of a change in the exchange rate on various macroeconomic variables. First, we consider the impact of the exchange rate on the various components of demand and on national income. Then, we analyze the impact of a change in the exchange rate on the balance of trade under two time frames – in one case, we allow enough time for an adjustment to take place and, in the other case, we consider the immediate impact of a change in the exchange rate.

THE EXCHANGE RATE AND OPEN-ECONOMY NATIONAL INCOME ACCOUNTING

We have just illustrated how the maintenance of a fixed exchange rate may have a dramatic impact on the economy if there exist pressures on the exchange rate to appreciate or to depreciate. These pressures compel interventions that, in turn, affect the amount of foreign currency reserves, thus influencing the level of the domestic money supply. It would be interesting to consider the impact of the adjustment mechanism on the economy if the country adopted a flexible exchange rate instead. Can we assume that the exchange rate has no impact on the economy and is no longer important when it is allowed to respond to the forces of the market? We must now investigate this question. We will discover through a review of national income accounting in the open economy that the performance of the economy remains highly dependent upon the price of foreign currency. Total domestic consumption, capital investment, and the trade balance are all functions of how much foreign goods cost. Whenever the exchange rate rises or falls, all three components of national income

---

8 As is well known, the U.S. complains bitterly about the Chinese peg; it is perceived to undervalue the renminbi, supposedly creating ever greater U.S. trade imbalances with China. We will examine the validity of this argument later on.

change, too. To see this more clearly, we first develop the open economy national income accounting identity formally.

In the closed economy, the national income accounting identity stipulates that the value of output is given by the domestic price level, P, where P is the domestic price level measured by the GDP deflator, multiplied by the amount of goods and services produced, Y, i.e. PY. This value must equal the total value of aggregate demand, which consists of consumption (C), capital investment (I), and government purchases (G):

$$PY = PC + PI + PG \qquad (13.3)$$

To extend the concept of national income accounting to the open economy, we extend our concept of aggregate demand to take into account domestic transactions with the rest of the world. First we include the aggregate demand for domestically produced goods and services from the rest of the world (exports). Next, we exclude domestic demand for foreign goods and services (imports); this demand consists of import demand for consumption goods, investment goods, and government purchases. To simplify matters, we break down consumption, investment, and government purchases into the demand for domestically produced goods and services and into the demand for imports:

$$
\begin{aligned}
PC &= PC_D + EP^*C_F \\
PI &= PI_D + EP^*I_F \\
PG &= PG_D + EP^*G_F
\end{aligned}
\qquad (13.4)
$$

where the subscript D indicates domestically produced goods and services, while the subscript F refers to imports. Imports are expressed in foreign prices, P^*; to obtain their value in terms of the domestic currency, imports must be multiplied by the exchange rate, E.

We can now rewrite equation (13.3) to account for international transactions, where we add exports PX, valued in domestic prices, and subtract imports (now valued in domestic prices too) that are part of total consumption, investment, and government spending:

$$PY = (PC_D + EP^*C_F) + (PI_D + EP^*I_F) + (PG_D + EP^*G_F) + PX - (EP^*C_F + EP^*I_F + EP^*G_F) \quad (13.5)$$

The simple closed economy equation of (13.3) has now become quite messy. We can simplify equation (13.5) significantly, however, by introducing a couple of definitions. First, let M be total imports (for consumer goods and services, investment goods, and government purchases of goods and services). Their total value can then be written as P^*M in terms of foreign currency and as EP^*M in domestic currency units. This simplifies the last bracket in (13.5) to:

$$EP^*M = (EP^*C_F + EP^*I_F + EP^*G_F) \qquad (13.6)$$

Next, we define the trade balance, TB, as exports minus imports

$$PTB = PX - EP^*M \qquad (13.7)$$

Using these definitions and dividing all the terms by the domestic price level, P, we can rearrange (13.5) into a simpler equation

$$Y = C + I + G + TB \tag{13.8}$$

At this point, you are probably asking: didn't I learn this in my first economics course? The answer is both yes and no. What you learned was simply that $Y = C + I + G + TB$. But, at the time, you probably did not focus on the fact that consumption, investment, and the trade balance are also dependent on the foreign price, P^*, as well as the exchange rate, E. This derivation serves as a subtle reminder that a country's national welfare is highly dependent on what happens outside of the national borders.

When foreign prices, P^*, or the value of foreign currency, E, changes, the values of consumption, investment, and the trade balance are also going to be altered – and this affects domestic income, too. To figure out by *how much* income is eventually affected, we must estimate first by *how much* the trade balance may change due to a change in the exchange rate.

THE MARSHALL–LERNER CONDITION

To be more precise and quantify the effect of the exchange rate on national income, we must understand exactly how the exchange rate affects the trade balance. We start off with a question that may seem to be altogether trivial: does a depreciation/devaluation result in an improvement in the balance of trade?[9] The question is seemingly trivial, since a depreciation renders exports cheaper to foreigners and imports more expensive to domestic agents. Why would the trade balance not improve?

To illustrate the problem, consider the example of British consumers' demand for foreign electronics. Assume that British consumers become interested in buying South-Korean electronics. The U.K. and South Korea both adhere to a flexible exchange rate regime, implying that, as British consumers' demand for South-Korean electronics increases, the South-Korean currency, the won, strengthens and the British pound depreciates. Will this depreciation improve the British balance of trade?

As the pound depreciates, British exports suddenly become more attractive to the South Koreans, who, thanks to the fact that they can now buy more British pounds with the same amount of wons, have more purchasing power for British goods than before: British exports thus tend to increase. At the same time, with the rising price of foreign currency, British consumers will want to curtail their imports of South-Korean electronics, because British purchasing power for South-Korean goods has eroded. Thus, the demand shock in favor of South-Korean electronics that ignited the depreciation of the pound in the first place is tempered by the rising price of foreign currency and imports fall. With export quantities rising and import quantities falling, then, it would seem that a currency depreciation improves the balance of trade.

---

9 Since a weakening of the domestic currency, i.e. an increase in the exchange rate E, is called a depreciation with a flexible exchange rate regime and a devaluation with a fixed exchange rate regime, the last two sections apply to either regime.

While we know the movements in export and import quantities, it is however unclear whether export earnings are rising and whether import payments are falling. This is because the value of imports (price times quantity) depends on the exchange rate. Now that we are looking into the role of the exchange rate, we find that by referring to quantities (number of units of imports and exports) we do not actually capture the full impact of the exchange rate on the value of the trade balance. A reasonable measure of the trade balance is not a long list of numbers of units we bought and sold abroad, but a measure of the value of the goods and services we traded as in equation (13.7) above. Reexamining (13.7), we recognize an important problem. If we assume domestic and foreign prices are held constant, as is warranted when domestic supply is very elastic in each country, we have

$$E \uparrow \Rightarrow X \uparrow, M \downarrow \Rightarrow PTB = PX(\uparrow) - E(\uparrow)P^*M(\downarrow) \qquad (13.9)$$

If the exchange rate rises (a depreciation/devaluation), we know for sure that the quantity of exports increases and the quantity of imports decreases. The problem is that the price of foreign currency E has also risen. Therefore we must consider what happens to the respective values of exports and of imports in terms of the domestic currency in order to include this term correctly in the framework of equation (13.8). From equation (13.9), we know that the value of exports in terms of domestic currency increases. What happens to the value of imports in terms of domestic currency is, however, not as straightforward: the domestic residents may be importing fewer units, but they are also paying more per unit. Therefore the value of imports in terms of domestic currency may not decline and it could even increase. The opposite movements in price and quantity thus render it unclear whether the value of the trade balance increases or decreases overall.

To resolve the ambiguity and clarify whether the value of imports rises or falls, Alfred Marshall and Abba Lerner independently derived the condition under which the trade balance will improve after a depreciation/devaluation of the domestic currency.

Marshall–Lerner Condition[10]

$$\partial PTB / \partial E > 0 \; iff \; | \, \varepsilon_x + \varepsilon_M \, | > 1 \qquad (13.10)$$

That is, the trade balance will improve if and only if the absolute value of the sum of the elasticities of demand for exports ε_x and imports ε_M exceeds unity.

The intuition behind this result is straightforward. If demand is highly inelastic, a large change in price will be met by a small change in the quantity demanded. When imports become more expensive and people do not reduce their import purchases (perhaps because people have no substitutes making the demand inelastic), the value of import payments can actually increase. We provide a numeric example of the mechanism with specific elasticities in the box below.

---

10 The formal derivation of the condition is presented in Appendix 1.

Impact of a Depreciation on the Balance of Trade

Let us illustrate this case with a specific example: we are attempting to measure the impact of a depreciation of the dollar against the euro on the U.S. balance of trade. Assume that P_M and P_X are normalized to unity so that we do not have to worry about changes in goods prices in the U.S. or Europe (this allows us to isolate the effect of changes in the exchange rate).

The depreciation affects the euro price of U.S. goods (making them cheaper for Europeans) and the dollar price of European goods (making them more expensive for the Americans). These effects are summarized in the two tables below. In both cases, trade is initially balanced with an exchange rate of E=$1/€ (second row). In the third row, the dollar depreciates to E=$2/€ and the trade balance is recalculated. First we will assume low elasticities of demand such that the Marshall–Lerner (M–L) conditions are not met:

Low elasticities						
$E(\$/€)$	P_X	X	P_M	$\$P_M = EP_M$	M	$\$TB = (P_X*X - EP_M*M)$
1	$1=€1	2	€1	$1	2	$2 – $2 = $0
2	$1=€0.5	3	€1	$2	1.9	$3 – $3.8 = $–0.8

We can even calculate the (arc) elasticity of import demand in this example. As the dollar depreciates from $1 to $2 per euro, the ratio of the percentage change[11] in import quantities over the percentage change in the import price is given by $\varepsilon_M = \%\Delta M/\%\Delta P_M = [(1.9-2)/1.95]/[(2-1)/1.5] = -0.0769$. Since the absolute value of the elasticity is smaller than unity, it is inelastic.

The elasticity of export demand (i.e. the foreign demand for domestic exports) is $\varepsilon_X = \%\Delta X/\%\Delta(P_X / E) = [(3-2)/2.5]/[(.5-1)/.75] = -0.6$ so it is also inelastic. The Marshall–Lerner condition refers to the absolute value of the sum of the two elasticities. In this example, the sum does not exceed unity and the condition is violated. Notice that the trade balance turns negative, –0.8, after the depreciation from $1 to $2 per euro; that was our predicted outcome as M–L was not met.

In our second example, we assume elastic import demand and export supply: the quantities of imports, M, and exports, X, change substantially in response to a depreciation of the dollar. In this case, the trade balance actually improves:

---

11 Calculated as end point less starting point divided by mid-point.

				High elasticities			
$E(\$/€)$	P_X	X	P_M	$\$P_M=EP_M$	M	$\$TB = (P_X*X–EP_M*M)$
1	\$1=€1	2	€1	\$1	2	\$2 – \$2 = \$0
2	\$1=€0.5	4	€1	\$2	0.5	\$4 – \$1 = \$3

The elasticity of import demand is $\varepsilon'_M = [(0.5–2)/\ 1.25]/[(2–1)/1.5] = –1.8$ so it is elastic, implying a large decline of imports. The elasticity of export demand is $\varepsilon'_X = [(4–2)/3]\ /\ [(.5–1)/.75] = –2$. The absolute value of the sum of the two elasticities exceeds unity and the trade balance turns positive, \$TB=\$3, just as the M–L condition predicts.

It is important to remember that *both* the export and the import sides have to be considered. Take, for example a country called Agraria. Suppose it is the sole exporter of coffee in the world, and it imports crude oil. As for most food items, the elasticity of demand for coffee is low – if you are a one-cup a day drinker, once you have had your morning coffee, it is unlikely that a price decline will lead you to drink a second, third, or fourth cup during the day. Agraria's coffee may be cheaper for the world coffee drinkers, but they may not increase their demand for Agraria's main export much; the depreciation does not generate a strong stimulus to the country's exports.

However, Agraria's import markets must also be considered. Agraria lacks any source of domestic energy and must import foreign oil. As its exchange rate depreciates, the cost of oil imports shoots up. With no energy substitutes on hand, Agraria simply purchases just about the same amount of oil – but now at higher prices since its currency has lost value. In these circumstances, it is almost certain that the depreciation results in a deterioration of Agraria's balance of trade. The increase in the value of exports is not large enough to compensate for the large increase in the cost of the oil imported.

THE J-CURVE EFFECT

Elasticities are not constant. In fact, economists make it a point to distinguish between short-run and long-run elasticities. Short-run elasticities are almost always significantly smaller (inelastic) than long-run ones, simply because in the long run economic agents have ample opportunities to find substitutes for commodities facing price increases.

As a result of highly inelastic demands in the short run, the Marshall–Lerner condition may never be satisfied in the short run, as both ε_x and ε_M are low. A depreciation (or a devaluation) may then lead to an immediate worsening of the balance of trade. In the long run, however, as agents find substitutes for foreign goods, the import demand elasticities rise, imports fall (while exports increase for similar reasons) and the goods balance improves. These dynamics are captured in Figure 13.9; time is represented on the horizontal axis and the goods balance on the vertical axis.

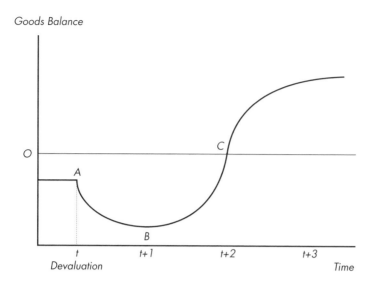

FIGURE 13.9 Goods Balance Adjustment to a Depreciation/Devaluation: The J-Curve

With a stretch of the imagination, one can see a J in the picture! The *y*-axis measures the goods balance and the *x*-axis time. Originally, this country faces a negative goods balance and hopes to improve the situation with a devaluation. The devaluation is expected to stimulate exports and discourage imports. However, this does not happen immediately as there are lags in the adjustment mechanism. The "J" shape illustrates these lags. Basically prices change immediately while quantity adjustments happen overtime. The devaluation takes place in *A*. Imports become immediately more expensive and the goods balance first deteriorates. Overtime, importers will buy fewer foreign goods and exporters will sell more domestic goods to the foreigners and (assuming *M–L* fulfilled): the goods balance will improve.

We can rationalize the J-curve effect with a concrete example. Assume that the U.K. faces a deficit in the goods balance with Japan (up to point *A*). Then, right after a depreciation/devaluation against the yen at time *t*, we observe that the volume of imports does not change: why is this so? The British importers of Japanese cars had entered into contracts to buy a specific quantity of Japanese cars in one month from now, so they cannot adjust their orders. Since the depreciation raises the domestic price of imports, total spending on Japanese imports rise. For similar reasons, the Japanese importers of British woolens cannot increase their orders much in the short run: so the small increase in earnings from British exports of woolens to Japan may be insufficient to compensate for higher spending on imports. The result is a worsening of the balance of trade from *A* to *B* at time *t+1*. Overtime, firms are able to adjust their contracts so the elasticities rise (a change in price has greater impact on the quantities) and the Marshall-Lerner conditions are met; the goods balance will eventually balance in *C* at time *t+2* and even turn into a surplus at time *t+3*.

Empirically, the price elasticities of import demand and export supply are hard to determine. As a result, data concerning the shape of the J-curve are not as precise as one would like for policy analysis. Estimates of how long it takes for the trade balance to improve after a depreciation range from three to six months. However, there also exist studies that do not even find the predicted negative short-term impact.

In the rest of the text, we will assume that 1. the Marshall–Lerner condition holds, so that a depreciation/devaluation results in an improvement in the balance of trade, and 2. the period considered is long enough to ignore J-curve effects.

Now that we understand thoroughly the various forms of exchange rate regime and their specific adjustment mechanism, we are in a position to construct models of the open economy. We start by considering short-run models where the foreign sector only consists in trade and, later on, we will extend the models to include international financial flows.

Summary of Key Concepts

1. Foreign exchange is just like any commodity: there is a supply of and a demand for foreign exchange and their interaction will simultaneously determine its price (the exchange rate) – assuming no interference by the government – and the quantity of foreign exchange traded.

2. Countries can choose between several different exchange rate regimes. At one end of the spectrum, the exchange rate is free to fluctuate to see its price determined by market forces – this corresponds to a flexible (floating) exchange rate. At the other end of the spectrum, the central bank sets the exchange rate – this corresponds to a fixed (pegged) exchange rate.

3. In a flexible exchange rate regime, an increase in the exchange rate is a depreciation of the domestic currency while a decrease is an appreciation. With a fixed exchange rate regime, these terms are replaced respectively by devaluation and revaluation.

4. The adjustment mechanisms to changes in supply of or demand for foreign exchange are fundamentally different under fixed and flexible exchange rate regimes.

5. With a flexible exchange rate regime, the balance of payments is always balanced through changes in the exchange rate.

6. With a fixed exchange rate regime, central bank must intervene constantly to equate the supply of and demand for foreign currency. It does so by buying and selling foreign currency reserves.

7. Interventions in the foreign exchange market on the part of the central bank affect the money supply.

8. The central bank can neutralize the effect that its foreign exchange intervention has on the money supply through sterilization, i.e. performing an open-market operation to change domestic credit and offset the impact of the foreign exchange intervention.

9. When foreign prices or the exchange rate change, the values of consumption, investment, and the trade balance are also going to be altered – and this affects domestic income, too.

10. The Marshall–Lerner condition tells us in what direction the trade balance changes when the exchange rate changes. It depends crucially on the magnitude of the export and import elasticities.

11. The J-curve shows that the short-run and long-run response of the trade balance to a change in the exchange rate may be fundamentally different.

CASE STUDY I

On Europe: Europe Feels Weight of Strong Euro
By Rachel Morarjee
The Financial Times, March 14, 2008

The euro smashed through new records this week in its advance against the dollar, spelling greater pain for many European companies. With markets no longer questioning whether the U.S. is in a recession but pondering how deep the downturn will be, the single currency reached a fresh high of $1.5688 against the dollar on Friday.

"The strengthening euro is certainly a burden for European equity markets. European companies become less competitive, not just in export markets, but in euroland markets as well," says Ralf Zimmermann, equity strategist at Sal Oppenheim in Frankfurt.

The problem of a strong euro is not new. Europe's currency has climbed more than 30 per cent against the dollar since the beginning of 2006 and 6.7 per cent against the dollar since the start of this year.

Policymakers are increasingly sounding the alarm over the currency's surge, signalling concern that it may cause economic damage. "In present circumstances, we are concerned about excessive exchange rate moves," Jean-Claude Trichet, president of the European Central Bank, said this week.

Over the past two years, European bourses have climbed in spite of the strong euro, driven by earnings growth, booming economies and restructuring, prompting some analysts to say that the traditional negative correlation between the euro and European equity market performance has broken down. That looks set to change.

"You've seen companies restructure, share buybacks, you've seen a dynamism of earnings per share rising by 20 per cent or more a year. Against that background, a couple of per cent off earnings because of a weak dollar just did not matter," says Roger Hirst, head of European equity research at Bear Stearns.

But with economies across Europe starting to slow, every percentage point counts and analysts expect the weakness of the dollar to bite more painfully. As a rule of thumb, a 10 per cent devaluation of the dollar against the euro will shave between 2.5 and 2.7 percentage points off earnings in Europe, analysts say.

In trade-weighted terms, the euro's gains have been less spectacular. The euro has risen 1.1 percent so far this year, according to the trade-weighted euro series provided by Datastream. Since December 31, 2006, the trade-weighted euro has risen 5.8 per cent, compared with a 16.6 per cent surge in the euro/dollar.

Even that is a cause for concern, says Jonathan Loynes, chief European economist at Capital Economics. "The appreciation of the euro over the last year has been particularly steep and when we have seen that rate of appreciation before, it has been accompanied by annual falls in exports," he says.

Britain is the eurozone's second-largest trade partner, so a weaker sterling and the slowing U.K. economy pose another threat to European corporates. "One should not underestimate the impact of the British pound. It's not only a dollar problem, it is a sterling problem," says Mr. Zimmermann.

According to Morgan Stanley research, North America accounts for 16 per cent of corporate Europe's revenues, emerging markets account for about 21 per cent of revenues, while trade within developed Europe accounts for the bulk of the rest. Europe's sensitivity to the U.S. economy has diminished over the past 10 years as the continent has become more exposed to Asia and Eastern Europe.

If growth in emerging markets (including Asia and the Middle East) remains strong, that could offset a weak U.S. economy, given how important the emerging economies have now become.

But Eastern Europe, which accounts for about 6 per cent of European corporate revenues, is not strong enough in isolation to offset the slowdown in dollar-based economies in the U.S. and Asia.

"It is not so much that we are at a tipping point in terms of the exchange rate, but rather that the dollar is very weak, the U.S. is in recession and global growth is slowing," says Ronan Carr, pan-European equity analyst at Morgan Stanley.

The blows from a stronger currency will not fall equally. Pharmaceutical companies are the most exposed because of the high level of sales in the U.S., and the relatively strong profitability of those revenues. Industrials, oils, media and chemicals are also highly exposed, while utilities and telecoms are relatively sheltered.

"Around a third of European earnings are dollar denominated, but in addition some companies are hit by having euro costs and dollar revenues. Many capital goods firms, EADS, automakers and some luxury goods makers have this problem," says Andrew Garthwaite, chief global equity strategist at Crédit Suisse. Even in the worst affected sectors it will become clear which companies are better prepared. For instance, French aerospace giant EADS, which has traditionally been seen as a bellwether for U.S. dollar exposure, has been laying the groundwork for a rising currency for years, hedging its currency exposure and moving its cost bases to the U.S.

Copyright The Financial Times Limited, 2008

CASE STUDY QUESTIONS

1. Elaborate on the distinction between the euro bilateral rise against the dollar and its smaller rise in terms of trade-weighted exchange rate.

2. The impact on Euroland's trade differs depending on the trade partners. Who are the important trade partners who will cause greater concerns for Euroland?

3. Explain the additional issues for Euroland resulting from the fact that a large chunk of Euroland foreign earnings are denominated in dollars.

4. How did some companies that bill in dollars, like EAD (Airbus' parent company), anticipating the fall of the dollar, cover themselves?

CASE STUDY II

China Slightly Loosens the Reins on its Currency's Market Fluctuation
By Keith Bradsher
New York Times, May 19, 2007

China's central bank announced Friday that it would begin allowing the country's currency to fluctuate more during each day's foreign exchange trading, but again rebuffed demands from the United States and Europe for a sustained rise in the currency.

The central bank also raised interest rates and demanded that commercial banks set aside more of their assets as reserves that cannot be lent. Both of the moves are aimed at reducing the risk of overheating in an economy that is growing at more than 11 percent and at taming speculation in domestic stock markets that have more than tripled since the beginning of last year.

The announcement came as top American and

Chinese economic policy makers prepared to meet next week in Washington in an effort to head off growing pressures from Congress to confront China over the widening American trade deficit.

But economists said that the latest policy moves, which take effect on Saturday, were unlikely to have any practical effect on China's soaring exports, while the initial reaction from Washington was cautious.

The People's Bank of China said in a statement posted on its website (http://www.pbc.gov.cn/english/detail.asp?col=6400&id=837) that it would allow the country's currency, known as the yuan, to rise or fall up to 0.5 percent in each day's trading. The current daily limit is 0.3 percent.

But the central bank gave a clear signal in its statement that the policy should not be interpreted as Chinese willingness to allow a run-up in the value of the yuan. The bank said it would continue to "keep the exchange rate basically stable at an adaptive and equilibrium level based on market supply and demand with reference to a basket of currencies."

The bank issued a separate statement quoting an unidentified spokesman as saying that the decision did not mean that the exchange rate "will see large ups and downs, nor large appreciations."

The People's Bank has not allowed the yuan to move the maximum allowed percentage on any day since it broke the yuan's peg to the dollar on July 21, 2005. The Chinese government allowed the yuan to rise 2.1 percent then, and has let it inch up by only another 5 percent over the nearly two years since.

In contrast, members of Congress from manufacturing states that have lost jobs during China's export boom have been calling for China to revalue by 25 percent or more. If China did allow the yuan to rise more quickly, Chinese exports would become more expensive in foreign markets and foreign goods would be more competitive in China.

Liang Hong, an economist in the Hong Kong office of Goldman Sachs, said in a research note that the wider trading band represented "a symbolic but laudable development in China's foreign exchange reform."

The initial reaction from Congress was chilly. "To widen the band is well and good, but if they don't use the band, nothing will happen," said Senator Charles E. Schumer, the New York Democrat who has called for steep tariffs on goods from China unless Beijing lets the yuan rise.

The Bush administration was also cautious but a little more welcoming. "This is a useful step towards greater flexibility and an eventual float of the currency," said Brookly McLaughlin, a Treasury spokeswoman. "It's important now that Chinese authorities use the wider band and allow greater currency movement within each day and over time."

Stephen Green, an economist in the Shanghai office of Standard Chartered Bank, said that China was likely to allow slightly faster appreciation in the next few days but that the long-term rate of appreciation would not change. There have been just two single-day rises of 0.16 percent and two single-day drops of 0.17 percent in two years, while the rest of the trading has fallen within an even narrower range, he added.

Widening the daily trading band is nonetheless the latest and most noticeable in a long series of steps by Chinese officials to gently awaken businesses to the risks that fluctuating currencies can pose. China pegged the yuan at 8.28 to the dollar from 1997 to 2005, lulling some businesses into ignoring currency risk.

In interviews last month at the Canton Fair, exporters from all over China said that they were paying closer attention to exchange rates. While Chinese export contracts are still denominated mainly in dollars, Chinese companies increasingly demand that their foreign customers agree to provisions requiring the buyer to pay extra if the dollar starts falling faster against the yuan.

Chinese officials acknowledge that there are arguments for faster appreciation of the yuan, but contend that this could threaten "social stability." Chinese workers making goods like textiles that compete with exports from even lower-wage countries could protest if currency appreciation makes their products uncompetitive and costs them their jobs.

Two-thirds of China's population still live in rural areas and the agricultural sector is barely competitive with imports at current currency levels, raising the prospect of increased rural unemployment if the yuan rose sharply and food imports surged.

The People's Bank of China also announced on Friday that it was raising the benchmark regulated rate for one-year bank deposits by 0.27 percentage point, to 3.06 percent, and increasing the benchmark rate for one-year bank loans by 0.18 percentage point, to 6.57 percent.

By raising deposit rates more than lending rates, the government showed confidence that the banks had put enough of their bad-loan problems behind them to survive on slightly narrower profit margins. Higher deposit rates also make it a little more attractive for Chinese families to put their savings in banks, instead of risking them in China's feverish stock markets. But raising domestic lending rates could make it harder for China to allow further appreciation of the yuan.

That is because the central bank is itself a borrower. It borrows yuan, by issuing bonds, to pay for its extensive interventions in currency markets, where it has accumulated $1.2 trillion in foreign exchange reserves, mainly dollars. The central bank earns a higher interest rate on American Treasury securities than it pays on yuan-denominated bonds at home. The authorities use this profit from the difference in interest rates to cover losses on the foreign exchange reserves, which are worth less and less in yuan as the yuan appreciates.

The semiofficial *China Business News* newspaper reported on Friday that the government had entrusted $3 billion to the Blackstone Group, the private equity firm, to invest abroad. Blackstone declined to comment; the company is in a "quiet" period before a planned initial offering on the New York Stock Exchange.

The central bank also ordered banks to hold 11.5 percent of assets as reserves effective Saturday, up from 11 percent. Many banks already have even larger reserves, however, as they have been swamped with deposits from China's brisk economic growth and large trade surplus, and have had trouble finding ways to lend this money.

CASE STUDY QUESTIONS

1. Why did China change its currency bands, and what are the expected consequences?

2. What is the use of a currency band?

3. Do you think China is likely to switch to a flexible exchange rate regime? Why or Why not?

Questions for Study and Review

1. Draw the supply and demand for yen with the dollar/yen exchange rate on the *vertical* axis. Americans' taste changes and they now import European cars instead of Japanese cars. Assume a fixed exchange rate regime and use your graph to answer the following questions with clear, in-depth explanations:

   a. Does the dollar appreciate, or depreciate, or stay put?

   b. How would the Federal Reserve have to intervene to stabilize the exchange rate?

   c. How would it sterilize the impact of its intervention?

2. When the Brazilian currency fell 55 percent against the dollar in the first few weeks of 2002, what was the expected impact on the trade balance?

    a. Immediately (in the very short run)? (Why? Be specific, use a graph)

    b. Six months later? (Why? Be specific, use a graph)

    c. How is the Marshall–Lerner condition related to your answers above?

3. The market for foreign exchange. Construct the demand for and the supply of euros using the U.S. demand for foreign imports and the European demand for U.S. exports. Assume only two trade partners: the U.S. and Europe. Also, assume only one import good, cars (VW) and one export good, computers (Macs).

    a. The U.S. demand for euros is derived from the demand for VW cars.

    Fill in the table below and use it to construct the U.S. demand for imports of VW cars and the U.S. demand for euros.

	E ($\$/€$)	P_{VW} in €	P_{VW} in $	M of VW (Quantity)	Value of M in € Demand for €
A	0.9	15,000		170	
B	1			160	
C	1.1			150	
D	1.2			140	
E	1.3			130	

Plot the relevant numbers on the following two graphs:

  i. The U.S. demand for VW (P_{VW} on the vertical axis and Q_{VW} on the horizontal axis).
  ii. The U.S. demand for euros.

    b. The supply of euros to the U.S. is derived from the foreign demand for U.S. Macs.

    Fill in the table opposite and use it to construct the foreign demand for U.S. Macs (the U.S. supply of exports) and the U.S. supply of euros.

    Plot the relevant numbers on the following two graphs:

  i. The foreign demand for Macs (P_{Mac} in euros on the vertical axis and Q_{Mac} on the horizontal axis).
  ii. The supply of euros to the United States.

    Is the supply of euros always upward sloping? Why or why not? Calculate the arc elasticity of foreign demand between *I* and *J*.

	E ($/€)	P_Mac in $ o	P_Mac in €	X of Macs (Quantity) Supply for €	Value of X in €
F	0.9	2,000		1000	
G	1			1200	
H	1.1			1400	
I	1.2			1600	
J	1.3			1700	

c. Put together the market for foreign exchange (S and D) and show the equilibrium exchange rate and the equilibrium quantity of € traded. What is the equilibrium exchange rate?

d. Now assume that, as a result of a change in taste, the U.S. public shifts some of its demand for cars from VWs to domestically produced Saturn. Show the impact on the foreign exchange market above. What happens to the U.S. exchange rate ($/€)?

e. Let us now assume that the U.S. and the Europeans agree together to peg their exchange rate at the level calculated in (c.). What happens to the exchange rate when the U.S. demand for cars shifts as in (d.) from European to U.S. cars?

f. Explain carefully the intervention process. What happens to the Federal Reserve Bank's foreign reserves? What is the impact on the money supply?

g. Finally, the Federal Reserve could counteract its effect on the money supply by using monetary policy. Describe the necessary open market operation.

4. Assume that the exchange rate between the euro and the pound is 1.5€/£ originally. Then the euro depreciates by 25 percent against the pound. The price of exports is €1 while the price of imports is £1. Due to the depreciation, European exports to the U.K. increase from 10 to 11 and its imports drop from 10 to 9.

a. What happens to the European balance of trade with the U.K.? Calculate the change in the European balance of trade.

b. Estimate the relevant elasticities (arc elasticities) to test whether the Marshall–Lerner condition is met.

References and Suggestions for Further Reading

Bradsher, K. (2007) "China Slightly Loosens the Reins on its Currency's Market Fluctuation," *New York Times*, May 19.
Broadus, J. and M. Goodfriend, M. (1996) "Foreign Exchange Operations and the Federal Reserve," *Federal Reserve Bank of Richmond Quarterly*, Winter: 1–19.

Chrystal, K. A. (1984) "A Guide to Foreign Exchange Markets," *Federal Reserve Bank of St. Louis Review*, March: 5–18.

Cross, S. Y. (1998) "All About The Foreign Exchange Market in the United States," New York: Federal Reserve Bank of New York, (http://www.newyorkfed.org/education/addpub/usfxm/)

European Central Bank, (2007) "ECB Foreign exchange operations," http://www.ecb.int/ecb/orga/tasks/html/foreign-exchange.en.html

Federal Reserve Bank of New York (2007) "US Foreign Exchange Intervention," *FedPoints* May. (http://www.ny.frb.org/aboutthefed/fedpoint/fed44.html)

Frankel, J.A., Goldstein, M., and Masson, P.R. (1991) *Characteristics of a Successful Exchange Rate System*, Occasional Paper No. 82, Washington: International Monetary Fund.

Ichikawa, M., Miller, M., and Sutherland, A. (1990) "Entering a preannounced currency band," *Economics Letters*, Elsevier, 34: 363–8.

International Monetary Fund (2006) "Annual Report on Exchange Arrangements and Exchange Restrictions," Washington: International Monetary Fund.

Klitgaard, T. (1999) "Exchange Rates and Profit Margins: The Case of Japanese Exporters," New York Federal Reserve Working Paper.

Mohsen B. O., Economidou, C., and Goswami, G. G. (2006) "Bilateral J-curve between the UK vis-à-vis her major trading partners," *Applied Economics*, 38: 879–88.

Morarjee, R. (2008) "On Europe: Europe feels weight of strong euro," *Financial Times*, March 14.

People's Bank of China (the), (http://www.pbc.gov.cn/english/detail.asp?col=64007id=837)

APPENDIX: THE MARSHALL–LERNER CONDITION[12]

The trade balance (in domestic prices) is expressed as $TB = PX(E) - EP^* M(E,Y)$. Assume that income Y is fixed and we set $P=P^*=1$. The trade balance is reduced to: $TB = X(E) - EM(E)$. Let us now convert the trade balance into units of foreign currency $(1/E)TB = TB^* = (1/E)X(E) - M(E)$ and differentiate with respect to the exchange rate E.

$$\frac{dTB^*}{dE} = -\frac{1}{E^2} X + \frac{1}{E} \frac{dX}{dE} - \frac{dM}{dE}$$

Now multiply the right hand side by E^2/X (>0) to highlight the elasticities

$$-1 + \frac{E}{X}\frac{dX}{dE} - \frac{E^2}{X}\frac{dM}{dE} = -1 + \frac{E}{X}\frac{dX}{dE} - \frac{E^2}{X}\frac{M}{E}\frac{E}{M}\frac{dM}{dE} = -1 + \frac{E}{X}\frac{dX}{dE} - \frac{EM}{X}\frac{E}{M}\frac{dM}{dE}$$

The elasticity of export and import demand are respectively:

$$\varepsilon_X = \frac{E}{X}\frac{dX}{dE} \quad \text{and} \quad \varepsilon_M = -\frac{E}{M}\frac{dM}{dE}$$

---

12 Assume that the country has no capital mobility.

The expression above can be rewritten as

$$-1 + \varepsilon_X + \frac{EM}{X}\, \varepsilon_M$$

The trade balance will increase (improve) if this term is positive. If we start from balanced trade $TB = 0$ or $X = EM$ the expression boils down to the M–L condition discussed in the chapter:

$$-1 + \varepsilon_X + \varepsilon_M > 0 \ or \ \varepsilon_X + \varepsilon_M > 1$$

Since we keep income Y fixed, the improvement corresponds to the shift upward of the X-M line that will be introduced in the next chapter.

Chapter 14

An Introduction to Modeling the Open Economy

LEARNING OBJECTIVES

By the end of this chapter you should be able to understand:

- why it is helpful to build models to analyze the impact of policy changes

- that we need to start with a very simple model involving strong assumptions and then extend the model by shedding or broadening the assumptions one by one

- that trade deficits may be due to fundamental factors other than trade barriers or exchange rates

- the link between national saving and the trade balance

- that the exchange rate regime has a profound influence on the effectiveness of public policy

- that a devaluation can be used as a policy instrument

- the impact of openness on a fiscal or monetary expansion

The basic elements of the open economy, the balance of payments and the exchange rate, have been introduced in Chapter 12. We have explained the adjustment mechanisms under various exchange rate regimes in Chapter 13. These are the building blocs we need to construct our first model of the international macroeconomy. We start with a simple model, because economists employ models to help understand solutions to problems that are too complex to work out explicitly. If a real-world problem cannot be solved at first, it is helpful to break it down into several components. This implies a simplification of the real world that helps us understand one specific part of the problem at a time. Once we have understood that one part, we can expand the model to render it more realistic allowing us to understand a broader section of the complex world. Brilliant model builders have a gift for choosing the crucial parts of the complex world that can be simplified to gain powerful insights.

How can we know whether our model is a good one? The test is simply to question how helpful our model is, or even whether it is helpful at all. In order to figure out whether our model is insightful, we must compare its predictions to data gathered from the real world. This is the path we shall follow in this chapter. We will start modeling the open economy by first developing the simplest model of the open economy and use it to analyze the impact of various economic policies under either a fixed or flexible exchange rate regime. We consider first the small open economy, too small to affect the rest of the world. The large open economy is discussed in the next chapter.

KEY FEATURES OF A BASIC OPEN-ECONOMY MODEL

We want to examine how our economy behaves when it is integrated into the global economy. How do changes in our international transactions, recorded by the balance of payments, affect domestic output and employment? Without introducing any additional assumptions, we know that aggregate demand, Z, must be adjusted to include the trade balance, TB, representing net foreign demand (exports, X, minus imports, M). Strictly speaking, we should include all the components of the current account, not just the trade balance. However, to simplify matters, we focus on the trade balance since it is by far the largest component of the current account and also the most visible one that is widely discussed in day-to-day affairs.

So aggregate demand is given by $Z \equiv C + I + G + TB$ where C is aggregate consumption, I is aggregate capital investment, G is government purchases of goods and services or government spending, and TB is the trade balance. The economy is in equilibrium when domestic production, Y, equals aggregate demand Z, or:

$$Y = C + I + G + TB \tag{14.1}$$

To specify the determinants of consumption, we follow John Maynard Keynes's idea that consumption consists of two parts: autonomous consumption, $\bar{C}$, and induced consumption. Autonomous consumption refers to the consumption that would take place if current year's income was zero – of course such consumption is only possible if consumers dissave, i.e. draw on their past savings. Induced consumption is the fraction of disposable income Y_D (defined as income minus net taxes or $Y - T$) that is used for consumption. The parameter c is called the *marginal propensity to consume*. It measures the increase in consumption resulting from a $1 increase in disposable income (so c must be positive and smaller than *1*). The Keynesian consumption function can then be written as:

$$C = \bar{C} + cY_D \equiv \bar{C} + c(Y - T) \tag{14.2}$$

In our simple model of the open economy, aggregate capital investment, I, depends negatively on the interest rate, i. Investment in new plants and factories decreases as the present discounted return from any investment project falls with an increase in the cost of borrowing, i:

$$I = I(i) \tag{14.3}$$

To round out our domestic demand, we note that it is common practice to assume that government spending, G, and net taxes, T, are fixed. Changes in either of these two variables will reflect changes in government's policy.

The last component of aggregate demand is the trade balance. In our first, simple model, we assume that exports, X, are exogenous i.e. they are determined outside of the model (denoted by a bar above the X). This is a simplifying assumption equivalent to stating that nothing changes in the rest of the world during the time span of the model.

$$X = P\bar{X} \tag{14.4a}$$

where P denotes the domestic price level. This is clearly a strong assumption and we will relax it later to see whether the model implications change when we introduce the determinants of domestic exports.

The simplest way to model domestic demand for imports is to assume that imports, M, are an increasing function of national income, just like any other demand. However, we also allow for an autonomous amount of imports, $\bar{M}$, which may represent government spending or private spending on essential imports. How much imports increase as income rises is determined by the nation's **marginal propensity to import**, $m<1$. More precisely, the marginal propensity to import is defined as the fraction of a change in income that is spent on additional imports. Combining autonomous import demand with the component of import demand increasing with income, we can write the domestic import demand function as:

$$M = \bar{M} + mY \tag{14.4b}$$

Since imports are purchased abroad, they are measured in units of foreign price P^* which must be converted into domestic prices by multiplying them by the exchange rate, E. The import demand function in terms of the domestic currency is then given by:

$$M = EP^* \left(\bar{M} + mY \right) \tag{14.4c}$$

Combining the import and export functions (14.4a, c), we obtain an explicit expression for the trade balance:

$$TB = X - M = P\bar{X} - EP^*(\bar{M} + mY) \tag{14.5}$$

To further simplify our model, we ignore inflation and assume that prices are fixed: $P = \bar{P}$ and $P^* = \bar{P}^*$. Such an assumption is motivated by the time span we are considering: we focus here on the short run, where the existence of price rigidities is a widespread belief. We also assume the absence of non-official capital flows, greatly simplifying the balance of payments: the BoP thus reduces to current and official accounts. Without capital flows, we can also ignore net income receipts and net unilateral transfers on the current account side and therefore the current account is approximated by the trade balance, $BoP = CA; TB$.

Clearly, this assumption is not realistic, but we explained earlier that we have to make somewhat unrealistic assumptions to build models simplifying the complex real world. In most modern economies, the financial account is not closed, and exports are not fixed. However, for now, these assumptions will make our life easier and allow us to acquire an intuitive understanding of the model before we relax the assumptions one by one to build a more complex model of the open economy. Finally, we have to specify the exchange rate regime that a country has selected. To keep matters simple, we will focus on the two polar cases: fixed exchange rates and flexible exchange rates.

A SMALL OPEN ECONOMY WITH FIXED EXCHANGE RATES

Under fixed exchange rate regimes, the central bank promises to intervene in the foreign exchange market to keep the exchange rate constant. It is therefore *not* the supply of and the demand for a foreign currency that determines its price (the exchange rate), but it is the central bank that, single-handedly, announces a fixed price for the foreign currency. The central bank must maintain the announced fixed price through sales and purchases in the foreign exchange market. In this chapter, we will also assume that the central bank sterilizes any effects of foreign exchange transactions to keep the money supply, M^s, constant.

Summary of Assumptions

1) Small open economy

Export demand	$X = P\bar{X}$
Import demand	$M = EP^*(\bar{M} + mY)$
Trade balance	$TB = X - M = P\bar{X} - EP^*(\bar{M} + mY)$

2) Fixed prices $\qquad\qquad\qquad\qquad P = \bar{P}$ and $P^* = \bar{P}^*$

3) Fixed exchange rates $\qquad$ $E = \bar{E}$,

4) Sterilization $\qquad$ $M^s = \bar{M}^s$

Overall, our model of the open economy may appear strange and oversimplified: it is as if we fixed everything! As we move through the subsequent chapters of this book, we will relax one assumption after another to examine whether and how the implications of our model change. The advantage of starting with the simplest possible model is that it allows us to build solid intuition about the very basic aspects of the open economy. Once we are comfortable with the fundamental components, we can increase the complexity and realism of our model by relaxing assumptions.

Our simple model already has an important implication. When a country's trade is balanced, $M = X$, the receipts for its export sales exactly equal the costs of its imports. Whenever trade is not balanced (e.g., $M \neq X$), the foreign exchange market is in disequilibrium because foreign exchange receipts from exports do not equal the payments necessary for imports. Take the case of imports exceeding exports (a trade deficit); then the amount of foreign currency necessary to pay for imports is greater than the amount of foreign currency earned from exports. In this case, the foreign exchange market is in disequilibrium – there is excess demand for foreign currency.

When the market for foreign exchange is in disequilibrium, the price of foreign exchange tends to adjust until supply equals demand. Under fixed exchange rate regimes, however, the price of foreign currency is held constant by the central bank and therefore it is not allowed to fluctuate to equate supply and demand. In the case we are considering, the country is running a trade deficit and the excess demand for foreign currency exerts upward pressures on the price of the foreign currency. To keep the exchange rate constant, the central bank must intervene; it sells foreign currency at the fixed exchange rate on the foreign exchange market in order to satisfy the excess demand and to prevent the price of the foreign currency from rising.

Our first observation underlines the following: under fixed exchange rates, there is an immediate connection between a trade imbalance, foreign exchange market imbalances, and central bank interventions. Next, we highlight the relationship between a trade imbalance and the other macro-economic variables in the economy.

Saving, Investment, and the Balance of Trade

To analyze the implications of our model on the broad economy, we need to rearrange some basic macroeconomic equations. Let us start with the following definitions:

National income Y is equal to disposable income plus net taxes:

$$Y \equiv Y_D + T$$

Private saving S^P is defined as the difference between disposable income and consumption:

$$S^P \equiv Y_D - C$$

Government saving S^G is defined as the difference between net revenues from tax receipts and government spending on goods and services:

$$S^G \equiv T - G$$

National saving S^N is defined as the sum of private and government saving:

$$S^N \equiv S^P + S^G$$

We can substitute these definitions into (14.1) and rearrange terms as follows: $Y = C + I + G + TB$ is rewritten as $Y - C - G - I = TB$ and we replace Y by $Y_D + T$ to get $Y_D - C + T - G - I = TB$ or $S^P + S^G - I = TB$.

We finally obtain an equivalent equilibrium equation for the economy:

$$S^N - I = TB \qquad\qquad (14.1a)$$

By simply rearranging the national income equilibrium equation using standard identities, we are able to highlight the link between the trade balance, national saving, and investment. At first, the result of our rearranging may seem surprising. Equation (14.1a) implies that whenever a trade deficit is observed, a country's investment exceeds its national saving. This is of course a very different story than what we are used to reading in the newspapers, where trade deficits are blamed on unfair trade practices or tariffs! Our result sheds a new light on the issue: intuitively, those countries whose consumers barely save and who run budget deficits will also lack the funds necessary to finance domestic investment. These funds must then be acquired from abroad. Specifically, the bricks and mortar for new factories, if not funded domestically, must be funded by the outside world. The stark implications of the simple model raise the question whether it has any real world relevance. The way we test our model is to look at real world data. Figure 14.1 is based on data from the U.S. Bureau of Economic Analysis' national accounts.

Since equation (14.1a) is an equilibrium condition, we would not expect the trade balance to be exactly equal to national saving minus investment *at all times*. In Figure 14.1, we are therefore looking for co-movement between S^N–I and the trade balance. The correlation between the two is 0.78 – which is quite high, given the simplicity of a model that does not account for many other crucial aspects of the real world. With these first insights about our simple model, we are set to examine how the model predicts the effect of economic policy in an open economy.

The Relationship between the Trade Balance, S^N–I, and National Income

To analyze the impact of economic policy in our model, we construct a graph that illustrates separately (a) the relationship between the trade balance and income and (b) the relation between S^N–I and income. Then, we use the equilibrium condition developed in (14.1a) $S^N - I = TB$ to determine the equilibrium level of income. We measure the trade balance and S^N–I on the vertical axis and national income on the horizontal axis.

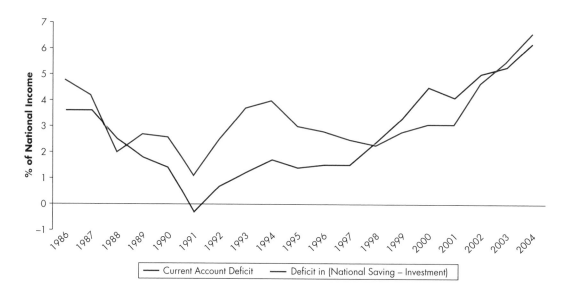

FIGURE 14.1 Co-movements between the U.S. Current Account Deficit and the Deficit in National Saving Less Investment

Note that $S^N{-}I$ is defined as business, private, and government saving minus net domestic investment.

Source: adapted from U.S. Department of Commerce, Bureau of Economic Analysis, and Marshall Reinsdorf (2005).

Although our model is simple, it relies largely on national account identities. While the implied relationship between the trade balance and saving/investment may be surprising initially, it is clearly observed in the data. Here we see that, between 1986 and 2004, the trade deficit movement is closely matched by the movement in the shortfall between national saving and investment.

First, we consider equation (14.5) that relates the trade balance to national income: $TB = X - M = \bar{P}\bar{X} - \bar{E}\bar{P}^* (\bar{M} + mY)$. Taking the derivative, $dTB / dY = -\bar{E}\bar{P}^*m$, indicates a negative relationship between income and the trade balance: $X{-}M$ is downward sloping in Figure 14.2. The absolute value of the slope of the line is a multiple of the marginal propensity to import. The intuition for the negative slope is straightforward. Our model assumes that exports are fixed, while the import demand function (equation 14.4c) indicates that imports increase when income increases. Thus, the trade balance must become more negative as income rises. All other variables in the equation (14.5), prices, exports, autonomous imports, and the exchange rate, are therefore variables that shift or rotate the $X{-}M$ line. Since in this model we have assumed that $\bar{P}$, $\bar{P}^*$ and $\bar{E}$ to be fixed, we can set each of them equal to *1* and, in this case, the slope of the $X{-}M$ line is simply the negative of the marginal propensity to import ($-m$).

Our second line in the $X{-}M/S^N{-}I$ and income space is the $S^N{-}I$ line. How do we derive the slope of this line? We know that national saving S^N is the sum of private and government saving. We first have to rewrite the private saving component of national saving as: $S^P = Y_D - C = Y - T - C$.

Then we substitute for the consumption function in 14.2 to rewrite private saving as:

$S^P = s(Y - T) - \bar{C}$ where we have used the property that the marginal propensity to save, *s*, equals one minus the marginal propensity to consume, c, i.e. $s=1-c$. The equation for national saving then becomes $S^N = s(Y - T) - \bar{C} + T - G$.

At this point, investment I is considered exogenous so $I = \bar{I}$. The equation of the S^N–I line finally takes the following form:

$$S^N - I = s(Y - T) - \bar{C} + T - G - \bar{I} \qquad (14.6)$$

From the last equation we find that the S^N–I line is upward sloping as drawn in Figure 14.2 since $d(S^N-I)/dY = s$. The intuition is that S^N–I increases as income increases because national saving (specifically private saving) increases as income rises. Autonomous consumption $\bar{C}$, taxes T, government spending G, and investment I remain as variables that shift the line in the X–M/S^N–I and income space.

Figure 14.2 summarizes the relationships between the trade balance, S^N–I, and national income.[1] The equilibrium of the economy occurs where the two lines intersect to determine equilibrium national income Y_0. In Figure 14.2, the equilibrium of the economy corresponds to a trade surplus. However, the intersection of the two lines (the equilibrium of the economy) could happen anywhere below, above, or on the horizontal axis, as we shall see when we examine policy implications, indicating either a trade deficit, or a trade surplus, or balanced trade.

We can now use our model and its graphical representation in Figure 14.2 to analyze the impact of various policy changes on the small open economy. We consider three forms of policy; fiscal policy, monetary policy, and exchange rate policy.

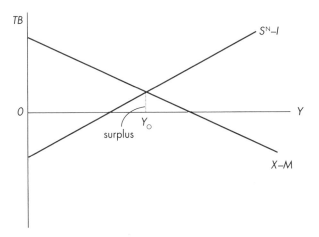

FIGURE 14.2 The Trade Balance, S^N–I, and National Income

The equilibrium condition for the economy $Y=C+I+G+X-M$ can be rewritten as $S^N-I=X-M$. The two curves S^N-I and $X-M$ will intersect because one is positively related to income (upward sloping) and the other negatively (downward sloping). The intersection of these two curves determines equilibrium Y_0. In the above graph, the equilibrium of the economy corresponds to a surplus in the trade balance. Indeed with fixed exchange rates, the equilibrium of the economy will not fall automatically at a level where the balance of trade is also in equilibrium.

---

1 To avoid cluttering the graph, we label the vertical axis simply trade balance, TB, representing both S^N-I and $X-M$.

Policy in a Small Open Economy with Fixed Exchange Rates

Models are meant to provide us with insights. At this point, our simple model has taught us that a shortfall in national saving over investment, i.e. $(S^N - I < 0)$, corresponds to a negative trade balance $(X - M = 0)$. The domestic economy cannot finance the totality of its imports with the revenue from its exports so the foreigners are lending the difference. These loans or inflows of foreign capital in the domestic economy help finance the shortfall in national saving over investment. This finding is totally consistent with the balance-of-payments accounts in Chapter 12; a current account deficit corresponds to a financial account surplus, i.e. to capital inflows. We also found that the trade balance tends to worsen as national income increases because demand for all goods, including imports, rises. The important use of the model is that it can help us analyze the effects of economic policy, specifically fiscal, monetary, and exchange rate policy.

Fiscal Policy

In this chapter, we investigate the effects of expansionary fiscal policy under sterilization. To simplify matters, we assume that we start from a point of balanced trade, $S^N - I = X - M = 0$. Suppose that the government decides to increase spending, $G\uparrow$. If G rises, government saving defined above as $T-G$ decreases to reduce national saving (the sum of private and government saving), $S^N \downarrow$. Thus S^N-I decreases and the S^N-I line in Figure 14.3 shifts down to the right. Since the new equilibrium of the

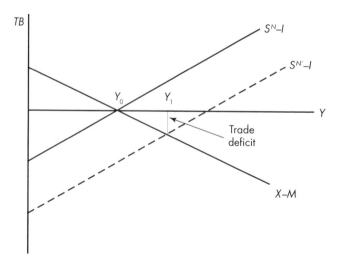

FIGURE 14.3 Increase in Government Spending in a Small Open Economy: Fixed Exchange Rates

An increase in government spending results in a decrease in government saving *(T–G)* and thus in national saving S^N. The S^N-I curve shifts down and the economy is stimulated, moving from Y_0 to a new equilibrium at Y_1. As the expansion encourages domestic demand for domestic as well as for foreign goods, imports also increase and cause a trade deficit to appear.

economy must correspond to $S^N - I = X - M$, Figure 14.3 highlights that the decrease in national saving is matched by a deterioration in the trade balance. How does that happen? From the national income identity, we know that an increase in government spending also increases national income. From our import demand function, we know that an increase in income then raises imports. Since exports are fixed, the trade balance must therefore deteriorate.

We can break down the mechanism of the model even further by highlighting each specific effect in response to expansionary fiscal policy. National saving is the only variable directly affected by the change in government spending; therefore the S^N–I line is the only line to shift (the X–M line stays put). Expansionary fiscal policy also increases national income with two effects. First, higher national income increases private saving: a movement along the S^N–I line. Second, the increase in national income causes domestic consumers to spend more, and some of this spending is on foreign goods. This effect is a movement along the X–M line. The economy moves from Y_0 reaching its new equilibrium at Y_1: a higher level of income in an economy that now exhibits a trade deficit.

That an increase in government spending has increased output is no surprise – we knew this from our introductory macro class. The new discovery is that the increase in government spending leads to a deterioration of the trade balance. This implication ties fiscal deficits to trade deficits![2] Intuitively, in an open economy, the increase in income generated by the increase in government spending leads to a higher consumption of imports, in turn leading to a deterioration in the trade balance.

The Small Open-Economy Multiplier

By opening the simple closed-economy model to international trade, we found that expansionary fiscal policy causes a decline in the trade balance. There is an additional, subtler implication, however. We can also compare how *effective* fiscal policy is in raising output in the closed and in the open economy. Basically we want to compare the extent of the national income expansion due to a \$1 increase in government spending in the closed and in the open economy. The formal evaluation of the effectiveness of fiscal policy in the closed and open economies can be undertaken by comparing the multipliers. Here we refer to the income and spending multiplier effect in macroeconomics that occurs when a change in aggregate demand causes a subsequent change in aggregate output in the economy.

Consider, for example, an increase in government spending without a corresponding increase in taxation. This increase in fiscal spending leads to higher income because the government purchases more goods and/or hires more government employees. The goods need to be produced and firms then need to hire more workers (or raise the wages of existing workers to entice them to work longer hours). A change in government spending therefore has a direct effect on income (the increased demand for goods) and an indirect effect (the increased income of the labor force) that, in turn, creates another increase in income though an increase in aggregate consumption demand.

---

2 See also the *New York Times* article, "America Is Borrowing Trouble," April 9, 2001, by Nobel prize-winning economists Franco Modigliani and Robert Solow, in Case Study II.

The open-economy multiplier can be derived using the national income equilibrium equation (14.1). As suggested before, if P, P^* and E are assumed to be fixed, we can as well set them up equal to 1, and the trade balance reduces to $TB = X - M = \bar{X} - \bar{M} - mY$.

After substituting for the consumption function (14.2) and the trade balance, the national income equilibrium equation becomes[3] $Y = \bar{C} + c(Y - T) + I + G + \bar{X} - \bar{M} - mY$.

We bring all the terms in Y on the left hand side $Y(1 - c + m) = \bar{C} - cT + I + G + \bar{X} - \bar{M}$ and solve for income

$$Y = \frac{\bar{C} - cT + I + G + \bar{X} - \bar{M}}{(s + m)} \tag{14.7}$$

Note that we have again used the definition that $s = (1-c)$. We can use the last equation to show that the change in income due to a change in government spending is $\partial Y / \partial G = 1/(s + m)$. So for every dollar that government spending increases, national income increases by $1/(s + m)$.

Small open-economy multiplier: $1/(s + m)$

Since the marginal propensity to save and the marginal propensity to import are both smaller than unity (as well as their sum since they are small), this implies that output increases by more than the dollar of new government spending. If the marginal propensity to save is 0.2 and the marginal propensity to import is 0.3, a 100 million dollar increase in government spending then raises income by $200 million, due to the multiplier effect.

In the closed economy, the fiscal policy multiplier is $1/s$, since the marginal propensity to import is zero, $m=0$ with no imports. The difference between the closed-economy multiplier and the small open-economy multiplier therefore depends crucially on the marginal propensity to import, m. As long as the marginal propensity to import is greater than zero, the open-economy multiplier is smaller than the closed-economy multiplier, $1/(s + m) < 1/s$. The greater the marginal propensity to import, however, the more dramatic the difference between the closed and small open economy is and the less effective expansionary fiscal policy is in raising output. A greater marginal propensity to import generates larger trade deficits (equation 14.5) as larger fractions of domestic income are spent on foreign goods. In sum, smaller increases in domestic output will materialize, because a larger fraction of every dollar of extra domestic income received will be spent abroad stimulating the foreign economy instead of the domestic economy.

This analysis reveals an important insight; expansionary fiscal policy not only worsens the trade balance, but it also becomes less and less effective at stimulating domestic output as the marginal propensity to import increases. In the closed economy, the entire increase in income is spent on domestic goods while, in the open economy, a fraction of this increase is spent on foreign goods; this fraction does not translate into an increase in income and employment at home. Therefore, in the open economy, the increased demand for domestic goods is smaller for any given change in government expenditures, implying a smaller multiplier effect.

---

3 To simplify matters we assume a flat tax, so that T is an exogenous policy variable.

Fiscal Policy and Crowding Out

In the previous section, we neglected to highlight one additional effect of the increase in government spending: it affects the interest rate. Since equipment investment depends crucially on the interest rate, we also need to discuss the "crowding-out" effect in the open economy. We have encountered the crowding-out effect in the closed economy, let us review the concept briefly below.

Whenever there is an increase in government spending, income rises (see Figure 14.3). The expansion triggers an increase in the money demand, as richer consumers want to buy more goods and need more money to do so. The surge in the demand for money results in a higher interest rate (the price of money). As the interest rate rises, equipment investment declines (see equation 14.3), so that the increase in government spending is said to "crowd out" private investment.

We can integrate crowding out into our model and in Figure 14.4 we illustrate its effect. In this case, the final equilibrium of the economy is at Y_1 and not at Y' where the economy would have reached its equilibrium had the interest rate not risen. Compared to Y', the new equilibrium corresponds to a lower level of output, since the rise in the interest rate caused the crowding out of investment, resulting in a smaller expansion.

To draw Figure 14.4, we simply modify Figure 14.3 (where we implicitly held the interest rate constant) to include the change in the interest rate and its adverse effect on investment (e.g. equipment, new plants) by firms. As interest rates rise and government spending crowds out private equipment investment, S^N–I shifts back to the level of output Y_1. The government's crowding out actually has a positive effect on the trade balance because the reduction in output due to lower investment results in reduced purchases of foreign goods.

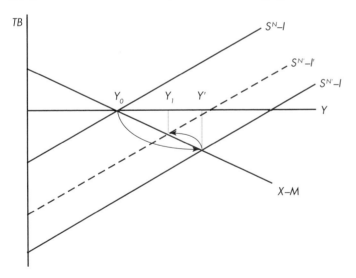

FIGURE 14.4 Fiscal Policy and Crowding out in a Small Open Economy: Fixed Exchange Rates

An increase in government spending raises income. Higher levels of income increase the demand for money (to undertake more financial transactions), which drives up the interest rate. The increase in the interest rate lowers equipment investment. Therefore expansionary fiscal policy "crowds out", or reduces, investment as indicated by the additional shift all the way to $S^{N'}$ – I'. In the open economy, crowding out has an additional implication: it reduces the trade deficit.

Monetary Policy

We can also use our simple model to examine monetary policy. In fact, our analysis of the crowding-out effects has already laid some important groundwork. An increase in the money supply lowers the interest rate and stimulates investment and output. The increase in investment, I, shifts the S^N–I line to the right. For a given level of national saving, the country must increase imports to acquire the additional domestic equipment demanded. As it stimulates the economy, the increase in investment raises national saving, but not sufficiently to meet the new demand for investment, so the trade balance still deteriorates.

The increase in income also increases overall spending on foreign goods worsening the balance of trade. In conclusion we find that both expansionary fiscal and monetary policies under fixed exchange rates without capital mobility result in increases in income just as in the closed economy. The new result is that both expansionary fiscal and monetary policies also cause deteriorations in the trade balance.

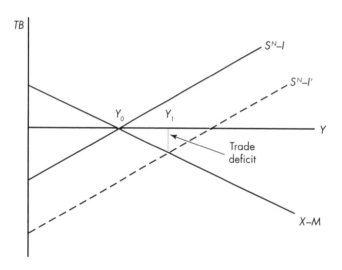

FIGURE 14.5 Monetary Policy in a Small Open Economy: Fixed Exchange Rates

Expansionary monetary policy has exactly the same impact as fiscal policy: it increases output, but also creates a trade deficit. Monetary policy works through the interest rate. An expansion of the money supply lowers the interest rate and shifts the S^N–I line down to the right because investment increases.

Devaluation or Revaluation

Whether the economy is closed or open, the country can use fiscal as well as monetary policy to achieve specific goals. In the open economy, assuming a fixed exchange rate regime, there exists an additional policy option: to change the official peg between the domestic currency and the foreign currencies. While the central bank promises to keep the price of foreign currency fixed, it may decide to undertake a one-time change in the level at which it keeps the price pegged. Instead of exchanging 2 units of domestic currency for 1 unit of foreign currency, the central bank may simply set a new price for the foreign currency; at the end of the day, the central bank may announce that, from now on, 3 units of domestic currency are now required to buy one unit of foreign currency. This example is equivalent to a one-time devaluation of the domestic currency.[4] Conversely, a decrease in the price of the foreign currency in terms of the domestic currency, i.e. fewer units of domestic currency needed to buy one unit of foreign currency, corresponds to a revaluation of the domestic currency.

We know from Chapter 13 that, after a devaluation, imports are more expensive for the domestic residents while the foreigners find domestic exports cheaper. The result is a decrease in the domestic demand for imports and an increase in the foreign demand for the country's exports, i.e. an improvement in the balance of trade.[5] This improvement leads to an increase in aggregate demand. The opposite is true in the case of a revaluation.

In terms of our TB/Y graph, the line directly affected by a change in the exchange rate, E, is the $X-M$ line. A devaluation shifts the line to the right thus increasing output (as foreign demand for domestic goods increases while domestic demand for foreign goods drops) while a revaluation shifts it to the left. The shift in Figure 14.6 illustrates that a devaluation increases income, due to an improved trade balance. A revaluation would have the opposite effect.

Using Figure 14.6, we can analyze the effect of a devaluation step-by-step. Assume that we start in equilibrium at Y_0 with balanced trade. The initial impact is an increase in the value of exports from X to X' while imports drop from M to M'. These are exogenous changes affecting $\bar{X}$ and $\bar{M}$. The

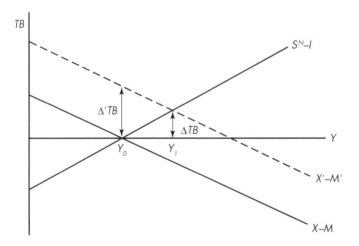

FIGURE 14.6 Devaluation in a Small Open Economy

As a result of the devaluation, exports, X, increase while imports, M, drop. The $X-M$ line shifts up as the devaluation improves the trade balance to increase output. The increase in income due to the devaluation also increases imports, so that the economy moves along the $X'-M'$ line until it reaches its new equilibrium Y_1.

---

4 i.e. a revaluation from the point-of-view of the foreign currency. So it is very important to specify which currency devalues or revalues with respect to which currency.

5 We assume all along that the Marshall–Lerner condition is fulfilled (see Chapter 13).

vertical shift of the *X–M* line measures the full impact $\Delta'TB$ of the devaluation assuming no change in income *Y*. However the increased demand for domestic goods by foreigners increases aggregate demand and stimulates the economy. As domestic income rises to Y_1, domestic consumers increase their import purchases, so that the final improvement in the trade balance $\Delta'TB$ will eventually be smaller than the initial shift of the S^N–*I* line.

A Well-Publicized Revaluation: The Case of China in 2005

A good example of the effects of a revaluation was provided by the Chinese Central Bank on July 22, 2005. On that date, the Bank of China changed the official price for the dollar from 8.2865 renminbi per dollar to 8.1211 – a 2 percent revaluation of the renminbi against the dollar. The Chinese central bank had kept the exchange rate against the dollar fixed for 10 years (1995 to 2005).

A second significant change that occurred on the same date concerned the selection of a new "anchor" for the renminbi. Instead of fixing the currency to the U.S. dollar only, the renminbi is now tied to a basket of eleven currencies with different weights for each one. Four currencies contribute to the bulk of the basket: 43 percent for the U.S. dollar, 18 percent for Japanese yen, 14 percent for the euro and 9 percent for the South Korean won. The large share for the U.S. dollar reflects the fact that China trades predominantly with two $-based economies, the U.S. and Hong Kong (Hong Kong also fixes its currency to the U.S. dollar). Since July 2005, the Chinese exchange rate has gradually appreciated against the dollar. By June 2007 the exchange rate had slipped to 7.66 renminbi per dollar.

Did the revaluation of the renminbi reduce the size of the U.S. trade deficit with China? Figure 14.7 below shows the evolution of trade in goods between the U.S. and China since 2000. The U.S. merchandise deficit skyrocketed over this period, and there is no evidence of improvement after the 2005 revaluation. To explain this, one might invoke the small extent of the revaluation. Many economists argue also that the renminbi is 10 percent to 30 percent undervalued.

There might be still another culprit. Recall that the trade deficit is determined by the intersection of the S^N–*I* and the *X–M* lines. The Chinese revaluation shifts the *X–M* line, but we have not considered what happened to S^N–*I* line over the same period. It turns out that personal saving in the U.S. declined to zero (!) in the late 1990s and then turned negative (!!) by 2005. Of course the massive U.S. budget deficit also constitutes negative government savings. In contrast the Chinese personal savings rate is about 30 percent of personal income and the government is running a massive fiscal surplus. Therefore net national saving in China is closer to 40 percent.

Figure 14.7 indicates that despite the July 2005 revaluation and the subsequent appreciation of the renminbi, the U.S. trade balance with China has deteriorated even further. Case Studies I and II address the recent trend in the U.S. to correct the U.S. trade deficit with tariffs. From our simple model it should be abundantly clear how futile such legislation would be.

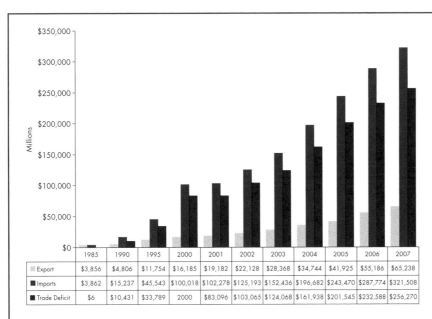

FIGURE 14.7 U.S. Trade With China, 1985–2007

Source: adapted from U.S. Census Bureau, Foreign Trade Statistics

This figure illustrates the trends in U.S. exports and imports with China as well as the resulting trade deficit. Although U.S. exports to China have increased substantially in the past 5 years, the trade gap between the two countries has exploded. The revaluation of the Chinese currency in 2005 has barely made a dent in the imbalance.

Policy with Fixed Exchange Rates: A Summary

The following table summarizes how key variables in the economy are affected by the impact of:

a) expansionary fiscal policy (an increase in government spending or decrease in net taxes),
b) expansionary monetary policy (an increase in the money supply),
c) a devaluation (an increase in the exchange rate) on the main variables in the model.

					Immediate effect on		Overall impact on	
	S^N	I	X	M	S^N–I line	X–M line	TB	Y
Increase in G or decrease in T	↓	–	–	–	Shifts right	–	↓	↑
Increase in M	–	↑	–	–	Shifts right	–	↓	↑
Devaluation	–	–	↑	↓	–	Shifts right	↑	↑

A SMALL OPEN ECONOMY WITH FLEXIBLE EXCHANGE RATES

In a world of flexible exchange rates, supply of and demand for the foreign currency determine its price (the exchange rate). The exchange rate fluctuates freely to maintain the equilibrium in the foreign exchange market at all times. We only have two small changes in our set of assumptions, a change in assumption 2) while assumption 5) about sterilization becomes irrelevant.

Summary of Assumptions

1) Small open economy

Exports	$X = P\bar{X}$
Imports	$M = EP^* (\bar{M} + mY)$

2) Flexible exchange rate $\qquad E \neq \bar{E}$
3) Fixed prices – short run $\qquad P = \bar{P}$ and $P^* = \bar{P}^*$

From our definition of the BoP, we know that, in a world without capital flows, BoP movements are entirely due to adjustments in the trade balance (or more generally, in the current account). Therefore we can derive an immediate, simple result: in a world without capital flows, the BoP is in equilibrium whenever the trade balance is in equilibrium.

Whenever the trade balance is positive, there exists an excess supply of foreign currency, since domestic residents sell more goods to foreigners than they buy from them. The excess supply causes the price of the foreign currency to fall; this is equivalent to an appreciation of the domestic currency. A negative trade balance will have the exact opposite effects.

The question is then how much of an appreciation or a depreciation will the country experience in response to a change in the trade balance? The simple answer is that the exchange rate rises or falls until equilibrium in the foreign exchange market is restored. This equilibrium is restored when the supply of foreign currency equals the demand for foreign currency. This can only correspond to a trade balance equal to zero (so $FA = 0$ too). The change in the price of the foreign currency takes place just about instantaneously. For instance, as soon as there is excess demand for the currency, its price will be bid up; those who need to buy the foreign currency (e.g. importers) are willing to pay a higher price for the foreign currency from those who hold the currency (e.g. exporters). Any disequilibrium will vanish rapidly as crowds of agents, around the globe, buy or sell the currency until the exchange rate adjusts to equate supply and demand and clear the market.

The insight that the exchange rate adjusts to assure a zero trade balance has a dramatic implication for our model. Recall that our open economy national income identity is that $Y = C + I + G + TB$. However, we have just learned that the exchange rate always adjusts such that the TB is zero. Hence with flexible exchange rates, and no capital mobility, the open economy national income equilibrium reduces to $Y = C + I + G$: this is precisely the national income equilibrium condition for the closed economy! The open economy under flexible exchange rates seems identical to the closed economy; as a result, fiscal and monetary policy have the same effect on output in either a closed economy or an open economy with flexible exchange rates (and no capital mobility). However, we need to compare the open economy with flexible exchange rate and with fixed exchange rates. We find that fiscal and monetary policies are more effective with flexible exchange rates because the impact of the policies on the demand for foreign goods is neutralized by the change in the exchange rate.

Flexible Exchange Rates and External Shocks

It is also important to highlight the powerful implication that the model suggests for flexible exchange rate regimes. Not only does the economy look like the closed economy, the flexible exchange rate also insulates the country from external shocks (such as in increase in the price of oil or a global recession). Imagine the rest of the world slips into a global recession. Foreign demand for domestic goods would drop and the domestic trade balance would deteriorate, resulting in a contraction of the domestic economy. In Figure 14.8, this is illustrated as a shift backward of the X–M line to X'–M.

Under flexible exchange rates, the negative trade balance triggers a depreciation of the domestic currency to restore equilibrium in the foreign exchange market. The depreciation stimulates exports and reduces imports – resulting in an improvement of the trade balance, and an expansion for the domestic economy. Equilibrium is restored once the domestic exchange rate has depreciated sufficiently to generate a zero trade balance. The X–M line shifts back to its original position, returning the economy to its original level of output: the global recession has been weathered by the flexible exchange rate regime with a swift depreciation of the domestic currency.

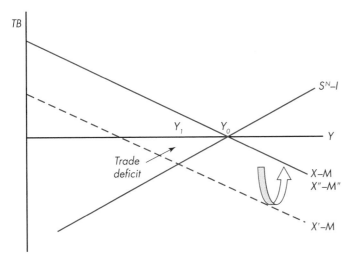

FIGURE 14.8 Insulation from a Foreign Disturbance with Flexible Exchange Rate

Flexible exchange rates insulate a country from foreign shocks. For example, a recession in the rest of the world would cause a decline in domestic exports from X to X' (shifting X–M line down to X'–M) generating a trade deficit. The trade deficit implies excess supply of the domestic currency (equivalently, excess demand for the foreign currency) and the value of the domestic currency falls. This depreciation continues until increased exports and decreased imports restore the balanced trade at Y_0.

Policy in a Small Open Economy with Flexible Exchange Rates

With flexible exchange rates, we only consider fiscal and monetary policy (by definition the central bank is not fiddling with exchange rate policy). The policy effects mirror those of the closed economy since the national income equilibrium equation is identical in the two economies. However, the adjustment process for the economy is slightly more intricate in the open economy than in the basic closed-economy model (taught in an intermediate macroeconomics class).

Fiscal Policy

As we have shown above, an increase in government spending shifts the S^N–I line down to the right. The resulting expansion of the economy brings with it a trade deficit. This is the end of the story with fixed exchange rates. However, with flexible exchange rates, a depreciation *has* to occur to restore the trade balance (Figure 14.9). This depreciation further stimulates the economy as the X–M line shifts to the right. Therefore fiscal policy under flexible exchange rates is highly effective. Instead of expanding output from Y_0 to Y', only, as would be the case with fixed exchange rates, the resulting economic boom leads to an output increase to Y_1.

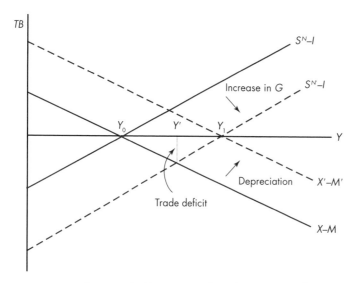

FIGURE 14.9 Increase in Government Spending in a Small Open Economy: Flexible Exchange Rates

As a result of the expansionary fiscal policy, S^N–I shifts right. A trade deficit generates excess supply of the domestic currency and the resulting depreciation shifts the X–M line to the right. The depreciation therefore enhances the impact of the fiscal expansion. The economy expands from Y_0 to Y_1, far beyond the level it would have achieved under the fixed exchange rates (Y').

Monetary Policy

Monetary policy affects the interest rate via a change in the money supply. The change in the interest rate, in turn, affects the level of investment I. Investment is of course a crucial determinant of S^N–I. Expansionary monetary policy lowers the interest rate and increases demand for investment. This shifts the S^N–I line to the right and income increases.

The increase in income raises demands for imports and the ensuing trade deficit triggers a depreciation under flexible exchange rates. The graph outlining these impacts is identical to Figure 14.9 with one exception: the cause for the original shift of the S^N–I line is an increase in the money supply resulting in an increase in investment I, instead of a decrease in national saving due to expansionary fiscal policy. So S^N–I shifts due to an increase in I rather than a decrease in S^N. Again we observe that, under flexible exchange rates, the trade balance adjusts automatically since the price of foreign exchange responds immediately to equate supply of and demand for foreign exchange. To the degree that this adjustment is immediate, the economy moves from Y_0 to Y_1 along the horizontal axis so that imports and exports are always balanced. In practice, even foreign exchange adjustments may take time and we have discussed a number of reasons why trade may not adjust instantaneously in our discussion of the J curve in Chapter 13. To the extent that the adjustment is not instantaneous, the movement from Y_0 to Y_1 might not take place exactly along the horizontal axis, but dip temporarily below the line to exhibit a trade deficit.

These two cases show clearly that, under flexible exchange rates, the expansion due to either fiscal or monetary policy is larger than under fixed exchange rates. Since there are no adverse effects due to the creation of trade deficits, the expansion is equivalent to what would have happened with the closed economy. In conclusion, the fiscal multipliers in this case are the same as the closed-economy ones.

Policy with Flexible Exchange Rates: A Summary

Impact of expansionary fiscal policy (increase in government spending or decrease in net taxes) and of expansionary monetary policy (increase in the money supply) on the main variables in the model.

					Immediate effect on		*Overall impact on*	
	S^N	I	X	M	S^N–I line	X–M line	TB = 0	Y^1
Increase in G or decrease in T	↓	–	↑	↓	Shifts right	Shifts right	–	↑
Increase in M	–	↑	↑	↓	Shifts right	Shifts right	–	↑

[1] Evidently the impact on income is greater than in the fixed exchange rate case.

We have developed the basic model for the small open economy without capital flows and with sterilization and considered the mechanics of fiscal and monetary policies under both fixed and flexible exchange rates (as well as devaluation with the fixed exchange rate case). Now we need to apply and extend the model. In the next chapter, we relax some of the assumptions. We need to investigate whether the economy can indeed sustain potentially long periods of sterilization as implied by our analysis above. After all, the trade deficits that we observed under fixed exchange rates above were not self-correcting. Then it would be valuable to extend our policy analysis by thinking in terms of the goals the policy makers want to achieve and by entertaining the thought that they could use more than one policy at a time. Finally, what happens if the domestic economy is large enough for its policies to affect its trade partners? These topics are left for Chapter 15 to examine.

Summary of Key Concepts

1. A crucial determinant of trade deficits is a country's lack of national saving. If the demand for investment exceeds national saving, a country must import goods from abroad to meet investment demand.
2. Since national saving is the sum of private and government savings (the budget surplus), both private citizens and government entities are to blame for a national saving shortfall.
3. Under fixed exchange rates, fiscal and monetary expansions stimulate output in the open economy, but they also cause a deterioration in the trade balance.
4. Since part of domestic income is spent on foreign goods, expansionary fiscal and monetary policies are not as effective as in the closed economy under fixed exchange rates. The small open-economy multiplier is smaller than the closed-economy multiplier.
5. A devaluation improves a small country's balance of trade and consequently stimulates its economy.
6. A flexible exchange rate regime insulates small open economies from foreign originated disturbances.
7. The impact of fiscal and monetary policy is greater with flexible exchange rates than with fixed exchange rates because economic policies are enhanced by simultaneous deprecia- tions or appreciations of the domestic currency.

CASE STUDY I

America is Borrowing Trouble
by Franco Modigliani and Robert M. Solow
New York Times, April 9, 2001

Many have criticized President Bush's proposal for a deep and lasting cut in income taxes, but hardly anyone has addressed its implications for what may well be the greatest potential danger facing the economy in the years to come: the large and growing deficit in our international trade balance. A massive, permanent tax cut would make the international economic position of the United States worse, not better. This is in addition to its other disadvantages.

The past decade has been one of exceptional

economic vigor: output increased nearly 40 percent, investment more than doubled and consumption grew just over 40 percent, pushed by a spending spree that reduced personal saving to near zero. But this rosy picture was accompanied by one worrisome development: throughout this period, spending grew faster than what the country earned, spilling over, in large part, into a growing trade deficit. By the end of 2000, the excess of expenditure over income had reached about 4 percent of America's gross domestic product and was apparently still on the rise.

For a country, just as for a family, there are only two ways of getting the money to spend more than one's income: borrowing it and selling assets. In the case of nations, the creditors and the buyers of the assets are foreigners. And indeed, throughout this prosperous past decade the United States sold more and more assets, like government bonds and shares in its companies, and went deeper and deeper into debt.

But why should one worry about this development? It is not serious as long as the debt is small and remains under control so as not to worry creditors. But if the debt is not under control, or if some event makes the debtor appear less creditworthy than before, the creditors may decide that they are not willing to finance a country's growing debt – for fear of a depreciation of the debtor's currency that lowers asset values in their own currencies. They may even want to liquidate part of their investment in search of diversification. If such a thing happened to the United States, there could be very unpleasant consequences for Americans.

Depreciation of the dollar would make imports so expensive and exports so cheap as to eliminate the trade deficit. But this depreciation would create a further motive for foreigners to liquidate their American assets, dumping the dollars so obtained in exchange for foreign currency. The size and power of the American economy has protected us from capital flight in shorter episodes of unfavorable trade balance, but there is no guarantee that this will remain true. Nor could the dollar be propped up through purchases by the Federal Reserve or the Treasury, since their small reserves of foreign currency would be woefully inadequate to stem the tide. (The United States reserves amount to some

$60 billion compared with a current trade deficit of $400 billion a year, just two months' borrowing.)

Thus a flight from the dollar would produce a deep devaluation and accompanying rise in the prices of imports and of things made with imports. At worst we might experience a wage and price spiral, calling for sharply higher interest rates. The final result could be falling investment and output, and high unemployment. And our weakness would be very likely to spread to other countries.

Few believe that this hard-landing scenario is an immediate threat. But there is good reason to believe that if nothing is done to change the current course, the probability of a costly ending will keep increasing. To avoid that danger, the administration and Congress should develop a plan that promptly stops the growth of the trade deficit, then reduces it to zero and possibly produces a positive balance, allowing for some repayment – and all this without an appreciable increase in unemployment.

The success of such a plan would rest on two main ingredients: a gradual reduction of total domestic expenditure relative to income – that is, a rise in national saving – and an increase in net exports.

These two components should proceed hand in hand; indeed, given the current level of demand for domestically produced goods and services, if we added to it by shifting more of our output to exports prematurely, the result would be inflationary pressures. Conversely, a reduction of domestic demand would have to be countered by an expansion of net exports to avoid creating a contraction in output and employment.

Unfortunately, there is no evidence that the administration and Congress are concerned with the balance of trade issue or are even aware of it. On the contrary, President Bush is galloping in exactly the wrong direction with his advocacy of using the likely (though by no means certain) large forthcoming budget surplus for a deep, permanent tax cut, rather than for retiring the debt or endowing Social Security – or both.

The president's proposal is just the opposite of the needed increase in national saving, and the consequences would be very negative. First, it would raise consumption by roughly one dollar for every dollar of tax reduction – which is precisely what the supporters of the bill claim to be its justification.

But, given the limitations on our labor force and our ability to produce, the rise in consumption would sooner or later produce some combination of the following unhealthy outcomes: significant inflationary pressures, in part undoing the tax rebate; a likely rise in interest rates to counter the inflation, leading to a reduction in investment; and a further increase in the trade deficit.

Can anyone really favor encouraging a further expansion of the recent spending spree at the expense of investment, the source of future growth? Or reducing taxes at the expense of a sharp addition to future taxes, required to service a much larger debt at higher interest rates? Or supporting a tax cut financed with money borrowed abroad, even in the favorable case in which foreign lenders would be prepared to finance a rapidly growing debt?

If Congress is acting responsibly, the least it can do is to postpone a deep permanent tax cut until this trade balance has turned positive.

But, some tax-cut proponents will argue, what if right now there is a clear danger of a significant economic contraction? If this were clearly the case – and it is still in doubt – then some measure to support demand might be appropriate. But the best approach would be to expand net exports, helping both domestic demand and the trade balance – perhaps by aiming at a controlled, limited devaluation of the dollar and by encouraging other countries, like Europe, to pursue more expansionary policies in their own interest.

It may even be justifiable to consider a modest, temporary tax cut, but with a warning that theory and evidence suggest that transitory tax cuts are likely to produce only limited, quick effects.

Franco Modigliani and Robert M. Solow are Nobel Prize winners in economics and professors emeriti at the Massachusetts Institute of Technology.

CASE STUDY QUESTIONS

1. Why are Modigliani and Solow against tax cuts?

2. What is the problem that Modigliani and Solow see with the trade deficit?

3. What is the problem that Modigliani and Solow see with the fiscal deficit?

4. Why do you think temporary tax cuts produce only limited effects on the economy?

5. Use the TB/Y diagram to outline the Modigliani–Solow argument. Can you devise a policy that would work better (i.e., provide economic stimulus while avoiding a trade deficit)?

CASE STUDY II

Greenspan Warns against Raising Tariffs on China
By Joseph Rebello and Elizabeth Price
Dow Jones Newswires and Wall Street Journal, June 24, 2005

Fed Chief Calls for Restraint in Congress, Urges Beijing to be Flexible on Currency
WASHINGTON – Federal Reserve Chairman Alan Greenspan warned Congress Thursday that a big increase in tariffs on Chinese imports would "materially lower" U.S. living standards and urged

lawmakers instead to let financial markets resolve trade imbalances with that country.

But, in testimony to the Senate Finance Committee, Mr. Greenspan said China ought to adopt a more flexible currency regime for the sake of its own economic stability and for the sake of "all participants in the global trading system."

The Fed chairman urged the Chinese government to act speedily to alter the fixed exchange rate system it has had for the last decade, saying "the sooner . . . the better."

Treasury Secretary John Snow also said China must introduce a more flexible currency system and open its economy to more imports in order to head off a dangerous wave of trade protectionism around the world.

"Nothing would do more damage to the prospects of increasing living standards throughout the world than efforts to inhibit the flow of trade," Mr. Snow said in prepared testimony to the Senate Finance Committee, where he was appearing with Mr. Greenspan. "However, it is incumbent on China to address concerns before mounting pressures worldwide to restrict trade harm the openness of the international trading system."

The Chinese government manages its currency through intervention and a system of capital controls that effectively pegs its currency at 8.28 yuan to the U.S. dollar. For nearly two years the Bush administration has publicly urged China to move to a more flexible system. China's leaders have said they want to do so, but can only move when the banking system reforms sufficiently to handle the adjustment.

The delay has provoked impatience in Congress, where a raft of legislative proposals would impose trade sanctions on Chinese imports in retaliation for the currency peg.

One bill, sponsored by Sens. Charles Schumer, a New York Democrat, and Lindsey Graham, a South Carolina Republican, would impose 27.5 percent tariffs on imports from China if Beijing doesn't allow its currency to appreciate within a period of 180 days. That measure, in an amendment to unrelated legislation, recently attracted 67 votes in favor – a very strong statement of support from both political parties. Messrs. Schumer and Graham agreed to withdraw it after Senate leaders promised a stand-alone vote this summer.

Mr. Snow said these proposals, if enacted, would not only harm the U.S. economy, but would also delay any action by the Chinese government to loosen its peg. "I cannot overstate my firm belief that resorting to isolationist trade policies would be ineffective, disruptive to markets and damaging to America's special role as the world's leading advocate for open markets and fair trade," Mr. Snow said. "Imposing trade penalties on China would likely provoke Chinese retaliation against U.S. exports as well," he added.

Mr. Snow repeated that China's currency peg has become "distortionary" to world financial markets and hinders China's ability to control inflation in the economy. He again said that the most effective strategy for reducing global trade imbalances is for Asian countries to allow more flexible currency markets, faster economic growth in Europe and Japan, and raising savings in the U.S.

Mr. Greenspan said that the U.S. government shouldn't dictate precisely how China should change its fixed exchange-rate system, saying Chinese authorities are better-equipped to find the right remedy.

Mr. Snow also said the U.S. budget deficit should fall to below 3 percent of gross domestic product this year, if Congress keeps spending under control. "We are also working to put in place innovative policies to increase the savings rate," he said.

Mr. Greenspan told lawmakers that a steep increase in tariffs would be counterproductive, hurting U.S. consumers without reducing the overall U.S. trade deficit. "The broad tariff on Chinese goods that has recently been proposed would significantly lower U.S. imports from China but would comparably raise U.S. imports from other low-cost sources of supply." "Prices of U.S. imports," he said, "would rise slightly" but "few, if any American jobs would be protected." "More generally, any significant elevation of tariffs that substantially reduces our overall imports, by keeping out competitively priced goods, would materially lower our standard of living," Mr. Greenspan said. "A policy to dismantle the global trading system in a misguided effort to protect jobs from competition would rebound to the eventual detriment of all U.S. job seekers, as well as millions of American consumers."

Mr. Greenspan played down the significance of the U.S. trade deficit with China, which reached a record $162 billion at the end of 2004. "The widening of the United States' bilateral trade deficit with China, measured gross, has been largely in lieu of wider deficits with other Asian economies, including Japan," he said. "Measured by value added, our bilateral deficits with China would have been far less, and our bilateral deficits with other Asian exporters would have been far more."

Under the circumstances, a decision by the Chinese government to revalue its currency – which is also known as the renminbi – would merely "redirect trade within Asia." He added: "Some observers mistakenly believe that a marked increase in the value of the Chinese renminbi relative to the U.S. dollar would significantly increase manufacturing activity and jobs in the United States. I am aware of no credible evidence that supports such a conclusion."

"Still," Mr. Greenspan said, "China should move quickly to change its exchange rate system – for its own good. To maintain that system, China has to purchase large amounts of foreign currencies and issue domestic-currency bonds to keep inflation from running out of control." "That task," he said, will become increasingly difficult for its central bank to perform." "Sterilization of continuing inflows of speculative funds will presumably become more difficult as the scale of these operations, already large, increases over time," Mr. Greenspan added, "It's better for China to let market forces regulate the currency because financial markets, if left free to continually reprice interest rates and asset values, will identify and respond to imbalances far sooner than a system based on administrative edict."

CASE STUDY QUESTIONS

1. Why would the U.S. be interested in raising tariffs on China? And what does a tariff have to do with an overvalued Chinese exchange rate? How would a flexible exchange rate solve the issue?

2. Is Mr. Snow really worried about inflation in China? Why do you think he wants a more flexible exchange rate in China.

3. Snow calls the Chinese exchange rate "distortionary." Who loses and who gains in the U.S.?

4. The article states: "Mr. Snow also said the U.S. budget deficit should fall to below 3 percent of gross domestic product this year, if Congress keeps spending under control. 'We are also working to put in place innovative policies to increase the savings rate,' he said." What does the budget deficit have to do with the Chinese exchange rate?

5. What do you think are "innovative measures to increase the savings rate?" And how is the saving rate related to the Chinese exchange rate?

Questions for Study and Review

1. In 1995, Mexico maintained a fixed exchange rate regime relative to the U.S. dollar. In the six months prior to the Mexican national elections in October 1995, the public debt increased by 30 percent.

   a. Use the *TB/Y* diagram to explain the effects of the increase in public debt. Be specific; highlight the effect of changes in the trade balance and output.

   b. Why do you think the Mexican debt increased? Use a graph.

2. From the Wall Street Journal Online News Roundup, "Foreign Exchange Section" WSJ May 3, 2002: NEW YORK: "The dollar fell sharply in Friday trading, with dealers clearly worried about the sustainability of the U.S. economic recovery. In midday trading, the dollar was at ¥126.93, compared with ¥127.88 late Thursday in New York, while the euro traded at 91.68 U.S. cents, up from 90.28 U.S. cents the previous session. In the U.S., the closely watched monthly employment report was weaker than expected, adding to the dollar's woes. For April, the unemployment rate rose to 6 percent, well above the 5.8 percent economists had forecast. 'The market's clearly bearish on the dollar,' said Mitul Kotecha, head of global currency strategy at Crédit Agricole Indosuez."

   a. If the statement that "dealers [are] clearly worried about the sustainability of the U.S. economic recovery" means that traders are worried that consumption expenditures in the U.S. will fall, what will be the effect on output, reserves, and the trade balance? Use the *TB/Y* diagram. Assume the U.S. has a fixed exchange rate.

   b. If the statement that "dealers [are] clearly worried about the sustainability of the U.S. economic recovery" means that traders are worried that consumption expenditures in the U.S. will fall, what will be the effect on output, the exchange rate, and the trade balance? Use the *TB/Y* diagram. Assume the U.S. has a flexible exchange rate.

3. Under fixed exchange rate regimes, when countries seek to improve their trade balance with fiscal policy, how is policy effectiveness influenced by the marginal propensity to import? Draw graphs to explain your answer.

4. On Oct. 30, 2000 the *Wall Street Journal* announced that "U.S. income growth slowed to 2.7 percent from 5.3 percent in the previous quarter. The 2.7 percent came in well below the forecast 3.5 percent." Assume Hong Kong and the U.S. are on a fixed exchange rate regime, while the U.S. and Europe are on a flexible exchange rate regime. As income growth in the U.S. decelerates, what do you expect to happen to:

   a. the U.S. trade balance with Hong Kong?

   b. U.S. reserves?

   c. the U.S. trade balance with Europe?

   d. Hong Kong output if the reduction in U.S. growth equals a reduction in U.S. autonomous consumption?

   Draw a graph to explain each answer.

5. Assume a small country is characterized by the following equations:

Consumption	$C = 220 + .7(Y-T)$
Investment	$I = 200$
Government spending	$G = 100$
Tax	$T = 100$
Imports	$M = 100 + .2Y$
Exports	$X = 400$

a. Calculate equilibrium income Y, the corresponding balance of trade TB, and government saving S_g using the usual equilibrium condition $Y=C+I+G+X-M$.

b. Construct the equations for the S^N-I line and for the $X-M$ line and equate these two equations to calculate equilibrium income Y (you should get the same result as in a.).

c. Calculate the impact of a fiscal expansion (an increase in G equal to 100) under fixed and then under flexible exchange rates using the $S^N-I/X-M$ approach.

   i. Fixed exchange rate regime – G increases from 100 to 200

   First construct the new equations for S^N-I and $X-M$ (if they have changed). Calculate the new level of output, the balance of trade TB, and government saving S_g. Illustrate your results with the $S^N-I/X-M$ graph.

   ii. Flexible exchange rates – same change in G starting from the original model

   What happens to the exchange rate? Construct the new equations for S^N-I. What is the value of $X-M$ with flexible exchange rates? Equate S^N-I and $X-M$ to calculate the resulting level of output. Illustrate your results with the $S^N-I/X-M$ graph.

   iii. Compare your results under fixed and flexible exchange rates.

6. Use the model below to find the impact of a devaluation in a fixed exchange rate regime. (Note that now the import and the export equations include the exchange rate.) Assume the following model of the economy:

Saving	$S = -80 + .2\,Y_D$
Investment	$I = 100 - 1000r$
Exports	$X = 500 + 50\varepsilon$
Imports	$M = 50 + .2\,Y - 100\varepsilon$
Government spending	$G = 100$
Tax	$T = 100$
Disposable income	$Y_D = Y - T$
Interest rate	$r = .05$
Real exchange rate	$\varepsilon = 1$

Where Y is domestic income. The interest rate is fixed. Prices are fixed.

a. Calculate the equilibrium level of income (Y^e) using the saving-investment/trade balance equilibrium condition.

b. Calculate the corresponding trade balance. Is trade balanced or do we have a surplus or a deficit?

c. Draw the corresponding $S^N-I/X-M$ graph and show your results (include the intercepts on the vertical axis of the two lines).

d. Now assume that the central bank redefine ε from 1 to 1.2. How do you call such policy?

e. Calculate the new level of income and the new trade balance. What is the impact of the devaluation on income and on the trade balance?

f. Illustrate the effect of the devaluation on the S^N–I/X–M graph and report your results.

g. Calculate the level of income consistent with balanced trade.

h. What exchange rate policy would you recommend to reach balanced trade? What would be the impact of that policy on output?

i. Assume that the level of income calculated in Questions 5 is below full employment income. Could you recommend a better policy to reach balanced trade, i.e. a policy that will not impact income adversely?

References and Suggestions for Further Reading

Bryant, R., Currie, D., Frenkel, J., Masson, P., and Portes, R. (eds) (1989) *Macroeconomic Policies in an Interdependent World*, Washington, D.C.: Brookings Institution.

Calvo, G. and Reinhart, C. (2002) "Fear of Floating," *Quarterly Journal of Economics*, 177: 379–408.

Caramazza, F. and Aziz, J. (1998) "Fixed or Flexible? Getting the Exchange Rate Right in the 1990s," International Monetary Fund, *Economic Issues*, 13 April.

Cooper, R. (1986) "Dealing with the Trade Deficit in a Floating Rate System," *Brookings Papers on Economic Activity*, 1: 195–208.

—— (1999) "Exchange Rates Choices," Harvard University. Reprinted in P. King, and S. Kumari King (eds) (2004), *International Economics and International Economic Policy: A Reader*, 4th edition, New York: McGraw-Hill.

Corden, W. M. (1994) *Economic Policy, Exchange Rates, and the International System* (chs 1–4), Oxford: Oxford University Press.

Dornbusch, R. (1980) *Open Economy Macroeconomics* (chs 11–12), New York: Basic Books.

Eichengreen B. and Razo-Garcia S. (2006) "The International Monetary System in the Last and Next 20 Years," *Economic Policy*, 21: 393–442.

Fischer, S. (2001) "Distinguished Lecture on Economics in Government: Exchange Rate Regimes: Is the Bipolar View Correct," *Journal of Economic Perspectives*, 15: 3–24.

Frankel, J. (1993) *On Exchange Rates*, Cambridge, MA: MIT Press.

Friedman, M. (1953) "The Case for Flexible Exchange Rates," in *Essays in Positive Economics*, Chicago: University of Chicago Press.

Gagnon, J. (1993) "Exchange Rate Flexibility and the Level of International Trade," *Journal of International Economics*: 269–87.

Girton, L. and Roper, D. (1977) "A Monetary Model of Exchange Market Pressure Applied to Post-War Canadian Experience," *American Economic Review*, 67: 537–48.

Helliwell, J. and Padmore, T. (1985) "Empirical Studies of Macroeconomic Interdependence," in R. Jones and P. Kenen (eds) *Handbook of International Economics*, Vol. II: 1107–1151, Amsterdam: North-Holland.

Johnson, H. (1970) "The Case for Flexible Exchange Rates," in G. Halm (ed.) *Approaches to Greater Exchange Rate Flexibility: The Burgenstock Papers*, 100–1, Princeton, NJ: Princeton University Press.

Kenen, P. (2000) "Fixed versus Floating Exchange Rates," *Cato Journal*, 20: 109–13.

Kenen, P.B. (1984) "Macroeconomic Theory and Policy: How the Closed Economy was Opened," chapter 13 in R.W. Jones and P.B. Kenen (eds) *Handbook of International Economics, Volume 1*, Amsterdam: North-Holland.

Levy-Yeyati, E. and Sturzenegger, F. (2005) "Classifying Exchange Rate Regimes: Deeds vs. Words," *European Economic Review*, 49: 1603–1635.

Li, Y. (2006) "Trade Balance: Numbers Can Be Deceiving," *China & World Economy* 14: 54–70.

McCulloch, R. (1983) "Unexpected Real Consequences of Floating Exchange Rates," *Princeton Essays in International Finance*, 154: 6.

Modigliani, F. and Solow, R. M. (2001) "America Is Borrowing Trouble," *New York Times*, April 9.

McKibbin, W. (1988) "International Policy Coordination," *Economic Record*, 64: 242–53.

Mundell, R. (1960) "The Monetary Dynamics of International Adjustment under Fixed and Floating Exchange Rates," *Quarterly Journal of Economics*, 74: 227–57.

—— (1961) "Flexible Exchange Rates and Employment Policy," *Canadian Journal of Economics and Political Sciences*, 27: 509–17.

—— (1963) "Capital Mobility and Stabilization Policy under Fixed and Flexible Exchange Rates," *Canadian Journal of Economics and Political Sciences*, 29: 475–8. These and other related articles by Mundell are gathered in his *International Economics* (1968) New York: Macmillan.

—— (1968) *International Economics*, (chs 17–19), New York: Macmillan.

Obstfeld, M. and Rogoff, K. (1995) "The Mirage of Fixed Exchange Rates," *Journal of Economic Perspectives*, 9: 73–96.

OECD (2001) "Saving and investment: determinants and policy implications," *OECD Economic Outlook* No. 70, December.

Poole, W. (2005) "How Dangerous is the US Current Account Deficit?," Economic Policy Lecture Series (Nov. 9), St. Charles, Mo.: Lindenwood University.

Rebello J. and Price, E. (2005) "Greenspan Warns Against Raising Tariffs on China," *Dow Jones Newswires and Wall Street Journal*, June 24.

Reinsdorf, M. (2005) "Saving, Wealth, Investment, and the Current-Account Deficit," *Survey of Current Business*, April, 85: 3.

Takayama, A. (1969) "The Effects of Fiscal and Monetary Policies under Flexible and Fixed Exchange Rates," *Canadian Journal of Economics*, 2: 190–209.

Taylor, M. P. (1995) "The Economics of Exchange Rates," *Journal of Economic Literature* 33: 13–47.

U.S. Census Bureau, Foreign Trade Statistics – Trade with China.

Vines, D. (1947) "Absorption Approach to the Balance of Payments," in *New Palgrave Dictionary of Economics*.

Chapter 15

Extensions of the Basic Open-Economy Model

Policy Effectiveness and the Large Open Economy

LEARNING OBJECTIVES

By the end of this chapter you should be able to understand that:

- in the long term, trade imbalances are unsustainable with fixed exchange rates

- countries have a number of policy options to correct trade imbalances – but each option has undesirable consequences

- policy makers must balance their pursuit of full employment with the goal of an external (trade) balance in an effort to conduct sustainable economic policy

- to meet a given number of policy goals, policy makers need an equal number of policy tools

- large open economies are linked through their trade balance. Policies in one country are transmitted to the trading partner via changes in the demand for imports and exports

- the impact of policies may be enhanced or dampened through repercussions in large open economies

In the analysis of our simple model with fixed exchange rates, we made two important discoveries. First, expansionary fiscal and monetary policies cause a deterioration of the trade balance. Second, the effectiveness of fiscal and monetary policy in raising output is smaller as compared to the closed economy (or as compared to the open economy with flexible exchange rates). We also found out that exchange rate policy, such as a one-time devaluation can stimulate output. The extensions presented in this chapter include new insights about sterilization (an assumption of the model) and the possibility of using several policies to achieve several goals. Finally we relax the small economy assumption and investigate what happens when two equally sized countries trade. We continue to assume the absence of non-official capital flows.

Crucial in our fixed exchange rate analysis in the previous chapter was the assumption of sterilization. However, as we wanted to focus on the basic mechanics of the model, we did not elaborate on this assumption. In the first part of this chapter, it is now time to revisit the sterilization assumption and to highlight the consequences of sterilization. We will relax the sterilization assumption and examine how the economy responds to policy under non-sterilization. In this case, the adjustment mechanism is described by the monetary approach to the balance of payments.

Up to now, we have discussed the impact of government policies, but we have not explained what a government hopes to achieve: we will now introduce the concepts of internal and external balance. Once we have defined goals for the government, we will present the Swan model showing how the policy makers can reach these two goals with two policies.

In the last part of this chapter, we relax yet another assumption: that of the small open economy. Chapter 14 highlighted that the open economy multiplier under fixed exchange rates is smaller than the closed economy one. Is this results-driven by our strong assumption of fixed (exogenous) exports in the small open economy? Recall that we found that the multiplier is reduced because some of the domestic income is spent on foreign goods, spending that cannot stimulate the domestic economy. What if we relaxed the fixed export/small open-economy assumption and allowed our imports to make foreigners richer so that foreigners spend more and buy more from the domestic economy? Then, by importing more, we would be able to export more and perhaps it could increase policy effectiveness! At this stage, it would be intriguing to relax the fixed export/small open-economy assumption and examine whether this assumption contributes to reducing policy effectiveness in the open economy. We will set up a two-country model where countries are linked through their balance of trade and focus on the concept of repercussions in *both* economies as a result of one country's policy changes.

STERILIZATION AND POLICIES TO MANAGE EXTERNAL DEFICITS

In a country with fixed exchange rates, a deterioration of the trade balance poses a serious problem to the central bank which has to urgently address the excess demand for foreign currency. The excess demand for foreign currency tends to drive up the price of foreign currency, but that price is supposed to be held constant by the central bank. To maintain the fixed exchange rate, the central bank must intervene in the currency market selling the foreign currency that is in excess demand (such a transaction is equivalent to buying the domestic currency that is in excess supply) until equilibrium between supply and demand is restored to the currency market.

To increase the supply of foreign currency on the markets, the central bank has to dip into its foreign currency reserves. However, the sale of foreign currency cannot go on forever, since the central bank eventually runs out of foreign currency reserves. Initially, the central bank may be able to borrow reserves from foreign banks (as Italy and Britain did during their 1992 currency crisis, when they borrowed billions from the German central bank). Among other examples of this practice is the case of Uruguay (in 2002), who borrowed billions from the U.S. central bank in futile attempts to stabilize its faltering fixed exchange rate regime. If such trade deficits persist and the central bank continues to require foreign reserves to stabilize the price of its currency, the central bank may have to turn to the International Monetary Fund[1] (IMF), the international reserve lender of last resort. The IMF is an institution under the United Nations umbrella designed to provide precisely those foreign currency reserve loans necessary to stabilize currencies.

Any additional foreign reserves that the central bank can procure from third parties allow the country to sustain the trade deficit a while longer. The borrowing cannot continue forever, however. Eventually, either the trade balance must revert back to zero (where supply equals demand for foreign currency) or the central bank will be forced to stop selling foreign currency (since it borrowed all it could and still ran out of reserves). If the central bank stops intervening in the foreign exchange market, the price of foreign currency immediately rises (and the domestic currency depreciates). As a result, as soon as the central bank stops intervening, the country effectively abandons its fixed exchange rate for a flexible exchange rate regime.

Henceforth, we analyze the options a government has to correct trade imbalances in order to avert a currency crisis. In Chapter 14, we highlighted policies that stimulate or cool down the economy. Since these policies also affect the balance of trade, we can now focus on their possible role in keeping trade balanced in the context of a fixed exchange rate regime.

---

1 The history and the role of the International Monetary Fund are discussed in Chapter 21.

"Drawing Lessons from the Mexican Crisis: Preventing and Resolving Financial Crises – the Role of the IMF"

Michel Camdessus, Managing Director of the IMF, May 22, 1995

Before considering the lessons of this experience, we must also be clear about how the crisis was resolved – I am confident enough to use these words today – and turned into a manageable problem. It was not resolved by the devaluation of December 20 [1994]. Nor was it resolved two days later when, after a further massive loss of international reserves, the peso was allowed to float. This merely delivered another blow to confidence, and the peso continued to depreciate sharply, as financial markets questioned Mexico's ability to service its short-term debt.

The fact is that confidence was not restored and the crisis was not resolved until two components were securely in place – a stringent adjustment program designed in close collaboration with the IMF, and a large-scale international financial rescue package in support of that program. This package has three elements. The IMF approved on February 1 [1995] an 18-month stand-by credit of $17.8 billion in support of Mexico's program for 1995–96, of which $7.8 billion was made available immediately. The other two elements, both dependent on Mexico's arrangement and policy understandings with the IMF are, of course, $20 billion in swaps and guarantees from the U.S. Exchange Stabilization Fund, and $10 billion of short-term support from the G-10 central banks through the Bank for International Settlements.

The IMF arrangement with Mexico is the largest ever approved for a member country, both in absolute amount and in relation to the country's quota in the Fund. Why such exceptional support? For a very simple reason, which is the very basic mandate of the IMF. Take Article I of our Articles of Agreement – it states that it is the IMF's mission: "To give confidence to members by making the general resources of the Fund temporarily available to them under adequate safeguards, thus providing them with opportunity to correct maladjustments in their balance of payments without resorting to measures destructive of national or international prosperity."

On January 31 of this year [1995], this was the problem: either large-scale financial assistance was put in place together with the support of the U.S. – and the IMF was the only institution in a position to extend it without delay – or Mexico had no solution other than to resort to "measures destructive of national or international prosperity," such as a moratorium on foreign debt or a reimposition of trade and exchange restrictions, with a major risk of the spread of such measures to a number of countries.

Source: *International Monetary Fund. Address at the conference of the Council of the Americas, May 22, 1995*

Policy Options

Assuming a country is interested in keeping its exchange rate fixed, we now explore the options available to its government wishing to correct a trade deficit and avert detrimental reserve outflows.

These options fall into two categories: **expenditure-switching** and **expenditure-reducing** policies. Both categories resolve the problem; however, as we shall see, both introduce serious downsides. We will discuss each in turn.

Expenditure-Switching Policies

Expenditure-switching policies entice domestic demand to switch from foreign imports to domestic goods. Such policies can be pure propaganda (such as "Buy American" or "Buy Local") or they can be tariffs and quotas that increase the price or reduce the quantity of foreign imports. Other forms of expenditure-switching trade policies are export subsidies[2] that entice foreigners into buying more domestic goods. The most effective expenditure-switching measure might be a one-time devaluation, since it involves an immediate price change for all imports and exports making imports less attractive to residents and exports more appealing to foreigners – a new way to look at a devaluation. All these policies improve the trade balance (assuming that the Marshall–Lerner conditions are fulfilled), because they switch demand from foreign to domestic goods.

The "Buy American Act"

The **Buy American Act** was passed by the U.S. Congress in 1933 at the height of the American depression. It mandates a preference for the purchase of domestically produced goods over foreign goods in U.S. government procurement. Interestingly, it has not been repealed until today!

The Buy American Act – (1) Restricts the purchase of supplies that are not domestic end products for use within the United States. A foreign end product may be purchased if it is determined that the price of the lowest domestic offer is unreasonable or if another exception applies, (2) Requires, with some exceptions, the use of only domestic construction materials in contracts for construction in the United States, and (3) Uses a two-part test to define a domestic end product. This test involves (a) The article must be manufactured in the United States; and (b) The cost of domestic components must exceed 50 percent of the cost of all the components.

Other "buy-national" legislative provisions exist separately from the Buy American Act requirements. These provisions can be found in the Agreements on Government Procurement; Government Procurement Policies and Practices; U.S.–Israel Free Trade Agreement; and in the U.S.–Canada Free Trade Agreement. Since then, the governments of most countries have followed the examined and instituted *"Buy Domestic"* legislation. To take the issue one step further, the U.S. State of Washington even forces its government to "Buy Local," that is to buy only from Washington State suppliers.

Source: Department of State – International Information Programs
(http://usinfo.state.gov/products/pubs/trade/glossac.htm#buyam)

---

2 Tariff, quotas, and export subsidies are discussed in the first part of this book when the theory of protection is developed (Chapter 5).

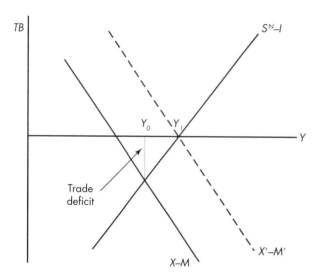

FIGURE 15.1 Expenditure-Switching Policies – A Devaluation

A devaluation increases the price of imports (for the domestic buyers) and decreases the price of exports (for the foreigners). Demand switches from foreign to domestic goods, the X–M shifts right, the trade deficit dwindles as the economy expands to Y_1. We assume that the Marshall–Lerner conditions are fulfilled.

By reducing imports and/or by increasing exports, expenditure-switching policies shift the X–M curve to the right (Figure 15.1)[3] from X–M to X'–M' because exports rise, $X'>X$, and imports fall, $M'<M$. This improvement in the trade balance also increases domestic production and domestic income from Y_0 to Y_1.

Expenditure-Reducing Policies

The alternatives to expenditure-switching policies are expenditure-reducing policies. Expenditure-reducing policies improve the trade balance by choking off domestic demand through lowering income. Reduction in government spending, increases in taxes, or contractionary monetary policy are such examples. Since a reduction in income is associated with fewer imports, expenditure-reducing policies improve the trade balance by curbing aggregate demand. However, expenditure-reducing policies target not only demand for imports, but the entire aggregate demand, so they have drastic effects: they not only reduce demand for imports, but the lower income also reduces demand for domestic goods! Therefore the improved trade balance comes at a cost: a decline in national income. This side effect cannot be popular among policy makers (more exactly among the citizens who elect them).

---

3 For students who have completed a course in international trade theory, we should also mention that some expenditure-switching effects may also have additional side effects that go beyond the TB/Y diagram as they distort relative domestic prices.

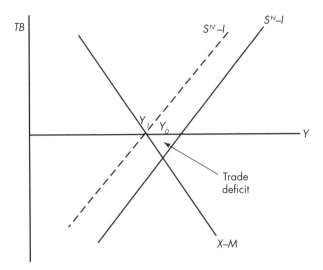

FIGURE 15.2 Expenditure-Reducing Policies

Expenditure-reducing policies raise national saving (because of reduced government spending or increase in taxes as shown in the above graph) or reduce investment (because of higher interest rates due to contractionary monetary policy). The trade balance improves, but national income falls, leading to a reduction in all purchases, not only purchases of foreign goods.

Figure 15.2 shows how expenditure-reducing policies can move a country out of a trade deficit at Y_0 to balanced trade, at the cost of lower income, Y_1. The S^N–I line shifts because expenditure-reducing policies could also be called "saving-increasing policies." By reducing government spending or increasing taxes, national saving rises, or alternatively through contractionary monetary policy, investment falls. Any of these effects shift the S^N–I line left.

Which Policy to Choose?

Neither expenditure-switching nor -reducing policies constitute a simple solution to correcting the trade deficit in order to maintain a fixed exchange rate regime. Expenditure-switching policies do raise output, but they turn out to be highly unpopular with trading partners, especially when they take the form of tariffs, quotas, or exports subsidies. Particularly, international organizations such as the World Trade Organization (WTO), the World Bank, and the IMF[4] do not look kindly at using barriers to trade to correct trade deficits. The rationale is that, if every country were to engage in such policies, global trade would dramatically fall and all countries would be worse off. These are some of the basic tenets we learn in the first part of this text. The WTO allows countries to "retaliate" with equal and opposite trade restrictions if a member country raises tariffs unilaterally; the rationale is

---

4 While the role of the World Bank and the IMF are discussed in Chapter 21 along with the IMF, the WTO is the subject of Chapter 9.

the hope of better behavior by the country that first introduced the barrier to trade (hoping to break the vicious cycle of protection at its root).

The less controversial forms of expenditure-switching policy are "buy domestic" campaigns or devaluations. Usually "buy domestic" campaigns have only limited impact. Devaluations are effective, but the problem here is that they have to be used judiciously. A country cannot change its "fixed" exchange rate frequently (say every few months), otherwise no one would ever believe that the exchange rate was actually fixed! Moreover, a devaluation of the domestic currency (improving the domestic balance of trade) is a revaluation for the trade partner (worsening the trade partner's balance of trade).

Expenditure-reducing policies can restore balanced trade without such negative impact on foreign countries, and they do not compromise the trust that the exchange rate is actually fixed. However, expenditure-reducing policies involve output contraction and increase in unemployment. For politicians, such policies are difficult to defend vis-à-vis their constituencies. With a fixed exchange rate regime, a policy maker facing a trade deficit is therefore in a bind. Either she upsets foreign trade partners and international organizations, or she incurs the wrath of her own constituency and possibly loses in the next election. Neither is an attractive choice.

If a devaluation is not possible, governments are usually left with few alternatives other than engaging in expenditure-reducing policies. This implies that only Y_1 in Figure 15.2 is attainable, raising the question of whether monetary or fiscal policies are actually effective in stimulating output under fixed exchange rates. Since negative reserve flows associated with trade deficits cannot be sustained forever, any initial change in fiscal or monetary policy aimed at increasing output must be followed by a subsequent contraction.

Clearly the government's favorite choice would be to engage in expenditure-switching policies. Such policies may work in an economy with a very small marginal propensity to import (since it will be easy to substitute domestic goods for foreign imports). On the other hand, in less-developed economies with high marginal propensities to import and low elasticities of import demand, this would be an especially unpopular choice, but possibly not as unpopular as reducing output to its original level.

Given the above discussion, the following question can be raised: assuming that a country initially enjoys balanced trade, why would it even engage in fiscal and monetary expansions when the final equilibrium under fixed exchange rates will eventually have to revert to the level of output in the beginning (as there seems to be only one level of output that corresponds to balanced trade)? One answer might be that policy makers in a country are not interested in maintaining the fixed exchange rate, or may have other policy priorities. Another observation of the real world reveals that political constraints entice policy makers into increasing output in the short term – possibly to win elections – and to deal with the economic fallout later.

In this context, it is important to add a note regarding the role of the IMF. The organization was created and designed to assist countries facing balance-of-payments difficulties or weathering currency crises by providing foreign reserve loans so that a fixed exchange rate could be maintained. The IMF provides assistance to allow countries to avoid frequent and dramatic currency devaluations due to temporary shocks. For instance, if a country runs a trade deficit and taps into the IMF coffers to collect short-term foreign currency loans, the country *still* has to deal with its trade deficit via expenditure-switching and -reducing policies. This is because the country cannot borrow forever from the IMF.

Moreover, just like any other lender, the IMF does not provide loans without strings attached. The IMF wants to see that the country is actually undertaking the reforms necessary to enable it to repay the loan.

Indeed in order to repay its loan, the country must not only eradicate the trade deficit, but it actually has to run a trade surplus to generate inflows of foreign currency allowing its central bank to build its reserves back up and repay the IMF. Over the years, IMF programs have often become synonymous with traumatic expenditure-reducing policies that leave bitter impressions on citizens, especially if they are unemployed. In this context, it is important to recognize that the IMF program simply alleviates symptoms caused by deeper economic predicaments that the country will have to address, with or without the IMF.

The Simple Policy Alternative: Non-Sterilization and the Monetary Approach to the Balance of Payments

Under fixed exchange rate regimes and in the absence of capital flows, we have discussed the need to maintain balanced trade to uphold equilibrium in the foreign exchange market at the fixed exchange rate. Without such equilibrium, there is no mechanism that prevents the economy from running out of foreign exchange reserves and being forced to forsake the fixed exchange rate regime. In light of these severe limitations, it seems odd that fixed exchange rate regimes were so prevalent in the latter part of the twentieth century, especially during times when capital flows were largely nonexistent (pre-1970s). Was this period a time of frantic expenditure-switching and -reducing policies by governments to maintain a trade balance?

It turns out that there is an alternative, exceedingly simple solution to maintaining fixed exchange rates, one that does not involve any policy interference at all! It involves relaxing our past assumption, the assumption of sterilization. If a central bank commits to non-sterilization, it basically allows the domestic money supply to fluctuate with any changes in reserves. We have introduced the mechanics of non-sterilization in Chapter 13, where we have shown that the monetary base (i.e. high-powered money) is equal to the sum of domestic credit (DC) plus foreign reserves (RES) valued in domestic currency units. By multiplying these expressions by the money multiplier μ, we obtained the money supply M^S:

$$M^S = \mu(DC + RES) \tag{15.1}$$

Note the immediate connection between the money supply, M^S, and the foreign currency reserves in the central bank, RES. The money supply rises whenever the central bank buys foreign currency from the public, since it has to pay for the foreign currency by handing out domestic currency. Therefore, every time the central bank buys foreign currency (at price E, the exchange rate) to add to its foreign reserves, RES, it hands out exactly ($\Delta RES=E^*foreign\ currency\ purchase$) dollars, increasing the money supply by $\mu(\Delta RES)$. For example, if the current price of a British pound is \$1.96 and the U.S. central bank buys 100 British pounds to increase its reserves, it has to create \$196 of new money to pay for it. As soon as these \$196 leave the U.S. central bank, the high-powered money in the U.S. increases by \$196 and the U.S. money supply by $\mu^*\$196$.

So how does non-sterilization resolve our policy problems under fixed exchange rates? It turns out that any trade imbalance automatically corrects itself overtime (!) if the central bank promises *not* to intervene to sterilize foreign currency reserve flows. The magic works through the change in the money supply. Let us reexamine the effects of monetary and fiscal policy under non-sterilization.

Monetary and Fiscal Expansion under Non-Sterilization

Recall the problem that the domestic economy faces after engaging in either fiscal or monetary policy expansion starting from balanced trade. In either case, the country incurs a trade deficit that is not sustainable forever because of the ensuing reserve outflow. From our discussion of the determinants of the money supply, it becomes apparent that, whenever the trade balance is negative, the central bank must sell reserves to keep the price of the foreign currency constant.

We now assume that domestic credit, DC, is not altered: the central bank adopts a non-sterilization policy. In this case, the trade deficit and the associated decline in foreign reserves translate into a proportional decline in the money supply. This is the situation in the economy at Y_1 in Figure 15.3. Now a powerful adjustment mechanism, devoid of any government interference, sets in. Overtime,

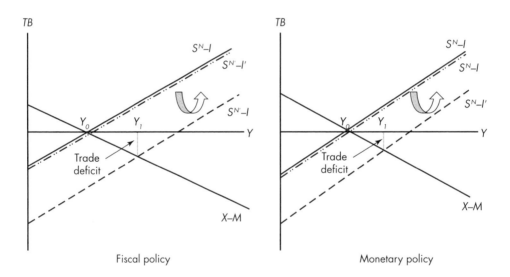

FIGURE 15.3 Fiscal and Monetary Policy with Non-Sterilization (Monetary Approach to the Balance of Payments)

Starting from balanced trade and under non-sterilization, any increase in output due to expansionary fiscal or monetary policy leads to reserve outflows that contract the money supply (equation 15.1). As a result, interest rates rise as long as the country maintains a trade deficit and investment decreases. In both cases the economy will get back to its original equilibrium overtime. In the case of monetary policy (on the right side of the graph), the interest rate dropped and then increased back to its original level too. So all the macroeconomic variables are also back to their original levels: there is policy neutrality. In the case of fiscal policy (on the left side of the graph), both the original expansionary fiscal policy and the automatic adjustment through a decrease in the money supply result in an increase in the interest rate. The final equilibrium will exhibit higher interest rates and consequently a different composition of aggregate demand (the original S^N–I line is now labeled $S^{N'}$–I).

as the money supply declines, interest rates rise and both capital investment and output fall. As output falls, the trade balance improves because the country buys fewer foreign goods.

Foreign reserves outflows will come to a halt only when the trade balance returns to zero. The economy thus keeps contracting until the trade balance is zero. This adjustment mechanism uncovers a surprising fact: under fixed exchange rates, in the absence of capital flows, fiscal or monetary policies are eventually ineffective in raising output. This result is also called policy neutrality. Under non-sterilization, the economy always returns all by itself to the original equilibrium from which the economy started *before* the initial fiscal or monetary expansion. The automatic adjustment associated with non-sterilization insures long-term stability for a fixed exchange rate system, a good outcome per se, but unfortunately, it implies that fiscal and monetary policy can only have a temporary impact on the economy.

This model of fixed exchange rates and non-sterilization in the absence of capital flows is known as the **monetary approach to the balance of payments**, although it might be more accurate to call it the monetary approach to the balance of trade. The hallmark of the monetary (or monetarist) approach is the complete absence of policy interference, since strong policy neutrality in the open economy implies that there are no long-term effects on output.

The alternative to non-sterilization is of course to have domestic credit change by exactly the amount that reserves change: this is the assumption on which Chapter 14 is based. This way, money supply is not affected by foreign reserves flows as the central bank sterilizes their effects. As we have seen above in the case of expansionary policies, sterilization allows the government to stimulate output in the short-term only as the country will sooner or later run out of reserves. At that time, the country must give up its peg (i.e. devalue its currency) or engage in expenditure-switching or -reducing policies.

INTERNAL AND EXTERNAL BALANCE: THE POLICY MIX

We can take our policy discussion one step further. The object of policy may not simply be to raise output by some amount. It may actually be to reach full-employment, or *internal balance*, in addition to keeping trade balanced, or *external balance*. How to achieve internal balance and external balance under fixed exchange rates can be succinctly analyzed in one diagram.

Jan Tinbergen (Nobel Prize winner in 1969) showed formally that in order to achieve two goals, the internal and the external balance, a policy maker must use two policy instruments. In Figure 15.4, we draw a vertical *FE* line indicating the level of full-employment income, Y_{FE}. As all the points on the horizontal axis correspond to balanced trade, the equilibrium of the economy should take place at the intersection of the vertical *FE* line and the horizontal axis: there, at Y_{FE}, both goals of internal and external balance are met.

Now assume that the economy is in equilibrium at Y_0 where it is plagued by both unemployment and a trade deficit. What should a policy maker suggest to alleviate these two concurrent predicaments? From the graph, we can see that to correct *both* problems, the policy maker must engage in expansionary policy (shifting out the S^N–I line) and a one-time devaluation (shifting out the X–M line) to correct the balance of trade deficit (the original trade deficit and that triggered by the expansion). The new $S^{N'}$–I (assuming fiscal policy) and X'–M' curves now intersect exactly at Y_{FE} where the

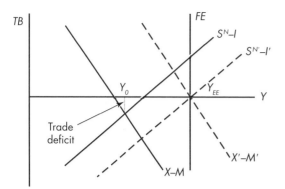

FIGURE 15.4 Internal and External Balance: The Policy Mix

Starting with unemployment and a trade deficit at Y_0, a policy maker needs two policy instruments to achieve external balance (balanced trade) and internal balance (full employment at Y_{FE}). A fiscal expansion stimulates output and employment (but worsens the trade balance) and a devaluation (X–M shifts) improves the trade balance (while also stimulating output) to fine-tune the economy into achieving internal and external balance.

economy benefits from full employment and balanced trade. This policy mix steering the country toward both internal and external balance is illustrated in Figure 15.4.

Why does a policy maker need to use two policies to reach two objectives: internal and external balance? The intuition is that each policy alone impacts on both the balance of trade and output; so the second policy must correct the impact of the first policy to achieve both goals. Figure 15.4 indicates that it will be most crucial for the policy maker to know exactly how much expansionary fiscal or monetary policy is needed and then exactly how large a devaluation is needed to exactly attain both goals. The process of reaching the internal and external balances using two policies can be succinctly summarized in the so-called Swan diagram, named after its creator, the Australian economist, Trevor Swan.

The Swan Diagram

The two policies considered are fiscal policy (a change in the government deficit, G–T) and exchange rate policy (devaluation or revaluation). We want to determine the policy mix that will allow a country to achieve both internal and external balance. We plan to represent the desired equilibrium in the (G–T, E) space so that each policy is represented respectively on a specific axis (Figure 15.4). Fiscal policy is measured as G–T (the budget deficit) – an increase corresponds to expansionary fiscal policy. Exchange rate policy is measured by the nominal exchange rate E – an increase is a devaluation of the domestic currency. Next we need to derive the lines that are associated with internal balance and external balance.

The internal balance line represents all combinations of fiscal policy and exchange rate levels that are associated with full employment, Y_{FE}. We pick point a in the (G–T, E) space where the economy is at its full employment level. Now let us engage in an experiment. If the government initiates expansionary fiscal policy, the economy moves beyond full employment (from a to b in Figure 15.5). In

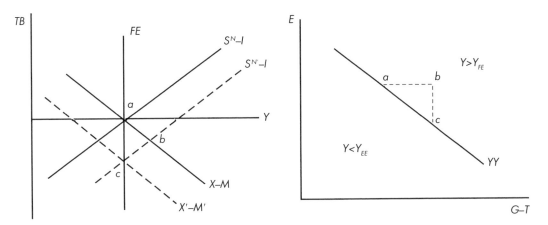

FIGURE 15.5 Construction of the Internal Balance Curve YY

From an internal balance equilibrium in *a*, expansionary fiscal policy sends the economy beyond full-employment in *b*. The contractionary impact of the revaluation restores full employment in *c*. So *a* and *c* are both points where a specific combination of fiscal policy and exchange rate correspond to full employment.

order to restore full employment again, the government must cool off the economy by revaluing its currency; indeed the stronger domestic currency reduces exports and increases imports. The adverse impact on the trade balance then dampens aggregate demand, moving the economy back from point *b* to point *c*, thus reversing the initial impact of the expansionary fiscal policy. The result of our experiment is that expansionary fiscal policy must be accompanied by a revaluation of the currency to keep the output level constant. So in our (G–T/E) space, the internal balance curve, YY, is downward sloping, pairing increases in G–T with decreases in E.

Similarly we can construct the external balance line associated with balanced trade in Figure 15.6. Again we pick any point, *d*, in the (G–T, E) space and assume it represents balanced trade. Then we examine the effects of a fiscal expansion: it results in a trade deficit at point *e*. To restore balanced trade, a devaluation is necessary; it stimulates the economy and moves it from *e* to *f*. We find that the external balance line, denoted by BB, is upwards sloping. This is because expansionary fiscal policy requires a devaluation to correct for the ensuing trade deficit. The construction of BB is illustrated below in Figure 15.6.

Finally we can combine the internal and external balance lines in one graph featuring our policy options on each of the two axes. The so-called Swan diagram in Figure 15.7 provides the one point in the economy where fiscal policy and exchange rate policy are consistent with both full employment and balanced trade, as the intersection of the two lines. Alternatively, the diagram can be used to indicate exactly how much fiscal and exchange rate policy have to change to move the economy from unemployment and a trade deficit, for instance, to internal and external equilibrium.

From any point other than *A*, the government can utilize the Swan diagram to design a policy action plan based on a combination of the two policies to eventually reach equilibrium *A*. Figure 15.8 illustrates such an example. We assume that the economy is in *B* – somewhere to the northeast of *A*. From our analysis summarized in the Swan diagram (Figure 15.7) we know that point *B* corresponds to a trade surplus and the economy is beyond full employment.

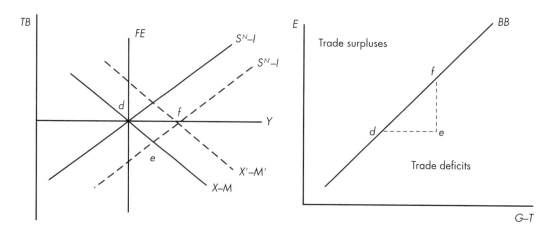

FIGURE 15.6 Construction of the External Balance Curve *BB*

Starting from external balance in *d*, an expansionary fiscal policy creates a trade deficit in *e*. A devaluation is needed to restore balanced trade in *f*. So *d* and *f* are both points where a specific combination of fiscal policy and exchange rate correspond to balanced trade.

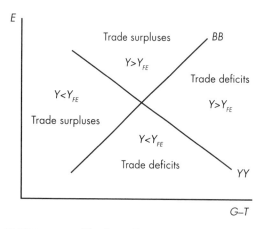

FIGURE 15.7 The Swan Diagram

The intersection of the internal balance curve, *YY*, and the external balance curve, *BB*, represents the one point where the economy achieves both full employment and balanced trade.

In this instance, the Swan diagram immediately highlights that the right policy prescription is a combination of contractionary fiscal policy and revaluation to return the economy to its internal and external balance. Note also that a revaluation alone would not succeed in restoring both equilibria as the economy would move vertically down to the *BB* line where there would still be over-employment. Similarly, contractionary fiscal policy alone would move the economy horizontally to the *YY* line where even larger trade surpluses would be present. Only a combination of the two policies can move the economy to *A*.

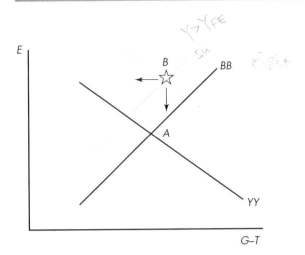

FIGURE 15.8 Policy with the Swan Diagram

To move from *B* to *A*, the graph clearly shows that *E* must decrease (a revaluation) and *G–T* must also decrease (through a cut in government spending or an increase in tax).

THE LARGE OPEN ECONOMY

We have now finished discussing policy options under fixed exchange rate regimes. We still need to tackle the issue of the robustness of one of our results. In the open economy models of Chapter 14, we showed that a fiscal expansion not only creates trade deficits, but is less effective at raising output than in the closed economy. In the closed economy, an infusion of government funds brings about an increase in income that can only be spent on domestic goods, while in the open economy, some of the increased income is spent on foreign goods. Basically, part of the additional income earned through the expansion of the domestic economy is diverted into increased demand for foreign-produced goods. The increase in imports was called a *leakage*, because income earned in the domestic economy leaks out abroad into demand for foreign-produced goods as import demand rises.

To simplify our analysis, we had assumed that our model focused on the "small open economy" where exports were fixed (exogenous). The portion of domestic income leaking out of the domestic economy corresponds then to the increase in import demand; these amounts do not find their way back into the domestic economy in the form of higher exports.

In this chapter, we have not always assumed a small open economy set-up. Earlier, we stated that various international agencies, like the WTO, the World Bank, or the IMF, may not approve of certain actions taken by countries to correct trade deficits as these actions might affect their trade partner(s) adversely; this is precisely what distinguishes small open economies from large open economies. Policies initiated in a large open economy will affect the trade partners. Let us now set up a new model and investigate the interactions, so-called **repercussions**, resulting from one country's policy changes.

We drop the small-economy assumption; our economy is now an equal player on the world stage. To simplify matters, we limit the world stage to two countries, linked together through their trade. The multi-country model has similar implications, but is more complicated to handle. Increases in domestic imports – translating into increases in exports from the point of view of the trade partner – are significant enough to increase aggregate demand in the foreign economy. In turn, this increase in demand stimulates the foreign economy, increasing their income. As a result, the trade partner feels richer: its aggregate demand is boosted, including its demand for imports of goods produced in the domestic economy, i.e. the exports of the domestic economy. In this case, it is clear that the increase in domestic imports eventually triggers an increase in exports. The two economies are linked through their balance of trade. In this global economy, one country's supply of exports is really the other country's demand for imports, allowing us to specify the domestic export demand function as:

$$X = \bar{X} + m^*Y^* \tag{15.2}$$

where asterisk superscripts denote variables associated with the foreign economy. In our previous specification for exports, $X = \bar{X}$, we had assumed that exports were exogenous and foreign income was not specified as a variable in the model. Now, when imports in the domestic economy increase, the foreign economy experiences an increase in income, Y^*, that stimulates its imports demand – the domestic exports, X. Domestic income spent on foreign imports finds its way back home in terms of increased exports. We are now able to summarize our assumptions and analyze the implications of the large open-economy model.

Assumptions

We maintain all assumptions from Chapter 14, including sterilization, but relax assumption 1) that exports are fixed (exogenous).

1) Large open economy $X = \bar{X} + m^*Y^*, M = \bar{M} + mY$
2) Fixed exchange rate $E = \bar{E}$
3) Fixed prices in both countries $P = \bar{P}$ and $P^* = \bar{P}^*$

We have simplified the model by setting the fixed prices and exchange rate equal to 1, allowing us to drop P, P^* and E from the import and export equations. Exports have now an important role in the functioning of the model. Any policy designed to stimulate domestic output increases not only the demand for foreign goods (domestic imports), but it will also increase domestic exports. The increase in imports raises foreign income, and, according to (15.2), increases domestic exports in turn. We must modify the national income equation for the domestic economy to integrate the new export equation. Then we develop an equivalent national income equation for the foreign economy.[5] Domestic national income is now:

$$Y = \bar{C} + cY + I + G + \bar{X} + m^* Y^* - \bar{M} - mY \tag{15.3}$$

---

5 To simplify the algebra we assume that taxes are zero (or flat) and that the rate of interest is fixed.

and can be rearranged as:

$$Y = \frac{\bar{C} + I + G + \bar{X} + m^* Y^* - \bar{M}}{s + m} \qquad (15.3a)$$

For the trade partner, we obtain the symmetric result:

$$Y^* = \frac{\bar{C}^* + I^* + G^* + \bar{X}^* + mY - \bar{M}^*}{s^* + m^*} \qquad (15.3b)$$

The two national income equations now highlight that the equilibrium level of income in one country depends on the level of income in the other country. This dependency underscores the interaction between the two large economies. If domestic income goes up as a result of expansionary fiscal policy, domestic imports rise. An increase in domestic imports is equivalent to an increase in foreign exports, which increases foreign income. As foreign income rises, foreigners consume more, resulting in an increase in their demand for imports. This increase in foreign imports is again equivalent to an increase in domestic exports and income. The powerful positive feedback mechanism continues on and on.

It is difficult to keep track of all the effects by simply looking at the equations. We can illustrate the interaction between the two economies with a graph (Figure 15.9) of the two national income

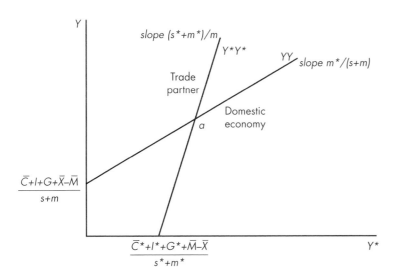

FIGURE 15.9 Global Equilibrium with Two Large Open Economies

The two economies are linked through their balances of trade that are always equal in absolute value, but have opposite sign. Since the domestic economy's export is the trade partner's import, a function of the trade partner's income, the domestic economy's income Y becomes a function of the trade partner's income Y*. In the large country model, the equilibrium condition for each country now includes the other country's income as an additional determinant, so it can be expressed as a function of the other country's income.

equations (15.3a,b) in the domestic and foreign income space (with domestic income on the vertical axis and foreign income on the horizontal). The easiest way to draw the two lines, YY for the domestic economy and Y^*Y^* for the foreign economy, is to calculate first their slopes and intercepts. We set Y^* equal to zero in 15.3a yielding $Y = (\bar{C} + I + G + \bar{X} - \bar{M})/(s + m)$ for the intercept of YY: this corresponds to national income equilibrium for the small open economy (see equation 14.5) when foreign income was ignored. The slope, dY/dY^*, in (15.3a), is $m^*/(s + m) > 0$. The domestic income line, YY, is thus upward sloping because an increase in foreign income raises domestic exports and therefore domestic income. We can now draw the YY line with a positive intercept.

To find the line representing foreign income, we follow an analogous method for determining slope and intercept, now using the equation for foreign income, (15.3b).[6] The flatter domestic income line, YY, corresponds to all the points where the domestic economy is in equilibrium for a given level of foreign income, Y^*. The steeper foreign income line, Y^*Y^*, corresponds to all the points where the foreign economy is in equilibrium given the level of domestic income, Y. The two lines intersect at point a, the joint equilibrium for both economies. This graph will greatly facilitate our analysis of policy in the large open economy.

Fiscal Policy in the Large Open Economy with Fixed Exchange Rates

The mechanism of fiscal policy in the large open economy model is illustrated in Figure 15.10 below. An increase in government spending in the domestic economy, ΔG, shifts the domestic income line, YY, up (its vertical intercept increases by the small open economy multiplier, mm_{so}, multiplied by the change in government spending, ΔG). It is immediately clear from the graph that both countries reach a higher level of income. Hence, the effect of an increase in domestic government spending benefits not only the domestic economy but also the foreign economy.

The intuition is that, since domestic income rises, domestic consumers buy more goods from abroad. This stimulates foreigners' income as their exports increase. This extra income translates into extra demand and foreigners spend some of it on additional imports (domestic exports). In turn, this new demand for domestic goods stimulates the domestic economy. This is a loop of repercussions between the two economies that will go on for a while, as shown in Figure 15.10 below, until the two economies reach a higher equilibrium.

Initially, the equilibrium for the two economies is at point a. The first blue arrow north indicates the effect of the increase in government spending on the domestic economy (at first only Y increases and Y^* is unchanged). Since domestic income has increased, the demand for imports increases too; these imports are exports from the point of view of the trading partner so foreign income rises along the horizontal arrow to the right. The repercussion effects are not complete yet: since foreign income increases (due to higher exports), foreigners save more and consume more goods, including goods

---

6 Here a technical note is in order. Note that the derivative dY^*/dY is given by $dY^*/dY = m/(s^* + m^*)$. To trace the slope in the Y/Y^* space, the slope of the foreign income line is the inverse of this derivative, $(s^* + m^*)/m$, since we show domestic income, Y, on the vertical axis and foreign income, Y^*, on the horizontal axis.

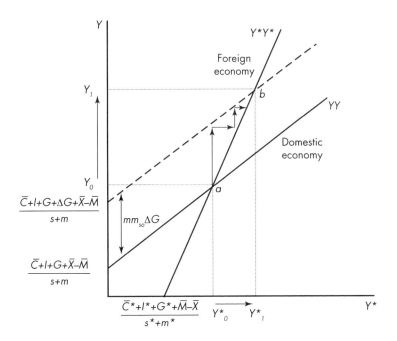

FIGURE 15.10 The Effects of Expansionary Fiscal Policy on Output with Two Large Open-Economy Model

The increase in government spending in the domestic economy will affect the domestic economy line by shifting it up. The other country is indirectly affected because the increase in demand in the domestic economy translates in an increase in exports for the other country. The other country's equilibrium line does not shift, but the adjustment takes place along its original line toward a higher level of income.

made abroad: their demand for imports (domestic exports) increases. From the point of view of the domestic economy, this increase in exports provides additional stimulation to the domestic income, illustrated by the vertical arrows. The increases become smaller and smaller as some of the increase in income is saved. The repercussions come to an end at point b, where both equilibrium income lines intersect again.

The Large Open-Economy Multiplier

The key question is: how much did income eventually rise due to the fiscal expansion? Is the domestic leakage observed with the small open-economy case fully returned to the domestic economy in the case of a large open economy? Some of the leakage is certainly eliminated, as the domestic economy's expansion also stimulates exports indirectly through the increase in foreign income.

To get a more accurate estimate of the extent of the leakage, if any, we need to derive the *large open-economy multiplier* that tells us exactly how much income rises due to a fiscal expansion. Equation (15.3a) depends on foreign income, defined in equation (15.3b). Substituting the expression for foreign income into (15.3a), and solving for domestic income, we obtain the large open-economy multiplier, mm_{lo}

$$mm_{lo} = \frac{1}{s + m - \dfrac{mm^*}{s^*+m^*}} \qquad (15.4)$$

Recall that the small open-economy multiplier, mm_{so}, derived in Chapter 14, was:

$$mm_{lo} = \frac{1}{s + m} \qquad (15.5)$$

Examining the two expressions, we can see that the large open-economy multiplier is larger than the small open-economy multiplier,[7] but smaller than the closed-economy multiplier, $mm_c = 1/s$, so we have:

$$mm_{so} < mm_{lo} < mm_c \qquad (15.6)$$

This result is significant. It verifies our previous finding: with a fixed exchange rate regime, an increase in government spending is not as effective in the open economy (whether small or large) as in the closed economy. In the closed economy, the entire amount of government spending is directed toward domestic goods, while in the open economy we have an increase in the demand for imported goods and thus a leakage. Even in the large open economy, there is a leakage, although smaller, as the increased imports do not trigger an equal amount of increased exports.

Why is there still a leakage in the large open economy? After all we have now allowed for feedback effects. The reason is that some of the increase in foreign income is saved and only a fraction of the increase in foreign consumption is directed toward foreign goods. However, by looking at the new multiplier, we see that the greater the foreign marginal propensity to import m^*, i.e. the more open the partner's economy, the greater the expansion for the domestic economy. Trading with a large very open economy is more beneficial!

In this section, we have discovered that large economies interact with each other through their domestic policies. In fact, the large-economy model conveys a more realistic picture of what happens between most of the large industrial countries. But we have only considered expenditure-changing types of policy. With fixed exchange rates, countries also use expenditure-switching policies (devaluation/revaluation). What would be their effects on the trade partner, knowing that the channel for these interactions is the balance of trade?

---

7 The third term in the denominator of the large open-economy multiplier is positive, making the denominator smaller than $s+m$ and the multiplier larger than the small open-economy multiplier.

Devaluation or Revaluation in the Large Open-Economy Model

We found out that a fiscal expansion in one country also stimulates its trade partner. What is the joint impact in the case of a devaluation? The devaluation stimulates domestic exports and reduces imports (assuming that the Marshall–Lerner conditions are satisfied). This implies that domestic income rises, while foreign income declines. In the small-country case, we have ignored repercussions on the trade partner's income; they were not significant since a small open economy, by definition, does not affect the rest of the world. On the other hand, the large open-economy framework allows us to examine the effect of a devaluation on the trade partner.

Let us assume that the domestic economy devalues its currency to improve its trade balance: domestic exports increase and domestic imports decrease thus shifting up the domestic income line, YY, by $mm_{so}(\Delta X - \Delta M)$. From the point of view of the trade partner, imports, M^*, increase (since $\Delta X \equiv \Delta M^*$) and exports X^* drop (since $\Delta M \equiv \Delta X^*$) so the foreign line, Y^*Y^*, shifts down by the same amount. Figure 15.11 shows that the two shifts result in the expected increase in income for the domestic economy and in a decrease in income for the foreign economy:

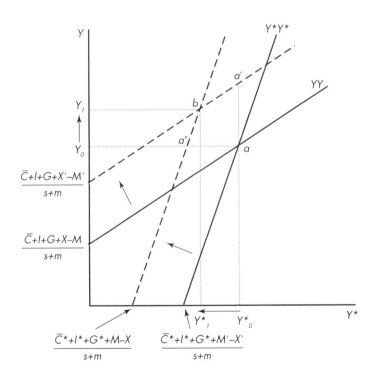

FIGURE 15.11 The Impact of a Devaluation with Two Large Open-Economy Model

In this case, the devaluation in the domestic economy is equivalent to a revaluation for the trade partner. The trade partner is directly affected and its equilibrium line shifts too. For the domestic economy, it is an improvement; for the trade partner, the impact is contractionary. As a result, instead of enhancing the improvement due to the devaluation in the domestic economy, the trade partner's contraction dampens its effect.

We now examine the adjustment process step-by-step. First the devaluation improves the domestic trade balance and gives the domestic economy a boost. Without any repercussion, i.e. without change in the trade partner's income, the domestic economy would move to a'. The foreign economy experiences an equal and opposite deterioration in its trade balance, moving to a''. The new equilibrium for both economies, b, must be somewhere between a' and a'' because the foreign trade partner benefits from the increase in income in the domestic economy (triggering higher imports so b is to the right of a'' relative to the horizontal axis) while the domestic economy is hurt by the decline in income abroad (translating into reduced exports so b is lower than a' relative to the vertical axis). The final joint equilibrium settles in b where income for the domestic economy is lower than in a', the small open-economy equilibrium.

In the case of a fiscal expansion, both countries benefited, and the repercussions enhanced the impact of fiscal policy at home and abroad. In the case of a devaluation in the domestic economy, both income lines shift in opposite direction; this highlights the exact opposite impacts on the two economies, thus mitigating the effectiveness of a devaluation. While the expansionary impact of fiscal policy is enhanced by the repercussions, the expansionary impact of a devaluation is reduced by the repercussions. The analysis of the effects of a revaluation in the domestic economy follows identical lines, except that all shifts and impacts will be reversed. The domestic economy's balance of trade and income will not be reduced as much compared to the small open-economy case, while the partner's balance of trade and income will improve.

Economists have estimated various multipliers assessing the impact of a fiscal expansion or of a devaluation in one country on its trade partners. Some of their results are presented in a box entitled "International Economic Interdependence Measure."

Policy in the Two-Country Model: Reinforcement and Conflict

In the two-country model, we can consider two forms of policy that the first economy might choose to carry out under fixed exchange rates: expenditure changing[8] and expenditure switching. As discussed at the beginning of this chapter, the policies could be used either to stimulate the economy or to correct a balance of trade disequilibrium.

Expenditure-Changing Policy in the Domestic Country to Stimulate the Economy

Assume that both countries are mired in a recession; they are both operating below the desired full-employment level. Then a fiscal expansion in the domestic country will trigger an expansion, albeit not as large, in the other economy. The repercussions further stimulate the partner's economy thus **reinforcing** the impact of the original policy in the domestic country. Policy makers would be eager

---

8 This is a more general term than expenditure-reducing policies to refer to fiscal policy.

to get precise estimates of the effect of a specific fiscal expansion on the income of each economy. Indeed economists have been able to use large models of the linked economies to do just that. The econometric results presented below testify to the importance of trying to predict accurately the extent of these repercussions.

Now assume that the domestic economy is suffering from a recession while the trade partner's economy is overheating. They are operating beyond full employment and wish to slow things down. Note that the model is considered in a short-run context – so prices are fixed and we do not mention actual inflation, but only inflationary pressures. In the domestic economy, the fiscal expansion is welcome. However, from the point of view of the partner's economy, the expansionary impact of the domestic fiscal expansion is not welcome. We have a **conflict**.

Expenditure-Switching Policy in the Domestic Country to Stimulate the Economy

Expenditure-switching policy, devaluation/revaluation, have the opposite impact on income in the two large countries. The above results will thus be reversed. When both countries are below full employment, a devaluation will help one country at the expense of the other that will sink further into its recession. Similarly, when they are both beyond full employment, the policy will be beneficial to one country, but harmful to the other. We have a *conflict*.

When the two countries need to correct opposite problems, then a devaluation or a revaluation will be welcome by both. We have *reinforcement*.

Policies to Correct a Trade Imbalance

Since any improvement in one country's balance of trade is identical to the resulting balance-of-trade deterioration borne by the trade partner, conflicts will be inherent. Devaluations to extend a country's trade surpluses will happen at the expense of the partner who might retaliate. Earlier, these policies were grouped under the "beggar thy neighbor" caption. Finally, we also saw that expenditure-changing policies just to fix the balance of trade are not practical.

International Economic Interdependence Measurements

Is it possible to measure the extent of the repercussions in the large open-economy model? Using extensive econometric models, economists have been able to estimate the open-economy multipliers either for fiscal policy or for a devaluation in one country. With their highly interlinked economies, the members of the European Union have been quite interested in the results of these studies. In the 1970s, the *Commission of the European Community* developed the *Meteor* model to appraise the economic interdependence of the member countries; the model was used to calculate the effect of a 1 percent increase in government spending in one country on income and on exports for all other member countries.[9] The results shown in Table 15.1 indicate that a 1 percent increase in government spending usually has a small effect on other countries' output (in the 0.1 to 0.5 percent rate), while it might increase exports of other countries significantly more, usually around 1–2 percent.

These numbers were confirmed by a study by the Organization for Economic Cooperation and Development in the 1980s. What was interesting about the OECD study was that it also calculated the effects of a real depreciation on trading partners. It is very significant to note that these effects

TABLE 15.1 Estimates of Policy Interdependence for E.U. Countries – Change in Government Spending

Percentage change in Income (Y) and Exports (X) induced by a 1% increase in government spending (G)

		France	Germany	Italy	Netherlands	U.K.	Belgium	USA
Effect on:								
France	Y	2.4	0.4	0.3	0.1	0.4	0	0.4
	X	−3.6	1.0	0.6	0.2	1.2	0.1	1.2
Germany	Y	0.8	3.1	0.7	0.2	0.9	0.1	1.0
	X	1.4	−1.3	1.1	0.3	1.5	0.1	1.7
Italy	Y	0.2	0.2	1.2	0	0.2	0	0.3
	X	1.6	1.5	0.7	0.3	1.8	0	1.9
Netherlands	Y	0.4	0.5	0.3	1.1	0.6	0.1	0.5
	X	1.2	1.1	0.7	−1.0	1.4	0.2	1.3
U.K.	Y	0.3	0.3	0.2	0.1	3.0	0	0.5
	X	0.7	0.6	0.4	0.1	−2.6	0	1.1
Belgium	Y	0.7	0.5	0.3	0.2	0.6	1.1	0.6
	X	1.9	1.6	1.0	0.5	1.8	−0.4	1.9

Header: *Initiating country*

Source: adapted from Meteor, Netherlands Central Planbureau for the E.E.C. Commission, 1977. Permission requested 11 August.

9 Hoare, T.F. (1977) "International Economic Interdependence, the Commission of the European Communities' Meteor Model," Directorate General for Economic and Financial Affairs of the EEC Commission.

TABLE 15.2 Estimates of Policy Interdependence for E.U. countries – Impact of a Real Depreciation

Percentage change in Income (Y) and the Current Account (CA) induced by a 10% real depreciation (2nd year)

Effect on:		Depreciating currency		
		U.S. $	German DM	Japanese ¥
U.S.	**Y**	0.5	0.1	0.2
	CA	3.7	0.3	1.3
OECD	**Y**	0.5	1.5	0.3
Europe	**CA**	1.4	2.2	2.0
Japan	**Y**	0.9	0.3	2.2
	CA	0.7	0.4	2.5
France	**Y**		0.2	
	CA		0.5	

Source: based on Table A7 (p. 82), OECD Economic Studies No. 1, Autumn 1983. See Larsen et al. *International Economic Linkages* (1983).

are all (!) positive. This implies that a real depreciation in the domestic economy leads to such a strong income effect in the country that it offsets the negative effect on the trading partner.

The advantage of the simulation approach using the above coefficients rests on the fact that one can estimate any kind of policy or shock impact on specific variables while fixing other key variables. Most of these studies were done in the seventies and the eighties. In the nineties, the preferred econometric approaches changed from estimating coefficients with large macroeconomic models to using co-integrating methods to analyze the impact of policy or of shocks. Also, the nature of the linkages changed – they became more complex as capital flows, freed from most national control, grew to be prevalent. Although these econometric methods are too complex to describe here, we can still mention some results from one such study by Centoni et al.[10] Their study covers the G7 countries (Canada, U.S., Japan, France, Germany, Italy, and the U.K.) over the 1974–2002 time span. They

---

10 Centoni, M., Cubadda, G., and Hecq, A. (2003) "Common Shocks, Common Dynamics, and the International Business Cycle," 4th Eurostat and DG Ecfin Colloquium on Modern Tools for Business Cycle Analysis, October, Luxembourg, European Parliament.

show that foreign shocks have much greater impact on the very open European economies than on the U.S. or Japan. They also find that, for France, Germany, and Italy, the impact of the foreign component on the business cycle fluctuations dominates over the domestic component, but that technological-type shocks have a much greater impact on the business cycle than fiscal/monetary shocks.

Up to now, we have been ignoring any autonomous movement of capital. To balance international payments, exports had to pay for the countries' imports. With a flexible exchange rate regime, the exchange rate would fluctuate to ensure that the currency market clears, automatically ensuring that exports would pay for the imports. Things were more complex when the country did not allow the exchange rate to fluctuate (i.e. with a fixed exchange rate regime), forcing the central bank to intervene (paying for excess imports over exports out of its foreign reserves) to keep the exchange rate fixed. Such assumptions were not too unrealistic when countries generally barred international capital movements.

However, by the late eighties, most countries had removed their capital controls; clearly, the models we have developed in these last two chapters have to be extended to integrate this development. First we need to figure out in what form these capital flows take place. In the next chapter, we return to the real world to address this first question. We describe the workings of the main international capital markets. In the following chapter, we focus on a specific type of operations on these markets, interest arbitrage, that we can readily format to integrate in our original model; we can then construct a new model of the open economy that incorporates not only international movements of goods and services, but also international movements of capital. We will find that, with this new generation of models, exports (or the central bank) do not have to pay for imports. Also the link between the balance of payments and the international investment position of a country will become clearer.

Summary of Key Concepts

1. Trade imbalances can be corrected with expenditure-switching or expenditure-reducing policies.
2. Expenditure-switching policies redirect domestic demand from foreign to domestic goods to stimulate foreign demand for domestic goods.
3. Expenditure-reducing policies lower the demand for imports by reducing total domestic demand.
4. These policies are limited as they may either aggravate the international community or have undesirable effects on the domestic economy. Eventually chronic trade imbalances cannot be sustained under fixed exchange rates.

5. There is a recourse: if a country commits to non-sterilization, no policy is needed to attain balanced trade. Eventually, an automatic adjustment will take place under the monetary approach to the balance of payments.

6. A country that wants to achieve balanced trade (external balance) and full-employment income (internal balance) requires two policies, for example fiscal expansion and a devaluation. These policy options are summarized in the Swan diagram.

7. The economies of large countries are linked through their balance of trade. Policies then have international repercussions in the sense that domestic fiscal expansions also affect output of the trade partners.

8. The fiscal multiplier in the large open economy is still smaller than in the closed economy, but it is larger than in the small open-economy case, due to the repercussions. Overall fiscal policy under fixed exchange rates without capital mobility is less effective than under either flexible exchange rates or in the closed economy.

9. In the two-country model, expansionary fiscal policy will affect both countries' income in the same direction, but a devaluation/revaluation in one country will have the opposite impact on the other country's output.

CASE STUDY 1

Switching Engines: Global Economic Growth has become Less Dependent on American Spending
David Simonds
The Economist, Feb. 22 2007

In recent years the American economic locomotive has pulled along the rest of the world, while frugal firms and households elsewhere have preferred to save not spend. So, at least, goes the popular wisdom. Signs that America's boom may be fading have therefore caused concern around the globe. Typically in the past, when America's economy has weakened, the rest of the world soon lagged. But this time – so far, anyway – looks different. The rest of the globe has speeded up even as the American engine has lost steam.

The figures are striking. The annual rate of growth of America's real domestic demand dropped from 4.4% in 2004 to only 1.9% in the second half of last

year. The main culprit was the sickly housing market: although consumer spending has held up better than expected, the construction of homes has collapsed. So is the rest of the world also wobbling? On the contrary, many other economies have put on a spurt. Japan's GDP grew by 4.8% at an annual rate in the fourth quarter, mainly thanks to stronger domestic demand. Granted, Japan's GDP figures are notoriously erratic, and this jump follows a poor third quarter. Even so, it was much stronger than expected and gave the Bank of Japan the confidence at last to raise interest rates by another quarter of a percentage point. Equally surprising was the euro area's annualized growth of 3.6%. GDP per person is now growing faster in the euro area than it is in America. Domestic demand is also booming in emerging economies in Asia, the Middle East and Russia.

All of this is helping America to sell more abroad. In the year to the fourth quarter, its merchandise exports rose by 15 percent in value, their fastest pace since 1988. By contrast, import growth slowed to only 4%. In 2006 as a whole, America's sales to China rose by a third, almost twice as fast as its (admittedly larger) imports from that country. Last year was the first since 1997 in which America's exports rose faster than its imports. America's trade deficit is still huge, but it began to narrow at the end of last year, amounting to 5.3% of GDP in the three months to December, down from 6.1% in the same period of 2005. Indeed, by the fourth quarter net trade with foreigners added to America's GDP growth rather than pulling it down.

A reason to be cheerful

The idea that the world economy was being pushed along in an American supermarket trolley was always an exaggeration: the $500 billion increase in America's current-account deficit over the past five years may seem huge, but it is equivalent to an annual increase of only 0.2% of global GDP. The difference now is that the rest of the world is doing more of the carrying.

Of course, countries like Japan, Germany, and China still run large trade surpluses, which means they are producing more than they buy. But it is the change in a country's surplus, not its absolute size, which adds to its growth. For example, China's current-account surplus hit a new record of around 8% of GDP last year. But according to Goldman Sachs, the increase in China's net exports accounted for 2.2 percentage points of the country's 11% GDP growth last year, down from 2.7 points in 2005. The investment bank thinks this contribution will shrink to 1.6 points this year. Most of China's growth comes not from exports but from domestic demand – and consumption is stronger than the official figures suggest.

These are early days, so don't get carried away. The real test of the rest of the world's stamina will come over the next year, as the negative wealth effects of falling home prices start to weigh on American consumer spending. But also take some confidence from the evidence thus far: the world economy may be able to cope without American shoppers.

CASE STUDY QUESTIONS

1. What is the impact of the slowdown in the U.S. economy and the increase in the growth rate of the Asian and European economies on U.S. imports and exports? Explain within the context of the model of the open economy.

2. What is the main source of growth in China: exports or domestic demand? Elaborate.

3. How do you appraise the importance of U.S. demand on world growth overall?

CASE STUDY II

The Fiscal Fallacy of Decoupling from America
Wolfgang Munchau
Financial Times, April 16, 2007

If the U.S. economy tanks, what will happen to the rest of us? Some investment bankers have argued that this time we can easily decouple from the U.S. This view is rooted in the assumption that the indefatigable Asian consumer and the resilient European corporate sector have made us all less dependent.

I do not buy this argument because it does not quite square with what we know about globalization. The world has become more, not less integrated, in terms of trade and financial linkages. The large world economies do not all have the same growth rates, nor do they share the same business cycles. But surely we are not fully decoupled. Some countries may be more shock-resistant than they used to be, but in a globalized world shocks also spread more easily. The answer depends on which of those two effects weighs more strongly. I suspect it is the latter.

When we talk about decoupling, we first of all need to be clear on what exactly we want to decouple from. The term only makes sense in the context of a U.S. recession, or sharp slowdown. There would be no need to decouple from a minor mid-cycle slowdown, the kind that is predicted by the Federal Reserve and other forecasters. If the U.S. economy were to go into recession, house prices would probably fall some more, as would equity prices. Corporate bankruptcies would probably go up, as would credit spreads. The exchange rate of the dollar against the euro and sterling would probably decline. A U.S. downturn is an economic and financial package deal, and it is this combined package that Asia and Europe would have to decouple from – if the decoupling theory is correct.

The good news is that our defences have improved. Many European countries have adopted an improved macroeconomic framework. Many members of the eurozone are now enjoying a previously unknown degree of macroeconomic stability. The U.K. has an independent central bank. Fiscal policy in Europe is far from perfect, but at least subject to a reasonably robust medium-term framework. And there is no question that Asian countries are also financially and economically more resilient today than 10 years ago.

The bad news is that in a globalized world there are more channels that can spread disaster. The classic trade channel is perhaps no longer the most important. Of course, U.S. consumers will consume and import less during a recession and this will affect global demand. But I suspect that the financial and asset price channels will turn out to be far more important.

One of the most potent promulgators of global shocks is the housing market. This may come as a surprise, since property markets are mostly local. But there is a surprisingly high degree of correlation between U.S. and European house price movements. As ever in such a debate, one has to be careful not to confuse correlation with causality. Of course, a decline in U.S. house prices does not actually cause a decline in European house prices, even if it precedes it. They have a common cause: cheap credit in the early part of the decade created housing bubbles on both sides of the Atlantic. The world's central banks pricked those bubbles by steering interest rates back towards neutral levels. In the present cycle, European interest rates followed U.S. rates with a lag of about one year. This suggests that the full impact on the European property market has yet to show through.

Another example is the U.S. subprime crisis, relating to junk mortgages to customers with poor credit ratings. Through some modern financial innovations such as collateralized debt obligations (CDOs), the impact of such local shocks is spread widely around the world. The spread of risk can be a source of stability, but it can turn into a source of instability if it spreads contagion. CDOs are complicated financial vehicles that buy in cash flows, such as mortgage payments, and turn them into tranches of securitised debt. These are then sold to global investors, such as hedge funds, which are lured by the high returns these instruments offer. To the extent that some of these CDOs contain significant chunks of subprime junk, this means that European investors are also indirectly exposed to the subprime crisis. Just talk to these guys about decoupling!

What about the equity markets? There is some research evidence to suggest that U.S. price movements actually cause price changes in Europe.* Also, I would suspect that European and Asian investors are not immune to a sudden change in expectations by U.S. investors about long-term profits growth.

Alan Ahearne, research fellow at Bruegel, the Brussels-based think-tank, argues that the reasons the Europeans will not decouple may come down to old-fashioned animal spirits. Rightly, or wrongly, he says, business leaders around the world see the U.S. as a locomotive for the global economy. Who wants to decouple from a locomotive?

I tend to go along with that view. The world economy is highly inter-dependent through a variety of real and imaginary channels. A sharp U.S. recession is the one event where decoupling is most needed, and least likely. If on the other hand U.S. growth remains robust, there is no need to worry about decoupling in the first place. Decoupling is either improbable or irrelevant.

* The latest IMF *World Economic Outlook*, Chapter 4 (www.imf.org).

Copyright, *Financial Times*, April 16, 2007.

CASE STUDY QUESTIONS

1. According to the theory developed in this chapter, is a recession in the U.S. expected to have an impact on the rest of the world through the trade channel? Elaborate on the trade channels.

2. Does Munchau think that the traditional trade channels are still that important? Explain.

3. What are the new channels described in the article? Indeed this article previews what will be covered in a later chapter when capital flows are taken into account.

Questions for Study and Review

1. On August 8 2002 Brazil received a 30-billion dollar loan from the IMF.

   a. Draw a graph to explain why Brazil may have needed the loan.

   b. Outline all other options (in the graph) that Brazil had in order to avoid having to take the IMF loan.

   c. If other options existed, why were they not attractive to Brazil?

   d. What type of policies are promised to the IMF in return for a reserve loan? Provide support for each policy you mention.

   e. How will Brazil ever repay the loan? Use a new graph.

2. Why is the IMF unpopular in exactly the countries to which it provides loans? Be specific in your economic reasoning and provide graphs for all parts of your answer.

3. In February 2002 Uruguay had a massive balance of payments deficit. What would be the effect on output if Uruguay had not allowed its exchange rate to float and had maintained a fixed exchange rate in June, while following monetary approach to the balance of payments? Draw a graph. Draw another graph indicating what happened after the country allowed the currency to float.

4. Imagine the U.S. was following the monetary approach to the balance of payments. Draw the effects of the increase in government expenditures associated with the 2001 Bush tax cut. Be sure to highlight the crowding-out effect. Given your answer, can you explain why the tax cut was eventually followed by a reduction in employment (and output)? Could this have been predicted last year?

5. In 2001, Argentina experienced a severe balance-of-payments crisis and defaulted on its government loans.

   a. Use the TB/Income diagram to outline *all* Argentinian policy options that could have created the crisis.

   b. Can you imagine why a country would engage in policies that create problems like the ones Argentina experienced?

   c. Use the *TB*/Income diagram to identify *all* policy options Argentina had at that point in time to get out of the currency crisis.

   d. Was it really Argentina's fault? The Brazilian economy currency had lost one third of its value against the dollar during the year prior to the Argentinian crisis. Could this have caused the Argentinian crisis? Use the *TB/Y* diagram.

   e. Which policies would the Argentinian government have had to engage in at that point in time to maintain its exchange rate regime, given that the Brazilian currency had lost value?

   f. Many journalists suggest that the Brazilian economic collapse in 2002 was actually due to the recession in Argentina, where Argentine consumers cut back on their consumption. How might this have lead to the crisis in Brazil? Use the *Y/Y** diagram to explain your answer.

6. Repercussions. Assume two large countries, Cascadia and Sierra. The real exchange rate is fixed. Cascadia's economy is described by the following equations:

Consumption	$C = 220 + 0.7(Y-T)$
Investment	$I = 200$
Government spending	$G = 100$
Tax	$T = 100$
Imports	$M = 100 + 0.2Y$
Exports	$X = 100 + 0.2Y^* - Y^*$ is Sierra's income –

   The economy is in equilibrium when income $Y = C + I + G + X - IM$. The specifications for the equations in Cascadia are identical to those of Sierra, i.e. they share the same values for the coefficients and the exogenous variables. As a result, Sierra's model is derived from the above model by taking all the asterisks from the variables with asterisks and adding asterisks to the variables without asterisks.

a. For each country solve for equilibrium income as a function of the other country's income.

b. Now you have derived a system of 2 equations with 2 unknowns (Y and Y^*)

Solve this system to obtain the simultaneous equilibrium income (a single number for each country) in each of the two countries.

c. Illustrate your results on the graph below with Y on the Y-axis and Y^* on the Y^*-axis. Draw curves I (for Cascadia) and II (for Sierra) corresponding to the above equations. Report the value of the intercepts and of the slopes and show the joint simultaneous equilibrium E for the two countries.

d. Calculate the balance of trade for each country.

e. Now assume that Cascadia uses expansionary fiscal policy: it increases G by 100. Show the effect on the above graph: the shift(s) of the relevant curve(s) and the new joint equilibrium income in E'.

f. Calculate the small open-economy multiplier m_{so}. This multiplier allows you to calculate by how much Y increases when G increases, assuming that Cascadia is small and cannot affect Sierra (i.e. no repercussions and Y^* does not change). So the increase in Y calculated with the small open-economy multiplier corresponds to the shift of Cascadia's $Y=f(Y^*)$ curve (it is the increase in its intercept).

g. What are the equations for curve I (Cascadia) and for curve II (Sierra) after Cascadia's fiscal expansion? What are the repercussions of Cascadia's expansionary fiscal policy on Sierra's income Y^*?

h. Calculate the multiplier for the large open-economy m_{lo} for Cascadia using the equation in the chapter and use the multiplier to calculate the new level of Cascadia's income. Then calculate Sierra's corresponding income after the repercussions have worked their way through and the two economies have reached a new simultaneous equilibrium.

i. Calculate the new balance of trade for each country.

Advanced:

j. Assume that Cascadia has a target level of output of 2,000. Assuming that the foreign government does not use any fiscal policy, what is the increase in government spending G in Cascadia necessary to achieve their target output?

k. Suppose that each country has a target output of 2,000 and that each government increases government spending (G and G^*) by the same amount. What is the common increase in G and G^* necessary to achieve the target outputs of the two countries? Solve for net exports and the budget deficit in each country.

References and Suggestions for Further Reading

Baxter, M. (1995) "International Trade and Business Cycles," in G. Grossman and K. Rogoff (eds) *Handbook of International Economics*, Vol.III: 1801–1864, Amsterdam: Elsevier.

Bryant, R., Currie, D., Frenkel, J., Masson, P., and Portes, R. (eds) (1989) *Macroeconomic Policies in an Interdependent World*, Washington, DC: Brookings Institution.

Bunkley, N. (2007) "Another Spin for 'Buy American,'" *New York Times*, June 14.

'Buy American Act,' Department of State – International Information Programs (http://usinfo.state.gov/products/pubs/trade/glossac.htm#buyam).

Calvo, G., and Reinhart, C. (2002) "Fear of Floating," *Quarterly Journal of Economics*, 177: 379–408.

Camdessus, M. (1995) "Drawing Lessons from the Mexican Crisis: Preventing and Resolving Financial Crises – the Role of the IMF," *Managing Director of the International Monetary Fund (IMF)*, May 22.

Centoni, M., Cubadda, G., and Hecq, A. (2003) "Common Shocks, Common Dynamics, and the International Business Cycle," 4th Eurostat and DG Ecfin Colloquium on Modern Tools for Business Cycle Analysis, October, Luxembourg, European Parliament.

Cooper, R. (1986) "Dealing with the Trade Deficit in a Floating Rate System," *Brookings Papers on Economic Activity*, 1986: 195–208.

—— (2001) "Is the U.S. Current Account Deficit Sustainable? Will it be Sustained?," *Brookings Papers on Economic Activity*, 2001: 217–26.

Dornbusch, R. (1987) "External Balance Correction: Depreciation or Protection?," *Brookings Papers on Economic Activity*, 1987: 249–70.

—— (1980) *Open Economy Macroeconomics*, New York: Basic Books.

Fischer, S. (2001) "Distinguished Lecture on Economics in Government: Exchange Rate Regimes: Is the Bipolar View Correct?," *Journal of Economic Perspectives*, 15: 3–24.

Garton P. and Chang, J. (2005) "The Chinese Currency: How Undervalued and How Much does it Matter?," Canberra: Australian Treasury *Economic Round Up*, http://www.treasury.gov.au/documents/1042/PDF/Spring_2005_Economic_Roundup.pdf.

Glain, S. (1998) "Japan's Inaction Hurts Other Asian Countries," *Wall Street Journal*, July 27.

Helliwell, J. and Padmore, T. (1985) "Empirical Studies of Macroeconomic Interdependence," in R. Jones and P. Kenen (eds), *Handbook of International Economics*, Vol. II: 1107–1151, Amsterdam: North-Holland.

Hoare, T.F. (1977) "International Economic Interdependence, – the Commission of the European Communities's Meteor Model," Brussels: Directorate General for Economic and Financial Affairs of the EEC Commission.

Hooper, P. and Marquez, J. (1995) "Exchange Rates, Prices and External Adjustment in the United States and Japan," in Peter Kenen (ed.), *Interdependence and the Macroeconomics of the Open Economy*, Princeton: Princeton University Press.

Johnson, H. (1958) "Toward a General Theory of the Balance of Payments," in J. Frenkel and H. Johnson (eds.), *The Monetary Approach to the Balance of Payments*, Toronto: University of Toronto Press.

Krugman P. and Baldwin, R. (1987) "The Persistence of the US Trade Deficit," *Brookings Papers on Economic Activity*, 1987: 1–55.

Krugman, P. (1992) "Adjustment in the World Economy," in P. Krugman *Currencies and Crises* (1–30), Cambridge: MIT Press.

—— (1998) "Latin America's Swan Song," (http://web.mit.edu/krugman/www/swansong.html).

Larsen, F., Llewellynm J., and Potter, S. (1993) "Estimates of Policy Interdependence for EU countries – Impact of a real depreciation," *International Economic Linkages – OECD Economic Studies No. 1*, Paris: OECD.

Lin, S. (2006) "Does it pay to go to the corners? An empirical evaluation of the bipolar view of exchange rates," *Economics Letters*, 92: 342–7.

McKibbin, W. (1988) "International Policy Coordination," *Economic Record* 64: 242–53.

McKinnon, R. (2001) "The International Dollar Standard and the Sustainability of the US Current Account Deficit," *Brookings Papers on Economic Activity*, 2001: 227–37.

Mann, C. (1999) *Is the US Trade Deficit Sustainable?*, IIE, Ch. 10.

Meteor (1977) *Netherlands Central Planbureau for the EEC Commission*.

Munchau, W. (2007) "The Fiscal Fallacy of Decoupling from America," *Financial Times*, April 16.

Mundell, R. (1960) "The Monetary Dynamics of International Adjustment under Fixed and Floating Exchange Rates," *Quarterly Journal of Economics*, 74: 227–57.

Norton, S. and Schlagenhauf, D. (1996) "The Role of International Factors in the Business Cycle: A Multi-Country Study," *Journal of International Economics*, 37: 85–104.

Obstfeld M. and Rogoff, K. "Perspectives on OECD Economic Integration: Implications for US Current Account Adjustment," Center for International and Development Economics Research, Working Paper Series 1006, 2006, UC Berkeley (http://www.kc.frb.org/PUBLICAT/SYMPOS/2000/rogoff.pdf).

Quiggin, J. (2004) "The Unsustainability of US Trade Deficits," *The Economists' Voice*, 1(3): 1–10.

Rodrik D. and Devarajan, S. (1992) "Do the Benefits of Fixed Exchange Rates Outweigh Their Costs? The Franc Zone in Africa," in I. Goldin and A.L. Winters (eds), *Open Economies: Structural Adjustment and Agriculture*, London: Cambridge University Press for CEPR.

Simonds, D. (2007) "Switching Engines: Global economic growth has become less dependent on American spending," *The Economist*, Feb 22.

Swan, T. (1963) "Longer Run Problems of the Balance of Payments," in *The Australian Economy: A Volume of Readings*, H.W. Arndt and M.W. Corden (eds), Melbourne: Cheshire Press. Reprinted in Caves and Johnson, *Readings in International Economics*, 1968, Homewood, IL: Irwin.

Weber, W. (1986) "Do Sterilized Interventions Affect the Exchange Rate?," *Federal Reserve Bank of Minneapolis Quarterly Review*, Summer 1986: 14–23.

Chapter 16

International Capital Markets

LEARNING OBJECTIVES

By the end of this chapter you should be able to understand:

- the reasons for the tremendous growth in global financial capital flows
- the different types of foreign exchange markets and their functions
- foreign exchange contracts, such as futures, options, swaps, and derivatives
- currency arbitrage and its impact on exchange rates
- strategies that limit firms' exposures to foreign exchange risk
- technical analysis, technical indicators, and short-term trading

This chapter serves as an introduction to international capital markets. The regulations that govern international capital transactions have changed profoundly since the 1970s. Most of these changes involved liberalizations of financial markets; consequently the amount of foreign exchange traded around the globe has grown dramatically.

Compounded with these volume upsurges, the diversity of the foreign exchange contracts traded on international capital markets has also increased. We track the recent innovations in the foreign exchange contracts and investigate the origins of what can only be called a spectacular explosion of international capital flows. Finally, the chapter reviews strategies that may be employed to price foreign exchange in the very short run.

INTERNATIONAL FINANCIAL FLOWS

After World War II, the monetary and exchange rate policies of industrialized countries was largely dictated by the Bretton Woods Agreement of 1944 (Bretton Woods details are discussed in Chapter 21). The Agreement did not allow free capital flows among nations. On the contrary, capital controls played an important role in managing the fixed exchange rate regimes that members of the "Bretton Woods Club" had agreed upon. Whenever exchange rates required adjustments, capital controls were an integral component of the adjustment mechanism.

Bretton Woods members thought capital controls were fundamental to the reconstruction and growth of the international trading system that had been devastated by a global depression, hyperinflation in Europe, and two world wars. As international trade recovered, however, it became increasingly difficult to distinguish between foreign exchange transactions for purposes of international trade (to pay for imports, for example) and capital transactions designed to take advantage of exchange rate misalignments.

An Extreme Form of Control: Currency Non-Convertibility

Capital flow restrictions were very tight in the past, as many countries prohibited currency convertibility, meaning that the public was not permitted even to hold balances in foreign currency. Currency non-convertibility is perhaps the most restrictive form of capital control as the government has the sole authority to hold foreign currency and to dole it out to government-approved importers. Such controls are essential in countries that fix their exchange rate at unrealistic levels. For instance East Germany used to fix their currency at par value with the West German DM (Deutsche Mark)

---

stipulating that one East German mark was worth exactly what a West German mark was worth. On the black market, however, the exchange rate was twenty East German marks for one West German mark, implying that, if anyone were allowed to hold foreign currency in East Germany, the value of the East German mark would fall dramatically.

The Growth of International Financial Capital Flows

The Bretton Woods Agreement was abandoned in 1973 and a period of unregulated exchange rates followed, resulting in an era of gradual international financial account liberalizations. The black line in the right panel of Figure 16.1 shows that total *annual* international capital flows increased dramatically, from less than half a trillion dollars in the early 1980s to over 6 trillion dollars in 2005. While world income also increased over that period, capital flows expanded much faster, rising from about 4 percent in 1980 to over 14 percent of world GDP in 2005. The left panel breaks down the total flows as percent of world GDP by type of flow. This illustrates that in the eighties, banking and other flows and, to a lesser extent, foreign direct investment made up the bulk of the flows. Since then, portfolio equity flows and, even more strikingly, portfolio debt flows have represented a growing share of the total while the banking share has not changed.

Increased international capital mobility went hand in hand with ever greater volumes of foreign exchange transactions. After all, the acquisition of foreign assets (denominated in foreign currency) requires foreign exchange. The **Bank of International Settlements** (BIS) oversees international monetary and financial cooperation and carries out regular surveys of *daily* international foreign exchange transaction volumes. According to the BIS, these flows increased from $590 billion in 1989 to $3,210 billion in 2007. Such volumes are staggering, especially when compared to the flows of

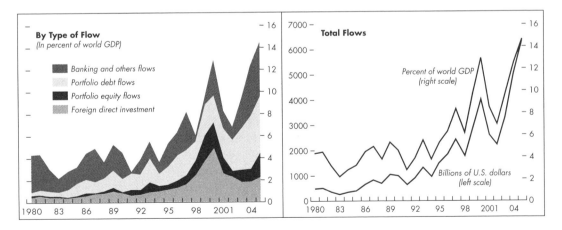

FIGURE 16.1 Global Capital Flows

Source: adapted from the *IMF Global Financial Stability Report* (2007)

daily global merchandise exports published by the World Trade Organization: $8.71 billion in 1989 and $38.08 billion in 2007. Global trade flows therefore constitute less than 2 percent of global foreign exchange transactions.

It is also striking that only a few currencies, often referred as **vehicle currencies**, are involved in most of the global foreign exchange transactions. As shown in Table 16.1, the dollar has been the most heavily traded currency by far. It was involved in 90 percent of the foreign exchange transactions in 2001, barely dropping to 88 percent in 2007; the euro's share is a distant second with a steady share of about 37 percent.

The fact that the dollar is by far the most traded currency reflects the popularity of U.S. assets and the depth of U.S. capital markets. Table 16.2 disaggregates U.S. net foreign asset positions to highlight the substantial share of U.S. assets that are owned by foreigners. In 2007, foreigners owned 19 percent of all U.S. long-term securities, including a staggering 57 percent of the U.S. government's treasury bills.

TABLE 16.1 Global Currency Turnover (in billion U.S.$)

	2001		2004		2007	
	Turnover	Share	Turnover	Share	Turnover	Share
Total (All Currency Pairs)	**1,173**	**100%**	**1,794**	**100%**	**3,081**	**100%**
Total U.S. dollar	**1,059**	**90%**	**1,591**	**88%**	**2,656**	**88%**
U.S. $/euro	354	30%	503	28%	840	27%
U.S. $/yen	231	20%	298	17%	397	13%
U.S. $/sterling	125	11%	248	14%	361	12%
U.S. $/Australian $	47	4%	98	5%	175	6%
U.S. $/Swiss franc	57	5%	78	4%	143	5%
U.S. $/Canadian $	50	4%	71	4%	115	4%
U.S. $/other	195	17%	295	16%	628	21%
Total euro (incl. U.S.$/euro)	**441**	**38%**	**662**	**36%**	**1,140**	**37%**
euro/yen	30	3%	51	3%	70	2%
euro/sterling	24	2%	43	2%	64	2%
euro/Swiss franc	12	1%	26	1%	54	2%
euro/other	21	2%	39	2%	112	4%
Other currencies	**26**	**2%**	**$42**	**2%**	**122**	**4%**

Source: adapted from Bank of International Settlements, *Triennial Central Bank Survey*, Table B. 5. Daily averages in April of each year. (http://www.bis.org/publ/rpfxf07t.htm)

TABLE 16.2 Share of Foreign-Owned U.S. Long-Term Securities (in billion U.S.$)

	1994	Foreign owned	2004	Foreign owned	2007	Foreign owned
Total	**15,697**	**8%**	**37,499**	**15%**	**48,718**	**19%**
Total U.S. gov't debt	**4,374**	**13%**	**8,336**	**25%**	**9,559**	**34%**
Treasury bills	2,392	19%	2,809	51%	3,454	57%
Gov't agency debt	1,982	5%	5,527	11%	6,105	21%
Total private debt	**11,323**	**6%**	**29,163**	**12%**	**39,159**	**15%**
Equity (stocks, funds)	7,767	5%	20,779	9%	27,768	11%
Corporate/Other debt	3,556	8%	8,384	18%	11,391	24%

Source: adapted from U.S. Department of the Treasury, *Report on Foreign Portfolio Holdings of U.S. Securities, Table 2* (2007). U.S. government agency securities include all securities issued by federally sponsored agencies and corporations, including the Government National Mortgage Association (GNMA).

Why are U.S. Assets such Popular Investments for Foreigners?

In 2006, the GDP of the European Union and the United States were almost identical with €11.9 trillion and €11.2 trillion, respectively. So why are investments in dollar so much more popular?

In Chapter 12 we presented data (Figure 12.1) illustrating the expansion of U.S. trade deficits over the past 25 years. From the definition of the balance of payments, we know that such deficits must be matched by equivalent financial account surpluses. Indeed, the U.S. has experienced large financial account surpluses generated by capital inflows, specifically sales of U.S. assets to foreigners. Capital inflows can also be seen as loans that foreigners extend to the United States. Therefore the country transitioned from being the world's largest creditor nation (a spot now held by Japan) to being the world's largest debtor nation as its trade and fiscal deficits ballooned in the 1980s (the evolution of the International Investment Position of the U.S. was presented in Table A12.3). These facts are confirmed in Table 16.2 showing the dramatic increase in foreign ownership of U.S. long-term securities.

Are we making two contradictory arguments in Chapter 12 and in Chapter 16? Did capital inflows increase because of the U.S. trade deficits, or did trade deficits increase because the dollar is the most attractive currency and the rest of the world is willing to have large current account surpluses with the U.S. to acquire these precious dollars and invest in the United States? The answer to this question requires a model of the open economy that features both international financial markets and international trade. This model is presented in the following chapters.

Euromarkets

Both the end of the Bretton Woods system and the ensuing capital market liberalizations resulted in an acceleration of international capital flows. But there was another key catalyst, too – the rise of **eurocurrency** markets. Eurocurrencies are defined as currencies held outside the jurisdiction of the issuing country's central bank. So a dollar held anywhere outside the U.S. is called a **eurodollar**, and a yen held anywhere outside Japan is a euroyen; there is even a euroeuro. In our discussion below, it is important to avoid the confusion that eurocurrencies may be somehow related to the euro (the currency of the European Economic and Monetary Union). The "euro" prefix indicates only that a currency is held in a nation where it is not the official currency.

The Birth of the Eurodollar

Curiously, the term eurodollar (and therefore the "euro" prefix for eurocurrencies) originated with the Soviet Union. In the 1950s, the Soviet Union became a major gold and oil exporter. At that time, eurocurrencies did not exist and foreign currency bank accounts were prohibited. Since gold and oil are both traded predominantly in U.S. dollars, the Soviet Union was forced to deposit its U.S. dollars in the U.S., where the funds were at risk of being frozen (or confiscated).

With the advent of the Cold War, the Soviet Union moved its U.S. dollar deposits to a Soviet-owned bank (today known as VTB Bank) with branches in France and the United Kingdom. Since VTB's telex address was EUROBANK, and since VTB was the first major source of dollars outside the U.S., foreign exchange traders soon referred to any dollar traded outside the U.S. as a EURODOLLAR.

(An abstract of VTB Bank's history can be found at http://www.vtb.ru)

The hallmark of eurocurrency markets is the ability of investors to hold funds denominated in a particular currency without having to be subject to the specific regulations of the country issuing the currency in question. For example, reserve requirements might differ across countries; this affects banks' profit margins and therefore the interest rates they can offer to customers. In fact, the BIS contends that eurocurrency markets came into existence precisely because investors were interested in circumventing domestic regulations. Nevertheless, eurocurrency markets provide investors with the convenience of depositing and borrowing foreign funds in a foreign country without being subject to the currency regulations that apply to these foreign funds in their own country.

From the late 1980s onwards, companies involved in international transactions began to borrow offshore, finding euromarkets a beneficial center for holding excess liquidity, providing short-term loans, and financing imports and exports. At that time, British banks started to lend dollars as an alternative to pounds in order to maintain their leading position in global finance, and London became the center of the eurodollar market. London's convenient geographical location (operating during Asian and American markets' active times) is also instrumental in preserving its dominance in the euromarket.

We have already seen that the dollar is by far the most traded international currency. It is no different in the eurocurrency markets. The dollar is so dominant among eurocurrencies that the term "eurodollar market" is often used interchangeably with eurocurrency market. The eurodollar constitutes about 66 percent of the daily eurocurrency trade. The attraction is understandable when we recall that these trades are not subject to any rules or regulations that govern domestic currency and/or bank deposits including taxes, restrictions on capital movements, or exchange controls.

FINANCIAL MARKETS AND INSTRUMENTS

The immense volume of global foreign exchange transactions has given rise to a variety of financial instruments that can be used to trade foreign currency. In this introduction to international financial markets, we focus on two basic markets and three prominent financial instruments. The two markets that we examine are the spot and forward markets, in which spot and forward contracts are traded. The two markets are bridged by foreign exchange swaps that generate the greatest daily foreign exchange trading volume.

Basic Foreign Exchange Contracts: Spot, Forward, and Swaps

Foreign currencies are traded in spot and forward markets. In the **spot market**, foreign exchange is traded for immediate delivery at a **spot price**, the price that is quoted when the contract is written. In Chapter 13, we described how the spot price is determined in countries with flexible exchange rates.

Alternatively, a forward contract can be written; in this case, two parties, a seller and a buyer, agree on a **forward price** *today* for a specific quantity of foreign currency that is to be delivered at a specified future date. The **forward market** is useful for firms expecting to receive foreign currency payments or having to make a foreign currency payment at some point in the future, but these firms want to insure themselves against changing exchange rates.

For example, a U.S. firm might expect payment, say €1 million, for goods delivered to a European customer in 3 months. The value of the €1 million *in terms of U.S. dollars* will fluctuate over the next three months. The firm may therefore be interested in purchasing a forward contract *today* that allows it to sell €1 million *in three months* at an exchange rate determined *today*. This forward contract would then provide the firm with the exact value of its future euro payments in terms of U.S. dollars. Its U.S. profits are no longer subject to an exchange rate risk.

Forward contracts are commonly written for 30, 60, or 90 days. Only sufficiently stable currencies are traded on forward markets, because currencies that fluctuate widely are too risky to trade with a forward contract. Table 16.3 reproduces a typical forward quote from the New York branch of the U.S. Central Bank, the New York Federal Reserve (which handles most U.S. foreign exchange transactions). The Table indicates a **forward premium** for the euro, since the forward price of the euro exceeds its spot rate. In contrast, the yen is selling at a **forward discount**. We develop the concepts of forward premiums/discounts further in the next chapter. Then we derive the concepts formally to show how they are related to changes in exchange rates as well as interest rates.

TABLE 16.3 Spot and Forward Exchange Rates (selected currencies – May 15, 2008)

Country	Currency	$ Price of foreign currency
Canada (Spot)	Can. dollar	0.9996
Denmark (Spot)	Den. krone	0.2069
European Monetary Union (Spot)	euro	1.5442
3 months forward	euro	1.5371
6 months forward	euro	1.5304
Japan (Spot)	yen	0.009506
3 months forward	yen	0.009555
6 months forward	yen	0.009601
Norway (Spot)	Nor. krone	0.1968
Sweden (Spot)	krona	0.1659
Switzerland (Spot)	franc	0.9466
United Kingdom (Spot)	sterling	1.9420

Source: adapted from New York Federal Reserve Bank data, New York Interbank Market, 10:00 a.m. Midpoints, May 15, 2008

A **foreign exchange swap** bridges spot and forward rates, since it allows traders to transfer funds that are denominated in two currencies at two different points in time. This sounds more complicated than it actually is. Think about it this way: most multinationals receive revenues in one currency on any given day, but need those funds to pay obligations in another currency on another day. Under this circumstance, swaps are a good instrument to minimize the foreign exchange risk.

Swapping Homes and Foreign Exchange: A Real World Foreign Exchange Swap

On January 1, 2008, the Vice President of an American multinational was promoted head of a newly acquired subsidiary in Munich, Germany. The U.S. multinational provides the VP with a nice bonus and promises to pay for her housing abroad. The VP is expected to stay in Germany for 3 years before returning to the U.S.

The company accountant finds a nice home for the VP in Munich that costs €500,000. The Munich housing market has been incredibly stable over the past years and the accountant expects to sell the home in three years for exactly the same amount, €500,000. Still, he is worried that the purchase of the house is exposing the company to exchange rate risk over the next three years. Since the euro is at an all-time high, he surmises that there is a good chance that the euro may fall over the next 3 years. This implies that the €500,000 may buy fewer dollars on January 1, 2011 than the amount of dollars he uses to buy the home today.

> The accountant initiates a currency swap. He writes a contract to buy €500,000 with dollars on January 1, 2008 (to buy the house) and at the same time agrees to sell €500,000 on January 2011 at a specified forward rate. Therefore the transaction involves a contract that specifies both a spot transaction and a forward transaction, therefore qualifying as a swap. For the cost of the price differential between the forward rate and the spot rate, the accountant has eliminated any foreign exchange risk for the multinational firm.

Insurance against this type of foreign exchange risk is so popular that swaps constitute by far the largest share of global foreign exchange transactions. Table 16.4 illustrates the change in the turnover of the three major types of foreign exchange contracts from 1989 to 2007. While forward contracts experienced the greatest increase in trading volume since 1989, swaps still constituted the largest daily trading volume with a staggering $1.7 trillion in 2007. That year, total daily global foreign exchange transactions (here the sum of spot, forward, swaps) exceeded $3.2 trillion. Note that global trade in goods was smaller by an entire order of magnitude. Table 16.4 shows that total daily financial turnover in 2007 was more than 80 times greater than daily world merchandise exports. In other words, only 1.19 percent of the financial turnover was used to settle merchandise trade transactions.

TABLE 16.4 Daily Foreign Exchange Volume and Goods Trade (in billions U.S.$)

	1989	1995	2001	2007	2007/1989 ratio
Global foreign exchange (FX) turnover	**590**	**1,190**	**1,200**	**3,210**	**5.4**
Spot	317	494	387	1,005	3.2
Forward	27	97	131	362	13.4
Swaps	190	548	656	1,714	9.0
Estimated reporting gaps	56	53	26	129	
Global merchandise exports	**8.49**	**14.15**	**16.95**	**38.08**	**4.4**
Ratio FX / Exports	**68**	**84**	**71**	**84**	

Sources: adapted from Bank of International Settlements and the World Trade Organization data. The financial data are daily averages for April of each year (adjusted for local and cross-border double-counting). The merchandise trade data are daily averages obtained from annual data.

Futures and Options

As international capital flows increased in volume, ever new exchange contracts were created to accommodate the needs and interests of currency traders. These contracts are labeled **derivatives**, indicating that they are some variation on spot, forward, and/or swap contracts. Formally, the term derivative refers to a financial instrument the value of which changes in response to variables specified in the underlying contract (such as timing, currency type, interest rates, etc.).

Derivatives are popular to offset complex financial risk exposures that multinational firms may face. Derivatives also offer a sophisticated means of speculating in currency markets. The diverse set of underlying assets and pay-off alternatives that has been developed over time has led to a huge range of derivative contracts that are traded today.

The most common foreign exchange derivatives are futures and options. **Futures** are very similar to forward contracts – the difference is that forwards are custom-tailored to the specific need of a specific customer (e.g., a British car dealer buying an €30,000 Italian Ferrari on May 15, 2008, to be delivered in three months, can buy the euros forward on the 3-month forward market – see rate on Table 16.3), while futures are standardized forward contracts that are written only for uniform quantities of currency to be exchanged at generic dates. The fact that future contracts are so standardized allows them to be traded at public exchanges, just like a stock. The Chicago Mercantile Exchange is the most active futures market, but other markets exist in New York and around the world.

Table 16.5 reports prices from the Chicago Mercantile Exchange for specific quantities of foreign exchange to be delivered at predetermined settlement dates. For instance, on Monday, July 21, 2008, a trader could buy a contract for €125,000 for delivery on September 8, 2008 for a **settlement price** (the closing price of the day) of $1.5847.

TABLE 16.5 Foreign Currency Futures (Chicago Mercantile Exchange, July 21, 2008)

Currency	Contract Size	Price Unit ($ per)	Settlement Date	Settlement in $
Japanese yen	¥ 12,500,000	¥100	8-Sep.-08	0.93980
Japanese yen	¥ 12,500,000	¥100	8-Dec.-08	0.94500
Canadian dollar	CA$ 100,000	CA$	8-Sep.-08	0.99820
Canadian dollar	CA$ 100,000	CA$	8-Dec.-08	0.99760
Canadian dollar	CA$ 100,000	CA$	9-Mar.-09	0.99710
Canadian dollar	CA$ 100,000	CA$	9-Sep.-09	0.99670
British pound	£ 62500	£	8-Sep.-08	1.99040
British pound	£ 62500	£	8-Dec.-08	1.97700
Swiss franc	CHF 125,000	CHF	8-Sep.-08	0.97980
Swiss franc	CHF 125,000	CHF	8-Dec.-08	0.98070
Australian dollar	AU$ 100,000	AU$	8-Sep.-08	0.96850

Currency	Contract Size	Price Unit ($ per)	Settlement Date	Settlement in $
Australian dollar	AU$ 100,000	AU$	8-Dec.-08	0.95730
Mexican peso	Peso 500,000	10 Peso	8-Aug.-08	0.98125
Mexican peso	Peso 500,000	10 Peso	8-Sep.-08	0.97775
Mexican peso	Peso 500,000	10 Peso	8-Dec.-08	0.96725
euro	€ 125,000	€	8-Sep.-08	1.58470
euro	€ 125,000	€	8-Dec.-08	1.57710
euro	€ 125,000	€	9-Sep.-09	1.55870

Source: adapted from Chicago Mercantile Exchange data

Options are more sophisticated derivatives than swaps or futures. There are two general types of options: calls and puts. If you purchase a **call option**, you purchase the right (but not the obligation) to buy a specific amount of foreign exchange within a specified period of time at a predetermined price (the **strike price**). A **put option** is similar, but it gives you the right to sell foreign currency.

Options involve **one-sided bets**, since buyers of options are not obliged to execute the currency exchange, while sellers must execute if buyers insist. For the right to exercise an option, the buyer must compensate the seller by paying a **premium**. Here it is very important to note that "purchasing the option" entails *only* the payment of the premium to the seller. That is, the buyer purchases the right to execute but does have to provide the actual funds to purchase the currency. For example, a call option to buy the pound for $2 in November 2007 might cost two cents; obviously this price *does not* include the actual cost of purchasing the pound. Indeed the actual purchase price of the foreign currency (if the option is to be executed) is also part of the options contract (see Table 16.6).

Real World Options: International Mergers and Acquisitions and Speculation

Foreign exchange options are popular instruments to ensure against a variety of uncertain outcomes. Imagine a U.S. firm in the midst of negotiating the purchase of a British firm for £1 million pounds, but the deal is not yet certain. The U.S. firm might be interested *today* in locking the dollar price of the pounds it will have to pay if the deal goes through. The U.S. firm could engage in a forward contract, but it would have to agree to *actually* buy the £1 million pounds at some future time. Because the purchase is still uncertain, however, the U.S. firm does not want to be held to such a contract in case the deal does not go through. Purchasing sterling calls totaling £1 million will protect the firm against an appreciation in the British pound before the deal is completed, but this will gives the firm a means of avoiding purchasing the sterling in the event the transaction does not occur.

On August 22, 2007, the spot rate for £1 was U.S.$1.9881, and the U.S. company was worried that the pound might appreciate and therefore increase the dollar price of the purchase. The soonest the firm expects the deal to close is in November, 2007. So the company accountant checks the foreign exchange options prices at the Chicago Mercantile Exchange (see Table 16.6). The quoted prices show that the premium for a call option at a $2 strike price, valid until November 2007, is about two cents (or exactly $0.0204). If the company decides instead to purchase a November $2.01 call option (so that it can buy pounds for U.S. $2.01 any time before November), the premium would be 1.66 cents.

Assume that the firm is worried that the pound might appreciate above $2.01 before the end of November; it will purchase November call options for $16,600 (1,000,000*0.0166) million allowing the firm to purchase £1,000,000 for $2,010,000 (1,000,000*2.01) if needed. The cost of purchasing the calls constitutes the maximum loss the firm could ever incur. The loss would materialize only if the pound spot rate never rose above $2.01 prior to November. In this case, the option is never worth exercising.

TABLE 16.6 Foreign Exchange Option Premiums (U.S.$/U.K.£ option contracts, Aug. 22, 2007)

Strike Price	Calls			Puts		
	Sept.	Oct.	Nov.	Sept.	Oct.	Nov.
2.000	0.0081	0.0139	0.0204	0.0177	0.0287	0.0351
2.010	0.0050	0.0105	0.0166	0.0246	0.0353	0.0412
2.020	0.0029	0.0078	0.0134	0.0324	0.0425	0.0497
2.030	0.0016	0.0057	0.0107	0.0411	0.0503	0.0552
2.040	0.0010	0.0041	0.0086	0.0505	0.0587	0.0630

Source: adapted from Chicago Mercantile Exchange data

An option is said to be **in the money** when it is worth exercising. This is when the strike price of the call (put) option is below (above) the current spot price. In our specific example, only when the spot price rises above $2.01 is the option worth exercising. While an option may be in the money, it *does not* imply that the U.S. firm has covered its cost (the $16,600 it paid to obtain the option). In our case, the spot price has to increase above $2.0266 ($2.01+$0.0166) to render exercising the option fully worthwhile.

Note that a November $2.01 put (the right to sell a pound at $2.01) was available at a 4.12 cent premium. The fact that the premium for the put is higher than that for the call suggests that the put is viewed as more likely to be exercised than the call, reflecting traders' expectations and other factors.

Finally, purchasing puts or calls is a means of speculating on the future of the spot exchange rate with a limited risk of loss. If, for example, a speculator believed that spot sterling would fall well below $2.00 before the end of November, purchasing a sterling put with a strike price of $2.00 for 3.51 cents is a way of gambling on that outcome without taking a large risk. The problem is that sterling will have to fall below $1.9649 for the gamble to be profitable because, although the strike price is $2.00, the speculator has already spent 3.51 cents on the premium or price of the option. With a contract size equal to £31,250, the total price of the option is $1,096.88 plus brokerage charges, which is the maximum loss that the speculator can experience. That will occur if spot sterling never goes below $2.00 before maturity, so it is never worth exercising. This put option is "in the money" (or, equivalently, "above water") whenever the spot exchange rate is below $2.00, but it is only profitable at spot exchange rates below $1.9649.

The variety and complexity of both domestic and international derivatives are limited only by the imagination of the officers of commercial and investment banks who are selling them in exchange for handsome fees. Beside currency futures and options, organized exchanges also trade interest rate as well as equity index derivatives. Derivatives were originally seen as a way of offsetting risks from previous financial exposures, but have increasingly become ways of speculating. Many investors have become involved in such derivatives without fully understanding the risks, and have absorbed large financial losses when markets turned against them. Beware potential investors: if you are told by a banker or broker that a particular investment or derivative contract offers the certainty of a large profit at virtually no risk, look for a new bank or brokerage firm. Neither international nor domestic financial markets offer opportunities for large profits at no significant risk. International derivative markets have reinforced this unhappy lesson for numerous investors in recent years.

The fundamental risk of an option is tied to its timing: many options expire unexercised and worthless. Therefore those traders or banks that sell (or "write") options are most likely to profit. At first sight, options may seem simple and attractive, but option pricing is quite complicated. It was not until 1973 that an optimal option pricing formula was formally derived (and the authors, Robert Merton and Myron Scholes, received the 1997 economics Nobel Prize for their work).

The importance of currency futures and options, as well as derivative markets in general, is growing rapidly. Table 16.7 shows that futures turnover was about ten times greater than options turnover in 2008. Interesting also is the geographic distribution of these trades: 90 percent of global futures and 40 percent of the global options are traded in the United States. By converting the annual data in Table 16.7 into daily figures, we can compare the futures and options turnover to the spot, forward, and swap turnover (shown earlier in Table 16.4). This reveals that futures and options corresponded to about 1 percent of the traditional foreign exchange turnover for 2004.

TABLE 16.7 Futures and Options Turnover (in billion U.S.$)

Currency	Futures				Options			
	2004	2005	2006	2007	2004	2005	2006	2007
Global	6,614.7	11,125.8	15,154.0	20,325.6	588.7	944.0	1,119.9	2,140.5
North America	6,080.9	10,258.4	13,684.8	17,653.6	346.1	449.0	453.1	621.7
Europe	12.5	36.6	45.7	106.6	3.0	7.8	10.4	7.6
Asia & Pacific	107.2	133.7	162.9	282.2	–	–	–	–
Other Markets	414.1	697.1	1,260.6	2,283.2	239.5	487.1	656.4	1,511.2

Source: adapted from Bank of International Settlements (BIS), *Quarterly Review.*

VARIOUS AGENTS AND THE FUNCTIONS OF THE MARKETS

Several types of traders use the forward/future markets regularly: currency arbitrageurs, importers and exporters, speculators, and interest arbitrageurs.[1] The dealings of these traders constitute the main sources of supply and demand for foreign exchange. Below we analyze the various functions of the main market participants: arbitraging, hedging, and speculating. To simplify, we ignore transaction costs in our examples.

Currency Arbitrageurs

Arbitrage is based on the simple principle of "buy low – sell high" to take advantage of price differentials in two or more markets. In the real world arbitrage is a bit more complicated, however. It not only involves buying low and selling high, but the transactions have to occur *simultaneously* in order to avoid exposure to the risk of price changes occurring between the two stages of the operation. International currency arbitrage can be loosely defined as an investment strategy that capitalizes on differences in currency prices in different locations or countries.

In response to imbalances in a currency's demand or supply, its price may differ in different locations around the globe. For example, there is a £/$ market in London as well as in New York. It is thus possible that the spot price might be slightly different in the two locations – allowing arbitrageurs to make a quick profit by buying low and selling high. Arbitrage thus ensures that prices realign quickly, such that no further risk-free gains exist. If such price differences exist, they are usually very small and it requires large sums to generate sizable gains.

---

1 Since interest arbitrage will provide the foundation for further economic models, it is described in the next chapter.

Take the example of the New Zealand dollar. On a given day, the price for the NZ$ could be U.S. $0.7190 in New York, but only U.S. $0.7186 in Wellington, New Zealand. That implies that one can gain by buying NZ$ in Wellington and by selling them in the New York. Since the margin is only U.S. $0.0004 per NZ$ traded ($0.7190–$0.7186=$0.0004), arbitrage requires huge foreign exchange trades, just to overcome transaction costs. In our example above, at least NZ $2,500 would have to be traded to overcome a $1 transaction cost (2,500*0.004=1); therefore this clarifies why currency arbitrage is usually carried out by banks or professional currency traders with access to large sums of capital. However by buying NZ$ in New Zealand, the price of the NZ$ increases and by selling them in the U.S., the opposite happens restoring *consistency* in the exchange rates.[2] Indeed currency arbitrage performs a crucial function on the currency markets. In the process, the banks harmonize the exchange rates in the different locations by buying where the price is low, thus appreciating the currency and selling where the price is high thus depreciating the currency.

Currency arbitrage can be quite complicated when trades involve more than two currencies. Take the example of **triangular arbitrage**, only possible when the spot rate differs from the cross exchange rate. Think about it this way: you should be able to obtain the €/¥ exchange rate by examining the spot rate in the *Wall Street Journal*. However you can also obtain the same exchange rate by examining the **cross exchange rate** that consists of, for example, the €/£ and the £/¥ exchange rates (since €/£ * £/¥ = €/¥). Differences between cross exchange rates and spot rates provide immediate profit opportunities and triangular arbitrage ensures that cross exchange rates are consistent with spot exchange rates. Since these price differentials are usually very small and temporary, complex forms of arbitrage involving more than three currencies can only be executed efficiently with computers. The world's fastest computers are therefore constantly scouring all possible cross rates in all trading locations for arbitrage opportunities that provide guaranteed profits.

Another source of arbitrage is the bid–ask spread. The **bid price** is the price at which banks buy foreign exchange and the **ask price** is the price at which banks sell foreign exchange. The difference between these two prices is the **bid–ask spread**. The size of this spread depends upon a number of factors: it is higher for currencies that are not traded much, for currencies that are volatile, or if the size of the transaction is small. For instance, for small transactions on August 16, 2007, the Bank of America quoted a 13 percent spread for the NZ$, while the Bank of New Zealand quoted only a 3 percent spread for similar sized transactions. Although the NZ$ is a strong currency, the market for U.S.$ in New Zealand is relatively more important and active than the market for NZ$ in the United States: so the Bank of America quotes a higher spread that covers its higher cost and provides a profit in the relatively illiquid U.S. market for NZ$.[3] The *intertrade* in foreign currency between banks is very active and the volumes are quite high, facilitating the matching of supply and demand for foreign currency.

---

2 Table 12.2 in Chapter 12 shows *consistent* cross exchange rates between the major currencies. For instance, the €/$ exchange rate, 1.352 is exactly the inverse of the $/€ exchange rate, 1.740 (assuming 3 decimals rounding).

3 When an American bank buys NZ$, there is no guarantee that the bank will find right away a customer wishing to acquire the equivalent quantity of NZ$. So the U.S. bank is not keen on holding the NZ$ and will sell them to another U.S. bank, which might in turn sell the NZ$ to still another U.S. bank.

Importers and Exporters

From the data presented earlier, we know that, in the new order of full international capital mobility, merchandise trade only represents a small proportion (1.25 percent) of total daily financial turnover. Although there are now new instruments available to importers and exporters, these traders have traditionally hedged on the spot and on the forward market to avoid the foreign exchange risk. For each transaction, there are two parties and only one will bear the foreign exchange risk; it all depends on the currency used in the invoice. Only the party that will have to pay (an importer) or to receive a payment (an exporter) in the foreign currency will have to convert to foreign currency and bear a foreign exchange risk. In this case, the importer will fear an appreciation of the foreign currency while the exporter will fear a depreciation that would cut into their profits.

Examples of Hedging Operations by Importers and Exporters

If a British importer of electricals, say Dixons, signs a contract today to import Japanese flat-screen TVs from Sony and to pay in Japanese yen upon delivery in three months, it is impossible for Dixons to predict exactly how much will have to be paid for the imports in terms of British pounds. The yen might vary widely in the next three months relative to the British pound. Instead of just hoping for the exchange rate to stay constant, the importer can avoid the uncertainties altogether and eliminate any exchange rate risk by hedging either on the spot or on the forward market. Basically, the function of **hedging** is to eradicate the foreign exchange risk.

To be more specific, whenever a payment in the foreign currency is anticipated, the risk of an appreciation of the foreign currency (i.e. a depreciation of the domestic currency) that would increase the cost of imports in terms of the domestic currency appears. There are two options available to the importer if he wishes to hedge these future payments to the foreign exporter. Immediately after signing the contract to import flat-screen TVs and pay a certain yen amount in 3 months, Dixons could immediately buy that amount of yen and deposit it in a bank account to earn interest for the next 3 months. In this case, the importer forgoes the interest rate on the British pound and earns instead the interest rate on the equivalent amount of yen (the differential between the two interest rates is either a cost or a gain depending on which interest is higher). By hedging, Dixons knows with certainty what the costs of the Japanese TVs are the day the contract is signed.

An alternative way of hedging is even simpler as it makes use of the forward market. The forward market gives the importer the option to buy Japanese yen for delivery in 3 months, at a price agreed upon today. That is, as soon as Dixons signs the deal to buy Japanese Sony TVs and pay in Japanese yen in 3 months, Dixons immediately enters into a second contract to buy the necessary amount of Japanese yen at a specific future date, i.e. in 3 months. The delivery of these yen will take place when Dixons needs them to pay for the imports, thus avoiding the foreign exchange risk since the forward exchange rate is known when the deal is struck. The forward exchange rate may be higher or lower than the spot rate. International traders can therefore use the spot or forward markets to insure themselves against any future exchange rate fluctuations by performing the exchange rate transaction at the same time the import/export contract is signed.

The actions followed by an exporter to avoid the foreign exchange risk are slightly more intricate to follow. Assume that Tissot, a Swiss watchmaker and exporter, is expecting payments in euros for selling watches in Italy. Tissot needs to sell *now* at a known rate the euros the company will receive in the future. If they wish to use the spot market, Tissot must convert the euros into Swiss francs now. How can they do that? Just by borrowing the euros and selling them *now* for units of Swiss francs at the spot rate. At this point, the Swiss exporter has hedged – Tissot has removed the foreign exchange risk through converting the foreign currency. Again the operation entails borrowing one currency (paying interest on the euros) and converting the euros into Swiss francs that Tissot can invest to earn interest – the differential between the two interest rates (euro and Swiss francs) will dictate the cost/gain. When Tissot receives the euros as payment in the future, all they have to do is to repay the euro loan.

Of course, Tissot could have used the forward market to achieve the same result. All that would be needed is to sell forward the amount of euros expected as payment. Similarly, as the sale of the euros takes place *now* at a known rate, the risk is removed.

Currency Speculators

Currency speculators enter foreign exchange markets with the intention of pursuing a pure gain. They aim at exploiting potential differentials between quoted exchange rates and their own expectations about what these rates will be in the future. They are willing to put up with the foreign exchange *risk* i.e. to take an **open position** on the markets. For example, a speculator may believe that the value of a currency will be rising in the future. This would lead the speculator to invest in the currency in hope that its appreciation would provide a future profit.

Speculators can use either the spot or the forward market. With fixed exchange rates, they can only use the spot market and, in the following box, we describe actions by speculators in the early nineties when they attacked the European currencies belonging to a joint peg. Speculation on the forward market is widespread as flexible exchange rate regimes are now the norm. A speculator compares the forward rate, representing an average of everyone's expectations, to his own expectations that are at odds with the crowd. If a currency is at a specific forward premium, i.e. the public thinks that the currency will appreciate in the future by a specific percentage, the speculator may believe that the currency may appreciate even more or maybe less than what is believed by the public and will act accordingly. In the first case, the speculator buys forward and sells at the future date. In the second case, the speculator sells forward and buys at the future date to fulfill his forward contract.

Speculators profit only when their expectations are correct – the penalty for a wrong guess is a financial loss. While speculation may deliver large gains or losses to speculators, they can also have (de)stabilizing effects on the entire market. For instance, if markets believe that a currency is weakening, but speculators think otherwise, the speculators' actions (currency purchases) may stop the downward slide to stabilize the currency. On the other hand, if speculators decide to go with an existing trend, their actions accelerate the rise or fall of a currency and add volatility to the price of a currency.

Destabilizing Speculation: The Aftermath of the European Currency Crises

In 1992, European currency markets were shaken when a number of currencies were the object of speculative attacks. Between September and October 1992, the Italian lira, British pound, Irish punt, Spanish peseta, and the Portuguese escudo all lost significant value although their exchange rate had previously been fixed against the German mark. For one reason or another, the notion had spread that these countries' fixed exchange rates were no longer supported by their economic fundamentals or were not consistent with the real exchange rates. Subsequently, large speculative sales forced the devaluations of these currencies. The U.K. even decided to float the pound and leave altogether the European exchange rate mechanism (ERM).

How can a speculator benefit from such devaluations? On the spot market, if he believes that the value of a currency could be falling or be devalued in the future, he sells the currency now to buy it back later on at a lower rate. These operations involve borrowing the currency at significant cost in order to sell it now. Then later, as the currency is devalued, he buys it back at a lower price. So when the public started to lose confidence in the Italian lira in summer 1992, a speculator would borrow 1,000,000 liras and sell them for DM1,323, accentuating the downward pressure on the lira. At the end of the year, after the lira had been seriously weakened, he could buy 1,171,958 lira with these DM (in summer 1992 the DM exchanged for 756 lira and at the end of the year the lira was devalued to 885 lira per DM). By selling the lira when the public expected the lira to devalue, he contributed to its decline.

Destabilizing speculation occurred again in 1993 when speculators also expected the French franc to depreciate, even though French fundamentals were solid. Efforts to rescue the French franc through concerted intervention with the Bundesbank failed as the volumes involved in the speculative attacks were massive. As a response to speculators, the Bank of France allowed the value of its currency to fluctuate by 15 percent. By the end of the year, however, the exchange rate was just about identical to its January 1, 1993 spot price. In this case, speculators increased the volatility of the French franc, but did not manage to substantively alter its price.

THE SHORT-TERM EXCHANGE RATE DETERMINATION AND TECHNICAL ANALYSIS

Economists are just about as good at forecasting minute-by-minute changes in exchange rates as meteorologists are at predicting the amount of rainfall tomorrow – probably not sufficiently accurate to place large financial bets. However, with trillions of dollars in daily capital flows, it is important to understand the basic principles that guide short-term currency transactions. In the very short term, changes in fundamentals (e.g., inflation, interest rates, unemployment) cannot be the major factors influencing foreign currency prices – they simply do not change often enough. Changes in fundamentals are discrete economic events, such as the announcement of a new record trade deficit in the

United States. This implies that even the most sophisticated traders, who work for the world's largest financial corporations, cannot rely on fundamentals to form expectations about the minute-by-minute exchange rate changes. These traders must develop alternative tools to form expectations about short-term market trends.

Tools used in short-term trading lack a clear economic component. They are designed to capture the "emotions of the price" or the "sentiment of the market." Economists, in contrast, seldom get emotional about prices, but seek to understand the fundamentals that determine long-term price levels. Minute-by-minute traders need to understand the psychology of the market place and they use technical analysis to "guestimate" what may happen in the market price. **Technical analysis** is a method of evaluating prices, including exchange rates, using statistics generated by market activity, past prices, and volume. The purpose is not to evaluate the intrinsic price of an asset (its true value), but to identify patterns in charts and summary statistics that provide hints uncovering in which direction the currency might move next. In the short term, traders are not interested in what "should" happen to prices in the long run (given economic fundamentals), but how best to provide a price quote when the next foreign exchange query arrives.

Technical analysis is based on three underlying principles: first the notion that prices reflect everything that is known to the market. These factors are, for example, supply and demand, political factors, or market sentiment. The second principle of technical analysis is that prices move in trends. Like a rolling stone, prices are prone to move in one general direction once they have started to move. Therefore technical analysts expend substantial efforts to identify trend patterns. Finally, technical analysts believe that history repeats itself. Some chart patterns have been recognized and categorized for over 100 years and the manner in which they have repeated themselves has led to the conclusion that human psychology changes little over time. Let us examine some prominent tools of technical analysis.

Candlestick Charting

Candlestick charts are visual summaries of price movements over a given period of time. Candlesticks were first developed in the market for Japanese rice contracts in the 1600s and they are perhaps the most popular technical analysis tool. They have become so popular that more and more generic financial graphs in newspapers and on the web are spruced up with the aid of candlesticks (for example the *Wall Street Journal's* weekly S&P500 graph). Just about every internet site that reports exchange rates also allows the user to chart not only spot prices, but also candlesticks.

A **candlestick** displays the open, close, daily high, and daily low prices (exchange rates) in one simple figure. In addition, the color of the candlestick indicates whether the currency was up or down for the day.

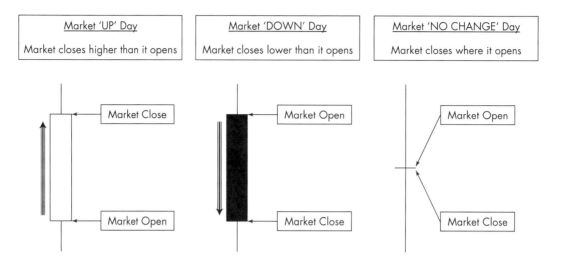

Whether the opening or closing exchange rate is on the top or bottom depends on the color convention of the graph. Darker colors indicate **down days** when the exchange rate falls from its open to its close. In this case, the vertical line on top of the body indicates the opening exchange rate and the bottom line indicates the closing exchange rate. In addition, there are specific candlestick patterns that have been associated with specific market events; the following four serve as prominent examples:

- A **Bullish** pattern is given by candlesticks that indicate an opening at (or near) the price low, then a significant gain, and finally a closing price near its high.

- A **Bearish** pattern is shown when the exchange rate opens at (or near) its high and drops substantially to close near its low.

- A **Hammer** indicates a reversal of a downward trend – but only if the hammer occurs after the exchange rate has fallen for several days. It is identified by a small body along with a large range.

- A **Doji** indicates a reversal of a trend and/or market indecision. The market meandered up and down during the day, just to finish at its opening price.

These four examples are just a few of the many different (over 20) candlestick indicators that are used in technical analysis.

How these candlesticks play out in a chart can be seen in Figure 16.2, which is an example of a daily candlestick chart for the dollar/euro exchange rate over a three-week period in 2008. Over that period, the exchange rate fluctuated about 2 percent and experienced three price trend reversals. Each time the trend reversed, the candlestick associated with the change is a Doji (circled). Careful analysis of charts and a keen eye to identify patters like Hammers or Dojis allows chartists to gain confidence in their exchange-rate predictions.

Price history – /USDEUR (5/12/2008 – 6/6/2008)

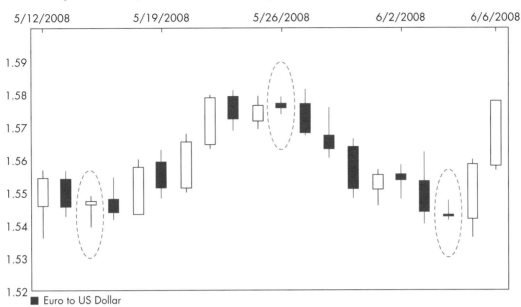

FIGURE 16.2 Dollar/Euro Movements Summarized by Candlesticks

Source: adapted from moneycentral data (moneycentral.com).

Trend Analysis

Aside from graphic price summaries provided by candlesticks, technical analysis also uses **trend analysis** to understand broad patterns in the data that manifest themselves over longer periods of time. A trend is simply a price movement in a general direction. We use the term "general direction," because the definition of a trend implies that there are price fluctuations.

"The trend is your friend" is a popular saying among technical analysts and one particularly effective method of identifying tends is a moving average. A "5-day moving average" is the average of the previous 5 days. Instead of averaging the exchange rate over more and more days as time goes by, a **moving average** is defined over a fixed period, and in the case above it is 5 days. This implies that each day the moving average adds one new observation (the most recent) and drops one observation (the oldest). Because exchange rates are constantly changing, the moving average also moves over time, but is less volatile than the spot rate. The longer the time-horizon of a moving average, the less volatile it becomes because the sum of past price movements gains ever greater weight.

The key usage of moving averages is to highlight changes in the direction of a trend by smoothing out short-term fluctuations (or "noise"). The most commonly used moving averages are for 20, 30, 50, 100, and 200 days and each time-horizon provides a different indicator for future exchange-rate movements. Typically, it is seen as a negative sign when the spot rate falls below its moving average. The opposite is true for spot rates that rise above their moving average – in this case further price increases are expected.

FIGURE 16.3 Moving Averages and Resistance Levels (dollar/euro exchange rate)

Source: adapted from Yahoo Finance data (yahoofinance.com).

Figure 16.3 provides a visual example of 50- and 200-day moving averages. The more volatile (black) 50-day moving average tracks the exchange rate better. The 200-day moving average (blue) instead is slow moving and therefore a better representation of the exchange rate's long-term trend. Each time the exchange rate pierces its 200-day moving average, it confirms a change in the long-term trend of the exchange rate in Figure 16.3. A piercing (when the short-term moving average cuts through the long-term moving average) from above signals a downward trend and a piercing from below is seen as an upward trend.

Support and Resistance Levels

Support/resistance levels act as floors or ceilings to future price movements. The **support level** is a price level below the current market price, thought to play the role of a price floor that keeps the price from falling any lower. A **resistance level** is a price level above the current market price, at which selling pressures are thought to be strong enough to keep the price from rising any further.

One of two events can happen when an exchange rate approaches a support/resistance level: either a support/resistance level acts as a reversal point, or if the support/resistance level is pierced, it can accelerate a trend. A reversal point exists when the exchange rate approaches the support/resistance level, but then bounces back to reverse its trend. Such reversals were observed several times in the dollar/euro rate in Figure 16.3. Between April and November 2007, the dollar/euro rate "tested" the 1.30 resistance level often, but always bounced back and never pierced it. The same was true for the 1.50 level between October 2007 and February 2008.

An accelerated trend occurred each time the resistance level was pierced in Figure 16.3, as shown by the large positive candlesticks following the piercing. In this case, the support/resistance levels can even reverse roles, meaning that the old resistance level becomes the new support. Indeed, the old resistance levels in Figure 16.3 for the dollar's depreciation have since become support levels that have not been tested, yet.

The scope of technical analysis is extensive and the sky is the limit on how many types of candlestick or statistical patterns can be employed to forecast prices in the absence of clear information provided by economic fundamentals. There are literally thousands of indicators available and it is up to the individual trader to find a successful subset of technical indicators that works for a particular portfolio. Some technical analysts claim to be extremely accurate and their choices profitable most of the time. Indeed, it is said that some successful traders arbitrage without knowledge of the economy, armed only with a deep understanding of technical analysis.

Formal statistical evaluations of technical analysis strategies have produced mixed results. In 2002, a search on *EconLit*, the database of all published economics articles, indicated that about half of the articles found some evidence in favor of some technical analysis indicators. "In favor" here means that, when one used a particular set of technical analysis tools, for a certain asset, over a certain period of time, one could have beaten the market average. In their survey for the *Journal of Economic Literature*, Menkhoff and Taylor (2007) come to the conclusion that "it is beyond question that, for major flexible exchange rates and over longer time periods, the use of technical analysis may provide very high returns. What is disputed, however, is whether the realization of these profits has to be bought at the cost of taking large risks and whether the profits can fully compensate for this additional risk." In essence the statement highlights that even a roulette player in Las Vegas can report great profit opportunities over a given period of time; the question is whether excessive risk is involved that may wipe out any gains in the long run. Nevertheless Menkhoff and Taylor (2007) point out that "technical analysis remains a passionate obsession of many foreign exchange market professionals; it is clearly an intrinsic part of this market."

While the exact profitability of technical analysis has not been proven in a systematic fashion, it is important to remind the reader that the goal of this chapter was twofold: first we sought to provide an introduction to the world of international finance using financial market data illustrating recent trends in foreign exchange markets. Here it was important to distinguish among different markets and market participants. Then we outlined the different functions of basic foreign exchange contracts and presented the types of contracts importers, currency traders, or speculators utilize to insure against currency risk.

Finally it is time to note that we have not yet discussed international bond markets. These markets are crucial to international finance since they are fundamental for so-called interest arbitrage operations. The next chapter introduces interest arbitrage, and establishes its link to exchange rates. This link can then be used to extend our formal open-economy model to include international financial flows.

Summary of Key Concepts

1. The massive expansion of international capital flows is due to the fall of the Bretton Woods system, financial market deregulations, and the rise of euro-currencies.
2. The daily flows of foreign exchange are approximately 100 times larger than the daily flows of merchandise trade.
3. Nine out of ten international financial transactions involve the U.S.$. The euro is a distant second with 36 percent of the transactions.
4. More than half of American treasury bills are held by foreigners who also hold about 20 percent of U.S. long-term securities.
5. Strong currencies can be bought and sold on a forward and futures markets at 1 month, 3 month, or 6 month. The forward markets allow companies to insure their international financial transactions against foreign exchange risk.
6. Currency futures and options are financial derivatives that multinationals and banks use to insure against currency risk.
7. Speculators do not insure against risk, instead they seek to assume risk for profit.
8. Technical analysis evaluates asset prices to understand minute-by-minute changes in the market. It uses statistics generated by market activity, past prices, and volume.
9. In the short run traders look for patterns in charts to determine the direction of any future movement in the price without any attempt to estimate its intrinsic price.

CASE STUDY

Marking the Dealer's Cards:
What Economists can Learn from Currency Traders
From *The Economist*, print edition November 24, 2005

You can make a career as an exchange-rate economist without ever crossing paths with a currency trader. The dealers who set the dollar's price and the professors who theorize about it are separate breeds, speaking different tongues and operating at quite different metabolic rates. This is how Richard Lyons, an economist at the Haas School of Business (part of the University of California, Berkeley), describes a day spent with a friend of trading stock.*

"Most of the time my friend was reading tea leaves that were, at least to me, not so clear. The pace was furious – a quote every five or ten seconds, a trade every minute or two . . . He looked over in the midst of his fury and asked me, 'What should I do?' I laughed. Nervously."

If asked that question at the start of the year, most economists, watching the steady deterioration of America's current-account balance, would have told a dollar trader to sell. That would have been costly. The greenback reached two-year highs against the euro and the pound this month – before slipping back a bit after the president of the European Central Bank indicated that higher euro-zone interest rates were on the way.

The currency market routinely confounds

economists. A classic 1983 study by Richard Meese and Kenneth Rogoff, then both at the Federal Reserve, concluded that macroeconomic models could not explain a currency's direction of travel, let alone how far it would go. One would do just as well to assume that next month's exchange rate will be the same as this month's. After another 20 years of interrogation, the macroeconomic data has confessed little more of value. A new review of the evidence** finds that some models, in some periods, beat tossing a coin. But not by very much.

Testing the tea leaves

If traders can learn nothing from economists, can economists learn anything from traders? No, is the customary answer. Economists traditionally assume that everything worth knowing about a currency is known by everyone; and that anything new is quickly embodied in the price. They imagine the market governed by an auctioneer, who finds the price that will square everybody's bids and offers before any actual trading takes place. Economists study the auctioneer, not the traders.

After his visit to the trading desks, however, Mr Lyons decided that dealers merited closer examination. He and Martin Evans, of Georgetown University, are part of a wider effort to model the currency market from "the trenches."*** We cannot understand how currencies behave, they argue, unless we study the thinking and behaviour of those who trade them.

The mythical auctioneer is notably absent from the models they construct. In his place stand the big currency dealers, who act as marketmakers, willing to buy or sell any amount of currency at their quoted prices. The marketmaker will take orders from a mix of clients – from American multinationals repatriating profits, to Asian central banks manipulating their currency – whose beliefs are as diverse as their motives.

These orders represent opinions, backed by money. As such, they convey useful information about what clients believe and how strongly they believe it. The marketmaker is privy to all of these opinions as they accumulate on its order books, while its clients know only their own. It is like a poker game in which only the dealer is allowed to see what each player throws into the pot.

What can be learned from peering over the dealer's shoulder? Messrs Lyons and Evans have access to six and a half years of data, ending in June 1999, from Citibank, one of the largest dollar dealers. The figures show the balance of orders flowing into the bank: on any given day, customers may buy more dollars from Citibank than they have sold to it, for example. This positive "order flow," as it is called, is valuable evidence of buying pressure that is visible only to the dealer.

Any such pressure will eventually be reflected in a stronger currency. What is surprising is how long it takes. Given that a trade is made every few minutes, a quotation every few seconds, one would think that any information in today's order flow would be swiftly incorporated into the dealer's quotes and the dollar's price. Whatever forecasting power the flow of orders possesses, it should be quickly exhausted.

It turns out, however, that the information in today's order flow will still be percolating through the market weeks afterwards. It takes time for a marketmaker to make sense of his orders, to distinguish signal from noise, plot from happenstance. It takes more time still for that insight to spread to the market as a whole, as dealers reveal what they know through their quotes and trades with each other. This hiatus creates an opportunity for forecasters. Messrs Lyons and Evans reckon that Citibank's order flow can predict almost 16 percent of the dollar's bobbing and weaving four weeks hence. That may not sound like a lot. But the macroeconomists cannot even explain what is going on today, let alone 16 percent of what will happen a month from now.

The two economists invoke Friedrich Hayek, who long ago pointed out that the economy runs on "dispersed bits of incomplete and frequently contradictory knowledge." These scattered insights, Hayek stressed, are communicated to everyone through shifts in market prices. But with the dollar, a big dealer's order books provide a sneak preview. If you can look into those books, you can infer something useful about the dollar next month. If not, then, like the rest of us, you can just flip a coin.

* *The Microstructure Approach to Exchange Rates,"* MIT Press, 2001.
** "Empirical Exchange Rate Models of the Nineties: Are Any Fit to Survive?," by Y.-W. Cheung, M. Chinn and

A. Garcia Pascual, *Journal of International Money and Finance*.
*** Many of their papers can be found at www.georgetown.edu/faculty/evansm1.

CASE STUDY QUESTIONS

1. Economists such as Meese and Rogoff believe that exchange rates follow a "Random Walk." What does that mean?

2. In this chapter, we show how the exchange rate is determined on the various markets. Are we inconsistent?

3. Who might actually have more impact on the exchange rate: the various people who need foreign currency or the currency traders?

4. What does this say about the idea of perfect immediate information held dear by economists and what really happens?

Questions for Study and Review

1. Suppose you are a U.S. bicycle dealer. You have signed a contract in which you agree to import 1,000 bicycles from a U.K. manufacturer and to pay £100,000 for them 6 months from today. How exactly can you use the forward exchange market to protect yourself against exchange rate risk?

2. What is the essential difference between an exporter and a speculator in the foreign exchange market?

3. Cross exchange rates calculation. The spot exchange rate between the $ and the Swiss franc is $0.7602/SF and the exchange rate between the dollar and the euro is $1.17/euro. Calculate the exchange rate between the euro and the Swiss franc as quoted in France.

4. The forward exchange rate (90-day) between the $ and the Swiss franc is $0.7613/SF and the forward exchange rate (90-day) between the dollar and the euro is $1.1659/euro. (Use the spot exchange rates quoted in question 3.)

    a. Are the markets expecting the Swiss franc to depreciate or to appreciate with respect to the dollar?

    b. Are the markets expecting the euro to depreciate or to appreciate with respect to the dollar?

5. Insuring against exchange rate risk, use the exchange rate data from the previous questions.

    a. Assume that Macy, a U.S. importer of Tissot Swiss watches, has to make a 1,000 SF payment in 90 days and wishes to use the forward market to insure against foreign exchange risk.

Explain carefully how they will do so and calculate how much the transaction will cost in terms of $ (assume no other cost).

b. Now assume that Macy uses the spot market to address the currency risk. The rate of interest on the dollar is 5 percent (annual basis) and the rate of interest on the Swiss franc is 4 percent (annual basis). Calculate the total cost of buying the Swiss francs on the spot market (assume no other costs).

c. Which alternative would you advise Macy to choose?

6. Speculation on the forward market. Use the data from earlier questions.

a. If a speculator believes that in 90 days the $/SF spot exchange rate is going to be $0.7610/SF, explain which actions he will take to speculate on the currencies.

b. Assuming that he plans to use $1,000,000 for his speculative activities, calculate his potential gain if his prediction is correct.

c. It turns out that 3 months later the spot rate is $0.7615/SF. Will he actually realize a gain or a loss from his speculative activities? Calculate it (show the sign).

7. Currency arbitrage. Assume that the exchange rate in New York is $1.1727/€ and in Paris it is 0.852€/$.

a. What actions will the currency arbitrageurs in the various banks (U.S. or France) take to realize a gain?

b. How much will they gain for each $1,000 traded? (assume no costs).

c. What will be the impact of their action on the $ price of the euro in New York? And on the euro price of the dollar in Paris? How long will this process continue?

References and Suggestions for Further Reading

Akram, F., Rime, D., and Sarno, L. (2005) "Arbitrage in the Foreign Exchange Market," *Central Bank of Norway Working Paper*, Oslo: Central Bank of Norway.

Bank for International Settlements (BIS) (2005) http://www.bis.org, Triennal Central Bank Survey, Foreign Exchange and Derivative Markets Activity in 2004, Basel, Switzerland.

Chicago Mercantile Exchange Group (CME), Chicago USA, http://www.cme.com.

Congressional Budget Office (2007) CBO Testimony by Peter R. Orszag director, Foreign Holdings of US, Government Securities and the US Current Account before the Committee on the Budget U.S. House of Representatives, June 26 Washington: CBO. http://www.cbo.gov/ftpdoc.cfm?index=8264&type=1.

Department of Treasury, Federal Reserve Bank of New York, Board of Governors of the Federal Reserve System (2007) Report on Foreign Portfolio Holdings of US Securities as of June 30, 2006, New York: Federal Reserve Bank. http://www.ustreas.gov/tic/fpis.html.

Egan, J. (2005) "Check the Currency Risk. Then Multiply by 100," *New York Times*, June 19.

Evans, M.D.D. and Lyons, R.K. (2002a) "Order Flow and Exchange Rate Dynamics," *Journal of Political Economy*, 110: 170–80.

—— (2002b) "Informational Integration and FX Trading," *Journal of International Money and Finance*, 21: 807–31.

Fieleke, N. (1985) "The Rise of the Foreign Currency Futures Market," *New England Economic Review*, March.

Froot, K. and Thaler, R. (1990) "Anomalies: Foreign Exchange," *Journal of Economic Perspectives*, 4: 179–92.

Lewis, K. (1995) "Puzzles in International Financial Markets," in G. Grossman and K. Rogoff (eds), *Handbook of International Economics*, Vol. III Amsterdam: Elsevier 1913–1972.

Lyons, R.K. and Moore, M. (2005) "An Information Approach to International Currencies," *NBER Working Paper* No. 1122 Berkeley: University of California.

Menkhoff, L. and Taylor, M. (2007) "The Obstinate Passion of Foreign Exchange Professionals: Technical Analysis," *Journal of Economic Literature* 45: 936–72.

Neely, C. J. (1997) "Technical Analysis in the foreign exchange market: A Layman's Guide," *St Louis Federal Reserve Review* Sept./Oct. http://research.stlouisfed.org/publications/review/97/09/9709cn.pdf.

Osler, C.L. (2000) "Support for Resistance: Technical Analysis and Intraday Exchange Rates," *Federal Reserve Bank of New York Economic Policy Review*, 6: 53–67.

—— (2003) "Currency Orders and Exchange Rate Dynamics: Explaining the Success of Technical Analysis," *Journal of Finance*, 58: 1791–1820.

Rhee, S.G. and Chang, R.P. (1992) "Intraday Arbitrage Opportunities in Foreign Exchange and Eurocurrency Markets," *Journal of Finance*, 47: 363–79.

Shleifer, A. and Vishny, R. (1997) "The Limits of Arbitrage," *Journal of Finance*, 52: 35–55.

Thornton, D. (1989) "Tests of Covered Interest Rate Parity," *Federal Reserve Bank of St. Louis Review*, July.

World Trade Organization (2006), International Trade Statistics 2006 http://www.wto.org/english/res_e/statis_e/its2006_e/its06_toc_e.htm, Geneva, Switzerland.

Chapter 17

Modeling International Capital Markets

LEARNING OBJECTIVES

By the end of this chapter you should be able to understand:

- why investors diversify their portfolio into foreign assets
- the risks involved in international diversification
- the mechanics and differences between covered and uncovered arbitrage
- the role arbitrage plays in the foreign exchange markets
- that capital flows can be integrated into a model of the open economy
- that the degree of capital mobility depends on the extent of capital controls imposed
- how the balance of payments equilibrium can be represented on a graph

Before integrating international financial investment decisions into a model of the open economy, we need to understand the incentives for capital to flow from one country to another. We can formalize the international financial investment decision by examining how best to allocate a financial portfolio across countries given the different returns and exchange rate movements over the investment horizon.

When we are referring to "capital flows," we are literally investigating the reasons why portfolio or foreign direct investment is undertaken abroad. Why exactly do investments move abroad in the first place? The main reason is related to arbitrage. Funds move from one country to another to generate the highest return for investors and, in the process, these financial capital movements equilibrate returns across countries.

In this chapter, we will first investigate the mechanics of capital movements, also called **interest arbitrage**. We also introduce the concept of **interest parity**, a situation where the returns on short-term assets invested in domestic or in foreign assets are equal; so this corresponds to equilibrium in financial markets. The theory of international capital market arbitrage is one of the crucial tenets of most international macroeconomic models. The second part of this chapter is therefore devoted to developing a framework that allows us to integrate capital movements into a formal model of the open economy.

INTERNATIONAL CAPITAL MARKET ARBITRAGE

The main principle behind international capital flows is based on standard economic behavior: capital flows from one country to another to maximize the expected returns for the investors. These international movements of capital are what we identify as interest arbitrage. Interest arbitrage is different from currency or locational arbitrage, both examples of price arbitrage, as explained in the previous chapter.

Interest arbitrage may involve exchange rate risk. Attracted by a higher interest rate abroad, arbitrageurs might invest their capital in an asset denominated in a foreign currency. If the foreign currency depreciates, the value of their investment falls. When their foreign investment is exposed to such exchange rate risk, it is said that the arbitrageurs' position is uncovered. Therefore, their financial operations correspond to **uncovered interest arbitrage**. We will show, however, that arbitrageurs have means to avoid such foreign exchange risk so that their foreign investment positions are covered (not exposed to risk). In this case, we refer to **covered interest arbitrage**.

Before developing the interest arbitrage models, an overview of the process and of the variables involved is in order. Let us first point out that we are looking at short-run models. From the brief description of interest arbitrage presented above, we can safely infer that, as the arbitrageur will want to compare the return on his investment in each country, he will need to know the short-term interest rate in each country. In addition, since he is considering exporting funds to another country in the event that the returns are higher there, he will have to convert the domestic currency into a foreign currency. This is not the finish of the story since, at the end of the period, when his assets mature, he is going to receive his investment plus interest in a foreign currency, so he will have to convert these proceeds back into the domestic currency. How does he do it and at what rate? This is where the distinction between uncovered and covered arbitrage appears: he can either rely on his expectations about the future exchange rate (uncovered) or use the forward exchange rate (covered). So the arbitrageur also needs information about exchange rates. To understand thoroughly how an arbitrageur decides where to invest his portfolio, we walk through the arbitrage process step-by-step. First, we consider uncovered interest arbitrage. Since the model for covered interest arbitrage is very similar, it will be easy to extend our explanations to that case later.

Uncovered Interest Arbitrage and Uncovered Interest Parity

Suppose that you wish to invest $1 either in the U.S. or in the U.K., and you are interested in the highest return. As mentioned above, the key variables you would want to scrutinize are the interest rates in both countries as well as the exchange rates between both currencies. Let us denote as i_t^{US} and i_t^{UK} the interest rates expressed as a decimal over the period of investment in the U.S. and in the U.K., respectively; in addition, E_t denotes the familiar spot rate at time t (in $ per £), while E_{t+1}^e is the expected exchange rate at time $t+1$ (more precisely, it is what investors believe at time t the exchange rate to be at time $t+1$). Here are your options:

> *Option A* If you invest the $1 in the U.S., you receive in period $t+1$ your original investment, $1, plus the return on your investment, $i_t^{US}*$1. So at the end of the period the total sum received is $1 *$(1 + i_t^{US})$. The rate of return is simply the U.S. interest rate.

> *Option B* If you invest the same $1 in the U.K., you must:

> 1. Convert the $1 into £ at the spot rate E_t: so your $1 turns into £$(1 / E_t)$
> 2. Invest the pounds in the U.K., earning i_t^{UK} interest
> 3. At the end of the period you receive your initial investment plus the U.K. interest payment, all in pounds, or £$(1 / E_t)(1 + i_t^{UK})$
> 4. Finally you have to convert your initial investment plus interest, denominated in British pounds sterling, back into dollars at the exchange rate at time $t+1$, E_{t+1}. Since E_{t+1} is not known when you enter into the investment operation at time t, you need to use your expectations about the exchange rate at time $t+1$, E_{t+1}^e. This yields total dollar receipts equal to $E_{t+1}^e (1 / E_t)(1 + i_t^{UK})$. In this case, since the transaction involves two conversions at likely different exchange rates, the expected rate of return is not simply the U.K. interest rate.[1]

---

1 In this case, the expected return can be calculated as the total sum received less the $1 investment or

$$E_{t+1}^e (1/E_t)(1+i_t^{UK}) - 1 = \frac{E_{t+1}^e (1+i_t^{UK}) - E_t}{E_t}$$

If you choose to invest in the U.K., your investment operation involves two exchange rates, E_t and E_{t+1}. Unless the exchange rate is fixed, implying $E_t = E_{t+1}$, it is safe to say that the exchange rates will be different at the beginning and the end of your investment period. So how do you decide where to undertake your investment? Here are the possible scenarios, and your decision points:

- *Case A*: $\$1(1 + i_t^{US}) < \$E^e_{t+1}(1 / E_t)(1 + i_t^{UK})$ invest in the U.K.
- *Case B*: $\$1(1 + i_t^{US}) > \$E^e_{t+1}(1 / E_t)(1 + i_t^{UK})$ invest in the U.S.
- *Case C*: $\$1(1 + i_t^{US}) = \$E^e_{t+1}(1 / E_t)(1 + i_t^{UK})$ you are indifferent between investing in the U.S. and the U.K.

This example highlights that capital flows in and out of countries, unless the equilibrium in Case C is reached. At this point, the returns in the two countries are the same; they are "at parity." In Case C, investors are indifferent between investing in the U.S. or the U.K.: they have no incentive to rearrange their portfolio between the two countries to seek greater returns. Case C is known as **uncovered interest parity**.

It turns out that, for the following reasons, Case C is actually the most likely case. Whenever the expected return is higher in the U.K. than in the U.S. (Case A) or vice versa (Case B), the forces of the market will ensure return towards parity (Case C). In Case A, capital will flow from the U.S. to the U.K., thus depleting the supply of capital and raising the interest rate, i_t^{US}, in the United States. At the same time, the capital inflows into the U.K. raise the amount of capital available and the U.K. interest rate, i_t^{UK}, falls. In addition, the capital flows affect the exchange rates. For example, in Case A, dollars are sold to buy pounds, and the dollar depreciates while the value of the pound increases so E_t increases. Investors also adjust their expectations and E_{t+1} decreases. This process of adjustment in interest and exchange rates continues until Case C is reached, where capital flows cease and an equilibrium is reached. An equivalent adjustment takes place in Case B. We can rearrange the expression in Case C to simplify the uncovered interest parity condition:

$$\text{Uncovered Interest Parity: } 1 + i_t^{US} = \left(\frac{E^e_{t+1}}{E_t}(1 + i_t^{UK}) \right) \tag{17.1}$$

To summarize the discussion, three factors influence the decision to invest internationally: (a) the domestic interest rate, (b) the foreign interest rate, and (c) the exchange rates (spot and expected future exchange rate).

We can derive additional insights out of the uncovered interest parity condition, by considering the dollar receipts from investing in the U.K., rearranging the right-hand side of equation (17.1), and adding and subtracting E_t in the numerator to find:

$$(1 + i_t^{UK}) \frac{E^e_{t+1} + E_t - E_t}{E_t} = (1 + i_t^{UK}) \left[1 + \frac{E^e_{t+1} - E_t}{E_t} \right]$$

This expression can be further simplified by defining $\varepsilon_t = \frac{E^e_{t+1} - E_t}{E_t}$ as the **expected rate of depreciation** of the dollar. Substituting for the expected rate of depreciation, we find that Case C can be rewritten as:

$$1 + i_t^{US} = (1 + i_t^{UK})(1 + \varepsilon_t) \tag{17.2}$$

If ε is positive, arbitrageurs expect the dollar to depreciate against the pound: indeed $\varepsilon > 0$ implies that $E_{t+1}^e > E_t$, so that more dollars are expected to be necessary to buy one pound at time $t+1$. If ε is negative, the dollar is expected to appreciate against the pound. Finally we can simplify (17.2) even further using the approximation

$$i_t^{US} \approx i_t^{UK} + \varepsilon_t \tag{17.3}$$

where we have multiplied out equation (17.2) and ignored the term $i_t^{UK}\varepsilon_t$ that is negligibly small. The approximation highlights the interpretation of uncovered interest parity: the arbitrageur can expect two possible sources of gain when investing abroad. These two gains are due to 1) the foreign investment earning higher interest rates and 2) the appreciation of the foreign currency over the life of the investment (equivalently the depreciation of the domestic currency corresponding to $\varepsilon > 0$). If the interest rates were identical at home and abroad, a potential appreciation of the foreign currency alone would make investing abroad more lucrative.

If ε is negative, the investor expects the foreign currency to depreciate over the life of the investment, and the gain from any positive interest differential could be wiped out. Any higher interest rate abroad must therefore be weighted against a possible exchange rate loss when the investment matures. The problem is that, while the interest differential is known at time t, ε is unknown since it is impossible to guess exactly how much the dollar will change in value with respect to the pound.

Testing the Uncovered Interest Parity Equation

Let us check the uncovered interest parity (equation 17.1) using data to examine its validity in the real word. A formal test of uncovered interest parity faces an immediate problem. To test it at time t, requires knowledge of the future exchange rate in the next period, i.e. at time $t+1$, E_{t+1}^e. Assuming that the period is a year, this data will not be available until next year. However we can still test the theory using historical data. We gather interest rate data for 3-month treasury bills for 2005 in pound sterling and in U.S. dollar and spot exchange rate data from January 2005 to March 2006 included. All these are average monthly data provided by the Bank of England. Since these are 3-month treasury bills, E_{t+1}^e corresponds to the exchange rate 3 months ahead, that is indeed unknown to the arbitrageur at the time – however we are using historical data to figure out how the equation fares. Parity corresponds to:

$$1 + i_{Jan\ 2005}^{US} = (1 + i_{Jan\ 2005}^{UK})(1 + \varepsilon)$$

$$\text{with} \quad \varepsilon = \frac{E_{Apr\ 2005} - E_{Jan\ 2005}}{E_{Jan\ 2005}} * 4$$

Indeed if the interest rates are quoted on an annual rate, the expected rate of depreciation over 3 months must be multiplied by 4 to correspond to an annual rate too.

It turns out that if you calculate and compare the receipts, interest and principal, on an annual basis of a $1 investment in a 3-month treasury bill in the U.S. or the U.K., uncovered interest parity is hopelessly off (the correlation between the last two columns is only 0.3).

There is actually a good explanation why economists would never expect to find support for uncovered interest parity in the data. It could only hold if people had crystal balls allowing them to perfectly forecast the exchange rate E_{t+1} at time t, when they undertake their investment. Uncovered interest parity (UIP) is therefore an interesting theoretical construct that *should* hold if investors had perfect foresight, but it is not very helpful for actual financial decisions.

TABLE 17.1 Uncovered Interest Parity Test

Date	E_{t+3} $/£	Date	E_t $/£	i_t^{UK}	i_t^{US}	$1 + i_t^{US}$	$(1 + i_t^{UK})(1 + \varepsilon_t)$
	Mo. Aver.		Mo. Aver.	% annual rate			
30 Apr. 05	1.896	31 Jan. 05	1.8764	4.66	2.34	1.0234	1.0903
31 May 05	1.8538	28 Feb. 05	1.8871	4.69	2.54	1.0254	0.9730
30 Jun. 05	1.8179	31 Mar. 05	1.9078	4.77	2.74	1.0274	0.8502
31 Jul. 05	1.7509	30 Apr. 05	1.896	4.7	2.77	1.0277	0.7265
31 Aug. 05	1.7943	31 May 05	1.8538	4.66	2.84	1.0284	0.9122
30 Sep. 05	1.8081	30 Jun. 05	1.8179	4.62	2.97	1.0297	1.0236
31 Oct. 05	1.764	31 Jul. 05	1.7509	4.46	3.21	1.0321	1.0759
30 Nov. 05	1.7341	31 Aug. 05	1.7943	4.41	3.44	1.0344	0.9040
31 Dec. 05	1.7462	30 Sep. 05	1.8081	4.4	3.42	1.0342	0.9010
31 Jan. 06	1.7678	31 Oct. 05	1.764	4.4	3.7	1.0370	1.0530
28 Feb. 06	1.747	30 Nov. 05	1.7341	4.42	3.88	1.0388	1.0753
31 Mar. 06	1.7435	31 Dec. 05	1.7462	4.43	3.88	1.0388	1.0378

Note: Since the interest rates are expressed on an annual basis, the percentage change in the exchange rate over the 3-month period is adjusted to an annual rate too.

Source: Bank of England – press@bankofengland.co.uk

In theory, the market mechanisms bringing about interest parity seem unassailable. Unfortunately, as shown with data, these uncovered markets are never at interest parity because arbitrageurs do not have perfect foresight. Our example with real data has established that basing international investment decision on uncovered interest arbitrage is a risky business! Maybe there is a better way to take advantage of interest differentials in different countries.

Covered Interest Arbitrage and Covered Interest Parity

While it is just about impossible for uncovered interest arbitrage to have reliable predictive powers, we will show that a simple variant of the formula will serve as a powerful investment guide. The only variable unknown in uncovered interest parity is the exchange rate in the next period, E_{t+1}. Markets have long found a way around the issue and forward markets do quote forward exchange rates, F_{t+1}, at time t. Thus while E_{t+1} is unknown at t, investors can simply substitute the forward exchange rate, F_{t+1}, to lock in, at time t, any future investment gain in a foreign currency.

The forward foreign exchange market was introduced in Chapter 16 where we found that it was widely used by various agents to circumvent the foreign exchange risk. An example of the forward exchange rate quoted *today* for transactions three months in the future can be seen in Table 16.3. With our knowledge of the forward exchange rate, our investment decision above is simply modified to:

- *Case A′*: $\$1(1 + i_t^{US}) < \$F_{t+1} (1 / E_t)(1 + i_t^{UK})$ invest in the U.K.
- *Case B′*: $\$1(1 + i_t^{US}) > \$F_{t+1} (1 / E_t)(1 + i_t^{UK})$ invest in the U.S.
- *Case C′*: $\$1(1 + i_t^{US}) = \$F_{t+1} (1 / E_t)(1 + i_t^{UK})$ you are indifferent between investing in the U.S. or the U.K.

Therefore, if the return on \$1 invested in the U.S. is higher than in the U.K., such as in Case B′, it would pay to move funds into the United States. In fact, this could happen even if the interest rate in the U.K. was greater than the interest rate in the U.S., as long as the increase in the value of the dollar over the period (as reflected by the forward rate) is large enough to wipe away the gain yielded by the interest differential in favor of the pound.

We can again rearrange the equation in case C′ to derive the **covered interest parity** condition.

$$Covered\ Interest\ Parity:\ 1 + i_t^{US} = \frac{F_{t+1}}{E_t}(1 + i_t^{UK}) \tag{17.4}$$

At time t, there are no unknowns in equation (17.4) in the sense that you can browse *The Financial Times* to look up the interest rates, the spot exchange rate, and the forward rate; therefore covered interest parity contains no risk as all positions are covered. The covered interest arbitrageur is not a speculator. Since anyone can trade using covered interest arbitrage, it is a key mechanism that determines interest rates and exchange rates across countries. Covered interest arbitrage is the mechanism that provides liquidity to foreign transactions and assures an orderly market place.

We can manipulate the covered parity equation in the same manner as the uncovered parity equation above replacing E_{t+1}^e by F_{t+1}. We now define $\frac{F_{t+1} - E_t}{E_t}$ as the **forward discount**[2] (FD) on the dollar with respect to the pound. The forward discount is the proportion by which a country's forward exchange rate exceeds its spot rate. Therefore, it implies that, when the market expects the dollar to depreciate, the equilibrium forward rate F_{t+1} exceeds the spot rate. In other words if FD is

---

2 Note that the forward premium/discount is usually presented in an annualized form and as a percentage to be consistent with the quoting of interest rates. For instance, if the forward exchange rate is quoted on a 3-month forward market, we multiply $\frac{F_{t+1} - E_t}{E_t}$ by 4 (annual) and by 100 (percentage).

positive, more dollars are needed to buy one pound on the forward market than on the spot market. If FD is negative, fewer dollars are needed to buy one pound on the forward market, so the dollar is at a **forward premium** with respect to the pound. From these definitions, it is clear that one cannot talk about a forward premium or discount without specifying the two currencies involved.[3] The covered interest parity condition can now be rewritten as:

$$1 + i_t^{US} = (1 + i_t^{UK})(1 + FD) \tag{17.5}$$

and the implied forward discount on the dollar corresponding to interest parity can thus be redefined as:

$$FD^p = \frac{(1 + i_t^{US})}{(1 + i_t^{UK})} - 1 \tag{17.6}$$

Let us use a specific example to highlight the forward discount: suppose the six-month interest rate is $i_{UK} = 6$ percent, and $i_{US} = 5$ percent in the U.K. and the U.S., respectively. From the U.S. investor's perspective, the implied FD^p on the pound is: $(1.05/1.06) - 1 = -0.0094$. Since this number is negative, the various agents on the forward market expect the dollar to appreciate (or equivalently, the pound to depreciate) so we can say that the dollar is a forward premium with respect to the pound. We can now derive the six-month forward exchange rate for the dollar, F_{t+6}, as we assume that covered interest parity is fulfilled (the markets are in equilibrium). If the current spot rate is $E_t = \$1.80/\pounds$, then the six-month forward rate should be: $F_{t+6} = E_t \times (1 + FD^p) = 1.80 \times (1 - .0094) = \$1.7831/\pounds$.

Again we can derive a handy approximation and use it to determine where an arbitrageur should invest his capital. As the interest rates and the forward premium are small decimal numbers, the covered interest parity condition (17.5) can be approximated as

$$i_t^{US} \approx i_t^{UK} + FD \tag{17.7}$$

The following example using annualized data shows how easy it is for an arbitrageur to compare potential investment opportunities. Assume that the interest rate in Switzerland is 5 percent and the interest rate in Germany is 7 percent, while the Swiss franc (SF) is at a 3 percent premium with respect to the euro (€) (or equivalently the euro is at a forward discount with respect to the Swiss franc). We have covered interest parity when $i_t^{Switz} \approx i_t^{Germ} + FD^{\,SF\ with\ respect\ to\ \text{€}}$ where $FD = -3$ percent. An interest arbitrageur sees immediately that he cannot take advantage of the higher interest rate in Germany to get a higher return, because the gain will be wiped away automatically by the greater loss he would face by investing in a currency, the euro, that is at a forward discount.

---

3 Since exchange rates are bilateral, we must point out that if one currency is at a forward discount with respect to another currency, the other currency is at a forward premium with respect to the first currency.

From the point of view of a Swiss investor, we have 5 percent>7 percent–3 percent. Conversely German arbitrageurs will invest in Switzerland as the premium on the Swiss franc will more than compensate for the lower Swiss interest rate.

In this example, we do not have interest parity. The returns are greater in Switzerland than in Germany so capital flows from Germany to Switzerland. How will the forces of the markets bring parity about? As capital flows from Germany to Switzerland, the interest rate in the Germany increases while the interest rate in Switzerland drops. As the arbitrageurs buy SF spot, and sell SF forward (i.e. buy euros forward), the Swiss franc appreciates now (E_t drops) while the forward Swiss franc depreciates (F_{t+1} increases) reducing the discount on the euro. So we start with $i_t^{Switz} > i_t^{Germ} + FD^{SF\ with\ respect\ to\ €}$, then we have $i_t^{Switz} \downarrow > i_t^{Germ} \uparrow + FD^{SF\ with\ respect\ to\ €} \uparrow$ bringing about interest parity.

To test whether covered interest rate parity actually happens, it is possible to collect actual interest rate differentials and forward premiums for various currencies. Pair up the data that occur at the same point in time and involve the same currencies, and compare the returns. We show an example of such an experiment in a box. Covered interest rate parity holds when covered interest arbitrage is not worthwhile (no profitable movement of capital is possible).

Empirical studies usually indicate that covered interest rate parity holds for industrialized countries with open capital markets, for instance the United States and the United Kingdom. While there are deviations from covered interest rate parity, these are often not large enough to make covered interest arbitrage worthwhile. These quirks are due to the characteristics of foreign financial investments (U.S. and Austrian government bonds are not exactly the same financial investment and so their interest rates are hard to compare), transaction costs (given by brokerage charges and commissions), political risk (as in the probability of repayment), and differential tax laws.

The formula we have developed corresponds to a situation where there is no special risk involved in investing abroad and no barrier whatsoever hindering the international flows of capital. This is an ideal situation far removed from the reality faced by interest arbitrageurs. Indeed some countries are riskier bets than others and countries also enforce various types of capital controls. So, if there are rules impeding arbitrage or imposing high costs on capital flows, these forward premiums may be quite high. If domestic default risk is rising relative to foreign default risk, the forward premium on the foreign currency (or equivalently the forward discount on the domestic currency) is also expected to rise.

Testing the Covered Interest Parity Equation

We can use the same U.S./U.K. data as above, just replacing E_{t+3} that was derived with historical data by F_{t+3}, also available from the Bank of England series, to check whether covered interest parity holds with two countries like the U.S. and the U.K., where the risk factor is minimal and capital mobility is high.

TABLE 17.2 Covered Interest Parity Test

Date	F_{t+3} \$/£	E_t \$/£	i_t^{US}	i_t^{UK}	$1 + i_t^{US}$	$(1 + i_t^{UK})(1 + FD)$
	Mo. Aver.	Mo. Aver.	% annual rate			
31 Jan. 05	1.8666	1.8764	4.66	2.34	1.0234	1.0247
28 Feb. 05	1.8778	1.8871	4.69	2.54	1.0254	1.0263
31 Mar. 05	1.8987	1.9078	4.77	2.74	1.0274	1.0277
30 Apr. 05	1.8879	1.896	4.7	2.77	1.0277	1.0291
31 May 05	1.8466	1.8538	4.66	2.84	1.0284	1.0303
30 Jun. 05	1.8118	1.8179	4.62	2.97	1.0297	1.0322
31 Jul. 05	1.7467	1.7509	4.46	3.21	1.0321	1.0346
31 Aug. 05	1.7911	1.7943	4.41	3.44	1.0344	1.0367
30 Sep. 05	1.8054	1.8081	4.4	3.42	1.0342	1.0378
31 Oct. 05	1.7625	1.764	4.4	3.7	1.0370	1.0404
30 Nov. 05	1.7333	1.7341	4.42	3.88	1.0388	1.0423
31 Dec. 05	1.7459	1.7462	4.43	3.88	1.0388	1.0436

Note: Since the interest rates are expressed on an annual basis, the forward discount over the 3-month period is annualized by multiplying it by 4.

Source: Bank of England (press@bankofengland.co.uk)

When we compare the total amount that an arbitrageur will receive (interest plus principal) in the U.S. and in the U.K. from a three-month treasury bill, the results fare much better than in the case of uncovered interest parity. Indeed the correlation between the two alternative approaches, invest in the U.S. or invest in the U.K., jumps from 0.3 with uncovered interest parity to 0.995 with covered interest parity, showing that covered interest parity is more likely to hold.

INTEGRATING INTEREST ARBITRAGE INTO THE OPEN-ECONOMY MODEL

In Chapter 14, we presented a simple Keynesian version of the open-economy model. Indeed the economy was open inasmuch as we allowed for international movements of goods and services. However we know from studying the balance of payments that, in addition to the current accounts, there are also financial accounts. Of course, in the 1960s and in the 1970s, most countries imposed strict controls on movements of capital so the model of Chapter 14, ignoring the financial flows that were not official, was adequate then to analyze the open economy.

As outlined in Chapter 16, things have changed dramatically and capital is now freer to move internationally, especially among industrialized nations. To be meaningful, the present-day open-economy model has to account for such movements of capital. The first part of this chapter led to the development of the interest parity model linking these international movements to some macroeconomic variables, namely interest rates and exchange rates. Since these variables are already included in the specification of the original Keynesian model, it should not be too difficult to incorporate the concepts conveyed by interest parity theory into a more encompassing international model of the economy.

We devote the rest of this chapter to formalizing the financial account and combining it with the current account equation developed in Chapter 14. This allows us to model an extended version of the international sector of the economy. In the next chapter, this international sector is integrated into the Keynesian model. This new version is renamed the Mundell–Fleming model.

To construct a behavioral equation explaining the movements of capital on a global scale, we draw on our previous analysis of the actions and motivations of interest arbitrageurs.[4] The interest parity condition implies that capital flows hinge crucially on difference in returns on investments across countries. First we reintroduce the financial account: recall that the financial account measures the *net* capital inflows into the domestic economy during a year. The simplest way to extend the basic open economy model is then to stipulate that the financial account (FA) depends on international interest differentials among other things. In addition, our equation for the financial account should consider that countries impose different types of restrictions on capital flows. Finally, financial markets in some countries are transparent and sound, but others are unstable and built on weak institutions, implying a difference in risk across countries. Considering these three factors, we formalize FA, the capital flows, as:

$$FA = \overline{FA} + k(i - i^*) + c(R^* - R) \qquad (17.8)$$

where $\overline{FA}$ is an exogenous coefficient measuring the magnitude of the net capital flows that are autonomous in the equation, k represents the degree of capital mobility that varies between zero (no

---

4 This implies that we only take into account short-term financial flows. From Chapter 12, we know that short-term flows are not the only components of the financial accounts. Our model does not take into account foreign direct investments and the accumulation of capital abroad. Such models have been developed in the literature, but are too complex for our purpose.

capital mobility) and infinity (perfect capital mobility), $(i - i^*)$ the interest differential, $(R^* - R)$ the differential between the foreign and the home country risk, and c the contagion probability discussed in detail below. The financial account is thus fundamentally dependent on differentials in both country returns and country risks.

The Financial Account under Fixed and Flexible Exchange Rates in the Mundell–Fleming Model

Capital flows are determined through uncovered arbitrage as shown earlier. Hence, capital inflows, i.e. the financial account balance, depend on the difference between the returns to investments in the domestic economy, namely i, and the returns to investments abroad, namely $i^* + \varepsilon$, where $\varepsilon = \dfrac{E^e - E}{E}$ denotes the expected rate of depreciation of the domestic currency. Under a fixed exchange rate regime, as long as the public does not expect a devaluation so that the current exchange rate is expected to remain unchanged, $\varepsilon = 0$, and exchange rate movements can be ignored. However, with a flexible exchange rate arrangement, the public may in general anticipate exchange rate changes, in which case exchange rate movements will be reflected in the equation. Specifically, the financial account would be positively related to the interest rate differential, $(i - i^*)$, negatively related to expected exchange rate, E^e, and positively related to the current exchange rate, E. In the special case that exchange rates change in a gradual, predictable way, it is plausible to assume that the expected rate of depreciation, ε, is constant and thereby included in the overall constant $\overline{FA}$. It will still be possible to consider devaluation or depreciation as a change in the value of the constant resulting in some shift of the balance-of-payments line. In Chapter 20, we will develop Dornbusch's overshooting model that explicitly introduces the dynamic adjustment of exchange rate expectations.

First, the equation for the financial account states that when domestic interest rates rise relative to foreign rates, the domestic economy experiences capital inflows. How large those capital inflows are depends on the degree of capital mobility, k. For OECD countries, the degree of capital mobility is high (k is large) as practically no control exists impeding the movement of capital: so capital flows are extensive whenever interest differentials appear. In contrast, controls that limit the mobility of capital (k is small) were prevalent after the fall of the gold standard and still subsist in many regions of the world. In the presence of capital controls, a small k may not allow for arbitrage, and so capital flows are reduced from a gush to a trickle. Think of capital controls as the faucet on a bathtub that can be adjusted from full (no control) to low (high control) stream, to control the flow of water. There have been numerous examples of severe restrictions on capital outflows in recent history. For example, Malaysia tried to weather the Asian financial crisis in the late 1990s by instating capital controls (see the next box entitled: Degrees of Capital Mobility and the Malaysian Crisis, p. 512.).

The second factor influencing capital flow is the risk differential: $(R^* - R)$ takes into account the fact that country-specific political and/or economic risks may scare off investors, no matter how large the rate of return. Contagion is often defined as a situation where an economic crisis in another country increases the probability of a crisis at home, even if the domestic economy is otherwise quite sound. The contagion probability, c, therefore scales how important country risk is to investors. The most likely transmission channel of contagion is international bank lending. Examples of contagion were abundant in the Asian crisis at the end of the 1990s. At that time, investors pulled large investments out of *all* Asian economies although *only a few* were actually in crisis. We will discuss detailed contagion examples later on in Chapter 23 on international currency crises.

In the real world, it is difficult to exactly identify changes in "risk," or to disentangle changes in risk from changes in the interest rate. Generally financial markets price all information (including risk) into the cost of funds so that changes in the interest rate reflect both changes in the supply and demand for funds as well as changes in information. This is the key insight for which Joseph Stiglitz received the 2001 Nobel Prize. Equation (17.8) can be interpreted as a way to separate in theory changes in the interest rate due to fluctuations in the excess demand for funds and those due to changes in country-specific risk.

The Balance of Payments Revisited

With our new equation explaining the financial account, we now revisit the balance of payments. We consider an economic interpretation of the balance of payments that allows the possibility for excess demand for or supply of foreign currency and, to distinguish it from the accounting approach of Chapter 12, we use the notation BP for this concept. We ignore the capital account, so the balance of payments is the sum of the current account, CA, and the financial account, FA: $BP = CA + FA$. In Chapter 14, the current account was narrowly defined as the trade balance, TB, exports, X, less imports, M. We retain the same specification ignoring prices and exchange rate so $CA = \bar{X} - \bar{M} - mY$. This formulation assumes a small-country case where exports are exogenous so $X = \bar{X}$ and a short-term time frame where prices are constant.

Substituting for the current account and the financial account in $BP = CA + FA$, we find:[5]

$$BP = \bar{X} - \bar{M} - mY + \bar{FA} + k(i - i^*) + c(R^* - R) \tag{17.9}$$

The introduction of the financial account has made this new equation representing the external sector more complicated compared to the specification in Chapter 14 where the financial account was ignored. There are now a multitude of factors that can cause an external imbalance, i.e. that make the value of balance of payments diverge from zero. Excess demand can result from either trade in goods, interest differentials, or risk differentials, as well as changes in income. The key is to find when the economy achieves external balance. **External balance** implies the absence of changes in reserves (under fixed exchange rates), or a stable exchange rate (under flexible exchange rates).[6]

---

5 Note that, in this expression, the exchange rate is implied in the trade balance as well as in interest parity, but to simplify our discussion we assume that it is constant and ignore it (see box entitled "The Financial Account under Fixed and Flexible Exchange Rates in the Mundell–Fleming Model" p. 508).

6 Introducing E explicitly in equation (17.9).

It is important to note that external balance is defined as *BP=0*: the only situation that entails zero excess demand for or excess supply of foreign currency, thus implying zero reserve flows (fixed exchange rates) or no need for adjusting exchange rate movements (flexible exchange rates). Since financial flows are now taken into account in our model, the definition of external balance is broader than in Chapter 15 where it only referred to balanced trade (export less import equal zero). This means that external balance does not require a zero current account balance anymore. For instance, trade deficits cause excess demand for foreign currency that can be sufficiently offset by foreign capital inflows wiping away the excess demand and restoring equilibrium on the foreign exchange market. In this case, *BP=0* is achieved with a negative current account balance offset by a positive financial account balance of the same absolute magnitude.

The External Balance Line

To integrate the external balance, given by *BP=0*, into an open economy model, we must first learn to plot it in the income and interest space (*Y,i*); this will allow us to combine it with the model we develop in the following chapters (Mundell–Fleming). The external balance line is thus defined as all the combinations of the domestic interest rate, *i*, and domestic income, *Y*, such that the balance of payments is in equilibrium. To derive the line, we set equation (17.9) equal to zero and solve for the interest rate, this yields:

$$i = \frac{(\bar{M} - \bar{X} - \bar{FA})}{k} + \frac{m}{k} Y + i^* - \frac{c}{k} (R^* - R) \qquad (17.10)$$

This equation may seem intimidating, but we can use it to derive the slope of the external balance line. Differentiating (17.10) with respect to income, *Y*, we find:

$$\frac{\partial i}{\partial Y} = \frac{m}{k} > 0 \qquad (17.11)$$

Since the derivative is positive,[7] the *BP=0* line is upward sloping in the interest and income space.

Alternatively, we can draw the same conclusion using intuition from a simple experiment (see Figure 17.1): we pick a point *a* in the interest-income space such that the current account and the financial account are both in equilibrium. Therefore *CA=0* and *FA=0*, consequently *BP=0* and point *a* lies on the *BP=0* line. Next, assume that the economy experiences a dramatic increase in income while the interest rate is held constant. The economy moves horizontally to point *b*. What do we know about point *b*? Income has increased, resulting in higher imports and a worsening of the trade balance (or *CA* in this model).

Since the interest rate has not changed, the financial account was not affected. This implies that *CA<0* and *FA=0* and therefore the balance of payments must be in deficit, *BP<0*. Since the starting

---

7 *m* is the marginal propensity to import so *0<m<1* while *k* varies between *0* and *∞*.

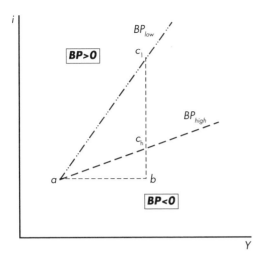

FIGURE 17.1 External Balance in Income and Interest Space

To derive the balance-of-payments line, we start with an equilibrium in the balance of payments (point a). Then we increase income while holding the interest rate constant. This is a horizontal movement from point a to point b. As income increases, the current account declines. To restore the balance-of-payments equilibrium, we need an increase in interest rates in order to generate capital inflows resulting in a financial account surplus. The financial account surplus exactly offsets the current account deficit at point c (c_l or c_h depending on the degree of capital mobility) to restore external balance. The area above (below) the $BP=0$ line therefore corresponds to a BP surplus (deficit).

The greater the degree of capital mobility, the larger the capital inflows resulting from any given increase in the interest rate: higher capital mobility therefore requires smaller increases in interest rates to offset current account deficits: this implies a flatter $BP=0$ line. The graph illustrates two different $BP=0$ lines, BP_{high} and BP_{low}, corresponding respectively to high and to low capital mobility.

point a corresponded to a balance-of-payments equilibrium (external balance), we must ask ourselves how we can return to such a situation. The trick is to raise interest rates enough to create capital inflows sufficiently large to offset exactly the current account deficit. This rise in the interest rate is represented by the vertical line from point b to point c_h. Since external balance is attained at both point a and point c_h, we can connect the two points and call it the external balance line, BP_{high}. This confirms that the $BP=0$ line is upward sloping. The experiment also taught us that the $BP=0$ line separates two regions with balance-of-payments deficits below the line and balance-of-payments surpluses above the line.

We can now analyze the steepness of the slope of the $BP=0$ line. From equation (17.11), we know that it is determined by the marginal propensity to import, m, relative to the degree of capital mobility, k. We will first assume that m, a small number that varies between 0 and 1, is constant and focus on k. *Higher* degrees of capital mobility (large k) generate *flatter* $BP=0$ lines as m/k is small. Conversely, *steeper* external balance lines are associated with *low* degrees of capital mobility (small k). In Figure 17.1, we can see that, when we assume high capital mobility, the increase in the interest rate to restore the external balance needs not be very large; indeed, with scant capital controls, a slight increase in the interest rate can trigger the large capital inflows necessary to offset the current account

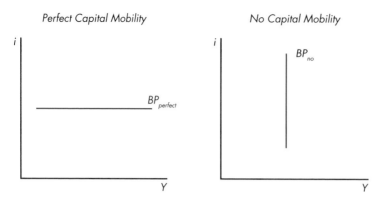

FIGURE 17.2 Perfect and No Capital Mobility

With perfect capital mobility, infinitesimal changes in the interest rate trigger infinitely large capital flows and the *BP* is horizontal. With no capital mobility, infinite changes in the interest rate would be needed to restore the slightest *CA* imbalance so that the *BP* is vertical.

deficit and bring the economy back on the flatter *BP=0* line named BP_{high}. Had we assumed low capital mobility due to extensive capital controls, large interest rate hikes would have been needed to secure the same amount of capital inflow in c_l – thus resulting in a much steeper external balance line, BP_{low}.

Economies with large marginal propensities to import exhibit relatively steeper external balance lines. Indeed, if we apply the *ceteris paribus* condition on k and focus on m, it is clear that a higher marginal propensity to import results in a greater current account deterioration when income increases. In order to restore the external balance, large capital inflows will be needed resulting in a steeper external balance line.

To sum up, small increases in the domestic interest rate generate sufficiently large capital flows to cover the current account deficit only if capital mobility is high. This results in flat external balance lines. If capital mobility is low, the rise in interest rates must be much larger and the external balance line is steep. We can extend the reasoning to the extreme cases of perfect capital mobility and no capital mobility. The perfect (or full) capital mobility line, $BP_{perfect}$ ($k \rightarrow \infty$), has a slope tending towards zero, thus it is horizontal while the no capital mobility line, BP_{no} ($k = 0$), has a slope tending towards infinity and is vertical (Figure 17.2). We will consider these two polar cases when we develop the complete models of the economy in the next chapters.

Degrees of Capital Mobility and the Malaysian Crisis

When the Asian crisis hit the South-East Asian countries in the late nineties, most countries relied on the IMF for advice and help. Malaysia, led by the Prime Minister Mahatir Mohamad, decided to draw its own course to deal with the crisis. The government felt strongly that speculative currency flows were mainly to blame for the crisis. They decided to resort on temporary capital control to ride the slump and get their economy back on track. They put together a package that many economists thought would be counterproductive as it could discourage investment in Malaysia and thwart the country's growth. However, the Malaysian government chose to impose *selective capital control*: they would stop capital flows leading to speculative activities, but still allow capital flows leading to the building up of their economy. The package consisted of the following measures:

The Malaysian leaders fixed the ringgit [the Malaysian currency] at 3.80 to the U.S. dollar to stabilize the exchange rate, thus effectively averting currency fluctuations and speculation while preventing a drastic depreciation of the ringgit with its costly consequences. To further prevent any currency speculation, they closed down the overseas trade of the ringgit and the Malaysian stock trading in Singapore.

They imposed selective controls on capital outflows. Short-term capital outflows by foreigners and local citizens were restrained by setting an initial one-year moratorium on outflows of foreign portfolio capital and financial assets in ringgit. For instance, they set a 10 percent tax on investment profits sent out of the country. Similar controls were set on capital transfers by local citizens and companies. However and most importantly, *no* restrictions were set on capital flows resulting from FDI or trade.

The very important aspect of these capital flows restrictions is that (i) the government focused them on the activities that could destabilize the foreign exchange market, (ii) they were temporary, (iii) they had minimal impact on the fundamentals of the economy since they did not apply to FDI or the settlement of trade.

This is an example of how capital controls can be devised in a selective manner to deal with specific problems. In this case the coefficient k in equation (17.9) was reduced from its original level (before the crisis), but capital flows could still happen, so k was not going to be equal to zero. In addition to various domestic economic measures, the package was successful in getting Malaysia out of the doldrums and the capital controls were eventually removed.

Source: adapted from *Global Trends* by Martin Khor and *Revisiting How Malaysia Overcame the Financial Crisis*, Third World Network, Jan. 18, 2004.

The External Balance Line under Different Exchange Rate Regimes

When we examined the slope of the external balance line in the previous section, we only engaged in one specific experiment that asked how the interest rate had to react to a change in income in order to maintain external balance. Implied in this experiment was that all other variables were held fixed (we enforced the *ceteris paribus* condition). It follows that the external balance line has been drawn assuming fixed exchange rate: E was one of the variables we held constant. Clearly, as long as the exchange rate does not vary, domestic policy changes cause movements along the external balance line, but the line does not shift.

To generalize the discussion, we now examine the $BP=0$ line under flexible exchange rates. Initially the economy is in equilibrium at the external balance point a in Figure 17.3. Now assume the

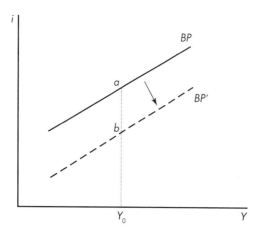

FIGURE 17.3 Impact of a Depreciation/Devaluation on the *BP* line

The depreciation improves the current account and generates a balance of payments surplus. The interest rate must fall so that an ensuing financial account deficit offsets the current account surplus. This implies that every point on the old *BP* line shifts down to *BP'*. Indeed point *a* is now in the *BP* surplus region, i.e. above the new external balance line, *BP'*.

occurrence of a depreciation of the domestic currency, *holding the level of income constant*. The term "holding income constant" implies that we can draw a vertical line at the original income level, Y_0 in Figure 17.3 without ever deviating to the left or right of it.

If the Marshall–Lerner condition holds, we know that a depreciation improves the trade balance and consequently the current account *CA*. This improvement in the trade balance immediately creates a surplus in the balance of payments – hence point *a* does not correspond to external balance anymore if there is a balance-of-payments surplus; it follows that the external balance line *BP* has actually shifted away from point *a*. In which direction did it shift? To return to external balance, the current account surplus needs to be offset with a financial account deficit. The financial account deficit is achieved through a decline in the interest rate all the way to point *b*: so *BP* must shift down to go through point *b*.

Note that we can pick any point along the original *BP=0* line and examine the effects of a depreciation. In each case, the conclusion will be that a lower interest rate is required to trigger the capital outflows necessary to return the balance of payments to equilibrium (external balance). Therefore we can state that a depreciation of the domestic currency causes the external balance line to shift down from *BP* to *BP'*.[8]

We could go through the same exercise to establish that an appreciation of the exchange rate leads to an upward shift in the external balance line. The development of the external balance line and the understanding of its mechanism are crucial for later policy analyses. Finally, since the mechanism of

---

8 As mentioned in an earlier footnote, equation (17.9) incorporates the exchange rate in an implied form. We know from Chapter 14 that both imports and exports, thus the current account *CA*, depend on the real exchange rate. To be more precise, the exchange rate is included in the Mbar and the Xbar terms, i.e. in the intercept of equation (17.10). A change in the exchange rate, either due to depreciation/appreciation or to devaluation/revaluation, will indeed shift the external balance line.

depreciation/appreciation with flexible exchange rates is equivalent to that of devaluation/revaluation with fixed exchange rate, this presentation applies just as well to these cases.

We can now integrate this new model of the international financial sector of the balance of payments into the *IS–LM* model of the economy to develop a truly international model of the economy including not only the balance of trade (as in Chapter 14 and 15), but also the financial account. In Chapter 18, we construct the new basic model and describe its mechanics under fixed exchange rates. In Chapter 19, we consider the case of flexible exchange rates and various extension of the model.

Summary of Key Concepts

1. Investors' goal is to maximize the returns on their portfolio. They compare the returns from investing at home to the returns from investing abroad. If they believe that the returns are higher abroad, they will invest in foreign assets.

2. Investing abroad involves not only the purchase of foreign assets, but also two foreign exchange transactions, one now and the other in the future.

3. Risk is an intrinsic part of investing abroad, since future exchange rates are unknown at the time an investor buys foreign assets. A simple way for an investor to protect investments from exchange rate risk is to use the forward market for the future foreign exchange transaction.

4. Uncovered interest arbitrage exposes investors to exchange rate risk, while covered interest arbitrage insulates foreign investments from foreign exchange risk by using the forward exchange market.

5. Ultimately international flows of capital depend on the different returns and also on the different risk levels involved in investing in various countries.

6. The external balance can be illustrated in the interest and income space. The external balance is upward sloping since current account deficits can be offset by capital inflows (a.k.a. financial account surpluses).

7. The extent of the controls on capital mobility determines how extensive a change in the interest rate needs to be to trigger the capital flows necessary to offset specific current account imbalances. The slope of the external balance line reflects the degree of capital mobility.

8. Since the international financial flows depend crucially on the capital controls and foreign exchange risk, our model of the financial account includes the degree of capital mobility (k) and risk (R).

9. The position of the external balance line is determined by the exchange rate. A change in the exchange rate results in a shift of the line (*ceteris paribus*).

CASE STUDY I

Carry on Speculating
From *The Economist* print edition, Feb 22, 2007

How traders have been triumphing over economic theory

NO COMMENT on the financial markets these days is complete without mention of the "carry trade," the borrowing or selling of currencies with low interest rates and the purchase of currencies with high rates. The trade is often blamed for the weakness of the Japanese yen and the unexpected enthusiasm of investors for the New Zealand and Australian dollars. But why does the carry trade work? In theory, it shouldn't – or not for as long as it has. Foreign-exchange markets operate under a state of "covered interest parity."

In other words, the difference between two countries' interest rates is exactly reflected in the gap between the spot, or current, exchange rate and the forward rate. High-interest-rate currencies are at a discount in the forward market; low-rate currencies at a premium. If that were not so, it would be possible for a Japanese investor to sell yen, buy dollars, invest those dollars at high American interest rates for 12 months and simultaneously sell the dollars forward for yen to lock in a profit in a year's time.

The potential for arbitrage means such profits cannot be earned. However, economic theory also suggests that "uncovered interest parity" should operate. Countries that offer high interest rates should be compensating investors for the risk that their currency will depreciate. In other words, the forward rate should be a good guess of the likely future spot rate. In the real world, uncovered interest parity has not applied over the past 25 years or so. A recent academic study* has shown that high-rate currencies have tended to appreciate and low-rate currencies to depreciate, the reverse of theory.

Carry-trade strategies would have brought substantial profits, not far short of stock market returns, although dealing costs would have limited the size of the bets traders could make. Academics have struggled for some time to explain this discrepancy. One possibility is that investors demand a risk premium, separate from the better interest rate, to compensate them for investing in a foreign currency. As this risk premium varies, it might overwhelm the effects of interest-rate changes.

For example, American investors might worry about the credibility of the Bank of Japan, but Japanese investors may regard the dollar as a "safe haven." This would drive the dollar up and the yen down. However, according to Andrew Scott, of the London Business School, it has been a struggle to find risk premiums that are large enough to explain exchange-rate volatility. So academics have been looking at the structure of foreign-exchange markets, to see if behavioral factors might be at work. One obvious possibility is that the actions of carry traders are self-fulfilling; when they borrow the yen and buy the dollar, they drive the former down and the latter up. If other investors follow "momentum" strategies – jumping on the bandwagon of existing trends – this would tend to push up currencies with high interest rates.

Financial Jaywalking

Such a strategy has its dangers. It has been likened to "picking up nickels in front of steamrollers": you have a long run of small gains but eventually get squashed. In the currency markets, this would mean a steady series of profits from the interest-rate premium that are all wiped out by a large, sudden shift in exchange rates: think of the pound's exit from the European exchange-rate mechanism in 1992.

The foreign-exchange markets have been remarkably calm since the Asian crisis of 1998 (when the yen rose sharply, hitting many carry traders). So a whole generation of investors may have grown up in a state of blissful innocence, unaware that their carry strategy has severe dangers. Inflation may provide an alternative explanation. The theory of purchasing-power parity (PPP) implies that high-inflation currencies should depreciate, relative to harder monies. In other words, while nominal exchange rates might vary, real rates should be pretty constant. And over the very long term, this seems to happen.

A study by the London Business School,[†] with ABN Amro, a Dutch bank, found that real exchange rates in 17 countries moved by less than an average of 0.2% a year over the period 1900–2006. Other things being equal (such as roughly similar real interest rates across countries) nominal interest rates should be higher in countries with higher inflation rates. So this should give support to uncovered-interest parity and deter the carry trade. Clearly, though, PPP has not been a useful guide over the past ten years, as the deflation-prone yen has declined against the dollar.

Perhaps the success of the carry trade reflects biases built up in an earlier era, during the inflationary 1970s and 1980s. Currencies prone to inflation back then, such as sterling and the dollar, have had to pay higher interest rates to compensate investors for their reputation. In fact, because inflation has declined, investors in Britain and America have been overcompensated for the risks – a windfall gain that has been exploited by followers of the carry trade. However, it is hard to believe that this effect could have lasted for as long as it has. So the reasons for the success of the carry trade remain a bit of a mystery.

What does seem plain, however, is that the carry trade tends to break down when markets become more turbulent. In such conditions, those who borrowed yen to buy other assets (such as emerging-market shares) might face a double blow as the yen rose while asset prices fell. If the turbulence were sufficiently large, many years' worth of profits from the carry trade might be wiped out. A steamroller could yet restore the reputation of economic theory.

* *"The Returns to Currency Speculation,"* by Craig Burnside, Martin Eichenbaum, Isaac Kleshchelski, and Sergio Rebelo.

† *Global Investment Returns Yearbook,* 2007.

CASE STUDY QUESTIONS

1. Why can't investors gain from covered interest arbitrage according to the theory?

2. Why should investors be able to gain from uncovered interest arbitrage?

3. "Empirical studies show that high rate currencies tend to appreciate while low rate currencies tend to depreciate." Do these findings go against the theory developed in the first part of the chapter? Explain.

4. How does carry trade work and what is its effect on the foreign exchange markets?

5. What are the risks of such strategies?

CASE STUDY II

The Domino Effect
From *The Economist*, print edition, July 3, 2008

Many currencies that are backed by a current-account deficit are now falling just as the dollar has
According to economic textbooks, the currencies of economies with large current-account deficits should depreciate relative to those of countries with surpluses. This will stimulate their exports and curb imports, thereby helping to slim the trade gaps. America has the world's biggest current-account deficit and the dollar has dutifully been falling since 2002. Oddly, however, the currencies of many other countries with large deficits had enjoyed big gains until recently. Now, at last, currency markets have started to see sense.

Britain, Australia, New Zealand, and Iceland all have large current-account deficits (along with many other American-style excesses, such as housing and credit booms). Yet over several years until mid-2007, their currencies perversely rose relative to those of economies, such as Japan and Switzerland, with big surpluses. For example, despite a current-account surplus of 4.9% of GDP last year, one of the biggest of any developed economy, Japan's trade-weighted exchange rate sank by 13% from the end of 2002 to mid-2007. New Zealand, where the deficit reached 8% of GDP (bigger than America's deficit of 6% of GDP at its peak), saw its currency gain 28% over the same period.

This paradox is the result of the "carry trade," a popular currency strategy that partly explains why trade flows are now dwarfed by cross-border capital flows. In a world of low interest rates, international investors were hungry for yield, and so piled into currencies that offered higher interest rates, namely those of Britain, Australia, New Zealand, and Iceland, as well as many emerging markets. Those higher interest rates paid by countries with large external deficits were supposed to compensate investors for the risk of currency depreciation. But as investors borrowed in low-interest currencies, such as the yen, to invest in high-yielding ones, this made the latter currencies stronger. That, in turn, prolonged global imbalances by making it easier for profligate countries to finance their current-account deficits.

But since the eruption of global financial turmoil last year and the dwindling appetite for risk, carry trades have started to unwind and it has become harder to finance deficits. As a result, current-account imbalances are once again exerting a powerful influence over currencies. The chart shows that the weakest currencies this year have been in countries with deficits, from Britain to South Africa. In contrast, the yen and the Swiss franc have perked up. The same chart a year or so ago would have shown virtually the opposite relationship.

Increased concern about current-account deficits is also causing investors to discriminate much more between emerging markets. A popular argument in recent years has been that developing economies are less risky because, unlike a decade ago, they are no longer dependent on foreign capital. It is true that emerging economies are forecast to have a combined current-account surplus of more than $800 billion this year, but this is more than accounted for by China, Russia, and the Gulf oil exporters. In fact over half of the 25 biggest emerging economies now have deficits. South Korea is running a deficit after a decade of surpluses. Brazil has also moved back into the red, despite record high prices for its commodity exports. Others such as India, South Africa, and Turkey have had external deficits for many years.

Sticking to our "mercantilist" guns

In an article last November, *The Economist* ranked 15 of the biggest emerging economies according to their economic riskiness. Based on the size of external and budget deficits, inflation rates and the pace of growth in bank lending, India, Turkey, and Hungary were deemed to be most vulnerable. The ranking

Moving back in line
Current-account balances and changes in exchange rates

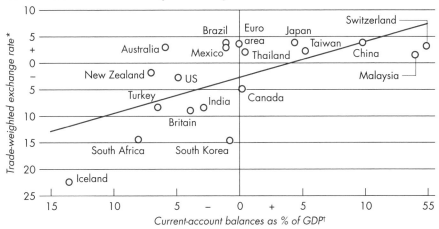

Sources: *The Economist*; BIS   *% change over last six months   †2008 forecast

attracted a lot of flak in India. An article in *The Times of India* accused *The Economist* of "mercantilist thinking at its worst" by treating a current-account surplus as good, a deficit bad. Agreed, a current-account deficit is not necessarily bad: an economy may be borrowing from abroad to finance investment that will lift future growth. Nevertheless, a large deficit does mean that an economy and its currency may struggle if foreign-capital inflows suddenly dry up.

And this is what has happened. This year foreign capital has gone into reverse at the same time as India's current-account deficit has widened sharply. Sharmila Whelan, an economist at CLSA, a brokerage firm, forecasts that India's current-account deficit will rise to almost 4% of GDP in the current fiscal year, and to 5.5% next year. Not only is the trade deficit soaring, largely as a result of higher oil prices; the overseas earnings of Indian IT services companies (two-fifths of which come from the financial sector) are likely to shrink this year.

The nature of the capital inflows financing a deficit also matters. Foreign direct investment (FDI) is less volatile than speculative capital inflows. If we assume that net FDI continues at last year's pace, then it would more than finance the expected current-account deficits in Brazil and Mexico this year. In contrast, net FDI might finance less than

one-third of India's deficit and only one-sixth of South Africa's, implying that their currencies are more at risk. The rupee has fallen by almost 10% against the dollar since late last year. Ms Whelan forecasts that it will drop by another 9% by March 2009.

Central banks in the developing world are now worried that falling currencies will exacerbate inflationary pressures. A year ago most emerging economies were intervening heavily to hold their currencies down; now many in Asia, including India, South Korea, Vietnam, and Thailand, are having to sell dollars to prop their exchange rates up. The prime exception is China, where hot money continues to pour in and where the current account has a massive surplus.

The longer that international investors remain risk-averse, the more attention they are likely to pay to current-account imbalances. A few currencies seem to have been overlooked: those of Australia, Poland, and Hungary have so far held up surprisingly well, despite their gaping external deficits. All three now look overvalued. They could be the next dominoes to fall.

CASE STUDY QUESTIONS

1. In the economy of Chapter 14, it was clear that a current account deficit would bring about a weakening of the currency. Explain why this did not happen in the past few years in a number of countries.

2. Why is this trend now being reversed?

3. Discuss the impact of the global financial turmoil of the last year and the role of risk in restoring "mercantilist" thinking about the external balance.

4. Elaborate on the difference between speculative financial flows and FDI volatility – how sensitive are they respectively to financial turmoil?

Questions for Study and Review

1. When the dollar depreciates,

   a. What should happen to international capital flows in and out of the U.S., according to interest arbitrage?

   b. What should happen to the return on financial investment/equity prices in the U.S., according to interest arbitrage?

   c. Write down an interest arbitrage equation you would expect to hold most of the time. Be comprehensive and specific!

2. For a long time, interest rate differentials between European countries were high. Use the concept of interest parity to explain how interest rates moved closer and closer together as more countries joined the European Exchange Rate Mechanism, eventually introducing perfect capital mobility.

3. Assume a country with flexible exchange rates has a financial account given by: $FA = \overline{FA} + TR$ $(i = i^*)$ where TR are transaction costs. Show how the $BP = 0$ line behaves in the i/Y space as transaction costs increase.

4. You open the *Wall Street Journal* and see that the spot rate is $1 for 100 yen. The interest rate in Japan on a one-year, yen-denominated deposit is 8 percent. The U.S. annual interest rate on dollar deposits is 5 percent.

   a. Provide a formula for the forward rate and calculate the forward rate.

   b. The forward rate that you find in the *Wall Street Journal* does not coincide with your calculations. Cite four reasons.

   c. The interest on a yen-denominated deposit in London is 11 percent. Can you explain the apparent lack of arbitrage?

5. Assume F_{t+1} increases:

   a. What would this say about people's expectations about E_{t+1}?

   b. Would capital flow into or out of the country?

   c. How exactly would the domestic balance of payments be affected?

   d. What would happen to the domestic/foreign interest differential?

   e. With flexible exchange rates between the domestic and the foreign economy, what would you expect might happen to E_t?

6. A one-year bond denominated in $ earns an interest rate of 5 percent per year. A one-year bond denominated in £ earns 7 percent per year and the exchange rate is $1.6714/£1. Assume that an investor can hedge on the forward market and that the 90-day forward exchange rate is $1.6602/£1.

   a. Calculate the forward discount on the dollar *on a yearly basis* (include the sign).

   b. Is the dollar at a forward discount or at a forward premium with respect to the pound?

   c. In which direction will capital flow?

   d. Calculate (in dollars) his return on the $1,000 invested *for 90 days* (i.e. the $ return he will receive by investing in the most profitable alternative whether $ or £).

7. Assume that the interest rate in the Netherlands is 10 percent, i.e. $i^* = 0.1$, the nominal exchange rate E between the U.S.$ and the euro is U.S.$1.30 /€ while the expected exchange rate in a year E^e_{t+1} is U.S.$1.32 /€.

   a. Is the euro expected to appreciate or to depreciate with respect to the U.S. dollar?

   b. Calculate the expected rate of appreciation of the euro.

   c. Calculate the expected return of U.S.$1 invested in the Netherlands (do not use the approximation).

   d. Use the above results and the equation describing the uncovered interest parity condition to determine the U.S. interest rate corresponding to interest parity.

   e. Now suppose that the U.S. interest rate becomes 12 percent, in which direction will capital flow?

8. Derive the $BP=0$ line when interest rates are on the horizontal axis and income is on the vertical axis.

9. How does the BP line change when the contagion coefficient "c" changes?

10. The $BP=0$ line corresponds to equilibrium on the foreign exchange market. With fixed exchange rates, it is defined in terms of the amount of intervention needed to stay on the $BP=0$ line. How much intervention is needed?

11. If it becomes riskier for Americans to invest in Algeria due to political turmoil in that country, what happens to the American $BP=0$ line (assume a two-country model).

References and Suggestions for Further Reading

Abidin, M. and Ahmad, Z. (1999) "The Financial Crisis in Malaysia: the Economic and Political Consequences," *Institute of South East Asian Studies*, 6.

Aliber, R. (2002) *The New International Money Game*, 6th edn, Chicago: University of Chicago Press.

Anker, P. (1999) "Uncovered Interest Parity, Monetary Policy and Time-Varying Risk Premia," *Journal of International Money and Finance*, 18: 835–51.

Bank of England, Statistics, http://213.225.136.206/statistics/index.htm.

Bansal, R. and Dahquist, M. (2000) "The Forward Premium Puzzle: Different Tales from Developed and Emerging Markets," *Journal of International Economics*, 51: 115–44.

Bekaert, G., Wei, M., and Xing, Y. (2002) "Uncovered Interest Rate Parity and the Term Structure," *NBER Working Paper #8795*.

Berk, J.M. and Knot K.H.W. (2001) "Testing for Long-Horizon UIP using PPP-Based Exchange Rate Expectations," *Journal of Banking and Finance*, 25: 377–91.

Burnside, C., Eichenbaum, M., Kleshchelski, I., and Rebelo, S. (2006) "The Returns to Currency Speculation," *NBER Working Paper 12489*.

Cavallo, M. (2006) "Interest Rates, Carry Trades, and Exchange Rate Movements," *Federal Reserve Bank of San Francisco Economic Letter*, 2006–31.

Chinn, M.D. and Meredith, G. (2004) "Monetary Policy and Long-Horizon Uncovered Interest Parity," *IMF Staff Papers*, 51: 409–30.

—— (1998) "Long-Horizon Uncovered Interest Rate Parity," *NBER Working Paper #6797*.

Deardorff, A. (1979) "One-Way Arbitrage and Its Implications for the Foreign Exchange Market," *Journal of Political Economy*, 87: 351–64.

Engel, C. (1996) "The Forward Discount Anomaly and the Risk Premium: A Survey of the Recent Evidence," *Journal of Empirical Finance*, 3: 123–92.

Faust, J. and Rogers, J.H. (1999) "Monetary Policy's Role in Exchange Rate Behavior," *International Finance Discussion Paper #652*.

Flood, R.P. and Rose, A.K. (1996) "Fixes: Of the Forward Discount Puzzle," *Review of Economics and Statistics*, 78: 748–52.

—— (2002) "Uncovered Interest Parity in Crisis," *IMF Staff Papers*, 49: 252–66.

Frankel, J. (1992) "Measuring International Capital Mobility: A Review," *American Economic Review*, Papers and proceedings, 82: 197–202.

—— (1993) "International Financial Integration: Relations between Interest Rates and Exchange Rates," in D. Das (ed.), *International Finance Contemporary Issues*, London: Routledge.

Galati, G. and Melvin, M. (2004) "Why Has FX Trading Surged? Explaining the 2004 Triennial Survey," *Bank of International Settlements Quarterly Review* 67–98.

Grabbe, J. (1999) *International Financial Markets*, New York: Elsevier.

Humpage. O. F. (2007) "The Yen Carry Trade," *Economic Trends*, Cincinnati: Federal Reserve Bank of Cincinnati.

International Monetary Fund, *International Capital Markets*, Washington DC: IMF various years.

Isard, P. (2006) "Uncovered Interest Parity," *IMF working paper*.

Lewis, K. (1995) "Puzzles in International Financial Markets," in G. Grossman and K. Rogoff (eds), *Handbook of International Economics*, Vol. III, Amsterdam: North-Holland.

Mark, N.C. and Wu, Y. (1998) "Rethinking Deviations from Uncovered Interest Parity: The Role of Covariance Risk and Noise," *Economic Journal*, 108: 1686–1706.

McCallum, B.T. (1994) "A Reconsideration of the Uncovered Interest Parity Relationship," *Journal of Monetary Economics*, 33: 105–32.

McGuire, P. and Tarashev, N. (2006) "The International Banking Market," *Bank of International Settlements Quarterly Review* (June) 11–25.

Taylor, M. (1995) "The Economics of Exchange Rates," *Journal of Economic Literature*, 33: 13–47.

Thornton, D. (1989) "Tests of Covered Interest Arbitrage," *Federal Reserve Bank of St. Louis*, St. Louis: Federal Reserve.

Chapter 18

Policy Under Fixed Exchange Rates

LEARNING OBJECTIVES

By the end of this chapter you should be able to understand:

- the mechanism of the open-economy Mundell–Fleming model
- the impact of sterilizing versus non-sterilizing in the very short run
- the importance of capital controls on policy outcomes
- the impact of capital mobility on domestic interest rates
- the effects of monetary and fiscal policy under fixed exchange rates
- the difference between devaluation to get an edge and devaluation as a last resort
- how to find the right fiscal and monetary policy to achieve full employment under fixed exchange rates

The models of the earlier chapters are now extended to the financial sector. In addition to considering the goods market and the current account only, the new models include the financial markets and the full balance of payments (current account plus financial account). The overall equilibrium of the economy is three pronged, involving the goods market, the financial markets, and the balance of payments (or external sector). The mechanics to achieve these three equilibria and the policy implications are elegantly captured by the Mundell–Fleming model. Robert Mundell (Nobel Laureate in Economics, 1999) developed the model with Marcus Fleming in the early 1960s while visiting the IMF.[1]

The so-called Mundell–Fleming model is simply the *IS–LM* model adapted to the open economy. To extend the traditional *IS–LM* model to the open economy, Robert Mundell and Marcus Fleming added one further element to the analysis, the balance-of-payments equilibrium, $BP = 0$. The closed economy *IS–LM* model thus turned into the open economy Mundell–Fleming model, allowing for an effective discussion of the effects of various economic policies in the open economy.

At first sight, the Mundell–Fleming model may seem uncomplicated, since we are simply adding the balance-of-payments equilibrium to the basic *IS–LM* model. However, the inclusion of the balance of payments generates additional assumptions allowing us to consider an array of different cases. We will use the Mundell–Fleming framework to analyze the effect of monetary policy, fiscal policy, or exchange rate policy on the economy. The outcomes will be shown to depend on (i) the exchange rate regime (fixed or flexible), and (ii) the degree of capital mobility (low, high, or perfect). A preview of all the possible cases that we will consider is provided in the box that follows.

Menu of the Potential Alternative Combinations of Assumptions Stipulated in the Specific Cases Presented in Chapters 18 and 19

First choose the exchange rate regime (in i.). Then pick the degree of capital mobility (in ii.). Finally, the impact of a specific policy (in iii.), given these assumptions (chosen from i. and ii.), will be assessed as a separate case below.

---

1 For a history of the Mundell–Fleming Model, that eventually led to the Nobel Prize for Robert A. Mundell, see "The History of the Mundell–Fleming Model: Keynote Speech," Mundell (2001).

---

i. **Exchange Rate**

■ Fixed (Chapter 18)
■ Flexible (Chapter 19)

ii. **Degree of Capital Mobility**

■ Low Capital Mobility, Steep *BP* (steeper than *LM*)
■ High Capital Mobility, Flat *BP* (flatter than *LM*)
■ Perfect Capital Mobility, Horizontal *BP*

iii. **Policy**

■ Monetary Policy
■ Fiscal Policy
■ Exchange Rate Policy

This chapter considers a fixed exchange rate regime and the next chapter (Chapter 19) examines the case of a flexible exchange rate regime. We also make some additional assumptions that will be relaxed later on: we first focus on the small-country case and assume a short-run model where prices are fixed. A two-country case as well as a flexible price adjustment will be developed in the next chapter.

Since the Mundell–Fleming (MF) model is an extension of the closed economy *IS–LM* model, we first review this basic model taught in intermediate macroeconomics classes and then add to it the international sector. The three markets considered in the MF model are: (i) the goods market illustrated by the *IS* curve, (ii) the financial (money-bonds) markets summarized by the *LM* curve, and (iii) the newly introduced notion of external balance or *BP=0* (see Chapter 17) represented by the *BP* curve.

A REVIEW OF THE BUILDING BLOCKS: THE *IS*, *LM*, AND *BP* CURVES

The *IS* curve is defined as the relationship between interest rates, i, and income, Y, such that capital *investment*, I, equals total *national savings*, S^N, (therefore the initials "*IS*"). When investment equals total savings, the supply of goods in the economy equals the demand for goods. In the open economy, this equilibrium in the goods market is achieved when domestic income Y equals total domestic demand for domestic goods – consumption, $C(Y)$, investment, $I(i)$, government demand, G, in addition to net foreign demand for domestic goods, X-$M(Y)$ – or

$$Y = C(Y) + I(i) + G + X - M(Y)$$

Note that we specify investment as dependent (negatively) on the interest rate, i, as this formulation provides the link between the goods and the financial markets. Since we first assume the small open-economy case, exports are exogenous, $X = \bar{X}$. Finally, since we are looking at fixed exchange rates, we do not need to specify the exchange rate, E, openly in the equation; instead, we consider this term implied in the X-M component. Given our definitions of the consumption and imports functions in Chapter 14, we can rewrite the previous equation as:[2]

IS:
$$Y = \frac{\bar{C} + I(i) + \bar{G} + \bar{X} - \bar{M}}{s + m} \tag{18.1}$$

The IS curve is downward sloping in the income and interest space (Figure 18.1), i.e. higher interest rates are associated with lower levels of output. Since higher interest rates discourage investment, reducing aggregate demand, a contraction in output, i.e. in income, Y, is then necessary to restore equilibrium in the goods market.

The LM curve depicts the financial markets defined as the money and the bonds markets. Since equilibrium in one market automatically warrants equilibrium in the other, we can concentrate on the money market. The LM curve is defined as the relationship between the interest rate, i, and income, Y, such that *money demand* (or *liquidity*, L) and *money supply*, M^S, are equal (therefore the

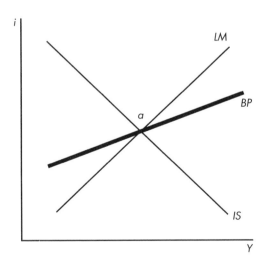

FIGURE 18.1 The Basic *IS–LM–BP* Model in Equilibrium - The Mundell–Fleming Model

At point a, the goods markets (*IS*), the financial markets (*LM*), and the foreign exchange market (*BP*) are all in equilibrium.

2 A similar equation (14.6) was derived in Chapter 14. The only difference is that it included tax, *T*. We ignore tax here – we shall be content to use change in government spending as our fiscal policy variable.

initials "*LM*"). The nominal domestic money supply, M^S, is a multiple of the central bank's issuance of domestic credit, *DC*, plus its foreign reserve holdings, *RES*, as shown in Chapter 13.

$$M^S = \mu(DC + RES) \tag{18.2}$$

Note that any change in foreign reserves impacts on the domestic money supply. Real money supply is given by $M^S/\bar{P}$, where $\bar{P}$ is the price level – the bar above *P* confirms our earlier assumption of fixed prices.

Nominal money demand, M^D, is derived according to the theory of liquidity preference: it depends on the transactions demand (increase in income, as richer people usually hold more cash balances on hand) and on the precautionary demand (decrease in the interest rate – a higher interest rate increases the opportunity cost of holding cash). The nominal money demand increases proportionally with the price level. Using a specific functional form, we can express the nominal money demand as $M^D = \bar{P}(\alpha Y - hi)$.

The real money demand can thus be expressed as $\alpha Y - hi$ where the coefficients α and h measure how sensitive money demand is to changes in income and the interest rate, respectively. Equilibrium in the money market (in real terms) then implies

$$LM: \qquad\qquad \frac{M^S}{\bar{P}} = \alpha Y - hi \tag{18.3}$$

The *LM* curve is upward sloping in the income and interest space of Figure 18.1 because an increase in income, *Y*, causes an increase in the demand for money. Since the supply of money is fixed, the price of money (the interest rate) rises to restore equilibrium on the money market.

Finally, the international sector is characterized by the balance of payments, *BP*, equal to the sum of the current account (*CA*) and the financial account (*FA*).[3] The external balance, *BP=0*, is reached when *the supply of and the demand for foreign exchange are equal* at the fixed exchange rate. When the foreign exchange market is in equilibrium at the fixed exchange rate, the level of foreign reserves (consequently the money supply) is stable as the central bank does not need to intervene to uphold the exchange rate. We have derived the external balance in Chapter 17, defining it in the interest and income space to be consistent with the *IS–LM* curves and we reproduce it here as equation (18.4)

$$BP: \qquad\qquad i = \frac{(\bar{M} - \bar{X} - \bar{FA})}{k} + \frac{m}{k}Y + i^* - \frac{c}{k}(R^* - R) \tag{18.4}$$

Simply expressed, the external balance defines the equilibrium in the foreign exchange market. In the previous chapter, we have shown that the external balance line, *BP*, is upward sloping when drawn in the interest and income space of Figure 18.1. We also discussed that its steepness depends on the degree of capital mobility measured by the coefficient *k*: fewer capital controls corresponding

---

3 For simplicity, we ignore the capital account as in the previous chapter and we let the balance of trade stand for the current account.

to a flatter external balance line. At the limit, the absence of any control on the movements of international capital, i.e. full or perfect capital mobility – corresponds to a horizontal external balance line.

Let us now review the essentials of fixed exchange rate regimes introduced in Chapter 13. Whenever the balance of payments does not equal zero, there is excess supply of (or demand for) the domestic currency on the foreign exchange market. In order to maintain a fixed price for the domestic currency, the central bank then has to intervene, buying or selling foreign currency. Any intervention by the central bank affects the quantity of foreign reserves held by the central bank and consequently the domestic money supply (as shown in equation 18.2).

From equation (18.3), we can see that changes in the money supply result in shifts of the LM curve. Therefore, it is crucial to clarify whether the central bank is allowed to sterilize or not. In Chapter 13, sterilization is defined as an open market operation by the central bank that neutralizes the effects of foreign reserve flows on the domestic money supply. The objective of such an open-market operation is to maintain a stable money supply at all times, so $\Delta M^S = 0$; as already explained in Chapter 13, it implies from equation (18.2) that any change in foreign reserves is offset by an opposite change in domestic credit, $\Delta RES = -\Delta DC$ (equation 13.2).

With the three main elements of the model identified, we now have a graph (Figure 18.1) in the i/Y space illustrating all the equilibrium points in each of the three sectors: the goods market (along the IS curve), the financial markets (along the LM curve), and the external sector (along the BP curve). Since there are three curves, all three will have to go through a common point, a, to reach a common equilibrium.

Now that we have developed the basic model, we can analyze the impact of monetary and fiscal policy on output under various degrees of capital mobility. Since we assume fixed exchange rates, we can also use the model to investigate how a devaluation or a revaluation would affect the economy. Recall that a devaluation/revaluation is a decision by the central bank to change the price of the domestic currency with respect to foreign currencies for some specific reason or goal, so it is a deliberate policy decision; we thus investigate so-called exchange rate policy. Finally, we will examine the most important aspect of the model for policy makers: how to use it to determine the right mix of fiscal and monetary policy to achieve full employment while maintaining the external balance.

MONETARY POLICY UNDER FIXED EXCHANGE RATES

We start with the unique equilibrium for the three markets: the goods market, financial markets, and the foreign exchange market (external balance). Suppose that, to facilitate the reasoning, point a in Figure 18.2 corresponds not only to an equilibrium in the balance of payments, but also that it represents balanced current and financial accounts ($CA=0$ $FA=0$ $BP=0$). An increase in the money supply then lowers the interest rate through the money market and *shifts the LM curve to the right* in Figure 18.2. The two graphs correspond to different degrees of capital mobility, but the basic mechanism is the same. As shown in the previous chapter, low capital mobility is associated with steep BP curves (left-hand graph) and high capital mobility with flat BP curves (right-hand graph). From the graphs, we can immediately determine the impact of the increase in the money supply. There are two distinct effects:

i. Income increases because capital investment, a component of aggregate demand, is stimulated by low interest rates (this is a movement along the *IS* curve). This increase in income raises imports, because imports are positively related to income in our import demand function. The increase in imports then causes a deterioration of the balance of trade.

ii. As the interest rate falls, financial capital flows out of the country since the return on financial investment is now greater abroad (recall our interest parity discussion). The larger the degree of capital mobility, the larger the capital outflows, and the larger the financial account deterioration.

Both the current and financial accounts decline; this implies that the balance of payments must be negative as the economy reaches point *b*. Indeed, the equilibrium in the goods and financial market at point *b*, where the *IS* and the new *LM'* curve now intersect, lies below the *BP* curve (the area of *BP* deficits).

The balance of payments deficit implies excess demand for the foreign currency (generated by importers and investors). In order to avert a rise in the price of foreign currency (a depreciation of the domestic currency), the central bank must intervene by tapping into its foreign currency reserves and selling them to the market at the fixed exchange rate. Importers and investors purchase foreign currency by selling their domestic currency to the central bank. As reserves fall, the money supply is reduced (see equation 18.2), thus affecting the economy. So the central bank has to decide whether

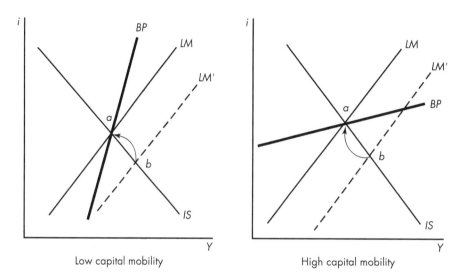

Low capital mobility   High capital mobility

FIGURE 18.2 Monetary Expansion under Fixed Exchange Rates, Low and High Capital Mobility

With low capital mobility, the external balance (*BP*) is steeper than *LM* and, with high capital mobility, *BP* is flatter than *LM*. In either case, expansionary monetary policy leads to a loss in foreign exchange reserves as the economy approaches point *b*, corresponding to a *BP* deficit. *Under non-sterilization*, the foreign exchange reserve outflows translate into a decrease in the money supply and *LM* must shift back until the three markets are again in equilibrium at point *a*. The adjustment will happen faster in economies with high capital mobility. Whatever the degree of capital mobility, monetary policy has no long-term effect on output under fixed exchange rates. Only *with sterilization*, can the economy remain, albeit temporarily, in *b*.

it plans to sterilize the reserve outflows or not, i.e. whether it wants to either sever or retain the direct link between reserves and money supply. We examine both cases.

Monetary Policy, Fixed Exchange Rates, and Sterilization

The reduction in the money supply mentioned above has a contractionary impact on the economy. The central bank may try to sterilize the effects of a balance-of-payments deficit on the money supply to stop the contraction, resulting from the intervention, happening. To do so, the central bank executes an open-market operation – purchasing bonds from the public – that exactly offsets the loss in foreign exchange reserves. This neutralizes the impact of the decline in reserves on the domestic money supply (there is no change in the money supply as $-\Delta RES=\Delta DC$). Why would a central bank want to sterilize? The answer is simple: by sterilizing the effects of the capital outflows resulting from the trade deficit, the central bank keeps the money supply constant at point b in Figure 18.2 and the economy can maintain its higher level of output.

Sterilization does not, however, solve the basic problem of the balance of payments deficit. It is not a long-term strategy. The longer the balance of payments deficits last, the more foreign exchange the central bank has to sell to keep the exchange rate fixed. Eventually, foreign reserves are depleted and sterilization is no longer an option.

Monetary Policy, Fixed Exchange Rates, and Non-Sterilization

When the central bank decides *not* to sterilize reserve outflows, the Mundell's income reserve-flow mechanism sets in (the mechanism was described in the monetary approach to the balance of payments in Chapter 15). There, the link between the foreign reserves changes and its impact on the money supply is not severed. As the central bank supports its exchange rate by selling foreign currency, reserves fall, and, in the absence of an open-market operation changing domestic credit, the money supply declines proportionately (equation 18.2). *The LM curve shifts back*, as the money supply contracts.

The decline in the domestic money supply continues as long as the foreign exchange market is in disequilibrium at the fixed exchange rate (i.e. as long as the country's balance of payments is negative, i.e. $BP<0$) and the central bank has to sell reserves (to intervene). The process comes to a halt only when the LM curve has shifted *all the way back* to its original equilibrium level at a, where external balance is restored, i.e. the foreign exchange market is in equilibrium at the fixed exchange rate and $BP=0$.

The decline in the money supply also raises the interest rate. The rise in the interest rate has two effects: income decreases (lowering the trade deficit), and the financial account improves because capital flows into the domestic economy, attracted by the higher interest rate. Both developments have a positive impact on the balance of payments. Ultimately, the interest rate must rise to its original level as the balance of payments is returned to its equilibrium, point a.

As is apparent from Figure 18.2, under fixed exchange rate regimes, monetary policy is neutral, and it cannot be used to affect the level of output permanently. Expansionary monetary policy simply sets in motion an automatic adjustment mechanism quite similar to the economic interactions described in the monetary approach to the balance of payments studied in Chapter 15. In sum, expansionary monetary policy leads to a negative balance of payments, that triggers reserve outflows; the impact on the money supply and on interest ultimately reverses the effect of the monetary policy.

Up to now, we have not tried to track the difference in the adjustment according to the various degrees of capital mobility. Figure 18.2 shows that, with either low or high capital mobility, the automatic adjustment mechanism will take place under non-sterilization, eventually wiping away the impact of the monetary policy. Nevertheless, the degree of capital mobility does matter in a subtle way. In the case of no capital mobility, that was covered in Chapter 15, monetary policy is reversed only through the trade effects, described above in (i) on p. 530; however, in this chapter, the financial effects, outlined in (ii), must also be taken into account.

What difference does it make whether capital mobility is low or high? As it turns out, the final outcome is the same, but the speed of adjustment is different. With low capital mobility, capital trickles out of the country as the interest rate falls from point a to b. With high capital mobility, capital gushes out of the country to create massive financial account deficits that translate into balance-of-payments deficits. The larger the balance-of-payments deficit, the faster the outflow of foreign reserves and the decline in the money supply. With high capital mobility, capital outflows will take place as soon as the interest rate starts dropping. Although the two graphs in Figure 18.2 seem very similar except for the slope of the BP curve, there is an important difference between the two cases: reserves are lost at a faster rate in the high capital mobility case, hence the adjustment back to the original equilibrium will also take place at a faster speed. Given this insight, we can infer what would happen in the case of perfect (or full) capital mobility.

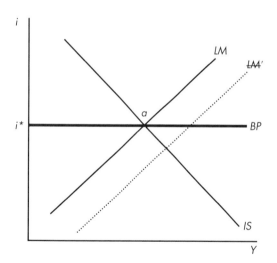

FIGURE 18.3 Monetary Expansion under Fixed Exchange Rates and Perfect Capital Mobility

Under perfect capital mobility, the external balance line (BP) is horizontal. An increase in the money supply can never succeed in shifting the LM curve to LM'. Under perfect capital mobility, any infinitesimal increase in the money supply must be reversed immediately because the interest rate cannot deviate from the world interest rate i^* without triggering infinite capital flows (or outflows) to maintain a balance-of-payments equilibrium.

With perfect capital mobility, the financial account effect dominates the mechanism. From the previous chapter, we know that the *BP* curve is horizontal at the world interest rate i^* in the small country case.[4] As soon as *LM* starts shifting to the right, the interest rate drops. With perfect capital mobility, the slightest interest differential triggers infinite capital outflows and immediate pressures on the domestic exchange rate to depreciate. This cannot be allowed with a fixed exchange rate system, so the central bank must intervene right away and *LM* cannot shift out: *LM′* does not exist except in the imagination of the policy maker! *With fixed exchange rate and perfect capital mobility, monetary policy does not work at all – the economy never leaves point a.* Note that it is not relevant to discuss the case of sterilization under perfect capital mobility. Sterilization is a form of monetary policy and we have just learned that the *LM* can never shift out under perfect capital mobility.

Currency Boards Revisited

This discussion makes it clear that, with fixed exchange rates (and non-sterilization), a country loses its sovereignty over its monetary policy. The higher the degree of capital mobility, the more powerless the central bank becomes. Acknowledging that, countries keen on pegging their currency on a vehicle currency while allowing full capital mobility often opt for a currency board to hold their peg. They are aware that the central bank has no power to carry out any independent monetary policy to meet specific domestic goals; its only role is to carry out intervention operations to uphold the peg. So the central bank might as well give up altogether trying to manage the money supply and let a currency board take care of managing the exchange rate through the money supply. In this case, there is no need for intervention and no adjustment mechanism, the currency board manages the money supply directly and picks the level that corresponds to a specific exchange rate. If the economy moves away from the *BP* line, all that the currency board does is to adjust the *LM* curve, so that the economy goes back to an *IS–LM–BP* equilibrium where the foreign exchange market is in equilibrium at the fixed exchange rate.

In conclusion, monetary policy is not a policy option under fixed exchange rates. Its impact is duly reversed and the greater the degree of capital mobility, the faster its effect is wiped away. Does this mean that policy makers have no way to stimulate their economy when capital is allowed to flow internationally? Maybe fiscal policy is more successful.

---

4 The equation of the *BP=0* line is $i = \dfrac{(\bar{M} - \bar{X} - \bar{FA})}{k} + \dfrac{m}{k}Y + i^*$

Perfect capital mobility corresponds to $k \to \infty$. In this case the first two terms on the right tends toward zero and i tends toward i^*. So with perfect capital mobility, the horizontal *BP* line must always stay put at $i=i^*$, the world interest rate.

FISCAL POLICY UNDER FIXED EXCHANGE RATES

An increase in government spending stimulates aggregate demand resulting in a rise in national income as *the IS curve shifts to the right.* To keep things simple, we again assume that both current and financial accounts are initially balanced at point *a*. The increase in income has two effects:

i.   It increases the demand for imports; this leads to a deterioration in the balance of trade and consequently in the current account.

ii. It raises the transactions demand for money; this constitutes a movement along the *LM* curve. Any increase in money demand, while money supply remains constant, raises the interest rate to keep the money market in equilibrium. The increase in the interest rate then generates capital inflows so the financial account improves.

To disentangle the effects on the balance of payments, we first note that the impact on the current account is negative while the financial account improves. Since the balance of payments is defined as $BP = CA + FA$, the overall impact of the expansionary fiscal policy on the balance of payments is ambiguous ($\Delta CA < 0$, $\Delta FA > 0$). To ascertain the net effect on the balance of payments, we have to identify whether the financial inflows offset the trade deficit or not ($|\Delta FA| >$ or $< |\Delta CA|$). Whether financial inflows are sufficiently large to offset the current account deficit depends crucially on the degree of capital mobility. Again we consider three cases: low, high, and perfect capital mobility to investigate whether capital movements in form of a trickle, steady flow, or flood generate different results.[5]

Fiscal Policy, Fixed Exchange Rates, and Low Capital Mobility

In countries with low degrees of capital mobility, the increase in the interest rate due to the increase in government spending generates only modest capital inflows. Figure 18.4, where the *BP curve is steeper than the LM curve*,[6] illustrates this case. The additional government spending shifts the *IS* curve to the right and the new equilibrium of the goods and money markets occurs at point *b*. Point *b* lies below and to the right of the *BP* curve in the area where *BP<0*. Due to numerous capital controls, the trickle of capital inflows (creating a financial account surplus) is insufficient to finance and offset the current account deficit. Thus the balance of payments slips into deficit (*BP<0*), causing excess demand for the foreign currency.

With excess demand for the foreign currency, there is pressure on the domestic currency to depreciate. The only way for the central bank to prevent the depreciation and uphold the fixed exchange rate is to intervene on the foreign exchange market. The central bank must draw on its reserves and

---

5 The case with no capital mobility was covered in Chapter 15.

6 To be more precise, the relative steepness of the *LM* and *BP* curves indicate the relative adjustment flexibility in the domestic money market and in the foreign exchange market.

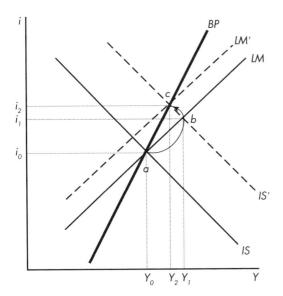

FIGURE 18.4 Fiscal Expansion under Fixed Exchange Rates and Low Capital Mobility

With low capital mobility, a fiscal expansion generates a balance of payments deficit as the economy moves from point a to point b. It happens because the financial account surplus triggered by higher interest rates is not large enough to offset the current account deficit generated by the increase in income as the economy moves to point b. To preserve a fixed exchange rate, the central bank has to sell foreign currency and the reduction in reserves lowers the money supply. The money supply contracts until the interest rate has risen sufficiently so that the financial account surplus exactly offsets the current account deficit. Note the increase in output from Y_0 to Y_2: therefore, fiscal policy is somehow effective in raising output under fixed exchange rates with low capital mobility.

sell the foreign currency on the foreign exchange market at the fixed exchange rate. This increases the supply of foreign currency, weakening it to equilibrate the foreign exchange market.

Just as in the case of expansionary monetary policy, the central bank could attempt to sterilize the effects of the foreign exchange reserve outflows to maintain a constant money supply. In this case, the economy can maintain its higher level of income at point b – but only temporarily. As we know, sterilization requires the central bank to inject domestic credit[7] to offset the loss of foreign reserves so that the *LM* curve stays put. However, since the balance of payments remains in disequilibrium, the central bank will eventually deplete its foreign currency reserves, demonstrating again that sterilization is not a long-term strategy. At that point, either the central bank has to stop sterilizing, or it will have to allow the exchange rate to adjust, as it can no longer satisfy the excess demand for foreign currency. However, if the country is truly committed to a fixed exchange rate, the only option is to stop sterilizing and the impact of intervention, as described below, cannot be avoided.

Under non-sterilization, the central bank sales of foreign currency reduce the foreign currency reserves, causing a decline in the domestic money supply. This *shifts the LM curve to the left*. The

---

7 This corresponds to an open market purchase of bonds from the the public.

decrease in the money supply raises the interest rate to higher levels, affecting both the current and the financial accounts. The higher cost of borrowing induces firms to cut their equipment investment, causing the economy to contract, thus lowering the trade deficit and improving the current account (a move along the new *IS* curve). Higher interest rates trigger further financial capital inflows and the financial account continues to improve.

Both effects have a positive impact on the balance of payments. To reach the new equilibrium where the goods market equilibrium, the money market equilibrium, and the external balance are achieved at point *c*, the interest rate must rise sufficiently until the financial account surplus exactly offsets the current account deficit.

The new equilibrium in the goods, money, and external markets at point *c* does not coincide with the original level of output at point *a*. Indeed fiscal policy is moderately effective in raising output under fixed exchange rates and low degrees of capital mobility since income increased from Y_0 to Y_2. We also note that, since we have moved from point *a* to point *c* on the *BP=0* line, the trade deficit has increased (due to a higher level of output Y), and it is now financed by larger capital inflows (the interest rate in *c* is higher than in *a*). The capital inflows are thus financing the trade deficit such that $FA = -CA$ to restore *BP=0*.

Fiscal Policy, Fixed Exchange Rates, and High Capital Mobility

In the case of high capital mobility, the *BP* curve is flatter than the *LM* curve as shown in Figure 18.5. An increase in the interest rate due to the increase in government spending generates massive capital inflows in countries with high degrees of capital mobility. The large capital inflows creating financial account surpluses more than compensate for the deficit in the current account at point *b*, so much so that there exists an overall balance of payments surplus, *BP>0*. The excess supply of the foreign currency exerts downward pressure on the price of the foreign currency. The central bank must therefore intervene to maintain the fixed exchange rate – this time by buying foreign currency in exchange for domestic currency to soak up the excess foreign currency supply. This implies that the domestic foreign reserves increase, in turn triggering a monetary expansion (see equation 18.2). *The LM curve shifts to the right.*

Again the central bank has the choice of sterilizing the reserve flows (and remaining at point *b*) or adopting non-sterilization. Sterilization implies that the central bank has to reduce domestic credit by selling bonds to the general public. With high capital mobility, such sales may have to be massive and may not be sustainable for any length of time. In this case, the rationale for sterilizing is unclear. Indeed, when the monetary expansion needed to restore the balance on the foreign currency markets at the fixed exchange rate is unleashed, the economy undergoes further expansion from point *b* to point *c*. In this respect, fiscal policy under fixed exchange rate with non-sterilization is highly effective.

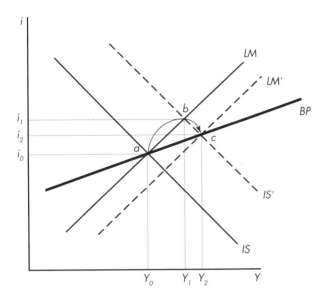

FIGURE 18.5 Fiscal Expansion under Fixed Exchange Rates and High Capital Mobility

A fiscal expansion shifts out the *IS* curve and increases income and the interest rate, moving the economy from point *a* to point *b*. With high capital mobility, the financial account surplus (caused by capital inflows triggered by the higher interest rate) more than offsets the current account deficit (created by the increase in income). To maintain a fixed exchange rate, given the balance of payments surplus, the central bank has to accumulate reserves and the money supply expands to restore equilibrium in the goods, money, and external markets. Under high degrees of capital mobility both the initial increase in government spending, and the ensuing monetary expansion fueled by capital inflows, stimulate the economy resulting in a sizable expansion.

Fiscal Policy, Fixed Exchange Rates, and Perfect Capital Mobility

Under perfect capital mobility, *the BP curve is horizontal* and the slightest increase in the domestic interest rate over the world rate i^* sets off infinitely large capital inflows. The balance of payments shoots into surplus and the excess demand for domestic currency (e.g. excess supply of foreign currency) explodes. The central bank must intervene immediately (setting up a parallel monetary expansion) to stop the domestic currency from appreciating. The central bank must acquire immediately the excess supply of foreign currency at the fixed exchange rate; this, in turn, increases the money supply and depresses the interest rate, ensuring that the domestic rate of interest remains at parity with the world rate of interest. Such adjustment results in maximum impact for the fiscal policy. In Figure 18.6, the economy goes directly from point *a* to point *c* without transitioning through point *b*. *The LM curve shifts to the right along with the IS curve.* With perfect capital mobility, sterilizing is not a policy option since sterilizing such large global capital flows is not feasible and the rationale for doing so is not clear.

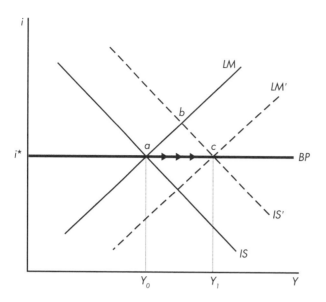

FIGURE 18.6 Fiscal Expansion under Fixed Exchange Rates and Perfect Capital Mobility

Under perfect capital mobility, the increase in output is maximized in the case of a fiscal expansion. The domestic interest rate must *always* equal the world interest rate; any deviation from such interest parity results in massive capital flows. To avoid that, the central bank must carry out a monetary policy that neutralizes at all time any deviation from the world interest rate. As a result, the *IS* and the *LM* curves have to shift together tracing the *BP* curve.

Comparing Open-Economy Models with and without Capital Mobility under Fixed Exchange Rates and Non-Sterilization

In Chapter 15, we studied a simpler model of the open economy with fixed exchange rates and non-sterilization; we also assumed no capital mobility. The key result was that neither fiscal nor monetary policy had any effect on output. Now that we have extended the model to include the international flow of capital and considered the various degrees of capital mobility, we find that monetary policy still does not affect output, but fiscal policy with non-sterilization can, after all, affect output. This happens, in the case of fiscal expansion, because current account deficits can now be offset, to a smaller or larger degree, by financial account surpluses.

In the absence of capital flows, the deficits created by a fiscal expansion cannot be financed at all and lead to equally large reserve outflows. With capital mobility, the fiscal expansion generates a current account deficit, but the higher interest rate causes capital inflows that essentially finance the current account deficit and allow the economy to maintain a higher level of output.

In 1979, Ireland became a member of a joint peg system with other European countries, meaning that they fixed their exchange rate. In the first half of the 1980s, Ireland experienced current account deficits at the same time as large capital inflows – FDI from the U.S. and European Union subsidies.

During this period up to the second half of the 1980s, the Irish government's prolific spending, taxing, and borrowing was out of hand. Capital inflows were the basic way to finance the budget deficit. After 1987, the Irish government adopted responsible policies and Ireland became the successful Celtic tiger we know now.

Why is Fiscal Policy more Effective in Raising Output than Monetary Policy under Fixed Exchange Rates?

We simplify the discussion by looking at expansionary policies and assuming that, initially, the economy displays balanced trade. Expansionary fiscal policy, as well as expansionary monetary policy, stimulates income, thus creating current account deficits. Under fixed exchange rates, current account deficits lead to a loss in foreign exchange reserves, triggering a contraction in the money supply. While expansionary fiscal and monetary policy have the same impact through the goods market side – creating balance of trade deficits and losses in reserves that have contractionary effects – their impact on capital flows is diametrically opposed.

Expansionary fiscal policy raises interest rates, generating foreign capital inflows that finance the current account deficit. If these capital flows are large (high capital mobility), not only will the current account deficit be fully financed, but these flows will contribute to further expansion in the economy. Expansionary monetary policy lowers the interest rate, causing capital outflows and further losses in foreign reserves as domestic investors want to move their assets abroad into a different currency. Therefore the LM curve has to shift back to its original level (the policy is neutral as all the real variables are back to their original level – see Table 18.1).

Another interesting way to look at this issue is to note that the IS curve is the instrument of fiscal policy while the adjustment mechanism takes place through the LM curve – these two curves are independent of each other. On the other hand, with monetary policy, the LM curve is involved in carrying out the policy and it is also shifting as a result of the adjustment process: it cannot play both roles effectively.

The Danger of a Pegged Exchange Rate: The Argentinian Crisis

In the 1990s, the Argentinian government passed a law fixing the peso to the dollar: the one-to-one peg was upheld by a currency board controlling the money supply directly. This was accompanied by other economic reforms – privatization and free movement of capital. Although the impact of such a move would be anti-inflationary, there were some dangers; chronic government deficits and a costly pension reform attempt pointed to a fiscal policy that was not prudent. As a result, the Argentinian international competitiveness suffered from an overvalued peso. Eventually, these policies triggered three years of recession and by 2001–2002 income per capita had dropped by

TABLE 18.1 Summary Impact of Monetary and Fiscal Policy under Fixed Exchange Rates

	K mobility	Effect on	LM	IS	BP line	Y	i	CA	FA	BP
Monetary Expansion	Low or high	Immediate	Shifts right	—	—	↑	↓	↓	↓	↓
		Intervention	Shifts back	—	—	↓	↑	↑	↑	↑
		Overall	Original level	—	—	Original level				BP=0
	Perfect	Immediate and overall	No shift	—	—	No change				BP=0
Fiscal Expansion	Low	Immediate	—	Shifts right	—	↑	↑	↓	↑	↓
		Intervention	Shifts left	—	—	↓	↑	↑	↑	↑
		Overall	Left of original	Right of original	—	↑	↑	↓	↑	BP=0
	High	Immediate	—	Shifts right	—	↑	↑	↓	↑	↑
		Intervention	Shifts right	—	—	↑	↓	↓	↓	↓
		Overall	Right of original	Right of original	—	↑	↑	↓	↑	BP=0
	Perfect	Immediate and intervention	Shifts right	Shifts right	—	↑	—	↓	↑	BP=0
		Overall	Right of original	Right of original	—	↑	—	↓	↑	BP=0

some 22 percent from 1998, unemployment had risen to around 20 percent, and the banking system all but collapsed. It is well known that international capital flows into emerging economies are quite fickle: capital flights were massive. As Argentina defaulted on its external debt, the IMF scrambled to come to the rescue, and they acted in rather inconsistent ways. Beset by similar woes, Brazil, Argentina's main export market, did not hesitate to forsake its dollar peg and float, seriously hurting Argentina's exports in the process. The Argentinian government was reluctant to give up their peg to the dollar; Argentina's policy makers were hoping for an automatic adjustment – decrease in the money supply and deflation – to sort out their problem.

However the severity of the economic crisis led to civil unrest and to the unavoidable devaluation of the peso. This development put a huge cost on the public; the Argentinian economy was highly dollarized with the bulk of loans and deposits denominated in dollar. To ease the pain on the debtors, the government allowed a one-to-one conversion on loans, but they set a different conversion rate for deposits: the outcome was a shambles. Eventually, the peso plunged to 3.18/$ resulting in major upheavals in the economy. Fortunately, the rejection of the dollar peg, coupled with more prudent policies, eventually paid off. By 2005, the economy had regained its 1998 level, the budget deficit had turned into a surplus, and the public debt was restructured. Exports strengthened and the country is now categorized as a managed floating economy by the IMF. A caveat is in order: the devaluation triggered an inflation spike resulting in a fall in real wages and a permanent increase in some basic prices; in sum, a redistribution effect causing greater income inequality and higher poverty.

EXCHANGE RATE POLICY

So far we have considered the impact of monetary and fiscal policy, but there is a third policy that governments can use to stimulate or slow down their economy under fixed exchange rates. The third policy is a devaluation or revaluation of the currency. This is not to say that the government allows the exchange rate to change and float freely. A devaluation or revaluation is simply a statement on the part of the government that instead of holding the price of foreign currency at exchange rate E_0, it will now hold it at exchange rate $E_1 \neq E_0$. It is a policy because the government changes the peg unilaterally from E_0 to E_1 for a specific reason.

An increase in the price of foreign currency is called a devaluation (more units of domestic currency are necessary to buy one foreign currency unit) and a decrease is a revaluation. A devaluation makes domestic exports more attractive and this is why countries, at times, engage in *competitive devaluations* to protect their domestic producers as well as giving their exporters an edge. In contrast, a *corrective devaluation* is one that aligns the nominal with the real exchange rate after periods of high inflation. We consider the economic theory behind these two forms of devaluation within the framework of the Mundell–Fleming model. We also assume that the Marshall–Lerner conditions are met: the devaluation results in an *improvement* in the balance of trade.

Competitive Devaluation

In this case, the economy is initially experiencing an overall equilibrium: at this specific level of output and interest rate, the goods market, the money market, and the foreign exchange market (*BP=0*) are in equilibrium. At the same time, however, the policymaker is faced with high levels of unemployment and wishes to stimulate the economy. The country can increase/redefine its peg from E^f_0 to E^f_1 (see Figure 18.7), hoping that the devaluation, by stimulating exports and discouraging imports, will generate a higher level of output and employment.[8]

---

8 This scenario is not altogether unrealistic. In the 1930s, countries attempted to escape the depression with competitive devaluation or so called "beggar thy neighbor" policies. Note that any gain from a devaluation comes at the expense of the trading partner in a large country setting.

To raise the price of foreign currency, the central bank simply buys foreign currency with domestic currency; this reduces the supply of foreign currency on the foreign exchange market, strengthening the foreign currency and weakening the domestic currency. The supply of foreign currency shifts to the left and the exchange rate increases to the desired new peg, E^f_1, as shown in Figure 18.7. The resulting increase in the foreign reserves and the ensuing increase in the monetary base can also be observed on the central bank's balance sheet on the right side of Figure 18.7.

We can also analyze the effect of a devaluation within the Mundell–Fleming framework. In Chapter 17, we demonstrated that a devaluation results in a downward shift of the BP curve. Now we add the new concept that, if the economy starts from a BP=0 equilibrium, the devaluation can only happen if the central bank intervenes. The intervention, consisting in an accumulation of foreign reserves (RES increases), causes an increase in the money supply (as the monetary base, MB, increases). So *both the BP and the LM curves shift out* with a devaluation. Figure 18.8 shows the two shifts.

The devaluation has also a third impact: it improves the current account and stimulates the economy. This is represented by a *rightward shift of the IS curve* as exports increase and imports are discouraged by the higher price of foreign currency. All three shifts result in a new equilibrium corresponding to an economic expansion from Y_0 to Y_1.

Will this new peg be permanent? Is it a better peg for the economy? What is the impact on the trade partners and their reactions? These are further questions that the model does not address. In the second case, the devaluation is seen as performing a correction. Indeed, competitive devaluation might be a thing of the past, but corrective devaluations have not been uncommon in recent times.

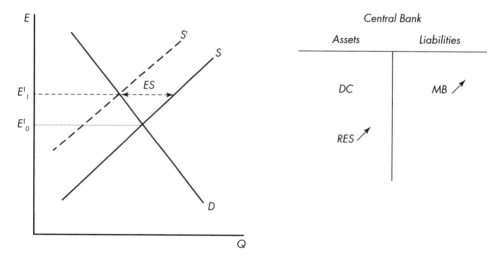

FIGURE 18.7 Impact of a Competitive Devaluation on the Foreign Exchange Market and on the Central Bank Balance Sheet

Starting from equilibrium on the foreign exchange market at E^f_0, the central bank announces a new peg corresponding to a higher price for the foreign currency, E^f_1. The central bank achieves this higher price by purchasing the foreign currency on the foreign exchange market, thus reducing its supply on the market. As central bank foreign reserves increase, so does the money supply.

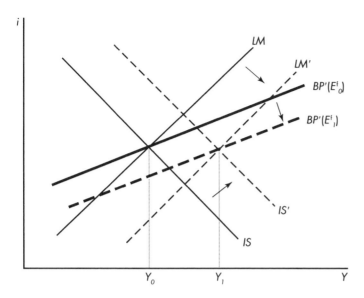

FIGURE 18.8 Economic Effects of a Competitive Devaluation (Starting from a Balance-of-Payments Equilibrium)

A competitive devaluation can be achieved only if the central bank buys foreign currency thus increasing the domestic money supply. This raises the price of foreign currency, shifting the external balance, *BP*, downward while the *LM* curve shifts to the right; the devaluation also causes an expansion in exports and a reduction in imports shifting the *IS* curve out.

Corrective Devaluation

In this case, the country is facing chronic imbalances at the fixed exchange rate and is unable to remain on the *BP* line. Basically, the country is trying to hold on to a fixed exchange rate regime while facing a severe balance-of-payments imbalance (either a large current account deficit, or a financial account deficit, or both). How could the country end up in such a situation? The country could have used expansionary policies unwisely and attempted to sterilize reserve flows or it might be facing chronic deficits resulting from a loss in international competitiveness. The country must keep intervening to maintain its fixed exchange rate, but since the intervention consists of selling foreign currency, the country's reserves will eventually be depleted. One solution to this quandary is to devalue the domestic currency. Again we can analyze the situation using a graph of the foreign exchange market together with a central bank balance sheet in Figure 18.9.

At the original fixed exchange rate, E^f_0, there is excess demand for the foreign currency, but the reserves are too low to satisfy this excess demand. As a result, the central bank can announce a new fixed exchange rate, this time at level E^f_1 where the foreign exchange market is in equilibrium. Note that, in this case, the central bank does not need to purchase any foreign exchange as in the case of a competitive devaluation. Here market forces drive the exchange rate up to E^f_1.

In the Mundell–Fleming model of Figure 18.10, we see that the devaluation has a positive impact on the economy. In this case, the initial position of the economy is at point *a*, where *IS* and *LM* intersect below the *BP* line so *BP*<0. At point *a*, the economy suffers from chronic balance-of-payments

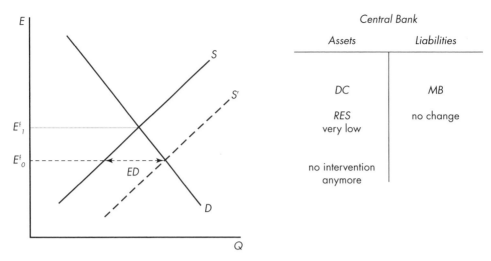

FIGURE 18.9 Impact of a Corrective Devaluation on the Foreign Exchange Market and on the Central Bank Balance Sheet

The foreign exchange market is in disequilibrium at the original peg E^f_0: the country has lost its international competitiveness and these imbalances are chronic. The country has sold most of its reserves to uphold the official peg E^f_0 and has no choice but to stop intervening and readjust its peg to be in line with the real external balance. The peg is moved to E^f_1, the exchange rate corresponding to equilibrium in the foreign exchange market. The money supply is not affected.

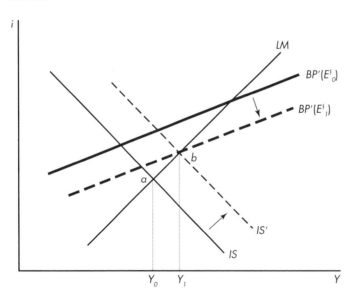

FIGURE 18.10 Economic Effects of a Corrective Devaluation (Starting from a Balance-of-Payments Disequilibrium)

BP shifts as the peg is redefined. There is no need to accommodate the devaluation with a change in the money supply because, in this case, the devaluation simply confirms the new equilibrium in the foreign exchange market. The *IS* curve shifts as the devaluation improves the balance of trade and the economy is stimulated.

deficits. The devaluation *shifts both the BP line and the IS curve to the right* (since it increases exports and decreases imports) as before, but the *LM* curve is *not* affected because there is no need for intervention in the foreign exchange market. The impact of the corrective devaluation is therefore also expansionary as income increases from Y_0 to Y_1.

Devaluations and Revaluations in Bretton Woods Era

In modern times, it has been more frequent for countries to devalue or revalue because it is necessary to do so. The Bretton Woods era (1945–1973) is replete with such instances; in this post-war international arrangement, all the currencies were pegged to the U.S. dollar. In essence, countries with high rates of inflation would lose their international competitiveness (e.g. France, Italy) and would have to devalue to regain it. This system worked fine and imposed some sort of monetary discipline on its members: countries that used their monetary policy unwisely, resulting in high inflation rates, had to devalue in shame.

However, in the 1960s, the U.S. rate of inflation also crept up and U.S. prices became significantly higher than German prices that were very stable. This situation was very unsettling for the Germans who had vowed to keep their inflation in check as a result of their traumatic experience with galloping inflation in the 1920s. If prices increase faster in the U.S. than in Germany, German goods become more desirable and Germany runs a trade surplus leading to an accumulation of reserves and an increase in the German monetary basis; the result being inflationary pressures in Germany. If Germany uses contractionary monetary policy to offset these pressures, the increase in the rate of interest leads to capital inflows, further accumulation of reserves, and further inflationary pressures: a vicious circle for Germany. The adjustment thus has to be effected through a revaluation. After a number of revaluations (1961, 1969), it became obvious to Germany that a flexible arrangement would be more suitable if the anchor, the U.S. dollar, persisted in its erratic performance, so they eventually allowed their currency to float against the $ in 1971.

TABLE 18.2 Summary Impact of Devaluation under Fixed Exchange Rates

	Type	Effect on	LM	IS	BP line	Y	i	CA	FA	BP
Devaluation	Competitive Start w/ BP=0	Immediate including intervention	Shifts right	—	Shifts right	↑	↓	↑	↓	—
		Impact on trade	—	Shifts right	—					
		Overall	Right of original	Right of original	Right of original	↑	↓	↑	↓	BP=0
	Corrective Start w/ BP<0	Immediate no intervention	—	—	Shifts right	↑	↑	↑	↑	↑
		Impact on trade	—	Shifts right	—					
		Overall	Original level	Right of original	Right of original	↑	↑	↑	↑	BP=0

THE POLICY MIX: INTERNAL AND EXTERNAL BALANCE

The universal economic aspiration of governments is to enjoy full employment. Unfortunately, we have seen that the goods and money markets equilibrium (the *IS–LM* intersection) may occur below or above full employment. Below full employment means that a lot of people do not have a job and above full employment means that there is excess demand for workers so that rising wages exert inflationary pressures on the economy.

If the *IS–LM–BP* equilibrium of the economy does not correspond to full employment, is it possible to attain full employment without relying on changes in foreign currency reserves and interventions in the foreign currency market? The problem for the policy maker is then to worry about two objectives: to bring the economy to *full employment*, e.g. the **internal balance**, and to ensure that this level of output is compatible with *BP=0*, e.g. the **external balance**, at the fixed exchange rate. We have discovered in Chapter 15 that, in order to pursue two goals, we need two policies and we discussed the policy mix in the case of the open-economy model without capital mobility. It is now time to look at the policy mix with the Mundell–Fleming model, i.e. assuming capital mobility.

We analyze the specific case where, initially, the economy enjoys external balance, but not internal balance. The *IS–LM–BP* curves intersect below full employment and the policy makers plan to remedy this situation with expansionary policies. Either expansionary fiscal or monetary policy can achieve this goal individually. However both policies affect the current account as well as the interest rate, and thus the financial account, in the process. With either expansionary policy, the current account deteriorates. However the two policies have opposite impacts on the rate of interest and,

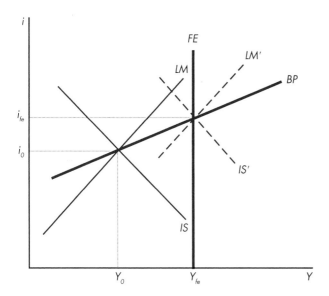

FIGURE 18.11 The Policy Mix

The right dose of monetary and fiscal policy can move the economy from a position of equilibrium in the three markets in Y_0 to the more desirable position in Y_{fe} where the economy is in equilibrium at full employment (*FE*). Monetary policy is used judiciously to adjust the interest rate so that external balance is retained in Y_{fe}.

consequently, on the financial account, worsening it with monetary policy and improving it with fiscal policy.

With expansionary monetary policy, the interest rate drops, triggering capital outflows. The overall effect is a deterioration in the balance of payments and internal balance is reached below the *BP* curve. In addition, the impact of the policy is reversed with non-sterilization. If we use fiscal policy only, the current account deteriorates while the financial account improves as the interest rate increases with expansionary fiscal policy. Whether the financial account improvement will be greater or smaller than the current account deterioration depends on the degree of capital mobility. So the final equilibrium of the economy at full employment can take place either above or below the *BP* curve.[9] Since one policy alone cannot achieve the goal of internal balance without losing the external balance, we must consider a policy mix. In Chapter 15, the policy mix consisted in fiscal and exchange rate policy. In the M–F model, we include monetary policy explicitly in the model by incorporating the *LM* curve. Exchange rates are fixed and they are not used as a policy instrument; so we pick fiscal and monetary policy to reach the internal balance, while maintaining the external balance.

By using both policies together (Figure 18.11), the country can engineer an expansion all the way to full employment at Y_{fe} and, at the same time, control the exact change in the interest rate allowing the economy to remain on the *BP* line, since the policies have opposite effect on the interest rate. The policy makers have to plan and calibrate carefully the amount of each policy needed to achieve the two

---

9 It would obviously be a stroke of luck if ΔCA were equal to $-\Delta FA$ at full employment.

goals. Since the *BP* curve is upward sloping, an increase in the interest rate is needed to maintain the external balance: the deterioration in the current account caused by the expansion must be matched by an improving financial account. Finally, since the economy reaches a new position with internal and external balance, there is no need for intervention and, consequently no painful reserve-flow adjustment mechanism – the economy can remain there. The policy makers have thus achieved the stated goal: full employment (FE) with internal and external balance, and no foreign exchange intervention.

However, Figure 18.11 does not really indicate precisely how we should use the two policies. It only illustrates the initial situation and the final situation with a higher interest rate and a higher level of government spending; the graph shows that, in principle, it should be possible to achieve both internal and external balance. In practice, it is not that simple. How does the policy maker know what is the right dose of each policy? Moreover fiscal and monetary policies work their way through the economy at very different paces – the lags involved in fiscal policy are longer; that would make the coordination very hard to achieve. So is there a method that would help the policy makers, in charge of the fiscal and in charge of the monetary policy, to figure out the best approach? A large amount of literature has been devoted to this question starting with Robert Mundell's original quest.[10]

The Policy Mix: Internal and External Balance in the Policy Space

An alternative representation of the policy mix is to develop a graph in the policy space that has fiscal policy and monetary policy on the two axes. We have encountered this type of graph before, when we drew the Swan diagram of Chapter 15. Figure 18.12 measures monetary policy (represented by

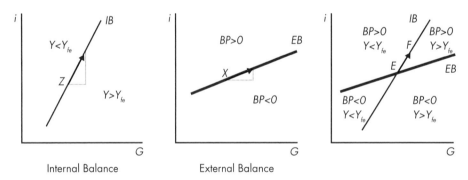

FIGURE 18.12   Construction of the Internal and External Balance

The *IB* and the *EB* lines correspond respectively to all the combinations of *i* and *G* that maintain the economy at full employment or in external balance (*i* and *G* measure respectively the extent of the monetary or fiscal policy exercised at the time). Each of the two lines, *IB* and *EB*, divide the space into two regions: unemployment and inflationary pressures for the *IB* line and balance-of-payments surplus and deficit for the *EB* line. The *IB* line must be steeper than the *EB* line, because starting from a *IB–EB* equilibrium in *E*, an increase in interest rate along the *IB* line to *F* brings about surpluses in the balance of payments, so *F* must lie above the *EB* line.

---

10 In his seminal article published in the IMF Staff Papers, in 1962, Mundell solves the assignment question.

the level of *i*, the interest rate) on the vertical axis and fiscal policy (given by the level of *G*, government spending) on the horizontal axis.

Internal balance and external balance are represented by two lines (*IB* and *EB*) in the policy space of Figure 18.12, showing all the combinations of the interest rate and government spending that result in internal or external balance respectively. Along the *IB* line, the economy is always at full employment ($Y=Y_{fe}$) and, along the *EB* line, the balance of payments is always zero ($BP=0$). The intersection of these two lines yields a unique solution: it indicates the size of the money supply (equivalent to the level of the interest rate) and the extent of government spending needed to reach both internal and external balance simultaneously.

The construction of the *EB* and the *IB* lines is very similar to the approach used in Chapter 15 to derive the *YY* and the *BB* line. A move out to the right on the horizontal axis corresponds to higher government spending, thus more expansionary policy. A move up on the vertical axis corresponds to higher interest rates (lower level of money supply), thus more contractionary monetary policy. If we start at a point *Z* in the left graph where the economy is at full employment and we increase government spending, the economy goes beyond full employment. To restore full employment, we need to use contractionary monetary policy: an increase in the interest rate. The internal balance line, *IB*, must be upward sloping. At the same level of government spending, any points above the *IB* line (with higher interest rate) correspond to a more contractionary monetary policy, so to a lower level of income, $Y<Y_{fe}$. Conversely, all the points below the *IB* line correspond to $Y>Y_{fe}$.

Similarly, we start with a point *X* on the middle graph where the balance of payments is balanced. A horizontal movement to the right of this point (at the same interest rate), i.e. an increase in government spending, will cause current account deficits. To restore the external balance $BP=0$, the financial account needs to improve and this is only possible with an increase in the interest rate. The external balance line, *EB*, is also upward sloping. If we carry out the same reasoning as above, we find out that points above the *EB* curve, corresponding to higher interest rate, exhibit surplus in the balance of payments, $BP>0$, while points below the *EB* line are in the balance of payments deficit area, $BP<0$.

Since both lines are upward sloping, we need to know where they stand relative to each other to complete the presentation on the right graph. Only then can we label the four quadrants delimited by the two lines according to their situation with respect to both balances (just as we did with the Swan diagram). The two lines intersect at a point *E* where both balances are achieved. If the economy moves up along the internal balance line from *E* to a point *F*, full employment is maintained; this is possible because the higher level of government spending is compensated by a more restrictive monetary policy, i.e. a higher interest rate. Since output is the same, the current account is not affected, but with higher interest rates, the financial account improves and the balance of payments turns into a surplus, i.e. a point *above* the external balance line. The *IB* line is thus *steeper* than the *EB* line and this does not depend on the level of capital mobility.

Now that we have constructed the policy mix graph, we are ready to use it to figure out the policies a government should implement to steer the economy toward an *IB–EB* equilibrium.

The Policy Assignment Question

In the last section, we analyzed a special case where the economy had external balance, it was on the *EB* line, but was not at full employment. We illustrated that a combination of fiscal and monetary policy can, in principle, bring the economy to E. However in our previous graph (Figure 18.11), we were only showing the initial and the final position. We were not showing how exactly we would reach E. More precisely we were not sketching the path that the economy should follow to get to E (although we hinted it in the explanations). The goal of the policy makers was to send the economy to the intersection point of the IB–EB lines. Still they had to use a policy mix to succeed. We now generalize the analysis by looking at any possible situation a country could find itself in: neither external nor internal balance, or one balance – but not the other.

We have two policies (fiscal and monetary policy) to reach two targets (internal and external balance). Which target should we assign to which policy? If we could answer this question, i.e. specify the correct **assignment**, we could provide a clue to countries that have one policy maker in charge of fiscal policy and another one in charge of monetary policy. In this case, it would be convenient to tell the policy maker in charge of money supply to worry uniquely about bringing the balance of payments into balance and to tell the policy maker in charge of fiscal policy to worry uniquely about restoring full employment. Could this division of labor work? If it did, that would also take care of the problem of varying speeds of adjustment with the different policies, since they are carried out independently of each other.

In fact, the formal model has shown that the idea of assigning a specific target to each policy really works. Let us try to figure out the correct assignment intuitively. Monetary policy affects the financial account directly through changes in the rate of interest. On the other hand, fiscal policy does not affect the current account directly. So overall, monetary policy seems to have a more direct impact on the balance of payments. Therefore, it would be a good bet to assign monetary policy to the external balance: this is the correct assignment. It is important to stress that we cannot switch the policy-target match around: if the government assigns the wrong target to a specific policy, the disequilibria would get worse.

Starting from disequilibrium at A in Figure 18.13, the correct assignment sends the economy back to equilibrium at E. There is a balance of payments surplus at A, so the central bank must cut the interest rate sending the economy on the EB line. External balance is restored on EB, but the government has to worry about inflationary pressures. The government thus cuts spending, restoring the internal balance as the economy moves to IB: in the process, a new smaller balance-of-payments surplus is created. Next it is the turn of the central bank to cut the interest rate again to restore the external balance. The economy is clearly converging towards E as each individual adjustment is smaller and smaller.

Let us now show an example of incorrect policy assignment. Starting from point B, the policy choices illustrated with arrows will not work. Cutting government spending to restore external balance and cutting the interest rate to bring the economy to full employment, brings further disequilibria. The starting point at B was a situation with balance-of-payments deficits and unemployment, so these are clearly the wrong policies.

Reality Check on the Policy Mix

The principle behind the policy mix, consisting in using both fiscal and monetary policies to reach two objectives, is straightforward and unassailable. Let us consider point B where the country suffers from a balance-of-payments deficit in addition to unemployment. According to the assignment directive, the central bank simply has to raise interest from the lower level at *B* to a higher level at *E* to deal with the balance-of-payments deficit. From a domestic point of view, this sounds like a very weird thing to do when the economy needs to be stimulated.

This would send the economy deeper into its recession as investment is stifled by the policy. The idea is to compensate this adverse impact on output with massive doses of expansionary fiscal policy as fiscal policy is assigned to fixing the internal balance. Not only would this increase the budget deficit, but it would be criticized as a blatant example of crowding out. How would business or the stock market react?! This is political suicide. Politicians are more worried about unemployment than about the balance of payments; as they ignore the external sector, their instincts lead them to conduct expansionary monetary and expansionary fiscal policy. Small very open economies may monitor closely their external balance; but by looking at the extent of the external imbalance exhibited by the U.S. economy in recent years, it is clear that large industrial economies are not willing to take action that might destabilize their domestic sector (note that the theory is developed in the context of the small open economy).

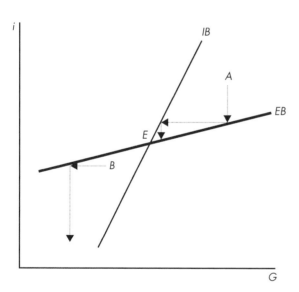

FIGURE 18.13 The Assignment

Starting from *A*, a situation with inflationary pressures ($Y>Y_{fe}$) and a balance-of-payments surplus ($BP>0$), the government assigns the correct tasks to its agencies: fiscal policy is devoted to fixing the inflationary pressures by cutting *G*, and monetary policy to fixing the balance of payments by cutting the interest rate. The economy will be shepherded to equilibrium in *E*. Let us see what happens if the government ignores the correct assignment: from another disequilibrium point *B*, where $Y<Y_{fe}$ and $BP<0$, had the government cut spending to restore the external balance and cut the interest rate to restore the internal balance, the economy would have been saddled with further disequilibria.

Not only does the assignment directive affect the composition of aggregate demand by using the interest rate as an instrument, but it also affects the composition of the external balance. In the process of moving toward full employment from point B, the current account deteriorates and the country receives large capital inflows to match these current account deficits: as a result, the country's level of international indebtedness increases and the greater foreign debt burden will involve greater interest payments to the foreigners. These developments may not be desirable either. This is a serious problem faced by the U.S. economy.

In this chapter, we have focused on the mechanism of the Mundell–Fleming model under fixed exchange rates and extended the model to appraise the impact of various policies. Then we considered the issue of attaining more than one goal with a policy mix. The next chapter will raise all the same questions under a flexible exchange rate arrangement, the prevalent system in the twenty-first century. The extensions of the model will cover the large open economy, a medium-run price adjustment model, and the policy mix under flexible exchange rates.

Summary of Key Concepts

1. With a fixed exchange rate, any policy that impinges on the foreign exchange market equilibrium requires intervention by the central bank to neutralize these effects.
2. The Mundell–Fleming model combines the goods and money market of the *IS–LM* model with the external balance, *BP=0*, developed in Chapter 17.
3. All three markets (the goods, money, and foreign exchange market) must clear for the economy to be in equilibrium.
4. While fiscal policy can have a lasting effect on output, monetary policy can only have a temporary effect under fixed exchange rates.
5. The higher the degree of capital mobility, the more effective fiscal policy will be.
6. The greater the degree of capital mobility, the faster the adjustment of the economy takes place.
7. If a country chooses to use devaluation as a means to stimulate its economy, the process will involve an intervention in the foreign exchange market followed by an adjustment in the money supply. The devalued exchange rate improves the trade balance, and the increase in the money supply stimulates the economy.
8. A devaluation can be used either to acquire a competitive edge or to acknowledge the fact that a currency may be too strong, causing chronic balance-of-payments deficits that are not sustainable.
9. If a country wishes to achieve full employment (internal balance) at the same time as external balance (*BP=0*) using two policy instruments, monetary and fiscal policies, it must assign a specific policy to a specific target to be successful.

CASE STUDY I

The Petrodollar Peg
From *The Economist* print edition, Dec 7, 2006

America should worry more about fixed exchange rates in the Gulf than the gently rising Chinese yuan

American politicians and businessmen view China's undervalued exchange rate and its huge current-account surplus as the main cause of America's vast deficit. Thus next week a high-powered delegation led by Henry Paulson, America's treasury secretary, will fly to Beijing to persuade China to take measures to reduce its surplus. But are they heading to the right place? At the global level, the biggest counterpart to America's deficit is the combined surpluses of the oil-exporting emerging economies. They are expected to run a total current-account surplus of some $500 billion this year, dwarfing China's likely surplus of $200 billion.

Counting only the Middle East oil exporters, the surplus has surged from $30 billion in 2002 to an estimated $280 billion this year. One reason why this gets much less attention than the smaller $160 billion increase in China is that only a fraction of it has gone into official reserves, which are publicly reported. Most of it is stashed in government oil-stabilisation or investment funds, such as the Abu Dhabi Investment Authority, which are much more secretive than the People's Bank of China – but which probably hold just as many dollar assets.

One big difference is that China is now allowing the yuan to rise against the dollar. The exchange rate is up by an annual rate of almost 7% since September. In contrast, the six members of the Gulf Co-operation Council, or GCC (Saudi Arabia, United Arab Emirates, Kuwait, Bahrain, Oman and Qatar), which account for virtually all of the Middle East's surplus, still peg their currencies firmly to the dollar. This is partly in preparation for the GCC's plan to adopt a single currency by 2010. But the bizarre result is that over the past four years of soaring oil prices, their real trade-weighted exchange rates have fallen.

The Gulf economies are running an average current-account surplus of 30% of their GDP, well in excess of China's surplus of 8 percent. Oil exporters cannot spend their windfall overnight and it makes sense for them to run a surplus when oil prices rise, as a buffer for when oil prices fall. Even so, one can have too much of a good thing.

It might be best for the Gulf states as well as the world economy if they abandoned their dollar pegs and shifted to some sort of currency basket. A more flexible exchange-rate regime would allow them to regain control of their monetary policies and so cool down their overheating economies. By pegging their exchange rates to the dollar, they have had to adopt America's monetary policy, leaving real interest rates too low (often negative) for such fast-growing economies. Credit is growing too rapidly, inflation is rising and the prices of assets, especially property in places such as Dubai, have exploded.

Official price indices almost certainly understate inflation. According to government figures, prices are rising in the UAE at an annual rate of 7%, but independent estimates put it at 15%. The dollar's slide against other major currencies is pushing up the price of imported goods. Only 10% of the GCC's imports come from America (compared with one-third each from Europe and Asia), so from a trade-weighted point of view, the dollar peg makes no sense.

In theory, a higher oil price should imply a rise in oil exporters' real exchange rates; and it is better if this occurs through a rise in the nominal rate rather than higher inflation. The main argument against allowing the exchange rate to rise is that it would harm the competitiveness of the non-oil sector in economies that need to diversify. However, pegging to the dollar has not always been a boon to the economies as a whole. When the dollar strengthened in the late 1990s, non-oil industries were squeezed at the same time that the price of crude was sliding.

This is another reason why pegging to a trade-weighted basket would make much more sense.

Oiling the world's wheels

Brad Setser, an economist at Roubini Global Economics, a research firm, argues that the dollar pegs of the Gulf states are also preventing some necessary rebalancing in the world economy. The recent depreciation of their trade-weighted currencies has raised the price of foreign goods and thus may be one reason why the increase in their imports has been unusually weak relative to the increase in exports. If, as seems likely, the dollar continues to fall, it will further drag down their currencies and thus keep external imbalances large.

A fully floating exchange rate would lead to too much volatility, but a bit more flexibility could usefully help oil exporters to adjust to fluctuations in oil prices. A trade-weighted basket, in which the euro had a large weight, would help to stabilise the real exchange rate of the GCC countries and so protect their competitiveness. It still would not ensure that oil exporters' currencies moved correctly in line with the oil price, however.

Some economists have therefore suggested that oil exporters should link their currencies in some way to the oil price. Currencies would rise when oil prices are high and fall when prices were weak. This would help to boost countries' external purchasing power and hence their imports when oil prices boom. It would also help to smooth the local currency value of oil revenues and hence government income, helping to avoid big deficits in bad times and huge surpluses in good times.

Oil exporters argue that they peg to the dollar because oil is priced in dollars and they want to avoid exchange-rate risk. But exchange-rate stability does not guarantee economic stability. On the contrary, a more flexible currency would allow economies to manage oil-price shocks better.

However, a rise in petro-currencies would not be a cure by itself for America's deficit (nor, for that matter, is a dearer Chinese yuan). The main solution to global rebalancing is for America to save more and for surplus countries, including both the oil exporters and China, to spend more. A rise in oil exporters' currencies could play a part in that.

CASE STUDY QUESTIONS

1. What kind of exchange rate regime have the six members of the Gulf Cooperation Council (GCC) adopted?

2. What is the state of their current account? How does it compare to China's? In what form are their foreign assets and how are they held?

3. What is the impact of the GCC's exchange rate regime on each country's monetary policy? Why is the GCC interest rate "too low" and what effect does this low interest rate have on their economies? Comment on the resulting imbalances and the effect on their real exchange rate.

4. Explain the downside for the GCC in moving to a fully floating exchange rate.

CASE STUDY II

Don't Revalue the Yuan
By Ronald McKinnon
Wall Street Journal, June 27, 2003

Treasury Secretary John Snow recently raised eyebrows when he suggested that "the Chinese government is interested in moving toward market-based, flexible exchange rates," and Washington would support such a move. His June 16 remarks caused a stir in the foreign exchange markets, and probably accelerated the conversion into yuan of privately held dollar assets in China – thus increasing the pressure on the yuan to appreciate from its current rate of 8.28 to the dollar.

That only goes to show how, with respect, Mr. Snow is wrong and moving to a flexible exchange rate is far from desirable. Under the present circumstances, floating the yuan would lead to repetitive appreciation. If China stops stabilizing the exchange rate, the yuan will float upward without any well defined limit – posing possibly severe domestic deflationary consequences.

Because further appreciations then become more likely, floating could have more serious effects than a one-time appreciation in the yuan. That is evident from the Japanese experience. From the 1970s through to the mid 1990s, a series of appreciations in the yen sent the Japanese economy into a deflationary tailspin and zero interest-rate liquidity trap, from which it has yet to recover.

Why would allowing the yuan to float freely lead to repetitive appreciation? China has become an important international creditor, with an ongoing balance of payments surplus from large inflows of foreign direct investment coupled with a small multilateral trade surplus. Because the dollar is the dominant international currency for borrowing and lending, that results in a continual buildup of liquid dollar claims on foreigners – a surprisingly high proportion of which are privately held, outside the direct control of the central government.

These ever-accumulating dollar balances need not disequilibriate the portfolios of Chinese savers holding both dollar and yuan assets as long as the yuan/dollar rate remains fixed within narrow band. That's because a stable exchange rate means Chinese savers will see dollar assets as just as safe as those in yuan.

But once the exchange rate begins to fluctuate (even if the yuan does not immediately appreciate), the dollar assets will look riskier and private holders will begin to dishoard them, forcing an appreciation in the value of the yuan. And this appreciation will repeat itself as China's balance of payments surplus – large inflows of FDI plus small current-account surpluses – continues to produce liquid dollar assets that China's private sector will be less and less willing to hold.

As the appreciation continues, domestic price levels in China – which are now finely balanced between inflation and deflation – will begin to fall. And as China's financial markets begin to anticipate an ever appreciating yuan and falling prices, interest rates will be pushed down to zero, making it impossible for the People's Bank of China to stop the deflation – very much like the trap in which Japan now finds itself.

There's already mounting evidence that China's modest internal interest rates – a deposit rate about 2 percent and a standard loan rate of 5.3 percent – have become too high. As dollars are converted into yuan, the People's Bank of China has been rapidly expanding its domestic monetary base so that the overall supply of new deposits of Chinese households and firms held by the commercial banks now greatly exceeds the demand for new loans. As in Japan, this puts the banks in a perilous position. And with interest rates unable to fall below zero, the room for rate cuts to correct this supply–demand imbalance is very limited.

While many observers ask what the right level for the yuan/dollar exchange rate should be, that's really missing the point. What's far more important than the precise exchange rate – whether it be seven, eight or nine yuan to the dollar – is that it remains stable, eliminating foreign-exchange risk and so making Chinese savers more willing to continue to accumulate an indefinite future stream of dollar assets.

Fortunately, the Chinese government has a lot of credibility invested in the present rate of 8.28 yuan per dollar, which it has now maintained since 1994. And it is important not to squander that credibility by making this central rate more "flexible."

Apart from mercantilist considerations, what is the main analytical argument used by supporters of an appreciation in the yuan? China has had a trade surplus since 1995, except for the first few months of this year when its trade happened to be roughly balanced multilaterally. However, many, if not most, economists believe that China's trade surplus could be reduced and even become negative – if an appreciation in the yuan made Chinese exports more expensive in dollar terms, so that fewer are sold abroad.

But this conventional wisdom is misplaced. China's trade surpluses reflect its surplus savings, just as America's huge ongoing trade deficit reflects the extraordinarily low net savings within the American economy – zero net personal savings and now large government dissaving from extraordinary fiscal deficits. Changing an exchange rate does not change these net savings propensities in any obvious way. However, in a deflationary world, if one country appreciates its currency against all its neighbors, the fall in its domestic-currency prices of tradable goods and services will create a downward deflationary spiral in prices and output with a consequent fall in imports. Thus, there is no predictable effect on China's net trade surplus from appreciating the yuan.

However Mr. Snow could be right if he defines flexibility more narrowly, allowing the market value of the yuan to fluctuate within a narrow soft band around 8.28 yuan to the dollar. This would have the big advantage of devolving the task of clearing of China's international payments to the clearing banks, and away from the People's Bank of China. But just as diamonds are forever, so too should be the central rate of 8.28 yuan to the dollar.

Go to http://www.djreprints.com/licencing/books.html

CASE STUDY QUESTIONS

1. What are McKinnon's arguments against a revaluation of the yuan?

2. Is McKinnon's primary argument based on Chinese or U.S. factors?

3. Why could a narrow revaluation find McKinnon's support?

4. Which part of the Chinese balance of payments is most affected by its exchange rate regime?

5. Outline the relationship between savings and the Chinese balance of payments.

Questions for Study and Review

1. Hong Kong managed to maintain its currency board during the East Asian crisis. During the crisis Hong Kong had severe reserve outflows and then exorbitant interest rates. Use the Mundell–Fleming model to show how that could occur. Start with a balance-of-payments equilibrium. Draw a graph.

2. If a country with a fixed exchange rate has an outstanding reserve loan from the IMF, what does the country need to do to repay it? Draw a graph of the exchange rate market and of the Mundell–Fleming model.

3. Be an economic detective. How could the above country have ever been in need of the reserve loan? Be specific. Use the Mundell–Fleming model and draw a graph.

4. You are a benevolent dictator in a small open economy with a massive government deficit, capital controls, and a large balance-of-payments deficit. Given your fixed exchange rate regime, describe the policies you can use to get the economy back to an internal and external balance. Provide diagrams that show your starting point and your final equilibrium.

5. Countries within the European Economic and Monetary Union have adopted a common currency, the euro, and a common monetary policy dictated by the European Central Bank. Can members raise their output using domestic fiscal and monetary policies? Use graphs to explain both policies.

6. A small country, Pecunia, under a fixed exchange rate regime, has achieved both internal (*IS–LM* intersection) and external balance. Pecunia trades a lot with the rest of the world. Pecunia's central bank does not sterilize, but it fears inflation. In addition, Pecunia only allows limited access to its capital market while its citizens need authorizations to invest abroad. The government plans to use fiscal policy (more specifically government spending) to ease the inflationary pressures on its economy.

   a. Spell out the policy carried out by the government.

   b. Use a graph slowing the *IS–LM–BP* to illustrate the impact of the policy – point *a* is the starting equilibrium. Show the shifts (if any) of the three curves *IS–LM–BP* resulting from the fiscal policy adopted.

   c. Break down the effect into two stages: (i) name the impact of the fiscal policy alone point *b*, (ii) name the final equilibrium point *c*. What can you say about the balance of payments in point *b*? Compare the level of income in *a*, *b*, and *c*.

7. A small country, Cascadia, has initially achieved internal and external balance. International financial capital flows are high but not perfectly mobile. Cascadia commits to a fixed exchange arrangement and defends it through intervention, but it does not sterilize. Cascadia elects a new prime minister who happens to be an excellent economist with an international reputation. As a result financial capital inflows increase dramatically and remain higher.

   a. What shift occurs to the *BP* curve because of the increased capital inflows?

   b. What intervention is necessary to defend the fixed exchange rate?

   c. As a result, how does Cascadia adjust back to external balance? What is the effect on its internal balance?

   d. Show all your results on a *IS–LM–BP* graph.

8. A small country, Alpenstein, has initially achieved both internal and external balance. Alpenstein prohibits international financial capital flows, so *FA=0*. Alpenstein has a fixed exchange rate

regime and defends it through official intervention; it does not sterilize. An exogenous shock occurs: foreign demand for Alpenstein's exports increases.

a. What is the slope of the *BP* curve?

b. What shift(s) occur in the *IS–LM–FE* setup because of the increase in foreign demand for its exports?

c. What intervention is necessary to keep the exchange rate fixed?

d. As a result, how does Alpenstein adjust back to external balance? What is the effect on the internal balance?

e. Show all your results on a *IS–LM–BP* graph.

9. Use the policy mix graph to show how the policy makers can bring an economy with balance-of-payments surpluses and unemployment to a stable level of output at full employment.

References and Suggestions for Further Reading

Argy, V. (1994) *International Macroeconomics: Theory and Policy*, New York: Routledge.

Bank of International Settlements (2001) "Comparing monetary policy operating procedures across the United States, Japan and the euro area," *BIS Papers 9*.

Bofinger, P. (1999) "The Conduct of Monetary Policy by the European Central Bank According to Article 105 of the Treaty versus the Real Economy," Working Paper, University of Würzburg.

Buckman, R. (2003) "Weak Dollar Won't Fix Huge US Trade Deficit," *Wall Street Journal*, May 22.

Buiter, W. H. (1999) "Alice in Euroland," *Journal of Common Market Studies*, 37: 181–209.

Enoch, C. and Gulde, A. (1998) "Are Currency Boards a Cure for All Monetary Problems?," *Finance and Development*, 35/Dec: 40–3.

European Central Bank (1999) "The Stability-Oriented Monetary Policy Strategy of the Eurosystem," *ECB Monthly Bulletin*, Jan: 39–50.

—— (2001) *The Monetary Policy of the ECB*, Frankfurt: ECB.

Fleming, J. M. (1962) "Domestic Financial Policies under Fixed and under Flexible Exchange Rates," *IMF Staff Papers*, 9: 369–79.

Frenkel, J. and Mussa, M. (1987) "The Mundell–Fleming Model a Quarter Century Later," *IMF Staff Papers*, 34: 567–620.

Friedman, M. (1988) "Lessons on Monetary Policy from the 1980s," *Journal of Economic Perspective*, Summer.

Hume, D. (1752) "On the Balance of Trade," reprinted in R. Cooper (ed.), *International Finance: Readings* (1969), Baltimore: Penguin Books.

International Monetary Fund (1996) "Currency Boards Circumscribe Discretionary Monetary Policy," *IMF Survey*, 5.

Issing, O., Gaspar, V., Angeloni, I., and Tristiani, O. (2001) *Monetary Policy in the Euro Area*, Cambridge: Cambridge University Press.

Kenen, P. (1985) "Macroeconomic Theory and Policy: How the Closed Economy Was Opened," in R. Jones and P. Kenen (eds), *Handbook of International Economics*, Amsterdam: North-Holland, II: 625–78.

Krueger, A. (2002) "Crisis Prevention and Resolution: Lessons from Argentina." Speech to National Bureau of Economic Research Conference on "The Argentina Crisis," Cambridge, MA (July 17). Available at http://www.imf.org/external/np/speeches/2002/071702.htm.

Krugman, P. (2000) "Reckonings; The Shadow of Debt," *The New York Times*, November 22.

Moreno, R. (2002) "Learning from Argentina's Crisis," *FRBSF Economic Letter*, Oct 18: 2002–2031.

Mundell, R. A. (1960) "The Monetary Dynamics of International Adjustment under Fixed and Flexible Exchange Rates," *Quarterly Journal of Economics*, 84: 227–57.

—— (1961) "The International Disequilibrium System," *Kyklos*, 14.

—— (1962) "The Appropriate Use of Monetary and Fiscal Policy for Internal and External Stability," *IMF Staff Papers*, 9: 70–7.

—— (1963) "Capital Mobility and Stabilization Policy under Fixed and Flexible Exchange Rates," *Canadian Journal of Economics and Political Science*, 29: 475–85.

—— (1968) *International Economics*, New York: Macmillan.

—— (2001) "The History of the Mundell–Fleming Model: Keynote Speech," *IMF Staff Papers*, 47: 215–27.

Mussa, M. (2002) *Argentina and the Fund: From Triumph to Tragedy*, Policy Analyses in International Economics, 67, Washington, D.C.: Institute for International Economics.

Niehans, J. (1968) "Monetary and Fiscal Policies in Open Economies under Fixed Exchange Rates: An Optimizing Approach," *Journal of Political Economy*, 76: 893–920.

Obstfeld, M., and Rogoff, K. (1995) "The Mirage of Fixed Exchange Rates," *Journal of Economic Perspectives* 9: 73–96.

Person, T. and Svensson, L. (1995) "The Operation and Collapse of Fixed Exchange Rate Regimes," in G. Grossman and K. Rogoff (eds), *Handbook of International Economics*, 3: 1865–1911, Amsterdam: Elsevier.

Semmler, W., Greiner, A., and Zhang W. (2006) *Monetary and Fiscal Policies in the Euro-Area: Macro Modeling, Learning and Empirics*, Heidelberg: Springer Verlag.

Turnovsky, S. J. (1977) *Macroeconomic Analysis and Stabilization Policy*, Cambridge: Cambridge University Press.

Chapter 19

Policy under Flexible Exchange Rates and Extensions of the Mundell–Fleming Model

LEARNING OBJECTIVES

By the end of this chapter you should be able to understand:

- the impact that fixed or flexible exchange rate regimes exert on the economy, according to the Mundell–Fleming model

- under which conditions, monetary and fiscal policies are more or less effective in reaching policy targets (such as full employment)

- the role of capital mobility in enhancing or reducing the effects of fiscal and monetary policy

- how policy can be used in a small open economy to achieve both internal and external balance

- how large open economies interact, and how fiscal and monetary policies then have global repercussions

- how price flexibility in the medium run affects the Mundell–Fleming adjustment mechanism

In the previous chapter, we examined fiscal and monetary policy under fixed exchange rates. The analysis generated an important new result. For a small country under fixed exchange rates, at best monetary policy can only be effective temporarily, that is when the country sterilizes foreign currency reserve flows. Eventually, however, a country must forsake monetary policy when it commits to a fixed exchange rate regime, because sterilization is only feasible as long as the country's foreign currency reserves are not exhausted. Capital mobility was shown to amplify the effect of fiscal policy on output.

A number of major industrialized countries still maintain a fixed exchange rate regime (a list is available in Table 13.1). The alternative to fixed exchange rates is to allow for a free-floating exchange rate, where market forces determine the prices of foreign currencies (for example in the U.S. and Japan). Most industrialized countries are now adhering to a flexible exchange rate regime.

In this chapter, we examine the effects of monetary and fiscal policies under flexible exchange rates. The approach will parallel that of the previous chapter considering the various level of capital mobility and assuming a small-country case. The first extension of the model delves into the situation where two large economies interact with each other. Finally, the assumption of fixed prices is relaxed and we analyze a traditional medium-run adjustment mechanism in the (small) open economy.

Before analyzing the impact of monetary and fiscal policy, let us quickly review the essentials of flexible exchange rate regimes. Recall that there will be excess supply of (or demand for) the domestic currency whenever the balance of payments is not in equilibrium ($BP{\neq}0$). Under flexible exchange rate regimes, central banks do not intervene to uphold the price of the domestic currency. Therefore, any imbalance in the market for foreign exchange results in an immediate change in the price of foreign exchange, relative to domestic currency. This simply says that whenever the balance of payments is not in equilibrium, the exchange rate must adjust, leading to appreciations or depreciations. These changes in the exchange rate continue as long as the balance of payments is not in equilibrium. Whenever equilibrium in the balance of payments is restored, $BP{=}0$, it must also be true that the exchange rate is no longer changing. Indeed in Chapter 17, we defined external balance under flexible exchange rates as a situation where the exchange rate was stable.

MONETARY POLICY UNDER FLEXIBLE EXCHANGE RATES

In the discussion below, the goods and money markets are initially in equilibrium where $BP{=}0$. In fact, with flexible exchange rates, the goods and money market equilibrium (i.e. the IS and LM intersection) always corresponds to external balance, since the exchange rate adjusts continuously to ensure that there is no excess demand for foreign currency, i.e. $BP{=}0$ at all times.

An increase in the money supply lowers the interest rate, as represented by the *rightward shift of the LM curve*. The drop in the interest rate then has two effects:

i. Income increases because capital investment is stimulated by the lower interest rates. This increase in income raises imports, affecting the current account negatively and thus causing a deterioration in the balance of payments.

ii. Financial capital flows out of the country because the return on portfolio investment becomes greater abroad as the domestic interest rate falls. Note that the greater the degree of capital mobility, the larger the capital outflows. Capital outflows also cause a deterioration in the balance of payments.

As both the current account and the financial account decline, the balance of payments that was originally in equilibrium must also turn negative. This balance of payments deficit sets in motion an adjustment in the financial market and in the goods market:

iii. A balance-of-payment deficit generates excess supply of domestic currency. Under fixed exchange rates, the central bank intervenes to offset this excess demand for foreign currency. Under flexible exchange rates, however, the central bank does not intervene in the foreign exchange market; market forces (supply and demand) determine a new price for the foreign currency. Excess demand for the foreign currency results in an increase in its price: the domestic currency thus depreciates. Recall from Chapter 17 that a depreciation of the domestic currency *shifts the BP line down to the right.*

iv. The depreciation improves the current account, since exports become cheaper to foreigners and imports become relatively more expensive for domestic consumers. This translates into greater activity in the domestic goods market. Domestic consumers purchase more domestic goods because they have become relatively cheaper and, for the same reason, foreigners also demand more domestically produced goods. This triggers an increase in the demand for domestic goods and the *IS curve shifts out*[1] *to the right.*

The extent of the *IS* shift depends on the magnitude of the current account improvement resulting from the depreciation. The scale of the depreciation depends on the magnitude of the balance-of-payments imbalance, thus on the volume of financial capital outflows. Therefore, we can state that the larger the capital outflows, the more dramatic is the deterioration in the balance of payments, causing a greater depreciation, and a larger shift in the *IS* curve. Since capital flows seem to be a crucial tenet, we must again examine the effects of different degrees of capital mobility on the effectiveness of monetary policy.

Monetary Policy, Flexible Exchange Rates, and Low Capital Mobility

Initially, the economy is in equilibrium at point *a*, the intersection of the *IS–LM–BP* curves (Figure 19.1). The monetary expansion shifts *LM* out to the right, resulting in a higher level of output and a

---

1 Note that the effect of a depreciation on the goods market is similar to that of a devaluation. This was illustrated in Chapter 17 and again in Chapter 18.

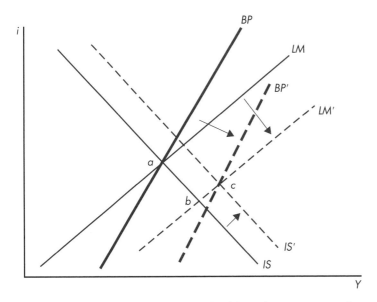

FIGURE 19.1 Monetary Policy under Flexible Exchange Rates and Low Capital Mobility

Expansionary monetary policy shifts *LM* to *LM'*. The economy moves to a higher level of income and a lower interest rate at point *b*. The higher income causes a current account deficit and the lower interest rate triggers capital outflows, resulting in *BP<0*. Excess demand for foreign assets and foreign goods generates excess demand for the foreign currency, raising its price. This depreciation of the domestic currency shifts the *BP* curve to the right and improves the balance of trade triggering an expansion that shifts the *IS* curve to the right too. These effects will happen until the economy regains its external balance, i.e. until the new *IS'* and *LM'* curves intersect at a point *c* where *BP=0* on a new *BP'* curve.

lower rate of interest at b. Both the current and financial accounts deteriorate causing an unambiguous deterioration of the balance of payments. Under low degrees of capital mobility, these deficits are relatively small because the capital outflows are small. The currency depreciates slightly to restore the external balance and the *BP* curve thus shifts to the right. As the exchange rate depreciates, the balance of trade improves and *IS* shifts concurrently to the right. In sum, the two curves, *BP* and *IS*, shift together to the right as the domestic currency depreciates until the economy is in equilibrium again, with *BP=0* happening at a higher level of income at c.

The monetary expansion under low degrees of capital mobility therefore shifts the output from point a to point b where both the current account and the financial account have deteriorated. The necessary depreciation is sufficiently large so that the ensuing improvement in the current account compensates for the capital outflows (the deterioration in the financial account). With low capital mobility, the extent of the needed depreciation does not have to be that large to restore equilibrium in the balance of payments so *IS* does not shift that much to reach the new equilibrium point c where *BP=0*: expansionary monetary policy generates a limited expansion. This is better than no impact: the outcome of expansionary monetary policy under fixed exchange rates with non-sterilization.

Monetary Policy, Flexible Exchange Rates, and High Capital Mobility

Under high degrees of capital mobility, the lower interest rate caused by a monetary expansion triggers larger capital outflows and therefore a larger balance-of-payments deficit at point *b*. A larger depreciation is needed to restore the equilibrium on the foreign exchange market. This implies a larger shift of the *IS* curve since demand for domestic goods increases even more. The greater increase in the demand for goods generates greater expansion in output. In Figure 19.2, we show exactly the same *IS–LM* curves and the same monetary expansion as in Figure 19.1, sending the economy to the same point *b*.

However, in the case of higher capital mobility, the depreciation needed to restore the external balance must be greater, because it must generate a greater current account surplus to compensate for the more extensive capital outflows affecting the financial account. The original expansion due to the increase in the money supply (the shift of *LM*) is the same in both cases as the economy moves from point *a* to point *b*. However the expansion resulting from the depreciation (i.e., the move from *b* to *c*) is larger in the case of high capital mobility. Therefore, under flexible exchange rates, a higher degree of capital mobility enhances the impact of monetary policy on output.

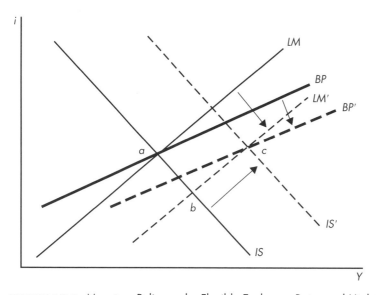

FIGURE 19.2 Monetary Policy under Flexible Exchange Rates and High Capital Mobility

With higher degrees of capital mobility, the *BP* curve is flatter than the *LM* curve. The original monetary expansion sends the economy to *b*, but the adjustment on the foreign exchange market needs be greater to compensate for the greater capital outflows. A larger depreciation generates more expansion and the economy moves to *c*. When comparing the two graphs, Figures 19.1 and 19.2, one can see that the movement from *a* to *b* is exactly the same, but *c* is farther to the right in this graph as *IS* shifts farther out.

Monetary Policy, Flexible Exchange Rates, and Perfect Capital Mobility

The perfect capital mobility case shows how extremely effective monetary policy is in influencing output in the open economy under flexible exchange rates. Under perfect capital mobility, the external balance line *BP* is horizontal: the domestic equilibrium interest rate cannot deviate from the interest rate in the rest of the world, because capital would immediately flow (in or out) until domestic returns equate foreign returns again. Since we are considering a small country, the *BP* curve is horizontal at the world interest rate, i^*. This means that the *BP* curve *does not shift* as a result of the depreciation. As soon as the balance of payments is turning to a deficit as a result of the monetary expansion, the exchange rate depreciates sharply because of massive capital outflows. This depreciation immediately sets off increased demand for domestic goods (from the residents buying import-substitutes and from the foreigners). The *IS* shifts out along with the *LM* curve to maintain the *IS–LM–BP* equilibrium, and this expansion takes place without any increase in the interest rate. When the *LM* curve reaches it final destination (determined by the size of the increase in the money supply), the *IS* curve will also stop shifting rightward.

As any increase in the money supply depresses the interest rate, the exchange rate needs to depreciate enough to trigger an increase in the money demand that matches the increase in the money supply so that the interest rate remains constant at the world interest, i^*. The mechanism works through the depreciation resulting in an increase in the current account that stimulates income and thus boosts the demand for money as the economy moves from point *a* to point *c* along the *BP* curve.

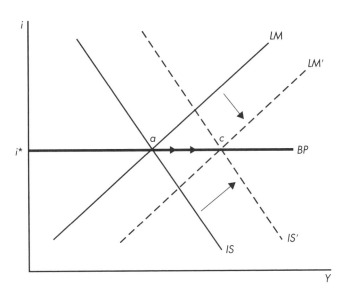

FIGURE 19.3 Monetary Policy under Flexible Exchange Rates and Perfect Capital Mobility

In this case, as soon as the domestic interest rate falls below the world interest rate, i^*, infinite capital outflows force a depreciation and thus the current account improves, triggering an expansion. So the *IS* and the *LM* curves shift together tracing the *BP* curve until the money supply has reached its new level. The economy experiences a substantial expansion from point *a* to point *c*.

The important insight is that higher degrees of capital mobility increase the effectiveness of monetary policy under flexible exchange rates. Note that this result is diametrically opposed to our finding under fixed exchange rates, where not only was monetary policy eventually ineffective in increasing output, but the speed at which the monetary expansion would be wiped away increased with a higher level of capital mobility. We thus find that a country faces an important policy trade-off when it chooses its exchange rate regime.

Canadian Monetary Policy in Late Nineties

The Canadian dollar depreciated sharply in mid-1998, leading the Bank of Canada to raise interest rates by a full percentage point to defend the currency. By early 1999, the recovery of the Canadian dollar to almost U.S. $0.70 was seen as threatening to export growth as well as to the continued growth of the economy. The Bank of Canada reduced interest rates by 25 basis points on May 4 1999, and announced that it was doing so because of the recent appreciation of the Canadian dollar. The Canadian dollar depreciated by 30 basis points in one day, so the Bank of Canada appears to have produced exactly the impact it wished. The flexible exchange rate allowed the Bank of Canada to pursue this course of action that would have been impossible with a fixed parity.

Source: Adapted from *The Wall Street Journal*, May 5, 1999, p. A–8.

In the previous chapter, we found that under fixed exchange rates, monetary policy was ineffective in raising output under any level of capital mobility. However, under fixed exchange rates, fiscal policy was effective, and its impact increased with the degree of capital mobility. It is time for us to examine how fiscal policy fares with flexible exchange rates.

FISCAL POLICY UNDER FLEXIBLE EXCHANGE RATES

An increase in government spending raises income and *shifts the IS curve to the right* as shown in Figure 19.4. This increase in income raises the transaction demand for money, driving up the interest rate. In addition, the increase in income stimulates the demand for imports, causing the current account to deteriorate. Finally, the higher interest rate generates capital inflows.

The crucial question is what happens to the balance of payments. If it improves, the domestic currency will appreciate; if it declines, the domestic currency will lose in value. Whether the balance of payments improves or declines depends on the relative magnitudes of the changes in the current and financial accounts. We encountered the same question in the case of fiscal policy with fixed exchange rates in Chapter 18. Again we must analyze the forces that determine these relative magnitudes to find out whether capital flows offset the changes in the trade imbalance or not. We therefore discuss again the same three cases, representing different levels of capital mobility.

Fiscal Policy, Flexible Exchange Rates, and Low Capital Mobility

If the increase in the interest rate generates only modest capital inflows, these inflows are insufficient to finance the current account deficit. As a result, the balance of payments deteriorates; there is excess demand for foreign currency, and, in the absence of central bank intervention, the price of the foreign currency rises: the domestic currency depreciates. The depreciation *shifts the BP to the right* and the goods market improves also, since the depreciation improves net exports. Therefore, *the IS curve shifts again rightward* along with the external balance line, *BP*, until a new equilibrium is reached where *IS–LM–BP* intersect.

Figure 19.4 shows this adjustment, highlighting that the *IS* curve shifts out not just once, but twice, in the same direction: the first shift is due to the expansionary fiscal policy, and the second shift is due to the improvement in the trade deficit brought about by the depreciation. Note that the lower the degree of capital mobility, the greater is the depreciation required to restore equilibrium in the balance of payments.

Under flexible exchange rates and low capital mobility, the expansionary impact of fiscal policy is therefore enhanced by a subsequent depreciation. Under fixed exchange rates, the impact of expansionary fiscal policy increased with capital mobility; in the next section, we examine whether this is also the case under flexible exchange rates.

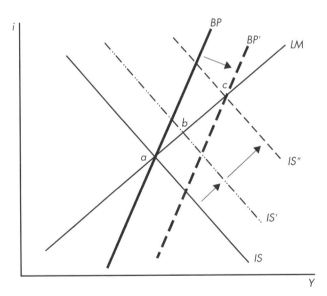

FIGURE 19.4 Fiscal Policy under Flexible Exchange Rates and Low Capital Mobility

Initially, the expansionary fiscal policy sends the *IS* curve to *IS'*. The new equilibrium of the economy (*IS'–LM*) at *b* corresponds to a deficit in the balance of payments (it is below the original *BP* curve) because the improvement in the financial account is not sufficient to offset the deterioration in the current account. A depreciation will take place to restore the external balance. As usual, the depreciation involves an improvement in the current account so both the *BP* and the *IS* curves shift to the right until they both intersect on the *LM* curve at *c* where the financial, goods, and currency markets are in equilibrium. Note that the *LM* curve stays put while the *IS* curve shifts twice.

Fiscal Policy, Flexible Exchange Rates, and High Capital Mobility

When capital flows are highly sensitive to domestic interest rate movements, the capital inflows caused by a fiscal expansion can be huge. With high capital mobility, these capital inflows are larger than the deterioration in the current account: the overall impact results in a balance of payments surplus (the new equilibrium of the economy at point b is above the original BP curve, so $BP>0$).[2] With a balance of payments surplus, there is excess demand for the domestic currency and excess supply for foreign currency as investors shift their financial assets into the domestic economy, selling their foreign currency investment. This drives down the price of foreign currency: the domestic currency appreciates.

The appreciation of the domestic currency *shifts the BP and the IS curves back* (to be precise, the *IS* shifts southwest and the *BP* northwest). The *IS* shifts back because the appreciation hurts domestic exports and creates a flood of foreign imports, reducing the amount of goods produced at home. The new equilibrium is achieved at point c; the appreciation has wiped away part of the improvement in income initially achieved by the increase in government spending.

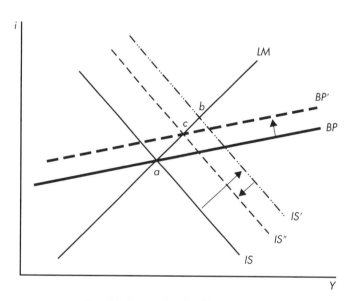

FIGURE 19.5 Fiscal Policy under Flexible Exchange Rates and High Capital Mobility

Expansionary fiscal policy shifts the *IS* curve to *IS′* and the economy moves from a to b. Point b is above the *BP* line and corresponds to $BP>0$: at b, the capital inflows induced by the increase in the interest rate more than compensate for the deterioration in the balance of trade. The external balance is in disequilibrium causing an appreciation that shifts the *BP* curve to the left (northwest). The increase in the value of the domestic currency has adverse effects on trade: the *IS* shifts back wiping away part of the fiscal expansion. A new *IS″–LM–BP′* equilibrium is reached in c. In this case, *IS* also shifts twice, but in opposite directions.

---

2 Again this happens because we depict high capital mobility as a situation where *BP* is flatter than *LM*.

It has become clear that increases in the degree of capital mobility have undesirable effects on the effectiveness of fiscal policy with flexible exchange rates. The ensuing appreciation of the currency has a negative impact on the current account, leading to a reduction in output. Although the expansion is not as large as with low capital mobility, some expansion still take place. The next query then is whether fiscal policy has any effect under perfect capital mobility.

Fiscal Policy, Flexible Exchange Rates, and Perfect Capital Mobility

With perfect capital mobility, the interest rate of a small economy cannot deviate from the world interest rates. Arbitrage immediately leads to massive capital flows, so that the returns in the two countries are equalized. With perfect capital mobility, a small economy has no choice but to adopt the world interest rate.

As soon as the government starts raising the level of fiscal spending, the domestic interest rate tends to rise. The slightest differential from the world interest rate generates massive capital inflows, as all the investors reshuffle their portfolio into the currency with higher returns, the domestic currency. This creates a massive demand for the domestic currency resulting in its immediate sharp appreciation until interest parity is restored. This forces the *IS* curve back into its original position where the domestic interest rate is equal to the world interest rate.

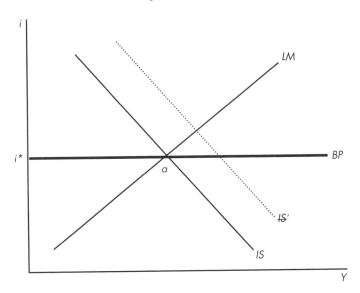

FIGURE 19.6 Fiscal Policy under Flexible Exchange Rates and Perfect Capital Mobility

The horizontal *BP* line cannot shift away from the world interest rate *i**. This means that the *IS–LM–BP* equilibrium can only take place at the world interest rate *i**. The slightest shift of the *IS* curve resulting from fiscal policy creates a wedge between the domestic and the world interest rates. This is not sustainable as infinitely large capital flows are triggered heralding an appreciation/depreciation that sends the *IS* curve straight back to its initial position. Basically, the *IS* curve cannot shift and the dotted *IS'* curve above cannot exist. Fiscal policy is powerless with perfect capital mobility.

Perfect capital mobility renders fiscal policy totally ineffective. The domestic interest rate cannot diverge from the world interest rate without creating huge capital flows with dire consequences on the exchange rate. The effect on the trade balance is immediate, negating the impact of the fiscal policy. With flexible exchange rate and full capital mobility, the *IS* curve cannot shift: it is stuck at its original position corresponding to the world interest rate.

As the degree of capital mobility reaches the highest levels, the policy makers in a small economy will find that fiscal policy is utterly unsuccessful in stimulating or slowing down the economy. All it will do is generate massive capital flows that impose dramatic adjustments in the exchange rate and in the trade balance.

Comparing Monetary and Fiscal Policy

With flexible exchange rates, any balance-of-payments imbalance causes exchange rate movements that have an immediate effect on the goods market through imports and exports. A depreciation is expansionary and shifts the *IS* curve to the right. An appreciation has the opposite effect. In addition, fiscal and monetary policies influence the interest rate in opposite directions, triggering capital flows that affect the financial account and consequently the balance of payments. How large the balance-of-payments imbalances are in response to monetary and fiscal policy under flexible exchange rates depends on the degree of capital mobility.

Expansionary monetary policy worsens both the current account, since income increases, and the financial account, since the interest rate drops. As the degree of capital mobility increases, the adverse impact on the financial account escalates, leading to larger balance of payments deteriorations. The ensuing depreciation generates large increases in domestic income.

Expansionary fiscal policy generates a current account deficit that can be financed by capital inflows. The more capital flows into the country, the smaller the balance-of-payments deficit, the smaller the size of the ensuing depreciation needed to restore equilibrium. When capital mobility is high, the balance of payments turns into surpluses causing an appreciation. Clearly a smaller depreciation, or worse an appreciation, has weak expansionary effect, or even initiates a contraction.

In conclusion, monetary policy is enhanced by higher capital mobility, but fiscal policy is handicapped.

Drawback of Policy-Making under Flexible Exchange Rates: Too Much Exchange Rate Volatility?

A flexible exchange rate regime can be appealing to central banks since it allows for effective monetary policy to achieve specific domestic objectives without having to worry about maintaining the exchange rate or intervening in the foreign exchange market. But would it be reasonable for central banks to worry about the appreciations or depreciations associated with domestically focused monetary policy?

Frequent movements in exchange rates are not welcomed by financial markets; they introduce uncertainties and affect both the trade in goods and international investments. Large countries, especially when they have a relatively small external sector, as in the case of the U.S., may not care. In August 2007, the chairman of the U.S. Federal Reserve Bank slashed the interest rate to stimulate the economy without being too concerned about the resulting impact on the dollar. The dollar soon reached record lows against its European and Asian counterparts.

In Europe, the European Central Bank (ECB) has adopted a policy of "benign neglect" with respect to the euro. The ECB's stated objective is keep inflation in check; it is *not* to maintain a stable price of foreign currency. Such a policy stance may not be desirable for countries whose economies consist of large export sectors, such as Germany. In fact, the sharp appreciation of the dollar in August 2007 hurt Germany growth as shown by the OECD's September 2007 downward revisions for expected German GDP growth in 2008.

Small countries, like Thailand, often rely to a large degree on trade-oriented growth and are therefore reluctant to undertake policy changes that imply large or frequent movements in exchange rates. Moreover, they believe that they have to protect themselves from severe depreciation in the trade partners' currency. Even if these countries are formally adhering to a flexible exchange rate regime, their central bank will carry out intervention operations to smooth out the impact of any domestic policy on the exchange rate. These informal exchange rate regimes are called *managed floats* or *dirty floats*.

Monetary Policy Works Better under Flexible Exchange Rates while Fiscal Policy is More Effective under Fixed Exchange Rates

When we compare the policies under different exchange rate regimes, we find that monetary policy is the least effective under fixed exchange rates, and fiscal policy the least effective with flexible exchange rates (although fiscal policy is moderately expansionary with lower levels of capital mobility). There is a very simple reason for this. With fixed exchange rates, the central bank is totally absorbed by the task of upholding the peg. The central bank cannot use changes in the money supply for domestic expansion/contraction. On the other hand, fiscal policy is free of constraints and can be used for domestic goals. With flexible exchange, the rationale is subtler as the market forces determine the price of foreign currency. Any imbalance in the foreign currency market, caused by monetary or fiscal policy, triggers a depreciation or an appreciation that will affect the balance of trade and shift the *IS* curve. As the *IS* curve is not stable, the policy maker cannot use fiscal policy very effectively to stimulate or slow down the economy. However nothing hinders the central bank, when using monetary policy for domestic purposes.

Up to now the analyses have been carried out in the context of a small economy and we found that, in the case of full capital mobility, a small country has no choice, but to put up with the world interest rate. This is not always an appealing choice and, as a result, small countries are often reluctant to lift all their capital controls. It will be interesting to see, however, how large countries fare. For instance, the U.S. and the U.K. have allowed very high levels of capital mobility for a long time. Why are these large economies so willing to do away with capital controls, while smaller countries often are reluctant to do so? Let us move forward and examine fiscal and monetary policy in large countries, i.e. countries large enough to affect the world interest rate.

TABLE 19.1 Summary Impact of Monetary and Fiscal Policy under Flexible Exchange Rates

	K mobility	Effect on	LM	IS	BP line	Y	i	CA	FA	BP
Monetary Expansion	Low or high	Immediate	Shifts right	–	–	↑	↓	↓	↓	↓
		Depreciation	–	Shifts right	Shifts right	↑	↑	↑	↑	↑
		Overall	Right of original	Right of original	Right of original	↑	↓	↑	↓	BP=0
	Perfect	Immediate and depreciation	Shifts right	Shifts right	–	↑	–	↑	↓	BP=0
		Overall	Right of original	Right of original	–	↑	–	↑	↓	BP=0
Fiscal Expansion	Low	Immediate	–	Shifts right	–	↑	↑	↓	↑	↓
		Depreciation	–	Shifts right	Shifts right	↑	↑	↑	↑	↑
		Overall	–	Right of original	Right of original	↑	↑	↓	↑	BP=0
	High	Immediate	–	Shifts right	–	↑	↑	↓	↑	↑
		Appreciation	–	Shifts left	Shifts left	↓	↓	↓	↓	↓
		Overall	Right of original	Right of original	–	↑	↑	↓	↑	BP=0
	Perfect	Immediate and appreciation	–	Cannot shift	–	No change				BP=0

THE LARGE OPEN ECONOMY UNDER FLEXIBLE EXCHANGE RATES

If we want to analyze a model of the modern economy where countries interact with each other through their external sector, it is more realistic to consider a situation where flexible exchange rates and full capital mobility are the norm. Think of it as the interaction between the U.S. and the European Monetary Union (EMU) area (the fifteen European countries that have adopted the euro as their currency), or the interaction between the U.S. and Japan.

Our economy is "large" in the sense that it experiences feedbacks or **repercussions** on the goods market as domestic imports affect foreign income and hence domestic exports. In addition, the economy is "large" in the sense that there exist feedback effects through international capital flows, such that the economy can affect the level of the world interest rates. These feedbacks rely on three transmission channels: exchange rate movements, foreign reserve flows, and trade flows.[3]

Our discussion focuses on *large* open economies with *perfect* capital mobility because it captures the situation of some of the largest economies in the global market place.[4] Perfect capital mobility implies perfect integration of world capital markets; it is also the easiest and most effective way to highlight the global policy feedbacks. To simplify things even further, we assume that the world consists only of *two* large economies. Again the model is easily extended to include any number of large countries, but the graphical representation would be problematic.

The assumption of two large open economies simplifies the analysis substantially: we know that whenever the domestic economy is running a current account deficit, the foreign economy (or the rest of the world) must run a current account surplus of the same magnitude. Similarly a financial account surplus in one country translates into a financial account deficit of the same magnitude for the partner's economy. This holds for each category of the balance of payments, and indeed for the balance of payments itself. We now investigate the impact of monetary and fiscal policy and continue to assume *fixed prices* as in the previous chapters. As usual, we start with current account, financial account, and thus balance of payments equal to zero (obviously in both countries).

Monetary Policy with Perfect Capital Mobility: Two Large Open Economies

Monetary policy has been shown to have a strong positive impact on output in the small open economy with flexible exchange rates. The increase in the money supply lowers the interest rate and stimulates output. The decline in the interest rate leads to capital outflows and the increase in output leads to a trade deficit. The shift of the *LM* curve, as indicated in Figure 19.7a, leads to a deterioration in the current account as well as in the financial account, unambiguously causing a balance of payments deficit, *BP<0*.

As we analyze the global economy, we must ask ourselves who the beneficiary of these capital outflows is. Another country must be getting capital inflows, i.e. an increase in its financial account, when the domestic economy is experiencing capital outflows. In a two-country world (domestic and foreign), it is obviously the foreign economy that is receiving the capital flows. Equivalently, if the domestic economy is experiencing a deterioration in its current account, this means that the foreign economy is exporting more to the domestic economy and importing less from it: this should register as an improvement in the foreign economy's current account. We start with a balance-of-payments

---

3 In Chapter 15, we studied these repercussions in the open-economy model with no capital mobility and derived a specific multiplier for the large open economy.

4 Obviously, perfect capital mobility is a utopia. For instance, the U.S. impose capital controls on international capital flows with various countries, e.g. Iran for political reasons. For the sake of the exposition, it is easier to assume the existence of perfect capital mobility. Note that it is possible to extend the model in the case of smaller degrees of capital mobility, using the mechanics and insights from the small open-economy Mundell–Fleming model.

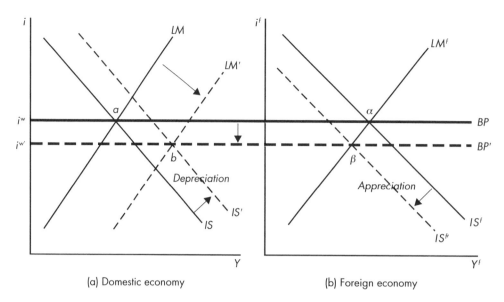

FIGURE 19.7 Monetary Policy in Two Large Open Economies with Perfect Capital Mobility

The increase in the money supply occurs in the domestic economy *only*: *LM* starts to shift, putting downward pressures on the interest rate. With perfect capital mobility, an immediate depreciation occurs keeping the parity between the interest rates. The depreciation further stimulates the domestic economy through an improvement in the current account. For the foreign economy, this translates into an appreciation and a deterioration of their current account: the result is a contraction and *IS^f* shifts back. This puts downward pressures on the interest rate at the same time as the depreciation in the domestic economy puts upward pressures on the interest rate. Overall the world interest drops to a new common level in *i$^{w'}$*. The domestic economy moves from *a* to *b* and the foreign economy from *α* to *β*. The monetary expansion in the domestic economy allows the interest rate to converge to a common lower level where both economies are in equilibrium.

equilibrium – at point *a* for the domestic economy on the left graph and at point *α* for the foreign economy on the right graph – the common or world interest rate, *i^w*, indicates the level of the original common horizontal *BP* line (Figure 19.7). The monetary expansion in the domestic economy puts downward pressures on its interest rate and stimulates its output; as a result, the financial account deteriorates and so does the trade balance. This affects the external sectors of the two economies in an opposite manner: an overall worsening of the balance of payments in the domestic economy is matched by an overall improvement in the foreign economy as *ΔFA+ΔCA<0* and *ΔFA^f+ΔCA^f>0*, so *BP<0* and *BP^f>0* (we denote foreign variables with "*^{f}*").

The balance-of-payment deficit in the domestic economy causes a depreciation of the domestic currency, while the balance-of-payment surplus abroad causes an appreciation of the foreign currency. The depreciation in the domestic economy shifts the *IS* curve out (northeast). In the foreign country, the depreciation of the domestic currency, corresponding to an appreciation of their own currency, shifts the *IS^f* curve back as the foreign economy's trade balance deteriorates.

The domestic expansion, generated by the depreciation of the domestic currency, puts upward pressures on the domestic interest rate.[5] In the foreign economy, the contraction, due to the decline

---

5 Note that the domestic interest rate would have dropped to a lower level where the *IS* and the new *LM'* lines intersect, but with perfect capital mobility, everything happens together and the domestic interest rate does not fall below *i^w*.

in exports, causes a fall in the foreign interest rate. The exchange rate will adjust until the interest rates in the two economies are equalized. At this point, capital stops flowing from the domestic economy to the foreign economy and the two economies have reached their respective new *IS–LM–BP* equilibria at a lower common rate of interest $i^{w'}$. The new external balance line *BP'*, horizontal at $i^{w'}<i^w$, lies below the original one.

Note that the domestic expansion is not as extensive as in the small-country case, since the domestic economy is large enough to actually lower the world interest rate; therefore domestic capital outflows are smaller than in the small economy and so is the current account improvement. More importantly, we observe that the domestic economy's monetary expansion causes a *contraction* in the trade partner's economy; the foreign economy experiences excess demand for its currency as capital is flowing into its economy to take advantage of its higher interest rate. This excess demand translates into the appreciation of the foreign currency that hurts exports and increases imports, reducing aggregate demand in the goods market.

Sometimes such policies are called **beggar thy neighbor** policies, because the domestic economy is expanding at the cost of a contraction in the foreign economy. On the other hand, the increase in the domestic money supply succeeded in *lowering* the world interest rate – a good thing per se! Let us investigate what happens in the case of a fiscal expansion in the domestic economy.

Implications of the Credit Squeeze in the Summer of 2007

The U.S., the U.K., and the European Monetary Union[6] are large open economies adhering to flexible exchange rate regimes (the U.S. dollar, the British pound, and the euro are freely floating with respect to each other). Capital mobility between these economies is close to perfect: indeed interest rates between the countries are not fully equalized, mainly due to different risks, taxation, and exchange rate expectations.

When the U.S. Federal Reserve Bank undertook a surprisingly large cut in its prime rate from 5.25 to 4.75 percent on September 18, 2007, to address liquidity shortages in the U.S. housing market, the dollar depreciated immediately to record lows against the pound and the euro. European central banks reacted immediately. Wary that inflation could pick up, the Bank of England had been gradually raising its interest rate to 5.75 percent; their reaction was to stop increasing their rate and leave it at 5.75. Likewise, the ECB had planned on a rate increase, but they held their rate at 4 percent although the President of the ECB, Jean-Claude Trichet, still very concerned about inflationary pressures, did not dismiss the possibilities of further rate hikes. Overall, by refraining from hiking up their own interest rate, the European central banks reacted to the U.S. policy without waiting for the impact of the repercussions to take place. They weighted the risk of inflation in their own economy against the handicap of trading against a very weak dollar and decided that they should not carry policies that would make their own currency even stronger. As an export-dependent region, a strong euro or a strong pound could seriously hurt Western European growth.

---

6 As the members of the European Monetary Union share a currency, the euro, they are considered as one large open economy.

Fiscal Policy with Perfect Capital Mobility: Two Large Open Economies

In the small open-economy model with perfect capital mobility, fiscal policy was shown to be totally ineffective in raising output. As discussed in the previous chapter, an increase in government spending raises the domestic interest rate, but as soon as the interest rate exceeds the world interest rate, massive capital inflows overwhelm the domestic economy. These inflows trigger a large appreciation of the currency, shrinking the trade balance to such an extent that the economy returns to its original equilibrium. Any equilibrium of the small open economy with perfect capital mobility *must* occur along the original, horizontal *BP* line at the given world interest rate.

With two large countries representing the world, the story is slightly different. We just found out in the case of monetary policy that the world interest rate is actually determined by the interactions between these two economies. So if one country carries out a policy that impinges on the domestic interest rate, the world interest rate will be affected, since it is determined by the equilibrium in both countries' financial markets.

Figure 19.8a shows how a fiscal expansion in the domestic economy shifts the *IS* curve out towards *IS'*. As the domestic economy carries out a policy that puts upward pressures on its interest rate, the world interest rate, that is determined as some sort of average in the two countries' financial markets,[7] will be affected, and, in this case, will rise: this will generate a new *BP* line lying above the original one. The mechanism is straightforward – as soon as the interest rate in the domestic economy rises above the foreign rate, the domestic economy experiences large capital inflows. The domestic currency appreciates causing a decline in the domestic trade balance until the new equilibrium is reached at point *b*.

These large capital inflows into the domestic economy must originate somewhere. The foreign economy is the source: investors attempt to sell their investments in the foreign economy and buy investments in the domestic economy to take advantage of (temporarily) higher returns. This creates excess supply of the foreign currency, leading to its depreciation. The foreign balance of trade improves and the (foreign) *IS^f* curve shifts to *IS$^{f'}$*. The improvement in the foreign goods market continues as long as the foreign currency depreciates, i.e. as long as the interest rate in the two countries diverges. The adjustment process stops when both economies are in equilibrium at the new world interest rate, $i^{w'}$.

Note that the entire adjustment hinges on the fact that the large open economy is able to raise the *world* interest rate via a domestic fiscal expansion. While a monetary expansion in a large country has contractionary impacts on the partners, a fiscal expansion has a positive impact on the output of the trading partners.

When we examined the large open economy in Chapter 15 (assuming fixed exchange rates and no capital mobility), we acknowledged that countries might have different economic objectives. One economy could be overheating and wishing for a contraction while another economy is in a slump

---

7 With perfect capital mobility, the financial markets of the two countries are perfectly integrated and this is where the world interest rate is determined. So it is obvious that anything happening in either (large) domestic market will impact on the world interest rate.

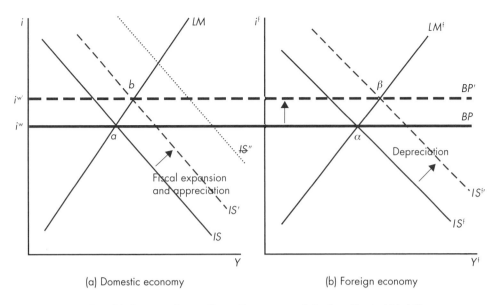

(a) Domestic economy   (b) Foreign economy

FIGURE 19.8 Fiscal Policy in a Large Open Economy with Perfect Capital Mobility

The fiscal expansion should send the domestic economy to *IS"*, but this can't happen because the resulting upward pressures on the interest rate trigger an immediate appreciation of the currency. The *IS"* curve does not exist and we cannot disentangle the expansionary fiscal effect from the resulting immediate and contractionary appreciation. The reason why the domestic economy can expand is due to the fact that the domestic appreciation translates into a foreign depreciation that stimulates the economy of the trade partner. There are consequently upward pressures on the foreign interest rate. The appreciation of the domestic currency combined with the depreciation on the foreign currency results in a higher interest rate, giving the domestic economy room for some expansion while also having expansionary effects on the foreign economy.

and hopes for stimulation. It is clear that when one large economy makes a domestic policy choice purely geared to fixing some specific domestic problem, the repercussions of the policy may or may not be welcomed by the partners. As an example, if the U.S. increases government spending to stimulate its economy when Europe is beset by inflation fears, Europeans will be unhappy; they would rather see the U.S. increase money supply.

We are hinting here that an expansion is not necessarily the ultimate goal for the policy makers. In fact, a more reasonable approach is to be equally concerned about both internal and external balance. We extend the approach to internal and external balance developed in the last chapter to the flexible exchange rate case in the appendix to this chapter.

Throughout this chapter and the last chapter, it seems that there was always a way to restore equilibrium in the economy without a change in prices. Basically, we were focusing on short-run models. However, given time, prices do change and would also contribute to the adjustment mechanisms. We should investigate these medium-run effects.

PRICE ADJUSTMENT IN THE MUNDELL–FLEMING MODEL

Until now, we have kept prices constant: not because we believe prices are constant in the world, but because it simplified our analysis. However we may believe that prices are fully flexible or that prices are sticky in the short-run, but will eventually change, given time. Since we have now presented a fully specified model of the open economy and analyzed the real effects of economic policies on the economy, it is time to relax our fixed-price assumption. When prices are flexible, government policies, whether changes in the nominal money supply or in government spending, affect the price level. This happens through an aggregate supply–aggregate demand mechanism. So, if we allow prices to fluctuate, we must develop a new comprehensive model for the open economy.

Effect of a One-time Increase in Prices on the Mundell–Fleming Model

Since the Mundell–Fleming model is basically an extension of the *IS–LM* model, it can be easily modified (just like the *IS–LM* model) to investigate the effect of fiscal or monetary policy when price changes are also considered in the adjustment. Prices in the basic *IS–LM* model enter via the money market, where the real supply of money in circulation, M_s/P, is immediately affected by the price level, P. Inflation, or an increase in the price level, P, lowers the real money supply. This insight makes the analysis very simple. This is good news since we have acquired a lot of experience with changes in the money supply and we are also fully familiar with shifts of the *LM* curve.

The impact of an increase in the price level is illustrated in Figure 19.9, representing two money-market equilibria and the associated *LM* curves. On the left graph, an increase in the price level from P_0 to P_1 shifts the real money supply, M_s/P, to the left and raises the equilibrium interest rate. As a result, the associated *LM* curve also shifts to the left from LM_0 to LM_1.

If we allow prices to fluctuate, we must also provide a comprehensive as well as theoretically and empirically sound mechanism that indicates in what manner prices change. First, we need to decide what degree of price flexibility should be assumed and explain why. The question of how fast and by what mechanism changes in the money supply translate into higher prices is not trivial. In their intermediate macroeconomic class (closed economy), students may have encountered models of perfectly flexible prices and other models that assume sticky prices. All these models were analyzed with the help of the aggregate supply and the aggregate demand curves. Both curves were illustrated in the price/income space. We now adapt the same approach to the open economy. When deriving these curves, the first question is to speculate whether they have to be modified to fit the open economy model.

The Open Economy Aggregate Supply Curve

The aggregate supply curve is derived from the interrelation of wages and prices in the labor market. It is drawn in the price/income space: for a given expected price level, the price level is an increasing function of income. The slope of the aggregate supply relation depends on the degree of price flexibility in the economy. In most intermediate macroeconomics courses, the sticky price model

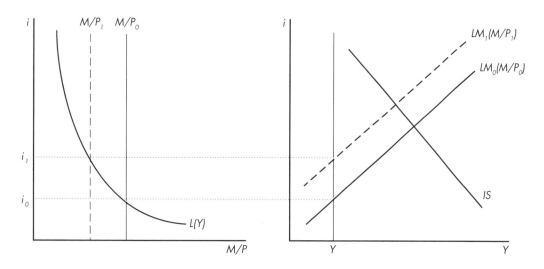

FIGURE 19.9 Impact of an Increase in the Price Level on the *LM* Curve

An increase in the price level corresponds to a cut in the real money supply M_s/P. Since the position of the *LM* curve depends on the real money supply, the *LM* curve shifts back from LM_0 to LM_1. Note that the identical shift in the *LM* curve would have been brought about if prices were constant while the nominal money supply (M_s) declined.

corresponds to the short-run Keynesian model of the economy. It is assumed that the adjustment is effected through changes in output rather than through changes in prices, so the economy can operate below or beyond full employment in the short run: the aggregate supply (*AS*) curve is perfectly elastic (horizontal).

Then, in the medium run, the labor market is introduced and prices are allowed to change gradually to bring about the adjustment of the economy overtime to its full-employment level. In this case, the *AS* curve is upward sloping; various degrees of elasticity determine its steepness. Perfect price flexibility implies a vertical *AS* curve – it is perfectly inelastic as price changes do not affect output.

In the earlier chapters, we have considered a *sticky* price model, where prices were fixed and the *AS* curve *horizontal* in the short run. We can now extend the Mundell–Fleming model and revise our analysis assuming that prices are no longer constant, but allowed to rise (or fall) over time and introducing the interplay with the labor market. In this case, the *AS* curve is *upward sloping*, but not vertical – the adjustment through prices is not immediate. In the next chapter, we consider *perfectly flexible prices* and a *vertical AS* curve. Finally, since the *AS* curve is derived from the domestic labor market, it can be considered a domestic entity: as a result, the aggregate supply curve in the open economy is no different from that in the closed economy. Is it the case with the aggregate demand relation?

The Open Economy Aggregate Demand Curve

Recall that aggregate demand, *AD*, depends not only on the domestic, but also on the foreign demand for domestic goods. To derive the *AS–AD* relationship in the open economy, we need to modify the closed economy *AD* curve and derive a new open economy *AD* relation.

In the closed economy, the *AD* curve is defined as all the combinations of prices and output such that both, the goods and the money markets, are in equilibrium: this corresponds to *IS–LM* intersection points. The open economy *AD* curve must integrate another dimension: *equilibrium in the balance of payments* (requiring *IS–LM–BP* intersection points). In addition, since the *BP=0* adjustment differs with fixed or flexible exchange rates, the resulting open economy *AD* curve also depends on the exchange rate regime.

In the closed economy case, we construct the *AD* curve by starting with an *IS–LM* equilibrium at a specific price level, P_0. Then we assume that the price level increases, shifting the *LM* curve back (see Figure 19.9). The new *IS–LM* intersection corresponds to a lower equilibrium output. So it is safe to draw the *AD* curve with a *negative* slope in the price and income space.

In the open economy, an increase in the price level also shifts the *LM* back, but this is not the end of the story. In Chapter 12, the real exchange rate was defined as $\varepsilon = EP^*/P$, with P^* and P the price levels in the foreign and domestic economy respectively. We also stated that an increase in the domestic price causes a real appreciation, bringing about a deterioration in the current account. In Chapter 14, we specified the current account as positively related to the *real* exchange rate – thus negatively related to the domestic price level. This tells us that both *IS* and *BP* shift leftward with an increase in the domestic price level as the current account deteriorates. The *IS* curve shifts back because the external component of aggregate demand (*CA*) drops. Likewise, since the balance of payments is the sum of the current account and the financial account, *BP* also shifts back and the deterioration in the current account must be met by an improvement in the financial account through an increase in the interest rate to restore *BP=0*. The contraction in output due the increase in prices is therefore larger in the open economy than in the closed economy as the current account is adversely affected. If the same increase in the price level brings about a larger drop in income in the open economy than in the closed economy, the open economy *AD* curve must be *flatter* than the closed economy *AD* curve; but both curves are *negatively* sloped (higher prices lead to lower output in either case).[8]

While the slope of the *AD* curve may differ, the *AS–AD* model for the open economy exhibits the same adjustment mechanism as the closed-economy model.

If the goods and financial markets are in equilibrium at the full-employment level, any policy change (or shock) that moves the economy away from full employment results in a change in prices that works through the *AS–AD* mechanism to eventually return the economy back to full employment. Once the external sector, represented by the current account as well as the financial account, has been integrated in the new open-economy *AD* curve, the mechanism of price adjustment in the medium run follows the same course as in the closed economy: the external effects are embedded in the new flatter open-economy *AD* curve.

Now that we have introduced a mechanism for price flexibility into the Mundell–Fleming model, the good news is that we do not have to revisit every one of the Mundell–Fleming cases considered earlier. In fact, we only need to reexamine the cases where policy worked well in the short run, i.e.

---

8 Note that the derivation and the slope of the *AD* curve is slightly different for the case of fixed exchange rates depending on intervention efforts on the part of the central bank and international reserve flows. It is still flatter than the closed economy *AD*.

fiscal policy with fixed exchange rates[9] and monetary policy with flexible exchange rates. As an example, since this chapter is devoted to flexible exchange rates, we present the case of monetary policy under flexible exchange rates. To do so, we return to our assumption of the small open economy to simplify the analysis.

Monetary Policy in the Medium Run under Flexible Exchange Rates and High Capital Mobility

We consider two applications of expansionary monetary policy. In the first case (Figure 19.10a), we assume that the economy is initially in equilibrium at its full-employment level (its medium-run equilibrium) and expansionary monetary policy is used to expand output even further. In this case, a wage–price spiral gets underway in the medium run bringing the economy back to its full-employment equilibrium. Alternatively, we have the case in Figure 19.10b, where the equilibrium in the goods, money, and external markets falls below full employment, and the government chooses to use expansionary monetary policy to restore full employment. In both cases, we draw the *IS–LM–BP* schedule above the *AS–AD* graph so that the axes measuring income Y in the two graphs share the same scale. A vertical line, *FE*, indicates the equivalent level of full employment in the two graphs.

What is the initial impact of an increase in the money supply with flexible exchange rates? We know that the resulting increase in output is enhanced by the depreciation needed to retain the external balance. Basically the *IS* (and the *BP*) curve also shift out, further stimulating the economy. The economy moves to Y_1.[10]

Case 1 – The Economy is Originally at Full Employment

In Figure 19.10a, the original level of output Y_0 coincides with full employment. In this case, the expansionary monetary policy shifts the *AD* curve out to *AD'* and the *LM* curve to *LM'*. The new *AD'–AS* equilibrium takes place beyond full employment in Y_1 (where *IS* and *LM'* intersect). Upward pressures on wages also raise prices, resulting in a contraction of the economy overtime until the economy is back to full employment. This contraction is driven by the increase in the price level. As prices rise, the *AS* curve shifts gradually left (and up) over time until it reaches *AS'* where aggregate demand and aggregate supply (*AS'–AD'*) intersect at the full-employment level (*FE*). The economy reached a new a medium-run equilibrium with a higher price level. This mechanism is illustrated in the lower panel of Figure 19.10a.

While the *AS* shifts back due to the wage–price spiral, the *IS–LM–BP* diagram is also affected by the increase in price. As illustrated in Figure 19.9, higher prices shift the *LM'* curve gradually back

---

9 Since monetary policy with non-sterilization under fixed exchange rate does not work at all, it would fail to affect the *AD* curve, so there is no point considering this case.

10 Some moderate price increase takes place since *AS* is upward sloping. We assume that *LM'*, *IS'*, and *BP'* final positions take the price increase into account, resulting in a smaller overall increase in the real money supply and a smaller depreciation.

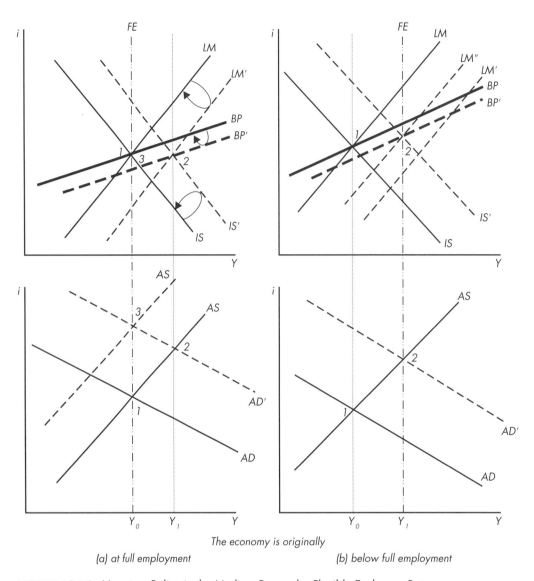

FIGURE 19.10 Monetary Policy in the Medium Run under Flexible Exchange Rates

First note that the aggregate demand curves shown in these graphs are the flatter open-economy aggregate demand curves that take into account the external sector. The left panel illustrates expansionary monetary policy from an initial full-employment level at Y_0. In the short run, the economy can move temporarily beyond full employment in Y_1 – labor works overtime, machinery is used around the clock resulting in some moderate price increases. The economy cannot remain at Y_1 as workers demand higher wages and inputs become scarcer. Eventually, increases in wages and input prices put pressure on the price level. This is the beginning of a wage–price spiral that will not relent as long as the economy is beyond full employment. The wage–price spiral initiates a contraction in the economy that will continue until the economy is back at full employment and there is no pressure on wages or prices anymore. In the right panel, monetary policy is used in an economy suffering from unemployment to bring it to full employment. This also results in a higher price level.

to its original level. The *LM* curve shifts because the real money supply drops; the *IS* shifts and the *BP* curves shift back because of the real appreciation. All three lines intersect again at the full-employment level of output (*FE*). To summarize, if the economy is initially at full employment, the impact of expansionary monetary policy under flexible exchange rates and high capital mobility is fully reversed in the medium run.

This is a stark reversal of our result under fixed prices shown earlier in the chapter. The crucial insight here is that we started from full employment. The *AD–AS* dynamics dictate that an economy (open or closed) can never be off its full-employment equilibrium in the medium run. Otherwise a price adjustment mechanism sets in and returns the economy to the original full-employment level.

Central Banks and the Compulsion to Control Inflation

Ever since the scary bouts of inflation faced by most of the western industrial economies in the 1970s and early 1980s, the central banks in the U.S., Canada, and Western Europe have been obsessed in using policy as soon as they detect the slightest hint of inflation. The European Central Bank (ECB), being the offspring to the German Bundesbank (known for its adamant anti-inflation stand), is very quick to respond with higher interest rates to any hint of rise in the harmonized rate of inflation of its fifteen members. Since the individual members' economies may face different kinds of inflationary pressures, the response of the ECB is not always welcome by all countries. In fact, the ECB is often accused of thwarting its members' growth rate by such cautious policies.

The most recent example of these dynamics is the French tension with the ECB, that reached a new high on September 15, 2007, when French president Nicolas Sarkozy accused the European central bank of helping speculators and hurting business by not cutting euro zone interest rates. Jean-Claude Trichet, the president of the European Central Bank, held rates constant in September and October 2007 saying that the ECB would "monitor very closely developments in the eurozone and that it was ready to counter risks to inflation, including higher energy prices."

Case 2 – The Economy is Originally below Full Employment

The second case assumes that the equilibrium of the economy does not correspond to full employment. In this case the central bankers could use monetary policy in hopes of moving the economy rapidly towards full employment. If they know the exact increase in the money supply needed to achieve this goal, they can succeed (but at a higher price level): the flatter open-economy *AD* curve will facilitate their task as the monetary expansion need not be as large to reach full employment. However, by interfering with the price adjustment mechanism, the policy makers forego the possibility of an automatic adjustment that would bring the economy to full employment over time through a fall in the price level.

Let us assume that the policy maker is impatient and wants to speed up the convergence to full employment (perhaps an election is near). This case is illustrated in Figure 19.10b. The expansionary monetary policy generates an increase in output and lowers interest rates (*LM* shifts to *LM'*). The increase in income causes a trade deficit and the decline in the interest rate, a capital outflow. As a result, the exchange rate depreciates, the *IS* curve shifts out to *IS'*, and the *BP* curve to *BP'*. In the lower graph *AD* shifts out to *AD'*; the ensuing rise in the price level eventually sends the *LM* curve back from *LM'* to its medium-run equilibrium level, *LM''*.

In Case 2, monetary policy is effective in stimulating an economy that is below full employment. However, without any policy intervention, an adjustment mechanism would have brought the economy to full employment with lower instead of higher prices. It is clear that an overheating economy could also be tamed with a cut in the money supply. Our analysis could be repeated to show the impact of all types of policy changes, domestic or external. Since the final analysis consists of looking at the interactions of the open economy *AD–AS* curves in the medium run, it would be repetitive to go through every case.

The last three chapters have developed a model of the small or large economy, under various exchange rate regimes allowing us to discuss the effect of policies or of policy mix in the short run. Only in the last section of this chapter, did we mention prices and the fact that they might change overtime. These chapters are grounded on the idea that prices are sticky in the short run and only change in the medium run. These are by no means monetarist assumptions; so we should also investigate the situation where prices adjust immediately to any change. The next chapter looks at models with fully flexible prices and the last part of the chapter investigates the dynamics of the adjustment mechanism.

Summary of Key Concepts

1. The primary difference between fixed and flexible exchange rates lies in the adjustment to a balance-of-payments imbalance. While this is the domain of the central bank (through intervention) with fixed exchange rates, market forces alone determine the price of foreign currency in a flexible exchange rate regime.

2. All adjustment mechanisms in the case of flexible exchange rates are ultimately driven by currency depreciations or appreciations. These changes in the price of foreign currency imply shifts of the *IS* curve (due to changing exports and imports) and of the *BP* curve.

3. Monetary policy under flexible exchange rates is very effective in raising output, and its effectiveness increases with the degree of capital mobility. Under fixed exchange rates monetary policy is ineffective in raising output.

4. Fiscal policy under flexible exchange rates becomes less and less effective as the degree of capital mobility increases. This result is exactly opposite to the effect of fiscal policy under fixed exchange rates.

5. A large open economy has the power to change the world interest rate. Two large countries without capital controls are linked inextricably through their current and financial accounts.

6. With perfect capital mobility, expansionary monetary policy in one large open economy results in a depreciation in that country's exchange rate. In a type of beggar thy neighbor

policy, the depreciations associated with the monetary expansion improve the domestic balance of trade, but hurt the foreign goods market. As the foreign currency appreciates, foreign exports become less competitive. The overall result is an expansion for the domestic economy and a contraction for the partner as well as a lower world interest rate.

7. With perfect capital mobility, expansionary fiscal policy in one country triggers massive capital inflows and an appreciation of the domestic currency. The overall result is an expansion for both economies as well as a higher world interest rate.

8. If we allow for medium-run price flexibility, the open-economy aggregate demand (*AD*) and aggregate supply (*AS*) model can be used to show that neither fiscal nor monetary policy is effective in raising output if the economy is already at full employment.

9. Medium-run price flexibility does, however, support economic policies designed to move the economy from a recession to full employment (at the expense of an increase in the price level).

CASE STUDY I

Insight: Currency Lessons Learned Since the Upheaval

By James McCormick, Global Head of Foreign Exchange Research at Lehman Brothers

Since the onset of the financial shock in July, economic and policy uncertainties have risen. But decisions by policymakers in the past few weeks have provided a rare moment to assess the economic implications of the market stress, and the various response functions we should expect from central banks.

We take three lessons about the outlook for currencies.

First, while debate rages about whether the Federal Reserve's 50 basis point rate cut was the right decision, one thing that should be clear is that the move was not dollar-friendly.

Historically, the worst combination for the dollar has been when U.S. yields have fallen vis-à-vis other currencies and equities and commodities have been rallying. This is the mix that has been building in

recent days and one that should persist in the coming weeks.

Indeed, the response by another set of policymakers – the Saudi Arabian Monetary Agency – has underscored the dollar risks. In spite of the peg to the U.S. dollar, the Saudis have not yet matched the Fed's rate cut, as the surge in oil prices continues to put upward pressure on inflation. Not surprisingly, there has been speculation that Saudi Arabia will follow Kuwait's example and drop the long-held dollar peg.

Admittedly, there are reasons to think we are near the end, not the beginning, of the dollar's five-year-old decline. The dollar is undervalued against many currencies, the poor business cycle news from the U.S. has been priced in, and any recovery should reveal a stock of assets in foreign-currency terms that look attractive. That said, we find it hard to imagine after the Fed's aggressive rate cut that these factors will help the dollar on a two-to-three-month horizon.

A second lesson from recent events is that there are macroeconomic implications from the financial stress, especially where the financial sector plays a significant role in the economy.

Take sterling. While the decision by the Treasury to guarantee deposits at U.K. banks has halted the decline, we cannot help thinking that the event will prove a turning point for the pound.

In a short period, the risks around U.K. policy have shifted from rate rises to rate cuts. Meanwhile, the turn in the U.K.'s macroeconomic picture has done nothing to dent the 15-year high in sentiment regarding sterling. History shows this is an ominous combination for a currency.

A final lesson is that the short-term outlook for carry-style trading strategies is positive.

For one thing, the choice by the Fed to cut by 50 basis points was an unambiguously short-run boost for riskier assets. In this environment, currencies such as the Swedish krona and Australian dollar look attractive, as both have maintained solid fundamentals. Oil-linked currencies like the Norwegian krone and, to a lesser degree, the Canadian dollar will also benefit. Asian currencies look cheap, especially with Chinese policymakers still tightening policy.

Further out, we are not convinced that we have returned to the carry-friendly days that existed before the August 2007 shock. Risk premia have increased and are unlikely to return to levels seen before the shock.

At the same time, the Fed's rate cut and U.K. policymakers' about-face after the recent run on bank deposits should say two things about the outlook: the global economy is turning down for the first time in several years at a time when economic optimism is high, and monetary policy uncertainty is on the rise after a prolonged period of near certainty of outcomes. Neither trend seems particularly supportive of a sustained carry-trade rally.

So while the short-run carry backdrop has been boosted by the Fed's decision, we still think the main impact of the summer's financial shock is that investors will have to pay more attention to the underlying fundamentals of G10 currencies. As a starting point, this shift should mean a more pronounced period of dollar weakness and a turn-down for the U.K. pound.

In a world of rising risk premia and falling growth, we also think the yen is entering a more persistent period of strength, even with the extreme market turbulence of this summer safely behind us.

CASE STUDY QUESTIONS

1. Which type of policy (fiscal or monetary) and which kind of exchange rate regime are discussed in the article? Given this exchange rate regime, what is your assessment of the impact of the Fed 0.5 percent rate cut on the U.S. dollar?

2. What should be the response of Central Banks in countries that fix their currency to the U.S. dollar like Saudi Arabia?

3. What is the outlook for the pound as a result of the U.K. banking problems?

4. Now that the world is entering a period of greater economic uncertainties, what are the important economic variables to watch when investing internationally?

CASE STUDY II

Preparing to Float
The Economist, June 25, 2008

Ukraine moves towards a free exchange rate

Exchange-rate moves by Ukraine's central bank in the past month signal that the country is moving towards a floating exchange rate that unifies the official and interbank rates – and so helps to check inflation, which is running at over 30 % year on year. Seemingly, the bank's management has fought off political pressure from exporters to make the change; and by acting now, it has a chance to hone its use of monetary levers before the country faces potentially serious economic and financial turbulence next year.

Shifting peg

Ukraine's inflationary problems – growth in consumer prices averaged 22% on year in the first quarter and is likely to exceed 30% in the second quarter – helped propel its central bank into action in late May, acceding finally to the recommendations of the IMF amongst others to change its exchange-rate policy. In the previous three years the country had maintained a de facto peg to the dollar, at HRN5.05:U.S.$1. As the U.S. currency declined against other major currencies, however, this helped to stoke import-price inflation in Ukraine and encouraged rapid growth in foreign-currency lending. On May 21st the board of the National Bank of Ukraine (NBU) announced a new official hryvnia exchange rate of HRN4.85:U.S.$1. The NBU had already refrained for several weeks from interventions in the interbank market that had previously kept the rate there within a tight informal corridor of HRN5.0 –5.06:U.S.$1. The NBU governor, Volodymyr Stelmakh, said that the appreciation could help reduce inflation by 3 percentage points in 2008.

Since the May 21st revaluation, which saw the currency strengthen by 4% against the dollar, the NBU has altered the official rate on ten occasions. The central bank has moved the currency in turns weaker, stronger, weaker and now stronger again: on June 23rd and 24th it traded at HRN4.8497:U.S.$1 on the official rate.

Moving target

By making small movements in both directions, the NBU is signalling its intention to move towards a more freely moving exchange rate. The first deputy head of the NBU, Anatoly Shapovalov, appeared to confirm this by stating that the previous policy of operating a de facto peg of the hryvnia to the U.S. dollar would be replaced by a flexible exchange-rate policy – presumably over the medium term. According to Mr Shapovalov, the intention is to move towards a floating official exchange rate. In the short term, the rate will not change every day, but will reflect prevailing market trends and the balance-of-payments position.

In tandem, according to Mr Stelmakh, the NBU intends to alter radically the way the domestic currency market functions, through the introduction of a "direct currency market." This would require commercial banks to conduct all their exchange-rate operations through the interbank currency exchange; banks currently tend to enter the interbank exchange with a net sum of currency deals concluded with clients internally. The aim of the proposed change is to make the currency market more transparent and to boost its trading volumes, in order to help to align the official exchange rate and the interbank trading rate more closely (on June 19th the interbank exchange rate was HRN4.74:U.S.$1). The interbank rate is currently estimated to account for 60–70% of the official rate, with the remainder reflecting the situation on international currency markets. To assist these changes, the NBU is prepared to extend the duration of the daily trading session at the interbank exchange and possibly to introduce 24-hour trading.

Battles won?

The move off the de facto peg of HRN5.05:U.S.$1 was fiercely resisted. The day after the NBU board announced the move, the bank's council, which is composed of members appointed by parliament and the president, exercised its right to veto the decision. It was the first such veto since independence, with the council's head, Petro Poroshenko, pointing to the likely negative impact on the country's already rapidly widening external deficit. The council's veto was subsequently overturned by the board.

The board's right to overturn the veto appears definitive and Mr Poroshenko's announced two-week deadline for reviewing the exchange rate has passed without major incident. It thus appears that Mr Stelmakh has won, despite strong pressure from Ukraine's exporters – the chairman of the parliamentary committee for industry, regulatory policy and enterprise has estimated that the revaluation could cost exporters HRN9bn (U.S.$1.9bn at the new official exchange rate). Since May 21st, exchange-rate policy has responded to market trends rather than political pressure.

Challenges ahead

The NBU's shift towards inflation-targeting, despite Mr Stelmakh's concerns that it could be undermined by a loose fiscal policy, is prudent given the context. Inflation is both imported and a result of domestic demand exceeding supply. On the demand side, the government has engaged in classic Keynesian pump-priming. And on the monetary front, there are large capital inflows which, given the fixed exchange rate, have led to rapid growth in money supply. Interest rate increases, sterilisation operations and increased reserve requirements have had limited success in stemming the tide.

The fixed exchange-rate was a useful nominal anchor, but it is no longer because of the capital inflows. As a small, open economy subject to exogenous shocks, policy shocks and transition shocks, the optimal situation for Ukraine is to maximise the number of levers at its disposal – hence the addition of exchange-rate flexibility.

The timing is pertinent because in 2009 Ukraine could suffer a terms-of-trade shock. Ukraine is Europe's fifth-largest consumer of gas (after Russia, the U.K., Germany and Italy), met mostly through imports from Central Asia at a price of U.S.$180 per 1,000 cubic metres. In March the Central Asians extracted a promise from Russia that they would receive a "European price" for their gas in 2009 – and currently this stands at around U.S.$340 per 1,000 cu metres. At this price, the metallurgy and chemicals enterprises that form the backbone of Ukraine's economy will suffer serious distress. Metallurgy alone accounts for around 40% of all export revenue and roughly a quarter of total industrial output.

If Ukraine did not move off the de facto dollar peg this year, there is a possibility that it would have been forced off in 2009. By making the change now, the NBU has time to learn how effective the various levers under its control are, while the country's businesses have some time to get used to life without the safety net of the dollar peg before Ukraine's external position becomes much more uncomfortable.

CASE STUDY QUESTIONS

1. Ukraine's currency, the HRN, has maintained a peg against the U.S. dollar in the last three years. Explain why the country's exporters are putting a lot of pressure on the Central Bank to keep the peg.

2. Why is the Central Bank so keen on loosening the peg and on revaluing the HRN against the dollar?

3. How has the Central Bank acted to loosen the peg?

4. Explain why, in a world with high capital mobility, a small open economy like Ukraine cannot control its inflation if it adheres to a fixed exchange rate system.

5. More precisely, why is it so important for Ukraine to be able to learn to use an independent monetary policy?

Questions for Study and Review

1. From its inception in 1999 to about 2002, the euro kept depreciating against the dollar.

   a. Show, with a graph, how European monetary policy could have been used to boost the euro and how that would have impacted on he U.S. economy.

   b. Draw a full employment line in your graph and discuss how this policy you have suggested would affect employment in Europe.

2. A small country, Pecunia, under a flexible exchange rate regime has achieved both internal (IS–LM intersection) and external balance. Pecunia trades a lot with the rest of the world, but allows only limited access to its capital market while its citizens need authorizations to invest abroad. Pecunia's central bank does not intervene at all. Pecunia is facing a serious housing slump and the central bank worries about its impact on its economy. If you were the president of the central bank, what would you do to deal with this situation?

   a. Spell out the policy carried out by the central bank (be specific).

   b. Use a graph showing the IS–LM–BP to illustrate the impact of the policy – name the starting equilibrium point a. Show the shifts (if any) of the three curves IS–LM–BP resulting from the policy adopted. Break down the effect into two stages: (i) name the impact of the policy alone, point b, (ii) name the final equilibrium point c.

   c. What is the status of the balance of payments in b? What will be the impact on the exchange rate? What will eventually happen to income – compared to its initial position in a?

3. Two large countries, domestic and foreign, under a flexible exchange rate regime, allow perfect capital mobility. The domestic economy, weary of inflationary pressures, cuts the money supply. Draw two graphs side by side showing the IS and the LM curves and the initial equilibrium for each country. Draw the relevant BP=0 curve and name all the curves and axes.

   a. Show the effect of the policy described above on the graph. Determine the initial world interest rate and the final one. Show all the shifts of the relevant curves in the two countries and the final two-country equilibrium.

   b. What will happen to the exchange rate in the domestic economy? What will eventually happen to income in each of the two countries?

4. The French and the German economies are very open to each other. They trade and invest freely in each other's economies. Assume that they had a flexible exchange rate regime at the time of the German reunification (in reality this was not the case). In order to finance the reunification of East and West Germany, Chancellor Köhl issued new government bonds – a form of expansionary fiscal policy.

   a. Draw two IS–LM graphs side by side, one for each country, to show the impact of the policy on the two countries. Draw the relevant BP=0 curve and name all the curves and axes on the graphs above. Name the original equilibrium point a for Germany and a* for France.

   b. Show the effect of the policy described above and the adjustment on the graph. Show the initial world (= Germany+France) interest rate as i and the final world interest rate as i'. Show all the shifts of the relevant curves in the two countries and the final two-country equilibrium (as respectively A and A^*) as Y'_G and Y''_F.

c. What do you expect the impact to be on the German DM? On the French franc?

d. What happens to the interest rate in the two countries eventually (from the original to the final situation)? And to income in each country?

Now let us start from this new equilibrium (the new interest rate is now i' and the new equilibrium income are Y'_G and Y'_F) and figure out what will happen when Germany uses monetary policy to fend off inflation.

e. Use a new set of graphs – one for each country. Draw the relevant BP' curve at interest rate i' and name all the curves and axes on the graphs above. Name the original equilibrium point A for Germany and A^* for France. Show the effect of the policy described above and the adjustment on the graph. Show the initial world interest rate as i' and the final world interest rate as i''. Show all the shifts of the relevant curves in the two countries and the final two-country equilibrium.

f. What do you expect the impact to be on the German DM? On the French franc?

g. What happens to the interest rate in the two countries eventually (from the situation in b to the final situation)? And to income in each country?

5. Switzerland adheres to a flexible exchange rate arrangement and allows very high to perfect levels of capital mobility. Unfortunately their economy is in a slump and their currency is too strong for the good of their economy. The exchange rate of 1.60 SF per euro overestimates the health of the Swiss economy. An exchange rate of 1.66SF per euro would be a better reflection of the Swiss fundamentals. Two problems need to be tackled at once with two policies.

a. Draw a graph showing the internal balance and the external balance as two lines in a space measuring, on the vertical axis, monetary policy as the level of interest rate i and, on the horizontal axis, fiscal policy as the level of government spending G. Show the position of the Swiss economy on the graph.

b. Suggest the correct assignment to restore both internal and external balance. Show the path on the graph.

6. In the mid 1990s, the Irish economy was at full employment. However since Ireland was planning to join the EMU, Ireland had a fixed exchange rate arrangement with the other members and had to follow its cue from the European Monetary Institute (EMI), the European organization that was harmonizing the monetary policy of the members. Most of the other members had sluggish economies so monetary expansion was the policy advocated.

a. What was the impact of the policy in the short run for Ireland?

b. Use the AD–AS diagram to show the effect of the policy on prices in Ireland in the medium run.

References and Suggestions for Further Readings

Argy, V. (1994) *International Macroeconomics: Theory and Policy*, New York: Routledge.

Black, S. (1984) "The Relationship Between Exchange Rate Policy and Monetary Policy In Ten Industrial Countries," in J. Bilson and R. Marston (eds), *Exchange Rate Theory And Practice*, Chicago: University of Chicago Press.

Boughton, J. (1989) "Policy Assignment Strategies with Somewhat Flexible Exchange Rates," in B. Eichengreen, M. Miller, and R. Portes (eds), *Exchange Rate Regimes and Macroeconomic Policy*, London: Academic Press.

Cooper, R. (1986) "Dealing with the Trade Deficit in a Floating Rate System," *Brookings Papers on Economic Activity*, 1986: 195–208.

Dornbusch, R. (1980) *Open Economy Macroeconomics*, New York: Basic Books.

—— (1987) "External Balance Correction: Depreciation or Protection?," *Brookings Papers on Economic Activity*, 1987: 249–70.

Dunn, R. (1983) "The Many Disappointments of Flexible Exchange Rates," *Princeton Essays in International Finance*, 154.

Fleming, J.M. (1962) "Domestic Financial Policies under Fixed and under Flexible Exchange Rates," *IMF Staff Papers*, 9: 369–79.

Frankel, J. (1993) *On Exchange Rates*, Cambridge, MA: MIT Press.

Frenkel, J. and Mussa, M. (1987) "The Mundell–Fleming Model a Quarter Century Later," *IMF Staff Papers*, 34: 567–620.

Friedman, M. (1953) "The Case for Flexible Exchange Rates," in *Essays in Positive Economics*, Chicago: University of Chicago Press.

—— (1988) "Lessons on Monetary Policy from the 1980s," *Journal of Economic Perspective*, 2: 51–72.

Helliwell, J. (1969) "Monetary and Fiscal Policies for an Open Economy," *Oxford Economic Papers*, 21: 35–55.

MacDonald, R. (1988) *Floating Exchange Rates: Theory and Evidence*, London: Unwin Hyman.

Mundell, R. (1962) "The Appropriate Use of Monetary and Fiscal Policy for Internal and External Stability," *IMF Staff Papers*, 9: 70–7.

—— (1963) "Capital Mobility and Stabilization Policy under Fixed and Flexible Exchange Rates," *Canadian Journal of Economics and Political Science*, 29: 475–85.

—— (1968) *International Economics*, ch. 17–19, New York: Macmillan.

Oudiz, G. and Sachs, J. et al. (1984) "Macroeconomic Policy Coordination among Industrialized Countries," *Brookings Papers on Economic Activity*, 1984: 1–75.

Sohmen, E. (1969) *Flexible Exchange Rates*, Chicago: University of Chicago Press.

Swoboda, A. and Dornbusch, R. (1973) "Adjustment Policy and Monetary Equilibrium in a Two-Country Model," in M. Connolly and A. Swoboda (eds), *International Trade and Money*, London: George Allen and Unwin.

Turnovsky, S. (1977) *Macroeconomic Analysis and Stabilization Policy*, Cambridge: Cambridge University Press.

APPENDIX:

The Policy Mix Revisited: Internal and External Balance

We are now going to use the model and the tools developed in the previous chapter to investigate the twin goals of internal and external balance when exchange rates are floating. However the problem is going to be different because external balance happens automatically through the forces of the market: exchange rates fluctuate continuously to keep the external sector balanced. So, with a flexible exchange rate, external balance is the norm. We have also shown earlier in this chapter that monetary policy was very effective at implementing government's goals as it induces changes in the exchange rate that reinforce the monetary policy. However, precisely because it does not control exchange rate fluctuations, the government may bring the economy to full employment, but at a new exchange rate that may not be entirely desirable: this new exchange rate may cause greater current account/ financial account imbalances or it might be very low/high historically. So we need to reformulate the question with the help of the case study below.

In September and again in October 2007, the Fed cut the interest rate to fend off a potential crisis in the financial markets that could trigger a recession in the U.S. economy. As expected, since the dollar is freely floating, it depreciated against the euro, the yen, and various currencies that are also freely floating. From a domestic point of view, the depreciation of the dollar is welcome as it also stimulates the U.S. economy and helps fight a possible recession. In this respect, monetary policy is indeed quite effective. However, the dollar is now historically very weak and other factors should be taken into consideration. The dollar is the main reserve currency of most central banks in the world – a weak dollar is not appealing and they might decide to shift their reserves from the weak dollar to the strong yen or the strong euro. Large sales of dollars on the world currency markets could be harmful to the U.S. economy. In addition, since Americans do not save much, the bulk of U.S. domestic investments, the source of future growth for the U.S. economy, are actually financed by the foreigners. What would happen if these capital inflows dry out because the U.S. returns are not appealing anymore?

So, perhaps, under a floating exchange rate, the policy makers may want to achieve full employment, but not at any exchange rate. Perhaps, the policy makers may wish to pick a certain exchange rate that is not going to be too low or too high. We asserted in an earlier chapter that, with flexible exchange rates, external balance meant that the exchange rate was stable (note that the dollar has been depreciating steadily in the past five years). This would indicate a certain harmony between the exchange rate and the fundamentals of the economy implying a more specific definition of external balance. So now that we have introduced the idea of a desirable target for the exchange rate, it becomes clear that to achieve that target and full employment, a policy mix similar to that developed in the last chapter is needed. Since we are constructing a model that fits the modern economy, we add the assumption of perfect capital mobility.

We construct the internal balance line, IB, where $Y = \bar{Y}$, and the external balance line, EB, where $E = \bar{E}$, given the assumptions of perfect capital mobility and the existence of target exchange rate, $\bar{E}$. Again the two policy instruments are monetary policy measured by the level of the interest rate, i on the y-axis, and fiscal policy measured by the level of government spending, G, on the x-axis. Since fiscal policy does not work with perfect capital mobility, the level of government spending has no impact on the internal balance and the IB line is horizontal. There is only one level of interest rate consistent with full employment. An increase in the money supply, putting downward pressures on the interest rate, triggers an immediate depreciation. This can only be neutralized by an increase in government spending, G: an increase in G puts upward pressures on the interest rate, triggering an appreciation. The EB line must be downward sloping. We can now draw these two lines in the i/G policy mix graph (Figure 19.11) and figure out the proper assignment to reach the intersection of these two lines, a. Again the two lines delimit four quadrants corresponding to all four combinations of imbalances. Inflationary pressures below the IB line, $Y > \bar{Y}$, and unemployment above, $Y < \bar{Y}$:

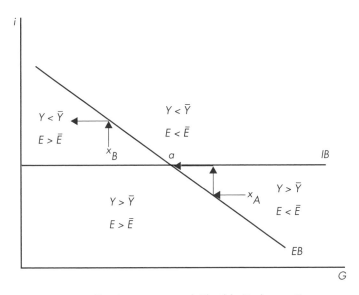

FIGURE 19.11 The Assignment with Flexible Exchange Rates

At A, the economy is beyond full employment and the exchange rate is too strong. The assignment required to converge towards equilibrium a is: fiscal policy to bring the exchange rate to the desired level, $\bar{E}$, and monetary policy to reach full employment. The opposite assignment used at B is incorrect and sends the economy further away from full employment and from the desired exchange rate. Note that the assignment is reversed compared to the assignment followed with fixed exchange rates.

indeed, if the interest rate increases at the same level of government spending, the economy drops below full employment. Similarly, starting from the desired level for the exchange rate $\bar{E}$, an increase in the interest rate, at the same level of government spending G, triggers an appreciation. Points above the EB line correspond to $E < \bar{E}$ and below, to $E > \bar{E}$.

Can we figure out intuitively which policy, fiscal or monetary, to attach to each goal, $E = \bar{E}$ or $Y = \bar{Y}$? It seems that, with flexible exchange rates, fiscal policy is not really independent of the exchange rate fluctuations. On the other hand monetary policy is quite independent. A good guess would be to devote monetary policy to maintain the internal balance and fiscal policy to target the exchange rate. This is what we do in Figure 19.11 where the economy, at point A, suffers from both inflationary pressures and too strong an exchange rate. The proper assignment duly brings the economy back to equilibrium a. The wrong assignment used at B makes things worse.

Another Reality Check: Restoring the External Balance

Is $BP=0$ an ideal goal? Maybe not always. For instance, the fact that the balance of payments will automatically readjust with flexible exchange rates does not mean that the composition of the external sector is not affected. If the new external balance happens at a different interest rate level, the new equilibrium may correspond to higher current account deficits matched by greater levels of capital inflows. As a result, the import-competing sector and the export sector might suffer. On the other hand, greater capital inflows imply that the domestic balance of international indebtedness will worsen and that future income payments to the foreigners will be higher.

Chapter 20

Perfectly Flexible Prices and Exchange Rate Dynamics

LEARNING OBJECTIVES

By the end of this chapter you should be able to understand:

- an economic concept, with a long history, named purchasing power parity, suggesting that the international price of commodities should be the same in all countries

- why prices of identical goods, converted into the same currency, are actually different in different countries

- that the idea of purchasing power parity, although controversial, is applied to compare international levels of living

- the importance of the assumption concerning price flexibility to explain the adjustment mechanism resulting from a shock

- the difference between two forms of analysis undertaken by economists: comparative statics and dynamics

- a major reason why exchange rates are so volatile in the short run

In earlier chapters, we assumed mostly that prices were fixed; indeed price variables were included in some of the models, but we would ignore changes in price and focus on other issues. However, in the last section of the previous chapter, prices are assumed to be sticky in the short run, but they adjust in the medium run: that approach allowed us to investigate how medium-run price adjustments would eventually modify the effect of policies deemed effective in the short run. The medium-run price adjustment assumption corresponds to an upward-sloping aggregate supply curve. In this chapter, we extend the idea of price flexibility to its utmost; perfect flexibility at all times. In making this assumption, we leave the Keynesian world of sticky prices in the short run and enter the world of monetarists, who believe that prices are absolutely flexible, i.e. they adjust fully and immediately to any change; the aggregate supply curve is vertical.

In this chapter, we discuss the existence and implications of perfectly flexible prices in international transactions. First we introduce the law of one price and the related concept of purchasing power parity. We investigate whether the empirical evidence supports international price flexibility in the short run and then whether purchasing power parity holds in the medium run. In the rest of the chapter, we develop models with flexible prices. First, we consider the monetary approach to the exchange rate based on fully flexible prices. Finally, we develop the so-called overshooting model, involving sticky prices in the short run and eventually flexible prices. In this last model, expectations are explicitly modeled and play a key role in the adjustment mechanism.

INTERNATIONAL ARBITRAGE AND PURCHASING POWER PARITY

A world governed by completely flexible prices must be a world where **arbitrage** is a powerful tool, immediately equalizing any differences in prices. Arbitrage is the age-old principle of "buy low, sell high." Arbitrageurs do not produce anything: they profit by exploiting the price differences of identical goods or financial instruments. In doing so, they equalize the prices. By buying where the price is low, they bid up that price; by selling where the price is high, they depress that price. This mechanism has already been discussed in the context of currency arbitrage: in Chapter 16, we explained how currency arbitrage brings about consistency in the exchanges rates quoted in various locations.

Domestic Arbitrage within Germany

If used convertible cars are cheaper in Berlin than in Munich, a profit opportunity arises. Why not fly to Berlin, buy a convertible, drive it to Munich and sell it there? If travel costs are small enough, and the initial price differential is high enough, this is a great way to make money. As more and more convertibles from Berlin are shipped to Munich, the price of used convertibles rises in Berlin and falls in Munich until the profit opportunity is arbitraged away.

If we believe in the principle of domestic arbitrage, there is no reason to believe arbitrage does not hold for international trade as well. Take any good or any service, a dozen eggs, for example. Domestic arbitrage ensures that the eggs in Berlin cost the same as in Munich; will they cost the same in Zurich, Switzerland (when expressed in the same currency)? In principle, **international arbitrage** should ensure it. Of course, there are limitations to perfect price equalization. This example entails shipping the eggs from one location to another; due to these additional transportation costs, prices cannot be perfectly equalized. To simplify the exposition, let us first abstract from such costs that hinder arbitrage.

In the case of international arbitrage, further considerations have to be taken into account. The price of the eggs in Berlin or Munich is quoted in euros while it is quoted in Swiss francs in Zurich. We have to convert one of the two prices quoted in order to compare it to the other in the same currency whether euros or Swiss francs. To do so, we use the nominal exchange rate quoted in the newspaper. Arbitrage then becomes a more complex operation when undertaken on the international markets. To introduce the process of international arbitrage, we start with a case involving a single commodity; this special case is known as the law of one price.

The Law of One Price

If we believe in international arbitrage, it must be true that, if a pair of Levi's blue jeans costs $24 in the U.S., and the exchange rate E is 1.50 dollars per euro, one would expect the price of a pair of Levi's in Germany to be €16, i.e.:

$$P^{US}_{jeans} = E_{\$/\epsilon} P^{G}_{jeans} \tag{20.1}$$

With this statement, we assume perfect arbitrage (no additional costs) and perfectly flexible prices.

The hypothesis that arbitrage would equalize the price of a commodity across countries is called the **law of one price**, meaning that there is only one price for a pair of Levi's blue jeans in the world (when expressed in the same currency). In different countries, this price is expressed in different currencies; if we want to find out the dollar price in foreign countries, we simply have to multiply the foreign price by the dollar price of the corresponding foreign currency. If the price of Levi's in the U.S. is lower than the euro price of Levi's in Germany converted into U.S. dollars using the nominal exchange rate, arbitrageurs will immediately see a profit opportunity. When $P^{US}_{jeans} < E_{\$/\epsilon} P^G_{jeans}$, arbitrageurs buy Levi's in the U.S. and sell them in Germany at a higher price (we had assumed no additional costs). As a result, the increase in the demand for Levi's in the U.S. raises the dollar price of Levi's in the U.S., while the increase in the supply of Levi's in Germany depresses the euro price of Levi's in Germany, bringing back parity between the two prices: the law of one price is restored.

International Arbitrage

A car costs £10,000 in the U.K. and the identical model costs $20,000 in the U.S.; if the exchange rate is £0.50/$1, the price of the car in the U.K. is equal to the price in the U.S. converted into £ (£10,000=$20,000*0.50). There is no arbitrage opportunity there. If today's actual exchange rate increases to £0.60/$1, it pays for Americans to purchase the car directly in the U.K.: this is because it only takes $16,666 at today's exchange rate to buy £10,000 that can be used to purchase the car in the U.K. in turn. If transporting the car to the U.S. costs less than $3,333, there is a profit opportunity.

As Americans are buying British cars to ship home, the total demand for cars increases in the U.K., putting upward pressures on the U.K. price; at the same time, the supply of cars increases in the U.S. putting downward pressures on the U.S. price. If we assume zero transportation costs, cars can be bought in the U.K. and shipped to the U.S. until the price of cars in the U.K. rises, for instance to £11,000 while the price of cars in the U.S. falls, for instance to $18,333. At these new prices, the profit opportunity disappears as £11,000 = $18,333 * 0.60, i.e.: $P^{UK}_{car} = E_{£/\$} P^{US}_{car}$ and the law of one price holds again.

There is another way to look at the law of one price. Assume that the two countries produce one good only, a pair of Levi's. If the price of Levi's is stable in the U.S. and in Germany and there is no arbitrage opportunity, then it implies that the nominal exchange rate is the ratio of the price in dollars and in euros of the Levi's, i.e.

$$E_{\$/\epsilon} = \frac{P^{US}_{jeans}}{P^G_{jeans}}.$$

Note that nowhere in the above discussion do we imply any causality between the relative prices and the nominal exchange rate.

Purchasing Power Parity (PPP)

The reasoning underlying the law of one price can be extended if we look beyond Levi's blue jeans at an entire shopping mall full of goods. If we talk of "prices" in general, we really mean a price index, such as the **consumer price index** (CPI). The consumer price index measures the change in the cost of a fixed basket of products and services, including housing, electricity, food, and transportation. The CPI is a measure of the price level that estimates the cost-of-living index for the citizens of a country. If we believe in international arbitrage, we believe that the price of each good in the basket adheres to the law of one price. As a result, the CPI basket, a weighted average of all these prices, also adheres to the law of one price (see box overleaf for caveats).

All countries calculate a cost-of-living index based on their own CPI. These indices are gathered and published regularly by international organizations and reprinted in various magazines such as *The Economist*. If we generalize the concept implied by the law of one price to the CPI and quote the domestic CPI as P_{CPI} and the foreign CPI as P^*_{CPI} we get

$$P_{CPI} = EP^*_{CPI} \qquad (20.2)$$

where E is the nominal exchange rate, quoted as the number of units of domestic currency in one unit of foreign currency. If the price of the CPI basket of goods and services is higher, say, in Switzerland than in Italy, i.e. $P^{SW}_{CPI} > E_{SF/\epsilon} P^{IT}_{CPI}$ Swiss residents will cross the border to buy Italian goods and services to take home. The overall increase in demand for Italian goods coupled with the increase in supply for the same goods in Switzerland, as the Swiss are taking them home, raises the price level in Italy and depresses it in Switzerland, until all arbitrage opportunities are exhausted. At this point, **purchasing power parity** (or PPP) is restored, i.e. $P^{SW}_{CPI} = E_{SF/\epsilon} P^{IT}_{CPI}$

We have extended the law of one price for one good to a price level (the CPI) for an aggregate of many goods and services (the basket). This new hypothesis is called **absolute purchasing power parity**. We can impart a further interpretation to this equation by extending the concept involved to more than two countries. We designate the CPI basket of goods and services as the reference basket. If P^{SW}_{CPI} is the price of the reference basket in Swiss francs, the price of each reference basket in each country (Italy, the UK, and Japan) is the same when converted into Swiss francs, i.e. $P^{SW}_{CPI} = E_{SF/\epsilon} P^{IT}_{CPI} = E_{SF/\pounds} P^{UK}_{CPI} = E_{SF/yen} P^{JAP}_{CPI} = \ldots$. This is a swooping assertion! This equation claims that if we know the price level (or CPI) in all the countries, we can derive the exchange rates between all the currencies.

It is critical to realize that both purchasing power parity and the law of one price are "hypotheses." They are only based on the assumption that prices are flexible due to goods and services arbitrage. However, some economists[1] have extended this notion into a theory of exchange rate determination. We can illustrate this new approach with an example: if the U.S. basket used to evaluate the U.S. CPI is worth $1,000 and the British basket used to evaluate the British CPI is worth £500, PPP predicts that the exchange rate between the dollar and the British pound is $2/£. A change in the relative price, for instance an increase in the U.S. price level (say to $1,200) implies a devaluation of the dollar to $2.4/£. This exchange rate determination approach, based on perfectly flexible prices, can be summarized by the following equation:

$$E = \frac{P_{CPI}}{P^*_{CPI}} \qquad (20.3)$$

---

1 For instance, Gustav Cassel at the beginning of the twentieth century.

We derived earlier an implied exchange rate between the dollar and the euro by using the law of one price, assuming that the countries were only producing one good. This new equation is indeed different as it is based on a basket of many goods and services called the **reference basket**.

Some Caveats Concerning the Reference Basket

First, does every single price in the basket increase in the same proportion or do some prices increase more and others less? If individual prices do not increase homogeneously, the CPI only measures the average increase in price and the perfect link with the law of one price is severed.

The second question is even more worrisome: is the reference basket used to calculate the CPI similar in all countries? The obvious answer is: not exactly. However proponents of the PPP approach still believe that changes in the ratio of the two CPIs will result in an exchange rate adjustment: an appreciation or a depreciation to compensate for the change in the relative CPI of the two countries.

The theory is pushed to the near absurd by *The Economist*: every year, *The Economist* constructs a Big Mac index and uses it to calculate an exchange rate based on purchasing power parity of the various currencies; then they compare it to the nominal exchange rate to stipulate whether a currency is overvalued, undervalued or correctly valued. (See Case Study II.)

We also observe that the three variables involved in the PPP approach – E, P and P^* – are the same three variables used in Chapter 12 to calculate the real exchange rate. The discussion of purchasing power parity might allow us to shed new light on the concept of the real exchange rate.

The Real Exchange Rate Revisited

In Chapter 12, the real exchange rate, e, was introduced as the nominal exchange rate, E, deflated by the relative price level (measured by the CPI) in the two countries or $e = EP^*/P$. With our new insights into purchasing power parity theory, we can now derive an alternative interpretation for the real exchange rate. The numerator of the fraction, EP^*, is the price of the foreign reference basket converted into domestic currency. The denominator is the price of the equivalent domestic reference basket P, in other words, the domestic CPI. So e, the real exchange rate, is the ratio of the prices of the two baskets.

Let us illustrate the concept of real exchange rate with an example: the U.S. is the domestic economy and the U.K. the foreign economy. P – the U.S. price of the domestic basket – is 100 and P^* – the U.K. price of the foreign basket – is 150 while the nominal exchange rate, $E_{\$/£}$, is 2, the real exchange rate, $e=(2*150)/100 = 3$. The meaning is now clear: three U.S. baskets of goods and services are needed to buy one U.K. basket of goods and services. This is akin to the notion of terms-of-trade. Here the term "real" is well taken: we are exchanging domestic goods for foreign goods, and not domestic units of currency for foreign units of currency – the latter refers to the concept of nominal exchange rate.

We know that a change in either price or in the nominal exchange rate affects the real exchange rate. For instance, an increase in the U.S. price level from 100 to 150 results in a fall in the real exchange rate from 3 to 2 [as $e=(2*150)/150 = 2$]; from the point of view of the U.S., this is a real appreciation since the U.S. only needs to give up two baskets to get one U.K. basket. As explained in Chapter 12, a real appreciation corresponds to a loss in international competitiveness for the country, because imports are stimulated and exports discouraged. An increase in the price level in the U.K. would cause a real depreciation for the U.S. – the U.S. would have to give up more baskets to acquire one U.K. basket: this is an improvement in the U.S. international competitiveness as imports will be discouraged and exports stimulated.

Just as the real exchange rate takes a new dimension thanks to the PPP theory, the concept of a real depreciation or appreciation projects a more realistic image. Indeed when we developed the import function in Chapter 14, we were trying to track the behavior of the importers; the explanatory variable we picked (among others) was not the nominal exchange rate, but the real exchange rate.

Reintroducing the real exchange rate allows us to make a final observation about PPP. If PPP holds, then the prices of the baskets have been arbitraged so $P=EP^*$ and the real exchange rate, e, is constant and equal to 1. Unfortunately, empirical studies are not supporting purchasing power parity well. We do not have to look far to illustrate this statement: in the 12 months from October 2006 to October 2007, the CPI in the U.S. increased by 3.5 percent while the CPI (named HICP) in the euro countries increased by 1.9 percent. If in October 2006, the exchange rate was \$/€1.2679, we can use the PPP equation to calculate the original CPI in the two places. Setting the CPI (an index) in the euro area to 100 in October 2006, we can derive the U.S. CPI at the same date as 126.79 ($P=1.2679*100$). Over the year the euro area CPI increases by 1.9 percent to 101.9 while the U.S. CPI increases by 3.5 percent to 131.23 (126.79*1.035). So if PPP holds in the short run, the dollar should only have depreciated to \$/€1.2878 ($P/P^*=131.23/101.9$) over the year. In fact, the dollar was quoted as \$/€1.4271 on October 1st, 2007 – a much greater depreciation than needed to uphold PPP. So we need first to subject purchasing power parity to a reality check and then figure out whether some variant of the theory might fare better.

Various Issues with Purchasing Power Parity

Up to now we have discussed the so-called concept of purchasing power parity. The whole idea was based on perfect price flexibility, abstracting from any factor that would hinder arbitrage. Reality is different. Everyone who has traveled abroad has realized that there are price differentials between identical goods across countries; generally these are greater than price differentials within the confines of a country. Worse even, historical data based on many centuries have also highlighted the existence of international prices differentials. So what is the problem with PPP? The answer is simple: there are a lot of hindrances to free arbitrage. Some are related to additional costs and barriers to trade, others are related to market structure or to the nature of the products traded. Finally free arbitrage may not happen immediately if one believes that prices are sticky in the short run and only adjust in the medium run.

i. Transportation Costs, Taxes, and Barriers to Trade

The first forms of hindrances relate to additional costs generated when commodities are traded. These hindrances do not rule out the possibility of gain through arbitrage. They just add a cost to the price of the good traded, leaving a wedge between the domestic price and the foreign price after all the arbitrage gains have been exploited. As a result, the prices will not be equalized. These costs could be so high as to wipe away any potential gain and make arbitrage prohibitive. In this case, the goods are not (internationally) traded and we will discuss this case below. Some of these costs, like transportation costs, are intrinsic to trading, while others, like taxes and barriers to trade, are the result of government interference. Transportation costs and taxes apply to either domestic or international arbitrage.

Barriers to trade are discussed in great details in the first part of this book and are relevant only to international arbitrage. They are the results of national government policies aimed at protecting some national sector. These barriers can take many forms: tariffs, quotas restricting the quantity traded, subsidies (either production or export subsidies), preferential contracts, and others. Protectionism in all its forms, particularly that of the rich industrialized countries (e.g. agricultural subsidies and fiercely protected defense contracts)[2] goes a long way in hindering international price convergence. Moreover, as the WTO (World Trade Organization) has put pressure on countries to remove tariff barriers, countries have come up with a host of non-tariff barriers to compensate for the loss of more direct protection. Specific health regulations, confusing forms to fill in, often aim at prohibiting the import of certain foreign goods. The non-tariff barriers have become quite important in impeding free trade, but it is much harder to estimate their exact costs.

Finally, there is a more subtle form of protection often exercised by governments that also distorts natural price convergence. In order to gain a cost advantage through undervaluation of their currency or simply to absorb some unexpected shock, central banks, supposedly committed to a floating exchange rate regime, do not hesitate to intervene in order to manage their exchange rate to their benefit.

ii. Market Structure

Arbitrage implies *no* interference in the forces of the market. Fully flexible prices are determined by the free interaction of supply and demand. The presence of monopolies distorts this perfect world as they set monopoly prices geared at maximizing monopoly rent. Basically, any market structure other than perfect competition interferes with arbitrage. Unfortunately, international trade is often carried out by large multinational corporations on markets that are far from being perfectly competitive.

---

2 It is interesting to mention how fiercely fought these contracts can be: when the U.S. Air Force needed to acquire a new fleet of refueling planes, they originally awarded the contract to EAD/Airbus, a European firm. After intense lobbying by Boeing, the original contract was deemed illegal by the GAO (U.S. Government Accounting Office) and scrapped.

iii. Nature of the Products: Product Differentiation and Innovation

The basic tenet of the hypothesis is price equalization. This idea makes sense only if the good or service considered is identical in the two countries. However not all goods traded are homogeneous. In the examples developed above, eggs would probably fit this requirement, but cars definitely do not. Cars are differentiated goods. In addition, countries have different standards imposed on the production of their manufactured products. So even if the cars were identical, the different standards would introduce differences between the domestic and foreign models thus creating a wedge between the prices. Note also that differentiated products are not usually traded in a perfectly competitive setting, since the products' differences impart a degree of monopolistic power to the producer – so trade then takes place in the imperfect setting of monopolistic competition.

Last, but not least, we should mention the role of innovation in creating price divergences. The Vernon's product cycle illustrates this evolution (see p. 114). Countries with high levels of technology will develop new products. At the beginning, these products will be non-standardized. Eventually, as the demand for these products increases and their production techniques become generally available, they will be produced, in standardized ways, by less technologically advanced countries – examples abounds in the IT industry.

iv. Non-tradables

We mentioned above that, if the cost of transporting goods internationally wipes away any potential arbitrage gain, these goods are not traded. For instance, if a cubic meter of sand needed to build a road is cheaper in Nova Scotia than in Devon, the sand will not be imported from Canada to London because the cost of transporting the sand would far outweigh the price differential. Sand is thus considered as a non-tradable, used only locally, in contrast to the tradables that are imported and exported. Many services are also non-tradable since they are performed or consumed locally (e.g. haircut, restaurant meal).

In fact, a substantial proportion of the goods and services consumed within a country are non-tradable. However their prices are included in the cost-of-living index: the CPI represents both tradables and non-tradables. If the prices of tradables and non-tradables move proportionately, PPP still holds. If not, PPP cannot reflect exchange rate movements properly. For instance, a developing country with export-oriented growth may experience greater productivity gains in its tradable than in its non-tradable sector. As the country's price of tradables is determined on the world market, it cannot change, but wages will increase in the tradable sector and consequently overall. The non-tradable sector, facing higher wages, will hike the price of the non-tradable. This result is in an increase in the relative price of its non-tradables; the country's CPI, consisting of both tradables and non-tradables, increases with respect to its trade partners. This triggers a real appreciation ($e<1$); PPP does not hold any more since we saw earlier that, when PPP holds, $e=1$.

Given such extensive exclusions, it seems quite preposterous to expect PPP ever to hold. Few goods are really traded under perfect competition, or are actually identical across countries, and on top of that, taxes (and other hidden restrictions such as safety standards) as well as transport costs rule out a lot of arbitrage. Finally, most services are non-tradable while many goods contain both tradable and non-tradable components. It seems that PPP is not a promising framework for explaining the fundamentals of exchange rate movements.

Ultimately, one can make a lot of adjustments to PPP. Actually, there is a lot of research taking place in this area of international macroeconomics – research focused on adjusting the PPP equation to deal with many of the problems mentioned above, such as the costs of trading, market structure, and the presence of non-traded goods. The PPP hypothesis remains popular among some economists who believe that arbitrage should be a key aspect of trade. However, the empirical evidence shows that deviations from PPP in the short run are large and volatile. It is clear that prices do not adjust in the short run: so PPP cannot explain short-run exchange rate movements as they follow a "random walk," a colorful term used by economists to admit their failing at explaining exchange rate volatility. We will see below that, despite its shortcomings, PPP is still an important concept in some specific areas of international macroeconomics.

Applications of PPP

Although PPP is controversial since it is not supported by empirical evidence in the short run, it has been applied in the past and is still used to investigate two issues: first, to set a realistic exchange rate after some shock and, second, to compare cross-country levels of living.

In order to figure out whether an exchange rate has become undervalued or overvalued with respect to another currency over a certain period, one can calculate the relative CPI for the two countries over the same period and compare it to their exchange rate movements. Gustav Cassel (1928) suggested such an approach to restore the exchange rate parities between the various warring nations' currencies after the First World War.

U.K. Return to the Gold Standard at the Pre-World War I Rate

The gold standard is a form of fixed exchange rate system whereby each country defines its currency in terms of gold. A fixed exchange rate between the currencies ensues. This system was prevalent before World War I. Both the U.S. and the U.K. suspended the gold parity during World War I. The economic disruption caused by the war had greater consequences in Europe than in America. The U.S. was able to rejoin the gold standard shortly after the end of the hostilities. Eventually, in the mid 1920s, the U.K. deemed that its economy had stabilized and that they could also rejoin the gold standard with the same gold price for the pound as before the war. However inflation in the U.K. had been greater than in the U.S. during the period. The ratio of the CPI in the two countries pointed to a weaker pound with respect to the dollar. The economic consequences of returning to the gold standard at the pre-World War I rate was harmful for Britain, leading to balance-of-trade deficits (due to an overvalued currency) and high rates of unemployment (due to the contractionary impact of the Bank of England intervention necessary to keep such a strong exchange rate). (These events are described in greater detail in the next chapter.)

PPP is quite popular in another realm of economics, unrelated to exchange-rate determination. PPP is used to compare different countries' levels of living. All countries report the value of their income in local currency – so how do we know which country is the richest and which one is the poorest? To compare levels of living, we focus on income per capita. We can always convert income per capita into one single base currency using the nominal exchange rate. However, since nominal exchange rates are very volatile and determined by traded goods only, among other problems, the result is not very meaningful specially when comparing very different economies (e.g. industrial versus agricultural or open versus closed). The best, albeit imperfect, method is to use the concept of PPP.

Basically the method is quite simple. To compare income in two countries, one must collect price and quantity data on every good and service in each of the two countries (sampling is necessary for practical reasons). Then we use the price structure of one of the two countries to recalculate income. Basically, we calculate income using the same set of weights, i.e. by multiplying the quantities in each country by the prices in the country we choose as the base. Since the price structure is not the same in the two countries as it reflects factors like taste, quality, etc. that are different in the two countries, we will obtain different results according to which country we use as base.[3]

International Levels of Living Comparison with PPP

We use a simple example with a two-good (bread and wine) and two-country model (Italy and the U.S.).

For each country, we calculate income per capita using its own currency as $\sum_i P_i^{IT} Q_i^{IT}$ and $\sum_i P_i^{US} Q_i^{US}$. The subscript i corresponds to good i and the superscript IT and US correspond respectively to Italy and the United States. We then compare income per capita using the nominal exchange rate to convert income per capita in each country into the same currency.

TABLE 20.1 Calculation of GDP Per Capita in own Currency

	Italy (per capita)			U.S. (per capita)		
	Price	Quantity	Consumption	Price	Quantity	Consumption
Bread	1.5€	50	75€	$3	60	$180
Wine	8€	10	80€	$12	12	$144
GDP (per capita)			155€			$324

---

3 This is the so-called index problem we encounter when calculating Paasche and Laspeyres indices. Note that the basic approach is identical to that used for inter-temporal comparisons.

Assume that the exchange rate is $1.25 per €. When we use the exchange rate to compare Italian versus American income, we get: $1.25*155 = $193.75 for Italy while U.S. income is equal to $324. This shows that the U.S. standard of living is 67 percent higher than Italy's (or that income in Italy is only 59 percent of the United States'). These results are indeed not realistic. Let us now compare the two standards of living with the PPP approach. We will use the U.S. prices to aggregate the quantities and then compare income in Italy and in the United States. We now compare $\sum_i P_i^{US} Q_i^{IT}$ and $\sum_i P_i^{US} Q_i^{US}$.

TABLE 20.2 Calculation of GDP Per Capita in Same Currency

	Italy (per capita)			U.S. (per capita)		
	Price	Quantity	Consumption	Price	Quantity	Consumption
Bread	$3	50	$150	$3	60	$180
Wine	$12	10	$120	$12	12	$144
GDP (per capita)			$270			$324

With PPP and using the $ prices to compare income per capita, we now find that U.S. income is only 324/270 = 1.2, i.e. 20 percent larger than Italian income – a more realistic comparison. Had we used the euro instead of the dollar to perform the comparisons, the results would have been slightly different, but the gap between the level of living of the two countries would also have narrowed to a more realistic order.

Purchasing power parity, with all its drawbacks, is still used extensively in the empirical literature, and *every time* you see *any* cross-country comparison *all* the variables have been adjusted by PPP to allow a representation in one currency. The Center for International Comparisons at the University of Pennsylvania has worked with the World Bank for many years to provide international data that are more meaningful than simple comparisons based on the exchange rates. Knowing the limitations of PPP approach, it is clear that these international comparisons should be regarded with a critical mindset. In addition, a fair amount of subjectivity enters in the actual construction of these PPP calculations. In Table 20.3, we show gross national income (GNI) per capita data for a sample of 12 different countries representing the spectrum from rich to poor countries. The first column corresponds to the UN data (using exchange rates at a specific point of time). The second and third columns are the World Bank data published in the World Development Indicators. The second column involves a correction of the UN data by using an average exchange rate. The third column is based on the PPP approach.

Table 20.3 shows that using PPP, rather than today's exchange rate, gives a more accurate picture of the relative levels of living, no matter how inaccurate the purchasing power parity assumption

TABLE 20.3 International Income Comparisons 2005, Exchange-Rate Based, and PPP Gross National Income (GNI)

	$ GNI per capita		
	Current exchange rate (U.S. dollars)	Atlas methodology (U.S. dollars)	PPP (international dollars)
U.S.	41,217	43,740	41,950
Ireland	41,336	40,150	34,720
U.K.	37,828	37,600	32,690
Australia	34,861	32,220	30,610
Spain	25,594	25,360	25,820
Saudi Arabia	13,119	11,770	14,740
Mexico	7,252	7,310	10,030
Turkey	3,580	4,710	8,420
Brazil	4,125	3,460	8,230
China	1,740	1,740	6,600
India	701	720	3,460
Haiti	429	450	1,840
Burundi	97	100	640

Source: adapted from United Nations, United Nations Statistics Division (unstats.un.org) and World Bank, World Development Indicators database (http://web.worldbank.org/WBSITE/EXTERNAL/DATASTATISTICS).

might be. It is clear that the method substantially lifts the level of living of the very poor countries to more realistic figures. For instance, an income per capita of $97 in Burundi, the last country in the list, is totally unrealistic – nobody can live on such a low income. The PPP correction from $97 to $640 makes more sense – the average income per capita in Burundi thus jumps from 1/425 to 1/65 of the average U.S. income per capita. On the other hand, the correction is performed at both ends, since the rich countries' levels of living are not as high as the non-adjusted data would convey.

Absolute versus Relative Purchasing Power Parity

Up to now, we have discussed a concept of absolute purchasing power parity where $P_{CPI} = EP^*_{CPI}$. Note, however, that the CPI depends on a specific reference year. The reference year is set as 100, but we do not know the extent of the deviation from PPP on that year. So it might be better to look at changes. Relative purchasing power parity requires that:

$$P_{CPI, t} / P_{CPI, t-1} = (E_t / E_{t-1})(P^*_{CPI, t} / P^*_{CPI, t-1})$$

If the rates of change are small this equation may be approximated by:

$$\frac{P_{CPI,\,t} - P_{CPI,\,t-1}}{P_{CPI,\,t-1}} = \frac{E_t - E_{t-1}}{E_{t-1}} + \frac{P^*_{CPI,\,t} - P^*_{CPI,\,t-1}}{P^*_{CPI,\,t-1}}$$

The term on the left hand side is the rate of inflation in the domestic country, π, while the last term in the right hand side is the rate of inflation in the foreign economy, π^*. Relative purchasing power parity thus requires that the percentage change in the exchange rate equal the inflation differential between the two countries or:

$$\frac{E_t - E_{t-1}}{E_{t-1}} = \pi - \pi^* \tag{20.4}$$

Since data on exchange rates and on rates of inflation are readily available through government statistics, it is easy to test the hypothesis of relative purchasing parity. We look at the British pound and the dollar and consider the rate of change of the $/£ exchange rate versus the inflation differential from the dollar over the 1975 to 2006 period (annual data). In Figure 20.1,

$$\frac{E_{\$/£,t} - E_{\$/£,t-1}}{E_{\$/£,t-1}}$$

is plotted on the x-axis and $\pi_{US} - \pi_{UK}$ on the y-axis. If relative PPP holds, these two terms are equal and the observation points are situated on the upward sloping dotted line.

Figure 20.1 does not support the PPP hypothesis. It is clear that the random walk assumption – the fact that PPP does not explain exchange rate movements – is not easily rejected, especially with shorter data sets. However there is a consensus in the literature that, if the data set is substantially extended, strong evidence that convergence will eventually happen usually appears.

Differentiated products, contracts, imperfect information, trade and transport costs all account, at least partially,[4] for deviations from PPP. If we examine more closely these reasons for the failure of PPP, however, we find that they are all to some degree short-run issues. After some length of time, one would expect these reasons for PPP failure to fade away. Overtime, production decisions can be altered and so can the product mix, allowing for less product differentiation. Contracts are rarely written for more than six months in advance. Substitutes can be produced to reduce monopoly power – perishable goods can be "arbitraged" by opening production facilities abroad. It is hard to imagine that imperfect information cannot be overcome in a matter of months or years, in our information society. Trade and transport costs remain, but we can easily adjust PPP to account for them, as they are constants. With the support of these arguments, why not posit that, although in the short run it is empirically unconfirmed, PPP holds in the long run.

To support this hypothesis empirically, economists had to use very long time series (up to 100-year). As a result, their data sets include both fixed and flexible arrangements – a potential problem

---

4 Problems associated with non-tradable, and various other issues not discussed here, associated with the extent of government spending or the existence of chronic deficits, are harder to suppress.

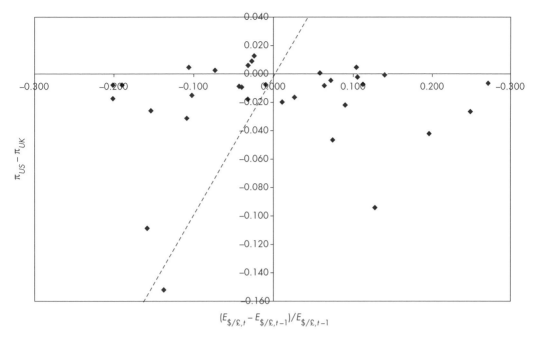

FIGURE 20.1 Purchasing Power Parity Test for U.K.–U.S. data (1975–2006)

Sources: adapted from the Bank of England and the U.S. Bureau of Labor Statistics.

The inflation differential is plotted on the *y*-axis and the rate of depreciation on the *x*-axis. Relative PPP holds when these are equal, i.e. all the observation points are on the upward-sloping dotted line. Out of 31 observations, no more than 3 are close to the line.

for the econometric estimation. These studies show that the **half-life** for the deviations varies between 3 and 5 years and, on average, the deviation from PPP damps out at a rate of 15 percent per year. In conclusion, PPP cannot be dismissed, given enough time for the adjustment to take place. At this point, the question is why does it take so long? In the short run, exchange rate volatility is mainly due to monetary and financial shocks, we know from earlier chapters that the adjustment is quite swift and that money is neutral. How do we square this fact with the snail pace of adjustment to PPP?[5] Rogoff, who noted the anomaly, answered this question by suggesting that, at this point, international markets are not yet integrated enough for prices to be equalized, especially in the short run.

The main conclusions of the above discussion are clear: PPP does not work in the short run, but cannot be rejected if enough time is given for prices to eventually adjust. Stating that deviations from PPP are temporary is akin to saying that prices are fixed, or "sticky" in the short run. However, in the medium run, prices become flexible and PPP becomes a reasonable assumption. This empirical evidence stresses the importance of developing a model that combines sticky short-run prices with flexible medium-run prices in order to examine the implications for the resulting exchange rate

---

5 This is the question raised by Rogoff in the "Purchasing Power Parity Puzzle."

movements. Robert Mundell's student, Ruediger Dornbusch, first constructed such a model in 1976, as the natural extension of the Mundell–Fleming model. We are quite familiar with the sticky short-run models, but not with the fully flexible price model proposed by the monetarist. To describe fully the mechanism of the Dornbusch model, we must first consider this approach too.

In the rest of the chapter, we present the monetarist approach to the exchange rate, indeed based on fully flexible prices; then we use the model to elucidate the occurrence of exchange rate "**over-shooting**" as we develop the dynamics of medium-run adjustments.

MONETARIST APPROACH TO THE EXCHANGE RATE

We must first set up a model illustrating the monetarist (or monetary) approach to the exchange rate. We assume fully flexible prices and a flexible exchange rate regime. The model involves two large economies, the domestic economy and the foreign economy. The variables for the foreign economy are denominated with an asterisk (*). With fully flexible prices, the economies always operate at their full-employment level. The equilibrium exchange rate is approximated by the PPP approach where $E = P/P^*$, i.e. we assume that investors expect the exchange rate to converge towards PPP which is equivalent to saying that PPP holds.

Exchange Rate Determination in the Model

We must first find how the price level is determined in this model. Let us consider the money market: the real supply of money is equal to M_s/P and the real demand, L, depends on the interest rate i and real income Y so it is equal to $L(i, Y)$. The money market is in equilibrium when: $M_s/P = L(i, Y)$. Rearranging the terms, we get:

$$P = \frac{M_s}{L(i, Y)} \tag{20.5a}$$

P is the price level that corresponds to equilibrium in the money market. The equivalent equation for the foreign country is:

$$P^* = \frac{M_s^*}{L^*(i^*, Y^*)}. \tag{20.5b}$$

From these two equations, we derive the relative price P/P^* that is equal to the exchange rate, $\bar{E}$, as PPP holds in the model.

$$\bar{E} = \frac{P}{P^*} = \frac{M_s/M_s^*}{L(i, Y) / L^*(i^*, Y^*)} \tag{20.6}$$

This equation illustrates that the exchange rate, $\bar{E}$, is the ratio of the relative supply of money over the relative demand for money in the two countries.

Implications of the Model

Some interesting implications can be derived from equation (20.6). We must first impose the *ceteris paribus* condition: we look at the impact of a change in one variable keeping all the other variables constant. If the domestic (nominal) money supply, M_s, increases, both the domestic price, P, and the exchange rate, $\bar{E}$, will increase proportionately, i.e. a 10 percent increase in the domestic (nominal) money supply will result in a 10 percent increase in the domestic price level, and a 10 percent depreciation – neither the domestic nor the foreign interest rate will be affected and the economy, as well as the foreign economy, will remain at its full-employment level. This result is essential to explain overshooting in the Dornbusch model below. The impact on the equilibrium with flexible prices of change in the other variables of equation (20.6) is also quite intriguing; we treat these cases in the Appendix at the end of this chapter. We can now impart another interpretation to this model. If one believes that prices are sticky in the short run, but eventually adjust overtime, the monetarist model can be considered as a long-run model of the economy.

EXCHANGE RATE DYNAMICS – OVERSHOOTING

One feature of the real world that is absent in the Mundell–Fleming model is the **intertemporal** dimension, i.e. showing what occurs across time. In essence, the model leaps from one equilibrium to another and we compare the two situations: we call this analysis "**comparative statics**." This approach provides an incomplete picture of the real world: it deprives us of any insights about the economic developments that occur during the transition. The duration of the transition may last from a few months to several years, so we should also be interested in the intertemporal process: the "dynamic adjustment" or simply the **dynamics**. Another substantial difference with M–F is that expectations, in the form of the expected rate of depreciation of the exchange rate, are now integrated in a more explicit manner in the model.

We assume fixed prices in the short run and fully flexible prices in the long run. The transition from the short-run to the long-run equilibrium takes place overtime through a gradual price adjustment. We assume that the foreign price level, P^*, is fixed and this will imply that the foreign money supply and the foreign interest rate, i^*, are also fixed (small-country case). We start with the long-run equilibrium where Y is always at its full-employment level and the price level is proportional to the money supply. There are no expectations about the exchange rate as it is determined by PPP and

$$E^e = E_t \text{ so } \delta = \frac{E^e - E_t}{E_t} = 0$$

The interest parity approximation $i = i^* + \delta$ is reduced to $i = i^*$ in the long run – note that the foreign interest rate, i^*, is fixed.

A Permanent Increase in the Nominal Money Supply

We now assume a permanent increase in the nominal money supply, M_s. As prices are fixed in the short run (sticky prices), the nominal increase translates into an increase in the real money supply, M_s/P, in the short run. As a result, the domestic interest rate, i, drops to keep the domestic money market in equilibrium. Evidently, the interest parity condition does not hold anymore and an immediate adjustment has to take place on that front too.

We must now figure out what happens to the expected rate of depreciation, δ. First there is a change in the expectations about the exchange rate, E^e: investors are aware that the result of a permanent increase in the money supply will be a proportional increase in price in the future and they also believe that the long-run exchange rate is approximated by PPP. So they expect a depreciation of the exchange rate that is proportional to the long-run increase in price. It is clear by looking at the interest parity condition below that since the returns on domestic investments, i, have dropped, the returns on foreign investments, the right side of the equation below, must also drop.

$$i = i^* + \frac{E^e - E_t}{E_t}$$

However E^e, the expected exchange rate, has increased as explained above, so E_t, the spot rate, must increase by a higher proportion for the right-hand term to decrease. Note that the spot rate, E_t, is the variable that has to change to bring the adjustment on the foreign exchange market with flexible exchange rates.

In sum, for the foreign exchange market to remain in equilibrium, we need a higher short-run depreciation of the currency than the long-run depreciation needed to bring the exchange rate to its new long-run equilibrium consistent with the higher price level and the higher level of money supply. This is the end of the short-run adjustment.

In the transition toward a new long-run equilibrium (the dynamics in the model), prices will gradually increase until their increase is proportional to the permanent increase in the nominal money supply; so the real money supply, M_s/P, will get back to its original level and, as a result, the interest rate will also get back to its original level (the neutrality of money emphasizes that all the real variables get back to their original level). The gradual increase in the interest rate ensures that the money market remains in equilibrium at all time during the transition back to the long-run equilibrium.

Adjustment on the Foreign Exchange Market

We must now consider the adjustment on the foreign exchange market. As the domestic interest rate increases, the returns on foreign investments – the right-hand side in the interest parity equation – must also increase. We assumed that the foreign interest rate was fixed, so let us concentrate on the expected rate of depreciation δ. No other change took place since the original permanent increase in the money, so the expected exchange rate, E^e, remains the same. Again the continuous adjustment on the foreign exchange market has to take place through a change in the spot exchange rate, E_t. It is clear that, for $E^e - E_t$ to increase, the spot exchange rate, E_t, has to drop, i.e. to appreciate. So, as the interest rate increases back gradually towards its original level where $i=i^*$ to keep the money market in equilibrium, the spot exchange rate, E_t, will have to appreciate gradually to keep the foreign exchange market in equilibrium until it is equal to E^e. When $E_t=E^e$, the expectations are fulfilled in the long run so δ, the expected rate of depreciation, equals zero. The speed of adjustment was discussed earlier and empirical studies estimate it at around eight years.

It is clear that the spot exchange rate, E_t, overshot its long-run equilibrium immediately after the permanent increase in the money supply (i.e. in the short run). It depreciated by more than was indicated by the expectations. So instead of depreciating during the transition from short to long run, it had to appreciate to correct for the excess depreciation that happened in the short run. The overshooting can be directly blamed on short-run price stickiness. Since prices did not contribute to the short-run adjustment, the slack fell on the interest rates, thus affecting both the equilibrium in the domestic money market and in the foreign exchange markets. Had the prices adjusted right away in the short run, the interest rate would not have changed and the exchange rate would have depreciated proportionally to the increase in the price level (according to PPP).

Extension of Model

There is a caveat. We have assumed that the permanent money increase was not affecting the level of output Y and that the economy was always at its long-run equilibrium. The forces eventually pushing the price level up in the transition were purely monetary (the gap between money demand and money supply). However if we consider a Keynesian short-run model, some expansion of the economy will take place when the money supply is increased. As Y increases, the demand for money also increases, putting upward pressures on the interest rate. This means that the interest rate does not have to drop quite as much in the short run to bring the money market back in equilibrium. In addition, the increase of Y beyond full employment will add to the eventual upward pressures on the price level. In this case, the overshooting will not be as large and the price adjustment back to long-run equilibrium will be faster. We could even imagine a situation where no noticeable overshooting takes place if the forces on the demand side are very strong.

We now revert to the original assumption where the price level starts adjusting before any output expansion and, therefore, overshooting happens. All these results are now illustrated in six graphs (Figure 20.2) summarizing the impact of an increase in the domestic money supply at time t_0. The graphs show the original level before t_0, the short run impact in t_0, and the path to the new long-run equilibrium overtime for the following variables: money supply, interest rate, real money supply, price, expected exchange rate, and spot exchange rate.

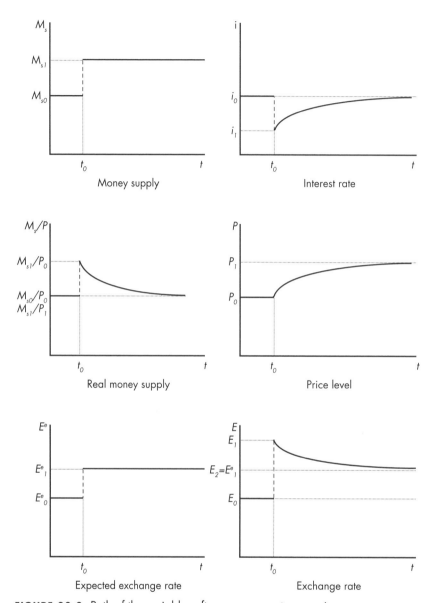

FIGURE 20.2 Path of the variables after a permanent money increase

An Illustration of the Model – The Dornbusch Overshooting Diagram

We start with a long-run equilibrium: the economy is at its full-employment level and all the financial markets are in equilibrium. The long-run equilibrium exchange rate is approximated by PPP. All the foreign variables are fixed. Prices are flexible in the long run and fixed in the short run. We assume a permanent increase in the money supply. Since there is no adjustment through prices in the short run, both the money market and the foreign exchange market will move to a new equilibrium (as these two markets are always in equilibrium). However this new equilibrium is not a long-run equilibrium. We want to illustrate how the economy moves from this short-run equilibrium resulting from the expansionary monetary policy to a new long-run equilibrium as prices eventually adjust.

The Dornbusch diagram (Figure 20.3) shows the exchange rate on the y-axis and the price on the x-axis. The long-run relation between the price level P (with P^* fixed) and the long-run equilibrium exchange rate that is approximated by the PPP relation is a 45° upward sloping line. As shown earlier, the equilibrium price is determined in the long run by the relative money supply divided by the relative money demand in the two countries. So this determines the position of the original long-run equilibrium price P_0. The vertical line $P=P_0$ intersects the PPP line at a point LR_0, the long-run equilibrium, allowing us to find the corresponding long-run exchange rate E_0 on the y-axis.

Now we assume a permanent increase in the money supply. The position of P_0 was determined by the ratio of the relative supply of money over the relative demand for money; as a result, in the long run, the increase in price from P_0 to P_1 as well as the increase in the long-run exchange rate from E_0 to E_1 will be proportional to the increase in M_s. So this determines the position of P_1 allowing us to find the new long-run equilibrium PR_1 and the new long-run equilibrium exchange rate E_1. However in the short run, the price does not change and remains at P_0. As explained earlier in the

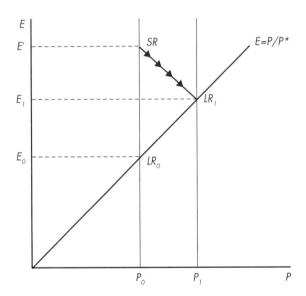

FIGURE 20.3 The Dornbush Overshooting Diagram

LR_0 is the original equilibrium where PPP holds as it is on the 45° lines where $E=P/P^*$. A permanent increase in the money supply will send the economy to LR_1 where PPP holds as price adjusts over time. From LR_0 to LR_1, the money supply, the price level, and the exchange rate increase proportionally. However, in the short run, prices are sticky and do not contribute to the adjustment. In order for the money market to remain in equilibrium, the slack will be taken by the exchange rate that will have to increase (depreciate) by more than proportionally to the increase in the money supply. So the exchange rate depreciates beyond its long-run equilibrium and will have to appreciate as prices start increasing to bring about the long-run equilibrium.

chapter, the exchange rate will thus overshoot its long-run equilibrium E_1 and depreciate all the way to E on the $P=P_0$ line (on point SR). When the price increases gradually in the transition to a new long-run equilibrium, the exchange rate will thus have to appreciate gradually to reach its long-run equilibrium E_1.

In our last theoretical chapter, we have extended the earlier models into a world where prices were flexible at all time and linked back to a very respectable area of economic thought: that of the monetarists. We have shown that there are important applications stemming from this hypothesis. More importantly, we have developed an important model of the modern economy, borrowing from both Keynesian sticky prices and monetarist flexible prices, to explain the volatility of short-run exchange rate fluctuations. The last three chapters follow an historical approach to describe the international monetary system, the European monetary integration experience, and finally, the more recent events surrounding the economic upheavals of many emerging economies.

Summary of Key Concepts

1. The Law of One Price states that if prices are fully flexible, identical goods should be identically priced on the world markets when their prices are converted into the same currency with the nominal exchange rate.
2. The notion is extrapolated to a basket of goods and services, the CPI (or price level). This is the basis for the concept of Purchasing Power Parity (PPP).
3. If it is true that the price of the basket is identical in various countries, then we can derive the nominal exchange rate as the ratio of the price levels.
4. All these statements are based on the assumption of perfect price flexibility at all times. There are so many reasons why this is not the case in the real world that PPP never holds in the short run: in fact, exchange rates are very volatile and follow a random walk.
5. Notwithstanding its many problems, PPP is used extensively for international levels of living comparisons.
6. However, in the long run, PPP is not to be dismissed, although it takes a long time for the exchange rate to converge towards the PPP estimates. PPP can thus be considered as an estimate of the long-run exchange rate.
7. A more realistic model might consider prices as sticky in the short run and flexible in the long run.
8. The Dornbusch overshooting model is based on such premises. The model states that, as a result of a monetary disturbance, the exchange rate will immediately overshoot its long-run equilibrium as prices do not contribute to the adjustment in the short run. A correction will have to take place when prices start to adjust in the long run. This model explains partially the high volatility of exchange rates in the short run.

CASE STUDY I

Soft Currency
July 26, 2007
From *The Economist*, print edition

The dollar is weak against a clutch of currencies that share many of its flaws

LONDON is never a cheap destination, but American visitors to Britain's capital this summer will find their wallets emptying a little faster than usual. A dollar now buys less British currency than it has for a generation. On July 23rd, the greenback slumped to $2.06 against the pound, its weakest level since 1981. Paris is scarcely cheaper for transatlantic tourists: this week the dollar sagged to €1.38, its lowest rate since the euro's launch in 1999.

The greenback has never been further out of favour on currency markets. The Federal Reserve tracks the dollar's value against a weighted basket of seven currencies that are commonly traded beyond their respective borders. This index, regarded as a good gauge of financial-market sentiment about the dollar, has fallen to an all-time low.

What lies behind the latest bout of dollar weakness? Part of the slump is cyclical, reflecting America's weak economy. GDP growth this year is expected to be lower in America than in the euro area, Britain, Australia and Canada, according to *The Economist*'s monthly poll of forecasters.

The origins of weak growth are a particular worry. Just as the trouble in America's housing market is a drag on the economy, the turmoil in the subprime-mortgage market weighs on the currency. Analysts at Goldman Sachs believe that lower overseas demand for corporate debt has put downward pressure on the dollar. The disquiet about mortgage credit in America, they suggest, may even have chipped away a little at the dollar's standing as a reserve currency.

High oil prices haven't helped either. Paul Robinson, a currency strategist at Barclays Capital, reckons that the dollar is the worst performing major currency during periods of rising oil prices. This might be because America uses more oil for each unit of output than other rich countries, so the higher cost of fuel hits growth – and thus the dollar – harder. American consumers are especially vulnerable, because low fuel taxes leave a thinner cushion between the cost of crude and retail prices. The spending of petrodollars also helps the dollar less than the euro, because oil-producing countries tend to import more from Europe than America.

So a steep oil price, a weak economy and an anxious credit market have all weakened the dollar. But America's growth prospects are not so poor and the subprime-mortgage market not so woeful – at least, not yet – that they can fully explain the dollar's recent sickliness.

Stephen Jen, currency economist at Morgan Stanley, suggests there might be more powerful forces driving the dollar down. A common fear is that Asia's central banks will diversify out of their large holdings of American debt. Mr Jen argues, however, that the biggest dollar diversifiers have been pension, insurance and mutual funds in America. These funds control assets worth $20.7 trillion, more than four times the size of the world's official currency reserves.

American mutual funds have gradually increased their overseas allocation of equities since 2003 from 15% to 22.5% of assets, says Mr Jen. If this portfolio shift mirrors the behaviour of all pension, insurance and mutual fund managers, it would imply an outflow from dollar assets of $1.16 trillion since 2003. That sum is not far short of China's entire hoard of official reserves.

Mr Jen argues that these capital outflows need not be a sign that asset managers are gloomy about prospects for either the dollar or the American economy. Rather they might reflect an underlying decline in provincialism, as investors gradually come to appreciate the dangers of relying excessively on home-country assets. A similar thing is happening, he says, in Japan where households are greedily buying overseas assets. If the dollar has suffered most, it is only because American institutions are the biggest pioneers of financial globalisation.

Yet wariness about the dollar may be part of the motivation to diversify. A regular survey by Merrill Lynch shows that global fund managers have been consistently negative about the dollar's prospects for the past five years. For most of that period, the same asset managers have expressed a wish to reduce the weight of American assets in their portfolios, though that urge was strongest three years ago. It is hard to disentangle diversification from desertion since each feeds on the other.

Don't deficits matter?

On the surface, the latest episode of dollar frailty seems to validate concerns about America's persistent current-account deficit and the associated build-up of overseas debt. Many economists welcome a weaker dollar which, by making America's imports dearer and its exports cheaper, helps narrow the country's external deficit. Indeed, the trade gap in the first five months of this year was smaller than in the same period in 2006.

But a closer look suggests that currency markets, rightly or wrongly, are blithe about trade imbalances. Some of the countries whose currencies have gained most at the dollar's expense, like Britain, Australia and New Zealand, have large external deficits and debts too. Australia's current-account shortfall has been more persistent than America's and, as a result, its net overseas debt last year was 60% of its GDP, compared with 19% for America.

New Zealand's debt ratio is larger still at 90% of GDP. Meanwhile the currency of the world's largest creditor nation, Japan, continues to languish – even against the dollar.

If anxiety about global imbalances is not driving currency markets, perhaps the dollar might rally once America's economy is back on its feet. It has, after all, fallen a long way already: on the Fed's broad trade-weighted index, the greenback is down 22% since its peak in 2002. According to the purchasing-power parities calculated by the OECD, the dollar is undervalued by 15% against the euro, 18% against the Australian dollar and 21% against the pound. Such divergences from fair value might not prove sustainable, particularly for the countries that have external financing gaps of their own to fill.

CASE STUDY QUESTIONS

1. Comment on the relation between the impact of high oil prices hitting the American economy and the depreciation of the dollar.

2. Are currency markets affected by chronic current account deficits? Besides the U.S., various other countries have large trade deficits – does this weaken their currency?

3. When compared to its purchasing power parity value, is the dollar overvalued or undervalued. How is the dollar purchasing power parity rate estimated?

CASE STUDY II

McCurrencies
May 25, 2006
From *The Economist*, print edition

Happy 20th birthday to our Big Mac index[6]

WHEN our economics editor invented the Big Mac index in 1986 as a light-hearted introduction to exchange-rate theory, little did she think that 20 years later she would still be munching her way, a little less sylph-like, around the world. As burgernomics enters its third decade, the Big Mac index is widely used and abused around the globe. It is time to take stock of what burgers do and do not tell you about exchange rates.

The Economist's Big Mac index is based on one of the oldest concepts in international economics: the theory of purchasing-power parity (PPP), which argues that in the long run, exchange rates should move towards levels that would equalise the prices of an identical basket of goods and services in any two countries. Our "basket" is a McDonald's Big Mac, produced in around 120 countries. The Big Mac PPP is the exchange rate that would leave burgers costing the same in America as elsewhere. Thus a Big Mac in China costs 10.5 yuan, against an average price in four American cities of $3.10 (see the first column of the hamburger standard table that follows this case study). To make the two prices equal would require an exchange rate of 3.39 yuan to the dollar, compared with a market rate of 8.03. In other words, the yuan is 58% "undervalued" against the dollar. To put it another way, converted into dollars at market rates the Chinese burger is the cheapest in the table.

In contrast, using the same method, the euro and sterling are overvalued against the dollar, by 22% and 18% respectively; the Swiss and Swedish currencies are even more overvalued. On the other hand, despite its recent climb, the yen appears to be 28% undervalued, with a PPP of only ¥81 to the dollar. Note that all emerging-market currencies also look too cheap.

The index was never intended to be a precise predictor of currency movements, simply a take-away guide to whether currencies are at their "correct" long-run level. Curiously, however, burgernomics has an impressive record in predicting exchange rates: currencies that show up as overvalued often tend to weaken in later years. But you must always remember the Big Mac's limitations. Burgers cannot sensibly be traded across borders and prices are distorted by differences in taxes and the cost of non-tradable inputs, such as rents.

Despite our frequent health warnings, some American politicians are fond of citing the Big Mac index rather too freely when it suits their cause – most notably in their demands for a big appreciation of the Chinese currency in order to reduce America's huge trade deficit. But the cheapness of a Big Mac in China does not really prove that the yuan is being held far below its fair-market value. Purchasing-power parity is a long-run concept. It signals where exchange rates are eventually heading, but it says little about today's market-equilibrium exchange rate that would make the prices of tradable goods equal. A burger is a product of both traded and non-traded inputs.

An idea to relish

It is quite natural for average prices to be lower in poorer countries than in developed ones. Although the prices of tradable things should be similar, non-tradable services will be cheaper because of lower wages. PPPs are therefore a more reliable way to convert GDP per head into dollars than market exchange rates, because cheaper prices mean that

---

6 The table for the hamburger standard for 2006 is available below.

money goes further. This is also why every poor country has an implied PPP exchange rate that is higher than today's market rate, making them all appear undervalued. Both theory and practice show that as countries get richer and their productivity rises, their real exchange rates appreciate. But this does not mean that a currency needs to rise massively today. Jonathan Anderson, chief economist at UBS in Hong Kong, reckons that the yuan is now only 10–15% below its fair-market value.

Even over the long run, adjustment towards PPP need not come from a shift in exchange rates; relative prices can change instead. For example, since 1995, when the yen was overvalued by 100% according to the Big Mac index, the local price of Japanese burgers has dropped by one-third. In the same period, American burgers have become one-third dearer. Similarly, the yuan's future real appreciation could come through faster inflation in China than in the United States.

The Big Mac index is most useful for assessing the exchange rates of countries with similar incomes per head. Thus, among emerging markets, the yuan does indeed look undervalued, while the currencies of Brazil, Turkey, Hungary and the Czech Republic look overvalued. Economists would be unwise to exclude Big Macs from their diet, but Super Size servings would equally be a mistake.

CASE STUDY QUESTIONS

1. What is the Big Mac Index supposed to tell us, according to *The Economist*?

2. What are the basic requirements for the law of one price to hold?

3. Are these requirements satisfied for the Big Mac Index?

4. Why do you think *The Economist* presents the index?

The hamburger standard for 2006

	Big Mac prices				
	In local currency	in dollars	Implied PPP* of the dollar	Actual dollar exchange rate May 22nd	Under (–)/over (+) valuation against the dollar, %
United States†	$3.10	3.10	–	–	–
Argentina	Peso 7.00	2.29	2.26	3.06	−26
Australia	A$3.25	2.44	1.05	1.33	−21
Brazil	Real 6.40	2.78	2.06	2.30	−10
Britain	£1.94	3.65	1.60†	1.88†	+18
Canada	C$3.52	3.14	1.14	1.12	+1
Chile	Peso 1,560	2.94	503	530	−5
China	Yuan 10.5	1.31	1.39	8.03	−58
Czech Republic	Koruna 59.05	2.67	19.0	22.1	−14
Denmark	DK127.75	4.77	8.95	5.88	+54
Egypt	Pound 9.50	1.65	3.06	5.77	−47
Euro area§	€2.94	3.77	1.05**	1.28**	+22
Hong Kong	HK$12	1.55	3.87	7.75	−50

Hungary	Forint 560	2.71	161	206	−12
Indonesia	Rupiah 14,600	1.57	4.710	9,325	−49
Japan	¥250	2.23	80.6	112	−28
Malaysia	Ringgit 5.50	1.52	1.77	3.63	−51
Mexico	Peso 29.00	2.57	9.35	11.3	−17
New Zealand	NZ$4.45	2.75	1.44	1.62	−11
Peru	New Sol9.50	2.91	3.05	3.26	−6
Philippines	Peso 85.00	1.62	27.4	52.6	−48
Poland	Zloty 6.50	2.10	2.10	3.10	−32
Russia	Rouble 48.00	1.77	15.5	27.1	−43
Singapore	S$3.60	2.27	1.16	1.59	−27
South Africa	Rand 13.95	2.11	4.50	6.60	−32
South Korea	Won 2,500	2.62	806	952	−15
Sweden	SKr33.00	4.53	10.6	7.28	+46
Switzerland	SFt6.30	5.21	2.03	1.21	+68
Taiwan	NT$75.00	2.33	24.2	32.1	−25
Thailand	Baht 60.00	1.56	19.4	38.4	−50
Turkey	Lire 4.20	2.72	1.35	1.54	−12
Venezuela	Bolivar 5,701	2.17	1.839	2.630	−30
Aruba	Florin 4.95	2.77	1.60	1.79	−11
Bulgaria	Lev 2.99	1.94	0.96	1.54	−37
Colombia	Peso 6,500	2.60	2,097	2,504	−16
Costa Rica	Colon 1,130	2.22	365	510	−28
Croatia	Kuna 15.0	2.62	4.84	5.72	−15
Dominican Rep	Peso 60.0	1.84	19.4	32.6	−41
Estonia	Kroon 29.5	2.40	9.52	12.3	−23
Fiji	Fiji $4.65	2.69	1.50	1.73	−13
Georgia	Lar14.15	2.31	1.34	1.80	−26
Guatemala	Quetral 17.25	2.27	5.56	7.59	−27
Honduras	Lempira 35.95	1.90	11.6	18.9	−39
Iceland	Kronur 459	6.37	148	72.0	+106
Latvia	Lats 1.35	2.47	0.44	0.55	−20
Lithuania	titas 6.50	2.41	2.10	2.69	−22
Macau	Pataca 11.1	1.39	9.59	7.99	−55
Moldova	Leu 23.0	2.75	7.62	13.2	−44
Morocco	Dirham 24.5	2.82	7.92	8.71	−9
Norway	Kroner 43.0	7.05	11.9	6.10	+127
Pakistan	Rupee 130	2.16	41.9	60.1	−30
Paraguay	Guatami 9,000	1.63	2,903	5,506	−47
Saudi Arabia	Riyal 9.00	2.40	2.90	3.75	−23
Slovakia	Koruna 58.0	1.97	18.7	29.5	−37

* Purchasing-power parity: local price divided by the price in United States.
† Average of New York, Chicago, Atlanta and San Francisco.
‡ Dollars per pound.
§ Weighted average of prices in euro area.
** Dollars per euro.

Questions for Study and Review

1. You are told that one of the reasons why PPP does not hold is the existence of tariffs and transportation costs. Later on in the chapter you are told that these two factors could be factored in because they are constant. Explain what would happen to international prices if tariffs and transportation costs were the only problem preventing PPP from holding.

2. Assume that Malaysia, like many developing countries, has a dual economy: a vibrant export sector where they manufacture computer components for various Japanese companies (tradable) and a sector that produces local goods only (non-tradable). Assume that PPP holds so their exchange rate is the ratio of their CPI over their trade partner's CPI, Japan.

   a. What is the original value of the real exchange rate?

   Then, new developments in computer technology allow Malaysia to produce the components at lower costs.

   b. What happens to wages in Malaysia's export sector? What happens to wages overall in Malaysia?

   c. What happens to costs and prices of the non-tradable? What happens to Malaysia's CPI? Explain. Finally what happens to the real exchange rate?

3. When you examine series constructed on the exchange rate approach and series constructed on the PPP approach to compare gross national income per capita, what can you say about the dispersion for the two series? What happens to the richer countries and what happens to the poorer countries when the level of living is estimated with the PPP approach?

4. *International Comparisons* An average consumer in Canada consumes 10 pounds of oranges, 4 loaves of bread, and 5 pints of beer. During the same period, the average Australian consumer consumes 6 pounds of oranges, 5 loaves of bread, and 6 pints of beer. Assume that the price of oranges in Canada is Can$2 per lb, a loaf of bread costs Can$3, and beer costs Can$4 per pint while the corresponding prices in Australia are respectively Aus$1 for oranges, Aus$4 per loaf, and Aus$5 for beer.

   a. Use the exchange rate between the two currencies to compare their standard of living using the Can$.

   (Find the exchange rate on the Website link http://www.x-rates.com/AUD/table.html)

   b. Now use the PPP approach with Canadian prices to compare their standards of living.

   c. Finally use the PPP approach with Australian prices to compare their standards of living.

   d. Comment on all three results.

5. Throughout the year in 1980, inflation in the U.S. was 13.5 percent while in the U.K. it was 18 percent. During that same year, the exchange rate, $/£, increased from 2.225 on January 1 to 2.292 on December 31. Find this point on Figure 20.1. Does this point meet the PPP criteria? Why or why not?

6. The central bank of Pecunia, a small country, decides to cut the money supply permanently by 10 percent. Assume a sticky price model in the short run, where prices eventually adjust in the long run. Explain what happens to the interest rate, the real money supply, the price level, the expected exchange rate, and the exchange rate in the short run. Describe the long-run adjustment for the above variables. Show all your results using the six graphs of Figure 20.2. Elaborate about the overall movements of the exchange rate (short run and long run) as a result of the contractionary monetary policy.

References and Suggestions for Further Reading

Balassa, B. (1964) "The Purchasing Power Parity Doctrine: A Reappraisal," *Journal of Political Economy*, 72: 584–96.

Cassel, G. (1928) *Post-War Monetary Stabilization*, New York: Columbia University Press.

Dornbusch, R. (1976) "Expectations and Exchange Rate Dynamics," *Journal of Political Economy*, 84: 1161–1176.

—— (1987) "Purchasing Power Parity," in J. Eatwell, M. Milgate, and P. Newman (eds), *The New Palgrave*, Vol. 3, New York: Macmillan.

Frenkel, J.A., Gylfason T., and Heliwell, J.F. (1980) "A Synthesis of Monetary and Keynesian Approaches to the Short-Run Balance of Payment Theory," *The Economic Journal*, 90: 582–92.

Frenkel, J. and Rose, A. (1996) "A Panel Project on Purchasing Power Parity: Mean Reversion Within and Between Countries," *Journal of International Economics* 40: 209–24.

Frenkel, J. and Johnson, H. (eds) (1976) *The Monetary Approach to the Balance of Payments*, London: Allen and Unwin.

International Monetary Funds (1977) *The Monetary Approach to the Balance of Payments*, Washington D.C.: International Monetary Funds.

Kravis, I. and Lipsey, R. (1983) *Toward an Explanation of National Price Levels*, Princeton Studies in International Finance, No 52. Princeton N.J.: International Finance Section, Department of Economics, Princeton University.

Lothian, J. and Taylor, M. (1996) "Real Exchange Rate Behavior: The Recent Float from the Perspective of the Past Two Centuries," *Journal of Political Economy*, 104: 488–509.

Rogoff, K. (1996) "The Purchasing Power Parity Puzzle," *Journal of Economic Literature*, 34: 647–68.

Samuelson, P. (1964) "Theoretical Notes on Trade Problems," *Review of Economics and Statistics*, 46: 145–54.

Summers, R. and Heston, A. (1991) "The Penn World Tables: An Expanded Set of International Comparisons, 1950–1988," *Quarterly Journal of Economics*, 106: 327–68.

Vernon, R. (1966) "International Investment and International Trade in the Product Cycle," *Quarterly Journal of Economics* 80:190–207.

APPENDIX: FURTHER IMPLICATIONS OF THE MONETARIST OR LONG-RUN MODEL

We will now interpret the monetarist model as a long-run model: this will allow us to derive further implications from the model. First we can simplify equation (20.6) reproduced below by making some assumptions specifying the form of the relations.

$$\bar{E} = \frac{P}{P^*} = \frac{M_s / M_s^*}{L(i,Y) / L^*(i^*, Y^*)}$$

becomes

$$\bar{E}=\frac{P}{P^*}=\frac{M_s/M_s^*}{Y/Y^*}\lambda(i-i^*)\qquad(20.7)$$

The term λ is a coefficient. We assume all the foreign variables fixed and focus on the domestic variables. We can draw the long-run domestic money market as a relation between the nominal money supply and the price level. Nominal money demand is positively related to P so upwards sloping and shifts with changes in the (real) interest rate or in Y. Since the long-run economy is always at its full-employment level, changes in Y are caused by supply-side shocks.

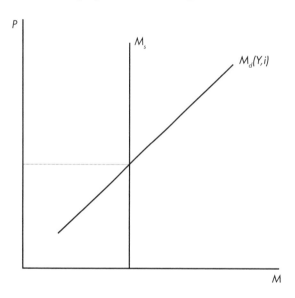

FIGURE 20.4 The Long-Run Money Market

Instead of the traditional representation of the short-run money market in the i/M space, we use the P/M space as P is the variable that adjusts in the long run. In this case the interest rate and income are the shift variables.

From this graph, it is clear that an increase in price and thus a long-run depreciation can be caused by various factors; monetary (Case 1) as well as real (Cases 2 and 3). The first case was presented in the main body of the chapter to explain the overshooting model. We present below examples of three shocks that would affect the price level and trigger a long-run depreciation.

Monetary shocks: impact on the money supply
Case 1. A permanent increase in the money supply.

Real shocks: impact on the long-run money demand
Case 2. An adverse supply shock reducing full employment Y to a lower level, e.g. an oil shock.
Case 3. An increase in the interest rate – due to some real disturbance (not monetary), e.g.

impact on the capital market of permanent disabling of the internet resulting in the inability to carry out financial transactions on the internet.

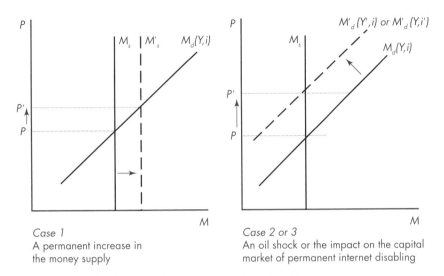

FIGURE 20.5 Shocks and Adjustment in the Long-Run Money Market

Case 1 corresponds to the situation discussed earlier in the chapter: the money supply is increased and M_s shifts to the right resulting in an increase in the price level and a long-run depreciation. In Case 2, Y full employment drops to Y' as a result of the oil shock. $M_d(Y,i)$ shifts to the left to $M'_d(Y',i)$ as the money demand is positively related to income: the money demand falls when income falls. The result is again an increase in the price level and a long-run depreciation. The same overall outcome takes place in Case 3. A real monetary shock (triggered by the loss of the internet) causes the interest rate to increase; M_d shifts to the left to $M'_d(Y,i')$ [instead of $M'_d(Y',i)$ with the oil shock] and the impact on the price level is equivalent.

Since we assume that all the foreign variables are fixed, any of the three cases will result in an increase in the price level and a long-run depreciation.

Chapter 21

The International Monetary System

A Brief History

LEARNING OBJECTIVES

By the end of this chapter you should be able to understand:

- the history of the international financial system over a century

- the development of currencies and exchange rates

- the gold standard and its basic adjustment mechanism

- the advantages and disadvantages of the gold standard – its heyday before World War I and its disappearance in the thirties

- how the Bretton Woods arrangement replaced the gold standard after World War II

- the weaknesses and demise of Bretton Woods

- the post-Bretton Woods experience with flexible exchange rates

- the issues relating to the "new international financial architecture"

In this chapter, we describe and analyze the evolution of the various exchange rate regimes over more than a century. Up to now, for the sake of clarity, the models developed in this textbook have been based primarily on the two extreme cases of fixed and flexible exchange rates. However, the list of exchange rate arrangements adopted by various countries now as well as in the past is extensive. Table 13.1 in Chapter 13 reproduces a table compiled by the IMF, cataloguing the various contemporary regimes.

First, we discuss the gold standard that prevailed until the beginning of World War I. The period between the two World Wars displayed a return to the gold standard for some countries only and a lot of instability overall. In the hope of eradicating such instabilities, the Bretton Woods system was introduced in 1944 as an international agreement between most industrialized countries. The demise of the Bretton Woods agreement in the early seventies heralded a decline in the prevalence of fixed exchange rate arrangements over flexible exchange rates. With the advent of greater international capital mobility and global financial integration, new types of instabilities have appeared. Greater efforts to regulate the new international financial architecture are now at the forefront of the news.

The Earliest Forms of Exchange Rates

The exchange rate is one of the most fundamental economic variables. With the development of ancient cultures came the need to exchange goods, i.e. to trade. This rudimentary level of economic development gave rise to the introduction of a currency – shells,[1] or any other precious, rare object – to facilitate the means of exchange and create a unit of account within that culture. As soon as a currency was established in a specific culture, trade between different tribes or cultures required a rate of exchange between these primitive forms of currency (e.g. how many of my pretty shells does it take to equal one of our precious goats?).[2]

Overtime, currencies based on shells or goats were replaced by currencies based on precious gems or metals, because these materials were not only rare but also durable. Sooner or later, all nations based their currency on gold and/or silver. "Based on" means that in order to avoid having to carry around large quantities of gold or silver, governments eventually printed paper money that could always be exchanged for a precious metal. In essence, the government promised to exchange a specific quantity of gold, say one ounce, for a specific quantity of paper currency, say $20.

---

1 Cowry shells were one of the most common form of money in many coastal countries or islands of the Indian and Pacific Oceans (used as late as the nineteenth century in certain areas).

2 Cattle of all kinds were also used as means of exchange. The word "capital" originally referred to the number of heads of a herd someone owned.

In most European economies, silver was the currency of choice during the Middle Ages: it was sufficiently abundant to serve as means of exchange, and appropriately rare to avoid massive bouts of inflation, since silver discoveries were scarce. Many countries also adhered to a bimetallic standard based on silver and gold. Silver was scarce until the sixteenth century; then massive silver discoveries in America forced most countries to give up silver and base their currencies on gold only. By the 1870s, some of the main bimetallic nations such as the U.S. moved to a pure gold standard.

THE GOLD STANDARD

The gold standard became the prevalent international monetary arrangement from the second half of the nineteenth century to World War I. Attempts at returning to that system after World War I were not successful. It was based on a number of principles, and it seems that after the war the conditions necessary for a successful monetary system did not exist any more. The heyday of the gold standard is considered to have lasted from 1880 to 1914.

The Gold Standard Four Crucial Principles

First and foremost, a government fixes the price of its paper currency to gold. In addition, it promises *always* to exchange paper money for gold at a fixed price. Second, the central bank fully backs all national banknotes and coinage with gold reserves. Third, the government allows the free import and export of gold. And fourth, prices and wages are fully flexible.

i. Determining the Official Price of Gold

If a country wants to introduce the gold standard, it must announce a price, P_G, at which it promises to exchange paper money for gold. As a result, citizens can stop carrying around the heavy gold: they can exchange their gold at the central bank for convenient banknotes at this set exchange rate.

ii. Backing Currency with Gold Reserves

As innocuous as it seems, fixing the price of gold in terms of units of domestic currency has some important consequences. A government cannot just say, 1 oz of gold is hereby declared to be worth $20 and then expect the forces of supply and demand to clear the gold market. What if the government issued $1,000 worth of banknotes, but only held 10 oz or $200 worth of gold? If everyone wanted to exchange their banknotes for gold, the insufficiency of the gold reserves would become immediately apparent. Once the first $200 of currency is exchanged for gold, there is no gold left for the people who still want to exchange their currency for gold. The whole system would collapse and the government would lose all credibility.

Clearly, each banknote must be backed with an equal amount of gold reserves. Citizens will exchange gold for paper money only if they believe that they can redeem their paper money for gold at any time in the future at the exact same price again. Consequently, the government cannot spend the gold it receives: it must hold it in reserve in case citizens want to convert their currency back into gold. Formally, the first two principles imply that the money supply, M^S, under the gold standard is given by:

$$M^S = P_G G \qquad (21.1)$$

i.e. the price of gold, P^G, times the amount of gold, G, held in the central bank's reserves.

iii. Free Trade in Gold

Assume that the U.S. and the U.K. are both on the gold standard; the central bank in the U.S. promises to exchange one ounce of gold for $20 and the central bank in the U.K. promises to exchange one ounce of gold for £4. The exchange rate or **mint**[3] **parity** (the term used during the gold standard period) between the two currencies can be immediately derived as $E = \$20/\pounds4 = 5$; i.e. one pound sterling buys five dollars. This exchange rate can only hold if gold is traded across the two countries. If the import and export of gold are prohibited, the exchange rate is meaningless as it would be impossible to establish an exchange rate based on gold.

iv. Prices and Wages Fully Flexible

This last condition is essential for the existence of a smooth adjustment mechanism. The system depends on perfect price/wage flexibility. Whenever a trade imbalance puts any pressure on the currency to differ slightly from the mint parity, a mechanism based on price flexibility ensures that the mint parity remains the equilibrium exchange rate.

A Devaluation is Ineffective Under the Gold Standard

If it becomes known that the amount of currency issued by a central bank exceeds the value of gold reserves, people would panic and attempt to exchange all their currency for gold. To make sure that every person who holds paper currency gets at least some amount of gold, the central bank could increase the price of gold to $P'_G > P_G$, say from $20 to $30. This implies that all of a sudden everyone holding currency is a little poorer in terms of gold ($20 now buys less gold than before).

A devaluation of the currency creates a **time consistency problem**. If the central bank were in the habit of devaluing regularly, only extraordinarily gullible people would be willing to carry the currency and believe the central bank's promise to keep the price of gold fixed. Indeed, the more often they are harmed by a devaluation, the less likely people are to hold that currency. They will abandon their currency for gold or other more stable foreign currencies. In summary, the gold standard only works if there is a long-run commitment to a specific price of gold and a stable 1-to-1 ratio between the currency in circulation and the gold reserves: this fosters the belief that the currency will not be devalued at any time.

---

3 A mint was the place where precious metals were minted into coins.

Adjustment under the Gold Standard

The simple rules of the gold standard carry some strong implications. Free trade in gold, together with the constant price of gold, has an important consequence. Imagine that the Conquistadors bring new gold to Spain. The central bank will deposit the gold in its reserves and issue currency in exchange. If the gold reserves increase by, say, 1 ton of gold, the money supply will increase proportionally. The discovery of new gold has resulted in an increase in the money supply, potentially leading to inflationary pressures.

Restrictions of the Model

The requirement that the government (gold) reserves be in a 1-to-1 proportion with the money supply implies that, under a gold standard regime, the impact of any increase in reserves on the money supply cannot be neutralized or *sterilized* by the central bank. Recall that sterilization involves offsetting changes in (central banks' foreign) reserves with changes in the domestic money supply. Central banks manage the money supply by altering the extent of domestic credit (DC) through open market operations. The mechanism of sterilization has been explained in Chapter 13. The central bank buys (or sells) assets such as treasury bills to increase (or decrease) the money supply. If we ignore the role of commercial banks and the money multiplier, equation 21.1 representing the money supply will then have to include domestic credit as shown below:

$$MS = P_G G + DC \qquad (21.2)$$

If domestic credit is added in the equation, the direct proportionality between the stock of money and the stock of official gold reserves is broken. Clearly, if the central bank sells treasury bills to the public to offset the impact on the money supply of the increase in gold, the central bank does not respect the one-to-one relation between money supply and gold reserves. Thus, non-sterilization is an essential tenet of the gold standard.

Changes in gold reserves are not only the result of new gold discoveries, they are also the result of trade imbalances. It is that one-to-one relation between the gold reserves and the money supply that allows an adjustment mechanism to take place. This basic adjustment is known as the "**Price-Specie-Flow Mechanism**." "Specie" is simply an ancient word for precious metals. This mechanism refers to the balancing of international trade via the flow of "specie" from one country to another.

David Hume and the Mercantilists

In 1758, the English philosopher, David Hume (reprint 1898), in his essay entitled "On the Balance of trade," developed the price-specie-flow mechanism to demonstrate the futility of the French **mercantilist** policies designed to amass maximum amounts of wealth in terms of gold and silver.

Mercantilism was an economic philosophy of the sixteenth and seventeenth century, based on the idea that a country should always run trade surpluses in order to accumulate financial wealth. To achieve such goals, trade policy consisted in high tariffs on imports and export subsidies, thus generating gold inflows. David Hume wrote his treatise to prove that mercantilism is theoretically inconsistent. Hume showed with his price-specie-flow mechanism how the gold standard would automatically eliminate trade imbalances, and that the trade surpluses under mercantilism could not be sustained.

The Price-Specie-Flow Mechanism

We consider a two-country model, the domestic and the foreign country. If the domestic country is running a trade surplus, it receives more gold for its exports than it has to pay for its imports. Recall that one of the tenets of the gold standard is free trade in gold allowing international transactions to be settled with gold. A trade surplus for the domestic economy thus generates gold inflows into the country. With non-sterilization, these inflows result in an equal increase in the money supply under the gold standard. Since the money supply rises while the productive capacity of the economy has not expanded, the price level rises. This increase in prices renders domestic products relatively more expensive compared to foreign goods, and foreign goods relatively cheaper. The result is decreased foreign demand for domestic goods (exports) and increased domestic demand for foreign goods (imports). As exports fall and imports rise, the trade surplus declines and the money supply increases at a slower pace. The inflationary pressures come to an end when the money supply stops rising: this occurs when trade is balanced.

A similar adjustment takes place in the foreign country. The domestic country's trade surplus is matched by an equivalent trade deficit in the foreign country. The trade deficit leads to a loss of gold, a decrease in the money supply, and a fall in the price level, bringing back the foreign country's competitiveness. When trade between the two countries is eventually balanced, gold stops flowing internationally (money supply and price levels stabilize in the two countries) and the equilibrium is restored.

Since, in this scenario, gold actually moves from one country to another to settle trade, additional costs, for transportation and insurance, are incurred. These costs create a wedge between the prices of gold in the two countries. The two limits of the wedge are referred to in the literature as the **gold export** and the **gold import points**. This simply means that, as the currencies are both defined in terms of their gold content, this wedge allows the two currencies to fluctuate around their mint parity in a small band corresponding to these costs.

In sum, under the gold standard, the central bank is allowing all changes in gold reserves to translate directly into equal changes in the money supply without trying to control the money supply or the price level. Every time the money supply changes, the domestic economy is at its whim. Basically, the central bank cannot manipulate the money supply (or the interest rate) for domestic purposes: in practical terms, it loses its sovereignty on monetary policy. This very simple and seemingly effective system is not without some drawbacks weighing against its obvious advantages.

A Modern Application of the Gold Standard: the Currency Board

The gold standard is not a totally obsolete form of exchange rate mechanism. There are several countries today that use a modern version of the gold standard called "currency board." We listed this system in Table 13.1 showing all the various exchange rate arrangements and we also mentioned it in Chapter 18 as a special form of fixed exchange rate (see p. 533). A currency board exists when the central bank issues money only in proportion to its foreign currency holdings as underlying asset. The currency board ensures that the currency peg to a strong currency, most often the dollar, is irreversible. Countries adopt such a system hoping that it will impart some degree of stability to their foreign sector. For example, Hong Kong is on a currency board based on the U.S. dollar, meaning that the entire Hong Kong money supply is backed by their U.S. dollar reserves. We make two modifications to equation (21.1). First, the country holds foreign currency reserves instead of gold and second, in a modern economy, the money multiplier, μ, is taken into account. This means that it is the monetary base that is backed entirely by the foreign currency reserves.

$$MS = \mu \, E \, ForeignCurrencyReserves$$

Instead of fixing the price of domestic currency to gold, currency boards fix the price of domestic currency to foreign currency. Simply speaking, currency boards fix the exchange rate. Under currency boards, central banks pledge to hold sufficient foreign currency reserves to back (fractionally) the money supply. So a version of the gold standard is alive and well in today's world in a number of small economies (such as Brunei or Estonia), and even in some more important ones (such as Hong Kong or Bulgaria).

Advantages and Disadvantages of the Gold Standard

The gold standard is seen to have two crucial advantages. First, it automatically ensures that *trade is always balanced* between countries. Second, it instills *fiscal discipline* in the economy. However due to its simplicity, *it lacks the flexibility necessary to deal with external shocks* such as fluctuations in the supply of gold or political upheavals of any nature.

Advantage 1: Balanced Trade

The automatic adjustment discussed above *always* restores equilibrium in the trade balance, should this equilibrium be disturbed. When international transactions mainly took the form of merchandise trade, balanced trade was regarded as desirable. In our modern global economy, where capital flows freely, balanced trade may not be that important. If countries have different growth rates or if they are developing economies, the question of trade balances/imbalances must be recast in a different light.

Advantage 2: Fiscal and Monetary Discipline

The gold standard instills fiscal discipline, because it does not allow the central bank to print money to finance government deficits. The central bank can only hand out currency in exchange for gold, never in exchange for government treasury bills. Does this mean that the government can never incur any debts? Not exactly.

The government can engage in deficit financing under specific conditions only: the total amount of the government debts must be covered by bond issues (such as U.S. treasury bonds) and all bond issues must be bought by *private* individuals and not by the central bank. If the central bank were to buy treasury bills, it would hand out dollars in exchange for something other than gold. This would immediately imply that *not* all the currency in circulation is backed by gold; the reserve requirement of the gold standard would be violated.

If the government dissaves (by running a budget deficit), other people in the economy have to save (to finance the deficit): the private citizens. Since the central bank cannot simply print money to purchase treasury bills, the government deficit is limited to the amount it can borrow from its citizens. The gold standard imposes fiscal discipline on governments. Moreover, central banks are precluded from the inflationary practice of printing money for the sole purpose of financing a fiscal deficit.

Disadvantage 1: Gold Supply and Demand Imbalances

Not all that glitters is gold. While the gold standard contains a foolproof, simple adjustment mechanism as well as imposing monetary and fiscal discipline, this simple exchange rate arrangement does not come without severe downsides. On the one hand, gold discoveries, like the Californian (1848) or Klondike, Alaska (1897) gold rushes, can lead to immediate inflation: if massive amounts of gold flood the market resulting in an increase in the money supply that is not matched by any increase in the economy's productive capacity, prices will rise.

On the other hand, periods of strong economic expansion (such as the industrial revolution) amplify the demand for money to accommodate the increase in output. Prices will remain constant provided that the money supply increases proportionally. However it would be a coincidence if gold discoveries were to increase proportionally to the increase in output just when needed. If the central bank does not have enough gold reserves to support an increase in the money supply, the excess demand for gold will cause deflation. This phenomenon occurred during the industrial revolution as gold discoveries did not keep pace with economic growth: prices fell by over 50 percent in the United States in the latter half of the 1800s, shaking the U.S. economy and resulting in unemployment. In general, inasmuch as the discrepancy between stagnating gold supplies and economic growth was not too drastic, this system tended to impart a deflationary trend on economies that was not unwanted.

Disadvantage 2: Political versus Economic Realities

The gold standard was never able to withstand episodes of war. Wars are times when sound economic policies give way to political necessities. After the government has soaked out all private savings by issuing treasury (war) bonds and selling them to the public to finance the military effort, the government has to resort to the central bank for further financing: then it is the turn of the central bank to buy the additional war bonds issued by the treasury. The central bank will pay with newly printed money. As shown in equation 21.2, domestic credit now becomes part – in addition to gold – of the reserves supporting the money supply: these operations clearly break the proportionality between currency and gold. The government has two options. First, it can restore the gold standard by resetting a mint parity that corresponds to a higher level of money supply supported by the fixed amount of gold: this is equivalent to a devaluation of the currency. Given that no economic statements by a government at a time of war can be truly credible, people know that the devaluation will not be unique and further devaluations are likely to follow if spending continues to exceed revenues: public confidence in the system is shattered and the gold standard system collapses. The other option is to leave the system altogether.

Disadvantage 3: Possible Adverse Economic Consequences

Theoretically, the adjustment mechanism under the gold standard is grounded on a crucial assumption: prices are fully flexible (they adjust immediately) and, as a result, economies are always at full employment. These assumptions correspond to the monetarist model developed in the previous chapter (see Figure 20.4). Since prices are nominal variables, their fluctuations[4] have no effect on the real variables and the economy is not affected by the adjustment mechanism – its impact is neutral. How realistic is this assumption? If prices do not adjust immediately, some of the burden of the adjustment will have to fall on other variables. In this case, a decrease in the money supply will result in an increase in the interest rate: the adjustment will then create losers and winners at least in the short run.

This is best illustrated with an example. Suppose two countries, Britain and the United States, adhere to the gold standard. A trade deficit for Britain sets up the following sequence: British gold flows to the U.S., the U.S. money supply expands while the British money supply shrinks. The reduction in the British money supply boosts the interest rate discouraging capital investment and leading to a contraction in the economy and consequently to layoffs. The economic contraction directly discourages imports. In addition, increased unemployment eventually depresses wages, and lower production costs lead to a reduction in the price of British goods. As British prices drop, British exports rise and imports fall even further until the trade balance returns to zero. The opposite will happen in the U.S. economy. In this case, the income-reserve flow mechanism described in Chapter 15 kicks in first, followed over time by the price-specie-flow mechanism, to complete the adjustment.

When countries tried to reinstate the gold standard after World War I, these painful economic adjustment aspects lessened the desirability of the system. We will highlight these problems in our post-World War I discussion.

---

4 We assume homogeneous price changes.

The Heyday of the Gold Standard – Pre-World War I

Well into the nineteenth century, most nations used a bimetallic standard: gold and silver.[5] However, England effectively adopted a gold standard in 1717 under the Master of the Mint, Sir Isaac Newton. Eventually England was the first nation to write the gold standard into law in 1819. The United States, although formally on a bimetallic (gold and silver) standard, switched de facto to gold in 1834 by fixing the price of gold at $20.67 per ounce – a price that was kept constant for 99 years. Like Britain, the U.S. did not write the gold standard into law until later (the law was passed in 1900). Most major countries had joined the gold standard by the 1870s.[6]

The period between 1880 and 1914 corresponds to the heyday of the system. The reasons for the success of the system during this period have been pinned to various factors. No major war took place in the period. Economies were open to trade and capital mobility was fairly unchecked. England held a key role in the system, as London was the main financial center for the system. Long-term capital flows from the richer and stable European economies to newly industrialized economies helped with the adjustment mechanism. The participants in the system were mainly the richer industrialized countries. When economic historians analyze the price fluctuations during the period, they note that although long-run prices were rather stable, their short-run variability was high. In fact, there were quite a few financial and banking crises during the period.

Another notable observation was that, in general, the price fluctuations were not large enough to fully credit the price-specie-flow mechanism for achieving the adjustment. This implies that governments might have reinforced the process by tampering with domestic credit: restricting it in the presence of a trade deficit and expanding it in presence of a trade surplus. In fact, a limited amount of gold was transferred internationally as countries would settle their balance of payments disequilibrium through capital flows.

The demise of the gold standard was a consequence of World War I. During the war, nearly all nations either placed restrictions on gold convertibility or issued non-convertible paper money. If the convertibility of gold is restricted, people can no longer exchange their paper currency for gold at the central bank. Once this happens, it becomes clear that the central bank does not have sufficient gold reserves to back all its paper currency and the system collapses. Spurred by the necessities of war, many countries had to relinquish the gold standard.

---

5 The official name of the British Pound used to be "Pound Sterling." Sterling is 92.5 percent pure silver, so the British currency was literally called "one pound of silver." Initially 240 pennies were coined out of a pound of sterling silver. But King Edward I (1239–1307) was the first to allow inflation and by the time Queen Elizabeth I (1533–1603) came to power, one pound of sterling silver already yielded 744 pence! Note that 310 percent inflation (going from 240 to 744 pence per pound of sterling silver) over 300 years is not bad, considering that just between 1969 and 1999 inflation in the U.S. was 354 percent!

6 Germany, 1871; Scandinavia, 1874; Holland, 1875; Belgium, Italy, Switzerland, 1873; France, Spain 1876; Austria, 1879; Russia, 1893; India, 1898.

RECONSTRUCTION AND EXCHANGE RATES AFTER WORLD WAR I

World War I ended in 1918 with the Treaty of Versailles. Most European countries found themselves in a dire economic situation. They were highly indebted, as they had to pay for past war expenditures that were financed through printing money. In addition, they needed to raise further funds for the current reconstruction efforts. Many governments continued to print money, resulting in chronic inflation. The situation was even worse for Germany, as a clause in the Treaty of Versailles involved the payment of war reparations to the victors. To meet all these commitments, the German government could only print paper money. The result was a period of extreme inflation (hyperinflation) in the 1920s.[7]

Longing for the monetary stability of the pre-World War I years, many countries decided to return to the gold standard. The U.S. was able to restore its gold parity in 1919, soon after the war ended. On the other hand, the countries plagued with hyperinflation, Germany and Austria, had no hope of joining the system any time soon. By 1928, most of the major currencies did eventually restore their parity to gold. We mentioned in the previous chapter the problem of reestablishing a realistic parity with gold and the use of purchasing power parity to determine it. Unfortunately, governments did not pay much heed to the advice of economists: Great Britain set the pound at too strong a level, leading to chronic trade deficits (see the following box), and France did the opposite, hoping that a weak franc would boost their international competitiveness. Sadly, these erratic settings did not enhance the general confidence in the gold standard. On the contrary!

Circumstances were different and some of the conditions necessary for the gold standard adjustment process to work smoothly were not in place anymore. Social laws had given more rights to workers, and democratically elected government could not afford to maintain fiscal discipline in light of labor unrest. Fiscal policy, barely used in the pre-World War I era, became a central tool of government policy; budget deficits made their appearance. Fiscal irresponsibility is anathema in a gold standard regime. In addition, it is well known that social laws reduce price and wage flexibility; thus another important tenet of the adjustment process had been weakened.

We are now used to active monetary policy: the central bank president is expected to keep the price level constant. The gold standard required exactly the opposite. Under the non-sterilization assumption, it stipulated that the central bank stays out of the business of managing the money supply, and simply serves as a storage facility for gold and as a printing press for a determined amount of currency. In fact, as mentioned earlier, under the rules of the game, central banks often facilitated the adjustment mechanism by reducing domestic credit in case of trade deficit and vice versa. Monetary policy for domestic purposes was not part of their mission. The role of central banks was secondary in the heyday period.[8] The post-World War I period saw a lot of economic distress: straightening out the problems in the domestic economy became more important than allowing the automatic adjustment to take place. Central banks in many countries (the United States and France)

---

7 This had a lasting impact on Germany's abhorrence of inflation (see Chapter 22).

8 However, most European countries had central banks during the heyday of the gold standard, and the U.S. was the only exception – its central bank, the Federal Reserve Board, was not created until 1913.

did intervene to sterilize the effect of the gold flows on the money supply: the non-sterilization rule was broken.

The British Attempt to Return to the Gold Standard

After years of rampant inflation, the British Chancellor of the Exchequer, Winston Churchill, returned Britain to the gold standard in 1925, hoping to conjure up the pre-World War I period of stability. His decision highlights another difficulty with the gold standard: how to choose the right gold parity. In the previous chapter (p 604), we suggested the use of the purchasing power parity approach to find a realistic parity. If the value of the domestic currency in term of gold is set too high, the mint parity or exchange rates with the other currencies will be too strong (overvalued). As a result, domestic residents will import excessively while their exports drop. A trade deficit will arise with dire economic consequences as implied by the price-specie-flow mechanism.

Winston Churchill and Prime Minister Stanley Baldwin insisted on a strong (overvalued) British currency. By choosing the pre-war gold parity for the pound, they set the exchange rate (mint parity) between the dollar and the pound to be identical to its pre-war rate, $4.87, although Britain's economy had been devastated by its war effort and the purchasing power of the pound had declined substantially. Economists, such as John Maynard Keynes, warned Churchill against overvaluing the pound. The Chancellor of the Exchequer failed to listen and referred to Keynes' suggestions simply as "feather-brained."[9]

The overvaluation of the pound was at the root of serious trade deficits, triggering gold outflows. The adjustment resulted in a monetary contraction. The conditions in the twenties were different than in the pre-World War I era. Prices fell and the interest rate increased. Instead of the expected boost to the economy from restoring a strong pound, the adjustment threw Britain into a recession. The demand for domestic goods dropped due to the initial deterioration in the balance of trade and the adverse impact on investment caused by the increase in the interest rate. The level of unemployment rose putting downward pressures on wages. As prices were not that flexible, especially downward, real wages fell. In addition, company defaults rose, unsettling banks and lending institutions. Economic historians estimate that more than half of the British unemployment in the 1920s was due to the over-valued exchange rate.[10]

The combination of increased unemployment and falling wages was an untenable situation in the early twentieth century, when labor laws and unions had taken firm hold in Europe. By the end of the decade, the British government decided it could no longer allow further reductions in wages and employment. In 1931, Britain abandoned the gold standard for good.

---

9 Keynes, J.M. (1931), p. 246.
10 Moggridge, D.E. (1972)

It is interesting to note that there was a scarcity of gold after the war. The European central banks, specially affected by the shortage, began to hold reserves in the form of strong currencies (dollar) that were redeemable into gold. The direct link between gold reserves and the domestic currency was thus broken; the system between 1925 and the early thirties had degenerated into a **gold-exchange standard**.

Most countries eventually had to leave the system. One of the last economies holding on to the gold standard was the United States. When President Roosevelt took office in 1933, unemployment had soared to nearly 25 percent. His inauguration took place literally in the middle of a third bank panic. Roosevelt immediately intervened. He declared a "banking holiday" that closed the banks to the public for eight days, to prevent further withdrawals. Then he took the U.S. off the gold standard between 1933 and 1934, when the dollar was redefined at a lower parity in terms of gold (from $20.67 to $35 per oz of gold).

The remaining years in the thirties were plagued by economic instability everywhere. The Great Depression began in the U.S. and spread to other industrialized countries, resulting in the collapse of their banking system. Every country tried to solve their domestic problems at the expense of their trade partners with so called "**beggar thy neighbor policies**." This included the competitive devaluations described in Chapter 18. Countries also tried to improve their balance of trade with protectionist trade policies: the U.S. passed the **Smoot–Hawley Act** with dire consequences for their struggling trade partners.[11] Retaliation by the other countries only made matters worse. By 1933, the overall level of international trade had dropped substantially and most countries suffered sluggish economies throughout the decade. During the inter-war years, countries experimented, not by choice, with all kinds of exchange rate setups. Most countries were unable to remain on the gold standard, so they tried to peg their currencies to a stronger currency, but would end up devaluing, by necessity (corrective devaluation) or just to gain an advantage (competitive devaluation). Other countries eventually floated their currencies. The intrinsic instability of the period was illustrated by wild reserves fluctuations for the pegged currencies and wild exchange rate fluctuations for the floating currencies. The whole international payments system fell into chaos, and trade as well as capital flows were severely curtailed.

The U.S. eventually got over the depression by the onset of World War II. The war effort provided a strong stimulus to the U.S. economy and, in contrast to the other countries involved in the war, the U.S. territory was not attacked so the U.S. did not have to go through a painful reconstruction period. On the other hand, the other economies were shattered by the war and it was clear that major planning was needed to restore the world economic order. Many understood that the economic upheavals following World War I were a major factor in the resumption of hostilities between the participants of that first war: the road toward a longer lasting peace was grounded on a stable economic order. The key question was how to ensure such economic stability. The informal and unstructured gold standard system had failed to restore international financial stability after the First World War; it had become obvious that the world now needed a new formal and more rigorously structured system.

---

11 The Smoot–Hawley Act raised tariffs to a record level on imports to the U.S. in 1930 (see Chapter 10 p. 500).

THE BRETTON WOODS SYSTEM

Bretton Woods is an American ski resort in New Hampshire: it became famous as the birthplace of the new international financial arrangement. Towards the end of World War II, finance ministers from forty-four nations met there to discuss a new international exchange rate agreement. The discussions were dominated by plans developed by Harry Dexter White (U.S. Treasury) and John Maynard Keynes (U.K. Treasury). Having learned that the absence of monetary or fiscal discipline can lead to economic instability and that post-war periods exert significant strain on governments, the participants sought to create a more stable international monetary system.

In the context of the Bretton Woods arrangement, the U.S. was to retain its gold parity at $35 per oz of gold while the other industrialized nations involved were to maintain a fixed exchange rate regime between their currency and the U.S. dollar. As a consequence of accumulating a lot of gold during the war, the U.S. was in a position to allow international convertibility of dollars into gold, but this privilege was restricted to foreign governments or central banks. Domestic convertibility was not permitted and U.S. citizens were not allowed, by law, to hold gold assets. From the point of view of Europeans, this system presented a welcome feature. As a result of the war, their gold reserves were nearly depleted and a one-to-one proportion between gold reserves and money supply was out of the question. **Fractional reserves** had become the norm anyway even before World War II. Lower reserve requirements in the European central banks freed important capital to rebuild Europe.

In addition to installing a new exchange rate regime, the Bretton Woods agreement established two new international financial institutions under the umbrella of the United Nations. The International Monetary Fund (IMF), was created to provide short-term (a maximum of two years) reserve loans to support central banks facing difficulties in maintaining their fixed exchange rate with dwindling reserves. The other institution, the International Bank for Reconstruction and Development (IBRD, also known as the World Bank), was originally charged with the reconstruction of Europe through loans for long-term development projects.[12] In this chapter, we focus mainly on the IMF, since it was the organization charged to oversee the new Bretton Woods international financial system. Developments at the World Bank and interactions with the IMF are the subject of the appendix at the end of this chapter.

Bretton Woods Main Tenets

1. On July 1, 1944, the U.S. dollar was defined in term of gold, at $35 per ounce of gold (the 1934 parity).
2. Member countries were to peg their currencies to the U.S. dollar, but did not need to hold (gold) reserves. Article IV stated that a member could alter the exchange rate of its currency only to

---

12 By the mid 1960s, the IBRD had accomplished its original reconstruction task. However, at that time, its U.S. director, Robert McNamara, decided to expand the charter of the bank to reduce poverty around the world, start an agricultural "green" revolution, and help developing countries with economic support.

correct a fundamental balance-of-payments disequilibrium, and only after consulting with the IMF.

3. All exchange transactions between member countries were not to diverge by more than ± 1% from the pegged exchange rate.

4. Upon entering the IMF, a country was to submit an exchange rate in terms of gold or the U.S. dollar.

5. If the IMF objected to changes in the exchange rate, but the member devalued anyway, that member became ineligible to use IMF resources.

6. Article VI allowed members to control capital movements in and out of their country to discourage speculation.[13]

7. Article VIII forbade members from setting any restriction on the current account. Existing tariffs were grandfathered.

8. Article XIV allowed a member country to retain the exchange controls that were in effect when the country entered the IMF. Once a member country abolished its exchange control, it could not re-impose controls again without IMF approval.

Originally, the IMF was designed to facilitate the operation of the Bretton Woods exchange rate arrangement. However the system lasted less than thirty years and was all but scrapped at the beginning of the 1970s. As a result, the role of the IMF had to be redefined afterward. During the Bretton Woods era, the IMF traditional role was to lend to countries experiencing balance-of-payments difficulties. In the Articles of Agreement (Purposes of the IMF), the IMF was established "to promote international monetary cooperation, exchange stability, and orderly exchange arrangements; to foster economic growth and high levels of employment; and to provide temporary financial assistance to countries to help ease balance of payments adjustment." The purposes are still the same but the IMF now focuses on "surveillance, financial assistance, and technical assistance" as world economic conditions evolve. The membership has also shot up from 44 to 185 countries by now. We will first describe the workings of the early IMF and the difficulties faced over the years.

Mechanism and Adjustment with the IMF/Bretton Woods

Foreign exchange reserves in the fund were held as gold, dollars, a few other reserve currencies, and as positions at the IMF, so the system was regarded as a gold-exchange standard. The primary purpose of the IMF was to lend hard currencies to countries experiencing excessive foreign exchange reserve losses. As an international fund, the IMF had to depend on its members' contributions; thus its activities were financed by the quotas contributed by the member countries. Each member was allotted

---

13 Non-convertibility of foreign currency meant that citizens who earned foreign currency had to redeem it at the central bank; they were not allowed to open private bank accounts to hold foreign currency.

a "quota" to pay into the fund – the size of national quotas being based on the size of their economies. Part of the quota had to be paid in gold or convertible foreign currencies, with the remainder in the form of each country's own domestic currency. The first part of the quota, known as the "gold tranche," counted as part of a country's reserves at the fund and could be borrowed without question. Each country could also borrow beyond its gold tranche under terms of conditionality; this implied that the country had to adjust its macroeconomic policies in order to repay the loan within a reasonable period of time.

Quotas and Voting Rights/Post Bretton Woods – Still Unsolved in the Second Millennium

The size of these quotas has changed over the year with the U.S. share falling while some other countries' share went up. The U.S. quota is now around 17 percent, Japan and Germany around 6 percent each, and France and the U.K. around 5 percent each. At the present time, a quarter of the quota must be paid in the form of special drawing rights (SDR) when a country joins and the other 75 percent can be called on at any time and paid in the country's own currency. The IMF can also borrow beyond the quotas from private banks or individual member's government.

The IMF decisions are made by a weighted voting system; the weights are determined by a country's quota. This is obviously not a very democratic approach, leading to much squabbling between members: there is a need to reallocate the quotas as they do not reflect the new economic strength of emerging economies. At a recent international meeting of the IMF in Singapore (September 2006), the members agreed to provide additional votes to China, South Korea, Mexico, and Turkey. Moreover there is also a consensus toward reviewing the underlying formula for calculating votes. Another issue concerns the EMU countries. Since these countries share a currency, the euro, and have a common monetary policy administered by one central bank, a single membership in the IMF and a single quota would make sense. Note that the sum of the individual EMU countries quota is larger than the U.S. quota.

The adjustment process foreseen by the Bretton Woods system had three stages, depending on the seriousness of payments problems.

1. For what were believed to be temporary or transitory imbalances, questionable policies were to be avoided, and financing was to be pursued. Deficit countries ran reserves down, surplus countries accumulated them, and both were presumed to sterilize.
2. For more serious problems, deficit countries were expected to adopt more restrictive monetary and/or fiscal polices, and surplus countries had an equal and parallel responsibility to adopt more expansionary policies. The system was explicitly designed to avoid the contractionary bias of the gold standard when surplus countries refused to expand and instead sterilized gold inflows, thereby forcing the deficit countries to carry severely restrictive policies.
3. For what were referred to as fundamental payments disequilibria, deficit countries were expected

to devalue, but only to do so after consultations with the IMF to ensure that the devaluation was not excessive or designed primarily for mercantilist purposes. The competitive devaluations of the thirties were not to be repeated. A country with a large and persistent surplus would be expected to revalue.

Weaknesses and Collapse of the Bretton Woods system

In the fifties and sixties, the system did not exactly function as expected by its charter. In fact, the arrangement eventually turned out to be deeply flawed. The fundamental causes of its demise are described below.

1. Merely financing disequilibria, and avoiding painful adjustment policies, went on for far longer than justified by the original plan. Central banks found ways to borrow from each other and thereby avoid conditionality. The quotas were expanded, making larger loans possible.
2. Surplus countries, expected to adopt expansionary macroeconomic policies to facilitate the adjustment, refused to do so. However, it would be hard to blame the German Bundesbank, a central bank committed to keeping low inflation through very conservative policies, for not abandoning its principles just to help out more profligate countries. The burden of the adjustment was thus placed mainly on the deficit countries, making the tightening of policies that they would have to pursue more severe. The intended outcome, that deficit and surplus countries would both contribute to the adjustment, was defeated.
3. There also was an intrinsic flaw in the system. This was not due to a lack of cooperation by the members as in the last section. This problem was called the N-1 question. There were N countries and thus N-1 independent bilateral exchanges rates to manage. As the dollar was pegged to gold, it was the responsibility of all the other members to keep their exchange rate pegged to the dollar. This meant that the U.S. never had to intervene on behalf of the dollar and could use their monetary policy for domestic purpose. This situation was very irritating to the European central banks. The central position of the dollar in the Bretton Woods era and its consequences are discussed in greater detail in Chapter 22 on European monetary integration.
4. By the end of the sixties, the post-war regime of open trade and capital flows was in serious danger of collapse. Despite the existence of large and chronic payments disequilibria (inflows), surplus countries were reluctant to revalue. They viewed an undervalued currency as useful in spurring exports and restricting imports, meaning that exchange rates were used for mercantilist purposes. Chronic deficit countries, like the United Kingdom, put off devaluations until a balance-of-payments crisis, triggering massive speculative capital outflows, compelled a parity change. It was obvious by the early 1960s that the sterling was overvalued at $2.80, but London fought off a devaluation until the fall of 1967, when its reserves were largely exhausted.

The U.S. Balance of Payments Difficulties

In the late forties, the United States had huge reserves and an unrivalled financial and economic position, in part because its capital stock had not been damaged by the war. The rest of the world lacked sufficient reserves, a situation that was referred to as a "dollar shortage." During the fifties, the United States started to run consistent payments deficits for two reasons: first, many countries had devalued sharply against the dollar at the end of the forties, thereby gaining a competitive advantage, and second, Americans were making large investments and loans in Europe and in the rest of the world. In the early fifties, the U.S. deficits were deemed desirable as they allowed countries with badly depleted foreign exchange reserves to build up their reserves again, thus stimulating world trade. By the end of the fifties, however, the U.S. deficits were sufficiently large as to create the impression of the so-called "dollar glut." Eventually, in the early sixties, the situation got worse and the United States faced a serious payments deficit.

In 1964, the United States adopted capital controls in the form of the **Interest Equalization Tax**: a tax levied on interest received from lending abroad aimed at discouraging capital outflows. This tax, combined with restrained U.S. macroeconomic policies, led to an improvement in the U.S. balance of payments and many observers thought the U.S. problem was largely solved. This relief was temporary. The Johnson administration got involved in a costly war in Vietnam in addition to increasing social welfare expenditures, under the Great Society program; all that without raising taxes. U.S. monetary policy remained relatively expansionary in the late sixties, despite large budget deficits. The results were predictable. The U.S. current account deteriorated, and capital outflows accelerated. The Johnson administration responded with a more thorough set of capital controls introducing a brief respite.

Dollar Glut and Demise of the System

If the original reserve shortage hampered trade and growth, the opposite, excess liquidity in the form of large dollar reserves held by the rest of the world, created serious potential problems: among these, world-wide inflationary pressures or a decline in the confidence in the dollar would wreak havoc in the system. In the arrangement, foreign central banks could redeem all their dollars into gold. As long as there was enough gold under Fort Knox, the site of the U.S. bullion depository, to support the foreign-held dollar reserves, everything was fine. But the Yale economist, Robert Triffin, anticipated that, eventually, this situation would turn around, as the gold supply was not increasing fast enough; then a loss of confidence in the dollar would occur. In fact, by 1970, the amount of foreign exchange outstanding exceeded the amount of gold reserves. A revaluation of gold (i.e. a devaluation of the dollar) was out of the question for two reasons: it would reduce the value of the foreign countries' dollar reserves and it would give an unfair advantage to the main gold producing countries, none other than the USSR and South Africa. Anticipating the problem, the international response led to the creation by the IMF of Special Drawing Rights (SDR) in 1967. The SDR did not help that much in this instance, but they still play a role in transactions between the IMF and the various members' central banks.

Special Drawing Rights (SDR)

Special drawing rights are baskets of strong currencies that were created in the sixties to supplement dollars and gold as international reserves. Since the introduction of the euro in 1999, they now comprise four currencies only: dollar, euro, yen, and pound ($, €, ¥, £). The weights of the four currencies are respectively 44% for the dollar, 34% for the euro, and 11% each for the yen and the pound. The exchange rate $/SDR is calculated using the exchange rate of the 3 other currencies with respect to the dollar and aggregating proportionately to their weight in the basket. The exchange rate as of August 27, 2008 was $1.57/SDR. The SDR interest rate is determined as a weighted average of the interest rates on short-term financial instruments in the markets of the currencies in the SDR basket. The use of SDR is restricted to central banks: they feature in the official reserves account of a country's balance of payments.

Eventually, in the late sixties and early seventies, doubts arose about the competence of the leadership of the Federal Reserve Board and the wisdom of U.S. fiscal policy decisions: it then became clear that the dollar gold parity could not be sustained. A massive speculative run against the dollar began, rapidly draining U.S. gold holdings. On 15 August 1971, the Nixon administration suspended gold sales, imposed a surtax on U.S. import tariffs, and urgently requested an international conference to negotiate new parities with the members' currencies. The **Smithsonian Conference** of December 1971 in Washington heralded a devaluation of the dollar relative to gold and a revaluation of the currencies of the surplus countries (Germany, Switzerland). To avoid a severe worsening of U.S. protectionism, the surplus countries went ahead with the proposal.

The new exchange rate schedule survived for just over a year. At the end of 1972, U.S. trade numbers were not much better, monetary policy was obviously too expansionary, and there was a perception that the Nixon administration was largely preoccupied with the Watergate scandal. The result was another speculative run on the dollar, and the adoption of floating exchange rates by the major industrialized countries in early 1973.

A BRIEF HISTORY OF THE FLOAT AFTER BRETTON WOODS

It is important to remember that the industrialized countries embraced flexible exchange rates in 1973, not by preference for such a system, but because Bretton Woods failed. The March 1973 adoption of flexible exchange rates by the major industrialized countries was widely expected to be temporary. Fixed exchange rates were still viewed as the normal and preferred system; it was thought that when the floating rates eventually settled in a narrow range, they could be re-fixed. Through the Committee of Twenty (C-20), the IMF had already begun discussions on a reform of the system.

The oil embargo of 1973, resulting in oil price hikes from $3 to $8 per barrel in 1974, changed everything. The **OPEC**[14] countries suddenly acquired a huge current account surplus (over $70

---

14 Organization of Petroleum Exporting Countries – a cartel restricting the supply of petroleum.

billion in 1975, declining to the $40 billion range in following years), and there was no way to predict how or where this money would be invested. In light of the payments instability that could result from shifts in OPEC investment patterns, as well as other uncertainties associated with higher oil prices, it did not appear feasible to return to a set of fixed parities. Flexible exchange rates then became the normal system for industrialized countries, despite widespread opposition among central bankers and finance ministry officials. This change was formalized in amendments to the IMF Articles of Agreement, adopted in Kingston, Jamaica, in 1976.

To be more precise, the **Jamaica Accord** allows countries to adopt whatever exchange rate regime they wish as long as it does not impact negatively on their trade partners. So as shown in Chapter 13 (Table 13.1), there now exist all shades of regime between fully floating and pegged exchange rates. Managed floats and **concerted** or **coordinated intervention**, unheard of during the Bretton Woods era, are now common practice. The majority of the countries follow some form of floating exchange rate and reserve the right to intervene in the foreign exchange markets when needed: many Asian countries make sure that their currency does not strengthen too much against the dollar. The **Plaza Accord** and the **Louvre Accord** in the eighties (see box below) were attempts, through intervention by the industrialized countries, to weaken a dollar that was deemed too strong in 1985 and to stop the slide of the dollar a few years later. By 2001, the newly introduced euro had lost about a third of its value against the dollar since its introduction in 1999. Intervention by both the U.S. Federal Reserve (Fed) and the European Central Bank rescued it. These three cases are examples of coordinated intervention taking place when an important currency seems to follow an erratic trend. In general, the industrialized countries go along with a so-called "**benign neglect**" approach; they carry out their monetary policy to achieve domestic goals without paying much attention to its impact on the currency. Indeed, fearing a recession, the chairman of the Fed, Ben Bernanke, has been cutting interest rates repeatedly in 2007, totally ignoring the negative impact of the policy on the already weak dollar.

The Dollar and U.S. Current Account Deficits since 1973

After leaving its gold peg, the U.S. dollar depreciated in 1973, then recovered in the following three years. By 1975–6, the new system had settled into a relatively stable pattern. Unfortunately, the dollar came under speculative attack in the summer and fall of 1978, necessitating, in late 1978, a rescue package organized by U.S. trade partners. In addition, worsening U.S. inflation continued to sap public confidence in the dollar's future.

In late 1979, the newly appointed chairman of the Federal Reserve Board, Paul Volcker, presided over a sharp tightening of U.S. monetary policy. In early 1981, in part because of increasing market confidence that Chairman Volcker's policies would succeed in breaking U.S. inflation, a large volume of capital began flowing into the United States and the dollar began a long appreciation. By the time it peaked in early 1985, the dollar had appreciated by over 60 percent in nominal effective terms and by approximately 40 percent in real terms resulting in huge current account deficits.

This appreciation can be seen as resulting primarily from an extremely unusual set of macroeconomic policies in the United States. The Kemp–Roth tax cut of 1981 combined with a large increase in military expenditure to produce large federal budget deficits. The unavoidable increase in U.S. Treasury borrowing coincided with a tight monetary policy, resulting in very high interest rates causing capital inflows that bid the dollar up to levels at which U.S. products became uncompetitive in world markets. The economy of the industrial and agricultural Midwest, particularly dependent on export markets, was shaken. On the positive side, the overvalued dollar forced U.S. tradable goods prices down and helped break the long-standing inflationary spiral of the late seventies.

In early 1985, the dollar started to depreciate due to an earlier easing of the U.S. monetary policy. In late 1985, the secretary of the treasury met with the finance ministers of the major industrialized countries at the Plaza Hotel in New York, where they agreed that the dollar was still too high and that coordinated intervention should be used to weaken it. Fearing an increase in American protectionism, the U.S. trade partners went along. The dollar continued to decline in 1986 and early 1987, leading to another meeting of the finance ministers at the Louvre in Paris; they concluded that existing exchange rates were approximately correct and that no further depreciation of the dollar was needed.

In the nineties, the dollar fluctuated moderately due to various economic or political events, rising overall. It appreciated further from late 1999 to the end of 2001, having risen by about 35 percent from its 1995–7 lows. Since then, the dollar has been in a free fall against the euro, the Canadian dollar, and the British pound; by August 28, 2008, it had stabilized around $1.48/€ from $0.90/€ eight years before. The dollar slide against the Asian currencies has not been as dramatic as these countries' central banks have intervened to maintain their international competitiveness (following a managed float system).

U.S. current account deficits, hovering in the $100–$200 billion range in the 1980s and early 1990s, worsened late in the decade, reaching levels of over $400 billion by 2001–2 and $711 billion for the year ending August 28, 2008. These deficits are ultimately the gap between U.S. investment and national savings rates. Investment has not been particularly high as a proportion of GDP, but national saving rates have been very low, even negative. During the eighties and early nineties, large public sector dissaving (budget deficits) offset much of an otherwise normal private saving rate. As the reduction in U.S. military expenditure, following the end of the Cold War, and large tax increases in 1990 and 1993 brought budget deficits down and even produced surpluses late in the decade, private saving rates declined. Unfortunately, the budget deficits have soared at the beginning of the twenty-first century, due to a policy of tax cuts when waging a war while private savings reached new lows; inevitably, the current account deficits have widened. Hopefully, the weaker dollar and a possible slowdown of the U.S. economy might reduce the extent of these current account deficits.

Since relinquishing its role as supervisor of the Bretton Woods system, the IMF has adopted new responsibilities. The Fund now exercises surveillance over the exchange rate policies carried out by its members. It has also underlined a number of specific principles to guide its members, expecting them to abide to these standards. For instance, members are not supposed to manipulate their exchange rates to gain unfair advantage over their trade partners or to prevent balance-of-payments adjustments (e.g. trying to maintain a surplus). Members should be considerate when they use other countries' currencies to intervene as these operations could destabilize other currencies. However, the IMF does not have the power to settle disputes nor to discipline countries that violate these rules. Basically, the IMF is not in a position to deal with international financial instability – it can only issue some guidelines hoping to reduce erratic exchange-rate-setting behaviour by its members.

However, in a world of high financial integration, the exchange rate becomes practically a secondary issue. The entities that have to be regulated are the international financial institutions, whether private or public, banks or others; often they are stateless or so-called multinational. In addition, the development of offshore finance has raised an important security aspect since 2001 (connected to terrorism laundering) that has added to the push for greater transparency and international standards. Debt crises and subsequent exchange rate instability have often been traced to imprudent and greedy behaviour by these international financial institutions. Fortunately, there is an international agency that exercises surveillance and drafts guidelines to regulate these institutions, the Bank for International Settlements (BIS). The problem is that the sprouting of all types of international financial entities and of new financial instruments has been so rapid and so extensive that it is a challenge to keep up with regulating them.

THE NEW FINANCIAL ARCHITECTURE: THE BASEL ACCORDS

The threat to the solvency of many large banks, brought about by the Latin American debt crisis of the early eighties, underscored the importance of imposing harmonized regulation on international banks. A rapid increase in international banking, as banks branched or set up subsidiaries outside the borders of their home countries, made it almost impossible for a single government or central bank to regulate its national banks. To avoid home country regulations, banks only had to set up subsidiaries in a jurisdiction with looser regulations. "Jurisdiction shopping" became a common practice as banks set up operations wherever they would escape stricter national regulations.

The world-wide collapse of banks in the thirties made it all too clear that an unregulated banking system was risky, leading to the idea of imposing international standards in bank regulation, at least for the industrialized countries.

Basel I

The bank regulatory authorities of the industrialized countries began discussions in 1986 at the Bank for International Settlements in Basel, Switzerland; they intended to coordinate their efforts to improve the soundness of the international banking system. The negotiations were directed at four issues facing international banks. Each of these issues potentially threatened bank solvency and the stability of the world's banking system:

1. *Capital adequacy.* Many of the largest banks had grown very rapidly throughout the seventies and eighties without selling additional common stock or retaining large earnings. As a result, their net worth declined as a percentage of their total assets; even rather modest losses, owing to bad loans, could thus threaten their solvency. An insolvency crisis could translate into enormous risks for government insurance agencies such as the Federal Deposit Insurance Company in the United States.

2. *Excessively risky loans.* Latin America was not the only area where risky loans, generating huge losses, had been made. U.S. banks lost large sums of money in Zaire and the Sudan. The decline in the U.S. commercial real-estate market, in the late eighties, inflicted large losses on banks from various countries, including Japan. Many banks simply did not appear to be sufficiently prudent in making large loans.

3. *Excessively concentrated loans.* Partially in order to reduce administrative costs, banks prefer making a few very large loans to making a large number of small ones. In addition, they often concentrate lending in a few industries or countries. Such concentration greatly increases the risk that the bank will fail if a single country or industry experiences serious financial problems. At one time Citibank had 75 percent of its net worth loaned in Brazil and over 100 percent of its net worth loaned in Latin America.

4. *Exposure from off-balance-sheet items.* International banks were becoming increasingly involved in foreign exchange forwards, futures, and options contracts, and many of these activities created potentially large risks that were concealed from the public. How could these risks be evaluated and limited?

The Basel Accord on Capital Adequacy of July 1988 began to address some of these problems. Most importantly, it set a minimum level of 8 percent for capital as a share of risk-adjusted assets. That 8 percent included both net worth and subordinated (non-deposit) debt. At least half of the 8 percent had to be stockholders' equity, including accumulated reserves. Loan types were ranked according to the degree of risk they carried, with loans to OECD governments least risky and loans to developing-country governments in the riskiest class. These risk weights were used to determine minimum capital requirements; if a bank makes more risky loans, it must maintain more net worth. The 1991 failure of the Bank for Credit and Capital International (BCCI) and the more recent problems of many large Japanese banks make it clear that the Basel Accord had not solved all the problems of excessive risk (and sometimes of fraud) in international banking, but the agreement was an important step in the right direction.

Basel II

Perceived inadequacies in the original Basel Accord led to negotiations to revise some of its terms. Basically, the new proliferation of securitization changed how banks did business. Instead of carrying loans in their balance sheet, they slice them and repackage them as tradable securities that are in turn sold on the financial markets. "Banks are now in the moving business, not in the storing business" according to *The Economist* (On Credit Watch, Oct 18 2007). Although it seems that securitization would allow banks to spread the risk more evenly, this did not happen as the banks chose to keep in their balance sheets those securities yielding the highest returns, i.e. the more risky ones. In addition, a host of new financial entities that were not bound by the rules of Basel I sprouted alongside the traditional banks, with the purpose of avoiding these rules.

What is now called "Basel II" was finalized in 2006 and it addresses some of these problems; unfortunately the pace of adoption of these new rules is sluggish. Basel II is based on three pillars: a more sensitive classification of risk, more disclosures by banks, and more overseeing power by regulators. The risk-weighted capital requirements on banks are now more intricate in order to accurately reflect the risks in various asset types. As mentioned above, Basel I treated loans to all OECD members as equally low in risk, without distinguishing between members (e.g. Turkey versus Switzerland) and viewed all loans to developing countries (e.g. Hong Kong) as being riskier than loans to any OECD member. In addition, Basel II requires far more public disclosure of their risk profiles by individual banks; this encourages the market (stockholders and depositors) to impose risk-reducing discipline. Basel II also expands the role of central banks and other financial authorities concerning prudential regulation while overseeing the risks that banks are allowed to undertake.

The challenge for Basel II was to balance the need for an enhanced international regulatory system that really does reduce the risk of major bank failures with the potential downside of a more complicated system that could stifle bank lending and burden taxpayers and bank stockholders. Unfortunately, the sub-prime crisis that sprouted in mid-2007 illustrated the shortcomings of the new rules. Basel II relies heavily on risk rating, but the institutions that are in charge of the rating (e.g. Moody, Standard and Poor) are also involved in the new securitization business. It was thus in their interest to boost these ratings. By summer 2007, this bias became apparent and these securities lost their appeals to investors, putting strains on the banks depending on the securitization process. A liquidity crunch resulted, affecting interbank rates, and requiring intervention by central banks.

Basically the root of the upheaval had little to do with the capital requirement rules and a lot to do with the need for more judicious financial supervision to avoid such an illiquidity crisis. At this point, regulators agree that Basel II needs to be scrutinized. First, in an effort to refine the ratings, the new rules gave more say to the rating agencies; this is part of the problem as the rating agencies' main sources of revenues come from the companies they rate. What is actually rated by these agencies presents another problem: the rating agencies focus mainly on whether a debt will be defaulted at maturity (credit risk) and not on liquidity management by individual financial institutions (the cause of the recent sub-prime crisis). In addition, some newly created forms of financial entities fall through the regulation net. Finally, each country seems to have its own approach towards banking supervision; different agencies are in charge and the degree of stringency varies. The question that regulators will have to answer is whether there is a need for more harmonized international supervision (with all the potential drawbacks).

Payment Crisis in Heavily Indebted Developing Countries

Another aspect of what may become a new financial architecture for international finance is a proposal by Anne Krueger, a former Deputy Managing Director of the IMF; could the concept of corporate bankruptcy be adapted to help heavily indebted developing countries facing a payments crisis. The purpose of such procedure is twofold: first, to avoid chaotic attempts by international banks to repossess their financial outlays before a country's foreign exchange reserves are exhausted; second, to institute some binding system for creditors allowing them to negotiate partial payments and/or longer-term structures for old debts. Bankruptcy laws in existence in various countries are being studied to find an effective solution to help sovereign nations that cannot service or repay their debts.

This chapter took us from the nineteenth century with the gold standard, through the more recent Bretton Woods era after World War II, and finally to the modern era. Now the main issues are not necessarily exchange rate problems, but rather the fear of international financial instability. These dangers can only be addressed through closer international cooperation to regulate the new stateless financial institutions. Individual countries have lost their sovereign power to regulate them. It is obviously in the interest of these institutions to work with their so-called regulator, the Bank for International Settlements, to avoid payments crises and their dreaded consequence, contagion, as the crisis spreads to other countries through the interwoven international financial grid. International financial crises will be the topic of the last chapter. In the meantime, we will pick up the history of the international monetary system in the seventies to present in the next chapter the unique experience of Western Europe in replacing Bretton Woods by a monetary union.

Summary of Key Concepts

1. The evolution of the standard from a bi-metallic standard (silver and gold) to a pure gold standard was achieved by the end of the nineteenth century.
2. With the gold standard, the value of national paper currencies would be defined in term of the weight of gold they could exchange for paper currency at the central bank. Since all currencies were defined likewise, their exchange rate or mint parity was simply the ratio of these weights of gold.
3. Central banks had to back any amount of currency in circulation by gold reserves and be ready to redeem the paper currency for gold.
4. In order to settle trade imbalances, gold could be freely traded internationally and the adjustment mechanism was crucially dependent on price and wage flexibility.
5. A deficit country would lose its gold reserves, resulting in a decrease in the money supply. With perfectly flexible prices, prices would drop and the country would regain its international competitiveness.
6. Under the rules of the game, not only were central banks not supposed to sterilize reserves changes, but they were expected to enhance the impact of the adjustment mechanism through credit loosening (surplus country) or tightening (deficit country).

7. From 1880 to 1914, the gold standard was quite successful at stabilizing its members' economies. Trade, as well as international capital flows, was not impeded by much control during the period.

8. The attempt to return to the gold standard after World War I was not successful and the industrialized nations fended off disastrous depressions in the thirties. The consequence was a resort to protection and competitive devaluations to try to solve domestic problems.

9. Aware of the importance of a stable world economic order as a crucial foundation for peace, the Bretton Woods arrangement was entered into by 44 countries at the end of World War II. The International Monetary Fund was to manage the system.

10. With Bretton Woods, the dollar was defined in terms of gold while the other currencies had to uphold a fixed exchange rate with the dollar. They did not need to hold reserves in terms of gold. This was a gold-exchange standard.

11. The dollar was the anchor in this system. As long as the U.S. economy was doing well, the system worked smoothly and was significant in helping the other countries rebuild their war-shattered economies. In the sixties, circumstances had changed and by the early seventies, for various reasons, Bretton Woods fell apart.

12. Efforts at salvaging the system were doomed and the world abandoned fixed for floating exchange rates.

13. Both nominal and real exchange rates have been far more volatile than had been expected when floating rates were adopted, and this volatility has been very disruptive, the 1981–5 appreciation of the dollar being particularly harmful to the tradable sector of the United States.

14. After the demise of Bretton Woods, the role of the IMF was recast towards "surveillance, financial assistance, and technical assistance" as world economic conditions evolved.

15. A new financial architecture, Basel I and II, has also been designed under the umbrella of the International Bank of International Settlements (BIS).

CASE STUDY I

Financial Reform – Reality Check at the IMF
April 20, 2006
From *The Economist* print edition

The fund needs a gentle overhaul, not a fundamental rethink

The International Monetary Fund cannot seem to win. Every financial crisis is the cue for the world's economic Pooh-Bahs to declare that the organisation desperately needs reform. This year there is a conspicuous lack of crises, and yet, as they prepare for the IMF's spring meetings this weekend, the great and the good are at it again. Mervyn King, governor of the Bank of England, says the fund's role is obscure. Tim Adams, the main international man at America's Treasury, has accused it of being "asleep at the wheel." Critics warn that the IMF faces irrelevance unless it reinvents itself radically.

That seems an extraordinary assertion. Less than a decade ago the world was rocked by emerging-market financial crises in which the fund was called on to save the day. Thanks to today's abundant liquidity, emerging economies have enjoyed easy access to private capital and hence no need for the IMF. But no one expects such liquidity to last forever. A temporary lack of fires does not remove the need for a fire brigade.

So what is really prompting the calls for reform? One disreputable reason to change is the internal workings of the IMF's budget. Bizarrely, the IMF makes money to pay for its staff only when it lends to countries in crisis. The lack of recent crises means the organisation faces a 30% drop in its income over the next two years. That suggests the IMF needs a new source of money, not a new role.

On two counts, however, the critics have a point. On the world's most intractable macroeconomic challenge, unwinding the imbalances between excessive borrowing in America and excess saving elsewhere, the IMF has almost no clout. Worse, many of the fund's potential clients in the emerging world are the most excessive savers.

They are doing their best to ensure that they never have to turn to the IMF again, by building up enormous foreign-exchange reserves, a hugely expensive and inefficient use of their resources.

Most financial bigwigs think the fund's future lies in helping to sort out the big global imbalances. Mr King wants the IMF to follow Keynes's dictum and offer "ruthless truth-telling" when countries are going wrong. Endless proposals offer advice on improving "multilateral surveillance" and on making the IMF's board more independent.

Sadly, the fund's ability to tell rich countries what to do is extremely limited. Rich countries have not borrowed from the IMF in decades and will be deaf to the fund's wise words unless it suits their own domestic interests. Only if the fund had the ability to punish non-borrowing members (as, in theory, it did in 1944), would the focus on "surveillance" amount to much. But no rich country will give the IMF that power. It is naive to believe the fund can become a global financial guardian.

The IMF's future – rather like its recent past – lies with emerging markets, where access to international capital is more precarious than you might think. Should global financial conditions become less forgiving, many countries – whether Indonesia, Hungary or even Brazil – might once again need access to the IMF's cash. Even the strongest would be better pooling risks within the IMF than going it alone by building up huge independent reserves.

For that to happen, emerging economies must believe the IMF represents them. This calls for a shift of power away from Europe. It is absurd that Brazil, China and India have 20% less clout within the fund than the Netherlands, Belgium and Italy, although the emerging economies are four times the size of the European ones, once you adjust for currency differences. Emerging countries are keen to contribute more cash (and thus get more votes), and they have the support of Rodrigo de Rato, the IMF's Spanish boss. The Europeans, too, should support this reform. A smaller voice in a useful organisation is better than power over a moribund one.

An IMFurance policy

With more sway over the fund, emerging economies could shift the organisation's priorities. One sensible idea, recently raised by the IMF's chief economist, would be to pool some of their reserves in the IMF, in effect, using it as an insurance facility that offers rapid access to cash if strong economies are hit by financial turbulence. Some rich countries worry about the perverse incentives that would create. It is a dilemma: the risk is real, but so is the cost of a crisis. If many of the fund's clients want such a scheme, rich countries should not block it.

Doubtless, the agitators want much more. But, unlike their grand ideas, giving emerging markets a bigger voice and useful products would at least make the IMF more useful.

CASE STUDY QUESTIONS

1. Why does the IMF clout diminish when the world is awash in liquidity and no financial crisis is looming?

2. Why are the IMF revenues lagging these days?

3. Is the IMF in a position to give advice to the richer economies? Why or why not? Shouldn't the IMF scold the U.S. for its excessive borrowing, low private savings, and for causing major global imbalances?

4. The IMF managing director is traditionally European while the chief economist is American – doesn't that sound like a rich countries' club? Comment.

5. Since the emerging nations are the main users of the funds, shouldn't they have more say in the running of the IMF? Comment.

CASE STUDY II

IMF Quotas – Monetary Misquotations
August 24, 2006
From *The Economist* print edition

A long-overdue shake-up at the IMF

THE IMF was founded during a moment of high statesmanship at Bretton Woods in New Hampshire. But when they divvied up the power in their new creation, its founders practised some low numerical arts. Each country's "quota" of votes was calculated according to an elaborate formula, which blended the economy's size, reserves, openness and volatility. But according to the man who invented it, this formula was a subtle contrivance, carefully designed to deliver a result pre-cooked by the Americans.

Singapore is a long way from New Hampshire. But as the fund prepares for its annual meeting in the Asian city-state next month, it is still trying to rid itself of the Bretton Woods formula and its many derivatives. This week, the fund's executive board heard the first formal proposal on quota reform since Rodrigo de Rato, the IMF Managing Director, unveiled his medium-term strategy to revamp the organisation last September.

The IMF's quotas are a distorted mirror of today's economy, partly because they must do three things at once. They determine how many votes a member can cast on the board, how much money it must put into the fund's coffers, and how many dollars it can take out before attracting penalty interest rates. They were last revised in January 1999. As a result, many countries are now underrepresented, even by the fund's odd formulas, and others find their clout falls far short of their weight in world output (see chart).

Mr de Rato wants to fix this problem in two steps over the next two years. First, he wants to sprinkle extra votes on a handful of underrepresented countries (probably China, South Korea, Mexico and Turkey, although he has yet to confirm this). Second, he wants a broader reallocation of votes and a new formula to calculate them.

This second step will be awkward, because votes cannot be taken from members that do not want to cede them. Quotas bring out the petty side of politicians, who obsess over every one of their 107,635 votes (the number cast by Britain and, curiously, by France as well), as if they were 107,635 square miles of territory.

The Americans want a new formula to give pride of place to GDP, the least arbitrary measure of an economy's weight in the world. It also suits America, which accounts for almost a third of world output, but casts only 17% of the votes. Yet such a formula would give many poor countries, which account for a tiny share of the world economy but a big share of the fund's work, still less say in its affairs.

To rectify this, each member may be given more "basic votes," a flat allocation, awarded regardless of economic size. These basic votes once made up over 15% of the total, but now represent just 2%, thanks to the IMF's growth. Tim Adams, who looks after international affairs at America's Treasury, seems happy to see these votes doubled or even tripled. "We don't want to see African voices dissipated any more than they are," he says.

Of course, a country's share of the vote does not translate one-for-one into a share of the power. Many big IMF decisions require an 85% majority. Hence a country with 15.1% of the vote is indispensable. A country with 14.9% can be sidelined.

Moreover, few decisions at the fund are ever put to a formal ballot. The executive directors, who meet around a U-shaped table about three days a week, are meant to reach their decisions by consensus. According to Leo Van Houtven, a former secretary of the IMF, a director's influence depends on more than the votes he wields. "Technical expertise is important, persuasiveness counts a great deal,

diplomacy, sense of timing, and length of service all have an impact." None of those virtues will appear in the fund's new formula. But they might just help to shape it.

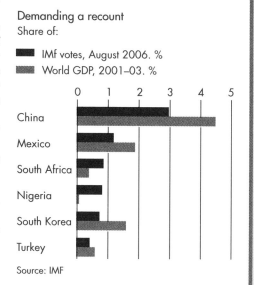

Demanding a recount
Share of:

■ IMf votes, August 2006. %
■ World GDP, 2001–03. %

China
Mexico
South Africa
Nigeria
South Korea
Turkey

Source: IMF

CASE STUDY QUESTIONS

1. Originally the IMF quotas were allotted according to a rather arcane formula, why did the designers choose that approach?

2. What are the three main activities for which the quota is taken into account?

3. Name some countries that are under-represented and some that are over-represented according to the actual quotas.

4. Is it possible to increase the quotas of underrepresented countries like China without revising the whole allocation and taking votes from, say, Belgium? Comment.

5. The U.S. quota dropped from 20 percent originally to 17 percent. Now, however U.S. GDP represents a third of world output. Should the U.S. quota be increased? Comment.

6. What about the EMU members (the euro country)? Should they merge their individual quotas? Comment.

Latest development: "IMF Executive Board Recommends to Governors Conclusion of Thirteenth General Quota Review," Press Release No. 08/02, January 4, 2008. "The Executive Board of the International Monetary Fund (IMF) has submitted a report to the IMF's Board of Governors recommending that the Thirteenth General Review of Quotas be concluded without an increase of quotas."

Questions for Study and Review

1. In 1870, as a consequence of their defeat in the Franco-Prussian war, the French were directed to pay 1 million francs-or in gold to the Prussians. Use your understanding of the gold standard adjustment to describe the economic consequences for the two countries.

2. Spain and bullionism. In the sixteenth and seventeenth centuries, as a result of colonizing South America, Spain acquired huge amounts of gold. However, it seemed that the more gold there was flowing from the Americas into Spain, the more gold there was flowing out of Spain to other European countries. Explain.

3. According to Gresham's law, bad money always displaces good money. What is the implication of this law for a bimetallic – silver/gold – standard?

4. We are in 1890: Great Britain and France are both on the gold standard. British exports to France exceed their imports from France. What will happen to the exchange rate between the pound and the franc? Describe the adjustment mechanism.

5. When Great Britain decided to go back on the gold standard in 1925, the Chancellor of the Exchequer chose the pre-1914 gold parity for the pound. Use the purchasing power parity concept introduced in the previous chapter to explain how he could have derived a more realistic parity.

6. In the thirties, countries tried to fend off the Depression and stimulate their economy with beggar thy neighbor methods. Explain the mechanism of a competitive devaluation (cf. Chapter 19). Since a devaluation produces a balance-of-trade improvement only at the expense of the trade partners, what action will the trade partners take? What is the resulting impact on the volume of trade?

7. What is the main difference between a gold standard and a gold-exchange standard?

8. Towards the end of the Bretton Woods era, the German currency (DM) was undervalued with respect to the dollar. What was the impact on the U.S./German balance of trade? What steps did Germany take, with the approval of the IMF, to solve the problem?

9. Exchange rate fluctuations since 1973 appear to be larger than warranted by the underlying economic circumstances in the nations involved. What reasons have been offered to explain this experience?

10. Explain how concerted intervention took place under the Plaza and under the Louvre agreements (cf. Chapter 13).

11. How did the role of the IMF evolve after the demise of Bretton Woods?

12. Explain why the IMF and the World Bank were perceived to be necessary for the Bretton Woods System.

13. Explain to your president why the gold standard will bring her fame in good times and disrepute in recessions.

14. If exports make up 75 percent of your country's GDP, what type of exchange rate regime should you have? What are the tradeoffs?

15. You are an economist advising an Asian country on its exchange rate regime choice. In a conference, its leaders tell you that domestic stability (full employment) is their first priority and that they have very large foreign currency reserves. What exchange rate regime do you recommend? Given your recommendation, what problems do you warn them they may encounter? When they ask how they can minimize these problems, what do you say?

16. What are the Basel Accords (Basel I and II)? What problems were the accords designed to address?

References and Suggestions for Further Reading

Bordo M. and Eichengreen, B. (eds) (1993) *A Retrospective on the Bretton Woods System*, Chicago: University of Chicago Press.

Branson, W. (1984) "Exchange Rate Policy after a Decade of Floating," in J. Bilson and R. Marston (eds), *Exchange Rate Theory and Practice*, Chicago: University of Chicago Press.

Crockett, A. (1997) "The Theory and Practice of Financial Stability," *Princeton Essays in International Finance*, 203: April.

Dornbusch, R. (1980) "Exchange Rates Economics: Where Do We Stand?," *Brookings Papers on Economic Activity*, 1980:143–85.

Eichengreen, B. and Flandreau, M. (eds) (1997) *The Gold Standard in Theory and History*, London: Routledge.

Frankel, J. (1996) "Recent Exchange Rate Experience and Proposal for Reforms," *American Economic Review*, Papers and proceedings, 86: 153–8.

Hume, D. (1898) "On the Balance of Trade," in *Essays: Moral, Political and Literary*, London: Longmans Green.

Keynes, J.M. (1920) *The Economic Consequences of the Peace*, New York: Harcourt Brace.

—— (1931) "The Economic Consequence of Mr. Churchill," in J.M. Keynes, *Essays in Persuasion*, reprinted (1991) New York: W.W.Norton.

McKinnon, R. (1996) *The Rules of the Game*, Cambridge: MIT Press.

Meese, R. (1990) "Currency Fluctuations in the Post-Bretton Woods Era," *Journal of Economic Perspectives*, 4: 3–24.

Moggridge, D.E. (1972) *British Monetary Policy 1924–1931: the Norman Conquest of Four Dollars & Eighty Six Cents*, reprinted (1992) London: Ashgate Publishing Company.

Nurske, R. (1944) *International Currency Experience*, Geneva: League of Nations.

Triffin, R. (1960) *Gold and the Dollar Crisis*, New Haven and London: Yale University Press.

APPENDIX: THE IMF VERSUS THE WORLD BANK – DIFFERENCES AND RECENT COLLABORATION

The blueprints for the International Monetary Fund (IMF) and the International Bank for Reconstruction and Development (IBRD) were drawn during the Bretton Woods conference at the end of World War II; the international treaty creating them was signed in 1945. A simplistic difference between the two concerns the level at which they operate. The role of the IMF was and still is to regulate the international financial system: as a result the IMF operates at the macroeconomic level. On the other hand, the role of the IBRD at first was to lend funds for reconstruction projects to the war-torn economies; it evolved into becoming a lender for development projects in the emerging economies. The IRBD became known as the World Bank, operating at the microeconomic level.

By convention, the head of the IMF is traditionally European while the head of the World Bank is American. When the Bretton Woods arrangement collapsed and when the World War II-torn countries recovered, both the IMF and the IRBD had to redefine their role. Eventually, they started to collaborate on specific issues such as poverty. Reconstruction is still a concern given the many wars going on in the world, but the original IBRD has been downgraded to a subset of the World Bank, along with other agencies, the International Development Association (IDA), the International Finance Corporation (IFC), The Multilateral Investment Guarantee Agency (MIGA), and the International Centre for Settlement of Investment Disputes (ICSID).

The World Bank has had a rocky history. In the past, when it helped developing economies, it was frequently blamed for ensuing problems: indeed the Bank often financed large flagship projects like dam building, that did not create long-run employment, and struggling economies would become more and more indebted. In the sixties and seventies, poorer developing countries benefited from rising commodity prices (their export good); so these countries felt confident about borrowing heavily from the Bank and other institutions in order to finance their development. Unfortunately, commodity prices eventually fell while energy prices (their import good) increased. These often mismanaged and corrupt economies found themselves in a dire situation and could not afford to pay the interest on their debts. To make things worse, they were allowed by the Bank to borrow just to service their debt: the interest payment burden dragged down these economies. The hope that their social and political institutions would rise to the challenge was unrealistic. This approach only resulted in a greater and greater international debt burden and a different tack was needed. In addition, when, in the eighties, the Bank engaged in debt-rescheduling problems, awareness about social and environmental concerns became a thorny issue, making the Bank even more unpopular. Basically, each time a new director was appointed, efforts at restructuring the bank were undertaken. The Bank now bears little similarity to its original blueprint.

The Bank has realized that governance and institutions in the borrowing country are a key element of successful undertakings. Currently, the World Bank approach has moved towards social type of projects such as education or health and, more importantly, the countries seeking help have to be genuinely involved in the designing of the projects: they should "own their reforms" and be responsible for their success. The countries must draw up their reform plans in collaboration with the World Bank, thus demonstrating the country's commitment to its reforms. The World Bank is then better disposed to provide technical assistance to carry the goals.

Starting in 1996, the World Bank in collaboration with the IMF started to provide debt relief to the very poor countries under the HIPC, the Heavily Indebted Poor Countries initiative. This program begun in 1996 as a collaboration between the World Bank's IDA and the IMF. The program was extended in 1999 to become the Enhanced HIPC including more countries and providing more debt relief faster. In 2005, the G8 (the group of rich industrialized countries) made a proposal for debt cancellation – the Multilateral Debt Relief Initiative (MDRI) would also provide additional financial aid in the form of grants (this new endeavor was tied to the Millennium Development Goal proposed by the UN); IDA is administering these goals.

By now, there are 41 countries in the HICP initiative, possibly eligible to receive debt relief. The conditions originally set for actually receiving debt relief had to be watered down eventually as they were too stringent. At the "decision point," countries must pledge to undertake a series of reforms (at the macro and micro level). Countries must "own" the reform effort and widespread consultation with the bank are essential to keep these countries on track.

Debt relief becomes irrevocable when the countries have satisfactorily implemented the planned reforms, i.e. are at "the completion point." Additional debt relief may be made available in case of unexpected external shocks. Out of these 41 countries (as of 2007), 22 are beyond the completion point, 9 have reached the decision point and are getting interim relief, and 10 are nowhere there (civil war, etc.). In 2006, IDA's participation in the Multilateral Debt Relief Initiative was approved: this means that IDA will cancel all debt outstanding and owed by HIPCs to IDA as of the end of 2003 as soon as these countries reach the "completion point."

What is the future of the bank? Many economists have pondered that question and are suggesting new directions in the running of the bank. World Bank economists are taking the position that it makes more sense to allocate the loans to countries open to reforms and only give advice to corrupt governments. A drawback of this approach is that the corrupt governments are usually in charge of the very poor countries and they will lose out in favor of slightly richer countries on the road to development and reforms. Another development is to move away from loans to straight grants and to stop making loans to richer countries like China or Russia.

Considering the relative success of these new programs, some economists think that there is a need for reassessing the basic lending practices of the World Bank. For instance there is an intrinsic dilemma resulting from the fact that, as a bank, the World Bank's revenues depend on the extent of its clientele. Indeed, the bank borrows at low interest rate (it enjoys AAA rating) from the world financial markets and lends at a slightly higher rate. So, there is an incentive to try to maximize the number of loans the bank extends, implying that some loans could be rather risky (a moral hazard problem). The structure of the bank could also be revamped: the Harvard economist, Ken Rogoff, believes that the World Bank should close some of its lending windows, specifically the IRBD and the IFC, and concentrate its efforts on the IDA that specializes in helping the HIPC. Since many of the World Bank decisions are very political, any adjustment along these lines will take a long time to be accepted and implemented.

Chapter 22

European Monetary Integration

LEARNING OBJECTIVES

By the end of this chapter, you should be able to understand:

- that oil shocks and unemployment in the seventies contributed to unite Europeans in adopting a common exchange rate regime

- how this system eventually evolved into greater monetary integration

- the difference between a system where exchange rate policy drives monetary policy and a system where monetary policy is openly harmonized

- the significance of the Maastricht Treaty in introducing a monetary union

- the impact of allowing full capital mobility in the European Community economies

- the basic conditions allowing a monetary union to be optimum

- what the European monetary union entails: the euro, the European Central Bank, and a common monetary policy

In the last chapter, we presented a brief history of the international monetary system and discussed the Bretton Woods arrangement that launched the modern post-World War II world economy. We now focus our attention on a specific group of countries in Western Europe. We pick up the thread towards the end of the Bretton Woods era and consider the impact of that system on the West European countries. We then describe how, after the collapse of Bretton Woods, these countries undertook various experiments attempting to develop a system that would replace Bretton Woods. In due course, they shaped their own exchange rate mechanism that was not unlike Bretton Woods, but avoided some of its obvious weaknesses. This mechanism had its own flaws and could not withstand shocks in the modern economy: basically a mere exchange rate mechanism was not a viable choice anymore. The options had narrowed to two alternatives: either forgetting about an exchange rate mechanism and floating or adhering to a more integrated system, a monetary union, with its own uncertainties. Eventually, most of Western Europe joined a monetary union, the European Economic and Monetary Union while a few countries, like the U.K., returned to a free float.

EUROPEAN ISSUES WITH BRETTON WOODS AND THE SNAKE

For the Europeans, the Bretton Woods system offered a valuable learning opportunity. The obvious problems with the system had to be avoided in the eventuality Bretton Woods failed. When this happened, the Europeans were ready with blueprints to experiment with. The first experiment was called, after the fact, the snake, illustrating how the joint float (see Chapter 13, p. 376) was snaking against the dollar over the years in graphical representations. This was followed by an exchange rate mechanism and eventually by a full fledged monetary union.

The European Economies under Bretton Woods

For the European countries, membership in the Bretton Woods system conveyed some desirable aspects. It imparted stability on two crucial economic variables: the exchange rate and the price level. Bretton Woods was a fixed exchange rate system so importers and exporters could carry out their international transactions without fear of exchange rate fluctuations. By reducing foreign exchange risk and uncertainties, this system facilitated international trade. This was all the more appealing to countries heavily depending on trade. In the previous chapter, we pointed out that the gold standard imposed monetary discipline on its followers. Bretton Woods was not a gold standard, but a gold-exchange standard, and through a slightly more roundabout process, it ensured that inflation would be low since the members' currencies were pegged to the dollar, and the dollar was pegged to gold.

This system worked quite well in the late forties and in the fifties when Europe was mainly preoccupied with reconstruction following World War II. The weaknesses of the Bretton Woods system became apparent in the sixties. The first two problems were presented briefly in the last chapter: they became known as *the confidence* and *the redundancy problems*. A third issue concerned the band within which a currency could fluctuate.

The Confidence Problem

The confidence problem was caused by the fact that, for all the member countries, with the exception of the United States, the dollar was the main foreign reserve asset. Therefore it was essential for these countries' central banks to hold dollars. In order to acquire these dollars, the members ran payments surpluses with the United States. This is equivalent to stating that the United States ran large trade deficits, thus providing the excess supply of dollars that could be accumulated by foreign central banks. Eventually, in the sixties, the realization that it might not be prudent to use as a main reserve the currency of a country plagued with a persistent trade deficit became apparent. Therefore, a possible loss of confidence in the dollar threatened the trust people had placed in the soundness of the system: any devaluation in the dollar-gold parity would undermine the member countries' reserves.

The Redundancy Problem

The second problem – the redundancy problem – is also referred to as the *n-1* question. It relates to a member country's sovereignty to use monetary policy for domestic purposes. Exchange rates are bilateral; they are the price of one currency in terms of another, so *n* countries can only have *n-1* independent exchange rates. All members of the Bretton Woods system had their currency pegged to the dollar, while the dollar was pegged to gold. So, as the dollar was the anchor in the system, the U.S. central bank, the Federal Reserve, did not have to intervene to support the U.S. exchange rate against any of the other currencies in the system. It was the task of all the other central banks to intervene in the foreign exchange market to keep their exchange rate pegged to the dollar. As a result the Federal Reserve could use its monetary policy for purely domestic purposes. The other countries had no choice but to forego the use of independent domestic monetary policy, as their monetary policy had to be devoted to maintaining parity with the dollar.

To work smoothly without the need for constant exchange rate readjustments, the countries participating in the system must share the same inflation rates. Indeed, any country carrying out a monetary policy resulting in higher inflation rates than the U.S. (and the other members) would lose its international competitiveness; when converted into dollars with the fixed exchange rate, its prices would be higher. To maintain its competitiveness, this country would need to devalue its currency; on the other hand, the dollar did not ever have to be devalued or revalued against any other currency. Basically, all the member countries had to align their monetary policy to that of the U.S., while the U.S. was directly pegged to gold. As long as the U.S. rate of inflation was low, this system worked to the advantage of the members. But in the sixties, U.S. inflation started to creep up, and countries with lower inflation rates than the U.S. experienced real devaluation and trade surpluses.

Germany and Bretton Woods

By the mid-sixties, Germany had lower rates of inflation than the United States. Since trade depends on the real Germany/U.S. exchange rate $(E^{DM/\$} * P^{US})/P^{GER}$ (cf. Chapter 13), the German currency underwent a real depreciation with respect to the dollar; the U.S. price level, P^{US}, increasing more than the German price level, P^{GER}. The resulting increase in their international competitiveness would create a trade surplus and Germany would accumulate dollar reserves, increasing their monetary base. If Germany chose not to sterilize, the resulting increase in the German money supply would be inflationary, a very unappealing consequence. On the other hand, sterilization would consist in a hike in the interest rate with various consequences: maybe discouraging domestic investments or maybe attracting foreign capital flows with further upward pressures on the Deutsche Mark. For Germany, the best solution to the quandary was for the DM to be revalued with respect to the dollar; Germany revalued against the dollar twice in the sixties and again in the seventies. The revaluation ensured that the decrease in $E^{DM/\$}$ would compensate for the increase in P^{US}/P^{GER}, thus stabilizing the real exchange rate and the trade balance. However a DM revaluation can be construed as a dollar devaluation; not a good omen for the anchor of the system.

The Fluctuation Band Problem

A third problem irritating the Europeans concerned the extent of exchange rate fluctuation allowed under the system. To avoid having to intervene as soon as the exchange rate deviated ever so slightly from its parity, it seemed reasonable to allow the exchange rate to fluctuate slightly around the parity chosen; central banks would not have to intervene constantly. It was agreed that central banks would only be expected to intervene when the exchange rate deviated by more than ±1 percent around parity; the no-intervention zone was called the "exchange rate band." A ±1 percent band implied that the maximum fluctuation between the dollar and any member's currency would not be greater than 2 percent. However, this also implied that the total fluctuation between two non-dollar currencies could be as high as 4 percent. This would happen if one European currency hit the floor of its band against the dollar while the other hit the ceiling of its band against the dollar. Europeans found the bands with the dollar too wide and reduced them to ±0.75 percent generating a 3 percent total band between two non-dollar currencies. In the early seventies, the Bretton Woods system was on the verge of collapsing (cf. Chapter 21) and a rescue effort, hammered out at the Smithsonian Conference in 1971, was launched. One of the tenets of these agreements consisted in widening the bands to ±2.25 percent to accommodate greater exchange rate fluctuations (resulting in a 9 percent total band between any two non-dollar currencies). A 9 percent band can be construed as a semi-flexible exchange rate – not at all the wishes of the Europeans.

The Pursuit of Exchange Rate Stability: The Snake

There were a number of reasons why the Europeans were keen to take part in an exchange rate system that guaranteed fixed exchange rates. As we learned in Chapter 21, their traumatic experiences with hyperinflation and widely fluctuating exchange rates in the interwar period had taught European policy makers the importance of stable exchange rates. The competitive devaluations practiced in the thirties to prop up their own economies resulted in a downward spiral for all. Indeed, the competitive advantage they would gain could only be at the expense of their trade partners who would then retaliate with the same policies. The increasing protectionism led to less and less trade overall; this was very unappealing. On the other hand, European countries have a long history of mutual trade, making a fixed exchange rate system highly desirable. The first step towards the establishment of a predictable trading system was the signature in 1957 of the Treaty of Rome creating the European Economic Community (E.E.C.) among six West European countries: Belgium, France, Germany, Italy, Luxembourg, and the Netherlands.[1] Although the Treaty of Rome did not specify openly monetary integration as a goal, some of the original articles did raise the need for coordination of macroeconomic and exchange rate policy including the possibility of mutual assistance for balance-of-payments difficulties through the Monetary Committee and various other advisory agencies created later on.

The E.E.C. was a customs union. In the framework of this trade arrangement, the six members agreed to remove gradually all tariffs among themselves and to establish a common external policy. Consequently they set uniform tariffs against imports from non-member countries. The E.E.C. also entered into a tangled system of agricultural price supports under the auspice of the Common Agricultural Policy (CAP): under this policy, the E.E.C. was fixing the prices of agricultural goods in the member countries. Settlements in agricultural trade were made in terms of **European Units of Account** (EUA). The EUA were defined in terms of gold, just like the dollar. As a result, any exchange rate change between two E.E.C. currencies resulting from a devaluation/revaluation against the dollar had to be neutralized to ensure that the agricultural prices remained the same in all the E.E.C. countries. This was possible through taxing or subsidizing these prices at the borders. The taxes/subsidies were called Monetary Compensation Amounts (MCA) creating a de facto dual exchange rate system: the green exchange rate for agricultural products (impervious of the impact of any devaluation/revaluation) and the normal exchange rate for the rest of E.E.C. trade.

Plans for a Purely European Arrangement

Aware for some time of the shortcomings of the Bretton Woods arrangement, the E.E.C. had started to look at alternatives as early as 1969. The European commission set up the Werner Committee to study the likelihood of monetary integration. At the European Summit at The Hague in 1969, two potential approaches for achieving further macroeconomic integration were tabled: through implementing a gradual coordination of all economic policies or through first coordinating the exchange rate and thus monetary policy, making the introduction of a common currency a natural outcome.

---

1 Eventually the E.E.C. would grow into the European Union (E.U.) comprising 27 member states.

The goals were the same, but the means were different. Would fiscal and monetary harmonization lead to a common currency or would exchange rate policy force monetary policy harmonization and also result in a common currency? Eventually the Werner Report in 1970 presented a synthesis of these approaches: convergence of economic policies as well as exchange rate and monetary harmonization. The first stage was envisioned as a period when both exchange rate and economic policies were to be coordinated. The bands of fluctuation were to be narrower between two community members than with the dollar – this represented the blueprint for the so-called **snake**, an endeavor by the E.E.C. to coordinate exchange rate policy in the seventies.

The Snake

In fact, the first European attempt at devising a more formal exchange rate harmonization scheme was a direct consequence of the Smithsonian Conference. The 9 percent band, mentioned above, between two E.E.C. currencies was not acceptable. It had to be somehow circumvented: the intra-E.E.C. band was thus restricted to 2.25 percent. The European moving band, its width fixed by the permitted range of fluctuation between member currencies, traced a snake-like path as it floated against the dollar; it was dubbed the "**snake in the tunnel**." The tunnel represented the band between the European currencies and the dollar. By March 1973, most European central banks stopped intervening to keep the parity with the dollar and chose to float freely against the dollar. The Bretton Woods system was doomed and the snake left the tunnel. Throughout the seventies, a number of various European countries participated in the joint float, linking their currencies together by limiting the range of exchange rate fluctuation between any two currencies in the group. As a result, the currencies of participating countries moved together relative to the dollar, rising or falling as a group. One salient innovation of the system was the creation of the **European Monetary Cooperation Fund** (EMCF)[2] to facilitate intervention for countries faced with temporary balance-of-payments problems. The EMCF would provide funds through its **Very Short Term Facilities** (VSTF). Although the snake symbolizes the European effort towards monetary integration in the seventies, it did not rise to the Werner Commission's hopes.

Demise of the Snake

The active participants in this scheme varied as countries joined or withdrew. Around that time, three new countries became members of the E.E.C.: the U.K., Ireland, and Denmark. Unfortunately the seventies were marred by oil shocks, resulting in high levels of inflation and unemployment in many European countries. As they attempted to use fiscal and monetary policy to return to full employment, many members had to drop from the joint float. Neither the U.K., who only stayed in the system for a few months, nor France who moved in and out at three different instances, nor Italy, were able to stabilize their currencies. The only countries remaining in the system were Germany and four smaller E.E.C. economies around its border (Belgium, Luxembourg, the Netherlands, and

---

2 The EMCF would eventually morph into the European Monetary Institute, precursor of the European Central Bank.

Denmark) in addition to two non-E.E.C. countries, Sweden and Norway. It was clear that a better system had to be designed if monetary integration was still a goal. The instabilities faced by most European currencies were too serious to be shored up by the VSTF. In the late seventies, Europeans undertook another attempt at erecting a stable currency system. The failures of the joint float led to the creation, after three European Council meetings, of the **European Monetary System** (EMS). In July 1978, the new **European Currency Unit**, the ECU, was introduced as a basket of European currencies and in January 1979, the EMS began to implement its **Exchange Rate Mechanism** (ERM).

THE EUROPEAN MONETARY SYSTEM AND ITS EXCHANGE RATE MECHANISM

The basic objective was to put together a monetary system that was not unlike Bretton Woods, but that would circumvent its major weaknesses. The E.E.C. members wanted a fixed exchange rate arrangement, but without the asymmetry intrinsic to Bretton Woods (the *n-1* problem). In addition, they saw the importance of dealing adequately with the issue of support for countries facing chronic balance-of-payments problems. It was clear that the very short-term assistance offered through Bretton Woods (and through the snake) was not sufficient to bring relief. Finally, there was the issue of removing capital controls[3] with the resulting danger of destabilizing currency speculation. During the Bretton Woods era, quite a few members had weak currencies, so the conventional wisdom was to place tight controls on their capital flows. However the gradual integration of the European economies in the seventies and the eighties called for freeing capital flows. In turn, the liberalization of capital would necessitate a higher level of mutual assistance in the case of a currency crisis.

Implementation of the New European System

We explain below the nature of the ECU and discuss the Exchange Rate Mechanism and the various funds created to support its operation. First a box summarizes the three main elements of the system.

The Basic Elements of the European Monetary System (EMS)

■ The ECU: a basket of members' currencies. The number of units of each currency in the basket corresponds to the weight of the currency in the ECU basket. By order of importance, the currencies included in the orginal basket (1979) were the Deutsche Mark, the French franc, the British pound, the Dutch guilder, the Belgium franc, the Italian lira, the Danish krone, and the Irish punt.

---

3 Currency convertibility was a different issue (see Chapter 16): it was eventually attained in the sixties in all E.E.C. countries, adding much flexibility to trade without introducing instability.

■ The Exchange Rate Mechanism (ERM): each country involved agreed to keep its bilateral exchange rates within a ±2.25 percent band around the bilateral central parity against any other member currencies. A wider band of ±6 percent was allowed for Italy and the new countries joining the mechanism. The ERM also entailed a formal intervention mechanism and a complex realignment scheme.

■ The various funds to finance intervention and help the members facing balance-of-payments difficulties were: the Very Short Term Financial Facilities (VSTFF), the Short Term Monetary Support (STMS), both under the umbrella of the European Monetary Cooperation Fund (EMCF) created in 1972, and the Medium Term Financial Assistance (MTFA) administered by the Council of Ministers.

The European Currency Unit

The European Currency Unit (or ECU) was the unit of account for the European Community (until it was replaced by the Euro). The ECU was designed as a basket of currencies; the weight of each currency would determine the number of units of each currency in the basket (the composition of the basket). These weights, the percentage of a currency value in the total value of the ECU, were based on the strength of various national economic variables. The ECU only existed in the form of balances – it was a virtual currency: the ECU never took the form of a physical currency (notes or coins) used in the individual member countries. The individual member countries continued to use their own national currency as unit of account and means of exchange; the ECU was a so-called **parallel currency**.

The exchange rate between the ECU and any non-E.E.C. currency could be calculated as a weighted average of the various exchange rates of the E.E.C. members. Since most of these exchange rates were pegged together within the Exchange Rate Mechanism (ERM), their movements against non-ERM floating currencies would be more or less synchronized. The original idea was to bestow on the ECU the role of anchor for the mechanism, substituting for the dollar in the Bretton Woods system. The notable difference was that the dollar was an independent currency pegged to gold while the ECU was a composite currency based on all the members' currencies. We will see below that, as the system evolved, the ECU did not really play that central role.

The Exchange Rate Mechanism

When the European Monetary System was launched, the European Economic Community included nine members: the original six plus the U.K., Ireland, and Denmark. The U.K. was a member of the European Monetary System and the British pound was included in the ECU, but, by choice, the U.K. did not take part in the Exchange Rate Mechanism until 1990. When the three Mediterranean countries (Greece, Portugal, and Spain) joined the European Community in the eighties, they were not in a position to participate in the ERM right away due to their high rates of inflation. Spain joined in 1989, Portugal in 1992, but Greece still had to wait (see Table 22.2).

TABLE 22.1 The ECU

Composition and weight for members' currencies in the ECU

Currency		BEF/LUF Belgium & Luxembourg*	DEM Germany	DKK Denmark	ESP Spain	FRF France	GBP U.K.	GRD Greece	IEP Ireland	ITL Italy	NLG Netherlands	PTE Portugal
March 1979	#	3.80	0.828	0.217	—	1.15	0.0885	—	0.00759	109.0	0.286	—
	%	9.64%	32.98%	3.06%	—	19.83%	13.34%	—	1.15%	9.49%	10.51%	—
Sept. 1984	#	3.85	0.719	0.219	—	1.31	0.0878	1.15	0.008781	140.0	0.256	—
	%	8.57%	32.08%	2.69%	—	19.06%	14.98%	1.31%	1.20%	9.98%	10.13%	—
Sept. 1989	#	3.30B 0.13L	0.6242	0.1976	6.885	1.332	0.08784	1.44	0.008552	151.8	0.2198	1.393
	%	8.18% 0.32%	31.96%	2.65%	4.14%	20.32%	12.45%	0.44%	1.09%	7.84%	9.98%	0.70%

Source: adapted from Eurostat

* Until 1989, Belgium and Luxembourg belonged to a currency union, so their data are merged. After 1989, the data for Belgium are presented in the left column and for Luxembourg in the right column.

The table shows the number of units of each currency in one ECU (#) and below the weight (%) of each currency in the ECU. These numbers were readjusted in 1984 to accommodate the addition of a new member, Greece, and again in 1989 to accommodate the addition of Spain and Portugal. The Luxembourg franc received its own weight in 1989. On December 31, 1998, the ECU was replaced by the euro at the going exchange rate between the ECU and the dollar (the weighted average of the exchange rates of each member with the dollar).

1. Intervention under the ERM

The Exchange Rate Mechanism was a fixed exchange rate regime, but currencies were allowed to vary within specific bands. All exchange rates were based on the ECU, the new European unit of account; as explained above, the value of the ECU was determined as a weighted average of the participating currencies. Each currency had a central parity vis-à-vis the ECU. These central rates were used to construct a grid of bilateral exchange rates. Whenever any *two* countries' exchange rate diverged by more than ±2.25 percent (or ±6 percent for Italy and later members), intervention by the *two* central banks was compulsory and unlimited: both central banks were to sell the stronger currency and buy the weaker currency.

However it was most likely that one of the two currencies involved in hitting the boundary of the band was the DM, as it was the strongest currency in the system. As a result, one expected the German central bank (the Bundesbank) to be regularly involved in shoring the weak currencies. This was the case because Germany had the lowest rate of inflation and consequently it was the strongest currency in the system; this was not caused by an asymmetrical flaw in the design of the system. With Bretton Woods, the U.S. Federal Reserve had no obligation to be involved in intervention operations to support the weaker currencies; in contrast, the ERM rules expected concerted intervention, making the system theoretically more symmetrical. Moreover financing for such intervention was unbounded: an unlimited credit line, the Very Short Term Financing Facilities (VSTFF) had to be made available by the strong currency central bank to the weak currency central bank.

What really happened was different. Countries could always intervene earlier to avoid hitting the boundaries of the band – these "intra-marginal" and unilateral forms of intervention were quite common. A country, seeing its currency depreciate, would sell a non-EMS currency (usually the dollar) to strengthen it – in fact intra-marginal intervention could be carried out with any form of foreign reserves. In this case, the country would not benefit of VSTFF. Not only was Germany weary of buying the currencies of weaker members to support them, but, whenever the Bundesbank had to do so, it would sterilize, thus derailing the adjustment mechanism. It is in this respect that the mechanism turned out to be asymmetrical. However the result was beneficial in imparting a deflationary bias to Germany's ERM partners. Since Germany was not going to bail out countries with higher rates of inflation, these countries has no other alternative but strive to emulate the German rates of inflation and, in the process, shadow Germany's monetary policy. In the eighties, France and Italy, welcomed this opportunity to fight their inflation problems. The other countries involved were very open small economies; they had no choice but follow the monetary policy of the larger economies. Basically in the eighties, the German Bundesbank dictated informally the monetary policy for the ERM members.

France and the ERM in the Eighties

For most of the decade, France was governed by a socialist president, François Mitterand. Earlier experiences with socialist governments had an undesirable impact on the French economy overall. The immediate social needs of the workers tended to take precedence over prudent fiscal and monetary policies. Thanks to France's association with the ERM, Mitterand was able to convince the French of the importance of a "franc fort," a strong franc: the French franc had to hold its own in the system and the only way to do so was to use conservative monetary policy and prudent fiscal policies, just like Germany. By shadowing the Bundesbank, the Banque de France was able to reduce the rate of inflation from 13 percent in 1980 to 2.7 percent in 1988. By the end of the decade, the French franc did not need to be devalued any more against the DM – it had become a strong currency.

In addition to intervention operations that were regularly carried out, the ERM had a very formal mechanism to devalue/revalue currencies.

2. Realignment under the ERM

Every so often, as countries real exchange rates diverged due to different rates of inflation, each central parity was recalculated to reflect the real exchange rate movements: this was called a realignment. In the first half of the eighties, most members would inflate at a faster rate than Germany. The result: a loss of international competitiveness and trade deficits putting pressure on these currencies to devalue. In the Bretton Woods system, such countries would devalue in a haphazard manner; often a bit more than needed to gain a competitive advantage. This was not permitted within the ERM and realignments were mostly formal and multilateral affairs involving thorough recalculations of all the pegs. The ERM members performed eleven realignments between 1979 and 1989; seven took place between 1979 and 1983 and none after 1987, thus illustrating that the inflation rates of the members had converged. This approach allowed a smooth and coherent adjustment for all the exchange rates and the ERM was characterized as a "**crawling peg**."

Additional Funds to Finance the System

The architects of the ERM sought to install a system that would deal effectively with countries experiencing chronic balance-of-payments problems. Both Bretton Woods and the snake boasted a short-term assistance mechanism to deal right away with temporary imbalances. The VSTFF, mentioned earlier and administered by the EMCF, were actually introduced in 1972 to facilitate balance-of-payments adjustments for the snake. However it had become clear that these funds were not sufficient to help countries facing more serious imbalances. So, in addition to the credit lines for intervention described above, the arrangement provided **Short Term Monetary Support** (STMS), also administered by the central banks and the EMCF, and, for chronic balance-of-payments difficulties,

Medium Term Financial Assistance (MTFA), administered by the council of finance ministers. The European Monetary Cooperation Fund acted as a clearing-house for the intervention mechanism: a specific proportion of each central bank's reserves was redeposited at the EMCF and used for these operations.

Economic Impact of the ERM on its Members

Did the ERM lower the volatility of the European currencies during the eighties? A number of studies set out to check this issue. Most studies agree that the ERM had a stabilizing impact on the participants' exchange rates, whether measured as bilateral intra-community rates or multilateral nominal rates.[4] Other economists note that the increased internal stability was paired with greater volatility between individual ERM currencies and the dollar.[5]

In addition, the ERM had an anti-inflationary impact on the member countries. Instead of using monetary policy to bring down inflation directly, the member countries used exchange rate pegging. It worked because the dominant currency in the system was the DM and Germany had the lowest rate of inflation. To remain in the ERM, all the other countries had to maintain their fixed peg to the DM. More precisely, this meant that, to avoid a "shameful" devaluation, they had to keep their *real* exchange rate vis-à-vis the DM stable. This was only possible by aligning their rate of inflation with Germany, thus shadowing Germany's monetary policy. Germany was dictating the monetary policy for the system and the other members gave up their sovereignty in this respect. This was a system where the exchange rate pegging was driving the monetary policy. The ERM succeeded where Bretton Woods did not for the reasons explained above – mainly a more balanced order, a more structured system, and more cooperation.

Monetary harmonization was actually taking place *in the background*, not in the open. The process was gradual as it took most countries a number of years to get their rate of inflation down to the German level. So realignments were frequent in the early eighties, but as the rates of inflation converged, by the end of the decade there was no need anymore for realignments.[6]

Finally, as the members of the ERM brought down their inflation rate, their international competitiveness was enhanced. Lower rates of inflation had favorable effects on their *real* exchange rate, thus making their goods more attractive to their trade partners. Eventually as the inflation rates converged within the ERM countries, real exchange rates between the members stabilized, thus evening out their mutual relative competitiveness, but their competitiveness vis-à-vis the rest of the world had improved due to the lower rates of inflation achieved.

Overall the ERM was successful in its first decade. The European countries were also fortunate to encounter favorable economic circumstances at the end of the eighties. However, potential causes of

---

4 See Ungerer (1983).

5 See Giavazzi et al. (1988).

6 The countries with higher rates of inflation would not get permission for a realignment right away. When the realignment eventually took place, the nominal adjustment would on purpose underestimate the real change (the opposite happened with Bretton-Woods where the process of devaluing or revaluing was unilateral). Indeed the ERM was used as a *counter-inflationary* instrument.

TABLE 22.2 Rates of Inflation of EMS Members and U.S.

Consumer prices – all items

Percentage change on the same period of the previous year

Annual

Country	1980	1985	1990	1995	2000	2005
Belgium	6.6	4.9	3.4	1.5	2.5	2.8
Denmark	12.3	4.7	2.6	2.1	2.9	1.8
France	13.6	5.8	3.2	1.8	1.7	1.7
Germany	5.4	2.1	2.7	1.7	1.5	2.0
Greece	24.7	19.3	20.4	8.9	3.2	3.6
Ireland	18.2	5.5	3.3	2.5	5.6	2.4
Italy	21.1	9.2	6.5	5.2	2.5	2.0
Luxembourg	6.3	4.1	3.3	1.9	3.2	2.5
Netherlands	6.5	2.3	2.5	1.9	2.4	1.7
Portugal	16.6	19.6	13.4	4.2	2.9	2.3
Spain	15.6	8.8	6.7	4.7	3.4	3.4
United Kingdom	18.0	6.1	7.0	2.7	0.8	2.0
United States	13.5	3.5	5.4	2.8	3.4	3.4

Source: OECD, based on data from http://stats.oecd.org

instability were looming and the leaders of the European Community were well aware that the system could not fend off a serious currency crisis. In reality, the ERM was merely a fixed exchange rate system where a concerted exchange rate pegging was driving the common monetary policy. The risk of a currency crisis is always possible with a fixed exchange rate regime and the various ERM funds would not be sufficient to prevent the worse outcomes: a massive devaluation or worse, expulsion from the system.

As a result, under the leadership of Jacques Delors, the then president of the Commission of the E.C.,[7] blueprints were drawn to replace the ERM by a system where the common monetary policy would be decided in the open, thus making a common exchange rate pegging system irrelevant. Basically they were visualizing a monetary union, involving a single currency and a common European central bank: a much higher level of monetary integration that would all but eradicate any danger of currency crises. They also drew a timetable, setting specific dates for reaching specific goals. Unfortunately, a number of events at the beginning of the nineties precipitated various currency crises and put in question the desirability or the feasibility of creating a European monetary union. The first event, the removal of the capital controls, had to happen and thus was expected; indeed freeing

---

7 The E.E.C. had been renamed the E.C.

the movements of capital made it imperative to design a better system. The other event was an unexpected historical occurrence, the German reunification.

THE 1992–3 EUROPEAN CURRENCY CRISES

We can apply the theory developed in Chapter 18 (Mundell–Fleming under fixed exchange rates) to the problem of removing capital controls and the theory developed in Chapter 15 (policy conflicts and reinforcements) to the German policy dictated by the needs of the reunification.

Theoretical Background

The removal of all capital controls was indispensable for the completion of the internal market between the members of the European Community. In order to reap all the benefits of their internal market, the members had to allow full capital mobility. Indeed, firms, banks, etc. had to be able to move capital freely from country to country to open branches and carry any business between each other. With full capital mobility and fixed exchange rates, countries fully lose any ability to use monetary policy in the short run, as shown in Chapter 18. In Figure 22.1, we illustrate the difference between monetary policy with no capital mobility, corresponding to the Bretton Woods era and the ERM through most of the eighties (left panel) and full capital mobility, corresponding to the last years of the eighties and the beginning of the nineties (right panel). In the first case, monetary policy works,

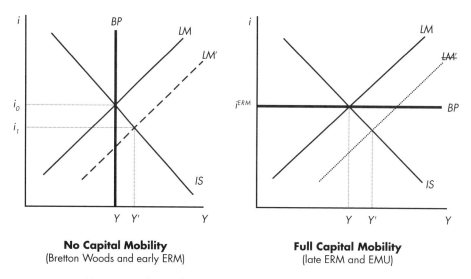

No Capital Mobility
(Bretton Woods and early ERM)

Full Capital Mobility
(late ERM and EMU)

FIGURE 22.1 Monetary Policy with Fixed Exchange Rates and Various Degrees of Capital Mobility

In the first graph, an economy *can* expand to Y' as long as it is willing and able to sustain (temporary) balance-of-payments deficits. In the second graph, an economy *cannot* expand to Y', because as soon as the interest rate drops below the ERM interest rate i^{ERM}, it faces unsustainable capital outflows.

provided sterilization is possible, while, in the other case, it is powerless. The fact that a combination of a fixed exchange rate regime, full capital mobility, and a workable monetary policy are inconsistent is sometime called the "unholy trinity."

Full capital mobility with a fixed exchange rate system also means that speculators can use the foreign exchange market for fast gains on currency trading, thus increasing the risk of currency volatility and market destabilization. A number of EC directives were passed in the late eighties gradually removing all capital controls still existing in the ERM countries, and, in the process, making the ERM currencies susceptible to speculative attacks.

The other problem has to do with policy repercussions between countries. Over the years, the other members of the ERM had no serious objections about shadowing the monetary policies of the Bundesbank; the German economy was strong and the Bundesbank was committed to low-inflation policies. However, the shock of the German reunification led to policies in Germany that were detrimental to the rest of the ERM countries. This illustrated the need to replace the system by a truly symmetrical arrangement. The economic demands created by German reunification were immense.[8] West Germany financed the rebuilding of the East by issuing and selling government bonds, thus tapping the global capital market. To avoid the inflationary impact of such a policy, the Bundesbank used a contractionary monetary policy. Unfortunately, at that time, the economies of the other ERM members, especially France, were slowing down; they needed the opposite: an expansionary monetary policy. However, the ERM was a system where the exchange rate pegging was the primary driving force. In order to remain within their band with the DM, these countries had no choice other than to shadow the German contractionary monetary policy. These were the first signs of tensions in the system.

This is illustrated in Figure 22.2 overleaf where the left panel corresponds to Germany and the right panel to France. On the left panel, the impact of issuing new bonds is depicted by the rightward shift of the *IS* curve and the anti-inflationary policy followed by the Bundesbank as a leftward shift of the *LM* curve. On the right panel, although the French equilibrium, Y^*_0, is below full employment, at Y^*_{FE}, France has no choice but to use contractionary monetary policy too in order to keep the French franc parity with the DM: the French economy ends up at Y^*_1, below its initial level, suffering further contraction.

---

8 After the fall of the Soviet Union in 1989, the territory forming the DDR or East Germany was integrated into the FDR or West Germany to reunify Germany. Economic development in East Germany was far behind that of West Germany, requiring a massive amount of financial support from West Germany.

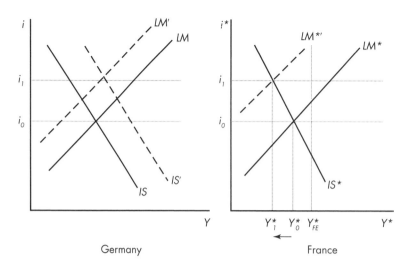

FIGURE 22.2 Policy Conflict

The German *IS* curve shifted to the right as the West German government increased spending to rebuild the East (the chancellor had promised not to raise tax to do so). At the same time, Germany used anti-inflationary monetary policy (an *LM* shift to the left) resulting in an increase in the interest rate from i_0 to i_1. In addition by tapping into the international supply of capital (the German government issued and sold bonds domestically and internationally), Germany put further upward pressures on the interest rate. By 1990, the French economy was starting to slow down and needed a stimulus. On the right panel, the French economy at Y_0^* needed a nudge to the right towards Y_{FE}^*. Instead, in order to keep its parity with the DM, France had no choice but to use a contractionary monetary policy resulting in further slowdowns. The consequences for France: a stagnation that lingered until 1994 and a run on the French franc in 1993.

The Currencies Crises

By the end of 1991, the members of the European Community agreed to the **Maastricht Treaty** (signed in 1992). The new treaty approved the establishment of a full monetary union, the **European Economic and Monetary Union** (EMU) and adopted a new name for the association: the **European Union** (E.U.), its present name. Maastricht had two other non-economic pillars for advancing European unity in a number of areas such as defense, justice, and home affairs (social policies and immigration). At that point, the plans for a monetary union were put in the open; a timetable to permanently lock the exchange rates of future members and then to eventually replace all the national currencies by one European currency were announced. So no further realignment was to happen before the final locking of the currencies at the end of the decade. Or, at least, these were the expectations.

However, the inflation rates had not fully converged and Italy still had higher rates than Germany (see Table 22.1); nevertheless, in 1990, Italy had given up the wider ± 6 percent band for the narrower ± 2.25 percent band. Italy's higher inflation was reflected in higher nominal interest rates resulting in one-way (hence possibly unstable) arbitrage operations, as the exchange rates were not expected to change. Large amounts of capital flowed into Italy. This created a very dangerous scenario: at the slightest hint that the monetary union might fail to happen or that, after all, a realignment (involving a devaluation of the lira) might take place, capital would flow out of Italy, triggering a currency crisis.

The Maastricht treaty was signed by all the nations involved in 1992, but several countries still required a referendum to ratify it. When the Treaty was rejected by a Danish referendum and barely ratified in France, the expectations of a smooth transition from ERM to EMU were shattered. The normal laws of arbitrage were reinstated and the lira was expected to devalue: this triggered the first currency crisis. Speculators borrowed lira and sold them for DM, in the expectation of being able to repay the loan by buying a devalued currency, thus making a gain. European central banks did not possess enough funds to defend the lira from speculators and the lira had to leave the arrangement. This was an ominous sign with regard to the stability of the exchange rate pact. Speculators then attacked the British pound: the pound had joined the exchange rate mechanism at too high a parity in 1990. The British pound collapsed on Black Wednesday September 16, 1992 and the U.K. withdrew from the ERM.

The financial upheaval continued in the following year: the Swedish krone, the Irish punt, the Spanish peseta, and the Portuguese escudo currencies had to be devalued. Finally, in July 1993, although the fundamentals of its economy were not showing any alarming signs, the French franc was the subject of speculative attacks. In response, the ERM widened its fluctuation bands to ± 15 percent, making any speculation unprofitable. Informally, the members kept the old bands (using intervention mechanisms) to keep in check the volatility of the ERM currencies until they would lock their currencies together. Contrarily to all the nay-sayers, this ploy worked and, as their economies bounced again, the potential members readied themselves for EMU by the second half of the decade.

THE EUROPEAN ECONOMIC AND MONETARY UNION

Surprisingly, the timetable of the Delors plan for EMU was eventually met, although the first stage (general tidying up of EMS, fewer realignments, removal of all capital controls, and a greater role for the ECU, the precursor of the new European currency) fell into rather rocky waters. The second stage concerned independence[9] (from any meddling by their government) of all the central banks, the creation of the European Monetary Institute (EMI) – the precursor of the European Central Bank – and a final listing of the admission criteria by 1994. Finally the introduction of EMU was scheduled for January 1999.

The Road to Completion

The Treaty of Maastricht, signed by the Head of States in 1992, was finally ratified by all the signatories by the end of 1993. A formal framework for the monetary union (EMU) along the Delors plan was set up. A common currency would replace the various national currencies; its name, the euro, was chosen in 1995 and a new institution; the European Central Bank (ECB), would be in charge of the common monetary policy. The criteria for admission, known as the **Maastricht criteria**, were agreed upon.

---

9 Just like the U.S. Federal Reserve, the German Bundesbank was totally independent in selecting the monetary policy that they deemed most efficient at stabilizing prices. On the other hand, central banks like the Banque de France and the Bank of England had their policy dictated by their ministries of finance; they were under constant pressure to meet the short-tem political needs of the government in power.

The Maastricht Criteria

i.   Inflation should not be higher than 1.5 percent above the average of the three members with the lowest rates of inflation.
ii. Interest rates should be within 2 percent of the three countries with the lowest rates.
iii. The ratio of the budget deficit over GDP should be less than 3 percent.
iv. The ratio of the debt over GDP should be lower than 60 percent.
v.   The ERM bands have to be tightened to ±2.25 percent for the countries still on a ±6 percent band and no devaluation should have taken place in the last two years.

The Maastricht admission criteria contained monetary and fiscal requirements. The monetary criteria ensured continuing convergence for inflation and interest rates of the members. The budget deficit and debt ratio criteria imposed fiscal discipline on the members. To ensure that countries not only met these criteria (iii. and iv.) at the onset of EMU, but also remain committed to uphold these criteria later on, a **Stability and Growth Pact**[10] (SGP) was agreed upon. The SGP establishes when a country breaks the rules on budget deficit ceiling (and debt ratio) and how to penalize it. The credibility of the new European Central Bank rested on it: monetary policy coordination for Europe could only work smoothly with prudent fiscal policies on the part of the members.

Note that there are no provisions for the withdrawal or expulsion of a member from the system (see later box, p. 680). The possibility of opting out was offered to a few countries reluctant to join the new system, but eventually all the members of the European Union met the criteria with the exception of Greece which joined the following year. The U.K. and Denmark decided on an official opt-out, while Sweden chose not to participate right away. Among the twelve new countries that joined the E.U. after 2000, Slovenia, Malta, and Cyprus have now adopted the euro, so a total of fifteen countries use the euro as their official legal tender.[11]

On the last day of 1998, the exchange rates of the eleven countries able and willing to join were fixed at their value in terms of the ECU (no further fluctuations were allowed). The euro, the new European currency, was introduced as a virtual currency at the ECU exchange rate ($1.17/€). The ECU (a basket of currencies) then disappeared. For a transitional period, national currencies continued to be used as the means of exchange, but for all practical purposes, they were just equivalent to some fraction of the single currency, the euro, as their exchange rates were locked. Prices would be quoted in both the national currency and the euro to accustom the public to the new currency. The euro in the form of coins and banknotes was not circulated before January 2002. After six months

---

10 It was imposed by Germany to allay the Bundesbank's fears that, deprived of the tool of expansionary monetary policy, irresponsible governments would replace it by unwise fiscal policy. Political reasons were very compelling: Germany might have dropped the idea of a common currency altogether without such a pact.

11 Belgium, France, Germany, Italy, Luxembourg, the Netherlands, Ireland, Greece, Spain, Portugal, Austria, Finland, Slovenia, Malta, and Cyprus.

of parallel existence, the national currencies lost their legal tender and were retired from circulation. The transition went smoothly as the countries were well prepared over the three years after the euro came into existence.

History of European Monetary Integration, 1969–99

What does monetary integration mean?

Harmonization of monetary policies of the members.
Establishment of a European Central Bank to carry out the common European monetary policy.
Creation of a common European currency.

The Seventies – Years of Economic Turmoil

High inflation – oil shocks.
Demise of the old international monetary system, Bretton-Woods, a fixed exchange rate system with the dollar as the anchor.
The snake in the tunnel and the snake out of the tunnel – first European effort to replace Bretton Woods.
Blueprint for a better system: the EMS and the ECU.

The Eighties – Closer cooperation within EMS/ERM

EMS/ERM – a concrete step towards economic discipline and responsibility.
Goal of members: to emulate German monetary policy and low inflation.
Intrinsic weaknesses of system: some asymmetry, no capital mobility.
End of decade: Grand design for the European Economic Monetary Union, the Delors plan, paving the way for a new Treaty, Maastricht.

The Nineties – Maastricht – shattered hopes for rapid monetary integration – then success.

The German reunification and recessions in Europe.
Capital mobility and resulting currency crises.
Diminished expectations followed by rapid success:
> **EMU introduced on time on January 1st 1999**
> Euro as balances – European Central Bank in charge of common monetary policy.

The euro (in specie) is introduced on January 1, 2002.

The Institutions of the European Economic and Monetary Union

The European Central Bank (ECB), established on June 1, 1998 and located in Frankfurt, replaces the European Monetary Institute and functions like the U.S. Federal Reserve in the sense that the national central banks are branches of the ECB. The combination of the ECB and the national central banks corresponds to the European System of Central Banks (ESCB). The ECB is headed by an Executive Board consisting of a president, a vice president, and four members representing six different countries: it sends instructions to the national central banks (now independent of their government) to carry out the policy. The governing council of the ECB consists of the presidents of the national central banks in addition to the six appointees of the Executive Board. The governing council determines monetary policy in a manner similar to that of the Federal Open Market Committee within the Federal Reserve System. The only objective of the ECB is price stability. There is no commitment about unemployment. Decisions are arrived at by majority vote. Monetary policy must be totally free from political interference and is the sole responsibility of the ECB. Exchange rate policy is the joint responsibility of the euro members of the E.U. council of finance ministers (the Eurogroup) setting the policy and the ECB running the day-to-day operations. Their approach results in "benign neglect,"[12] since an exchange rate policy is not so important anymore. Finally, the national central banks (or the finance ministries) are in charge of banking supervision.

When the Europeans designed their grand project, there were practically no modern examples on the scale of the E.U. to follow. Small countries, like Belgium and Luxembourg, had experimented with currency union. The integration of Germany into a nation originated with the formation of a currency union, within the Zollverein, but this happened in the nineteenth century. The Europeans were indeed pioneering a new international financial system. Fortunately, economists had researched the issue and a body of literature on "**Optimum Currency Areas**" was available. The practical aspects of implementation had to be considered: the institutions were created, but how would the system work in the real world?

Economic Analysis: The Theory of Optimum Currency Areas

The introduction of a monetary union brings obvious benefits at the microeconomic level. Competition is stimulated through price and wages transparency. The absence of currency conversion costs and exchange rate fluctuations (no need for hedging costs) is the source of large savings. Finally, businesses have access to a greater capital market, lowering the cost of borrowing and of investing.

Further projected benefits of a monetary union include low inflation and currency stability as well as overall macroeconomic stability. Are such expectations warranted? It is clear that the ECB has credibility: it has been able to keep inflation low and its two consecutive presidents have ignored any

---

12 However in September 2000, shortly after its introduction, the euro had to be shored-through concerted intervention between the ECB and the U.S. Federal Reserve to stop a steep fall that was shaking its credibility.

pressure from national governments. However the success of EMU still hinges on another economic question: the feasibility of the EMU as an optimum currency area. In the 1960s, Robert Mundell (Economics Nobel Laureate 1999) and Ronald McKinnon developed the theory of optimum currency areas. The theory investigates how to determine the ideal area over which either a single currency or rigidly fixed exchange rates should prevail and be successful: basically, countries joining a currency area should have similar economic structures (same economic cycles) and high mobility of capital and labor (as a buffer). The first condition ensures that all the members' needs for a specific policy, either contractionary or expansionary, will be synchronized – this is essential with a "one monetary policy for all" system. This condition is not unrealistic. The EMU core members have similar economies, they trade a lot together, and they are highly integrated: their interactions will generate similar economic cycles. To join, newer members will have to harmonize their economy with the core members.

The second condition provides a buffer in case the economy of a country/region is not cyclically synchronized with the other members. A member country may be affected by an asymmetric shock (for instance, an external shock like the German reunification or a supply shock like the Dutch flood disasters of the fifties) or a member country may have faster (e.g. Ireland) or slower (e.g. Italy) growth. A normal adjustment mechanism in such a case would involve prices and wages. However, as members of a monetary union, countries share the same monetary policy and the same rate of inflation. Their price levels are linked in principle so they cannot use a price/wage adjustment at the national level to correct their specific shocks. Capital and labor mobility must provide the buffer, making up for the inability to adjust price/wage when needed.

Capital movements are now unhindered, but what about labor mobility in the E.U.? If we consider the United States as a currency area comprising fifty different states, labor can move readily from a depressed state/region to a booming one. Unfortunately, labor mobility is low in the E.U. for a number of reasons: language barriers, social barriers, heavy regulations, labor market rigidities. Many studies have compared labor mobility in Europe and in the U.S. illustrating the lack of mobility in Europe. Without labor mobility, national/regional recessions have to be dealt with by some form of fiscal federalism to help the country or the region affected by an asymmetric shock. Unfortunately the E.U. budget is small, so fiscal transfers are limited. In the U.S., local shocks are met by a presidential declaration of "disaster area" and federal funds will flow into the area. Moreover, in Europe, certain regions suffer from chronically low economic development and the small fiscal transfers provided may not be sufficient to help these areas.

In sum, most economists agree that, at this point, EMU is not really an optimal currency area. Does EMU possess the potential of becoming an optimal currency area? Some of the key problems that need to be corrected are labor market rigidities and fiscal rigidities. Many of the EMU members have made extensive efforts to free their labor market from all the regulations at the root of their high natural rates of unemployment. Germany has been able recently to bring down its wage costs and thus regain its international competitiveness. Some countries are also making huge strides in introducing greater fiscal flexibility in their laws. These adjustments are easier to implement in smaller countries such as the Netherlands. Countries have reaped substantial gains from such efforts in terms of higher rate of growth and lower natural rate of unemployment. Others are not doing as well (see case study: Beggar thy neighbour).

There are two further causes for concern. First, increasing trade and deepening economic integration in EMU will result in greater regional specialization. Specialization will make regions more susceptible to an asymmetric shock either due to a slackening of demand or to a natural disaster. For instance the European aircraft industry is more and less congregated around Toulouse, France, so the economy of the region is closely tied to its ups and downs. The second problem was basically self-inflicted by the designers of the system. It stemmed from the imposition of the Stability and Growth Pact. In the process of strengthening the overall credibility of the ECB, the EMU members lost much flexibility to deal with their own specific regional or sectoral business cycles using national fiscal transfers. As Portugal found out, the punishment for not meeting the criteria was too harsh and basically counterproductive. Fortunately, the implementation of the SGP has now been watered down, mitigating the potential ill effects of the policy. National governments have more or less regained the ability to use their budget in a countercyclical manner, i.e. by increasing expenditures when times are bad, followed by more restrictive policies when the economy picks up.

Leaving the Euro?

Once a member of EMU, can a country just resign? Indeed, there are no provisions for possible withdrawal in the treaty. But is it possible from a practical point of view? It would depend on the reasons why a country wanted to give up the euro to reclaim its original currency. If the country is not under duress, it might be possible, albeit costly. If the country is facing serious economic problems, it may not be realistic. Why would a country leave the system? Probably because the euro has become too strong for its economy and the country has lost its international competitiveness. Since it cannot devalue the euro, it would be appealing to bring back the old national currency and devalue. For instance, since the introduction of the euro, Italian labor costs have risen faster than German labor costs as the Italian government has not been able to control wages; in addition, labor productivity has not increased at the same pace as in Germany. Italy's export industries are struggling and a devaluation would be most welcome. Why can't Italy bring the lira back and devalue? Italian debt, private or public, is now denominated in euros and a devaluation of the lira would result in a huge increase in the debt (when denominated in lira) and a greater burden to service it. Everyone would expect to be repaid in euros and nobody would want to hold lira, as they would expect further devaluations, leading to dire consequences on the interest rate. Leaving the euro would definitely be problematic.

Implementation of the ECB Common Monetary Policy

What is the best way to carry out the common monetary policy in different nations? How does the transmission of the monetary mechanisms at the level of so many different countries work? These were key questions. The ERM member countries used to trust the German Bundesbank in setting up the targets; unfortunately this had dire consequences at the time of the German reunification. When the ECB inherited this role, it was expected to set up overall targets for the EMU currency area as a whole, not for specific countries. A fundamental and well-understood tenet of the policy is to ignore issues related to unemployment: the only objective of the ECB is to keep inflation down. This implies strict independence of the European System of Central Bank (including the national central banks) from the national governments.

The ECB could target the money supply, the inflation rate or a combination of both. Measuring aggregate money supply for the EMU economies as a whole might be difficult. Instead, the ECB mainly targets an index of average inflation in the member countries called the Harmonized Index of Consumer Prices (HICP). The ECB's governing council has defined price stability as "a year-on-year increase in the Harmonised Index of Consumer Prices (HICP) for the euro area of below 2 percent." It aims to maintain inflation rates below, but close to, 2 percent over the medium term. The actual policy is carried out by the national central banks: they conduct open market operations to keep the interest rate within a specific range.[13]

How smoothly, evenly, and quickly is the common monetary policy chosen transmitted into each national economy? This question is of great concern to the three nations who chose not to join EMU at its onset. Let us first consider Denmark: the Danish economy is highly integrated with the economies of the EMU members and the bulk of its trade is carried on with these nations. Its business cycle is very much in phase with the euro area and, although the Danes chose by referendum to keep their own currency, they shadow the monetary policy dictated by the ECB. In sum, the Danish currency fluctuates with the euro and, de facto, it is pegged to it. However, the Danes have not formally given up their sovereignty on their monetary and exchange rate policy. The cases of Great Britain and Sweden are different: these economies are not as integrated with the EMU economies as the Danish economy, and their business cycles are not really synchronized with the EMU members. For these countries, the concern whether "one-size-fits-all" monetary policy actually "fits-all" is genuine. The box below goes a long way to explaining why it might not be in the interests of these two countries to join the EMU: they do exhibit institutional and structural differences with the bulk of the continental European economies. In addition, these countries have strong ideological beliefs against losing any form of national sovereignty. The British are proud of their currency, the pound, and giving it up is very unappealing.

Institutional and Structural Differences between Countries

There are a number of factors that might result in different responses to monetary policy in the different economies. First, the extent and the speed of transmission may be different from country to country for the following reasons.

- If an economy is very open, as the monetary policy chosen affects the exchange rate, the policy will have secondary impact through the balance of trade that could be unwelcome. Tight

---

13 The ceiling is the overnight rate of borrowing by banks from the central bank and the floor is the rate at which banks with surplus cash deposit overnight funds.

monetary policy → higher interest rates → appreciation → deterioration in the balance of trade → greater contraction.

- If an economy is more oriented towards heavy industry than towards services, the monetary policy will have a greater impact on investment. Tight monetary policy → higher interest rates → greater fall in investment demand → greater contraction.

In addition, the structure of the banking system, the lending approach, business customs, are all relevant issues affecting the speed of transmission of monetary policy.

- If businesses are borrowing mainly through the capital market (e.g. the U.K.), transmission will be slower. If they are borrowing through banks, it will be faster as the change in the rate of interest will affect borrowing directly.
- On the other hand, if the banks have close relations with business and tend to shelter business from interest hikes, as in Germany, they will slow down the process.
- Another significant difference between countries is the ratio of fixed versus variable interest loans. In countries where variable loans are prevalent, the transmission will evidently be faster (e.g. the U.K., Austria).
- A last point concerns the extent of the use of consumer credit. In countries, like the U.K., where credit cards are used without restraint, any interest hike will be rapidly transmitted into higher interest payments on the card resulting in faster transmission of the policy. In countries where consumers are reluctant to purchase on credit (Mediterranean countries), the transmission is slower.

Source: adapted from *The Economist*, "Can one size fit all?," May 26, 1998.

Criticism and Assessment of the System

The institutional weaknesses of EMU are clear to the British. The system is too centralized and the decision process is not transparent enough. In addition, although policy makers have to testify to the European Parliament, the British feel that accountability is lacking. Of course, the same criticisms can be leveled against the U.S. Federal Reserve.

Independence or Accountability? Which is More Important?

Decisions about inflation targeting have a long-run scope. It is thus important to decouple such decisions from the political process that is likely to focus on short-run electoral issues such as unemployment. The consensus is that independent central banks are more likely to succeed in taming inflation without undue consequences on growth. For these reasons, one crucial precondition for EMU was to impart independence to the central banks of the member countries so that, in turn, the ECB would independent. In its first ten years, the ECB has not disappointed the public in this respect; however a serious criticism has been leveled regularly (and often by the British) at the bank: its lack of transparency and accountability. Indeed the ECB must report regularly to the European Parliament (EP), but this is a mere formality as the EP has no sway on its policies.

The French President, Nicolas Sarkozy, who is holding the E.U. presidency for the second half of 2008, has put forward a proposal to deal with this problem. First, the ECB should publish minutes of the meetings of the governing council reporting the rate-setting discussions. Second, the euro subset of the council of financial minister, the Eurogroup, should have its own permanent secretariat that would interact directly with the ECB.

Obviously, the president of the ECB, another Frenchman, Jean Claude Trichet, is not sold on the idea. The ECB is different from any national central bank in the sense that the decision makers on the governing council hold various nationalities. If the deliberations were made public, there would be a danger that they would become reluctant to go ahead with decisions that could be good for the eurozone as a whole, but not so good for their own country. Similarly, the second proposal could result in a group of finance ministers banding together to bully the ECB. In sum, these two reforms could result in a loss of independence for the ECB.

Enter two famous European economists, intimately versed in the workings of the ECB, Francesco Giavazzi and Charles Wyplosz. They argue that without accountability, independence is not such a desirable quality. Accountability can only be tracked through transparency, i.e. through the publication of minutes. It is clear that, without published minutes of the deliberations, a bank could make unwise decisions and cover up its incompetence. Giavazzi and Wiplosz believe that more openness would improve the ECB policy effectiveness. From a practical point of view, the criticism leveled against Sarkozy's first proposal can be easily dealt with by publishing the deliberations while maintaining the anonymity of the discussants. They also dismiss the potential drawback of the second proposal by stating that the disagreements between the various national central banks are much greater than between anyone of them and the ECB – and, in addition, the ECB has shown by now that it does not let itself be bullied by national governments.

Source: adapted from "Sarkozy calls for more accountable ECB," by Ben Hall and Ralph Atkins in Frankfurt, *The Financial Times*, July 21, 2008; "A Trojan Horse," *The Financial Times*, July 22, 2008; and "Sarkozy is right to call for an end to secrecy," by Francesco Giavazzi and Charles Wyplosz, *The Financial Times*, July 24, 2008.

A potentially more serious problem is the fact that EMU is not an optimum currency area. Members are occasionally out of synch with the other EMU countries (the pack). Without labor mobility or the opportunity to devalue their currency, countries that detect a lowering of their cost competitiveness relative to the other members – due to higher inflation or weak productivity growth – find themselves in a very difficult position. The adjustment back into the pack can be very slow (see case study below). The big question is whether the EMU will become an optimum currency area as time goes by. With almost ten years of operation (and data), economists are starting to carry out empirical studies to answer this crucial question. On the positive side, the ECB has acquired a high level of credibility due to its ability to keep overall inflation low. The euro capital market is developing and the euro is playing an ever more important role as a reserve currency. Central banks all over the world have diversified their reserves, switching from dollars to euros. The euro has eventually been able to capture some of the benefits of seignorage[14] that, formerly, were reaped mainly by the dollar. The euro has established itself as a strong currency[15] reaching record rates against the dollar.

The road towards European monetary integration was not always smooth. Indeed at the beginning of the nineties, once capital was allowed to flow freely, most Western European countries fell prey to international speculators, eager to exploit any potential weakness for gain. Europe got over these bad times and the threat of destabilizing speculation has receded. However many other countries or groups of countries of the world have also faced such speculative attacks. The next chapter is devoted to the modern international financial crises around the world and to the so-called risk of contagion.

Summary of Key Concepts

1. In its first 15 years, the Bretton Woods international exchange rate system was successful in stabilizing the war-torn European economies. By the sixties, the system, with its blatant asymmetries, started to have detrimental impacts on some of its European members. The system eventually collapsed in the early seventies.

2. The Europeans favor pegged exchange rate systems because these systems impart stability when countries trade a lot between each other. So they introduced, in the seventies, their own pegged system to replace Bretton Woods, the so-called snake. The oil shocks of the period, coupled with the inability of some of the members to use correct policies to deal with supply shocks, resulted in stagflation (high inflation and high unemployment). The demise of the snake led to the design of a better exchange rate system, the ERM, under the auspices of the new European Monetary System.

3. In the eighties, the new system was eventually successful in bringing inflation down towards Germany's low rates. Countries were pegging their exchange rates on each other and these fixed parities could only hold if the members harmonized their monetary policy. So exchange rate pegging was driving the monetary policy of the members who shadowed the German Bundesbank. The system had good financing facilities to help countries with

---

14 Seignorage is the benefit accruing to a government when it creates money, the government liability: the money is held by the public, but the public does not earn interest on money. The same applies when the money issued by the government of one country is held as reserves in the central bank of another country, interest free. For the issuing country, it is like borrowing without cost.

15 From its beginning, the euro was expected to be a strong currency, but the unusual strength of the dollar coupled with the disappearance of the DM led to speculative pressures that caused it to depreciate from $1.17 to about $0.85 by the end of 2000. After concerted intervention with the U.S. Federal Reserve, as mentioned earlier, the euro recovered promptly.

temporary balance-of-payments difficulties as long as speculators were not permitted to enter the international capital markets. This was done through strict capital controls.

4. By the end of the eighties, further integration within the countries of the European Community hinged on the removal of the capital controls, thus putting the system at risk. Aware of the potential problems, the European leaders designed a new system, a monetary union with one common currency and one central bank to carry the monetary policy. Such a system would obviously eradicate any possibility of currency crisis.

5. The capital controls were dismantled, but the new system could only be introduced in stages, with 1999 as the completion date. In the meantime, various upheavals, political and economic, resulted in the dreaded currency crises of the early nineties. Amazingly, the project survived and the common European currency, the euro, was introduced in 1999 as scheduled.

6. In its first ten years, the system, now encompassing 15 countries, has been resilient. There is a body of economic literature describing the basic conditions that a monetary union has to meet to be optimum. These conditions include similar economic structure, high mobility of labor and capital, and fiscal federalism to help countries affected by an asymmetric shock. Unfortunately, the European labor markets are notable for their rigidities and the E.U. budget is much too small to be of much help. So the question must be reframed by asking whether the EMU will become an optimum currency area in the future.

CASE STUDY

Beggar Thy Neighbour
January 25, 2007
From *The Economist* print edition

Germany's economy has regained its lost competitiveness, but it may come at the expense of Spain, where wages are rising fast

The economy of the euro area is basking in a rare period of optimism. Growth forecasts ended the year higher than at the start of the year, the first time this has happened since 2000. The growth differential with America's economy has narrowed and is expected to contract further this year. But in an economy that comprises 13 diverse nations, such blessings are rarely unmixed. A particular concern is that the recent resurgence at the euro zone's core could portend a protracted slump at its periphery.

Germany has been the source of much of the recent good news in Europe. For so long a laggard in the euro area, its economy is now growing faster than the regional average. Unemployment, though still high, has dropped sharply in the last two years. The latest survey from Ifo, a Munich economic-research institute, shows that business confidence remains close to a 15-year high. Exports and business investment are doing well. Understandable doubts remain about the durability of Germany's revival: consumer spending has so far failed to take off convincingly.

Yet arguably the German economy is on a sounder footing than at any time since reunification. Germany's recovery in cost competitiveness has been crucial to its reviving fortunes. Declining real wages and a modest upswing in productivity have together produced a sustained drop in unit labour costs. Lower wage costs, in turn, have helped boost exports and jobs.

Hope for a lasting German recovery is mixed with concern about the outlook for countries where wage discipline has been less strict. In Italy and Portugal, for example, a combination of strong wage increases and weak productivity growth has undermined cost competitiveness.

The same cocktail of higher wages and sluggish productivity clouds the outlook for one of the fastest-growing European economies: Spain. In the last decade, its economy has expanded by an average of 3.7% a year, nearly twice the rate for the whole euro zone. Spanish demand has been driven by housing and credit booms that are vulnerable to higher interest rates. But high labour costs may in the end prove to be Spain's undoing. In a report published this week the OECD, while applauding Spain's "remarkable" performance, noted that its relatively high inflation had undermined its competitiveness.

Olivier Blanchard, of the Massachusetts Institute of Technology, sees Spain as a plausible next victim of what he calls "the rotating slumps under the euro." In his view, the euro area is characterised by a succession of booms and busts, each in a single country. A typical stop–go cycle starts with a localised increase in demand, which in turn leads to higher wages, lost competitiveness and finally to a protracted downturn. Since short-term interest rates in the euro area are not tailored to individual countries' cycles, monetary policy can attenuate neither boom nor bust.

In Mr Blanchard's model, the slump migrates across the currency zone according to shifts in relative wage costs. A long period of above-average wage growth that goes unmatched by productivity gains will eventually leave a country at a significant cost disadvantage.

Germany's recent history shows how hard it is for a member of the euro club to recover from a cost-induced slump. Devaluation might have been an obvious remedy, but can only be achieved by leaving the currency union. The only other solution is to drive down wage costs relative to those in competing countries. This option is also costly: Germans have paid the price in terms of high unemployment and stunted growth. Cost reduction is also painfully slow. Workers are resistant to pay cuts, so the necessary reduction in real wages relies on a long period of below-average inflation. This kind of wage discipline has underpinned Germany's revival.

An increase in productivity growth, a more recent trend, has given German competitiveness a further boost. Output per hour in Germany rose by 2% last year, according to a report published on January 23rd by the Conference Board, a business organisation. Such vigour has put further distance between Germany and its trading partners to the south. Spain's performance is particularly dismal. Output per hour there fell by 0.5% last year, continuing a negative trend that dates back to the mid-1990s.

For Mr Blanchard, Spain is at a potentially dangerous point in the relative-cost cycle. Wages are still rising at a rate roughly twice the euro zone's average and well ahead of productivity growth. Spain's real exchange rate is up by nearly a quarter since 2000 (see chart). But so far the economy shows few symptoms of ill health. GDP probably grew by 3.6% last year and forecasts for this year suggest only a modest slowdown.

One clear sign of something amiss is Spain's current-account deficit, which widened to 8.8% of GDP last year, estimates the OECD. Such imbalances can reflect shifts in competitiveness and warn of trouble ahead – especially, perhaps, in a currency union where the costs of wage adjustment are high. Within America, by contrast, cost imbalances are resolved less painfully, because workers are willing to move from depressed states to where jobs are more plentiful.

Portugal's ballooning trade deficit in the late 1990s was a symptom of declining competitiveness and the economy has yet to recover from the subsequent bust. Spain now has the second-largest current-account deficit in the world in dollar terms and looks dangerously overheated. Germany's resurgence has set a challenge for the euro zone's southern members. Without the option of devaluation, their medium-term outlook looks less than rosy.

North–South divide
Real effective exchange rates
Based on relative unit labour costs, 1993=100

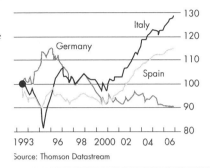

Source: Thomson Datastream

CASE STUDY QUESTIONS

1. This article raises the issue of cost competitiveness in Germany and in Spain. Compare the situation in the two countries.

2. Through the EMU, with a common monetary policy, one would hope for convergence of the inflation rates of the various members. Is this the case for Spain? Explain why or why not.

3. What are Blanchard's "rotating slumps under the euro"? Describe their various stages.

4. Explain why the common monetary policy cannot help specific countries in a slump. What about a devaluation?

5. What is the only painstaking slow solution for Spain? Germany has also put up with it and finally its economy has picked up. How did they do it?

6. Basically this article hinges on the fact that the currency union (EMU) is not optimum. Two basic points are raised: member countries may have different cycles and cost imbalances cannot be solved through movement of labor. Elaborate on these points.

Questions for Study and Review

1. The euro was introduced in January 1999 at $1.17 per euro. Its value dropped steadily to around $0.82 per euro at its lowest. Fearing a currency crisis, the ECB (along with the FED) decided to intervene in September 2000. Describe the concerted actions of the ECB and of the FED. What was the impact on the euro and on the dollar?

2. At the end of the 1980s, the inflation rate in most ERM member countries had converged towards the low and stable German inflation rate of 2 percent. In addition, the real interest rate for all the member countries was equal to 3 percent. However the Italian inflation rate was still a few points higher and the public expected it to remain 2 percentage points above the German rate.

a. What was the nominal interest rate in Italy? And in Germany?

b. As the exchange rate between the Deutsche Mark and the lira was permanently locked and not expected to change to prepare the countries for EMU, in which direction was capital flowing? Italy to Germany or Germany to Italy?

c. These flows were called convergence plays. However at the beginning of the nineties, some worrisome events took place, such as the Danish rejection of the Treaty of Maastricht, calling into question the feasibility of a future EMU.

   i. What kind of pressure did these new developments put on the lira? (to appreciate or to depreciate?)
   ii. Describe how the investors and the speculators reacted? What eventually happened to the lira and to Italy's participation in the system?

3. The existence of a European Economic and Monetary Union implies that the European Central Bank must be completely in charge of the European monetary policy. The monetary policy agreed upon by the ECB is now carried out by the various national central banks. What important *qualification* had to be acquired by these national central banks in order to become part of the European System of Central Banks? Elaborate.

4. What is the fundamental difference between the "ECU" and the "euro" as European monetary instruments?

5. Assume that a Mediterranean volcano blows up, damaging a large region of an EMU member country. Explain what may or may not (but should) happen to stabilize the economy of the region.

6. In order to finance the reunification of East and West Germany in the late eighties, the German government issued new bonds to finance the reconstruction and modernization of East Germany.

   a. What was the potential effect of such action on German prices?

   b. What policy did the German central bank, the Bundesbank, carry out to alleviate these effects.

7. The lira and the Belgian franc are participating in the ERM with the +/– 2.25 percent band, i.e. the currencies are allowed to fluctuate by this percentage around the central parity (the official peg). Assume that the *central parity* between the Belgian franc and the lira is 31.5 lira per Belgian franc and that, within a year, the *market exchange rate* between the two currencies increases from 31.8 lira per Belgian franc to 32.3 lira per Belgian franc (BF).

   a. Which of the two currencies has appreciated?

   b. Calculate whether this new exchange rate (32.3 Lira/BF) is still within the acceptable band for these two ERM currencies.

   c. If the currencies are out of the acceptable band, explain the mechanism of compulsory intervention necessary to bring the two currencies back into the band. Answer in terms of the action of each central bank, the Bank of Italy and the Bank of Belgium.

    d. Assuming that the movements in the exchange rates were due to different rates of inflation, which country had the lower rate of inflation?

    e. What is the impact of intervention on the real exchange rate of the country that has the lower rate of inflation? (a real depreciation or a real appreciation?)

    f. What is the effect on its international competitiveness?

8. The so-called "unholy trinity" problem. Explain with the use of graphs and references to Chapter 18 why an exchange rate system, including pegged exchange rate, full capital mobility, and the use of monetary policy for domestic needs, cannot work. Apply the theory to the EMS experience from 1989 on (German reunification and removal of capital controls in France and Italy).

References and Suggestions for Further Reading

Artis, M. (1992) "The Maastricht Road to Monetary Union," *Journal of Common Market Studies*, 30: 299–310.

Blanchard, O. (2006) "Portugal, Italy, Spain, and Germany: The Implications of a Suboptimal Currency Area," New York: WEL–MIT meeting.

De Grauwe, P. (1994) "Towards European Monetary Union without the EMS," in *Economic Policy*, Cambridge: Cambridge University Press: 149–85.

—— (1994) *The Economics of Monetary Integration*, Oxford: Oxford University Press.

Economic Report of the President (1999) Executive Office of the President of the United States, Washington: Government Printing Office: 291–305.

Eichengreen, B. (1993) "European Monetary Unification," *Journal of Economic Literature*, 31: 1321–1357.

Eichengreen, B. and Wyplosz C. (1998) "The Stability Pact: More than a Minor Nuisance?," *Economic Policy*, 26: 65–113.

Giavazzi, F., Micossi, S., and Miller, M. (eds) (1988) *The European Monetary System*, Cambridge: Cambridge University Press.

Giavazzi F. and Giovannini, A. (1989) *Limiting Exchange Rate Flexibility: The European Monetary System*, Cambridge, MA: MIT Press.

Higgins, B. (1993) "Was the ERM Crisis Inevitable?," *Economic Review*, Kansas Federal Reserve, 78/4: 27–40.

McKinnon, R. (1963) "Optimum Currency Area," *American Economic Review*, 54: 717–25.

Mundell, R. (1961) "A Theory of Optimum Currency Areas," *American Economic Review*, 52: 657–65.

Padoa-Schioppa, T. (1988) "The EMS: A Long-Term View," in F. Giavazzi, S. Micossi, and M. Miller (eds), *The European Monetary System* Banca d'Italia, Centre for Economic Policy Research, Cambridge: Cambridge University Press.

Padoa-Schioppa, T., et al. (1987) *Efficiency, Stability and Equity*, Oxford: Oxford University Press: ch. 8 and ch. 12.

Portes, R. and Rey H. (1998) "The Emergence of the Euro as an International Currency," *Economic Policy*, 26: 305–43.

Swann, D. (1992) "Economic and Monetary Union," in *The Economics of the Common Market*, 7th ed., London: Penguin (ch. 7: 199–245).

Tew, B. (1992) "Onwards to EMU," in *The Single European Market and Beyond*, D. Swann (ed.), London: Routledge (ch. 8: 193–211).

Thygesen, N. (1993) "Towards Monetary Union in Europe," *Journal of Common Market Studies*, 31: 447–72.

Tsoukalis, L. (1993) *The New European Economy*, Oxford: Oxford University Press.

Ungerer, H., Evans O., and Young P. (1983) *The European Monetary System: The Experience*, Washington: International Monetary Fund.

van Ypersele, J. and Koeune J. C. (1985) *The European Monetary System*, Cambridge: Cambridge University Press (chapters 2 and 3).

Chapter 23

International Financial Crises

LEARNING OBJECTIVES

By the end of the chapter you should be able to understand:

- the different sources of currency crises in the 1970s, 1980s, and 1990s
- the characteristics and consequences of the "Debt Crises" in the 1980s
- how the Brady plan revitalized international capital flows in the 1990s
- the origins of the "East Asian Crisis" in 1997, how it started and spread
- the difference between speculative attacks and contagion
- IMF bailouts and moral hazard during currency crises

Our study of the international macroeconomy has highlighted that both international trade and international financial flows have a profound impact on domestic economic performance. While the International Monetary Fund was explicitly created to manage exchange rates and prevent destabilizing international capital flows, it has not always been successful. The period of financial liberalization since the 1970s has been accompanied by a number of severe currency crises in developed and developing countries. This chapter provides an account of the recent currency crises and their causes. We focus especially on the origins of the Debt Crisis in the 1980s and the Asian Financial Crisis in the 1990s.[1]

THE 1970S OIL SHOCKS: FINANCIAL FLOW IMBALANCES AND THE ORIGINS OF THE DEBT CRISES

In the wake of the **Organization of the Petroleum Exporting Countries'** (OPEC) **oil embargo** in 1973, world oil prices quadrupled. The surge in the price of this crucial raw material had two important effects. Due to the highly inelastic demand for this commodity, oil exporters experienced a huge surge in oil revenues. OPEC countries' current account surpluses increased tenfold from a combined $5.4 billion in 1973 to $54.9 billion in 1974. At the end of the 1970s their current account surpluses exceeded $100 billion. A group of prominent economists (Jeffrey Sachs, Richard Cooper, and Stanley Fisher in Sachs et al., 1981) reported that oil importing developing countries' combined current account deficits ballooned from $7.3 billion in 1973 to $82 billion in 1980.

The bonanza of the oil exporters was therefore the demise of the oil importers who experienced acute inflation (due to rising energy prices) which caused massive recessions and unemployment. As oil importers struggled to deal with recessions, their fiscal deficits also spun out of control. Tax revenues declined as the economies fell into deep recessions. Any attempts by governments to mitigate the recessions and postpone expenditure-reducing policies only exacerbated both the fiscal and the trade deficits. These deficits needed to be financed and soon these countries started to accumulate foreign debt at breathtaking rates. Most of these countries were under fixed exchange rate regimes; therefore the immediate consequence of the massive balance-of-payments deficits was the danger of running out of foreign currency reserves. Country after country started to experience currency crises and financial markets responded with *speculative attacks* on currencies.

---

1 Ying Tang provided excellent background research for this chapter.

Speculative Attacks: How Speculators Make Money Attacking Currencies

How do speculators "attack" a currency and how can such an attack generate profits? Assume a speculator expects a country's currency will be devalued in the near future. Assume also that this speculator is willing to place a bet that the currency will eventually be worth less. Let's take the example of Thailand in 1997, which had pegged their currency (the Thai baht, THB) to the U.S. dollar before the Asian Crisis and examine how speculators may profit by attacking that currency.

1. The speculator borrows THB100. At an exchange rate of 10 THB/$, this would be equivalent to borrowing $10.
2. Then the speculator sells the THB10 in exchange for dollars.
3. If other speculators are also expecting the THB to fall, they will also start to borrow THB and sell them for foreign currency.
4. As more and more speculators start selling the baht, the Thai central bank is in danger of running out of reserves; it may no longer be able to uphold its peg to the dollar. If the baht selling continues, the central bank will have eventually to allow the exchange rate to float and the baht will depreciate.
5. Once the central bank runs out of reserves or decides to stop defending its exchange rate, the currency depreciates immediately, say from THB10 to THB20 per dollar.
6. To repay the initial loan of THB100, our speculator in 1) now only needs $5 to buy THB100! Thus, the speculator has made a profit of $5 (ignoring interest rates).

When Thai interest rates are low, speculators can easily engage in such attacks and hold out for long periods of time, waiting for the central bank reserves to deplete. Note also that speculators are even able to earn interest on their dollar deposits, which offsets the borrowing cost in Thailand. The smaller the interest differential between the Thai and U.S. interest rates, the less costly is the attack. That is why countries who find their currencies under attack often raise short-term interest rates dramatically (in the case of Hong Kong in 1997, interest rates rose up to 280 percent during the crisis). Exorbitant interest rates do deter speculators, but also they spell the demise of any domestic equipment investment.

One may think that it is difficult for currency speculators to gamble against central banks. But one speculator, George Soros, achieved considerable fame after his large bets against the British pound led to the depreciation of the mighty pound sterling. It is said that on Wednesday, 16 September 1992, he sold 10 billion pounds sterling in one night and booked an estimated $1.1 billion in profits. Eventually, Soros would clear $2 billion after the dust settled and the British pound had fallen to its lowest point. His actions earned him the title "the man who broke the Bank of England." By his own account, George Soros is quoted as saying:

Our total position by Black Wednesday had to be worth almost $10 billion. We planned to sell more than that. In fact, when Norman Lamont [then head of the British Central Bank] said just before the devaluation that he would borrow nearly $15 billion to defend sterling, we were amused because that was about how much we wanted to sell.

(The Times, October 26, 1992)

A MODEL OF CURRENCY CRISES: KRUGMAN'S MODEL OF SPECULATIVE ATTACKS

The first model of currency crises reflects the economists' view in the 1980s that the causes of currency crises could always be found in "fundamental disequilibrium." The term fundamental disequilibrium indicates that domestic policies are not compatible with a specific exchange rate regime. The best example of such disequilibria was, of course, when countries attempted to maintain fixed exchange rate regimes while oil prices skyrocketed and foreign currency reserves evaporated.

The Krugman (1979) crisis model explains why rational investors would start to sell a currency *even though the country has not yet run out of foreign reserves.* The model pertains to economies with fixed exchange rate regimes (so the change in the exchange rate is zero by definition, $\Delta E = 0$). To understand why speculators would attack a currency *before* the country runs out of reserves, we have to understand the economic situation *before* the attack.

To limit the complexity of the analysis, Krugman makes some simplifying assumptions. First, domestic inflation ($\Delta P / P_{-1}$) is determined by changes in the domestic money supply ($\Delta M^S / M^S_{-1}$), or:

$$P = mM^S \rightarrow \frac{\Delta P}{P_{-1}} = \frac{\Delta M^S}{M^S_{-1}} \tag{23.1}$$

Note that the subscripts are necessary because percentage changes are always calculated with reference to an earlier base period. In addition, Krugman reminds us that money supply in an open economy is determined by domestic credit, DC, and foreign currency reserves, RES, and that changes in the money supply are given by:

$$\Delta M^S = \Delta DC + \Delta RES \tag{23.2}$$

Then Krugman assumes purchasing power parity, or $P = EP^*$,

$$P = EP^* \rightarrow \frac{\Delta P}{P_{-1}} = \frac{\Delta E}{E_{-1}} + \frac{\Delta P^*}{P_{-1}} \tag{23.3}$$

If the exchange rate is fixed, $\Delta E = 0$, and foreign prices stay constant, $\Delta P^* = 0$, equation (23.3) implies that the domestic price level is also fixed, $\Delta P = 0$, or purchasing power parity would be violated. But if domestic prices are fixed, $\Delta P = 0$, equation (23.1) tells us that the money supply cannot change either, $\Delta M^S = 0$.

If the money supply is fixed, $\Delta M^S = 0$, the very definition of the money supply in (23.2) implies that it must be true that any decrease in foreign reserves must be accompanied by an equal increase in domestic credit, or $\Delta DC = -\Delta RES$, since $\Delta M^S = 0$ in equation (23.2). We can now examine a country on the brink of a currency crisis. Let us say that the country has experienced a recession, tax revenues have fallen, and the government deficit has risen. If domestic credit is used to finance the fiscal deficit we immediately know that the central bank must simultaneously sell reserves to maintain a fixed money supply (recall that $\Delta DC = -\Delta RES$). But since foreign currency reserves are finite, everyone knows that the central bank must eventually run out of reserves – it is only a matter of time.

Under such conditions, investors won't wait passively to absorb capital losses the day the central bank runs out of reserves and the currency depreciates. They spring into action *today* trying to reduce their holdings of the currency since they expect an imminent depreciation. Their sales of the currency drain the central bank's foreign currency reserves even faster and the time leading up to the crisis is shortened. While it seems that speculators started to attack the currency *before* the crisis, the mechanics of the model highlight that the crisis was really pre-programmed and foreign exchange traders simply executed a rational strategy given the fundamental disequilibrium.

Note that the selling of domestic currency can be "self fulfilling." More recent models of financial crises talk about the *herd behavior* of foreign exchange traders. When they observe large sales (which may or may not have been rational, or based on fundamental disequilibria), they simply follow the crowd and the sheer amount of sales overwhelms the central bank and depletes its foreign currency reserves. The larger international financial markets have become relative to the reserve holding of central banks, the more likely it has become that such herd behavior unhinges fixed exchange rate regimes.

THE END OF CAPITAL FLOWS: DEBT CRISES IN THE 1980S

Until the 1980s, sovereign debt (the bonds issued by governments), was considered the safest investment possible. Who, for example, would ever imagine that the U.S. government could (or would) default on its own debt? In the 1970s, it was inconceivable that *any* country could default on its debt. However, by 1979 developing country debt had reached $359 billion. The U.S. itself was, however, also trying to deal with the effects of the oil shocks and raised interest rates sharply to reduce inflation in the early 1980s. As a consequence, the real interest rate that many developing countries had to pay on their foreign debt jumped to an unprecedented 16–20 percent. Many developing countries were unable to pay that much interest and proceeded to take on more foreign debt, simply to make their interest payments. This increased developing-country debt to $552 billion by 1982. Even worse, the eminent economist, Anne Krueger reported that a staggering 58 percent of total current account deficits in developing countries in 1982 were generated by interest payments alone (Krueger, 1987).

Soon the deeply indebted countries started to realize that the exorbitant interest rates would never allow them to repay their debt. Often the interest payments on foreign debt were several times larger than the entire value of countries' annual exports! The debt crisis started in August 1982 when Mexico announced that it simply could not generate sufficient foreign currency to service its debt. The Mexican central bank had run out of foreign currency reserves and it could make no further payments on its foreign debt. Other Latin American countries soon followed into default, among them, Argentina and Brazil. In early 1983, Venezuela, Chile, Peru, Ecuador, and Paraguay also stopped debt payments.

As sovereign nations were unable to repay their debt, foreign investment in these countries came to a halt. This was the beginning of a great stalemate: foreigners would not invest in countries that did not repay debt, because they were afraid they would never see their money again. On the other hand, the countries in default would never be able to repay any debt, if their economies did not improve and this would be hard to achieve without international investment. In response, U.S. Treasury Secretary Nicholas Brady crafted the "**Brady Plan**," which proposed that defaulting countries would return to their debt payments in exchange for a partial debt reduction and new foreign loans.

The Brady Plan constituted a win-win situation for borrowers and lenders. It rescheduled debt with longer maturity (to reduce the annual payments), and the World Bank and IMF agreed to guarantee some debt (which lowered the risk premium and the interest rate). This allowed for lower interest rates and lower annual payments. At the same time, foreign lenders could finally hope to receive some return on their investment. In summary, the Brady Plan left debtor countries with lower payments on less debt while foreign lenders were guaranteed repayment of a large fraction of their original loan. The Brady Plan jump-started the recovery of countries hit by debt crises and also the return to global international lending.

THE RESURGENCE OF CAPITAL FLOWS TO "EMERGING MARKETS" IN THE 1990S

Soon after the Brady Plan took hold, the term "**emerging markets**" became the buzz word in financial markets in the 1990s. After the return of global lending, several countries were judged to be on the cusp of becoming industrialized, especially in Asia. These countries were seen as financially vibrant: they provided great profit opportunities (and high returns on capital) supposedly because of unusually high growth rates that these countries expected in the near future. Even better, the typical emerging market nation was running a balance-of-payments surplus, as most of them based their growth on export-led development strategies. While economists were initially elated that global lending resumed, it would soon become clear that the capital flows of the early 1990s might have been excessive.

Most emerging markets were in Asia, and Asian economies did grow a lot faster than industrialized nations in the early 1990s. In addition, the Brady Plan introduced financial account liberalizations, which led to additional capital flows, as predicted by the Mundell–Fleming model. How these capital inflows affect the economy depends on the exact exchange rate regime, as we will see below.

THE EFFECT OF CAPITAL INFLOWS IN THE MUNDELL–FLEMING MODEL

In the following exercises, we examine the effects of capital inflows using the Mundell–Fleming model. First, we examine the case of fixed exchange rates, and then move to the case of flexible exchange rates. In response to the Brady Plan, a number of countries removed their capital controls,

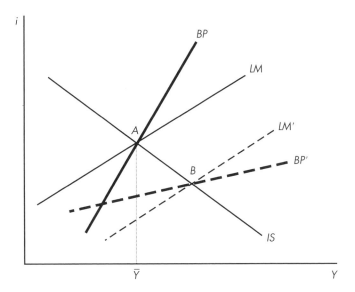

FIGURE 23.1 Fixed Exchange Rates and Capital Inflows

Greater capital mobility induces more capital inflows at any given interest differential. The external balance line rotates, implying a flatter slope and a lower level of interest necessary to maintain external balance at any given level of output (compare the interest rate necessary to assure external balance at output level $\bar{Y}$). Capital inflows that cannot be sterilized must then increase the money supply to create a monetary expansion.

resulting in an increase in the degree of capital mobility, k. Therefore, these inflows caused an increase in their financial account balance.

We can start at an equilibrium point A, in Figure 23.1, that represents the intersection of the goods market, money market and external balance equilibriums. Recall that the financial account equation in Chapter 17 was given by:

$$FA = \bar{FA} + k(i - i^*) + c(R^* - R) \qquad (23.4)$$

The equation shows that, for any interest differential, the liberalization of the financial account (larger k) induces financial capital inflows. Chapter 17 also explained how financial liberalizations rotate the $BP=0$ line to flatten its slope.

Starting in equilibrium at point A, we assume that massive capital inflows result in a balance of payments surplus ($BP>0$). This balance-of-payments surplus causes excess demand for domestic currency, which exerts upward pressure on the price of domestic currency. The only way to avoid an appreciation is to sell domestic currency and reduce its excess demand. This increases the domestic money supply (LM shifts down) as the central bank accumulates foreign currency reserves. The new equilibrium is reached when the LM curve intersects with the external balance line at point B. At point B, there is no longer upward pressure on the domestic currency and therefore no need to increase the money supply further.

The disadvantage at point B could be that the increase in money supply can be inflationary. If output is already at its potential output level at point A, any increase in output overheats the economy (driving up wages and the prices of factor inputs) to increase overall price pressures. Oil exporters like Indonesia faced exactly this dilemma between either inflationary pressure or an appreciating currency in the early 1990s.

In the case of flexible exchange rates, the central bank does not have to intervene and the exchange rate adjusts automatically to excess demand and supply of domestic currency. How such an economy is affected after a financial liberalization is presented in Figure 23.2.

As capital flows into the country, there is excess demand for domestic currency and the BP line rotates to BP'. Under flexible exchange rates, the capital inflows constitute excess demand for the domestic currency, which causes its immediate appreciation (BP' shifts to $BP''=0$). This appreciation represents a loss of international competitiveness for the domestic exporters to reduce the trade balance. The trade deficit increases in response to the appreciation, and the reduced production in the goods market shifts the IS curve to IS', until the economy reaches its new equilibrium, point C.

The adjustment under flexible exchange rates is thus quite different than under fixed rates. Indeed under fixed exchange rate, financial liberalizations hold the risk of an appreciation, which then results in an economic boom and perhaps inflation. Under flexible exchange rates, the currency appreciates, which reduces exports, raises imports and lowers domestic production.

Some argue, however, that the large capital flows to emerging markets had an altogether different reason. It has been proposed that the IMFs involvement in the Brady Plan had generated a so-called "**moral hazard**" on the part of international investors. The Brady Plan had essentially revealed that international institutions, such as the IMF, were willing to broker bail-out plans and assume debt risk when debt crises occurred. Some argue that this constituted an implicit insurance in future debt

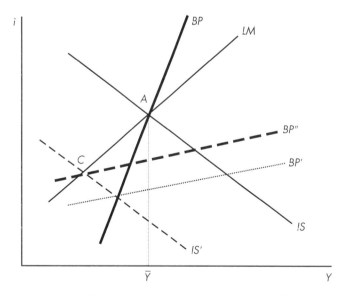

FIGURE 23.2 Flexible Exchange Rates and Capital Inflows

Capital inflows cause an appreciation under flexible exchange rates. This appreciation has an adverse effect on domestic exports. This reduces output.

crises, leading to excessively risky lending today. In this example moral hazard is present when banks engage in excessively risky loans, or do not sufficiently monitor the country's risk or project risk. If the project performs well, the bank would make a lot of money. If the project went into default, the expectation of banks was now to be bailed out by international institutions.

Moral Hazard

Moral hazard is an economic term that describes how the redistribution of risk changes people's behaviors. "Redistribution of risk," is best explained using the example of car insurance: buying collision insurance redistributes the risk of having to pay for a totally destroyed car from drivers to insurance companies. This may then lead to a change in the behavior of the driver (who may now drive more recklessly and without fear of monetary penalty if the car were to be totally destroyed). To avoid moral hazard, insurance companies introduce "deductibles" that force the driver to co-pay in the event of an accident. The co-pay then induces safer driving by sharing the accident risk.

Moral hazard occurs in global financial markets when international agencies, such as the IMF, World Bank, or G7 countries provide implicit or explicit bail-out guarantees or rescue packages for commercial lenders. It induces lenders to engage in excessively risky loans and may therefore cause excessive capital flows.

THE END OF EXUBERANT INTERNATIONAL LENDING: THE ASIAN FINANCIAL CRISIS

The Asian Financial Crisis in 1997 was the largest, but not the only currency crisis in the late 1990s. Since then, the Czech Republic (1997), Russia (1998), Brazil (1999), Ecuador (2000), Turkey (2001), and Argentina (2002) have also experienced severe currency crises. The Asian Crisis unfolded after the region had seen several decades of remarkable economic performance. The IMF reported that these countries were such a success that Asia had attracted almost half of total international capital inflow to developing countries (Guitián, 1998). The Asian economies maintained high interest rates that were exceptionally attractive to foreign investors. At the same time, several Asian economies (i.e., Thailand, Malaysia, Indonesia, the Philippines, Singapore, and South Korea) experienced much higher growth rates of GDP than did the rest of the world.

In a public speech by IMF Managing Director Michel Camdessus just four months before the crisis, the East Asian economies were praised as representing "the essence of globalization – open, dynamic economies that continue to amaze the world with their rapid economic growth and development" (IMF Survey, 1997). Only a few months later, these very same economies were sucked into the largest financial crisis in the past century, requiring the most monumental bail-out plan the IMF ever devised.

Unlike the currency crises in the 1980s, East Asian countries did not experience "bad fundamentals" or large macroeconomic imbalances before the crisis. Many Asian central banks did not openly fix their exchange rate, but followed a so-called "**dirty float**" that required constant intervention to maintain an exchange rate that was generally pegged to the dollar and/or the yen. Today economists agree that the sources of the East Asian financial problems originated in weaknesses in their financial institutions that were overwhelmed by the capital inflows. Financial institutions lacked "social infrastructure" (the manpower to supervise banks efficiently) and the governance of these institutions was at times subject to "crony capitalism" (where the political elite engages in questionable financial dealings). A combination of inadequate financial sector supervision under fixed exchange rates led banks and corporations to borrow excessive amounts of international capital. Much of this excessive debt was short-term and denominated in foreign currency. In addition, government cronies (for example the Indonesian President Suharto's son) started strings of doomed enterprises financed by foreign capital.

In early 1997, international investors started to worry that they might be overexposed in Asia: the crisis struck Thailand first, which was arguably the weakest of the East Asian economies. Thai exports had been weak since 1996, which led to a decline in investment, and Thai real GDP growth dropped from 8.6 percent in 1995 to 6.4 percent in 1996. This change from extraordinarily high to just simply high growth rate alerted foreign investors to move their money out of Thai investments and look for better opportunities elsewhere. While the foreign capital inflows had financed much of the Thai expansion, capital outflow now spelled the demise of Thailand's economic fortunes.

In May 1997, speculators attacked the Thai currency and the Thai central bank suffered a massive outflow of foreign currency reserves in an attempt to prop up its currency. As speculation persisted, the Thai central bank ran out of reserves on July 2, 1997 and had to allow the baht to devalue. Within days of the baht devaluation, speculators moved to attack the Malaysian ringgit and by the end of 1997, the ringgit had lost 50 percent of its value. Then investors turned to the Indonesian rupiah. Unlike Thailand and Malaysia, Indonesia suffered from inflation, but on the positive side, it had a trade surplus, and over $20 billion in foreign currency reserves. Nevertheless, the rupiah came under severe attack in August 1997 and a few days later the rigid Indonesian exchange rate regime was abandoned in favor of a free float. By mid 1998, the Indonesian rupiah had lost 85 percent of its original value. Ultimately the speculation spread to South Korea, the world's eleventh largest economy. No one would have imagined a year earlier that speculators could bring down the Korean currency. By December 12 1997, the Korean currency could, however, no longer be defended and the Korean central bank abandoned its tightly controlled exchange rate for a free float. As foreigners pulled out their investments, not only did the demand for currencies fall, but also the demand for domestic stocks. Figure 23.3 shows how dramatically currencies and equities fell in the key Asian Crisis Economies.

All afflicted countries (except Malaysia) turned to the IMF for assistance, and received loans to implement economic plans that were supposed to mitigate the damage. These plans included the bitter medicine of higher interest rates to limit the exchange rate depreciation, efforts to avoid large fiscal deficits (a euphemism for tax increases), and "structural" reforms that were to address institutional weaknesses. All of the troubled countries went from growth rates in excess of 6 percent in 1996 to severe contractions in 1998.

The speculative attacks were not only restricted to the four countries mentioned above. The currencies of Hong Kong and Taiwan were also attacked, but here speculators got burned. Taiwan held the largest currency reserves in the world in 1997. In the second wave of speculative attacks, the Taiwan new dollar was attacked in October 1997. Unwilling to spend their foreign currency reserves on speculators, the government immediately floated the currency.

Bilateral U.S. Dollar Exchange Rates

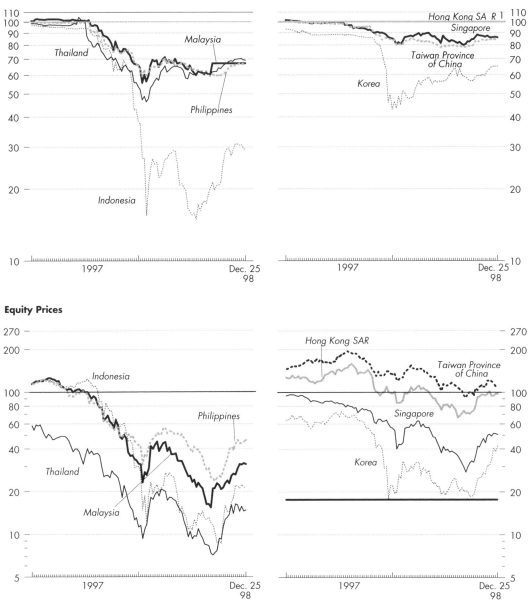

Equity Prices

FIGURE 23.3 Overview of Exchange Rate and Equity Prices during the Asian Crisis

Source: "The Asian Crisis: Causes and Cures," in *Finance and Development*, June 1998, Volume 35, 2. Copyright International Monetary Fund.

Vertical scale is in logs – January 1998=100.

Speculators began attacking the Hong Kong dollar first in July, and then again in October 1997. However, they were in for another surprise. Unlike Taiwan, which had floated its currency immediately, the Hong Kong Monetary Authority (HKMA) staunchly defended their currency board. At one point, the HKMA raised interest rates to an astronomical 280 percent. In the face of such staggering interest rates, speculators had to abandon their attacks or risk incurring heavy losses. The 280 percent interest rates had, however, serious repercussions on the Hong Kong economy as most mortgages were based on variable and not fixed interest rates. Additionally, the local stock market was spooked by the actions of the HKMA and plunged 13.7 percent on October 28 1997.

In the case of Hong Kong, speculators' expectations of the HKMA's ability to successfully defend their currency board were proven to be incorrect. They had miscalculated and had not expected the monetary authority's willingness to put up with high interest rates and economic turmoil to keep the exchange rate pegged. Thus, the speculative attack on the Hong Kong dollar did not have the self-fulfilling characteristics of the previous attacks.

CONTAGION

How did the Thai currency crisis spread like a wildfire from country to country, all the way to South Korea, the eleventh largest world economy some 7,000 miles from the original crisis epicenter? Why would any speculator attack the Taiwanese economy, which held the world's largest currency reserves? The domino effect of spreading crises (like the flu) has become known as **contagion**.

There are several prevailing views of why the contagion spread across Asian economies. One view is that once investors had seen one country abandon the peg under pressure, they expected other countries with a similar cultural background also to stop defending their currencies. There was no specific new information that fueled the contagion; it was simply a change in attitude by investors. The 1997 Thai crisis caused investors to switch from the previous interpretation of the East Asian economies' growth records as an "Asian miracle," to the notion of moral hazard and excessive overinvestment that required the rebalancing of their international portfolio.

Another interpretation of East Asian contagion is that all attacked economies were inherently linked by their trading system. Countries that compete in the global market place are uniquely affected by devaluations. For example, one country's devaluation represents a loss of competitiveness of its trading partner, forcing it to devalue to maintain its exports. For example, when Thailand devalued, other Asian countries lost their competitive edge and their exports became relatively more expensive.

The third explanation for contagion is based on financial linkages between countries. For example, a wave of bankruptcies in Thailand may have triggered the speculative attack on Taiwan, since Taiwanese investors had unusually large investments in Thailand, which was expected to reduce the profitability (and stock price) of Taiwanese companies. Even worse, when investors are burned in one country, they may have to liquidate their remaining investment positions in other countries, which plunges yet more countries into financial disarray.

Overall it is safe to say that the integration of international capital markets has led to a profound interdependence of international economies. Excessive capital flows as in the early 1990s led to swift, large capital flow reversals that left the economies in shambles. On the other hand, debt crises and the absence of international capital flows deprive countries of the essential investments necessary for development. Over time economists have come to conclude that transparency, solid regulations and strong institutions are key components to support international capital flows.

THE AFTERMATH OF THE EAST ASIAN CRISIS: THE ECONOMICS OF RESERVE ACCUMULATION

One key lesson from the financial currency crises in the 1990s was that no matter how large the economy may have been, the country's currency will be attacked if its exchange rate is misaligned. While Krugman associated currency attacks with fundamental disequilibria, the 1990s proved that contagion was also a formidable source of currency crises, even in countries where fundamentals were not in disequilibrium (see Hong Kong and Taiwan). The second lesson of the East Asian Crises was that global capital markets were too large and acted too fast for the IMF to provide expedient relief in order to prevent economic collapse. In the "Self-Help Guide for Emerging Markets" the eminent economist Martin Feldstein outlined the options available to countries that wanted to insure themselves from future speculative attacks, especially those unrelated to economic fundamentals. Asian nations immediately learned from the crises and took their economic fortunes into their own hands. Since the Asian Crises, the new strategy has been for countries to literally "self insure" against future crises, attacks, and contagion.

The simple insurance mechanism has been to accumulate foreign currency reserves at a scale that has never been observed before. Huge foreign currency reserves are held by Asian economies today to provide the necessary resource to deter and fend off any possible currency attack. In 2006, foreign exchange reserves held by developing nations reached an all-time high, and today it is not unusual to see levels of foreign currency reserves in emerging market economies exceed those held by advanced countries (in relation to their incomes or trade). Harvard economist Dani Rodrik reports that foreign currency reserves represented a staggering 30 percent share of GDP in developing counties in 2004, while they represented less than 5 percent of GDP in industrialized nations (Rodrik, 2006).

Figure 23.4 shows, however, that reserves are strikingly and unevenly distributed across counties. The largest level of reserves is held by China ($1.8 trillion), but reserves comprise only about 3 percent of Chinese GDP. Japan's reserves, $1 trillion, constitute 25 percent of Japanese GDP. It is clear, however, that all the Asian crisis countries feature not only large absolute sums of reserves, but their reserves usually exceed 20 percent of GDP, as well.

Insurance is seldom free and the accumulation of reserves is particularly costly. Central banks usually hold their foreign exchange reserves in secure assets, such as U.S. Treasury bills, that carry some of the lowest returns. Therefore foreign currency reserves feature an important opportunity cost: if the government used the funds to invest in its own country's economic development, it could generate a sizable social rate of return. This social cost (the difference between the U.S. Treasury rate of return and the estimated country's social return on investment) is thus the cost of insurance against speculative attacks. Rodrik (2006) argues that the social cost is about 1 percent of GDP for developing nations, but hastens to point out that this tremendous cost might be justified given that currency crises might impose even greater social costs.

Another reason for the fantastic increase in foreign currency reserves held by Asian nations might be the attempt to prevent the home currency from appreciating as the countries recovered from the

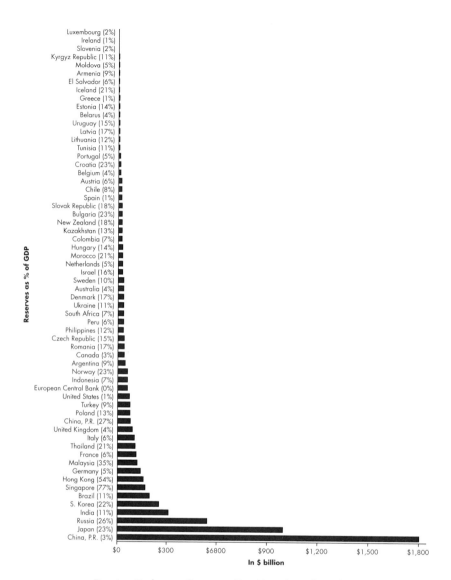

FIGURE 23.4 Foreign Exchange Reserves: Total Levels and % of GDP

Source: adapted from IMF data.

May 2008 levels of foreign currency reserves and 2007 levels of PPP adjusted GDP. Total reserves on the vertical axis and reserves as percent of GDP in brackets next to the country name.

Asian crisis. When a country runs large balance-of-payments surpluses, there exists excess demand for its currency and, in the absence of central bank intervention, the currency would appreciate. This dynamic would render exports more expensive and it has been suggested that some central banks intervene to stop this trend. In the case of an Asian nation, the central bank would have to purchase foreign currency (the dollar) and issue domestic currency to negate the excess demand for domestic currency. In the process, the country is subject to inflationary pressures (since its money supply rises) as it accumulates an ever larger stock of reserves.

Note that the argument that a country might "falsely" establish its competitiveness by purchasing foreign exchange and keeping its own currency "cheap" is essentially mercantilist in nature. Mercantilism sought to maximize the export earnings of a country rather than national income. In this application of twenty-first-century mercantilism, central banks intervene to keep exports cheap, imports expensive, and hold large sums of money in the bank instead of spending them on domestic development. The country most often identified as following this development strategy is China, with over $1.8 trillion in reserves.

RESERVE ACCUMULATION AND INTERNATIONAL COMPETITIVENESS IMPLICATIONS

Enormous reserve accumulation, especially on the part of China, can have curious implications that pertain not only to the Chinese economy. Since reserves are in U.S. dollars, the massive dollar purchases hold the value of the dollar artificially high. Given the massive trade deficit in the U.S., economists had long expected a stronger depreciation of the dollar. However, the large reserve accumulation in Asia has prevented this depreciation thus far.

There is also a direct effect of Asian countries' foreign reserve accumulations on the U.S. economy. Figure 23.5 indicates that U.S. Federal Reserve started to raise the discount rate and the federal funds target rate in June 2004. While the bond yields and mortgage rates usually respond swiftly to such changes, the graph below shows that even after two dozen increases in the federal reserve rates, mortgage and bond rates still do not register a significant effect. Some say this trend may be heavily influenced by the Chinese (and other Asian nations) purchases of U.S. Treasury bills, which keeps the demand for such securities high and therefore their return (which the inverse of the price) low.

This implies that potentially much of the U.S. housing boom, the refinancing of mortgages, and the ferocious consumption spending on the part of U.S. consumers may have been driven by low interest rates that were, in part, fueled by Chinese/Asian purchases of U.S. treasury bills. Some argue that Asian nations lent the U.S. the funds to continue to consume beyond its means and to sustain its enormous fiscal and trade deficits.

The final aspect that has to be considered is the impact of actually holding over 1 trillion in reserves. Once reserves become this large, it becomes difficult for a country to "divest" its dollars. If the Chinese central bank chose to divest its dollars quickly the price would fall so rapidly that the value of its reserves would only be a fraction of the original $1.8 trillion. Alternatively, as soon as speculators guess that the Chinese Central Bank is intending to sell a significant chunk of its dollar reserves (no matter how slowly) speculation against the dollar would lead to its sharp drop. Any decline of the dollar, therefore, reduces potentially a large share of the reserves. This highlights that those reserves that are being held for insurance against excessive capital flows will be hard to spend in crises, since it would reduce the insurance value itself.

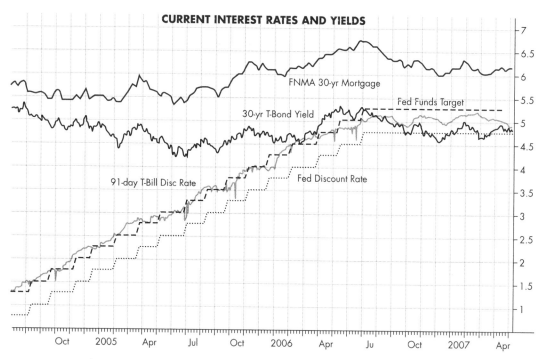

FIGURE 23.5 The Interest Rate Disconnect (U.S. Federal Reserve, Mortgage and Bond Rates)

Source: Alston Boyd, Economic Director, Martin Capital Advisors, LLP, with thanks (http://www.martincapital.com/chart-pgs/CH_RTSSH.HTM)

Summary of Key Concepts

1. Fluctuations in the price of oil (or other key items such as grain or rice) can generate current account fluctuations that may lead to balance-of-payments and debt crises.
2. Almost all major Latin American countries experienced a debt crisis in the early 1980s. Many defaulted on their foreign debt because their total exports were at times smaller than the interest payments on their debt.
3. The debt crisis of the 1980s was resolved by the Brady Plan that forced concessions (debt and interest reductions) from commercial banks in exchange for a return in Latin American countries' debt service.
4. The Brady Plan also restored international lending by guaranteeing part of the countries' foreign debt and by amortizing the debt payments over longer time horizons.
5. Prior to the 1997 Asian crisis, emerging markets had received huge capital inflows. When growth slowed in the late 1990s, investors withdrew their funds only to find out that a number of financial institutions (particularly banks) had already been in precarious financial conditions.

6. After the Asian crisis, many Asian countries sought to "self insure" themselves against dramatic capital outflows. This implied a massive accumulation of reserves, which have risen to unprecedented levels in Asia.

CASE STUDY I

Guilt by Association
Pamela Druckerman, *The Wall Street Journal*, Oct. 14, 2002.

Can the concept of financial contagion be tossed into history's dustbin? The Clinton administration certainly didn't think so. When financial crises roared throughout emerging markets in Asia, Russia and Latin America during the 1990s, the U.S. was quick to back big financial bailouts as firewalls to keep the situation from spreading. Officials saw contagion – the guilt by association that makes one nation prone to economic upheaval just because another one is in crisis – as a force to be reckoned with.

When the Bush administration took over, it insisted those days had ended. To prove the point, the U.S. steadfastly withheld aid when Argentina fell into a financial crisis late last year. Contagion, U.S. officials said, was just a passing intellectual fashion, made obsolete by better market information and the benefits of experience. "We need to retire that fashion like a hula hoop," Treasury Secretary Paul O'Neill said. Many economists aren't buying that line, though. They say contagion may be less virulent, since fewer countries have fixed exchange rates, which can come violently unpinned in a crisis and deal a cataclysmic blow to stumbling economies. But they warn that contagion is still a factor and say that, despite the administration's official stance, it is still worrying Washington.

When Argentina's state finances collapsed in December in the largest-ever bond default by a government borrower, other South American financial markets rumbled. But they experienced nothing like the earthquakes that once brought a string of nations around the globe near financial collapse. Is that a sign of contagion's demise? Not so, say some economists. They say Argentina's crisis was so many years in the making that investors had plenty of time to react calmly, instead of stampeding out of other markets in a panic, as they've done in the past. They also point to the spread of financial problems with Argentina's Latin American neighbors this summer, and to the U.S. reaction.

Contagion concerns may have made investors quicker on the trigger in Brazil, whose bonds and currency fell off a cliff this summer. Of course, a major catalyst for Brazil's crisis was the surprising popularity of Workers' Party presidential candidate Luiz Inacio Lula da Silva ahead of the Oct. 6 election; investors were concerned that he would undo pro-market reforms if he was elected. (As it turns out, Mr. da Silva won about twice as many votes as his nearest rival, but faces an Oct. 27 runoff election.) But with Argentina in default on much of its government debt, investors also focused on whether Brazil could sustain payments on its own debt, regardless of the outcome of the balloting. "Seeing Argentina, nobody wanted to take chances and give Brazil the benefit of the doubt," says Walter Molano, head of emerging-markets research at BCP Securities Inc., a brokerage firm in Greenwich, Conn.

In August, the U.S. threw its support behind a $30.4 billion International Monetary Fund package for Brazil. It also backed a smaller package to bolster the wounded banking system in Uruguay, which got caught in Argentina's downdraft. Some economists say those moves belie the administration's professed confidence that contagion is obsolete. However, U.S. officials have barely budged in the contagion debate. Mr. O'Neill acknowledged that "intense external pressures" from its neighbors on tiny Uruguay compelled the U.S. to intervene on its behalf. But he and John Taylor, U.S. Treasury undersecretary for international affairs, attributed Brazil's troubles to the domestic issue of pre-election jitters. "There's been nothing like the Russian contagion in Argentina's crisis," Mr. Taylor said on a visit to Mexico in August after the IMF package was put together for Brazil. "There's been virtually no impact."

U.S. officials point out that interest rates, the usual measure of whether countries have been tainted by a crisis elsewhere, hardly moved in the emerging markets as Argentina's economy went into a tailspin. By mid-January, yields on Argentina's foreign bonds had soared, reflecting investors' perception of risk on the debt. But bonds from Mexico, South Korea, the Philippines and even Brazil were mostly steady. And bonds in Malaysia and Russia actually strengthened, driving their yields down. Interest rates have since edged still higher in Argentina and have more than doubled in Brazil. But rates climbed only temporarily in other developing countries in response to Brazil's problems.

In the Asian nations, as well as in Russia and Mexico, rates are still near their January levels. Economists say interest rates don't tell the whole story, though. "There are a lot of different channels for contagion," says Morris Goldstein, senior fellow at the Institute for International Economics in Washington. For one, economists point to direct-investment trends. The Institute of International Finance, a Washington group representing commercial banks and financial firms, estimates investment in hard assets like factories in emerging markets will fall 16 percent to $113 billion this year, in part because of Argentina's troubles and its government's reaction. The government ordered a host of dollar denominated contracts, bank accounts and retirement funds to be swapped into pesos, in most cases violating investment contracts and implying steep losses for companies. Electricity companies, for instance, were forced to charge their customers in pesos rather than dollars, even after the peso had lost much of its value. "People are much more concerned about making longer-term investments, and they're reviewing contracts backwards and forwards," says David Gould, director of global economic analysis for the Institute of International Finance. There is a sense among international investors, he says, that once a country opens its markets, "it doesn't mean they're open forever."

Analysts also are wary of the argument that better market information has helped render contagion obsolete. Investors certainly have more information to chew on these days. In 1999, the IMF and the multilateral Bank for International Settlements imposed new financial disclosure standards on borrowing governments, on the assumption that well-informed investors are less prone to making rash judgments. To comply with the new standards, central banks around the world have built Websites offering daily data on their foreign-exchange and gold reserves and on government debt levels, information they once doled out a few times a year. Those who buy and sell emerging-market bonds praise the improved disclosure, saying they're less likely to be blindsided by things like debt tucked away inside state enterprises. But economists don't believe that these advances ensure that the U.S. won't have to intervene again at some point to stop contagion. "Information is always going to be imperfect in the markets," says Barry Eichengreen, economics professor at the University of California at Berkeley and author of a book on financial crises. "There may be times when the markets don't get it right, or when the outcome is so uncertain we're reluctant to leave markets to their own devices."

CASE STUDY QUESTIONS

1. Outline the various channels through which contagion can occur. Be specific.

2. How do you (or the article) imagine that contagion can start and stop?

3. Where would you draw the line between contagion and weak economic fundamentals?

4. How is contagion linked to risk and capital flows in this article?

CASE STUDY II

Who's in Charge of Determining U.S. Interest Rates? It May Be Beijing
By Floyd Norris, *New York Times*, May 19, 2005

In Washington these days, complaining about China has become standard operating procedure. The Bush administration calls on China to allow its currency to rise and Congress talks of punishment if China does not do so. Be careful what you wish for. As speeches of low-level Chinese bureaucrats are read with care for hints as to just when China will allow its currency to rise, perhaps it would be better for Americans to ponder the impact of China's current policies.

Some might wonder just why the American politicians are upset. The way things work now, China sells to the world most everything the world wants and then buys United States Treasury securities. That helps hold down interest rates and stimulates consumer spending. You can understand why China might not like to keep doing that forever. Those Treasury securities do not pay much interest, and they are sure to decline in value, measured in Chinese yuan, when that currency rises. But the largest vendor financing program ever has stimulated both the Chinese and American economies.

In Washington, the theory is that China's keeping the yuan low increases America's trade deficit. But the benefits to United States exporters from a modest rise in the Chinese currency would most likely be small, while the effect of higher interest rates could be larger if China cut back on its purchases, particularly if other Asian central banks decided that they, too, wanted to sell dollars. If that were to happen, the impact could be acute in the housing market. Investors in housing stocks have been nervous for some time, happy to see ever-higher profits but worried that the good times must end someday and fearful that they could be left holding the bag when that happens.

One stock where those conflicting emotions have played out is Pulte Homes, a home builder active in 27 states. Last fall, its share price fell when it reported problems in Las Vegas, which was perhaps the most overheated market in America. But price cuts there got homes selling again, and the stock has resumed its ascent. Pulte filed its quarterly report with the Securities and Exchange Commission last week, disclosing that its inventory of land continues to grow. Some of that land is owned, while the rest is controlled via purchase options that give Pulte the right to walk away – forfeiting what it paid for the option – if home sales soften.

Kathleen Shanley, a bond analyst at Gimme Credit, points out that Pulte's inventory of land is concentrated in areas where home prices have been rising rapidly and that the company's cash flow is negative, even as profits soar, because of all the land it is buying. Pulte has been borrowing money even as it buys back stock at high prices. When things were at their worst in Las Vegas, Pulte was seeing cancellations of home purchases that amounted to 75 percent of new sales. "The risk of similar, and perhaps more prolonged, regional downturns should not be ignored," Ms. Shanley wrote in a note to clients.

Rising interest rates could be a cause of such downturns. Homeowners with fixed-rate mortgages would be relatively immune, although they could find it harder to sell if they needed to, and the flow of cash from mortgage refinancings would dry up. But many buyers, particularly in some of the hottest markets, have resorted to floating-rate mortgages, some of them paying only interest.

Alan Greenspan, the Federal Reserve chairman, has less power over interest rates than he once did. Perhaps the real decision maker will be Hu Jintao, the Chinese president, as he weighs the pressures to free his currency and stop accumulating Treasury securities. In the words of Robert J. Barbera, the chief economist of ITG/Hoenig, "Hu's in charge here."

CASE STUDY QUESTIONS

1. Explain the link between China's exchange rate and U.S. interest rates.

2. Explain the link between China's trade surplus and U.S. interest rates.

3. Who is benefiting from the Chinese trade surplus and exchange rate regime in the U.S. and in China?

4. How is Europe affected by the accumulation of reserves in Asian economies?

5. Why do you think every country does not follow the exchange rate management that the Chinese instituted?

Questions for Study and Review

1. If China maintains its large trade surplus, but allows its exchange rate to be market determined, what do you think will be the impact on the U.S.$/Yuan exchange rate? What would be the impact on U.S. interest rates?

2. In what ways is the Asian debt crisis similar to, and different from, the difficulties which Latin America experienced in the early 1980s?

3. If one developing country experiences a payments and debt crisis, explain through which linkages the crisis might spread to other countries in the region?

4. Why would a rise in the Chinese exchange rate help the U.S. or European markets? Exactly who would it help and who would it hurt?

References and Suggestions for Further Reading

Boorman, J., Lane, T., Ghattas, M.S., Bulir, A., Gjosh, A., Haverman, X., Mourmouras, A., and Phelps, S. (2000) "Managing the Financial Crisis: The Experience in East Asia," IMF Working Paper 107.

Chinn, Menzie D. (1998) "Before the Fall: Were East Asian Currencies Overvalued?," NBER working paper 6491.

Chiodo, A.J. and Owyang, M.T. (2002) "A Case Study of a Currency Crisis: The Russian Default of 1998," St. Louis Federal Reserve Review, 11.

Doraisami, A. (2005) "The Political Economy of Capital Flows and Capital Controls in Malaysia," Journal of Contemporary Asia, 35: 249–63.

Eichengreen, B., (1999) "The International Monetary Fund in the Wake of the Asian Crisis," University of California-Berkeley Working Paper.

FDIC, (1997) "Chapter 5: The LDC Debt Crisis," in History of the Eighties – Lessons for the Future, FDIC's Public Information Center.

Feldstein, M. (1999) "A Self-Help Guide for Emerging Markets," Foreign Affairs, 78: March/April.

Fischer, S. (1997) "Closing Remarks: What Have we Learned?," in G. Perry, G. Calvo, W. M. Corden, S. Fischer, Sir

A. Walters, and J. Williamson, *Currency Boards and External Shocks: How Much Pain, How Much Gain?* Washington, D.C.: The World Bank.

Guitián, M. (1998) "The Challenge of Managing Global Capital Flows," *Finance and Development*, 35: June.

Haggard, S. (2000) *The Political Economy of the Asian Financial Crisis*, Washington, D.C.: Institute for International Economics.

Haggard, S. and MacIntyre, A. (2000) "The political economy of the Asian financial crisis: Korea and Thailand Compared," in G.W. Noble and J. Ravenhill (eds), *The Asian Financial Crisis and the Architecture of Global Finance*, Cambridge: Cambridge University Press.

IMF (1997) "Globalization in Asia: Challenges for Regional Cooperation and Implications for Hong Kong," *IMF Survey*, March 26: no. 5.

IMF Staff (1998) "The Asian Crisis: Causes and Cures," *Finance and Development*, June 35: 2.

IMF External Relations Department (1999) "The IMF's Response to the Asian Crisis," Factsheet, January http://imf.org/external/np/exr/facts/asia.htm.

Kindleberger, C.P. (1978) *Manias, Panics, and Crashes: A History of Financial Crises*, New York. Basic Books.

Krueger, A. O. (1987) "Debt, Capital Flows, and LDC Growth," *The American Economic Review*, Papers and Proceedings 77: 159–64.

Krugman, P. (1979) "A Model of Balance-of-Payments Crises," *Journal of Money, Credit, and Banking*, 11: 311–25.

—— (1998) "Saving Asia: It's Time to Get Radical," *Fortune*, September 7: 75–80.

Mishkin, F.S. (1999) "Lessons from the Asian Crisis," National Bureau of Economic Research. Working Paper Series. Working Paper No. 7102. April.

Mohanty, M.S. and Turner, P. (2006) "Foreign exchange reserve accumulation in emerging markets: what are the domestic implications?," *Bank for International Settlements Quarterly Review*, September.

Nanto, D.K. (1998) "CRS Report: The 1997–1998 Asian Financial Crisis," CRS Report for Congress, February 6, http://www.fas.org/man/crs/crs-asia2.htm.

Rodrik, D. (2006) "The Social Cost of Foreign Exchange Reserves," NBER Working Paper 11952.

Sachs, J. and Solomon, R. (1981) "The Debt of Developing Countries: Another Look," *Brookings Papers on Economic Activity*, 1981: 593–607.

Sachs, J. (1998) "The IMF and the Asian Flu," *The American Prospect*, 37: 16–21.

Sachs, J. D., Cooper, R. N. and Fischer, S. (1981) "The Current Account and Macroeconomic Adjustment in the 1970s," *Brookings Papers on Economic Activity*, 1981: 201–82.

Sachs, J.D. and Woo, W.T. (1999) "The Asian Financial Crisis: What Happened and What is to be Done," University of Michigan Working Paper.

Saxena, S.C. (2004) "The Changing Nature of Currency Crises since the 1970s," *Journal of Economic Surveys*, 18: 321–50.

Vasquez, I. (1996) "The Brady Plan and Market-Based Solutions to Debt Crises," *Cato Journal*, 16: 233–43.

Glossary

Absolute advantage The argument, associated with Adam Smith, that trade is based on absolute differences in costs. A country exports those products for which its costs, measured in terms of labor hours, are lower than costs in other countries.

Accommodating transactions Those items in the balance-of-payments accounts that occur in order to offset imbalances in the total of the remaining items. Flows of foreign exchange reserves are the dominant accommodating transaction. See *Autonomous transactions*.

Ad valorem tariff A tariff that is measured as a percentage of the value of the traded product.

Affiliate A business established in one country that is controlled by a company incorporated in another country.

Agglomeration The concentration of production in one location to achieve the external economies of scale possible when additional production by one firm allows costs of production for other firms in the industry to decline.

Antidumping duty A tariff imposed by an importing country to offset a foreign firm's practice of selling at a lower price in the importer's market than at home or at a lower price than its cost of production.

Appreciation An increase in the value of a currency, measured in terms of other currencies, in a regime of flexible (floating) exchange rates. If the dollar/sterling exchange rate moved from $1.50 per pound to $1.25, that would be an appreciation of the dollar as fewer dollars would be needed to buy one pound. The opposite is called a *depreciation*.

Arbitrage Purchase of a good or an asset in a low-price market and its riskless sale in a higher-price market. If arbitrage is possible, prices should either be equalized or differ by no more than transport or transactions costs.

Arbitrageur A person who engages in arbitrage.

Articles of Agreement of the IMF The founding document of the International Monetary Fund that defines the Fund's functions. Agreed to at the Bretton Woods conference in 1944 and amended since then.

Ask price See *Spread*.

Autarky A state of complete self sufficiency and the absence of trade.

Autonomous transactions or accounts Those items in the balance-of-payments accounts generated by commercial or financial reasons, and not to balance other items. The sum of the autonomous items is offset by accommodating items. International trade and long-term capital flows are autonomous transactions. See *Accomodating transactions*.

Balance of payments A set of accounts that represents all transactions between residents of one country and residents of the rest of the world during a period of time, normally a year.

Balance of trade Also called balance on goods and services in the U.S. International Transactions Accounts. Defined as exports minus imports of goods and services. If positive, the country has a trade surplus and if negative, a trade deficit. In the models developed in the text, the balance of trade is called net export NX.

Balance on current account In addition to the balance of trade, it includes net income receipts (income received from assets this country's residents own abroad minus income payments to assets in this country owned by foreign residents) and net unilateral current transfers (gifts received by residents of this country minus gifts made to foreign residents). Note that a trade deficit does not necessarily imply a current account deficit, if the country has substantial investments abroad and thus receives large income payments – this has often been the case for the U.K.

Balance on merchandise trade Also named balance on goods in the U.S. International Transactions Accounts. Defined as exports minus imports of goods. It does not include trade in services. The more technologically advanced countries, like the U.S., may have a deficit in their goods balance and a surplus in their services balance.

Balance on services Defined as exports minus imports of services.

Bank for International Settlements (BIS) A financial institution located in Basel, Switzerland, which provides a range of services to the central banks of the industrialized countries. The BIS was founded in 1930 to manage problems arising from the German reparations payments following World War I. Representatives of the central banks of the industrialized countries frequently meet at the BIS for consultations on monetary and exchange-market policies. The members have been involved recently in drafting guidelines for international banking known as Basel I and Basel II.

Barter exchange ratio The amount of one good that must be given up to obtain a unit of another good. A difference between the domestic barter exchange ratio within a country and the international barter exchange ratio creates an opportunity to gain from trade.

Barter line A line that represents a country's consumption possibilities frontier when trade is possible. Its slope equals the international barter exchange ratio.

Basel I and II Ongoing attempts by the Bank for International Settlements members to impose international standards regulating the international banking system.

Beggar thy neighbor policies Trade or exchange rate policies carried out by a country that enable it to gain at the expense of its partners, e.g. a competitive devaluation.

Benign neglect This general term can be used to convey a specific policy: in the context of a central bank, it refers to the complete lack of intervention on the foreign exchange market to influence the exchange rate.

Bid price See *Spread*.

Bilateral exchange rate The price of a foreign currency in terms of units of domestic currency.

BP line or BP=0 line Combinations of interest rates and levels of domestic output that will produce equilibrium in the balance of payments.

Brady Plan A plan, named after the U.S. Secretary of the Treasury who initiated it in 1989, to ease the Latin American debt crisis by encouraging banks to write off some of these debts and lengthen those maturities that remained.

Brain drain The movement of scientists, engineers, medical personnel, and other highly educated people from developing to industrialized countries, which results in a loss of public investment in education for the developing country.

Bretton Woods Agreement The conclusion of the Bretton Woods conference, held at a resort of that name in New Hampshire during the summer of 1944. The World Bank and the International Monetary Fund were created by the Bretton Woods Agreement. The term "Bretton Woods system" is often used to describe the international monetary system of fixed exchange rates that prevailed until the crises of 1971 and 1973.

Buy American Act Passed by U.S. Congress in 1933; it mandates a preference for the purchase of domestically produced goods over foreign goods in U.S. government procurement.

c.i.f. Cost, insurance, and freight. This measurement of the value of imports includes the cost of the goods itself, insurance, and freight.

Cable transfer A means of transferring foreign exchange from one economic agent to another. An electronic message instructs a bank to transfer funds from the account of one party to that of another.

CAFTA A free trade area between the U.S. and various Central American countries that was implemented in 2006. Renamed DR-CAFTA after the Dominican Republic joined the negotiations in 2004.

Call An option contract that allows the owner to purchase a specified quantity of a financial asset, such as foreign exchange, at a fixed price during a specified period. The owner is not required to exercise the option. The price at which the option can be exercised is known as the "strike price."

Candlestick charting A graphical presentation to show the behavior of an exchange rate over a trading day.

Capital account This balance of payments account records capital transfers and the buying and selling of non-produced and non-financial assets. This is a new account introduced in 1999 to bring the U.S. balance of payments in line with international standards.

Cartel A collusive arrangement among sellers of a product, which is intended to raise the price of that product in order to extract monopoly rents.

Ceteris paribus The *ceteris paribus* condition is invoked to analyze the specific impact in a model of a change in one variable only. The *ceteris paribus* condition (Latin for "all other things equal") ensures that the other variables are kept constant.

Clean floating exchange rate An exchange rate solely determined by market forces. The central bank never intervenes – buying or selling foreign exchange – to influence the exchange rate. This is in contrast with a *dirty floating exchange rate*.

Clearing House International Payments System (CHIPS) The electronic system among banks in New York and other major foreign financial centers, which is used to transfer foreign exchange, that is, to complete foreign exchange market transactions.

Closed economy An economy that does not trade, one that is in a state of autarky.

Commercial policy Government policies that are intended to change international trade flows, particularly to restrict imports.

Common market A group of countries that allows the free movement of goods, services, capital, and labor among members, and shares a common external tariff schedule. The European Economic Community, created in 1957, is the most successful example.

Common property resource A resource for which use by one individual reduces the amount available for other individuals, but one from which no individual can be excluded.

Community indifference curve A curve that shows all the combinations of two goods that provide the community with the same level of welfare, that is, to which the community would be indifferent. A set of these curves can be used to show increases in community welfare as more goods are made available.

Comparative advantage The argument, developed by David Ricardo in the early nineteenth century, that mutually beneficial balanced trade is possible even if one country has an absolute advantage in all goods. If there is a difference in the relative cost of two goods in the two countries, each country will gain by exporting the product for which it has comparatively lower costs.

Comparative statics Comparing two different equilibria taking place at different times. See *Dynamics* in contrast.

Computable General Equilibrium model (CGE) An economic model that allows equilibrium values of prices and quantities in input and output markets to be calculated, given assumptions about consumer preferences, production technologies, initial factor supplies, competition, and government policies.

Concerted intervention See *Intervention*.

Conditionality The policy under which the International Monetary Fund makes large loans (drawings) to member countries only if they pursue exchange rate and other policies that can be expected to improve the borrowing country's balance-of-payments performance and make the repayment of the loan possible.

Conflict or policy conflict In the context of this book, a situation where the policy followed by a country to correct a specific problem ends up worsening the problems faced by the trade partner.

Consumer price index (CPI) An index based on the price of a representative basket of goods and services consumed by an average urban consumer. See *Reference basket*.

Consumers' surplus The difference between what a consumer would be willing to pay for a product and its market price.

Contagion The transmission of a balance-of-payments or debt crisis from one country to similar countries, often in the same region, that did not experience the original shock suffered by the first country. In 1997, Thailand had such a crisis, which soon affected Malaysia, Indonesia, and South Korea.

Countervailing duty A tariff imposed by an importing country which is intended to increase the price of a good that has benefited from a foreign subsidy.

Covered interest arbitrage A foreign currency trade involving an asset with a fixed interest rate (e.g. a government bond) together with a matching forward contract that hedges the currency risk associated with the trade. Inconsistencies between interest rates and forward rates may allow for a riskless gain.

Covered interest parity A situation where the forward discount on a currency, measured as an annual rate, is equal to the local interest rate minus the foreign interest rate.

Crawling peg An exchange rate system in which an official fixed parity is declared. The fixed parity is redefined occasionally to maintain balance-of-payments equilibrium and/or offset differing rates of inflation among countries. The members of the exchange rate mechanism overseen by the European Monetary System followed such an arrangement.

Credit A transaction that results in a payment into a country. Exports, receipts of dividend and interest payments, and purchases of local assets by foreigners are all credits in a country's balance-of-payments accounts.

Crowding out The argument that government spending does not stimulate output because it crowds out or discourages other private transactions, perhaps through higher interest rates resulting from government borrowing.

Currency band A situation where the central bank allows the currency to fluctuate within a fixed band, but intervenes if the currency hits the floor or the ceiling of the band. The width of the band determines whether this regime is closer to a fixed or to a flexible exchange rate regime.

Currency basket A currency unit defined as a weighted average of a bunch of actual currencies. The Special Drawing Rights (SDR) issued by the International Monetary Funds and the European Currency Unit (ECU) are examples of such virtual currencies. Another example is a country's choice to peg its currency to a weighted average of a group of currencies.

Currency board An exchange rate arrangement such that an institution, the currency board, is charged with upholding the strictest form of a fixed/pegged exchange rate. Either the central bank or an independent monetary authority can administer the currency board. The currency board regulates the domestic money supply so that is backed by a specified amount of foreign reserves. A currency board requires all central bank objectives to be subordinated to the exchange rate target.

Currency mismatch A situation faced by an enterprise or a government that borrows heavily in one foreign currency without holding offsetting assets in that currency and without hedging. Their position is uncovered as a devaluation of the domestic currency would cause large losses. If such currency mismatches are widespread, the local economy may experience a large number of bankruptcies. Argentina experienced this circumstance in 2002, as did Thailand in 1997.

Currency substitution The argument that national currencies are often viewed as substitutes and that firms switch from holding one currency to another in response to changes in expected yields and risks.

Current account A country's total receipts from exports of goods and services (including income receipts) minus its local expenditures on imports of goods and services (including income payments) plus *net unilateral transfers* such as gifts and foreign aid (gifts to us minus gifts from us) over a specific period (generally a year) – it is a flow.

Customs union A group of countries that allow free trade in goods and services among members and maintain a common external tariff schedule.

Deadweight loss The loss from a tariff or other restrictive policy that is a gain to nobody. A pure efficiency loss.

Debit A transaction that results in a payment out of a country. Imports and purchases of foreign securities are debits in a country's balance-of-payments accounts.

Debt/equity swap An exchange that occurs when a bank sells financial claims on a foreign government to another firm at a discount, and that firm allows the debtor country to pay the debt in local currency, which it uses to finance a direct investment in the debtor country. Frequently used in Latin America to ease the burdens of excessive debt.

Deficit A negative record for any of the balances, i.e. the sum of the credit entries is smaller that the sum of the debit entries. The opposite is a *surplus*.

Depreciation A decrease in the value of a currency, measured in terms of other currencies, in a regime of flexible (floating) exchange rates. If the dollar/sterling exchange rate moved from $1.50 per pound to $1.75, that would be a depreciation of the dollar as more dollars would be needed to buy one pound. The opposite is called an *appreciation*.

Devaluation A decrease in the value of a currency, measured in terms of other currencies, in a regime of fixed (pegged) exchange rates. This happens only if a government or central bank changes the fixed exchange rate or parity or peg for its currency. The opposite is called a *revaluation*. A devaluation may be performed to gain an edge (competitive devaluation) or to restore a overvalued peg to a more realistic level (corrective devaluation).

Developing country A country that has not attained the high level of income per capita earned in countries that have already industrialized. World Bank statistics group countries into high-income, middle-income and low-income categories; IMF trade statistics refer to industrialized and developing country groups. The WTO refers to specific provisions applicable to developing countries but does not define the term.

Dirty (or managed) floating exchange rate An exchange rate mainly determined by market forces. However, the central bank intervenes – buying or selling foreign exchange – when deemed necessary to influence the exchange rate. This is in contrast with a *clean floating exchange rate*.

Discount rate The rate at which a cost or benefit that occurs one year in the future must be reduced to express it in terms of its equivalent current money value.

Dispute Settlement Body In the World Trade Organization, all member countries meet as the Dispute Settlement Body to accept or reject reports of dispute settlement panels and appeals.

Doha Development Agenda The issues to be addressed in a round of multilateral trade negotiations begun in 2001 by a WTO ministerial meeting in Doha, Qatar. A stated intent of the round was to address the concerns of developing countries.

Dornbusch model See *Overshooting*.

Dumping The practice of selling a product in an export market for less than its price in the home market or for less than its cost of production (usually its average total cost).

Dutch disease The tendency of a natural resource discovery or increase in its price to result in a less competitive position for a country's manufacturing sector.

Dynamics Focusing on the path followed over time from one equilibrium to another. See *Comparative statics* in contrast.

Economic geography A field of study that has recently focused on the way costs of transportation and communication interact with economies of scale and market size to determine wages and the pattern of production.

Economic union An agreement among a group of countries to allow the free movement of goods, services, capital and labor among members, to maintain a common external tariff, and to achieve some degree of unification in their budgetary and monetary systems.

Economies of scale Production conditions such that long-run average costs decline as a firm's output increases. Economies of scale can exist when fixed costs are particularly important in an industry, when doubling all inputs results in more than double the output, or when learning by doing is possible.

Edgeworth–Bowley box An analytical diagram developed by Francis Edgeworth and Arthur Bowley that allows one to demonstrate the efficient allocations of goods between individuals or factors of production between industries.

Effective exchange rate Also called *trade-weighted exchange rate* or *multilateral* exchange rate The weighted sum of all bilateral exchange rates (in index form): the weight is the proportion of trade with the country in total trade.

Effective rate of protection A measurement of the amount of protection provided to an industry by a tariff schedule which allows for tariffs on inputs that the industry buys from others, as well as for the tariff on the industry's output. The measure indicates the percentage by which the value-added in producing a product under the tariff regime differs from value-added at world prices of inputs and output.

Efficiency locus In the Edgeworth–Bowley box, the allocation of goods between two individuals (or factors of production between two industries) that allows one individual to attain the highest possible level of welfare (the maximum production of one good) without reducing the welfare of the other individual (production of the other good). Also called the "contract curve."

Embargo A complete prohibition of trade with a country. U.S. trade with Cuba, for example, has been under an embargo.

Emerging economies/markets Developing economies expanding the role of the markets – originally former socialist countries moving from central planning to a market economy. It describes a nation's socioeconomic activity as being in the process of rapid industrialization. The term "rapidly growing economies" is an alternative designation.

Escape clause Temporary protection allowed for industries that experience serious injury from imports. Granting escape clause relief does not require a demonstration that trade is unfair.

Euro The currency of the European Economic and Monetary Union (EMU). In January 1999, the euro was introduced as a virtual currency. Three years later, it became a physical currency replacing 12 national currencies (including the Deutsche Mark, the French franc, and the Italian lira). It is now legal tender in 15 European countries.

Eurobonds Bonds denominated in the currency of one country and sold in another country, e.g. dollar-denominated bonds sold in Europe.

Eurocurrency See *Eurodollar*.

Eurodollar or eurocurrency Deposits in a specific country denominated in a currency other than that country's currency. Originally referred to dollar deposits in Europe.

Euromarkets Markets for eurocurrencies such as the eurodollar or euroyen.

European Central Bank (ECB) Established on June 1, 1993, the ECB is located in Frankfurt, Germany. Its management structure is very similar to that of the U.S. Federal Reserve System, with the governors of the national central banks sitting on the Governing Council, along with six members of the Executive Board, and acting as the Federal Open Market Committee does in the United States. The ECB and the national central banks form the European System of Central Banks (ESCB).

European Community See *European Economic Community*.

European Currency Unit (ECU) Created in 1978 to facilitate the mechanism of the European Monetary System. A basket of European currency – the weight of each currency in the basket was determined by a number of variables including GDP. In January 1, 1999, the ECU exchange rate determined the exchange rate for the newly created euro and the ECU disappeared.

European Economic and Monetary Union (EMU) A monetary union sporting a single currency, the euro and a common central bank, the European Central Bank (ECB), administering the common monetary policy for the members. As of 2008, the EMU had 15 members, but new members are added regularly as they meet the basic criteria for admission.

European Economic Community (EEC) An association of European countries, negotiated in 1957, that agreed to free trade among its members and imposed a common external tariff on trade with non-members. In 1967 the EEC joined with the European Coal and Steel Community and Euratom to become the European Community (EC). In 1993 an agreement to achieve even closer economic cooperation was ratified in Maastricht; the EC was renamed the European Union (E.U.) and the agreement paved the way for the European Economic and Monetary Union (EMU). As of 2008, the E.U. membership reached 27 countries.

European Monetary Cooperation Fund (EMCF) Created in 1973 to help finance balance-of-payments difficulties for countries involved in the snake. This institution assumed different names over the years, but can be considered as the precursor of the European Monetary Institute.

European Monetary System (EMS) The gradual harmonization of the monetary systems of the members of the EC starting in 1979. Fixed exchange rates and coordinated monetary policies existed until 1992–3 when the system encountered major problems. The EMS became a full monetary union for a subset of countries in January of 1999.

European System of Central Bank (ESCB) See *European Central Bank*.

European Union See *European Economic Community*.

European Unit of Account (EUA) A EEC currency used for agricultural settlements between the EEC members and pegged to gold. Created with the EEC in 1957, it was replaced by the ECU in 1978.

Exchange market intervention See *Foreign exchange market intervention*.

Exchange rate arrangement See *Exchange rate regime*.

Exchange Rate Mechanism (ERM) The arrangement through which the members of the European Monetary System pegged their exchange rates to each other in a parity grid.

Exchange rate regime The convention a country adopts to determine its exchange rate. The country may let the markets determine the exchange rate at all times (flexible or floating exchange rate) or the country may set the exchange rate and uphold it through central bank intervention (fixed or pegged exchange rate). Between these two polar cases, countries may adhere to a host of hybrid systems.

Expected rate of depreciation of a currency Expected percentage change in the exchange rate of a currency (measured as the number of units of this currency in one unit of a foreign currency) over a specific period.

Expenditure-reducing policies Policies aimed at reducing demand overall in order to reduce imports and improve the balance of trade. Example: contractionary fiscal policy. A more general term to refer to these policies would be expenditure-changing policies.

Expenditure-switching policies Policies aimed at enticing demand to switch from foreign imports to domestic goods in order to improve the balance of trade. Examples: buy domestic propaganda, tariffs/quotas, devaluation.

Export tariffs Taxes or tariffs that are applied to export receipts. Such tariffs are frequently used by developing countries as a revenue source, but have the effect of discouraging exports of the taxed products.

Export-led growth Policies based on the rapid growth of exports sales to encourage economic growth. Widely used in East Asian countries.

External balance The balance of trade is balanced (Keynesian model). More generally, foreign reserves flows are zero (Mundell–Fleming model under fixed exchange rates), or the exchange rate is stable (Mundell–Fleming model under flexible exchange rates).

External economies of scale Greater production by one firm in an industry allows costs of production for other firms in the industry to decline. This benefit from greater production represents a positive externality that an individual firm will ignore in deciding how much to produce. In such circumstances some advocate a subsidy to give the firm an incentive to expand output.

Externality Benefits or costs from a transaction that affect those who are not parties to the transaction. A positive externality from more flu vaccinations given is better health for those exposed to inoculated individuals. A negative externality from greater steel production is additional pollution and lower environmental quality of individuals in the same air shed.

f.a.s. Free alongside ship. This measurement of the value of exports includes the price of the goods shipped to the side of the ship, but without loading costs.

f.o.b. Free on board. This measurement of the value of exports includes the price of the goods loaded on the ship, but without the cost of international shipping and insurance.

Factor endowment The quantities of labor, capital, land, or other factors of production available to produce in a country. The Heckscher–Ohlin theory assumes these quantities are fixed irrespective of the factor reward earned at home or abroad.

Factor intensity reversal A situation in which industry A is more labor-intensive at one set of relative factor prices, but industry B becomes more labor-intensive at another set of relative factor prices. Factor intensity reversal can occur when it is easier to substitute one factor for the other in industry A than it is in industry B or vice versa.

Factor-price equalization The argument that international trade based on differences in relative factor endowments, as predicted by the Heckscher–Ohlin theorem, will eliminate international differences in factor prices. An important condition is that the factor endowments of the two countries, while different, are similar enough that both countries are incompletely specialized in producing the same two goods.

Financial account A country's total receipts from the sale of financial assets to foreign residents minus its total expenditures on purchases of financial assets from foreign residents. These assets include both debt and equity instruments. Before 1999, this account was referred to as the capital account.

Fixed (or pegged) exchange rate A country sets the price of the foreign currencies in terms of the domestic currency and intervenes on the foreign currency markets to uphold this exchange rate.

Flexible (or floating) exchange rate An exchange rate determined at all times by the free forces of the foreign exchange market: it corresponds to equilibrium supply and demand on that market.

Floating exchange rate See *Flexible exchange rate*.

Foreign direct investment Acquisition of a controlling interest in a firm in a foreign country and the investments that firm makes. A frequently applied standard to represent a controlling interest is ownership greater than or equal to 10 percent of the firm's shares outstanding.

Foreign exchange market intervention Purchases or sales of foreign exchange by a central bank intended to uphold a fixed (pegged) exchange rate or to affect the fluctuations of a flexible (floating) exchange rate then referred to as a managed or dirty floating exchange rate.

Foreign exchange reserves Equivalent to the *official reserve transactions* (ORT) in the balance of payments. These assets are held by the central bank and can be used to intervene on the foreign exchange markets to support a fixed or managed floating exchange rate. In the U.S. balance of payments, these are named "U.S. official reserve assets" consisting in gold, Special Drawing Rights, the reserve position in the International Monetary Fund, and foreign currencies.

Foreign exchange swap A purchase of a currency in the spot market and its simultaneous sale in the forward market (or vice versa). See *Swap*.

Foreign trade multiplier See *Open-economy multiplier*.

Forward discount Percentage change between the forward exchange rate and the spot exchange rate expressed as an annual rate: if the forward markets indicate a depreciation of the currency over the period, it is called a forward discount.

Forward exchange market A market in which it is possible to purchase foreign exchange for delivery and payment at a future date. The quantity and exchange rate are determined at the outset, but payment is made at a fixed future date, frequently in 30, 60, or 90 days.

Forward premium Percentage change between the forward exchange rate and the spot exchange rate expressed as an annual rate: if the forward markets indicate an appreciation of the currency over the period, it is called a forward premium.

Fractional reserves Less than a one-to-one proportion between reserves and monetary base.

Free rider An individual who cannot be excluded from the benefits of a good or service for which she does not pay.

Free-trade area A group of countries that maintains free trade among members, but each country maintains its own tariff schedule for trade with non-members. NAFTA (including Canada, the U.S., and Mexico) and CAFTA (including the U.S. and Central American countries) are such examples.

Free-trade zone An area within a nation where manufacturing can be carried out with imported parts and components on which no tariffs have been paid. The output must be exported to retain duty-free status. Many developing countries establish free-trade zones, also known as export processing zones, as a way of encouraging export activities that require intermediate inputs, without eliminating protection for domestic industries that produce such inputs for the rest of the economy.

Futures market for foreign currencies A market that is similar to the forward market except that all contracts mature on the same day of the month, a secondary market for the contracts exists, and the amounts of money in the contracts are smaller. Futures contracts are traded in commodity markets rather than through commercial banks.

General Agreement on Tariffs and Trade (GATT) An agreement reached in 1947 that established principles to govern international trade in goods. Also, until 1995 the GATT was an organization based in Geneva to administer this trade agreement, to settle trade disputes between member countries, and to foster negotiations to liberalize trade. It was replaced by the World Trade Organization in 1995.

Generalized System of Preferences A preferential trading arrangement in which industrialized countries allow tariff-free imports from developing countries while maintaining tariffs on the same products from other industrialized countries.

Globalization The outcome of very rapid increase in communication, trade, investment, and the transfer of ideas among countries internationally.

Gold exchange standard In this system, reserves are not only held in the form of gold, but also in the form of strong currencies directly pegged to gold, like the dollar between 1919 and 1973.

Gold export and gold import points Band around the mint parity between which a currency will fluctuate in the gold standard. The wedge corresponds to the cost of shipping the gold (transportation and insurance).

Gold standard A monetary system in which a government or a central bank maintains a fixed price of gold in terms of its currency by offering to purchase or sell gold at a fixed local currency price. Exchange rates are then determined by relative national prices of gold.

Goods Balance See *Balance on merchandise trade*.

Half-life Assuming a dampening of deviations overtime until they become insignificant, half-life corresponds to half of that time.

Heckscher–Ohlin theorem The argument, developed by two Swedish economists in the 1920s, that international trade patterns are determined by differences across countries in their relative endowments of factor inputs. Each country will export those products that require intensively its relatively abundant factors of production. Sometimes referred to as the *factor endowments* theory of trade.

Hedge In finance, a hedge is an investment that is undertaken to reduce or cancel out the risk associated with another investment. If the risk cannot be canceled out, hedging is designed to minimize exposure to an unwanted risk while still allowing the business to profit from an investment activity.

Hedging Undertaking a financial transaction that cancels or offsets the risk existing from a previous financial position.

Homothetic tastes Preferences such that an increase in income results in the same proportional increase in the quantity demanded of all goods.

Immiserizing growth Economic growth that is so strongly biased toward the production of exports, and the world demand for these exports is so price-inelastic, that the world price falls sufficiently to leave the country worse off than it was before the growth occurred.

Import-substitution industrialization A development policy in which economic growth is to be encouraged by repressing imports and by encouraging the domestic production of substitutes for those imports.

Industrial strategy The argument that the growth of industries within an economy should not be left to market forces but should instead be guided by government policies. The government should choose industries that have strong prospects and encourage their growth, perhaps by maintaining barriers to imports.

Industrial targeting Government policies to promote a specific industry.

Infant-industry protection The argument that an industry's costs will be high when it begins production, and it will need protection from imports to survive. If provided with a period of protection, the industry's costs will decline and it will be able to prosper without protection.

Intellectual property rights Legal protection of property developed through research and other creative efforts. Forms of protection include patents, copyrights, and trademarks.

Interest Equalization Tax In order to discourage capital outflows that were adversely affecting the U.S. balance of payments, the U.S. set a 15 percent tax on interest paid by foreign borrowers between 1963 and 1974.

Interest arbitrage Interest arbitrageurs choose to invest in assets denominated either in domestic or in foreign currencies in order to maximize their returns (covered) or their expected returns (uncovered).

Interest parity A situation where the returns on short-term assets invested either in the domestic or in a foreign currency are equal. Corresponds to an equilibrium in the market. See also *Covered interest parity* and *Uncovered interest parity*.

Internal balance The economy is at full employment.

International arbitrage Same as arbitrage, but in an international setting. See *Arbitrage*.

International Bank for Reconstruction and Development (IBRD) An institution founded in 1944 at the Bretton Woods conference. Located in Washington D.C., it was originally set up to finance reconstruction after World War II. Once this primary goal was achieved, it focused on development projects in poor countries. This institution also carries on research and provides advice in the area of development economics. Also known as the "World Bank."

International Finance Corporation A division of the IBRD which carries on equity financing of private projects in developing countries.

International investment position A calculation by the U.S. Bureau of Economic Analysis to measure the cumulative value of all domestic investments abroad (official and private) and all the foreign-owned investments in the domestic economy. A positive balance indicates a country that is a net creditor with respect to the rest of the world, a negative balance points to a net debtor (the present situation for the U.S.).

International Monetary Fund (IMF) An institution that was founded at the Bretton Woods conference in 1944. Located in Washington D.C., across the street from the IBRD, it lends money to countries facing large balance-of-payments deficits. It also oversees the exchange rate system and provides research and advisory services for member countries in the areas of monetary economics and international finance.

International Transactions Accounts Official name of the U.S. Balance of Payments recorded by the Bureau of Economic Analysis, U.S. Department of Commerce.

Intertemporal Taking place across time or across different periods.

Intervention See *Foreign exchange market intervention*. Central banks of industrialized countries might band together to stabilize an important currency through concerted/coordinated intervention.

Intra-industry trade Trade that occurs when a country both exports and imports the output of the same industry. Italy exporting Fiat automobiles to Germany and importing VWs from Germany is an example of intra-industry trade.

IS line Combinations of interest rates and output levels such that saving and intended investment are equal, resulting in equilibrium in the goods market.

Isoquant A curve representing all the combinations of two factors of production that can produce a fixed quantity of a product. A set of isoquants can be used to represent a production function for two inputs.

Jamaica Accord In January 1976, an agreement on an amendment of the Articles of IMF was negotiated allowing floating exchange rate arrangements, whether freely floating or managed floating, previously banned by Bretton Woods. All form of pegs are also permitted (except to gold).

J-curve effect After a devaluation or depreciation, a country's balance of trade may deteriorate for a brief period of time before improving enough to offset the deterioration.

Joint float A group of countries tie their exchange rate together (a pegged regime), but allow the group of currencies to float freely against third currencies. The European snake in the seventies is such an example.

Keynesian open economy model A macroeconomic model of the goods market that includes explicitly the trade sector as *net export* (exports minus imports).

Kyoto Protocol A 1997 agreement from the United Nations Climate Change Convention held in Kyoto, Japan that established targets for reductions of CO_2 emissions by most high-income countries.

Labor theory of value The view of the classical economists that commodities should exchange for one another in proportion to the number of hours required in their production.

Large open-economy multiplier See *Open-economy multiplier* for general description. It is larger than the small open-economy multiplier as it allows for repercussions: the expansion in the first economy results in greater demand for imports produced by the trade partner's economy, thus stimulating the partner's economy. In turn, the partner's expansion results in greater demand for imports produced by the first economy, triggering further expansion.

Law of one price The argument that international differences in prices for the same commodity are automatically arbitraged away by trade. If the exchange rate is €1.32 per £, a product that costs £1 in Great Britain should cost €1.32 in Austria. This law is based on a number of unrealistic assumptions.

Learning curve A relationship showing the tendency for a firm's marginal cost of production to fall as its cumulative output rises. This relationship has been especially important in aircraft and semiconductor production.

Least developed countries Designation by the United Nations of the most economically and socially vulnerable countries. The 2008 criteria included gross national income per capita less than $750, with the lowest measures of human development based on health and education. Countries in this grouping cannot exceed 75 million in population. Fifty countries were listed in this category in 2008.

Leontief paradox The 1953 research finding by Wassily Leontief that U.S. exports were more labor-intensive than U.S. imports, which contradicts the predictions of the Heckscher–Ohlin theorem.

Letter of credit A document issued by a commercial bank that promises to pay a fixed amount of money if certain conditions are met, such as the delivery of exported goods to a customer. If firm A wishes to purchase goods from firm B in a foreign country, firm B may require that firm A to provide a letter of credit for the amount of the purchase. If such a letter is provided, firm B is guaranteed by a known commercial bank that it will be fully paid a certain number of days after firm A takes delivery of the goods.

LM line Combinations of interest rates and output levels that clear the financial markets (money and bonds markets), given the level of the nominal money supply and of price (i.e. given the level of the real money supply).

London Interbank Offer Rate (LIBOR) The market-determined interest rate on short-term interbank deposits in the Eurodollar market in London, frequently used as the basis for floating interest rates on international loans. A country might borrow at LIBOR plus 1 percent, for example.

Long position Owning an asset or a contract to take delivery of an asset at a fixed price with no hedge or offsetting position. A long position is profitable if the price of the asset rises.

Louvre Accord In 1987, Britain, France, Germany, Japan, and the U.S. agreed to stop any action leading to further depreciation of the dollar – the dollar had fallen by 30 percent since the Plaza Accord in 1985 through concerted intervention. See *Plaza Accord*.

Maastricht criteria The monetary and fiscal criteria a country must meet to be admitted into the EMU.

Maastricht Treaty A treaty signed by the members of the European Community in Maastricht, the Netherlands, on February 7, 1992 and implemented in November 1993. In addition to closer cooperation on the political front (with the Common Foreign and Security Policy pillar and the Justice and Home Affairs pillar), this treaty heralded the onset of a European Economic and Monetary Union (EMU) with a common central bank, a common monetary policy, and a common currency.

Managed floating exchange rate Equivalent to *dirty floating exchange rate*.

Maquiladora A factory that uses imported inputs to assemble a final product. In Mexico, the firm does not need to pay a tariff on the imported inputs as long as it exports the assembled product.

Marginal propensity to import The fraction of a change in income that is spent on imports.

Marginal rate of substitution The rate at which an individual or a group of people would be willing to exchange one good for another and be no better or worse off. Equals the ratio of the marginal utilities of the two goods, which equals the slope of an indifference curve. Also, the rate at which a firm would be willing to substitute one input for another and still maintain the same level of output. Equals the ratio of the marginal products of the two factor inputs, which equals the slope of an isoquant.

Marginal rate of transformation The rate at which an economy can transform one good into another by moving productive resources from one industry to another. Equals the ratio of the marginal costs of the two goods, which equals the slope of the production-possibility curve.

Marginal utility The additional utility or improvement in welfare that an individual experiences from consuming an additional unit of a good.

Marshall–Lerner condition In order for a devaluation to improve a country's balance of trade, the sum of the elasticity of demand for imports and for exports (in absolute value) must be greater than one.

Median voter model A model that predicts a group decision will be determined by the preferences of the median voter, as when half of the group would prefer a higher level of spending on a public good and half of the group would prefer a lower level of spending on that good.

Mercantilism A seventeenth-century school of thought asserting that a government should actively discourage imports and encourage exports in order to accumulate gold reserves. It also entailed strict regulation in other aspects of the economy.

MERCOSUR A common market including Brazil, Argentina, Uruguay, and Paraguay.

Mint parity Term used for the exchange rate with the gold standard – corresponds to the ratio of the gold content of two currencies on the gold standard.

Monetary (or monetarist) approach to the balance of payments A view of the balance of payments, or the exchange rate, that emphasizes excess demands for, or supplies of, money as causes of exchange market disequilibria. An asset market approach to the balance of payments in which domestic and foreign assets are viewed as perfect substitutes – this is not presented in this textbook.

Monetary base The total volume of member bank reserve accounts and currency created by a central bank. The monetary base, sometimes known as "high-powered money," is central in determining the money supply of a country as it corresponds to a specific fraction of the money supply. The ratio between the money supply and the monetary base is called the money multiplier.

Moral hazard An institutional or legal situation that, perhaps unintentionally, encourages irresponsible behavior. If, for example, the IMF always provides financial rescue packages to indebted developing countries resulting in the lenders being fully compensated or "bailed out," banks in industrialized countries may feel encouraged to act less than prudently: the expectation of an IMF "bail-out" encourages irresponsible lending, making a later debt crisis more likely.

Most-favored-nation status (MFN) A country promises to offer the country having most-favored-nation status the lowest tariff that it offers to any third country. Tariff reductions made within the British Commonwealth and the GATT were based on this principle.

Moving average Instead of focusing on the movements of individual data points in a time series, data points are averaged over a specific number of observations and we now focus on the movement of this average over time. Each data point, instead of being the data for this specific observation will correspond to an average of, say, the last two observations.

Multi-Fibre Arrangement (MFA) A system of bilateral quotas in the markets for textiles and garments in which each exporting country was allowed to send a specified quantity of various textile or garment products to an importing country per year. MFA quotas were eliminated in 2005.

Multilateral exchange rate See *Effective exchange rate*.

Multinational Corporation A business organization that produces goods or services in more than one country.

Mundell–Fleming model An open-economy model that extends the goods market and the money market model (IS–LM) to include trade and international capital flows.

NAFTA See *North American Free Trade Agreement*.

Negative externality Action by one party that leaves another party worse off, but the first party bears no cost for this effect.

Net exporter A country that exports more than it imports, with reference to all trade, or trade in a certain good, or trade that embodies a certain factor input.

Net exports Same as the balance of trade, i.e. exports minus imports.

Net income receipts See *Balance on current accounts*.

Net unilateral transfers See *Balance on current accounts*.

New International Economic Order An agenda of proposals advanced in the 1970s by developing countries to improve their trade and development prospects. In addition to trade preferences for developing countries, the agenda called for a system of price support programs for primary products exported by developing countries. Fears of enormous costs and resource allocation inefficiencies led the industrialized countries to resist this and other parts of the NIEO program.

Newly industrialized countries (NICs) A group of previously poor countries that experienced very rapid economic growth during the 1970s and 1980s, as they shifted from the production of agricultural commodities to manufactured goods. Their exports to industrialized countries grew rapidly. South Korea, Taiwan, Hong Kong, and Singapore were the original NICs, but in the 1990s China, Thailand, Malaysia, and Indonesia were added to that group.

Nominal effective exchange rate See *Effective exchange rate* – calculated with nominal bilateral exchange rate.

Nominal exchange rate The exchange rate determined on the foreign exchange markets, whether freely or through intervention.

Nontariff barrier Any government policy other than a tariff which is designed to discourage imports in favor of domestic products. Quotas and government procurement rules are among the most important nontariff trade barriers.

Non-tradable A good or service that is not traded internationally (usually due to high transportation costs).

Nontraded good See *Non-tradable*.

North American Free Trade Agreement (NAFTA) An agreement to establish a free-trade area consisting of the United States, Canada, and Mexico. A U.S.–Canada free trade area began operations in 1989, and was extended to Mexico at the beginning of 1994.

Offer curve A curve that illustrates the volume of exports and imports that a country will choose to undertake at various terms of trade. Also known as a "reciprocal demand curve."

Official reserve transactions Transactions carried out by the central bank. The main reason for such transactions is to intervene on the foreign exchange markets in order to affect the nominal exchange rate (mainly with a fixed or a managed floating exchange rate regime).

Official reserve transactions balance A measurement of a country's balance-of-payments surplus or deficit that includes all the items in the current account and all the items in the financial accounts that are not official reserve transactions. It used to be known as the "official settlements balance of payments" and in IMF statistics is reported as the "overall balance."

Oil embargo See *Organization of Petroleum Exporting Countries* and *Embargo*.

Oligopoly An industry in which a few firms account for a large share of total sales.

Open-economy macroeconomics Macroeconomic models that explicitly include foreign trade (e.g. *Keynesian model*) or foreign trade and international capital-flow sectors (e.g. *Mundell–Fleming model*).

Open-economy multiplier The Keynesian fiscal multiplier adjusted to allow for the existence of foreign trade. Since part of the stimulus resulting from a fiscal expansion will be diverted into greater demand for foreign-produced goods (imports), a so-called "leakage" takes place and the final expansion will not be as large: the open-economy multiplier is not as large as the closed-economy one. There is a distinction between the *small open-economy* multiplier and the *large open-economy multiplier* (see entries on these terms).

Open-market operations The purchase or sale of domestic bonds by the central bank to alter the size of the money supply in the economy.

Open position To take an open position on the foreign exchange market, i.e. to be willing to put up with the foreign exchange risk.

Opportunity cost The cost of one good in terms of the amount of another good that could have been produced with the same factors of production.

Optimum currency area The area within which a single currency (or rigidly fixed exchange rates) and a common monetary policy can operate successfully. Theory pioneered by Mundell and McKinnon.

Optimum tariff A tariff that is designed to maximize a large country's benefits from trade by improving its terms of trade. It is optimal only for the country imposing the tariff, not for the world.

Options In currency markets, one-sided transactions where one party purchases the right to buy (*call*) or to sell (*put*) a specific amount of foreign currency. See *Call* and *Put*.

Orderly Marketing Agreement An agreement between an importing and exporting country that typically limits the physical volume of a good that can be imported

Organization for Economic Cooperation and Development (OECD) An organization consisting of the governments of industrialized market economies, headquartered in Paris. It publishes statistics on international trade and financial flows, and carries out research on these countries.

Organization of Petroleum Exporting Countries (OPEC) An organization of oil producing and exporting countries. It can be regarded as a cartel as they regulate the supply of oil for export (embargo) in order to regulate its price. See *Embargo*.

Overshooting A condition that occurs when the price of an asset, such as foreign exchange, moving towards its permanent equilibrium happens to jump beyond it in the short run, before coming back to that permanent equilibrium. Associated with Rudiger Dornbusch's analysis of the response of a floating exchange rate to a shift in monetary policy.

Par value The central value of a fixed (pegged) exchange rate, denominated in terms of a foreign currency or gold. The exchange rate is allowed to fluctuate within a band around its par value. Bretton Woods and the Exchange Rate Mechanism of the European Monetary System set par values for the members' exchange rates.

Parallel currency A currency that exists alongside another currency – both currencies have legal tender. Example: the euro and the DM for a short period in 2002.

Pegged exchange rate Equivalent to *fixed exchange rate*.

Plaza Accord In 1985, the central banks of Britain, France, Germany, and Japan agreed with the U.S. Fed to bring down, through concerted intervention, the value of the dollar that had appreciated substantially in the early eighties. See *Louvre Accord*.

Policy assignment model A model of balance-of-payments adjustment under fixed exchange rates (and also flexible exchange rates) allowing the economy to reach both the desired level of domestic output and payments equilibrium through the use of fiscal and monetary policies. Associated with J. Marcus Fleming and Robert Mundell.

Portfolio balance model A view of the financial account or of the overall balance of payments that emphasizes the demand for and supply of financial assets. Concludes that capital flows in response to recent changes in expected yields rather than in response to differing levels of expected yields. In this asset market approach to the balance of payments, domestic and foreign assets are viewed as imperfect substitutes.

Portfolio investment Purchase of stocks or bonds in a foreign country.

Prebisch–Singer hypothesis The argument developed by Raul Prebisch and Hans Singer that developing countries face a secular decline in their terms of trade due to a trend toward lower prices for primary commodities relative to prices of manufactured goods.

Predatory dumping Temporary dumping designed to drive competing firms out of business in order to create a monopoly and raise prices.

Preference similarity hypothesis The observation that trade in consumer goods often occurs because a product that is popular in the country in which it is produced can most easily be exported to countries with similar consumer tastes or levels of income per capita. Associated with Stefan Burenstam Linder.

Preferential Trade Agreement An agreement by two or more countries to impose less stringent restrictions on their mutual trade than on their trade with countries that do not join the agreement.

Primary product An agricultural or natural resource commodity that is sold without further processing.

Principle of second best The argument that when it is not possible to remove one economic distortion, such as an imperfectly competitive product or factor market, eliminating another distortion, such as a tariff, may not increase economic efficiency. Many arguments for protection are based on this principle. Associated with Richard Lipsey and Kelvin Lancaster.

Prisoners' dilemma Based on the situation where two prisoners are interrogated separately, and each has an incentive to confess and obtain a lighter sentence by implicating the other. In trade policy settings such incentives make cooperative action to reduce tariffs or subsidies less likely.

Producers' surplus The difference between the price at which a product can be sold and the minimum price which a seller would be willing to accept for it.

Production function A graphical or mathematical representation of all the combinations of inputs which will produce various quantities of a product. Can be represented with an isoquant map if only two inputs exist.

Production-possibility curve A graphical representation of all possible combinations of the maximum output of one good for a given level of output of the other, determined by an economy's currently available technology and factors of production.

Purchasing power parity (PPP) – absolute The argument that the exchange rate between two currencies should be equal to the relative price of a specific basket of goods (CPI) in the two countries. If the price level in Switzerland is 200 and the price level in France is 100, the exchange rate should be SF2 = €1. Associated with Gustav Cassel.

Purchasing power parity (PPP) – relative This theory contends that the rate of change in the exchange rate between two currencies is equal to the inflation differential in the two countries.

Purchasing power parity theory The belief that the exchange rate will reach its purchasing power parity level in equilibrium.

Put An option contract that allows its owner to sell a specified amount of a financial asset, such as foreign exchange, at a fixed price during a specified period of time. The owner of the option is not required to exercise the option. The price at which the asset can be sold is known as the "strike price."

Quota A government policy that limits the physical volume of a product which may be imported per period of time.

Quota rents The extra profits that accrue to those who have the right to bring products into a country under a quota. Equal to the difference between the domestic price of the product in the importing country and the world price, multiplied by the quantity imported.

Real effective exchange rate The nominal effective exchange rate adjusted for differing rates of inflation to create an index of cost and price competitiveness in world markets. If a country's nominal effective exchange rate depreciated by 5 percent in a year in which its rate of inflation exceeded the average rate of inflation in the rest of the world by 5 percentage points, its real effective exchange rate would be unchanged.

Real exchange rate The nominal exchange rate deflated by relative prices (ratio of the two CPI) in the two countries. The relative price of a basket of goods in two countries expressed in the same currency.

Real interest rate The nominal interest rate minus the expected rate of inflation. Current saving and investment decisions should be based on the real interest rate over the maturity of the asset.

Real money supply A nation's money supply divided by the price level in that country. The real money supply represents the purchasing power of the nation's money supply; it is critical in determining the demand for goods and services, as well as for financial assets, in a monetarist model.

Reciprocal demand curve A curve that illustrates the volume of exports and imports that a country will choose to undertake at various terms of trade. Also known as an "offer curve."

Reference basket A fixed assortment of goods and services the price of which is used as a base to construct a price index like the CPI.

Reinforcement or policy reinforcement A situation where the policy followed by a country to correct a specific problem ends up correcting (partially) the problems faced by the trade partner.

Relative factor endowments The relative amounts of different factors of production which two countries have. India has a relative abundance of labor, while the United Kingdom has a relative abundance of capital. In testing the Heckscher–Ohlin theory, economists express the country's endowment of a factor relative to the world supply of that factor; if this ratio showing its supply of the factor exceeds the country's share of world income, an indication of its demand for a factor, the country is relatively abundant in this factor.

Relative factor intensities The relative amounts of different factors of production that are used in the production of two goods. At a given wage–rental ratio, the capital–labor ratio in clothing production is smaller than in oil refining; clothing is relatively labor-intensive, and oil refining is relatively capital-intensive.

Remittances The transfer of a foreign worker's earnings to her home country.

Rent seeking The attempt to receive favorable government treatment that results in higher income for an individual. Subsidies and trade barriers create higher returns or rents for immobile factors in those industries.

Repercussions Two large open economies trading with each other affect each other's economies through their trade sector (net exports). The impact of a policy change by one country (fiscal or devaluation) affects the partner's economy and in turn affects the original economy: these impacts go back and forth until an new equilibrium for the two economies is reached.

Resistance A price level above the current market price, at which selling pressures should be strong enough to overcome buying pressure and keep the price from going any higher.

Revaluation An increase in the value of a currency, measured in terms of other currencies, in a regime of fixed (pegged) exchange rates. This happens only if a government or central bank changes the fixed exchange rate or parity or peg for its currency. The opposite is called a *devaluation*.

Rybczynski theorem The argument, associated with Thomas Rybcyznski, that if the supply of one factor of production increases, when both relative factor and goods prices are unchanged, the output of the product using that factor intensively will increase and the output of the product using the other factor of production intensively must decline.

Services balance See *Balance on services*.

Settlement accounts or transactions Correspond to the resulting payment for or receipt from a deal.

Settlement date The date at which payment is made and an asset received. Normally two business days after the trade is agreed to for spot foreign exchange transactions. If British Petroleum purchases euros from the Deutsche Bank on Wednesday, payment will be made in both directions on that Friday, which is the settlement date.

Short position Having a liability or a contract to deliver an asset in the future at a fixed price with no hedge or offsetting position. A short position is profitable if the asset declines in price, and vice versa. A short position in sterling would exist if someone owed a sterling debt without offsetting sterling assets, or if that person had sold sterling in the forward or futures market while not holding offsetting sterling assets. See *Long position* in contrast.

Single Market Program An initiative agreed in 1986 by the European Economic Community to eliminate remaining barriers to the free flow of goods, services, labor, and capital among member countries.

Small open-economy multiplier See *open-economy multiplier* for general description. The small open-economy multiplier is smaller than the large open-economy multiplier as the latter allows for repercussions. See *large open-economy multiplier*.

Smithsonian Conference As the confidence in the dollar as anchor of the Bretton Woods system waned, a conference was called by President Nixon; it took place in December 1971 at the Smithsonian Institution where representatives from ten industrialized countries agreed to revalue their currency against the dollar and widen the bands.

Smoot–Hawley tariff A very high level of tariffs adopted by the United States in 1930 that caused a dramatic decline in the volume of world trade. It is widely believed to have worsened the great depression.

Snake Name given to the joint float followed by a number of European countries in the seventies.

Snake in the tunnel The earlier version of the snake that was implemented right after the demise of Bretton Woods. In this version of the snake, the joint float was pegged to the dollar, creating a tunnel.

Society for Worldwide Interbank Financial Telecommunication (SWIFT) An electronic system maintained by large international banks for transmitting instructions for foreign exchange transfers and other international transactions.

Special Drawing Rights (SDRs) A foreign exchange reserve asset created by the International Monetary Fund in 1969 to supplement the existing exchange reserves of member countries. The SDR is a basket of currencies based on a weighted average of the U.S. dollar, the euro, the yen, and the pound sterling. It is used as a unit of account by the IMF and various other international organizations.

Specie flow mechanism A balance-of-payments adjustment mechanism in which the domestic money supply is rigidly tied to the balance of payments, falling in the case of deficits and rising when surpluses occur. Associated with David Hume.

Specific factors model A factor of production is specific to an industry, or immobile when its productivity in one industry exceeds its productivity in other industries at any price. A specific factors model predicts that immobile factors that produce import-competing goods will be harmed by free trade. The text refers to the case where capital is immobile between industries, but labor is mobile, as a specific factors model.

Specific tariff A tariff that is measured as a fixed amount of money per physical unit imported – $500 per car or €10 per ton, for example.

Speculation In finance, the assumption of risk in return for an uncertain possibility of a reward. By definition, only positions that involve negligible risk represent "investments" rather than speculation.

Speculator A person engaged in speculation. See *Speculation*.

Spot market or spot exchange market The market for an asset, such as foreign exchange, in which delivery is scheduled within one or two days.

Spread Difference between the *ask price* (price at which a bank will sell foreign exchange) and the *bid price* (price at which a bank will buy foreign exchange).

Stability and Growth Pact A commitment by the members of EMU to uphold the two Maastricht fiscal criteria (budget deficit no larger than 3 percent and debt no larger than 60 percent of GDP), even after being admitted to the EMU.

Statistical discrepancy Also known as "net errors and omissions." Logically, all the entries in the balance of payments must sum up to zero, but many of the entries are estimates of actual transactions that contain many errors so this is unlikely to happen. The statistical discrepancy is the number that must be entered in the balance-of-payments accounts of a country to make all the entries sum up to zero. The statistical discrepancy number is frequently placed at the end of the table and is simply the sum of all the other entries in the account with the sign reversed.

Sterilization A domestic monetary policy action designed to offset the monetary effect of a balance of payments disequilibrium in the context of a fixed exchange rate arrangement. Through *intervention* to uphold the fixed exchange rate, the central bank alters the size of its foreign reserves (on its asset side) thus affecting the domestic money supply. The impact of intervention can be offset through an *open market operation* that restores the money supply to its original level. The policy of allowing intervention to affect the money supply is called non-sterilization.

Stern Review A report prepared under the direction of Sir Nicholas Stern in 2006 that reviewed the economic consequences of global warming.

Stolper–Samuelson theorem The argument that in a world of Heckscher–Ohlin trade, free trade will reduce the income of the scarce factor of production and increase the income of the abundant factor of production in each country. Associated with Paul Samuelson and Wolfgang Stolper.

Strategic trade policy The argument that trade policy, including subsidies and import restrictions, should be used to encourage the growth of domestic industries that the government believes can earn above-average profits or benefit from external economies of scale in production. This approach often involves trying to choose industries in which rapid technical advances are likely and where growing world markets exist.

Strike price The price at which an option can be exercised before the expiration date. Such an option is said to be "at the money" if the strike price equals the current market price, and "in the money" if the market price exceeds the strike price, so a call option is worth exercising. A call option is "out of the money" if the current market price is below the strike price, so the option is not worth exercising.

Structural funds Monies allocated by the European Union to promote convergence in levels of development among the various regions. Recipient regions generally suffer from high unemployment and poor infrastructure. Related to Cohesion Funds, also intended to achieve this same goal but distributed to nations whose per capita income is less than 90 percent of the Community average.

Subsidy A negative tax or tariff (a payment by the government).

Sunset industry A mature industry that faces such intense import competition that its output declines.

Support A price level below the current market price at which buying interest should be able to overcome selling pressures and keep the price from going any lower.

Surplus A positive record for any of the balances, i.e. the sum of the credit entries is greater that the sum of the debit entries. The opposite is a *deficit*.

Swap A transaction in which one security or stream of income is exchanged for another, frequently with a contract to reverse the transaction at a date in the future. Also see *Foreign exchange swaps*.

Tariff A tax on imports or exports imposed by a government. Tariffs are frequently a major source of revenue for developing countries, but are primarily used to protect import-competing industries in industrialized countries.

Tariff rate quota A trade restriction which places a low tariff rate on a fixed volume of a good imported per period of time and a higher tariff rate on imports above that level. There may be no tariff imposed on the fixed volume, and a tariff above that level.

Technical analysis A method followed by traders to study the price and volume data for a specific exchange rate and used to create charts to "guesstimate" movements in the exchange rate.

Terms of trade The ratio of a country's export prices to its import prices. For a small country, higher terms of trade imply larger benefits from trade, and vice versa.

Time consistency problem Due to constraints on economy policy at different points in time, policymakers may not implement what they regard originally as the best option.

Trade Adjustment Assistance (TAA) The provision of financial aid to industries injured by growing imports or to their employees. When tariffs are reduced, trade adjustment assistance may be promised for import-competing industries.

Trade balance See *Balance of trade*.

Trade creation An efficiency gain that results from the formation of a free trade area or a customs union: more efficient firms from another member country displace less efficient local producers in the domestic market and imports increase.

Trade diversion An efficiency loss that results from the formation of a free trade area or a customs union: less efficient firms from a member country displace more efficient producers from a non-member country. It occurs because of the discriminatory nature of the tariff regime. The member country faces no tariff in the import market, whereas the non-member still faces a tariff.

Trade expansion An efficiency gain that results from the formation of a free trade area or a customs union: as the consumers in the domestic economy are able to buy goods at a lower price, they can expand their consumption.

Trade-weighted exchange rate See *Effective exchange rate.*

Trade-related investment measures (TRIMs) Government policies in which foreign direct investments in a country are allowed only if the investing firm promises to meet certain trade performance goals. The Uruguay Round agreement prohibits TRIMs that require firms to use a certain amount of domestically produced inputs or maintain a certain balance between imports and exports.

Transfer pricing The practice of using false or misleading prices on trade documents in order to evade *ad valorem* tariffs or exchange controls, or to shift profits within a multinational firm from a high-tax-rate jurisdiction to a low-tax-rate jurisdiction. Also known as "false invoicing."

Uncovered interest arbitrage A form of arbitrage that involves the conversion of the domestic currency into the foreign currency to take advantage of a higher interest rate on foreign currency investments. The interest arbitrage is "uncovered" because the return on the investment is denominated in foreign currency and hence the return is exposed to foreign exchange risk (the foreign currency may depreciate during the period of the investment).

Uncovered interest parity The expected rate of depreciation of a currency (see definition), measured as an annual rate, is equal to the local interest rate minus the foreign interest rate.

Unilateral transfers (net) Subset of the current account defined as gifts/foreign aid to the domestic economy minus gifts/foreign aid from the domestic economy.

United Nations Conference on Trade and Development (UNCTAD) A U.N. organization that also holds conferences every four years with the intent of building consensus on development policies. Its focus has changed since the 1960s as thinking about the development process has changed. The organization carries out analytical research and policy analysis, and it provides technical assistance to developing countries regarding participation in the world trading system. In the 1970s the New International Economic Order agenda for reform of the world economy grew out of its conferences.

Uruguay Round A round of negotiations on trade liberalization held under GATT auspices completed in 1993. The agreement reached reduced tariffs and addressed trade practices not previously covered by GATT rules. It also replaced the GATT with the World Trade Organization.

US Trade Representative (USTR) An official of the executive branch of the U.S. government who is responsible for carrying on negotiations with foreign governments on foreign trade issues. Previously known as the "Special Trade Representative."

Vehicle currencies A (strong) currency that is most commonly used to settle international trade transactions, even if it is not the national currency. Examples: the dollar or the euro.

Vernon product cycle The observation that a high-income country that develops a new product or production process may have a strong export position only for a limited time. When the technology becomes standardized and available abroad, and production requires factor inputs that are relatively abundant in other countries, the innovating country may even become a net importer of the product. Associated with Raymond Vernon.

Voluntary export restraint (VER) An agreement by a country to limit its export sales to another country, frequently in order to avoid a more damaging protectionist policy by the importing country. Sometimes known as an "Orderly Marketing Agreement" (OMA). VERs are severely restricted by the Uruguay Round agreement.

Walras's law The idea that excess demands must net out to zero across an economy in a general equilibrium framework, because if there is an excess demand in one market, there must be an offsetting excess supply in another market. Associated with Leon Walras.

Welfare The well-being of an individual or a country.

World Bank See *IBRD*

World Trade Organization (WTO) A successor organization to the GATT established in 1995, as agreed upon in the Uruguay Round. The WTO provides a stronger administrative framework, more streamlined dispute resolution provisions, and a trade-policy review procedure, all of which suggest more effective implementation of the agreements reached.

Index

eBooks – at www.eBookstore.tandf.co.uk

A library at your fingertips!

eBooks are electronic versions of printed books. You can store them on your PC/laptop or browse them online.

They have advantages for anyone needing rapid access to a wide variety of published, copyright information.

eBooks can help your research by enabling you to bookmark chapters, annotate text and use instant searches to find specific words or phrases. Several eBook files would fit on even a small laptop or PDA.

NEW: Save money by eSubscribing: cheap, online access to any eBook for as long as you need it.

Annual subscription packages

We now offer special low-cost bulk subscriptions to packages of eBooks in certain subject areas. These are available to libraries or to individuals.

For more information please contact webmaster.ebooks@tandf.co.uk

We're continually developing the eBook concept, so keep up to date by visiting the website.

www.eBookstore.tandf.co.uk